Shem Pete's Alaska

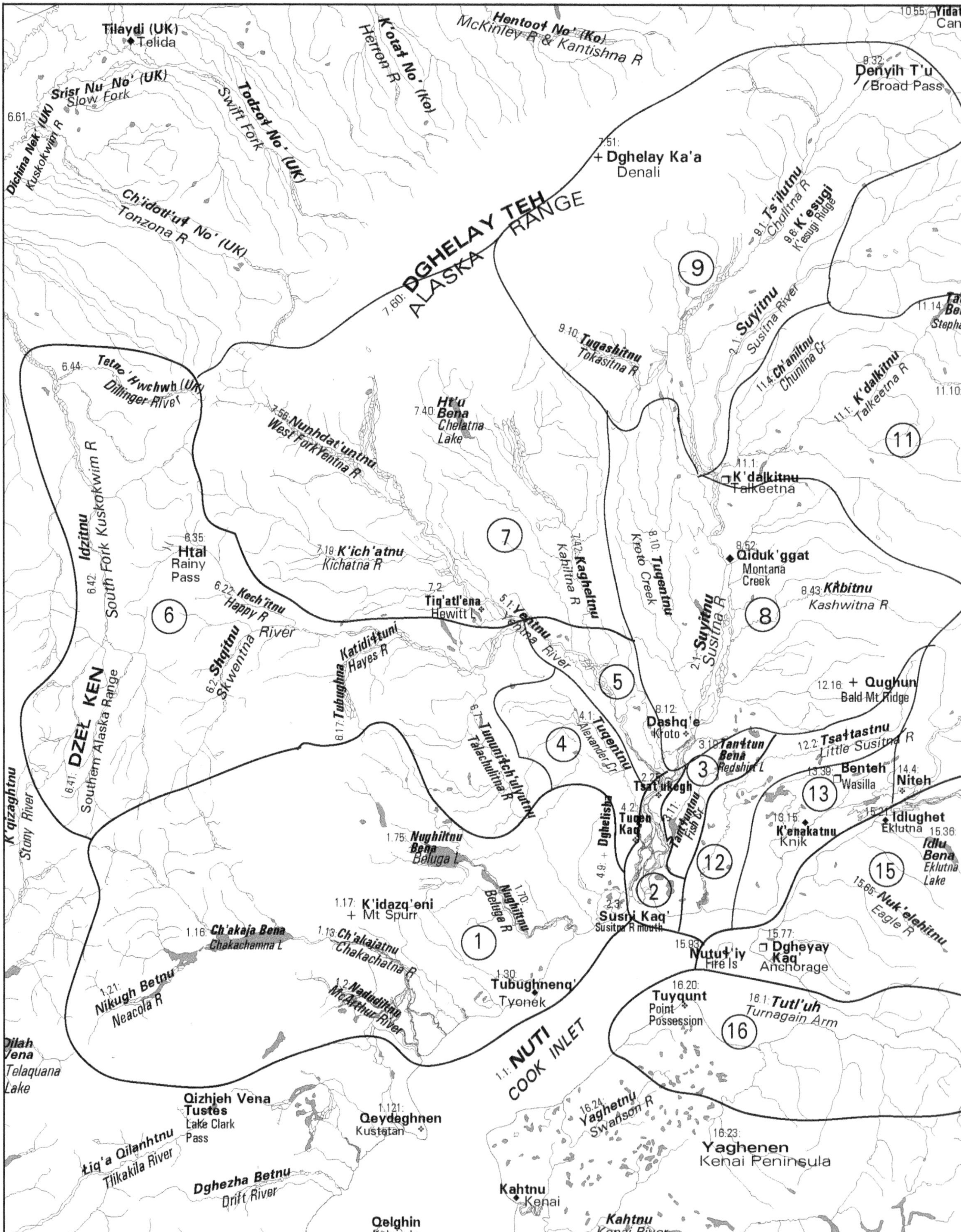

Tilaydi (UK)
Telida
Hentoot No' (Ko)
McKinley R & Kantishna R
K'otat No' (Ko)
Herron R
9.32: Denyih T'u
Broad Pass
6.61: Dichina Nek' (UK)
Kuskokwim R
Srisr Nu No' (UK)
Slow Fork
Todzot No' (UK)
Swift Fork
7.51: Dghelay Ka'a
Denali
Ch'idotl'ut No' (UK)
Tonzona R
7.60: DGHELAY TEH
ALASKA RANGE
9.1: Ts'ilutnu
Chulitna R
9.6: K'esugi
K'esugi Ridge
9
2.1: Suyitnu
Susitna River
9.10: Tugashitnu
Tokositna R
11.14: Tat Ben
Stepha
6.44: Tetno' Hwchwh (UK)
Dillinger River
11.4: Ch'aniltnu
Chunilna Cr
11.1: K'dalkitnu
Talkeetna R
11.10
7.56: Nunhdat'untnu
West Fork Yentna R
7.40: Ht'u Bena
Chelatna Lake
11
11.1: K'dalkitnu
Talkeetna
Idzitnu
South Fork Kuskokwim R
6.35: Htal
Rainy Pass
7
7.19: K'ich'atnu
Kichatna R
7.42: Kagheltnu
Kahiltna R
8.10: Tugentnu
Kroto Creek
8.52: Qiduk'ggat
Montana Creek
6.42
6.22: Kech'itnu
Happy R
7.2: Tiq'atl'ena
Hewitt L
5.1: Yentnu
Yentna River
2.1: Suyitnu
Susitna R
8.43: K'ibitnu
Kashwitna R
6
8
6.2: Shqitnu
Skwentna River
6.17: Tubughna Katidiltuni
Hayes R
5
12.16: Qughun
Bald Mt Ridge
DZEL KEN
Southern Alaska Range
6.41
6.7: Tununitch'uiyutnu
Talachulitna R
4.1: Tugentnu
Alexander Cr
8.12: Dashq'e
Kroto
4
3.10: Tanltun Bena
Redshirt L
3
12.2: Tsaltastnu
Little Susitna R
13.39: Benteh
Wasilla
14.4: Niteh
K'qizaghtnu
Stony River
2.2: Tsat'ukegh
4.2: Tugen Kaq'
3.11: Tanltuntnu
Fish Cr
13
13.15: K'enakatnu
Knik
15.21: Idlughet
Eklutna
15.36: Idlu Bena
Eklutna Lake
1.75: Nughiltnu Bena
Beluga L
4.9: Dghelishla
12
15
2
1.70: Nughiltnu
Beluga R
15.65: Nuk'elehitnu
Eagle R
1.17: K'idazq'eni
Mt Spurr
2.3: Susni Kaq'
Susitna R mouth
1.16: Ch'akaja Bena
Chakachamna L
1.13: Ch'akajatnu
Chakachatna R
1
15.93: Nutul'iy
Fire Is
15.77: Dgheyay Kaq'
Anchorage
1.21: Nikugh Betnu
Neacola R
1.2: Nadudiltnu
McArthur River
1.30: Tubughneng'
Tyonek
16.20: Tuyqunt
Point Possession
16.1: Tutl'uh
Turnagain Arm
16
Qilah Vena
Telaquana Lake
1.1: NUTI
COOK INLET
Qizhjeh Vena Tustes
Lake Clark Pass
1.121: Qeydeghnen
Kustatan
16.24: Yaghetnu
Swanson R
16.23: Yaghenen
Kenai Peninsula
Łiq'a Qilanhtnu
Tlikakila River
Dghezha Betnu
Drift River
Kahtnu
Kenai
Kahtnu
Kenai River
Qelghin
Kalgin Is
10.55: Yidat
Cant

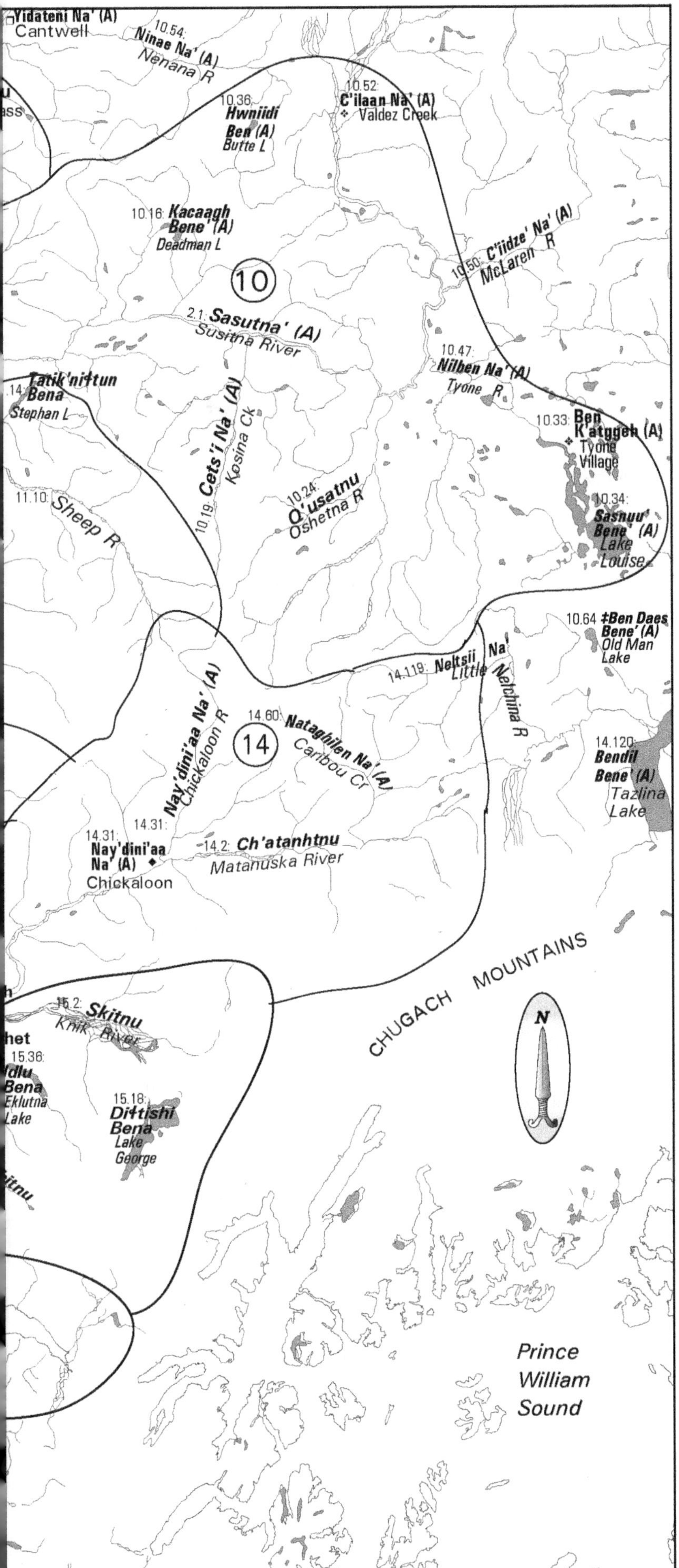

MAP 1

Chapter guide to *Shem Pete's Alaska* and major Dena'ina place names in Upper Cook Inlet

MAP BY MATT GANLEY AND JAMES KARI

Chapter drainage boundaries

(10) Numbers in circles are chapter numbers

Chapter number

Place number

Dena'ina name in bold

8.43: **Kiłbitnu**

Kashwitna R

U.S. Geological Survey place name

Scale

20 miles

Front:

1 Pete Trefon Sr.
2 Clyde Trefon
3 Pete Trefon Jr.
4 Liz Balluta
5 Peter Kalifornsky
6 Sava Stephan
7 Jim Kari
8 Shem Pete

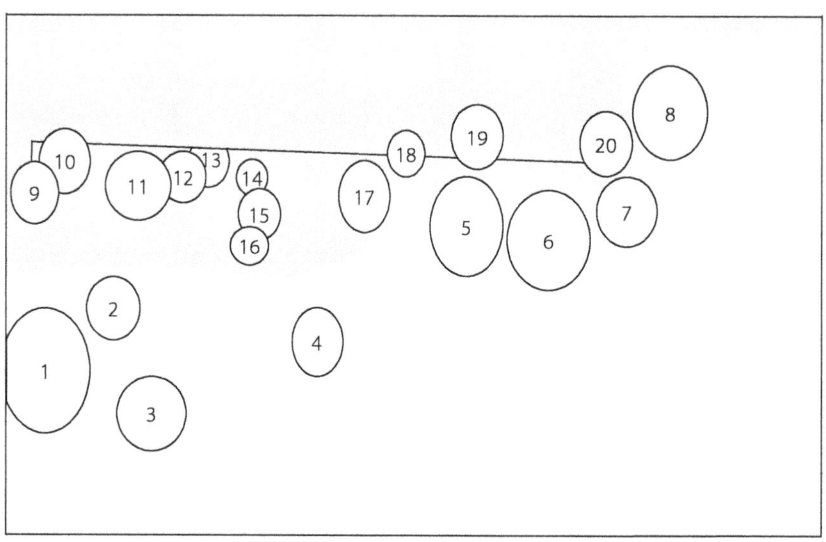

Back:

9 Ada Trefon
10 Chuck Trefon
11 Harry Balluta
12 Duane Balluta
13 Sophie Balluta
14 Natasya Chambers
15 Margaret Balluta
16 not identified
17 Albert Wassillie
18 Jeanne Carltikoff (Willis)
19 Melvin Trefon
20 not identified

Not visible to left: Antone Evan and Macy Hobson

Playing **ch'enlahi**—the hand game—in Nondalton, April 1, 1976, a seminal moment for Dena'ina cultural renewal. Shem Pete, then 79 years of age, led the gambling songs for the Cook Inlet players, Peter Kalifornsky and Sava Stephan, while Antone Evan led songs for the Nondalton players Pete Trefon and Macy Hobson.

PHOTO BY JOAN TENENBAUM

Shem Pete's Alaska

The Territory of the Upper Cook Inlet Dena'ina

2016 Edition

by **James Kari** *and* **James A. Fall**

Principal contributor
Shem Pete

Additional place names and commentary by

Daniel Alex
Mike Alex
Nickafor Alexan
Emma Alexie
Alexandra Allowan
Tommy Allowan
Harry Balluta
Pete Bobby
Sergei Californsky
Maxim Chickalusion
Nellie Chickalusion
Ella Chuitt
Fedora Constantine
Peter Constantine
Miska Deaphon
Bobby Esai
Hester Evan
Fred Ewan
Betty Gilcrist
Charlie Hubbard
Peter Kalifornsky
Ben Neely
Dick Mishakoff
Jim McKinley
Katherine Nicolie
Billy Pete
Alec Peter
Henry Peters
Annie Ronning
Fedosia Sacaloff
Dick Secondchief
Morrie Secondchief
Jim Sinyon
Johnny Shaginoff
Mary Shaginoff
Alberta Stephan
John Stephan
Leo Stephan
Pete Stephan
Sava Stephan
Terry Stephan
Frank Stickwan
John Stump
Jake Tansy
Arthur Theodore
Bailey Theodore
Lillian Theodore
Mike Theodore
Andy Tyone
Jack Tyone
Jim Tyone
Katie Wade

PUBLISHED BY THE UNIVERSITY OF ALASKA PRESS WITH THE ALASKA NATIVE LANGUAGE CENTER

Revised second edition

Second edition

First edition
1987
Alaska Native Language Center, University of Alaska and The CIRI Foundation.

Address correspondence to:

University of Alaska Press
Fairbanks, Alaska 99775-0120

Library of Congress Cataloging-in-Publication Data

Names: Kari, James M., editor of compilation. | Fall, James A., editor of compilation. | Pete, Shem, approximately 1896-1989, contributor. | Alex, Daniel, contributor. | Alaska Native Language Center.
Title: Shem Pete's Alaska : the territory of the Upper Cook Inlet Dena'ina / [compiled and edited] by James Kari and James A. Fall ; principal contributor, Shem Pete ; additional place names and commentary by Daniel Alex [and 51 others].
Description: 2016 edition, revised second edition. | Fairbanks, Alaska : The University of Alaska Press with the Alaska Native Language Center, 2016. | "Second edition 2003, University of Alaska Press; first edition 1987"–Title page verso. | Includes bibliographical references and indexes.
Identifiers: LCCN 2016017304 (print) | LCCN 2016017707 (ebook) | ISBN 9781602233065 (paperback : alkaline paper) | ISBN 9781602233072 (e-book)
Subjects: LCSH: Dena'ina Indians–Alaska–Cook Inlet. | Names, Dena'ina–Alaska–Cook Inlet. | Names, Geographical–Alaska. | Names, Geographical–Alaska–Cook Inlet. | Dena'ina language–Glossaries, vocabularies, etc. | Alaska–History, Local. | Cook Inlet (Alaska)–History, Local.
Classification: LCC E99.T185 S54 2016 (print) | LCC E99.T185 (ebook) | DDC 916.4/34–dc23
LC record available at https://lccn.loc.gov/2016017304

Printed in the United States of America

Translations from Dena'ina Athabascan
Shem Pete
Billy Pete
Katherine Nicolie
Sava Stephan
James Kari

Maps
Matt Ganley, Map Alaska: www.map-alaska.com

Music transcriptions
Thomas F. Johnston, University of Alaska Fairbanks

Design
Dixon J. Jones, UAF Rasmuson Library Graphics

Front cover
Lynx Lake and lakes west of Willow, photo by Fred Hirschmann AK-6838. See Plate 5 and Fig. 61.
Inset photos: top, see page 394; bottom left to right, see Plate 24, Fig. 3, Plate 9 and Map 17.

Back cover
See Fig. 5.

Vignette backgrounds
Close-up of dentalia shell necklace worn by Shem Pete at the Cook Inlet Region, Inc. potlatch on October 17, 1985. Dentalia shells are called **k'enq'ena** and the necklace is called **t'uyedi.** Photo by Kathy Kiefer.

Detail of a large birchbark basket, the elegant utility vessel of the Dena'ina, called **lch'ehi** or **q'ey lch'eha.** This basket was made by Emma Alexie of Lime Village. Digital image by Kim Armstrong, UAF Rasmuson Library Photographic Unit.

Preparation of the 2003 edition was funded in part by a grant from the State of Alaska, administered by the Department of Community and Regional Affairs, through the 1985 Cultural Heritage Program of Cook Inlet Region, Inc. Funding was also provided by Cook Inlet Region, Inc., and by Alaska Native Language Center, College of Liberal Arts, University of Alaska, Fairbanks, and a grant in 2001 from The CIRI Foundation.

Contents

List of Maps and Tables VII
Foreword by William Bright XI
Preface to the 2016 Edition XII
Preface to the 2003 Edition XIII
Introduction to the 1987 Edition XV
Acknowledgments XVII
Terminology and Format XVIII
Symbols, Abbreviations, Common Dena'ina Words XIX
The Dena'ina and Ahtna Sound Systems and Alphabets XXI

Introduction **1**
- **Shem Pete Ełan Shit'i,** 'I Am Shem Pete' 1
- Billy Shem Pete 6
- Sava Stephan, Sr. 8
- The Dena'ina Language Area, Dena'ina Dialects, and Prehistoric Migrations, *by James Kari* 10
- ‡Prehistory of the Greater Upper Cook Inlet Region *by Douglas Reger and Brian T. Wygal* 15
- The Russian Presence in Upper Cook Inlet, *by James Kari and James A. Fall* 17
- Upper Inlet Dena'ina Regional Bands, Subsistence Patterns, and Traditional Leaders, *by James A. Fall* 22
- Upper Inlet Dena'ina Bands and Band Names, *by James Kari* 27
- Dena'ina Place Names and Territorial Knowledge, *by James Kari* 30
- A Note on Map Production for *Shem Pete's Alaska, by Matt Ganley* 36

1 Western Cook Inlet **49**
- Chief Simeon Chickalusion, 1880–1957 59
- **Tanik'edi,** a Dena'ina Technique for Salmon Fishing in Cook Inlet, *by Nickafor Alexan* 64
- Beluga Hunting in the Tyonek Area, *by James Kari and James A. Fall* 75
- **Quyushi Uqu Ch'el'ani,** Beluga Hunting, *by Shem Pete* 78

2 Lower Susitna River **81**
- The Wrangell Map of 1839, *by James Kari* 85
- Early Historic Dena'ina Log and Pole Buildings, *by D. C. Beard* 94
- **Susitnu Htsukdu'a**—The Susitna Story, *by Shem Pete* 96

3 Fish Creek **99**
- Notes on Dena'ina Watercraft, *by James Kari* 102
- **Baytnidahen** and Red Shirt, *by Shem Pete, translated by Billy Pete* 106

4 Alexander Creek Drainage **109**
- **Ghuliy**—Potlatch Wealth, *by James Kari* 115

5 Lower Yentna River **119**
- Shem Pete, Dena'ina Singer and Composer, *by Thomas F. Johnston* 125

6 Skwentna River to the Rainy Pass Area **131**
- **Htal**—the 1932 Trip to Rainy Pass, *by Sava Stephan* 140
- ‡Introducing the Proto-Dene *Lex Loci* with Selected Dene Place Names South and West of the Alaska Range, *by James Kari* 144

7 Upper Yentna River, Lake Creek, and Kahiltna River **149**
Archaeological Investigations at **Tiq'atl'ena Bena** (Hewitt Lake), *by R. Greg Dixon* 151
1919 Trip from Susitna Station to the Johnson Creek area and Hewitt Lake, *by Shem Pete* 164

8 Middle Susitna River **173**
Traveling with the Kroto Creek Band in the 1920s, *by Katherine Nicolie* 177
Q'u Nuch'tutnał Dini Sht'a 179
The Story of **Beł Dink'udlaghen**: The One Who Swam Back Inside with Them (the Salmon), *by Shem Pete* 184
Wasilla Stephan of Montana Creek, *compiled by James Kari, with an excerpt by Russell Annabel* 195

9 Chulitna River **201**
‡Names for Denali in Alaska Native Languages and the Denali Name Change of 2015 *by James Kari* 211

10 Upper Susitna River **215**
A Trip from Tyone Village to Knik in 1912, *by Jim Tyone* 223
‡Recent Advances in Ethnogeographic Research Methods, *by James Kari* 231

11 Talkeetna River **235**
Ch'anqet' and the Mountain People, *by Shem Pete* 240
John Shaginoff 257

12 Little Susitna River **259**
No Room in the Homeland...Willow's First Citizen Looks for Home, *by James Kari and Priscilla Russell* 264
Being With Shem Pete, *by Priscilla Russell* 265

13 Western Knik Arm **271**
Knik Archaeological Excavations, *by Fran Seager-Boss* 281

14 Matanuska River **289**
Basdut—Old Man Ezi, *told in Dena'ina by Shem Pete, translated by Billy Pete* 293
Chief Ezi, *by Alberta Stephan* 295
The Chickaloon Ahtna Country, *by Katie Wade and the Chickaloon Village Traditional Council* 298

15 Eastern Knik Arm and the Anchorage area **313**
Dach' Idlughet Hyighiyih—How Eklutna Got Its Name, *by Shem Pete* 326
Early Days in Anchorage, *by Shem Pete and Sava Stephan* 335

16 Turnagain Arm and Point Possession **343**
Captain Cook's Arrival in Cook Inlet in 1778, *by James Kari* 345
Nutul'iy ch'u Tutl'uh—Fire Island and Turnagain Arm, *by Shem Pete* 348
Unhsah Tahna'ina—The First Underwater People, *by Fedosia Sacaloff* 357

2003 BIBLIOGRAPHY 358
‡2016 BIBLIOGRAPHY 367
GEOGRAPHIC NAMES INDEX 370
PERSONAL NAMES INDEX 379
SUBJECT INDEX 386

List of Maps and Tables

Tables

Table 1	The Dena'ina sound system	xx
Table 2	The Ahtna sound system	xx
Table 3	Discrepancies in orthographies for three Athabascan languages in *Shem Pete's Alaska*	xxi
Table 4	Upper Inlet Dena'ina **Qeshqa** (Chiefs)	26
Table 5	Upper Inlet Dena'ina and Some Neighboring Bands	28
Table 6	The cartography of Upper Cook Inlet relevant to Dena'ina place names reconstruction	33
Table 7	Summary of the place names inventory in *Shem Pete's Alaska*	37
Table 8	Toponymic generic terms in Dena'ina and Ahtna	38
Table 9	Semantic analysis of place names in *Shem Pete's Alaska*	40
Table 10	Place names on the 1839 Wrangell map (eastern portion)	87
Table 11	Dena'ina terms for songs and dances	126
‡Table 12	Diachronically significant Dene place names south and west of the Alaska Range	145
Table 13	Shem Pete's family on the 1920 census for Susitna Station	171
Table 14	Athabascan names for Denali/Mt. McKinley	211
‡Table 15	Summary of thirteen routes by Jake Tansy and nine by Jim Tyone	232

Maps

Map 1	Chapter guide to *Shem Pete's Alaska* and major Dena'ina place names in Upper Cook Inlet, *by Matt Ganley and James Kari*	front of book
Map 2	The Dena'ina language area showing dialects and surrounding languages, *by Matt Ganley and James Kari*	392–393
Map 3	Oblique landform map of Alaska with the Dena'ina language area, from Alpha et al. 1988	11
Map 4	Cook Inlet Basin and the Dena'ina Language area in relief, *by Matt Ganley*	11
‡Map 5	Distribution of Na-Dene languages, *by James Kari*	12
Map 6	Detail from the 1884 Petroff map: Upper Cook Inlet	19
‡Map 7	Upper Inlet Dena'ina regional and local band names, *by James Kari*	29
Map 8	Shem Pete's lifetime travels, *by Karen Pearson*	30
Map 9	Hydronymic districts in Northern Athabascan languages, *by Dixon Jones*	39
Map 10	Detail from 1940 Kroll's map of Alaska: Upper Cook Inlet	44
Map 11	Western Cook Inlet (Chapter 1 Dena'ina place names map), *by Matt Ganley*	48
Map 12	Two USGS quad maps with names for **K'idazq'eni Łi'a**	53
Map 13	Inset map of Tyonek area (Dena'ina place names map), *by Matt Ganley*	57
Map 14	Detail from the1794 Vancouver map of Cook Inlet	63
Map 15	Detail from the 1911 Brooks map: Upper Cook Inlet	73
Map 16	Lower Susitna River (Chapter 2 Dena'ina place names map), *by Matt Ganley*	80
Map 17	Wrangell map of 1839 (eastern portion)	86
Map 18	Fish Creek (Chapter 3 Dena'ina place names map), *by Matt Ganley*	98
Map 19	Alexander Creek (Chapter 4 Dena'ina place names map), *by Matt Ganley*	108
Map 20	Detail from the Eldridge and Muldrow map of 1898: Lower Susitna River	111
Map 21	Lower Yentna River (Chapter 5 Dena'ina place names map), *by Matt Ganley*	118
Map 22	Detail from the 1899 Herron map: Tyonek to Kichatna River	120
Map 23	Skwentna River (Chapter 6 Dena'ina place names map), *by Matt Ganley*	130
Map 24	Detail from the 1898 Spurr map: Skwentna River to South Fork of Kuskokwim River	132
Map 25	Aboriginal band distributions for the Upper Kuskokwim–Kantishna River, *by Edward Hosley*	144
‡Map 26	Selected Upper Kuskokwim and Dena'ina names west of the range and in Cook Inlet Basin, *by James Kari*	147
Map 27	Upper Yentna River (Chapter 7 Dena'ina place names map), *by Matt Ganley*	148
Map 28	Map of the Hewitt Lake site, *by Greg Dixon*	152
Map 29	Detail from the 1899 Herron Map: Kichatna River to Dillinger River	155
Map 30	Detail from the 1910a Sleem Map: Iditarod Trail and Peters Hills	157
Map 31	Detail from the 1995 Kroll map: McKliskan	158
Map 32	Detail from the 1906 Herning map: Upper Yentna River	161
Map 33	Middle Susitna. River (Chapter 8 Dena'ina place names map), *by Matt Ganley*	172
Map 34	Inset map: Kroto Creek settlements and place names *(base names map by Dan Foster)*	176
Map 35	Detail from the 1900 Meiklejohn Map: Kroto Creek to Talkeetna	193

Map 36 Chulitna River (Chapter 9 Dena'ina place names map), *by Matt Ganley* 200
Map 37 Detail from the 1916 Alaska Engineering Commission map: K'esugi Ridge 203
Map 38 Detail from the 1910a Sleem Map: Peters Hills and Chulitna River 204
Map 39 Detail from the Eldridge and Muldrow map of 1898: Talkeetna to Broad Pass 209
Map 40 Athabascan names for Denali/Mt. McKinley, *by James Kari* 212
Map 41 Upper Susitna River (Chapter 10 Dena'ina place names map), *by Matt Ganley* 215
Map 42 The Dickey sketch map of 1896 217
Map 43 Jim Tyone's 1912 travel route: Tyone Village to Knik 225
Map 44 The 1904 Moffit sketch map with *SPA* feature numbers 231
‡Map 45 Comparison of two sets of travel routes: thirteen by Jake Tansy and nine by Jim Tyone 233
Map 46 Talkeetna River (Chapter 11 Dena'ina place names map), *by Matt Ganley* 234
Map 47 Detail from the 1900 Meiklejohn Map: Talkeetna River and Chickaloon River 255
Map 48 Little Susitna River (Chapter 12 Dena'ina place names map), *by Matt Ganley* 258
Map 49 Detail from 1906 Herning map: Lower Susitna River to Knik Arm 260
Map 50 Detail from 1910b Sleem map of Willow Creek Mining District: Knik Arm 268
Map 51 Western Knik Arm (Chapter 13 Dena'ina place names map), *by Matt Ganley* 270
Map 52 Detail from the 1899 Johnston and Herning Map: Knik Arm and lower Susitna River 275
Map 53 Old Knik in 1912 as drawn by Stanley Herning 283
Map 54 Detail from Davidson 1915 cadastral map of Cottonwood Creek area 286
Map 55 Matanuska River (Chapter 14 Dena'ina place names map), *by Matt Ganley* 289
Map 56 Detail from the 1900 Meiklejohn Map: Matanuska River 291
Map 57 Detail from the Mendenhall map of 1898: Matanuska River 296
‡Map 58 Four Dena'ina/Ahtna-origin names on Waring 1936 305
Map 59 Detail from the 1906 Herning map: Matanuska River 306
Map 60 1885 Ahtna Sketch map annotated by Henry T. Allen 310
Map 61 Eastern Knik Arm and Anchorage area (Chapter 15 Dena'ina place names map, *by Matt Ganley*) 313
Map 62 Detail from the Mendenhall map of 1898: Eagle River 329
Map 63 Detail from the 1910a Sleem map: Anchorage area and Turnagain Arm 340
Map 64 Turnagain Arm (Chapter 16 Dena'ina place names map), *by Matt Ganley* 343
Map 65 The 1778 chart of Cooks River, *by James Cook* 345
Map 66 Detail from the 1884 Petroff map: Middle Cook Inlet 355

FIGURE 2

Urban Anchorage offers strikingly beautiful views of Cook Inlet Basin. A goal of this book is to make people aware of the Dena'ina place names that surround us so that the names can be learned. In photo captions we will mention Dena'ina place names in **boldface** and the feature number [chapter.number] of places in the photograph.

A view from the hillside above Anchorage to the north showing **Nuti** (13.1) Knik Arm, and the profile of the high mountains of the Alaska Range. **Dghelay Ka'a** (7.51) Denali is about 140 miles to the north of the Anchorage area.

PHOTO BY BOB BUTTERFIELD, COURTESY OF NATIONAL PARK SERVICE

Foreword

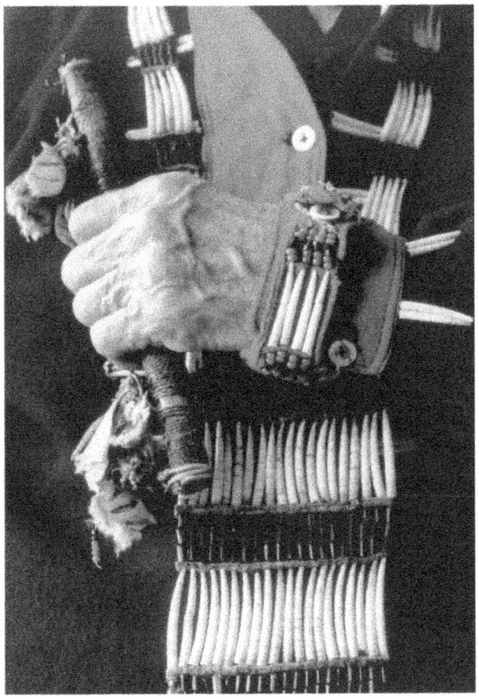

FIGURE 3
This photo of Shem Pete with his chief's regalia was taken on "Shem Pete Day," sponsored by Cook Inlet Region Inc. on October 17, 1985. This photograph was used on a poster for CIRI's fourteenth annual meeting in 1987 and on the cover of the first edition of this book.
PHOTO BY KATHY KIEFER

This volume was an instant classic when it was first published in 1987. Shem Pete's experience and wisdom as an elder of the Dena'ina Athabascan Indians shine through this work like the sun—as do the skill and devotion of James Kari, James Fall, and the other Dena'ina and Anglo-American people who contributed to making the book a reality.

I don't know of any other book like this one. It is organized as an ethnogeography: an account, in both Dena'ina and English, of all the places that Shem Pete had visited in his native land, the Upper Cook Inlet country. We learn the history of each place, who lived there, and what the fishing was like. But this book is even more than an encyclopedia of Dena'ina geography: integrated with that information, we are also given stories, songs, maps, pictures, personal reminiscences, and all the richness of traditional Dena'ina life.

So we have a volume that offers a vivid picture of Native Alaskan culture, history, geography, and language, with added glimpses of oral literature and music. It puts us there. Furthermore, this revised edition is not just a routine update: it is a significant expansion and is even richer than the original. All Native American peoples—indeed, all traditional communities in the world—would be fortunate and proud to have this kind of record of their life and culture.

William Bright
University of Colorado, Boulder

‡*William Bright passed away on October 15, 2006. His last book was* Native American Place Names of the United States, *University of Oklahoma, 2004. Bright was noted for his contributions to knowledge about place names and their linguistic importance for California's Native tribes.*

Preface to the 2016 Edition

Shem Pete's Alaska (SPA) is a reconstructed ethnogeography of the Upper Cook Inlet dialect of the Dena'ina language area. Its format, use of sources, and methodologies are in the *ethnogeographic* research tradition that was fostered by Franz Boas (e.g., Harrington 1916, Waterman 1920, and Boas 1934; summary article: Affable and Beeler 1996). As the 2003 edition of *SPA* was going out of print, we decided to prepare a Revised Second Edition that can be reprinted in the future without further revisions.

Fall (2009) and Langdon and Leggett (2009) discuss how the previous editions of *SPA* have influenced Dena'ina scholarship and Dena'ina cultural identity. The most visible recognition of Dena'ina identity was the naming of five meeting rooms with Dena'ina place names at the Dena'ina Civic and Convention Center that opened in 2008 in downtown Anchorage. Since 2003 Dena'ina place names have appeared on signs in Chugach State Park, in Denali State Park, in Municipality of Anchorage parks, along several Anchorage trails and viewpoints, and on the University of Alaska Anchorage campus. The CIRI corporate website displays Dena'ina village names, and CIRI's Tikahtnu Shopping Center showcases the Dena'ina place name for Cook Inlet. In 2009–2010, KNBA radio produced a program called "Dena'ina Lifeways" with twenty-six short radio segments that featured narrative segments by Shem Pete, Billy Pete, Peter Kalifornsky, and Fedosia Sacaloff, many of which appeared in the 2003 book. The website about Southcentral Alaska history by Coleen Mielke has made extensive use of the book (Mielke 2000). In 2015 the first chapter of Charles Wohlforth's official book for the city of Anchorage's centennial was titled "Shem Pete: a place called *Dgheyay Kaq'*."

The 2013–2014 exhibition and book *Dena'inaq' Huch'ulyeshi: The Dena'ina Way of Living* at the Anchorage Museum was a landmark event for Dena'ina cultural revitalization (Jones, Fall, and Leggett 2013). Dena'ina language and anecdotes from the 2003 *SPA* were prominent throughout. The seven-year process to develop the exhibition and catalog brought together an energized group of Dena'ina who planned the informative educational exhibit that was enthusiastically explored by young and old.

The 2016 edition has these features:

- Twenty-eight place name entries have been added; this edition has 1,002 numbered features.
- All place name entries were reviewed. Over one hundred name entries were revised: a few spellings or word divisions were changed; some variant names were added; various locations were corrected; all literal translations were reviewed; the sixteen chapter maps were reviewed and modified as needed. Some new conventions and symbols are added. Revisions to the name entries are marked with ‡.
- Numerous place name annotations have been added citing current scholarship on Dena'ina, Ahtna, and Upper Kuskokwim language, ethnography, and archaeology. New information is marked with ‡.
- Parts of the introduction and other articles have been rewritten for clarification, to cite recent sources, and to present updated terminology.
- Two revised articles are "Prehistory of the Greater Upper Cook Inlet Region" and "Names for Denali in Alaska Native Languages and the Denali Name Change of 2015."
- Two new articles replace two from the 2003 edition: "Introducing the Proto-Dene *Lex Loci* with selected Dene Place Names South and West of the Alaska Range"* and "Recent Advances in Ethnogeographic Research Methods."
- Sixteen new photographs and five maps have been added or substituted for figures in the 2003 edition. Many figures have expanded captions.
- Cross-references to feature names, maps, and figures are much more detailed.
- New references are presented in a 2016 Bibliography
- The three indexes have been updated.

In sum, the 2016 edition has a wide range of new and revised information as well as indexing and cross-referencing features that will enhance the book's utility for research or as a field guide.

Our friend and mentor Shem Pete continues to inspire us.

---

* The theory Kari calls the "Proto-Dene *Lex Loci*" (PDLL or 'word/law of location') is based upon historical linguistic inferences from ethnogeographic data from contiguous Alaska Dene languages. While the PDLL requires a book-length presentation, the main article on pp. 144–147 is adapted to *SPA*'s atlas format with cross-references to various topics, place names and figures.

Preface to the 2003 Edition

Shem Pete (1896–89), the colorful and brilliant raconteur, was the foremost Dena'ina cultural broker of his time. The wide appeal of the first edition of *Shem Pete's Alaska* can be attributed to Shem's enduring influence, and to the book's formula: a survey of the landscape of Upper Cook Inlet through Dena'ina place names blended with comments by Shem Pete and other experts as well as citations from the early historic documents about Dena'ina life in Upper Cook Inlet.

Although the 1987 edition of *Shem Pete's Alaska* went out of print by 1988, the book has been the basic reference work and field guide on the Dena'ina people and territory of Upper Cook Inlet. The impact of the first edition is seen in the many references to it in Alaskana books and in the press, in the archaeological survey work in Upper Inlet that was prompted by the names and annotations in the first edition, and by the Dena'ina place names that have appeared in guide books, brochures, and maps, as well as on signs in several state parks and in Denali National Park and Preserve.[1] Hikers, snow machiners, and tour guides have used the book on outings. Many people have memorized and learned to pronounce sets of place names, and a few persons have named homesteads, businesses, non-profit groups, and websites from names and words in *Shem Pete's Alaska.*

Technically, *Shem Pete's Alaska* is an annotated and mapped ethnogeography of traditional Dena'ina place names. The place names in the book are a *reconstructed composite place name network* from the vantage points of the life experiences of Shem Pete and other Dena'ina and Ahtna speakers. Our goals for the second edition have been to review all of the primary and secondary sources, to update the Dena'ina place name inventory, to add more place annotations and photographs, to compare and analyze the early historic maps of Upper Cook Inlet, and to draft new place name maps. We examined our own notes from the 1970s and 80s and the Upper Inlet Dena'ina audio tape collection (Kari and Fall 1990) for additional Dena'ina place names, refinements in locations, and comments on Dena'ina land use and important events. Sava Stephan has been the main source on technical aspects of Dena'ina transcription and translation.

The second edition presents names for 974 places in the same sixteen-chapter organization. We have added 253 Dena'ina, Ahtna, or Upper Kuskokwim named places, and we have revised the locations, spellings, or translations for more than 75 places. We have included all of the articles and stories from the first edition, and we have revised the introduction and added fourteen stories or articles, including two epic Dena'ina stories by Shem Pete. We reviewed and refined many locations by traveling in the Upper Inlet and in the course of developing the digital shaded relief place name maps by Matt Ganley.

The following are the key features of the research for the second edition: A) This is a long-term research program spanning more than twenty years. The materials for the book have been revisited after fifteen years. B) The place names data have been consolidated and analyzed in conjunction with linguistic work on the Dena'ina and Ahtna languages. C) Locations of places have been critically reviewed, and the mapping has been developed through several stages. D) Annotations for places are based upon the overall ethnographic record for the Dena'ina, including historic sources and folkloristic materials (oral interviews and transcribed narratives). Our research methods and techniques are discussed in detail on pp. 41–44.[2]

We noted in the introduction to the first edition that documentation of Upper Inlet Dena'ina place names is incomplete. This continues to be the case, especially if we compare the Upper Inlet Dena'ina record with some unpublished Athabascan ethnogeographic materials in other parts of Alaska. An increase of more than 25 percent in the number of named places and the addition of the attractive place name maps have resulted in a much more comprehensive and authoritative record of Dena'ina presence in the Upper Cook Inlet country. The materials from *Shem Pete's Alaska* provide context for many of the central issues in contemporary Alaska, and it is our hope that the book will reach a wide audience.

1. For example, the Matanuska-Susitna borough recently produced a poster for Alaska Historic Preservation Week that featured place names from the first edition (Petal 2002).

2. Afable and Beeler (1996) is a review article on place names research in the Native American languages of North America, and it is useful to make a few comparisons between the materials in *Shem Pete's Alaska* and works of a similar nature. Two publications somewhat like this book in breadth and format are Harrington's *Ethnogeography of the Tewa Indians* (1916) and Waterman's *Yurok Geography* (1920). Two major research efforts on Native place names in Alaska are Jetté's (1910) unpublished work on Koyukon names and Bergsland's (1959, 1994:587–653) thorough compilation of Aleut names. Since the 1970s there has been a fair amount of ethnogeographic research in Alaska Native languages; however, much of this work is unpublished or is in the "grey literature" often with unconsolidated data and ad hoc cartography. The first and second editions of *Shem Pete's Alaska* are the only Alaskan publications that combine Native language place name research with mapping and extensive annotations.

Introduction to the 1987 Edition

This book is about the territory of the Dena'ina (Tanaina) Athabascans of the Upper Cook Inlet region of Alaska based upon interviews with Dena'ina people who know it well. In 1986 there remain about twenty-five speakers of the Upper Inlet dialect of the Dena'ina language. Most of them are over sixty. The foremost expert on the traditional Dena'ina of Upper Cook Inlet is Shem Pete, himself Dena'ina, who was born at **Yusdishlaq',** near Susitna Station, in about 1896.

Shem is one of the most versatile Native storytellers and historians in late twentieth-century Alaska. Since 1974 he has worked with James Kari of the Alaska Native Language Center at the University of Alaska recording many aspects of Dena'ina language and culture. Since 1978 Shem has also collaborated with James A. Fall of the Alaska Department of Fish and Game, Subsistence Division, recording Upper Cook Inlet Dena'ina ethnohistory and land use. Shem has tape-recorded more than sixty-five hours of narrative and music. His published stories (Pete 1975, 1977, 1980a, 1980b) showcase his rare talent. However, only about one-third of Shem's tape-recorded material has yet been transcribed and translated.

This book contains an introductory section followed by sixteen chapters grouped by stream drainage in which 711 places and about 720 Native place names in the upper Cook Inlet region are listed, mapped, and annotated (see Map 1). These names, recorded by Kari and Fall between 1974 and 1986, were provided by thirty-six Dena'ina and Ahtna speakers from these areas. Included with the place names are comments about the places by Kari and Fall from notes, recordings, and published and unpublished secondary sources. Portions of this material have appeared elsewhere (Kari 1977a, 1977b, 1978b, 1982a, 1982b; Kari and Kari 1982; Fall 1981, 1987). For additional perspective there are also several essays, vignettes, maps, and photographs illustrating Dena'ina history and culture, and several stories and songs by Shem Pete and others.

The editors have made considerable effort to recover place names in all areas that Dena'ina bands formerly used. However, there are many lost Native place names in areas such as the Knik River valley, the Talkeetna Mountains, and the Chulitna River. Thus, the comments and annotations about the places are not complete. There is much more that can and should be said about Dena'ina history and land use. Nevertheless, the names and commentary presented here convey important information about the traditional economy, population centers, transportation, and beliefs of the Dena'ina.

Because the Dena'ina and other Alaska Native peoples kept no written records, oral traditions in the form of stories, songs, and place names, for example, were a major source of knowledge and instruction for the young and old alike. Passed from one generation to the next, these traditions contained accumulated Dena'ina knowledge of the world around them. As this book demonstrates, place names and the stories associated with geographic features are fine examples of the rich and varied Dena'ina oral heritage. Shem Pete and the other contributors to this book are among the last people who convey the wisdom of the oral tradition. The depth and breadth of their understanding of their traditional territory illustrate the remarkable memories of these Dena'ina elders. That Shem and others remember so much also evidences the former vigor of Upper Inlet Dena'ina culture.

Here, in the south-facing basin beneath the tallest mountains in North America, the Dena'ina can demonstrate that they have used virtually all lakes with good fisheries, all major stream basins, all of the more accessible passes through the Alaska Range, and most of the foothills and ridges at the base of the Central Alaska Range and the western slopes of the Talkeetna Mountains. The detailed texture of this ethnogeography is of special significance now that most of the described territory is no longer being used by Dena'ina people. Because more than half of Alaska's growing population lives in the region surveyed in this book, it is certain that the facts and lore presented herein will remain important to future generations of Alaskans.

Acknowledgments

We present this book with heartfelt gratitude to Shem Pete and to the forty-five other Dena'ina, Ahtna, and Upper Kuskokwim people who contributed information on the geography of Upper Cook Inlet. For the first edition we are especially indebted to Shem Pete, Billy Pete, Katherine Nicolie, Johnny Shaginoff, and Mike Alex, all of whom have passed away, for the time they spent with us describing the country that they knew.

For the second edition we give special thanks to Sava Stephan for his many contributions and for his patient guidance with Dena'ina translation and transcription.

For the first edition we also thank Lydia Hays, of The CIRI Foundation, who was instrumental in getting this project started. We also appreciate the work by Kathy Kiefer and others at Cook Inlet Region, Inc., and by Lorraine Basnar Elder of Alaska Native Language Center. Thanks also go to ethnomusicologist, the late Thomas F. Johnston of the University of Alaska Fairbanks, for his musical transcriptions. We remain indebted to Priscilla Russell for facilitating the work with Shem and for the use of her research materials and photographs. For the second edition thanks go to Matt Ganley for his careful work on the digital cartography; to Richard Veazey of UAF Rasmuson Library for his photographic work; to Jeff Davis for his help with the extensive writings of Russell Annabel; to the Chickaloon Village Traditional Council for their help in typing up several recorded narratives and for permission to use a selection of photographs; to Dixon Jones of UAF Rasmuson Library for book design and layout; and to Pam Odom, 'Nanne Myers, and Jennifer Collier of the University of Alaska Press for editorial suggestions and encouragement.

In addition to the many Dena'ina people who contributed to this book, Jim Fall wishes to thank the following for their contributions or general encouragement: Ron Stanek, Dan Foster, Bill Simeone, Nancy Yaw Davis, J. Arthur and Emily Fall, Catharine McClellan, Glenn Bacon, T. Weber Greiser, Doug Reger, Bill Workman, Karen Wood Workman, and Greg Dixon. We also thank the following persons for their contributions and help: Isaac Stephan, Leo Stephan, Alberta Stephan, Katie Wade, Lillian Theodore, Betty Gilcrist, Tom Taylor, Fran Seager-Boss, Mark Stasik, John Ritter, Alan Boraas, Dianne Gudgel-Holmes, Chuck Holmes, Hollis Twitchell, Katherine Arndt, Rose Speranza, A. J. McClanahan, Bill Schneider, Roberta Sheldon, Lydia Black, Walter Van Horn, Fred Hirschmann, Randi Hirschmann, Bradford Washburn, Mike Krauss, Tom Alton, Keith Basso, William Bright, and Tom Thornton.

Jim Kari gives special thanks to Adeline Kari and her children Princess, Evon, Odin, and Hassan for their encouragement and support.

We acknowledge with thanks a grant for work on the first edition to Cook Inlet Region, Inc., from the State of Alaska, Department of Community and Regional Affairs during 1985–1986. Between 1974 and 1986 the Alaska Native Language Center, University of Alaska, Fairbanks, supported much of Kari's work on this material. A Vilas Graduate Fellowship from the University of Wisconsin-Madison partially supported Fall's work with Shem Pete, Billy Pete, and other Dena'ina in 1978 and 1979. The Division of Subsistence, Alaska Department of Fish and Game, conducted research during 1980–1984 that provided information about historic and contemporary uses of places in the Tyonek area. A grant from the Alaska Humanities Forum entitled "Upper Cook Inlet Den'aina Oral Traditions," supported Jim Fall's work with Shem Pete, Billy Pete, and Katherine Nicolie in 1987–1990. A contract from Denali National Park and Preserve, "Native Place Name Mapping in Denali National Park and Preserve," sponsored Kari's work with Sava Stephan in 1998–1999. Research sponsored by the U.S. Fish and Wildlife Service in 2000–2001 advanced our knowledge of western Ahtna geography. Grants from The CIRI Foundation in 2001 contributed to the preparation of the second edition.

‡2016 Acknowledgments. We wish to thank Amy Simpson, Krista West, and James Englehardt at the University of Alaska Press, Larry Kaplan at ANLC, and UAF Provost Susan Heinrichs for support for the 2016 edition of *SPA*. We have truly enjoyed working with UAF graphic designer Dixon Jones on both the 2003 and 2016 editions. We wish to recognize Aaron Leggett for his contributions to Dena'ina studies and his help with this edition. Isaac Stephan helped us with photo and location identifications. We thank Coleen Mielke for sharing her important historical research with us. Work on Ahtna in 2012 and 2013 benefitted from Ahtna language expertise by Fred Ewan, Charlie Hubbard, Andy Tyone, and Bill Simeone. Work on Upper Kuskokwim and the Miska Deaphon texts in 2014–2015 was assisted by Betty Petruska, Steve Nickolai Sr., Nick Alexia, Teresa Hanson and Ray Collins. We thank Alan Boraas, Brian Wygal, Katherine Krasinski, Ben Potter, Monty Rogers, and Gerad M. Smith for summaries of recent archaeological work. Kari also recognizes Gerad M. Smith for his assistance with GIS mapping and database formats for place names in several Dene languages. We also thank members of the Knik Tribal Council, the Native Village of Eklutna, the Native Village of Tyonek, and Chickaloon Village Traditional Council for their continuing interest and encouragement.

Terminology and Format

Following the nine-part introduction, the book is divided into sixteen chapters, each of which covers a portion of the Upper Cook Inlet Dena'ina dialect area. Map 1, at the front of the book, is an index map of the sixteen chapter-areas in Upper Cook Inlet. In each chapter numbering begins with 1 at the downstream section of each area and proceeds upstream. Maps with each chapter are keyed to the numbers. The features from the first edition retain the same numbers. Features added to the second edition have been given ascending numbers and are noted by the symbol §. The persons who were the sources of the names and annotations for each area are noted at the beginning of each chapter.

Here are two examples of entries for place names from chapters 1 and 2:

1.39 K'enq'a Bena • 'Fishing Hole Lake'
Congahbuna Lake, locally "Peter's Lake" or "Bird's Lake"

The FEATURE NUMBER and DENA'INA PLACE NAME in the entry heading are in **boldface**. The LITERAL TRANSLATION of the name is in plain roman type within single quotation marks. The LOCATION OR OFFICIAL MAP NAME of the place is in *italic type.*

This lake has a *Dena'ina-origin name* (Congahbuna) as well as two *locally used unofficial names,* that are shown within quotation marks "Peter's Lake" or "Bird's Lake."

It is helpful to keep distinctions in mind between *a)* true Dena'ina place names as reported by Dena'ina speakers; *b)* official place names on file with USGS (which can derive from different languages such as English, Russian, Dena'ina, or other Native languages); and *c)* locally used names, which are usually English names and which do not appear on USGS maps. Frequently there are Dena'ina names for places that have no official or locally used names and for these we give a description of the place's location. The location and mapping of many places is approximate. Most of the principal consultants had difficulty reading maps. If a place could not be located on a map, its number is given in parentheses.

2.3 Susni Kaq' • 'Sand Island Mouth'
Susitna Delta area, including Big Island and the west channel of the lower Susitna
Shem Pete: "«They say that all the ducks lay their eggs at **Susni Kaq'** as far up as **Qałnigi Denuch'dnel'usht**. They have lots of beluga and hooligan there. They put up lots of fish too. There were many smokehouses. There were many dry spruce with limbs [used for drying fish]». "They didn't have **nichił**, they just dry fish there. Hundred of them. Smokehouses right along here to toward the mouth of Alexander Creek, over a four-mile area [on the west channel]."

In his epic biography of Chief Diqelas Tukda of Alexander Creek, Shem Pete describes how the chief died at **Susni Kaq'** in June of 1906, just as the beluga were running (Pete 1977).

Comments about a place may follow an entry's heading. The comments are preceded by the author's or speaker's name. Comments within both double quotation marks and European quotation marks (*guillemets* "« »") were made in Dena'ina and have been translated (e.g., "«They say that all the ducks…»" above). Those within only double quotation marks ("…") were made in English (e.g., "They didn't have **nichił**…" above). Statements not enclosed in any quotation marks are by the editors. The term **nichił** frequently appears in the annotations. A **nichił** is a traditional Dena'ina winter house consisting of a log frame covered with bark, with the floor of the structure dug down into the ground a few feet. The presence of **nichił** indicates habitation of an area in the winter. See Fig. 15.

‡For this edition literal translations have been reviewed. Many have been revised.

Two symbols used in 2016 literal translations are:

- Ω (omega) morphemes in names with Dene structure that are opaque or unclear in meaning; e.g., see 6.42, p. 142.
- ∞ (infinity) for what may be substrate names from a previous language; see 6.2 and 16.18 and Table 12.

Symbols, Abbreviations, Common Dena'ina Words

Throughout the Book

‡	new names, additions, or revisions in the 2016 edition.
§	new or revised names in the 2003 edition
« »	sentence translated from Dena'ina
[..]	comment inserted by editors
(1.33)	numbers in parentheses are features that could not be located or mapped
SPA	*Shem Pete's Alaska*
"Kanchee Point"	name in quotes, an unofficial place name or locally used name
[**Tuk'ebeq'tnu ?**]	name in brackets has a reconstructed spelling, and was not re-elicited
"Shuna"	‡name cited as in its source

In Dena'ina Language Stories

¶	paragraph break (in Dena'ina texts)
italic type	English translation of a Dena'ina sentence

Frequently Used Dena'ina Words

qeshqa	headman, band leader
nichił	Dena'ina winter house
tsukdu	a story, legendary or non-fiction

Dena'ina Dialect Abbreviations

U	Upper Inlet
O	Outer Inlet
Il	Iliamna
I	Inland

‡Language Abbreviations

A	Ahtna
Ath	Athabascan
DY	Dene-Yeniseian
K	Koyukon
PA, PD	Proto-Athabascan or Proto-Dene
PDLL	Proto-Dene *Lex Loci* (theory abbrev.) See other PDLL symbols on p. 144
Tc	Tanacross
UK	Upper Kuskokwim
UT	Upper Tanana

Symbols on Maps

) (	mountain pass
— —	linear feature, ridge
❖	former Dena'ina settlements or sites
◆	contemporary Dena'ina settlements
❑	other contemporary settlements
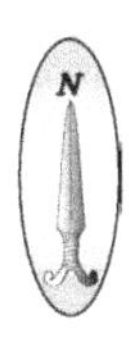	north symbol, an iron dagger with fluted hand guards, called **tl'usts'eghi** in Dena'ina, was a trade item in Cook Inlet in the nineteenth century. Graphic by Matt Ganley.

Cross-Reference Policies

a. Dena'ina place names and places are referred to by the Dena'ina name in bold, the chapter and feature number, e.g., "see **K'esugi** (9.7, K'esugi Ridge)."

b. Maps are referred to by map number, e.g., "see Map 15."

c. Photos and other illustrations are referred to by figure number, e.g., "see Fig. 11."

d. Page specific citations, e.g., "see pp. 33–34."

e. References to the color plates in the center of the book are by plate number: "see Plate 9."

‡f. On the first page of each chapter (e.g., Chap. 1, p. 49) is a summary of additions and revisions to the chapter in 2003 and in 2016.

TABLE 1. THE DENA'INA SOUND SYSTEM ‡Also see Kari 2007:xxiii-xix

Upper Inlet dialect

Consonants

MANNER OF ARTICULATION	labial	alveolar	lateral	alveo-palatal	palatal	front velar	back velar	glottal
				PLACE OF ARTICULATION				
Stops								
plain	**b**	**d**	**dl**	**dz**	**(j)**	**g**	**gg**	**'**
aspirated		**t**	**tl**	**ts**	**(ch)**	**k**	**q**	
glottalized		**t'**	**tl'**	**ts'**	**(ch')**	**k'**	**q'**	
Fricatives								
voiced			**l**	**z**	**(zh)**	**(ŷ)**	**gh**	
voiceless			**ł**	**s**	**(sh)**	**(x)**	**h**	**hh**
Nasals and glides	**m**	**n**			**y**			

Vowels

long	**i a u**
short	**e**

TABLE 2. THE AHTNA SOUND SYSTEM

Upper Inlet dialect

Consonants

MANNER OF ARTICULATION	labial	alveolar	lateral	alveo-palatal	front velar	back velar	glottal
				PLACE OF ARTICULATION			
Stops							
plain	**b**	**d**	**dl**	**dz**	**g**	**gg**	**'**
aspirated		**t**	**tl**	**ts**	**c**	**k**	
glottalized		**t'**	**tl'**	**ts'**	**c'**	**k'**	
Fricatives							
voiced			**l**	**z**	**y**	**gh**	
voiceless			**ł**	**s**	**yh**	**x**	**h**
Nasals and glides	**m**	**n**			**ng**		

Vowels

	long		short	
	front	back	front	back
high	**ii**	**uu**	**i**	**u**
mid		**oo**	**e**	**o**
low	**ae**	**aa**	**a**	

The Dena'ina and Ahtna Sound Systems and Alphabets

The Dena'ina alphabet can be displayed in a chart (Table 1) that indicates how and where in the mouth the sounds are produced. Many sounds, such as the glottalized consonants which are written with a following apostrophe, have no English equivalents. Stephan (2005) is a set of Upper Inlet Dena'ina literacy exercises with a recording by Sava Stephan.

As noted on the chart in parentheses, there are several sounds that are found in the other Dena'ina dialects that are not distinct in the Upper Inlet dialect. These are: **dz** vs. **j**, **ch** vs. **ts**, **ch'** vs. **ts'**, **s** vs. **sh**. Upper Inlet speakers favor the palatal (ch, j) pronunciation. Upper Inlet also lacks the front velar fricatives, **ŷ** and **x**. We have adopted the convention for the Dena'ina language of spelling words in Upper Inlet with the sounds that are found in the other dialects.

The Ahtna language is presented extensively in *SPA*. By way of comparison, the Ahtna sound system is presented in Table 2. The main discrepancies in the two writing systems are 1) the front and back velars, where the Dena'ina **k**, **k'**, **q**, **q'**, **h** correspond to Ahtna **c**, **c'**, **k**, **k'**, and **x**, and 2) Dena'ina has a simple four vowel system, whereas Ahtna has ten vowels, five long vowels (written with double letters), and five short vowels.

Chapters 6 and 7 include several place names from the Upper Kuskokwim language that are written in the practical alphabet for that language. Table 3 summarizes the sounds in practical writing systems for these three languages which are "contradictatory," i.e., they are the same or similar sounds but have distinct symbols in these alphabets. If there were a common writing system for all the Athabascan languages, there would be a minimal number of such discrepancies. A congruent symbol is presented at the right of Table 3.

TABLE 3. DISCREPANCIES IN ORTHOGRAPHIES FOR THREE ATHABASCAN LANGUAGES IN SHEM PETE'S ALASKA

Dena'ina	*Ahtna*	*Upper Kuskokwim*	*congruent/ phonetic*
k	**c**	–	**k**
k'	**c'**	–	**k'**
q	**k**	**k**	**q**
q'	**k'**	**k'**	**q'**
h	**x**	**h**	**x**
i	**ii**	**e**	**i, ii**
e	**e**	**i**†	**e, ə**

† ‡Note that UK vowels **i** (schwa) and **e** (high front) are the opposite values of Dena'ina **i** and **e**.

A note on Upper Inlet Dena'ina stress

The suprasegmental system in Dena'ina dialects has not been studied in depth. The Upper Inlet dialect has a stress system that is somewhat distinct from the other Dena'ina dialects. Here are some place names from the book with hyphens for syllable breaks and with the primary stress marked with capital letters.

a. *One-word place names, with stress on the final syllable*
h-TAL
qu-GHUN
k'e-nu-qa-k'i-tne-TANT
tanł-TUNT
sdak'-dal-'IY
ta-K'AT

b. *One-word place names, with stress on the next-to-last syllable*
tu-QA-shi
tu-qa-SHI-tnu
tanł-TUN-tnu
h-NI-di
nu-GHIL-tnu
ben-tu-łi-k'a-LA-shi
bech'-di-DATL'-tnu
h-ni-ts'uk'-NI-lut

c. *Two-word place names, with stress on the first word the same as for the single word; and stress on the second word if one syllable or next-to-last syllable if two syllables*
tu-QA-shi KAQ'
tanł-TUN BE-na
qu-GHUN BET-nu
dghe-LAY KA-'a

FIGURE 4

Shem Pete's mother, **Balasgulya** or **K'eludghiłna** (center), stands in front of her smokehouse at Susitna Station circa 1915. The other adult women are Nayna, Mary, and Annie. **K'eludghiłna** is holding Mary's child.

PHOTO COURTESY OF ALEXANDRA ALLOWAN

Introduction

Shem Pete Ełan Shit'i

'I Am Shem Pete'

Shem Pete's[1] residence history was:

1896/1898–1934 Susitna Station and Red Shirt Lake
1934–39 Tyonek
1939–43 Anchorage
1944–78 Nancy Lake
1978–79 Willow
1979–87 Tyonek
1987–89 Anchorage

"The way I raised when I was a little kid, as far as I remember, I just going to tell you that. My own story, though. How I raised. I was raised pretty hard. Well, I born in Susitna Station. And my father was an Indian chief—used to be. And he married first. They got six kids. And he was getting pretty old and he needed help. You know, he getting old and he lose his wife. So, he married my mother. And I don't know when... and they lived together I don't know how many years, I was born. I don't even remember my father. When I was two years old he died, and my mother raised me. I remember when the oldest one—his boy, my brother—used to be chief [Chief Evan]. My father was married to some young girls before [in previous marriages]. He got six boys. I'm the last one.[2]

"My mother's name was **K'eludghiłna.** [Her name means] everything she pass 'em out. Everything, she just give it away, Billy's [Shem's son's] grandma. She give everything away just for nothing. She don't keep it. That's the way Billy is. He just like his grandma. He give everything that he got. She feeding everybody. She take care of a lot of kids, that woman.

"I was born [about] 1900. My mother raised me. And I was raised tough. Until I was two years old my mother raised me at Red Shirt Lake.[3] At Red Shirt Lake fish run from July until November month. Good easy place to get by. She raised me. She stayed with me there until I got old enough [so] I can walk around, follow my mother. She can't kill no game. She can't [go] trapping. We stay there maybe ten years. A lot of fish. I was raised on fish. I'm not ashamed of that, 'cause I was raised on fish. I like the fish yet. We don't waste nothin.' Even the fish in the stomach of big fish. We don't waste nothin' when I was a kid.

"When I was eight years old I started working in a restaurant [in Susitna Station]. I wash the dishes, peeling onions and potatoes. And I get fifty cents a day. And I would work ten hours a day, five cents an hour. I work for three years, to help my mother. Well, you know the restaurant, a big restaurant. Bread and good meat.... And that cleaned stuff, they put it in a box. Moose bones that they don't cut all the meat off of it, they put it into a box, and after I get through working, I put it on my shoulder and take it home and give it to my mother. My mother help lots of people too. And bread, a little bit dry, they put it in the big box, meat and bones. And my mother make a soup. I work there three years.

"And before I was in school, white man talking to me. My mother tell me, 'Sing!' That thing I know it. 'You tell that white man, "Sing."' Well, that white man talk to me. I said, 'Sing. Sing.' Well, that's all [I knew in English]. I talk in my own language. Those white people talking to me and I can't understand them. Well, they call me 'Shem.' They can't understand 'Sing.' They call me 'Shem' after that.[4]

"And pretty soon school started at Susitna. They took me back down to Susitna Station. [We] got a cabin, my mother and I. And I went to school. I'd never heard no

1. This sketch of Shem Pete's life was compiled by James Kari based upon two tape-recorded autobiographical narratives, one from 1976 and one from 1985, and from additional notes by James Kari, Priscilla Russell, and James Fall. The addendum for the second edition was written by James Fall and includes several other sources.

2. Shem never heard his father's Dena'ina name. He says that his father's name was simply Pete, and he was of the **K'kalayi** clan. Shem's mother, Balasgulya or **K'eludghiłna** 'Mother of One Who Passes Around Food,' was born circa 1870 and died in 1918. She was of the Nulchina or 'Sky Clan.' Consequently, Shem Pete is Nulchina too. See photo of Balasgulya on opposite page. There was some confusion over Shem's birth date. With Alaska Native Services his birth date was listed as July 14, 1900. Shem usually stated his birth date was 1898. Based on his earliest memories we think that he had been born earlier, in 1896.

3. See Chapter 3, "**Baytnidahen** and Red Shirt," for more detailed descriptions of life at Red Shirt Lake.

4. In another account of this story, Shem says that when he was little and didn't speak English, his mother told him that if white people should talk to him, he should say in Dena'ina "**Sh'in**" 'I don't know.' One day the white storekeeper told him to "Sing," (he used to sing all the time) and Shem replied "**Sh'in.**" Afterwards the storekeeper started calling him Shem. In the Old Testament, Shem is Noah's oldest son. The storekeeper was probably Jim Cleghorn, the ACC storekeeper at Susitna in the late 1890s. Shem Pete's Dena'ina name was **K'etech'ayutiłen**, which is a hunting name meaning 'One Who is Bringing It [Gun] Among Game.' Shem's baptismal name, Derenty (or Terentij), is Russian. He pronounced this *Delindin.* A lake near the Little Susitna River, Delyndia Lake (12.7), is named after Shem.

FIGURE 5

Shem Pete near **Tudli Bena** (12.12, Nancy Lake) at his winter trapping location with a rack of beaver pelts. Photo taken by Julius Kallander, Jr., in the 1950s. For many years Julius and Billy Pete were trapping partners.

PHOTO COURTESY OF FEODORIA KALLANDER PENNINGTON AND BETTY GILCRIST

white man English talk, nothing. I learned about three years, ABCs. All by myself, ABC it take me three years to learn. When I walk around in the street there, in the village, I sing a song: 'A..., B..., C..., A, B, C!' so I don't forget. I don't want to forget, so I sing that song.

"And the oldest of his [Shem's father's] kids, after he [father] die they make him chief.[5] He was pretty old and he died too, when he got old. My brothers take me up there [Rainy Pass and upper Yentna] when...I was young. And I killed a caribou. But [when] I went out there fourth trip, I got .30-30. Oh, boy, I got something! I got little cannon, I thought. And I shoot the caribou, down they go. When I used to be shooting with .22, they stagger around, and I just keep on shooting.... That time I was a man already, 14 or 15 year old. And, boy, I kill quite a few caribou. That's how we get the caribou. We need the skin in them days. They dry them up nice, and they sell them two dollars per skin. Sometimes they get one or two hundred caribou. The last time I went up there, when I got .30-30, we were nine men. We went up there.... We bring lots of caribou skin, and plenty caribou meat.... Anyway, we take our meat down to Susitna Station—caribou meat, moose meat. We put it in a cache.... And the potlatch come. One hundred skin or more they piled up in the middle. Blankets and money—oh, gee, over one thousand dollars it might be.

"But them days, them other days, why, the Natives they do their [own] ways. Now, we got the judge and marshals. They told us the way they wanted it. But the way before was the way we wanted to live in. And then the youngest, my brother,[6] not really my brother, they were my father's kids. His name was **Beq'e Nuqeydghulya Tukda** ['Father of One Who Does Not Pay Attention to Insults,' Chief Ephim]. He was a tough man. His name means 'He Make Himself Clear.' That's his name, Indian. That man was over seven feet tall, Indian. They make him chief. [That's] the last time... they had chief at Susitna. Ephim died in 1916. And they want to make me chief. But I give up. I don't want it. I told them, 'The white man's good enough now.' I just took care of the church.[7]

"There used to be a lot of people at Susitnu, at least 700, 600 Natives. And whooping cough, that one came along and it killed quite a few. Quite a few. And then measles come. Hit Susitnu. That killed quite a few. Then the third time, 1918, the flu come. That wiped them out, about

5. Chief Evan, see 5.8 and Figs. 64, 76, and 77.

6. Chief Ephim, see Fig. 53.

7. In the early 1930s Shem was the last church warden at the Russian Orthodox chapel at Susitna Station.

600 of us. When the flu hit in 1918, Susitna was a lot of people. I go back to Susitna Station [from Anchorage] to go to school. And a big flu there. First week when the flu hits there we lose thirty-six. I lose my mother the first day. Then, from there on, we lose lots of people. They just walk on the trail in Susitna Village. They fall down all over. We drag them inside to the house. Yes, we lose lot of people. It pretty near cleaned up all the Susitna people. A lot of people. We must have lost over a hundred Native. Good people. Gee whiz, we get pretty lonesome. We're only a few people left. That's three times lots of people died [on the lower Susitna River].[8]

"I got married in 1920 in Talkeetna. And I got a boy [Billy Pete]. Anyway, we stayed there [at Susitna Station] for quite a while. My mother used to tell me, 'Don't go after those girls that are coughing. Leave them T.B. girls alone.' But she [Inge, his wife] went after me pretty strong.[9]

"And anyway, we stay there [at Susitna after 1918] several years. And ... three family left. They move down to Tyonek [in 1934]. [Simeon] Chickalusion come up there [to Susitna]. He's so lonesome. Just a very few Tyonek people was there. He took us. We be eleven of us. Brought us down. Not many people down Tyonek, except for three [Susitna] girls and each girl had ten, eleven kids. Right there was thirty. Them young girls, they had the kids. There was six, seven Tyonek people left, that's all. They all the Susitna people. They grow up. And there's lots of Susitna people down Tyonek.

"He [Simeon Chickalusion] want me in Tyonek. He want to give me his daughter too. He don't want me to monkey around in Anchorage. He was a smart man. He pick us up in Susitna. He's the one who brought us to Tyonek.[10]

"In 1936 I made big money as the boss for the animals for a movie they were making in Anchorage. They had hundreds of rabbits and porcupines, some bears, and an eagle. I told them what to feed them animals and how much. I'd feed rabbits to that eagle. That bear was always hungry. We got meat from the butcher shop for it.

"I used to ... stay there [in Tyonek]. For six years I stay there. Pretty hard place to get by. No trout. No fur. Tyonek was pretty small. Not many there. And we stay here for a few years, and we lose him [Simeon Chickalusion]. Already my boys, Billy and Sava [Stephan], they do a lot of work, just like when I was a kid.[11] They work for them old peoples around there. They hunt for them. They hunt the ducks, hunt all over. Sava [Stephan] little fella. They was only six hours different. Billy born first. And six hours later, Sava born too.

"Boy, I'll tell you when we lost our boss [Simeon Chickalusion], we really thought Tyonek's no more. We don't know what to do. We're still here yet, after him. But now, I don't want [to be] chief, I told them. But they give me the chief clothes—dress, beads, feather hat, rattle. Chickalusion give me that. The last man here. He was the boss for us here in Tyonek. They give me all his clothes—beads on his clothes, feather hat, the rattle, neck beads.[12] They tell me, 'You're the last one gonna be chief for us.' I told them, 'The white people do the place. They tell us do that and do this. Not this way. Not this way ... I'm not going to be good chief. I won't go for that.' So they let me out.

"So I move away from there. I move up to Nancy Lake [in 1944]. I build a home there. I build three cabin. At this new one, I stay there. After I left, they hit the oil right in the village [Tyonek], and they want to get me back. They said they're going to build me a home. When I left, I said I'd never turn around again. I'm going to stay out. I'm going to build a home at Nancy Lake. I get by pretty good over there. Lots of fur, lots of fish. Tyonek, we can't get nothing. I stay at Nancy Lake. Over thirty years I stay there. I like that place.[13]

"I know lots of creeks and lakes, all over the hills and mountains. I know quite a few from **Yach'ditnu** [2.6] at the mouth of the Susitna River all the way up to Happy River [6.22]. I know quite a few names in that part of the country.

"I tell lots of stories. I know a lot of songs. I sing a song. Every Tuesday I teach the whole village [Tyonek]. The young generation—about ten years, twelve years old—they dance for me. And I sing. I know the old songs. Way back. One hundred or more old songs. I sing to them, the young generation, the small kids. They talk native. Before that they never talk native. They learn the English. Now they tell me 'Chada [Grandpa] come! Hey, Chada, come!' They all jump on me when I come down Tyonek. I like to dance for you people, all you ladies and gentlemen. And I dance like hell too. I pretty good.

"Well, I know lots more to say, but I think I talk too much. Cause I can't talk pretty good English neither. I like to talk my own language. Well, that's enough for a while. **Q'u dutdgheshcheł.** ['Well, I'm going to shut up now.']

---

8. Shem was one of three young men who did most of the grave digging at Susitna in the winter of 1918–1919.

9. Shem Pete's wife, Inge, was one year younger than Shem and was of the **K'kalayi** clan. Her Dena'ina name was **Tulałen**, 'The One Who Will Be.' Their son, Billy, was born in 1920. In 1922 they had a daughter, Mary. Inge died in Anchorage in May of 1925 and was buried in the Sixth Avenue cemetery. Sava Stephan recalls that his father brought him to Inge's funeral. Afterwards, in 1926, Shem had a potlatch for her in Eklutna. Shem's daughter Mary died in 1940. See also pp. 164–172, a narrative in which Inge traveled with Shem up the Yentna River in the fall of 1919.

10. Shem was the oldest of the eleven Susitna people who moved to Tyonek on May 14, 1934. Shem recalled that Simeon Chickalusion told him that he thought that Shem should be buried in Tyonek.

11. Sava Stephan of Tyonek is Shem's nephew, whom he addressed as **shgguya** 'my child.' See pp. 8–9.

12. See pp. 115–117 on Shem's dancing gear.

13. See pp. 264–265, Chapter 12, "Willow's First Citizen Looks for Home." Shem moved back to Tyonek in 1979.

FIGURE 6

Young Martha Alexan and Shem Pete singing at the Tyonek guesthouse in 1981. Shem related two sources for his first name. One is that it was reinterpreted from the English word "sing," and the other that it was reinterpreted from the Dena'ina word **sh'in** 'I don't know.'

PHOTO BY PRISCILLA RUSSELL

Addendum for the 2003 edition—The pending publication of the first edition of *SPA* was celebrated by "Shem Pete Day," culminating with a special program at the Anchorage Museum of History and Art on October 17, 1985, co-sponsored by CIRI Inc. and the Cook Inlet Historical Society. Several hundred people attended. The event was well covered by Anchorage newspapers (McKinney 1985, Fattig 1985). Many key contributors to the book attended in addition to Shem and Billy Pete, including Katherine Nicolie, Sava Stephan, Tommy Allowan, Fedora Constantine, and Peter Kalifornsky (see Fig. 10). Shem performed several Dena'ina songs and danced wearing his regalia. The Tyonek Singers and Dancers, whom Shem and Billy helped to establish, also performed.

In 1987, Shem and Billy moved from Tyonek to an apartment at the Robert Rude Housing Project in Anchorage, mostly to be closer to health care facilities. Shem continued to work with Jim Kari and Jim Fall in reviewing, translating, and annotating recorded narratives. They added additional recordings to the collection (Kari and Fall 1990). Several more of Shem's stories have been published, including "Shq'uła Tsukdu," (The "Whistler" [Hoary Marmot] Story) (Pete 2000) and "The Hunting Dog" (Pete 1989).

In June of 1989 Shem Pete was chosen as CIRI's first Shareholder of the Year by a panel of five CIRI shareholders (CIRI 1989). The *CIRI Newsletter* noted: "Shem Pete was nominated by Max Chickalusion, Sr., who described Shem as an Athabascan storyteller . . . and the oldest friend of the people of Tyonek and the Big Susitna areas. Shem is recognized for his lifelong dedication to preservation of Dena'ina history and traditions in the Cook Inlet region. . . . He is a composer, historian, traditional dancer, and geographer, recognized for his unparalleled expertise of Dena'ina places and names in the Cook Inlet region."

By the time of this award, however, it was obvious that Shem's health was failing. He was unable to attend the CIRI meeting to accept the award himself, and Billy accepted on his behalf. On July 2, 1989, Shem Pete passed away at the Alaska Native Medical Center in Anchorage. The next day, his obituary appeared on the front page of the *Anchorage Daily News* (Hulen 1989a).

The funeral took place in Tyonek on July 4. Billy Pete chose to have the "top coffin" or grave house painted blue rather than white, the usual color in Tyonek, "to stand out." Blue is also the primary color of Shem's **Nulchina** Clan.

The Village of Tyonek and CIRI sponsored a memorial potlatch for Shem Pete in Tyonek on October 7, 1989. A biography of Shem by Lydia Hays, vice president of CIRI was included in the potlatch program. This event was featured in the *Anchorage Daily News'* "We Alaskans" Sunday supplement under the title "Death of a Storyteller: Goodbye, Shem Pete" (Hulen 1989b). During the potlatch, people who knew Shem were asked to share some of their memories. The following statements are from CIRI 1990.

Bonnie McCord of Tyonek, who helped organize and run the potlatch: "We have gathered here today to memorialize Shem Pete, who died on July 2, 1989 at the age of nearly 95 years. Shem was important for us as father, friend, relative, and respected tradition bearer of our Dena'ina Athabascan ways. We share in the loss of this important person from our midst, but also realize that we each must accept the individual responsibility to carry on the Dena'ina tradition of our heritage."

Lydia L. Hays, then vice president of CIRI Inc.: "He had a strong sense of adventure and curiosity about the world. Over the years with his remarkable memory he became a rich treasure of knowledge about the Dena'ina world and values. He welcomed the world with courage and lived in it to the fullest. He is an inspiration to all who seek the rewarding journey of a proud Dena'ina man" (Hays 1989).

Jim Fall: "As I think back to the times I sat with him and learned stories and traditions, I remind myself that it would be a mistake to think that he was just talking to me during that time. And really what Shem Pete was doing was talking to all of us. And he had this day in mind when he was talking to me. And Billy will remember this quite well: when Shem ended a story, when the tape recorder was off, he would say how important that story was; that people would have an interest in that story, and that people should know that story because some day they might hear that story and they might save their lives with that story. And so, this [memorial potlatch] isn't an end at all. This is just a renewal, an acknowledgment of Shem's generosity, because that concern that he had for all of us is going to continue as we learn from him through what he's left with us."

Peter Ezi, president of Eklutna Village: "When I was very young in the Nancy Lake area, we used to come up there and trap for beaver. One of the things I haven't read in no book about Shem is that he wasn't only a friend to man. He could have chickadees land on his shoulder. Dogs: he knew how to train dogs, and, I mean, he was a nature lover.... When I go into his house, it's a house that had a welcome written all over it, and in his fish camp. I grew up admiring the person."

Paul Theodore of Knik: "It don't make no difference—any village, when people die, the first one to show up was old Shem. He'd come walk in the door. They give him tea, coffee. That's a surprising thing, you know, people respecting the dead the way he did. It don't make no difference, wintertime, summertime. He showed up. I never see too many others, the way that he show up there. Without being around, he'd know what's going on, you know. You'd never know where he'd come from and when he'd come. He just appeared the morning of the funeral. He'd show up. Show his respect. Spend a few days and go back wherever he came from. I really remember that part of him. Showing respect for people that's beyond this world."

Leo Stephan of **Niteh** and Eklutna, member of the CIRI Board: "[Shem Pete] wanted to pass on all of the history of the people here to the young people. He loved young children. He wanted them to have the history. Shem and I and also Billy went and did some prospecting. We did some trapping. We fished on Point Possession for over 30 years together. And the thing that strikes me the most and made a deep impression on me was the generosity of Shem. He was a very colorful person. He would talk to you seriously, and then he would also joke with you and sometimes you have to make the distinction whether he's serious and when he's not serious. But most of all, he was a true Athabascan."

In January of 1990 the Alaska State Legislature drafted a statement "In Memoriam, Shem Pete." The statement concludes, "He is noted for his determination to pass on what he knew to the younger generation. It was important to tell stories over and over. Lasting are his words, 'Who's going to tell the stories when I'm dead?'...His voice is quiet now, but Shem would want the story of his people to go on. Goodbye Chada."

FIGURE 7

Shem Pete, the master storyteller, visiting the University of Alaska Fairbanks in May of 1983. Shem sprinkled his narratives with provocative ideas. The first line of his epic biography of Diqelas Tukda (Pete 1977:1) is: **"Q'udi qenaga nch'uk'a hghilet,"** 'the language of the present time does not exist,' his indirect way of stating that the Dena'ina language of our times is weak in comparison to the high language of his ancestors.

PHOTO BY JAMES KARI

‡*The status of the Shem Pete story and audio collection*—The Shem Pete Collection is one of the largest and most varied collections by a major storyteller for any Alaska Native language. The original tapes and digital files of Shem and Billy Pete and Sava Stephan are at the Alaska Native Language Center/Archive at the University of Alaska Fairbanks. In 2015, for Shem Pete the ANLCA catalog has 69 recordings recorded between 1974 and 1988 (about 57 hours). The Sava Stephan Collection consists of 27 recordings made between 1994 and 2004. Our current index has about 160 narrative segments by Shem. Recent work consolidated and verified the tapes and digital files. One goal is to coordinate audio and text file names. A priority for the Shem Pete Collection is to edit and geo-reference all of his non-fiction narratives (place names, land use, ethnographic descriptions, events, biographies).

Bill Shem (Billy) Pete

Billy Shem Pete[14] was born at Susitna Station on January 18, 1920, the same day as Sava Stephan. Because Billy's and Sava's mothers were the daughters of sisters, the boys were considered brothers in the traditional Dena'ina kinship system. They were both members of the **K'kalayi** Clan. Shem Pete addressed both of them as **shgguya** ["my child"].

Although in his early years he lived mostly at Susitna Station, after the death of his mother when he was about five years old, Billy spent most summers in Anchorage with his grandmother Annie (his mother's mother), his sister Mary, and his "brother" Sava. They lived in a rented house and visited Dena'ina fish camps at **Tak'at** [15.75], **Chansh Kaq'** [15.83, the mouth of Chester Creek], and **Nuch'ishtunt** [15.91, Point Woronzof]. In an interview published by the CIRI Foundation in 1986 (McClanahan 1986:95), Billy recalled: "I been back and forth between Anchorage and Susitna ever since I was a six-month old, I guess. So, in reality, I was almost raised in Anchorage. And I was raised among the white people in Anchorage—white kids—ever since." Billy's strong bicultural and bilingual skills dated from his early experiences in Susitna Station, Tyonek, Anchorage, and other Upper Cook Inlet communities. Billy's grandmother, with whom he spoke in Dena'ina, taught him many of the traditions, history, and stories (**tsukdu**) of the Upper Inlet people.

Later Billy recalled traditional Dena'ina education: "When it would get to be evening, one old-timer would start telling stories. When he tells stories about an hour, he tell another old-timer, 'Your turn to tell story.' It went around like that." (Fattig 1985). Billy drew upon this education decades later when he helped his father recall, translate, and comment upon this vast collection of Dena'ina oral traditions. Billy moved to Tyonek with most of the Susitna Station Dena'ina in 1934. He fished at Granite Point that summer and attended school at Tyonek for three months, but then returned to the Susitna River to trap that winter. In an interview conducted by Nancy Yaw Davis in Anchorage on August 19, 1994, Billy recalled: "I went to school for three months [at Tyonek]. I was about fourteen then. And when I had cerebral hemorrhage, they gave me a reading test and everything down at ANS hospital here [in Anchorage]. And they told me I had [the equivalent of] two years college education then. That is, after I got dumb from having cerebral hemorrhage. I was self-educated. I used to take a big bunch of books. I used to trap all the time and I'd take my dictionary and go out in the woods and stay out there two or three months at a time. And when I catch enough fur, I used to go to Willow and send my furs out."

FIGURE 8

Billy Pete displaying his subsistence catch of king salmon on the beach at New Tyonek in 1984.

PHOTO BY JAMES FALL

Billy moved to Anchorage in about 1935. He worked at the Emard cannery there and also worked in canneries in Bristol Bay, where, as in many of his jobs, he was selected as a foreman. He also worked for twenty-five cents an hour as a section man for the Alaska Railroad for three seasons, and helped build the airstrip at Elmendorf Air Force Base. Also, "In World War II, why I was down to Whittier. I helped on that Whittier tunnel.... Beside that, I used to be down at Seward. I used to work on the boats all the time down at Seward for quite a little while" (McClanahan 1986:94).

In about 1944, Billy and Shem moved to Nancy Lake, where they lived in three different cabins until 1978. In

14. Based on J. Fall and J. Kari notes and also McClanahan 1986:92–96 and Fattig 1985.

the 1940s into the 1960s, Billy trapped lynx, mink, beaver, marten, and coyote around Red Shirt Lake, in the area that today is the Nancy Lake Recreation Area. He pitched his tent at the former village site of **Tanltunt** [3.18] at the lake outlet. He ran his trap line using cross-country skis rather than a dog team.

When he was about forty, while on his trap line, Billy suffered a stroke. After pulling a sled loaded with fifteen beaver pelts (the legal limit) over six miles for sixteen hours, he managed to get himself to the Alaska Railroad and flag down a train for help. He remarked, "I used to be as tough as the horses." After paying his fare, he rode in the baggage car into Anchorage and checked into the hospital. Several years later, he had a second stroke and had to learn to walk again.

Billy and Shem fished at the outlet of Red Shirt Lake, where they caught fish with a twelve-foot gill net. They caught sockeyes, cohos, and steelhead that they brought back to their Nancy Lake cabin for use over the winter.

Billy and Shem fished commercially for salmon at Point Possession from the 1940s until the mid-1970s when Billy sold his limited entry permit due to back problems. During those years, they camped at their site beginning in May. Billy fished "an outside location" with the set net staked in a sandbar and stretched out to deep water where it was secured with an anchor. A favorite story of Billy's concerned the time he and Shem caught "a blue whale" in his salmon net.

At Nancy Lake, Billy killed a moose every year, plus beavers and black bears. Billy and Shem often had some young men from Eklutna, Tyonek, or Anchorage staying with them. They'd cut wood and trap with Shem around Nancy Lake.

Right after fishing in the fall, Billy and Shem usually "just took off" to the Talkeetna Mountains, or sometimes Susitna Mountain and Beluga Mountain [4.18], for two to ten weeks. They prospected for gold, taking only "beans and flour" with them, shooting spruce grouse, ground squirrels, and porcupines, and catching trout. Billy said, "It was fun in the mountains. We'd go there just to pass the time and enjoy life." Billy recalled that they never found much gold, just a nugget once in a while.

Billy moved with his father back to Tyonek in 1979. There, he enjoyed subsistence salmon fishing and hooligan fishing. Billy helped reestablish the Tyonek Singers and Dancers. Due to Shem's failing health, Billy moved with his father back to Anchorage in 1987 to the Robert Rude Housing Project. He continued to contribute to the teaching of Dena'ina traditions and subsistence skills. For example, Billy was a "Native resource person" at the Bureau of Land Management's "Trailside Discovery Camp" (pre-school to sixth grade) at the Campbell Creek Science Center in Anchorage. He taught children how to drum, how to make snares, and told them stories. Billy worked with Jim Fall on an Alaska Humanities Forum Grant to translate and annotate the collection of Dena'ina tapes, and record new stories with Shem (Fall 1990).

Billy Pete often downplayed his Dena'ina language skills, claiming that he had to return to Tyonek as an adult to learn the language over again. Despite his modesty, Billy's bilingual skills, his self-education, and his extensive knowledge of Dena'ina culture and oral traditions combined to make him a key expert, a precise translator, and an essential partner with his father in the preservation of the Upper Cook Inlet Dena'ina culture and history.

Of particular interest to Billy were the survival skills conveyed in Dena'ina stories and oral traditions. As he explained in The CIRI Foundation interview (McClanahan 1986:95): "If I run up against it out in the woods, if it snows on me about one or two foot, I can just simply take my ax and hew out my snowshoes that they used to call "banjoes." It only takes about couple hours to build those. As long as you got a rope of some sort, you can make yourself a pair of snowshoes with just an ax. Just hew them out.... Just tie it on your foot and go home. And that's about all." One of Billy's favorite stories was "The Hunting Dog Story" (Pete 1989), in which an entire village is saved due to the foresight of the younger of two brothers, who packs a starving dog on his back in a search for food, despite the protests of his brother that it's just a waste of time and energy. The dog locates the den of a black bear, which the brothers kill and bring back to their village. Billy summarized the moral of the story as, "So you can bet your life the dog's going to save your life sometime."

After the death of his father, Billy Pete became very lonesome living in Anchorage. At the urging of Emil McCord, Sr., Billy moved back to Tyonek in September 1989 and lived in a small house on the bluff overlooking Cook Inlet. He continued to help the Tyonek Singers and Dancers to learn traditional Dena'ina songs. In August 1994, in what was perhaps his last recorded interview, Billy worked with Nancy Yaw Davis to preserve information about **Tak'at** [15.75], the site of a traditional Dena'ina fish camp in Anchorage.

Billy Pete passed away in Tyonek on June 7, 1995, where he was buried next to his father. The village sponsored his memorial potlatch on July 15, 1995.

Sava Stephan, Sr.

"Sava Stephan, Sr.,[15] now a retired commercial fishermen and trapper, was born at Susitna Station on January 18, 1920, just six hours after his cousin Bill S. Pete was born. Mr. Stephan is a shy man, but his strong interest in his Native culture and heritage becomes apparent even in a short conversation" (McClanahan 1986:102).

Sava's father was Anderson Stephan of Kroto Creek village and his mother was Inga Stephan, also from Kroto Creek village. Inga's full maiden name was Evgenia Ephim, and she was Shem Pete's wife's mother's sister's daughter. Anderson Stephan and Shem Pete were close friends. In fact, Shem and his wife, also named Inga, and Anderson and Inga were married in a double wedding in Talkeetna in 1919. Sava's mother died in1927. Shem's wife had died in 1925. After Shem and Anderson lost their wives, they often would travel together with young Billy and Sava. (See Fig. 77, with Anderson, Inga, and Sava with a group at **Bentalit,** the Lake Creek site; also see Figs. 55 and 180 for Anderson's picture.)

Sava recalls: "I don't remember when I first went out hunting. (Laughs.) I started walking with my dad when I was about five years old. I can hardly walk in snowshoes. But I been with him all the time after that since I started putting the snowshoes on. I been trapping with him all the time. Every year. I was with my dad, all the time. I didn't go to school or nothing. Because he was takin' me out trapping. I think I was trapping since I was seven years old. I was traveling with him. All that time I was out trapping with him. Until they brought us down here [to Tyonek], we started fishing. Then I quit trapping, and my dad died down here [in Tyonek], too. Since then I'm still in Tyonek, and that's all we can do—fishing. I never can go out trapping or nothing since my dad died."

On many occasions when he was a child, Sava would stay in Anchorage, usually with two older Dena'ina women who lived on lower Chester Creek.

"Our grandma **Nachikda**. I don't even remember her name, [adds later] **Hu'idilna** my real Grandma name. She stay in Anchorage when there was only one street. I can't talk because I was too young you know. I hardly remember. «We stayed in town with our grandmother [Shem's wife's mother].» I don't even remember her name «She was a Susitna person, our grandmother, I also saw our grandfather, and we stayed in Anchorage with our grandmother.» Mary Pete and Billy Pete and myself. One Fourth Avenue running, only one street. From Chester Creek all the way up to Anchorage we walk. That's far.

"We used to walk with our grandmother. «Our grandmother would walk with us and tell us stories.» She look at me and say **nq'ak'nanshtun**, "«I've been missing you.»" She wanted me to tell stories. Well I don't know how to tell stories anyway. But I talk like hell anyway."

15. Compiled by James Kari from taped interviews and notes with Sava Stephan and from McClanahan (1986:102–105).

FIGURE 9

Sava Stephan in the early 1990s.

PHOTO COURTESY OF THE MARY CONRAD CENTER

In 1934 Sava was one of eleven Sustina Station residents who moved to Tyonek at the invitation of Chief Simeon Chickalusion. "My parents was there—Anderson Stephan, my father's name. My mother's name is Inga. Used to be all my uncles is there [at Susitna Station]. 'Thirty-four, I think they move down here when everybody die off from Susitna. Move us down here and we still here yet.... There was only us left there. I think that's why they move us down here.... When I first came down here I was only twelve years old." [*sic;* Sava was fourteen years old when the Susitna people moved to Tyonek.]

In 1938 Sava married Anna Chickalusion, the daughter of Simeon and Annie Chickalusion. Their first of seven children, Sava Jr., was born on January 1, 1940. Sava's wife Anna died in 1948. Today Isaac Stephan, who resides in Anchorage, is Sava's one surviving child. Sava's father Anderson passed away in 1963.

As his many observations throughout *Shem Pete's Alaska* attest, Sava Stephan has had a remarkable career as an all-around outdoorsman, boat captain, and traveler. He is the last Dena'ina to have gone on a fall hunting trip to Rainy Pass (Chapter 6), he had trapping and traveling experience in the Kroto Creek area (Chapter 8), and after he moved to Tyonek, Sava traveled extensively with his father-in-law Simeon

FIGURE 10

Sava Stephan, Shem Pete, and Billy Pete on Shem Pete Day, Oct. 17, 1985.

PHOTO COURTESY OF THE CIRI FOUNDATION

Chickalusion and other Tyonek people throughout the middle Inlet (Chapter 1). Also whenever Sava has stayed in Anchorage he has been with the key Dena'ina people there, and he has many interesting observations on Dena'ina life in the town setting (Chapter 15 and pp. 335–337).

"Buster Ephim was married to one of those Susitna people, Nellie, and Olga, two sisters. We was with him all the time, me and Billy Pete. He was a little bit older than us. He died, I don't know when he died. We hop around with him any place he go. By rowing some time, sometime we got two kicker. We always go to Tyonek.

"Buster Ephim taught me about going across the Inlet. He taught me how to go. He make captain out of me. He teach me how. I used to go across the Inlet from Tyonek from across to Fire Island and back across to Susitna River, all the way around. And Little Susitna come in. I go up that creek. I go hunt moose around there. Sometime I pass that railroad track. I go from Anchorage to Tyonek or Anchorage to Point Possession or down to Kenai. From Point Possession I rowed all the way to Kenai one time. I row right along the beach. I bought another kicker and hook it up. All the Kenai people like me. They say, "Hello my friend." They took me around Kenai, the whole city. And I didn't spend no money."

Sava has a congenial personality. His nickname is **Duggel**, the Russian word for 'handle.' Sava explained "I used to haul that cooking utensil. They called me **Duggel** cause I used to handle them cooking utensils. Joe Nicoli, guy from Kroto Creek, named me that."

Throughout his life, Sava has been helping out the Dena'ina people. For more than thirty years Sava served as **dichuk,** or church warden, for the Orthodox Church in Tyonek. He helped to found the Tyonek Singers and Dancers. In 1990 Sava fell, injuring his spine, and for the past thirteen years he has been in nursing homes in Anchorage. He remains very active and attends many events in the Anchorage community. For more than ten years he has been the main source for technical translations with Shem Pete's complex and multi-faceted story collection. Sava also has helped on two language materials, a set of Upper Inlet Dena'ina literacy exercises (Kari and Stephan 1994) ‡and *Upper Inlet Dena'ina Language Lessons* (Stephan 2005).

With a long career as a versatile worker and as a careful listener and student of Dena'ina traditions, Sava Stephan has become in his senior years the recognized expert on the Upper Inlet Dena'ina people. He has made truly enormous contributions to Dena'ina language and culture.

‡Following the publication of the 2003 edition of *SPA*, Sava continued his major contributions to Dena'ina language and culture. In 2003 CIRI acknowledged Sava's contributions with the CIRI Shareholder of the Year award. In 2004–05 Sava participated in several Dena'ina language classes at the Alaska Native Heritage Center. Sava Stephan passed away at age 93 on June 1, 2013. He was buried in the Tyonek village cemetery, near Shem and Billy Pete.

The Dena'ina Language Area, Dena'ina Dialects and Prehistoric Migrations

by James Kari

The Dena'ina language area (Maps 2, 3, and 4) is strikingly diverse in geography. The language is in a westward leaning horseshoe-shape that is bifurcated by the Alaska Range and Cook Inlet. It is about ‡51,000 sq. miles in area.[16] West of Cook Inlet Basin on the other side of the Alaska Range, the language area has three major streams in the Kuskokwim drainage, as well as the upper Mulchatna Rriver, Lake Clark, and the northern half of Iliamna Lake. This marked diversity in geography and climate has contributed to the cultural and linguistic diversity within Dena'ina.

The geography and geology of this part of Alaska and the study area of this book, the Upper Cook Inlet, have been described in several sources (Wahrhaftig 1965, Williams 1958). Most of the Upper Cook Inlet is in the physiographic unit called the Susitna Lowland. The Susitna lowland is bordered in the north by the tall mountains of the Central Alaska Range and on the east by the Talkeetna Mountains. The small-scale orientation maps for this book are of Upper Cook Inlet, Map 1, at the front of the book, and of the Dena'ina language area and Cook Inlet Basin, Map 2, on pp. 392–393.

The Dena'ina aboriginal population, which has been estimated at 3,000 to 5,000 prior to Euro-American contact, was likely higher than that of any other Northern Athabascan language group. The Dena'ina had one of the richest resource bases in Alaska. The Dena'ina are the only Northern Athabascan people with territory on salt water, and no other Northern Athabascan people had such an abundance of land and water foods.

Language and dialect groupings and language boundaries attempt to show the best and earliest information on language affiliation, traditional land use, and boundaries. All of the Dena'ina dialects (Map 2, pp. 392–393) are mutually intelligible, although full understanding is difficult between speakers from widely separated areas, such as Lime Village and Susitna, or Kenai and Eklutna, or Kenai and Lime Village. Below is a classification of Dena'ina dialects and the main villages in which they are (or were) spoken in the twentieth century. In 2003 we can report that there is only a small number of older generation speakers in the Upper Inlet, Outer Inlet, and Iliamna dialects. The Inland dialect has fewer than fifty speakers.

16. ‡Since the early 1980s, as was stated in Kari and Kari (1980), the size of the Dena'ina language area has been underestimated by about 20 percent. Computer calculations show that Dena'ina territory is about 51,000 sq. mi. in area, about the size of the state of Louisiana (Kari 2013:xix).

I. Upper Inlet dialect (Tyonek, Alexander Creek, Susitna, Kroto Creek, Montana Creek, Knik, Eklutna)

II. Lower Inlet dialects
   a. Outer Inlet dialect (Kenai, Seldovia, Kustatan, Polly Creek)
   b. Iliamna dialect (Pedro Bay, Old Iliamna)
   c. Inland dialect (Nondalton, Lime Village, Stony River)

Map 2 shows the dialect boundaries within Dena'ina and the surrounding Native language boundaries as well as the main Dena'ina villages of the historic and modern periods. Maps 3 and 4 are relief maps that give some sense of the spectacular landscape of southcentral Alaska. The Dena'ina have been in some approximation of the language area shown in Map 1 for perhaps 1000 years BP (before the present time). A challenging problem for Alaskan prehistory is to determine at what times and from where the Dena'ina expanded into this language area. When looking at the Dena'ina dialects and the fascinating geography of Cook Inlet basin, it is important to see Dena'ina as being at the end point on the North Pacific of the great Athabascan language family of North America (Map 5).

The following is quoted from Kari (1996b:51–53):

> A variety of facts are available that offer clues to Dena'ina regional prehistory. A pervasive theme is that Cook Inlet Basin has been a magnet environment that is very rich in subsistence resources.... There is a core of truly distinct features that all Dena'ina dialects share so that we can conclude that the language had a distinct proto-stage, i.e., there was a *proto-Dena'ina language* of some unknown antiquity in a smaller territorial expanse. Briefly, the shared core of features includes a vowel shift, several features of verb morphology and morphophonemics, and numerous pan-Dena'ina vocabulary innovations.

‡The topical vocabularies in the 2007 Dena'ina Topical Dictionary provide highly detailed context on Dena'ina adaptations to the geographically distinctive language area. Kari 2007:xxii:

> This array of interesting comparative and regional issues in Dena'ina vocabulary, such as the great number of dialect variants, the elite [i.e. esoterogenic] replacements, and the reanalyzed roots, indicate that the D. have been at the archaic periphery of the Athabascan language family in North America. These vocabulary patterns reflect long-term occupation of the Inland dialect area, and territorial expansion in order to annex lands and resources in what is the most resource-rich region of the contiguous Northern Athabascan languages.

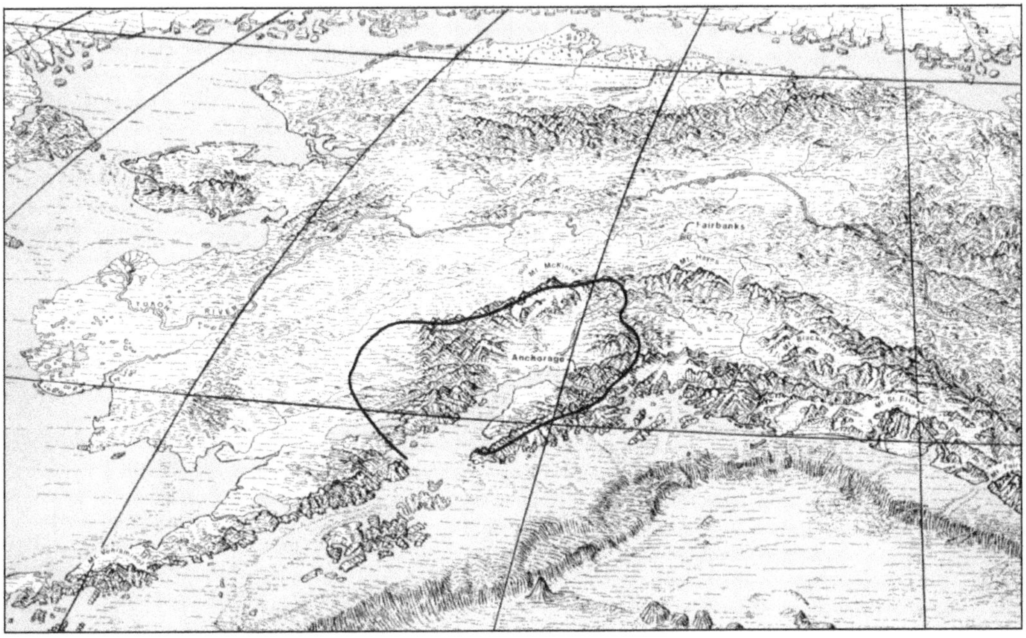

MAP 3

(Above) Oblique landform map of Alaska with the Dena'ina language area.

MAP FROM ALPHA ET AL. 1988

MAP 4

(Below) Dena'ina language area in relief, with language and dialect boundaries.

MAP BY MATT GANLEY

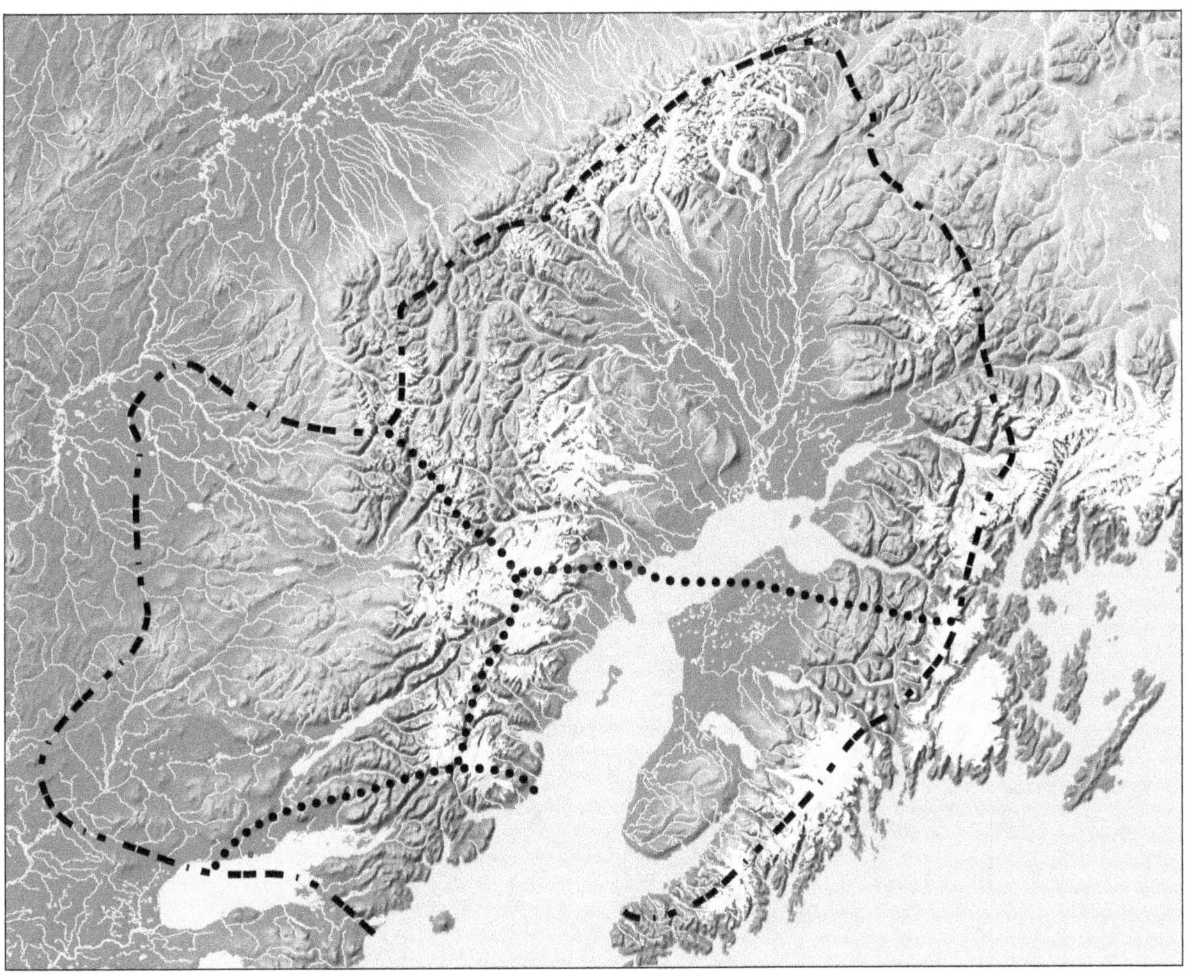

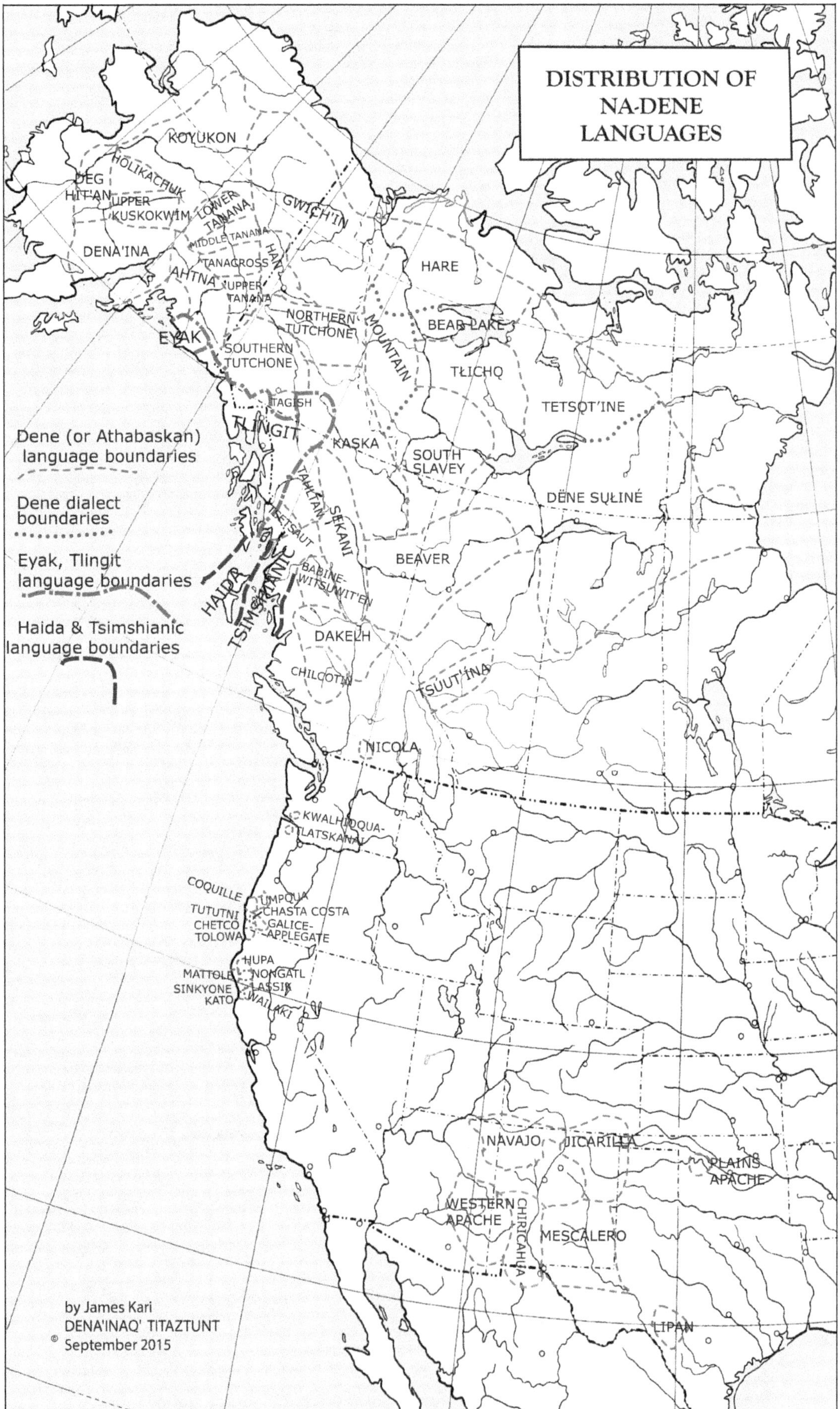

‡MAP 5

Distribution of Dene, Eyak, and Tlingit Languages.

Na-Dene consists of the Athabascan family plus Eyak and Tlingit. Since 2005 the term "Dene" has been used more than "Athabascan" to refer to the language family.

MAP BY JAMES KARI

The geographical position of the four Dena'ina dialects (termed Inland, Iliamna, Outer Inlet, and Upper Inlet, Kari 1975) is significant. I have suggested that the Dena'ina, prior to their expansion into Cook Inlet, were west of the Alaska Range in the upper Stony River area and perhaps also the South Fork of the Kuskokwim River. The Dena'ina first entered the Cook Inlet Basin through Rainy Pass or Ptarmigan Pass and established several clusters of villages in the Upper Inlet (e.g., the lower Skwentna River area, Kroto Creek, lower Susitna River, Knik Arm, Tyonek).

The extensive Ahtna areal influences on the Upper Inlet dialect attest to the relative priority of the Upper Inlet move. Subsequent to this expansion there was a move through Merrill Pass, Lake Clark Pass, or Telaquana Pass into Lower Cook Inlet via the Kustatan area (the most central point in the entire language area), and then across to the northcentral Kenai Peninsula (the core area of the Kenai Peninsula Dena'ina), and then south into Kachemak Bay. This move may have been coordinated with the Dena'ina expansion into the northern shores of Lake Iliamna via Lake Clark.

Dena'ina internal differentiation indicates that the dialects have been separated within their historical language area by both time and geographical barriers. Within the Dena'ina dialects, there is asymmetry in intelligibility. The Upper Inlet dialect can be rather difficult for Kenai or Nondalton speakers to understand, whereas Upper Inlet speakers can understand the other dialects more freely. This is due to the major consonant mergers in Upper Inlet Dena'ina which create a blurring of many forms and homophony and ambiguity from the points of view of the other dialects. For example, in Outer Inlet and Inland dialects these three stems are distinct: **yegh** 'downward,' **zegh** 'to scrape,' and **zhegh** 'to be serrated.' However in Upper Inlet all three stems are pronounced the same, **yegh**. There are also differences in prefix orderings in the verbs in the Dena'ina dialects that are consistently maintained and that serve to impede dialect intelligibility.

It seems likely that the first Dena'ina bands in the Upper Inlet operated on both sides of the Alaska Range using the salmon resources at the Dena'ina sites in the lower Skwentna River near its confluence with the Yentna River. These could be the oldest Dena'ina sites in the Upper Inlet dialect area. The Dena'ina next may have occupied the lower and middle Susitna River region, the Tyonek area, and Knik Arm. The story of the Salmon Boy told by Shem Pete (see Chapter 8) is set at the group of sites on lower Kroto Creek. This story implies that there was a time when the Dena'ina did not have reliable salmon runs and that Kroto Creek was a focal place for the harvest and ritualization of salmon. The name for the Tyonek area, **Tubughnen** 'Beach Land,' is so basic that it implies that this was the first beach on the inlet that the Dena'ina occupied. Few other beaches on Cook Inlet are named in Dena'ina.

FIGURE 11

A view from Anchorage of **Dghelishla** 'little mountain,' (4.9, Mt. Susitna). The most familiar, functional, and distinctive landmark in Upper Cook Inlet is this 4,396-foot tall mountain which has been dubbed "The Sleeping Lady," a name that is not based upon a Dena'ina name or legend. (See also the discussion at 4.9.) The Dena'ina used this mountain for navigational orientation just as boat and airplane pilots do today. **Dghelishla** is in numerous photographs throughout the book.

PHOTO BY PRISCILLA RUSSELL

Many lexical (i.e., vocabulary) and cultural patterns, as well as shared phonological patterns, link Upper Inlet Dena'ina to Ahtna (Kari 1977a). The clan migration stories of both the Upper Inlet Dena'ina and the Ahtna depict movements of people from the Copper River to Cook Inlet. Many of the Ahtna and Dena'ina of the twentieth century (such as Shem Pete, Jim Tyone, Johnny Shaginoff, and Simeon and Olga Ezi) used to speak both languages. Intermarriage was common and there is a zone of bilingual place names and joint land use on their shared border in the Talkeetna, Matanuska, and upper Susitna areas. In Chapters 10, 11, 13, and 14, about 56 place names are given in both Dena'ina and Ahtna and more than 160 names are in Ahtna. The Ahtna have borrowed the Dena'ina name for the Susitna River, **Sasutna'** (with the **-tn-** cluster for 'stream') from Dena'ina **Susitnu,** implying that Dena'ina occupation of the Susitna preceded that of the Ahtna. A few other place names with **-tna'** in modern **Ahtna** territory on the upper Susitna imply that Dena'ina territory formerly extended east of the Talkeetna Mountains (see 10.20, 10.27). The Ahtna have also borrowed the Dena'ina name for the Matanuska River (see 14.1). In the nineteenth century the Ahtna expanded north and west into the upper Nenana River and the Talkeetna Mountains. Given the size of the Upper Inlet dialect area and the wide array of diffusions between Upper Inlet and Ahtna, it seems safe to conclude that Upper Inlet Dena'ina and Ahtna have been closely associated for some time, perhaps 1,500–2,000 years.[16a]

We find no evidence through Dena'ina vocabulary, place names, or narratives of co-occupation with bilingualism and co-residence in any part of Cook Inlet by both the Dena'ina and an Eskimo people. Upper Inlet has the fewest number of Eskimo-origin loan words of the four Dena'ina dialects (twelve of the fifty-eight Eskimo-origin loans are in the Upper Inlet, Kari 1994:328–33).

The Dena'ina arrival on the western Kenai Peninsula is now well documented archaeologically (Reger and Boraas 1996). ‡Reger (2013:70) states, "On the Kenai River 37 radiocarbon dates from 16 sites show that the first significant occupation occurred in about AD 1000 to AD 1200." However, in the Upper Cook Inlet there is still no comparable dating of sites. The research analogue would be to have comparable test dates for the known site complexes in the Knik area (Fish Creek and Cottonwood Creek), the lower Susitna River sites (Alexander Creek, Susitna Station), the Wasilla Lake district, the lower Kroto Creek area, and the lower Skwentna River-Yentna River. It appears from the general distribution of these undated site complexes that the Upper Inlet Dena'ina population throughout Upper Inlet could have been very large, for example in the year 1700, and that they could have occupied these site districts for much longer than the Dena'ina sites on the Kenai Peninsula. Consider also Osgood's (1937:18) statement that Knik Arm was "a once populous region."

The Upper Inlet Dena'ina have their own view of the occupation of their territory in their ethnohistoric traditions (which have been extensively recorded by Shem Pete). They have a sense of long-term occupation of the Upper Inlet, but they do not claim to have been in their modern territory forever. Shem Pete stated that the Dena'ina from Knik Arm would say that when the people first lived on lower Knik Arm the banks in the Point McKenzie-Anchorage area were close enough that a **bashla**, ulu knife, could be tossed back and forth during the fish run (see 13.3).

Shem Pete was adamant that the Dena'ina did not jointly occupy any of their modern territory with their arch rivals, the Alutiiq.

‡Key points for this edition and for the Proto-Dene *Lex Loci* theory (PDLL, see pp. 144–147):

- Nichols 1992 and Fortescue 1998 characterize the coast of the North Pacific as an ancient multilingual diffusion corridor (also Kari 2010b:209, 211, 213). Cook Inlet Basin was occupied by other vanished languages, and there are signs of substrate non-Dene languages in Dena'ina vocabulary. Notable are the esoterogenic coinings (i.e., obfuscations) for common words, such as water, blood and fire (symbolized as ¤ in Kari 2007:xxi-xxii).
- When we compare substrate influences for all twelve Alaska Dene languages (Kari 2010b:207): "Cook Inlet Basin is likely the only part of Alaska where Athabascans have expanded into lands that were previously occupied by non-Athabascans."
- On pp. 146–147 we present the striking toponymic evidence for a set of founding place names that reflects the initial Dene (Athabascan) arrival and a Proto-Dena'ina homeland in the **Htsay Nenq'** area (plateau at upper Stony, Holitna, and Mulchatna Rivers) perhaps by 10,000 years BP. The Dena'ina place names network expanded around Cook Inlet Basin in phases. Some layers of names and trajectories can be detected. It is notable that the Dena'ina vigorously rejected substrate place names in favor of their rule-driven Dene names.

16a ‡Kari's views on Dene and Na-Dene prehistory have altered since the Dene-Yeniseian Hypothesis (Vadja 2010, see p. 144) and by archaeological assessments of Northern Archaic sites on the Upper Susitna River. Ben Potter (2010:151–152) has noted "There does seem to be consensus that once established, Northern Archaic represents continuous populations, perhaps linked with Na-Dene (Workman 1978), given the extended dichotomy between interior-focused Northern Archaic and various coastal groups (related to Arctic Small Tool and/or Norton tradition) from ~5000 cal BP to recent times. Northern Archaic tradition subsistence economy was focused on terrestrial hunting (principally caribou) and fishing." Kari now estimates that Upper Inlet Dena'ina-Ahtna interactions span 5,000 years or longer.

‡Prehistory of the Greater Upper Cook Inlet Region

by Douglas Reger and Brian T. Wygal

(new for the 2016 edition)

Doug Reger has conducted archaeological investigations throughout Cook Inlet and Southcentral Alaska and is now retired from the Alaska Department of Natural Resources.

Brian T. Wygal is an assistant professor of anthropology at Adelphi University in New York and has sixteen years of archaeological experience in the Susitna and Tanana valleys of Alaska.

The prehistoric archaeological record for the Upper Cook Inlet area has expanded in the past fifteen years, building on knowledge gained from previously documented sites. Excavations have occurred at the Beluga Point site on Turnagain Arm, at the Fish Creek site on Knik Arm, and at the Hewitt Lake site in the Yentna River drainage. Excavated sites along the Kenai River, the middle Susitna River, and upper Matanuska River are peripheral but add to interpretations of Upper Cook Inlet archaeology.

The first entry of people into the Cook Inlet Basin has yet to be discovered; however, the earliest known sites date between 10,000 and 7500 years ago in the surrounding mountains and upstream along the Susitna River. The Beluga Point site on Turnagain Arm (Reger 1996, 1998), sites in the Kenai Mountains (Reger and Pipkin 1996), in the Matanuska River canyon (Hadleigh-West 1996) and two sites located in the middle Susitna Valley (Wygal and Goebel 2012) contain stone tools left behind by highly mobile hunter gatherers. These small groups relied heavily on large land mammals for the major part of their subsistence as suggested by sites occupying high ground and overlooking prime hunting areas. Like their neighbors to the north, these early colonizers produced thin razor sharp microblades from specialized cores made from high quality stone.

The archaeological evidence from the greater Upper Cook Inlet region after the time of the microblade cultures is confusing, probably because several different groups occupied the area at the same time. A site in the Kenai Mountains (Reger 1998), several along the upper Susitna, and one along the middle Susitna River (J. Dixon et al. 1985; Wygal and Goebel 2012) indicate users of notched and/or lanceolate stone points were present in the basin about 6000 to 3000 years ago. Known as the Northern Archaic tradition, these hunter gatherers focused intensively on hunting caribou and sometimes moose primarily in upland areas. Like the original colonizers of Interior Alaska, Northern Archaic people also used microblade technology in some locations but not in others. While there have been discussions concerning a connection between the Northern Archaic and later Athabascan groups, convincing archaeological evidence has yet to materialize (Esdale 2008:6–7). In fact, so little is known about the Northern Archaic that some researchers question the term's efficacy entirely (Anderson 2008:177).

At the Beluga Point site overlooking Turnagain Arm, people bearing a distinctive stemmed chipped stone projectile point and high-shouldered knife appeared during the Northern Archaic period (Reger1998). These stemmed points are more similar in style to those used by earlier coastal cultures. Individual artifacts such as the chipped knives show influences from the Alaska Peninsula that were also moving into the Cook Inlet Basin. Because no slate occurred with those artifacts, the stemmed points probably pre-date the technique of grinding slate into tools, which appeared in Cook Inlet shortly before 4000 years ago. At 4200 years ago, people using ground slate spear points and knives camped at Beluga Point (Reger 1998), and similar artifacts have been found as far as the Upper Yentna River drainage (R.G. Dixon 1996), probably via trade networks. The ground slate artifacts look like tools from the Ocean Bay culture of Kodiak Island and coastal Southcentral Alaska. People who ground slate to make tools occupied coastal and lower river valleys while hunters using notched points may have used the upland and flanks of the mountains surrounding Upper Cook Inlet to continue hunting land animals. Currently, archaeologists are focused on understanding the degree to which these differences represent seasonal exploitation of environments by one group or entirely different cultures.

The Kachemak Culture spread over much of the Cook Inlet drainage from 3000 to 1000 years ago (Workman and Workman 2010). In the Upper Inlet, Riverine Kachemak moved up major rivers and along the coast. By 2000 years ago, Riverine Kachemak may have reached as far north as Hewitt Lake near the confluence of the Yentna and Skwentna rivers (Schneider 2013). Evidence from the Kenai Peninsula shows Riverine Kachemak people relied on salmon fishing as a staple of their diet, but they also harvested land animals (Reger and Boraas 1996; Reger 1998; Workman and Workman 2010). Small, notched pebble sinkers attached to nets were used in large rivers and were common artifacts from that culture. The fishing sites contained many tools and debris from salmon harvests, and caches containing salmon bone were found inside houses excavated into the ground surface. These people ground slate to form ulus and spear points; chipped stone arrow points were also common. Physically, the Riverine Kachemak people were probably related to the coastal peoples from Kachemak Bay and Kodiak Island (Reger and Boraas 1996).

While clearly an ancient language, Athabascan-speaking Dena'ina can be archaeologically identified in the Upper Cook Inlet Basin for the first time between 1500 to 1000 years ago. Sites from the last 1000 years include fish camps and villages with large multi-room houses. These houses were excavated partially into the ground and had earthen embankments around the walls and central fire hearths in the main room, often with a single side room addition. Tools were made mostly of wood and bone with limited use of stone, and a few slate points and ground adzes have been found. Copper artifacts, mainly pins, awls, and arrow tips, occur in Dena'ina sites. Copper was probably obtained through trade with Ahtna groups in the Copper River Basin from AD 1000 to 1700 (Cooper 2012). While copper tools were most common among the Ahtna, they also have been found in the Fish Creek site near Knik, at the Beluga Point site on Turnagain Arm, and along the Kenai River. Further evidence illustrating an Ahtna-Dena'ina connection is the occurrence of a distinctive form of underground caches in both areas. Similar salmon caches were identified along the lower Deska River at Kroto Creek, the Kenai River, and along the middle and lower Copper River, among other areas.

Very recent sites contain glass trade beads and iron implements marking the arrival of western traders around AD 1778. The distribution of known Dena'ina village sites revolves around salmon bearing streams of Upper Cook Inlet with additional village sites further inland along major confluences with the lower Susitna River, such as at Kroto Creek, Yentna River, and Deshka River, in addition to smaller tributaries such as Fish Creek and Cottonwood Creek entering Knik Arm. Dena'ina also established villages along large lakes including Wasilla Lake, Nancy Lake, and Big Lake. The strong presence of Dena'ina at large inland lakes extended south and west with substantial villages reported at Kijik on Lake Clark and eastern Iliamna Lake (VanStone and Townsend 1970). The size and distribution of late Dena'ina sites in the Upper Cook Inlet area suggests a considerable population thrived there.

Remains of animals harvested by Dena'ina hunters and fishermen indicate more dependence on small and medium game than in earlier times. Ptarmigan, snowshoe hare, red squirrel, porcupine, beaver, moose, sheep, and caribou were hunted. Locations of villages and seasonal camps at good fishing locations show that salmon and trout harvests were similarly important resources for the Dena'ina.

An occupation at the Beluga Point site, radiocarbon dated between 800 and 600 years ago, suggests neighboring Eskimo-Aleut groups continued to influence the archaeology of Upper Cook Inlet at the same time as Dena'ina. Ground slate tools, polished adze bits and stone scrapers appear identical to artifacts from Prince William Sound. Other evidence for Eskimo-Aleut influence on the Upper Inlet occurs at the Fish Creek site along Knik Arm, where a labret and gravel-tempered-pottery were found. The labret and pottery are thought to represent an Eskimo-Aleut occupation (Dumond and Mace 1968) but could also indicate direct trade with Dena'ina. De Laguna (1934:141) also speculated about an Eskimo-Aleut presence at the Fish Creek site on the basis of a ground stone lamp recovered in 1913 by a local farmer. While the discovery of Eskimo-Aleut technology in Dena'ina territory may indicate trade or technological diffusion by neighboring groups, their significance indicates contact with Eskimo-Aleut cultures if not a direct presence of people from more southerly coasts.

In summary, the earliest archaeological evidence in the Cook Inlet Basin points toward Interior Alaska for the origin of the first people following the melting of vast Ice Age glaciers. After that time, hunters and fishers apparently came from the Pacific coastal areas and Bristol Bay as well as from the Interior. Over time, these two groups traded, inter-married, and sometimes conflicted with each other. The first well-documented wide spread culture in Cook Inlet, the Kachemak culture, varied in form according to the environmental setting of the population. The Marine Kachemak along the Lower Cook Inlet shores traced material ties to Kodiak Island, while the Riverine Kachemak people were strongly influenced by Bristol Bay and more northern coastal people. The rich resources of Cook Inlet, particularly the upper and middle areas, have long been a place where many outside ideas merged to form a succession of changing cultures.

The Cook Inlet Basin has been used by succeeding groups of Native Peoples and was frequented by more than a single group at a time. The evidence thus far suggests that differing groups may have occupied interior mountain areas and coastal areas throughout much of the post-glacial time. That pattern holds the possibility that people ancestral to the historic Dena'ina have been present in Interior Alaska long before AD 1000. Unfortunately, archaeological evidence alone is currently insufficient to clearly pinpoint the source for a Dena'ina migration into the greater Cook Inlet region.

‡Archaeological summaries and references added to the 2016 edition are on pages 14, 68, 142, 146, 153, 182, 216, 238, and 280.

The Russian Presence in Upper Cook Inlet

by James Kari and James A. Fall

Although there were some Russians and creoles on the Kenai Peninsula beginning in the 1780s, there is little evidence of any permanent occupation or formal exploration of the territory of the Upper Inlet Dena'ina by Russians or other non-Dena'ina people during the entire period of Russian colonization. It seems that the Russians had no direct control over the Upper Inlet Dena'ina or their lands, although they did influencethe Dena'ina people in major ways by introducing western trade goods and, later, after the 1840s, the Orthodox religion (Fall 1981, 1987).

The first Euro-Americans to contact the Dena'ina were British. The Cook expedition spent a week in Cook Inlet in 1778 (see Chapter 16). Russian forts were established at Kasilof and Kenai in the 1780s and 1790s. We know that the first twenty or twenty-five years of Russian-Dena'ina contact were extremely violent, especially on the Kenai Peninsula (Bancroft 1886:338ff). There is evidence that some Dena'ina in the Tyonek area led a rebellion. (See 1.44, 1.45, and 1.48 on the Dena'ina rebel named **Quq'ey**.) This culminated in the late 1790s when Russian forts at both Iliamna and Tyonek were attacked by the Dena'ina and at least 20 Russians and 100 natives were killed (Tikhmenov 1978:46; Fall 1981:65, 68; ‡Stafeev, n.d., ‡Boraas and Leggett 2013). The 1794 map in Vancouver 1801 actually notes the "Russian Factory" in the Tyonek area prior to its destruction (see Map 14). Violent reprisals against the Dena'ina followed. Stafeev (n.d.) stated that nine Dena'ina men were assassinated in Kenai during the summer following the attack on the Tyonek fort.[17]

There is no evidence of a permanent Russian post or store, other than the short-lived fort at Tyonek in the1790s, anywhere in Upper Cook Inlet until the time of the 1867 purchase of Alaska by the United States (Davis 1965:14). From the Dena'ina point of view, the Upper Inlet was entirely their territory until Americans began to enter in search of gold in the mid-1880s. Brooks (1953:175–76, 235) noted that, "Russian trade routes were almost entirely confined to the Pacific and Bering Sea littoral.... They appear...to have paid small heed to the great Susitna valley."

Shem Pete did not acknowledge any Russian exploration of the Susitna River. He commented, "They [Russians] had their headquarters in Kenai. They killed lots of people, and they took their women. They didn't move into the [Dena'ina] villages. They [were] scared the Dena'ina would kill them. They didn't trap much [on the Kenai Peninsula]. They [Dena'ina] never let the Russians up there [up the Susitna River]. They [Russians] were too cheap [in trading]. They [Dena'ina] don't allow them. They kill them. Not even ten or twenty in a group go there, because too many natives." Shem Pete added (from Fall and Greiser (1986)): "They know what they done down the Inlet. They took all the fur and run for nothing. They take their clothes. They took the fur away from the Natives. They kill em off and take em back."

The two earliest records of Dena'ina participating in long-distance interior trade are from the 1790s. An Ahtna story told by Fred and Katie John (Kari 1986:75–86) is an account of the killing of a party of Russians on the upper Copper River in the Tanada Creek area, probably in the winter of 1794–95. A person identified as a Cook Inlet Dena'ina man named **C'uket Ta'** 'father of he buys things' played the key role in setting up the ambush of the Russian party. In the spring of 1797, Russian trader Dmitrii Tarkhanov, the first person to provide written historic records of the Copper River, recorded from the mouth of the Tonsina River a brief description of trade that takes place at Tazlina Lake between the Ahtna and a people that cross themselves from the left and who come to trade and hunt at Lake Baltybel [Tazlina Lake] (Grenov 1997:9–10; ‡Black 2008; see also 14.120). These visiting people must be Cook Inlet Dena'ina.

In reviewing the nineteenth-century maps of Cook Inlet and the Upper Inlet area, we find that mapping of Cook Inlet progressed very little after Cook's map of 1778 and Vancouver's of 1794. The only map for the entire nineteenth century showing any detail of the Susitna River and points north in Upper Cook Inlet is the1839 Wrangell map (Map 17, discussed in detail in Chapter 2), yet the eastern portion of this map is a compilation of Dena'ina or Ahtna sketch maps and place names *and is not based on actual Russian exploration.* The eastern portion of the Wrangell map is the most extensive and conclusive record of Dena'ina and Ahtna geographic information (villages, trails, and long-distance trade) for the early nineteenth century. Later maps of Cook Inlet and the upper Cook Inlet basin, such as the Teben'kov (1848), Holmberg (1854), Dall (1870), and Petroff(1884, Map 7 below), are much less detailed than the 1839 Wrangell map.

Russian attempts to explore the upper Cook Inlet area were minimal. There are some sketchy records indicating that a man named Bazhenov ascended the Matanuska River to the Copper River in the company of Dena'inas in about 1805 (Doroshin n.d.:38). The only Dena'ina report of any Russian presence in the upper Cook Inlet region is

17. Shem Pete recorded several stories about the early years of Russian-Dena'ina conflict. His accounts of skirmishes at Tyonek, Knik, Point Possession, and Kenai, when they are transcribed and translated, will be valuable contributions to our understanding of this period of Cook Inlet's history.

the statement by Talkeetna Nicholie that a Russian once died on the Kichatna River (Browne 1956:4, 179; see 7.18).

It has been alleged that in 1834 a Russian named Malakhov was the first white man to ascend the Susitna River (Spurr 1900:93; Brooks 1953:235). No first-hand account of Malakhov's trip has been found. Arndt (1985) recently translated orders written in October 1843 by A. K. Etolin for Petr Malakhov, who traveled in Alaska during the summer of 1844 rather than 1834. Etolin's orders reveal the vague notions the Russians in Kodiak and Sitka had of upper Cook Inlet and trails to the Copper River. Etolin directed Malakhov "to explore the course of the Sushitna River from its mouth to the place where it joins or discharges from Lake Plavezhnoe [Tazlina Lake]" (Russian-American Company Records 1844:No. 647). Therefore, Malakhov was not a source for the detail on the earlier 1839 Wrangell map (Map 17).

In 1844, Etolin wrote that Malakhov had been unable to find Plavezhnoe Lake and that he had reached "the place where the Mountain Kolchane descends to Sushitna village" (Russian-America Company Records 1844, No. 647). In 1847, the geographer Teben'kov commented that "the last camp of Malakhov at latitude 62° 50' longitude 148° 46' on the Sushitna River also explains nothing. And thus the Sushitna River, like the Copper River, awaits absolute definition which...is impossible to accomplish quickly" (Russian-America Company Records 1847, No. 325). This reading places Malakhov in the Devil Canyon area at his northernmost point.[18]

According to Nancy Davis, "For the Russian period, most if not all trading and missionization contact took place in the Middle and Lower Inlet areas" (1965:14).

FIGURE 12

Shem Pete's knowledge of place names intersected with the earliest written records from Upper Cook Inlet when, in the mid-1970s, we made the connection between a lake spelled on the 1839 Wrangell map as "Takniltubena" and **Tatik'niłtun Bena,** (11.14, Stephan Lake). This lake, viewed here from north to south, is at the border of the Ahtna-Dena'ina languages and is important in Dena'ina/Ahtna prehistory. See pp. 85–87 and Map 17 for a detailed discussion of the Wrangell map.

PHOTO COURTESY OF COOK INLET REGION, INC.

The Russians in Alaska were few in number, and they concentrated on developing trade in the interior areas by working through native middlemen. In the Upper Inlet area, as summarized in Fall 1981 and 1987, this trade was conducted through middlemen who were the Dena'ina **qeshqa** 'rich men' or leaders. There is very little information about Russian presence along Knik Arm in the early nineteenth century, and there are no records of permanent year-round posts there. The following quote from Khlebnikov, from the 1820s, indicates that only a winter post, *zimov'e* in Russian, was on Knik Arm and that it was occupied by a Dena'ina from Kenai. The location is probably at **Niteh** on the lower Matanuska River (see 14.4). This is a good account of the role of the native middleman in the early nineteenth century.

18. Teben'kov's comments were included in the orders given to Ruf Serebrennikov, who was killed by Upper Ahtnas in June 1848 near Slana when he was exploring and mapping that area. An Ahtna account of the Serebrennikov incident by Fred and Katie John appears in Kari (1986:107–115).

> In September is sent from the redoubt [Kenai] in a baidarka with trade goods a reliable Kenaitze to Knik where he winters with his countrymen. To him they bring near and far their furs. He himself visits for this and goes on the Sushitna River where beaver is most abundant. In April he leaves with the furs in a baidara to Nikolaevsk [Kenai] redoubt. The oarsmen are Kenaitze of those villages with which he traded. They remain for the summer at the redoubt for company work, preparation of fish, and dragging out wood (Liapunova and Fedorova 1979:80–81, Khlebnikov 1994).

Although there is little evidence of Russians residing in upper Cook Inlet, there was considerable Russian impact upon Dena'ina culture. We do not yet know the extent of mixed marriages in the early periods. In the Kroto Creek area a group of fair-skinned, red-haired Dena'ina speakers has been reported by Shem Pete (see 8.12). It seems that Russian-Dena'ina contact and intermarriage with a creole native-Russian population increased considerably after 1850. The Dena'ina had access to a wide variety of Russian trade goods, and they adopted the Orthodox religion. Kenai was the main supply point for the Russian trade goods that entered other areas around Cook Inlet. Orthodox priests were based in Kenai after 1845, and the first visits by priests to the upper inlet area may have occurred after this time (Tikhmenov 1978:383). The first Orthodox chapels at Knik, Eklutna, and Susitna Station were probably built in the 1870s after the U.S. purchased Alaska. In 1881 priest Hiermonk Nikita visited Tyonek, Knik and Susitna (Townsend 1974:10–11). Sheldon, a physician writing in 1906, stated, "The aborigines living on the shores of Cook Inlet and the Susitna River have in their veins much Russian blood" (Sheldon 1908:269).

In the 1860s and 1870s the Upper Inlet area was still a very isolated part of Alaska. Dall, writing in the late 1860s, summarized what little information he had available (1870:272–273). The Russian-American historian Ivan Petroff, writing in the 1870s, stated that the natives of the Susitna River and Knik Arm still dressed in skin clothing and lived in traditional houses (Petroff 1900:280).

Petroff (1900:160) wrote,

> What the country north of Cook Inlet is like no civilized man can tell, as in all the years of the occupation of the coast by the Caucasian race it has remained a sealed book. The Indians tell us that the rivers lead into lakes and that the lakes are connected by rivers with other lakes again, until finally the waters flow into the basins of the Tanana and the Yukon; but conflicting with this intermingling of the waters are stories of mountains of immense altitude visible for hundreds of miles. The natives living north of this terra incognita give, however, a similar description, which may be accepted until reliable explorers are enabled to penetrate this region.

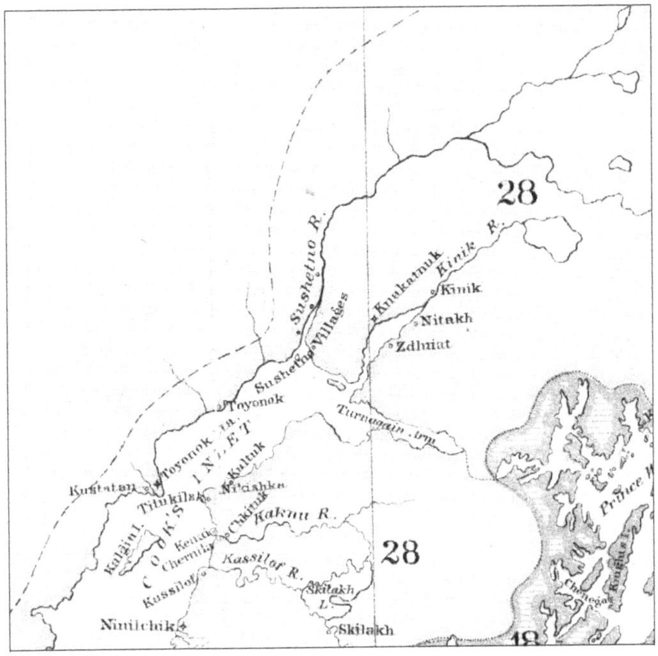

MAP 6

Detail from the 1884 Petroff map: Upper Cook Inlet.

The map from Petroff 1884 that appeared with the 1880 census has virtually no detail for the interior of Southcentral Alaska. All communities shown are on or near tidewater.

Recent publications by Andrei Znamenski provide perspective on the Orthodox church activities in Upper Cook Inlet. According to Znamenski, "Before the 1880s Russian Orthodoxy had relatively little influence on Tanaina society" (1996:30). In the 1880s there was renewed activity, and in Cook Inlet a series of chapels serving Dena'ina communities was built. In the Upper Inlet churches were built at Tyonek in 1882, at Knik in 1889, at Susitna Station in 1890, and at Eklutna in 1897 (Zamenski 2000:7). All of the chapels had native church wardens and readers. Typically the communities were visited rarely by priests and all services were conducted by the church wardens and readers. Znamenski also notes that none of the Russian missionaries to the Dena'ina knew the Native language. The services were held in Russian and Dena'ina interpreters assisted (Znamenski 2000:16). The first Orthodox priest to reside a full winter in Upper Cook Inlet was Nikolai Mitropolsky at Old Knik in 1888–89 (Znamenski 1998:6), and priest Ioann Bortnovsky resided in Cook Inlet from 1897–1907 and left detailed letters and records. Znamenski writes:

> Bortnovsky stands out among other missionaries to the Dena'ina, not only because he stayed in their country for eleven years, but because he caught Dena'ina society in a most dramatic period of its

FIGURE 13

(Right) Shem Pete constructed numerous Russian Orthodox crosses. This one was made for a funeral at Eklutna in 1976. Shem called his dog "Gemuk."

PHOTO BY PRISCILLA RUSSELL

FIGURE 14

(Below) A Russian Orthodox baptismal ceremony for the Kallander children at the family home in Anchorage in 1957. Front row: Bobby, Sammy, Norman, Betty, and Mary Kallander. Back row: Mrs. Mike Oskolkoff, Jimmy Kallander, Alice Debbie Fullenwider, Margaret June Baird, Lay Reader Mike Alex, Gronia Baird, Feodoria Kallander.

PHOTO COURTESY OF FEODORIA KALLANDER PENNINGTON AND BETTY GILCRIST

history. Still recovering from the toll on its population taken by the 1884 influenza epidemic, the Dena'ina faced a massive influx of newcomers. American and Scandinavian gold miners, cannery workers, road and railroad construction teams, and American soldiers altered familiar Native landscapes. Some of these newcomers intermarried with Dena'ina and gradually changed the ethnic composition of the traditional Athapaskan villages.

Although the Dena'ina did not forsake their occupations of hunting and fishing, income accumulated from their work as hired laborers began to contribute significantly to their livelihood. They became part of the new economy as guides, hunters, mail carriers, and laborers. As a result of these interactions, first with Creoles of Russian-Aleut origin, and later with Euro-Americans, the Dena'ina reshaped their identity, incorporating numerous elements from the culture of the newcomers. It appears that the Dena'ina adopted the Russian Church as part of a strategy of accommodation to the new challenges and that the church eventually became integral to indigenous culture. Since the end of the eighteenth century, Orthodox Christianity had been the only European religion with which the Dena'ina were familiar. Most important, the rich ceremonialism of Orthodoxy, along with the lack of excessive social control, apparently matched Dena'ina cultural expectations. It might be suggested that for the Dena'ina, Russian Orthodoxy became a convenient bridge that connected their old traditional and new American worlds (Znamenski 1998:4–5).

According to Alaska Commercial Company records, by 1876 some Americans were arriving at Tyonek and heading out in search of gold. In 1887 J. N. Johnston went up the Yentna River. He is thought to have been the first American to do so (Fall 1981:93–94). The man called **Sdigel** 'Glass' in the place name on the lower Susitna (see 2.12) is said by Shem Pete to have been the first white man, also an American, to ascend the Susitna. There were no documented explorations until the mid-1890s, when parties of prospectors began to ascend the Susitna basin. The Spillum and Ladd party of 1893–94, described in Bayou 1946, may be the first American group on the Susitna. In 1895 James Germanson may have been the first American up the Matanuska River (Powell 1910:325). In 1896 William Dickey stated that "no white man has ever been over seventy-five miles above Susitna Station.... The country is known only by the reports of the Indians who come down it yearly with furs" (Cole 1979:3). Dickey also said, in 1897, "The largest unexplored region in the United States is the country north of Cook Inlet" (Moore 1981:10).

Throughout the nineteenth century the main language of trade in Cook Inlet was Russian, and many of the Dena'ina spoke Russian as a second language. If we examine the Russian words that have been borrowed by the Dena'ina, we get a revealing picture of the nature of Dena'ina-Russian contact. Over 500 Russian loanwords have been recorded in the Kenai dialect of Dena'ina, and in the Upper Inlet dialect about 250 have been recorded, most of which have been supplied by Shem Pete. Shem Pete knew a fair amount of conversational Russian. Some Upper Inlet Dena'ina Russian loanwords are for foods, such as coffee, tea, used tea leaves, flour, syrup, sugar, pepper, mustard, and potato. Others are for clothing, such as suspenders, ribbons, shoes, and several kinds of hats; various tools, such as ax, grindstone, key, and file; various types of boats and boat terms, such as dory, schooner, baidarka, anchor, and oarlock; and religious and social terms, such as church, second chief, church warden, sin, and icon. There are even a few loanwords from Siberian Native languages, words such as *galeq* 'paper' and *chubudushga* 'silver fox.'[19]

Professor Lydia Black, specialist in Russian-America and Alaska anthropology and a native speaker of Russian, recalls her first meeting with Shem Pete: "Shortly after I arrived in Fairbanks, in January1983, Dr. James Kari asked me to come up to his office. He liked me to meet someone. I climbed up a flight of stairs and entered. Two men were visiting. I barely took a step or two when the older of the two gentlemen rose and asked, no, stated, in perfect Russian: *Madam, vy russkaia* (Madam, you are a Russian). I admitted to the fact. Delendii (it was he) bowed over my hand, and we proceeded to converse about this and that. I thought that if I have encountered Delendii in Moscow, neither his manners nor his speech would ever betray him as an Alaska Native. I also remember, that his son, who accompanied him on this visit, pulled on his coat and whispered (for all to hear) 'They are not supposed to know'—referring to Delendii's command of the Russian language. This is one of the fondest memories I have of this grand man, the renowned elder of the Dena'ina nation."

In retrospect, it seems that we underestimated Shem's ability in the Russian language. He did not make an effort to speak Russian when he was with Russian speakers in the Orthodox community or when visiting with Fedosia Sacaloff in Kenai, who was fluent in Russian. It is quite interesting if in fact Shem Pete was concealing his knowledge of Russian.

---

19. The loanwords are presented in Kari (1977a, 1994, and ‡2007).

Upper Inlet Dena'ina Regional Bands, Subsistence Patterns, and Traditional Leaders

by James A. Fall

In the nineteenth and early twentieth centuries, the Upper Inlet Dena'ina comprised several regional bands. These included the **Tubughna** of the northwest shores of upper Cook Inlet, the **Susitnuht'ana** of the Susitna River drainage as far upstream as the mouth of the Yentna River, the **Yentnuht'ana** of the Yentna River drainage, the **Dashq'eht'ana** of the middle Susitna drainage up to the mouth of the Talkeetna River, and the **K'enaht'ana** of Knik Arm and the Matanuska River. Within each regional band were several villages, each containing multi-family dwellings called **nichił**. The houses contained groups of kin—usually men of the same clan, their wives, and children. Leading each **nichił** or group of **nichił** was a **qeshqa** 'rich man.' The qeshqa organized his **ukilaqa** 'his clan helpers' into cooperative hunting and fishing groups. In addition to this economic role, **qeshqa** instructed the young, settled disputes, and organized warriors for battles with the **Ułchena** (the Alutiiq and preceding peoples)[19a]. The village served as a base for the Dena'ina's resource harvesting activities. It was occupied for much of the year and contained many caches of preserved foods. Table 4 lists the Upper Inlet Dena'ina **qeshqa** by name, place of residence, and clan affiliation. Table 5 and Map 8 summarize the regional and local bands and band names in the middle and upper Cook Inlet areas. Also see the more detailed summaries of each band's activities presented in Chapters 1, 2, 5, 9, 10, and 13.

Traditionally, each Dena'ina individual belonged to one of about twelve named matrilineal clans. The clans were grouped into two unnamed moieties or "sides." *Matrilineal* means that men and women were members of their mother's clan. In other words, membership in a clan passed only through the female line. The clans and moieties were exogamous; individuals were required to marry a person of another clan in the opposite moiety. For example, **Nulchina** (Sky Clan) men were prohibited from marrying **Nulchina** women. Additionally, they could not marry **Tulchina** (Water Clan) women because the **Nulchina** and **Tulchina** clans are in the same moiety, or the same "side." Instead, **Nulchina** and **Tulchina** men could marry women of clans of the opposite moiety, clans such as **Chishyi** (Red Paint Clan) and **K'kalayi** (Fishtail Clan). Associated with each clan was an origin story. Sometimes these stories were linked with specific places (see, for example, 4.9 and 14.21). In addition to regulating marriage, clan membership shaped residential units, hunting and fishing groups, political positions, and inheritance of material goods (see Osgood 1937:128–131; Fall 1981:220–233, 409–427; Kalifornsky 1984:20–21).

The seasonal round of all the regional bands centered on salmon fishing in the spring and summer from camps near the villages, and big game hunting in the fall, often in upland areas. Figure 16 summarizes the general seasonal round for Upper Inlet Dena'ina bands of the nineteenth

19a Kari (2007:77) now treats **Ułchena** as the D. name for one or more early peoples (Norton, Kachemak) and Alutiiq, (Kodiak, or Koniag). This is based on the range of glosses given for the term (a "Southeastern people" in Iliamna and Nondalton) and place names that refer to them such as Roadhouse Mountain on the N side of Iliamna Lake. See p. 147.

FIGURE 15

Nichił, the Dena'ina winter house. This diagram of the Dena'ina winter house is based upon Osgood (1937:58).

DRAWING BY KATHY KIEFER

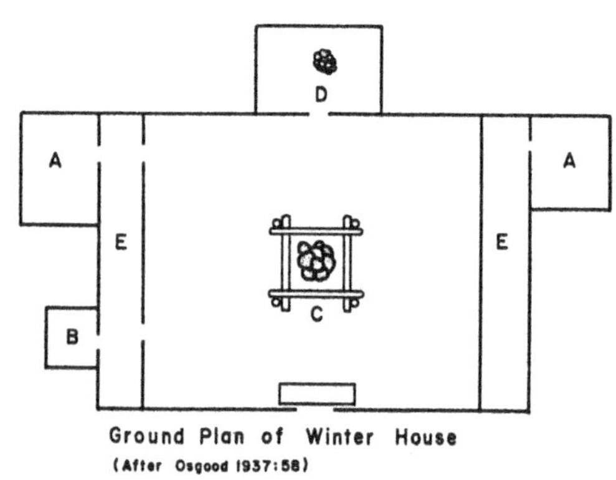

century. However, each regional band followed its own particular pattern of subsistence activities, shaped by the availability of different kinds of resources. Traditional stories (**tsukdu**), place name and land use narratives, and written ethnohistorical materials all provide information about these seasonal rounds (see summary in Fall 1987:31–38; Alexan 1965; Kari 1982a, 1982b; Kari and Kari 1982; Fall, Foster, and Stanek 1984:20–23; and ‡Stanek, Fall, and Holen 2006, and Evanoff 2010:66).

Dena'ina elders today stress that subsistence resources around Tyonek were diverse and abundant in the past. The Tyonek area was known as **Ełnen Bunkda** 'The Mother of the Earth' because of the rich marine products available locally. It was contrasted with the Susitna River drainage, called **Ełnen Tukda** 'The Father of the Earth,' where large land mammals and furbearers were more readily accessible.

A new round of subsistence harvests began for the **Tubughna** and **Susitnuht'ana** in **Nut'aq'i n'u** 'Geese Month' (April). Many kinds of migratory birds were snared or shot with blunt arrows at local marshes, lakes, and river mouths. The territory around **Susni Kaq'** (2.3), the mouth of the Susitna River, was especially important in spring for hunting and for trade. Extended family groups operated **tay'in** 'fish traps' for trout, and they harvested beaver with spears or deadfalls.

In late April, families moved from the winter villages to fish camps along Cook Inlet and the Susitna River. They harvested large numbers of hooligan (eulachon) with dip nets and from them prepared hooligan oil. These Dena'ina also hunted marine mammals from the camps. Harbor seals were hunted from kayaks (**biqidin** or **baydargi**) with harpoons or with clubs. Beluga were hunted from **yuyqul**, beluga spearing platforms. The Dena'ina rendered beluga fat into oil, and they dried and stored beluga meat for winter use (see p. 76; Pete 1980b; Alexan 1965). The **Tubughna** obtained razor clams in the spring by either traveling south to Redoubt Bay or Tuxedni Bay or trading with the **Qezdeghdna** or **Qeydeghtna** of lower Cook Inlet.

The Dena'ina harvested the greatest numbers of salmon beginning in late May and June. June is referred to as **Łiq'aka'a n'u** 'King Salmon Month.' King and sockeye salmon were caught with dip nets from **tanik'edi**, pole platforms that extended directly into the inlet above the tidal flats (see pp. 64–65). Salmon were also caught in basket traps and weirs in small streams and lake outlets. The Dena'ina especially used these methods for harvesting silver salmon in late August and September during fall hunts. Most of the summer was spent fishing and preparing a large supply of dry salmon for winter use. The **qeshqa** of each multi-family house or village directed the harvesting, processing, and storing of salmon.

Hunting land mammals was also an important activity for the **Tubughna** and **Susitnuh'tana,** although their access to big game was more limited than that of other upper Cook Inlet Indians. Elders report that moose were rare in the Tyonek area until the 1940s. The Dena'ina hunted caribou, sheep, and bear in the mountains west of Tyonek near Chakachamna Lake (1.16). They hunted bear and fished for silver salmon in the fall in the Hiline Lake-Beluga Mountain (4.20) area north of the villages. Groups of **Tubughna** traveled through **Tubughna Katidiłtuni** (6.17, Hayes River Pass) to hunt caribou and sheep in the Rainy Pass area and to trade with the Yentna River (5.1) and Susitna River Dena'ina. As they returned to their winter villages on Cook Inlet, the **Tubughna** hunters cached meat along their trails for use during winter hunting trips. The **Susitnuht'ana** traveled along the Susitna and Yentna rivers and on trails north of the Skwentna River to reach caribou hunting grounds. It is likely, however, that the lower Susitna River Dena'ina obtained much of their caribou meat and hides through trade with the **Yentnuht'ana** and **Dashq'eht'ana**.

Early winter, from November to January, was usually a period of rest in the winter villages of the **Tubughna** and **Susitnuht'ana.** People visited other communities, traded, told stories, and held potlatches. November is called **Qatggentdałna** 'Visitors.' Hunting partners made short trips of one to several days for moose, bear, ptarmigan, hare, and porcupine to supplement the diet of dried fish, meat, and oil. Fresh fish, mostly trout, were harvested through the ice of local lakes. Furbearers, such as marten, were harvested for raw materials, potlatching, and trade. If food supplies ran low in January, February, or March, village groups sometimes dispersed to lakes in new hunting and fishing areas. Specially trained dogs were used to seek out brown and black bear dens. In April, with the anticipated return of waterfowl, hooligan, marine mammals, and salmon, the sparse season ended and the seasonal cycle began again.

In contrast to the people of the lower Susitna and Tyonek areas, the **Dashq'eht'ana** and **Yentnuht'ana** of the middle Susitna and Yentna rivers were more oriented to resources of the inland regions and mountains. They did not hunt marine mammals in the spring themselves, for example, but traded for these products at **Susni Kaq'.** Nevertheless, these inland regional bands depended heavily on salmon, especially the early king salmon. They fished intensely throughout the summer. In fall, the **Dashq'eht'ana** traveled north to the Tokositna (9.10) and Chulitna (9.1) rivers, or east to the Talkeetna Mountains to hunt moose, ground squirrel, and especially caribou. They floated down the rivers with their catches in caribou or moose hide boats to spend the winter at their villages. Winter was an important time for trade with other Dena'ina.

The annual cycle of the **K'enaht'ana** of Knik Arm and the Matanuska and Knik river drainages was generally like

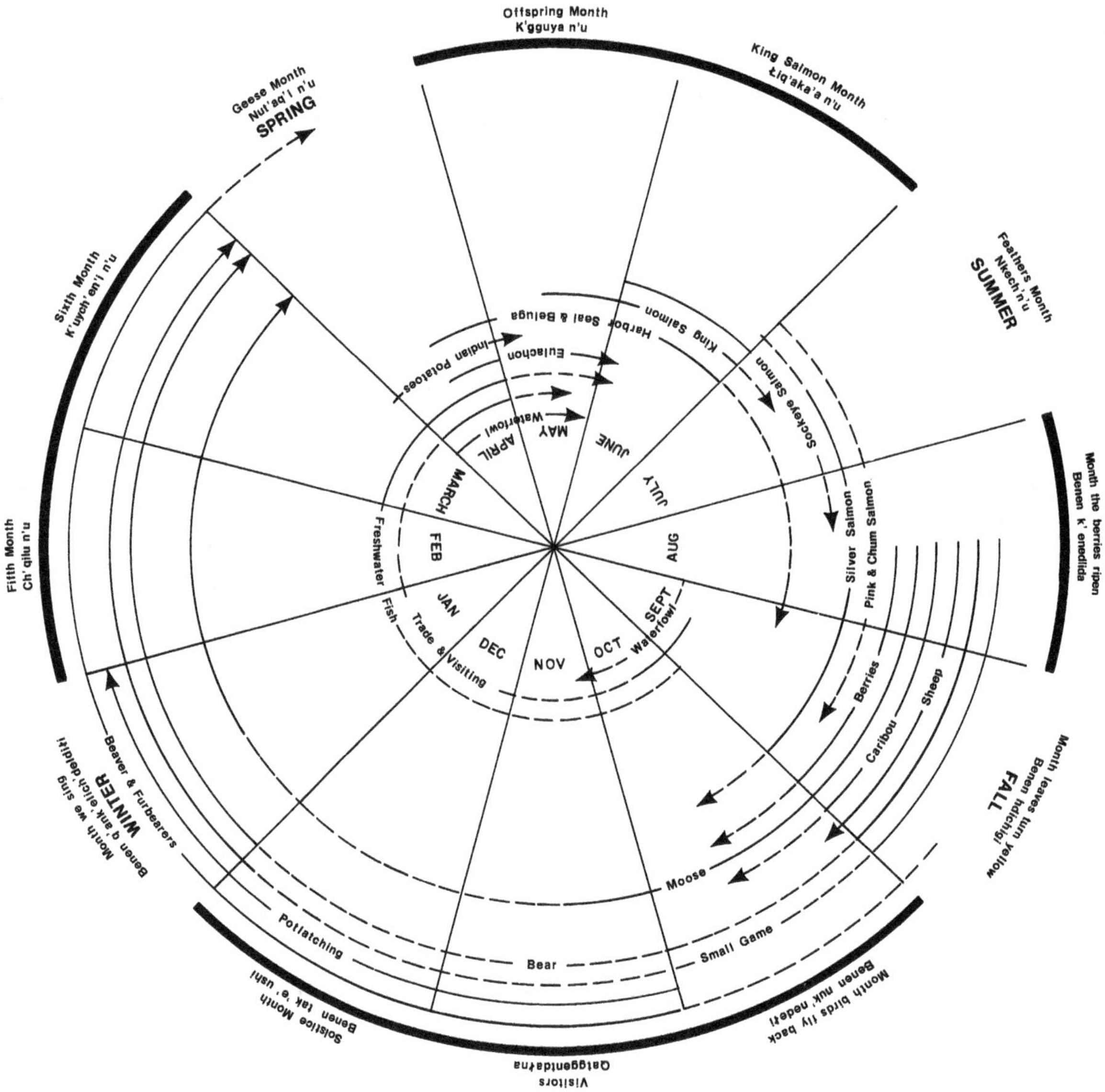

that of the Susitna River Dena'ina. Some Knik Arm people traveled to the mouth of the Susitna River in spring to harvest hooligan, seal, and waterfowl. Others traded with the **Susitnuht'ana** for hooligan at **Dilhi Tunch'del'usht Beydegh** 'Point Where Hooligan are Transported' (13.3, Point Mac-Kenzie). Many **K'enaht'ana** moved from their winter villages to lower Knik Arm, including the present-day Anchorage area, in April and May to harvest king salmon with dip nets from **tanik'edi** (see pp. 64–65 and 15.75). Later in the spring and summer, sockeye and silver salmon were available in many Knik Arm tributaries. The Knik Arm Dena'ina caught these fish in basket traps and with weirs and dip nets. They stored dried salmon in caches near the winter villages.

Like the other regional bands, the **K'enaht'ana** hunted primarily in late August and September. Some Knik River and Eklutna people journeyed into the Chugach Mountains for sheep, bear, ground squirrels, and probably caribou. Other Knik Arm Dena'ina hunted caribou in the Talkeetna Mountains. They traded caribou meat and hides with the **Tubughna**, receiving dried fish and marine mammal products in return. The remainder of their winter and early spring subsistence activities resembled those of the Susitna River regional band.

FIGURE 16

The Dena'ina seasonal round.

DRAWING BY DAN FOSTER

The descriptions that Dena'ina elders provide of the traditional Upper Inlet Dena'ina economy highlight the seasonal periods of abundance in spring, summer, and fall, followed by months of relative scarcity in the winter. Elders maintain that large supplies of food were harvested, processed, and stored during the seasons of plenty for later use and for trade. These oral traditions illustrate the important role of the Dena'ina leaders, the **qeshqa**, in subsistence

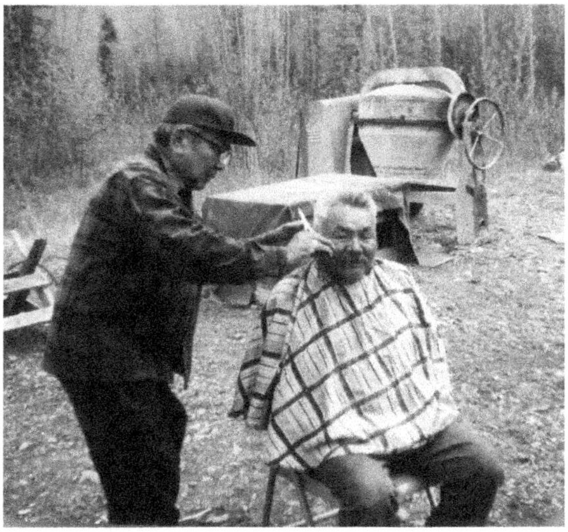

FIGURE 17

(Above) Chief Mike Alex, giving a haircut to Billy Pete at Eklutna in 1976.

PHOTO BY PRISCILLA RUSSELL

FIGURE 18

(Right) Chief Chilligan Phillip or "Big Chilligan," originally from Susitna and later chief of Tyonek, and his wife, Olga, in the late 1920s. Shem said that his Indian name was **Beghuduch'di'ishen,** meaning 'we refrain from talking about him.' See 1.13 regarding Chilligan's use of the Chakachamna Lake area.

PHOTO COURTESY OF ALEXANDRA ALLOWAN

activities. Billy Pete says that in addition to organizing the harvests, the **qeshqa** in each village was "the master of the cache," for he collected the products of his followers' hunting and fishing efforts, and distributed these foods back to them during the lean times in the winter. The **qeshqa** was also the overseer of inter-village trade, as the late Nickafor Alexan of Tyonek explained:

> At one time the old Chief of Tyonek was a friend with the chief of Knik. The two Chiefs had made an agreement to sell food between each tribe. The agreement was for the Tyonek Chief to sell the Knik Chief dried and smoked fish, because the Knik people couldn't catch enough. As for the Tyonek Chief, he could trade fish for caribou hide, moose hide and dried meat and sinew, because the Knik people lived a lot closer to the mountains where there is a lot of meat to hunt. The two Chiefs call each other "Shluchin," which means, be friends always, no matter what became between them" (Alexan 1981:1).

In summary, the Upper Inlet Dena'ina enjoyed a diverse and often abundant resource base. Groups of kin, organized by **qeshqa**, worked hard to store foods during seasons of plenty. Trade among villages in different parts of the Upper Cook Inlet area linked the regional bands together in a network of exchange of food and other important products.

TABLE 4. UPPER INLET DENA'INA QESHQA (CHIEFS)

Compiled by James A. Fall and James Kari

For Dena'ina accounts of important **qeshqa** and middlemen, see Shem Pete's epic biography of **Diqelas Tukda** of Alexander Creek (Pete 1977) and also Shem Pete's description of chief Dusgeda Tukda from Knik in Fall (1987:49). Several of these chiefs are pictured in this book.

	Place	Chief's name	Clan name and moiety (A or B)	Time span
1	**Tubughnenq'** (Tyonek)	Chadaka'a	(B)	Early nineteenth century
		Nunk'ilash	(B)	Mid nineteenth century
		Nugheldu‡ Tukda	Chishyi (A)	Mid nineteenth century
		Beni‡'a Ch'ulyałen	Chishyi (A)	1840s–c. 1918
		Big Chilligan (aka Chilligan Philip, Fig. 18)	Chishyi (A)	Died 1931
		Simeon Chickalusion (Fig. 35)	Tulchina (B)	1880–1957
2	**Tuqen Kaq'** (Alexander Creek)	Wasihdi Tukda	Chishyi (A)	Mid nineteenth century
		Diqelas Tukda	Chishyi (A)	1830s to 1906
3	**Tsat'ukegh** (Susitna Station)	Pete	K'kalayi (A)	Died c. 1900
		Evan Duyeq (Figs. 63, 76, 77)	Nulchina (B)	Died c. 1910
		Beq'e Nuqeyedghulya Tukda (aka Ephim) (Fig. 54)	Nulchina (B)	Died 1916
4	**Tani'i** (opposite Susitna Station)	Ts'inst'a Gga Tukda	K'kalayi (A)	Late nineteenth century
5	**Tsuk Qayeh** (lower Yentna River)	Tsuk Qayeh Ka'a Iden	?	Late nineteenth century
6	**Dashq'e** (Kroto Village)	K'eghudu	Nulchina (B)	Died c. 1910
		Chijuk (aka Tsilałen) (Figs. 17, 113, 114)	Nulchina (B)	Died 1930s
7	**Tanłtunt** (Red Shirt Lake)	Baytnidahen	K'kalayi (A)	Died c. 1905
		K'eł Nuts'ehen (aka Red Shirt)	K'kalayi (A)	Died c. 1917
8	**K'dalkitnu** (Talkeetna area)	Denyishla Iden	K'kalayi (A)	Died c. 1905
		Ch'k'idetnishen (aka Talkeetna Nicholie) (Figs. 148, 149)	Dghelay Teht'ana (A)	c. 1860–1918
9	**K'enakatnu** (Knik)	"Bowen Affanassia"	?	Died 1890s
		Affinassa	Nulchina (B)	Died 1890s
		Dusgeda Tukda	Chishyi (A)	1830s–c. 1910
		Qatsen (Stepankda) (Fig. 220)	Nulchina (B)	Died 1915
		Tenqa (Aruf)	?	Died 1913
10	**Benteh** (Wasilla Lake)	Bentehen (title) Chief Wasilla (Fig. 176)	Nulchina (B)	Died 1907
11	**Chuqilintnu** (lower Wasilla Creek)	Benitnanilchinen	?	Died several centuries ago
12	**Niteh** (Matanuska)	Nitehen (title), Qa Dyiluggen	Chishyi (A)	Died nineteenth century
		Betsik'nughesalen	Chishyi (A)	Died nineteenth century
		Basdut (Simeon Ezi) (Fig. 182)	Chishyi (A)	Died ‡1935
		Billy Ezi, Sr. (Fig. 181)	Tulchina (B)	1898–1971
13	**Nuk'din'itnu** (Chickaloon)	Chiklu	Tulchina	Late nineteenth century
14	**Idlughet** (Eklutna)	Nicolie	Chishyi (A)	1880s
		Beł K'ighi‡'ishen (Eklutna Alex)	Chishyi (A)	1865–1953
		Mike Alex (Figs. 14, 17, 203)	Nulchina (B)	1908–1977
15	**Ch'aghałnikt** (Point Possession)	Chiklu	Tulchina	Died c. 1900
		Jimmy Nikolai	?	Died 1930s
		Billy Nikolai (Fig. 231)	?	Died 1952

No **qeshqa** names are remembered for the villages on the upper Yentna River.

Upper Inlet Dena'ina Bands and Band Names

by James Kari

Ethnonyms are names for groups of people. In Dena'ina and other Athabascan languages, this is an important vocabulary domain. At this time sixty-one ethnonyms for Dena'ina groups have been recorded (Kari 1996b:56–57; ‡Kari 2007:73–76). The expert speakers know only a subset of these ethnonyms, and some band names have been lost. There is, for instance, no recorded name for the people of the Kachemak Bay region. The most general term of self-desgination for Dena'ina speakers of all dialects is **Dena'ina**, 'the people.' The term *Tanaina* (as in Osgood 1937) is from this term. In addition there are other recorded names for neighboring Athabascans, the Alutiiq, and the Central Yupik.

FIGURE 19

An unidentified "Susitna mother and child," in 1906.

PHOTO BY FREDERICK A. COOK

In the Dena'ina language the set of band names serves as an index system to the geography and people of the entire region. The band names are hierarchically organized and are usually based upon place names, regional and local, so that an individual could have had two to three band affiliations. For example, the same person could have had these regional and local band affiliations:

Sustina River Dena'ina: **Susitnu Ht'ana**
Middle Susitna River Dena'ina: **Dun'ena**
Kroto Village Dena'ina: **Dashq'e Ht'ana**

There is special status accorded a main village or a drainage system for which there is an ethnonym with **ht'ana.** For example, in the lower Susitna River there were numerous settlements that were part of the seasonal round. But the suffix **ht'ana** is only applied to the Susitna Station, Alexander Creek, lower Yentna Old Village, and Kroto Creek sites. Analogously, there are regional band names for the Yentna River Dena'ina and the Susitna River Dena'ina, but not for the Matanuska River Dena'ina or the Knik River Dena'ina. The nineteen Dena'ina regional band names (for the whole language area) must be of some antiquity.

The following passage from a 1985 narrative by Shem Pete shows how the band names are used in speech:

> Iydluytnu Qayeht'ana ghu k'a qeył dghinih ha t'qighit'a.
> *They were called 'the plural objects river village people' [Eklutna people].*
>
> You know from Susitnu Station, Yusdishla Qayeht'ana, Dashq'e Qayeht'ana, ighi Tsuk Qayeh qayeht'ana.
> *You know from Susitna Station there are the 'little point people' [site on island in Susitna River], then the 'on the shoal people' [Kroto people], and the 'old village people' [lower Yentna Old Village people].*
>
> Ndaha village yeh hq'u qayeht'ana heł dghinih.
> *Wherever there was a village they called them 'the village people.'*
>
> That's the way it is from Kenai to Eklutnu to Matanuska, Niteh, Nitehen, Iydlughet, Iydlughe Ht'ana, K'enakatnu Ht'ana.
> *'Among the Islands,' [Matanuska site], 'the person of among the islands' [was the chief there], at 'by the plural objects' were the 'by the plural objects people' [Eklutna people], and the '?-stream people' [Fish Creek-Knik village people].'*

Table 5 and Map 7 display the Dena'ina band names in the Upper Cook Inlet.

TABLE 5. UPPER INLET DENA'INA AND SOME NEIGHBORING BANDS ‡SEE ALSO KARI 2007:73–77

The regional band names are numbered with Roman numerals here and are shown on Map 7 within circles. The prominent village band names are numbered with regular (arabic) numerals here and on Map 7.

I	Kustatan and West-Lower Cook Inlet Dena'ina	**Qezdeghtna** (OI) **Qeydaghetna** (U)	'peninsula people'
II	Tyonek Dena'ina; also Cook Inlet Dena'ina	**Tubughna** (O), **Tebughna** (U), **Tuvugh Ht'an** (I)	'beach people'
III	Susitna River Dena'ina	**Susitnuht'ana** **Dustnay** (Ahtna)	'sand river people' 'people out in front'
1	Alexander Creek village Dena'ina	**Tuqen Kaq' Qayeh Ht'ana**	'clear water mouth village people'
2	Susitna Station Dena'ina (two names)	**Yusdishla Qayeht'ana,** **Susitnu Qayeh Ht'ana**	'little point village people' 'sand river village people'
IV	Rainy Pass area Dena'ina	**Shandała Nununk'dnilghuyna**	'people who holler to make migrating birds fall down'
V	Yentna River Dena'ina	**Yentnuht'ana**	'backbone river people'
3	Lower Yentna Old Village people	**Tsuk Qayeh Qayeh Ht'ana**	'old village village people'
VI	Middle Susitna Dena'ina	**Dun'ena**	'near upriver people'
4	Kroto Creek Dena'ina	**Dashq'e Ht'ana**	'on the shoal people'
5	Montana Creek village people	**Qiduk'ggat Ht'ana**	'frozen overflow people'
6	Talkeetna village/river people	**K'dalkitnu Ht'ana**	'food is stored- river- people'
VII	Talkeetna Mountains Ahtna-Dena'ina	**Dghelay Teht'ana** (U) **Dzełyi Ht'ana** (Talkeetna)	'mountain people'
VIII	Western Ahtna	**Htsay Ht'ana,** **Hwtsaay Hwt'aene** (A)	'small timber people'
7	Chickaloon Dena'ina	**Nuk'din'itnu Ht'ana,** **Nay'dini'aa Na' Hwt'aene** (A)	'bridge goes across people'
8	Wasilla area Dena'ina	**Benteh Ht'ana**	'among the lakes people'
9	Fish Creek-Knik village people	**K'enakatnu Ht'ana**	'?- stream people'
IX	Knik Arm area Dena'ina	**K'enaht'ana**	possibly 'vision people'
10	Matanuska village Dena'ina	**Niteh Ht'ana**	'among the islands people'
11	Eklutna village Dena'ina	**Iydlughet Ht'ana, Idluytnu Qayeh Ht'ana**	'at plural objects village people'
X	Turnagain Arm Dena'ina	**Tutl'uht'ana**	'headwaters people'
12	Point Possession Dena'ina	**Tuzqunt Ht'ana** (O) **Tuyqunt Ht'ana** (U)	'still water people'
XI	Kenai Peninsula Dena'ina; Swanson River Dena'ina	**Yaghenenht'ana** (OI) **Yaht'ana, Yaghedna** (U)	'good land people'
13	Nikiski area Dena'ina	**Qeghnenht'ana** (O)	'adjacent land people'
XII	Kenai Dena'ina, Kenai River people	**Kahtnuht'ana** **Nkahtnuht'ana** (IIU)	'river mouth river people'
‡XIII	Ahtna, Copper River people	**Utnuht'ana**	'beyond river people'

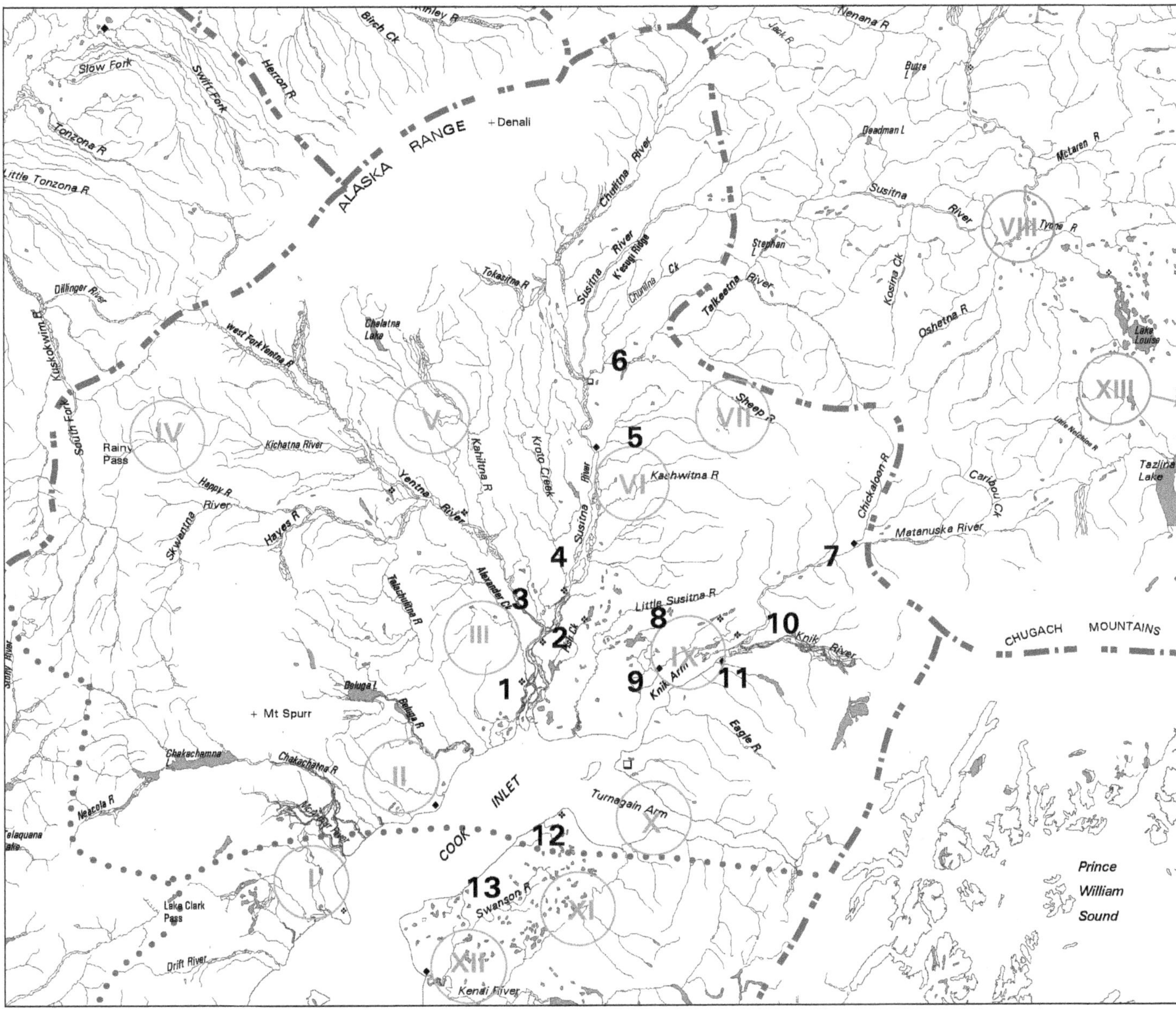

‡MAP 7

Upper Cook Inlet Dena'ina regional and local band names.

Circled Roman numerals for regional bands, arabic numerals for local bands.

MAP BY JAMES KARI

Dena'ina Place Names and Territorial Knowledge

by James Kari

Some features of orally transmitted Dena'ina place names

Shem Pete's knowledge of the Dena'ina geography of upper Cook Inlet was extremely impressive. He knew from memory more than 650 of the 1,002 place names in this book. He had been to most of the places he named, and he also knew many other Native (Dena'ina and Ahtna) names in areas beyond his personal travels. (See Map 8.) Shem was the sole source of about 350 of the names listed in the book. He was fond of listing the names. He discussed and recorded names for some areas on a dozen or more separate occasions. He was consistent in his pronunciation of the names and in the sequencing and location of the places. Shem also very consistently stated that he did *not* know certain areas, which is another measure of the integrity of the data he did report. In Rainy Pass, for example, he knew the series of mountains and streams as far as he had traveled (Chapter 6), but the sequence stops abruptly at **Qułch'ishtnu** (6.40, Styx River).

‡For the overall Dena'ina language area (Maps 2 and 4) there are over 2300 Dena'ina place names on record in 2015 (Kari 2010a). The three most complete published sources on Dena'ina names are this volume, Kalifornsky 1991 for the Kenai Peninsula, and Evanoff

MAP 8

Shem Pete's lifetime travels.

This map presents the boundaries of the Upper Inlet Dena'ina dialect area (dashed line), which is about 25,000 square miles in area, and also shows the outer extent of the places Shem traveled on foot or by boat (solid line), an area of more than 13,800 square miles. Two academic reviews of the book noted that Shem Pete's place name inventory and estimated lifetime travel map are among the most extensive in the ethnogeographic literature for Native North America (Afable and Beeler 1996:185–86) and for elsewhere in the world (Hunn 1994).

MAP BY KAREN PEARSON

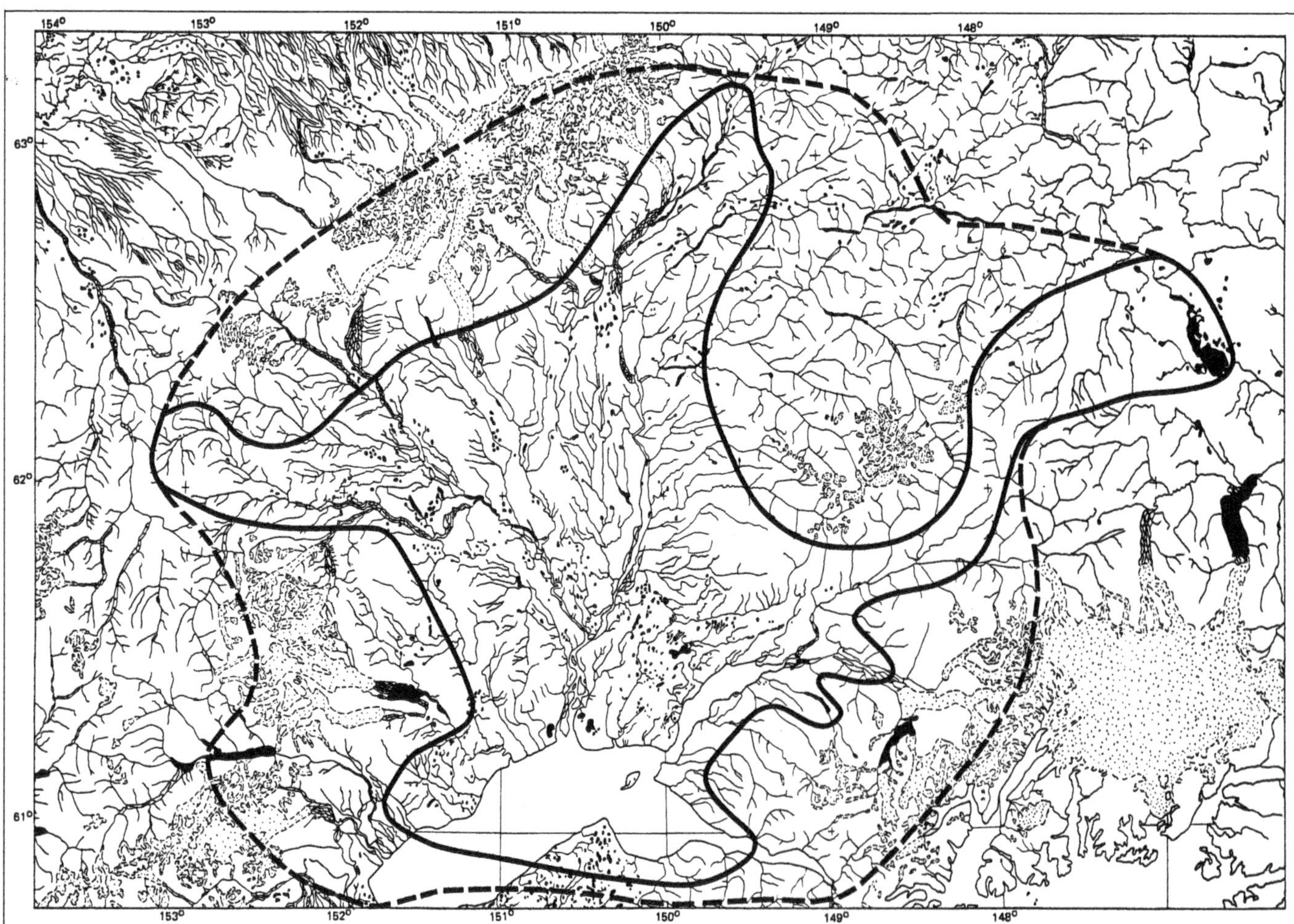

2010 for portions of the Inland and Iliamna dialect areas. By way of comparison, Upper Inlet Dena'ina place name records are not as detailed and complete as those for Inland Dena'ina (Nondalton and Lime Village), Ahtna, Koyukon, or Gwich'in.

There are several features of Dena'ina (and other Athabascan) place name knowledge that deserve special mention. The conventions for transmitting the names and the numerous patterns in structure and distribution in sets of names indicate that the Athabascans have an "official" geographic names system. For the Dena'ina and the ancient Athabascans place names were an essential component of their land and life. The Dena'ina (and other Athabascans) apply names in a systematic and parsimonious way over entire drainage systems and regions (Kari 1989). A set of names was vital for navigation and orientation through a band territory. The names were carefully passed on through the generations and across the clan and language boundaries. ‡Also see *watershed tenure*, pp. 144–147.

Consider that the last speakers of the Upper Cook Inlet dialect of Dena'ina who have reported names for this book learned about them while traveling in the country or, in some cases, from listening to stories. The speakers report these place names with great care and with obvious affection for the associations between the names, the ancestors, and the land. These oral place names are independent of the historic place names; i.e., they have been used almost exclusively by speakers of Dena'ina (or Ahtna or one of the other neighboring Athabascan languages). The names are strictly reported from memory and are not learned from maps or written records. Speakers repeatedly confirm sequences of names. There has been very little disagreement about place names among the forty-five or more speakers of Dena'ina or Ahtna who have contributed the names to this book. Significantly, places with forgotten names are left unnamed. New names are never coined by individuals, and Dena'ina places are almost never named after people.

The oral place names are quite stable and conservative over time. Between Athabascan languages, a single set of names extends across language and dialect boundaries with regular phonological adjustment. For example, in Chapters 10, 11, 13, and 14, forty-five names that occur in both Ahtna and Dena'ina are pronounced according to the sound systems of each language. Of the sixty or so Dena'ina place names that were recorded before 1845, all but five or six were known by Shem Pete or other speakers in the late twentieth century. The vast majority of the Dena'ina names that have been recorded in the Upper Cook Inlet region are clearly aboriginal; that is, they were used by the Dena'ina prior to historic contact.

The speakers of Dena'ina and Ahtna are fond of the place names, in part because the meanings are usually analyzable. Sequences of names are a stimulating mix of fact and imagery and can be enjoyed as folk poetry. It is fascinating to learn, for example, that the Peters Hills (7.46) are **K'enuqak'itnetant** 'Where an Animal Is Crouching and Revolving,' or that a creek on the Chulitna River (9.3) is **Qichi Qinghiłneqt** 'The Old Lady Made It That Far,' or that the name of the Stephan Lake site (11.13), **Tatik'niłtunt,** means 'Where a Game Trail Goes into Water.'

Virtually all of the Upper Cook Inlet Dena'ina and Ahtna place names are composed of Athabascan roots and morphemes. There appear to be no non-Athabascan place names on these lists, even though in the ancient past the Dena'ina must have been incursive into Cook Inlet Basin. For the Dena'ina place names have been essential for orientation and boundary marking. Accordingly, the geopolitical and ideological function of Athabascan place names is an extremely interesting area for the study of Athabascan prehistory. Some individual place names served as boundary markers, see for example 10.28 and 10.35, two mountain boundary markers west of Tyone Lake. More broadly, patterns in the Athabascan generic terms for 'stream' and 'mountain' have served to mark regions. (See Map 9.)

‡In the past ten years place name records have advanced for eight Dene languages surrounding the Alaska Range. Ahtna geography is the most advanced of any Alaska Native language (see Kari 2008, 2010b, 2011, 2014 and Kari and Tuttle 2005). Kari generalizes that all Alaska Dene share a highly functional and rule-driven SIGN+GENERIC *generative geography* (see pp. 144–147 and the PDLL theory).

The role of Native geographic knowledge in early travel, exploration and cartography in Upper Cook Inlet

Shem Pete's Alaska is referenced to a wide array of published and unpublished sources and maps on the Upper Cook Inlet. We have made a concerted effort to find every written source or mention of Dena'ina place names in the study area. We have also cited sources that mention Dena'ina people and their activities during the late nineteenth and early twentieth centuries when the Dena'ina were still using large portions of their territory.

The early historic interactions with the Dena'ina by Russian officials and by the U.S. military and the USGS, as well as by special interest groups such as merchants, miners, mountaineers, and hunters, can be characterized as "commercial intelligence gathering" (as discussed in Sterritt et al. 1998:194). The citations from the historic sources and the selection of early cartography of Upper Inlet in *Shem Pete's Alaska* demonstrate a vigorous Dena'ina knowledge of the landscape of Upper Cook Inlet. In the first Russian sources on the Cook Inlet Dena'ina

(Wrangell 1839 [1980], Map 17) and early American sources on exploration in Upper Cook Inlet in the 1890s and early 1900s, we can trace the key role that Dena'ina and Ahtna knowledge of geography played as non-Native miners, businessmen, hunters and clergy first came into the Upper Inlet.

The Dena'ina and Ahtna head men were recruited as guides, gave trail-route and travel instructions, drew sketch maps, and recited networks of Dena'ina place names. The 1839 Wrangell map is the most remarkable early source. (See Map 17 and the discussion there.)

The naturalist-artist Henry W. Elliott, writing in the mid-1890s, described Dena'ina ("Kenaitze") overland travel patterns.

> The Kenaitze are ardent hunters, nevertheless, and spend most of their time and energy in the chase of land animals—making long journeys into the interior, and gloomy recesses of mountain cañons and defiles, to follow and find the fur-bearing quarry peculiar to their country. They have regular tracks of main travel, where, like the stage stations on our frontier post-roads, at intervals they have erected shelter-huts, in which they live with their families for months of the year at a time (Elliott 1897:91).

This passage from William Dickey, writing in 1896 on the middle Susitna River above Talkeetna, indicates the broad regional or small-scale sense of the territory that the expert Dena'ina or Ahtna men knew:

> Much interested in the geography of this country, and finding the Government charts so unreliable, we gathered all the information possible from the Indians and the few whites who had, during the summer, prospected on the upper river. The Kuilchaus [**gheltsana** the Dena'ina term for interior Athabascans] drew for me a map of the river, holding the pencil by the extreme end, and much amused with their first experience with pencils and paper. When they reached as far in the drawing as they had ever been on the river they drew their pencil around back and shook their heads, and we could not get them to venture any further opinion as to the river beyond. Their only way of estimating distances was by sleeps, as they had no conception of what a mile was; in fact, they did not know what the words Indian or white signified. One of the Knik tribe, an intelligent and prosperous Indian who trades with the interior Indians and who travels every winter in the interior country, drew a map showing the relation of the upper Copper, Sushitna, and Tanana rivers. He makes, as do all the interior Indians, the three rivers in close proximity at their head waters (Dickey 1897b, in Washburn 1951:87).

In 1898 Lieut. H. G. Learnard commented on Dena'ina territorial knowledge in the Talkeetna area: "All seem to have a good idea of distance, which is expressed in so many sleeps, and also a fair idea of the geography of the country as regards important features. They are the best of hunters and can see and locate game when a white man would not think there were any in the vicinity" (Learnard 1900:666).

Similarly, Lieut. Joseph Herron, traveling in 1899, offers these important details about Athabascan trail systems:

> In exploring my route I found that there already existed throughout its length winter sled trails cut out, blazed and in regular use by the Indians and coinciding with or paralleling my trail throughout. I have indicated these on the maps of this report. These trails represent the result of a knowledge of the country accumulated during many generations, as well as the labor of many Indians. They follow direct lines and traverse advantageous ground. These can be economically followed, connected and plainly marked, and made ready for general use (Herron 1901: 54).

See also p. 122 and Figs. 76 and 77, where geologist Josiah Spurr in 1898 encountered Shem Pete's stepbrother, Chief Evan, who gave him directions and a sketch map of the Yentna and Happy river drainages.

For perspective, we should note that there are some deleterious accounts about Athabascan geographic knowledge, some of which seem to keep reemerging. This topic is dealt with in more detail in Kari (1999:22–23).

Hudson Stuck wrote in 1914, "It is true that the little handful of Indians on the Sushitna River, who never approached nearer than one hundred miles to the mountain, have another name for it. They call it *Traléika,* which, in their wholly different language, has the same signification" (Stuck 1914:viii). Stuck's claim regarding the lack of travel near the Alaska Range by the Susitna Dena'ina is inaccurate. The Dena'ina made use of the frontal foothill system across the base of the south side of Central Alaska Range. The earliest encounters with Dena'ina men in the Alaska Range produced the earliest toponymic documentation, such as Eldridge and Learnard in 1898 and the names "Talkeetna," "Chunilna," "Chulitna"; Spurr in 1898 and the names "Yenlo" and "Kliskon"; or Herron in 1899 and the names "Kahiltna" and "Kichatna"; or Cook-Browne in 1906 and the names "Tokasha" and "Kanicula." These names certainly were part of the aboriginal Dena'ina place names system.

The prominent geologist Alfred H. Brooks in his monograph *The Mount McKinley Region* made a number of claims about "the Alaskan Indian," i.e., the Athabascans.

> Much of the range formed an almost impassable barrier between the hunting ground of the Cook Inlet natives and that of the Kuskokwim Indians. It [the Alaska Range] does not seem to have been named,

> for the Alaska Indian has no fixed geographic nomenclature for the larger geographic features. A river will have half a dozen names, depending on the direction from which it is approached. The cartographers who cover Alaska maps with unpronounceable names, imagining that these are based on local usage, are often mislead (Brooks 1911:22).

Brooks never did first-hand ethnographic research with Athabascan people, and he was discussing a subject on which he had no relevant expertise. There is in fact a well-established Athabascan name for the Alaska Range (7.61 Dena'ina: **Dghelay Teh**, Lower Tanana: **Deghiloyi Ti**). The main passes of the Central Alaska Range, Broad Pass and Rainy Pass, were traversed in aboriginal times, probably with regularity, and we have documented sequences of Athabascan names and travel in virtually all of the accessible passes throughout the Alaska Range. The streams, small or large, have *a single name* that may have differing pronunciations from the vantage point of different language areas. The variant pronunciations of shared Athabascan place names are strong proof of the antiquity of the oral names. Athabascan place names from the oral tradition are vastly more conservative and stable than are Alaska's official map names.

Cartographic sources on Dena'ina place names

We present many examples of the Upper Inlet cartographic record, including many rare and obscure sources. ‡Cartotoponymy is the study of names attested on maps. In Table 6 the maps we analyzed for *SPA* are grouped into eleven types.

The maps which have made the largest contributions to Dena'ina toponomy are the 1839 Wrangell map, the USGS and military survey maps of 1898 and 1899, and the USGS quad maps of the 1950s and 1960s. The most interesting

TABLE 6. THE CARTOGRAPHY OF UPPER COOK INLET RELEVANT TO DENA'INA PLACE NAMES RECONSTRUCTION

		Cartographer/author	Date of field work	Date map published	Map no. in *Shem Pete's Alaska*
1	Ship-based maritime cartography				
	coastal Native presence only, no overland exploration				
		Cook	1778	[1967]	65
		Vancouver	1794	[1801]	14
		Teben'kov	1830–50	1852	
2	Early continental cartography				
	some incorporate Native sketch maps and toponyms				
		Wrangell	1820–35	1839	17
		Zagoskin	1842–45	1967	
		Dall	1867	1870	
		Petroff	1880	1884	6, 66
3	Early historic sketch maps				
	noting Native presence and some Native toponyms				
		Dickey	1896	1897	42
		Johnston and Herning	1895–99	1899	45, 52
		Herning	1898–1906	1906	32, 49, 59
4	Early historic privately published regional topographic maps				
	showing commercial developments (mining, roadhouses, trails) and incorporating some Native sketch maps and toponyms				
		Cook	1906	1907, 1908	
		Sleem	?	1910a	30, 38, 63
		Sleem	?	1910b	50
5	Native-drawn sketch maps with annotations or toponomy				
	very few early Native sketch maps are known for Cook Inlet Basin				
		Allen	1885	1887	60
		Moffit	1904		44

TABLE 6 (CONTINUED)

			Cartographer/author	Date of field work	Date map published	Map no. in *Shem Pete's Alaska*
6		U.S. Army expedition topographic maps of main travel routes				
		some Native toponyms provided by Native guides				
			Meiklejohn	1898–99	1900	35, 47, 56
			Herron	1899	1901	22, 29
7		General Land Office cadastral maps				
		large scale maps showing property ownership, trails; a fine source for locating early historic Native trails and structures				
			Davidson	1911–1912	1915	54
8		United States Geological Survey maps				
	a	Early USGS expedition topographic maps,				
		excellent topography, some Native toponyms, especially for major streams				
			Eldridge and Muldrow	1898	1900	20, 39
			Mendenhall	1898	1900	57, 62
			Spurr	1898	1900	24
			Brooks	1902	1911	15
	b	USGS localized geological and topographic maps				
		few Native names noted				
			Moffit (upper Susitna)	1910	1912	
			Capps (Yentna distict)	1911	1913	
			Capps (Willow Creek)	1913	1915	
			Capps (Skwentna)	1926	1929	
			‡Waring (Anthracite Ridge)	1931	1936	58
	c	modern USGS quad maps; Orth 1971; GNIS files on Alaska place names				
		many minor Native-origin names recorded from 1950s to1970s				
				1950s–1970s		12, 58
	d	unpublished USGS field maps, sources for numerous Native-origin names				
		most not available but frequently cited in Orth 1971				see Chp. 14:14.100–102
9		Commercially produced multi-purpose Alaska maps				
		many unofficial names are noted; some have unique information on Native-origin names				
			Rand McNally		1890s to present	
			Kroll Map Co.		1910s to present	10, 31
			Alaska Road & Recreation maps		1970s to present	
			Imus Geographics		2000	
10		Expository cartography on Dena'ina				
			de Laguna (sites)	1930	1934	
			Townsend (sites)		1981	
			Kari and Kari (place names)	1980	1980	
			Kari and Fall (place names)	1981–86	1987	
			Kari, Fall, and Ganley	2001–2003	this volume	chapter maps, e.g., 11, 16, 18, etc.
11		Draft field maps and place names lists for Dena'ina and Ahtna place names				
		marked or labeled USGS maps				
			Kari		1974–2001	Fig. 21

maps for depiction of Dena'ina presence, what I call "incipient cartography," are Herning (1906) and Sleem (1910). These maps lack the accuracy of the early USGS maps, but they incorporate some Native-drawn sketch maps, and they display many details about the Native trail systems, sites, and structures.

The anaylsis of Dena'ina place names

By way of introduction we present some terms and general principles about Dena'ina place names. The place names follow regular grammatical patterns and usually have clear, analyzable meanings. Dena'ina place names typically have a two-part or binomial structure: **Tatik'nitun Bena** (11.14 Stephan Lake, Fig 12 above), 'Game Trail Goes Into Water Lake,' or **K'enq'a Bena** (1.39) 'Fishing Hole Lake,' where the first word is a ‡*sign* (or specific) term, which can be a verb or a noun, and the second word, **bena** 'lake,' is a generic term, which identifies the type of feature in the place name. Some names have a structure noun+ verb+generic, such as **K'da T'el'iht** (1.8) 'where antlers are gathered' (antlers + are gathered + **t** where, place of).

‡There are some one-word place names, usually nominalized verbs, such as **K'idazq'eni** (1.17, Mt. Spurr) 'the one that is burning inside.' A key principle of Athabascan place naming is that names occur in *sets* for a group of related geographical of features. In our research we tried to generate these sets of names. For example there is the glacier name at Mt. Spurr 1.91, **K'idazq'eni Łi'a** that is based upon the name **K'idazq'eni**. Or Prairie Creek Tatik'niłtuntnu (11.11), and **Tatik'niłtun Bena** Stephan Lake (11.14) which share the sign **Tatik'niłtun** 'Game Trail goes into Water.' About 400 names in this book are in sets of two or more names.

There is a fairly extensive inventory of Dena'ina place names in Upper Cook Inlet, and the names can be studied and analyzed at several levels: 1) we can examine and categorize the meanings of the names; 2) we can study the structure of the names, for example how the generic terms are used to create sets of names; 3) we can look at

FIGURE 20

The principle of the clustering of Dena'ina names into sets is evident in this view from the summit of Pioneer Peak of **Skitnu** (15.2, the Knik River valley) and **Skitnu Łi'a** (15.15, Knik Glacier). Grouped with these two names, at the center of the frame, is **Skitnu Dghelaya** (15.16, Mt. Goode). The mountains in the upper left of the frame are called **Ch'atanhtnu Dghelaya** (14.58, Mt. Marcus Baker and nearby mountains) since they are at the head of **Ch'atanhtnu** (14.2, Matanuska River).

PHOTO BY LORRAINE BASNAR ELDER, 1982

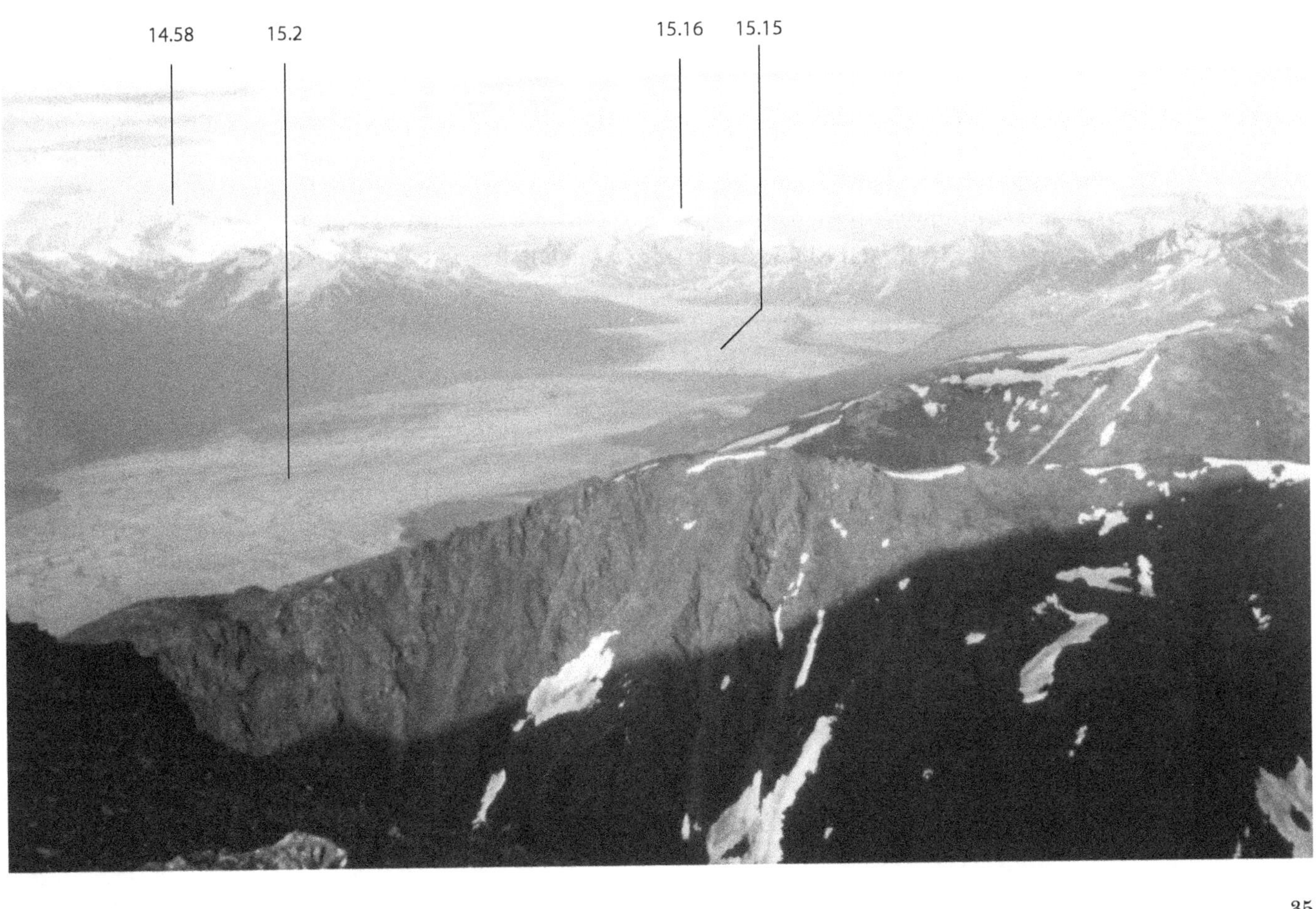

A note on map production for *Shem Pete's Alaska*

by Matt Ganley

Matt Ganley is a vice president for Bering Straits Foundation, and is also the owner of Map-Alaska. He received his MA (Anthropology) in 1991 from the University of Alaska Fairbanks, where he has completed coursework for a Ph.D.

The maps produced for each chapter of *Shem Pete's Alaska* are important for understanding the relationship of place names to topography. As a research component for this volume, the use of detailed topography and hydrography allowed significant refinement of name placement. For the reader and student, the relief maps provide a visually stimulating means for learning place names and understanding the interaction of Dena'ina names and topography.

The choice of material for creating the base maps for this volume presented some challenges. Mapping software and digital data were used to generate the shaded relief and hydrographic layers. Initial placement of Dena'ina toponyms over these base maps was based on the maps contained in the first edition of *SPA*. Individual locations were then refined or corrected as necessary during multiple review sessions with Dr. Kari for name and number placement.

All topographic detail was derived from the 1-degree or 15-minute series Digital Elevation Models (DEM) available from the USGS. These files were merged, converted to UTM projections, subsets were derived for each area, and the topography projected as grayscale reflectance maps. Cleanup was necessary in the final images. Vector data was readily available for hydrography and glacier coverage in 1:1,000,000 or 1:63,360 scale Digital Line Graphs (DLG) from USGS. Like the DEMs, these files were merged and subsetted, and re-projected after initial conversion into Data Exchange format (DXF). For the glacier coverage, the vector outlines were filled, exported, and converted to a raster imagery, which was then placed over the topographic reflectance maps.

The use of the two topographic resolutions of one degree or fifteen minute series DEMs created continuity between Dr. Kari's original working maps and the final maps for this volume. It was relatively easy to use the USGS 1:250,000 or 1:63,360 quad sheets for crosschecking the locations of specific toponyms. Using the 1:63,360 vector coverage for hydrography (USGS DLG) resulted in accurate placement of drainage-based toponyms. The maps were first prepared within a projected file to retain accurate geo-spatial name distribution. These coverages were then converted to a combined vector (hydrography/text) and raster (topography) format for the final maps.

Throughout the volume the reader will notice that the maps for each chapter are not consistent in scale. Given the choice of standardizing a scale for all maps or providing the best detail for each particular area, it was decided that the latter was more appropriate. It was found, as one would expect, that there was a correlation between the distribution of names and the level of topographic detail needed to convey the specific Dena'ina knowledge of the landscape. In areas where the names were dispersed, a more generalized base was used for clarity of representation. Conversely, where names occurred with great frequency, a more detailed topographic and hydrographic model was necessary. In some rare cases it was necessary to impose a detailed hydrographic model over a more generalized topographic model to create a sensible map, as for the Anchorage area (Map 61 in Chapter 15).

In Alaska, most research concerning indigenous toponyms has been conducted using standard USGS map sheets. While the majority of elders and community members are familiar with these maps, future research should consider using more "realistic" devices for eliciting information about place and landscapes. Shaded relief or reflectance maps can represent the landscape in a manner more consistent with our visual perception and experience of landforms. As technology continues to accelerate towards faster and more compact means of 3D representations, the use of rendered viewsheds, oblique imagery, and shaded relief during the interview process may allow the collection of more elaborate toponymic information and rich travel narratives.

the distributions of names for what they can tell us about Dena'ina settlement, travel, and land use; and 4) there are a few other patterns in the Dena'ina names that make one wonder if these occur for some reason. There is some duplication in names. There are three mountains called **Dghelishla** 'little mountain' (4.9, 10.6, and 11.9). See also Fig. 70 in Chapter 4 where we discuss what appears to be a coordinated *ensemble* of names for a group of six hills, ridges, and mountains between Mount Susitna and Beluga Mountain. See also pp. 144–147.

In Table 7 we summarize the overall inventory of place names in *Shem Pete's Alaska,* including language of origin and numbers of bilingual names. In 7A we count the distinct named places in the book, but we do not count all the variant forms for one place, such as distinct dialect variants and bilingual names. At name entries we state when Shem Pete or other speakers have speculated or offered their best guess about a name. In 7B the term ‡*reconstructed names* are those place names where as editors we assigned a name without other verification from speakers. Non-traditional names are Dena'ina names that have been recorded or suggested in the historic period which are not true oral place names (see 15.85, 15.86, 15.97, and 15.99). 7C summarizes the number of names in the book that are from Dena'ina and the other neighboring Athabascan languages and the bilingual and multilingual names.

TABLE 7. SUMMARY OF THE PLACE NAMES INVENTORY IN SHEM PETE'S ALASKA

A. Total named places	
first edition (1987)	720
second edition (2003)	974 (+26%)
revised second edition (2016)	1,002 (+2.8%)
B. Types of names and editorial decisions	
unique names	605
names in sets of 2 or more	395 (40%)
names not mapped	8
reconstructed names (by editors)	15
non-traditional names	6
C. Language of origin and bilingual naming	
Dena'ina	753
Ahtna	163
Dena'ina-Ahtna	56
Upper Kuskokwim	6
Dena'ina-Upper Kuskokwim	11
Dena'ina-Ahtna-UK-Lower Tanana	2
Ahtna-Lower Tanana	2
Dena'ina-Ahtna-Lower Tanana	1
places noted without a Dena'ina name	9
English	1*
substrate ∞ (from unknown language)	2

*See 15.82; the Dena'ina names for "Anchorage," **Angits** and **Tan** are from English words.

Toponymic generic terms, the morphemes that appear regularly in place names, are the main landscape concepts recognized in the language. These terms are key to memorizing sets of Dena'ina place names. When we see Dena'ina and Athabascan place names recorded on early historic maps, the variations in the generic terms across the Athabascan languages can give us clues as to the specific language or dialect that was being used when a name was documented. For example, in Chapters 6 and 10 we trace the Dena'ina 'stream' term **-tnu** with a **-tn-** cluster, in some Upper Kuskokwim and Ahtna stream names. Such names in these two neighboring Athabascan languages imply that in some time in the past these drainages were in Dena'ina territory.

Table 8 displays the toponymic generic terms that are most common in Upper Inlet Dena'ina and Western Ahtna place names. These terms classify the landscape and facilitate the memorization of sets of names. ‡Generic terms range in their geometry from linear features, points, polygons, and areas. These are symbolized on the table.

When we compare place names across the various Athabascan languages, some remarkable patterns emerge that reveal the antiquity of some generic terms and some striking geopolitical functions of names for streams and names for mountains. Map 9 shows that in the Northern Athabascan languages there are seven mutually exclusive stems for 'stream' that have overt boundary marking functions. I refer to these as *hydronymic districts.* (See Kari 1996a, 1996c.) The Western Alaska term for 'stream' is reflected in the Dena'ina stem **-tnu** and the Ahtna stem **-na'.**

It also interesting that the terms for 'mountain' have some regional patterns across Athabascan languages, though these are not as clear-cut as the seven mutually exclusive terms for 'stream.' The Dena'ina and Ahtna terms for 'mountain' **dghelay** and **dghelaay,** respectively, are used in their territories south of the Central Alaska Range. The term **dghelay** has a noticeable boundary-marking function when compared with the mountain names with **ddheł** or **dleł** in the Athabascan languages of the Tanana River Valley to the north. The cognate word, **dzeł,** is uncommon in Dena'ina place names but is somewhat more common in Ahtna place names. It appears that the Tanana Valley Athabascan place name 7.62 **Deghiloyi** for 'Alaska Range' extended its meaning to 'mountain' in the languages positioned south or west of the Alaska Range. This place naming shift may signal the onset of early movements into new territories south of the Alaska Range. Thus place names were basic to ancient Athabascan land tenure, and shifts in place naming for 'mountain'

TABLE 8. TOPONYMIC GENERIC TERMS IN DENA'INA AND AHTNA ‡also see Kari (2007:121–147 and 2008:17–26)

Symbols: specific place ↘ linear feature ⇔ local area, polygon ⊙ regional area ○ - hyphen indicates possessed form of noun

	type of feature	Dena'ina (Upper Inlet)	Ahtna
A	Common verb suffixes or enclitics in place names, VERB+ENC		
	in, at area ⊙○	**-h**	**-x**
	at, where, specific place ↘	**-t**	**-den, -de**
	by, at, near ⊙ ↘	**-gh**	**-gha**
	relative suffix, that which is VERB' ⊙ ↘	**-i**	**-i**
B	Common areal nouns or postpositions in place names, NOUN + PP		
	in a region, over an area' ○	**-teh**	**-tah**
	below, beneath ⊙	**-t'uh**	**-t'aa**
	on, at a place ↘	**-q'**	**-k'et**
	on a flat surface, ‡area of resource ⊙	**-quq'**	**-kaak'e**
	along the distance of ⇔	**-ghuy**	**-ghaay**
	tip of, point of ⇔	**-ki**	**-cii**
	at the end, limits of ⇔	**-lugh**	**-laaghe**
C.1	Common geographic noun roots: Water features		
	stream (primary) ⇔	**-tnu**	**-na'**
	stream (as noun) ⇔	**k'etnu**	**c'ena'**
	stream mouth, confluence ↘	**-kaq', dukaq'**	**-caeq'e**
	headwaters ⊙	**-tl'u, tl'ughu**	**-tl'aa**
	lake ⊙	**ben, -bena**	**ben, -bene'**
	enclosed lake ⊙	**dałtuni**	**dełtaani**
	glacier ⇔	**łi, -łi'a**	**łuu, -luu'**
	stream from hillside ⇔	**ch'adinłeni**	**ts'ediniłeni**
	stream into head of lake	**dinłent**	**diniłende**
	lake outlet stream ⇔	**q'estnu**	**k'ese**
	straight stream plain or channel ⇔	**tuyan, -tuyana**	**tayen, -tayene'**
	slough on stream ⇔	**-q'eghtsi, nineq**	**–**
C.2	Common geographic noun roots: Land features		
	mountain ⊙	**dghelay, -dghelaya'**	**dghelaay, -dghelaaye'** **dzeł, -dzele'**
	hill ⊙	**tes, -tesa'**	**tes, -tese'**
	ridge, esker ↘	**ses, -yits'a**	**ses, -yese'**
	plain, clearing ⊙	**ken, -kena'**	**cen, -cene'**
	swamp ⊙	**tl'egh quq'**	
	riverbank ↘	**bes, -besa**	**bes, -bese'**
	island ⇔ ⊙	**ni, -ni'a**	**nuu, -nuu'**
	shoal, low island ⊙	**dash**	**daes**
	gorge, canyon ⇔	**denyit**	**dyii**
C.3	Common geographic noun roots: Man-made or man-utilized features		
	village ⊙	**qayeh**	**kayax**
	trail ⇔	**-tena, tinitun**	**tene**
	pass, portage ⇔	**-tustes**	**-tates**

MAP 9

Hydronymic districts in Northern Athabascan languages.

‡The hydronymic district was the first key concept for Kari's theory of Dene prehistory "The Proto-Dene *Lex Loci*" ('word/ law of location,' or PDLL) that is introduced on pp. 144–147. Some concepts presented in Kari (1996a, 1996c, and 2010b) that are central to the PDLL theory are *hydronymic districts* (seven regional terms for 'stream' in Northern Dene languages), *reverse hydronymns* (use of a minor hydronymn to highlight streams such as **-niq'ə** instead of **-na'** in Western Alaska), and *oronymic districts* (where PA ***dzəł** 'mountain' shifts to ***dəghilayi** south and west of the Alaska Range, see. 7.61). The hydronym **niq'ə** literally means 'on the upstream.' The **na'/ niq'ə** hyronymn boundary on the Tanana River is at Delta River and Goodpaster River. Kari (1996a:463): "the **na'/ niq'ə** innovation is only one piece of evidence of the gradual westward/ downstream expansion of the Athabaskans into western and Southcentral Alaska. The Tanana River, with four [to five] smallish language areas gives every indication of having been the ancient center of Northern Athabaskan culture." Also introduced on p. 144 is the PDLL term *watershed tenure* that includes hydronymic districts and several other pragmatic/ intentional place naming devices that are detectable in Alaska Dene place names.

MAP BY JAMES KARI AND DIXON JONES

and 'stream' seem to reflect deliberate policy changes by Athabascan bands (Kari 1996a).

Whereas generic terms in place names are important for understanding how the Dena'ina (and other Athabascans) classify their geography, the ‡*signs* (or specific terms) in the place names reveal a great deal about environmental interests and cultural values. The various types of name meanings, such as birds or water conditions (or hydrology), can be traced as one reads through the lists of names. In Table 9 we summarize the meanings in the specific terms for the 1,002 names in the book. For this summary we treat a set of names only once. We group here 605 names into general classes of meaning.

The above grouping is based upon a couple of operational principles, and sometimes the distinctions in name meanings is a judgment call. Names that are partially analyzable were placed in categories, such as hydrology. Some names seem to have a clear meaning but what they refer to is moot; e.g., **Qułtsadi** 'That Which is Pounding (Hammering) Upward' (6.54, Kohlsaat Peak) might refer to the geology or to a human or animal activity. The count for geological feature names lumps together names that range from being graphic and descriptive of a landform to being metaphoric and/or abstract, e.g., **Tuqashi** (9.19) 'objects that fall in water' vs. **K'esugi** (9.7) 'the Ancient One.' Material culture groups names that refer to man-made products including structures and implements. Customary activities are names that refer to recurrent activities such as **Dach'qelqiht** 'Where We Spend the Spring,' (7.7) or a resource harvest activity such as **Nutsahdnghitses** 'Rocks Dammed Across' (7.8). Human events are names which appear to derive from a single incident such as **Tununiłch'ulyutnu** 'River Where People Killed Each Other in Water' (6.7).

TABLE 9. SEMANTIC ANALYSIS OF PLACE NAMES IN SHEM PETE'S ALASKA

A	Natural history		
	Animals	30	5%
	Fish	18	3%
	Birds	8	<1%
	Vegetation	43	7%
	Insects	3	<1%
	Hydrology	123	21%
	Terrain and geology	157	26%
	Weather	12	1%
	Direction	19	2%
B	Human activities		
	Material culture	34	6%
	Foods	6	<1%
	Trails	22	2%
	Customary activities	54	9%
	Significant human events	15	2.5%
	People	6	<1%
	Historic events or activities	6	1%
	Mythological events	6	1%
C	Others		
	Opaque or unanalyzable -Ω- or -?-	11	1%
	‡Partially analyzable	7	<1%
	‡Ambiguous (two or more meanings)	5	<1%
	Class not clear	9	<1%
	‡Substrate -∞-	2	<1%

Here are some interesting facts about the meanings of Dena'ina place names. Very few of the names are unanalyzable or *opaque* (-Ω-, 11, or 1 percent), seven are partially analyzable. Unanalyzable names, such as **K'ich'atnu** (7.19), or **K'enakanen** (13.1), do not contain recognizable stems or verb forms, and expert speakers such as Shem Pete tended not to give meanings for them. Nevertheless they sound like and feel like Dena'ina place names. There are no Eskimo-origin names in Upper Cook Inlet. ‡In the 2016 edition we treat two names as *substrate* names from an unknown language ∞, 6.2 Skwentna River and 16.8 Dipper Lake and stream, both with the stem **shqit**. There are a few names with Russian loan words such as a lake **Gidara Q'dalchini** 'The One Made Like a Guitar' (16.40) (which is placed in the hydrology category).

It is striking how few of the Dena'ina names refer to people—only six, one being **Chikdashla Bena** 'little grandmother's lake' (1.54, lake by Tyonek cemetery). Only two names refer to people by name: **Dghełtayi Betnu** 'Creek of the One That Is Strong' (15.9, Jim Creek) is said to refer to Indian Jim's personal name, and the other is **Delindin Bena** (12.8, Delyndia Lake) which is based upon Shem Pete's Russian name. Thus the record shows that the Dena'ina did not name places after people. The personal naming system, for religious reasons, was kept distinct from the place name system.[20]

Only one percent of the names are clearly related to historic events or activities. For example, the name **Sdigel Qak'ighałnikt** 'Where Glass Pitched a Tent' (2.12) is said to refer to the first white man, an American, to ascend the Susitna River. Two names refer to historic coal mining (1.40 and 5.7)

Another pattern that is rare in Dena'ina place names is overt reference to mythological events. Even though the Dena'ina and especially Shem Pete had a vast repertoire of **tsukdu,** stories of the distant times when animals and

20. One name, **Dusgeda Tukda Ti'iltant** (12.4) 'Where Father of Dusgeda was Carried Out,' does contain a personal name, but this is Shem Pete's way of referring to this site on the Little Susitna River. Strictly speaking, this is not a true Dena'ina place name, and in this typology I treated it as a human event.

humans spoke, very few place names of the Upper Inlet Dena'ina refer to their mythology. One such name seems to be **Ggih Qughijaq Bena** 'Lake Where a Monster Came Up' (13.28, White Lake). Places that have strong associations with mythology such as **Nutsada'iy** (14.59, Lions Head) on the upper Matanuska River, have naturalistic names, in this case 'Rock That Is Standing.' Also a place with a fantastic-sounding name, **K'enuqak'itnetant** 'Where an Animal Is Crouching and Revolving' (7.46, Peters Hills), does not have a myth reported for the name, but instead Shem Pete states that this is the natural impression the mountain gives as one is walking around it.

In general, Alaskan Athabascan legendary stories (the Dena'ina **tsukdu**) do not often refer to specific geographic names, and few place names make overt references to legends. On occasion Shem Pete annotated place names with **tsukdu**. The Salmon Boy Story (pp. 184–190) is an example of a prominent legend tied to a specific area, lower Kroto Creek. Shem Pete's style of annotation for place names in his country is factual and refers to human events, land use, and environmental conditions. To summarize, the Dena'ina place name system, as reflected in the meanings summarized in Table 9, emphasizes naturalistic descriptions of places and resources that facilitates practical orienteering by the memorization and association of names with features.

Yet another way to study Dena'ina place names is for distributional patterning. The chapter maps in *Shem Pete's Alaska* can be reviewed for patterns such as: 1) the relative density of names in favorite places (such as Chapter 8 on lower Kroto Creek); 2) the sequence and placement of named places on travel routes (e.g., Chapters 2, 3, and 5 along the lower Sustina and Yentna Rivers have named places that reflect overnight camps by the rivers or along ridges and eskers with established trails); 3) the types of features the Dena'ina tend to name versus those they tend *not* to name; or 4) the contrast in areas where names are well known versus those that are poorly known and have gone undocumented, ‡such as in the Talkeetna Mountains (Chapter 11).

Ethnogeographic methods for *Shem Pete's Alaska*

‡The Dena'ina geography of Upper Cook Inlet has been researched off and on for more than forty years. It is instructive to review the stages of this work and the techniques that produced cumulative advances in the Upper Inlet Dena'ina place names records. *SPA* combines linguistic methods (citations of vocabulary and narrative) with ethnographic and historical sources in the drainage-based atlas format. The exemplary work of the Northern Athabascan ethnographic research tradition is Helm 1981, the Subarctic volume of the *Handbook of North American Indians*. In the 21st century primary ethnographic

FIGURE 21

Shem Pete and James Kari making a presentation on Dena'ina place names at a conference in Anchorage in 1981. ‡Tobias (2009:331–333) has a useful review of our methods for this book. He calls our approach an "in depth salvage toponymy study." Tobias contrasts our methods with those typical of land-use-and-occupancy studies.

PHOTO BY PRISCILLA RUSSELL

research on Northern Dene is not feasible. On the other hand *SPA*'s ethnogeographic methods are highly synthetic and inter-disciplinary.

Beginning in 1974 we began researching Dena'ina place names in Upper Cook Inlet with Shem Pete and our other consultants. We put the names on slips of paper and in lists, and these lists were revised, updated, and marked on USGS maps. Kari and Kari (1982) listed and mapped 373 Dena'ina names in Upper Inlet. This was expanded to the 720 places that were presented in the 1987 edition of *Shem Pete's Alaska*. We began work for the second edition by listing and updating all of the Dena'ina place name files. We then reviewed these lists section by section with Sava Stephan and several other Dena'ina or Ahtna speakers. For the second edition 252 named places were added and more than 75 other places had some revision in location, spelling, or translation. All along we were frequently revising our editorial decisions, especially about locations of names. We had to factor in Shem Pete's and Sava Stephan's limited eyesight and lack of map-reading skills and our lack of familiarity with and access to much of the country that Shem knew. ‡The cornerstone of an ethnogeographic research program is the cumulative drainage-based place names list. For Alaska Dene languages, the shared constantly informative rule-driven generative geography can be reconstructed by the cultivation of archival sources and by repeated reviews of place names lists with the most expert speakers.

Researching in a depopulated language area where there are few expert speakers like Upper Cook Inlet places many constraints on the fieldwork and the record. In some cases Shem Pete and the other speakers could state with authority the exact name, location, and meaning of a feature. In other cases all that we have to work with is sketchy evidence, perhaps from a map or historic source. The Upper Inlet Dena'ina geography is more speculative and is not as authoritative in detail and precision if we compare the present corpus with the work I have done on Inland Dena'ina (Nondalton and Lime Village), Ahtna, or Upper Tanana. In those three Athabascan language areas there has been more on-going use of the land and the Native place names in the twentieth century, there have been more experts who know adjacent and overlapping areas, and there have been more opportunities to refine the place name lists and to verify locations. For example, in Chapter 1 there are many lakes and streams near Tyonek where no name was known by ten or more speakers queried. In chapter 12, the Little Susitna River drainage has many features in areas that Shem traveled through all his life that have no recorded Dena'ina place names. In the Talkeetna River we are fortunate to have the few names recalled by Shem and Johnny Shaginoff, but many major features, such as Disappointment Creek and Sheep River, have no known names.

Some examples of specific techniques and advances in the Dena'ina geography are presented herewith.

A) Newly elicited or remembered names. Sava Stephan has been the major contributor of Dena'ina names recorded ‡between 1987 and 2002. Quite a few names were recalled by Sava as we reviewed lists of names or as we inquired about features for which there still were no Dena'ina names. Leo Stephan and Katie Wade also added previously unrecorded names. Several names in Chapters 10 and 14 were brought in from the Ahtna place names lists (Kari 2002 ‡and 2008). Examples: 1.94, 1.95, 8.74, 8.75, 8.76, 10.50–56.

B) Names that occurred in recorded narratives by Shem Pete and others that were not available in 1987. The Jim Tyone travel story (in Chapter 10) yielded several previously undocumented names along the Matanuska River. Examples: 3.29, 3.32, 8.68, 14.115–116, 16.25.

C) Names from Shem Pete that we had misplaced or had not filed and that did not appear in the first edition. Examples: 8.93, 9.36, 9.37, 9.38, 15.118, ‡and 10.59, 10.60.

D) Names prompted by documentary sources. Several Dena'ina names mentioned in writings by Annabel, Spurr, and others were added; e.g., 8.84, 8.85, 8.87, 6.45, 16.46. Our examination of historic maps produced other leads, e.g., 8.86, 7.59. Four Dena'ina- or Ahtna-origin stream names we had not noticed before on the Matanuska River (14.100–102, 14.124, and Map 58)were all recorded by

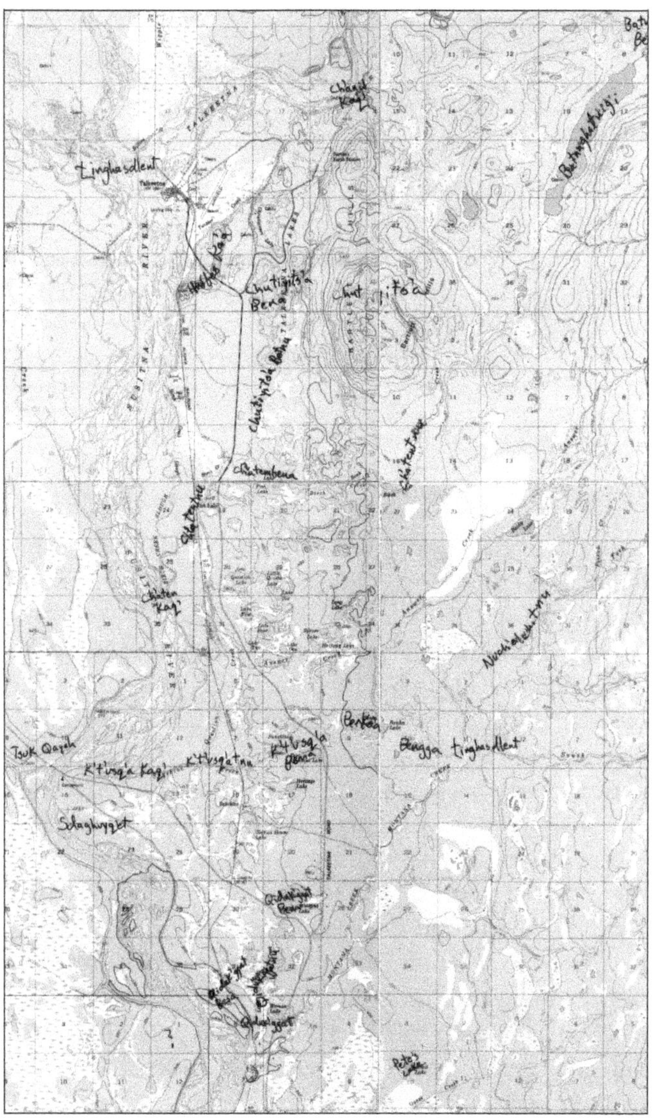

FIGURE 21

Kari's laminated field maps with Dena'ina place names from the Talkeetna area. The most effective way to map and correct Native place names is to write names on laminated maps. During our work with Shem Pete we did not have extensive mapping using this technique.

FIGURE 23

Łich'antnu Łi'a (1.77, Capps Glacier) with the feature **Łik'a Kin'i** (1.116, 'dog's head') the nunatak on the right, a name obtained by back-translating from the map name "Dogshead Glacier." See also Plate 3.

PHOTO COURTESY OF COOK INLET REGION, INC.

USGS in 1931. Even though we could not re-elicit these, they were added to the lists. An interesting example is **Łik'a Kin'i** 'dog's head' (1.116, Dogshead, Fig. 23), the nunatak northeast of Capps Glacier. This is a Dena'ina-translation place name that we noticed on the draft Tyonek quad sheet that is on file at the National Archives in Anchorage. USGS topographer Tom Taylor (p.c.) recalled that he had recorded this name with Nickafor Alexan at Tyonek in 1958; the name was re-elicited with Sava Stephan. ‡In 2016, **[Dnigi Ghi]** (9.40 Moose's Tooth) was reconstructed.

E) Names generated by applying the rules of the Dena'ina/Athabascan naming system. Probably 60 percent of the 252 names added to the second edition were generated by such rules. These include derived names for many stream mouths, outlet streams, or mountains, e.g., 8.70–8.73. The name for Ruth Glacier (9.18) **Dghelay Ka'a Łi'a** is a logically correct generated name. By this principle, some recent man-made features, such as Westchester Lagoon in Anchorage (15.126), have Dena'ina place names in *Shem Pete's Alaska.*

F) Names generated by mapping decisions. As we marked drafts of the chapter maps on the digital shaded-relief base maps by Matt Ganley, we had the opportunity to visualize the names in the chapter and to see geographic lacunae. At this stage many map locations were refined and a few more names were generated; e.g., 3.27, 4.25, 6.47. We consider this "loop" between the lists of names and the final cartography to be an especially important stage for review of the inventory and for coordination of the named features with their map locations.

G) Revised place name pronunciations. The Native-origin names on the USGS maps served as prompts for asking Shem Pete about specific names. At times in the first edition all we could report was Shem Pete's best guess of a name. At times we have found more plausible Dena'ina place names. For example, for the Dena'ina-origin name Nagishlamina River (1.19), Sava feels that **Nahq'ashla Betnu,** 'Little Lookout Stream,' is plausible and sounds familiar to him. This was changed from **Nuq'shla** 'little bar' in the first edition. See also the anecdote for 9.16 **K'enik'ela** and Fig. 123.

H) Translation or etymological refinement; e.g., 1.24 **Sdidahtnu**, 'Calves Become Cramped River,' an interesting translation offered by Sava Stephan. ‡For the 2016 edition Kari reviewed all the literal translations.

I) Location revision via local expertise. In the Talkeetna area, the remapping of 8.52 **Qiduk'ggat** to the site at the mouth of Little Montana Creek, via Lillian Theodore, led to two other generated names, 8.88 and 8.89. Alaska Range mountaineer Dave Johnston and NPS pilot-ranger Hollis Twitchell offered more likely locations for 9.7, 9.21, and 9.26. We assume that Shem knew names for the more accessible mountains adjacent to the Chulitna River and not the higher peaks such as Moose's Tooth. A revision in the location of one name can have a ripple effect on locations of adjacent names.

J) Editorial speculation. Perhaps 10 percent of the 1,002 names are based upon some level of speculation. Shem Pete, Sava Stephan, and others have given their best recollection of a name in someone else's territory, or their rendition of a written name; e.g., 1.20, 6.50. In some cases, such as 9.16 **K'enik'ela,** we feel that we improved over our speculation of 1987. ‡For fifteen names we have provided a reconstructed spelling of the name (using [...]), though we have no other verification for the name. For example, 15.113 Metal Creek is possibly **[Yuyantnu]** 'Cloud Creek,' based upon Russell Annabel's translation of the Dena'ina name in some of his writings. ‡See also pp. 231–233 on some recent ethnogeographic methods such as the use of databases and place-intensive narratives.

The status and recognition of Dena'ina place names

Alaska's maps and historic records have layers of place names from different periods of Alaska's history. The names are from international languages such as Spanish, Russian, French, and English as well as from various Alaska Native languages. This book is a compilation of the oral Dena'ina place names of Upper Cook Inlet. Shem Pete had a dual place names system. He knew hundreds of Dena'ina place names that he learned through traveling or from listening to other Dena'ina people. He also knew many Russian-origin place names, and he knew hundreds of English names that had been newly coined and used by English speakers early in the twentieth century. Two distinct classes of place names are the *official place names* on maps that are recognized by USGS, and the *locally-used place names,* some of which appear on privately published maps or guidebooks or in historic sources, and some of which are only known by word of mouth. For example, the stream 1.29 has the Den'ina name **Ch'elehtnu,** which has the official name Old Tyonek Creek, but locally this is usually called "Robert's Creek." A fascinating aspect of the early historic maps of Upper Cook Inlet is their depiction of place names, many of which are otherwise forgotten. For example, Map 50 (Sleem 1910b) has many defunct place names around Knik Arm (e.g., The Island,Wasillas Cabin, Wasillas Cache, Grassy Ridge.)

The official record of place names in Alaska and in the United States is maintained by the U.S. Geological Survey in what is called the GNIS, the Geographical Names Information System. For Alaska the GNIS contains all place names that are on the USGS Alaska quad maps with coordinates, feature type, and description. The first compilation of place names in Alaska was Marcus Baker's *Geographic Dictionary of Alaska* (1906). Donald Orth's *Dictionary of Alaska Place Names* (1971) is a frequently used source on Alaska's place names, listing more than 26,000 names throughout the state. The most current records of Alaska place names are available from USGS, either on their website or in a digital file. The names of streets, roads, subdivisions, and buildings are *not* included in the GNIS.

In Alaska *unofficial place names* are commonly coined and used by many groups such as business owners, pilots, hunters, fishermen, mountain climbers, and snowmachiners. Some unofficial names acquire official status, especially if they are printed on privately published maps. The Kroll Map of Alaska, published about every ten years since the 1910s, is an interesting record of many unofficial place names for cultural features such as trails and roadhouses. (See Map 10 below, a section from the Kroll Map of the 1940s). The popular Alaska Road & Recreation Maps of Southcentral Alaska contain hundreds of unofficial place names, for example, for roads, boat landings, fishing holes, and roads.

Looking at Dena'ina-origin place names that appear in the GNIS as official place names in the study area of *Shem Pete's Alaska,* we count about 90 Dena'ina or Ahtna-origin names. This count excludes names such as Tanaina Peak, which is not a traditional Dena'ina name. Also excluded are places on the maps named after Dena'ina chiefs—such as Wasilla, Chickaloon, Red Shirt, or Kroto—which are not traditional Dena'ina place names. The Dena'ina-origin names were established in two eras. The well-known names for large streams and villages and a few hills and mountains derive from the 1890s to the 1910s: Tyonek, Eklutna, Chester, Yentna, Susitna, Kashwitna, Kahiltna, Chuitt, Talkeetna, Tokasha, Yenlo, Kliskon, or Yukla. A second period during which Dena'ina-origin names were recorded was the 1950s and 1960s, when USGS topographers made the effort to gather place names from local experts. In 1958 Tom Taylor of USGS recorded and submitted about sixteen Dena'ina names in the Tyonek and Kustatan areas. These are for lesser known features such as Skeetna Lake, Kaldachabuna Lake, and Congahbuna Lake. A small number of official names are based upon translations of Dena'ina names, such as Dogshead Glacier (1.114) and Birchwood (15.58).

MAP 10

Detail from 1940 Kroll's map of Alaska: Upper Cook Inlet

The Kroll map of Alaska has been published at about ten year intervals since the 1910s. Here is a detail from the study area of this book from the Kroll map of the late 1940s. This map is a source on unofficial and historic place names, especially for commercial enterprises such as roadhouses, mines, freighting trails, boat landings, bays, and inlets. The Kroll maps tend to retain many of these place names on their maps long after the sites have been abandoned.

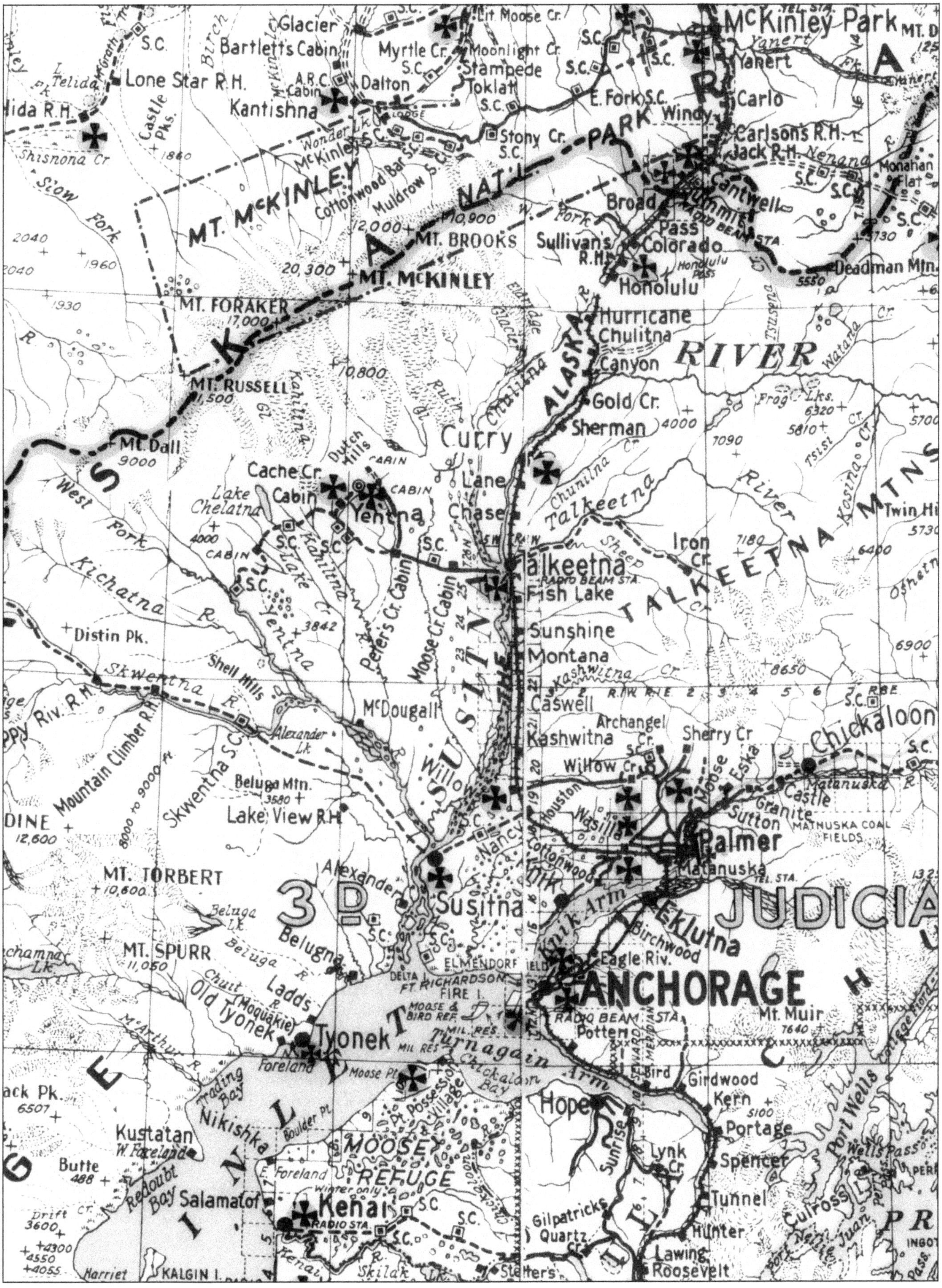
McKinley Park
Glacier
Bartlett's Cabin
Myrtle Cr.
Moonlight Cr.
Stampede
Lone Star R.H.
Dalton
Toklat
Kantishna
Yanert
Carlo
Windy
E. Fork S.C.
Stony Cr.
Carlson's R.H.
Jack R.H.
Nenana
Cantwell
Monahan Flat
MT. McKINLEY NAT'L PARK
Cottonwood Bar
Muldrow
Broad Pass
Summit
Colorado
Sullivan's R.H.
Honolulu
MT. BROOKS
MT. McKINLEY
20,300
12,000
10,900
Deadman Mtn.
MT. FORAKER
17,000
Hurricane
Chulitna
Canyon
RIVER
MT. RUSSELL
11,500
10,800
Gold Cr.
Sherman
Curry
MT. Dall
9000
West Fork
Cache Cr. Cabin
Dutch Hills
Lake Chelatna
Yentna
Lane
Chase
Talkeetna
Iron Cr.
Fish Lake
TALKEETNA MTNS
Kichatna R.
Distin Pk.
Sunshine
Montana
Skwentna R.
Shell Hills
McDougall
Caswell
Archangel
Kashwitna
Sherry Cr.
Chickaloon
Mountain Climber R.H.
Skwentna S.C.
Beluga Mtn.
3580
Lake View R.H.
Willow
Houston
Wasilla
Matanuska
Castle
Granite
Sutton
Palmer
MATANUSKA COAL FIELDS
MT. TORBERT
10,600
Alexander
Susitna
3D. JUDICIAL
Knik Arm
Eklutna
Birchwood
Eagle Riv.
MT. SPURR
11,050
Beluga R.
Belugna
ELMENDORF FIELD
FT. RICHARDSON
FIRE I.
ANCHORAGE
Ladds
Old Tyonek
Tyonek
Mt. Muir
7640
Potter
Turnagain Arm
Chickaloon Bay
Moose Pt.
Foreland
Trading Bay
Bird
Girdwood
Kern
Hope
Portage
Port Wells
Nikishka
Kustatan
W. Foreland
MOOSE REFUGE
Sunrise
Lynk Cr.
Spencer
Butte
488
Redoubt Bay
Salamatof
E. Foreland
Kenai
RADIO STA.
Tunnel
Gilpatricks
Quartz Cr.
Hunter
Culross
Lawing
Roosevelt
KALGIN I.
Skilak Lk.
INLET

FIGURE 24

Bradford Washburn has been photographing the Alaska Range since the 1930s. This Washburn photo of the Central Alaska Range, taken from an elevation of 2000 feet above the town of Talkeetna on February 26, 1979, was selected because it can be captioned with 17 Dena'ina place names. When we highlight Dena'ina place names in the high mountains of the Central Alaska Range, we are looking at the perimeter of the Dena'ina place name network. The cardinal points and lines in the Dena'ina name system are located downland in the outlier hills and the main streams of Upper Cook Inlet Basin. See also Fig. 125 for a similar view in summer.

PHOTO USED WITH THE PERMISSION OF BRADFORD WASHBURN, #8381

1 **K'enuqak'itnetant** (7.46, Peters Hills)
2 **K'enik'ela** (9.35, Avalanche Spire)
3 **Be'u** (7.49, Mt. Foraker)
4 **Begguya** (7.50, Mt. Hunter)
5 **Ben Ka'a** (9.13, Benco Lake)
6 **Tuqashi** (9.14, Tokasha Mts)
7 **Dghelay Ka'a** (7.51, Denali)
8 **Dghelay Ka'a Łi'a** (9.18, toe of Ruth Glacier)
9 **Ts'ilu Dghelaya** (9.17, mt. east of Ruth Glacier)
10 **K'esugi Ken** (9.6, Curry Ridge)
11 **Łi Tayena Dghelaya** (9.36, Mt. Deception)
12 **Ts'ilutnu** (9.1, Chulitna River)
13 **Suyitnu** (2.1, Susitna River)
14 **K'dalkitnu** (11.1, Talkeetna River)
15 **Łinghasdlent** (8.66, "The Forks," confluence of three rivers)
16 **Hnibes Ka'a** (8.65, "Ski Hill")
‡17 **Dnigi Ghi** (9.40, Mooses Tooth)

As in most of Alaska, the Native-origin place names in Upper Cook Inlet were established with little control for linguistic accuracy. There are many gross distortions of Dena'ina names, such as Mount Yukla on the Eagle River (from **Nuk'elehitnu**) or Chuitkilnachna Creek south of Tyonek (from **Ch'k'e'uła Betnu**). There are also mislocated Native-origin map names, such as 10.18, Mount Watana. The corresponding Ahtna source name, **Debetse'**, is on the north side of the Susitna River. At times the presence of a Native-origin names on maps is purely accidental, as with Chester Creek (15.84) in Anchorage, from **Chanshtnu** 'Grass Creek,' and Goose Creek (10.23) on the upper Susitna River, from **Gguus Kulaen Na'** 'Creek Where There Is Celery.' One ‡facetious and completely bogus "Native name," Bulchitna (7.35), was established in 1954. In addition, there are some coined Dena'ina-origin names that are not traditional Dena'ina place names. Four mountain names in the Chugach Range above Anchorage—Kanchee, Knoya, Koktaya, and Tikishla—were suggested by the Mountaineering Club of Alaska in the 1960s (see Chapter 15, also Porco 1985). In 1984 members of the Mountaineering Club submitted the name "Kidazqeni Glacier" (1.91) off Mt. Spurr. ‡In 2000 Chugach State Park staff submitted a name "Thachkatnu Creek" based on **Łach Q'atnu** (15.33). Kari had suggested a spelling "Thachkatnu" in Carberry 1979. At that time special characters like ł and q', were not endorsed by the USBGN or the Alaska State Board. In 2015 the correctly spelled Dena'ina name—Łach Q'atnu Creek—was recognized by the Alaska State Board.

Another complication is that the well-known privately published maps such as the Kroll Maps and the Alaska Road & Recreation Maps often introduce and then promote recently coined names for unnamed features. A recently published map of Chugach State Park by Imus Geographics (2000 and 2006) has a variety of Dena'ina place names. Some names are from the first edition of *Shem Pete's Alaska* with Dena'ina names in parentheses shown after the official name, e.g., *Turnagain Arm (Tutl'uh)*. The map also has quite a number of unofficial Dena'ina-origin names for mountains used by the Mountaineering Club of Alaska: Delgga Mtn., Yudi Peak and others.

To summarize, the official recognition of Dena'ina place names is meager. Only a small number of Dena'ina place names are commonly used, such as the major steam names (Yentna, Susitna, Talkeetna, Chester) or village names (Tyonek, Eklutna). The official and locally used unofficial names in Upper Cook Inlet and Southcentral Alaska are overwhelmingly in English. We estimate that about 35 percent of the places in *SPA* have no official name.

In 1982 the Alaska legislature adopted a guideline for the Alaska State Board of Geographic Names that states that the Board "shall consider using Alaska Native place names for geographic features that have not been previously named using Native language writing systems accepted by the Alaska Native Language Center" (Laws of Alaska, 1982:CSSB 727(SA)). In 1994 the U.S. Board on Geographic Names adopted a guideline that allows for the use of special alphabetical symbols and diacritics in place names so that they names can be established with accurate spellings in established local Native language writing systems. In 2002 the Alaska State Board of Geographic Names and also the U.S. Board approved a respelling for "Kidazqeni Glacier," with the apostrophes for the glottal stops, as "K'idazq'eni Glacier" (1.91). They also approved a new name "K'esugi Ridge" (9.7). These names adhere to the spellings of the Dena'ina writing system so that the public can strive for more accurate pronunciations of the names.

The Dena'ina place names of Upper Cook Inlet are intrinsically fascinating. They memorialize the Dena'ina people and their life ways. We have seen from the first edition of *Shem Pete's Alaska* that Dena'ina place names are being used in a variety of ways—in education, in tourism, in outdoor travel, on signs and brochures, and in the naming of businesses and websites. We envision that many people will be memorizing and using sets of Dena'ina names and that more Dena'ina place names will become official place names. We also envision that learning Dena'ina place names will be enhanced with maps, posters, and signs, along with audio files to help with pronunciation. Our friend and mentor, Shem Pete, wanted all of us to perpetuate these names.

‡In 2016 we note the many creative ways that Dena'ina place names have flourished and have significant public visibility in Anchorage and in Upper Cook Inlet. The Dena'ina Center opened in 2008 with five meeting rooms named for Dena'ina villages. Dena'ina language was used throughout the 2013 exhibit Dena'inaq' Huch'ulyeshi at the Anchorage Museum. An interactive map of Anchorage with twelve Dena'ina names from the 2013 exhibit is now in the Alaska Gallery at the Anchorage Museum. Since 2003 Dena'ina place names have appeared on signs in Chugach State Park, Denali State Park, in several Anchorage Municipality parks, and on the UAA campus. The CIRI corporate website has Dena'ina village names. Knik Tribal Council has given Dena'ina names to some street names in subdivisions on Knik lands. Dena'ina place names are being used for businesses and non-profits (e.g., Bentalit Lodge, Skitnu Bahai Camp, Tuqashi Institute). The official recognition of Dena'ina place names on USGS maps has advanced rather slowly. In the 2016 reprint we make note of two new authentic Dena'ina and Ahtna names, Ch'akajabena Mountain (1.127) and Nen' Yese' Ridge (10.62); two name changes, Tsaani Creek (9.41, from Squaw Creek) and Upland Kacaagh Lake (10.16, from Deadman Lake); and two names with revised spellings, Ch'akajabena Lake (1.16) and Łach Q'atnu Creek (15.33).

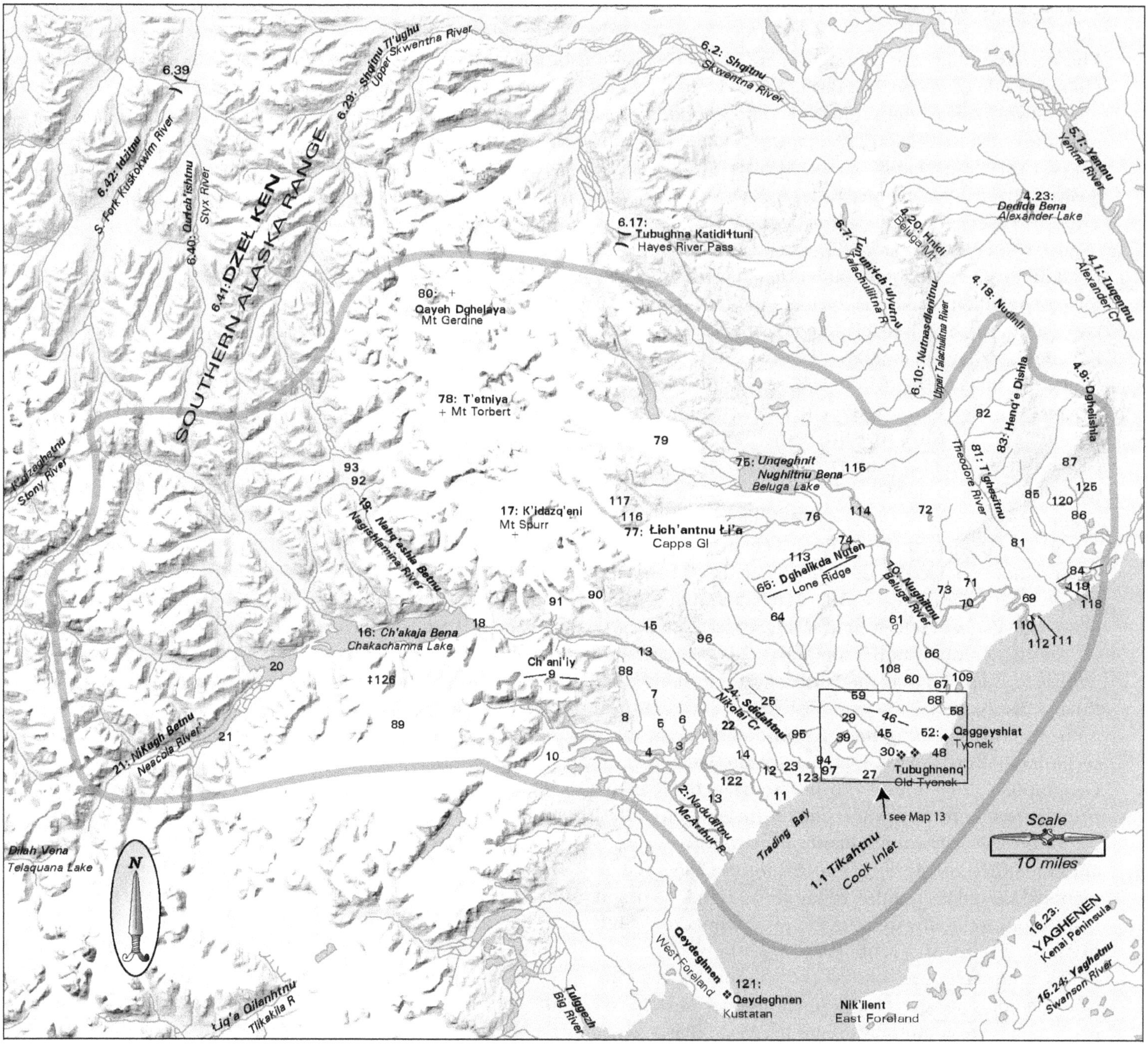

MAP 11

Place names map of Western Cook Inlet, showing Nos. 1.1 to 1.127.

MAP BY MATT GANLEY

1

Western Cook Inlet

McArthur River to mouth of Susitna River

Although our survey of place names begins north of the McArthur River, it should be noted that the Dena'ina place names extend south along the west side of Cook Inlet to the lower end of Kamishak Bay. Iliamna Lake Dena'ina were traveling up the beach to the Alaska Commercial Company post at Tyonek in the 1880s. Many Dena'ina villages and camps were located in the Kustatan area. See Cook Inlet Historic Sites Project (1975:101–120) and Chickalusion (1982) for information about the Kustatan area. After about 1930 Dena'ina villages at Kustatan and Polly Creek were abandoned. Tyonek people still journey by boat down the inlet for spring clam digging at traditional camp sites at Point Harriet and Little Jack Slough (Fall, Foster, and Stanek 1984:129–134).

There has been some question about where the prehistoric boundary between the Outer Inlet and Upper Inlet Dena'ina dialects was. For convenience, the Alaska Native Language Center map (Krauss 1982) places it at Tyonek, where both dialects are now present. The 1778 Anderson vocabulary, collected on the Cook expedition somewhere between Kustatan, Tyonek, and Point Possession, has both the Upper Inlet and Outer Inlet dialects. The 1883 Jacobsen word list (1977), the first collected at Tyonek, was in the Outer Inlet dialect. Kustatan residents, such as the Chickalusions, have spoken the Outer Inlet dialect. Long-time Tyonek families, such as the Chuitts and the Trentons, have spoken the Upper Inlet dialect. Today's speakers of Dena'ina state that the Upper Inlet dialect has been dominant at Tyonek.

Shem Pete: "«A long time ago they called Tyonek **Ełnen Bunkda** 'Mother of the Earth' because there are lots of things to eat all the time: clams, fish, beluga, seal, grease, and oil [products that women process]. But they call Susitna River **Ełnen Tukda** 'Father of the Earth' because they always had lots of fur, lots of caribou meat, dry meat, dry fish, but not much oil» [products that men obtain].

"They used to get lots of grub at Tyonek.... They never used to go hungry because there was lots of seals and belugas. [In spring] everybody [in Tyonek] begins making oil and grease. They put up lots of grease for everybody [in the inland villages]. They all come down to Tyonek to get oil and this grease. They keep coming, keep coming getting oil. They bring all kinds of fur blankets, parka squirrel, whistler, lynx, marten.... And lots of caribou and black bear meat and beaver meat so they could buy all this oil. Those big beluga guts all full of oil. The Tyonek people were rich from oil and **baba** [dry fish] too.... They used to have regular road down to Tyonek...for grease and seal meat, fish. And this story is from long time ago, before Russians or anybody came to this country.... It was way before my time."

Sources: (south of Tyonek) Peter Constantine, Maxim Chickalusion, Terry Stephan, Pete Bobby; (north of Tyonek) Alec Peter, Shem Pete, Sava Stephan, Nickafor Alexan, Tommy Allowan, Ella Chuitt, Nellie Chickalusion, Fedora Constantine

2003 revisions: names added 1.88–1.125; locations revised 1.69, 1.113; Dena'ina names revised 1.19 and 1.75.
‡2016 revisions: names added 1.126, 1.127; names revised 1.50, 1.58, 1.59, 1.85, 1.92, 1.93, 1.97; figures added 36A, 49A.

Peter Constantine: "In spring when the parka squirrels came out, the men would go to the mountains to hunt, and the women stayed home and fished for trout in the streams with fish traps. The men went to Chakachamna or to Rainy Pass for caribou."

1.1 Tikahtnu or **Nuti** • 'Ocean River,' 'Saltwater'
Cook Inlet
The first name is mainly used in the Outer Inlet area. The second name is most commonly used in the Upper Inlet area. See Kari and Kari (1982:84–89). Note that the Dena'ina also use their river-oriented directional system when referring to places on Cook Inlet. For example, bays on the inlet are named with the word **kaq'** 'river mouth' (Kari and Kari 1982:43–45).

Baily Theodore commented to Kari in January of 1977 that on a clear day and at the right angle **Tatnintin** is visible from Knik. This is 'ridge extending into water,' Cape Douglas, which is the most southerly Dena'ina place name that has been recorded.

§1.121 Qezdeghnen *(O)*, **Qeydeghnen** *(U)* • 'Peninsula Land'
Kustatan Peninsula, Kustatan village site, West Foreland
A name first documented as "Kustatan" in the 1880 census by Petroff (Map 66), this peninsula is the most central point in the Dena'ina language area. Being on the trails along the west side of the Inlet, near several passes through the Southern Alaska Range, and the main navigational point in middle Cook Inlet, Kustatan has played a key role in Dena'ina prehistory. Kustatan was the site of the remarkable Kustatan Bear Story that took place here in the winter of 1895–96 (Chickalusion 1982, Kalifornsky 1991:286–310). Several village sites are described in Cook Inlet Historic Sites Project (1975:109–110). On Sleem (1910a) this is "Kostaka." ‡Stanek, Fall, and Holen (2006:63–67) present a nice profile of Kustatan village.

Elliott (1897:87): "So precipitous is this mainland shore of Cook's Inlet that at only two small points of the most limited area is there any low land to be found, and these spots have been promptly utilized by the Kenaitze Indians as sites for their villages of Tyonok and Kustatan."

‡Kari has suggested that three Dena'ina eco-regional names with **nen** 'land,' 1.121 Kustatan Peninsula, 1.30 Tyonek area, and 16.23 (Swanson River and Kenai Peninsula), have the feel of being an *ensemble of founding regional place names.* See Table 12 and Map 26.

1.2 Nadudiltnu • 'Current Flows Down-River'
McArthur River
This is and has been a major hunting and trapping area for Tyonek and Kustatan people. Use of this area by Kustatan people is presented in Chickalusion 1982. Contemporary harvest of beluga, seal, moose, beaver, and waterfowl in this area is documented in Fall, Foster, and Stanek 1984.

Trading Bay, the arc of coastline between West Foreland (or Kustatan Peninsula) and North Foreland, was so named in 1786 by British Captains Nathaniel Portlock and George Dixon in recognition of the early contact period of the 1780s and 1790s when British, Spanish, and Russian sailing ships came into Cook Inlet to engage in trade with the Dena'ina.

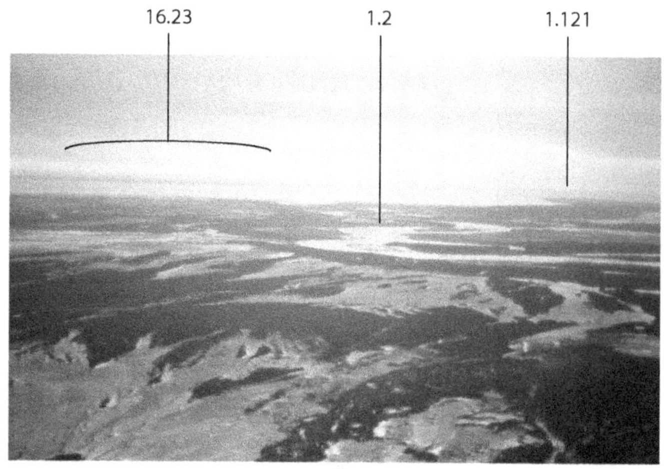

FIGURE 25

Looking south from **Nadudiltnu** (1.2, McArthur River), **Qezdeghnen** (1.121, Kustatan Peninsula) is visible on the west shore of **Tikahtnu** or **Nuti** (1.1, Cook Inlet). On the far horizon is the shore of **Yaghenen** (16.23, the Kenai Peninsula).
PHOTO COURTESY OF COOK INLET REGION, INC.

In the summer of 1786, while in Trading Bay, Capt. Nathaniel Portlock wrote observations about his surroundings. Unrau (1994:21), citing Portlock (1789:120): "Several small canoes from a town near the south point of Trading Bay approached the ships. In one of the canoes was a Native whom Portlock had nicknamed 'the Factor' because of his help in procuring furs for the British during their stay in Trading Bay."

When in Trading Bay in 1794 the Vancouver ship was approached by two Dena'ina men in a small canoe. Vancouver wrote:

"One of these, whose name was *Sal-tart*, possessing some apparent superiority over the rest, presented me with some martin [*sic*] skins, and received in return some iron, beads, a few other trinkets, and a small quantity of snuff and tobacco, all of which he seemed to value very highly. These people appeared to be acquainted with the Russians, of whose language they seemed to speak several words; but our very confined knowledge of that, as well as our total ignorance of their native tongue, prevented our acquiring the information which, from the intelligent appearance of these very civil and well-behaved strangers, we might otherwise have been enabled to obtain" (Unrau 1994:25 citing Vancouver 1801).

1.3 Nughi'ukda • 'Extends Down Poorly'
Noaukta Slough
The suffix **-kda** in Dena'ina suggests something that is poor, shabby, or dilapidated, usually in an affectionate

FIGURE 26

On the lower right hand edge is **Nughi'ukda** (1.3, Noaukta Slough) cutting south off of **Ch'akajatnu** (1.13, Chakachatna River). ‡1.126 is **Ch'akaja Bena Dghil'u** (Ch'akajabena Mountain). The ridge **Ch'ani'iy** (1.9) is south or left of 1.13. At the upper right edge of the scene is 1.78 **T'etniya**, Mt. Torbert.

PHOTO COURTESY OF COOK INLET REGION, INC.

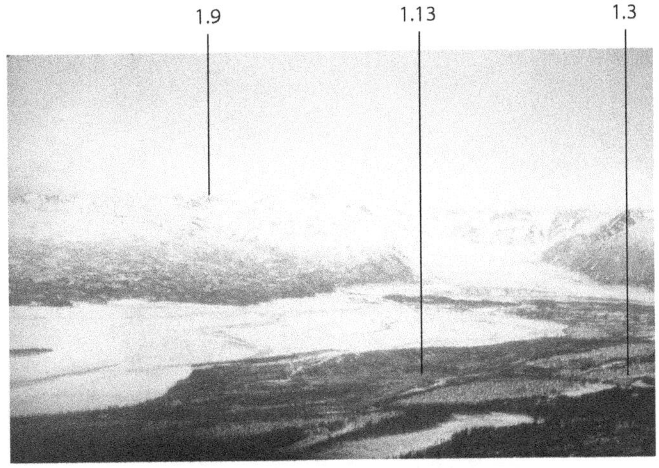

FIGURE 27

Looking north from above **Nadudiltnu Łi'a** (1.10, Blockade Glacier), is the officially unnamed ridge **Ch'ani'iy** (1.9), and the valley of **Ch'akajatnu** (1.13, Chakachatna River).

PHOTO COURTESY OF COOK INLET REGION, INC.

or humorous sense. Some other place names with the **-kda** suffix are 1.102, 1.65, and 7.14.

1.4 Tuk'nudghetl' • 'Broken Water'
long lake north of McArthur River

1.5 Tutnelchik • 'Yellow Water'
*lake and stream north of **Tuk'nudghetl'** (1.4)*

1.6 Tubughnen Nuch'utdałi • 'Let's Go Back to Tyonek'
creek into Noaukta Slough from the north
As the name indicates, this stream is on a sled trail between Tyonek and the base of the Alaska Range.

1.7 K'daghutnu • 'Antler Velvet Creek'
*creek at base of **Ch'ani'iy** (1.9), flowing south*

1.8 K'da T'el'iht • 'Where Antlers Are Gathered'
*camp at base of **Ch'ani'iy** (1.9)*
This was a key hunting and trapping area for Kustatan and Tyonek people until the mid-twentieth century. The late Harry Trenton (of Tyonek) made his camp here.

1.9 Ch'ani'iy • 'The One That Extends Out (from range)'
"McArthur" ridge between McArthur River and Chakachatna River
Peter Constantine said that this was a major hunting area of both Kustatan and Tyonek people. He said that Big Chilligan, chief of Tyonek in the 1920s, had a trapline here which was then later used by Harry Trenton.

§1.88 Ch'ani'iy Betnu • 'Stream of the One That Extends Out (from range)'
stream at "McArthur" ridge between McArthur River and Chakachatna River

1.10 Nadudiltnu Łi'a • 'Current Flows Down-River-Glacier'
McArthur Glacier and/or Blockade Glacier

§1.89 Nadudiltnu Dghelaya • 'Mountain of Current Flows Down-River'
mountain south of Chakachamna Lake and at the head of McArthur Glacier

1.11 Tach'nach'ninchett • 'Where Someone Put a Man's Head Underwater'
south fork of Cottonwood Slough
Peter Constantine and Maxim Chickalusion say that this name derives from a story about a fight between two men over a single fish.

1.12 Tudesi Betnu • 'Driftwood Creek'
Cottonwood Slough

1.13 Ch'akajatnu • 'River Where Tail Comes Out'
Chakachatna River
Several Tyonek families currently hunt and trap in the Chakachatna River area.

§1.122 Jateghił'iy Betnu • 'Stream of Water That Divides'
Middle River, "Allowan River"
A name called by Peter Constantine and located by Sava Stephan.

1.14 Betnu Ch'ełitnu • 'Stream That Flows Down'
creek into Middle River from north
Robert Allowan of Tyonek had a camp here. A dog trail used to follow this stream.

1.15 Ch'atanalch'elt • 'Where Clear Water Comes Out'
Straight Creek
Simeon Chickalusion, Peter Constantine, Robert Allowan, and Maxim Chickalusion have had hunting

FIGURE 28

Ch'akajatnu (1.13, Chakachatna River), near the base of **K'idazq'eni** (1.17, Mt. Spurr) in June of 1927.

Capps (1935:34): "Before the advent of the whiteman the natives of Tyonek were accustomed to make summer hunting trips into the headwaters of the Chakachatna basin."

STEPHEN R. CAPPS JR. COLLECTION, (#4-5 1229), ARCHIVES, ALASKA AND POLAR REGIONS DEPT., RASMUSON LIBRARY, UNIVERSITY OF ALASKA FAIRBANKS

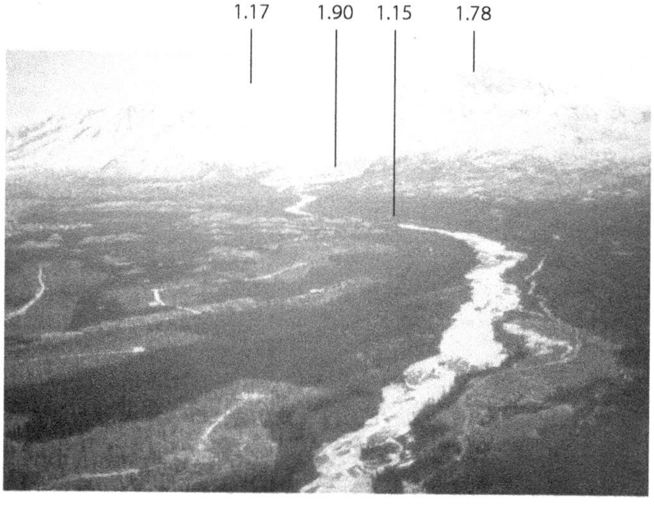

FIGURE 29

Ch'atanalch'elt (1.15, Straight Creek) and **Ch'atanalch'elt Łi'a** (1.90, "Straight Glacier") flow out from between the mountains **K'idazq'eni** (1.17, Mt. Spurr) and **T'etniya** (1.78, Mt. Torbert).

PHOTO COURTESY OF COOK INLET REGION, INC.

FIGURE 30

The cone of volcano **K'idazq'eni**, (1.17, Mt. Spurr), 'the one that is burning inside,' in 1977.

PHOTO BY PRISCILLA RUSSELL

and trapping camps here. It is said that the water here is sulphurous.

§1.90 **Ch'atanalch'elt Łi'a** • 'Where Clear Water Comes Out Glacier'
"Straight Glacier"
Wilson and Crews (1999:29): "The glacier has not been set foot upon, so far as we know, unless by Indians, who have a name for it, "Ch'atanalch'elt" ('where clear water comes out')."

‡1.126 **Ch'akaja Bena Dghil'u** • 'Tail Comes out Lake Mountain'
Ch'akajabena Mountain, on south side of Ch'akajabena Lake
This name was submitted in 2005 by a mountaineering group that attempted to ascend this mountain.

1.16 **Ch'akaja Bena** • 'Lake Where Tail Comes Out'
‡Ch'akajabena Lake (the official name since 2005), formerly Chakachamna Lake
In the nineteenth century, Chakachamna Lake was a key area for caribou, Dall sheep, and ground squirrels for the Tyonek and Kustatan people. Fall salmon, late silvers that were dried and frozen (**nudelbay**), also were processed here. The Chickalusion family continued to use this area into the 1920s. Big Chilligan was the last Tyonek man to hunt here regularly. See Fig. 18.

When the Capps geological party landed here on one of the first airplane flights into the area in 1927, it was reported in a *United States Daily* article that there were few signs of any recent human use. They noted "scattered camp stakes which had been driven into the ground by Indians long ago."

The names Chakachamna and Nagishlamina were reported to geologist Capps in 1927 by Big Chilligan of Tyonek, who was their guide in this area (Orth 1971:197, 669).

Nickafor Alexan (n.d.) in his account of "The Fifth Chief of Tyonek: Chilligan Phillip," noted the following about Chilligan's use of this area: "He used to go beyond Mount Spurr for caribou hide and meat quite a few time. He kill lots of brown bears and black bear. He used to go up to the mountain every summer after fish, to get mountain squirrel, because in the olden days if they get many squirrel they would eat the meat and make parky out of the skin. They used to make money on that too."

The trails through Merrill Pass (**Tutnutl'ech'a Tustes**) and Telaquana Pass (**Dilah Vena Tustes**) met at upper Chakachamna Lake. These were the main passes used between Tyonek and Kustatan and the Stony River. The Lime Village Dena'ina state that Chief Chickalusion and others would come from Kustatan through these passes with seal and other marine products and that they would travel to the inlet to trade and visit. Late winter was the main season for travel through here. It appears that no Dena'ina people have walked through these passes since about 1925 (Kari 1978a:3; Kari and Kari 1982:55–57; Alexan 1981:1; Capps 1935:13).

Billy Pete reported that this lake has late fall fish, silvers and sockeyes that are "really red and ready to die." Tyonek people dried these fall fish for winter use. Peter

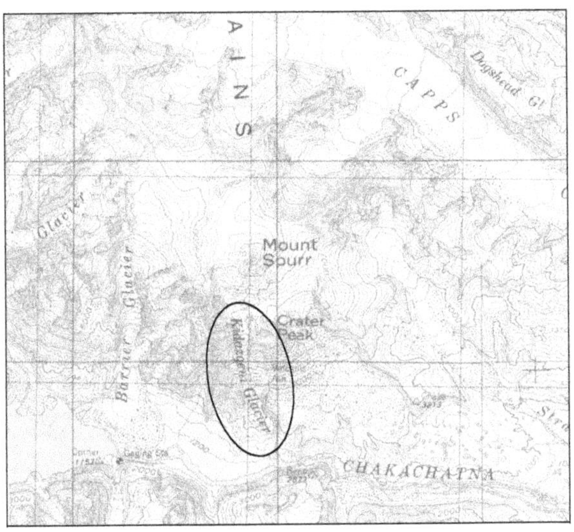

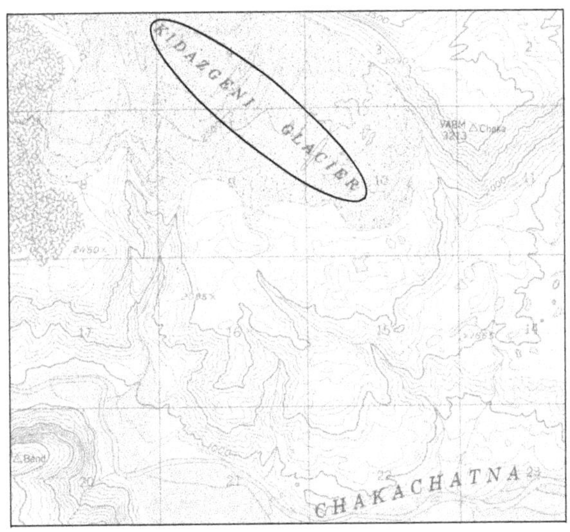

MAP 12

Wilson and Crews (1999:29) observe that on the Tyonek 1:250,000 quad map—the limited revised version of the 1985 map (left)—the newly named "Kidazqeni Glacier" was placed on the wrong glacier. They had proposed that the name be placed on the larger double pronged glacier to the east of Crater Peak. Adding further irony, on the Tyonek B–6 1:63,000 quad map of 1985 (right), the name is placed on the correct glacier, but the name was misspelled as "Kidazgeni."

In 2002 the Alaska State Board on Geographic Names and the U.S. Board of Geographic Names approved the respelling of this name to K'idazq'eni Glacier. The glottalized consonants—**k'** and **q'**—will present a more accurate version of the name to the public.

Constantine recalled that hunting for moose, sheep, and caribou was good in the country surrounding this lake.

1.17 K'idazq'eni *(O)*, **K'idayq'eni** *(U)* • 'That Which Is Burning Inside'
Mount Spurr

§1.91 K'idazq'eni Łi'a • 'Glacier of That Which Is Burning Inside'
Kidazqeni Glacier, (as of 2002) K'idazq'eni Glacier
Wilson and Crews (1999:29) summarize how this feature became an official name in 1984:

> The other Dena'ina name in use in the Tordrillos is "Kidazqeni" (streamlined and anglicized from K'idazq'eni), as mentioned above. This Native name for Mount Spurr, however, has unfortunately already been overridden by Josiah Spurr's cognomen. In 1984, K'idazq'eni was officially attached instead to a prominent double-barreled glacier on Mount Spurr's southern flank—the Kidazqeni Glacier.

1.18 Qichiqa Ta'a • 'Old Ladies' Soup'
stream and hot spring into Chakachamna Lake near outlet
Pete Bobby of Lime Village heard from his father about this hot spring and campsite near the base of Mount Spurr.

1.19 §Nahq'ashla Betnu (Dena'ina name revised) • 'Little Lookout River'
Nagishlamina River
The name recorded by Capps in 1927 seems to have the Upper Inlet term for **nahq'a** 'lookout.' This name sounds familiar to Sava Stephan. The two following names, for a lake and a hill, are implied. This stream connects to the upper Skwentna River, and this route would have been used for fall hunting in the nineteenth century.

§1.92 Nahq'ashla • 'Little Lookout'
‡possibly hill at head of Nagishlamina River

§1.93 Nahq'ashla Bena • 'Little Lookout Lake'
pond at head of Nagishlamina River
‡In 1927 Capps obtained this name from Chief Chilligan, and we surmise that the lookout and pond names are at the pass between this stream and the South Fork of the Skwentna River.

1.20 Hni Bena • 'Island Lake'
Kenibuna Lake

1.21 Nikugh Betnu • 'Big Island River'
Neacola River
This name and 1.20 were reported by Pete Bobby of Lime Village. Chilligan River into Chakachamna Lake was named for Chief Chilligan who accompanied geologist Capps on his 1927 survey. "Named for Chief Chilligan of Tyonek 'who built a cabin on this river in about 1896'" (Orth 1971:210). See Fig. 18, a photo of Chief Chilligan and his wife Olga.

1.22 Ch'k'e'uła Betnu • 'River Where We Chew Something'
Chuitkilnachna Creek
The name refers to the eating of waterfowl. This is a prime waterfowl hunting area. Note the highly altered USGS place name.

1.23 Ken Ka'a • 'Big Flat'
flat south of the mouth of Nikolai Creek
This is known as a waterfowl and moose hunting area.

1.24 Sdidahtnu • 'Calves Become Cramped River'
Nikolai Creek
The name Stedatna Creek, a sidestream of Nikolai Creek, comes from the Dena'ina name for Nikolai Creek. This traditional waterfowl hunting area is still used by Tyonek residents.

Sava Stephan: "That way they were talking about that place «a person is walking and stepping there» snow lifting and thawing so, **sdidaq** «one gets cramped,» **shedeq'** «it is cramped, in the calf» that's what it means, in snowshoes, when we really going on snowshoes fast. That snow is just flying like this, when frozen ice hits in the back of the calf muscle."

§1.123 Sdidahtnu Kaq' • 'Calves Become Cramped Mouth'
mouth of Nikolai Creek

§1.94 K'ta'atnu • 'Soup Creek'
first small creek from the north into Nikolai Creek
Name recalled by Sava Stephan.

§1.95 Batuk'elehtnu • 'Fish Run into It-Stream'
Stetatna Creek
Name recalled by Sava Stephan.

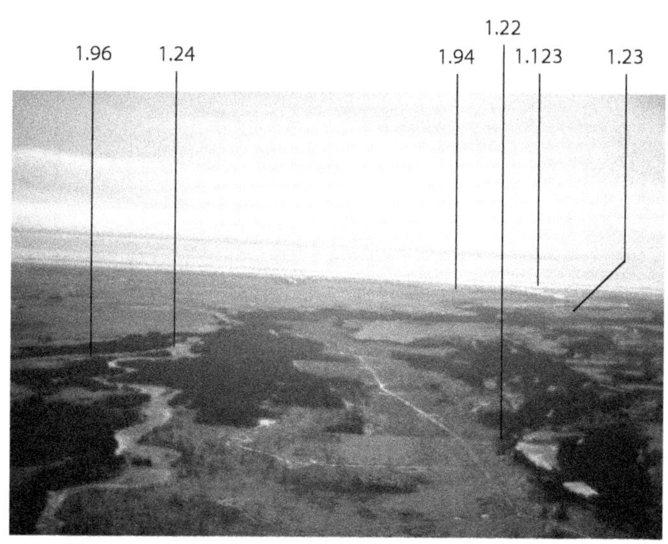

FIGURE 31

The stream in the left foreground is **Sdidahtnu** (1.24) Nikolai Creek and the stream in the right foreground is **Ch'ek'e'uła Betnu** (1.22) Chuitkilnachna Creek. At the left side of the photo, flowing into Nikolai Creek is **Nuntalyiytnu** (1.96). Near the shore of the Inlet on the right side of the photo are features **K'ta'atnu** (1.94), **Sdidahtnu Kaq'** (1.123) Nikolai Creek mouth, and **Ken Ka'a** (1.23), the flat south of the mouth of Nikolai Creek.
PHOTO COURTESY OF COOK INLET REGION, INC.

1.25 Nuntnalyiy • 'Objects That Extend Across'
"Bald Hills" north of Nikolai Creek
This is a noted game lookout and hunting area.

§1.96 Nuntnalyiytnu • 'Stream of Objects That Extend Across'
stream from "Bald Hills" into Nikolai Creek

§1.97 Ts'ahlatnu, Ch'ahlatnu • '-Ω -Stream'
small creek north of the mouth of Nikolai Ck
Name recalled by Sava Stephan.

1.26 Qunduk'elyasht • 'Where Things Are Brought Up'
beach at south boundary of Tyonek Reservation
The place name refers to the carrying of freight up from the beach at this point. The modern salmon camps used by Tyonek people extend from here north to **Tank'itnu** (1.45), Tyonek Creek.

1.27 Badi Dulyasht • 'Where Umiaks Are Brought Up'
Granite Point
Badi is the Dena'ina word for the large Eskimo-style umiak. See also the discussion of boats on pp. 102–104. Sometimes also called **Baqay Dulyasht** 'Where Birchbark Canoes Are Brought Up.' According to one story told by Shem Pete, a Russian schooner anchored here. Before the crew could land, the boat sank because of the work of a Dena'ina medicine man. Many died here.

Sava Stephan has discussed various Tyonek-area sea foods: "It look like a bell, stick to the rock. I took my oars and stick between the rock and his mouth you know. I throw it down, and I get em out. I put it in the boat. I don't know what they call that, under the rock. I know **baggila** [mussels, blue mussel *Mytilis edulis*] too, I seen that. I sit down on the beach and I used to eat **baggila**. At Granite Point. I used to fish down there at Granite Point when I was a kid with my dad. And old Bobby Stephan used to wait. I gather lots of things like that, I haul it up to him and I let him eat **baggila**. **Chuq'ush** [butter clams, *Saxidomus giganteus*] some as far as Granite Point. **Qiy'in** [razor clams, *Siliqua alta*] we would got to Point Harriet or Polly Creek. **Dgheljema**, [red neck clams, *Spisula sp.*] I heard about. They don't come up that far. **Ch'eghesh**, [sea urchin, species uncertain] I heard about but I never see them. We use **tsanagha** [sea anenome, species uncertain]. That used to be around the Inlet. **Tsanagha tuyułkesi** [floating sea anenome, species uncertain]. **Qanałggi** [sea snails, species uncertain] they used to have lots at Beluga River. They used to have lots. They call it "beans." About that big around, we used to just smash them and eat that. We used to call it "beans." «They would be abundant.» Tide drifting out, back and forth.

"At Tyonek I thought they were crazy, sit around the beach eating that, just like a cap, **tutsighił'iy** [jellyfish, species uncertain]. Everybody all the ladies sit around the beach, walk around the beach, they pack them to one place and everyone sit on the beach eating that. I tried it, raw. I didn't care much for that. I walked around the point, "Lighthouse" they use to call it. I got a fish camp below there from Tyonek. «We would eat jellyfish.» About that big around, just like a cap and about that thick. In summertime, fall time, before king [the king salmon run], we walking the beach there and them Tyonek boys there, they grab em and they tear something off and they eat them right there. «They would say, let's eat jellyfish.» They walk the beach."

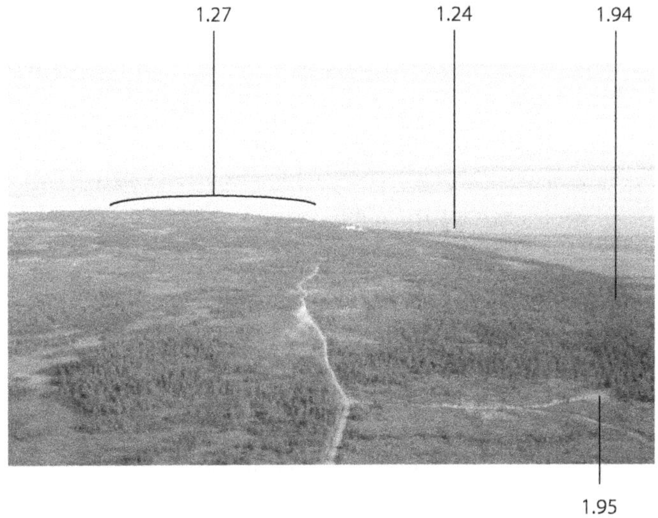

FIGURE 32

Looking east from above 1.27 **Badi Dulyasht**, Granite Point. About a half mile to the south is 1.26 **Qunduk'elyasht**. On the right edge in the flat are features **K'ta'atnu** (1.94) and **Batuk'elehtnu** (1.95).
PHOTO COURTESY OF COOK INLET REGION, INC.

"At Tyonek we would stay on the beach for hooligans [oulachon, *Thaleichthys pacificus*]. Come ashore on high water mark and all over on high water mark, «They twist (getting stranded) in the water, the hooligans swim ashore, they twist in the water» in the high water mark, on the beach. They get stranded. «They would say the hooligans got twisted up the beach, the hooligans are stranded on the upland.» «Tyonek people would come and gather them, and pack them back and bring them inside and they would roast them and boil them. I saw that.» That was at my fish camp, they used to have village down there. The village was swamped with them. Then they move up to where the village is now.

"«I saw them eating **dgheyay**, needlefish [*Gasterosteus aculeatus*].» Its right behind [after] hooligans. «They would put in dipnets and they were really full.» They drag it ashore and boy oh boy. They got that pot on the fire. Tyonek. Up Susitna too. We used to go for them right at Susitna Station, and some place Alexander Creek up. I see that hooligan [school] about two feet wide along the beach, and we just get on top of it, so thick."

1.28 Qitlaq'at • 'Muddy Place'
Beach north of Granite Point

§1.98 Qitlaq'i Besa • 'Muddy Place Bank'
Hill at beach north of Granite Point

§1.99 Qitlaq'i Bena • 'Muddy Place Lake'
Small lake north of Granite Point
According to Sava Stephan this lake was used by Nestor Constantine.

§1.100 Nelnitnu • 'Steambath Creek'
Seasonal creek below Granite point, before Nikolai River
This is perhaps the name that appeared on the 1910a Sleem map as "Netnu."

§1.101 Nelnikda Ey'unt • 'Where There Is a Dilapidated Steambath'
Small lake behind Granite Point
Names 1.99, 1.00, 1.101, and 1.102 were contributed by Sava Stephan.

§1.102 Nelnikda • 'Dilapidated Steambath'
Hill above lake, just south of ***K'enq'a Betnu***

1.29 Ch'elehtnu • 'Spawning Stream'
Old Tyonek Creek, locally called "Robert's Creek"
According to Fall (1981:406), the oldest of the historic Tyonek village sites was located here. De Laguna noted a site here (1934:139).

In about 1875 an Alaska Commercial Company store opened here, and people from several surrounding locations consolidated here (Fall, Foster, and Stanek 1984:27). This was the first permanent store in the upper Cook Inlet area.

In 1883 Johan Jacobsen, who was collecting artifacts for a Berlin museum, visited this site. "I obtained clothing of caribou and elk [moose] skin and wooden bows and arrows as well as several other interesting objects" (Jacobsen 1977:193). The forty-three-word vocabulary he recorded for material culture items is, interestingly, in the Outer Inlet dialect, with phonemes **z** and **zh**.

This has been a beluga hunting area. Peter Constantine reports that his father killed beluga here. This is the site of many contemporary fish camps; it is a king salmon stream (Chickalusion and Chickalusion 1979:7), and an important source of silver salmon in the fall and early winter.

1.30 Tubughnenq' • 'Beach Land'
Old Tyonek; regional name for the area between Beluga River and Granite Point
This place name has been applied to the three main historic village sites: Old Tyonek, Tobona or Second Tyonek, and New Tyonek. See also Fall (1981:404–408).

Cook Inlet Historic Sites Project (1975:103): "Once part of a continuous village or a closely related group of villages which stretched from Beluga to Granite Point. Houses were built along the creek close to the high tide line."

FIGURE 33

(**a**, right) A view of **Tubughnenq'** (1.30) Old Tyonek in 1898.
(**b**, below) An unidentified group of Dena'ina at **Tubughnenq'** Old Tyonek in 1898.

PHOTOS BY GEOLOGIST W. C. MENDENHALL, COURTESY OF U. S. GEOLOGICAL SURVEY PHOTOGRAPHIC LIBRARY, DENVER. MENDENHALL 1900:338

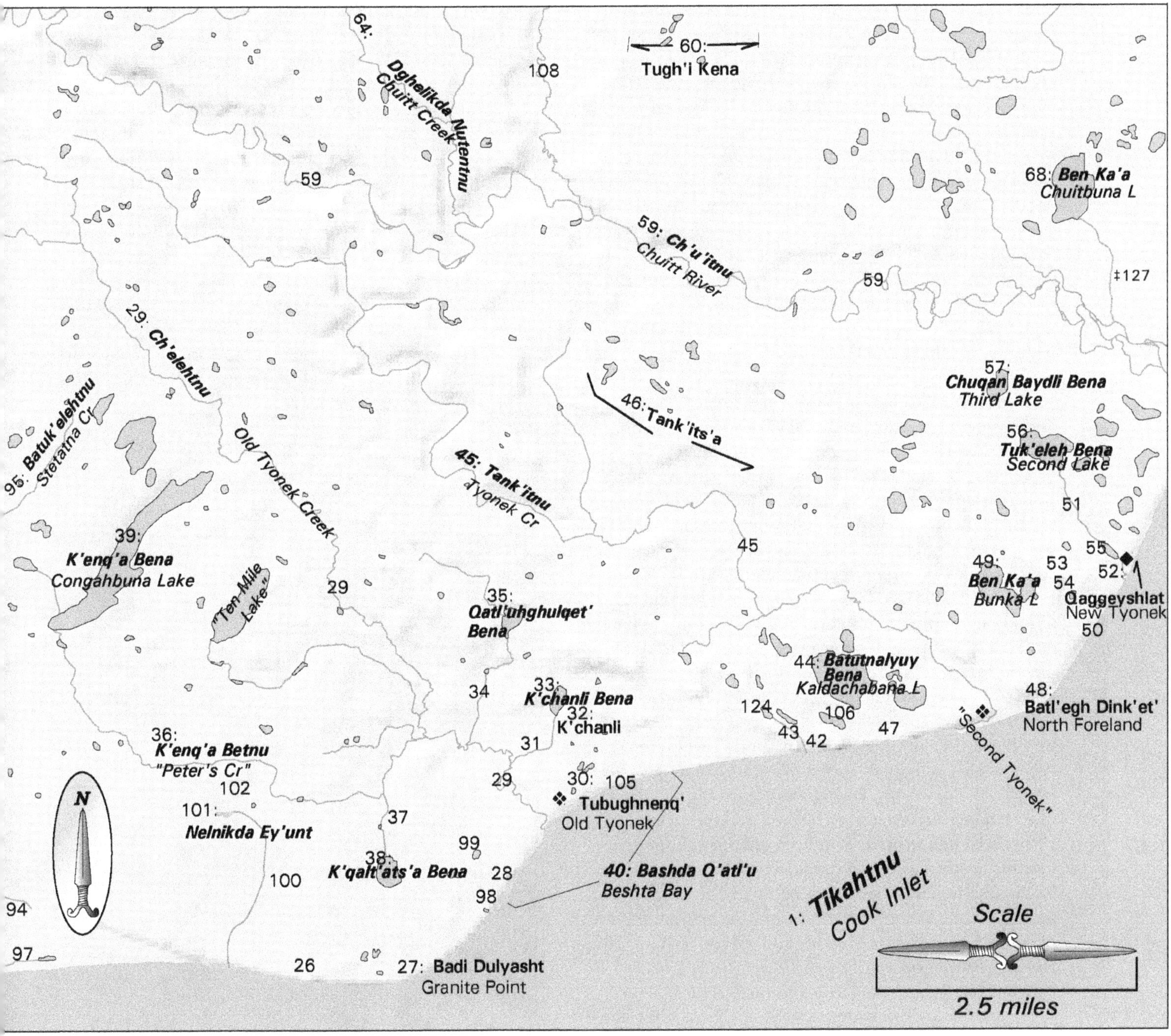

MAP 13

Inset map of Tyonek area. Nos. 26–64, 94–108 and ‡127.

‡Stanek, Fall, and Holen (2006) is a good current source on Tyonek cultural history, subsistence, and contemporary life. A color land stat map of Tyonek and a list of place names appeared in Evanoff (2010:149–153).

MAP BY MATT GANLEY

Kari and Kari (1982:96) speculated that the simplicity of this place name **Tubughnenq'** suggests that this was the first beach on Cook Inlet occupied by the Dena'ina. ‡The name seems to be an overt proclamation. See Table 12 and Map 26. The name Tyonek does not mean "little chief" as has been reported (e.g., Baker 1906:645; Orth 1971:1001). That interpretation comes from a comparison of the word Tyonek with the surname Tyone, which derives from a Siberian Russian loanword toyón meaning 'chief.'

Fall (1987:50–51) described the important role of **Benil'a Ch'ulyałen**, Chief Pete of Tyonek, who ran the Alaska Commericial Company store in the last years of the nineteenth century.

Shem Pete: "«I'll tell you about the Tyonek chief. They used to call him Pete. He was a good man. He took care of everybody. Everybody listened to him, whatever he said, whenever he gave an order. His name was **Benil'a Ch'ulyałen**. There's nobody else that remembers him now.»"

Two village names from the Tyonek area, "Nogosnik" and "Chnedakits," that are listed in the Wrangell collection (Arndt 1985) have not been re-elicited.

Wilfred Osgood, a biologist, recorded various natural history notes at Tyonek in the summer of 1900. "Paper birch: At Tyonek it surpasses all other trees in point of numbers.... Judging from the size of the Indian birch baskets, trees a foot more in diameter are to be found" (Osgood 1901:55). "Ground squirrel. They are said to be abundant...in the mountains lying some 60 miles back of Tyonek. While in Tyonek an Indian brought in a lot of one hundred spermophile skins from these mountains to be used in making parkas and other articles of native wearing apparel" (*op. cit.*: 63). "Beaver: a limited number are secured every season along the streams in the mountains about 60 miles inland from Tyonek" (*op. cit.*: 63). "Least weasel. The natives regard the capture of one of these rare animals as a piece of great good fortune. One old Indian who frequently visited our cabin told us that his brother who had caught one when a small boy had in consequence become a 'big chief'; he assured me that since I had caught one I must surely be destined to become a man of great wealth and power" (*op. cit.*:70, cf. Fall 1987:58–60).

Glenn at Tyonek in 1898 commented (1900a:647): "The ease with which the natives of Cook Inlet can obtain their living is most remarkable. It reminds one of the divine provision made for the children of Israel in their wanderings.... In the case of these Indians fish are so abundant that the waves actually wash them on the shore, where only a few minutes of each day is required to gather more than a sufficiency. Besides, the same waves wash upon the same beach coal in abundance...."

Pierce (1996) summarized the contents of a journal maintained by V. V. Stafeev, a former Russian-American Company employee who remained in Alaska to work for American trading companies. Stafeev was stationed at Tyonek from 1884 to 1888 while he worked for the Alaska Commercial Company (see also Fall 1987:50). In 1888, Stafeev wrote that the Tyonek Dena'ina spent much of the winter, four or more months, away from the village "in temporary huts in the woods" trapping furs for sale (Pierce 1996:176). In May 1885, Stafeev (Pierce 1996:178) recorded what he called the first visit by Ahtna to Tyonek:

"They held a ceremony: upon leaving their baidarkas they loaded their guns and went dancing to the toion's house. There the Tuiunok men were standing, also with loaded guns. When the [visitors] drew close they suddenly rushed at the group of Tuiunok men firing. They crossed and went on firing. In this manner the greeting ended."

Znamenski (1998:5) notes that the first year-round lay reader for the Orthodox church in Tyonek was Nikolai Kuliktukta who was appointed in 1899.

Alexandra Kaloa described the move from Old Tyonek in 1931 due to high swells and threat of flooding (McClanahan 1986:89).

FIGURE 34

The late Peter Constantine of Tyonek knew many Dena'ina places, especially in the Kustatan area. Peter spoke the Kenai dialect of Dena'ina, and he was the last resident of Kustatan village.
PHOTO TAKEN IN 1979 BY PRISCILLA RUSSELL

Chief Simeon Chickalusion, 1880–1957

Compiled by James Kari and James Fall

Simeon Chickalusion was the son of Peter Chickalusion of Kustatan. His older brother Theodore was the last prominent shaman of the Outer Inlet Dena'ina. At the turn of the century, the Chickalusions were probably the most well-known family among the Dena'ina because of their far-reaching travels in Cook Inlet and through the southern Alaska Range. Tyonek elder Nickafor Alexan wrote a short biography of Simeon Chickalusion, "Sixth chief and Governor of Tyonek." Simeon Chickalusion became chief of Tyonek in 1931 when Chief Chilligan Phillip died.

An article by Phyllis D. Carlson (1972) drew upon Alexan's account:

> Simeon Chickalusion had been born in Tyonek on April 10, 1880. Soon after... his family had moved down the Inlet to Kustatan where his father was chief. When Simeon was seventeen, he attended the Russian church school at Kenai, and later, mined for gold in Hope and Sunrise on the Kenai Peninsula. Still later he worked on boats and sailed as far west as Kodiak and the Barren Islands. Soon after his marriage to a Tyonek woman, he moved with his family from Kustatan back to Tyonek so his four children... could attend school... [This took place in 1928.]

Chickalusion was a good spokesman with the outside world, for he had worked with white men, knew their ways, and could speak their language. He could also speak Russian and, of course, could talk with the natives in their own tongue.

FIGURE 35

Chief Simeon Chickalusion and his wife, Annie, in 1938.

PHOTO COURTESY OF PHYLLIS CARLSON

Gillette (1978), also drawing upon Alexan's account, wrote, "When the village moved from Susitna Station to Tyonek [in 1934], he [Simeon] told each family what to do, where each house was to be built.... He helped them arrange to buy a tractor and sawmill.... Villagers recall how he always endorsed the old ways of self-sufficiency, of living off the land instead of buying things from the store. He thought they ought to be out picking berries and wild greens and taking sap from the trees instead of buying corned beef, cookies, and pop."

Billy Pete remembers Chickalusion: "Chickalusion was chief down here. Don't matter what it was—if you wanted cup of tea, or if you needed a hand, or anything at all, he'll get right out there and help you. Don't matter what it was. He'll get right out there and help you. He'll boss the whole thing—how to build a house. He'll just walk around and tell everybody how to do things. If somebody didn't know anything about how to do a certain job, why he'd go and tell them how to do it. And they did it that way."

Sava Stephan: "I got along with old chief Chickalusion, chief in the village here. I got married to his daughter. He make we work on the church there and everything else" (McClanahan 1986:105).

"After I got married I started to travel with Simeon (Chickalusion). We used to stay at his upper and lower cabin at Granite Point. Pretty quiet guy. He had two boats. I did not go out in woods with him too much cause my wife had crippled legs. His wife [Annie] did not speak English. She was from Polly Creek. He was easy going guy. I used to be with him all the time. I was married to his daughter. I spent many years going around with him. All over he goes to. Trapping. On the back there, way back of Kustatan. McArthur River way up the river, **Nadudiltnu**. We go up there and winter over there some place. I was married then. Before that I never go no place. The whole family would go, his family and my family. His wife.... I'm not a Cook Inlet man yet. I'm from Susitna, I don't know much about Cook Inlet. I been fishing around there since 1930." Q: "You just spoke Dena'ina then?" "Yeah." Q: "What did Simeon talk about?" "Well he used to tell us stories about **delgga** [raven], about how people understand **delgga** when he holler over us and people answer him back. We just hear about that, that's all."

Cornelius Osgood noted in 1931 that Simeon Chickalusion was the recognized authority on Dena'ina culture at Tyonek. "Simeon was fifty-one, and was born at Tyonek, as was his mother, though his father was from Kustatan farther down the coast. I had the feeling that he knew a great deal more than I was able to record from him during my brief stay at this place" (Osgood 1937:24–25).

Peter Kalifornsky of Kenai, whose mother, Agrafena, was sister to Simeon and Theodore Chickalusion, says that the family name comes from the Dena'ina personal name **Begh Chik'el'ishen** 'The One Who Kills Game for Him.' One pass, from Drift River to Twin Lakes on the upper Mulchatna River, is called **Chikalushen Tustes,** a very unusual place name for Dena'ina, because it contains the family's personal name. (See also 16.12 for comments on the similar but unrelated name "Chickaloon.")

Simeon Chickalusion was **Tulchina,** Water Clan. The Susitna River chiefs' gear—necklaces, shirt, rattles, and headdress—had been passed on to Simeon by Big Chilligan in 1930. Simeon then presented these articles to Shem Pete in 1957 (see pp. 115–117), which signified that Shem Pete was then the traditional chief of the Upper Inlet Dena'ina.

Shem Pete addressed Chickalusion as **shingha** 'older brother,' because Chickalusion was Shem's older clan cousin. In 1959 Shem hosted a potlatch in Tyonek in memory of Simeon Chickalusion. At the potlatch Shem introduced the following mourning song, now a prominent song in the repetoire of the Tyonek singers.

‡FIG 36A

Annie and Simeon Chickalusion, Sava Stephan, Sr., at right with young Isaac Stephan in 1949 at 1.42 **Qitanaghiłdeqt**, Simeon's fish camp.

FROM THE PAULINE ALLOWAN COLLECTION

Chickalusion Mourning Song

by Shem Pete

Ełnen gini dghiłkegh ch'u shughu
Tubguhnen qenga k'ghilat'i.
Tyonek's reputation is over this whole wide world.

Una'iy shingha ka'a.
Come to me my big older brother.

Una'iy shingha ka'a.
Come to me my big older brother.

[other verses]

Ełnen gini dghiłkegh ch'u shughu nkilaqa
qenga k'ghilat'i.
The reputation of your workers is over this whole wide world.

Ełnen gini dghiłkegh ch'u shughu
nch'enaqa qenga k'ghilat'i.
The reputation of your children is over this whole wide world.

Ełnen gini dghiłkegh ch'u shughu nkununa
qenga k'ghilat'i.
Word of your hunting luck is over this whole wide world.

Ełnen gini dghiłkegh ch'u shughu ntiya
ka'a qenga k'ghilat'i.
Word of your great strength is over this whole wide world.

Ełnen gini dghiłkegh ch'u shughu ndleq'a
qenga k'ghilat'i.
Word of your laughter is over this whole wide world.

Ełnen gini dghiłkegh ch'u shughu nqeshqa
qenga k'ghilat'i.
Word of your wealth is over this whole wide world.

Ełnen gini dghiłkegh ch'u shughu n'ushla
qenga k'ghilat'i.
The reputation of your little wife is over this whole wide world.

FIGURE 36

Music to the *Chickalusion Mourning Song.*

MUSIC TRANSCRIPTION BY THOMAS F. JOHNSTON

1.31 K'chanli Betnu • 'Grass Is There Creek'
outlet stream into Old Tyonek Creek from north

1.32 K'chanli • 'Grass Is There'
hill north of Old Tyonek
Peter Constantine remarked that the large number of old house pits on the hills back from the Inlet is evidence of the defensive-oriented arrangement of the old Dena'ina villages. From here they could view approaching traffic on the Inlet and were able to withstand attacks from their archenemies, the Alutiiq (Pacific Gulf Eskimo).

Contemporary Tyonek residents trap furbearers in this area.

1.33 K'chanli Bena • 'Grass Is There Lake'
lake two miles north of Old Tyonek
Sava Stephan: "That lake is gone now, they drained out the water."

§(1.103) Ts'atuk'enaltset • 'Water Rushes out Fast'
location uncertain near ***K'chanli***
Name via Mrs. Nikanorga and Archie Sunrise, from Kari's field notes.

§(1.104) Ts'atuk'enaltset Bena • 'Water Rushes out Fast Lake'
lake near ***K'chanli****, location uncertain*
Name via Mrs. Nikanorga and Archie Sunrise. Recognized by Sava Stephan.

1.34 Q'atl'uhghulqet' Betnu • 'Overturned Trees Creek'
outlet stream into Old Tyonek Creek

1.35 Q'atl'uhghulqet' Bena • 'Overturned Trees Lake'
Lake north of ***K'chanli Bena***

1.36 K'enq'a Betnu • 'Fishing Hole Creek'
outlet stream of Congahbuna, locally known as "Peter's Creek"
Peter's Creek is named after the late Peter Constantine. Constantine said that the flat south of here is known to be a dangerous place to travel during summer. Once a woman got lost here and her body was later found in the inlet.

1.37 K'qalt'ats'a Betnu • 'Water Lily Creek'
outlet stream into "Peter's Creek" from south

1.38 K'qalt'ats'a Bena • 'Water Lily Lake'
lake north of Granite Point
This is a trout fishing site. The mislocated place name Kaldachbuna Lake, for "Blood Lake" (1.44), is based upon this name.

1.39 K'enq'a Bena • 'Fishing Hole Lake'
Congahbuna Lake, locally "Peter's Lake" or "Bird's Lake"
From 1930 until 1951 the late Peter Constantine (whose nickname was "Bird") stayed here regularly while trapping. He had a cabin here. Prior to 1930 this place was used by Nikafor Alexan. It is a popular trout fishing lake today. Many other lakes in this area have been used by Tyonek people, but the Dena'ina place names are no longer remembered. Sava Stephan: "At **K'enq'a Bena** Nickafor's [Alexan] wife built a cabin."

1.40 Bashda Q'atl'u, Bashda Ch'atł'utnil'u • 'Coal Bay' or 'Coal Extends Out from Head (of stream)'
Beshta Bay
Glenn (1900:720): "In Cook Inlet there is an abundance of very satisfactory coal.... That used by us was mined by the Indians just below Tyoonok from a vein that crops out from above the high-water mark. The vein reaches down as far as the low water mark, and probably farther."

This is the site of most of the modern Tyonek fish camps. People gather beach coal for fuel in the camps. Sergei Californsky (Kari 1980:38) described building a cabin here. A gravesite is noted here in Cook Inlet Historic Sites Project (1975:103).

§1.105 Tsaqent'u • 'Beneath Burning Rock'
coal vein in Beshta Bay
Name reported by Sava Stephan.

(1.41) (no Dena'ina name)
Moquawkie Indian Reservation
The name Moquawkie does not correspond to any of the known Dena'ina place names in the area. This name was established in 1915 when the Tyonek Indian Reservation was formed.

The name has a pejorative connotation locally, as it is only used by non-Dena'inas. Peter Constantine: "I've been asked about this name many times. I don't know what it means." Billy Pete humorously speculated about the name's origin: "That Captain Cook, he came to Tyonek and saw them talking Dena'ina. I think he told them, 'You guys talk like ducks.' So he called them Moquawkie [from quack-quack] Indians. He's the one that named them."

William Bright (personal communication) noted that this appears to be an Ojibwa language name meaning 'bear land.' Ojibwa is the Algonquian language of Wisconsin and Michigan. The place name might have been coined during the founding of a reservation by a playful whiteman. It is like the name "Milwaukee," cf. Ojibwa /makwa/ 'bear,' /aki/ 'land.' Perhaps archival research can shed light on how and why the name was suggested for the Tyonek reservation.

1.42 Qitnaghiłdeqt • 'Where It Is High'
draw at Simeon Chickalusion's fish camp. See Fig. 36a.
Chief Simeon Chickalusion located his fish camp here in about 1930. Prior to that time he fished at Kustatan.

§1.106 Qitnaghiłdeq Betnu • 'Stream of Where It Is High'
small creek at draw at Simeon Chickalusion's fish camp
Sava Stephan: "That come out of lake there."

1.43 K'etnu Ka'a • 'Big Creek'
creek south of Maxim Chickalusion's fish camp

§1.124 K'etnu Ka'a Bena • 'Big Creek Lake'
small lake at head of creek south of Maxim Chickalusion's fish camp

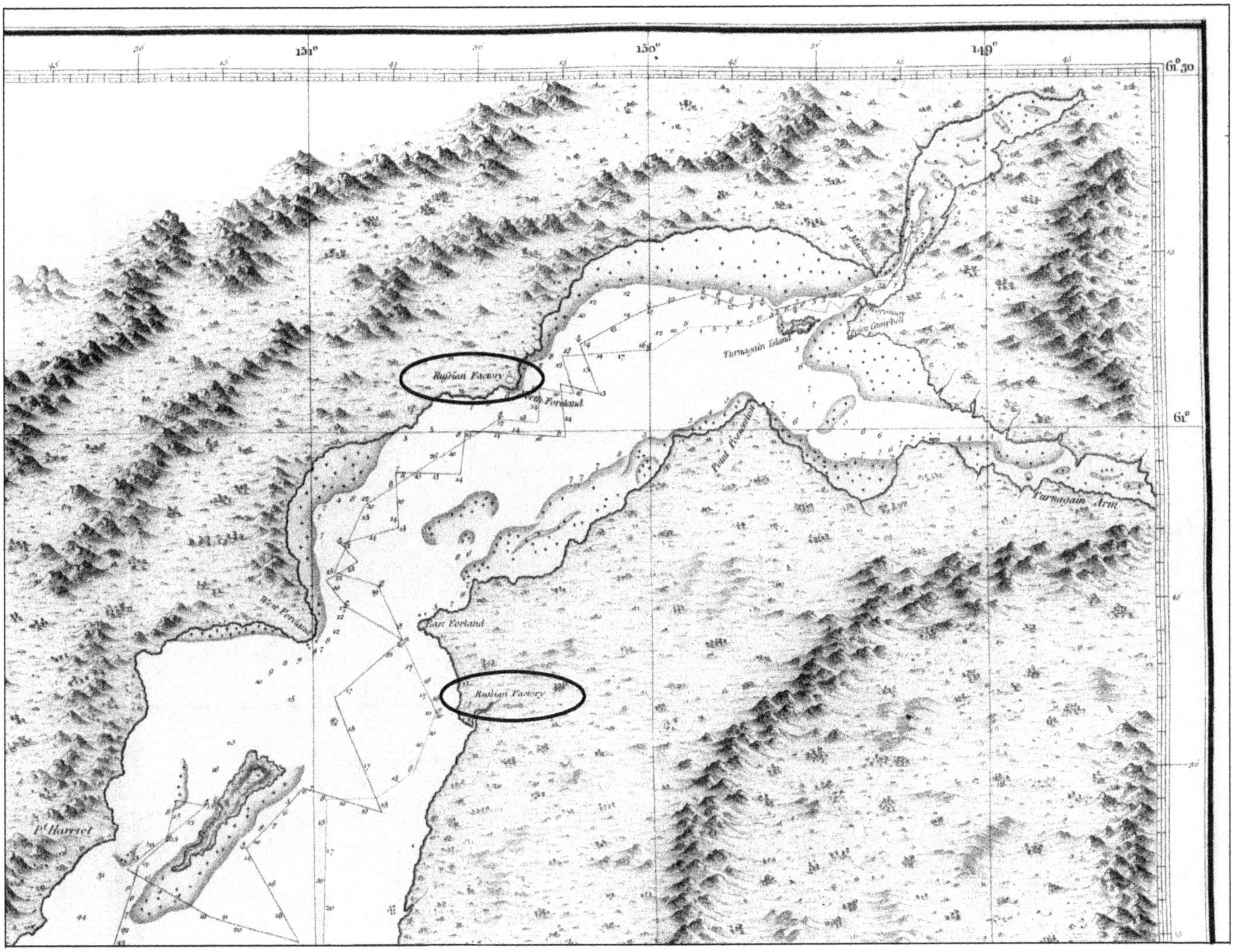

1.44 Batutnalyuy Bena or **Batunk'elyashi Bena** • '‡People Were Put into the Water Lake' or 'In It Things Are Washed Lake'

Kaldachabuna Lake, locally known as "Blood Lake"

Apparently the name **Batunk'elyashi Bena** is the modern name. Shem Pete said that the original name is now avoided. The map name Kaldachabuna comes from the Dena'ina name for lake **K'qalt'ats'a Bena** (1.38) south of Old Tyonek. Alexan calls this lake "Big Lake" (1981:6–7).

Kaldachabuna Lake is of major historical importance to Tyonek people as the home of the warrior **Quq'ey** and his brother **‡Betuyelash** (Cook Inlet Historic Sites Project 1975:106–107; Alexan 1981). It is said that one should not drink the water of this lake because many people were killed in it.

‡From Shem Pete's **Quq'ey** story: «Where they have the name Batutnalyuy Bena it (lake) had no outlet. Blood washed over there and an outlet was made. The blood did this.»

(1.107) Banilqek'ejehi Bena • 'Lake That They Ran into Together'

lake near "Washtub," location uncertain

MAP 14

Detail from the1794 Vancouver map of Cook Inlet.

Vancouver's 1794 map of Cook Inlet with his 1801 report is an excellent example of British maritime cartography. This is an advance over the 1778 map by Cook (Map 65), with numerous soundings in the inlet and more detailed mountain profiles. The cultural details are especially important. Note the "Russian Factory" at North Foreland as well as at the mouth of the Kenai River. The Vancouver party gave several names on this trip, including Points Harriet, Woronzof, MacKenzie, and Campbell. There are no Native-origin place names, however.

ARCHIVES, ALASKA AND POLAR REGIONS DEPT., RASMUSON LIBRARY, UNIVERSITY OF ALASKA FAIRBANKS

Tanik'edi, a Dena'ina Technique for Salmon Fishing in Cook Inlet

by Nickafor Alexan

Nickafor Alexan of Tyonek was an accomplished Dena'ina storyteller and a close friend of Shem Pete's. Late in his life, in the 1960s, he recorded several important Tyonek-area stories. These were re-published in Alexan 1981. This account of the ***tanik'edi*** *fishing technique first appeared in Alexan's article "How Tyonek People Used to Eat" in the Alaska Sportsman in 1965. The name tanik'edi means 'object that is stretched out in the water.' Nickafor Alexan has various unpublished writings that are at the Archives of the University of Alaska Anchorage.*

"First they go in the woods and get the small trees, roots and all, about twenty of them. They trim the branches from the trees and then they dig holes in the beach and put this tree's roots down and pile heavy rocks round them. And then after they got all the trees set up about ten or twelve feet apart down the beach they get smaller tree with roots and set that on ebb side, or rather south side. They pile heavy rocks on them and lean this smaller trees against that larger trees and tie it together with roots. [Spruce] roots was only rope they used mostly. After all this trees sat up, then they get poles and lay them on ebb side about two feet apart and tie them with roots very tight all the way to top Then they have few larger pole on side top of trap to walk on.

"I understand there is lots of work on them, but all the village people work together. If any person not sick but if he don't work on that trap, they won't let him fish on that trap. So everyone have to work. When the trap are finish they make their scoop [dip net], about four feet long, two feet wide, and one and half feet deep, made of roots. And have strong five or six feet pole for handle. And then when they think fish are coming they sit on the lower poles, sat their scoop down low in the water. When tide coming in and come up to first or bottom pole, they move up to next pole. That way they could fish from low water to high water. A person that don't sleep good will get most fish those days."

Early documentation of the **tanik'edi** is in Bean 1887 which has a fine drawing and caption by the well-known artist-naturalist Henry W. Elliott from the 1880s shown in Fig 38. Elliott (1897:87) also wrote: "The upper waters of Cook's Inlet are said to be quite remarkable for their barrenness of fish–salmon only being plenty in the running season, ascending all the numerous rivers and rivulets; the reason most likely is due to the turbid upheaval of the bottoms everywhere by that violent tidal bore which prevails, recurring twice every twenty-four hours. The Indians here employ a curious trestle or staging of poles, which they use in spearing salmon, and netting them from its support."

FIGURE 37

(Opposite, top) This drawing of a **tanik'edi** by Diane L. Theide accompanied Nickafor Alexan's article in *Alaska Sportsman*, January 1965. Used by permission of Alaska Northwest Publishing Co. The caption read "When one get first fish, they holler with cheer so much all the people come down to the beach and scooping up all over in the water"—Nickafor Alexan.

FIGURE 38

(Opposite, bottom) An excellent drawing by Henry W. Elliott of two **tanik'edi** being used near Old Tyonek in the early 1880s. Men are depicted at the outer ends of the racks standing in canoes and holding dipnets.

Note the buildings on shore and the distant outline of Mt. Susitna.

FROM ELLIOTT 1897:87

A name mentioned by Terry Stephan, but not reconfirmed.

1.45 Tank'itnu • 'Fish Dock River'
Tyonek Creek, and "Second Tyonek" site or "Tobona"
This place name refers to the **tanik'edi** 'log fish dock' (see pp. 64–65) that the Dena'ina used in the inlet at the mouth of this creek prior to 1880. This was one of about five sites in the Tyonek area where these dipnetting docks were used.

After Old Tyonek (1.30, near Old Tyonek Creek), was abandoned in about 1900 because of tidal erosion, the main village was located here. It was occupied until 1932, when high tides precipitated the move to the modern Tyonek village site (Cook Inlet Historic Sites Project 1975:105; Fall 1981:407).

Ella Chuitt said that during the 1918 flu epidemic thirty-seven children died here.

1.46 Tank'its'a • possibly 'Fish Dock Ridge'
ridge north of Tyonek Creek
The late Peter Constantine noted that many house pits are along this ridge and that it was a lookout point.

1.47 T'ghes Ka'a Hnidaghi'ut • 'Where a Big Cottonwood Is Standing'
locally called "Cottonwood," site on the beach south of Tobona
A village was located here in the time of the warrior **Quq'ey**. Alexan (1981:20) refers to Cottonwood as "the first village, where the Tyonek people had fish hanging on racks to smoke and dry." Paul Chuitt of Tyonek had a fish camp here.

1.48 Batl'eghdink'et' • 'Sedge Extends Against It'
North Foreland, also called "Lighthouse," near Paul Chuitt's fish camp
In April 1794, the English Captain George Vancouver entered Cook Inlet in the sloop Discovery. A contingent of Vancouver's men under the command of Lt. Whidbey visited a trading station of the Lebedev-Lastochkin Company at North Foreland, labeled "Russian Factory" on the map (Map 14) accompanying Vancouver's report (Fall 1981:65; 1987:17). Following is an excerpt of Vancouver's description of the visit by the British sailors to the Russian outpost, which, according to this account, had been built around 1790 (Vancouver 1801:206–207).

"The ebb tide having commenced by the time they had reached the north Foreland, our party stopped for the night close in the vicinity of the Russian establishment, mentioned by those [natives] who had visited the ship in the large open boat, to which our gentlemen received a most friendly invitation.

"At this station there was only one large house, about 50 feet long, 24 wide, and about 10 feet high; this was appropriated to the residence of nineteen Russians, under the direction of an elderly man, who conducted our party into the house by a small door that was its only entrance, and seated them at a table near the upper or further end of the habitation, where a repast consisting of fried fish and cranberries was produced....

"By the assistance of a very indifferent interpreter, Mr. Whidbey understood that the Russians had been at this station nearly four years, yet there was not the least appearance of cultivation, although in the summer season the soil most probably was capable of producing many useful articles of food. This, however, seemed to be of little moment to the European residents, as they appeared to be perfectly content to live after the manner of the native Indians of the country.... So far as any conclusion could be drawn from this short interview, the Russians seemed to live upon the most intimate terms of friendship with the Indians of all description, who appeared to be perfectly satisfied in being subjected to Russian authority."

However, conflicts between the Dena'ina and the Russians did arise, and the Dena'ina destroyed the fort in the late 1790s, precipitating violent reprisals (Tikhmenev 1978:45–46). Afterwards, there do not appear to have been any major Russian posts established in the Upper Cook Inlet area.

Local stories of the warrior **Quq'ey** are set during the 1780s and 1790s. Two written accounts of this period have appeared, one by Nickafor Alexan (1981:1–9), and one by the Russian trader Vladimir Stafeev. Stafeev's account from the 1860s has been translated from Russian (Stafeev n.d.) and is summarized in Mishler (1985a:20). According to Alexan, the warrior **Quq'ey** is said to have killed fifty Russian soldiers at this fort. Afterwards he was killed by other Dena'ina. ‡Boraas and Leggett (2013) compare three sources on the battle at Tyonek (Stafeev, Alexan, and Pete).

The precise location of this fort, which was said by Vancouver (1801:205–207) to be 50 feet long and 24 feet wide, has not been determined. Peter Constantine said that Dena'ina moved back into this area after the Russians abandoned the post.

1.49 Ben Ka'a • 'Big Lake'
Bunka Lake or locally "Big Lake"
In the past, women put fish traps here in the spring for trout and king salmon while the men hunted in the uplands (Chickalusion and Chickalusion 1979:2).

1.50 Qałnigi Dnilent • 'Where Current Flows to the Rocks'
beach south of New Tyonek
Many Tyonek people set their salmon nets here. This is also the main butchering place in the contemporary beluga hunts. See Figure 39.

1.51 Qaggeyshlat Betnu • possibly 'Creek of Little Place Between the Toes'
Indian Creek, through New Tyonek
Many medicinal plants, including cow parsnip, are found on this stream. This used to be a duck and goose hunting area.

FIGURE 39

(Top) **Qałnigi Dnilent** 'Where Current Flows to the Rocks' (1.50), south of New Tyonek, in 1981.

PHOTO BY PRISCILLA RUSSELL

FIGURE 40

(Center) The photo is taken near **Qaggeyshlat Betnu** (1.51) at modern Tyonek, **Qaggeyshlat** (1.52).

PHOTO BY PRISCILLA RUSSELL

FIGURE 41

(Bottom) Aerial view of Tyonek. Modern Tyonek occupies the site known as **Qaggeyshlat** (1.52). The creek just south of the village is **Qaggeyshlat Betnu** (1.51).

PHOTO COURTESY OF COOK INLET REGION, INC.

1.52 **Qaggeyshlat** • possibly 'Little Place Between the Toes'
New Tyonek
Sometimes called by the variant name **Ggaggashlat** 'Little Birds Place.'

This is the modern site of Tyonek, developed in the 1930s. De Laguna (1934:139) said that this place is an old village site. Chief Simeon Chickalusion initiated the move here from the site at **Tank'itnu** (1.45). The Susitna Station people moved here in 1934. A description of the site and its structures is in Cook Inlet Historic Sites Project:104–108.

Nickafor Alexan described Chickalusion's role in founding the new village in his story "Sixth Chief and Governor Of Tyonek" (Alexan n.d.).

"Tubughna: The Beach People" is a film produced by Frank and Jo Brink on behalf of the people of Tyonek. It focuses on the village's history, especially the changes that took place after Tyonek received money for oil and gas exploration leases on its property in the 1960s. The film features Shem Pete leading the community in singing a traditional Tyonek dance song.

1.53 **Chikdashla Betnu** • 'Little Grandmother Creek'
creek above Tyonek cemetery

1.54 **Chikdashla Bena** • 'Little Grandmother Lake'
small lake behind Tyonek cemetery
Tyonek residents report house pits in this area.

1.55 **Qaggeyshla Bena** • 'Lake of Little Place Between the Toes'
First Lake, at west end of New Tyonek

1.56 **Tuk'eleh Bena** • 'Spawning Lake'
Second Lake
This is both an ancient and modern fishing site for rainbow trout and silver salmon (Chickalusion and Chickalusion 1979:3).

1.57 **Chuqan Baydli Bena** or **Chuqan Bazdluyi Bena** • 'Lake in Which There Are Beaver Lodges'
Third Lake
This is a beaver hunting and trout fishing area (Chickalusion and Chickalusion 1979:4).

1.58 **Ch'u'itnu Hdakaq'** • '-Ω- River Mouth'
mouth of Chuitna River, Ladd
Fall (1981:406): "One small village that survived into the 1910s was located at the mouth of the Chuitt River." This was the northernmost of the four larger historic villages in the Tyonek area. Of this place, de Laguna (1934:139) wrote, "The modern village is on an ancient site, Ts'ui'tna."

In 1896, the priest Bortnovsky from Kenai wrote, "At Chubutnu only one Indian family lives permanently; the others come here to work for the Ladd Company [saltery]" (Townsend 1974:19).

The two families associated with this site are the Chuitts and Chilligans. Many people died here in a measles epidemic in 1913. ‡Boraas et al. (2015:62–68) have compiled documents and photos on the Ladd Station Dena'ina village.

FIGURE 42
Shem Pete at the Russian Orthodox church at Tyonek in 1983.
PHOTO BY PRISCILLA RUSSELL

‡The proposed Chuitna Coal Mine project by PacRim Coal, LP, has resulted in extensive research on the Chuitna River drainage in the past ten years (Braund & Assoc., Boraas et al. 2015). Literature reviews discuss the geology, salmon biology, historical, and ethnographic sources (Boraas et al. 2015). "A large archaeological site complex (TYO-132) is located at the Ch'u'itnu near [and on both sides of] its mouth, parts of which were occupied from the early 1600s to early 1800s (Braund & Assoc. 2007; Boraas et al. 2015). The village is probably the one referred to as "First Village" in Alexan (1981). The site area contains over 40 house remains and well over a hundred underground cold storage pits for storing salmon and other foods for winter." Separate archaeological surveys in 2007, 2012, 2013, and 2014 resulted in the formation of the Ch'u'itnu Archaeological District. Boraas et al. (2015:38–41) list ten significant sites with fourteen radiocarbon dates that range between AD 1450 and AD 1896. Also noted are several cremation and burial sites. Rogers 2015 is an important analysis of the use of Dena'ina lithics and lithic artifacts from the large collection obtained by Braund and Assoc. from the Ch'u'itnu Archaeological District.

1.59 **Ch'u'itnu, Ch'ubetnu** • '-Ω- River'
Chuitna River, Chuitt River
The meaning of this name is obscure to all of today's speakers. Shem Pete speculated that it may be related to the word **ch'ibu** 'sadness.' ‡Kari had noted a possible etymology with the stem **ch'u** 'odor, ordorous.' This name was misspelled in Kari (2007:114) as "Ch'u'it'nu." The lower Chuitt River has long been a popular fishing area. Before contact with non-Natives, the Dena'ina would fish here, walking downstream holding dip nets. Fish traps and fish pits were located along the river (Chickalusion and

Chickalusion 1979:5). The fall run of silver salmon in the Chuitt River has been especially important.

The majority of contemporary Tyonek hunting activity is centered southwest of the village, from the Chuitt River to south of McArthur River. It seems that this southward and westward orientation for modern Tyonek subsistence activity is in part a reaction to increased hunting pressure by non-Natives in areas north of Tyonek, especially north of the Beluga River. Prior to the 1920s, the Tyonek Dena'ina used the areas north of Tyonek extensively (Fall, Foster, and Stanek 1984:178).

Most of the place names in the Chuitt and Beluga drainages were reported by the late Alec Peter in 1976 when he was about ninety-one years of age.

Sava Stephan: "Those seals would go up Chuitt River to eat jellyfish. Chuitt River I walked all the way up there to that lake. My dad used to pack a canoe up there and go all over the lakes up there. Long time ago my dad used to be champion moose hunter. Tyonek boys didn't know much about moose hunt. My dad used to know lots about camping. He kill moose for them. Late fish go up to Chuitt Lake. Sometime they set net and get that late fish. Nothing but old fish get in there. The old fellas used to like that late fish, getting old. They used to like that when it's dry. **Nudelbay**. Dried old fish. They used to hang them up on a spruce tree, the old fish. **Nudelbay**."

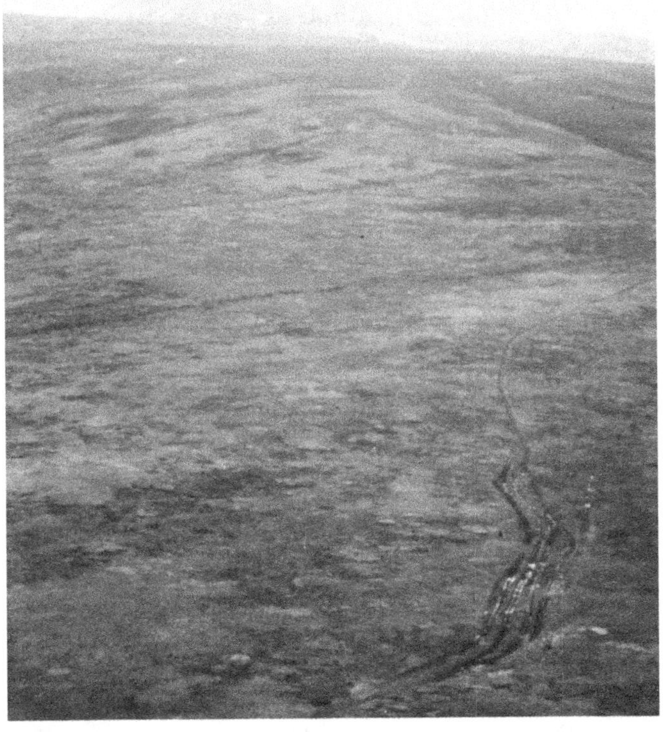

FIGURE 43

Dghelikda Nuten 'No-Good Mountain Trail,' (1.65), Lone Ridge. The stream to the right is **Dghelikda Nutentnu** (1.64), Chuitt Creek.

PHOTO COURTESY OF COOK INLET REGION, INC.

§1.108 **Tugh'i Betnu** • 'Sandbar Creek'
Lone Creek

1.60 **Tugh'i Kena** • 'Sandbar Flat'
flat east of Lone Creek
This place is near Pat Chuitt's old camp. It is visible from the Chuitt River.

1.61 **Tugh'i Bena** • 'Sandbar Lake'
lake at head of Lone Creek
Ella Chuitt: "«Pat Chuitt had a camp on this lake.»"
Billy Pete: "We used to go for moose in winter time from Tyonek to Paul Chuitt's camp, and then to Beluga Mountain."

(1.62) **Tsał Bena** • 'Box Lake'
lake, location uncertain, in Chuitna drainage
Ella Chuitt said that this is the nearest to Tyonek of three lakes in the Chuitt River drainage that she remembers.

(1.63) **Suluna Deqejeq Hnitunt** • 'Where Saltfish Is Stored'
on trail toward Beluga River, location uncertain
Peter Constantine said that the Chuitt family kept saltfish in a barrel here for use on the **Dghelikda Nuten** trail (1.65).

1.64 **Dghelikda Nutentnu** • 'No-Good Mountain Trail Creek'
Chuitt Creek
This was the principal upland hunting country in the Tyonek area. This ridge was used in the fall for hunting ground squirrel and large game. In the past beaver were hunted in many of the lakes in this area. The names of the many of these lakes are no longer remembered.

1.65 **Dghelikda Nuten** • 'No-Good Mountain Trail'
Lone Ridge
There was a major trail for hauling meat between Tyonek and **Dghelikda Nuten**. The trail begins near the Tyonek pump house and ascends to the uplands along the Chuitt River to Lone Ridge. Formerly this trail branched from Lone Ridge to the north crossing the Beluga River to the upper Talachulitna River. The "Indian winter trail" on the Herron map of 1899 (Map 22), from Tyonek to the Skwentna River, is the first documentation of this trail. See 6.10 for further discussion by Herron.

1.66 **Tuk'elehtnu** • 'Spawning Stream'
Three Mile Creek
‡Boraas et al. (2015:80–86) present a compilation of hunting and fishing areas used by Tyonek families on the Chuitna River and the Threemile Creek drainages.

1.67 **Tuk'eleh Bena** • 'Spawning Lake'
Tukallah Lake
This lake has been a fishing site for red and silver salmon as well as Dolly Varden and rainbow trout (Chickalusion and Chickalusion 1979:3).

1.68 Ben Ka'a or **Ch'u'itnu Bena** • 'Big Lake' or '-Ω- Lake'
Chuitbuna Lake
Ella Chuitt said that the Chuitt family used to have houses here. This is an important area for moose hunting and trout fishing.

‡**1.127 Ben Ka'a Betnu** • 'Large Lake Stream'
outlet stream of Chuitbuna Lake
‡Boraas et al. 2015. "Salmon were caught using weirs in a tributary stream complex that drains **Ben Ka'a,** a lake north of the TYO-132 site complex, or from beach fishing such as described by Alexan (1965)."

§**1.109 Batuk'iydlaghi** • 'The One in Which Fish Swim into the Water'
Viapan Lake
Name recalled by Sava Stephan: "Viapan Lake, we landed there all the time. That's what they used to call **Batuk'iydlaghi Bena**."

Brooks (1911:16) described the Tyonek-Susitna beach trail in 1902: "The route lay along the western shore of Cook Inlet, over a gravel beach at the foot of a series of gravel bluffs which rise fifty to one hundred feet above the water.... This strip, limited by the inlet on one side and by the precipitous escarpment on the other, gave excellent opportunity to break in the pack horses."

Sava Stephan: "Once I went in eight hours from Susitna to Tyonek in winter with dogs. January. I had nine dogs. Dogs go by themselves on clear ice. Just little bit run through the snow, on the beach. Old lady was riding in sled. I make about three trips with a load. I haul house logs with a bobsled. I go with Pedro Goozmer. Or when walking in spring. It's twelve miles from Beluga to Tyonek. They had camps all over there. Always camp at Beluga River mouth. From there it take me a day, two days to come down from Susitna. If ice go out I go on the sand. Sometime be nice and slick ice. Two day trip." (See also 1.84 on travel along the beach trail.)

§**1.110 Nughiltnu Kaq', Nughil Kaq'** • 'Mouth of River That Flows Down'
mouth of Beluga River
Sava Stephan: "«At Beluga River [mouth] ice was floating, pretty thick, we were going back and forth across it, and it was pretty good. We went over it and we had made ice poles. And we were probing across.» **Aya aya ya**, we almost froze to death. On the middle of Beluga River you know we can't get across. The pole was too short, we can't hit the bottom with it. We were on snowshoes. We can't get ashore, we can't get across. Finally «It floated off on us. and we hit the beach. It carried us in the current. So we came to shore.» I was with Wilson Nikolai."

1.69 Ts'inal'unt • 'Where a Protrusion Sticks Straight Up'
hill on north side of Beluga River (location revised)
The first wooded bend up the Beluga River on the north side. This is a landmark and campsite with firewood at the junction of the summer/winter beach trail from the mouth of the Susitna to Tyonek and the upland trail to the Skwentna River. This "Indian Trail" on the 1911 Brooks map (Map 15) goes up the southern side of the Theodore River, along the west slope of Beluga Mountain to the Skwentna River. The Brooks party went through here in June of 1902. Also the Cook party went on this trail in 1903 (Cook 1904, 1907).

§**1.111 Ts'inal'un Bena** • 'Lake of Where a Protrusion Sticks Straight Up'
small lake lake near hill north of Beluga River, possibly Seeley Lake
Name confirmed by Sava Stephan.

§**1.112 Ts'inal'untnu** • 'Stream of Where a Protrusion Sticks Straight Up'
creek off hill on north side of Beluga River

1.70 Nughiltnu • 'River That Flows Down'
Beluga River
Shem Pete: "«**Nughiltnu** is close to **T'ghesitnu** (Theodore River, 1.81). There are no house pits there.»"

Nickafor Alexan (1981:18): "It is said that [Chief] Pete used to have long logs sticking out of Beluga River close to the hills, and when the belugas came in there at high tide to go up the river, he would spear the belugas."

Passing the Beluga River in 1898 Spurr (1950:8) noted, "We came to a deep "tide-drain" a moat-like channel of water caused by the flow and ebb of the strong tides from the inlet, back and forth over the muddy flat." The Dena'ina term for this type of tide drain is **tl'ik'ts'itnu**.

Going through here in 1910, Browne (1956:81) commented on the importance of beluga in the local diet and the rich salmon and fowl resources of this stream. This area is presently used by Tyonek people for beluga and waterfowl hunting. In the past, bear hunting was popular here.

1.71 Q'aghiltnu • 'Stream That Flows Into (River)'
Olson Creek
This name was reported by Alec Peter, and later confirmed by Sava Stephan.

1.72 Q'aghil Bena • 'Lake of Stream That Flows In'
narrow lake at head of Olson Creek

1.73 Esni Ghiłent • 'Where Current Flows Through Cottonwoods'
Coffee Creek

§**1.74 K'q'uya Bena** • 'Sockeye Salmon Lake'
Bishop Lake

§**1.113 K'q'uya Betnu** • 'Sockeye Salmon Stream'
Bishop Creek
Ella Chuitt has heard of this place, which is said to be "way up" at the upper end of the Chuitt family's territory. The name was also reported by the late Alec Peter.

§**1.114 Unqeghdut Nughiltnu Bena** • 'Downstream Lake of Flows Down River'
Lower Beluga Lake

FIGURE 45

Felt Lake off the upper Beluga River has no recorded Dena'ina name. Beyond the lake is **Nughiltnu** (1.70), Beluga River. In the distance is a nice view of the group of upland features presented in Chapter 4.: **Hnidi** (4.20, Beluga Mountain), **Nudinli**, (4.18) **Henq'edishla** (1.83, Little Mt. Sustina), and **Dghelishla** (4.9, Mt. Sustina). See Fig. 70.

PHOTO COURTESY OF COOK INLET REGION, INC.

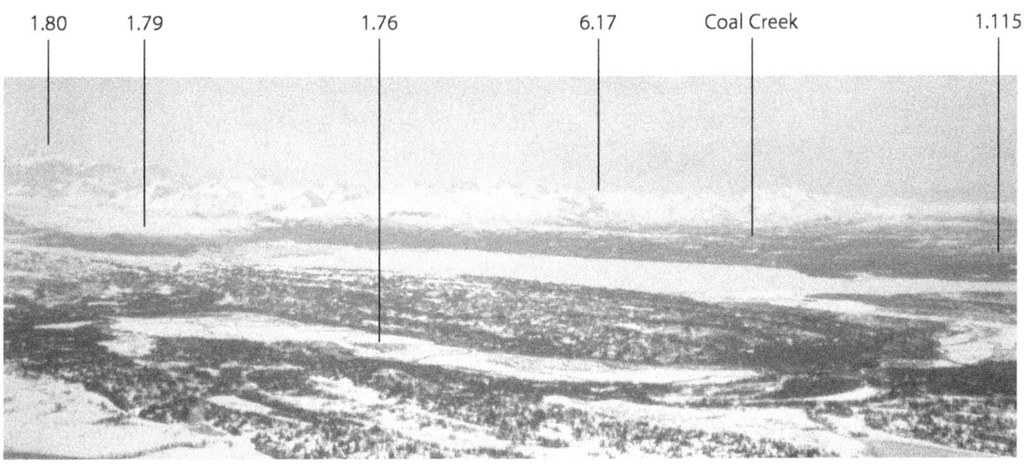

FIGURE 46

Unqeghnit Nughiltnu Bena (1.75) Beluga Lake in winter. At the right edge of the photo, east of the lake outlet is **Tahelitnu** (1.115) Drill Creek. South of Beluga Lake is **Łich'antnu** (1.76) Chichantna River. At the head of the lake is **Nughiltnu Łi'a** (1.79), Triumvirate Glacier. The large mountain above here is **Qayeh Dghelaya** (1.80), Mt. Gerdine. See 6.17 and Plate 4, Coal Creek and **Tubughna Katidiłtuni** (Hayes River Pass), north of Beluga Lake.

PHOTO COURTESY OF COOK INLET REGION, INC.

§1.115 Tahelitnu • 'Hard-packed Snow Trail Creek'
Drill Creek (revised location)
Mentioned by Shem Pete and not mapped but subsequently located by Sava Stephan. As the name reveals, this was on a winter trail that led north on the west side of Beluga Mountain.

Sava Stephan: "**Tahelitnu**. I heard about that. Some place behind that Susitna Mountain. I know it go into Beluga Lake or Beluga River. Something like a frozen road. **Tiqeli naghelten** 'snow trail is frozen.'"

1.75 Unqeghnit Nughiltnu Bena • 'Upstream Lake of Flows Down River'
(upper) Beluga Lake
Beluga Lake and the upper Beluga River have not been widely used by the Tyonek people since the 1920s. Chief Pete (**Benił'a Ch'ulyałen**) (ca. 1830–1918) was the last **qeshqa** to use this area extensively. Chief **Nunk'ilash** of Tyonek is said to have died when hunting at Beluga Lake (Alexan 1981:15).

Shem Pete: "When I was a kid, Robert Allowan took me from Susitna Station over there to Beluga Lake. We just travel around. We come back on **Nutnasdlenitnu** (6.10) then go back on top of the mountain and come back to Susitna Station. All April we travel around hunting beaver. Every place we stop we find beaver. We had a good dog team."

According to the late Peter Constantine, Steve Chuitt was the last Tyonek person to trap and hunt regularly at Beluga Lake. Peter Constantine last traveled here with Chuitt in 1931. After the development of Anchorage in the 1920s, the Beluga River drainage was used by various non-Natives. As a result, most Tyonek people tended to use the areas south of Tyonek for subsistence activities.

1.76 Łich'antnu • 'Creek from Glacier'
Chichantna River

1.77 Łich'antnu Łi'a • 'Glacier of Creek from Glacier'
Capps Glacier

§1.116 Łik'a Kin'i • 'Dog's Head'
Dogshead, the nunatak northeast of Capps Glacier
This Dena'ina translation name was reported to Tom Taylor of USGS in 1958 by Nickafor Alexan. The name was confirmed by Sava Stephan.

§1.117 Łik'a Kin'i Łi'a • 'Dog's Head Glacier'
Dogshead Glacier

1.78 T'etniya • 'That Which Makes Noise'
Mount Torbert

1.79 Nughiltnu Łi'a • 'Glacier of Flows Down River'
Triumvirate Glacier
It was here, according to Shem Pete, that **Benił'a Ch'ulyałen**, Chief Pete of Tyonek, found a giant porcupine quill, inside of which he walked around. He thus obtained power (Fall 1987:59).

1.80 Qayeh Dghelaya • 'Village Mountain'
Mount Gerdine
This name and Mt. Torbert (1.78) were reported by Alec Peter but are not known by any other speakers.

1.81 T'ghesitnu • 'Cottonwood River'
Theodore River
An "Indian Trail" up the south bank of the Theodore River and to the Talachulitna River is marked on the 1904 and 1907 Cook maps, the 1911 Brooks map (Map 15), a 1914 Bureau of Soils map of Cook Inlet, and the 1910a map by Sleem.

Brooks (1911:17): "Returning, we reached the base

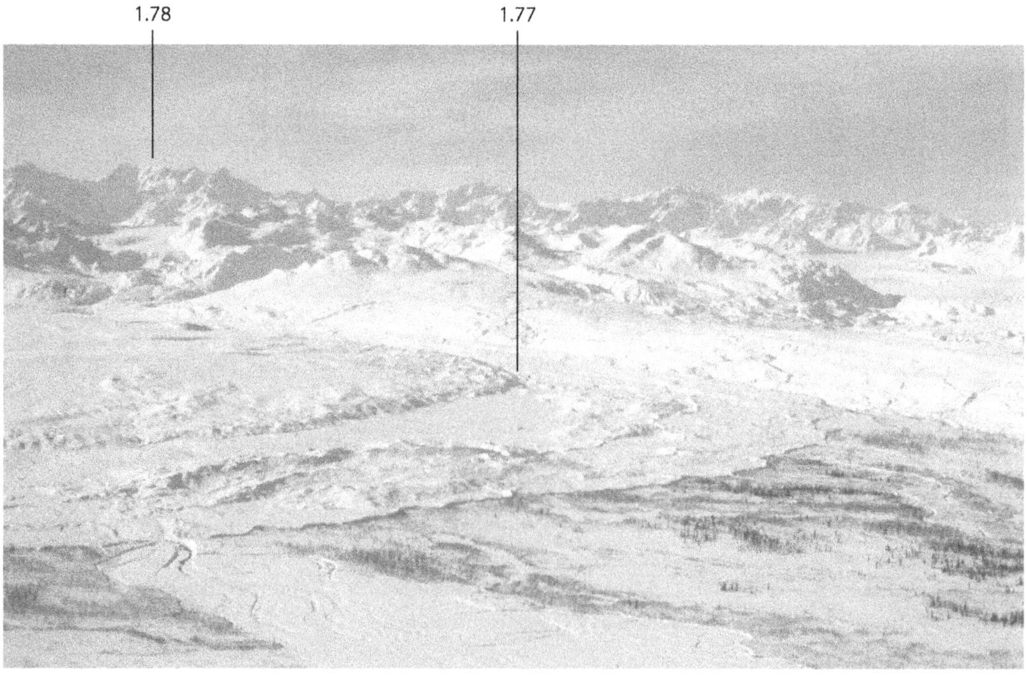

FIGURE 46
Łich'antnu Łi'a (1.77, Capps Glacier), with the higher Tordrillo Mountains. **T'etniya** (1.78, Mt. Torbert) is at the left side of the picture.
PHOTO COURTESY OF COOK INLET REGION, INC.

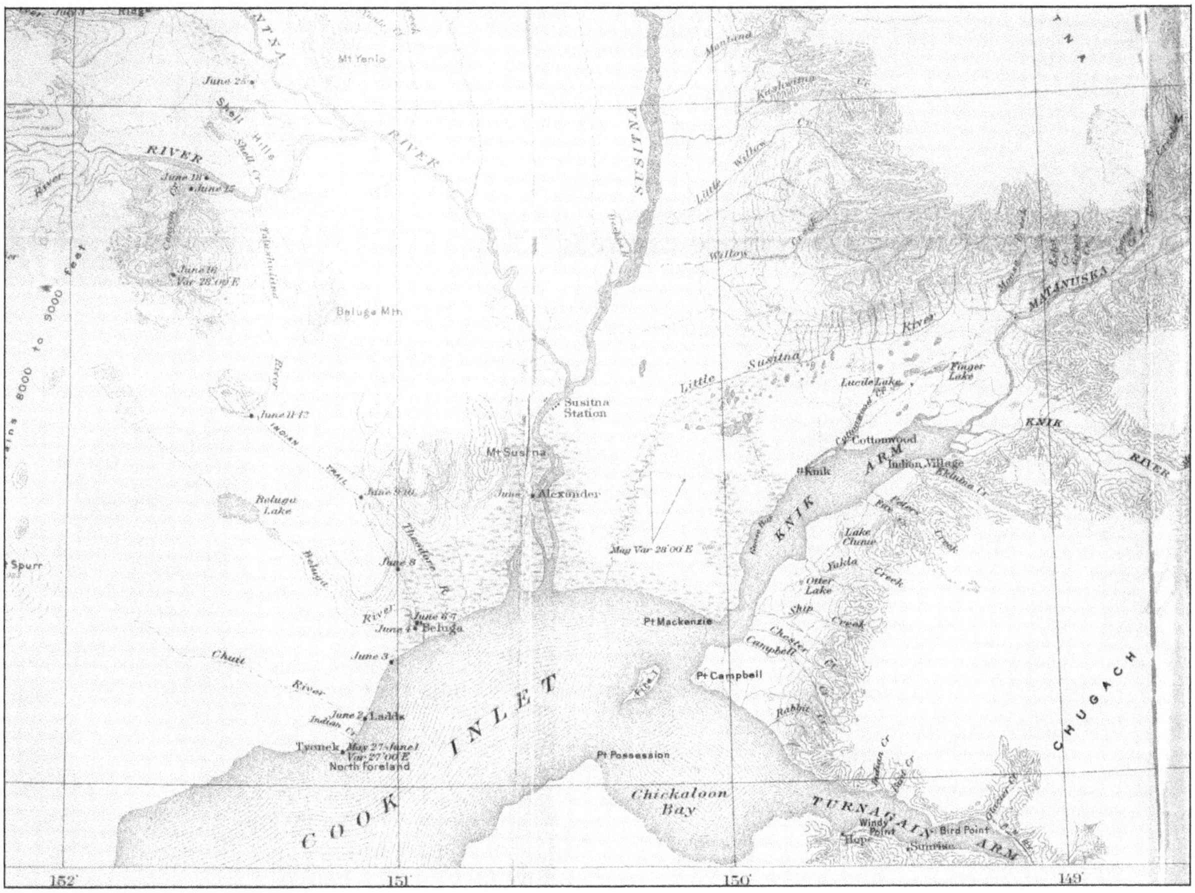

camp on Beluga River on June 7. The trail choppers had found the old Indian trail of which we had heard rumors at Tyonek, and thereby had been able to establish a route for 7 or 8 miles. On the 8th the reunited party resumed the march, dispatching Eberhardt and Anderson with the boat to a rendezvous on the Skwentna. The trail led northwestward over a gravel plateau which sloped up gently toward the mountains, interrupted here and there by knobs of granitic rocks.... Many swamps retarded our progress and severely taxed the strength of the horses, but good grass was abundant. The many lakes and ponds were breeding grounds of waterfowl, and the camp larder was much improved by contributions of duck, geese, and sand-hill crane, as well as grouse. June 13 brought us to the foothills of the range, and for several days we made rapid progress over a country thickly covered with grass and studded with parklike groves of trees. In these highlands many large brown bear were seen. The Indian trail vanished above timber line, and on descending to the lowland of the Skwentna Valley we were compelled to do continuous chopping in order to penetrate the dense grove of alder, spruce, and birch."

Capps (1929:78) described this same trail: "The Geological Survey expedition landed its horses at a point 2 miles above the mouth of the Beluga River... and with light loads proceeded northward around the head of the Talushulitna River [Talachulitna River, 6.7], reaching the Skwentna some miles above the mouth of Canyon

MAP 15

Detail from the 1911 Brooks map: Upper Cook Inlet.

With the annual surveys conducted by the Alaska branch of the United States Geological Survey, professional cartography in Alaska advanced rapidly between 1898 and 1915. Alfred H. Brooks was chief Alaska geologist for the USGS between 1903 and 1923. Brooks' 1911 map entitled "Reconnaissance Map, Mt. McKinley Region Alaska" was based upon his 1902 circumnavigation of the Central Alaska Range (‡Brooks 1904). This detail from upper Cook Inlet shows the Brooks' party's camping positions and a trail from Tyonek to the "Indian Trail" along the Theodore River to the Skwentna River (see 1.81). ‡Brooks (1904:412): "At the Beluga River the course lay inland, and by good fortune an Indian trail lightened the labor of the axmen; but it was designed to be used in the fall and winter when the ground was frozen." By 1911 much of the topography of Southcentral Alaska, the larger streams and ridges and mountains, had official names with conventionalized spellings on the USGS maps.

‡Information and sources from *SPA* pertinent to the proposed Donlin Gold Pipeline route that were *not* cited in the 2015 Donlin draft EIS (US Army Corps of Engineers, 2015) include: Chapter 1, Beluga River, Theodore River, and the Mt. Susitna area; Chapter 4, the Alexander Creek drainage and the Beluga Mt. area; and Chapter 6, the Talachulitna, Skwenta, and Happy Rivers, Rainy Pass, and South Fork of Kuskokwim. Also not mentioned in the 2015 EIS was Collins (2004) on Upper Kuskokwim ethnography and language.

ARCHIVES, ALASKA AND POLAR REGIONS DEPT., RASMUSON LIBRARY, UNIVERSITY OF ALASKA FAIRBANKS

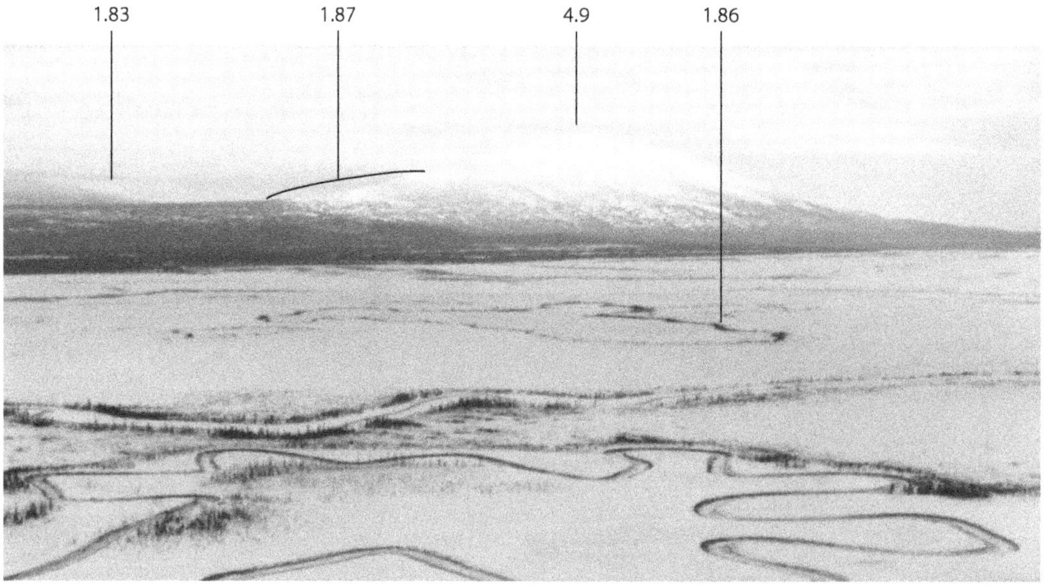

FIGURE 48

Tl'equkena (1.84, Chedatna Lakes Flat) with **Dghelishla** (4.9, Mt. Susitna) in the background. The ridge tapering south of 4.9 is **Ch'chihi Ken** (1.87). Just visible is **Henq'edishla** (1.83, Little Mount Susitna). In the foreground is **Ch'qi'untnu** (1.86, Ivan River).
PHOTO BY PRISCILLA RUSSELL

Creek.... About 10 days should be allowed for traversing the 70 miles from Beluga to the Skwentna."

1.82 Henq'e Dishla Betnu • 'Creek of the Little Upland One'
creek into Theodore River west of Little Mount Susitna

1.83 Henq'edishla • 'The Little Upland One'
Little Mount Susitna
See Fig. 70 in Chapter 4.

1.84 Tl'equkena • perhaps 'Back Surface Flat'
Chedatna Lakes Flat between Beluga and Susitna rivers
The trail across this flat between Tyonek and the lower Susitna was well traveled. The old trail was on the upland side, along the edge of the timberline. The trail was especially used for the grease trade in winter. Shem Pete said that the old people said that caribou used to be caught on this flat in the distant past.

Shem Pete composed his love song, **Ada Beghuynisdi**, as he walked through here in 1915; see pp. 126–127.

§1.118 Tl'equkena Bena • perhaps 'Back Surface Flat Lake'
Chedatna Lakes between Beluga and Susitna rivers
Note that the name Chedatna Lake derives from the Dena'ina name for Lewis River, 1.85.

§1.119 Tl'equkena Betnu • 'Back Surface Flat Creek'
stream through Chedatna Lakes
Sava Stephan: "I used to go from Susitna to Tyonek. I covered all these lakes, along the beach too. **Ts'idatnu,** Theodore River, Beluga River I been through there lots of times. **Tl'equkena**, there a creek running through there, and way down next to Cottonwood there is a little creek by Beluga Field under the ground, **Tl'equkena Betnu**."

1.85 Ts'idatnu • '-Ω- River'
Lewis River

§1.125 Dghelishla Ch'adinłeni • 'The One That Flows from Little Mountain'
upper north fork of Lewis River off of Mt. Susitna

1.86 Ch'qi'untnu • 'We Found a Place Creek'
Ivan River
Shem Pete: "«That creek that flows from it [**Ch'chihi Ken**, 1.87], close to **T'ghesitnu** (1.81), is **Ch'qi'untnu**.»"

This seems be the place reported by Learnard (1900:653) as "Chuitnacocks" [**Ch'qi'untnu Kaq'**], said to be one mile below the mouth of the Susitna.

Shem Pete said that his brother was here in 1906 when he saw a large sternwheeler enter the Susitna River, the first such boat he had seen.

1.120 Ch'chihi Ken Betnu • 'Stream of Ridge Where We Cry'
creek from sloping ridge south of Mt. Susitna, into Ivan River

1.87 Ch'chihi Ken • 'Ridge Where We Cry'
sloping ridge south of Mt. Susitna
Shem Pete: "«That big ridge going downriver from **Dghelishla** [Mount Susitna, 4.9] all the way to Beluga, they call **Ch'chihi Ken.** They would sit down there. Everything is in view. They can see their whole country.» Everything is just right under them. They think about their brothers and their fathers and mothers. They remember that, and they just sit down there and cry. That's the place we cry all the time, 'cause everything just show up plain. That's why they call it **Ch'chihi Ken**" (Kari and Kari 1982:1).

Beluga Hunting in the Tyonek Area

by James Kari and James A. Fall

FIGURE 49

This drawing of the **yuyqul** is by Leonard Savage.

FROM THE FIRST PRINTING OF SHEM PETE'S BELUGA HUNTING STORY (KARI 1980), REPRINTED WITH PERMISSION OF THE NATIONAL BILINGUAL MATERIALS DEVELOPMENT CENTER

The Dena'ina of Cook Inlet are the only Athabascans who have regularly hunted whales. The large whales (order Cetacea), called **tałin** in Dena'ina, that entered the Inlet were not hunted, but stranded whales were harvested (Osgood 1937). In fact, the place name for Polly Creek village is **Tałin Ch'iłtant** 'Where We Found a Whale.' The small, white beluga whales (*Delphinapterus leaucas*) were hunted regularly by the Dena'ina between May and August. Aboriginally, this was done mainly at stream mouths on the broad tidal flats on the western shore, from the mouth of the Susitna River to the Chuitna River and also in the Kenai River area. It is only there in the broad, shallow mudflats that the **yuyqul**, beluga spearing tree, could be implanted. After the introduction of powerful firearms, the Dena'ina abandoned this unique technology, and beluga were shot at river mouths. (See, for example, Kalifornsky 1975 and Pete 1977.)

In the literature on Dena'ina culture traits, Wrangell, Petroff, Osgood, and others have stressed that certain items of Dena'ina material culture were borrowed from Eskimo peoples, and that their marine adaptation was rudimentary. Dzeniskevich (1981) is a recent restatement of this assertion.

However, there is evidence that coastal resources of Cook Inlet were, and are, well integrated into the Dena'ina seasonal round of subsistence activities. (See especially Fall, Foster, and Stanek 1984.) For example, the Dena'ina fishing dock, **tanik'edi**, for dipnetting salmon in tidewater (which was not documented in Osgood 1937, but see the description by Nikafor Alexan on p. 64; cf. Fall 1987:34), is a Dena'ina innovation and not a borrowing.

Likewise, the Upper Inlet Dena'ina method of catching the beluga with the **yuyqul** seems to be unique in North America. It cannot be classed as method or implement that the Dena'ina borrowed from the Eskimo or Aleut people (such as, for example, the bidarka or kayak). It appears to be an extension of the hunting strategies behind the Athabascan elevated game lookout, called **dehq'a** in Dena'ina (Fall 1981:192). Furthermore, operation of both the **tanik'edi** and the **yuyqul** require specialized knowledge of Cook Inlet currents and tides as well as the movement of beluga and salmon in marine waters. Even the word **yuyqul** is intriguing in that it contains the stem **qul**, which is not used in any other word in any of the Dena'ina dialects, and seems to be rare in other Alaskan Athabascan languages. But note that in Navajo a cognate stem, **kaal**, is used in the verb theme 'to place rigid objects in a series' (Young and Morgan 1980:423).

There are good data available now on traditional Dena'ina water transport, vastly more than Osgood (1937:67–69) had access to, which further illustrate the effective Dena'ina adaptation to both marine and riverine environments. (See further discussion in Chapter 3.) Dena'ina used sealskin kayaks extensively in inland areas throughout their territory. Kayaks were known to be durable on overland portages. It now appears that the use and manufacture of kayaks and umiaks by the Dena'ina has considerable antiquity. Although the Dena'ina are said to have been timid in contrast to the Eskimo in handling the kayaks and umiaks, no one can claim that handling boats in Cook Inlet is easy. This elaboration in Dena'ina water transport can be contrasted with that of the Ingalik (Osgood 1940:380), who had access to sealskins from nearby Norton Sound, yet did not use kayaks or umiaks within their territory.

Shem Pete's masterful and intricate description of the Dena'ina beluga hunting technique, on pp. 78–79, is based upon accounts by some of the last eyewitnesses, including Chief Pete of Tyonek, and **Bidyaka'a** of Tyonek, the last Dena'ina to use the **yuyqul**. The story first appeared in Pete (1980b:6–12). The text is slightly revised here.

Although Shem's is not an eyewitness account, it is richly detailed, containing many of the terms for cultural items that have long been obsolete. For comparison and corroboration, Wrangell's description of Dena'ina beluga hunting, recorded in the 1830s, is presented below.

> In shallow places near the shore, in currents from entering steams where beluga pursue fish, poles are driven in on which the hunters seat themselves and watch the fish. As soon as the whale has drawn near enough, the Kenay throws a pole with an arrow, that is to say, a harpoon head attached to a pole one and a half sazhens long and attached to a thong ten sazhens long with an inflated bladder on the end; the beluga, impaled with the harpoon head, quickly swims away and the bladder in the water shows the location of the animal to which the the hunter, jumping into his prepared baidarka, sets out in pursuit and grasping the shaft, which in the meantime has freed itself from the harpoon head, inserts into it a slate knife, stabs the beluga a few more times, and at last brings it lifeless to the shore (Wrangell 1970:12).

FIGURE 49

Shem Pete sorts butchered beluga blubber on the beach just north of Tyonek in 1981.

PHOTO BY PRISCILLA RUSSELL

Another early mention of Dena'ina beluga hunting appeared in Steensby's (1917:43) survey of Eskimo whale hunting techniques.

> The coast of Cooks Inlet, the large indentation west of the Kenai Peninsula is not inhabited by the Eskimo, but by a Kenai tribe closely connected, the Ingaliks [*sic* the Dena'ina]; the members of which like their kinsmen on the Lower Yukon. have been strongly influenced by the Eskimo culture. They use the kayak for hunting White Whale, which, in rather large numbers, resort to the lower parts of the bay. The animal, however, is not hunted direct from the kayak, but the hunter places himself on a staging of poles erected in the water, from which he hurls his lance, which has a slate head. When an animal is hit, he gets his boat which he has ready and pursues it. Large whales, which also visit the bay, are not hunted by the Indians. When, in August, the whale hunting and the salmon fishing, which are carried on at the same time, are ended, they wander up in the mountains, where they hunt

reindeer and mountain-sheep. In September or October they set out in canoes, which they have covered with reindeer hides, down the Suchitna River back to Cooks Inlet, where the winter is passed in earth covered-winter houses which, judging from Jacobsen's description, are of quite the same kind as the Eskimo houses on the Yukon and in Kadiak. This, then, is the third case of a non-Eskimo neighboring tribe adopting the Eskimo culture.

One of the more interesting findings of recent research at Tyonek by the Alaska Department of Fish and Game, Division of Subsistence, is the renewal of interest in beluga hunting. Prior to 1940, beluga meat and blubber were a major part of the Tyonek diet. It is estimated that six or seven beluga were harvested per year in the 1930s and 1940s. In the following decades the beluga was rarely pursued, but since 1979 the hunt has been revived, and the meat and blubber have been shared widely in the village (Fall, Foster, and Stanek 1984:167–173). ‡For a recent summary of beluga hunting and uses of beluga in Tyonek in the late 20th and early 21st centuries, see Braund and Huntington (2011).

A brief technical description of beluga butchering at Tyonek appears in Fall, Foster, and Stanek 1984:172. Tommy Allowan of Tyonek was in charge of the butchering process in the 1970s and 1980s; he learned this skill from Chief Simeon Chickalusion. The Dena'ina have numerous technical terms for beluga as well as for seal anatomy and butchering. These are of some interest in that they show the extension of the language into specialized marine activities.

Nickafor Alexan summarized the uses of beluga: "The Indians those days used to use the beluga's oil and eat the meat of the belugas they kill. Also they used to eat the blubber, boil all the fat into oil, put all the meat up to dry for the winter, and take all the sinew string for bow. Because the [beluga] sinew string is much stronger" (Alexan 1981:18).

Shem Pete adds: "The big beluga guts, they fill them right up with oil and blubber, strings of blubber, mixed them up with beluga oil."

Beluga products were important items in the trade between the "beach people" of Tyonek and the more land-oriented Dena'ina of the middle and upper Susitna and the Yentna rivers (Fall 1987:35).

In the 1990s, the beluga population in Cook Inlet underwent a steep decline, at least in part due to hunting by non-Dena'ina Alaska Native hunters based in Anchorage. In May 2000, the National Marine Fisheries Service (NMFS 2000) designated the Cook Inlet beluga stock as depleted under the Marine Mammal Protection Act. In the environmental impact statement (EIS) prepared as part of the development of a plan for the management and recovery of the Cook Inlet belugas, the NMFS acknowledged the traditional use of beluga by the Upper Inlet Dena'ina, citing the oral traditions provided by Shem Pete, as well as the continuing hunting traditions in Tyonek (NMFS 2000:26–27; Mahoney and Shelden 2000). The EIS concluded that allowing a limited subsistence hunting opportunity during the recovery of the beluga population should be a management goal in order to maintain these traditional uses (NMFS 2000:66). In the early phases of the recovery plan, subsistence hunting of belugas was limited to hunters from Tyonek, in recognition of the well-documented historical depth of the cultural traditions associated with beluga hunting in the village.

‡However, the Cook Inlet beluga population has continued to decline, and the population was listed as endangered under the Endangered Species Act (ESA) in 2008. All subsistence hunting was closed until at least 2018, but the population failed to show any signs of recovery. The draft recovery plan published in 2015 (NMFS 2015) discussed a range of threats to recovery, including catastrophic events (such as mass strandings and oil spills), habitat loss and degradation, noise, disease, reduced prey populations, and pollution. Although listed as a "threat of low relative concern," under the ESA, NMFS will not authorize a subsistence hunt if the activity is "likely to jeopardize the continued existence of the Cook Inlet beluga whale population" (NMFS 2015:88).

Quyushi Uqu Ch'el'ani
Beluga Hunting

by Shem Pete

"Nacheyakda'ina quyushi uhu qul'ih.
Our grandfathers used to hunt beluga.

Ch'ubetnu Tubughnenq' qech' tabagh quyushi qughidił.
Beluga come near the beach between Chuitna [Chuitt] River and Old Tyonek.

Ch'bala beggats'a dnaghelt'ayi sht'a qunuhggats'hghighi'uk ch'q'u
They used to dig up a spruce tree with a big root structure and

beggats'a ghini badahdalqeyh t'qeyeghiłik.
they hewed out the root structure [into a perch].

Tsenqeydghiłtuk' ch'u belutuna ghinhdi łuq'u qeyech'anqeyedghigits'.
They carried it down to the water, and they tore off all the inner bark.

Qeydełt'ich' ch'q'u yethdi heyetnełggush.
They peeled it and then they dried it.

"Łduntutset gheli hdi yuse gheli nintutset sht'a quhqelash ch'u hq'aqeydeyeł.
At low tide, when the tide had gone quite far out, they would dig a hole and put it [tree] in.

Ch'bala lu hniqeyduyeł hq'aqeydełchet.
They stuck the top end of the spruce in a hole, and they stood it up.

Dnigi deyes k'qałen ghini tuq'i nilanh qeyełtl'ił ch'q'u jahtl'in eł naltlah t'qeyeł'ish.
They braided three strips of moose skin and smeared it with pitch.

Ch'q'u ch'bala lu ghu hniqeydghitseyi ghu tl'ił ghini yutgge sht'a benyestkeyh ghu t'qeyeghił'ik.
They tied ropes onto the spruce that was standing there.

Ch'u tl'ił ghini dnaghelt'ayi sht'a bech'annayk'et'h t'qeyeghił'ik.
They had many ropes extending out in different directions.

Ch'qiluna k'uych'ena hyighitih, ts'iłq'i tl'ił.
Five or six people held one rope.

Yethdi ggaqeydełnesh dghu tl'ił ghini łuq'u hyitih ch'u qeyenenish ch'u ggaqeydełchet.
Then they stood it [tree] up when they pulled on all the ropes and they held onto it.

Ch'q'u tl'ił ghini łuq'u hyitih.
They held onto those ropes.

Ch'q'u yethdi ts'i'un hnidi'ush hnuq'u tl'ił ghini benułtu hnitsanaltsadi yi'enhyeyish tl'ił ghin.
And then when it [tree] was sticking straight up, they tied the ropes to stakes.

Yach'en elugh yin k'a qenhyuyish hyitih ch'q'u yina kiq'u ts'iłt'an ghunen qeyuyish.
They held on [to the ropes] on the other side while one man tied up those that were still untied.

Dach' ghunen diq'u qeyuyish qugheshť'a qiłket hnuq'u yethdi yina kiq'u qenhyiłkis.
Thus he tied them to stakes very well, and it was secure when they tied it over and over.

Yuyqul k'atnili qeynułtu dghiłchik.
They made a pole ladder for the spearing tree.

"Q'uyethdi bantadusht hnuq'u yuyqul deduhna ghuna nik'uhdel'ush.
When the tide came in, they took out [in a canoe] the ones who would sit in the spearing tree.

Qeyeqadghilggesh ch'u yuyqul ghini qeyalggesh beggats'a badahdalqeyi ghini.
They climbed up the spearing tree and got into the hewed out roots of the spruce tree.

Tiqeshi ghin łuq'u qeyeduqeyedełdeł tiqeshi k'ghenidi ghini k'elises bedinghilin tl'ił benaltl'inh łu.
They passed up to them spears with bladder drags tied onto them with braided sinew ropes.

Qutsaghił'i k'deyes bighejetl'i k'eghenidi t'ghit'a łu.
It is said that the drag was an inflated sealskin.

Bedinghilin tl'ila yaghelisht'a quhnaghits'egh t'qeył'ish.
They coiled the braided rope neatly.

Ts'iłghetna ch'qilu beq'edi betetneshi łu betl'ila k'ghila łu.
The rope was said to be twenty-five fathoms long [measured by outstretched arms].

‡FIGURE 49A

At the 2013–14 Dena'ina Exhibit at the Anchorage Museum perhaps the most spectacular display was a life-size replica of the **yuyqul**, the beluga spearing platform, based on Shem's description. After the exhibition closed, the yuyqul replica was put on permanent display at Anchorage's Ted Stevens International Airport.

PHOTO BY AARON LEGGETT

"Nishhqugh nintudushi dghu quyushi łiq'a tl'uyeh ch'adeł.
At halftide, the beluga come after the salmon.

Quyushi qeye'idelqay łu.
Then they speared a beluga.

K'ghenidi tuhyiłdeł hch'abesyiłchesh.
They threw the drag into the water and it [beluga] pulled it away.

Hnuq'u ki dahdi qughena qudeł yiki q'u k'a qeydelqay.
Whenever it swam up by them, they speared it another time.

Yeqech' ghu t'qet'ih ch'u dahdik'a aqeydelqay.
They did that and they would spear it several times.

Yungget dghu baydalgi at hdalts'ina dendałteyna quyushi ghin qeyeł k'uhnedeł.
Up there on shore, strong men who sat in bidarkas went out together in their boats after the beluga.

Kiq'u qeye'idelqay yi kiq'u hk'uhnedeł.
They speared the beluga too as they went out.

Yethdi quyushi ghini qeyetl'uyeh neqash ch'u
Then they caught up with it in the chase and

k'ghenidi ghini hyiłket yethdi hch'abesqubełchesh.
they grabbed the drag and it [beluga] pulled them behind it.

Tahyełneh gheli.
They really tired it out.

Niłghenaq'u qunudleh qadelchet k'eldunahdi tl'ił hyitih qeyenenish.
Now and then it swam back up and surfaced, and some of them would hold onto the rope and pull on it.

Tahyełneh ch'q'u q'aditin eł nuhyiggat ch'u qubelaq'aydelyesh.
They tired it out, and they stabbed it with the spear and they caught it.

"Qeyats'ena qeyk'eneggesh.
They strung a rope through its jaw.

Daha tabagh hech' daghiłggech' besqeytelish.
They started to drag it to whatever beach was close by.

Niqahyiłtash.
They brought it ashore [above the tide line].

Nił'unihyilash.
They butchered it.

Nughelkidi hyighush.
They cut the blubber into blocks.

Yethdi baydalgi q'eduhyilash yethdi nuhqitdel'ush.
Then they loaded it onto bidarkas and transported it back.

Qayeht'ana niłtehyel'ih.
They divided it among the villagers.

Paul Chuitt betukda, Bidyaka'a qeyełnihen, quyushi chich'eł'ishi qeshqa ghila.
They said that Paul Chuitt's father, who they called Bidyaka'a, was the one who was the chief of beluga killing.

Yen undaden yuyqul beq'e dghiduhen ghila.
He was the last one who sat on a beluga spearing tree [in about 1880]."

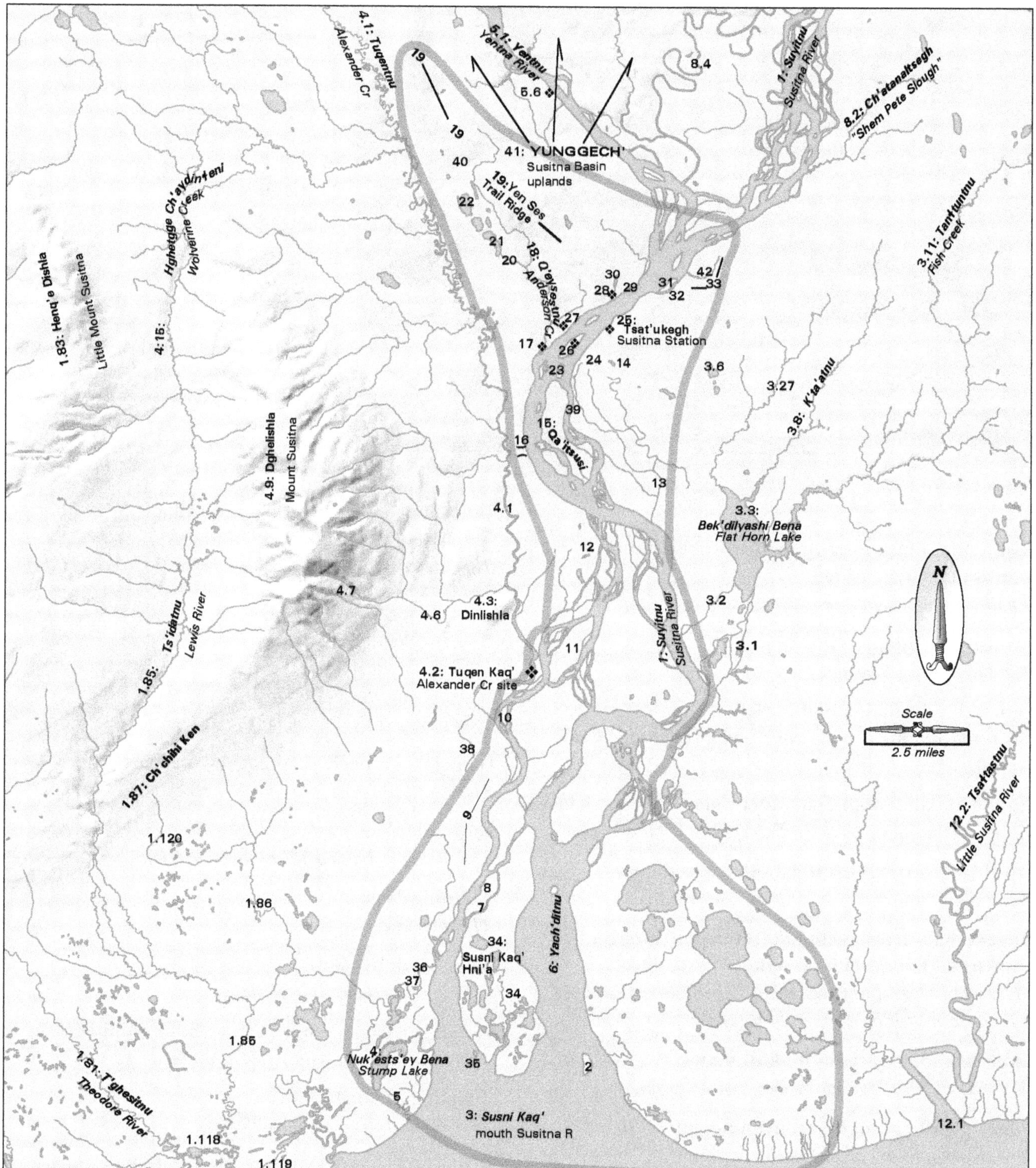

MAP 16

Place names map of the lower Susitna River, showing Nos. 2.1 to 2.44.

MAP BY MATT GANLEY

2 Lower Susitna River

From mouth to Yentna River

Shem Pete: "Those Natives used to put up lots of grub.... All summer long they put up lots of fish and lots of grease, and seal grease and all the grease they can get a hold of for winter, down **Susni Kaq'** [Susitna Delta, 2.4]. They had lots of caches [at their winter villages]. They come down there [to **Susni Kaq'**] with skin boats. They put up lots of beluga grease and blubber and during the winter lots of Tyonek people came up there, and Knik people, and Kroto people, Alexander people—everybody visit them. They have a lot of fun. They used to live good.

"The Susitna people put up all the fish they could at Susitna Station then they followed the fish to Whiskey Lake [7.10], or **Tanłtunt** (Red Shirt Lake, 3.18), or **Bentalit** (Fish Lake Creek, 5.21), any place they know there's lots of fish. They put them up until it's time to go up into the mountains. They let some people stay with the fish so nothing happen. Captain of the **nichił** (**qeshqa**) tell each person where to go—to Yenlo Hill or Rainy Pass, all over. Some stay in the mountains until November month, and then they haul everything back down in skin boat or on the ice. They take everything back to the main camp. From November month until January they visited back and forth, everybody settled down. Then they had to start hunting again for bear holes. They scatter out, up to the mountains."

Billy Pete: "Subsistence goods were always brought back to the main year-round village. These villages were the sites of the main salmon fishing, and the main food caches were kept here."

Spurr (1900:66–67): "On the Sushitna River, in the 30 miles between its mouth and the junction of the Skwentna,

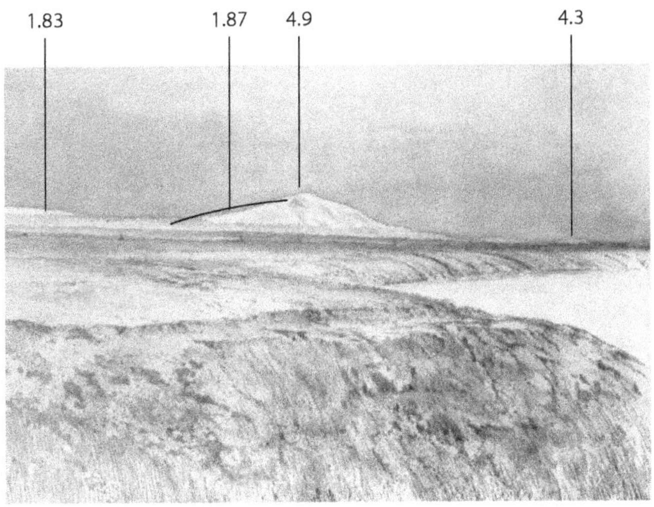

‡FIGURE 50A

Photo engraving of Beluga Flats taken in 1898, just north of **Nughil Kaq'** (1.110) the mouth of Beluga River, with **Dghelishla** (4.9), Mt. Susitna and **Ch'chihi Ken** (1.87) in the distance, as well as **Henq'e Dishla** (1.83, Little Mt. Susitna), and **Dinlishla** (4.3, Dinglishna Hill).

FROM ELDRIDGE 1900:10

Sources: Shem Pete, Billy Pete, Alexandra Allowan, Katherine Nicolie, Tommy Allowan, Sava Stephan, Nellie Chickalusion

2003 revisions: names added 2.34–42; location revised 2.19.
‡2016 revisions: names revised 2.1 and 2.26; figure moved 50A.

FIGURE 51

Aerial view looking up **Susni Kaq'**, (2.3, the west side of the mouth of the Susitna River). The lake in the center of the frame is **Nuk'ests'ey Bena** (2.4, Stump Lake). The outline of **Dinlishla**, (4.3, Dinglishna Hill) can be seen east of **Dghelishla** (4.9, Mt. Susitna). Browne (1956:101): "The name of the Susitna River will serve as an example of a descriptive name that is historical as well; Susitna means in the language of the Susitna Indians, 'the river of sand' or 'the sandy river.' No name could be chosen that better describes the natural peculiarities of this great stream, and at the same time it will perpetuate through centuries to come, not only the name of one of the Alaska tribes, but a sentence from their language as well."

Glenn (1900a: 641, 642): "The Sushitna River is filled with islands and innumerable sand bars, as is shown on the enclosed map prepared by Sergeant Yanert. In fact the word "Sushitna" means sand. The Sushitna valley and river have been used as a winter trail by the Tanana Indians for years. There is but little doubt that a trail for summer use can be found in this valley."

PHOTO BY PRISCILLA RUSSELL

there are two small villages of the Sushitna natives, one about eight miles from the delta [Alexander Creek] and the second and larger one clustered around the trading post [Susitna Station] a few miles below the mouth of the Skwentna [*sic*, i.e., Yentna River]. Those two villages number only a few hundred people."

2.1 Suyitnu, Susitnu *(Dena'ina);* **Sasutna'** *(Ahtna);* **Sosutno'** *(Upper Kuskokwim);* **Sosudeno'** *(Lower Tanana)* •
'Sand River'
Susitna River
‡In Dena'ina both pronunciations are used. In the Lower Tanana, Upper Kuskokwim, and Ahtna names the vowel **-u-** is curious, and makes those names more opaque in meaning. Sometimes the Susitna River is also referred to as **Ts'iti** 'The Major River.' The Dena'ina of the Susitna are called **Susitnuht'ana.** This term is usually applied to the people of the villages on the lower Susitna, below the Yentna River, but sometimes the term is also applied to the Kroto Creek Dena'ina (or **Dashq'eht'ana**) or the Yentna River Dena'ina (or **Yentnuht'ana**). The Ahtna pronunciation of this name, with the stem for 'river' as **tna'** (which is usually simply **na'** in Ahtna place names), implies that this name is of Dena'ina and not of Ahtna origin, and that Dena'ina occupation of the Susitna drainage preceded that of the Ahtna.

The first written mention of the Susitna River was

by Gavriil Davydov in 1802–1803. He noted that the Dena'ina would travel up the Susitna in June, and "after a twelve-day journey they catch sight of the Sushitna bending to the right amongst the mountains.... After fourteen or fifteen days' journeying they usually reach the mountains. Here the Kinai meet up with the inhabitants of the Copper River" (Davydov 1977:199).

Shem Pete said that in the 1880s, six hundred Dena'ina populated the lower Susitna River.

An early mention of king salmon fishing on the Susitna River in 1880 appears in Bean (1887:90). "Mr. Fisher" [a fishery agent based in Kenai] gives the following notes on the chowichee or king salmon [*O. tshawytscha*]:

"The run of salmon in 1880 at Kenai was very light until July 20. Prior to that date the, fish were running largely at Tyonik, about seventy miles up Cook's Inlet from Kenai, and also up the Sutchitna (Sushetno) River at the head of the inlet.... The Suchitna, (Sushetno) River Indians, who, owing to scarcity of fish heretofore in their river, always bought their winter supply of smoked and dried fish from the natives of Tyonik, caught such an abundant supply in 1880 as to enable them to sell to their former purveyors.'"

2.2 Buk'ghidaggi or **Tuy'ingga** • 'That Which Is Eroding' or 'Little Island'
Delta Island in lower east channel

2.3 Susni Kaq' • 'Sand Island Mouth'
Susitna Delta area, including Big Island and the west channel of the lower Susitna
Shem Pete: "«They say that all the ducks lay their eggs at Susni Kaq' as far up as **Qałnigi Denuch'dnel'usht** (2.8). They got lots of beluga and hooligan there. They put up lots of fish too. There were many smokehouses. There were many dry spruce with limbs [used for drying fish].»

"They didn't have **nichił**, they just dry fish there. Hundred of them. Smokehouses right along here to toward the mouth of Alexander Creek, over a four-mile area [on the west channel]."

Susni Kaq' was the site of spring trade fairs. Shem Pete summarized these events in Fall (1987:34–35): "[The upper Susitna Dena'ina] used to bring all kinds of parka squirrel coats and blankets. They used to bring lots of fur clothes and blankets to the mouth of the Susitna River...and start trading and buy lots of oil.... King salmon was good and rich down there, and they trade and buy them.... And a whole bunch of dry hooligans to take home.... From all over they came to the mouth of the Susitna River in springtime. It was a regular meeting place. The Tyonek people wanted to get fur so they came there too."

In his epic biography of Chief **Diqelas Tukda** of Alexander Creek, Shem Pete described how the chief died at **Susni Kaq'** in June of 1906, just as the beluga were running (Pete 1977).

In May of 1898 Spurr (1950:11) was stranded for nearly two weeks at the mouth of the Susitna as the ice broke up: "We moved our camp to a better location on the opposite (west) side of the river, where we found an empty Indian house and bath-house. This camp was used by the Indians who come here in the summer to fish."

Sava Stephan: "**Dgheyay** [needlefish, *Gasterosteus aculeatus*] we used to have lots at Susitna, early in the spring. Little before hooligan [oulachon, *Thaleichthys pacificus*] come up. Hooligan so thick up Susitna River, about four feet wide, we could just about walk on it. We put a canoe on top there and canoe drive right on top. **Dgheyay** catch right on the beach. My grandma made a big scoop for it, she take us down the beach and drop it in the water, lay sideways, and she take it up flat like this and she pull it ashore, that thing is full of needlefish. «The needlefish came ashore in bunches, The needlefish are running» they used to say. Hooligan used to go right up, all the way past Talkeetna. All the rivers were chuck full of hooligans and needlefish. Even around Alexander Creek we seen them floating around on the beach. They's not very big. All stuck together about five or six feet long. They all stick together and drift in, in the fall time. We open them up and we used to eat them."

At Susitna Station in 1896 William A. Dickey (1897b:82) wrote: "While building boats we witnessed the annual run of candlefish [hooligan], a species of smelt so fat when dried they will burn like a candle. The natives stand on the bank with rude dips made of willow roots and catch quantities of them, which are dried on long racks in the sun. Indeed the river was so full of the fish that it was impossible to dip a bucket into the water without catching some of the little beauties."

Learnard (1900:673–74): "So thick, indeed, are their schools [of hooligan, smelt] that with every outgoing tide one finds them cast upon the beach unable to get back into the water, rendering it an easy matter to gather up a water bucket full in five or ten minutes, selecting only those that are alive. They are so thick in fact that the squaws, when enterprising enough, can catch great quantities by dipping an ordinary basket into the water.

"During the month of May and part of June candle fish run in countless thousands up all the streams flowing into Cook Inlet. The candle fish belong to the smelt family, are about 6 to 8 inches in length, and are very oily. After each tide, when these fish are running, the Indians pick them up from the beach. These are then dried by the natives and put away with the dried salmon as part of the winter's food supply. Nearly every part of the fish is preserved, the bones, the head ostensibly for the dogs, but are generally used by the Indians, as the supply is usually insufficient."

§2.34 Susni Kaq' Hni'a • 'Sand Island Mouth Island'
Big Island in the Susitna Delta
The series of fish camps was on the west side of Big Island.

§2.35 **Tuyu'ułi** • 'That Which Is Floating'
island or bar at mouth of Susitna, in west channel, possibly Barrel Island
Sava Stephan: "That's a seagull island at mouth of Susitna. They picked seagull eggs on it."

2.4 **Nuk'ests'ey Bena** • possibly 'Spit Extends Across Lake'
Stump Lake
Shem Pete: "«**Nuk'ests'ey Bena** flows into the mouth of the Susitna. Out on the islands swans are nesting.» I think it is named for a spit of spruce trees."

2.5 **Nuk'ests'ey Betnu** • possibly 'Spit Extends Across Creek'
Stump Lake outlet

§2.36 **Bech'didatl'tnu** • 'We Come up to It-creek'
Beluga Slough
Sava Stephan notes that this was on the winter trail to Tyonek.

§2.37 **Bech'didatl' Bena** • 'We Come up to It-lake'
lake off Beluga Slough, perhaps halfway along slough, on north side

2.6 **Yach'ditnu** • 'That Side River'
east channel of lower Susitna River
This channel was not used as frequently as the west channel.

Shem Pete: "This used to be the main channel long ago."

Katherine Nicolie: "On this side of the Susitna there was no place for buildings."

Both the 1906 Herning map (Map 49) and the 1910a Sleem map (Map 62) show two structures marked "fish camp" on the east bank at the mouth of this channel.

2.7 **Qałnigi Denuch'dnel'ushtnu** • 'Creek Where Rocks Are Transported'
slough on the west side of Big Island
Eldridge noted in 1898 (1900:9) "The Sushitna River has formed a large delta, which is now cut by three or four channels of considerable size, the westernmost being used by the Indians on account of shortness, depth, and the opportunity afforded, in reaching it, of landing on the shore of the inlet in case of storm or high winds."

2.8 **Qałnigi Denuch'dnel'usht** • 'Where Rocks Are Transported'
island at the northwest end of Big Island
The name refers to the gathering of rocks used for cooking or for heating steambaths. Smokehouses extended in a line on this island and on the slough and were used extensively in spring and summer.

2.9 **Ch'bala Ch'anił'ut** • 'Where Spruce Extend Out'
ridge along Susitna south of Alexander Creek, northeast of Casper Slough
Shem Pete: "Just spruce tree come into the river there. Lots of spruce on west channel."

Sava Stephan: "**Ch'bala Ch'anił'ut**, I been through there, all over."

§2.38 **Ch'bala Ch'anił'utnu** • 'Where Spruce Extend Out-Stream'
stream west of ridge 2.9

2.10 **K'tl'ila T'el'iht** • 'Where Indian Potato Is Gathered'
island south of Alexander Creek mouth
Shem Pete: "«From here a series of hills extends on upriver.»"

An important vegetable, Indian potato (the root of *Hedysarum alpinum*, **k'tl'ila** in Dena'ina), was gathered in spring and fall here. See P. R. Kari (1991:126–27) on the Dena'ina uses of **k'tl'ila**.

Sava Stephan: "**K'tl'ila** [Indian potato] they used to eat that, I eat them at mouth of Susitina on that little island there. I dig em out a big pile like that. I brought it back to Tyonek. Boy my grandma used to like that. That's all we eat there was **k'tl'ila** and **k'dghaya, bach dghaya** [seagull eggs]. And **tsahduya** [marsh violet, *Viola epipsila*] that's all we used to have to make tea out of. We go to that island we make pile of **tsahduya**, we make tea out of that, eat seagull eggs and **k'tl'ila**. No animals, we're lucky we get moose.

"We travel around like that (in a canoe). When we see a bunch of "beans" [**qanałggi,** sea snails, species uncertain] I get some in canoe, lots. I pile that up in my lap and I eat some of that. Even in the little lakes they used to have them, little pond."

See also 4.2, Alexander Creek village site.

FIGURE 52

Henry George, Nora McCord, Tommy Allowan, Billy Pete, and Irene Ephim at Susitna Station in 1926. Henry George continued to stay at Sustina Station on into the 1950s and was one of the village's last residents.

STEPHEN R. CAPPS, JR. COLLECTION (#1209), ARCHIVES, ALASKA AND POLAR REGIONS DEPT., RASMUSON LIBRARY, UNIVERSITY OF ALASKA FAIRBANKS

The Wrangell Map of 1839

by James Kari

Rear Admiral Ferdinand von Wrangell was governor of Russian Alaska between 1830 and 1835. He stimulated exploration in Alaska's interior, and he compiled information on the native peoples and geography of Alaska. His report and map, *Russian America, Statistical and Ethnographic Information* (Wrangell 1980), which was first published in German in 1839, is the best ethnographic sketch from the Russian period of the Natives of Alaska.

The map in Wrangell's report (Map 17) was compiled from several sources, including different sketch maps made by Alaska Natives who worked the trade routes as colonial agents. Wrangell's was the most detailed map and accurate of that time of interior Alaska and the Susitna and Copper rivers. It was not until 1887, with the publication of Henry T. Allen's map of his 1885 exploration of Alaska, that a more refined map of portions of Interior Alaska was available. If we compare the best subsequent map done forty-five years later, the Petroff map of 1884 (Map 6), the Petroff map has much *less* information for the southcentral interior area than does this earlier map by Wrangell. ‡Postnikov and Falk (2015:314–322) have an excellent discussion of Wrangell's geographical research effort.

There are several significant facts that can be summarized about the western half of the Wrangell map for Cook Inlet and Copper River. Most of the information was based upon information relayed by Native men rather than by direct exploration by Russians. Most of the names in the Southcentral Interior can be matched with documented Dena'ina or Ahtna place names. Table 10 on page 89 is a numbered list of names that correspond to the numbers on Map 17.

Here are some other important points about the Wrangell map:

1) This was the foremost map of Southcentral Alaska of that time. The stream drainages, relief of portions of the Alaska Range, and trails are very detailed. Note that some village locations are indicated by dots, e.g., three dots for villages on the right-hand bank of the Susitina River seem to indicate Alexander Creek (4.2), a site opposite Susitna Station (possibly 2.28), and Kroto Creek village (8.12).

2) Inaccurate and incomplete aspects of the map suggest that the information about the Susitna and Copper rivers was supplied by Dena'ina or Ahtna traders and that the area probably had not yet been explored formally by Russians (as had the coastal features). More important, it seems that the Athabascan traders who controlled these routes conveyed only a limited amount of information about geographic features and trails. There are even hints that they conveyed *misinformation* about their country. Note, for instance, that the largest tributary of the Susitna River, the Yentna River, is left off the map. Also note that the named lakes 16 and 17, Butte Lake and Deadman Lake, are reversed (See 10.16 and 10.36.) Was this intentional misinformation?

3) I suspect that the source for most of the Dena'ina names was a Dena'ina man from the Knik Arm area. This would be the most central location for what was conveyed. The northernmost village name, "Titlokat," and an easterly name, "Nutatlgat," are each about 300 miles by trail from Knik Arm. These distances are quite remarkable. The Wrangell map is strong evidence of the extensive role that the Dena'ina had in the trade of this period.

4) Of the seventeen Athabascan-origin names in Southcentral Alaska that appear on the Wrangell map, all but two have been documented by modern speakers of these languages. This demonstrates the stability of the Athabascan place names over time. ‡One spectacular addition in 2016 from a Shem Pete text is 10.59, **Ht'u Ben,** possibly Square Lake on the upper Oshetna River.

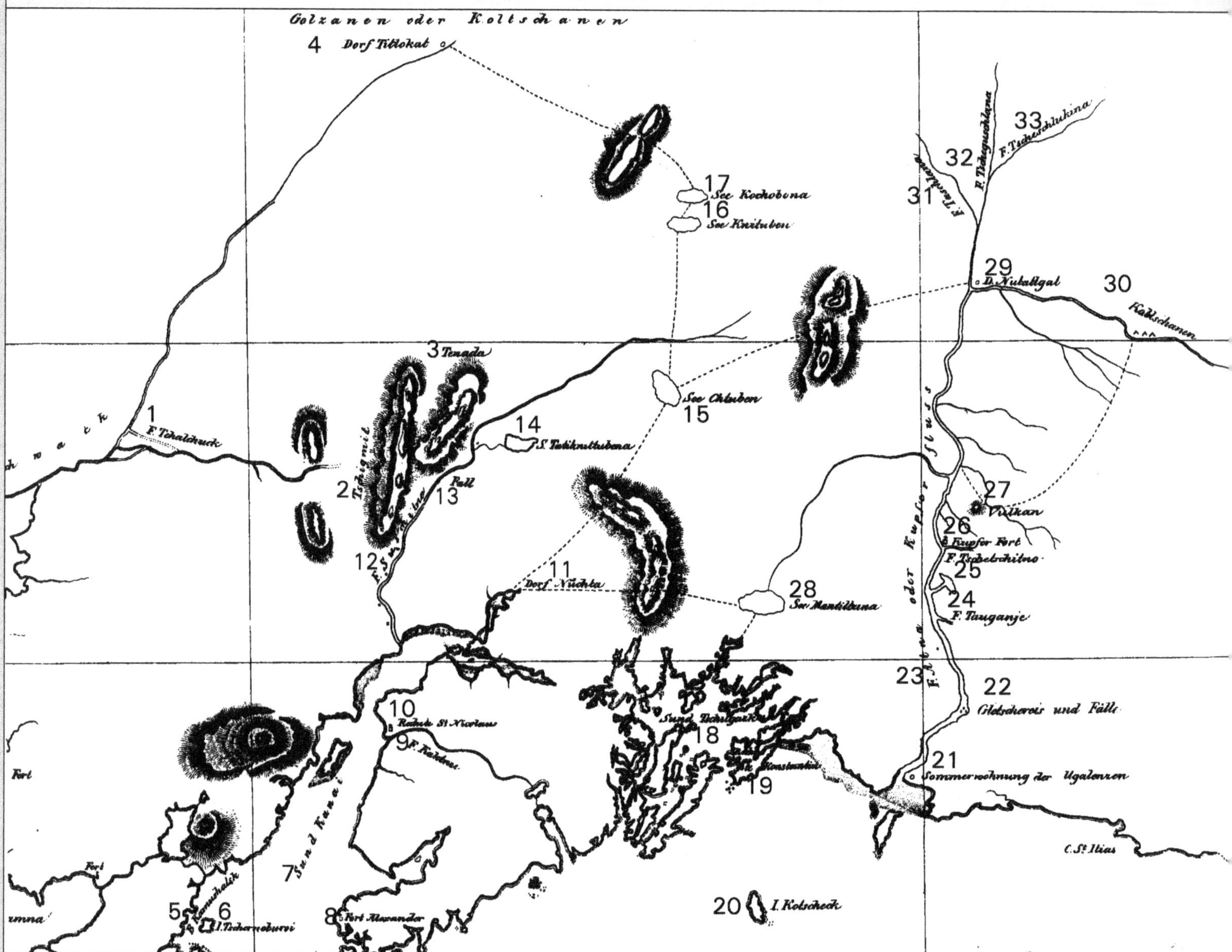

MAP 17

Wrangell map of 1839 (eastern portion).

ARCHIVES, ALASKA AND POLAR REGIONS DEPT., RASMUSON LIBRARY, UNIVERSITY OF ALASKA FAIRBANKS

TABLE 10. PLACE NAMES ON THE 1839 WRANGELL MAP (EASTERN PORTION) ‡WITH *SPA* FEATURE NUMBERS.

Key

"map name" = *source language*: **name transcribed,** 'translation of name' (feature indicated)

Westerly

1. "F. Tchalchuck" = *Central Yupik*: **Teggalgum,** 'stone (river)' (Stony River)
2. "Tschigmit" = *Central Yupik*: **Cirmit,** 'mountains' (Southern Alaska Range)
3. "Tenada" = *Deg Hit'an*: **Dengadh,** 'the high one' (7.51, Denali, Mt. McKinley) See also Kari (1986b).
4. "Dorf Titlokat" = *Dena'ina*: **Titl'u Kaq',** 'headwaters-mouth village' (10.38, Toklat village)
   "Glozanen oder Koltschanen" =*Dena'ina/Ahtna*: **Gheltsana** 'Tanana Valley Athabascans' (Same as 30 below)

Cook Inlet

5. "Kamushahk" = *Alutiiq*: **Qameksaq** '?' (Kamishak Bay)
6. "I. Tschernaburi" = *Russian*: 'black -' (Augustine Is.)
7. "Sund Kenai" = *German*: (Kenai Sound)
8. "Fort Alexander" = *English/German*: Fort Alexander (English Bay)
9. "Kahnu" = *Dena'ina*: **Kahtnu,** 'river mouth river' (Kenai River)
10. "Redut St. Niklaus" = *Russian*: Redoubt St. Nicholas (church name)
11. "Dorf Nuchta" = *Dena'ina*: **Niteh,** 'between islands village' (14.4, Matanuska site)

Susitna River

12. "F. Suschitno" *Dena'ina*: **Susitnu,** 'sand river' (2.1, Susitna River)
13. "Fall" = *German*: 'fall, waterfall,' (10.12, Devil Canyon)
14. "S. Tatikniltunbena" = *Dena'ina*: **Tatik'niłtun Bena,** 'game trail in water-lake' (11.14, Stephan Lake)
15. "See Chluben" = *Dena'ina* **[‡Ht'u Ben]** (10.59, possibly Square Lake off Oshetna River)
16. "See Knituben" Dena'ina: **Hnidi Ben,** 'upstream lake' (10.36, Butte Lake)
17. "See Kochobena" = *Dena'ina*: **Qughkugh Bena,** 'large area lake' (10.16, Deadman Lake)

Note that 16 and 17 are reversed, ‡i.e., Butte Lake is north of Deadman Lake

‡Note the trail through mountains between 16–17 Butte Lake toward 4 Toklat suggests that this is the pass trail on Wells Creek to Yanert Fork, the shortest trail to the north. This trail is described in detail by Jake Tansy of Cantwell (Kari 2010b:59–64).

Prince William Sound / Copper River

18. "Sund Tschugark" = *German:* Chugach Sound (Prince William Sound)
19. "Redut te Konstantin = *Russian:* Constantin Redoubt (Constantine Harbor on Hinchinbrook Island)
20. "I. Kothchech" = *Alutiiq:* **Qucuaq,** '-?-' (Middleton Island)
21. "Sommer Wolunung der Ugalanzen" = *German*: 'summer home of the Ugalentz (Eyak)' (Eyak site, perhaps Alaganik)
22. "Glatschiris and Falls" = *German*: 'glaciers and falls' (Miles, Childs Glaciers)
23. "F. Atna ordor Kupfer fluss" = *Ahtna/German*: '**Atna**' ‡'Beyond River' (10.64, Copper River)
24. "F. Tauganye" = *language and name not known* (possibly Bremner River)
25. "Tschetchitno" *Ahtna:* **Tsedi Na',** 'copper river' (Chitina River)
26. "Kupfer Fort" = *German:* 'copper fort,' (perhaps **Tsedi Kulaende** 'copper village')
27. "Vulkan" = *German:* 'volcano' (Wrangell Volcano, Mt. Wrangell); note the trail around the Wrangell Mountains which was well traveled by the Ahtna.
28. "See Mantilbana" = *Dena'ina/Ahtna*: **Bendiil Bene',** 'lake flows-lake' (14.120, Tazlina Lake)
29. "Nutatlgat" = *Dena'ina:* **Nutał Kaq',** 'roasted salmon mouth' (Batzulnetas, Tanada Creek site)
30. "Kolschanen" = *Upper Ahtna:* **Keltsaane** (name of Upper Tanana people)
31. "F. Taschlana" = *Ahtna:* **Tezdlen Na',** 'swift current river' (Tazlina River)
32. "F. Tschiguschlana" = *Ahtna*: name not recognized
33. "Tscheschlukina" = *Ahtna*: **Tsiis Tl'edze' Na',** 'ochre paint river' (Chistochina River)

2.11 Dehgega Inejaht • 'Where Silverberries Are Picked'
island east of Alexander Creek village, one-half mile upriver
The word **dehgega** refers to the berry *Elaeagnus commutata,* known in English as silverberry. See P. R. Kari (1991:92) on the uses of **dehgega**.

2.12 Sdigel Qak'ighałnikt • 'Where "Glass" Pitched a Tent'
upper end of slough on west side of Susitna River, flowing southwest toward Alexander
Shem Pete: "This is four or five miles below Susitna on a little spit. **Sdigel** was the first white man to go by there. He set a tent there. He picked up a tent there at that fish camp."

The man nicknamed **Sdigel**, the Russian word for 'window pane,' is said to have been an American. Shem Pete estimates that he camped here in perhaps the 1870s, when Shem's mother was a girl. Fall (1987:21) examined Alaska Commercial Company records and noted that a few American prospectors were ascending the Susitna as early as 1876.

2.13 Q'ebengga Betnu • 'Creek of Little Lake on the Flat'
swamp and small stream into the Susitna

2.14 Q'ebengga • 'Little Lake on (Flat)'
lake one mile south of Susitna Station

2.15 Qa'itsusi • possibly 'Tiring'
large island north of Bell Island Slough extending two miles south of Susitna Station
Shem Pete: "**Qa'itsusi** is a little above **Sdigel Qak'ighałnikt**. Pretty good size used to be. All go away now. Just a little island."

Billy Pete: "**Qaqitsas**, there is a long stretch and they get tired there. I think that's what it means."

This island is said to be a good place for gathering Indian potatoes in the spring and fall.

§2.39 Qa'itsusi Betnu • possibly 'Tiring Stream'
slough on east side of island north of Bell Island Slough

2.16 Tus Nuch'k'elyasht • 'Portage Where We Carry Things Across'
portage between Susitna River and Alexander Creek opposite Pierce Creek

FIGURE 53

Beq'e Nuqeydghulya Tukda, Chief Ephim, Shem Pete's step-brother, was chief of Susitna from about 1911 to 1915. Photo courtesy of Nellie Chickalusion. Shem Pete: "That Susitna chief [Evan] had a brother. He was a big man, seven feet tall. His name was Ephim, his Russian name. My brother. My father's kids, there were six. He was the last **Duyeq**. All the white men liked him. He was a tough man. His name **Beq'e Nuqeydghulya Tukda** means 'He Make Himself Clear.' That's his name, Indian. That man was over seven feet tall, Indian. They make him chief. [That's] the last time . . . they had chief at Susitna. Ephim died in 1916."

In the 1910 census for Susitna Station Ephim is listed as Big Ephim, age 45. Several Tyonek residents possess copies of this photograph. Shem Pete, Alexandra Allowan, Fedora Constantine, and Nellie Chickalusion positively identified the individual in the photo as Chief Ephim, "the last Susitna Station duyeq."

Some confusion has arisen about the identity of the man in this picture. In a recent publication on the Copper River this same photo has been identified as Chief Nicholai of Taral (Simpson 2001:13, neg. #380.98.52, Anchorage Museum of History and Fine Arts). The copy at the Anchorage Museum is part of the Mike Alex Collection and is identified as "Chief Nickoli," but does not indicate a location. Mike Alex was the village chief at Eklutna and a former chief there was named Nickoli. However, Dan Alex, Mike Alex's son and the grandson of Chief Ephim of Susitna Station (his mother's father) positively identified this photo as his grandfather Ephim, stating that the identification as "Chief Nickoli" is an error. Also, Ken Pratt's 1998 article on Chief Nicholai of Taral reproduces the only known photograph of Nicholai, taken at Taral in 1898–99, with all persons identified (from the Francis Pope collection, UAF #66-15-723). None of the early sources on Chief Nicholai of Taral describe him as lean and tall, the exact description Shem Pete provided of his brother Ephim.

This name is likely the same as the one recorded in the Wrangell notes of the 1830s as "Tuchkitnil'tash" (Arndt 1985).

Shem Pete: "This portage is about a half-mile long. Sleds and canoes were taken across here. They left most of the canoes on the Susitna side. They took one to cross Alexander. That's where they used to go up to the mountains."

2.17 Q'ey Ses Kaq' • 'Birchbark Mouth'
site at mouth of Anderson Creek
Sava Stephan: "That's my dad's fish camp, He put up dog fish one year. He put up four cache, about mile and half below Susitna Station."

Two of Sava Stephan's father's brothers drowned near **Q'ey Sestnu** when Sava was small. They capsized in a sail boat. "I was a little kid when my dad use to come down there. His brother made a fish camp there and build a house there. They make a sail boat on a canoe, and they was in there when they drowned. We came down there from Susitnu. We see them and they were behind us them two brothers. And not even two hours time they were dead, my dad's brothers. They didn't go very far, not 150 feet away from that fish camp when they drowned. One got to shore, one didn't know how to swim. He went back out for him and he [too] drowned."

2.18 Q'ey Sestnu • 'Birchbark Creek'
Anderson Creek
Anderson Creek was named after Anderson Stephan, Sava Stephan's father (see Figs. 54, 78, and 180).

It was here that Shem Pete's step-brothers, Evan and Ephim, were raised. This was a winter village until perhaps 1870 and was used as a fish camp by Susitna Station people until the 1930s.

Shem Pete summarized the life at the Anderson Creek site (cf. Fall 1981:375–378): "«The last large Dena'ina **nichił** on the Susitna was at **Q'ey Sestnu**. One hundred and twenty years ago it was here. They had a trail through here from **Tuqentnu** (Alexander Creek) to Susitna Station. The house was across the creek from the trail from **Tuqentnu.** The west side of **Q'eyses** leads to the mountains and here there were no **nichił**. On the east side **nichił** extended downstream from the lake outlet. That's the information that I heard. They say there were lots of houses there.»"

2.19 Yen Ses • 'Backbone Ridge'
Trail Ridge
This name is related to the name for Yentna River, **Yentnu.** The Dena'ina liked to maintain trails on low ridges or eskers that parallel major rivers. This ridge was a hunting area for moose and porcupine. The trail led west to **Sdak'dal'iy** (5.8) on the Yentna River.

Shem Pete: "They used to have lots of good luck hunting there."

2.20 Kala Ch'aq'a Betnu • 'Narrow Fish Tail Creek'
Yensus Lake outlet
This was a major hunting area.

2.21 Kala Ch'aq'a Bena • 'Narrow Fish Tail Lake'
Yensus Lake
Shem Pete: "Those three little lakes all got name [**Q'eyses Bena, Kala Ch'aq'a Bena, Ha Bena**]."

2.22 Q'eyses Bena • 'Birchbark Lake'
lake at the head of Anderson Creek
A regularly used trail went from Susitna Station to this lake.

§2.40 Q'ey Ses, or **Q'ey Ses Tesha** • 'Birchbark' or'Birchbark Hill'
hill or ridge northeast of 2.22
We are assuming this is a distinct hill, a spur off Trail Ridge

2.23 Dehi Beq'e De'uhi • 'The One with a Cache upon It'
island one mile south of Susitna Station
Shem Pete: "The Aleuts come up there lot of times, just for fight. There nobody expect they got a cache on the middle of that island. They put in dry fish and everything. They hide it, you know."

2.24 Q'eghtsigga • 'Little Slough'
spring quarter mile south of Susitna Station.
This spring used to be on a slough on the east bank, which washed away in the early years of this century. Sava Stephan: "**Q'eghtsigga**, that's right next to my house at Susitina."

2.25 Tsat'ukegh • 'Beneath the Big Boulder'
Susitna Station village and hill
Sava Stephan: **"Tsat'ukeght** that was right next to store, big rock. There's rock sticking out like that, all the way out, its about forty feet long sticking out into middle of the river. They had a road going up it."

Shem Pete: "«Upriver from **Tsat'ukegh** the **nichił** extended to **Qałnigi T'el'iht** (2.31). It was completely full of houses. At **Tsat'ukegh** when the fires started in the morning, the smoke was like a big cloud of fog. I did not see that. A trail went to **Ken Tiditunt** (2.33). On the upriver [east] side there was the trail on **Nqadink'et'i** (3.7) and that trail met the [Susitna] river.»"

Shem Pete's stepfather and two older brothers were the last three chiefs of Susitna Station between 1895 and 1917. See Fig. 53.

Shem Pete: "At Susitna Station, my brother was a rich man. He was a storekeeper for seven or eight years. He was a rich man. His name was **Duyeq** [Chief Evan]. That was my brother. He was a big chief [from 1900 until 1910]. He didn't go broke. He was a rich man when he died. I was a big boy already when he died."

After 1895 Susitna Station grew for about two decades as a supply route on the Iditarod Trail. Shem Pete describes Susitna Station in the era from 1910 to 1916 as a "jumping place" with the miners going through here to Cache Creek or to Iditarod. Susitna Station is also described in Fall (1981:375–378). About 150 people are listed for Susitna Station for the 1880 and 1890 censuses. Glenn (1900:724) stated that 183 Indians were there in 1899. In 1910 the village's population had grown to

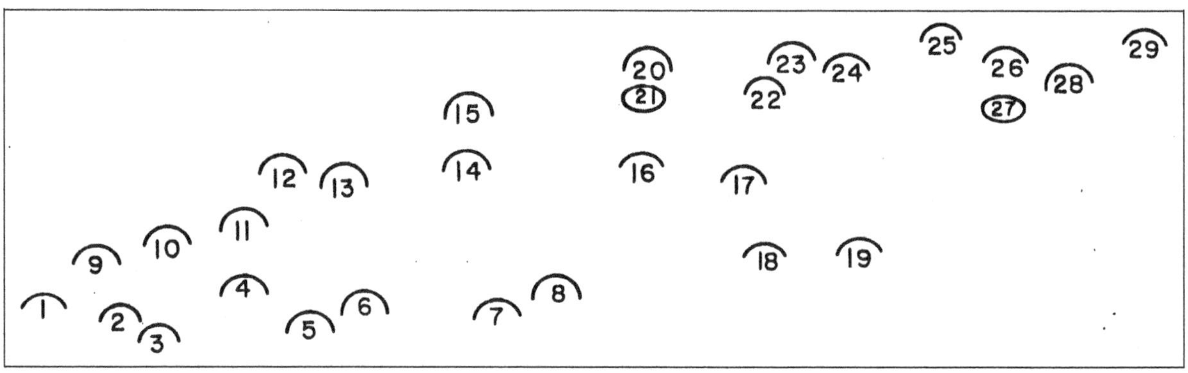

FIGURES 54 AND 55

The Dena'ina of Susitna Station and Kroto Creek circa 1931. This photo, courtesy of Nellie Chickalusion, shows almost all of the residents of Susitna Station and Kroto Creek in the 1930s.

1. Tommy Allowan
2. Sava Stephan
3. Billy Pete
4. Wilson Nicolie
5. Fedora Constantine
6. Nayna Snodgrass
7. Olga Stephan
8. Nellie Chickalusion
9. Alec Nicolie
10. Vasca Ephim
11. Joe Nicolie
12. Bobby Stephan
13. Anderson Stephan
14. Henry George
15. Yacob Stephan
16. **Chijuk**, chief of Kroto Village
17. **Nidinłna** (Christine)
18. Nora McCord
19. Mary Pete
20. Katherine Stephan
21. Richard Stephan
22. Pete Allowan
23. Alexandra Allowan
24. Katherine Nicolie
25. Annie Jacko, Billy Pete's maternal grandmother
26. Mattie Ephim
27. Mattie Ephim's daughter
28. Irene Ephim
29. **Tuts'**

Not pictured: Shem Pete, Nicolie Barbol, Robert Allowan, **Chadashla** (Anderson Stephan's father).

257 persons with 74 being Native or Dena'ina. Many Dena'ina, including Shem Pete's family, evidently were not counted in the 1910 census. The 1920 census lists only 48 persons for Susitna Station, 43 of whom seem to be Dena'ina. Shem Pete and his new wife Inge are listed in the 1920 census. (See Table 13, p. 171.)

Catherine Bayou (1946) recounted the story of the Spillum and Ladd party of nine men who went up the Susitna River in the fall of 1893 and winter of 1894. This seems to be the first documented trip by Americans up the Susitna River. The party carried a large food supply, an outfit for whipsawing lumber, and a team of fourteen sturdy malemutes. They made it to Sustina Station without any trouble, but then the river began to freeze and they had to wait for it to freeze solid enough for dog team travel. Bayou writes: "Jim Cleghourn, a fine old gentleman, was in charge of the ACC store at Susitna.... The Susitna Indian chief was in charge of the other store in the village. Chris says he was one of the wisest Indians he's ever met. He spoke little English, never read books nor magazines, and had never been away from his village; but he was onto the ways of the white man. If you couldn't understand his words, you could understand their meaning by the motions he made as he talked. Chris would often go to his store just to listen to him, and he got to know him rather well.

"Pretty soon," said the old chief, "there be not much more Indian left. No squaws, too. White man fix. Yeah, white man all over the same thing. He destroy Indian for his own good. Long time from now, oh yes, long long time, white man have big war. He not only hurt Indian, he hurt himself. All over world everybody fight. Me be dead by that time. Maybe you too." (*Cf.* Shem Pete's story on pp. 96–97.)

As the Dickey party ascended the Susitna in 1896, Dickey (1897a) stated that no white man had been upriver farther than seventy-five miles above Susitna Station, and that one-third of the boats used by miners in these attempts had been lost.

In June of 1896 priest John Bortnovsky of Kenai wrote this about his visit to the "second Susitna village,"

"The second Susitna village is smaller than Toyonok. It consists of about fifteen houses.... Contrary to the common opinion that the Susitna Indians are more savage and stern than the Indians of other villages, they are more industrious, more thrifty and foresighted than others.... The total population of the three villages on the Susitna River is 199 (102 male and 97 female). There are 38 children of school age" (Townsend 1974:19).

Bortnovsky also wrote in 1897: "During this winter I also had a desire to visit the inhabitants of the Sustina village. In 1897 more than half of them did not receive confession and communion because they were away on their hunting trips. Unfortunately I was unable to meet them. This year the Sustina natives were not able to store enough iukola [dried fish]. As a result they had to leave their homes and go hunting, which forced them to lead the life of pure nomads before the rivers and lakes broke up. However, by Christmas they descended the mountains to their village" (Znamenski 1998:15).

Browne, who stayed at Susitna Station in 1906, 1910 and 1912 prior to mountaineering in the Mount McKinley area, said "Now Susitna Station is the nearest settlement to the Alaska Range on the Susitna side. It also forms the only port of entry and departure for the men who have penetrated the great wilderness between the Susitna River and the Tanana" (Browne 1956:216).

In June of 1906 Browne wrote, "There were many Indians about, and scaffolds lined the banks weighted down with long fringes of dried hooligans. The Susitna birch-bark canoes were everywhere, flitting light as leaves through the swift water (Browne 1956:23)."

The 1918 influenza epidemic decimated the Dena'ina population. When anthropologist Cornelius Osgood visited Susitna in 1931, he described the people as "melancholy" (Osgood 1937:18). In 1934 over thirty Susitna people moved down to Tyonek at the invitation of Chief Simeon Chickalusion. Shem Pete was the oldest of the people who moved. The post office was discontinued in 1943.

One Dena'ina commercial activity stimulated by the towns of Knik and Susitna Station in the early 1900s was the manufacturing of high-quality snowshoes. Russell Annabel (1987:349) described the Dena'ina snowshoe. "He was a good snowshoe man, and he had a pair of six-foot Susitna webs made by a Tena Indian who was rated a master artisan. The webs were light—5½ pounds—and the birch frames were flawless, with perfect balance, and the babiche filling was fine and closely woven."

In 1910 Browne noted, "The camp had changed to quite a little village. The A. C. Co. had erected a large store and warehouses, but Indian cabins were still in evidence" (Browne 1956:83).

Annabel's "Mishka's Beads" (Field and Stream, October 1939b) is a charming story, probably fictionalized, of the Susitna Station community awaiting the arrival of the first salmon in May in the 1920s.

In 1926 William Beach (1931:116, 153) noted while at Sustina Station, "There are several imposing buildings, a good-sized school and church. Both are now closed as the government has closed the school, and I imagine there is not sufficient population to keep the church going." Beach shot movie film at Sustina. "I ground out some movie film of the Indians, all of whom were more than anxious to be pictured." Beach's film has not been located.

The last storekeeper and postmaster at Susitna Station was Rowland R. Healy (Ernest A. Ross of Everett Washington, letter to Kari in 1989). Ross lived at Susitna Station from 1927 to 1935 and knew Shem Pete as well as his children Billy and Mary Pete. Shem often mentioned Mr. Healy. Ross recalled that Healy was "the benefactor and best friend of all the Susitna Natives."

A few Dena'ina remained at Susitna Station and died

FIGURE 56

Looking southwest from Susitna Station in 1926. The rock point **Tsat'ukegh** (2.25) is at the left. On the opposite bank of the river is location **Bes Delggeyat** (2.27). The profile of **Dghelishla**, (4.9, Mount Susitna) is in the background.

STEPHEN R. CAPPS, JR. COLLECTION (#83-149-2483), ARCHIVES, ALASKA AND POLAR REGIONS DEPT., RASMUSON LIBRARY, UNIVERSITY OF ALASKA FAIRBANKS

there in the 1960s. One of the most poignant stories Shem Pete has told about Susitna Station is that of the funeral for Nikolai Barbol, the last man to be buried here. Barbol, who stayed on after the others moved down to Tyonek in 1934, died in the winter of 1965. Shem Pete flew there from Tyonek with five other Susitna people.

Shem Pete: "And the last man died at Susitna was Nikolai Barbol. He died. So that was the last one. I was up there at his funeral. I get into Anchorage. I heard he, the last man, died. So I jump in an airplane. Went to Susitna Station. Tommy Allowan, Sava Stephan, and Tommy's mother [Alexandra Allowan], Chickalusion's wife, and Paul Chuitt's daughter [Polly], and me, six we was, got to visit Nikolai. The last man died."

Barbol's body was still in his cabin. They froze the body and then buried it at the "new graveyard" out by Jimmy Ephim's old house. Shem Pete conducted the funeral. Barbol was four years younger than Shem.

2.26 Yusdishlaq', Yusdishla *(Dena'ina)*, **‡Esdesladi** *(Upper Kuskokwim)* • 'On the Little Point'
island and village site midriver opposite Susitna Station (now washed away)

This was an old village site as well as the location of the first Alaska Commercial Company store and modern cabins of the 1890s. Shem said that the first Orthodox church on the Susitna River was built here on this island. He estimates that this was in the 1860s or 1870s. There were no other Orthodox churches anywhere else in the Susitna drainage.

Shem Pete: "«**Yusdishlaq'** was too small for all the people there.»"

Shem Pete commented in the **Inda'i** story: "At Susitna Station there was a little island across there about a mile or two long. There was so many houses on that island there was no room on it. So they moved over to the east side. They started moving across there, one by one."

The buildings on **Yusdishlaq'** were destroyed by a flood on September 6–8, 1898. ‡Aaron Leggett found an 1899 article by A. Beverly Smith who described and photographed Susitna Station in the summer of 1898.

Learnard (1900:654) described this place in 1898, just before the flood. "The party reached the Alaska Commercial Company's store.... The store stands on an island in the middle of the river, which at this point is about three-quarters of a mile wide and 90 feet deep in places. Several Indian cabins stand near the store, with others on both sides of the stream a short distance above the store."

Shem Pete: "«When the ice jam broke up at **Untuhtay'unt** [8.33, a tributary of Kroto Creek], the water got really deep. The water even went up **Tsat'ukegh** (2.25, hill). **Yusdishlaq'** was swamped by ice when the ice went out.» Biggest ice breakup in history. Everything washed away. Must have been 90 years ago. My mother was about 15 or 20 years old. She run to the bank and seen that ice coming down. She start hollering, and everybody woke up and saved their life. **Yusdishlaq'** was washed away. House and everything. There used to be big village there. Three stores. Three different company. I born on that

‡FIGURE 56A

Photo taken during the flood at Susitna Station on Sept. 6, 1898, probably by A. Beverly Smith.

B2014.013.002, TRON ANDERSEN COLLECTION, ANCHORAGE MUSEUM

island. After that people moved to **Tsat'ukeght**. More higher place. **Yusdishlaq'** no high no place."

2.27 Bes Delggeyat • 'At the White Bank'
riverbank across from Susitna Station
Shem Pete: "That's a graveyard right across from **Tsat'ukegh.**"

Shem Pete said that he found a coffin washing away there when he was six or seven years old.

2.28 Tani'i • 'Point That Extends into the Water'
point and site opposite and north of Susitna Station
This seems to be the second village on the right bank of the Susitna River marked by a dot on the 1839 Wrangell map (Map 17).

Shem Pete: "«There used to be four or five **nichił** on **Tani'i**. My father's brother, who was a medicine man, stayed there.»" The medicine man who told the Susitna prophecy story (Pete 1975) lived at **Tani'i** in the 1880s.

"Right across Susitna Station they got a big trail towards Alexander Creek."

Alexandra Allowan told the following story about the two points on opposite sides of the Susitna, **Tsat'ukegh** and **Tani'i** (2.28). "«These rocks, **Tsat'ukegh** and **Tani'i** used to move back and forth alongside one another. They killed people if they fell in near them. **Yubugh Tayqan** ['The One Who Paddled Around the World'] kicked one of them upriver. Then he turned around and kicked the other one downriver. Then they came to be on opposite sides of the river. They are rocks on the water. They used to kill people. He kicked them apart.»"

2.29 Ha Betnu, Hatnu • 'Grease Creek'
Leech Lake outlet stream
Shem Pete: "«There were **nichił** on **Ha Betnu.**»"

2.30 Ha Bena • **'Grease Lake'**
Leech Lake
Billy Pete: "They cached a lot of grease there so the Aleuts wouldn't take it away (when they raided Dena'ina villages). Grease was very important. Everything they eat, they eat with grease."

2.31 Qałnigi T'el'iht • 'Where Rocks Are Gathered'
island on east bank above Susitna Station
Shem Pete: "«Cabins extended one after the other, all the way from **Qałnigi T'el'iht** to **Tsat'ukeght**.... Up at **Qałnigi T'el'iht** there was a big village on the trail near **Ken Tiditunt** (2.33).»"

2.32 Qałnigi T'el'ihtnu • 'Rocks Are Gathered-Creek'
slough on east bank above Susitna Station

§2.41 Yunggech' • 'Toward the Uplands'
general Susitna Basin upland area towards the Alaska Range
A regional place name, contributed by Sava Stephan.

2.33 Ken Tiditunt • 'Where Trail Comes to the Flat'
swamp northeast of Susitna Station
Shem Pete: "«This trail led from **Qałnigi T'el'iht** east to Red Shirt Lake.»"

§2.42 Ken Tidituntnu • 'Trail Comes to the Flat-Stream'
creek through swamp northeast of Susitna Station

Early Historic Dena'ina Log and Pole Buildings

by D. C. Beard

Dena'ina log and pole building techniques are very interesting and are not well documented. *Shelters, Shacks, and Shanties* by D. C. Beard (1914) is the classic book on early American log and pole buildings that has been used by generations of Boy Scouts for building a wide variety of camp shelters and cabins. Two chapters in Beard 1914 describe caches and a cabins from the Susitna River. Beard knew some of the early American outdoorsmen who went up the Sustina River such as Belmore Browne and Herschel Parker, who attempted to climb Denali in 1906 and 1912. However, his descriptions are so detailed that he may have spent some time around Susitina Station. Beard's references to Susitna caches and cabins hearken back to a time when the Dena'ina and the first American outdoorsman were sharing woodlore and building techniques. Some fine woodcraft was being practiced on the Susitna River in the early twentieth century. Beard (1914:78–80):

> The "Belmore Browne" cache consists of a pole or a half log placed in the fork of the two trees on top of which goods are held in place by a rope and the whole covered with a piece of canvas lashed together with eyelets, like a shoe (Fig. 103).
>
> The "Herschel Parker" cache is used where the articles to be cached are in a box. For this cache two poles are lashed to two trees, one on each side of the trees (Fig. 104), and across the two poles the box is placed.
>
> We now come to more pretentious caches, the first of which is the "Susitna," which is a little log cabin built on a table with four long legs. The poles or logs composing the legs of the table are cut in a peculiar fashion, as shown in the diagram to the left of Fig. 107; this is intended to prevent animals from climbing to the top; also, as a further protection, pieces of tin are sometimes tacked around the poles so as to give no foothold to the claws of the little animals.
>
> Fig. 106 shows two other methods sometimes adopted to protect small caches and Fig. 108 is still another method of using logs which have the roots still attached to them for supports. Such logs can be used where the ground is too stony to dig holes for posts.
>
> Fig. 109 shows another form of the Susitna cache wherein the goods are packed in a box-like structure and covered with tent-cloth tightly lashed down.

Beard (1914:191–194) is a chapter entitled "How to Build a Susitna Log Cabin and How to Cut Trees for the End Plates." What Beard calls "The Susitna Log Cabin" has a roof with curved end plate rafters made from a spruce tree with a curved root. This is an adaptation in the use

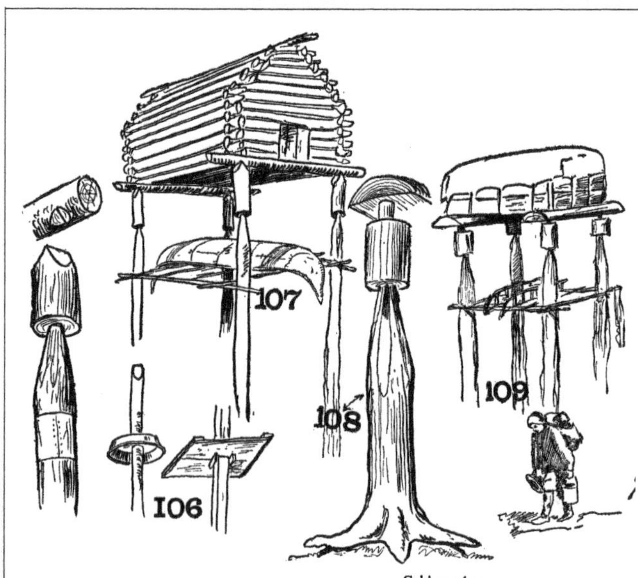

Cabin caches.

FIGURES 57 AND 58

Drawings by D. C. Beard, used with permission of Charles Scribner's Sons.

The Susitna log house.

FIGURE 59 Drawing by D. C. Beard, used with permission of Charles Scribner's Sons.

of what the Dena'ina call **k'ghehda**, **k'egheda**, a curved branch or tree trunk. **K'ghehda** from spruce or birch had several uses—as upright props for structures, as curved boat ribs, and as rafter logs. Beard's Figs. 266 and 267 show how the Susitna Dena'ina constructed a cabin roof with the **k'eghehda** as a rafter.

> Still farther north the Susitna house explains the origin of the overhanging eaves. Of course the Susitna, as here drawn, is not exactly the same as that built by the natives on the Susitna River, but the end plates (Fig. 263) are the same as those used in the primitive houses of the Northwest.
>
> Fig. 264 shows a standing fir-tree and also shows what cuts to make in order to get the right-shaped log for an end plate. Fig. 265 shows the method of scoring and hewing necessary in order to flatten the end of the log as it is in Fig. 266. Fig. 267 shows the style in which the natives roof their Susitnas with logs. The elbows at the end of the plates (Fig. 266) serve to keep the logs of the roof (Fig. 267) from rolling off, but the Susitna log cabin which we are building is expected to have a roof (Fig. 268) of thatch or a roof of shingles, because we have passed the rude shacks, sheds, and shelters used for camps and are now building real houses in which we may live. The Susitna may be built of round logs or of flattened logs (le carréage), in which case we can use the General Putnam square notch (Fig. 263) for joining the ends of our logs. In raising the roof, erect the ridge-pole first.... If the logs are round you must notch the rafters and side-plates as shown by the diagram between Figs. 263 and 267; the dotted lines show where the rafter and the logs come together. Nail your rafters to your ridge-pole and fasten them to the side-plate with wooden pegs or spikes.... If the roof is to be shingled, collect a lot of poles about four inches in diameter, flatten them on both sides, and nail them to the rafters not more than two inches apart, allowing the ends of the sticks to extend beyond the walls of the house at least six inches....
>
> The Susitna form of house is the one from which the old Long Island farmhouses were evolved although the old Long Islanders copied theirs from the homes they left in Holland, but we must remember that even the effete civilization of Europe once had a backwoods country a long, long time ago, and then they built their houses from the timbers hewn in the forests as our own ancestors did in this country; consequently, many of the characteristics of present-day houses which seem to us useless and unnecessary are survivals of the necessary characteristics of houses made of crude material.

Susitnu Htsukdu'a: The Susitna Story

by Shem Pete

This is the story about the Susitna people that Shem Pete told most often. Each time he would tell this prophecy, which was made in the 1880s, Shem emphasized different details and issues. The first published version of this story was in Pete (1975). The version here was told in English in the fall of 1978 at the Anchorage Museum of History and Art as part of the Captain Cook Commemorative Lecture Series. This is reprinted from Exploration in Alaska, Captain Cook Commemorative Lectures *(Shalkop 1980:196–197). Some slight revisions and notes have been added here. Pete (1975) has been reprinted in the original bilingual version in Cole et al. (1985:24–26).*

"I came from Susitna Station. That's where I born, and my father was a chief. He had a brother.[1] He was a big medicine man in Susitna. Used to be living there. There was a medicine man in Susitna. There were a lot of people all over there. And he told them Susitna Station people, 'And pretty soon all you people gonna die and not even one going to be alive around here.' I never seen him.[2] 'You people all gonna die,' he said. They pretty near clubbed him.

"They told him, 'We was over six hundred people here.' A lot of people. A lot of village. Out at Alexander Creek, and Susitna Station on the island there. I don't know how many hundreds. And on the west side of the Susitna another big village, about a mile long, just lined up the cabins. A lot of Indians still alive yet.

"He said, 'The way I look at it is I'm a medicine man—don't forget my word. Remember my word. Someday it may help you. I'm going to be gone too. And pretty soon measles maybe gonna be come. And this your skin gonna be stretched all over your body, see.' He don't know that was the measles. 'Your body gonna be crippled all over,' he said. 'Some of them gonna make them blind. Quite a few gonna die of that sickness, and after that pretty soon you people gonna hear about a fight down in the States some place [World War I]. And that sickness come from down south. And that gonna kill lots of people. You people used to walk around on the trail are just gonna lay down, and you people don't know to die. You people gonna die though.' So now when the flu coming [1918] I see thirty-five people one week we lose. That was just the beginning.

"And he told them, those people, 'Don't eat too much white man grub. Use your own grub. Put up lots of fish. Put up meat. Pretty soon, I don't know, after the flu, I see the airplane *grgrgrgrgr*, and I see the train, *whoowhoowhooooo, whoowhoowhooooo.* I hear that too. On the ground, the bare ground got a wheel. Just like a boat go, go fast. Then there—after a little while, *whoowhoo-whooooo-whoowhooooo.*' He copy that. He hear that [train whistle].

FIGURE 60
Cover of the first edition of **Susitnu Htsukdu'a**, published in 1975 by the Alaska Native Language Center, University of Alaska Fairbanks.

1. Shem Pete notes that this man's name was **Ts'inst'a Gga Tukda'**, 'Father of the Little Old Lady.'

2. Shem is establishing that the reason he can tell this story is that he was not exposed to this ominous curse.

"'So that Susitna Station gonna be nothing left like it is today. You'll be all gone, not even one.' I didn't see him. They would say, 'No no no no!' There was over six-hundred people here. There were kids born, about fifteen, twenty kids born. 'How many we lose a year you think?' He said, 'Two, three.' Average is about three person die every year. 'Yahyah, about fifteen, twenty kids. We just increasing right along. We can't die it all.' He told us, 'I see nothing left from that sickness come. You people just like burn the grass down. Gonna be killing all, everybody. Now remember, who got little money gonna buy some matches, buy ammunition. Buy axe, buy file. Pretty soon gonna be something happen. Listen careful,' he said.

"'There gonna be white man gonna be just like this sand,' he pick it up in his hand, the sand. 'You fellows gonna be not living one place. Few here, few there, all over just scattered along like little berries between them white people. You all the Native not gonna be staying one place. Be here, there, all over Alaska. So I think, What the white man gonna eat out of? They can't live on the berries. They don't know how to hunt. It's gonna be tough for the white man. Listen to me. And all the white men they gonna see something happen. *Grgrgrgrgrgr* airplane gonna be just like mosquitoes. So they all gonna get into the airplane. Then they gonna pick it up and take them all back to the States.'

"'And listen, put up lots of fish. And put the matches away. Put the ammunition away. Put up a file and an axe. Pretty soon no more white man in this Alaska. I never seen one. You people, how many gonna be left here? Go up to Rainy Pass country.' He told them, 'Don't stay too long. Soon as the white man gone, you just take off and take a little fish. When you get there, lots of caribou, lots of game, lots of sheep. And you people so far you can go. And after I go away, you people gonna live quite a long time. So listen to me, now you gonna see that Susitna gonna be not even one left,' he told them.

"Well, that's true. What now, not even one Indian of all the young people in the Susitna. There's nothing. There's nobody left. So just few ones that were left, in 1930s Chief Chickalusion of Tyonek pick us up, about dozen of us altogether. He put them in the dories and take 'em down to Tyonek. Now the young Susitna people increasing. Maybe more than two hundred people now. Lots of Susitna Indians down in Tyonek. Tyonek Indians only about five or six left. The Susitna Indians take it over now. Lots of Susitna people down in Tyonek.

"Now I got not much to tell you. Who could believe that story? That pretty soon white man be no more. All gonna go back down to the States. Nobody, not even one, gonna believe me right now in this house. But I believe it though. That's why I just telling the young generation, the young Native, around here they could hear me, they could listen to me. I don't like this story gonna be gone. I don't want nobody to forget that story. My father's brother, the medicine man, what he told, that came true, everything. He don't know the plane, and he holler like a train, '*Whoowhoowhooooo-whoowhoo.*' And he holler like a airplane, '*Grrgrgrgrgr.* They go up in the air. They just like mosquitoes. They gonna fly anywhere in this doggone Alaska. Pretty soon they gonna quit. No more grub. What they gonna eat? They can't. They all gonna go back down the States. And you people can't get no more grub. I see that. Listen to me!' he said.

"So I like to put up that story. That happened quite a while ago. Who gonna believe me? But I believe it though. Well that's all I'm gonna tell you now. Ladies, gentlemen, I thank you."

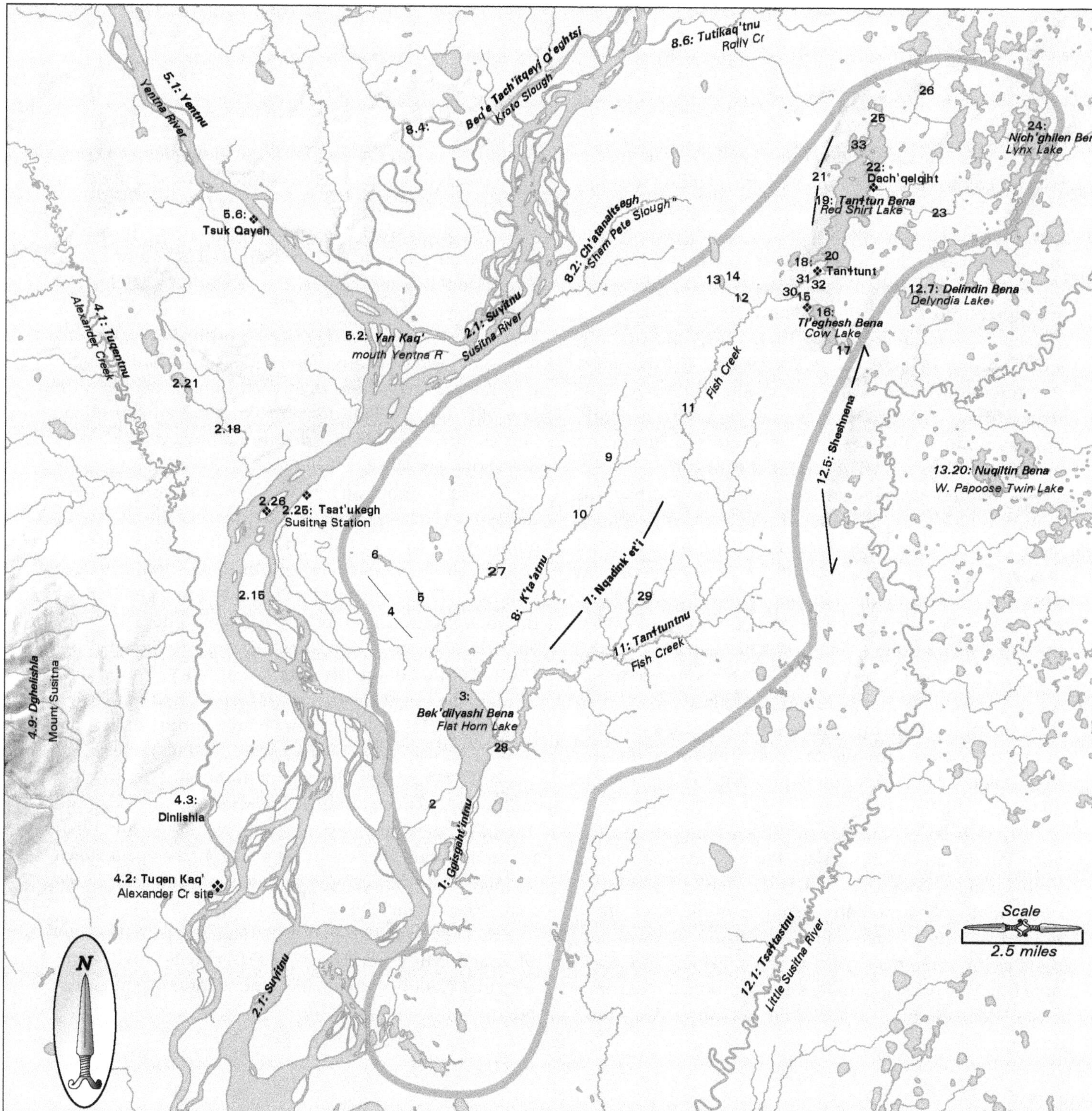

MAP 18

Place names map of Fish Creek, showing Nos. 3.1 to 3.33.

MAP BY MATT GANLEY

3 Fish Creek

3.1 Ggisgaht'intnu • 'Iron Pyrite Creek'
lower Fish Creek, southernmost outlet of Flat Horn Lake, locally "Cheechako Gold Creek"
The Dena'ina term for pyrite literally means 'it looks like fish scales.'
Shem Pete: "«It flows into the Susitna about two miles up. They used that for hunting beaver.»"

3.2 Bek'dilyashi Betnu • 'Creek of Things Are Carried to It'
outlet of Flat Horn Lake, north of lower Fish Creek

3.3 Bek'dilyashi Bena • 'Lake of Things Are Carried to It'
Flat Horn Lake
This was an important site for salmon fishing.
Shem Pete: "«Below Susitna at **Bek'dilyashi Bena** there were many **nichił**. They pack canoe or skin boat into that lake [from the Susitna River].» That's what the name means. They had a regular summer trail there. Just grab the canoe and take off for there."
Billy Pete: "Lots of fish in there and lots big Indian house used to be around there. That's about two hundred years ago. There were no **nichił** there when I was a boy. July and August they get lots of fish, but they always had trap out for **bat** [lake trout, *Salvelinus namaycush*]. Also lots of ducks and geese and beaver. Last one to have a house there was Victor Antone's father, maybe fifty years ago. That was their second main camp."

3.4 Shq'ach'egh Kena • 'Shortcut Flat'
large flat between Flat Horn Lake and Susitna Station

3.5 Gega Bena Betnu • 'Berry Lake Creek'
stream into north end of Flat Horn Lake

3.6 Gega Bena • 'Berry Lake'
lake two miles east of Susitna Station
The timbered area on the east side of **Gega Bena** to **K'ta'atnu** was a popular moose hunting area.

§3.27 Bek'dilyashi Dinłent • 'Where It Flows into Things Are Carried to It'
stream into Flat Horn Lake from northeast

3.7 Nqadink'et'i • 'Foot Path Extends'
low ridge from Flat Horn Lake to Cow Lake and to Susitna Station
Shem Pete: "«About four miles from Susitna [Station] is a ridge. Its name is **Nqadink'et'i**. We had a portage there.»"
Billy Pete: "It's a little hill about three or four feet high and about a hundred yards wide all the way across that flat to **K'ta'atnu.**"

3.8 K'ta'atnu • 'Soup Creek'
creek into northeast end of Flat Horn Lake
Shem Pete: "There was no fish in that creek. They never use it except as hunting ground."

3.9 K'ta'atnu Tl'u • 'Soup Creek Headwaters'
upper 'Soup Creek'
Billy Pete: "They used to go up to Shem Pete Creek [8.2 on Susitna River]. They go across that little flat, and they get to Red Shirt Lake, **Tanłtunt**. They had a regular trail over there. The trail it show yet. The trail is west of the lakes on higher ground. It curves around small lakes west of lower Red Shirt Lake. «The summer trail is deep.»" The trail crosses **K'ta'atnu Tl'u.**

3.10 Nuk'dalyut • 'Where a Bridge Extends Across'
bridge across upper 'Soup Creek'
Shem Pete: "They had their own bridge. Spruce trees, a bunch of them they throw in. They make bridge to go across **K'ta'atnu.**"
This is the southern trail between Susitna Station and Red Shirt Lake. Shem mentions that they used to slide canoes across here in spring before breakup. Also discussed in Fall and Greiser (1986):C2.

§3.28 Tanłtun Kaq' • 'Mouth of Enclosed Object [bag] Is Set in Water'
mouth of Fish Creek, on Flat Horn Lake

Sources: Shem Pete, Billy Pete, Sava Stephan

2003 revisions: names added 3.27–33.
‡2016 revisions: figure added 67A.

FIGURE 61

An important lake district for the Sustina Dena'ina is shown here in this aerial photo taken just east of **Tanłtun Bena** (3.19, Red Shirt Lake) and the site of **Tanłtunt** (3.18). In the foreground is **Nich'ghilen Bena**, (3.24, Lynx Lake). **Unqeghnit Skitnu Bena,** (12.24 Butterfly Lake, so-shaped) is in the upper left. To its west is **Delindin Bena** (12.7, Dylindia Lake, named for Shem Pete by his Russian name). The southernmost end of **Tanłtun Bena** (3.19) is at the right edge of the picture in a line straight below **Dghelishla** (9.1, Mt. Susitna). The thin outline of a lake to its left is **Tl'eghesh Bena,** (3.16, Cow Lake), which has many ancient Dena'ina house sites.

PHOTO BY FRED HIRSCHMANN AK-6838

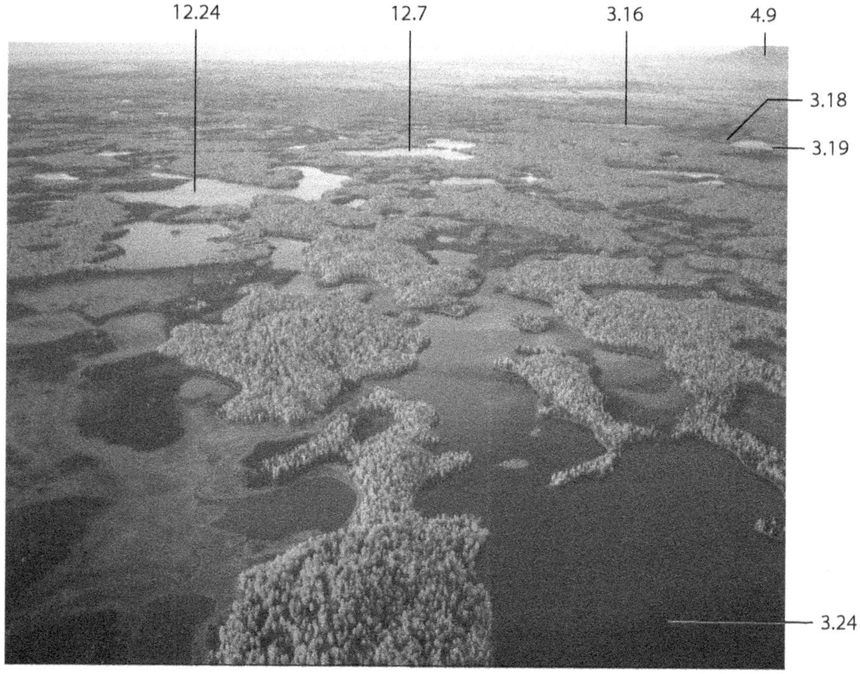

3.11 Tanłtun Betnu, Tanłtuntnu • 'Creek of Enclosed Object [bag] Is Set in Water'
middle Fish Creek, from Flat Horn Lake to Red Shirt Lake
Shem Pete: "Lots of salmon in that creek, the one that come up to Red Shirt Lake. There used to be **nichił** all along it."

§3.29 Nqadink'et'i Betnu • 'Foot Path Extends'
stream into lower Fish Creek
The name is derived from **Nqadink'et'i** (3.7)

3.12 K'enuq' Q'estsiq' • 'Mineral Lick Outlet'
creek (or former creek) into Fish Creek from 'Mineral Lick Lake' or Out Lake (3.13)

3.13 K'enuq' Bena • 'Mineral Lick Lake'
two lakes three miles west of Red Shirt Lake outlet, now known as Out Lake

3.14 K'enuq' Qiy'unt • 'Where There Is a Mineral Lick'
campsite by Out Lake
The name indicates that this place was a hunting site. Moose and caribou tend to gather at such mineral licks.

Fall and Greiser (1986): Billy Pete: "They always used to come up here to kill moose. Over this way they had a regular moose hunting ground. There's a bunch of little lakes going this way [west]. Right on this ridge here there's a bunch of little lakes. And they used to hunt moose over there. Moose just stayed in that area."

§3.30 Tl'eghes Bena Q'estsiq' Hq'adghiłent • 'Where Leech Lake Outlet Current Flows Down'
site where Cow Lake outlet stream meets Fish Creek

3.15 Tl'eghes Bena Q'estsiq' • 'Leech Lake Outlet'
Cow Lake outlet stream
Shem Pete: "«There were **nichił** from **Tanłtun** [Red Shirt Lake] to **Tl'eghes Bena** [3.16], and they also extended to **Tudli Bena** [Nancy Lake, 12.12]. I saw the house pits. They are overgrown with grass. The grass is four or five feet tall.» We seen 'em."

The houses were on the east side of this stream about a mile and a half below the lake.

3.16 Tl'eghes Bena • 'Leech Lake'
Cow Lake
Shem Pete: "«There were also **nichił** here north and south of the lake outlet.»"

3.17 Tl'eghesh Bena Bidiłtuni • 'That Which Is Connected to Leech Lake'
small lake southeast of Cow Lake
A trail starts at the upper end of this lake and leads north to the Little Susitna River.

3.18 Tanłtunt • 'Where Enclosed Object [bag] Is Set in Water'
Red Shirt Lake outlet village site
Shem Pete: "«The trail went from Susitna Station to **Tanłtunt** [about twelve miles]. Another trail came from Knik and Big Lake.»"

Fall (1981:382): "The village stretched from the outlet of Red Shirt Lake for one-half mile downstream along both banks."

According to Shem Pete, the last **nichił** in the Upper Inlet area was used here, probably until about 1900.

Shem Pete stayed here before 1900. He said his

mother carried him here while he was an infant. There used to be three different Dena'ina villages on Red Shirt Lake—one at this site, one at Lynx Creek mouth, and one at the head of the lake. Shem's mother worked all summer here cutting and drying salmon that were caught in the fish trap.

Shem and Billy Pete continued to fish and trap lynx, marten, beaver, and otter in this area after 1918. This area, now part of the Nancy Lake Recreation Area, was Billy Pete's primary trapping location in the early 1940s. He camped at the former village site and checked his traps on cross-country skiis. See also Fall (1981:382–384) and Reger (1983 [1978]).

During a visit to Red Shirt Lake in 1986, Shem and Billy provided further commentary on Dena'ina uses of the area (Fall and Greiser (1986)):

Shem: "There used to be at **Tanłtunt,** before white man, before Russians come, there was a big village there. **Nichił**. Big house for all the people living around here. And sweathouse. There's a partition all the way around they say. People living there, lotta people."

Billy: "There was probably a dozen of them, dozen of those [**nichił**].... And on that side of that side of Red Shirt Lake, all along there, I don't know how many **nichił** they had at once.... All the way to where that creek [**Nich'ghilentnu**; 3.23] comes out right in middle of the lake."

Shem: "All the way they used to pack with dogs to there, on **Shesh Nena** [12.5]. All the way." This is a reference to the "Hunting Dog Story," which explains how when food supplies ran low in the late winter, hunters packed starving dogs on their backs, who detected bear dens from which the hunters took the animals (see Pete 1989).

Billy: "They just stayed the year round because it was easy to get by up there. All they did was wait for fish, and they'd go out—moose, not moose—but moose just came up 200 years ago or so...."

Billy: "[Shem] was only two [years old] when he came here. This house there was standing up yet. I seen that house [in the 1930s]."

Shem: "It was a log cabin. They like to have a fire in the middle. They get by easy with that thing. Big **nichił** all over. Used to be all the time, whole lot of fish."

Billy: "This is a pretty good creek. Just put it [trap or net] across the creek here. Right down here I used to catch lots of fish over there."

§3.31 Hchił Nughik'at' • 'Weir Fence Is Stretched Down'
weir site at ***Tanłtunt***
The following exchange between Billy and Shem was recorded by Fall and Greiser (1986) during a visit to Redshirt Lake:

Billy: "Susitna Station, Yentna people, and Kroto people used that Red Shirt Lake to get fish, just about. Way up until late in December month those steelheads used to come up there. And all fall, from around."

Shem: "They get all winter fish there."

Billy: "Around August month until way late in December they used to put up fish. Red salmon and silver salmon used to come up there and they put those up. And then those steelheads start running way late in fall. They're bigger than red salmon, uh, silver salmon. Natives call it silver salmon. But I took a look at it, I know they're steelheads."

Shem: "In one spot they put the bridge across, the natives, they had no net they put in **tay'in** [fishtrap] and a scoop [dip net] big long, full of fish. That big around."

Billy: "They [fishtraps] were about four feet high, I guess, four feet long, four feet diameter eight to ten feet long. And they used to get it all full of fish and they roll it up the hill over here, side of the hill, and over there. The chiefs say, "You take that many fish, and you take that many fish." And maybe all that fish, well, each guy get about a hundred fish or so. And they cut that fish up and put it up. They used to have big smokehouses all over these places here. Not only one you know, maybe a dozen big smokehouse. They fill it right up with fish. And the rest they bury them all over around here, across."

FIGURE 62

Billy Pete and Shem Pete visiting a house site at **Tanłtunt** (3.18), the Red Shirt Lake village site (3.18) in 1978.
PHOTO BY PRISCILLA RUSSELL

§3.32 Łiq'a Hq'atnełt • 'Where Salmon Are Poured'
fish holding pit on bank at ***Tanłtunt***
Shem: "Lot of holes [fish caches] all over."

3.19 Tanłtun Bena • 'Enclosed Object [bag] Is Set in Water'
Red Shirt Lake
Shem Pete: "«That's the best lake in Alaska. It has the biggest fish. Fish are still running when the snow falls.»"

Fall (1981:383): "On Red Shirt Lake itself **nichił** were constructed along the easternshore; the western shore was too steep for permanent habitation."

For a time at the turn of the century, Dena'ina caught trout in the winter at Red Shirt Lake and took them by sled to Susitna Station for the restaurant there.

Notes on Dena'ina Watercraft

by James Kari

It is germane to summarize the modes of water travel that the Upper Inlet Dena'ina used in pre-contact times and how these are reflected in the accounts of Dena'ina travel throughout *Shem Pete's Alaska.* Aboriginally the Dena'ina had four main types of boats. Two of these craft were Athabascan in origin, the **baqay,** the birchbark canoe, and the **elgheji**, the skin boat. Two craft made with sealskin were modeled after Eskimo boats: the **biqidin,** the kayak-style boat, and the **badi**, a large umiak-style boat. For the Dena'ina kayaks and umiaks complemented but did not replace birchbark canoes, moose skin boats, and rafts. The summary of water transportation for the Dena'ina in Osgood (1937:67–70) remains excellent. Osgood noted "a problem is first to ascertain how far the Eskimo kaiak and umiak had penetrated into the Tanaina area at the time of historic contact, and second to determine to what extent the birch bark canoe and moose skin boat had been retained" (op.cit.:67). ‡For more information on Dena'ina watercraft see Kari (2007:242–46), and Jones, Fall, and Leggett (2013:175–179).

The **baqay** is the traditional Athabascan-style birchbark canoe. Birchbark canoes were frequently used in the lake districts between the Susitna River and Knik Arm (such as Big Lake, Nancy Lake and Red Shirt Lake; see Plate 5 and Fig. 61) as well as on the Kenai Peninsula. See Spurr's mention of Dena'ina use of the birch canoe in 1898 at 5.7 and 5.8. Spurr made this generalization about birch bark canoes in 1898. "The uninhabited character of the country is probably due partly to the lack of game, as mentioned before, but also to the character of the Skwentna [Yentna], which is so rapid and dangerous that it is not a good stream for birch canoes. The Indians do not settle permanently in any place which they can not readily reach in canoes" (Spurr 1900:67). Several Dena'ina place names refer to the birchbark canoe, or the harvesting of bark for canoes (see names 7.52, 8.49, 13.54, and 16.14). Birchbark canoes were used into the 1920s.

The **elgheji** or skin boat was a temporary craft made with raw moose or caribou skins stretched over a pole frame. The word **elgheji** refers to the frame and means 'the one that is ribbed.' It was used to freight loads of meat downstream on larger sidesteams such as the Yentna or the Kashwitna rivers following upland hunting trips. The skin boat was never used on the Inlet. In May of 1898 geologist Spurr noted "In ascending the [Yentna] river at the end of May we met many of these natives returning from the

FIGURE 63

‡Nora McCord (left) and her siblings at her grandmother Annie Ephim's house, standing in front of a **baqay**, a birchbark canoe, at Susitna Station, late 1920s or early 1930s.

PHOTO COURTESY OF ALEXANDRA ALLOWAN

FIGURE 64

This classic photo of a Dena'ina man in a three-hold baidarka was taken by F. H. Rojec on the Susitna River, probably just above the confluence with the Yenta River in late May or early June of 1910. Rojec was the photographer for the 1910 Mazama expedition which attempted unsuccessfully to climb Denali. We discuss this photo again in Chapter 5 as we think that the man shown is likely Chief Evan, Shem Pete's step-brother.

Harry Balluta of Nondalton commented on this picture, noting that the double upturned prow on the Dena'ina bairdarka was called in Dena'ina **k'eł k'itughił'u** which means 'into the bay with it.' This prow was so-called to ensure luck in hunting when turning into a bay.

PHOTO USED WITH PERMISSION OF THE MAZAMAS, PORTLAND, OR., NEG. NO. VM1993.031.N002

FIGURE 65

Dena'ina men from Point Possession village, Billy Nicholai (left) and Johnny Nicholai in their gas engine-powered sailboat in the late 1920s near Knik.

PHOTO COURTESY OF FEODORIA KALLANDER PENNINGTON

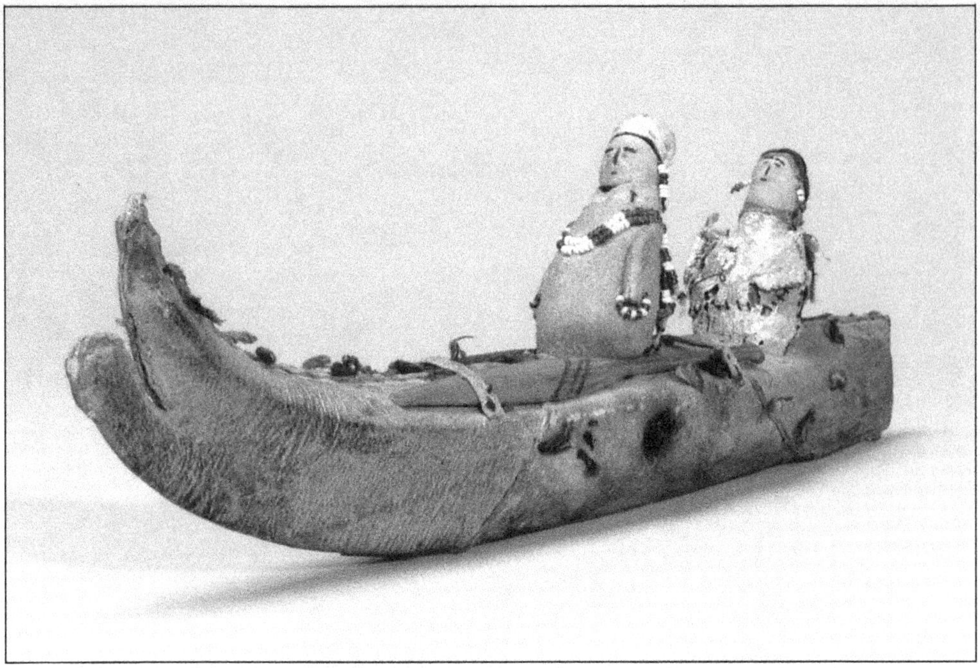

FIGURE 66

This model baidarka with human figurines was made at Susitna Station in about 1915. Rupert Axley Moon, a teacher at Susitna Station in 1915–16, collected this model, and the maker is not named. Walter VanHorn (p.c.) notes that this is the only example of a baidarka that has been collected from the Dena'ina area, there being no full-size boat in any collection. The figurines are a man and woman dressed in Dena'ina-style skin tunics.

PHOTO BY WALTER VANHORN AND THE ANCHORAGE MUSEUM OF HISTORY AND ART

hunt, running down the river with their furs, meat and families in rude boats made by stretching moose skin over wooden frames" (Spurr 1900:66–67). See other mention of the use of the **elgheji** at 6.10, 6.22, 7.23, and 8.43. The **elgheji** was used as recently as the 1930s.

The Dena'ina manufactured three different styles of kayaks (one-, two-, and three-hole craft) or baidarkas. Shem Pete, in a discussion on boats in February of 1985, summarized that the **biqidin** was the main mode of travel on Cook Inlet and on the lower Susitna and lower Yentna rivers. The Dena'ina would would go in the **biqidin** as far upstream as **Tiq'atl'ena** (7.2 Hewitt Lake), **Tuqentnu** (8.10 Kroto Creek), and **Tanłtunt** (3.19, site at Red Shirt Lake). Shem noted that these were the fastest and most versatile craft. They had terminology for all parts of the vessel. They would oil the skins of the **biqidin** with seal oil, and they would last a long time. The Dena'ina could drag them and bring them places that the **baqay** (birchbark canoe) could not go.

The Upper Inlet Dena'ina baidarka was patterned after the Pacific Eskimo-style baidarka (as described in Zimmerly 2000:29–37) and was made of sealskin on a birch frame. The Dena'ina baidarka was used in the Upper Inlet until the 1910s. Hodge (1907:717) in the entry for "Knik" [Old Knik/Eklutna] states, "They use the birch bark canoe on the inland rivers but purchase skin bidarkas of the Kenai Nikishka people to fish and travel along the coast." The only Dena'ina place name that refers to the kayak or baidarka is in the Iliamna dialect area: Iniskin Bay is **Viqidin Ts'iznigitnu** 'where we hold the kayak.' We are fortunate to have two examples of the Dena'ina baidarka (Figs. 64 and 66).

The **badi** or umiak were the main craft the Dena'ina used for traveling in Cook Inlet with people and gear. They were probably last used in the 1880s. Shem Pete related several accounts of use of the **badi** on Knik Arm (see 12.1) and Turnagain Arm (see 16.11) and in the uplands, even as far as **Tiq'atl'ena** (7.2), Hewitt Lake. Two Dena'ina place names, 1.27 **Badi Dulyasht**, Granite Point, and 15.92 **Ułchena Bada Huch'ilyut,** Campbell Point, refer to the umiak-style boat. Also **badi** is the general term for any kind of boat for the Upper Inlet and Outer Inlet Dena'ina.

The log raft called, **hnes**, was used for one-way travel on the larger rivers,and was never used on the Inlet. See the description of the use of small rafts made by Talkeetna Alec in 1910 at 9.12. Also see the description by Sava Stephan at 6.3.

The Dena'ina also have numerous terms for an array of post-contact water craft such as dories, scows, schooners, sloops, and various motor boats and fishing boats. In Shem Pete's narrative in Chapter 7, the party was tracking a lumber dory from Susitna Station to above the Skwentna River and then came downstream with the current. See also the description of Alec's skill at lining and steering a loaded boat on the Chulitna River in 1910 at 9.4. Sava Stephan in his autobiography (see 0.3) makes several references to his career as a boat captain throughout the Upper Inlet.

FIGURE 67

Shem Pete surveys the fishing site at **Tanłtunt,** Red Shirt Lake Village (3.18), in 1978.
PHOTO BY PRISCILLA RUSSELL

3.20 Beq'estsiq' Tuyu'uli • 'Object Floating at the Outlet'
island at Red Shirt Lake outlet

3.21 Tanłtun Tesha • 'Hill of Enclosed Object [bag] Is Set in Water'
ridge on west shore of Red Shirt Lake
This is described as a lookout and hunting area.

During a visit to Red Shirt Lake in 1986 (Fall and Greiser (1986)), Billy Pete offered these additional comments on **Tanłtun Tesha** and the uses of resources in the first several decades of the twentieth century.

Billy Pete: "This hill, like this, they climb up and after that they get to the flat, and they just go across the flat. They used to have summer trail here. And when they catch bunch of spruce hens, they used to pack it down to where they got their canoe and go down with four or five dozen spruce hens. And they used to sell them two bits a piece to one of them restaurants [at Susitna Station]. They weren't restaurants, they were roadhouses, they used to call them.... And anybody who ever want to buy spruce hens [spruce grouse], they just threw down two bits apiece. They bring down maybe four to five dozen spruce hens. Sell all of them. That same day they used to go back up to Red Shirt Lake. They start catching some more trout, and stuff like that. And the sack of flour used to be dollar. Dollar a sack of flour."

3.22 Dach'qelqiht • 'Where We Spend the Spring'
site where Lynx Creek enters Red Shirt Lake
Shem Pete said there was a spring camp and small village on the bay on both sides of the mouth of Lynx Creek. This was also used as a summer fish camp.

Fall and Geiser (1986:C2): "This is a former village site at the outlet of Lynx Creek, where it enters Red Shirt Lake. There were **nichił** (multi-family birch bark houses) south of this outlet on a small bay. On the flat near the creek (where the helicopter sat down) was a fish camp, where there were open-sided smokehouses. There also were **nichił** on the north side of the creek."

3.23 Nich'ghilentnu • 'Creek That Flows Swiftly'
Lynx Creek
One of the three bands on Red Shirt Lake lived at the mouth of Lynx Creek. Many **nichił** were located further up this creek. Shem Pete reported that these houses were abandoned long ago.

Shem Pete: "That's where lots of Indian camps used to be."

Billy Pete: "It's a swift creek. That's why silver salmon go up there. They lay their eggs in swift water only. There were lots of fish there in wintertime. This was an important place for hunting bear from a **dehq'a** [elevated lookout] when the bear were eating salmon."

Fall and Greiser (1986:C2): "People operated a fish trap in **Nich'ghilentnu,** Lynx Creek."

3.24 Nich'ghilen Bena • 'Lake of Creek That Flows Swiftly'
Lynx Lake
This area may be seen in Plate 5.

§3.33 Nik'uleht • 'Place That Fish Swim To'
a sockeye spawning location along a gravel beach on upper Red Shirt Lake, possibly bay on northwest end of lake
Fall and Greiser (1986), Billy Pete: "They used to have I don't know how many **nichił** over here, there was one over here, and over on the second point I showed you. And then towards Cow Lake, and then this side of the lake, they used to have **nichił** all over, all the way up to where that bridge coming out this way, to **Nik'uleht** where the fish come."

3.25 Tanłtun Dinłent • 'Where It Flows into Enclosed Object [bag] Is Set in Water'
site at north end of Red Shirt Lake where upper Fish Creek enters lake
According to Shem Pete, a separate band of Dena'ina lived here at the upper end of Red Shirt Lake.

3.26 Tudli Benach' Titaytuntnu • 'Creek on Trail to Cold Water Lake'
upper Fish Creek, above Red Shirt Lake
Many small lakes on upper Fish Creek, in the present Nancy Lake Recreation Area, including the newly named Shem Pete Lake, have no recorded Dena'ina names. A trail along upper Fish Creek led to **Tutikaq' Bena** (8.8, North Rolly Lake).

Baytnidahen and Red Shirt

by Shem Pete, translated by Billy Pete

Shem Pete: "At **Tanłtunt** [Red Shirt Lake] there was a rich man. His name was **Baytnidahen.** He had a camp just where the main trail went. Every time somebody came through, they stopped there. His name was **Baytnidahen**. He was my little father. He was **K'kalayi,** a different tribe [clan]. He wasn't my real father, so I just called him "my little father." My brother was **Nulchina** and he was **K'kalayi,** that man at **Tanłtunt.** He helped all the people. He let them stay overnight. He had two big copper cooking buckets. When lots of people came, he got out those two big buckets. They brought one big bucket inside, and he started cooking for them. He was a good rich man.

"He made a song when he was going to get married. He trapped for two years way up the Yentna River. That big skin boat, he brought it back full of furs. He brought that back down to Susitna Station. He sold the furs. They made a big tent for him. He bought lots of clothes, rolls of cloth, rolls of calico. He rolled it out all around the tent on the ground.

"[He said] 'I made a song. I called you people here to help me sing this song I made.' After they sang, he gave them five yards of calico apiece. The woman he was going to marry was a pretty woman. Her father's name was **Batninch'ey.** She was nice looking. The song he made for that woman I am going to sing now.

"He said, 'I thought I was going to have the woman to help me make a living, but she got married to someone else.' He told this to the people. 'I hoped that was the one I was going to marry.'

"That woman was crying too, and dancing and everything. He told everybody to come to the tent. They all had that cloth around them, calico and cloth like that. They were hanging onto that cloth and standing, and they were crying with him. In other words, they were singing that song with him, that song, my 'little father' made:

[verse one:]
That's the woman I thought I was going to marry.

[verse two:]
That's the one I thought was going to cook for me.

[verse three:]
That's the one I thought was going to keep me happy.

[verse four:]
That's the one I thought was going to sleep with me.

"That Red Shirt was next to the chief. His name was **K'eł Nuts'ehen.** They made him **yagashchik,** second chief [of Susitna Station]. He was a smart man. He [Red Shirt] married that man's [**Baytnidahen's**] daughter. He stayed with that man for I don't know how many years, and then that man **Baytnidahen** died. So he [Red Shirt] took over that place. He did just like that man. He took care of everything that went by that place, **Tanłtunt.** He stayed there until he died, in 1916 or 1917, and they buried him over there. This was Red Shirt. Now that village has gone to waste.

"I was raised there too, but now I'm too old. That's why I am staying at Willow now. I'm just an old man. Red Shirt used to help everybody that came through. When he was at Susitna Station he used to work for one dollar a day. He used to buy a sack of flour and pack it down to his house at Susitna Station. He had another house there. He told his wife to bake bread, the whole fifty pounds. He used to truly like his wife because she was prettier than any other woman at Susitna Station. He used to go around the village and get all the kids. The little ones, he pack them home, maybe two or three at a time. He used to give the kids bread, and after they ate bread he used to tell stories. He used to tell us stories.

"'I used to do this a long time ago,' he said.

"He made believe he was in the story, the one doing those things, and we used to laugh at him. He used to tell a bunch of different stories, and then we go to sleep. He used to tell lots and lots of stories. My mother used to get worried. She knew where we were so she would go over to that house. We were all sleeping. My mother packed me back and took me home.

"I used to call him [Redshirt] brother-in-law. Everbody liked him. He was a good man. He stayed at **Tanłtunt** for a long time. He used to put fish trap across [just below the outlet on Fish Creek]. He built a bigger smokehouse than the one they had. He put up lots of fish for the people there, just like **Baytnidahen.** Sometimes in October month or so, when the silver salmon are all gone, he caught trout next. When all the salmon were gone, he made a different trap for trout. He used to have a trout trap over there [in Fish Creek]. They used trout until the salmon came back again. And then they started putting up fish for winter. Red Shirt built a big smokehouse. In spring they made dry fish for winter. All summer long. He built a big smokehouse,

‡FIG. 67A

This fine photo was taken in 1917 of the Susitna Station people and school teacher Katherine Kane. This is the last group photo of Susitna Station people prior to the devastation of the 1918 influenza epidemic. Shem Pete, then age 21, seems to be in the photo in front of the right-most window (see arrow).

B2013.049.5, KATHERINE KANE MANUSCRIPT, ANCHORAGE MUSEUM

and he filled it right up with smoked salmon. He stayed at Red Shirt Lake, and he took over his father-in-law's place. Just because he was on the main trail, everybody came to him and made good use of that place. They stayed there two or three nights. People came there from Susitna, Kroto, Knik, and Alexander Creek. They all stayed there two or three days. They helped him cutting wood. They used to take their winter catch of furs to Knik to George Palmer. He used to pay the highest price for furs. That's the only one they used to sell furs to.

"Red Shirt was the last one to stay at Red Shirt Lake. Red Shirt had lots of people staying with him. There was lots of fish, and they ate it year round. It takes lots of work to get lots of fish. Forty or fifty people stayed there. It was an easy place. Bear, moose, spruce hen, beaver; they could get all those things. It was a main highway. It was just like a roadhouse there.

"There was a big bar on the east side of the lake, right in the middle. Cabin all around to the mouth of that creek they used to be living. That's where I raised, by the cabin. I see the frame yet [in 1978], where they build that house. Anybody can see the big ring around on top there. They pack 'em up, the big logs. They tie 'em up rope. Two, three, four rope. They stand 'em up and out the flag on top, American flag on top, alongside the graveyard.... About sixty years ago [in 1918] the last time someone got buried there.[1]

"I'm seventy-six years old now. I'm not going to live too long anymore. But it's all right. That's a good place for the young generation. Could get by there. Look at myself here. My mother raised me.... I was raised on fish."

When he was a small boy about five years old, Shem Pete stayed up late into the night listening to Red Shirt tell stories (**tsukdu**). Shem recalled that over the course of several nights, Red Shirt began to tell him the story of **Yubugh Tayqan**, an eight-day cycle of stories about the culture hero 'the one who paddled around the world.' Young Shem kept falling asleep and Red Shirt kept waking him up. Eventually Shem's mother found him and carried him home. This is why Shem did not remember the entire set of stories in the **Yubugh Tayqan** cycle.

1. Shem noted that Red Shirt died in about 1913 or 1914 at about the age of fifty. A man named Evan Red Shirt, age thirty, is on the 1910 census at Susitna Station.

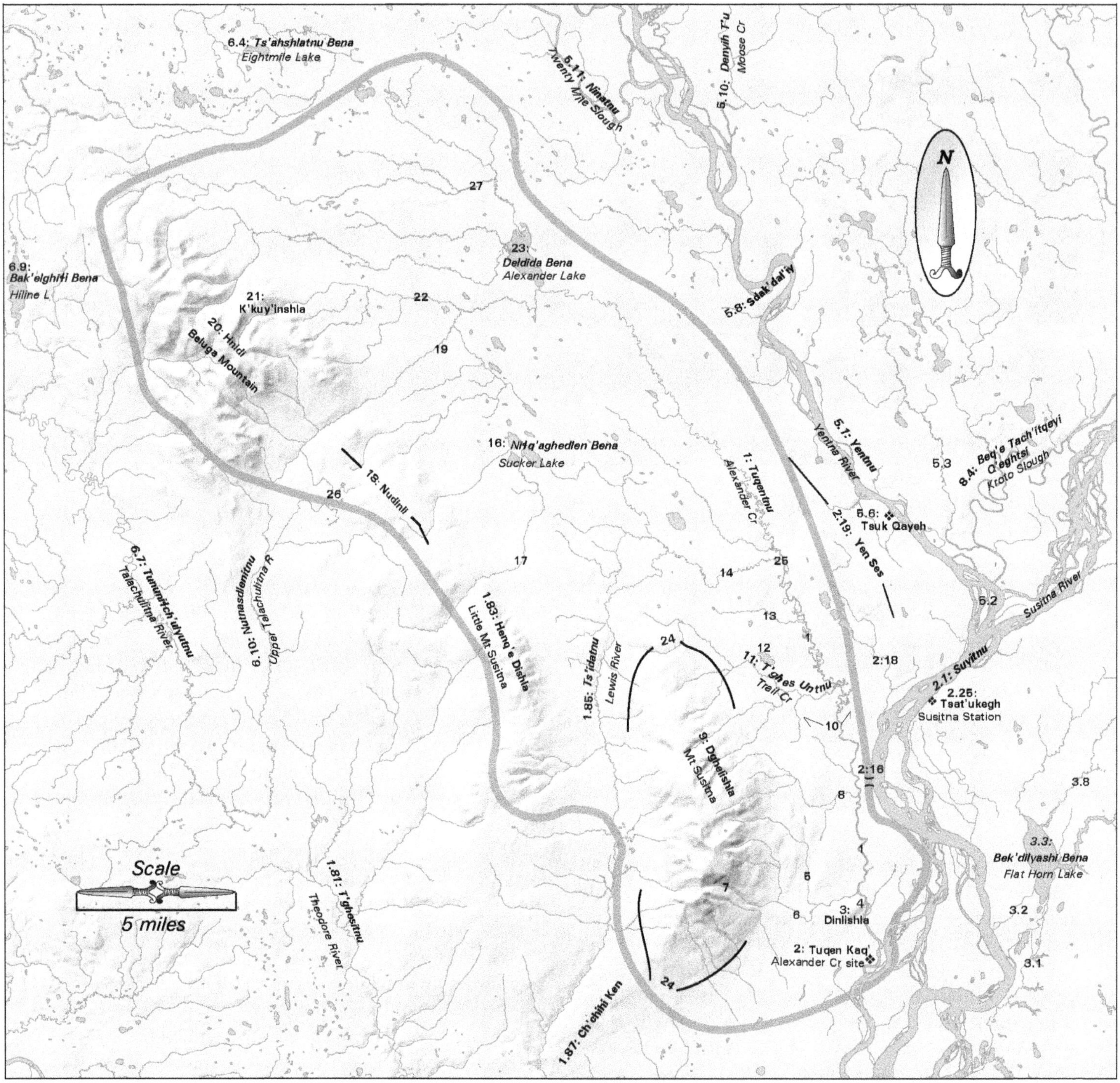

MAP 19

Place names map of Alexander Creek, showing Nos. 4.1 to 4.27.

MAP BY MATT GANLEY

4 Alexander Creek Drainage

from the mouth to Beluga Mountain

4.1 Tuqentnu • 'Clearwater Creek'
Alexander Creek
This was a major salmon fishing stream for the Alexander Creek band (Fall 1981:185). Alexander Creek and Kroto Creek (8.10) have the same Dena'ina name.
(Eldridge 1900:10) "Eight or ten miles upstream spruce appears, increasing rapidly to Alexander (Taguntna, Indian) Creek, from which point northward it is an important growth both in quantity and size." (See Map 20.

In 1898 Learnard (1900:654) noted that this stream was named after the chief who lived one quarter of a mile above the mouth of the stream. Alexander and **Diqelas Tukda** were the same person (Fall 1981:373).

Shem Pete: "«There were **nichił** at the mouth of Alexander Creek and all the way up.» They make a good living there."

Browne (1956:17) wrote in 1906: "Some foodless Susitna natives glided past in their tiny birch-bark canoes on their way to a moose range on the headwaters of the Alexander River."

The 1975 CINA (p. 91) survey reports for Alexander Creek "Numerous rectangular pits and house depressions. Located on historic trails to the interior."

Fall and Greiser (1986): Shem Pete: "**Tuqentnu**, right across from... they make one [weir] there too. That river pretty big you know. Small four, five pounds [fish] they get it. They would catch hundreds of fish. They use three or four **tay'in** [fishtraps]."

4.2 Tuqen Kaq' • 'Clearwater Mouth'
Alexander Creek village site
This seems to be the first village on the Susitna River marked on the 1839 Wrangell map, Map 17.

In Shem Pete's rendition of the culture hero cycle about **Yubugh Tayqan**, an eight-day cycle of stories about 'the one who paddled around the world,' the hero's travels end when he returns home to **Tuqen Kaq'** after passing **Tsat'ukegh** and **Tani'i** further up the Susitna River.

"At **Tuqen Kaq'** one chief was **Wasihdi Tukda**. I don't know his Russian name. He was a good man. He was a rich man, but he went broke somehow. The medicine men broke him. They kept wishing him bad luck, and the medicine men broke him. When his boy died, he had not much money left, and he told his wife, 'Let's kill ourselves.' She told him, 'Go ahead if you want to.' And he did. And they found him. Chickalusion [perhaps Peter Chickalusion, Simeon Chickalusion's father] found his body down Kalgin Island, way down the inlet. He brought his body to Kenai and buried him in the Kenai church graveyard. That's the story I'm telling you."

The funeral of **Diqelas Tukda**, chief of Alexander Creek, at **Tuqen Kaq'** in 1906 is described in Pete 1977:21–22. "«The boats extended in a line from the mouth of the Susitna to Alexander Creek.... His [**Diqelas Tukda**'s] house was visible upon the hill.... It was sticking out over the bank shabbily.... The boats kept landing, and they carried them into the timber. **Tuqen Kaq'** was a tiny place.»"

Shem Pete: "Nikolai Barbol's father stayed at Alexander Creek. He had lots of kids, and he put up lots, tons of grub, two or three caches of fish for the kids. He had a garden. Nikolai Barbol and Henry George [his younger brother] later moved up to Susitna Station."

In the 1910 census sixteen persons, all Dena'ina, were listed at Alexander Creek. Chief Evan, age fifty-three, is noted as the chief. In the 1920 census two persons, both non-Native, are listed at Alexander Creek. Shem Pete said that the last Dena'ina person to be buried at Alexander was Yentna Evan in 1921 or 1922.

CINA 1975:91: "Gravesite with two Russian Orthodox crosses. Small rectangular depressions in the vicinity. Likely associated with Alexander Creek village site.... Recorded as a village site by de Laguna and Petroff."

Shem Pete: "In 1906 they seen a big sternwheeler. They were hunting at **Dghelishla** [Mount Susitna, 4.9]. My daddy is up there. They seen that big sternwheeler

Sources: Shem Pete, Billy Pete, Sava Stephan

2003 revisions: names added 4.24–27.
‡2016 revisions: figure replaced 72.

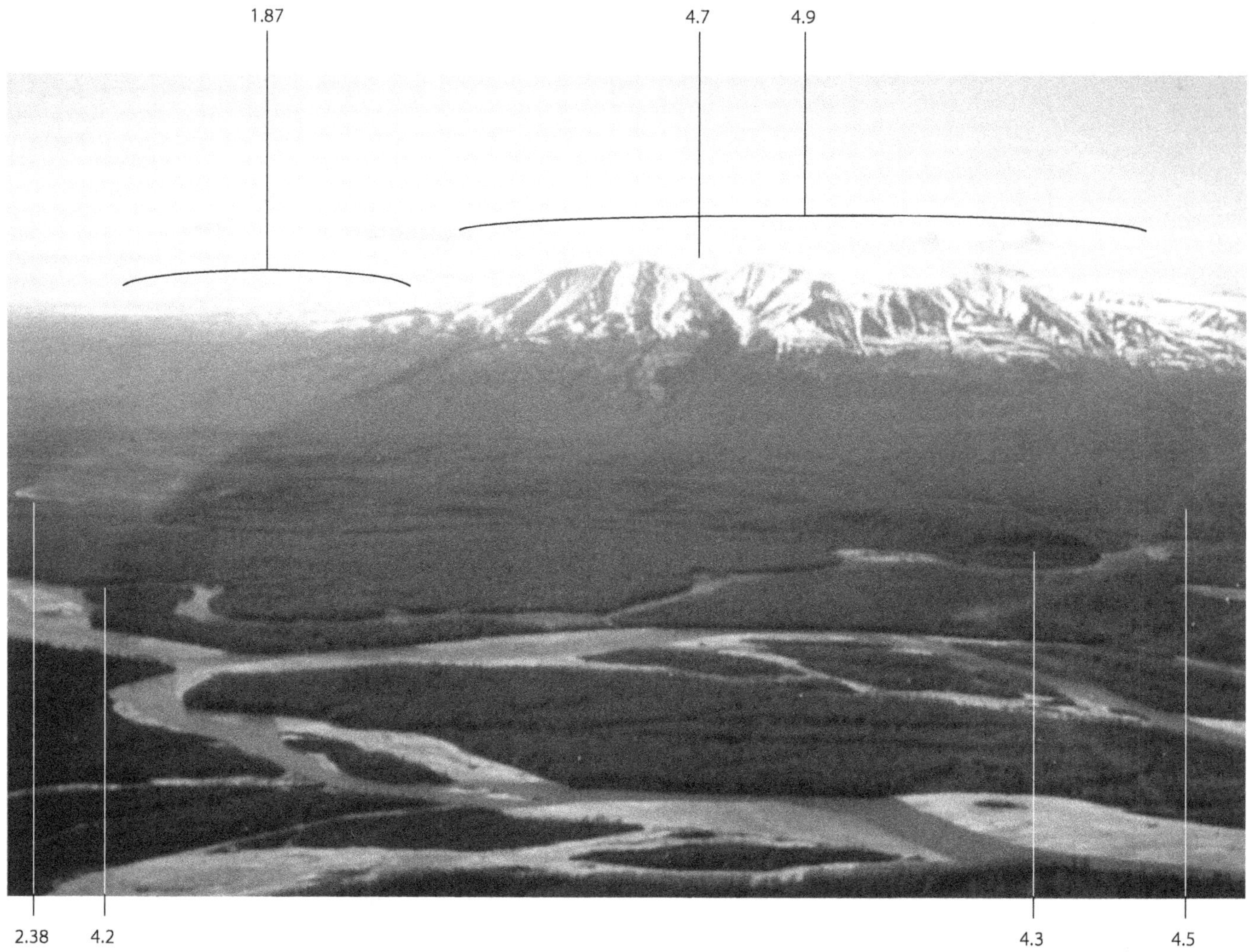

FIGURE 68

Tuqen Kaq', (4.2, the mouth of Alexander Creek), with **Dghelishla** (4.9, Mount Susitna). The notch is **Tsedi Bak'ilani** (4.7, South Peak Canyon). Tapering to the south is **Ch'chihi Ken** (1.87). The relief of **Dinlishla** (4.3, Dinglishna Hill) is noticeable above the bank of Alexander Creek. 4.5 is **Dinlishlatnu** (Granite Creek).

Tuqen Kaq' is frequently referred to as a very rich location, probably the best in the Susitna basin. As noted in Fall (1981:182–183, 372–375), the Dena'ina "describe it as a 'rich place' with salmon, trout, spruce hen, rabbits, beaver, and berries in abundance. The people of this reportedly large village 'never had trouble getting grub.'... Apparently the Alexander Creek Indians were the most sedentary of all of the **Susitnuht'ana.**"

Shem Pete: "They had fish traps right at Alexander Creek. They had fish all year round. They don't go nowhere for nothing."

PHOTO COURTESY OF COOK INLET REGION, INC.

coming up the river. They saw it out in the inlet. Come into the mouth of Alexander Creek. «Those American women [on the boat] got scared.» They [Shem's father's party] came back. The sternwheeler was still there yet. 1906." Shem added that this boat carried the first livestock that the Susitna people had seen. He said a large party left Susitna to cross the Alaska Range to the Iditarod gold fields. Shem may be referring to the Cook party of 1906, which brought in twenty packhorses and ascended the Yentna River. See Cook (1908).

Sava Stephan: **"Ts'inun** [lit. 'straight across'] is wind from Turnagain Arm direction. Boy, that seal like it when it blowing, rough weather like that in Susitna River. They just jumping up and down all over. They all come into Susitna River. We see that head popping out right there, right there all over. Especially them little ones.... I hunt seal at mouth of Susitna. At Alexander Creek, seal goes in there at low tide, when it go dry there's a whole big pile of them. I used to go up there all the time."

4.3 Dinlishla • 'Little Ridge'
Dinglishna Hill
See Fig. 70.

4.4 Dinlishla Ełch'ish Ka'a Eł Deqiy'un • 'Big Bracket Fungus Sticking out from Little Ridge'
rock (?) protrusion on Dinglishna Hill
Shem Pete: "«There was a big fungus, maybe fifty feet around, and it took millions of years to grow. They used to come to it, and even if they want to go home, they make a circle and come back to the same place.» They do that for half a day, then they get home somehow. They chopped all over it [the fungus], lots of axe marks on it. «Before they left it, they would pay it [with a gift]. It was so big, as big as the inside of a house. One punk.» That was funny ashes."

See P. R. Kari (1991:184–85) on the use of the ashes of bracket fungus or artist fungus (*Ganoderma* and *Fomes spp.*), which are mixed with snuff or tobacco and placed in the mouth.

4.5 Dinlishlatnu • 'Little Ridge Creek'
Granite Creek above the north end of Dinglishna Hill

4.6 Tsedi Bak'ilanitnu • 'Creek in Which There Is Copper'
creek from South Peak Canyon on Mount Susitna

4.7 Tsedi Bak'ilani • 'The One in Which There Is Copper'
South Peak Canyon
Shem Pete: "That one big cut is **Tsedi Bak'ilani**. Way before the Russians came they found a big [piece of] copper walking around. It looked like a big porcupine. He [the man who found the copper] peed on that copper walking around. They found that maybe four hundred or five hundred years ago, before the Russians came to Alaska. A rich man's cousin hunted around **Dghelishla** [4.9]. He saw that copper kinda walk around, come alive, I don't know. It gave him luck. That's where that chief got lucky. That porcupine copper died. He got lucky. They cut a little piece and make arrow point. They got rich outa that copper. They sell that."

Billy Pete: "They pound it [copper] with another rock to make it harder and make knife out of it. They take a big rock and put copper there. These people were called **nuk'qetset** ['They pound it']. They were just like blacksmiths. For thousands of years they had blacksmiths. They used flint, and then they found copper, and it was better. They could make any kind of shape by pounding the copper. Some people got very good. They were very valuable. They had a cache out in the woods so he could survive. He [the coppersmith] would stay out in the woods in case a war tribe came. Someone would run out and tell them. They'd hide all the copper and stuff like that. He'd run away and hide himself somewhere else. He was a very important, valuable man."

4.8 Etl' Ghiłgetnu • 'Rotten Beaver Dam - Creek'
Pierce Creek
Shem Pete: "«The creek flowing down upland from **Dinlishla** comes out near the mouth of Alexander Creek, **Etl' Ghiłgetnu.** There is a rotten beaver dam there. Just grass in there. It is good trapping for fox there.» "This

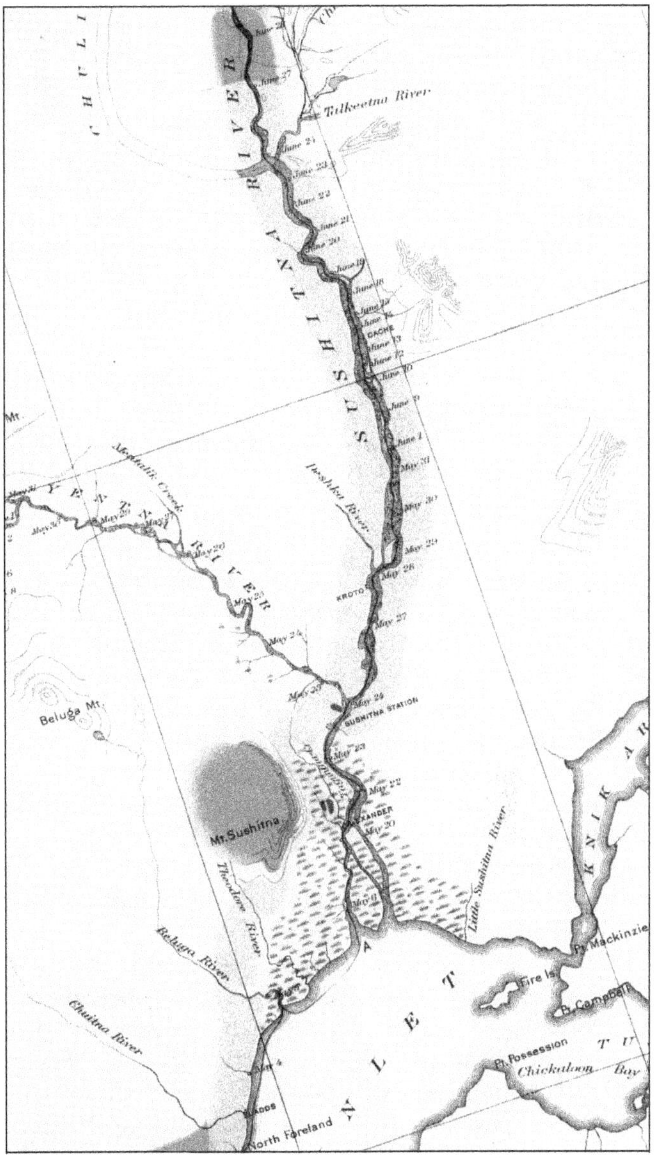

MAP 20

Detail from the Eldridge and Muldrow map of 1898: Lower Susitna River.

The map from George Eldridge's 1900 report shows the dates and trails taken by both the Eldridge and Spurr parties in May of 1898. Of note here is the relief for 4.3 Dinglishna Hill next to Mount Susitna and the Dena'ina name for Alexander Creek, noted as "Taguntna." Sherwood (1965:175) summarized the detailed instructions for mapping that were given to USGS geologists Eldridge and Robert Muldrow which show the quality of work that was expected of the first professional USGS cartography of this area. Eldridge was to determine topographic features with a continuous stadia line over the route and by sketches of adjacent country made with a plane table. Latitude stations were established at twenty-five mile intervals. Observations were also recorded on climate and minerals. Sherwood notes, "For a pioneer reconnaissance this was an ambitious order." Map 39 is another detail from this map.

is a little creek about three or four feet wide. «The trail from **Tuqen Kaq'** to **Dghelishla** went up here.»

"The Alexander Creek people had a regular road going up the mountain, three or four feet wide. It took two hours to get there and they had all day to hunt. They come back with ground squirrel and bear."

Brooks wrote in 1902, when he climbed Mount Susitna to take measurements of the height of Mount McKinley, "From this point [Alexander Creek village] we followed an Indian trail, winding in and out among swamps and lakes, through spruce forests and across several streams on old beaver dams, to Mount Susitna" (Brooks 1911:16–17).

In 1906 Browne (1956:160) left Alexander and climbed Mount Susitna. "We found an old Indian trail that led us through beautiful deep woods broken now and then by beaver meadows."

4.9 Dghelishla • 'Little Mountain'
Mount Susitna
Dghelishla is a sacred mountain to the Dena'ina. It is quite obvious to Dena'ina speakers that that the name 'Little Mountain' is paired opposite the name for Denali [Mount McKinley], **Dghelay Ka'a** 'Big Mountain.' A third mountain that might also be part of this set is Bald Mountain in Talkeetna, also called **Dghelishla**. The ridge on the southern flank, **Ch'chihi Ken** (1.86), is a mourning place. There are several stories of people obtaining power on Mount Susitna (e.g., Pete 1977). Kalifornsky (1984:20–21, 1991:205) wrote that the **Nulchina** 'Sky Clan' first landed in Cook Inlet at Mount Susitna when they descended on a frozen cloud.

Mildred Jacobsson's *Legend of Sleeping Lady* (1976), and Ann Dixon's *The Sleeping Lady* (1994) are not authentic Dena'ina stories. Dixon (1994:1) has a disclaimer. "The origin of the story is unknown. It may have begun with homesteaders or prospectors in Southcentral, Alaska, perhaps between the 1930s and the 1950s.... Many people believe that the legend of the Sleeping Lady is Native Alaskan in origin. While "Susitna" is an Athabascan word, the story is not a Native legend, according to Shem Pete, the now-deceased Dena'ina elder who spent much of his later life documenting Dena'ina culture and legends."

Billy Pete: "This mountain, **Dghelishla**, they call 'Sleeping Beauty.' I don't know for what reason. I read on a piece of paper that there was a legend behind that. That there was a warrior who went to war, and his woman lay down in the brush and went to sleep. There is no such [Dena'ina] story as 'Sleeping Beauty.' I don't think so."

§4.24 Dghelishla Qakenu • 'The Base of Little Mountain'
general area of the lower slopes surrounding Mount Susitna
Name contributed by Sava Stephan.

4.10 Ken Ka'a • 'Big Flat'
flats north of Pierce Creek on both sides of Alexander Creek

4.11 T'eghes Untnu • 'Cottonwood Den Creek'
Trail Creek

FIGURE 69

One of the foremost Dena'ina experts, Emma Alexie of Lime Village, with **Dghelishla** (4.9, Mount Susitna), in the background. Taken at **Nuch'ishtunt** (15.91, Point Woronzof) in 2001. The kuspuk that Shem Pete is wearing in Fig. 42 and Plate 1 was made by Emma, as was the birchbark basket used in background screens in this book, e.g., pp. 106–107.

Shem used to call Emma **Jiggi** which means 'princess, favorite child.'

PHOTO BY JAMES KARI

Shem Pete: "«**T'eghes Untnu** flows into the main [Alexander] creek.»"

4.12 T'eghes Untnu Bena • 'Lake of Cottonwood Den Creek'
lake north of Trail Creek

4.13 Sts'is Ch'eght • 'Blocked by Rocks'
creek between Trail and Sucker creeks

§4.25 Nilq'aghedlen Kaq' • 'Current Flows Together Mouth'
mouth of Sucker Creek

4.14 Nilq'aghedlentnu • 'Current Flows Together Creek'
Sucker Creek, Sucker Lake outlet stream
Shem Pete: "«This flows out of **Nilq'aghedlen Bena** [4.16].»"

4.15 Hghetgge Ch'aydinleni • 'One That Flows out from in Between'
Wolverine Creek
Shem Pete: "«We used to catch grayling in **Hghetgge Ch'aydinleni**.»"

4.16 Niłq'aghedlen Bena • 'Flows Together Lake'
Sucker Lake
Nichił and fishing areas are said to be located here.

Shem Pete: "Nobody go hungry at that lake."

Robert Allowan of Susitna and Tyonek trapped at Sucker Lake and Sucker Creek until the early 1930s.

4.17 Nudinli Betnu • 'Creek of Ridge That Extends Across'
upper Sucker Creek
Shem Pete: "«We used to catch trout in **Nudinli Betnu**.» Pretty good size creek."

4.18 Nudinli • 'Ridge That Extends Across'
ridge between Beluga Mountain and Mt. Susitna
Shem Pete: "This is a long, low mountain, just like a bridge, to run across from Susitna Mountain to **Hnidi** [4.20, Beluga Mt.]. We used to go along the ridge from mountain to mountain. Lots of little lakes there [referring to the Wolf Lakes area]."

§4.26 Nudinli Bena • 'Lake(s) of Ridge That Extends Across'
Wolf Lakes

4.19 Hniditnu • 'River of the One Upriver'
Bear Creek
Shem Pete: "«That one that flows from between those mountains flows into **Deldida Bena**» [4.23]."

4.20 Hnidi • 'The Upriver One'
Beluga Mountain
In 1899 Herron (1901:113) recorded the name of this mountain as "Snee-dee." See Map 22.

Shem Pete: "Some young people stayed all winter up on Susitna Mountain and Beluga Mountain, and the connecting ridge, **Nudinli** [4.18]. They got all the meat they wanted and just stayed there all winter. There was lots of ptarmigan and marten for fur. They used the marten fur for blankets. They were pretty expensive, so people stayed up there to trap them. They'd stay until March and then come back to their women with furs and

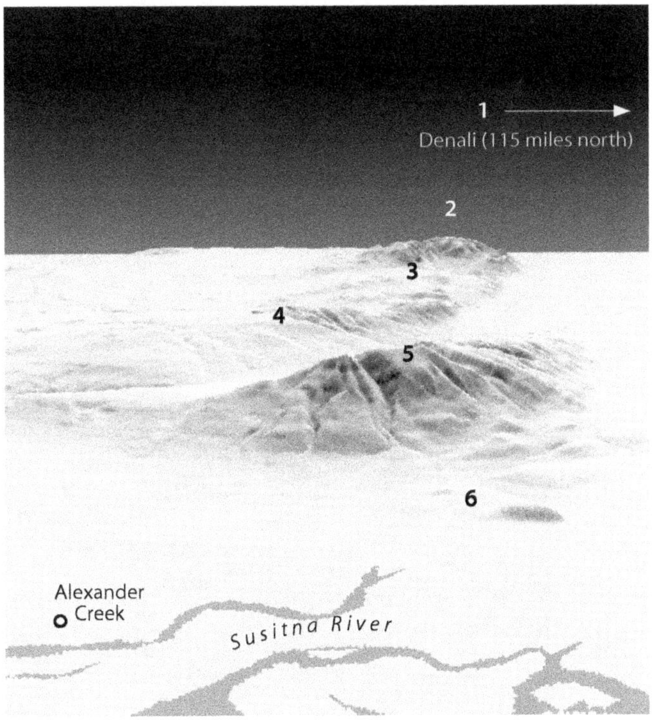

FIGURE 70

‡Dena'ina place names (and those in other Dene languages) can be studied and analyzed at several levels. About 95 percent of Dena'ina names in this book have clear meanings. On occasion in Dene languages we find a group of names that have coordinated meanings that can be viewed as a *place name ensemble*. These five place names plus the name for Denali have shared meanings that link them together as a set of names. Consider these six features: 3 and 6 have the term **dinli** 'ridge that extends;' 4, 5 and 6 have the suffix **-shla** 'little;' 2 and 4 use directional stems 'upland' and 'upriver.' These five names can be easily memorized and used for trail orientation walking in either direction. A place name ensemble reflects planning and pragmatism at the time the names were first coined. Furthermore, there is the over-arching link between the names 5, **Dghelishla** 'little mountain,' and 6, **Dghelay Ka'a** 'big mountain' (Denali), in the center of the Alaska Range. It is possible these two names were planned out this way when they were first coined in the ancient past. Also see *watershed tenure*, pp. 144–147.
PROJECTION BY MATT GANLEY

	Name	Translation	Geographic Feature	Linked stems	
1	**Dghelay Ka'a** (7.51)	'Big Mountain'	Denali, 115 miles north, elev. 20,320'	**dghelay** (*cf.* 5)	**ka'a** (*cf.* 4,5,6)
2	**Hnidi** (4.20)	'The Upriver One'	Beluga Mt., elev. 3,639'	directional **hnidi** (*cf.* 4)	
3	**Nudinli** (4.18)	'Ridge That Extends Across'	ridge at upper Sucker Creek, elev. 2,209'	**dinli** (*cf.* 6)	
4	**Henq'edishla** (1.83)	'The Little Upland One'	Little Mt. Susitna, elev. 3,035'	directional **henq'edi** (*cf.* 2)	**shla** (*cf.* 1,5,6)
5	**Dghelisha** (4.9)	'Little Mountain'	Mt. Susitna, elev. 4,396'	**dgheli** (*cf.* 1)	**shla** (*cf.* 1,4,6)
6	**Dinlishla** (4.3)	'Little Ridge That Extends'	Dinglishna Hill, elev. 479'	**dinli** (*cf.* 3)	**shla** (*cf.* 1,4,5)

porcupine meat on sleds. The women made coats from the marten skins. This was before they started trapping for profit, before the Russians came. They made big bunches of **ał** [deadfalls], and caught lots of beaver in the early fall, smoke the meat, then start catching marten. And when they come back home, they'd take a rest and then go back to the mouth of the Susitna River to get geese in the spring."

Shem Pete: "When I was just a kid, before Billy was born, Tommy's [Allowan] father, Robert Allowan took me from Susitna Station over there towards Beluga Lake [1.75]. We travel around. We come back on **Nutnasdlenitnu** [6.10] then go back on top of the mountain and come back to Susitna Station. All April we travel around hunting beaver. Every place we stop we find beaver. We had a good dog team."

Billy Pete: "Used to be no moose around Tyonek. We used to go winter time from here [Tyonek] to Paul Chuitt's camp and then on to Beluga Mountain."

4.21 K'kuy'inshla, K'kuy'ingga • 'Little Heart'
point 2130' elev., east of Beluga Mountain

4.22 K'kuy'inshla Betnu • 'Little Heart Creek'
Texas Creek

4.23 Deldida Bena • 'Tree Squirrel Lake'
Alexander Lake
Shem Pete: "«From the upper end of **Deldida Bena** the streams divide, and the trail goes to **Ts'ahshlatnu** [Eightmile Creek, 6.3] and Skwentna. There used to be **nichił** at the outlet of **Deldida Bena** a long time ago. **Tuqentnu** [Alexander Creek] is this outlet stream.» On the east side there's an island and across from there were two or three **nichił**."

Until the 1970s Shem and Billy Pete used Alexander Lake as an access point to the Beluga Mountain area to the west. They would spend a week to ten days hunting, prospecting, and fishing for grayling in the uplands. Billy Pete: "All you need is a little hook and some snares to survive in that country. We caught lots of big grayling and spruce grouse."

§4.27 Deldida Bena Dinłent • 'The One That Flows into Tree Squirrel Lake'
Deep Creek into Alexander Lake

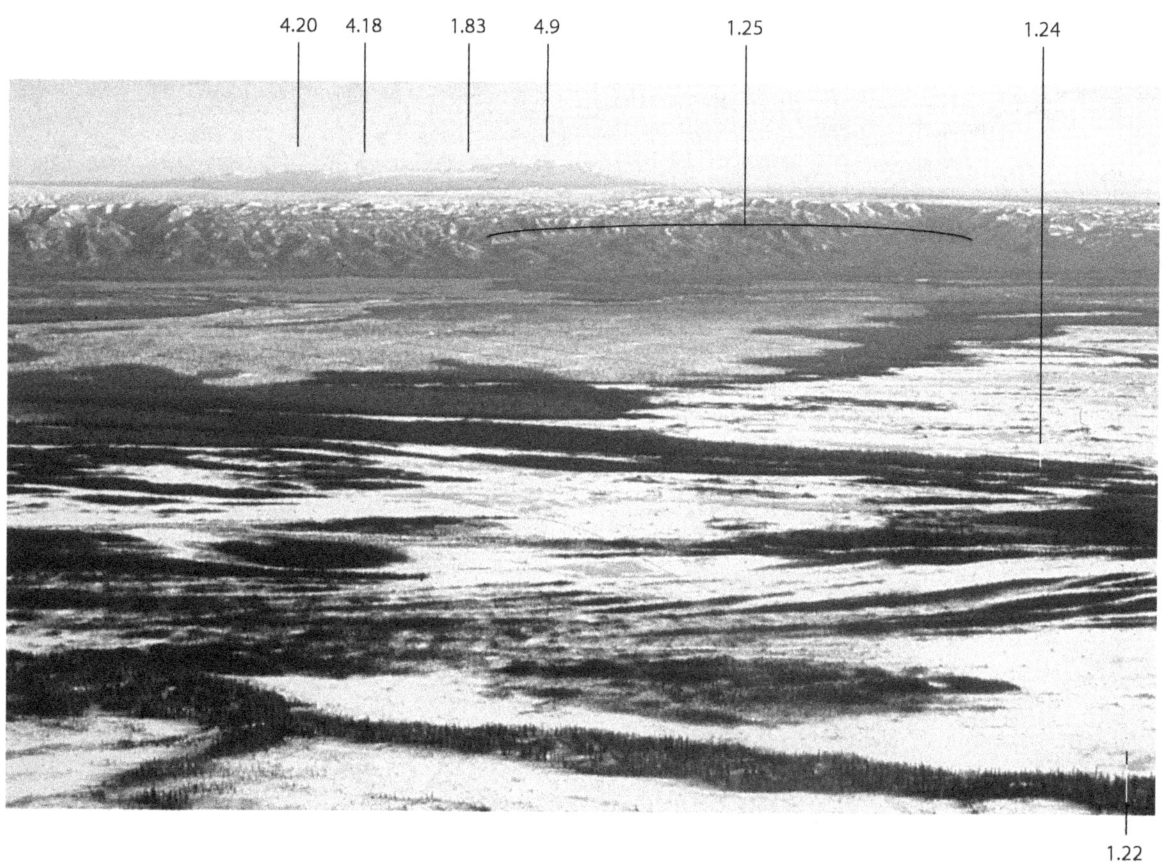

FIGURE 71

A low-altitude photo from south of Tyonek looking north. The view is above **Ch'ek'e'uła Betnu** (1.22, Chuitkilnachna Creek), and next stream is **Sdidahtnu** (1.24, Nikolai Creek). The ridge at the upper side of the view is **Nuntnalyiy** (1.25, locally known as "Bald Hills") which runs parallel to Nikolai Creek. On the upper edge of the frame is the distant outline of **Hnidi** (4.20, Beluga Mt.), **Nudinli** (4.18), **Henq'e Dishla** (1.83, Little Mt. Susitna), and **Dghelishla** (4.9, Mount Susitna). *Cf.* Fig. 70.
PHOTO COURTESY OF COOK INLET REGION, INC.

Ghuliy—Potlatch Wealth

by James Kari

In 1957, following the death of Simeon Chickalusion, Shem Pete received Dena'ina heirlooms that originally belonged to various prominent Dena'ina from the lower Susitna River and Tyonek. In the 1960s these articles were held for safekeeping by Don and Tina Rozell of Willow. In September 1976 Shem Pete transferred these items to the Anchorage Museum of History and Art. Since then, on several occasions, he has performed Dena'ina songs while wearing these articles. A videotape of him wearing these items while singing the Chickalusion mourning song was made in 1979 (Alaska Native Language Center, Talking Alaska Series, No. 6).

Shem Pete: "That Susitna chief had a brother. He was a big man, seven feet tall. His name was Ephim, his Russian name. My brother. My father's kids, there were six. He was the last duyeq [chief, see Fig. 64]. All the white men liked him. I have clothes that belonged to him. His clothes. Those clothes, they gave them to me. I use them sometime. I have my brother's hat, two pair, two hats, a rattle. I got the beads. I got four feet long old-fashioned [dentalium] beads. And I got old-fashioned Native dress. They make that themselves. They put all the beads on it. I put it on, that. I used to be dancing. But now, I don't want [to be] no chief, I told them. But they give me the chief clothes—dress, beads, feather hat, rattle. Chickalusion give me that. The last man here. He was the boss for us here in Tyonek. They give me all his clothes—beads on his clothes, feather hat, the rattle, neck beads. They tell me, 'You're the last one going to be chief for us.' I told them...'I'm not going to be good chief. I won't go for that.' So they let me out. I'm not so rich so I don't like those clothes. I'm not chief. I'm just Shem Pete. That's good enough."

The five articles of clothing, now at the Anchorage Museum of History and Art, are described on the following pages based upon information on file at the museum.

‡FIGURE 72

Five photos of Shem were found in a box in Shem Pete's cabin in Willow in the early 1990s and were donated to the Knik Tribal Council. In this unpublished photo of Shem in about 1970, he is wearing his headdress, necklace, and shirt and is holding the pair of rattles at Nancy Lake.

PHOTO COURTESY OF KNIK TRIBAL COUNCIL

1. **Sukna dghak**: beaded wool shirt

Description: dark blue wool shirt with standup collar, long sleeves, red cuffs, secured with shell buttons and a red panel approximately half-way down the front of the shirt. Just above the cuffs are ten dentalium shells sewn in pairs. Down the front are sewn twenty-eight dentalium shells in pairs.

History: This is a potlatch dancing shirt. It was made at Susitna Station about 1900. It was originally owned by Chief Ephim, the last chief of Susitna and Shem Pete's older brother. When Ephim died in about 1916, the shirt was given at a potlatch to Big Chilligan of Susitna (and later of Tyonek). When Big Chilligan died in 1931, the shirt was potlatched to Simeon Chickalusion, the chief at Tyonek. Upon Chickalusion's death in 1957, the shirt was potlatched to Shem Pete.

2. **T'uyedi:** dentalium necklace.

Description: dentalium shell necklace with dentalium shell pendant made up of 119 shells, with 19 in the bottom string and 20 in the following five strands. Between each string of shells are 60 opaque red glass beads. The bottom of the pendant is finished in 74 red glass beads and red woolen cloth. The necklace has 39 dentalium shells separated by solid black beads.

History: The dentalium necklace was used at potlatches as part of the dancing outfit. This necklace was made either at Kroto Creek or Susitna Station probably between 1880 and 1900. The earliest known owner of the necklace was Big Chilligan. It was potlatched to Simeon Chickalusion in 1931 and to Shem Pete in 1957.

3. **Nk'itl'ił:** dentalium wristlets

Description: A string of loosely woven red wool folded over and sewn together on three sides. Strung on one side of the fabric are four single strands of sinew thread strung with alternating blue and black beads and dentalium shells. Centered on each piece is a shell button.

FIGURE 73

(Left) Shown here is item 1, the beaded wool shirt, and item 2, the dentalium necklace.

PHOTO COURTESY OF THE ANCHORAGE MUSEUM OF HISTORY AND ART (#78.35.1)

FIGURE 74

(Right) At top is item 5, the eagle feather headdress; at center is item 4, the puffin beak rattles, and item 3, the dentalium wristlets. Wrapped around these is a dentalium necklace that belonged to Nickafor Alexan of Tyonek. This necklace was presented to the museum by his daughter, Leona Deck of Tyonek.

PHOTO COURTESY OF THE ANCHORAGE MUSEUM OF HISTORY AND ART (#78.35.2, 78.35.3AB, 78.35.5)

History: The wristlets were also part of a potlatch dancing outfit. These were made in Tyonek in about 1905 by Mrs. Ely Stephan. They were potlatched to Shem Pete upon Ely Stephan's death in 1951.

4. Ch'dulali: puffin beak rattles

Description: Thin, round, wooden rods wrapped with braided sinew. Suspended from each rod are four bunches of puffin beaks hung on separate rawhide thongs which are joined at one end and woven under the sinew wrappings on the rods. There are about twenty puffin beaks on each rod. Feathers are fitted into the beaks.

History: The pair of rattles was used by the shaman in curing ceremonies. This set was originally owned by Shem Pete's stepfather, Susitna Pete. They were potlatched to his son Evan in about 1902. In about 1917 they were given to Big Chilligan. Simeon Chickalusion received them in 1931, and Shem Pete obtained them in 1957. Osgood (1937:177–178) describes the use of these rattles.

5. Chijeł: eagle feather headdress.

Description: Goose and eagle feathers attached together into red woolen cloth head band with twisted sinew ties. The feathers stand upright. Some quills have fluffs attached to them with sinew.

History: This was used by the shaman in curing ceremonies. The origin of this headdress is unknown. The earliest known owner is Big Chilligan. It was given to Simeon Chickalusion in 1931 and to Shem Pete in 1957.

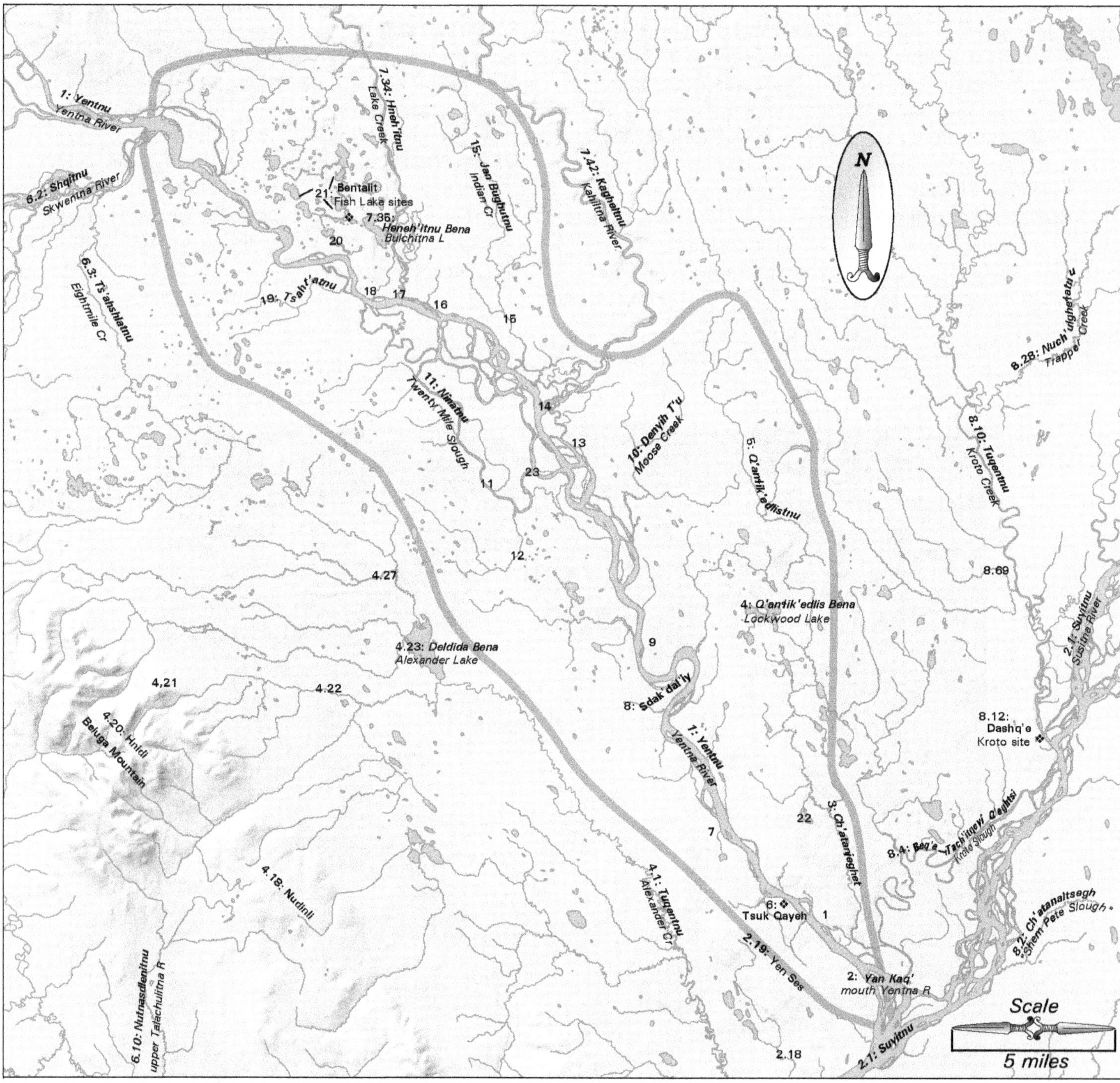

MAP 21

Place names map of the lower Yentna River, showing Nos. 5.1 to 5.23.

MAP BY MATT GANLEY

5 Lower Yentna River

from mouth to Skwentna, excluding the Kahiltna River and Lake Creek drainages

Shem Pete: "Whenever the **Tiq'atl'ena** [Hewitt Lake, 7.2] people needed anything, they had big **badi** [umiak, large skin boat], and they'd come down to Alexander Creek to trade for beluga grease, seal oil, hooligan oil, fish head oil, and they gave the Alexander Creek people caribou skins and marten skins. They helped each other, for they were the same people. The Yentna people took rain proof beaver-skin blankets, marten-skin blankets, "whistler" (marmot) blankets, and other things to the mouth of the Susitna River to trade for beluga oil, seal oil, fish head oil, hooligan oil, and maybe dry fish and seal meat and beluga meat, because they didn't have them fresh up there. They brought down all those different animal furs and bought oil with it. They used to bring all kinds of parka squirrel coats and blankets. They used to bring lots fur clothes and blankets to the mouth of the Susitna River and start trading and buy lots of oil. Two or three boat loads. In one or two weeks they got back home. And they got whole big bunch of dry fish. King salmon was good and rich down there at the mouth of the Susitna River, and they trade and buy them. They got good, rich fish to take home; real fish from salt water. And whole bunch of dry hooligans to take home. They brought back five or six **badi** [umiaks] made of sealskins. They traded for sealskins too."

5.1 Yentnu *(Dena'ina);* **Yanatno'** *(Upper Kuskokwim)* •
possibly 'Backbone River' or 'Straight Channel River'
Yentna River
Analysis of the name is moot. The stem is **yen** and not **yan,** as in **Yan Kaq'** (5.2), the mouth of the Yentna River. Also the Upper Kuskokwim name for Yentna River is **Yanatno'.** See also the related name **Yen Ses** (2.19, Trail Ridge).

The Yentna River was a major travel corridor for the Susitna Dena'ina. The absence of this river on the otherwise detailed 1839 Wrangell map (Map 17) suggests that this stream was deliberately not reported to Wrangell. The Yentna was the home of a regional band centered in several villages in the Skwentna area. These were the **Yentnuht'ana**. Fall (1981:386) comments that by the late nineteenth century the Yentna River village sites were no longer occupied in the winter as population consolidated at Susitna Station. Shem Pete did not remember any chiefs' names from the upper Yentna villages.

As Spurr ascended the lower Yentna River in May of 1898, he wrote, "We met Indians continually coming down the river in boats made of moose skin stretched over rough wooden frames; they were returning from their spring hunt up the river" (Spurr 1900:47). After these encounters on the lower Yentna, Spurr's group did not see any Indians until they descended the South Fork of the Kuskokwim River two months later.

Spurr (1900:66–67): "In the whole length of the Skwentna [Yentna] there is not a single permanent habitation, only temporary camps being found, which are used as stopping places by the natives from the villages mentioned in their fall and spring hunts. In ascending the river at the end of May we met many of these natives returning from the hunt, running down the river with their furs, meat and families in rude boats made by stretching moose skin over wooden frames; but after this we saw no living being for nearly two months, until we had descended the Kuskokwim over a hundred miles. The uninhabited character of the country is probably due partly to the lack of game, as mentioned before, but also to the character of the Skwentna [Yentna], which is so rapid and dangerous that it is not a good stream for birch canoes. The Indians do not settle permanently in any place which they can not readily reach in canoes."

In 1898 Learnard (1900:655): "About three miles above the company store a large river flows into the Sushitna, and is called Yentna (Yedno) by the Indians, and by some white men the "Johnson" [*sic* "Johnston"

Sources: Shem Pete, Billy Pete, Katherine Nicolie, Sava Stephan

2003 revisions: names added 5.22, 5.23; place relocated 5.18; names with revised spellings 5.9, 5.13.
‡2016 revisions: names revised 5.2, 5.14; map revised 22.

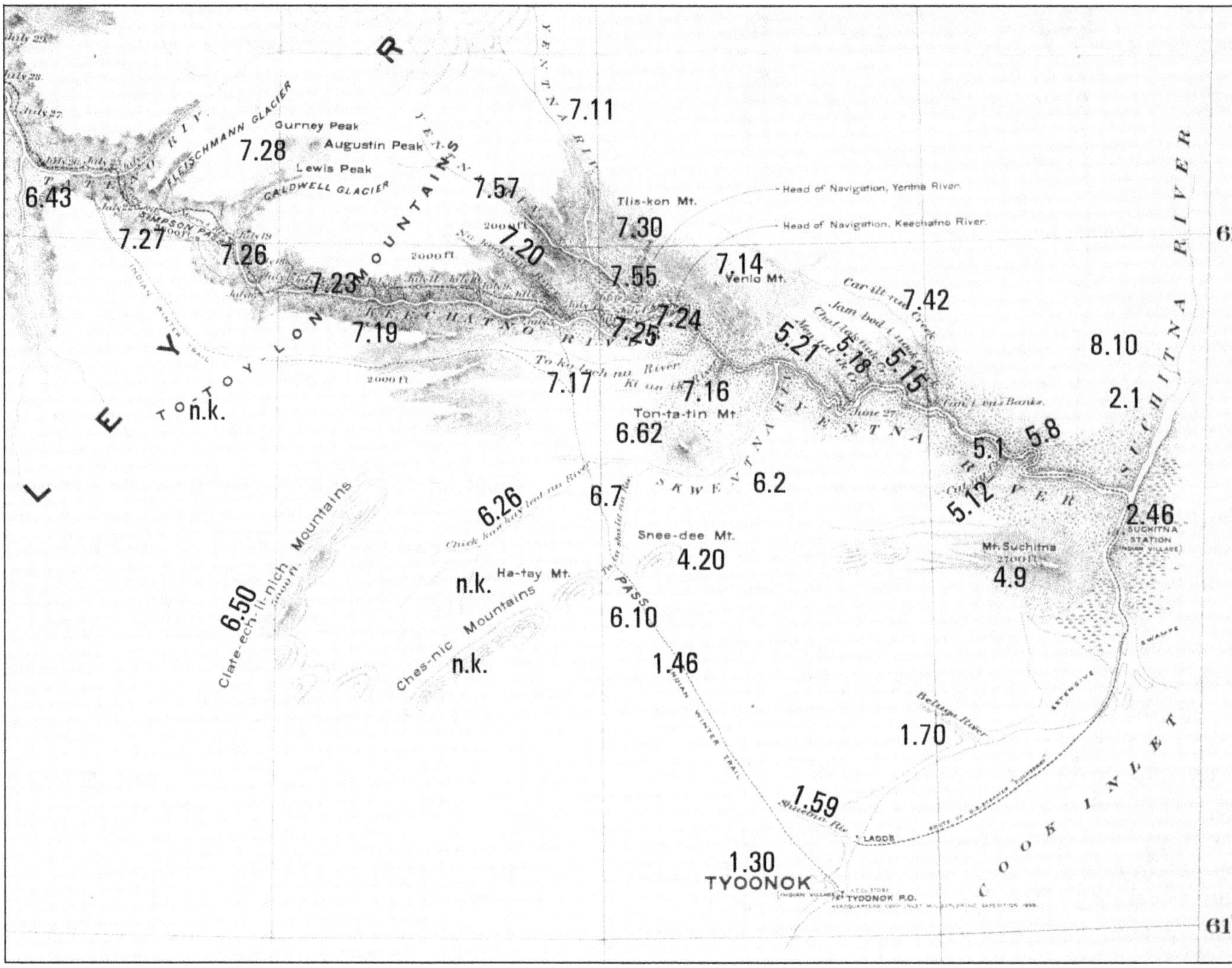

MAP 22

‡Detail from the 1899 Herron map: Tyonek to Kichatna River, with feature numbers in *SPA*. Cf. Map 29, p. 155.

With Shem Pete, the Herron report and map (partially shown in Maps 22 and 29) was the most important source for the re-elicitation of place names. Herron documented ‡twenty-nine Dena'ina place names between Tyonek and the Kichatna River. The northern portion of this map (not shown in Maps 22 or 29) presents another ‡fifty place names from Upper Kuskokwim or Koyukon. This map has such good detail on Dena'ina place names on the Yentna River because Lieut. Herron traveled the first leg of his journey in June of 1899 from Susitna Station by steamboat accompanied by his Dena'ina guides Stepan and Slinkta. These place names and trails were recorded at this time of relatively comfortable passage.

Herron wrote (1901:6–7): "I was transported by Captain Glenn on the steamboat to the head of navigation of the Yentna River, hitherto unexplored farther than its junction with the Skwentna River, and to the head of navigation of a branch river designated by the Indians and called by them the Keechatno, hitherto unknown and unexplored; and at the latter point I was to begin my overland exploration to the Yukon River, this starting point having been decided upon by the Indians in my consultations with them at Suchitna Station."

Herron (1901:19): "A council of Indians was convened to discuss the country into which I was to go. However, on the subject of their own country they promptly rejected the proposition to seek a pass over the divide via the Yentna River, stating positively that the Yentna heads in glaciers and that there is no way to get around them. The Indians knew very little about the country beyond the divide, by reason of their territory and hunting, trapping and fishing grounds being restricted, by the oldest traditions and customs among the tribes, to the country east of the divide, and with certain limits, for the same reasons, in the other directions."

Ray Collins (‡2004:59–65) offers interesting comments on the Herron expedition: "This [above] statement indicates that the Athabascans living at Susitna Station had a clear awareness of their band territory boundaries, and that these were defined by "the oldest traditions." The people of the Upper Kuskokwim most likely had the same awareness of their boundaries in relationship to those of the other people living around them."

on the 1899 Johnston and Herning map, Map 52] in honor of the first white man to ascend it. Mr J was with the party and from him I obtained the following information concerning it. He said he had ascended it about two hundred miles, and that there were two passes over the mountains from the headwaters to the head waters of the Kuskokwim, which were used by the Kuskokwim Indians when they came to the Sushitna store to trade."

5.2 Yan Kaq' • '‡Straight Channel Mouth'
mouth of Yentna River
The stem **yan** may be from **tuyan**, 'straight stream course.'

5.3 Ch'atanjeghet • possibly 'Clear Water Comes Out'
Fish Creek
‡Meaning suggested by SP. The verb stem here: **jegh** or **dzegh** is unique for Dena'ina. Shem Pete: "«There were **nichił** there. Lots of fish come out of there. Here were **nichił,** smokehouses, and many people there.»"

Sava Stephan: "We were staying at **Ch'atanjeght** «We spent the winter. And the ice went out on us.» **Ayayaya.** My mother she brought us out to the bank to wait. **Qa'elnesh.** [I remember that]. And ice is pulling out. When ice pull out we were on top the hill, but it feels like an earthquake. When the ice hit the ground. That ice is pretty strong. When it hit the ground you know just like caterpillar push the ground."

§5.22 Ch'atanjegh Bena • possibly 'Clear Water Comes Out-Lake'
lake on Fish Creek
Source: Shem Pete, a name overlooked for the first edition, and confirmed by Sava Stephan.

5.4 Qanłik'edlis Bena • 'Lake Where Dogs Drag Something Around'
Lockwood Lake
Billy Pete: "We go there in one day. That's half and half people's country, Kroto and Susitna. They use it for hunting bear."

Katherine Nicolie: "My brother and them used to go there spring and fall to get ducks and swans. From there you get to Yentna."

5.5 Q'anłik'edlistnu • 'Creek Where Dogs Drag Something Around'
creek from north into Fish Creek
Shem Pete: "«This flows into **Ch'atanjeghet.**»"

5.6 Tsuk Qayeh • 'Old Village'
sites three and a half miles up the Yentna, on the south bank
Shem Pete stated that there are two different sites here, about one half mile apart.

Shem Pete: "«They say that there was a big village there. There were **nichił.** It is above **Ch'atanjeght** about three and half miles on the left side going up. The people from **Tsuk Qayeh** died off long ago. The one called **Tsuk Qayeh Ka'a Iden** ['The Big Person from Old Village'] founded that village.»"

FIGURE 75
Jim Fall and Shem Pete on the banks of the Yentna (5.1) opposite **Ch'atanjeghet** (5.3), Fish Creek, on Sept 3, 1982.
PHOTO BY GLENN BACON

Shem Pete states that long ago people here had died of starvation. Then the village was reoccupied.

Fall (1981:387): "People from here used to fish upstream at **Bentalit** [5.21] as this was not a good fishing site."

Billy Pete: "They would cut trees for one to five miles around. Then they moved 30 miles away, and then leave it for 50 or 60 years until the trees grow back. Then they moved back in. They stay close to where there's lots of fish."

5.7 Bashda T'el'iht • 'Where Coal Is Gathered'
*three miles above **Tsuk Qayeh** on the south bank of the Yentna*
Shem Pete: "This place had once been a village with lots of **nichił** (Fall 1981:387). Big Evan had his village there. They didn't use the coal though. Just a nice place to stay.

"«The last man [from **Bashda T'el'iht**] was **An Ka'a** [Big Evan]. He moved back in after the trees grew back up. He died at Susitna Station. He died in 1912 or 1910.»

"«Big steamer go up there. They load that steamboat

with coal. They [Dena'ina] worked for that the whole summer. Maybe for $2.50 a day. The Dena'ina they don't use it [coal]. Now a short time ago Bill Dennison overloaded his scow and he tip over. He got killed from that coal. There's lots of coal there.»"

In May 25, 1898 in this area Spurr (1950:21) noted: "On this day we met several Indians returning from hunting, the first party was that of Stefano, second chief of the Susitna Indians. In his birch canoe he had with him his squaw and two children, a dog, and some furs. Stefano had never been to the head of the river but drew a sketch of the river, so far as he knew and understood it. Next came the canoe of another Indian, the head Susitna chief, both with furs and squaws and brown-eyed blubber-faced, often almond-eyed children. None of these Indians spoke a word of English. Madison [Spurr's guide], who had lived among them, talked with them in a Russian-Indian jargon, but the communication was none of the best. We could get no geographical information, they replying "don't know" to all questions."

5.8 Sdak'dal'iy • 'Point That Is Extending'
large bend on Yentna River
Shem Pete: "That's the biggest bend. «They say that there was a big spruce there that would strike the water and would kill people. That **Yubugh Tayqan** [The One Who Paddled Around the World] shot it with an arrow and killed it. Then the people could portage over it.

"«They had a trail to **Sdak'dal'iy.** The ridge **Q'eyses** [Trail Ridge, 2.19] extends up to **Sdak'dal'iy**. There are no **nichił** there at **Sdak'dal'iy**. Right in the middle of that **Sdak'dal'iy** there is warm water. It don't freeze in the winter. The dogs can drink there.»"

Hooligan are said to run up the Yentna River as far as **Sdak'dal'iy**.

A map-making encounter in this area on May 26, 1898, between Spurr and Evan (Shem Pete's step-brother) seems to be the source of the Dena'ina names that appear on the 1900 Spurr map, such as "Mentaklit" and "Kohlsaat." See Map 24.

FIGURE 76

"The Susitna Chief," probably Evan Duyeq, Shem Pete's oldest stepbrother, in 1906.

Shem Pete: "At Susitna Station, my brother was a rich man. He was a storekeeper for seven or eight years. He was a rich man. His name was **Duyeq** [Chief Evan]. That was my brother. He was a big chief [from 1900 until 1910]. He didn't go broke. He was a rich man when he died. I was a big boy already when he died."

In the 1910 census it is moot as to which person is Chief Evan. A Chief Evan listed at Sustina Station is said to have been seventy years old in a family of six. The most likely person is a Big Evan listed as being forty-five in a family of four. There is also an Evan Longhair, age forty. Complicating the identification is a Chief Evan, age fifty-three on the roster for Alexander Creek village

PHOTO BY FREDERICK COOK

FIGURE 77

This is a cropped close-up of Fig. 64, the 1910 photo of the man in the baidarka on the Susitna River. The man bears a close resemblance in body and facial features to the man in the 1906 picture. Chief Evan is the prominent Dena'ina cultural broker from 1900 to 1910. He is mentioned in numerous historic sources from the mid-1890s until about 1910, and he was actively engaged in the travel and trade that took place in Susitna Dena'ina territory. We feel that this is the same man in both the 1906 and 1910 photos.

PHOTO BY F. H. ROJEC, USED WITH PERMISSION OF THE MAZAMAS, PORTLAND, OR., NEG. NO. VM1993.031.N002

Spurr (1950:22–3): "Resuming our upward struggle the next day, we met more Indians coming down the river from the hunt. There was Ivan, the brother of the Susitna chief, in his birch canoe, a strapping fellow with aquiline nose and shock of black bush hair. He drew a map for us and promised to come back after he had gone to the station with his furs, but he never did. Presently he was joined by another tall Indian, this time the chief's son-in-law. He had a skin boat with wood ribs which disgorged children of all sizes and many dogs. The tall Indian grinned and glared. He offered some beaver meat for some bread, but we could spare him none, so gave them a little tea, sugar, and flour and made them happy. My spectacles seemed to fascinate them."

§5.9 Tsaqent'u (revised spelling) • 'Beneath the Fire Rock'
high banks on the north side of the east side of the Yentna, two to three miles above the large bend
Shem Pete: "**Tsaqent'u** is a big bank. There are big hills on both side the creek."

5.10 Denyiht'u • 'Enclosed Canyon'
Moose Creek
Shem Pete: "«There are salmon there. They camped there for salmon.»"

§5.23 Ninatnu Kaq' • 'Slough River-Mouth'
lower mouth of Twenty Mile Slough

5.11 Ninatnu • 'Slough River'
Twenty Mile Slough
Shem Pete: "«That **Ninatnu** starts below **Bentalit** [5.21]. They come down it in one night. They paddle from the upriver end in one day.» They use that for bear hunting." This is Katherine Nicolie's former trapping area.

5.12 K'etnu • 'Creek'
Kutna Creek
Not a traditional Dena'ina place name, but the generic name for 'creek' which was interpreted by Herron (Map 22) as a place name "Cutnu" for the first creek from the west above **Sdak'dal'iy** (5.8). This was then placed on USGS maps on as a tributary of Twenty Mile Slough.

5.13 possibly **[Tsani Bes]** • possibly 'Cliff Riverbank'
"Cani Vus Banks" (on Herron, Map 22)
Shem Pete did not recognize this name. Herron located it just below the Kahiltna River on the east bank.

5.14 Kagheltnu Hdakaq' • ‡'Mouth of River That Flows from Upstream'
mouth of Kahiltna River
See 7.42–7.51 on the Kahiltna River drainage.

5.15 Jan Bughutnu • 'Horizon Creek'
Indian Creek
Herron lists this as "Jam-bod-i-nook Creek."

Shem Pete: "«We get to **Jan Bughutnu** by a trail from the Kahiltna. We paddle down it.»"

5.16 Nił'atesh'it'ut • 'Where Hills Come Together'
hills on Yentna River just below McDougall
Shem Pete: "This is on the west side below McDougall."

5.17 Hneh'itnu Kaq' • 'Upland Creek Mouth'
mouth of Lake Creek, McDougall
See 7.34–7.41 on the Lake Creek drainage.

Shem. Pete: "«Nickli [Nagley] had two stores at McDougall.»" The former community of McDougall is described by Cole (1983:83–84).

Sava Stephan: "McDougall, another one [trip] I did, McDougall to Susitna I come down on the ice, ice skate. They had mail. Airplane don't land there. I pack that mail up to McDougall and I came back down same day, about four hours round trip. Ice skate."

5.18 Ch'atanił'ut • 'Where Water Flows Out'
§*creek and bluff above McDougall (revised location)*
This name corresponds with Herron's "Chatlaknuk Creek" from the east between **Jan Bughutnu** (5.15) and **Bentalit** (5.21).

Katherine Nicolie: "There are lots of fish there. And lots of bear sign. I was scared all night when we camped there [in 1932]."

Shem Pete: "«There is a **nch'eł'eni** [Brush Man, or Woodsman figure] there out in the woods. When they paddle by there, it grabs them. It left a mark of three fingers on the side of the boat. They feared it. They pulled their boat ashore there. It is still alive now.»"

5.19 Tsaht'atnu • 'Beneath Rocks Creek'
creek above upper end of Twenty Mile Slough
Shem Pete: "«Nobody paddles there. There are rocks and rapids. They don't paddle there.»"

5.20 Bentalitnu • 'Creek of Flowing Lake Water'
Fish Lake Creek
Spurr (1900) (Map 24) records this as "Mentalik." It is called "Men-tal-ik Creek" on the 1901 Herron map (Map 22).

5.21 Bentalit • 'Where Lake Water Flows'
Fish Lake villages
Shem Pete: "«**Bentalit** is a series of connected lakes. A large number of salmon come out of there. When the ice goes out, they put nets in the water and catch salmon. They catch steelhead under the ice. They can save themselves [from starvation] quickly there.' From the mouth of **Bentalit** the **nichił** were just crowded together going upriver. There were lots of people there.»

"They got lots of smokehouses all over, way far up. Big Native village, used to be. They catch fish early there. A big bunch of Natives, they moved there in the springtime. Right after the ice pulled out. It was the one spot where they catch fish early. Lake after lake, all lined up a long ways. They fish the whole summer and fall. A lot of fish. They put fish traps between each of the lakes. They live on trout all winter. They catch red salmon and silver salmon up there, but they go down to the main [Yentna] river to catch king salmon. Before the Russians came,

there were lots of Indians there. No moose. I think about a hundred years ago moose came to this part of Alaska. All they know is caribou and bear. Not much meat [on a bear]. A little over a hundred pounds. That doesn't last long if there's lots of people. They hunted the bear all the time. They had good dogs for hunting. They stayed at **Bentalit** year round. Maybe five or six villages along that creek."

Shem Pete noted that when he was a child, people were still living here in spring and fall but not in winter. This was also a camping place on the journey from Susitna Station to Rainy Pass. This area is described in Fall (1981:387–388).

FIGURE 78

Inga Stephan, Sava Stephan, Anderson Stephan, Bobby Stephan, and Nellie Chickalusion on a late fall moose hunt on the Yentna River, perhaps at **Bentalit** (5.21), circa 1925.

Sava Stephan re: photograph at **Bentalit:** "I hardly remember that. My dad had three houses there. **Kagheltnu** [near Kahiltna river]. When I was about two years old my mom and dad used to stay up there with us."

PHOTO COURTESY OF ALEXANDRA ALLOWAN

Shem Pete, Dena'ina Singer and Composer

by Thomas F. Johnston

Shem Pete had a very large musical repertoire. He tape-recorded over seventy-five songs that represent a wide array of musical genres. As a lead singer, Shem was extremely imposing. When singing in a group he usually determined the sequence of songs, and in his colorful and didactic way, he called out the key words to be used in the subsequent verse. He was known to alter the mood of an entire evening by his choice of songs. After moving back to Tyonek in 1979, the Tyonek singers and dancers, under Shem's tutelage, expanded their repertoire to include many of the traditional songs of the Cook Inlet Dena'ina.

Lydia Hays wrote in 1989 for Shem Pete's potlatch: "Shem was talented in other ways. He knew many songs; he had audio-recorded over 75 songs for educational purposes on such subjects as medicine, dance, mourning, gambling, rowing and love. Of that number, at least ten songs are of his own composition.... They are Dena'ina culture through and through."

The late Thomas F. Johnston was an ethnomusicologist at the University of Alaska Fairbanks, who specialized in the analysis of Eskimo and Athabascan music. In his survey of the music of Alaska Natives, Johnston visited Tyonek and Kenai in 1976. In 1978 Johnston and Kari recorded Shem Pete singing a large portion of his song repertoire in Fairbanks. Johnston transcribed about a dozen of Shem Pete's songs. Johnston's 1979 article is a summary of Dena'ina music.

Every folk society has its spokesman, someone versed in tradition and in the channels of oral transmission which sustain that tradition. Shem Pete is not only a remarkable singer and one of the last carriers of that Dena'ina culture which has its roots in the precontact era, but also is a propagator and disseminator par excellence. The stories, songs, and compositions of Shem Pete set an extraordinary "literary" standard in the folklore and folkways of Alaska Natives, embodying the pathos, tragedy, and humor of a virile hunting society overtaken by the industrial age and the wage economy.

Shem Pete's songs feature twelve or fourteen bars of music repeated many times, carrying a basically unchanging songtext each time, although one noun or verb may change in spontaneous, improvised variation. The song texts are concerned mainly with respect for elders, achievements of forefathers, and the personal traits of revered kin; thus there are numerous kinship terms. Shem has composed songs for special occasions, such as the death of a chief.

Shem employs gradual pitch rise throughout the unfolding of a song, and this should be considered a form of musical development. Upward fourth leaps are common, but major second and third ascents and descents are even more common. Minor seconds are rare, as are the large scalar intervals. For emphasis, Shem frequently pushes a quarter note onto a following short eighth note ascending at a phrase, rather like the "e" sound at the end of lines of French poetry.

The microtonal melodies and irregular quarter note rhythms of his compositions are archetypical Athabascan and thus constitute a unique cultural code, a crystallization of Dena'ina musical values bearing shared emotional meaning for all of his people. In the songs of Shem Pete live ancient values of deference to elders and traditional kinship ties, affinity with the land, and oneness with wildlife. The human message is inerrantly matched to the rugged contours of his linear vocal melodies and to the sturdy rhythmic propulsion of his songs, which, together with the dance that they accompany, function at important social events to express Dena'ina-ness.

FIGURE 79

In a videotape made in 1979, "Talking Alaska, Dena'ina," Shem Pete and Billy Pete performed "Ada Beghuynisdi," the Chickalusion mourning song, ‡and Mike Alex's mourning song while Shem wore the Upper Inlet chiefs' regalia.

TABLE 11. DENA'INA TERMS FOR SONGS AND DANCES (‡ALSO SEE KARI 2007:302)

dance, lively potlatch dance	**k'ejesh**	love song	**k'q'ak'eliga**
he/she is dancing (fast lively)	**k'eljesh**	medicine song	**janja k'eliga** (UI) **janju k'elik a** (O)
dance, solo motion-style dance	**k'enduxi** (I), **nidush** (UO)	mountain song	**dghili k'eliga**
he/she is dancing solo, motion-style	**niyush**	mourning song	**chegh k'eli** **k'q'achegh k'eliga** (L) **yun'eh k'eli** (NL) **yunggedi k'eli** (U)
a type of dance (style uncertain)	**yutsedi** (Talkeetna)	potlatch song	**htitl' k'eliga**
masquerading during Orthodox Christmas holiday	**maskarada, maskalada**	protection song	**shesh k'eliga** **shesh k'eli** **na'uch'ehi** (O)
dancing staff	**qentsi tets'a** (U)	war song	**k'eghun k'eliga** (OUIl) **k'ughun k'eliga** (I)
feather headdress	**chijeł**	‡women's mountain squirrel song	**qunsha k'eliga**
song	**k'eli, k'eliga; k'elik'a** (O)	‡church songs	**silgu k'eliga**
refrain in song	**niqayday'uni** (U)	‡lullaby	**ch'q'ayna k'eliga**
he/she is singing	**k'deli**	‡rowing song	**taniłggadi k'eliga**
ancient song	**htsast'a k'eliga**	‡song within a story	**sukdu k'eliga**
dancing song	**ndux k'eli** (NL) **ndush k'eli** (OUIl) **k'enduxi k'eliga** (NL)		
gambling song	**ch'enlahi k'eliga**		

Ada Beghuynisdi
Her Dear Thoughts

By Shem Pete

Shem composed this song for a girlfriend in Tyonek in 1915 as he walked the trail between Tyonek and Susitna Station.

Bek'u nutayeshtnu ch'ghu shi Heł shnughelnik shi. Ada ada beghuynisdi. Ada.	*Because I am about to leave her,* *she remembers me in the evening.* *Dear, dear (precious), her thoughts,* *Dear one.*
Beghu iyeshchit ch'ghu shi Heł shnughelnik shi. Ada ada beghuynisdi. Ada.	*Because I am starting to love her,* *she remembers me in the evening.* *Dear, dear (precious), her thoughts,* *Dear one.*
Q'adanset ch'ghu shi Heł shnughelnik shi. Ada ada beghuynisdi. Ada.	*I just realized that* *she remembers me in the evening.* *Dear, dear (precious), her thoughts,* *Dear one.*

FIGURE 80 Music for love song.

MUSIC TRANSCRIPTION BY THOMAS F. JOHNSTON

Beɬ hnaghesht'ihi ch'ghu shi	*Since I used to play with her,*
Heɬ shnughelnik shi	*she remembers me in the evening.*
Ada ada beghuynisdi.	*Dear, dear (precious), her thoughts.*
Ada.	*Dear one.*
Beɬ dgheshnih ch'ghu shi	*Because I used to speak with her,*
Heɬ shnughelnik shi.	*she remembers me in the evening.*
Ada ada beghuynisdi.	*Dear, dear (precious), her thoughts,*
Ada.	*Dear one.*

Heyula

A Tyonek Dance Song

This lively dance song was first sung in Tyonek in about 1906. It is the best-known song of the Cook Inlet Dena'ina. There are no actual words in the song.

FIGURE 81 Music for "Heyula."

MUSIC TRANSCRIPTION BY THOMAS F. JOHNSTON

FIGURE 82

The Tyonek dancers in 1981. Back row: Bonnie McCord, Fedora Constantine, Billy Pete, Theodore (Chad) Chickalusion, Sergie Californsky; front row: Sava Stephan, Keith Constantine, Shem Pete.

Cole et al. (1985:23): "Shem Pete has also been teaching—history, songs, legends, dances—to a young generation of Dena'ina. 'He has told us "We're not going to be around forever," we have to learn these things now,' says Bonnie McCord, president of the village of Tyonek. 'This information will remain important to future generations of Alaskans, thanks to Shem Pete and others.'"

PHOTO BY ISAAC STEPHAN

FIGURE 83

Sergei Californsky, Shem Pete, and Maxim Chickalusion playing the Dena'ina hand game, **ch'enlahi,** in Tyonek 1980. The **ch'enlahi** game has four players in teams of two. One pair hides two sets of marked and unmarked sticks in their hands while singing a series of songs. The opposing team tries to guess for the set of unmarked sticks. If the guessing side guesses correctly, they win the point, and it is their turn to sing and to hide the sticks.

PHOTO BY PRISCILLA RUSSELL

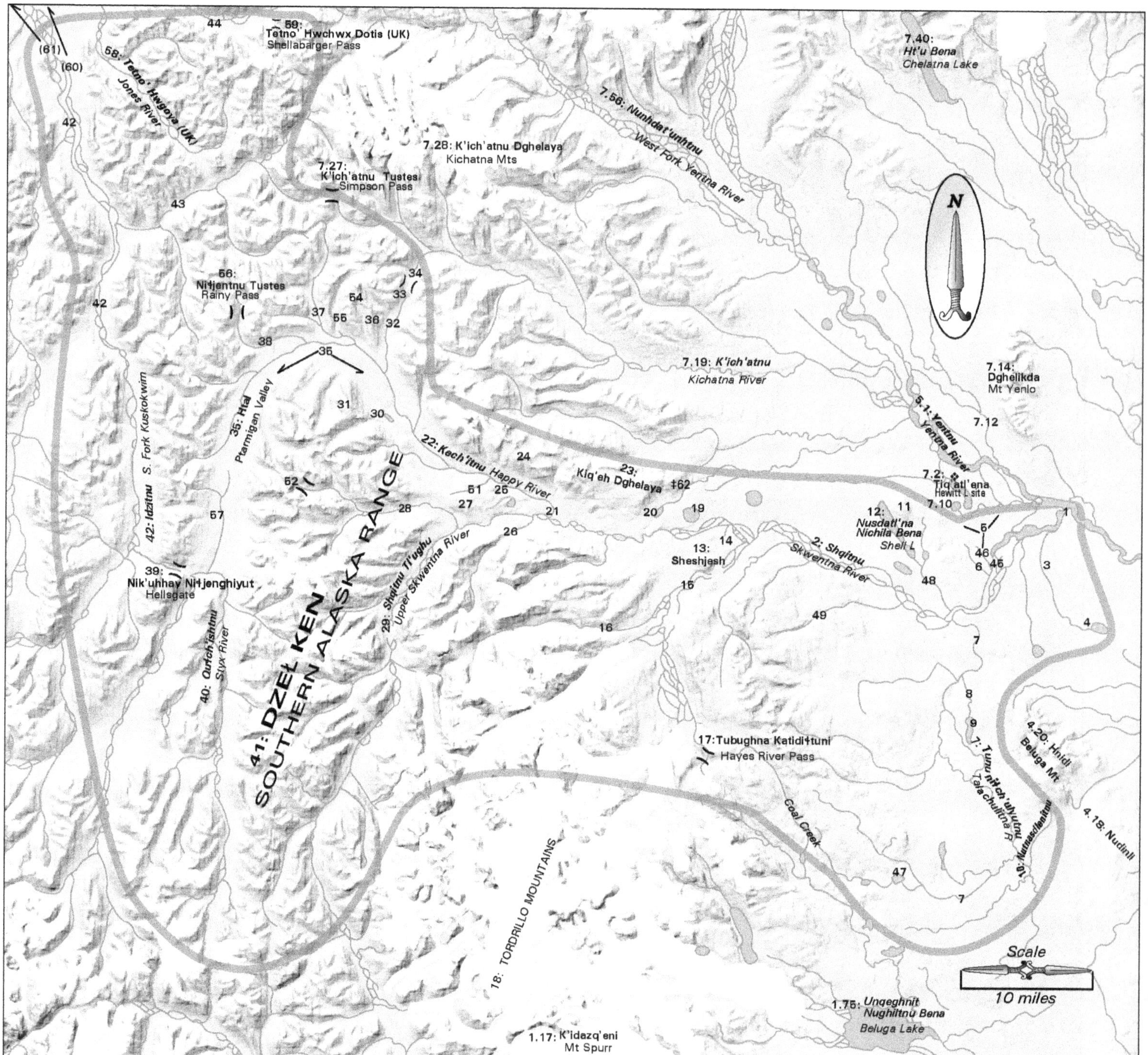

MAP 23

Place names map of the Skwentna River, showing Nos. 6.1 to 6.62.

MAP BY MATT GANLEY

6 Skwentna River to the Rainy Pass Area

6.1 Shqitnu Hdakaq' • ‡'-∞- River Mouth'
mouth of Skwentna River

6.2 Shqitnu • ‡'-∞- River'
Skwentna River
The word **shqit** appears in three widely separated Dena'ina place names. Its meaning is uncertain. ‡This could be a *substrate* place name from an unknown language; these are rare in the Dena'ina place name corpus. Also see Table 12, p. 147, and 16.18, p. 352. A translation of 'sloping ridge river' was once offered by Pete Bobby of Lime Village.

Sava Stephan: "We see seal all the way up to Skwentna. All the way up. We just shoot em. They go up with the salmon."

6.3 Ts'ahshlatnu • 'Little Sinew Creek'
Eightmile Creek
Shem Pete: "«Close to **Deldida Bena** [Alexander Lake, 4.23] is a creek that flows from **K'kuy'ingga** [4.21]. Its name is **Ts'ahshlatnu.**» "It's ten or twelve feet wide and full of fish. There were big **nichił** there."

Fall (1981:388) noted that there was a fish camp located here and that the stream has a good silver salmon run.

Sava Stephan, on his 1932 trip to Rainy Pass: "«At **Ts'ahshlatnu** we crossed a lake in a raft.» I thought to myself, 'I hope I don't get on that wooden raft no more.' Gee whiz, I lay down across that raft and go down, and I stand up like that. I was so scared. My dad don't care. He's paddling, and we were going across. I can even see the bottom. Rocks. I was about eleven years old. I been through there. «We started off on the raft. They had made a canoe too. We were going across, we were keeping toward shore. But we could not make it in the canoe. Then he made a raft.» Must a been a pretty big lake when they make a raft and go across. I hardly remember."

6.4 Ts'ahshlatnu Bena • 'Little Sinew Creek Lake'
Eightmile Lake

6.5 Kentuhdiłk'el Kena • 'Eroded Flat'
flat north of lower Skwentna River

§6.45 Q'ech'elt'at • possibly 'Changing'
portion of lower Skwentna River, about five miles above the mouth
This name was reported to Spurr in 1898, probably by Chief Evan. However, this name did *not* appear on Spurr's 1900 map (Map 24). The name is well known to Sava Stephan. The difficult passage through here prompted Josiah Spurr to write a ballad, "The Snag Flats of the Katcheltat" (Spurr 1950:37ABC).

§6.46 Q'ech'elt'atnu • possibly 'Changing Stream'
creek from north into Skwentna River

6.6 Kentuhdiłk'elt • 'Where Water Eroded the Flat'
creek into Skwentna River from north
Shem Pete: "«Here we pass close by **Tiq'atl'ena** [Hewitt Lake site, 7.2].»" A trail went from here toward the Hewitt Lake area.

6.7 Tununiłch'ulyutnu • 'River Where People Killed Each Other in Water'
Talachulitna River
Shem Pete: "There were three guys. Two were **Nulchina** and one was **K'kali**. They had a big war among each other. And the three of them—two brothers and one **K'kali**—got away some way or another. And they were going way up in that country. They only had one parka squirrel coat. They had just jumped out of the house and just took off out of the **nichił**. They got that far, to **Tununiłch'ulyutnu**. They only had one parka squirrel coat. There was three of them, and they took turns wearing that coat. And the two **Nulchina** got scared of that **K'kali**, because he was a 'champion.' And they told that **K'kali**, 'Give me that parka.' And when he was taking it off over his head, they

Sources: Shem Pete, Billy Pete, Sava Stephan, Miska Deaphon

2003 revisions: names added 6.45–61; location names revised 6.16, 6.24, 6.25, 6.36; spelling revised 6.44.
‡2016 revisions: name added 6.62; names revised 6.1, 6.2, 6.15, 6.17, 6.29, 6.42, 6.43, 6.61; figure deleted 92; map revised 25; map replaced 26.

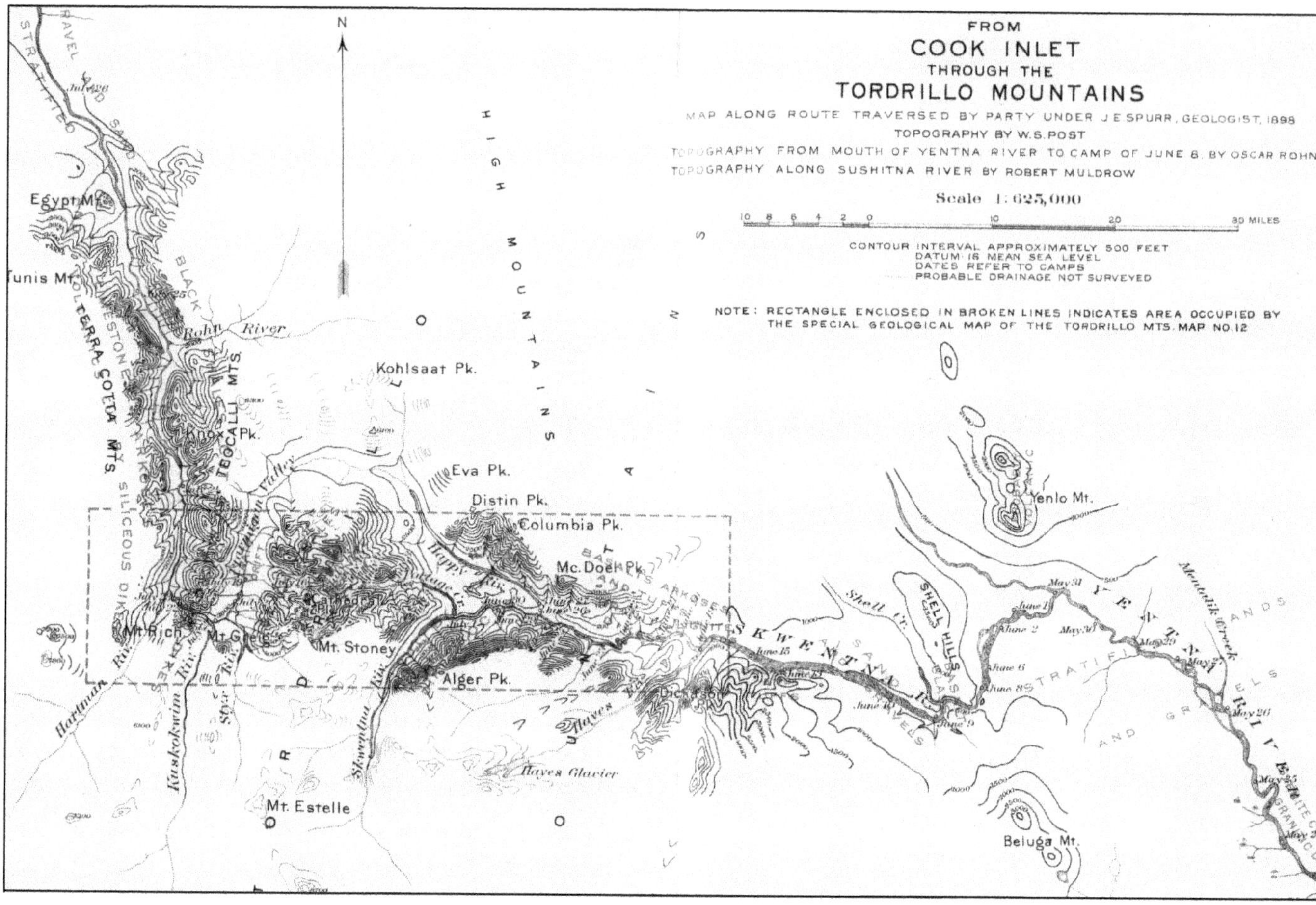

MAP 24

Detail from the 1898 Spurr map: Skwentna River to South Fork of Kuskokwim River.

Josiah Spurr, traveling without Dena'ina guides but following the Native trail in May–June of 1898, coined several names on the Yentna and Happy River drainages. Dena'ina-origin names, such as Mentalik, Yenlo, and possibly Kohlsaat, were apparently called for him by Chief Evan as he drew a sketch map on the lower Yentna River. See 5.8, and Figs. 76 and 77.

Spurr took the Happy River trail toward Rainy Pass in 1898, following the sketch map made by Chief Evan. Spurr (1900:102) wrote "One of the maps drawn by the Indians—the one which seemed the most likely—depicted the head of our stream, rising in swampy ground, with a low portage from it over to the opposing headwaters of the north-flowing drainage." It is interesting to compare Spurr's 1898 map with Herron's 1899 map; see Map 29, p. 155.

FIGURE 84

A winter view of **Tununiłch'ulyutnu Bena** (6.47, Judd Lake), at the head of the Talachulitna River. To the northeast in the distance is a nice view of **Hnidi** (4.20, Beluga Mountain). In the foreground is Coal Creek above Beluga Lake.

PHOTO COURTESY OF COOK INLET REGION, INC.

stabbed him in the back with a big knife. That's the time they got the name from. They killed each other at the mouth of that creek. So they called it **Tununiłch'ulyutnu.**

"Very deep water in this river. Around 1900 all the beaver froze to death because of cold winter. All streams froze except **Tununiłch'ulyutnu**. There the beaver lived and they came back from there. "«Salmon go up that river to **Bak'elghiłi Bena** [Hiline Lake, 6.9].»"

"There's a big waterfall [series of rapids] on that creek, near where it empties into the Skwentna River. There's a canyon and a waterfall there. They put skins on a pole and several guys would carry their stuff there—meat, skins, berries, grease. Then they could float home [down the Skwentna and Yentna] from there.

"Only one guy came down that waterfall with his skin boat. He was named Big Evan, **Evan Ka'a**, or **Anka'a**. He had his wife and kids with him. He always went up there, from his village on the lower Yentna River. He just got tired of packing his boat and supplies all down around the waterfall. So he just got in the **elgheji** [moose-skin boat]. He told his wife, 'If I don't come down, see that Beluga Mountain? You know the way we go. Take the kids. Pack lots of grub and go to the mouth of Alexander Creek.' «He got back in his skin boat and jumped over the waterfall. He made it. He was the only one who ever did that.»"

The 1911 Brooks map (Map 15) has this as "Talashulitna River" and in 1921 Hubback (1929:148) called this the "Chusalitna River."

6.8 Bak'elghiłi Betnu • 'Creek in Which Something Is Clubbed'
Hiline Lake outlet stream

6.9 Bak'elghiłi Bena • 'Lake in Which Something Is Clubbed'
Hiline Lake
Here the Alexander, Susitna, and Tyonek people fished for fall salmon and made fermented fish. Game was also abundant, and at nearby Beluga Mountain (4.20) the people hunted for bear, ground squirrel, and marmot. The Alexander people came north via **Nutnasdlenitnu** (6.10) or **Tununiłch'ulyutnu** (6.7) and returned with their food supplies via the Yentna River. The area seems to have been jointly used.

Billy Pete's grandmother (his mother's mother) dried and smoked silver salmon at this lake in the fall.

Shem Pete: "«That lake is full of silver salmon. There are **nichił** there. They dug big pits there for salmon. They clubbed the fish there.»"

Billy Pete: "There's always silver salmon come up to that

lake. They used to go to [Hiline] Lake. They used to take a club and club the fish" (from Fall and Greiser (1986)).

"«**Yagu** [Shem's mother's second husband] used to hunt bear at **Bak'elghili Bena**. He killed them from the water, wading in the water. He killed four or five every fall plus a hundred beaver. After fishing they would stay there two or three months.

"«One old man from Tyonek used to go there for brown bear, for the grease. He went there with thirty or forty **kilaqa** [helpers]. His helpers carried the grease to Susitna, and he got rich from it. He got killed. One time he had a muzzle-loader rigged as a bear trap [at Hiline Lake], and he was crawling around, and he accidentally shot and killed himself.»" The above story was told to Shem by Chief Pete of Tyonek.

§6.47 Tununiłch'ulyutnu Bena • 'Lake of River Where People Killed Each Other in Water'
Judd Lake

6.10 Nutnasdlenitnu • 'River That Flows Back Again'
uppermost fork of Talachulitna River from Beluga Mountain
The north-south flow of this stream, in contrast with the south-north flow of **Tununiłch'ulyutnu**, allowed for special options when traveling in this area.

Shem Pete: "«On the other side of **Hnidi** [Beluga Mountain, 4.20] is a creek that flows that way, toward the rising sun. It flows around **Hnidi** and flows back in an upriver direction. That is **Nutnasdlenitnu**. **Hnidi** is its headwaters.»

"The Susitna River people killed caribou and bear along **Nutnasdlenitnu**. They got lots of meat in that country. They reached that country overland along trails. But they caught too much there to pack it all back to their villages. So they used small **elgheji** [skin boats], maybe six feet wide by fifteen feet long, long shape, with round bottoms. They used raw caribou and moose hides to cover the frames. In the swift water, they steered with poles. So they came down the river in skin boats and brought back whatever they could use. They went all the way around by water, back down to the Susitna River. At this waterfall on the **Nutnasdlenitnu**, the people had to pack their belongings around. They packed the hides and frames around the waterfall and all the stuff they had with them—meats, skins, berries, and grease. Then they floated home from there."

The "Indian winter trail" on Herron's map (Map 22) extends from Tyonek up the Chuitt River to the Talachulitna River to the Skwentna River. Herron (1901:49): "My Suchitna Indians showed me the mountains Hatay [not known] and Sneedee [**Hnidi**, Beluga Mountain, 4.20] and acquainted me with the pass in between them. The Indian trail to Tyoonok runs through this pass. This pass adds to my route the advantage of a direct all-land connection to Tyoonok."

In 1902 the Brooks party traveled from Tyonek to the Alaska Range up the Theodore River and then into this drainage. Brooks noted that this trail was visible below the timberline (1911:17, Map 15). The 1903 Cook party also took this trail (Cook 1904, 1907). Another trail went to Tyonek via **Tahelitnu**, Drill Creek, and Beluga Lake (see 1.113).

6.11 Nusdatl'na Nichila • 'Ghosts' House'
Shell Hill
Shem Pete: "«At the head of **Tiq'atl'ena** [Hewitt Lake, 7.2] is a big hill, **Nusdatl'na Nichila**.»"

See Fig. 93, with Shell Hill in the distance beyond Hewitt Lake.

6.12 Nusdatl'na Nichila Bena • 'Ghosts' House Lake'
Shell Lake
The name of a mountain that Herron noted in this area on his 1901 map (Map 22), "Ton-ta-tin," is not recognized by today's Dena'ina speakers.

§6.48 Nusdatl'na Nichila Betnu • 'Ghosts' House Stream'
Shell Lake outlet stream

§6.49 Denyihtnu • 'Canyon Creek'
Canyon Creek
Name provided by Shem Pete in a text.

6.13 Sheshjesh • 'Saved,' 'Rescued'
Porcupine Butte
Shem Pete: "«On the downriver side of **Tubughna Katidiłtun** [Hayes River, 6.15], **Sheshjesh** sticks up sharply.» Nobody climb up on that though."

"«That is a good place for bear hunting.» There's lots of bears and porcupines on that hill, so when people get hungry, they go there."

6.14 Shesh Bena, Seshjesh Bena • 'Saved Lake'
Red Salmon Lake

6.15 Tubughna Katidiłtuni Betnu • 'River of Tyonek People's ‡Upriver Trail'
Hayes River
Beach (1931:153) noted that Indian Jimmie of Susitna Station got swamped near Hayes River in 1926.

6.16 Denyih T'u • 'Enclosed Canyon'
§Spring Creek into Hayes River (revised location).

6.17 Tubughna Katidiłtuni • 'Tyonek People's ‡Upriver Trail'
Hayes River Pass
See Plate 4. The name is significant as an indication of an important travel corridor for the Tyonek people to their caribou and Dall sheep hunting areas in the upper Skwentna River. ‡This trail name implies out-bound travel from Tyonek. In 1898 Glenn (1900:715) said that there was a "high trail with firm footing" used by the Indians between the mouth of the Skwentna River and Tyonek. No living Dena'ina have used this trail. The Chuitts were the last Tyonek people to use it, according to Shem Pete. On Herron's 1901 map (Map 22) "Indian winter trail" is the Tyonek to Talachulitna River trail via Lone Ridge. See 6.10 above and 1.65.

Dena'ina names on Herron's map in this area which

are not known today are "Ha-tay Mountain," "To-toy-lon Mountains," and "Ches-nic Mountains" (Map 22).

6.18 (no recorded name)
Tordrillo Mountains
This name was given by Spurr in 1898 to the general section of the Alaska Range from Hayes River through Portage Pass. For a time we thought this could be a Dena'ina-origin name with the word **dghelay** 'mountain.' The name "Tordrillo" is not recognized or used by Dena'ina speakers.

Rodman and Crews (1999:32–37) did extensive research on this name, examining Spurr's field notes. We concur with their conclusions; i.e., that Spurr probably misspelled a Spanish name "tordillo," meaning 'dark,' 'dun,' or 'dappled.' In Spanish this is also the name of a small, dull-colored thrush. There is no evidence to support the suggestion that the name was given at an earlier date by Spanish explorers.

FIGURE 85
"Pass over the Tordrillo Mountains." Photo-engraving by Josiah Spurr (1898:52).

6.19 Hnidi Bena • 'Upriver Lake'
lake, possibly Finger Lake
Shem Pete: "«**Hnidi Bena** is on the lower [river side] of **Kiq'eh Dghelaya** [6.23].»"

6.20 Kiq'eh Dghelaya Bena • 'Point Mountain Lake'
Red Lake

‡6.62 "Tontatin," [Tuntaytin] • 'Elongated Ridge That Extends to Water
ridge north of Red Lake
On the Herron map (see Map 29, p. 155) this is a plausible Dena'ina name that was not recognized by Shem Pete.

6.21 Kech'itnu Hdakaq' • 'Mouth of Feathers River'
mouth of Happy River

6.22 Kech'itnu *(Dena'ina)*, **‡Ts'ik'etno** *(Upper Kuskokwim)* • perhaps 'Feathers River'
Happy River
‡Mentioned twice by Miska Deaphon on a 1982 recording, apparently for Happy River. The UK name is noteworthy as is seems to be reshaped from Dena'ina **Kech'itnu.**

Shem Pete: "«We go to **Htal** [Rainy Pass-Ptarmigan Valley] on **Kech'itnu.** We cross the river holding onto a pole.» The strongest one puts the pole on his shoulder and gets in front. Pretty rough. Swift. «It is bad. The water comes up to their waists, and then flows up over their shoulders.» Jump right up, water so fast. «It is bad where they cross.»"

Ascending the Happy River on June 28, 1898, Spurr (1950:43) noted: "The river we were ascending till two days back—the Squentna of Katcheltat—ran on far into the alpine mountains of great height and ruggedness [looking to the upper Skwentna Canyon, 6.29], and the canyon on which we were camped ran twenty or thirty miles ahead into the same mountain range. Afterward we sighted another tributary of the Squentna, running into the mountains to the west, which I determined to try for passage into the Kuskokwim. Along this valley on the hillside we thought we saw the smoke of two fires. At first we decided to walk to them, supposing them to be the camps of Kuskokwim Indians, but as the sun was low now we thought we could not find them if we went. Away back on the mountain side above our camp a fire was burning, we thought must have been set by some Indian. While Madison and I were up in trees looking over the country, we thought we heard shots, which we concluded came from Indian hunters."

Shem Pete referring to the Spurr party: "When white man make trail, they had some Indians show them the only spot where they could get through. The white men were happy to find that pass. That's why I think they called that **Kech'itnu** 'Happy River.'"

Herron did not follow the Happy River trail in 1899, but it is marked "Indian winter trail" on his 1901 map (Map 29).

6.23 Kiq'eh Dghelaya • 'Point Mountain'
McDoel Mountain, or ridge elev. 3862' "Wolverine"
Shem Pete: "«Crossing there, there is **Kiq'eh Dghelaya**. From there the mountains extend in an upriver direction.» That's good trail, no hill. Lots of onion [wild chives, *Allium schoenoprasum*] there. I camped there at the edge of that point. It's an old camp from two, three hundred years ago."

6.24 Beq'e Nutistuni • 'The One with a Trail on It'
§Columbia Peak and surrounding ridges (revised location)
Shem Pete: "Pretty steep, that mountain. Almost touch your nose on that with a heavy pack."

The trail goes on the north side of the Happy River, on the slopes of this mountain.

6.25 Beq'e Nutistin Bena • 'Lake of the One with a Trail on It'
§Lake on Iditarod Trail above Shirley Lake (revised location)
Shem Pete: "All the time moose come into there. We catch moose there."

6.26 possibly **[Chik'a Qilantnu]** • 'Wood Is There River'
Chickak River
This may be "Chick-kaw-kay-lent-na River" on the Herron map (Map 29). This name is not known by today's speakers.

§(6.50) Łiteh Neli or **Łiteh Nelni** or **Nelni Betiy'uni** • 'Steambath Among Glaciers' or 'Steambath That Is Attached'
mountain on upper Skwentna River, location uncertain
A name recorded by Herron as "Cla-te-linich" and cited in Baker (1906:186, 371). Recalled by Sava Stephan: "I think they had a steambath at that place. **Nelni, nelni betiy'uni,** «a steambath. a steambath that is attached.» They called it that on **Shqitnu**."

6.27 Sandalyut • 'Where Objects Are Standing'
Long Lake Hills
Shem Pete: "«Those two standing together they call **Sandalyut**. Those rocks are about the same height. They are a man and wife side by side. She is turned downriver away from him. I saw that.»"

Nellie Chickalusion: "If they have good luck hunting, they move together. Or else they move apart. When they [hunters] pass by the rocks, they pay it something."

§6.51 Sandalyutnu • 'Objects Are Standing-Stream'
creek above Long Lake Hills into Happy River

6.28 Tus Nuch'k'elyashtnu • 'Stream of Where We Carry Things Through the Pass'
Portage Creek
On the return from Rainy Pass, the Dena'ina descended the Happy River, then portaged over to Portage Creek. It was at this point that the Dena'ina assembled skin boats and began their return trip down the Skwentna River. See Fall (1987:35).

Shem Pete: "«They made skin boats and departed. There is a big waterfall there [on Skwentna River near Portage Creek], and we shot down it. We went under the water and disappeared. They laughed that it was just like we died and we're still alive. Just that place is no good. We go into a canyon then we come out at **Kech'itnu** [Happy River, 6.22].»"

Sava Stephan discussed the river crossing in this area on the way to Rainy Pass in 1932: "They crossed the river. My dad packed. I packed just as much as my Dad. I was a small kid, on my back. He put that bag on top of another bag. My pack he put that on there. Then he make a pole about 16 feet long. Alec Nicoli is the biggest and the tallest. They go above, against the tide. Bobby is on the middle and my dad is the last. They put my pack on his pack, and he hold me over here. I walk in water all the way up to my neck. And then I pulled. And he hold my hand like this, and I float on my back and my dad is dragging me across. He dragged me all the way across the river."

§6.52 Tus Nuch'k'elyasht • 'Where We Carry Things Through the Pass'
Portage Pass
In 1898 the Spurr party crossed to the Kuskokwim drainage through Portage Pass off the upper Skwentna River (Spurr 1900:47–67). They were traveling without Native guides but were following sketch maps made by Susitna people they met at Susitna Station and on the lower Yentna River. Spurr and his party thought that they were the first white men to cross through this pass. Spurr noted "thanks to the Indian maps" they found this particular pass. See Map 24.

While on Portage Creek the Spurr party (1950:50) had the sense that they were being watched by Indians: "At night a fire started up on the opposite side of the

FIGURE 86

Looking down **Shqitnu Tl'u** (6. 29, the upper Skwentna River), just above Black and Tan Creek, in 1926. The mountain **Łiteh Nelni** 'steambath among glaciers' (6.50) may be in this part of the upper Skwentna River.

Capps (1935:34): "The Susitna natives formerly hunted in the upper Skwentna Basin, but for the last 30 years these expeditions have been given up." Capps (1929:78): "Occasionally a native family makes a hunting trip up the Skwentna, going up on foot and later descending the river in rough boats covered with the skins of animals killed during the hunt. Even such temporary visits have been rare in recent years."

STEPHEN R. CAPPS, JR. COLLECTION (#83-149-2412), ARCHIVES, ALASKA AND POLAR REGIONS DEPT., RASMUSON LIBRARY, UNIVERSITY OF ALASKA FAIRBANKS

FIGURE 87

Looking up **Shqitnu Tl'u** (6.29, the upper Skwentna River) from an elevation above Tumbling Creek in 1926.

Capps (1929:74): "The winters are said to be severe in the upper Skwentna Basin, and strong winds prevail, particularly near the mountain passes. It is reported to be difficult to keep trails open." Capps (1929:77): "The upper valley of the Skwentna River is so little visited by men, either white or native, that its animal life is almost undisturbed."

STEPHEN R. CAPPS, JR. COLLECTION (#83-149-2413), ARCHIVES, ALASKA AND POLAR REGIONS DEPT., RASMUSON LIBRARY, UNIVERSITY OF ALASKA FAIRBANKS

creek, in the place where we saw fire on our walking trip of four or five days before. It is probable that there were Indians there. But if there were any Indians in this whole country, we never saw them. It may be that these mysterious hunters, if any were there, saw us. I cannot solve this mystery, and indeed we did not think much about it."

Hubback (1929:182–3) wrote in August of 1921: "Porterage Creek [*sic*] is a small tributary of the Skwentna and no doubt obtained its name because there was an old trail from the Skwentna to the Kuskokwim over the divide between Porterage and the Styx."

6.29 Shqitnu Tl'u • ‡'-∞- River Headwaters'
upper Skwentna River
Shem Pete had no knowledge of Dena'ina people traveling up the Skwentna River and over to Chakachamna Lake.

When the Capps party surveyed and mapped the upper Skwentna in the summer of 1926, several newspaper articles appeared that claimed that this valley had, at that time, probably never been seen before by white men. *Anchorage Daily Times* (Sept. 18, 1926): "Mr. Capps saw several signs of natives but none of whites. Even the few signs of native camps were 20 or 30 years old."

6.30 Kech'itnu Bena or **Bendiltunt** • 'Feathers River Lake' or 'Where There Is a Lake'
Puntilla Lake
Somewhere in this area was a camp where the women would stay while the men went up further into the pass.

In this area an "Indian cabin" is marked on the right bank of Happy River on the 1910a Sleem map (Map 30).

In 1930 Beach (1931:175) noted that, "Pontella's cabin was so named from the trapper who originally built it. In the days when the pass was in use, the musher would stop at Puntella's and telephone to the pass for weather conditions, and when he started, Pontella would advise about the Pass." This implies that **Bendiltunt,** once suggested by Shem Pete, ‡was influenced by the actual name Puntilla.

6.31 Bak'nin'iy • 'Caribou Fence'
mountain, caribou fence, and village site possibly north of Puntilla Mountain
Shem Pete: "**Bak'nin'iy**, that's a high mountain. Nobody can climb that mountain. Above there is the pass. That's a big village, used to be. I don't know how many miles that fence they make for caribou. About ten miles pretty near. «From the one they call 'caribou fence' I don't know how many miles it is to 'updraft stream,' (6.40) straight across. It might be four or five miles. Up to there they put poles together and they made a big fence. It went right up against 'caribou fence mountain.'»" This was a major caribou hunting site. The Upper Inlet Dena'ina caribou fence is described in Osgood 1937:33.

6.32 Chuqitnu • 'Beaver Lodge Creek'
Moose Creek
From here the trail comes to **Htal** [Ptarmigan Valley].

Shem Pete: "Lots of fox up there. When the sun shines you can't breathe because of the stink [of the fox droppings]."

6.33 Ch'dat'ana Bena • 'Grayling Lake'
Moose Creek Lake
Shem Pete described approaching here from the Kichatna River [7.19]: "«Up the canyon of the **K'its'atnu** on a ridge there is a lake. It is called **Ch'dat'ana Bena**. As a boy I went there.»"

6.34 Chuqitnu Tustes • 'Beaver Lodge Creek - Pass'
pass from Moose Creek to upper Kichatna River
Shem Pete: "«**Chuqitnu** has a trail over a pass.»"

§(6.53) Qunsha Betnu • 'Arctic Ground Squirrel Lake'
creek in this area on right side going up
Name recalled by Sava Stephan.

FIGURE 88

A view of the upper Skwentna River (6.29) with a caribou in 1926.
STEPHEN R. CAPPS, JR. COLLECTION (#83-149-2429), ARCHIVES, ALASKA AND POLAR REGIONS DEPT., RASMUSON LIBRARY, UNIVERSITY OF ALASKA FAIRBANKS

6.35 Htal *(Dena'ina);* **Hwtal** *(Upper Kuskokwim)* • 'Wide Place'
Ptarmigan Valley and the Rainy Pass area
The term **Htal** applies to the long wide valley known as Ptarmigan Valley. It has been the custom of Shem Pete and others to refer to **Htal** in English as "Rainy Pass."

Shem Pete: "«From **Bak'nin'iy** to Ptarmigan Pass (6.39) there was a village.» There were many people there, lots of people. Nobody knows how many thousand Natives that catch caribou there. Not much timber there. "«It does not snow much, and there are lots of caribou there.»

"The people there they call **Shandała Nununk'- dnelghuyna** ['People Who Cause the Migrating Birds to Fall by Hollering']. Those geese when fly over, fall time, they all holler. Maybe geese go up twenty or thirty miles. **Nichił** is just up close, all along that river I guess. They make scare the geese. They holler for miles, and the geese they get all scared. Pretty soon they just get tired, and they fall down. They pick 'em up. They eat 'em up too. Of course. Yeah. Good geese. I wouldn't let 'em go. **Shandała Nununk'dnelghuyna**, they were year-round citizens up there."

These people maintained caribou fences and specialized in hunting. Shem Pete has remarked, "They don't know where they come from, but they talked Dena'ina." These people do not fit into the clan origin stories that Shem knows. See further discussion on pp. 144–146.

In the Susitna prophecy story, Shem Pete's uncle instructed people to return to **Htal** to live off the land after the white people are forced to leave Alaska (Pete 1975, and pp. 96–98).

6.36 K'eghunagga • 'Little Ridge' or 'Little Hump'
mountain on north or west side of Rainy Pass, possibly ridge extending south from Kohlsaat Peak (revised location)
Shem Pete: "On the west, right hand side is the biggest mountain. It looks like a moose's back. «I don't know the English name. There is a cave there. Two guys came there, and they saw an animal. They say that there are ground squirrels as big as a brown bears. It is like a bench there and they were laying on it. That guy came out and told about it, and he was all out of breath. It is still there, on the right hand side of **Htal**. It is really dark there. When they crawled inside, they saw it. "This happened not long ago. It is still sitting there. It is upstream at **Htal** 'wide place' on the right hand side. It is straight across there, and it looks like a real true [ground squirrel] fur coat.» [It is] just straight up and down «there across from the river bar. Also the next place upstream they would climb up and look for game.» I know exactly where it is. «I know that place.»"

§6.54 Qułtsadi • possibly 'That Which Is Pounding (hammering) Upward'
Kohlsaat Peak
The name Kohlsaat first appears on the map in Spurr 1900 (Map 24). However, this name is listed in Orth 1971:536 as a "local name reported in 1958." The name may have been called for Spurr by Chief Evan when they drew a map from the vantage point of the lower Yentna River. Shem Pete did not recognize the name. Sava Stephan confirmed the name as given here, adding that he heard Bobby Stephan mention it. However, William Bright (personal communication) points out that *kohlsaat* in German means "cabbage seed," and perhaps this name was simply coined by Spurr and his group.

§6.55 Qułtsaditnu • 'Stream of That Which Is Pounding (hammering) Upward'
stream off Kohlsaat Peak

FIGURE 89

Htal (6.35, Ptarmigan Valley) near **Niłjentnu Tustes** (6.56, Rainy Pass) in 1926.

STEPHEN R. CAPPS, JR. COLLECTION (#83-149-2471), ARCHIVES, ALASKA AND POLAR REGIONS DEPT., RASMUSON LIBRARY, UNIVERSITY OF ALASKA FAIRBANKS

6.37 Chish T'el'iht • 'Where Ochre Is Gathered'
possibly Threemile Creek
Shem Pete: "«On the slope of **K'eghunagga** there is ochre. There is a creek running through. **Chish tl'ech'a** ['blue ochre' (cinnabar)] is there.» Just like rubber. You cut in there and quicksilver shoots out."

Shem Pete: "**Chish** [red ochre] was obtained in the Rainy Pass area. They took only half a teaspoon full and put it just like oil in a moose skin bag. It dried and turned black. They sold it all over to up north people."

6.38 Niłjentnu *(Dena'ina)*; **Nełdzin No'** *(Upper Kuskokwim)* • 'Pass Creek'
Pass Creek
The trail through Rainy Pass goes here. This route was first mapped in 1902 by A. H. Brooks who coined the name Rainy Pass. Brooks (1911:18) wrote: "At length we reached the headwaters of the river, and on July 12, in a dense fog, we crossed a pass, expecting to find the Kuskokwim waters beyond; but on the following day the stream that we were descending proved to be still on the coast side of the divide. Here the killing of a moose provided a welcome change of diet, and for two months thereafter we were almost always able to procure fresh meat. Before a route could be chosen from this point it was necessary to reconnoiter. Three men spent a day and the greater part of a night exploring in different directions, and at length found a pass which had long been used by the natives as a route between the Kuskokwim basin and the Cook Inlet region. Rainy Pass, as we called our new discovery, lies to the south of Simpson Pass discovered by Herron. It has an altitude of about 2,950 feet and undoubtedly affords opportunity of piercing the southern part of the Alaska Range. This region appeared to abound in white Alaskan [Dall] sheep."

§6.56 Niłjentnu Tustes *(Dena'ina)*, **‡Nełts'in** *(Upper Kuskokwim)* • 'Pass Creek Pass'
Rainy Pass
Mentioned by Miska Deaphon on a 1982 recording.

§6.57 Htal Betnu • 'Wide Area Stream'
Ptarmigan Creek

6.39 Nik'uhhay Niłjenghiyut • 'Where Nik'uhhay [Nikolai] Went Through the Pass'
Hellsgate, called by Shem Pete "Ptarmigan Pass"
Shem Pete: "That's the first man make a pass there. He was an Iditarod Indian. «The **Gheltsana** [Upper Kuskokwim Athabascans] did not come across the pass. The one they call **Nik'uhhay** went through there. And they call it **Nik'uhhay Niłjenghiyut.**» That was a little while after the Russians come, because they called him Nikolai already." It is interesting that Shem could estimate this date and that the person who came through this pass was an "Iditarod Indian."

This is one of the only Dena'ina place names that is based upon a personal name.

Shem Pete: "On the left-hand side there is a valley [location uncertain]. It's like sunshine there all the time, even at midnight. It's a rock. That's radium. They afraid to go over there. My father stopped his kids from going over there. I know where that cut is." Six years earlier, before Shem was there, it was covered in a rockslide.

6.40 Qułch'ishtnu • 'Updraft River'
Styx River
Shem Pete: "«The Susitna people would say 'wind blows upward.' It is windy there all the time. 'Updraft stream' is on the upstream side of **Htal.** It is a really big level place. The river bar there is really flat. The Americans did not know the area upstream of **Htal.** The people of long ago came there, a person of long ago came there. They would see game animals there.»" This is the last in the sequence of names that Shem Pete called through here.

The location of this place name is speculative, but we assume that Shem Pete in his travels reached a stream into the South Fork drainage. From Hubback's 1921 account (below) we find that Dena'ina were still using the lower Styx River in the 1920s. It is also interesting that Shem Pete stated that the Americans did not know

Htal—the 1932 Trip to Rainy Pass

by Sava Stephan

Sava Stephan went on a caribou hunting trip to Rainy Pass in the fall of 1932. He was then twelve years old. He was with his father Anderson Stephan, his uncle Bobby Stephan, and his grandfather Alec Nikolai. The following short story was dictated by Sava Stephan in 1979 and appeared in Kari 1980:23–24.

Htalch' q'angheshduk shi shcheyakda eł.
I went to Rainy Pass with my grandfather [Alec Nikolai].

Qelun ts'ełq'i uq'edi heyi shi.
I was eleven [twelve] years old.

Yeh q'anch'udeł. Yentnu hkach'dghinik.
We walked around there. We went up the Yentna River in a boat.

Chada shch' quynghiyet ghenuy gga.
Grandfather chased a small caribou up towards me.

Shihdi beda igheshten.
I held on to its horns.

Niqaghelqełi gheshtił.
I was carrying a pistol.

Nch'u k'dełteł.
It did not fire.

Ghenuy ghinihdi shtunuhudalt'eq'.
That caribou ran off.

Beda yan igheshten.
I was just holding its horns.

Further comments by Sava on the 1932 trip to Rainy Pass. See also 6.3 and 6.28 for other anecdotes by Sava from this trip.

"Trail was going up. We got on that trail and come down. There were caribou. My dad sit down and he shoot one caribou. And that caribou just stared at us, standing one place. Staring at us. He gonna hurt us. We start walking away, and we hide [behind] stumps and stuff. And that thing there looked just like caribou. Then he got back on line. Soon as he got to the line, he goes up on top the mountain. Part of it (the caribou herd) was down the hill, at the foot of the hill. The caribou [herd] end was down the foot of the hill, and the top of the caribou [herd] was on top the hill, over the mountain. It [the herd] was that long. So that might be about 500 or 600 caribou in Rainy Pass. My dad shoot at one caribou. Said he might hurt us so we quit. Soon as he said that caribou jumped right back up in line and go up the hill.

"First caribou I seen I thought they were crazy. [I was with] Old Bobby Stephan, and Alec Nickolai and my dad. They shoot at that caribou, the biggest caribou, they call it **nin'ijuy.** Old caribou, big as a moose. They shoot and shoot. And then they cripple it. He got a horns about that long. They hang on to it. And old Bobby and my dad and Alec Nikolai they got on top of it. His knife is about that long. And he took it out, and he cut his horn. Soon as he hit it my dad flew about ten feet away from him. That caribou just shook him like this and he flew. I thought they were crazy. They crippled it, and then they try to kill it with knife. I had no place to hide. No stumps, nothing in the mountain. They kill it anyway, and I was glad. I was pretty good size boy, about fourteen years old [*sic*, SS was twelve years old]. I was packing. More than my dad. Whatever he got I pick it up and put it in my packsack.

"I think about that all the time. I wish I had been a little bigger and a little older than that."

FIGURE 90

A drawing illustrating Sava Stephan's story by Leonard Savage, from the first printing of this story (Kari 1980).

COURTESY OF THE NATIONAL BILINGUAL MATERIALS DEVELOPMENT CENTER

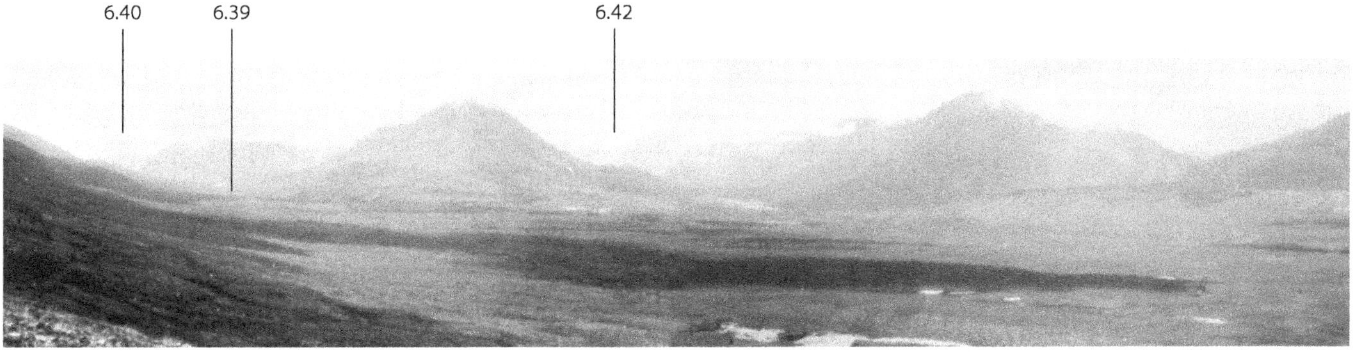

FIGURE 91

The south end of Ptarmigan Valley past Rainy Pass, in the Ptarmigan Creek drainage **Htal Betnu** (6.57) in 1926. The valley in the distance to the left is **Nik'uhhay Niłjenghiyut** (6.39, Hellsgate), and beyond this is the lower valley of **Qułch'ishtnu** (6.40, Styx River) and **Idzitnu** (6.42, the South Fork of the Kuskokwim River).

STEPHEN R. CAPPS, JR. COLLECTION (#83-149-2467), ARCHIVES, ALASKA AND POLAR REGIONS DEPT., RASMUSON LIBRARY, UNIVERSITY OF ALASKA FAIRBANKS

beyond Ptarmigan Valley; i.e., there were areas beyond the Iditarod Trail traffic that the Dena'ina still regarded as their hunting country.

When the Spurr party crossed through Ptarmigan Valley on July 18, 1898, on their first day descending a Kuskokwim drainage, just above the junction of the Styx River with Ptarmigan Creek, Spurr (1950:58–59) wrote: "The next day in the afternoon I was able to bestir myself, and discovered a well-marked Indian trail following down above the stream." On July 21 Spurr noted: "At the end of the Indian trail, where we had camped, there had been an extensive and long-established Indian camp. There was a banya, or log sweat-bath house, and I found a pair of fine [Dall] mountain-sheep horns which had been chipped as if to make spear-heads. I still have these. On the portage trail which led to this camp we found comparatively fresh mocassin tracks.... We had not seen even an Indian since the 30th of May.

"The Indians who had been hunting in the region of this pass and who had remained a long time in the camp which we found, had probably had a winter camp here and had left the country at the time of the break-up or soon before, having come up when all was frozen and hard. They were evidently Kuskokwim Indians."

Writing in 1921 Hubback (1929:182–83) described what is the most westerly documentation of an Upper Inlet Dena'ina hunting party, on the Styx River in the Kuskokwim drainage, in the early twentieth century. Hubback wrote: "Our camp was 3000 feet above sea-level. In the evening we saw about three miles from us, at the mouth of a canyon, a wisp of smoke. We knew that there were no prospectors in that part of the country, and we suspected that some Indians whom we had seen on the Skwentna River, and who stated that they were going up to the headwaters of the Skwentna to hunt for their winter moose meat, might have found their way into the canyon, which we believed, and afterwards found correct, provided a pass into Porterage Creek from the valley of the Styx....

"We found out subsequently that they had killed some dozens of young caribou; in fact, we saw evidence of the destruction of two small caribou, where merely the skins had been taken and the meat left. In one place we found a pile of meat and close to this meat were the udders of a young cow caribou. Possibly the udders had been cut out to destroy the identity of the sex of the skin should any questions be asked. The Indians killed these caribou, specially selecting females and young, because they wished to utilize the skins for snowshoe webbing. I understand that the thicker hides of the older animals are not so suitable; possibly are not so easy to prepare for the purpose for which the Indians take the skins."

6.41 Dzeł Ken • 'Mountain Base'
The Alaska Range, especially the southern Alaska Range
‡Both 6.41 and 6.42 are on Table 12, see discussion on p. 146. This regional name is most commonly used in the Lime Village and Lake Clark areas. Note that Brooks incorrectly stated, "It [the Alaska Range] does not seem to have been named, for the Alaska Indian has no fixed geographical nomenclature for the larger geographic features" (1911:22).

6.42 Idzitnu *(U-Dena'ina)*, **‡Izitnu** *(I-Dena'ina)*; **‡Edze No'** *(Upper Kuskokwim)* • '-Ω-River'
South Fork of Kuskokwim River
‡In the 1987 and 2003 editions we neglected to cite significant differences between the Upper Inlet, Inland Dena'ina and Upper Kuskokwim names for the South Fork of the Kuskokwim River. The Upper Inlet and Upper Kuskokwim forms use high front vowels **-i-** (UK **-e-**) and the consonant **-dz-**, but the Inland Dena'ina name has **-z-**. The name is a classic example of an opaque (**Ω**) Dene place name. All three forms are ambiguous and are not readily translated by expert speakers or linguists. This is an archaic Dene hyronymn. The name recorded by Herron in 1900 as "Echeatnu" corresponds with U-Dena'ina **Idzitnu.**

In 1844 the Russian explorer Zagoskin wrote, "The Kenai [Dena'ina] people travel on the winter trail to meet the Ttychannanika [Kuskokwim River, see 6.52 below] natives who for their part assemble to trade with them at the place called Itstsynno [South Fork of the Kuskokwim]" (1967:272).

6.43 ‡[Duditnu] *(Dena'ina),* **[Dode No']** *(Upper Kuskokwim)* • 'Downriver River'
‡Tatina River, locally "Rohn River"
‡The Herron party crossed through Simpson Pass on July 23, 1899 (Herron 1901:34). Currently "Rohn River" is the locally used name for this stream (Ray Collins p.c.); Rohn River was named by Spurr in 1898 for geologist Oscar Rohn. Kari now thinks that the UK name "Tateno" was told to Herron by Chief Sesui. The reconstructed name 'downriver river' is plausible. However, neither Shem Pete nor Upper Kuskokwim experts such as Bobby Esai recognize a name similar to "Tateno."

Herron (1901:35) commented, "The Indians knew very little about the country beyond the divide, by reason of their territory, and hunting, trapping, and fishing grounds were restricted, by the oldest traditions and customs among the tribes, to the country east of the divide." On July 28th just above Egypt Mountain Herron's guides told him that they knew the country no further, and they went back home to Susitna. The Herron party subsequently had much difficulty. They were later rescued by Chief Sesui of the Telida band of the Upper Kuskokwim people.

‡Two sites with hearths, bone and lithics on the lower Tatina River were found along the Donlin Gold pipeline corridor. The site MCG-0060 dates from ca. 4500 BP and MCG-0057 dates from ca. 4300 BP. These are recommended for further work (US Army Corps of Engineers 2015: 3.20:20).

§6.58 Tetno' Hwgoya *(Upper Kuskokwim)* • via Dena'ina 'Little Water River'
Jones River
‡This name and 6.44 have the Dena'ina syllable for water, **ti-** (UK **te-**) instead of UK **tu**. This fact plus **-tno'**, indicate that these two stream names were first named by Dena'ina speakers.

6.44 Tetno' Hwchwh *(Upper Kuskokwim)* • via Dena'ina 'Big Water River'
Dillinger River
Herron named this stream Dillinger for one member of his party, and he did not record a Native name for this stream (See Map 29).

Collins (2000) has the following account by Miska Deaphon of the 'people in the mountain' at a hill east of the Dillinger River called **Ts'enan Naz'one** (also in Kari 1999:95).

"Up there is the mountain they call **Ts'enan Naz'one.** On the west side of that one out there a small mountain sticks out. They walked up to that one. They used to say there were **Dził ye Hwt'ana** (Hill-People) inside that mountain. They came to a place they called the "doorway" of the Hill People's home. Then whatever they are carrying in their packs–dry fish eggs or dry fish–everyone takes some from their packs. They would put a little piece of that dry fish or fish eggs in the place they call the Hill-People's doorway. Then they would talk to them and say, 'In return for whatever you people use of this you will help people, because this is what we have down below and here we are giving it to you to eat.' Then they would put those things in the doorway. They named the things that are around there also—caribou, sheep, black bear, moose and porcupine. 'You will help people with these things,' they said, and then they put the things in there."

§6.59 Tetno' Hwchwh Dotis *(Upper Kuskokwim)* • 'Big Water River-Pass'
Shellabarger Pass (see Plate 7 and Fig. 98)
The Upper Kuskokwim place name for Shellabarger Pass from the Dillinger River to the West Fork of the Yentna is **Tetno' Hwchwh Dotis** (Kari 1999:95). Upper Kuskokwim people state that Susitna Dena'ina ventured west of the Alaska Range to hunt sheep on occasion, either through Rainy Pass, Simpson Pass, or Shellabarger Pass.

§6.60 Toy'draya' *(Upper Kuskokwim)* • 'Water Heart'
Egypt Mountain, (not shown on Map 23 but see Maps 24, 29, and 30)
Upper Kuskokwim Athabascans have, in recent years, recorded stories and place names from the South Fork area (Schneider, Gudgel-Holmes, and Dalle-Molle 1984:15; Collins 1985, 2000; Kari 1999). Mishka Deaphon of Nikolai had gone up the Post River as far as Post Lake and was familiar with the Rainy Pass country. Several of the names he knew coincided with those reported by Shem Pete.

There are several sources concerning Dena'ina trade and hunting west of the range in the historic period. Mishka Deaphon and Bobby Esai of Nikolai have identified Egypt Mountain on the South Fork, **Toy'draya'** in their language, as the place where Susitna Dena'ina came to trade with the Upper Kuskokwim or to hunt sheep (Collins 1985:362, Kari 1999:95, Collins 2000). Hosley (1966b:42–43) adds more details on Dena'ina activities west of the Range, summarizing from Zagoskin:

Zagoskin related that in 1842 the Kinaytz (Tanaina) began traveling into the headwaters of the Kuskokwim across the Alaska Range, thereby reducing the fur trade at Kolmakov Redoubt by over one-third. The Tanaina were acting as agents of the Redoubt of Nicholaevsky on Cook Inlet (Zagoskin 1847:MS.118). Again in 1844, Zagoskin mentions meeting natives from the upper Kuskokwim who were traveling to the mouth of the Holitna for the purpose of informing the administrator that the natives would not be coming down river to trade "as they had already sold their fur to the Kenay toen [chief] 'Kusloma' who came by orders from Nicholaesky Redoubt" (Op. cit., p.130). And still later he notes that the "Kenaytz natives at winter time by the Togtigchatno creek (South Fork of the Kuskokwim [JK: actually the Middle Fork and Windy Fork of Big River, in UK **Tohwdechoh No'**]) make their trips in upper place [probably Rainy Pass] to the Ttigannanik [6.61 **Dichina Nek'a** UK] people, who also come for trade with them to the meeting place which is called Itz-tzino (6.42 UK **Edze No'**), which lies close to the mouth of the Togtigchagno" (Zagoskin 1847:MS133). See also Shem Pete's (1977) account of the Dena'ina **qeshqa**, **Diqelas Tukda,** who traveled with his uncle from Alexander Creek village to the Kuskokwim River trade with the **gheltsana**.

Collins (2004): "Miska Deaphon told of people meeting some Tanaina Athabascans who were hunting sheep near Farewell. They related that the American people had opened a trading post at Sustina Station on the Cook Inlet of the Alaska Range. Later that winter people from Nikolai walked over to the store. They went through Rainy Pass pulling sleds on which they carried mink, beaver and marten skins. These were traded for about fifty cents each and they purchased their first .30-30 rifles, some ammunition and pilot bread (M. Deaphon, personal communication)." Upper Kuskokwim people continued to travel to the store at Susitna Station until about 1918. Shem Pete remembered the long-haired **gheltsana** visiting at Susitna Station. Shem learned a few of the songs that he sings from the **gheltsana**. See also Pulu (1975:32) and Fall (1987:18–19, 48–52).

§6.61 Dichina Nek' *(Upper Kuskokwim)*; **Kenaniq'** *(Dena'ina)* • 'Timbered River'
Kuskokwim River (not shown on Map 23)

The Dena'ina name is from speakers at Lime Village. Shem Pete did not know this Dena'ina name for the Kuskokwim River.

‡As of 2015 there are 810 recorded Upper Kuskokwim place names (Kari 2015). There is evidence that Dena'ina occupied some of UK territory and that Dena'ina place names were coined earlier than those in Upper Kuskokwim. Typically UK has the stem **no'** for 'stream' whereas Dena'ina stream names always have **-tnu**, with a distinctive **t-**. There are about ten names with **-tno'** reported by UK speakers: **Tsalatno'** Selatna River, **Tochotno'** Tokotna River as well as **Tetno'** Jones River (6.58) and Dillinger River (6.44). It appears that in early times Dena'ina bands had territory north to the South Fork of the Kuskokwim.

‡In the fall of 2014 anthropologist Ray Collins of McGrath established an archival collection at the Alaska Native Language Center/Archive of his Upper Kuskokwim notes and recordings which date from1963. Highly significant is a group of 31 recordings made by Chief Miska Deaphon (1903–1984) of Nikolai. In 1980–81 Deaphon self-recorded his own memoirs. These texts are monolingual, slowly paced, and feature detailed accounts about hunting, wildlife, places, and trails throughout the UK language area. The Deaphon audio collection has perhaps best land use narratives for any Alaska Native language.

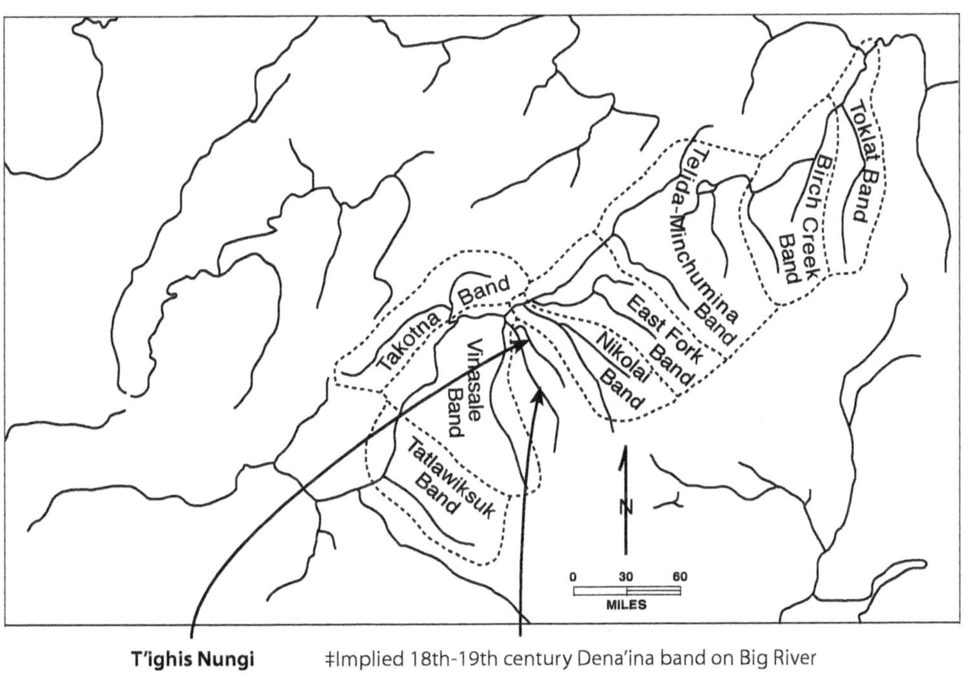

MAP 25

Aboriginal band distributions for the Upper Kuskokwim-Kantishna river drainages.

Hosley (1966a: 87–89) and Collins (2004:41–42) present information about a Dena'ina "strong man" who had a fortified village on the Windy Fork of the Big River at **T'ighis Nungi** (UK name) in the early 19th century. After some hostilities, Upper Kuskokwim men conducted a raid, killing several people and driving them out of Big River.

AFTER EDWARD HOSLEY 1966A:86

‡Introducing the Proto-Dene *Lex Loci* with Selected Dene Place Names South and West of the Alaska Range

by James Kari

For further study on PDLL refer to discussions and examples on pages xii, 14, 39, 141, 154, 214–215, 217, 221–222, 227–229, and 309.

Since 2010 I have been taking notes and lecturing on a theory of Dene prehistory I call the "Proto-Dene *Lex Loci*" ('word/law of location,' or PDLL). This theory is based upon historical linguistic inferences from place name networks and other linguistic patterns from contiguous Alaska Dene languages. With this article, Table 12-ABC (three groups of place names selected for their traits of significance), and with annotations and cross-references to entries in *SPA*, we can provide a brief introduction to the PDLL.

The PDLL was prompted by the Dene-Yenseian Hypothesis. Edward Vajda's 2010 article presented grammatical and lexical evidence that the Na-Dene languages of North America are genetically related to Ket and other extinct Yeniseian languages of western Siberia. The symposium volume (Kari and Potter 2010) provided discussions and initial scientific support that a Dene-Yenseian language stock was located in Beringia, c. 14,000–15,000 yrs. ago. One consequence of the DY language stock is that Proto-Na-Dene must have been in Alaska by 12,000–14,000 BP. For background reading see Kari 2010b that discusses the *geolinguistic conservatism* of the Dene (or Athabascan) language family, and a "slow chronology" for the Na-Dene in Northwest North America, with Tlingit and Eyak branching off at early dates from the other Dene languages.

The PDLL theory has accelerated in the past ten years with advances in place names coverage for eight contiguous Dene languages surrounding the Alaska Range (Ahtna, Dena'ina, Upper Kuskokwim, Upper Koyukon, Lower Tanana, Middle Tanana, Tanacross, Upper Tanana); there are nearly 9,000 names on record in similar database formats. (See p. 232, re: a database field "match" that tags names of significance.)

We can reconstruct for Proto-Dene a bipartite SIGN+GENERIC naming system. The more detailed place names lists are very informative. We find technical hydrological or geological naming. Lithic prospecting is indicated by place names for certain stones or minerals. On occasion we can detect band movement trajectories, name provenance (where a name was coined), founding place names φ, or environmental change ₪. Early Dene bands used clever variations of the SIGN+GENERIC formula to coin names for certain streams, landmarks, and favored habitats. I use the term *watershed tenure devices* for several intentional, pragmatic naming devices such as hydronymic districts and reverse hydronymns (p. 39, Kari 1996a, 1996).

For Table 12 I selected significant names for three subregions south and west of the Alaska Range. Table 12A-B-C has three regional diachronic layers with a convention Å^2-Å^3-Å^4. Table 12A has oldest group of selected names, Å^2, Ahtna in the Upper Susitna River (mainly in Chapter 10 of *SPA*); 12B has the next oldest, Å^3, Upper Kuskokwim or Dena'ina names along the western piedmont of the Alaska Range; and 12C, Å^4, has eight place names that stimulate discussion about phases of the Dena'ina occupation of Cook Inlet Basin.

This is the current outline of *PDLL traits of diachronic significance* (some traits are not presented in Table 12). A selected name can be noted for two or more traits.

1. Locational, overt, or contextual information in the Dene place names networks: overtly informative ☼, environmental change ₪, founding place names φ, boundary markers ‖, pass-markers ≍, favorite themes (lithics ⮝, anatomy ♡), contextually informative (clan-origin locations, myth locations(c)).
2. Watershed tenure (WT) devices: pragmatic SIGN+GENERIC patterns that enhance memorization and recognition of features
   2.1 Generic WT: hydronymic districts, reverse hydronyms: ↕, double reverse hydronymns (»-↕), regional generic terms (Dena'ina **-tnu** 'stream').
   2.2 Sign WT: patterned duplications ≡, x≡; geo-duplicates g≡ (noticeable local place name duplications), name ensembles ✋, pairs », resemblent pairs ≈.
3. Dene historical linguistic traits: Dene lexical archaisms Å; semantic opaqueness Ω (esp. hydronymns); irregular sound correspondences in bilingual Dene names ≠; morpheme or stem irregularities m≠ (ellipsis, contractions); substrate place names ∞; regional comparisons of substrate, irregular & opaque names.

PDLL is a stimulating theory for Dene and Na-Dene prehistory due to the interplay between the selection of significant names among the rule-driven Dene name networks, and the traits that span a wide range of information types. These three regional case studies demonstrate how the PDLL leads to hypotheses on relative antiquity, temporal benchmarks, and trajectories for Alaska Dene band movements

TABLE 12. DIACHRONICALLY SIGNIFICANT DENE PLACE NAMES SOUTH AND WEST OF THE ALASKA RANGE

Å² *SPA#*	lng	first Copper R Basin names	location, Maps 41, 55	literal	PDLL traits	comments; other sources
10.64	A	'Atna'	Copper River	beyond river	☼	coined in Tanana Valley
10.63	A	Ben Daes Bene'	Old Man Lake	shallows lake lake	x≡	7 distant duplicates, Healy L., Mentasta L, cf. ⑧
10.29	A	Hwtsaay Nene'	West Ahtna Uplands	dwarf tree country	x≡	3 PA duplicated ecoregions, cf. ⑨
10.62	A	Nen' Yese'	Nen' Yese' Ridge	land ridge	₪, »	also **Nen' Yese' Ggaay** (esker N of Glennallen)
10.61	A	K'ey Tsaaygha	hill N of Tyone R	by dwarf birch	≡	same as name for Hogan Hill
10.24	A	Sasnuu' Bene'	Lake Louise	sand island lake	₪, g≡	same as Summit Lake
10.12	A	Nataghił'aade	Devil Canyon	current flows down	≡	same as Baird Canyon, see Fig. 135A,
10.28	D A	Yusdikda, 'Usdicde	Lone Butte	dear one far ahead	‖, ≈	cf. 10.35, both with **nes,** overt boundary marker
10.35	A	Xensdii	ridge W of Tyone Lake	the next one ahead	≈	cf. 10.28, both with **nes**
14.71	A	Siz'aani	Gunsight Mountain	inside me, my heart	≡	also mt. at Copper Glacier, Figs. 190, 190A
14.1	A D	Ts'itonh Na' Ch'atanhtnu	Matanuska River	trail comes out river	≠	reanalyzed in both A and D

TABLE 12A. EARLY AHTNA NAMES (Å²) ON THE UPPER SUSITNA RIVER

A case study on the Tanana River with 45–50 names shows that the Tanana Valley has the oldest Dene place names within the current corpus. When we summarize *all* linguistic documentation for the Tanana Valley Dene languages and Ahtna in Copper River, there is little substrate linguistic data; there is no linguistic evidence of non-Dene languages having been present in the circum-Alaska Range uplands. Kari 2010b:207, "For the Copper River Basin and the Ahtna language area a strong case can be made for long-term occupation without the presence of any other non-Athabascans."

Table 12A has eleven Å² Ahtna or Dena'ina names in Western Ahtna country. We can point to strong evidence that the Dene entered Copper River from the Tanana Valley (and not the reverse) and that names were coined both before and after Glacial Lake Ahtna was at its maximum: 11,000–10,000 BP. The name 10.64 **'Atna'** 'Beyond (the range) River' Copper River is overtly informative, i.e., the provenance of this name was the Tanana Valley. The initial evidence about early Dene band movements came from three upland ecoregion names with a rare term for 'dwarf trees,' PA *$*h^wttha\hat{:}x$* 'dwarf tree' which is a true Dene lexical archaism. Kari (1993:242): "These three names suggest an ordering or seriation of band movements: 1st Ketchumstock uplands, 2nd Susitna-West Fork Uplands [10.29], 3rd Mulchatna-Holitna-Stony River Plateau ⑨."

Several patterned duplications ≡, and geoduplicates g≡, indicate that the Dene/Ahtna were naming places in Copper River Basin prior to and following the breeching of Lake Ahtna c. 10,700 BP (Shimer 2009, Reger et al. 2012). Citing just six place names, the pre-/post Lake Ahtna evidence is unequivocal. See the annotations for 1) geoduplicates **Sasnuu' Bene'** (10.34 Lake Louise and Summit Lake), 2) a patterned duplication **K'ey Tsaaygha** (10.61 hill on Tyone River and Hogan Hill, the island of Lake Ahtna; and 3) the two Lake Ahtna shoreline names, a patterned pair **Nen' Yese'** (10.62) and **Nen' Yese' Ggaay.** See other Å² name annotations 10.12, 10.60, 10.61, 10.63, and 10.64 and others not on Table 12 (7.61, 10.57, 10.58, 14.70, and 14.71). There are many affinities between Ahtna names and place names in Tanana Valley (e.g., five mountains that are named for a shiny ochre).

Å³ Map 26	lng	founding names W of Alaska Range	location, Map 26	literal	PDLL traits	comments; other sources
① 6.61	UKD	Dichina Nek' Kenaniq'	Kuskokwim R	stick river	-↨, φ	∃ 1st order stream w reverse hydronymn
②	UK	Tsat'asr Nek'	Highpower Ck	stone charcoal stream	»-↨,⅄, φ	∃ linked reverse hydronymn
③ 6.42	D UK	Idzitnu, Izitnu Edze No'	South Fork Kuskokwim R	Ω stream	Ω, ≠, ≍, φ	iconic, ambiguous, see 6.42
④	UK	Mazr'a Nek'	Kuchaynanik Ck	stone type stream	»-↨,⅄, φ	∃ clever, double reverse hydronym cf. ⑥
⑤	UK	Hwtsash Nek'	Creek on Middle Windy Fork	ahead/first stream	-↨, φ	∃
⑥	D	Vazh'atnu	North Babel River	stone type stream	»-↨,⅄, φ	∃ clever, cf. ④
⑦	D	K'qizaghetnu	Stony River	Ω "distant" stream	Ω, ≠	ellipsis, irregular
⑧	D	Ven Dash Vena	Tundra Lake	shallows lake lake	x≡	cf. Old Man Lake 10.63, Mentasta L, Healy Lake
⑨	D	Htsay Nenq'	Stony-Holitna-Mulchatna Plateau	"first land"	x≡, ≠, φ	ancient homeland; cognate w A.10.29, also in Tc 'dwarf tree land'
⑩ 6.41	D	Dzeł Ken	Southern Alaska Range	mountain base	x≡	same as UT pass at Nabesna-Chisana-White R
⑪	D	Nduk'eyux Dghil'u	Telaquana Mt	game enters mountain	☼	rare mythic place name; Kari 2007:ii
⑫	D	Tałchatnaq'	Hook Ck	muskrat stream	≠-↨, φ	∃, irregular sound for 'muskrat'
⑬	D	Vałts'atnaq'	Mulchatna R	Ω-stream	Ω -↨, φ	∃, irregular and opaque

TABLE 12 B FOUNDING DENE NAMES WEST OF ALASKA RANGE (Å³)

Thirteen Å³ names on Map 26 are ordered north to south along the west piedmont of the Alaska Range. These Å³ names appear to be a set of initial pioneering Dene place names. From the corner of the Central/Southern Alaska Range to Mulchatna River is a set of seven reverse hydronyms (Map 26: ①, ②, ④, ⑤, ⑥, ⑫ and ⑬); a trail of *linked founding place names* (first presented in Kari 1996a:458–59).

The Upper Kuskokwim name for Highpower Creek ② illustrates ancient Dene geographical naming ingenuity. Highpower Creek at the northwest corner of the Alaska Range was the first sidestream in the Kuskokwim drainage to be named with a reverse hydronym: **Tsat'asr Nek'** (in UK). The Dene also gave a name **Tsat'asr No'** to a small tributary of Highpower Creek, the same sign 'black rock' with the dominant hydronym **-no'**, a clever device that flags this confluence as a trail intersection. I call this a *double reverse hydronym* (»-↨). Note that two streams to the south ④ and ⑥ are another double reverse hydronymn. The south-most founding name, Mulchatna River **Vałts'atnaq'** is conspicuous; the syllables **vał-ts'at** are opaque. Two stems for 'stream' **na'** and **niq'** were blended into **naq'**. The name for Hook Creek to the north **Tałchatnaq'** has this same blended stem. Opaque and irregular hydonymns (Ω or ≠) are relevant to the PDLL.

One other likely founding place name is **Nduk'eyux Dghil'u** Telaquana Mountain (see Kari 2007:ii). This is an overtly informative name (☼) 'game enters mountain,' and a rare instance of a Dene place name referencing a sacred myth, an emergence story. A connection between the Dene of the upper Tanana River and the west piedmont is indicated by the extra-territorial duplication (x≡) of the UT names **Ddhäł Chin** and Dena'ina **Dzeł Ken** Southern Alaska Range. The Upper Tanana name refers to the valley and passes that connect the upper White-Chisana-Nabesna Rivers. This pair of x≡ cognates at opposite ends of the Alaska Range horseshoe is striking. The most conspicuous Å³ names show meta-pragmatism: the trail of eight reverse hydronyms, the two x≡ distant duplications for ecoregions **Htsay Nenq'** and **Dzeł Ken.**

The Inland Dena'ina regard **Htsay Nenq'** as the ancestral homeland (Balluta 2008). The Stony River was the first sockeye salmon that early Dene named. Wherever Dena'ina coined stream names, they have the unique Dena'ina stem **-tnu**. Also there are suggestions of an early "westward Dena'ina spread" based on numerous stream names with syllables ending in **-tneq** in Yupik, and **-tno'** in Lower Koyukon, and Deg Hit'an. The initial place names in this Proto-Dena'ina homeland could have been coined 10,000 years ago. The arrowheads, bone points, & microblades at the Lime Hills Cave site (Ackerman 1997) that date from ca. 8100–9500 are situated in time and space to represent this early Dene presence.

Å⁴ *SPA#*	lng	notable Cook Inlet names	location Map 26	literal	PDLL traits	comments; other sources
⓮	D	Ułcha Dghil'u	Roadhouse Mountain	a people's mountain	∞	**ułcha, ułchena** an ancient people, Norton-era, true substrate p.n.
⓯ 6.2	D	Shqitnu	Swentna River	∞-stream	∞	possible substrate p.n. in D; **shqit** in two others 16.18 and hill in Kenai
⓰ 7.19	D	K'ich'atnu	Kichatna River	Ω-stream	Ω	opaque ancient name, see 7.19
⓱ 1.30	D	Tubughnenq'	Tyonek area	beach land	☼, φ, ✋	founding ensemble, overt proclamation
⓲ 1.121	D	Qezdeghnen	Kustatan Peninsula	peninsula land	φ, ✋	founding ensemble
⓳ 16.23	D	Yaghenen	Kenai Peninsula	good … land	φ, ✋	founding ensemble, **yaghe-** an innovation
⓴ 16.23	D	Unhghenesditnu	creek at Kalifornsky	farthest ahead stream	☼, ‖	boundary name, cf. **nes** in 10.28,10.35
㉑	D	Ggasilatnu	Kasilof River	∞ stream	∞	true substrate p.n. in D

TABLE 12C. SOME SIGNIFICANT DENA'INA NAMES AROUND COOK INLET (Å⁴)

There have been some vanished languages and place names around Cook Inlet, however the Dena'ina vigorously rejected substrate names. Eight names around Cook Inlet point to distinct layers of naming in Cook Inlet Basin. We can note three substrate place names (∞): ⓮ **Ułcha Dghil'u** Roadhouse Mountain refers to a vanished people who were at Iliamna Lake (perhaps at c. 3000–4000 BP). The name **Shqitnu** ⓯ Skwentna River stands out as a likely substrate name. (There are two other Dena'ina names with the stem **shqit). Ggasilatnu** ㉑ Kasilof River has a substrate word with D. **-tnu.** Opaque hydronymns such as ③ South Fork of the Kuskokwim, and ⓰ Kichatna River stand out as likely founding place names (φ) that mark several passes (≍).

Three ecoregion names with **nen** 'land' on the shore of Cook Inlet ⓱, ⓲, ⓳ have the sense that they were coined as an founding ensemble of names, with an implied trajectory from west-to-east. This set of names branded the first Dena'ina coastal habitats. We can speculate about the date of this ensemble. Three names—⓳, ⓴, ㉑—on the Kenai Peninsula show that the Dena'ina moved south after arriving at the Swanson River area. The overt boundary name for the small stream at Kalifornsky ⓴, only ¼ mile from the mouth of a substrate name **Ggasilatnu** ㉑, implies there was communication between the first Kenai Peninsula Dena'ina and the last Riverine Kachemak people, which could be dated at c. 1000–1100 BP (Reger & Boraas 1996).

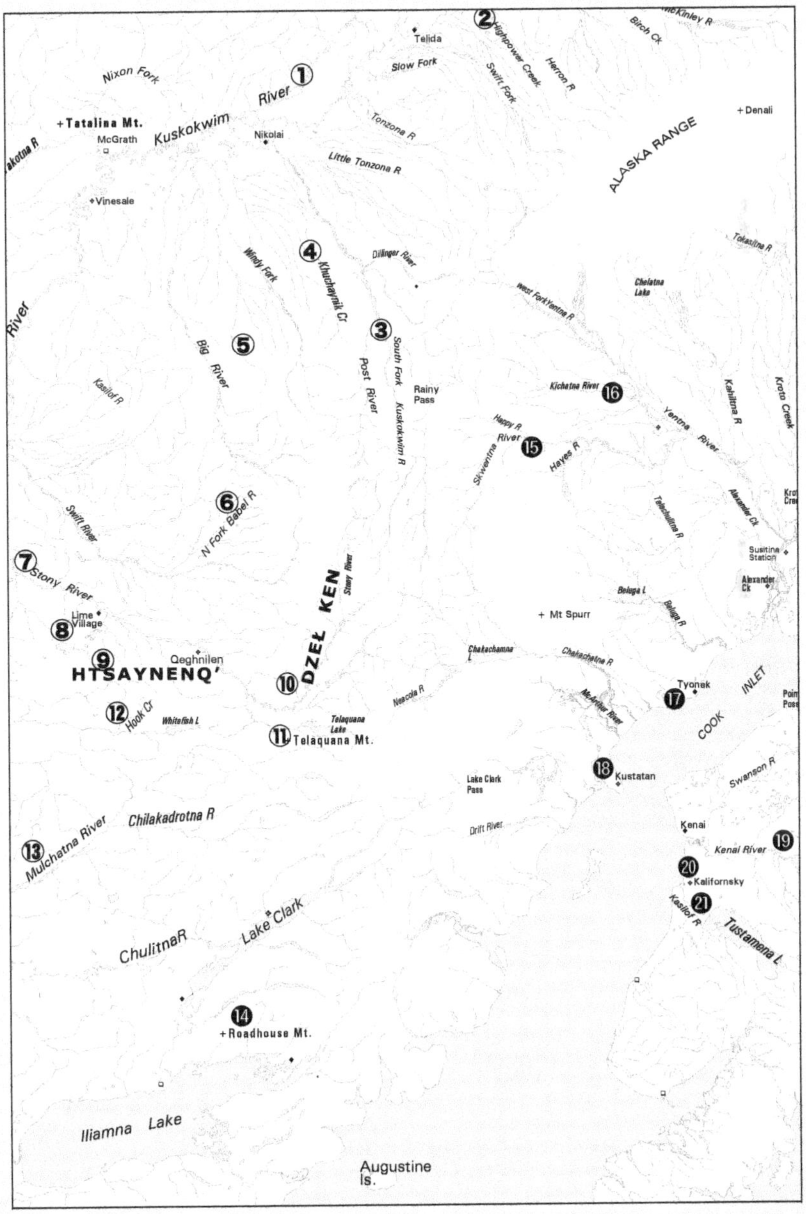

MAP 26

‡Selected Upper Kuskokwim and Dena'ina names west of the range and in Cook Inlet Basin.

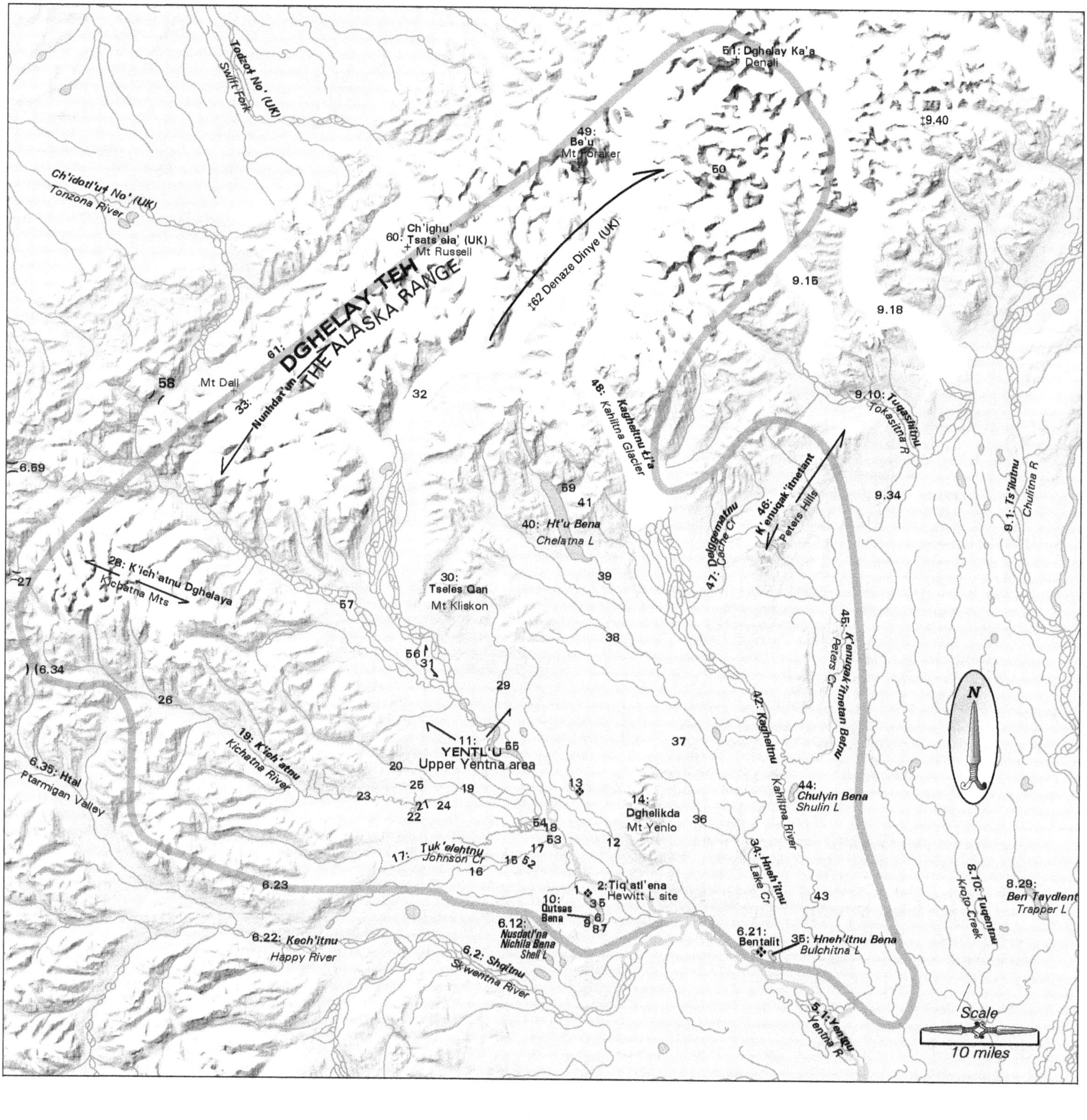

MAP 27

Place names map of the Upper Yentna River, showing Nos. 7.1 to 7.62.

MAP BY MATT GANLEY

7 Upper Yentna River, Lake Creek, and Kahiltna River

above the mouth of the Skwentna River, and the drainages below Denali

The materials presented in Chapters 6, 7, and 9 demonstrate that the Dena'ina made extensive use of the lands at the base of the high mountains of the Central Alaska Range.

Doroshin, who traveled with Dena'ina in the Kenai Mountains in 1848, wrote, "In the mountains every step, every motion, almost every word is underlain with certain traditional rules.... In the mountains they are very taciturn, and they sing no other songs besides the mountain songs.... In the mountains 'knife' is called **k'nidultihi**, otherwise **k'izhak'i**" (Radloff and Schiefner 1874:vii). At times Shem Pete talked about the unique language that was used by the Dena'ina when hunting in mountain areas. He noted that many common words were taboo. For example, instead of saying **k'enuy'a** for beaver, they would say **nan**, which usually means 'moss.'

There are several accounts in this book that show the Dena'ina and other Athabascans responding to the energized atmosphere of the mountains. Miska Deaphon's account of the tiny 'people in the mountains' at 6.44 is a very graphic example. See also comments by John Stump on Denali at 7.51, and Katherine Nicolie on proper behavior when in the mountains at 8.45 and 12.16.

7.1 Tiq'atl'ena Betnu • 'Timbered Area Notch - Stream'
outlet of Hewitt Lake Hewitt Lake, just above the mouth of the Skwentna River
Shem Pete: "Whenever the **Tiq'atl'ena** [Hewitt Lake, 7.2] people needed anything, they had big **badi** [umiak, large skin boat], and they'd come down to Alexander Creek to trade for beluga grease, seal oil, hooligan oil, fish head oil, and they gave the Alexander Creek people caribou skins and marten skins."

7.2 Tiq'atl'ena • 'Timbered Area Notch'
Hewitt Lake village site Hewitt Lake village site, near lake outlet
The stem **tiq'a** means 'timbered area,' and the stem **tl'en** means 'barbed' or 'notched.'

This had been a permanent village until the late nineteenth century (Fall 1981:176–177, 388–389). It was also a base camp for hunting in the Rainy Pass area. The people from the upper Yentna villages specialized in catching furbearers such as ground squirrel, beaver, and marten, and in making fur clothing. The Wrathall site (TAL-049) is on the northeast end of the lake. See Dixon 1996:93–108 and pp. 151–153 and the site map, Map 28.

Shem Pete: "They used to catch fish early at **Tiq'atl'ena**. There was lots of people there year round. They used to catch lots of bear there. The people at **Tiq'atl'ena** and **Qutsas Bena** [7.10] always had a lot to eat. That's the place they used to have a camp, and they used to have a big village there too. My mother used to pack me over there, and when I was old enough, I used

FIGURE 93
Tiq'atl'ena Bena (7.3, Hewitt Lake) looking west toward **Nusdatl'na Nichila** 'ghosts' house,' (6.11, Shell Hills).
PHOTO BY GREG DIXON, JUNE 1992

Sources: Shem Pete, Billy Pete

2003 revisions: names added 7.52–7.61; location name revised 7.18.
‡2016 revisions: names added 7.62; names revised 7.10, 7.19, 7.20, 7.42, 7.48, 7.54, 7.61; map revised 29.

to walk over there with them. They used to put trap across there for trout, in May month, early in the spring. After they caught trout, salmon came up next, so they put in king salmon trap and red salmon trap. They made the holes in the trap big enough so the small fish could go up the creek. They tried to save everything that they didn't need right away. The salmon came up there in late May and they caught them with traps in June month. They also caught rainbow trout and Dolly Varden char. This was right near **Tiq'atl'ena**. People stayed at each lake [Hewitt and Whiskey lakes]. There were big villages where the fish are. **Nichił** all over the place. To the east of **Tiq'atl'ena** was another big village. There were big villages on the flat places on the lake. Three flat places had villages."

7.3 Tiq'atl'ena Bena • 'Timbered Area Notch - Lake'
Hewitt Lake
Shem Pete said that this was the "second best lake," after Red Shirt Lake, and that it was sometimes called **K'unkda Bena** 'Mother of the Lakes.'

Shem Pete: "**Nichił** were on the east side but not on the west side. Too much hill there. There were **nichił** that reach from **Sdak'dal'iy** [7.5] there down to the lower end. For about two miles I think. At the head of the lake too there were **nichił** very close together."

Billy Pete: "Even a short time ago we used that lake for about a month. We hunt moose up there. Lots of bear. 1931 I think."

(7.4) Qałnigi Ka'a Dnay'unt • 'Where There Is a Large Rock'
large rock in or by Hewitt Lake

7.5 Sdak'dal'iy • 'Point That Extends'
point on east shore of Hewitt Lake
The site TAL-050 is just south of here. Shem Pete: "«There are big spruce on that point. The **nichił** extended all the way down from **Sdak'dal'iy**. From there a trail started down to the water and the trail from the Yentna ended, a portage.» They got to have that trail you know. «The trail went from the head of **Tiq'atl'ena** to the Yentna.»"

7.6 Qutsas Tus Nuch'k'elyasht or **§Qutsas Bena Tus Tighitunt** • 'Where We Carry Things Across to Qutsas' or 'Portage Trail to Qutsas Lake'
portage from Hewitt Lake to Whiskey Lake
Shem Pete comments that this was a main trail joining the several camps.

7.7 Dach'qelqiht • 'Where We Spend the Spring'
outlet of Whiskey Lake
Shem Pete: "«**Dach'qelqiht** is the outlet of **Qutsas Bena** [7.10]. It flows in on the left-hand side. From here the lake is visible.» I been there a lot of times. People were there all the time in the spring."

7.8 Nutsahdnghitses • 'Rocks Dammed Across'
site on Whiskey Lake outlet stream
This was a fishing site. The place name indicates that a rock weir was used here.

FIGURE 94

Looking westward to **Tiq'atl'ena Betnu**, (7.1, the Hewitt Lake outlet stream), toward **Dach'qelqiht** (7.9, the Whiskey Lake outlet stream). Near here are the fishing sites 7.8 **Nutsahdnghitses** and 7.9 **K'enq'a**.

PHOTO BY GREG DIXON, JUNE 1992

7.9 K'enq'a • 'Fishing Site'
fishing location on Whiskey Lake outlet stream

7.10 Qutsas Bena • '-Ω- lake'
Whiskey Lake
Shem Pete: "«There is a fishing site on **Qutsas Bena**. They stay there living on trout. They save themselves on that. They say that they used to spend the spring there. They put a fish fence in **Qutsas Bena**, and they took a lot of trout. There are big salmon in **Qutsas Bena** and **Tiq'atl'ena** [7.2].» There were **nichił** all around the lake. Lots of bear also. People hunt bear day and night. **Tiq'atl'ena** was so full of people. They leave **Qutsas Bena** open for bear."

7.11 Yentl'u • 'Backbone Headwaters'
upper Yentna River area
This is a regional place name and the source of the name Yenlo.

Shem Pete: "«At **Yentl'u** the Susitna people used to kill sheep easily. There were lots of sheep there. They see them upriver. When it gets cold they bring them downriver. When I was a child, the one called **Yagu** had a younger brother. His name was **K'eł Nuts'ehen** [or Red Shirt, see pp. 106–107]. His Russian name was Basili. **Yagu** and two others had no wives. **Yentl'u** was their property. They killed a lot of sheep. They gathered them easily. Every fall they went there when I was a kid. **Yentl'u** was **Yagu**'s and his brother's country. They would take out those sheep backbones and dry the meat. The brought many [sheep] downriver. There is not much water in **Yentl'u** for the sheep [to be transported in boats].»"

7.12 Keshch'a Betnu • 'Feathers Creek'
Donkey Creek
King, sockeye, and pink salmon run in this creek (Roy 1987).

Archaeological Investigations at Tiq'atl'ena Bena (Hewitt Lake)

by R. Greg Dixon

Greg Dixon has extensive experience at archaeological excavations throughout Southcentral Alaska. He has worked at the Alaska Office of History and Archaeology and is retired from the National Park Service.

According to Shem Pete and other Dena'ina, **Tiq'atl'ena Bena** (7.3, Hewitt Lake) was an important seasonal camp in the early twentieth century and, before that, the location of several year-round Dena'ina villages. Recent archaeological investigations have revealed abundant evidence of historic and prehistoric occupation and subsistence uses there (Lee 1987:1; Dixon 1990; Dixon 1996: 93–107). Stone, bone, wood, ceramic, glass, metal and other artifacts, along with surface depressions likely indicating locations of former dwellings and cache structures have been found at two locations along the east side of the lake (AHRS Sites TAL-049 and TYO-085). Cultural indications have also been noted at another locality on the west side of Hewitt Lake (with no AHRS assignment). An uninvestigated fourth site (TYO-050), located on the east side of the lake south of TAL-049, is reported to contain cultural remains.

Former Hewitt Lake residents Judy and Dallas Nichols found a large greenstone splitting adze head on their property near the northeast end of the lake. It had been sharpened on one end by grinding and polishing and had a single notch pecked into it to facilitate its hafting to a handle—as is documented to have been done elsewhere in the Cook Inlet area by the Dena'ina (Osgood 1937: 103). The Nichols also discovered a second similarly shaped, but smaller, pecked and polished adze.

At the Nichols' invitation, in July of 1987 archaeologists R. Greg Dixon and Susan Lee made a brief field investigation aimed at documenting the precise origin of these adzes. Although no further information on these adzes was obtained, they noted many other indications of prehistoric and historic uses of the Hewitt Lake area (Lee 1987). These included a small shallow surface depression that was suggestive of the location of a former Dena'ina dwelling, along with numerous pieces of "fire cracked rock," remains of heated stones commonly used by Dena'inas to heat water for cooking and for creating steam in sweat baths (Osgood 1937:45, 59). They also found a small chert end scraper that is similar to others documented to have been used by Dena'ina elsewhere for cleaning skins (Osgood 1937: 103), and small chert and quartzite debitage flakes (waste products from stone tool manufacturing).

Later, eight more small chert scrapers, eight chert flake cores, two pumice abraders, a basalt hammer stone, a basalt net weight, and other stone tool fragments were also found on the Nichols property. A number of worked and unworked mammal bone fragments, a bone button, seventeen small glass beads of varying colors and shapes, eighteen glazed, decorated ceramic fragments, and other historic items were also found there. The beads and ceramic fragments bore similarities to others commonly traded to Natives in Alaska (cf. Ketz 1983). Rectangular and circular surface depressions of sizes and shapes suggestive of former locations of semi-subterranean Dena'ina dwellings and cache pits were also observed on several other nearby properties. The total evidence of past cultural uses along the northeast end of Hewitt Lake was spread over an area about 800 meters long by 30 meters wide. A summary description of this site evidence was entered into the Alaska Heritage Resources Survey under the AHRS identification number of TAL-049.

In 1990, Dixon (1990) found additional evidence of past cultural activity at the south end of Hewitt Lake, along the east bank of Hewitt Creek (the outlet of Hewitt Lake) directly opposite the confluence of Whiskey Creek. A test pit placed inside an irregularly shaped depression revealed fire cracked rock about 1.5 centimeters below surface, along with fragments of burned and unburned mammal bone (including beaver mandibles and a leg bone), calcined bone fragments, two chert waste flakes, and a small piece of red ocher. A summary description of these finding were included in the AHRS file under identification number TYO-085. See Fig. 94, the Hewitt Lake outlet.

In 1992, Dixon undertook more extensive investigations of the depressions noted on Mr. Grant Wrathall's property, two lots northwest of the Nichols' (TAL-049). Between the lake bluff and bordering spruce forest to the east, he located thirteen or fourteen large, square or rectangular surface depressions which were suggestive of the locations of former Dena'ina houses (**nichił**). Sixty-two smaller, circular, cache sized pits ranging from 50 centimeters to 1.5 meters in diameter, and extending from 40 to 60 centimeters deep were also found, and this series of depressions continued on the neighboring properties to the northwest and to the southeast.

MAP 28

Wrathall site map.

GREG DIXON

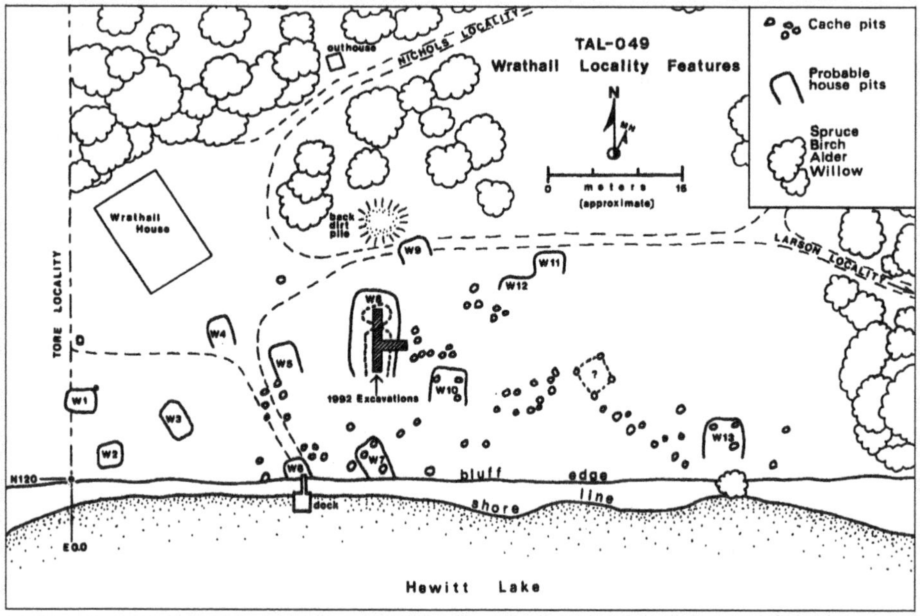

One of the larger depressions on Mr. Wrathall's lot, designated the "W8 feature," had overall outside dimensions of approximately 10 meters by 6 meters. A roughly 7 meters by 4 meters secondary depression within the larger depression contained internal configurations that suggested the location of a bench or sleeping platform constructed in the dwelling as described in Osgood's ethnography of the Dena'ina (1937: 58, 62). The secondary depression within the W8 Feature also had a roughly 2 meters diameter depression attached to its north end that was suggestive of a sweat bath as is reported to have commonly been attached to Dena'ina dwellings (ibid).

Dixon selected the W8 Feature for exploratory excavations, and with the assistance of Karen W. Workman, a grid system was laid out over it and a 1 meters by 8m, north to south oriented trench unit opened through its approximate center. A 1 meters by 4 meters excavation unit projecting to the east from the middle of the north-south trench unit was also opened later with the goal of transecting possible feature walls and benches.

Excavations in both units were carried out to sterile ground, which was reached about 130 centimeters below the surface. Among the important features exposed in the tests were two approximately 50 centimeters diameter unconfined hearths about 70 centimeters apart near the center of the secondary depression. Both appeared to have been based in the same probable cultural floor, and both contained abundant wood ash, charcoal, fire cracked-rock, burned and unburned wood, and few small artifact fragments. Each also contained portions of articulated salmonid vertebra, ribs, and a number of small fragments of mammal bone. Both hearths also contained birch bark lining at their bases.

Evidence found in the area of the suspected sweat bath at the north end of the W8 feature supported the conclusion of its use as such. Dense accumulations of fire cracked rock were found along with interspersed layers of sand, charcoal, pieces of burned and unburned wood, and occasional artifact fragments.

At the conclusion of excavations, detailed drawings of the soil stratigraphy exposed in all test units were made. These illustrate a complex of cultural activities in the W8 feature, along with numerous interspersed layers of tephra (volcanic ash). Two or more living floors in the W8 feature were suggested, along with other internal features such as posts.

While the profile drawings were being completed, Mr. Jim Thurston, his wife, and son stopped by. They reported depression features on their property on the west side of the lake. In Dixon's follow up investigations of these, two oblong shaped depressions about 2 meters by 3 meters in size and 30 centimeters deep were noted. Due to time constraints, no testing or other investigation of these features was attempted.

A total of 3,554 cultural and non-cultural items were collected from the W8 feature in 1992. These include 135 complete or fragmented stone artifacts; three items of carved bone; 216 small chert, basalt, slate, and quartzite debitage flakes; soil and radiocarbon samples; and a large number of fauna and plant remains.

Noteworthy artifacts include multiple small chert scrapers and flake cores, a flaked basalt projectile point, a small flaked black chert knife with a handle fashioned into it, and an iron knife blade or other such object that contained stains on one end indicating being hafted or inserted into a handle. Also, a blue tubular glass bead was found associated with elements of a bear paw, which in turn occurred beneath a wooden post.

Fragments of ground slate projectile points with diamond shaped cross sections were also found, along with small ground slate rods or burnishers, fragmented flaked and ground slate ulus, and flaked basalt bifaces. Use of a groove and snap manufacturing technique was indicated on a few of the slate and bone artifacts.

Rough bifacially flaked basalt preforms and coarsely made choppers were also found in the 1992 excavations,

FIGURE 95

The site pit at the northeast end of Hewitt Lake TAL-049 site pit, facing west. Initial structural evidence, possibly associated with a dwelling room wall, revealed in the 1992 testing of the W8 depression feature at the "Wrathall" locality.

PHOTO BY GREG DIXON

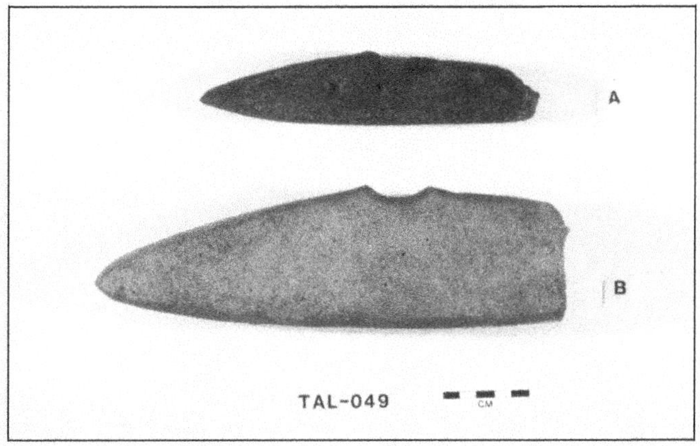

FIGURE 96

Stone adzes from the "Nichols" locality of the TAL-049 site, at the northeast end of Hewitt Lake, Alaska:
A: Pecked and polished, single notched diorite (?) "hunters" adze.
B: Pecked and polished, single notched greenstone (?) "splitting" adze.

PHOTO BY GREG DIXON

along with grinding slab fragments, a possible stone pick, and 91 small, bi-notched pebble net weights.

Many well-preserved fauna remains were encountered in the W8 Feature, with beaver and bear dominating. Moose or caribou, and a number of unidentified small mammal bones or fragments were also present, along with antler fragments and fish bones. Numerous birch bark fragments were also present throughout the cultural deposits.

Twenty-eight samples of charred remains were collected from the W8 feature for radio metric dating purposes, along with tephra and other soil samples. Dr. John P. Cook of the Bureau of Land Management graciously funded a radiocarbon sample analysis (BETA 67021) of material collected from the lowest W8 soil level containing cultural remains. The raw C-14 date of 4410 90 BP (Dixon 1996:102) obtained from this, fits well within a series of radiocarbon dates for sites throughout the central Gulf of Alaska presented by Mills (1994). Associated with this dated soil level were two fragments of a ground slate projectile point that had a diamond shaped cross section. This artifact, combined with the associated date, presents intriguing possibilities that earliest cultural uses at Hewitt Lake may have been by people associated with the Ocean Bay II culture, as at Pedro Bay on the Alaska Peninsula (Townsend 1970) and at the Sylva site in Kachemak Bay on the Kenai Peninsula (Workman et al. 1993).

A 10 centimeters thick layer of tephra which originated from the now extinct and glacier covered Hayes volcano, located in the Tordrillo Mountains about 70 kilometers southwest of Hewitt Lake (Begét 1993 personal communication), was encountered in the W8 Feature excavations. These deposits occurred from 96 centimeters to 1.06 meters below the surface in all units. This tephra, which has been dated to 3650 BP (Riehle and Bowers 1990; Begét 1991: 188) provides another valuable date marker for the cultural remains found in the W8 feature and elsewhere in the region.

In conclusion, abundant evidence of prehistoric cultural remains is now documented for sites along Hewitt Lake. The archaeological investigations at **Tiq'atl'ena Bena** have revealed utilization of that area by Native peoples beginning over 3600 years ago and continuing to around the AD 1930s. Definition or clarification of such questions as the cultural affiliation of the ethnic group(s) formerly living there, their origins and interrelations with neighboring groups, seasonality and dates of uses, and the function(s) of various features discovered in sites along the lake await further studies.

‡Archaeological work at Hewitt Lake site TAL-049 was continued by William H. Schneider 2013. Regarding the TAL-049 site on the NE shore of Hewitt Lake he writes (op. cit.:132): "TAL-049 is over half a mile long and contains over 60 cultural depressions but only 14 square meters have been excavated within a single feature." Schneider summarizes that Ocean Bay II peoples were at TAL-049 about 4400 years ago, that Riverine Kachemak peoples may be at this same site at 2000 B.P., and that more recent occupations are by the Dena'ina.

FIGURE 97

Dghelikda (7.14, Mount Yenlo) is beyond **Yentnu** (5.1, Yentna River), at the confluence of Hewitt Creek.

Shem Pete: "They call it **Dghelikda** 'Funny Mountain' because there are trees up there. The caribou at **Dghelikda** are really pretty. They used to kill those up on that mountain. These skins were given only to the best people, they were so pretty. That's what they call '**Dghelikda** caribou.' There are lots of bear up there."

PHOTO BY GREG DIXON

7.13 Keshch'a Bena • 'Feathers Lake'
Donkey Creek Lake
This is said to a have been an important Dena'ina village long ago. This is the village site in the war story **Jiggi Baneyaht** 'Where the Princess Is Raised.' Fall (1981:389–390): "The sons and daughters of **qeshqa** were brought up at this village because it was 'hidden' far from the Inlet and safe from raids." Once this village was attacked by Alutiiq coming up the Yentna River via Mount Yenlo. A man and woman escaped and warned the Dena'ina downriver, who killed the Alutiiq as they returned. After this battle, the village was not reoccupied. No use of the area in the twentieth century is remembered.

7.14 Dghelikda • 'Odd Mountain' or 'Funny Mountain'
Mount Yenlo
The name Yenlo is from **Yentl'u**, 7.11.

"«**Diqelas Tukda** [chief of Alexander Creek] built a rock cairn on that ridge on the side toward the [Yentna] river. When they went up the river in canoes, it looked like a man standing up there. It should still be standing there.»"

§7.52 Baqay Nilyasht • 'Where Birchbark Canoes Are Left'
canoe landing site near Red Creek mouth
Shem Pete: "«**Baqay Nilyasht** is at **K'qiy'un Kaq'**. They used to come up there in canoes or bidarkas. They start packing from **K'qiy'un Kaq'.** After going a long way by boat, they would leave canoes here and walk to **Htal** [Rainy Pass].»"

Above here the streams were too swift for canoe travel.

During the retaliatory raid in the **Jiggi Baneyaht** story [7.13], watchmen were placed here by the canoes.

7.15 K'qiy'un Kaq' • 'Mouth of Place Is There'
Red Creek mouth

7.16 K'qiy'untnu • 'Creek of Place Is There'
Red Creek
Herron records this as "Ki-un-ik Creek." It is on the trail to Rainy Pass leading overland from Red Creek to **Kiq'eh Dghelaya.**

7.17 Tuk'elehtnu, Tuk'eleh Betnu • 'Fish Run Creek'
Johnson Creek
The 1901 Herron map (Map 29) calls this "To-ko-loch-nu River."

§7.53 Tuk'eleh Kaq' • 'Fish Run Mouth'
mouth of Johnson Creek

7.18 K'eyghashtnu • 'Fish Is Harvested Creek'
§possibly spawning ponds above Johnson Creek and below the mouth of the Kichatna (revised location)
Shem Pete did not know first hand of any Dena'ina fishing here, but he speculated that this must have once been a fishing stream. Roy 1987 indicates that pink, sockeye, and king salmon run here.
Shem Pete: "«Harvest something stream" the one that is on the downstream side of where they call mouth of Kichatna.»"

§7.54 K'its'atnu Kaq' • '-Ω- River'
mouth of Kichatna River

7.19 K'its'atnu • '-Ω- River'
Kichatna River
‡This stream name appears on Table 12 as a stellar example of an opaque place name (Ω). The morphemes **k'i-** and **ts'a-~ch'a-** can be any number of prefixes or compounds.

Shem Pete: "«Upriver from **K'eyghashtnu** is **K'its'atnu.** We went that far.»"

The Herron party went this far by boat, and then began ascending the Kichatna (Keechatno) River on foot on July 1, 1899 (Herron 1901:28).

In 1910 Talkeetna Nicholie told Belmore Browne that a Russian trader had died years before in the swamps on the Kichatna River (Browne 1956:4,179.) Browne states that the Russian was trying to climb Mount McKinley, but it is more likely that he was trying to cross the Alaska Range through Simpson Pass. There are no corroborating records of this incident. This is the only information we know of about Russians traveling in the Yentna River drainage.

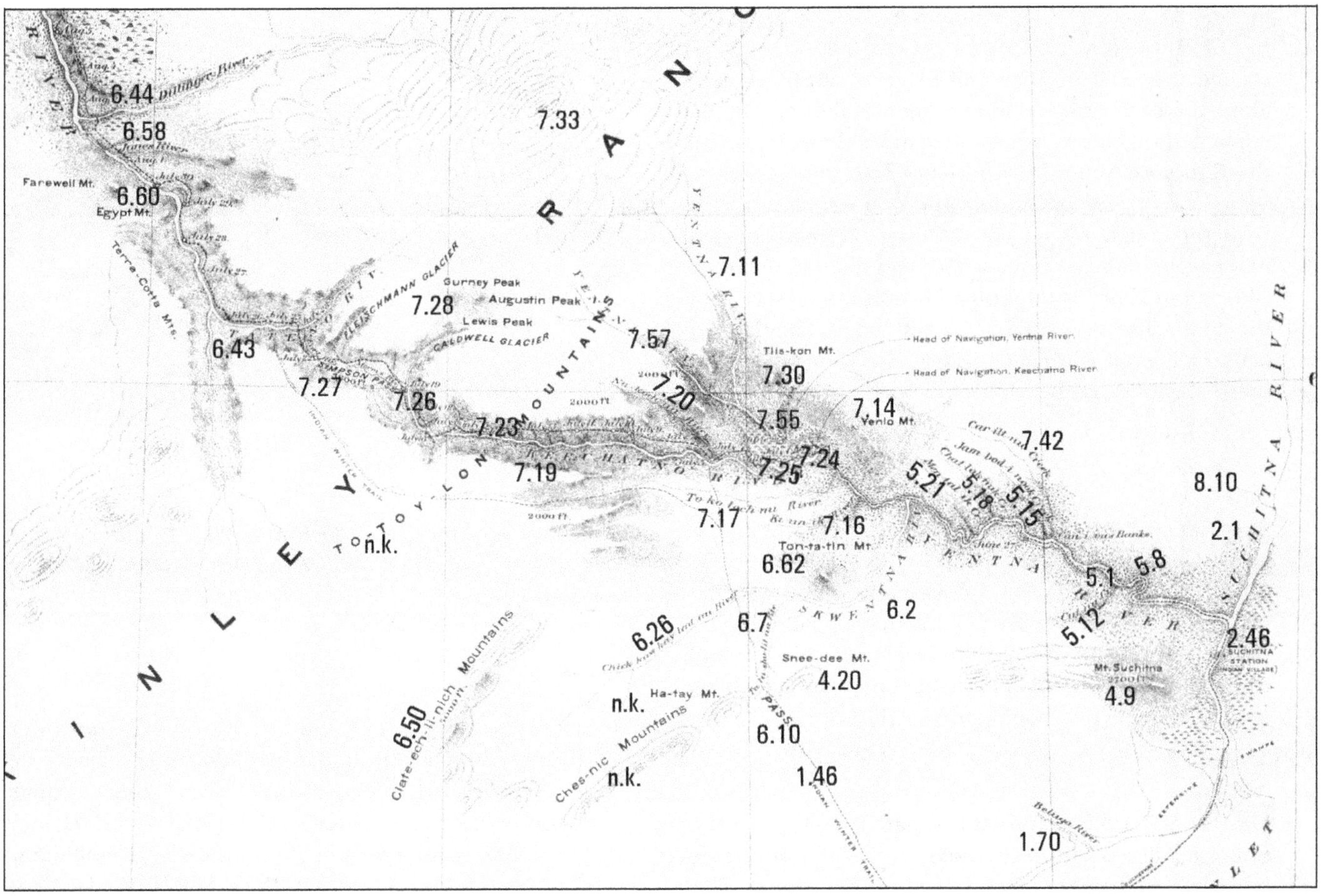

‡7.20 "Nakochna," [Nanquq'tnu, Nunquhtnu?] • possibly 'Moss Surface Creek' or 'Across Surface Creek'
Nakochna River
Shem Pete was not certain about the accuracy of this name, first recorded by Herron in 1899. He initially thought the name might be **Nukats'tnu,** but he later rejected that name.

Herron (1901:30): "The Nakochnu River…marks the point where the Indians cache their canoes, or the head of Indian canoe navigation." Ray Collins (2000) offers comparisons with the Upper Kuskokwim Athabascan upland travel patterns: "where 'the Indians cache their canoes' or 'the head of canoe navigation.' Such locations are also designated in the upper Kuskokwim, on the South Fork and on the Middle Fork of Big River. Thus all the river routes to the mountains are known. Head of canoe navigation was noted. From that point all travel was on foot when going into the mountains. On return trips skin boats might be used to float downstream from areas closer to the headwaters."

7.21 Gega Betnu • 'Berry Creek'
outlet of Gega Bena (7.22)
Shem Pete: "«Below **Gega Bena** it [creek] flows through a canyon. Once my older brother, **Beq'e Nuqeydghelya Tukda** [Chief Ephim], shot a bear there, and it fell down into that canyon. He went down there and brought up the meat.»"

‡MAP 29
Detail from the 1899 Herron Map: Kichatna River to Dillinger River, with *SPA* feature numbers.

Herron's map from the Kichatna River to the Dillinger River is the first mapping of Simpson Pass. The last Dena'ina place name Herron recorded is the "Tateno" River and on July 28th the Dena'ina guides returned to Susitna. Herron named the Jones and Dillinger rivers for members of his party. Several names (Farewell Mt., Egypt Mt., and Terra Cotta Mts.) were coined one year before by Spurr. See also Map 24 (Spurr) ‡and notes at 6.43 and 6.62.

7.22 Gega Bena • 'Berry Lake'
lake on south side of middle Kichatna River
Shem Pete: "I went in that lake. Our face is all blue. «Berries were touching the water.»"

Shem Pete: "They catch lots of bear there. There's lots of blueberries that place. All around the lake they see bear and they kill them. They just went up to that lake to look for black bear and then they went on to **Htal.**"

7.23 K'its'atnu Tayena • '-Ω- River Straight Stretch'
straight stretch on the canyon of the Kichatna River
Shem Pete: "«Going upriver we go into **K'its'atnu Tayena**, and on the left-hand side there is **Gega Bena.** I have gone that far [on the Kichatna].»"

When intending to hunt in the **K'its'atnu** country, Susitna Station Dena'ina traveled up the Yentna in canoes to **Tiq'atl'ena** (7.2). The women stayed there while the men continued in the canoes to Gold Hill, where they cached the canoes. They walked upstream from here along the east bank and hunted moose. Billy and Shem explained that it is not possible to travel downstream on the **K'its'atnu** above its confluence with the Nakochna River with canoes, only with **elgheji** (moose skin boats). In negotiating this stretch of water, a strong man kneeled in the front of the boat and a "stronger man" in the back, who was in charge and shouted orders over the roar of the rapids. They steered the boat with poles. They landed at the Nakochna River and had tea. They then proceeded on to **Tiq'atl'ena**, where they joined the women.

7.24 K'ghultishi • 'That Which Protrudes'
hill on south side of Kichatna River (‡location revised on Map 27)
Shem Pete: "That is a landmark for the Natives. It is above **Gega Bena**."

On the second day on the Kichatna about six miles upstream, the Herron party camped at a small hill "Pol-tish-ee." Three miles above here, Herron wrote, "An old camp and blazes showed where the Indian Ivan had been on a hunting expedition" (Herron 1901:30).

7.25 [Nen ?] • 'Land'
Nin Ridge
Herron (1901:30) recorded this name, saying that the opposite hill was known as "Tesch" (**tesh** 'hill'). Both may be truncated forms of actual Dena'ina place names. This would be along the aboriginal trail.

Brooks (1911:18): "At first our course lay along the east of the Kichatna by the route that was followed in 1899 by Lieutenant Herron, of whose mention is made elsewhere. Herron's trail had in many places been destroyed by undercutting of the river bank and had to be pieced out by chopping through the alder thickets. After three days, which netted only about 10 miles air line, we came to bench bordering the east side of the valley, 50 feet above the river, which offered excellent traveling. An Indian trail was discovered leading through an open parklike stretch known as Nin Ridge. Everywhere appeared thick patches of red-top grass, the finest the writer has ever seen in Alaska."

Shem Pete: "There's lots of gold there. You could get rich there."

7.26 K'its'atnu Tl'u • '-Ω- River - Headwaters'
canyon on upper Kichatna River
Shem Pete: "«Up the **K'its'atnu** there is a canyon. They did not put the women in the canoes there.» Too rough."

7.27 K'ich'atnu Tustes • '-Ω- River - Pass'
Simpson Pass
See Map 30. Following this trail, Herron's 1899 expedition ascended the Kichatna to Simpson Pass. Herron's guides told him that they knew the country no further and, six days later, after reaching the South Fork of the Kuskokwim River, both of the guides went back home to Susitna (Herron 1901:35). See 6.43. Shem Pete once

FIGURE 98
Kichatna Spires on the right at **K'ich'atnu Tl'u** (7.26, the upper Kichatna River area) in the area of **Tetno' Hwchwx Dotis** (6.59, Shellabarger Pass).
PHOTO BY MARK STASIK

stated that the Upper Kuskokwim people did not come through this pass into the upper Yentna River.

The Frederick Cook party went from Tyonek through Simpson Pass in 1903 (Cook 1904, 1906). In 1930 Beach (1931:190), near Simpson Pass, saw the "still visible trail of Lieut. Joseph S. Herron in 1899. This ill-fated expedition discovered Simpson Pass and then wandered about the Kuskokwim. His Indian guides had deserted him one night."

Note that in this area there is also a pass to Moose Creek Lake toward the upper Happy River and Rainy Pass. See 6.33 and 6.34.

7.28 K'its'atnu Dghelaya • '-Ω- River Mountain'
Kichatna Mountains
Shem Pete: "They didn't use that mountain."

§7.55 Tseles Qan Kaq' • 'Ground Squirrel Lodge Mouth'
mouth of Clearwater Creek
This is listed on Herron's map (Map 29) as "Gliskon Kok Ck."

7.29 Tseles Qantnu • 'Ground Squirrel Lodge Creek'
Clearwater Creek
Shem Pete: "«The one that flows from **Tseles Qan** has clear water. It flows beneath **Dghelikda** [Mount Yenlo].»"

7.30 Tseles Qan • 'Ground Squirrel Lodge'
Mount Kliskon
Herron wrote this name as "Tlis-kon."

Shem Pete: "I been up there. It's a pretty mountain. Lots of parka squirrel."

This is frequently mentioned as a game lookout and hunting area. The name is interesting as the word **tseles** for ground squirrel is not used in Dena'ina but is used in the adjacent Ahtna and Upper Kuskokwim languages. The name may imply bilingualism and intermarriage

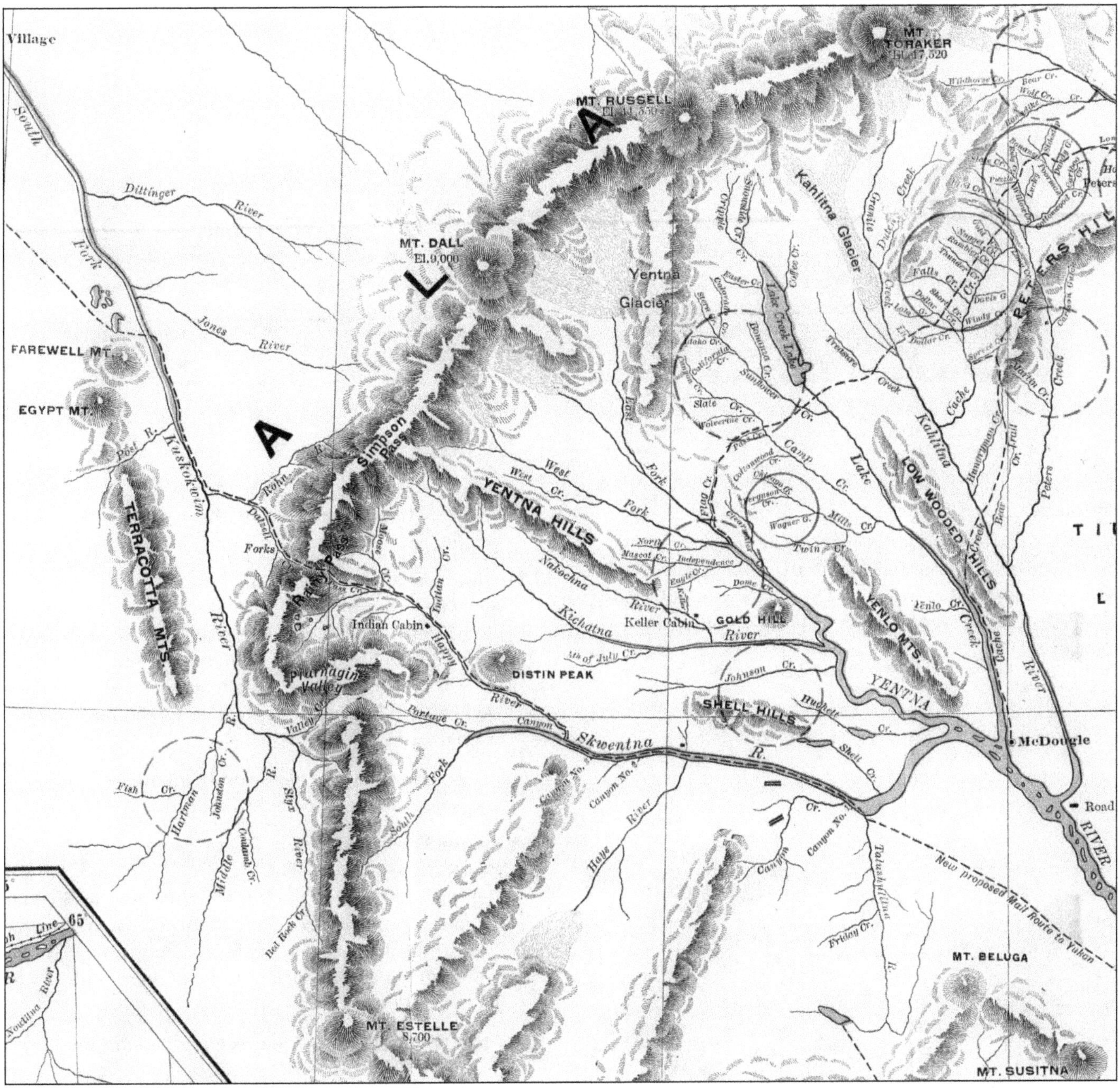

MAP 30

Detail from the 1910a Sleem Map: Iditarod Trail and Peters Hills.

This detail shows the Iditarod Trail up the Happy river and through Rainy Pass and the mining districts in the Yentna River drainage. The west-east trail from the upper Yentna River, across the upper Kahiltna to the Tokositna, appears here between Flag Creek and the Peters Hills and also on the Capps map (1913:8). Shem Pete believed that this was an aboriginal trail. A discussion of the 1910a Sleem map is with Map 63.

ARCHIVES, ALASKA AND POLAR REGIONS DEPT., RASMUSON LIBRARY, UNIVERSITY OF ALASKA FAIRBANKS

FIGURE 99

A view from **Tseles Qan** (7.30, Mount Kliskon). The valley in the foreground is the head of **Tseles Qantnu** (7.29, Clearwater Creek). Beyond this is Mount Fairview, in the hazy distance is **Dghelikda** (7.14, Mount Yenlo). Photo taken by Stephen R. Capps in the summer of 1911.

FROM THE STEPHEN R. CAPPS, JR. COLLECTION (#344), COURTESY OF THE ALASKA AND POLAR REGIONS DEPT. ARCHIVES, UNIVERSITY OF ALASKA

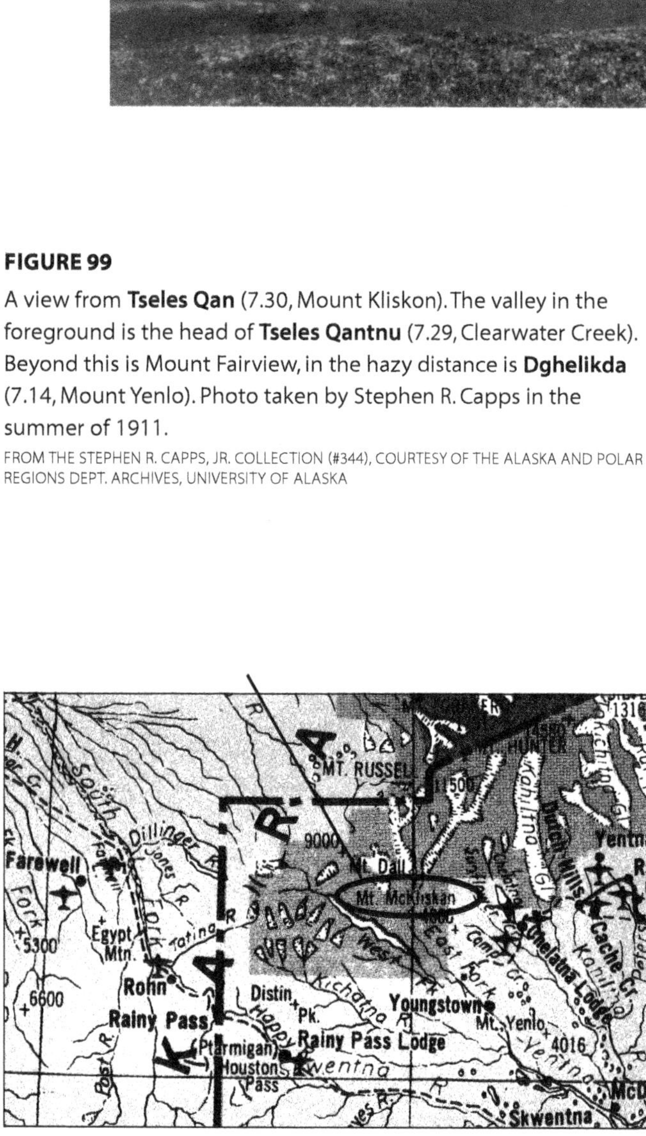

MAP 31

This close-up of the 1995 edition of the Kroll map of Alaska has "Mount Kliskon" mountain impishly labeled as "Mount McKliskan."

REPRINTED COURTESY OF KROLL MAP COMPANY, INC., SEATTLE

between the Dena'ina and the Upper Kuskokwim people.

7.31 Dusdikda • 'No-Good Point'
island in Yentna River, 12–13 miles above Skwentna
Shem Pete: "«The one they call **Dusdikda** extends upriver. They used to drive moose along it. The river there is brown in color. That's a big island above **Tseles Qan** [Mount Kliskon]. That's as far up the Yentna River as I have gone.»"

§7.56 Dusdikda Betnu • 'No-Good Point Stream'
slough on west side island in Yentna River

7.32 Yentnu Łi'a • 'Backbone River Glacier'
Yentna Glacier
Herron (1901:19): "They [Dena'ina men at Susitna Station] promptly rejected the proposition to seek a pass over the divide via the Yentna River, stating positively that the Yentna heads in glaciers and that there is no way to get around them."

§7.57 Nunhdat'unhtnu • 'Objects Extended in Line-River'
probably West Fork of Yentna River
Name confirmed by Sava Stephan. The pass at the head of the West Fork, Shellabarger Pass, was probably used on occasion by the Dena'ina. In the Upper Kuskokwim language this pass is named **Tetno' Hwchwx Dotis** (see 6.59) based upon the name for the Dillinger River.

7.33 Nunhdat'unh • 'Objects Extended in Line'
Central Alaska Range between head of East and West Forks of the Yentna River and Mount Dall
Shem Pete: "«Extending to the west from Mount McKinley is **Nunhdat'unh**, the mountains all over there.»"

The name cited by Herron for the main part of the southern Alaska Range, "To-toy-lon," is not recognized by today's Dena'ina speakers.

Sava Stephan: **"Nunhdat'un,** my dad told me there's a

people up there, don't talk our language. Native [were] up there. He knows there. He been up through there, but not me. They may have been Upper Kuskokwim people.» My dad and Shem Pete went through there."

§7.58 Ch'idotl'uł No' Dotis *(Upper Kuskokwim)* • 'Braided String River - Pass'
Mystic Pass
This name is based upon the Upper Kuskokwim name for the Tonzona River (Kari 1999:99).

William Beach in 1925 while near Mt. Dall and Mystic Pass at the head of the Tonzona River suggested that some Dena'ina had been obtaining sheep via Mystic Pass. Beach (1931:90–91, 94): "Capps had described the head of this stream and as there was a very interesting glacier toward the head of another stream on the left-hand side which he called Surprise Glacier, owing to its being unobserved until you came directly upon it, I was particularly anxious to see it.

"At the extreme head of the main stream there was a break in the mountains and a fine low pass which should lead down to the head of the Yentna on the south side of the range. So far as is known this pass had been undiscovered until this year when Capps explored it and went through to the south side. For many years the Indians from the south side of the range would go up to the head of the Yentna and return with sheep. This puzzled the Alaskans, as no sheep had ever been seen on the south side, so it is fair to presume that this pass must have been known to the older Indians and used by them. As we had seen many meat racks that had not been used for years, we felt sure that our suspicion was correct....

"Rainy Pass could not be over forty to fifty miles away, which meant three days travel at best. On all the mountains I could see many sheep."

7.34 Hneh'itnu, Heneh'itnu • 'Upland Creek'
Lake Creek
A trail ascending the east bank of Lake Creek to Chelatna Lake is shown on the 1906 Herning map (Map 32). A lateral trail is shown on Sleem (1910a) (Map 30) going up Flag Creek, crossing Lake Creek, and to the Peters Hills.

Fall and Greiser (1986): Billy Pete: "Right after the ice goes out by the Lake Creek they used to start catching fish. They used to have a **nichił** over there. At the Lake Creek."

7.35 Hneh'itnu Bena, Heneh'itnu Bena • 'Upland Creek Lake'
Bulchitna Lake
Billy Pete: "Bulchitna. Somebody named Charley Nelson, a Swede, he died around 1934 or 1936. He used to stay right at McDougall for about forty years. He found that lake and said 'Oh bullshit,' and that's the name of it." Orth (1971:166) states that Bulchitna Lake was first published as such in 1954.

7.36 Dghelikda T'uh Ch'adinłeni • 'The One Flowing from No-Good Mountain'
Yenlo Creek

7.37 K'kuy'ingga, §K'kuy'inshla • 'Little Heart'
Willow Mountain

7.38 Hdaq K'ilantnu • 'Creek Where There Is Mineral Pigment [ochre]'
Camp Creek
This is on a trail from Kroto Creek to the upper Yentna via **Tseles Qan** (7.30), Mount Kliskon. **Hdaq** is said by Shem Pete to be the lowest grade ochre pigment.

7.39 Ht'u Bena Q'estsiq' • 'Outlet of Beneath [the range] Lake'
upper Lake Creek, between Chelatna Lake and Camp Creek
It was in this area on Sunflower Creek that the Browne

FIGURE 100

A view taken from **Ch'idotl'uł No' Dotis** (7.58, Mystic Pass) at the very head of the Tonzona River, looking west down into the upper west fork of the Yentna River. Taken in 1925 by Stephen R. Capps, Jr. This photo may have been taken on the very day that Capps coined the name "Mystic Pass." ‡Bobby Esai stated that Mystic Pass was used occasionally during falltime by both the Dena'ina and the Upper Kuskokwim people.

STEPHEN R. CAPPS, JR. COLLECTION (#83-149-2370), ARCHIVES, ALASKA AND POLAR REGIONS DEPT., RASMUSON LIBRARY, UNIVERSITY OF ALASKA FAIRBANKS

FIGURE 101

(Above) **Ht'u Bena** (7.40, Chelatna Lake), viewed from the ridge on the west side of the lake. The mountain on the east side of the lake is **Ht'u Bena Dghelaya** (7.41). **Ch'alentnu** (7.58, Coffee Creek) is the valley on the left. Photo taken in the summer of 1911 by Stephen R. Capps, Jr.

STEPHEN R. CAPPS, JR. COLLECTION (#83-149-1197), ARCHIVES, ALASKA AND POLAR REGIONS DEPT., RASMUSON LIBRARY, UNIVERSITY OF ALASKA FAIRBANKS

FIGURE 102

(Right) **Chulyin Bena** (7.44, Shulin Lake) on the left above **K'enuqak'itnetan Betnu** (7.45, lower Peters Creek), near its confluence with **Kagheltnu** (7.43, Kahiltna River). In the distance can be seen **Yentnu** (5.1, the Yentna River).

PHOTO BY FRED HIRSCHMANN, AK-6824

FIGURE 103

Ch'alentnu (7.58, Coffee Creek) and its outlet into **Ht'u Bena** (7.40, Chelatna Lake), looking to the south. Roger Robinson of the National Park Service is in the foreground.

PHOTO BY MARK STASIK

and Cook party met Susitna Pete in 1906. (Shem Pete calls this man **Tsel Ch'a'ilk'elen**. See 7.47.) Pete then joined them as they crossed the southern base of Mount McKinley to the Tokositna River, where Susitna Pete was the source of several of the Dena'ina names recorded by Cook and Browne (Cook 1908:163–174; Browne 1956: 48–59). Pete is pictured following p. 162 of Cook's book. He was joined briefly by his wife, whom Browne described as a "typical Susitna Indian woman." Shem Pete said that this woman was his step-sister.

7.40 Ht'u Bena • 'Beneath [the range] Lake'
Chelatna Lake
This name first appeared in Herning (1906) as "Chelintna Lake" (Map 32) and Capps (1913) as Chelantna Lake. Shem Pete did not recognize the name "Chelatna." On the 1910a Sleem map this is given as "Lake Creek Lake" (Map 30).

Shem Pete: "«My brothers used to go there, to where they call it **Ht'u Bena**.» I heard about it, but I didn't see it. «My brothers carried a birchbark canoe from **Dghelikda** [Mount Yenlo] and they brought it over the flats. And they put it in that lake. On the lower end it is a brown color. Where it enters the mountains [above] it is a black color. One lake has two colors. Where it enters the mountains there is a [giant] leech. It is as tall as the mountain when it sticks its head out. Sometimes it is higher than the mountain. On the lower end where it is brown there is a [giant] brown bear. It is a good-natured animal. Where the water is black, however, when a caribou swims there, it disappears. The leech swallows it. It kills things that it smells. On the lower end where it is brown, nothing happens there. The caribou swim straight across there. When the caribou go into that lake, they [the Dena'ina] put in the canoe that they had brought, and they stab them. That's what I heard about it, **Ht'u Bena**.»"

Browne (1956:48): "While fording the beautiful stream called Lake Creek by the miners, Susitna Pete told us an interesting story. He said that in the lake at the head of the stream there lived an enormous fish. The fish was so large that it could eat caribou. A friend of his once followed four caribou so relentlessly that they were forced to swim the lake to escape, and while the hunter stood on the mountainside sadly watching his escaping quarry, the huge fish rose to the surface with a hissing sound and—swallowed the caribou."

§7.59 likely **[Ch'alentnu]** • 'Current Flows Out-Stream'
Coffee Creek
This name is suggested by the spelling on the 1906 Herning map "Chelintna Lake" (Map 33) and Capps (1913) as "Chelantna Lake" which imply this plausible name for the main stream entering into the east side of Chelatna Lake, Coffee Creek.

7.41 Ht'u Bena Dghelaya • 'Mountain of Lake Beneath [the range]'
mountain, elev. 4660', east of Chelatna Lake

7.42 Kagheltnu • ‡'River That Flows from Upstream'
Kahiltna River
Shem Pete states that this name is shortened from **Kaghilentnu**. He also said that the Kahiltna River is too swift to navigate in a skin boat with a large load of meat. Other streams, such as Kichatna, Talachulitna, and Happy River, were much more navigable with the traditional skin boats. Therefore, people hunted up this river in the late fall until freeze-up and then traveled downstream on the ice (Fall 1987:35).

The trail from McDougall, up the Kahiltna River to Cache Creek and over to the Tokositna River, was traveled by Shem Pete in about 1904. This trail is indicated on maps by Herning 1906 (Map 32), Cook 1907 and Sleem 1910a (Map 30). Shem maintained that this was an aboriginal Dena'ina trail. The use of this trail during the gold rush period is summarized by Cole (1983:85–88).

7.43 Qałnigi Keght • 'At the Big Rock'
large rock, perhaps twenty miles up the Kahiltna River, on the east bank
Shem Pete: "«We go into the crevices there. Rocks are cracked in different directions. We walk around on the inside. There is porcupine dung eight to ten feet thick

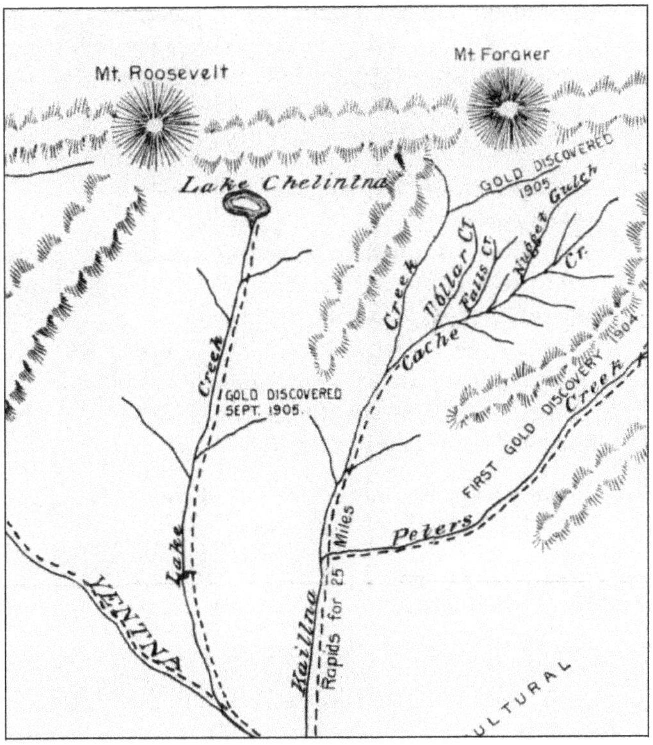

MAP 32

Detail from the 1906 Herning map: Upper Yentna River

This detail in the upper Yentna River on the 1906 map of Central Alaska by O. G. Herning, the storekeeper at Knik, shows what is now known as Chelatna Lake as "Lake Chelintna."

ARCHIVES, ALASKA AND POLAR REGIONS DEPT., RASMUSON LIBRARY, UNIVERSITY OF ALASKA FAIRBANKS

FIGURE 104

K'enuqak'itnetant (7.46, Peters Hills). Photo taken in 1911 by Stephen R. Capps, Jr.

STEPHEN R. CAPPS, JR. COLLECTION (#262), ARCHIVES, ALASKA AND POLAR REGIONS DEPT., RASMUSON LIBRARY, UNIVERSITY OF ALASKA FAIRBANKS

inside it. It does not snow beneath there. Beneath there was a camp. The campfires of the old people are under there.» They save them rock axes for souvenir.

"«The church warden at Tyonek took that woman **Sidel Bunkda,** and they went marten trapping at the Kahiltna River. When he called for her to come, she wouldn't quit [trapping]. She went all around that rock, and they took off in sleds, leaving her behind. They heard her calling, '**Sidel**, my grandfather, **Sidel**, my grandfather.' When they started back for Tyonek, she became frightened, and she jumped off the rock and landed in the snow. She didn't die.» She don't care she die. That's all about it, that **Qałnigi Keght**."

7.44 Chulyin Bena • 'Raven Lake'
Shulin Lake
Shem Pete was not certain about this name, which was reported in 1958 by USGS (Orth 1971:871). This is the Outer Inlet Dena'ina name for raven.

When the Cook party crossed the upper Kahiltna River in this area in 1906, they camped "at a point where eighteen years before the Susitna chief [Pete] had hunted moose" (Cook 1908:163).

7.45 K'enuqak'itnetan Betnu • 'Creek of Animal Is Crouching and Revolving'
Peters Creek

7.46 K'enuqak'itnetant • 'Where an Animal Is Crouching and Revolving'
Peters Hills
Shem Pete: "That just like an animal to them. Just like kneeling down animal. «As you walk around it, it looks just like a big animal lying there. Upriver from that mountain **K'enuqak'itnetant,** we come to **Tuqashitnu** [Tokositna River].» We go across the country there through the bite. Pass there." See 9.9.

7.47 Delggematnu • 'Ptarmigan Creek'
Cache Creek
Shem Pete: "«**Tsel Ch'a'ilk'elen** [Susitna Pete, Shem Pete's former brother-in-law] had a village on **Delggematnu**. He found gold up there. He worked there a good many years.» He drink water, he see gold down in **Delggematnu**. He made a cache up there." Susitna Pete's camp on Cache Creek is mentioned by Cook (1908:174).

Shem Pete recalled traveling through here by sled in March of about 1904. They could not catch any caribou.

7.48 Kagheltnu Łi'a • ‡'Glacier of River That Flows from Upstream'
Kahiltna Glacier

§7.60 Ch'ighu' Tsats'ela *(Upper Kuskokwim)***;** possibly **[K'ghitsala]** *(Dena'ina)* • 'Fang'
Mount Russell
Name contributed by Nick Dennis of Nikolai. Mount Russell is visible from the south, but we never obtained a Dena'ina name for it.

‡7.62 Denaze Dinye *(Upper Kuskokwim)* • 'The Tall One Canyon'
south mountain wall between Mt. Russell and Mt. Foraker
In a remarkable narrative told by Miska Deaphon of Nikolai in 1981, in 1919 Deaphon, Carl Susui, and Carl's wife walked from Telida to the head of Swift Fork into the upper Tonzona River Basin, returning to Telida (Deaphon 2015). «Upland up above and from upstream is a gorge, chasm. **Denaze Dinye** 'tall one's canyon,' the chasm extends upland from the upstream side, it seems to extend down to the treeline below.»

7.49 Be'u • 'His Wife,' **‡Ts'udots'in Denaze** *(Upper Kuskokwim)* 'Downstream Tall One'
Mount Foraker
Shem Pete: "«On the east side of **Dghelay Ka'a** sits his [Mt. McKinley's] wife.»"

Upper Kuskokwim uses directionals 'downstream' and 'upstream' to distinguish the two largest mountains in the range.

7.50 Begguya • 'His Child'
Mount Hunter
Shem Pete: "«In the middle is their child.»"

7.51 Dghelay Ka'a *(U)*, **Dghili Ka'a** *(OI)*, **Dghelaay Ce'e** *(Ahtna)* • 'Big Mountain'
Denali (formerly Mount McKinley) and the high mountains of the Central Alaska Range
The Dena'ina names for Mount Susitna (4.9) and Denali, in their very simplicity, **Dghelishla,** 'Little Mountain,'

and **Dghelay Ka'a**, 'Big Mountain,' stand out among the Dena'ina geographic names as a pair of iconic place names. See further discussion of Denali names on pp. 211–213. See 9.18 Ruth Glacier, which we now consider to be **Dghelay Ka'a Łi'a**.

Brooks, Stuck, Spurr, Browne, Cook, and others have recorded the Upper Inlet Dena'ina name variously as "Traleika," "Traleyka," "Doleika," "To-lah-gah." Brooks (1911:22): "[T]he tribes on the east side of the range, who seldom, if ever, approached it, termed it Traleyka." Note that the name "Traleika Glacier," a branch of Muldrow Glacier on the north face, coined by Washburn in 1945, is based upon this Dena'ina name for Denali. This is not an aboriginal name for this feature. Such a name for a glacier would have been more appropriate on the south side of the Range, i.e., for Ruth Glacier, see 9.18.

Annabel (1997e:338): "Things I wonder about. How come we're told that "Denali" is the Injun name for Mt. McKinley? Every Injun I know in the area calls the mountain "Delaykah," which means simply, "That big peak over there."

The late Jennie Peters of Cantwell quipped to Kari in 1978: "We don't call it 'Denali.' That's what white people tell us that we call it."

Sheldon (1908:271–272, 277): "The Susitna Indians place the origin of man near Mt. McKinley and the raven as creator.... The big peak marks the beginning of the world; here man first began existence, and from here he spread to the utmost reaches of the earth.... The mountain god is regarded as a protector, helping the Indian in his troubles. If an Indian ventures into the high mountains and appeals to the spirit, he is supposed to be received cordially and is given direct advice for his future conduct."

Browne (1956:4): "If you can earn the confidence of the aged Indians they will tell you of days when the earth was covered with water, and how a god who was chasing his eloping sweetheart threw a rock with intent to kill, and how that rock rose above the falling water and stands to this day—the incomparable Doleika."

Metcalf (1910: 256): "To the Russians it was known as "Bolshoy," to the natives of Cook Inlet as "Traleika," both signifying high or "big" mountain. The Indians have a strange myth concerning it, believing it to be the birthplace of mankind; the Creator has His workshop near its base, and there, even to this day, is busy fashioning with His hands the human race. While thus engaged He assumes the form of a raven. The great peak thus marks the beginning of the world, when mankind has migrated to the utmost reaches of the earth."

The late John Stump remarked that the clouds on top of **Dghelay Ka'a** are said to be the smoke of the fires of **dghelay dnay**, the legendary 'mountain people.' John Stump: "Same thing that big McKinley mountain, they're people too. All the Indians say when they [the mountain people] build a fire you see their smoke—those clouds on top. All Indians will say 'We'll be glad they built a fire. Gonna warm up.' And it did too. And when it's all clear up there, no smoke on the mountains, they's gonna get cold. And they do too. They're people, three of them. They used to be people. When they see cloud, they say, 'By God, they're waking up. They're building a fire.'"

These clouds in the mountains that are said to control the weather are called **yuq' qiteni** 'the ones that hold the [other] clouds.'

§7.61 Dghelay Teh, *‡(Dena'ina),* **Digheloye Te** *(Upper Kuskokwim),* **Deghiloyi Ti** *(Lower Tanana),* **Dghilaayi Tah** *(Ahtna)* • 'Among the Mountains'
The Alaska Range
This is the regional name that applies to the entire Alaska Range as well as to the adjacent mountain ranges, such as the Talkeetna Mountains.

‡Kari (1996a:463) first discussed the shift in the Athabascan/Dene names for 'mountain' and 'Alaska Range.' "The central Alaska term for 'Alaska Range' has extended its meaning to 'mountain' in the language positioned either south of west of the Alaska Range [Ahtna, Dena'ina, Upper Kuskokwm, and Deg Hit'an].... One might speculate from the loci of the original name for 'Alaska Range' compared with the areas with the extended meaning 'mountain,' that an Athabaskan place name conference or negotiation among chiefs on this issue took place in the lower Tanana River area."

FIGURE 105

Be'u (7.49, Mount Foraker) viewed from Granite Creek on the upper Kahiltna River. Photo taken in 1911 by Stephen R. Capps, Jr.
STEPHEN R. CAPPS, JR. COLLECTION (#298), ARCHIVES, ALASKA AND POLAR REGIONS DEPT., RASMUSON LIBRARY, UNIVERSITY OF ALASKA FAIRBANKS

1919 Trip from Sushitna Station to the Johnson Creek area and Hewitt Lake

by Shem Pete

In the nineteenth and early twentieth centuries, the Dena'ina of the lower Susitna River villages traveled up the Yentna and Skwentna rivers and their tributaries in the late summer and early fall to hunt caribou in the Rainy Pass area. After caching their watercraft, the men continued on foot. Following a successful hunt, they constructed skin boats (**elgheji**) by covering wooden frames with the raw hides, and floated downstream with their winter supply of meat to the villages. As a boy and young man Shem Pete participated in many of these hunts with his older brothers and other Dena'ina men.

With Shem Pete on this particular trip in August 1919 are Yagu Stephan (Tommy Allowan's father), Tsilgi or Chilligan (the senior person and group leader and Yagu Stephan's brother), Chilligan's mother and younger brother (unnamed in the story), Shem's fiance (named **Tulałen** or Inge, who was pregnant), Inge's mother (who is listed as Joko, age 60 on the 1920 census, see Table 13), and two young children. Shem's account begins three days out of Susitna Station without mentioning the point of departure. They had tracked the boat up the Yentna somewhere above Johnson Creek (7.18) where they started out on the trail for Rainy Pass.

This is a true life adventure narrative told with precise detail and great emotion. This is the only story in which Shem names and discusses his wife. This story validates Shem's credentials as an Alaska outdoorsman.

Recorded on October 14, 1983, in Fairbanks; translated on September 21, 1996, with Sava Stephan. Seventeen and one-half minutes in length.

1920, 1920 [1919]. My name is Shem Pete, I was gonna get married to the, to Billy's mother. And then so pretty soon ready to put. Two more months she gonna, she supposed to be go, but January month she have that baby. We went up, going up on the dory.

Ighi dora ghini betl'ila eł nch'edał ighi.
We were going with a dory by (tracking) rope.

Ighi Tommy betukda ghun shi Chilligan, Tommy betukda bingha ghun shi, Tsilgi ghin qeył dghinih.
So Tommy (Allowan's) father, Tommy's father's older brother, Chilligan was called Tsilgi.

Yen eł ch'taydatl'.
We went with him.

Ch'u nayna nuquq'ushi ghuda.
Because he was to spend the fall season with us.

Ch'u "Three days nch'idatl'i eł q'u nch'uk'a natl'uyiyul.
And we had been going for three days, and no one was following (closely) after us.

Beghala dghiłdes ch'u yes tunuch'delggesh.
His (Chilligan's) pack was heavy, and we were going up on ahead.

Yet ch'ninu ch'u nch'uk'a na'eł shih nutałghatl'.
We stopped there and it was not quite dark yet on us.

Biqu hngheł'ani qubeł chich'enah iyni nulnesh ch'u naqanushełdanełtuk' ch'u.
I went to look for him, in case someone had been sick, and I took a gun and ran back.

Bet'uynugheshjuł ken q'u jitshla qugheltishi hq'u.
And I met up him on a flat by a little knoll.

Ghunen idałq'en ch'u qendugh qiłtan k'i.
He (Tsilgi or Chilligan) had a fire burning, and he lay on the floor (of a cabin, house).

Bedzik'ni'u ch'u ki daghelnik [??] benaq'a k'a hditdal.
His ears were aching [inaudible], and his eyes had turned red.

Shkin'i, shkin'i, shi nik'ni'u!" ni.
"My head, my head has a pain!" he said.

Ch'u łuq'u nushełdghełtesh ch'u nutałghatl' ch'u.
So I ran about (to get wood) and it was getting dark.

Ch'bach'etl'a ghini nghalggeni banik'nesdzel.
I chopped off some jack spruce, dry ones.

Hdakat nubesdelchesh ch'u chik'a daghiłkugh daghettunh tl'uh.
I dragged this up to the doorway and made a big pile (of wood) in back.

Yethdi shan qilan.
It was summer (August).

Q'u nushełdayeltuk' ch'u sha'a nutułgheli k'u.
And then I ran back before it would get dark on me.

Q'u nutałghatl' hnik'dulnen.
It was getting dark and the sun had set.

Yus shełndeltush, q'u nch'uk'a nishich"elsil gheli ch'u
So I ran on ahead, and I had not gotten too exhausted and

Tuk'eleh Betnu ghu qetnih yet ch'ach'idał łiq'a qudeł.
we had left from where they call 'fish run stream' (7.18, Johnson Creek) and salmon (silver salmon) were jumping.

Yet idiłdi already ts'iłq'i łiq'a chiłyuq.
There he (Yagu Stephan) had already caught one salmon.

Yada k'a chiyiłyuggi di ighi Stephan qeył dghinih, Tommy ghun tukda.
He had got it somehow, that guy they called Stephan, Tommy's father.

Stephan, Yagu qeył dghinih.
Stephan, they called him Yagu.

Ch'u "Dudushdich'en q'u nughiłghatl'," dach' qubeł deshni,
"On the downstream side it is dark," and I said to them,

"Nch'uk'a nabeł yetułquli q'ent'a qil.
"He will not dawn with us, it looks serious.

"Bekin'i banik'di'u ch'u benaq'a k'a benana ghundi deł t'enijuq," qubeł deshni.
"His head is aching and his eyes and face are bloody," I told them.

Tsukan gheli q'u bunkda ghun sheł nutashju.
Early in the morning his mother came back with me.

[This is ambiguous, but apparently this was Chilligan's mother.]

Yanahdi dehq'aka'a duch'qiy'un.
And then there we put up a big rack.

I had new tent, q'udidi tent nughełkes.
I had a new tent, I had brought a new tent.

I take that woman, dek'isen ghunen ghe nigheshuyi ghuda qubeł tayeshu.
I had brought that woman, I had gone with them because of the woman that I was going to marry.

FIGURE 106
Shem Pete near **Delggematnu** (7.47, Cache Creek) in 1977.
PHOTO BY PRISCILLA RUSSELL

Ch'u dehq'a łu nich'qiłtan ch'u beghnu shi shyagh'a.
And we lay him down by the rack with my gear.

Balatga new one ghin, bach'iyaghałchet all the stuff, trap and everything.
We wrapped all my stuff in that new tent.

Ch'u nayna kiq'u nach' ghin ch'ighetneq ch'u yeh nuch'tasdatl', q'u gheli qil gheli eydlan.
So then we brought more things over to us, and we started back there, he was nearly dead.

Hełch'en hnuq'u qil eydlan. Qil eydlan ch'u ki daghiset.
In the evening he died. He died and it was a long ways off.

Dehq'a duch'qi'un nich'qinilu dghu hał ch'u t'eł'an.
We had put things on the rack that we had built, I used a pack.

Grub ghini na'a qilal two three days, you know ch'u.
We had had no grub for two or three days, you know.

Ch'u bunkda ghun jenutghelnesh, three days jani k'a gheli hał nch'k'iłdatl'.
And I had carried his (Chilligan's) mother on my back for three days, all day long we had been packing.

Daghiset ghu dudiset, batnalyiy ka'a ch'dałchin ch'u yuset dghu yuset dghu.
It was a long way, and it got even farther and we made a big bier (or stretcher).

Bisanesyel q'es ghiduh da'ildatl'.
I stood up with her sitting on my shoulders as she sat up on my neck.

Be'u ghunen ts'iłch'en yesaneyel, yet ts'iłch'en ghedunhdi bekela ghun Yagu, Jacob Stephan, Yagu Stephan, yen nundghelyesh.
His wife stood on one side and on the other side was his younger brother, Yagu Stephan, as the time passed.

Ts'iłq'i jani k'a gheli nunch'ghalnik.
We had been carrying him (his body) for one whole day.

Niłghena gheli q'u beł nikench'dełgget qebenq'e ch'u.
One after the other we took turns carrying him on that (bier).

Q'ut'un idiłti łuq'u gheli nelnitl'. Nelnitl' ch'u kenq'e qugheltishi qenuch'ghalnigi ghu na'eł nughiłghatl'.
The next morning he (the body) was all swollen. He was swollen, and we brought him to a knoll on that flat when it got dark on us.

Qubunkda ghun na'ełni, "Qeshqa ghuna ki nch'uk'a yaghelich' k'a beyaga nighesneshna shina shida.
Their mother said to us, "Those chiefs could not have buried his body as nicely.

Gu q'u ełnench' banłchit," na'eł ni.
"Put him here in the ground," she said to us.

Duguli k'i łu nuch'ulał. Hnihdełnen, foot and a half hqugh nihdanłnen. Qałnigi nitsik'aghelał danłnen.
We had brought axes. I chopped down a foot and half. I chopped while bringing out rocks.

Nestsał nestsał, jani q'e gheli, hełch'en jetshlaq'a łuq'u blistered t'iłal.
I chopped and chopped all day long, and by evening I was all blistered.

Belaq'a, shlaq'a ch'atanineq. Nuk'ghełk'el ch'u ditali k'dgheshghun ch'u
His palms and my palms had become blistered. I split some (wood) and made boards and

ts'endatt'un t'ełuq ghu ch'u beyashiga nuk'dnayełchin ch'u gelis ghin nudayełchin ch'u.
I made them thin and I made his coffin and I made a cross.

Ghu hnik'danełnenh hqugh shi shghedeh hqugh nch'uk'a didiset hqugh q'u.
I had dug down there and according to my height it was not that very deep.

Maybe two foot and half, three foot hqugh k'a shi qałnigi nidnashjel ch'u.
I had chopped down maybe two and half feet, three feet, but bedrock was extending there.

Yet'u qałnigi beq'e nuch'eytnayagh.
And with that we pushed rocks upon him.

Ch'bala dendałkeghi shi dendałkeghi ghini about eight or ten inch hqugh dendałkeghi ghini.
Then big spruce, spruce as big a me, about eight or ten inches thick.

Chik'a ka'a benaqach'dayel ch'u yi beduldetl' ye ki bear ch'ak'nuchit k'a nch'u t'qilil.
We piled big logs around him, and they were pinned together so that a bear would not be able to tear it open.

K'enaqak'anay'u qidaghiłkegh ch'u baqak'nay'u ch'iluq.
We made a big fence to go around him.

Ndahdi two three days k'ashi ch'eghutnu, no eat nothing, nch'uk'a yada grub q'atl'a nch'uk'a nuch'ilkeł.
We had worked for two or three days with nothing to eat, we had not brought enough food.

Na'eł q'uqidaq ch'u ch'u ełnen bach'niłchet, bech'anach'dalggey.
We were getting concerned, and we buried him and we left him.

K'unde gheli ghu qil. Łik'aqa łuq'u k'unde qubeł nihdalnen.

The starvation became serious. All the dogs were starting to die of starvation.

Ch'u ełyuni nijaq', iyni ka'a eł .32 special new one sh'iyna k'ilan.

And some spruce hens landed, my gun was a new one, a big .32 special.

Beł k'dełtetl ch'u yi qa nghiset nch'uk'a k'elqeł.

I shot one and on that they lived, but I did not eat.

K'eyaga egh ghgheshtnu ch'u ch'u q'ut'un idiłti yus ghu balgas ghu nich'niłggat, ch'anch'itdatl'.

From where I had been working on the body, the next morning we got back to where we had left the boat.

Baqay k'a yedi yet ch'iy eytun baqay ch'ghijaq' ch'u yun'e Johnson Creek K'eyghastnu dudusdich'en K'ich'atnu Kaq' qetni yeh taynik.

The boat was laying there, and we caulked the boat and then we went upstream to Johnson Creek ‡7.18, to 'harvest fish stream' ‡7.54 the one that is on the downstream side of where they call mouth of Kichatna.

Johnson Creek ghu kaq' ghu Tuk'eleh Kaq' ghu qetni dghu dghaynigi dey'un.

At the mouth of Johnson Creek, 'fish run-mouth' ‡7.53, was a cache.

Baqach'ghidatl'i ełdi marigu potato chips ghini maybe four, five, six cans t'uhdaydlu.

We climbed up it and inside were some milk and potato chips, maybe five or six cans.

Eagle Milk ghinihdi, five, six case yet t'uhdnałtun. Mergansina yegh t'uh qilch' taydlan, ch'ighetneq.

There were five or six cases of Eagle Milk. The Americans at this place had nearly died, and we took these.

Ki ch'ghunesh dghu yeh, q'u yet yunun qayahdast'it łdi. Yunun qutsagheł'i qughiban ki, tana'iltlet hnuq'u.

We kept on going by boat (downstream), and then across the way something appeared. Across there a seal swam up to the surface and then dove back under.

Sh'iyna dus bik'dnghełnen k'nich'en dayeshdu. Łuq'u hnes daghełtey.

I loaded some shells into my rifle, and I sat up in the stern. I was stronger than the others.

Tommy tukda shla ghundi shq'ay daghiłkegh. Q'u be'u k'ilan.

Tommy's father [Yagu] was a little guy, he was shorter than me, he had a wife.

Ch'u naghena hda ki qugheltlet hnuq'u iyni beł k'dayełtetl'.

And when it [the seal] came up near us, I shot it with the rifle.

Betsiduq' q'u beł bullet ghu behinaghestses.

I scraped the top of his head with a bullet.

Bekin'a łuq'u gheli bedeyes hdnilal, bets'ena yan ayahdast'it.

He head was all devoid of skin, just the (skull) bone was visible (SP chuckles).

Benich' hnighiqan ch'u ighi Stephan Stephan Yagu iy bit'a łyeł.

He brought the boat behind it and Stephan, Yagu Stephan grabbed its flipper.

Deghi łuq'u beyu'eł ghuda ch'u yeluh hnu duguli eł.

Since it tried to bite him with its teeth, and he held an axe.

Bedeyes k'a hnisen nothing.

It had no skin (on its head), nothing.

Yets'ena ghini tsaytnatset, ch'u tsaynghałnen ch'u chiyiłyuq. Yiten ch'u beł niqaghanshnik ch'u.

He pounded its skull, he hit it several times and he killed it. He grabbed it and I steered ashore with it.

Yungge nik'nełch'aq'.

I rolled it on up above (onto the bank).

Ki nch'uk'a q'alkik. Nagh'inqel'an k'undet k'u

It had not stopped raining. We were exhausted and starving.

Yunit yunit ghu cache ghin k'i ch'ghaynik ch'u potato chip, Eagle brand milk yi k'undet qilch' taydlan.

We went upstream to that cache and for the potato chip, and Eagle brand milk, as starvation had started to get serious.

Beqa ch'itujesh t'nt'a ch'ighetneq ch'u

We could survive on this and we took it and

qutsaghił'iy ghini benich' nuch'hnutqani eł q'u ba ta'iltutl'.

as we came back down up to the rear end of that seal the water level had risen up to it.

Dach'u all the time na'eł ełkun. Tugheltеł.

All the time it was raining on us. The water was raising.

Ch'u ki gini nuch'k'niłch'aq' ch'u baqay ghini tagh'i beghech ihech'dghinłggat bach' k'eyeghiłch'aq' ch'u.

So we rolled it down, and we shoved it up over the oars and the gunwale railing of that boat and we rolled it into it (the boat).

Beł nik'unuch'hnghatqan.

And we started out away from shore again with it.

Dek'isna ghuna qukut' qukut' qubedach'hnghinqan dghu.

We kept those women covered (in a tarp) while going in the boat.

FIGURE 107

Be'u (7.49, Mount Foraker) and **Dghelay Ka'a** (7.51, Denali). Photo taken above the Collinsville mine area with **Hdaq K'ilantnu,** (7.38, Camp Creek) in the foreground.

PHOTO BY MARK STASIK

Hełch' ch'u q'u yach'u qubek'ełch'ish. Yet ełch'ey yan.
By evening they had gotten wind-exposed. It was so windy.

Nobody can get up. Gunda k'undet ghu qil gheli.
No one could get up, now the starvation was so bad.

Qutsagheł'i ghin ch'adach' ghu ch'eł'an ch'u dghiłkegh gheli.
We had to do something with that seal, and it was really large.

Nateya qilal. Ghu ch'eghi'anh hnuq'u nunch'idiltey gheli, we strong.
Our strength was gone. At the time we had seen it, we had regained strength, we were strong.

Łu nuquch'ghalkit. Quch'k'ełch'ah. Ch'u nch'uk'a qit'a'ideshniyi ninya ghini.
So we brought it ashore. We rolled it up. And I had not known anything about this kind of animal.

Begguna ghini beghundelnesh ch'u ghet baqadayełen, ch'u bedeyes ghin ts'iłde q'u deghenst'us.
I cut off its arms and it cut it in (falling into a pot), and I cut along the skin on one side.

Ch'u yus qubetuynghełt'ech'.
And I put this out on the fire for them.

Yet ighi potato chip ghini my wife, Tulałen ghunen, nalgheji tuk'ehniłqet' ch'u nuyniłbu' ch'u yus seal eł sinałt'a.
And my wife, that Tulałen, put those potato chips into boiling water, and she stirred that and she was roasting that seal on the fire.

Maragu can't help, "Maragu elqat da yagheli ch'u maragu si tuniłtl'it ch'u."
The milk could not help, "If I could eat the milk that would be fine, pour some for me."

Shlaq'adghichet.
And she gave that to me.

"Ha q'u seven days yet gu hninayyul gin tiltlut," shełni
"So, seven days have passed here, drink this," she told me.

Ch'u galduha nghalggeni hdi qutsagheł'i niqubeyiłach
So she cooked for them the dry potatoes and the seal.

Beta'a ghin tunult'it gheli, del tughetneli ch'u.
The soup got really thick, a blood soup.

One cup yan telch'eh ch'u yach' qahdelyash.
And I drank just one cup, and I lay down there.

Ch'anikna na'eł nughedeł, nughedełna, yina ghuna k'i k'ta'a qubidgheltl'et hnuyu yach' quhduttuk'.
The young people who were going with us, when I gave them some of the soup, they collapsed.

Shik'a I never eat for seven days, nch'u ghu nch'u k'elqeł.

I had not eaten for seven days, I had not eaten anything.

Galduha nghelqet'q'u yach' qidghelnen. Ch'u anyway naytałqun hnuq'u q'ut'un hdulnen bedeyes ch'adanłkits.

I ate potatoes and then fell asleep. And anyway at dawn in the morning I removed the skin (of the seal).

"Bedeyes ghin nch'u qideqet'i shi," tsukdi k'isen sh'u ghu Tulałen ghun bunkda shełni.

"That skin is worthless," that old lady, my wife Tulałen's mother told me.

Beghusch'diłtani eł nughidlah dghelyan, about two three inch fat on his back.

When we skinned it it was so fat, about two or three inches of fat were on its back.

Ch'u łuq'u beq'eh ghin betsen ch'ighetneq ch'u yetdu nuch'enasdul yet.

And so we took all the fat and the meat, and we stayed there another night.

K'qelqat ch'u nik'unuch'ghatnik. Tiq'atl'ena qeyłnihi eł nuch'dghitnik.

They ate and we set out again in the boat. We got back to the place called 'timbered lowlands gap' (Hewitt Lake site, 7.2).

Łiq'a bak'ilan. Bear chich'ełyuq. Bech'eshjesh gheli yethdi.

There were salmon in it. We killed a bear. We were really safe there.

Łiq'a nk'ilan gheli gee whiz. Dach' gheli q'u tudełni gheli.

There were lots of salmon. They were really splashing in the water.

Łiq'a ch'elqat, bear ch'u ch'elqat, qutsagheł'i gha ghini hyiłkash ch'u ha eł łiq'a ch'elqat.

We ate the salmon, we ate the bear, and we rendered that seal fat, and we ate that salmon with grease.

Ch'eshjesh, natsen natsen nuk'esdlan.

We were safe, our flesh, our flesh got restored.

Ch'u ighi yagheli ki nik'unch'eghatnik, niłnuch'eghutnik.

So that was good and we set out again by boat, and we made it back.

Bude q'u niłnuch'eghutnik naqeshqa ghun.

We had returned without him (Tsilgi or Chilligan), without our leader.

Billy ghunhdi yet hey January month shgguya eydlan. Q'u yethdi bek'idlana gga, shgguya iydlan.

And that Billy, my son was born that winter in January month. So then he was a newborn, my son.

Bunkda ghundi t.b. hał eł qiydnałdu.

His mother got t.b., and she (Shem's wife, Inge) got injured carrying a pack.

Elugh k'a yełkit dghu.

I had not yet married her though.

Hundred pound of sugar dek'isen gga ghu dghildes ghu nch'uk'a hughu qeyeł yiłghal.

There was no reason for her to have packed a hundred pounds of sugar, that small woman.

Beł yach' qidulnen. Bejagh q'u daydlut' ch'u t.b. t'yiluq, ch'u shqil eydlan.

She had fallen down with that. Her chest got infected and she got t.b. and she died.

Five years yan beł gheshdu, ghu shi qil eydlan t.b. yighetneq ch'en.

I stayed with her only five years. When she died, t.b. took her away.

Anchorage hdi hospital tudayel'un ch'u Anchorage yethdi shqil eydlan.

I transported her by boat to the Anchorage hospital and then she died in Anchorage.

[Shem's last expression here is charged with emotion. He says literally 'and then I died in Anchorage.']

Q'u k'i ch'adach' ghu heł nutghelnek? Nuqelnek nch'uk'a shqil ghu nuqelnik t'i

But why should I tell you about this? This is not for the telling.

I don't like to talk about my wife.

Q'u dutdgheshcheł.

Now I am going to shut up.

(Pause, segment added later that day.)

Sh'u ghila'en ghunen ghinhdi ighi Inge qeył dghinih.

The one that was my wife was called Inge.

Q'u about March month, no February month, shgul janq'u nugheyuł

So in March month, no in February month, she was going to school.

"Shik'a gunen ghe niniyush," sheł qetni. Yetdhi Mr. Miller qeył dghinihen Native Native boss, superintendent ghila.

"You should marry this person," the superintendent told me, the one they called Mr. Miller.

Quyu ch'u Susitnu ht'ana t'qinult'a, before flu ch'u.
He had come up when the Susitna people had been numerous, before the flu.

Ch'u Mr. Miller ghunen, "Dahna q'u Sam Pete yeghe nighiyuni dehni gundi k'isen?"
And that Mr. Miller said, "How many of you say that Sam Pete should marry this girl?"

Łuq'u gheli gganqelchet. Ch'u nuhnastsut.
Everyone all stood up. And they sat back down.

"Tahdna q'u nch'u ghe nighiyu idini?"
"Now do you want him to marry a Russian?"

Shi yi ts'iłt'an yan begganlnik "I don't want to marry, I'm too young."
So just I stood up by myself, "I don't want to marry, I'm too young."

K'i ts'iłt'an k'a gganelnik.
So just I had stood up.

They win, they make me get married.

Dog team Iditarod Trail yeh, freighting t'esht'an, I make money.
I was freighting on the Iditarod Trail, I make money.

Ch'u Mr. Coffee qeył dghinihen Judge Talkitnu ye eydu. Daghiset from Suyitnu Station.
And the one they called Mr. Coffee was a judge staying in Talkeetna, that was a long way from Susitna Station.

Tiq'a naqulahi ghuda yet yun'e Talkitnu qech'iydatl'.
We went upstream to Talkeetna to get married.

[Shem's expression to get married is interesting and means literally 'to become part of the timbered lowlands.' The implication is that the man in the uplands becomes united with the woman in the lowlands.]

Anderson, Sava betukda, gu Tulałen ghunen, yen k'a yen be'u ghunen k'a dek'isen ghun yighetneq ch'u qech'idatl'.
Anderson, Sava's father, he too had a wife, and he took brought her, and we went there (to Talkeetna).

Ch'u tiq'a naqiluq.
And he married us.

[Shem was older than Anderson. They got married in a double wedding in Talkeetna in 1919.]

Yagheli q'udiki I tell you my wife's name, Inge qeył dghinih q'u.
That is good now, I'll tell you my wife's name, they called her Inge. (Shem sobs.)

Beghe qgheshnak k'a nch'u ideshne.
I don't care to talk about her.

FIGURE 108

A sunset silhouette of the Central Alaska Range looking to the west from Talkeetna Alaskan Lodge. The mountain at the left edge (and about 100 miles in the distance) is **Nunhdat'un** (9.33, Mt. Dall and associated mountains between the heads of the East and West Forks of the Yentna River), the pyramidal peak is (possibly) **K'ghitsala** (7.60, Mt. Russell). At the right edge is **Be'u** (7.49, Mt. Foraker).

PHOTO BY JAMES KARI

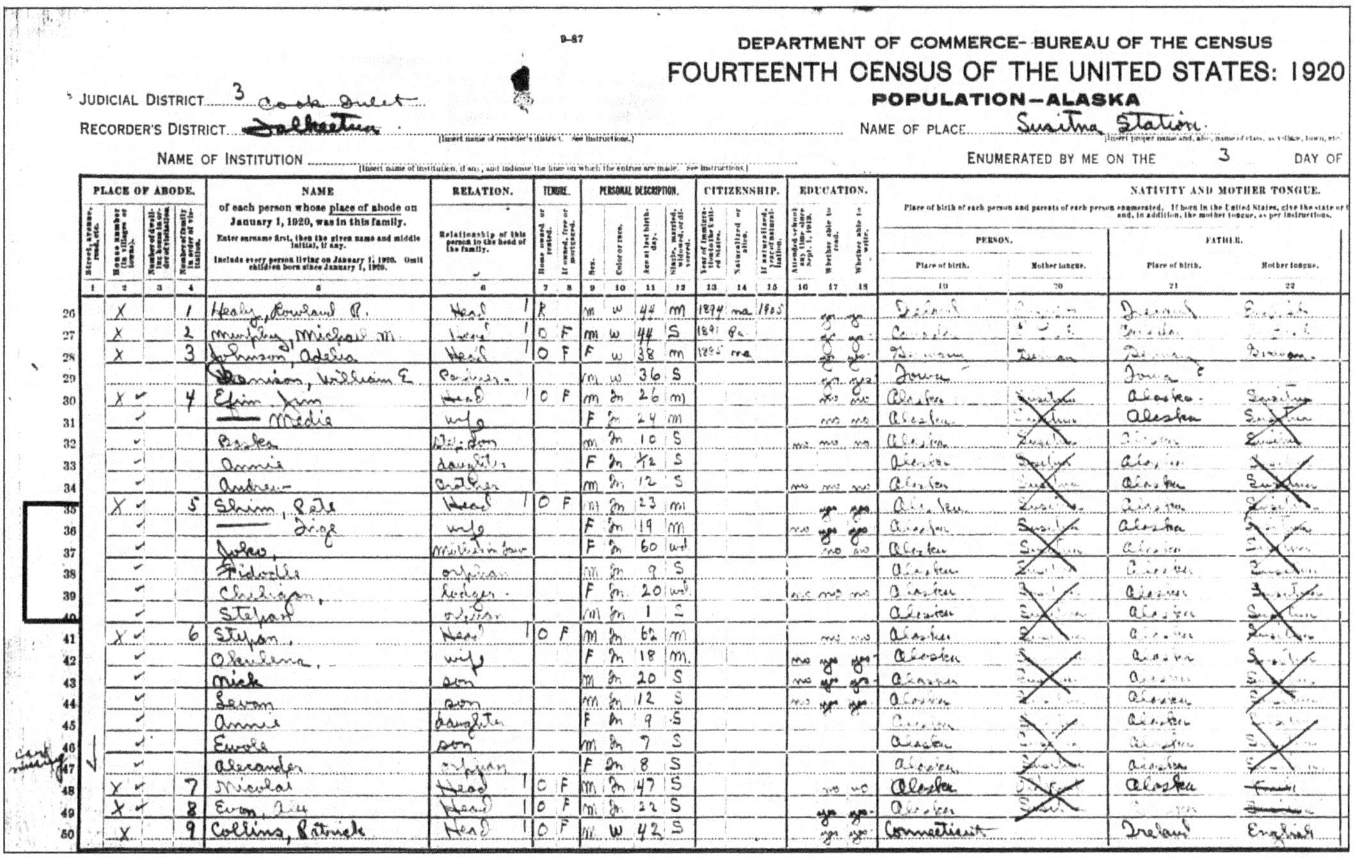

9-87

DEPARTMENT OF COMMERCE–BUREAU OF THE CENSUS

FOURTEENTH CENSUS OF THE UNITED STATES: 1920

POPULATION—ALASKA

JUDICIAL DISTRICT 3 Cook Inlet

RECORDER'S DISTRICT Talkeetna

NAME OF PLACE Susitna Station

NAME OF INSTITUTION

ENUMERATED BY ME ON THE 3 DAY OF

Line	House no.	Family no.	Name	Relation	Tenure		Sex	Color or race	Age	Marital	Place of birth (person)	Place of birth (father)
26	X	1	Healy, Rowland R.	Head	R		m	w	44	m	[illegible]	[illegible]
27	X	2	Murphy, Michael M.	Head	O	F	m	w	44	S	[illegible]	[illegible]
28	X	3	Johnson, Adelia	Head	O	F	F	w	38	m	[illegible]	[illegible]
29			Denison, William E.	Partner			m	w	36	S	Iowa	Iowa
30	X	4	Efim, Jim	Head	O	F	m	In	26	m	Alaska	Alaska
31			—— Media	wife			F	In	24	m	Alaska	Alaska
32			Barka	[illegible]			m	In	10	S	Alaska	[illegible]
33			Annie	daughter			F	In	4/12	S	Alaska	Alaska
34			Andrew	brother			m	In	12	S	Alaska	Alaska
35	X	5	Shim, Pete	Head	O	F	m	In	23	m	Alaska	Alaska
36			—— Inge	wife			F	In	19	m	Alaska	Alaska
37			Jokes	Mother-in-law			F	In	60	wd	Alaska	Alaska
38			Fidoshe	orphan			m	In	9	S	Alaska	Alaska
39			Chelagan	lodger			F	In	20	wd	Alaska	Alaska
40			Stepan	[illegible]			m	In	1	S	Alaska	Alaska
41	X	6	Stepan	Head	O	F	m	In	62	m	Alaska	Alaska
42			Olaulena	wife			F	In	18	m	Alaska	Alaska
43			Nick	son			m	In	20	S	Alaska	Alaska
44			Sevan	son			m	In	12	S	Alaska	Alaska
45			Annie	daughter			F	In	9	S	Alaska	Alaska
46			Ewole	son			m	In	7	S	Alaska	Alaska
47			Alexander	orphan			F	In	8	S	Alaska	Alaska
48	X	7	Nicolai	Head	O	F	m	In	47	S	Alaska	Alaska
49	X	8	Evan, [illegible]	Head	O	F	m	In	22	S	Alaska	[illegible]
50	X	9	Collins, Patrick	Head	O	F	m	w	42	S	Connecticut	Ireland

TABLE 13. SHEM PETE'S FAMILY ON THE 1920 CENSUS FOR SUSITNA STATION.

Shem Pete (whose name is written as "Pete Shim")and his wife Inge and their household of six persons are listed on the 1920 census for Susitna Station. This census was taken on February 3, 1920, so this would have been a few months after the events described in this story.

‡Since 2000 Wasilla historian Colleen Mielke has developed an impressive and influential website, "Matanuska-Susitna Valley, Alaska, Researching Our South Central Alaska Roots." The site features primary records on the people and history of Upper Cook Inlet. Currently she has over 70 articles at the site. Mielke has typed and posted censuses; church, court, and commercial records; obscure newspaper articles; citations from O.J. Herning journals; and biographies of prominent early Upper Cook Inlet people. All of the Dena'ina settlements and the historic towns of Cook Inlet are given coverage, and also those of other areas such as Prince Willam Sound and Bristol Bay. See http://freepages.genealogy.rootsweb.ancestry.com/~coleen/ south_central_alaska.

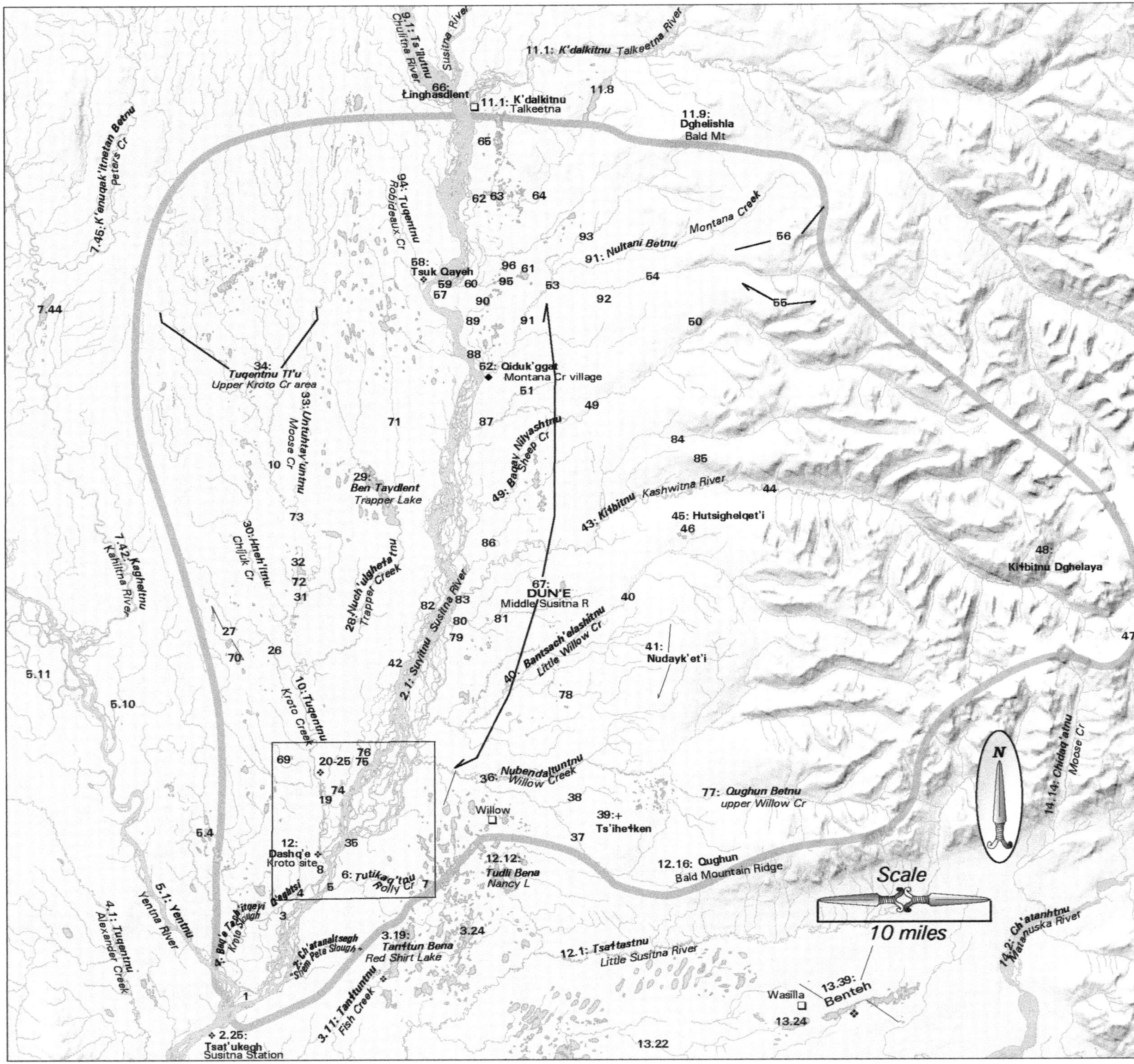

9.1: Ts'ilutnu
Chulitna River
Susitna River
11.1: K'dalkitnu Talkeetna River
66: Łinghasdlent
11.1: K'dalkitnu
Talkeetna
11.8
11.9: Dghelishla
Bald Mt
7.45: K'enuqak'itnetan Betnu
Peters Cr
94: Tuqentnu
Robideaux Cr
58: Tsuk Qayeh
91: Nultani Betnu
Montana Creek
7.44
34: Tuqentnu Tl'u
Upper Kroto Cr area
62: Qiduk'ggat
Montana Cr village
33: Untuhtay'untnu
Moose Cr
29: Ben Taydlent
Trapper Lake
49: Baqay Nilyashtnu
Sheep Cr
43: Kitbitnu Kashwitna River
45: Hutsighelqet'i
7.42: Kagheltnu
Kahiltna River
30: Hneh'itnu
Chijuk Cr
28: Nuch'ulgheta'tnu
Trapper Creek
48: Kitbitnu Dghelaya
67: DUN'E
Middle Susitna R
2.1: Suyitnu Susitna River
41: Nudayk'et'i
40: Bantsach'elashitnu
Little Willow Cr
5.11
5.10
10: Tuqentnu
Kroto Creek
36: Nubendaltuntnu
Willow Creek
77: Qughun Betnu
upper Willow Cr
Willow
39: Ts'ihetken
14.14: Chidaq'atnu
Moose Cr
5.4
12: Dashq'e
Kroto site
6: Tutikaq'tnu
Rolly Cr
12.12: Tudli Bena
Nancy L
12.16: Qughun
Bald Mountain Ridge
Scale
10 miles
4.1: Tuqentnu
Alexander Creek
5.1: Yentnu
Yentna River
4: Baq'e Taq'itgeyi
Kroto Slough
B'eghtsi
2: Ch'atanaltsegh
"Shem Pete Slough"
3.19: Tantuntnu Bena
Red Shirt Lake
3.24
12.1: Tsaltastnu
Little Susitna River
14.2: Ch'atanhtnu
Matanuska River
3.11: Tantuntnu
Fish Creek
Wasilla
13.39: Benteh
13.24
2.25: Tsat'ukegh
Susitna Station
13.22
47
N

8

Middle Susitna River

from Yentna River to Talkeetna town, including Kroto Creek (or Deshka River) drainage

Katherine Nicolie: "They [Katherine's family] stay at Kroto all winter and spring. They stay for fish in summer. End of July they leave Kroto for the [Talkeetna] mountains. Go back to Kroto in October before ice." See also Katherine Nicolie's story on pp. 77–78.

Shem Pete: "«Kroto people used **K'esugi** [9.7, K'esugi Ridge] to **Qughun** [12.16, Bald Mountain Ridge]. They used that area.» They went up Willow, Montana, and Caswell creeks to the mountains. They catch caribou in that mountain. Every summer they stay waiting for caribou. They catch caribou, they make a skin boat and go down to Kroto. The Yentna was too far for them."

Billy Pete: "Instead of making shortcut, they just go all the way through. Those people, just visit their friends. Like at Nancy Lake, big bunch of **nichił** over there. They had to see them before they go to Talkeetna. Instead of a straight line from A to B, they make about a 500-mile extra trip to visit all their friends. Maybe it take them a month to get there."

Browne (1956:78): "Your northern red man is a master of the craft of travel. After the salmon-run on the lower rivers has filled their caches with food for man and dog, they await the freezing of the waters. When the icy covering has formed, their dogs pull their belongings to the moose pastures and caribou ranges of the interior. Here they hunt and trap the long winter through, and after the spring sun has sent the ice booming towards the sea, they sew up their winter skins into boats and drift with dignity to their summer homes. Here the boats are dismantled, and the skins—none the worse for their immersion—are tanned. When their winter's fur catch is traded, they can await the autumn salmon run in peace."

MAP 33

(Opposite) Place names map of the middle Susitna River, showing Nos. 8.1 to 8.96.

MAP BY MATT GANLEY

§8.67 Dun'e • 'Intermediate Distance Upstream'
the middle Susitna River area, from above Yentna River to Talkeetna River
This regional place name also is in the ethnonym, **Dun'ena**, for the middle Susitna Dena'ina people.

8.1 Beq'e Tach'itqeyi • 'On It We Sink into the Water'
island at the confluence of the Yentna River with the Susitna River

8.2 Ch'atanaltsegh • 'Yellow Water Flows Out'
creek into Susitna River on east side two miles above the mouth of the Yentna, locally called "Shem Pete Slough"
Shem Pete: "«On the Red Shirt [Lake] side at **Ch'atanaltsegh** I built a cabin in 1926. Katherine Nicolie used that. They used to leave canoes and boats there, and here was the well-known upper trail, to **Tanłtunt** [3.18, Red Shirt Lake site]. It crossed **K'ta'atnu** [3.8]. There is a swamp there.» Then to **Tanłtuntnu** [3.11 Fish Creek]. They carry everything across that bridge." (See 3.10).

Katherine Nicolie last used this cabin in 1934 when she was trapping out of Kroto Creek village.

Billy Pete (Fall and Greiser (1986):C2): "This place was not a fish camp. It was mainly used December through March for beaver and lynx trapping."

Billy Pete said the canoe landing was on the right side of the creek where it flows into what was once a slough. The birch bark canoes were left in a "high cache," that is, in racks in the trees. Billy caught his first "rabbit" (snowshoe hare) here when he was about five to seven years old. According to Billy, the cabin site has since washed away.

From here was a "summer trail" to **Tanłtunt** to take

Sources: Shem Pete, Billy Pete, Katherine Nicolie, Alexandra Allowan, Annie Ronning, Pete Stephan, John Stephan, Sava Stephan, Lillian Theodore

2003 revisions: names added 8.67–8.96; locations revised 8.36, 8.51, 8.52.

‡2016 revisions: names revised 8.43 8.44, 8.47, 8.48, 8.83, 8.84, 8.85, 8.86; map revised 35.

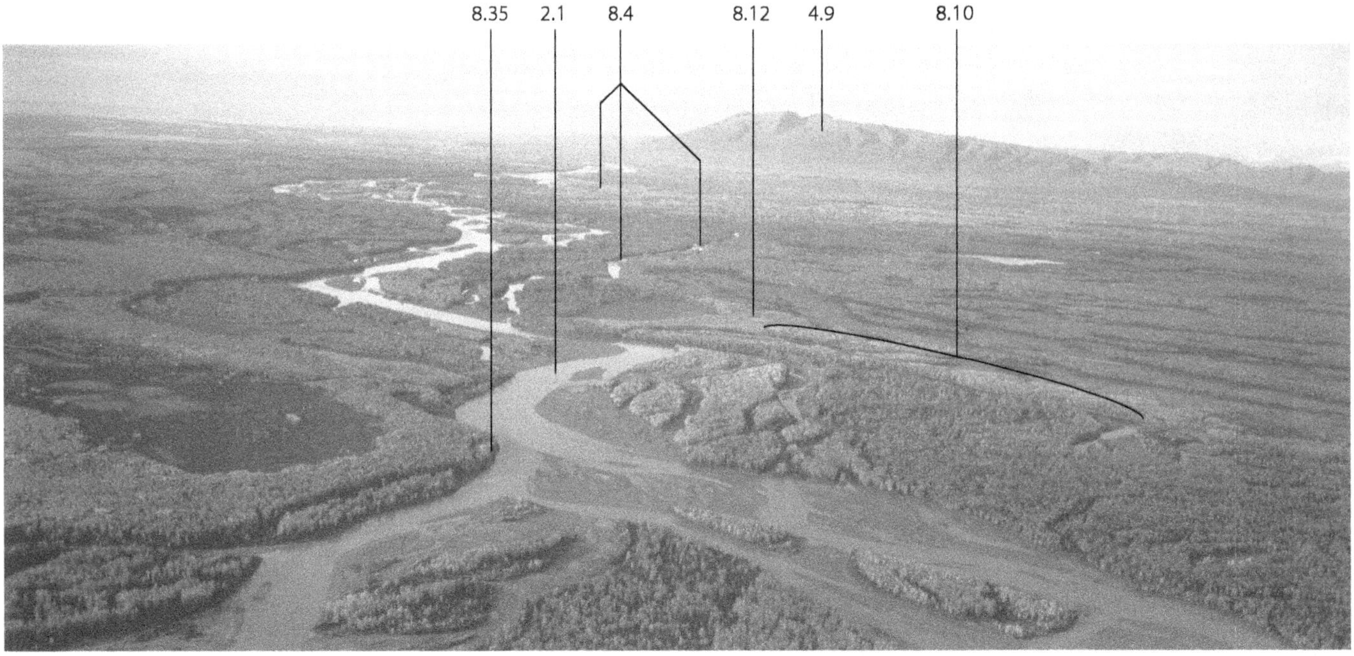

FIGURE 109

Portion of an aerial view looking to the south above **Suyitnu** (2.1, the Sustina River), several miles above the mouth of Kroto Creek. The drainage of **Dashq'e Betnu** or **Tuqentnu** (8.10, Kroto Creek) is just above the more conspicuous **Beq'e Tach'itqeyi Q'eghtsi** (8.4, Kroto Slough). The site of **Dashq'e** (8.12, Kroto Village) is on the south bank. The lake to the west of the slough is Whitsol Lake. In the distance is **Dghelishla** (4.9, Mt. Susitna). On the east bank at the junction of the two large branches is 8.35 **Niqaghelełt**. See Plate 9 for the full aerial view.

PHOTO BY FRED HIRSCHMANN AK-6833

FIGURE 110

Billy Pete holding his "lynx stick" on September 3, 1982, near Red Shirt Lake outlet. He left the stick some thirty years before when he trapped here.

PHOTO BY GLENN BACON

trout in the spring. After Susitna Station became a commercial center (1890s), with restaurants and stores, the Dena'ina transported trout along this trail to Susitna Station and sold them to restaurants. Another trail crossed here going north to Kroto village.

Shem and Billy provided more commentary on the Dena'ina's use of this area during a visit to Shem Pete's Slough in 1986, recorded by Fall and Greiser (1986):

Billy Pete: "About fifty-five years ago [Shem built a cabin here]; no, more than that, I guess. I was only five years old when he built that house; no, about seven, I think, about seven years old when they built that house. [Note: this makes it about 1925 to 1927.] And I was trying my best to help him, and pretty soon I managed to catch a rabbit when it snowed and I could see the rabbit tracks. It dragged me back out in the woods, and when it get tired, I'd drag him, and pretty soon I managed to get him in the house."

Q: How long did you use this cabin?

Billy Pete: "Oh, about fifteen to twenty years. Katherine Nicolie used it for a long time too. Katherine Nicolie and Wilson, they used that. They used to trap beaver along here and all over out there. And they used to trap mink along here."

Q: What time of year would they use the cabin?

Billy Pete: "From around December month until March month, I guess."

Shem Pete: "Katherine Nicolie used to go out over this country. [Shem then explained that this had been a cremation site.] Oh way back, hundred years ago those people died. Well they knows that we come back to the cabin. Katherine say "What the hell is that?" she say. Yeah, she didn't like it. No, she did not stay here, but she trapping in this river here.

"She trapping for a good many years. She had them dogs and they chased them guys away. I look around. There were dead people there. I hear them dead peoples. That Katherine Nicolie, I don't think she liked it.... They quit though. They leave us alone; for three or four days. I don't know what they doing. They burned them. Dead people. They come back, when somebody comes nighttime. We don't know how long ago.... Might be one hundred or two hundred years ago."

8.3 Ch'bat'ashghet • 'Spruce Charcoal Place'
one mile south of upper end of Kroto Slough
Shem Pete: "«Seven miles up from Susitna Station, above Shem Pete Creek, is **Ch'bat'ashghet**. There is wood there, and» they make lunch there. They build a fire going up to Kroto. That's all they use 'em for. No **nichił**. «It's on the trail to **Dashq'e**» [8.12]."

8.4 Beq'e Tach'itqeyi Q'eghtsi • 'Slough on Which We Sink into the Water'
Kroto Slough
Billy Pete: "We had a little camp over there, and we used to trap on Kroto Slough. It is full of beaver on that creek. We used to go about ten miles down it in the spring. About half a dozen guys used to go there to catch brown bear and black bear. The bears used to look for fish back bone and stuff like that. I believe that was a pretty important slough for them."

8.5 Tutikaq' • perhaps 'Descending Water Mouth'
mouth of Rolly Creek

8.6 Tutikaq'tnu • 'Creek of Descending Water Mouth'
Rolly Creek
Billy Pete: "**Tutikaq'tnu** goes below Kroto about three miles. I used to trap beaver all along there. There are lots of little lakes all along there."

8.7 Tutikaq' Bena • 'Lake of Descending Water Mouth'
North Rolly Lake
Billy Pete: "Northwest from Nancy Lake is a little lake on top of a hill. Right from there a creek begins, **Tutikaq'tnu**. That's about a half-mile long lake, that last lake. I used to trap beaver and lynx. That's about all it's good for. I used to catch my limit in about four or five days in that area."

8.8 Qek'telchet • 'Where Fish Swim over Ripples'
point one mile south of Kroto village
Katherine Nicolie: "This was the main boat landing for Kroto."

8.9 Dashq'e Kaq' • 'On the Bar Mouth'
mouth of Kroto Creek

8.10 Tuqentnu, Dashq'e Betnu • 'Clearwater Creek' or 'On the Shoal Creek'
Kroto Creek, Deshka River
Both Dena'ina names and both English map names have been used interchangeably. Sleem 1910a (Map 38) has this as Deshka-Kroto Creek.

Learnard (1900:655, 670): "The vicinity of the stream is much frequented by them [the Dena'ina] in the winter as a hunting ground.... The finest timber seen in the Susitna valley was found in the vicinity of Croto Creek."

This stream was the focal use area of the Kroto Creek band, especially on the lower six or seven miles. This is reflected by the density of place names on Map 34 (Fall 1981:380). "One Tanaina man [Shem Pete] maintains that winter houses were once found all along the lower four or five miles of Kroto Creek on the bluffs, with fish camps down the hill along the stream. Many graves can be found along this portion of the creek." Several archaeological sites have been recorded by Reger (1983), and more recently the Matanuska-Susitna Borough Cultural Resource Division has surveyed sites in this area (Seager-Boss, p.c.).

Thomas (1900:735): "At Croto creek, about 15 miles up the river from Sushitna Station, are about twenty Indians. They are intelligent, healthy, and dress as if they were in good circumstances for Indians. They were nearly all away fishing when we stopped there. The amount of fish hung up to dry showed they would not go hungry this winter."

8.11 Tl'et' Qelchentnu • 'Fart Smell Creek'
creek from west just below Kroto village

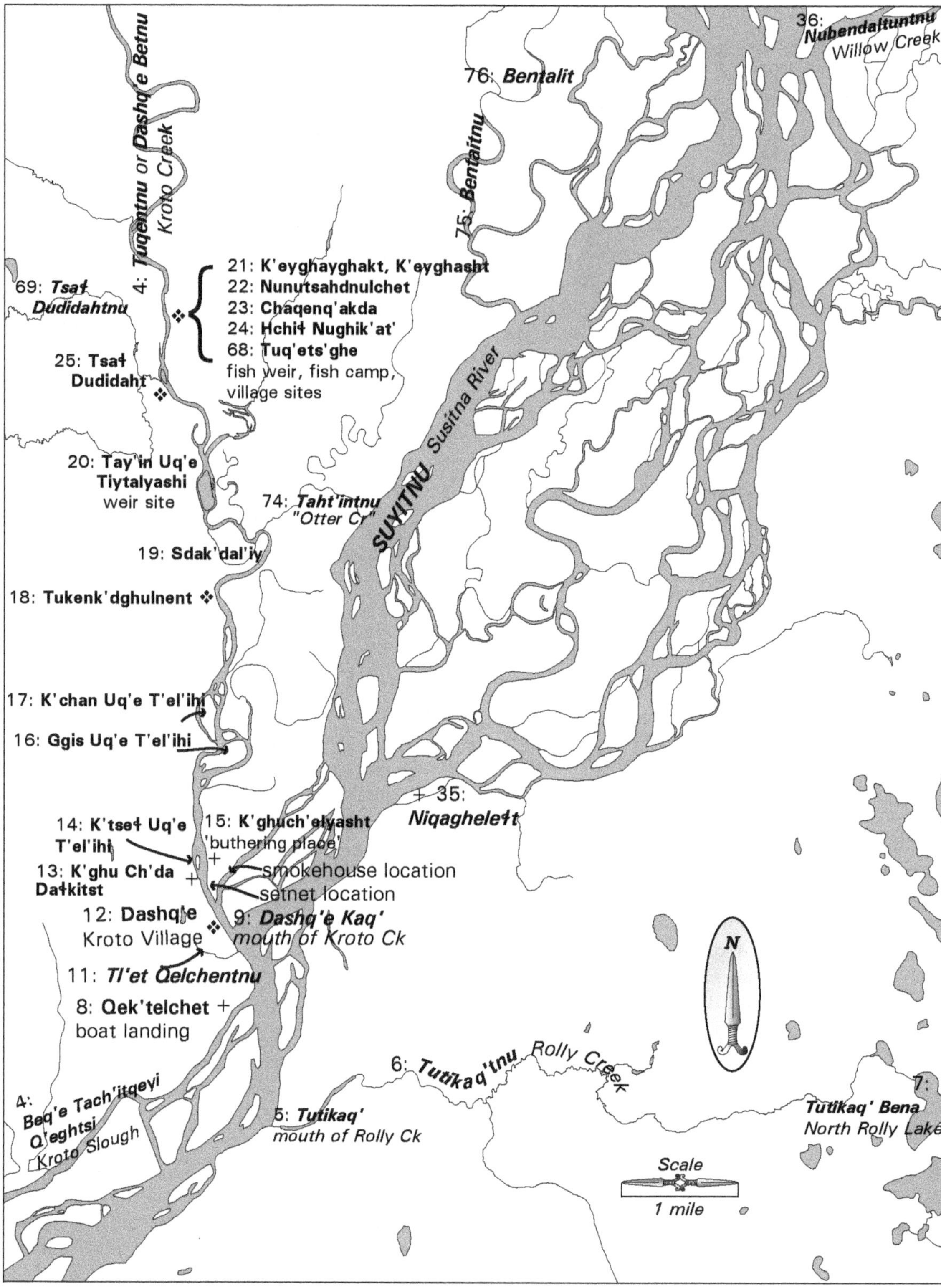

MAP 34

Kroto Creek settlements and place names.

The lower four miles of Kroto Creek has the highest density of Dena'ina names in this book. Fall (1981:379–382) attempted to correlate the named places with locations. This map from Kari and Fall (1987:158) was reproduced in the review article on Native American place name research by Afable and Beeler (1996:186).

BASE MAP BY DAN FOSTER

Traveling with the Kroto Creek Band in the 1920s

by Katherine Nicolie

Katherine Nicolie was born in October of 1914 in Talkeetna. Her parents were Talkeetna Nicholie and Christine Nicolie. According to Shem Pete, Katherine's Dena'ina name was ***Bałaytninłna,*** *which means something like 'mother of the one that passes beads around.' Katherine was the authority on the Kroto-Talkeetna Dena'ina dialect and an expert hunter and fisher. Katherine passed away in May of 1990.*

"We leave Kroto after fish all put up and mama made a bunch of dog pack out of canvas, and we travel in canoe as far as the mouth of Willow Creek. That was in August after the kings are gone, and we had put in a cache [at Kroto]. Filled one cache with kings. That was enough. We lived at Willow for a while. I don't know how long. We pass that 'Sight See Lake' [Kashwitna Lake by the Parks Highway]. And we take off for the top of the mountain. And we climbed the mountain. They made a nice camp. And then mama start killing ground squirrels. The traps were cached up there. My brother [Alec Nicolie] and my stepfather left us at the camp, and they hunted for caribou at **Kiłbitnu Tl'u** [8.44], the head of the Kashwitna. After they got enough caribou to eat, we go down the canyon to Kashwitna. They just got two—just what they could pack, just what they could live on. They never quit hunting until they got three moose.

"Mama clean the skin. She sew them together. They made a skin boat out of it, and then they drift down. Before we get to the mouth of Kashwitna, ice start coming down. This was October. Even with the ice coming down, finally we hit the Susitna River. Right through the ice we made it

FIGURE 111

Katherine Nicolie as a woman of about twenty-three years of age. Lillian Stephan Theodore is in front of Katherine. Taken at the Willow Section house in 1938 or 1939. The other children are not identified.

PHOTO COURTESY OF LILLIAN THEODORE

to Kroto. They made lots of dry meat, dry fish. It took over a week to drift down. Come home. Feel good.

"They used to put up lots of stuff and didn't worry until freeze-up. And then they start hauling groceries again. At Susitna Station they got sugar, flour, dry fruit, tea. They got rice from Talkeetna, plus beans, coffee, tea, good instant milk, cocoa, dry onions in a can, salt and rock salt. They'd get enough moose and beaver, and then they hunted more beaver."

"Me and my sister, those days we were tough girls. We get in a canoe only about this narrow, paddle. Go on the river, go up the river and just about shoot all the beaver we want. We make our own money. And the folks, oh, so proud of us. And we skinned the beaver ourself. We kill it. And, boy, it's good to be trained that way.... I used to go take a tent after I lost my sister. Well, I had my own team, too, you know. Old man make snowshoes for us. Camp any place, all by myself. Trap. I don't think I can do it any more. Well, I be scared. (Laughs.) Scared of people. I'm not scared of animal," (This paragraph is from McClanahan 1986:133). [Katherine once commented that she killed her first moose when she was thirteen years old.]

"It was 1926. In November we left Kroto for **Qughun** Mountain [Bald Mountain Ridge, 12.16]. We came down the Kashwitna River. They started killing beaver and moose. That's all we had to eat. They made a skin boat and came down to Kroto. The ice was just thick enough that they could walk to Willow, and it had snowed already. He [**Chijuk**, Katherine's stepfather, Figs. 112 and 113] took those three boys to pick up all the beaver, his own and all. He told them they had to take them to town. They went to Willow and put them on the train.

"The game warden was on the train, so they didn't load the beaver skins. The old man went on the train. He got out at Matanuska. He told the boys to wait for the passenger train which was coming behind. The first one had been a freight train with one coach. But the game warden followed him on the passenger train. When they unloaded the beaver skins in Anchorage, he [the game warden] took them to jail. The game warden's name was Gadwalter. The old man got ninety days for having ninety beaver. He was lucky he didn't get more. He refused to tell them who he was going to sell them to. He didn't speak English and didn't understand well either. Only my oldest brother could speak some English.

"The next morning they let the boys out, and just one came back. Just the youngest one came back to Kroto, and the old man is crying, and the oldest one [Alec Nicolie] stayed in town with him. As soon as he came back, mama found out there's something wrong. She asked him if he got picked up, and he said yes. The oldest one stayed in town for one week and found out he got ninety days. He went to town all the time because the old man was crying. When he came back without him he felt bad, and he [Alec] made that song. That's the one everybody is singing now (see below).

"The last time we went up the Talkeetna Mountains was [the winter of] 1928–29. We went up Little Willow Creek. But my [youngest] brother got sick, so we came back early. The ice was too thick at the mouth of Little Willow. We went in a slough and got stuck there. So we unloaded the boat and left it there. We packed out what we could. We went to Kroto and got a tent. Made a frame. But my younger brother, who was sick, didn't want to go to Kroto. They [stepfather and older brother] took him to Anchorage and then to Talkeetna. My mom's uncle [Talkeetna Alec] wanted him up there. My brother died in May. He fell from a tree while playing. Chilligan came up from Tyonek to help the old man. He couldn't help the boy, but through his medicine Chilligan convinced the old man [**Chijuk**] not to kill himself in grief. This boy was his very own son."

Q'u Nuch'tutnał Dini Sht'a

Dick Mishakoff, originally from Kenai, recorded this song in 1961 in Tyonek with Clark Davis. This was one of the most well-known songs in the Dena'ina repertoire.

Mishakoff made these comments about the song: "This is a song that came from Kroto. They were the ones who made this song. They made this song because their dad got some beavers out of season, and he was selling it in Anchorage, and then he'd buy some groceries. So he took some beavers into town, town of Anchorage, you know, and then he got caught with it and so he got in jail. So, this boy said there was two brothers and two sisters, and their mom was with them. They were waiting for him and they found out he was in jail, so they took it real hard. So, they made this song here. That's when they made that potlatch [at Kroto] that time. Then there's a lot of people up there and it cost them a lot of money."

Q'u nuch'tutnał dini sht'a

Now you say, 'We are about to return'

SUNG BY DICK MISHAKOFF

Q'u nuch'tutnał dini sht'a.
Heyo hey.
A heyo heyo hey
Heyo yo ki hey.
Q'u Anchorage town dini sht'a.
Heyo hey.
A heyo heyo hey
Heyo yo ki hey.

Now you say 'we about to return'.
Heyo hey.
A heyo heyo hey
Heyo yo ki hey.
Now you say, 'Anchorage town.'
Heyo hey.
A heyo heyo hey
Heyo yo ki hey.

Katherine Nicolie said that this was a beaver stream and pond.

8.12 Dashq'e • 'On the Shoal (or Bar)'
Kroto village
This name was first recorded as "Tishku" in Wrangell's notes of the 1830s (Arndt 1985). This may be the third dot on the right bank of the Susitna on the 1839 Wrangell map (Map 18).

The village site is reported in de Laguna (1934:139), Cook Inlet Historic Sites Project (1975:96), and Fall (1981:379–382), as well as the maps by Sleem (1910a) (Map 31), Meiklejohn (1900) (Map 36) and Herning (1906) (Map 49). In the 1910 census twenty persons, all Dena'ina, are listed at Kroto village. It appears that the village was not surveyed for the 1920 census.

This was the main village of the Kroto Creek band and was the last Dena'ina village occupied on the Susitna River. Fall: "The last two **qeshqa** in the area, **K'ghudu** and **Chijuk**... both... had houses at Kroto" (1981:381). Kroto was abandoned in about 1937 following the death of **Chijuk**. Katherine Nicolie told how **Chijuk** disappeared in July 1937 when he did not return from a bear hunt. The dogs came back, and her mother tried to follow his tracks, but they disappeared and no one would help her search for him. His body was never found. After this, Christine and Katherine moved to Point Possession.

Shem Pete: "There was a rich man at Kroto. His name was **K'ghudu** in Dena'ina. White men called him Kroto. He was a rich man. He was Charlie Kroto's father. He's got lots of relations at Tyonek now. That's why they call that place Kroto now. He was a good man on this earth. He had lots of people staying with him, maybe one hundred or so. He didn't have to do anything, trapping or anything. Those rich people never had to do anything. They had others staying with them, and they told them what to do. That's what they used rich people for. About one hundred years ago they stayed in one big house, like a community hall. There were partitions between the families. About seventy-five years ago that all changed. The chief said, 'Build a house for that man,' and they did. He also said, 'Take that woman. Let her be your wife.' Because he was a big chief, he did that. Seventy-five years ago, they had to listen to the chief. They have all died off now. He died too. Kroto chief was his name. White men called him Kroto chief."

Shem Pete told a story about **Inda'i**, a man from the Copper River or Canada, who traveled in the winter to **Dashq'e** to obtain matches, long before Shem was born. He spent the summer there and in the fall returned home with trade goods. Shem Pete in the **Inda'i** story tells of the founding of the village at **Dashq'e**:

"«That place they used to call Kroto. That was a big village. There were two different villages about two miles apart. Northern Kroto people, southern Kroto people.

FIGURE 112

Chijuk (center), chief at Kroto Village, with his wife Christine or **Nidinłna**, both wearing dentalia necklaces, and Christine's son, Joe Nicolie, circa 1933. The small child is not identified. Photo courtesy of Alexandra Allowan. **Chijuk** and family were the last residents of Kroto Village. The chief was Katherine Nicolie's step-father. He had two Dena'ina names, **Chijuk** 'curly hair,' or **Tsilałen** 'the one that moves his head.'

PHOTO COURTESY OF ALEXANDRA ALLOWAN

They had a village [upriver?] and one man [K'ghudu] moved south because he had a lot of kids. They built a big house for him and he stayed there. Lots of people came down and built houses around his house. That was a big village there. And now today there's nothing there. Not even one house. There's no Indians there now.»"

In 1906 Sheldon described houses at Kroto: "Since the time of the Russians and iron implements, a big log hut or barabara has generally been adopted. The barabaras now at Kroto and other places are about eighteen feet square, constructed of logs, with gable roof in which a big slit is left in the centre for smoke to escape, and long fireplaces on the floor to one side" (Sheldon 1908:272).

In the spring of 1912, Browne (1956:219–220) described spending the night at Kroto village. He was hosted by Shilligan (Chilligan), Chief Kroto's brother, a medicine man.

Billy Pete: "Those Kroto people looked like white men, white skin with red, curly hair and whiskers. Long before the Russians. That was the only place around Cook Inlet where there was curly-haired, red headed people."

Katherine Nicolie: "Pete Alec's father's cousin had a house on top over here, on that ridge [west of Kroto village]. That's where Pete Stephan's father lived. They were born right here, before they moved to Montana Creek."

8.13 K'ghu Ch'da Dałkitst • 'Where a Fur Blanket Is Lying'
creek and flat three-quarters of a mile above Kroto village
Shem Pete: "From the mouth [of Kroto Creek] you can see up to **K'ghu Ch'da Dałkitst**."

Katherine Nicolie did not recognize this name.

8.14 K'tseł Uq'e T'el'ihi • 'On It Fish Spreader Sticks Are Gathered'
island in Kroto Creek near first fishing site
Katherine Nicolie: "There's nothing but little alders and cottonwoods. They're skinny and tall. We used to haul that in a little boat. They dry it, and Mom peel it, and the old man make a fish rack. We hang 'em up. They had a big smokehouse. It was nice."

Here the Nicolie family set a net for king salmon in a place where murky water of the Susitna mixed with clear water of Kroto Creek.

8.15 K'ghuch'elyasht • 'Butchering Place'
place above fishing site where game was butchered
Katherine Nicolie: "This is where old man [**Chijuk**] used to land bear. We used to call it **K'ghuch'elyasht**. We never land there after we grow up.

"On this island [between Kroto Creek and Susitna River] there was another house, the old house. John Stephan's father's father used to have a smokehouse over there. When we were small we saw that smokehouse. It was standing up yet on this island. He just come right across here where he had a net, not down at our place."

8.16 Ggis Uq'e T'el'ihi • 'Where Celery Is Gathered'
island in Kroto Creek
Ggis is the Dena'ina name for wild celery or cow parsnip (*Heracleum lanatum*).

8.17 K'chan Uq'e T'el'ihi • 'Where Grass Is Gathered'
island in Kroto Creek

8.18 Tukenk'dghulnent • 'Where Roots Washed Out'
place about three miles up Kroto Creek
This place and the next seven places are located within a two-mile area on Kroto Creek, in an area of high aboriginal population. See Map 35.

8.19 Sdak'dal'iy • 'Point That Extends'
bend and point on west bank of Kroto Creek
Cache pits are reported here.

8.20 Tay'in Uq'e Tiytalyashi • 'Fish Trap Is Floating upon It'
small island in Kroto Creek, four miles up

8.21 K'eyghayghakt, K'eyghasht • 'Where Fish Is Harvested'
fish trap site on Kroto Creek
Katherine Nicolie: "Summertime, you know, come out in the Deshka River, we'll put up lots of fish. And we was pretty small when we learn how to cut fish, even, helpin' Mom. We used to put up fish in summertime.... He [**Chijuk**] had a big smokehouse. And he made a net himself—fishnet, by hand. We had a little skiff. I don't know where they found it. My brother and them, they go hunt a big rock. They use it for anchor out there. They put the net out and catch lots of king salmon. We was too small to help Mom. Mom was sittin' down the creek all day to cut fish, cut fish. And she filled all that smokehouse, all by herself.

"And then he [**Chijuk**] make a little money. He either goes to Anchorage or Talkeetna, sell the fur. And then they break trail from Deshka River to Willow. It's twelve miles through the woods. Then they haul the groceries in. I don't know how many trips they makes in the winter before they get enough for summer.... And then, 1932, we learned a little more. Just to travel, you know. We were big enough to travel then, go back and forth to Talkeetna in summertime on the train. From Deshka River go up and canoe—paddle. And then walk six miles to get in the train. Get in the railroad track, and then put shoes on. And that's how we learned to talk English. Little at a time. Little at a time" (McClanahan 1986:132,134).

8.22 Nunutsahdnulchet • 'Where They Put Rocks Across'
site five to six miles up Kroto Creek
Learnard (1900:655): "About 6 miles up from its [Kroto Creek's] mouth the Sushitna Indians have a fishing village, used in the summertime."

Shem Pete: "Thousands of people used that fish trap."

This particular site had special significance both as a fishing site and as a site associated with the symbolic story **Beł Dink'udlaghen**, pp. 184–190. Osgood (1937:148–149) presented the story in brief as told by Eklutna Jim. Osgood noted that the first salmon rituals were still observed in the Susitna villages in the 1930s.

Special care was taken with the first king salmon, and a feast was given.

Katherine Nicolie: "You have to put up fish fast. The fish run stays for only a few days." Katherine Nicolie added that she thinks that **Nunutsahdnulchet** was just a seasonal camp and not a winter village like Kroto. She believed that her step-father, **Chijuk**, was born here.

8.23 Chaqenq'akda • 'Shabby Smokehouse'
site on east bank of Kroto Creek, near a spring
Katherine Nicolie and her younger sister used to travel up here in a canoe from the village at the mouth of Kroto Creek. Katherine Nicolie: "We saw some old sticks, just worn out ones, sticking out here and there. There's another place here where a beaver dammed a pond. It came to [became] a lake now. Mom said it wasn't there. Beaver made it. Now there swans and ducks have lots of fun. Last time I was there is 1940."

8.24 Hchił Nughik'at' • 'Fish Fence Extends Down'
fishing site on Kroto Creek, five miles up

§8.68 Tuq'ets'ghe • 'By the Spring Water'
spring water site in vicinity of main Kroto Creek fish camp
Location mentioned by Shem Pete in the Salmon Boy story.

Shem Pete: "«A really big spring flows in here. They used that spring water. There were many **nichił** here. They harvested fish here. There were many people here, a little ways from the fish trap.»"

8.25 Tsał Dudidaht • 'Where Coffins Fall Down'
cemetery site on Kroto Creek, about five miles up on west bank
Shem Pete: "That means dead man's box wash out. It slides there. Graveyards wash out all the time. «There were **nichił** there too.»"

Katherine Nicolie said that graves extend from here down to the mouth of Kroto Creek.

§8.69 Tsał Dudidahtnu • 'Where Coffins Fall Down'
stream from west, about five miles up

8.26 Uq'e Tsits'ełdatl'i Betnu • 'Creek of On It Someone Went in Fear'
creek into Kroto Creek from west from hill (below)

8.27 Uq'e Tsits'ełdatl'i • 'On It Someone Went in Fear'
ridge between Kroto Creek and Kahiltna River
Billy Pete: "That's a good-size hill. When they had a war with the Aleuts, two brothers ran away on that hill so they couldn't find them."

Here at the ridge it is said that the Kroto Creek band maintained a hideaway with caches of grease, dry meat, and fish, in case of an attack from the Alutiiq (Fall 1981:380).

Shem Pete: "«Joe Nicolie [Katherine Nicolie's brother] had a house there, on that hill.»"

[The following was translated by Billy Pete] Shem Pete: "«This is an important name. A ridge here is called **Uq'e Tsits'eldatl'i**. That's when Aleut [Alutiiq] attack them, and they run to that hill. There is a lake there and they got all the water they needed. It means "We got scared and we run up that hill there." Nobody found that hill [i.e., the **Ułchena** never found it], so when anything happen, Aleut or somebody come, they run to that hill and nobody find them. They had caches there with lots of grease so they could stay there for a month if they had to. They keep the caches hidden.»"

§8.70 Uq'e Tsits'ełdatl'i Bena • 'On It Someone Went in Fear-Lake'
lake on ridge 8.27

8.28 Nuch'ulghełatnu • 'Creek That Turns Back Around'
lower Trapper Creek
The name refers to the meanders in this creek, which Shem Pete said are "Just like moose guts."

Shem Pete: "«This creek flows out of **Ben Taydlent**.»"

"Katherine [Nicolie] used to hunt in a canoe there, like a man. She caught lots of beaver up there. She went up there by herself."

Katherine Nicolie said that her stepfather would travel from Kroto to Trapper Creek and back in one day in order to spear king salmon.

‡The Trapper Creek Overlook site contains important archaeological evidence from the middle Susitna Valley (Wygal and Goebel 2012). Recent research has documented a series of small-scale occupations deposited through repeated visits to the site starting as early as 12,400 years ago and culminating around 4,500 year ago (Wygal and Krasinski, p. c.).

8.29 Ben Taydlent, Ben Taydlena • 'Lake Where Current Is'
Trapper Lake
Shem Pete: "«This is where they would come up in bidarkas and start out walking on the trail up into the mountains. They could paddle that far in a canoe it seems.» Pretty swift water. They got waterfall too. They pack that bidarka up. «At **Ben Taydlena** they catch trout year round. There was a **nichił** and a small village at the lake outlet they say.» According to Shem Pete, this area was good for caribou hunting fifty or more years ago.

"At a big island on the lower end, old man Toughluck [a Dena'ina man from Talkeetna] had a house on that lake."

Lillian Theodore also notes that George Toughluck had a cabin at Trapper Lake. She went there with her father when she was young. She recalls that his small cabin was at the south end of the lake near the outlet. Toughluck worked at Caswell, then moved to Talkeetna. Lillian's father, Wasilla Stephan, used to go in the direction Trapper Lake sometimes.

§8.71 Ben Taydlentnu • 'Lake Where Current Is-Stream'
stream flowing into Trapper Lake from Rocky Lakes

8.30 Heneh'itnu • 'Upland Creek'
§Chijuk Creek from west into Kroto Creek, two miles below Neil Lake outlet
A recently named stream from the name **Chijuk,** the

chief of Kroto village in the 1930s. See 8.12 and Figs. 112 and 113.

Shem Pete: "It's a long creek, go way up. «This one flows down from the upper area. It flows into **Tuqentnu** [8.10] downstream from **Benteh**» [8.32]."

Alexandra Allowan recalled that her family used to walk there in wintertime to trap. Then they would come back down in spring in a skin boat. This was on a trail system leading north to the upper Kahiltna River.

8.31 Nilq'aghedlent • 'Where Streams Join'
confluence of Neil Lake outlet and Kroto Creek

8.32 Benteh • 'Among the Lakes'
Neil Lake
Shem Pete: "«That's where Anderson Stephan used to trap.»"

Katherine Nicolie: "Anderson never did use that place after his two brothers drowned there. That's Mrs. Allowan's uncles.

"That **K'ghudu** [Chief Kroto], that **Benteh**, that's his trapline."

§8.72 Benteh Betnu • 'Among the Lakes Stream'
Neil Lake outlet stream and also inlet stream

§8.73 Untuhtay'un Kaq' • 'Mouth of Washed-Out'
mouth of Moose Creek

8.33 Untuhtay'untnu • 'Washed-Out Creek'
Moose Creek
An ice jam on this creek in 1898 caused major flooding downstream at Susitna Station (Learnard 1900:663). See 2.26.

8.34 Tuqentnu Tl'u • 'Clear Water Creek Headwaters'
upper Kroto Creek area

8.35 Niqagheleɬt • 'Where Current Is Swirling'
*bluff and eddy on the Susitna River, one mile above **Dashq'e**, on the east bank*
Shem Pete: "«This is visible upriver from **Dashq'e**. They named it **Niqagheleɬt**. There was a big camp there.» They used to haul supplies up there for the railroad. In 1917 we see the first boat, big steamer. Go 'Choo! Choo! Choo!' Big steamboat. Go up to Kroto [to **Niqagheleɬt**]. I went up there, and they take me up to Talkeetna. They put the rails and everything. They freighting all summer."

Railroad ties were hauled to this point during the construction of the Alaska Railroad.

§8.74 Taht'intnu • 'Otter Creek'
first creek above Kroto Creek on west bank
Sava Stephan: "Otter Creek is below **Bentalitnu**. «I had a cabin there.»"

§8.75 Bentalitnu • 'Creek of Flowing Lake Water,' or 'Lake Waves Creek'
second creek above Kroto Creek on west bank

§8.76 Bentalit, Benteh • 'Where Lake Water Flows,' or 'Among the Lakes'
small lakes between Kroto Creek and the Susitna River
This happens to be the same place name as **Bentalit**, 5.21 Fish Lake village off the Yentna River.

‡Katherine Nicolai: "**K'ghudu** he really owned that **Benteh**. Yeah, that **Benteh** that's his and that's his trapline. And then, well all that's Anderson's."

Sava Stephan: "I stayed up there with my dad, for two year, when 4–5 years old.

"I hardly remember. From Kroto Creek its about two miles up at fish camp. That's where we used to stay. He had a trapline straight back of that place. **Bentalitnu.** We had a trapline below him.

"We call it Otter Creek. I build a cabin up there when I was kid. **Bentalit** should be around three quarters of a mile above Kroto. **Bentalitnu.** Otter Creek is below **Bentalitnu**. Above there there are lakes connected together, we used to call **Benteh**.... Shem Pete and Billy Pete was there to the cabin. From the cabin to Willow Creek we come to, we walked there, two miles, me and Billy.... I was running dogs, with a sled. I'll bet they wish they had a camera. «They were running. The dogs were running.» Run like heck on the ice. Took us about two hours, maybe one hour from Kroto Creek to Susitna. Slick ice all the way down. I come down."

"We used to have a trapline at **Benteh**. Those lakes, about five or six of them connected. My dad used to chop hole in ice and set a net there, he used to pull them out, take them out of the net, (**bat,** lake trout). Then I used to pack that home. Everybody used to eat that fish, **lih**, that's that whitefish. They're wide, about that big wide. That's all they used to eat in Kroto Creek. I was there almost a year. Up the creek, up **Tuqentnu,** [Kroto Creek] clear water, they go up the creek a ways, and they use hook. And they bring out just like nothing, Katherine Nicolie and Inga, two sisters used to pack fish home. Trout. They eat it, boil it, bake it, fry it."

8.36 Nubendaltuntnu • 'Stream That Lakes Extend Across'
§lower Willow Creek and Peters Creek
A fall fishing location for the Kroto Creek band was at the mouth of Willow Creek. Fish were stored here in underground caches before people went hunting in the Talkeetna Mountains. This is noted in Reger (1983:7).

Fall and Greiser (1986): Billy Pete: "They start from early in the spring and when they get enough grease, why then they start fishing. By that time fish comes up. And they make those fish traps... on those creeks like that Little Willow [Creek] and Big Willow [Creek]."

Shem Pete: "**Tay'in** [fishtrap], only what they use to get the fish, no other way to get them. Or spear them."

Capps, in his survey of the geology of the upper Willow Creek mining district, said that there were no permanent settlements of Natives in upper Willow Creek, but that hunting and trapping trips were undertaken by Natives throughout the area (Capps 1915:20).

Snider (1966:120) "In 1888 two miners who were working in the Glory Hole in Juneau made the trip from Juneau to Knik, then an Indian village, to trap fur and

The Story of Beł Dink'udlaghen: The One Who Swam Back Inside with Them (the Salmon)

by Shem Pete

Told by Shem Pete at Willow, Alaska, on February 27, 1979. The story is 11 minutes, 40 seconds in length. Translated by Billy Pete, Sava Stephan, and Jim Kari.

Background by James Fall: This was one of Shem Pete's favorite stories and, judging from the number of times he talked about it, one that he considered especially important. The story explains the origins of Dena'ina rules about how to handle salmon in order to show respect to the fish and ensure their future return. Osgood (1937:148–149) links a version of this story to the origin of the "first salmon ceremony" of the Dena'ina villages of the Susitna River.

> The giving of the ceremony of the first salmon in the Tanaina area centers among the villages of the Susitna River. The purpose of the performance is to celebrate and assure the necessary supply of this seasonal fish which is particularly important economically due to the lack of sea mammals.
>
> At the beginning of the run of king salmon each year when the first are caught, an annual ceremony takes place. The natives lay down fresh grass in front of the houses and carefully spread the salmon upon it. The fish are never brought into the house. Then the people take a sweat bath and put on their best clothes, painting and decorating their hair. After that a "lucky" weed, found near the timberline, is burned. When these preparations have been carried out, the people gather on the fresh grass. They clean and cook the fish without breaking the backbone, throwing the entrails back into the water—because the salmon want their clothes. Then the people eat together. Those, however, who have suffered nose bleed in the sweat bath must wait until the fish are one day old before eating.

When Shem first mentioned this story to me, he called it "The man who came back with the salmon and got in the fish trap." He explained that it is about a "medicine man" from Kroto and took place about "three or four hundred years ago." According to Shem, this story occurred "where they had a fish trap on Kroto Creek about four miles up from the mouth." This is the place Katherine Nicolie called "Old Smokehouse." Shem called it **Chaqenq'akda**, 'shabby smokehouse' [8.23]. After he finished telling the story for taping, Shem added that he did not know how this man died and "that's one drawback" to this recorded version. There's more to this man's story, Shem said. Billy Pete agreed that the story might have been a little longer, but he was only ten when he'd last heard this story from his grandmother and could not remember any more of it. Katherine Nicolie was of the opinion that Shem had combined elements of two stories into one narrative, one concerning the Salmon Boy and the other about the exploits of a renowned shaman from the Kroto Creek area.

The setting of the story, at the concentration of sites on lower Kroto Creek (Map 34), implies that the Dena'ina had come from a place that did not have reliable salmon runs and that Kroto Creek was the focal place for the harvest and ritualization of salmon. Nickafor Alexan of Tyonek (1981:26–27) wrote an English language version of this Dena'ina story. Similar Salmon Boy legends told by the Ahtna of Copper River appear in Simeone and Kari (2002).

The plot and phrasing of the story are complex. Shem tells how the Salmon Boy brought the salmon to the people and more generally how other animals were created for the people due to the rituals the Salmon Boy taught them.

Synopsis: In the beginning the people had no salmon. A boy turns into a fish. Then the salmon come to them for the first time. So the boy swims back out to the ocean with the salmon. After staying with the salmon, he flies back with the geese to the Kroto Creek area. He turns into a salmon and goes back out a second time. When he returns he leads the salmon to Kroto Creek and the Dena'ina develop their salmon fishery there at specific places. Then the Salmon Boy turns into a human and gives them instructions on how to place him up by the bank to ritualize the catch of a small king salmon. While on the bank the Salmon Boy begins to transform himself into different types of animals. Also he shows them how to do a winter solstice ceremony in the steambath, which then brings the arrival of the migrating fowl, the land animals, and the sea animals.

Numerous comments were added by Billy Pete when Fall and Pete first translated the text, and we have provided other notes for context.

Ighi daghiłggech'i hnaga heł nuhtghelnek.
I'm going to tell you a short bit of language.

Beł Dink'udlaghen be'iyi dighila'en.
His name was, "The One who Swam Back Inside With Them."

Yen łu beł nulank'taldatl' ighi.
He is one that swam out with the migrating fish [to the ocean].

Hchił ghin dudushdich'en hch'aniyu yethdi shagela gga, nutiha gga dighila, denshin.
This person came to downstream side of the weir/bridge and there were two pretty trout.

Beni'ilnit. "Shi k'a ch'adach' tsa t'eshjuq tsadi," iyniyen.
He was surprised. He thought, "I wish I could be like that."

[BP: He was wishing,"I wish I was one of those little trout."]

Ighi pretty soon yeshquq' a'iltu'.
Pretty soon he was [in the water] alongside them.

[BP: He became one of those trout.]

Tuq'i nlan ch'u gee they were having yagheli qubeł qiydlan.
There were three of them, and they were having a good time.

Yeh yeqech' ch'u heł nugheleh heł nugheleh ch'u.
So he was swimming around with them and swimming around with them.

Łiq'a ghini, łiq'aka'a beqilal.
[At that time] those sockeye salmon and the king salmon did not exist.

Yethdi spring q'udi nutsahdnaniłnen ch'u.
So then in the spring they [the people] put a dam across.

[The stream is Kroto Creek or Deshka River.]

Tay'in qiydlu łiq'a nułtu.
They had fish traps there for salmon.

Łiq'a, łiq'a ka'a qubedighilagh.
A salmon, a big king salmon swam into them [into their trap].

Qeshjesh.
They were saved.

Hnuq'u shani q'u k'qiydalghan, deqeyqadi.
That summer they put up fish as their food.

El'ekna ghuna, el'ekna k'ghila.
Those medicine men, there were lots of medicine men.

El'ekna qit'a qidiniy łdi łiq'a eydlan, shagela gga eydlan.
The medicine men thought [that they had made medicine], and that he had become a salmon, or that he had become a small trout.

Łiq'a ghini nulanteldeł.
Those salmon go back [home, back to the ocean].

Łiq'a ghin nulanteldeł yehdalnenh hnuq'u hyighetneq ch'u danaqeyghiłghel.
At the time when the salmon start back home, they took him and they put him in [their boat].

Beł nulank'taldatl'.
They went home with him.

Yeh q'u heł hey ghiyet. Hey ghiyet ch'u
He spent the winter out there [in the ocean] with them. He spent the winter and

next spring hnuq'u nut'aq'i na ghuna early ghuneh nuhnedeł.
and the next spring, those geese came back early.

Naq'eltani tuniyu.
He had joined God.[1]

Yina ghun q'etnaghiju.
He [the boy] had come back upon them [the geese].

Q'uda beł nunk'dnasdatl'.
Now he flew back with them [geese].

Qubenaqank'nadatl'.
They [geese] had made their return trip to them.

Dashq'e ghu hnuqinit hdi. "Gudi," hełni, ghidu ch'u qeył naqadnudeł ch'u
He recognized 'on the shoal' [8.12]. "Here," he told them that he had lived here, and they flew in a circle with him and

naqa..., naqa naqen[deł].
they flew around and circled around [Kroto village, 8.12].

Ghunenhdi, ghunenhdi dach'u "Woooo!" nih.
And he himself hollered "Woooooooo!"

[Billy explained that the boy was making a different call than the geese.]

Qubech' yił.
He hollered to them [to those natives].

"Wooo!" hełnih.
He hollered to them, "Wooooooo!"

Qandadashnesh ghił ni n'ulkit nch'uk'a t'ite'
He made that sound, but they could not catch him.

[Billy:"Because it was almost impossible to catch a goose alive then."]

1. Billy Pete and Sava Stephan have been puzzled by this statement. It is atypical of Shem Pete's storytelling to invoke Christian themes. Billy suggested leaving it out. It seems that Shem is using the word **Naq'eltani** 'God' in a pre-Christian sense.

FIGURE 113
Chijuk and **Nidinłna** (Christine) with a lumber canoe on the Susitna River near Kroto Creek.
PHOTO COURTESY OF LILLIAN THEODORE

Hnudutnik.
They couldn't make it.

Shani k'a gheli nuch'k'ulkitni yehnudutnik.
They tried to catch him all summer, but they could not do it.

[Billy: "Because he was a wild goose he couldn't just walk back up to people, to his brothers and sisters."]

So kiq'u kiq'u łiq'a ghini nulantaldatl'.
Pretty soon, [fall time was coming] and the salmon were starting to go back.

Nulanteldał hnuq'u nuhyighetneq, danaqiyghiłghel.
When they were returning [to sea], they took him again, and they put him in [their boat].

Beł nulank'taldatl.
He went home with them.

Nextsh yet t'uh heł hey ghiyet.
Next he spent the winter at their place with them [with the salmon].

So... łitl'en nuqisdlan hnuq'u,
And when spring time came again,

łiq'a gudeh nulanteldał hnu qedeq (hyighetneq) danaqeyghiłghel.
when the fish were coming back up this way, they took him and put him back in [the skin boat and started back up this way].

Danaqeyghiłghel ch'u.
They put him back in [the boat].

Dashq'e, Dashq'e k'a hnuqiditni.
*He recognized 'on the shoal' [**Dashq'e**, 8.12] again.*

[Billy commented, "Each fish [salmon] belongs to a certain creek and lake, and he stayed with the bunch from Kroto."]

Yunit ghu kiq'u Dash diduset ts'ełq'i ghunit K'eyghasht dghu heł dghinih hq'u.
Upstream near to "The shoal," was another place that they called 'Fish Harvest Place' [8.21].

Ighi yedghu deghułi ghuliy nunuk'hniyiy ch'u łiq'aka beqił'en.
And there they would stretch something [a weir fence] across, and they would wait for king salmon.

[Shem: I don't know how many **nichił** there were where they used to put up fish on a big island. There used to be a big island. I used to go up there. It's become pretty small now.]

Tay'in tanahnilu.
They had put the fish traps in the water.

Dehdalts'i.
They just sat up there [and waited].

"Łiq'a dighilagh," qetni.
"Salmon have swum in [the fish trap]," they said.

Gee qeshjesh.
Gee, they were saved.

Łiq'a deggech'a hdeqil qiydlan.
They had the fresh fish that they had been lacking.

Qeshjesh ch'u ghini łiq'a nich'ahnibeł dghuh qeynił'ih łuq'u.
They were saved, and they rolled it [the big fish trap] up and they looked at them.

Kiq'u łiq'a tay'in qahni'un ch'u.
And again they then set the salmon trap.

Kiq'u łiq'a qeych'aniłtl'it.
And again they dumped out some salmon.

Ts'iłt'an ghun qebenił'an łdi łiq'a k'uch' t'et'an q'u betihtełtan.
One guy was looking at them, and one salmon among the others was acting strange.

"Ch'adach' tsa beduyesghiłt'eq' tsadi," yitni.
It [that fish that looked different] was thinking, "I wish someone would throw me in" [the bin].

[Billy: "I wish he'd pick me up and put me in the grass someplace."]

Yunit gudi yegh ni'ilgguk ch'u yighetneq tik'u qeyghiłt'eq'.
That man walked here upstream to him [that fish], picked him up, and threw him out [in the grass someplace.]

K'echan tuyniłt'eq'.
He threw him into the grass.

Ch'u ts'iq'u yet ltan.
And he was just laying there [dead].

Dach' łuq'u qeyuqu hnił'an ch'yan t'ghit'a ch'ghuhdi.
That is how everyone was always looking for him [for the Salmon Boy, the fish that looked different.]

[Billy: They were always ready for him.]

Beł dink'udlagh.
He had swum back in [to the trap] with them [the salmon].

[Billy: And that bunch of fish he was with went in the fish trap.]

Ch'u yeghe yet nu'iju, hk'uch' kiq'u lchin ki.
And when he came back to him [the fish in the grass], it looked different.

Ghu beggesh qiseni ighetneq ch'u yet'uh nik'ni'et.
He took a clean [caribou skin] and put it under it [the little skin].

Dghiłchek'a gga.
It was a small one [the Salmon Boy].

Ki nu kiq'u q'udi yenuynidalnen, ki hk'uch' t'ent'a.
And when he thought of him again, that fish was different again.

[Billy: It had taken a different form.]

Ch'adach' ghu t'et'an, t'et'an ch'u ninya ka'a t'iłah ka t'iłah ch'q'u.
And he [that Salmon Boy] just kept doing that and doing that, and so the large animals were created.

Pretty soon quht'ana gga kiq'u eydlan.
After a while, he turned into a little human being again.

Ghedghu dehq'a qidu ch'u dunuhqi'un ch'u yaghelisht'a duhqiłdatl'.
They built a little rack and they put things in there nicely.

[Billy: A good caribou skin and whatever they figured he needed.]

Yet duhyiłghel.
They put him [the Salmon Boy] up there.

Ch'u niłghena q'udi nuhqinil'ish.
And one after another they would go to look at him.

Itełqun ughasht'a gheli udi nuyilggesh ghu nuynil'ish.
Early in the morning a man would go alone and look at him there.

Beł dnayi ghila q'u shida.
Maybe that was one of his relatives.

Ch'u k'uch' t'et'ih, kiq'u yet nuydilah quht'ana gheli nlana gga.
And he kept changing to form the different kind of animals, though he was a real human, a small person.

[Billy added that he was getting a litter bigger each time.]

Yedghu yet dełtan.
He was laying there.

Ch'u kiq'u yenu'iju bech' qinash.
He went to him again, and that guy talked to him.

"Q'u nuneshju shit'i," yełni. "Aa'," yełni.
He said to him, "I have come back," and he [that man] said to him, "Yes."

Nił'i ghenasht'a henda nuch'tułchiłi t'qit'a," ni
"Pretty soon perhaps we'll make something," he said.

Ch'u hełch'te ghuda beł k'delghish.
Every evening something [animals] called to him.

[Billy: These were geese, ducks, swans, all the birds.]

Q'u qit'a nunasdzit gheli.
Pretty soon he recognized everything.

[Billy: He knew who he was and everything.]

FIGURE 114

Shem Pete leading a song in the traditional fashion with several Dena'ina experts, at Tyonek in 1981: Maxim Chickalusion, Sr. (back to the camera), Peter Kalifornsky, Sergie Californsky, Pete Bobby, Shem, and Sava Stephan. Sava and Sergie are holding a birch plank drum that Maxim is hitting in time with a short birch post. This is the aboriginal Dena'ina drum as described by Osgood (1937:121).

PHOTO BY PRISCILLA RUSSELL

Ch'u q'u q'etjitshla nu'ilkagh.
And then he got a little bigger.

[Billy: Maybe three or four feet tall.]

Yet jan hnuq'u t'iłkagh.
That day he became real big.

Qeyyelgha yek'a, ki ch'ada qubech' tuhdałnen.
Those people were putting up dry fish and soon everything came back to them.

[Billy: He stayed out in the brush by himself all the time and pretty soon he knew everything, what he knew before.]

Ch'u łiq'a eł duhghidatl' gheli ch'u,
They put up lots of salmon and,

Dashq'e yunit ghu, Nunutsahdneltset h'iyi daghila, Chaqenq'akda h'iyi daghila dghu
Upstream of Kroto Village was the place named 'where they put rocks across' [8.22] and the place named 'Shabby Smokehouse' [8.23].

Tuq'ets'ghet k'i heł hdghinih.
They also used to call a place 'At the Spring Water' [8.68].

[Billy: **Chaqenq'akda** [8.23] 'shabby smoke house' is a place on the east bank of Kroto Creek, about five to six miles up from the mouth. Another site in this general area is **Nunutsahdnelchet** [8.22], 'where they put rocks across.']

Ye Tuq'ets' ghini kisht'a łiq'a nunudeh hnuq'u
When lots of salmon were coming to "Spring Water,"

łiq'a q'inch'a ch'et'ihi ghini.
there would be those eels [literally 'salmon roe females'].

Di łiq'a ghini ch'u denłtsuy ka'a gheli baquldeł.
Among the salmon there used to be a lot of big narrow things [eels] that came up to them.

[Attaching themselves to the salmon coming from below.][2]

"Łiq'a nuch'dnul'ił," hdghinih.
They would say, "We're going to see [lots of] salmon again."

Ghu nelni t'uh ghełghulih tuhnałq'esh ch'u
They scrubbed that floor inside the steambath house and

[Billy: They washed it good and burned lots of medicine they used to have, like **ggis**, wild celery roots, to purify the bath house.]

qubeyi qidiłtlet ch'u qeyyaga ch'u yet nuhyiltan ch'u yet hłneq' qiqeyghulkit.
so they went into his [Salmon Boy's] place and brought his body back [into the bath house] and lay him on the floor [in the bath house].[3]

[Billy: They put clean grass and everything clean underneath him. Caribou skin or something too.]

Ch'u ts'iłt'an yan q'u nelni t'uh ghu łtah.
He was all alone in the bath house, laying there.

2. Billy: "Every morning they used to run there to look to see if the two eels were there. If they see them, they tell the older people, and they know there's going to be lots of fish." I [JF] asked for a description of these giant eels. Billy said that they were one foot in diameter and about fifteen to twenty feet long. Eels are called **łiq'a q'inch'a**.

3. On March 1, 1979, Billy and Shem explained that this was an annual performance by this shaman, which he did because he had once died. Billy believes that the shaman followed an evolutionary pattern during his transformation. Water creatures came first, algae to one-celled animals to fish. Then all kinds of animals that make noises. He said, "That's the way life began, and he followed the same pattern." Shem said that the last animals they heard were "winter animals," and "then he came dancing out of the bath house." Shem said that the shaman made a special song that he sang as he exited the bath house but "we never did hear the song." This was because after the shaman's death, the song was not sung again because "they were afraid he might come back." Billy also maintained that the shaman's old body each year drifted down the inlet and was eaten by fish.

Ghu ch'adach' ghu beł idelghish.
And then there was some kind hollering noise passing by.

[Cranes and all the waterfowl, he could hear them all in the bath house calling in the bath house.]

Pretty soon quk'uljik.
Pretty soon, he came out dancing.

Quk'uljik iłdi kisht'a betsitu'iltutl'.
When he came out dancing, there was lots of feathers in his hair.

[Billy: A bunch of feathers were falling off of him.]

Kisht'a betsitu'iltutl' ch'u el'ek yuh ghu.
His head was all full of feathers in his hair, and he was making medicine.

Ehe, qeył delghesh, qeył delghesh
Yes, they were hollering [singing] with him, they were hollering [singing] with him.

Yeghe ch'u t'an t'an ch'u quht'ana gheli nusdlan
He kept doing that and doing that [dancing and singing with the waterfowl], and he got to be a real person again.

Qubech' qenash gheli dujuq.
And he really talked to them.

Yen shughu beł dink'udlaghen be'iyi daghila.
That is the one whose name was "the one who swam back inside with them."

[Billy: "The man that came back with the fish and got into the fish trap."]

Ki taltashen heł dghinih.
They also used to call him, "Taltashen" ['The one that was put in water'].

N'uyi jaghidaq hnuq'u, gu łiq'a ka'a qełchish ch'u denghilin eł lghal eł t'ehyił'ish ch'u.
At the winter solstice here they would make the salmon [with this ritual] and they used to bundle him up with a sinew "beluga" rope.[4]

Biłni ghu tuhyełt'eh.
They [took him and] threw him in the water.

Yalih, yalih ch'u yet tl'ił ghini qyeduquq' ghu qeyn-ghełchesh.
He kept swimming in there, and swimming in there, they were tugging [on that rope] up above.

[Billy explained, "Pretty soon, when he stopped pulling on that rope, they pulled it back up and he was gone. I suppose he became a little trout again."]

Nelni ghini, nichił ka'a gheli nelni bekini'uh t'ghit'a.
There was always a bath house connected to each big nichił [winter house].

Nelni bekidghi'u tuydełq'ash gheli ch'u łuq'u hełch'teh dughu qenda hteyush hnuq'u,
They scrubbed the floor of the steam bath and in the evening when they got it all ready,

qudulyi łuq'u gheli tsahduya, qendagh hchaq'a k'ilan łu idayq'enh t'ehghił'ik łu.
they put medicine, sage, in each corner of the floor [of the steam bath] and burned them.

[Billy: And they all sat in the **nichił** and waited.]

Dach' nuhqulnek shughu nuqelnek t'i.
I am telling this the way they told me this story.[5]

Ghu nelni yan hq'u yagheli tqeł'ish.
They cleaned that bath house up real good.

[Billy: And just waited for him.]

Pretty soon yada k'ilan, k'delghish qbe'uh ghu.
Pretty soon, there was something, there was a noise nearby them.

[Billy: They heard everything—swans, geese, bear, caribou—all the land animals.]

Nut'aq'i ghudehdi eł, yada k'ilan, quggesh yada dghiłney jetshla k'ilan łuq'u delghesh.
All the water fowl and everything, the swans of different sizes, all of them were hollering.

[Billy: Everything that's on the beach—ducks, **nut'aq'i,** (waterfowl]. Everything, all the waterfowl, they all were calling.

Ndał ch'da hudehdi eł k'delghish, k'delghish.
And cranes and all the waterfowl kept calling, and calling.

[Billy: All the geese and everything that flies, they all quack.]

Łuq'u nunudełi ghu ni delghish delghish ch'delghish.
All the birds kept calling, and calling, and calling.

Ch'u łuq'u gheli qubiduhdghises.
Then everything, all sounds diminished.

Ighi ghenuyi ghudehdi, bear ghuhdi k'delghish.
Then the caribou and bear and everything called next [the land mammals].

4. Billy explained that this happened every the winter solstice, **n'uyi jaghidaq**; the shortest day of the year. He added that "The Indians kept good track of the days."

5. Shem here is indicating that he was not an eyewitness to these events, but is passing on the story exactly as he heard it.

FIGURE 115

Billy Pete (left) and Gilbert Kallander working on an outboard motor at Point Possession in the 1950s.

PHOTO COURTESY OF FEODORIA KALLANDER PENNINGTON

Qunsha ghudehdi eł.
The ground squirrels also [called].

Shq'uła ghudehdi eł.
The whistlers [called] also.

Ghu nuqetnih, qetnih qetnih ch'u
They kept making their sounds like that, making sounds, and making sounds and

ghal yeduhdistlaq' hnuq'u nelni t'uh ghu,
when it quieted down, there in the bath house,

tunuggech' ka'a gheli qadahdelchet.
they heard big swells [like the ocean, in the bath house].

Bełni ghin yełtetl'.
Water was striking the place.

Qutsaghił'iy ghudehdi, quyushi ghuhdi k'delghesh biłni at yada ninya nlan.
Then the seals and belugas hollered, all of the water animals.

Łiq'a qudełi ghuhdi ił.
And the salmon were jumping.

Yaghelisht'a qetnih, qetnih, qetnih ch'u.
They kept making their sounds nicely, making sounds, and making sounds.

Ighi nelni ghini ighi biłni duhdistlaq' hnu quk'eljesh.
And when the water quieted down at the bath house, he came out dancing.

Quk'eljesh ghu qeył k'delghish, qeył delghish qeył delghish ch'u.
As he came out dancing, they [the animals] kept singing with him, singing with him [all night].

Q'u yidultash gheli.
He came right back to his own body again.

Quht'ana nusdlani kiq'u.
He came back to be human again.

Dach' łu t'ghet'an łu.
That's is how he did this.

Yi ki q'udi gu hq'u yan ba nuhtghelnek.
That's as far as I'm going to tell this story.

Q'u dutdgheshcheł.
I'm going to shut up now.

prospect for gold in the mountains now known as the Willow Creek District. Presumably they came by water. These were the first men to discover gold. The names of these first gold discoverers, who lived for a while in old Kinik, were W. J. Morris and his partner, H. Herndon."

§8.77 Qughun Betnu • 'Hump Stream'
upper Willow Creek, above Peters Creek
See also 12.16, **Qughun** Bald Mountain.

8.37 Hech' Nuydlentnu • 'Creek That Flows Back and Forth (meandering)'
Deception Creek

8.38 Ts'ihełken Betnu • 'Pitch-Dark Ridge Creek'
creek into Deception Creek from ***Ts'ihełken***

8.39 Ts'ihełken • 'Pitch-Dark Ridge'
ridge, elev. 1500', noted as triangulation mark "Bullion" at base of Bald Mountain Ridge (12.16)
According to Shem Pete, 'Pitch-dark' refers to the contrast between the timbered zone here and the open country of Bald Mountain Ridge. This ridge was in the center of the site that was proposed for a new Alaska state capital at Willow in the 1970s.

8.40 Bantsach'elashitnu • 'Stream of Someone Gave Rocks to Him'
Little Willow Creek
The name refers to the practice of warming food by dropping hot rocks into containers. The trail used by the Kroto band in the Talkeetna Mountains crossed the upper reaches of this stream.

§8.78 Nudayk'et'i Betnu • 'Timberlines Extend Down-Stream'
Iron Creek

8.41 Nudayk'et'i • 'Timberlines Extend Down'
ridge and peak elev. 3186' "Willow" south of Little Willow Creek
Katherine Nicolie: "We go through **Nudayk'et'i** from **Qughun** [Bald Mountain Ridge, 12.16]. We go up to **Qughun**, and they don't kill anything. Then from there we go across **Bantsach'elashitnu** [Little Willow Creek, 8.40]. Then we keep on, go follow the mountain. And there is a nice-looking place there. They stop there. They hunt for a while. Lots of blueberries.

"Before we go down to canyon on Kashwitna. That nice looking mountain. That's the one they call **Nudayk'et'i**. That's my stepfather's country." It was here that Katherine Nicolie hunted for ptarmigan with a bow and arrow when she was a little girl. She recalled meeting some of the Talkeetna Dena'ina up here, who came from the direction of Montana Creek.

8.42 T'ghes Tuhdatbut Tayena • 'Cottonwood Bleached in Water-Straight Stretch'
stretch of the Susitna River below the Kashwitna River
The name refers to gray-white colored cottonwood driftwood. This is where the woman **Ch'anqet'** from the Talkeetna Mountains was stranded in the snow in about 1903–04. See pp. 244.

§8.79 Qatna'iy • 'That Which Stands Against a Place'
rock bluff on E side of Susitna, W of Kashwitna Section House
Sava Stephan: "**Qatna'iy**, that's same place they call Otter Creek, my new trapline, I don't know what they call that name now. I build trapline cabin over there. My dad call it Otter Creek, **Qatna'iy yehdi** big hill standing up, just like a rock. I almost got attacked by a wolf there. My shells got stuck in barrel.... **Qatna'iy** that's a little hill, that's all. We kill moose on top of that. All I do is put it in that skin and slide it down the hill."

§8.80 Q'is Kaq' • 'Birchbark Mouth'
mouth of 196 Mile Creek or Grey's Creek

§8.81 Q'istnu • 'Birchbark Stream'
196 Mile Creek, now called Grey's Creek
Reduced from **q'eyses** 'birchbark.'

§8.82 Hnibes • 'Embedded River Bank'
Kashwitna Knobs
Sava Stephan: "**Bentalit,** that's where my trapline was. **Hnibes** is above Kroto Creek about seven mile up. It's right on the river, on the Susitna, on left side going up. Wilson Nicolai had a cabin right back of **Hnibes.** I used to snowshoe around back there. My Dad's dad was up at **Benteh**, we had 19 dogs, we used to walk to Talkeetna in one day. Three cabins we passed at **Benteh.** That was my Dad's place, then it passed to me."

§8.83 Kiłbitnu Kaq' • '‡Boy Canyon River Mouth'
mouth of Kashwitna River
Cook Inlet Historic Sites Project (1975:96): "At the confluence of the Kashwitna and Susitna Rivers. According to informants the area was good for beaver. A winter village is the likely type of habitation. From informants it was a place to stay during hunting times. Pits have been reported in the state's survey of historical sites in the Kashwitna area."

8.43 Kiłbitnu • '‡Boy Canyon River'
Kashwitna River
‡In several Dene languages **bi-** literally 'inside it' refers to canyon.

Alexandra Allowan made one trip up the Kashwitna River when she was very young. She recalled seeing Native camps on the Kashwitna.

‡Katherine Nicoli: "No **nichił** in that country. Too rough a place for people I think."

Sava Stephan: "In fall time [1924 or so] I come down in a skin boat when I was a little kid, **Kiłbitnu.** With my dad and that **Tsitnelggeyen** [Simeon Ezi, who was married to Sava's father's sister]. We had been up in the mountains. We come down Kashwitna from the mountain, not very far to the mountains. **Kiłbitnu** we come down in the creek, my dad and **Tsitnelggeyen**. We came at the Willow Creek near that pump station and from there we come down to Kroto Creek and then down

FIGURE 116

Looking southwest down **Kiłbitnu Tl'u** (8.44, '‡Boy Canyon River Headwaters,' the upper Kashwitna River). Photo by Stephen R. Capps, Jr., in 1913.

STEPHEN R. CAPPS, JR. COLLECTION (#83-149-1991), ARCHIVES, ALASKA AND POLAR REGIONS DEPT., RASMUSON LIBRARY, UNIVERSITY OF ALASKA FAIRBANKS

to Susitna Station. I barely remember that. I was two or three years. Just three of us went."

Annabel (1997d:328): "Over yonder in some cottonwoods the Kashwitna moose had a kind of spa. Well-hidden, known only to a few Indians and sourdoughs, the lick consisted of a brackish hot spring and about a half acre of brindle-colored mud. I have no idea what minerals apart from salt were in the water and mud, but they must have added up to a prime moose tonic. Judging from the sign, moose had been coming here for centuries. Their trails through the timber were like country roads. Shed antlers gnawed on by porcupine lay everywhere in the lush waist-high grass. Piles of bones attested to kills made by Indians and wolves."

8.44 Kiłbitnu Tl'u • '‡Boy Canyon River Headwaters'
upper Kashwitna River
Shem Pete: "«The one called **Kiłkda** was from Susitna Station. He found gold there. Every summer he used to bring Americans up there. They paid him fifty dollars in gold for the trip. He found gold in the mountains. He went up there every summer. I saw him. He died [of the 1918 flu] in my presence.»"

Bailey Theodore: "A long time ago they used to go around for caribou there. They had a cache at the mountain, where the Kashwitna comes out of the mountain. He [**Kiłkda**] told my father that he found gold up there."

The trails on the 1906 Herning map (Map 49) are interesting. A winter trail going northwest from Knik is shown crossing the Little Susitna River, going on the west side of Nancy Lake, then crossing Willow Creek, and Little Willow Creek to the Kashwitna River. Also a trail is shown ascending the south bank of the Kashwitna and crossing Little Willow and Willow creeks where it would join with several trails. See also 14.20 regarding a trail from King River to the upper Kashwitna River.

§8.84 "Yus-Tel-Tay-Uh-Na" [Yus ?-tay'uhtnu] • 'Stream of -?- Ridge That Extends Ahead'
North Fork of Kashwitna River
A place name from Russell Annabel (1939a): "Yus-Tel-Tay-Uh-Na. One ridge over from a creek that drains into the Kashwitna." This pronunciation by Sava Stephan is speculative. The syllable -Tel- from Annabel looks irregular.

CINA (1975:96): "Mr. Dunder related to us his knowledge of a village site on the North Fork of the Kashwitna River. This site was also confirmed by Jim Dryer, a friend of Mr. Dunder. Dryer also related the existence of an old Indian trail which linked this village and Chickaloon."

§8.85 ‡[Yus ?-tay'uh] • possibly 'Ridge That Extends Ahead'
ridge south of North Fork of Kashwitna River

8.45 Hutsighelqet'i • 'Bald-Headed One'
mountain, elev. 4482', "Whitna," between Little Willow Creek and Kashwitna River
Katherine Nicolie: "From **Nudayk'et'i** we stop at another mountain over that way. Nothing on top. And there's a big lake by it. That's what they call **Hutsighelqet'i**. And they ain't supposed to call it all the time neither. They say it comes to be bad weather. They used to tell us not to call it."

8.46 Hutsighelqet'i Bena • 'Bald-Headed Lake'
small lakes on mountain, "Whitna"

8.47 Kiłbitnu Łi'a • '‡Boy Canyon River Glacier'
Kashwitna Glacier

8.48 Kiłbitnu Dghelaya • '‡Boy Canyon River Mountain'
mountain, elev. 6730', at head of Kashwitna River

§8.86 Q'uch'u'itnu • ‡'Stone Point -?- Stream'
possibly Caswell Creek
See Map 35. ‡Note the similarity with **Ch'u'itnu** (1.59), the name for Chuitna River. The only mention of Dena'ina living in Caswell we have seen is via C. Mielke (2012). A report at National Archives dated 1/29/1945

by Dr. Hoehn, a physician in Palmer: "Johnny Toughluck living at Caswell is married to a native woman who already had several children."

8.49 Baqay Nilyashtnu • 'Creek Where Birchbark Canoes Are Left'
Sheep Creek
According to Pete Stephan, the name refers to the practice of leaving canoes here while groups went hunting in the mountains to the east. Sheep Creek is too shallow for hauling loads of meat.

8.50 Bak'enin'iy • 'Caribou Fence'
caribou fence in gap between mountains "Sunshine" and "Wolverine" north of Sheep Creek
Shem Pete: "«**Bak'nin'iy** is upland from Montana Creek.» Two mountains close together. «They made a fence there for caribou.» Wasilla Stephan used to use that area."

The caribou fence here was last used in the late nineteenth century.

8.51 K'eł Tuqishlatnu, §Łtuqenshlatnu • 'Creek in Which Things Drift' or 'Little Clear Creek'
a tributary or slough of Goose Creek (location revised)
The second name is from Pete Stephan in 1976. The first name is from from Shem Pete.

§8.87 Tunadlut' • 'Murky Water'
Goose Creek, lower Goose Creek
The name "Toonaklut" is mentioned in numerous stories by Russell Annabel (e.g., 1997c:185). Annabel's homestead was located here (Davis 2002). The name was confirmed by Sava Stephan and Lillian Theodore.

8.52 Qiduk'ggat • 'Overflows and Freezes'
§Montana Creek village, mouth of Little Montana Creek (location revised)
Kari (1999:14): "In the Montana Creek area we refined a location of the place name **Qiduk'ggat**. Lillian Theodore states that this name applies to a site at the mouth of Little Montana Creek. Therefore the lake at the head of this stream, Little Montana Lake, is a new name to the list."

Montana Creek became a small Dena'ina village in about 1915 when the railroad construction was underway. Trails go west from here to Trapper Lake and east toward Larsen Lake and the western Talkeetna Mountains.

Seager-Boss (1996:33) "A native village site was established at Montana Creek in 1915, when it was still a construction camp for the Alaska Railroad (Kari and Fall 1987: 165). Many native inhabitants in the Talkeetna area may have abandoned their traditional village homes and congregated at railroad camps in the hopes of gaining cash paying jobs. A similar relocation to railroad outposts took place at Nancy Lake and Kashwitna with the Kroto clans of the Susitna (Fall 1981)."

Katherine Nicolie: "Montana Creek didn't have nothing to stop there for unless we go up to the mountain. That's a new place. That start when the railroad start. Not an old place."

Pete Stephan noted that he knew the country north

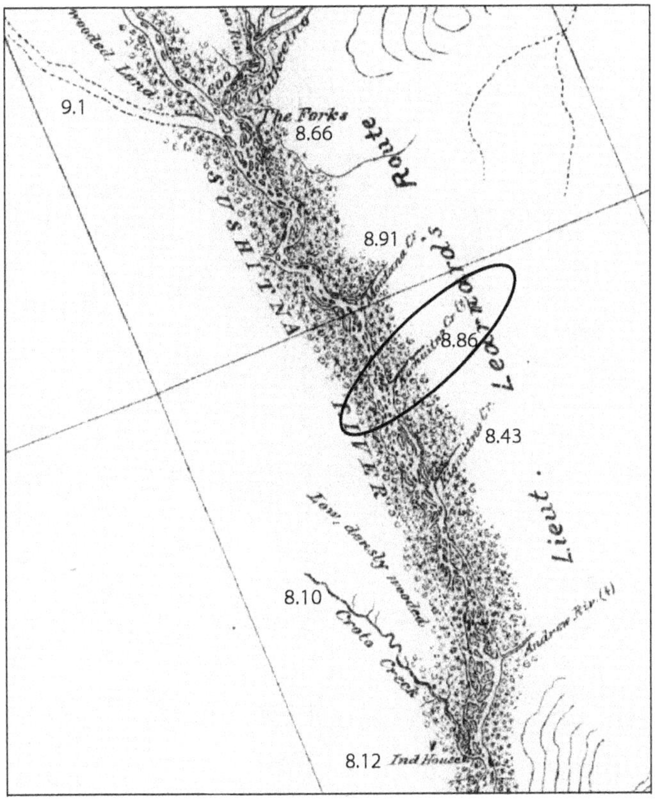

MAP 35

Detail from the 1900 Meiklejohn Map: Kroto Creek to Talkeetna with *SPA* feature numbers.

The stream "Kochuitna ?" between Kashwitna River ("Kismitna River") and Montana Creek prompted the name **Q'uch'u'itnu**, possibly Caswell Creek (8.86). Sava Stephan said that this pronunciation sounded familiar to him. This name is not mentioned anywhere else in the reports by Learnard, Yanert, and others. "Ind. House" at lower right is Kroto Village (8.12).

ARCHIVES, ALASKA AND POLAR REGIONS DEPT., RASMUSON LIBRARY, UNIVERSITY OF ALASKA FAIRBANKS

FIGURE 117

Tunadlut' (8.38, Goose Creek).

PHOTO BY JEFF DAVIS

FIGURE 118

(Above) On the bed of the Susitna River near the mouth of Montana Creek are Bobby Stephan, Lillian Stephan Theodore, and Susie Stephan, ca 1939.

PHOTO COURTESY OF LILLIAN THEODORE

FIGURE 119

(Right) Susie Stephan, Bobby Stephan, and Lillian Stephan Theodore near Montana Creek cemetery in the late 1930s.

PHOTO COURTESY OF LILLIAN THEODORE

and east of here best, but he did not know the area to the west on the other side of the Susitna, including many streams quite near Montana Creek. Pete Stephan had traveled extensively between here and Stephan Lake.

In 1980 the Montana Creek cemetery was surveyed by the Cooperative Park Studies Unit. In addition to the ten visible graves, signs of fifteen housepits and about 150 cache pits were located here (Cooperative Park Studies Unit 1980).

Lillian Theodore notes that the lower channel at the mouth of Montana Creek was known as "Pete's Slough" for her uncle Pete Stephan (see Fig. 124). She adds that Wasilla Stephan would fish at Montana Creek for silvers, pinks, and kings, as well as grayling and whitefish. He had smokehouses at Pete's Slough and on the north side of the creek. He would go up to Sunshine for the sockeye run. He would cross the Susitna River after the ice went out and hunt muskrat and beaver at a small lake and creek on the point across from the mouth of Montana Creek.

Annabel (1997e:327): "Our Susitna Denna Indians are the solidest of solid moose fans. For example, consider a Denna funeral I once attended. Old "Moose Meat" Nick Stepan, of Montana Creek, had passed on. He'd been a valued friend of mine. I had hunted moose with Nick since I was a kid. He showed me how to make moose hock moccasins and weave moose-babiche snowshoe filling. He got me started using a dried moose bladder for a tobacco pouch. He taught me that a moosehide, hair side up, is the world's best cold-weather mattress. He proved to me that the jaw muscles are the choicest meat on a moose carcass. And that a bit of its gall lends superb flavor to a moose steak.

"Nick's oldest son, Mishkah, gave the eulogy. 'We know there's plenty moose where you are now, Papa,' Mishkah said as we stood around the plank coffin. 'Big moose. Fat moose.' Mishkah's voice broke, then he added, 'Good to eat and fun to hunt, by gosh. You are lucky, Papa.'

"A mighty fine send-off, I thought."

§8.88 **Qiduk'ggat Besa** • 'Overflows and Freezes Bank'
ridge along Susitna River above mouth of Montana Creek

§8.89 **Qiduk'ggatnu** • 'Overflows and Freezes Stream'
Little Montana Creek

§8.90 **Qiduk'ggat Bena** • 'Overflows and Freezes Lake'
Little Montana Creek Lake at junction, formerly "Old Mans Lake"

§8.91 **Nultani Betnu** • 'Animal That Is Lying Down'
Montana Creek, Middle Fork of Montana Creek

Wasilla Stephan of Montana Creek

compiled by James Kari, with an excerpt by Russell Annabel

Wasilla Stephan of Montana Creek was an expert hunter and woodsman. He was born in 1888 at Kroto Creek, and he died in 1970. His father was from Nenana. His daughter, Lillian Theodore, has lived in the Montana Creek area all her life. Lillian has supplied other facts about Wasilla Stephan's knowledge of the country. See for example 8.52 and 8.53.

The prolific adventure writer Russell Annabel was a friend and neighbor of Wasilla's who lived several miles downstream at Goose Creek from the late 1920s until 1953. Several of Annabel's stories feature Wasilla Stephan and his activities as a hunter and woodsman (Annabel 1948:77–78, 1997d:22). Lillian recalls that her father and Annabel would visit frequently, that her father would speak some Dena'ina language with Annabel. She also recalls that Annabel frequently took notes when they talked. Jeff Davis (2002:199–201) profiles Wasilla Stephan in his book-length biography of Annabel.

The following is an excerpt from a story entitled "Brawn as in Bruin" (Annabel 1997b: 241–42), originally published in 1954 in Hunting Yearbook. *Lillian Theodore notes that Wasilla's smokehouses were at Pete's Slough and on the north side of the mouth of Montana Creek, see 8.52 and Fig. 121.*

But I think the best crack I ever heard on the subject of bear strength was made by my friend Wasilla Stepan. Wasilla is chief of a fading tribe of Susitna-Denna. He lives three miles north of my place and, in summer, makes his living drying salmon, which he sells to dog mushers. Tall and dignified, the only chief I ever knew who looks like one, he came down to Goose Creek one September morning to make an apology. He wouldn't be able to fill an order Tex [Cobb] and I had given him for a bale of dried silver salmon, he informed us, unless we could wait another ten days. There had been a little trouble at his camp, he said. Bear trouble. In fact, he said, he was going to have to build a new fish house, on account of the former one was in ruins. Over a pot of tea he told us the awful misadventure that had happened.

For several nights in a row, Wasilla said, a brown bear had prowled about the fish house obviously working up courage to enter and pull down the racks of drying salmon. A tin-roofed affair, twenty feet square and open on all sides, the fish house stood on the bank of the Susitna River 200 yards from Wasilla's summer cabin. Wasilla didn't have a

FIGURE 120

Nick Oskolkoff (left) and Wasilla Stephan in 1965 at **Niteh** (14.4, Matanuska village site). Nick Oskolkoff was originally from Kenai and lived at **Niteh** in the 1960s. Nick's Dena'ina name, according to Shem Pete, was **Nuhunulgak**.

PHOTO COURTESY OF LILLIAN THEODORE

FIGURE 121

Wasilla Stephan's smokehouse at Pete's Slough in 1950.

PHOTO COURTESY OF LILLIAN THEODORE

watchdog, he explained, and he had been reluctant to stand guard over the fish house at night with a rifle. Like most of the Tena people, he had a strong aversion to being abroad after nightfall. Moreover, he pointed out, he was an old man, and when he had put in a hard day splitting salmon and tending his nets, needed rest.

So he did the next best thing. He set a snare for the bear. It was no ordinary snare. It was a length of quarter-inch steel cable, strong enough to have garroted a cape buffalo. Painstakingly and with veteran trapper's skill, he set it in the brush directly behind the fish house and tied it securely to a leaning, fire-killed spruce snag. With a heap of fish gurry for bait it was a deadly contrivance, and Wasilla went home that night assuring himself that his bear troubles were practically over and done with.

Fate threw him a curve. Along toward midnight he was awakened by an astonishingly loud tinny crash in the direction of the fish house. Pulling on his pants and moccasins, he hastened out with his rifle to investigate. It was an overcast night with rain and an icy wind blowing off the glaciers of Mt. McKinley. As the old chief eased into the fish house clearing he heard the bear bawl, then saw the shadowy outline of the animal fighting the snare.

Wasilla carried a .405 and he had learned through hard-won experience that the way to kill a bear is to keep blasting as long as the bear moves and then shoot him a couple of times for luck. It prevents incidents. So tonight he emptied the .405.

Of course, the whole thing was very unsporting, but then Wasilla isn't a sportsman. He is an old man making his living on the bank of a wilderness river, and the bear was out to give him trouble. Had given him trouble. When he went over to the fallen animal, Wasilla told us, he saw for the first time that the fish house now had two sections. The brown bear, throwing his great weight and strength against the cable snare, had pulled over the spruce snag to which the snare was fastened. And the snag had fallen across the tin roof of the fish house – that was the crash he had heard—cleaving the roof in half. All the fish racks were knocked down and rain was pouring in on them.

"So that's why," Wasilla said, "I won't be able to bring you that bale of silver salmon like I said I would."

"He musta been a heck of strong bear," Tex said.

"I guess so," Wasilla said, shrugging. "But did you ever hear of a weak bear?"

Which, I think, ties up the subject of bear strength.

FIGURE 122

Upper Montana Creek, with **Nultani Betnu** (8.90, the Middle Fork of Montana Creek) in the center. The slopes of **Nultani** (8.56) are above.

PHOTO BY JEFF DAVIS

Annabel (1953:35) offers this etymology of this name: "Then we moved into the mountains, to the lake-dotted headwaters of a clear-water creek the Indians call Nolletana—Stream-Running-Through-Bald-Mountains."

8.53 Łinghasdlent • 'Where Streams Join'
confluence of the north, middle and south forks of Montana Creek
Pete Stephan reported that there are house pits in this area.

A story by Annabel (1997d:22) gives an elaborate account of a "first salmon ceremony" event Annabel claimed to have witnessed on Montana Creek.

8.54 Tsit'untali Betnu • 'Thin Wide Head Creek'
South Fork of Montana Creek
Annabel's story "Old Grizzlies Die Hard" (1987:138–149) is a gripping story about a Montana Creek bear hunter he called "Billy No-Dogs" who knew some arcane bear hunting techniques and rituals. No-Dogs, accompanied by Annabel, killed an aged grizzly that had an "ancient weapon point, holy to the Denna Indians, that he had carried for years in his shaggy carcass." Sava Stephan does not recall anyone by this name, and he has not heard this story, though he thinks it sounds plausible.

§8.92 Nuch'dalyut • 'Where We Bring Things (Branches) Back'
Wasilla Stephan's cabin location off the South Fork of Montana Creek
Source: Johnny Stephan via Mike Theodore and Lillian Theodore. Lillian Theodore notes that for hunting Wasilla Stephan would mainly go to the east. **Nuch'dalyuch'** was at head of the "Old Indian Trail" that went up mountains between the South Fork of Montana Creek and Sheep Creek. Wasilla Stephan had cabins at **Nuch'dalyut** off the South Fork of Montana Creek, and also at "Pete's Lake" (Emil Lake). Johnny Stephan's cabin was past the Wilson farm on South Fork.

Sava Stephan "**Nuch'dalyut** is between Talkeetnu and Montana, that's where John Stephan had a cabin. He was trapping over there. Took him about two hours to walk back over there. I think his father [Wasilla Stephan] built that. [The name means] 'Like we pack back home branches.' Like packing back dry alders. I think I stayed with them about a year. Wassila, his wife and his wife had a sister. She come from Kroto Creek. And her brother's name of Scottie. They used to call youngest brother Alec **Q'untsila.** The older brother was Scottie and the oldest one was Pete Stephan. They used to call him **K'nuy'a Gga** (little beaver). He was in the army."

8.55 Tsit'untali Dghelaya • 'Thin Wide Head Mountain'
mountains, elev. 4559' and 5344', south of South Fork of Montana Creek
Shem Pete: "«**Tsit'untali** is below **Nultani**.»"

This is locally known as "Table Top."

8.56 Nultani • 'Animal That Is Lying Down'
series of mountains on upper middle fork of Montana Creek

FIGURE 123

Looking northeast from the upper reaches of Montana Creek.

STEPHEN R. CAPPS, JR. COLLECTION (#83-149-2010), ARCHIVES, ALASKA AND POLAR REGIONS DEPT., RASMUSON LIBRARY, UNIVERSITY OF ALASKA FAIRBANKS

Shem Pete: "**Nultani** looks to them like an animal lying there."

John Stephan said that the name Montana (Creek) is an anglicization of the Dena'ina name **Nultani**. Pete Stephan referred to this in English as "Snowshoe Hill."

§8.93 Nuch'elehitnu • 'Stream of Fish Swim Around a Corner'
North Fork of Montana Creek
Name and translation from Sava Stephan.

8.57 Sdaghuyq'et • 'On the End of the Point'
point on Susitna River between Montana and Sunshine creeks

§8.94 Tuqentnu • 'Clear Water Creek'
Robideaux Creek
This name is from Pete Stephan in 1976. The name was omitted on later typed lists and did not appear in the first edition.

8.58 Tsuk Qayeh • 'Old Village'
site opposite mouth of Sunshine Creek
Shem Pete: "I think it's close to the mouth of Sunshine Creek. They call it Old Village." The exact location is unknown. This is another site used by the Mountain People.

8.59 K't'usq'a Kaq' • 'Mouth of Fish Cutting Hole'
mouth of Sunshine Creek
Shem Pete: "They cut fish in the mouth of that creek. They camp for the fish."

Two areas with numerous Dena'ina fish cache pits have been located in this area by the Matanuska-Susitna Borough Cultural Resource Division (Seager-Boss 1996:37–41).

8.60 K't'usq'atnu • 'Fish Cutting Hole Creek'
Sunshine Creek
Shem Pete: "Lots of fish in that creek."

Katherine Nicolie: "They put up silvers there."

Graves of children of the Nick Nicolie family are located near the Sunshine Section House (Seager-Boss 1996:57).

§8.95 K't'usq'a Bena • 'Fish Cutting Hole Lake'
Sunshine Lake

8.61 Ben Ka'a • 'Big Lake'
Benka Lake

§8.96 Ben Gga • 'Small Lake'
small lake next to Benka Lake
Name contributed by Lillian Theodore.

8.62 Ch'aten Kaq' • 'Mouth of Trail Comes Out'
mouth of Birch Creek on Susitna River
Shem Pete: "**Ch'anqet'** would bring that dry meat down [from the Talkeetna Mountains] to **Ch'aten Kaq'.** They put up lots fish there."

Katherine Nicolie: "They were catching some king salmon at the mouth."

8.63 Ch'atem Bena • 'Trail Comes Out - Lake'
Fish Lake

Katherine Nicolie: "My father and his brothers used to stay there. They had a fish trap there. Old timers. Annie Ronning's [Katherine's cousin's] father, all my uncles. Everybody used to have their own place. Build some kind of house. Before white people, they say my father had a house there. After he died [in 1918], Mom never did go back. They had all kinds of trout. They use it in spring and fall. In fall when trout goes back to the lake, and then when they coming down in the spring. They had a bridge. I remember when Mom took me there one time. We was watching to see if trout go in trap. They had a place box-like. They pull it [fishtrap] out, and they dump it. They say everybody used to travel through and stop there just for the trout."

Annie Ronning's father, **Shik'u** or Nick Nicolie, is buried here.

8.64 Ch'atentnu • 'Trail Comes Out - Creek'
Birch Creek, and also Fish Lake outlet stream

8.65 Hnibes Ka'a • 'Big Embedded Bank'
ridge one mile south of Talkeetna, "Ski Hill"
Shem Pete: "That's part of **Chuti Yits'a** [see 11.2]."

See 11.2, 11.21, and 11.22 on the Talkeetna Lakes, which could have been placed in this chapter.

8.66 Łinghasdlent • 'Where Streams Join'
"The Forks," area at confluence of Chulitna and Talkeetna rivers with the Susitna River

This is known as "The Forks" on early maps, a translation of the Dena'ina name (see Map 35.)

Shem Pete: "«One open place above Talkeetna. All creeks come into one open area.»"

FIGURE 124

(Right) Pete Stephan, Bobby Stephan, and Lillian Stephan Theodore at Montana Creek section house in early 1940s. Pete Stephan contributed several names in the Montana Creek-Talkeetna area in 1976.

PHOTO COURTESY OF LILLIAN THEODORE

FIGURE 125

(Below) Aerial view from above "The Forks" or **Łinghasdlent** (8.66, the confluence of the Chulitna, Susitna and Talkeetna Rivers). The river in the center of the frame is **Ts'ilutnu** (9.1, Chulitna River); the rivers at plane's tail wing are **Susitnu** (2.1, the Susitna River) and **K'dalkitnu** (11.1, the Talkeetna River). On the horizon is a clear view of **Dghelay Teh** (7.61, the Central Alaska Range) and the mountains **K'ghitsala** (7.60, Mt. Russell), **Be'u** (7.49, Mt. Foraker), **Begguya** (7.50, Mt. Hunter), and **Dghelay Ka'a** (7.51, Denali). Also in view is **Dghelay Ka'a Łi'a** (9.25, Ruth Glacier). ‡7.62 added in 2016, **Denaze Dinyet** the canyon wall beneath Mt. Foraker, via Miska Deaphon Cf. Fig. 24, a similar view of the Alaska Range in winter.

PHOTO BY SHARI GEORGE

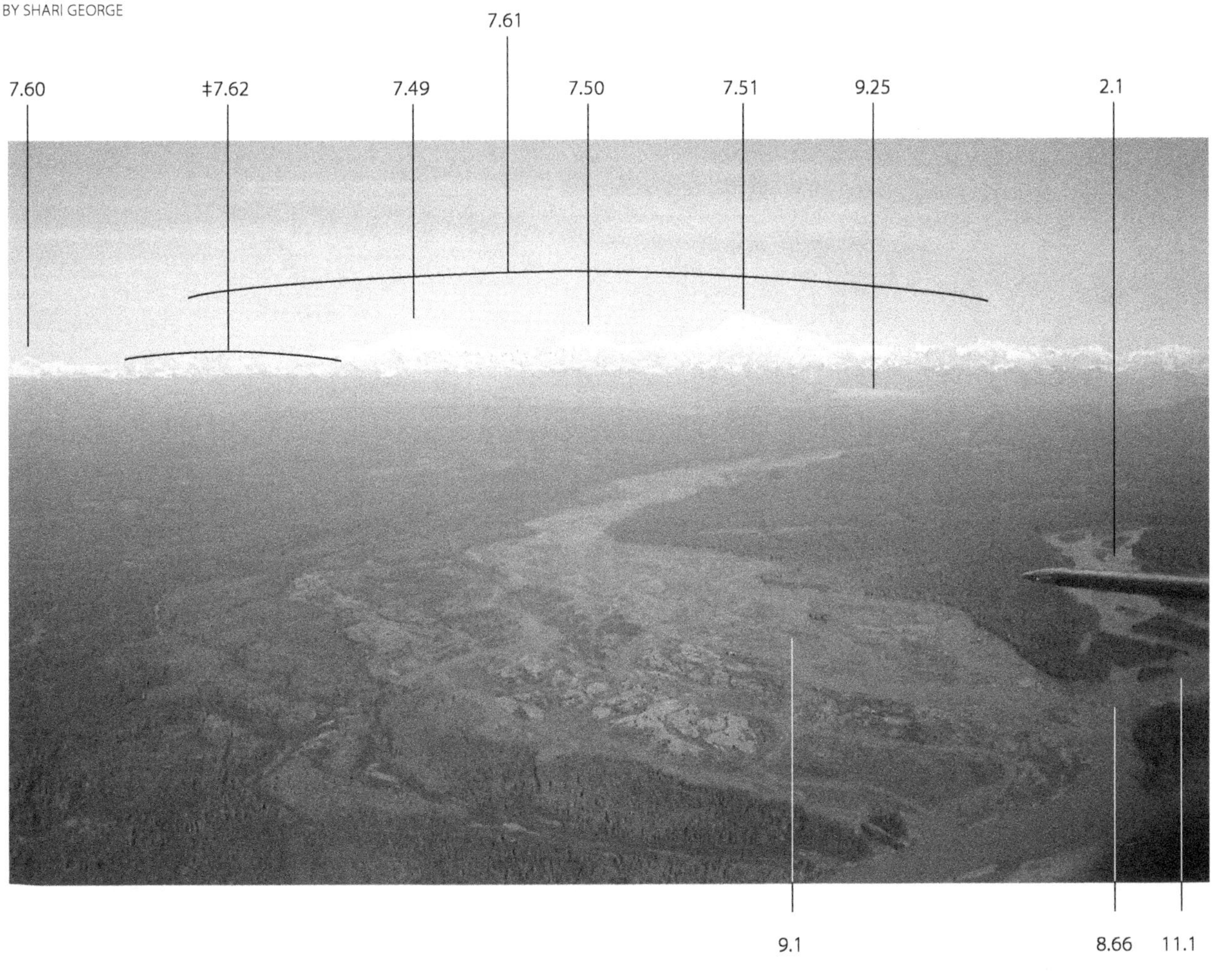

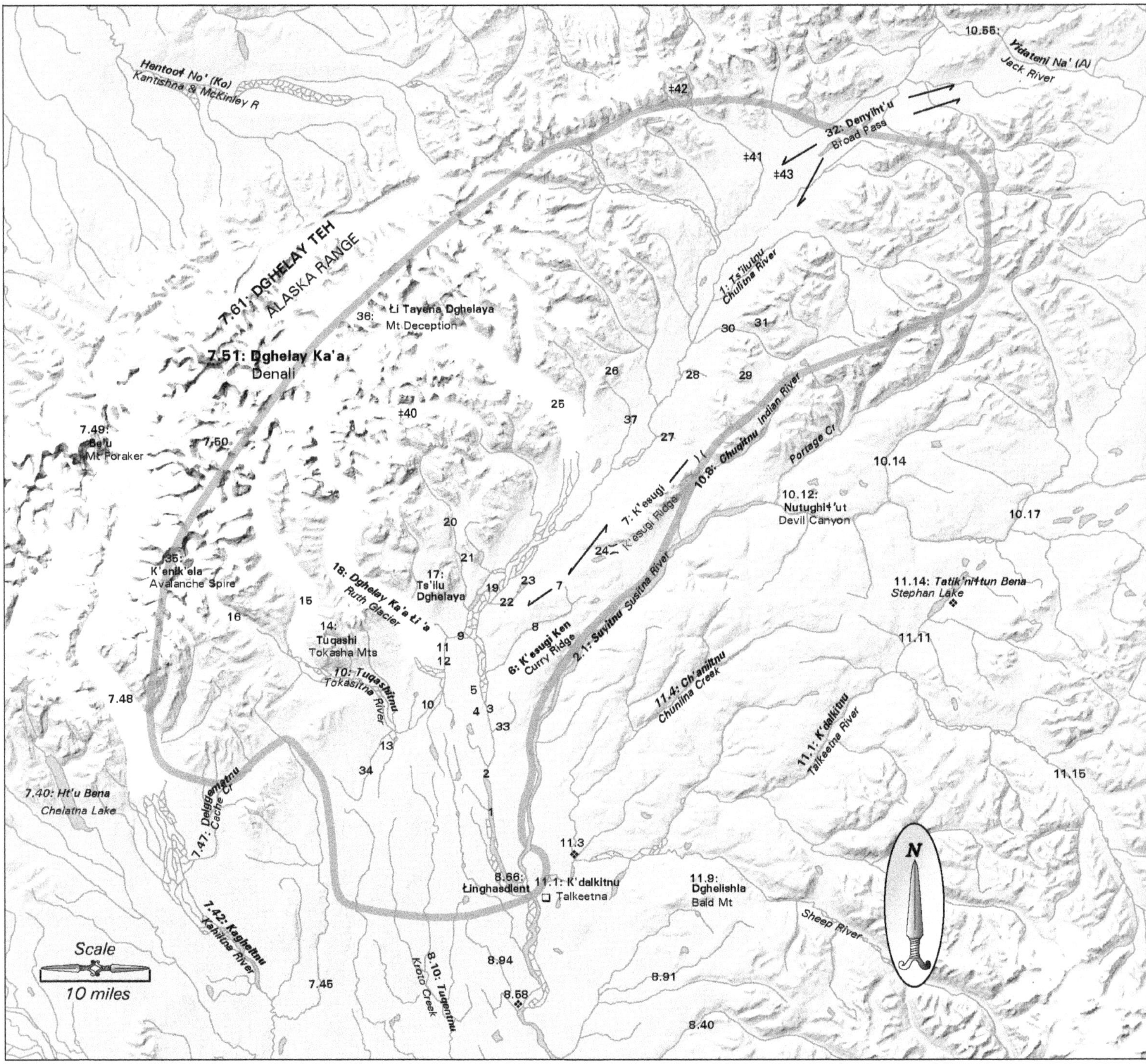

MAP 36

Place names map of the Chulitna River, showing Nos. 9.1 to 9.44.

MAP BY MATT GANLEY

9 Chulitna River

9.1 Ts'ilutnu *(Dena'ina)*, **Tsulatna'** *(Ahtna)* • possibly 'Straight Hand River;' 'Tongue River'
Chulitna River
‡Shem was consistent in his pronunciation **Ts'ilutnu**. In 1987 we had translated this as 'Forearm River' but **ts'ilu** is not a match with **-ts'ila** forearm. The Ahtna name was reported by Jake Tansy and was perhaps influenced by the pronunciation of "Chulitna." Usually river names have shared names and meanings across the Athabascan language boundaries.

Shem Pete: "«Upriver from **Łinghasdlent** [The Forks at Talkeetna, 8.66] and upriver from where they call it **Tuqashitnu** [Tokositna River, 9.10] there is a stream that flows out from a glacier. I remember that name. **Ts'ilutnu.**»"

Places on the Chulitna River were better known to Shem Pete than are the parallel areas on the Susitna River. Shem said that the Chulitna River is more navigable in a skin boat than is the adjacent portion of the Susitna. He learned these names mainly by traveling here with **Ch'ek'idetnishen**, Talkeetna Nicholie, who was 60 years Shem's senior.

The 1904 Moffit map (Map 44) has the Chulitna River at its northwest limits.

Ascending the Chulitna in 1910, Browne wrote: "One detachment [of Indians] had passed us.... They had drifted past us in boats made of the green skins of moose and caribou. The primitive canoes were loaded to the gunwales with men, women, children, and dogs, and in the bow of each sat an Indian man tapping the river bottom with a slender pole and searching the channel for dangers that might wreck his frail craft" (1956:178).

In 1912 Browne met Talkeetna Nicholie, his two wives, and his son-in-law, Stephan, on the Chulitna. Browne describes bartering with Stephan for moose meat (1956:223–224).

Katherine Nicolie: "My little brother was born in 1922. We go way back up towards McKinley Mountain where **Ts'ilutnu** comes. They come down in skin boat down to Talkeetna. Then from Talkeetna back to Kroto. That's the last time I remember. And they had all kinds of names to the places up there. I wish I could remember all. After they cross **Ts'ilutnu**, they camp there and old man trap and hunt beaver from there. My brother Alec was there. Mom used to put us in sled and haul us around.... They say all the Susitna people used to go up that way for hunting."

9.2 Nil'atesh'it'ut • 'Where Hills Come Together'
adjoining hills on Chulitna River near Denali State Park boundary

§9.33 K'esugi Ken Betnu • 'Base of the Ancient One-Stream'
creek off Curry Ridge, above Blair Lake

9.3 Qichi Qinghiłneqt • 'The Old Lady Made It That Far'
perhaps stream from Blair Lake
Shem Pete: "«**Qichi Qinghiłneqt** is on the right-hand side going up.» Kinda canyon there. Rock cut inside there. «It is like a den there. There is a cave. That is where that old lady got to. She camped there and those things as big as swallows—bats—were flying around. They grab something above and hang down.» She wasn't scared 'cause she all done in. **Qichi Qinghiłneqt**. Old lady. I think that was **Ch'anqet**' [see p. 240]."

9.4 Tuch'etl'ghi'ut • 'Where Brush Extends into the Water'
area on west bank of Chulitna River, fifteen miles up from its mouth, §possibly "Railroad Creek"
Shem Pete: "You can't go through those alders. Just like curly hair. On left-hand side going up. I been up and down that creek a good many times, 1913, 1914, 1915."

Katherine Nicolie: "Another place on **Ts'ilutnu** just alder sticking in the river, all tangled up one. Alder just look like my hair tangled up. They name it **Tuch'etl'ghi'ut.**"

Sources: Shem Pete, Katherine Nicolie, ‡Jake Tansy, and Charlie Hubbard

2003 revisions: names added 9.33–9.39; locations revised 9.4, 9.5, 9.7, 9.26; Dena'ina names changed 9.16, 9.18.
‡2016 revisions: names added 9.40–9.43; name renumbered 9.44; map revised 37.

C. E. Rusk (1910:13) with the 1910 Mazama party bound for the Tokasitna River and Ruth Glacier wrote: "Only one hope remained. That was to return to Talkeetna and make another effort to secure aid from the Indians who had previously refused to go with us. There we again launched the "hog trough," as one member of the party dubbed the boat, and, leaving Rojec and Cool in camp, Ridley and I, feeling somewhat as though we were taking life in hand, started for Talkeetna, which we reached in about an hour's time, Through the intercession of Mr. J. B. Dyer, the Alaska Commercial Company's Agent, Indian Aleck agreed to help us up to the Tokositna, although he had previously expressed the opinion that our boat was "no good." Aleck was the only Indian available at Talkeetna at that time.

"Next morning, with Aleck in command of the boat, we made back to our camp, and the Indian soon demonstrated his skill in the swift water. All we had to do was to pull, either on the oars or on the line, and Aleck would do the rest.

"We loaded the boat to the last pound we thought it would carry, frequently heeding Aleck's caution of 'Maybe too hebby.'

"...At Five Mile Canyon we had before us a difficult bit of water, for the river here was confined in a narrow, deep channel between precipitous walls from one hundred to two hundred feet in height, and in many places perpendicular or even overhanging. We would line up one side as far as possible—then it was pull for the opposite side, and pull hard, too, for there was always a point above which we must land and we just had to make it. Once or twice it was necessary for the man nearest the bow-doubly stirred to action by Aleck's 'Queek, Queek!'—to spring to the straight face of the rock, secure a precarious hold and catch the boat before it could sweep upon the rocks below. Frequently, too, it was necessary for one man to climb up over a perpendicular point and receive the rope as it was passed around to him by the man behind. But we had good luck, and in five hours we were through. There was never an hour, except when we were in camp, that we were not wet to the skin."

9.5 K'echan Yela • 'Grass Mountain'

hill without trees, above ***Tuch'etl'ghi'ut****, possibly hill 1007 feet north of bridge over Parks Highway*

‡The name is notable as the only instance of a stem **yela'** as a landform term in Dena'ina. This is similar to **-yele'** 'ridge' in Koyukon and the Toklat dialect of Lower Tanana.

Katherine Nicolie: "Another ridge way up there. We used to watch it. Mom haul us in sled. One hill with no trees. All grass. Just big hill. Nice. They call it **K'echan Yela**."

9.6 K'esugi Ken • 'Base of the Ancient One'

§Curry Ridge, the southerly lobe of ***K'esugi*** *(revised location)*

Shem Pete: "«There at **K'esugi Ken** we kill fourteen bear» before we quit. 1914 I kill seven, «and Little Bobby's older brother also killed seven.»"

‡In 2015 the new state campground at Parks Highway mile 137 was named K'esugi Ken Campground by Alaska State Parks.

9.7 K'esugi • 'The Ancient One'

K'esugi Ridge, ridge between the Susitna and Chulitna rivers, from Blair Lake to Chulitna Pass, between mile 132 and mile 166 on the Parks Highway

Shem Pete: "«Kroto people used **K'esugi** to **Qughun** [Bald Mountain Ridge, 12.16]. They used that area.» They catch caribou in that mountain. Every summer they stay waiting for caribou. They catch caribou, they make a skin boat, and go down to Kroto.

"«**K'esugi** was Little Bobby's [Stephan] father's mountain. He would go there for caribou. They used it in the fall. When he was young, he went to work [hunting] at that mountain, Little Bobby's little father.

"«We went up **K'esugi**. Up there we came to some caribou. We killed caribou. We packed them down to the people staying at **Quht'anagga K'etnu K'ilant** [Gold Creek, 10.5, in 1914].»"

In October of 2002 the U.S. Board on Geographic Names accepted K'esugi Ridge as the official place name for this ridge. Docket 380 of the USBGN states: "This proposal is to make official the name K'esugi Ridge for a 38 km (24 mi) long ridge in Denali State Park. The proponent... reports that this name is of Dena'ina origin and translates as 'The Ancient One'.... The Dena'ina people used the ridge for hunting. The feature is also named, although without the writing mark, in the 2000 edition of DeLorme's *Alaska Atlas and Gazetteer* (the 1992 edition of the same publication erroneously labeled it 'Keshgi Ridge').

"...A search of the Internet resulted in numerous references to Kesugi Ridge [*sic*], primarily by adventure travel organizers and hiking and outdoors groups. One outdoors recreation website referred to the ridge as K'esugi Ridge. The proponent suggests that the use of the apostrophe in the proposed name 'will promote awareness of the Dena'ina pronunciation with [the] glottalized k'.' The ridge is used today by hikers, and offers spectacular views of Denali/Mount McKinley and surrounding mountain ranges."

9.8 Nelnikda Ey'unt • 'Where There Is a Shabby Steambath'

Troublesome Creek

Shem Pete: "On east side is **Nelnikda Ey'unt**. I saw it [remains of a steambath]. Must be old camp there. They hunt bears up there all time, Susitna and Kroto Indian. Lots of bear."

9.9 Tuqashi Kaq' • 'Mouth of Things That Fall into Water'

mouth of Tokositna River

Shem Pete: "«There is a pass to **Tuqashi Kaq'** by **K'enuqak'itnetant** [7.46, Peters Hills].»"

Rusk (1910:14) with the Mazama party of 1910 wrote: "We arrived opposite the mouth of the Tokositna on the forenoon of the 10th [of June 1910]. Here Aleck seemed

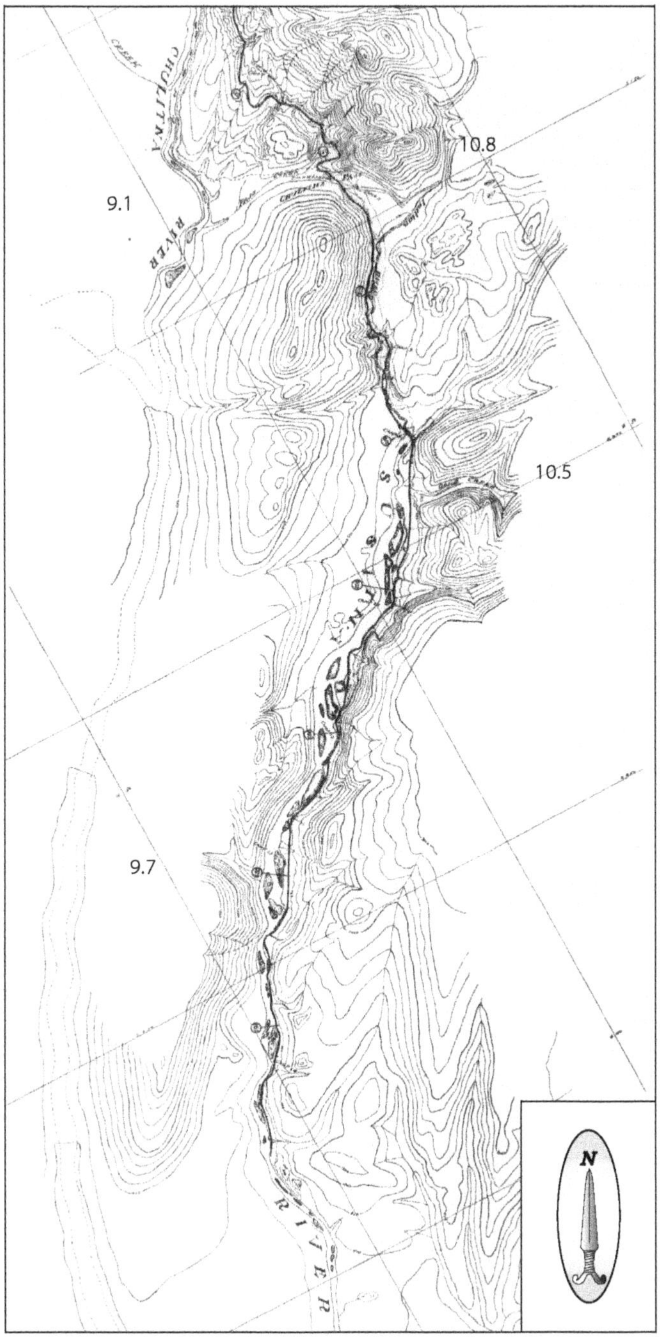

MAP 37

Detail from the 1916 Alaska Engineering Commission map: K'esugi Ridge, ‡with *SPA* feature numbers.

The topography of **K'esugi** (9.7) as well as streams **Ts'ilutnu** (9.1) Chulitna River, **Chuqitnu** (10.8) Indian River, and **Quht'ana Gga K'etnu K'ilani** (10.5) Gold Creek are displayed on this 1916 map for the Alaska Railroad survey by the Alaska Engineering Commission. It is also shown in relief on the 1910a Sleem map (Map 38).

ARCHIVES, ALASKA AND POLAR REGIONS DEPT., RASMUSON LIBRARY, UNIVERSITY OF ALASKA FAIRBANKS

to develop a superstitious fear, and he tried to persuade us to go on up the Chulitna, where, he said, there were many caribou. Finding that he had already taken us quite a distance past the mouth of the Tokositna, we demanded that he immediately cross us to the mouth of that stream. With the Indian still demurring, we ran across a turbulent channel to an island. Aleck declared we could not take our boat up to Tokositna.

"...As it was evident that the Tokositna was a better stretch of water than we had had on the entire trip, here was no apparent cause for Aleck's strange behavior. I returned to my companions, and, after eating lunch, all got into the boat and we swept downstream into the mouth of the Tokositna, Aleck apparently bordering on a state of terror. When we had once started up that stream his fears vanished and he began to whistle and sing and to exhibit all symptoms of a man who had just emerged safely from a terrible danger and felt happy over his deliverance. Doubtless some superstition of his tribe, regarding this place, had gripped him."

9.10 Tuqashitnu • 'Stream of Things That Fall into Water'

Tokositna River

The name Tokositna was first recorded by Brooks in 1902 as "Tokochitna" (Baker 1906:630). In 1906 Belmore Browne said that, according to Susitna Pete, this name translates as 'The River That Comes from the Land Where There Are No Trees' (1956:49). Shem Pete and James Kari note that the name derives from the verb theme 'plural objects fall,' referring to the rocks that continually fall from the steep Tokasha Mountains.

Shem Pete traveled to the Tokositna River in the spring of 1904, from Susitna Station to the Yentna River, up the Kahiltna River and Cache Creek, then over the divide past **K'enuqak'itnetant** [7.46, Peters Hills] to the Tokositna. This trail is shown on the 1906 Herning map, the1910a Sleem map (Maps 32 and 30), and the 1913 Capps map.

9.11 Ch'etl'uch'ghilyasht • 'Where We Hold Things (Boats) in Water'

rapids on Tokositna River, five miles above mouth

Shem Pete: "«We came there [via Peters Hills].» We don't like **Ch'etl'uch'ghilyasht**. We move down below. We spent the winter. In spring we make a skin boat, and we go down to Talkeetna and way down to Kroto. «We spent the spring there. They don't want that waterfall.» I was about eight years old. «I roasted ptarmigan.» I had bow and arrow, no gun yet."

9.12 Tuqashi Tayena • 'Straight Stretch of Things That Fall into Water'

section of Tokositna River

Rusk (1910:15) at their camp on the Tokasitna River near foot of Ruth Glacier in June of 1910:

"With little difficulty, we proceeded about two miles up the Tokositna and pitched our permanent camp on the north bank of the river near the mouth of a small

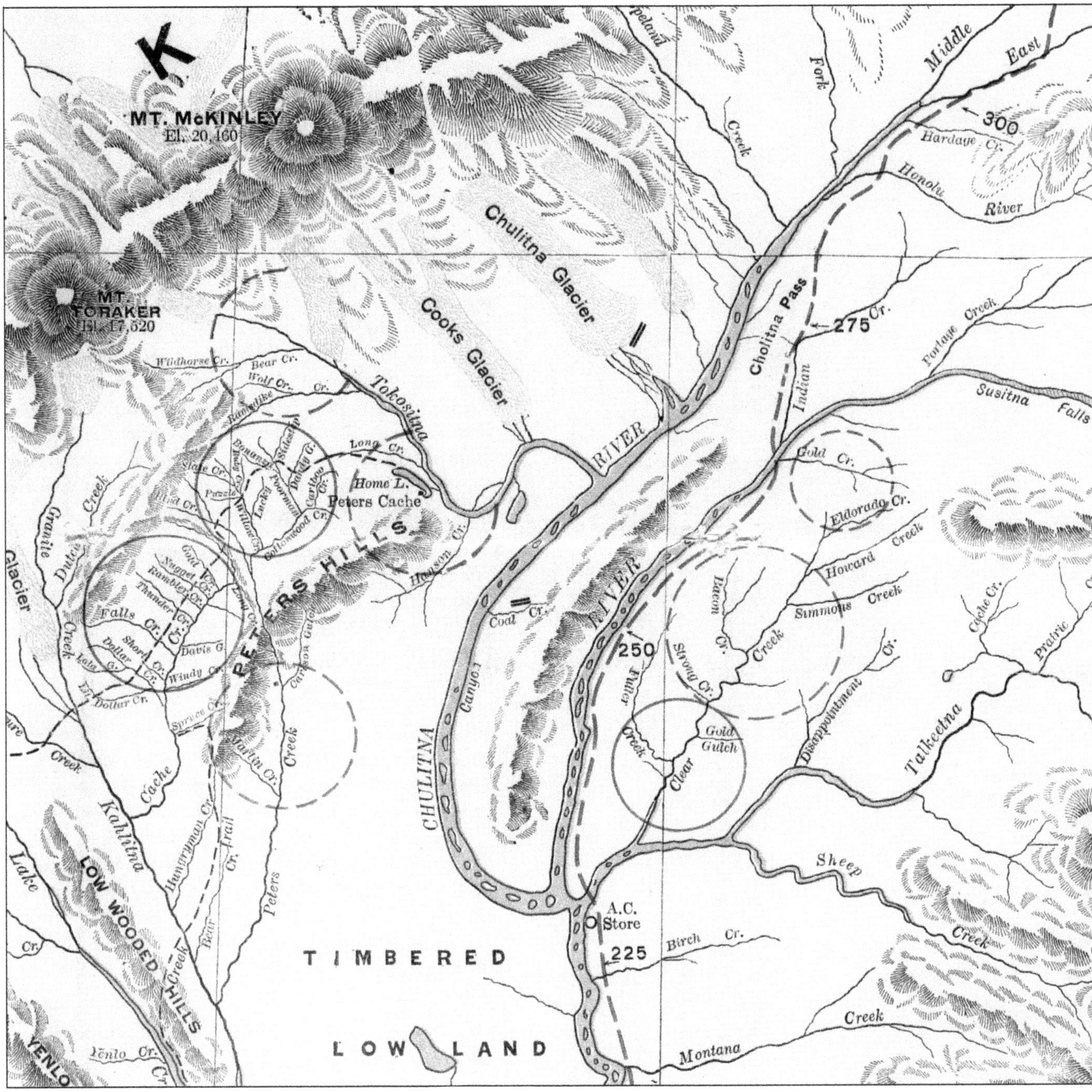

MAP 38

Detail from the 1910a Sleem Map: Peters Hills and Chulitna River.

The 1910a map by D. H. Sleem featured mining districts and trails. This detail shows the Cache Creek and Clear Creek mining districts. Typical of the mining districts was the trend toward establishing English place names. Only the major stream names that had been established ten or twelve years earlier have Native-origin names (Kahiltna, Tokositna, Chulitna). Chunilna Creek (11.4 **Ch'aniltnu**) is here called "Clear Creek," but on Map 39 (Eldridge and Muldrow 1900) this is "Chinalnda Creek." It can be interesting to compare how cultural interests are reflected in the newly coined names for the mining districts on the 1910 Sleem map with the Dena'ina place names. "A. C. Store" is at Talkeetna townsite.

ARCHIVES, ALASKA AND POLAR REGIONS DEPT., RASMUSON LIBRARY, UNIVERSITY OF ALASKA FAIRBANKS

glacial stream. It was an ideal camping spot, with plenty of good wood and water, and we came to think of it as home for over a month.

"Next morning our Indian built a little raft—with about as much surface as a good ironing board-out of spruce logs. He had previously agreed to return to Talkeetna, secure another Indian and come up the river in a canoe, with a lot of additional supplies for us.

"'When will you be back, Aleck?' I asked.

"'I t'ink fibe days," he answered, after which he got aboard his raft and went bobbing, like a cork, around the bend, out of sight.

"We never saw Aleck again.

"Our supplies, both for our base camp and for the mountain work, were very limited, and much depended upon the return of the Indians.

"Given the logistics, it was hardly possible for Aleck or anyone else to resupply the group."

9.13 Ben Ka'a • 'Big Lake'
Bunco Lake

§9.34 Ben Ka'a Betnu • 'Big Lake's Stream'
Bunco Creek

9.14 Tuqashi • 'Things [Rocks] That Fall into Water'
Tokasha Mountains

9.15 Tuqashitnu Łi'a • 'Glacier of Things That Fall into Water River'
Tokositna Glacier
Shem Pete: "«That glacier extends upriver from **Tuqashi.**» That's a big one. Big glacier."

This is the site of a story recorded by Shem Pete about a Dena'ina woman who was captured by the **Łi Dnay** 'Glacier People.'

9.16 §K'enik'ela Łi'a (name revised from first edition) • 'Glacier of the One That Has Broken Off'
Kanikula Glacier
Shem Pete: "Left-hand side a little one [glacier]. **Hni Qula**, no danger. They weren't scared, but dangerous one on the right-hand side [Tokositna Glacier]."

In Kari and Fall (1987:177) we speculated that Kanikula Glacier (formerly Little Tokasitna Glacier), based upon the pronunciation of the anglicized place name and Shem and Billy Pete's suggestion, was **Hni Qula Łi'a**, meaning 'no fear, unafraid glacier,' though Shem Pete did not actually know this name first hand. The name was originally recorded by Belmore Browne from Susitna Pete in 1906 and also has been spelled as Kahnicula or Kanicula (Browne 1956:49, Orth 1971:494). The new information is Bradford Washington's recollection (p.c. to Kari in 2000) that Browne pronounced this name as [kenikela], where the next-to-last syllable has a schwa-type vowel and not [u], as we had assumed in our discussions with Shem and Billy Pete. A likely etymology is with the Dena'ing verb **k'el** 'to break.' Sava Stephan is comfortable with a name **K'enik'ela Łi'a** 'that which breaks off-glacier,' a plausible Dena'ina name for a major glacier.

§9.35 K'enik'ela • 'The One That Has Broken Off'
Avalanche Spire

9.17 Ts'ilu Dghelaya • possibly 'Straight Hand Mountain'
elev. 4270', known as "Alder," west of Chulitna River

9.18 §Dghelay Ka'a Łi'a (revised name) • 'Big Mountain - Glacier'
Ruth Glacier
Kari (1999:73): "I have recently concluded that this is the logical name for Ruth Glacier, i.e., this is how the largest

FIGURE 126

Tuqashi, (9.14, the Tokasha Mountains), viewed here from Pirate Lake in 1999.

PHOTO BY JAMES KARI

FIGURE 127

In the distance is **K'enik'ela** (9.35) Avalanche Spire and **K'enik'ela Łi'a** (9.16, Kenikula Glacier) (formerly called Little Tokashitna River and Glacier). Photo taken in 1917, by Stephen R. Capps, Jr.

STEPHEN R. CAPPS, JR. COLLECTION (#83-149-1168), ARCHIVES, ALASKA AND POLAR REGIONS DEPT., RASMUSON LIBRARY, UNIVERSITY OF ALASKA FAIRBANKS

FIGURE 128

Ts'ilu Dghelaya (9.17, the unnamed mountain at the lower end of Ruth Gorge and west of the Chulitna River), viewed from Pirate Lake in 1999. At the right edge of the frame is **Betnu Detniyitnu** (9.20, Coffee Creek).

PHOTO BY JAMES KARI

FIGURE 129

Łi Tayena (9.25, upper Eldridge Glacier) above Fountain River. We have concluded that Mount Deception (dominant peak on the left) is **Łi Tayena Dghelaya** (9.36).

PHOTO BY PETER G. SANCHEZ, COURTESY OF NATIONAL PARK SERVICE

FIGURE 130

Looking north into **Betnu Detniyitnu** (9.20, upper Coffee Creek Valley) toward Coffee Glacier and the mountains Broken Tooth and **[‡Dnigi Ghi]** (9.40 Moose's Tooth) on upper left side of the frame. The mountain on the left foreground between Spink Lake and Coffee River may be **Detniyi** (9.21).

PHOTO BY MARK STASIK

glacier of an associated mountain would be named following the rules of the Dena'ina place name system."

Shem Pete: "«There is a big glacier that goes across there. They took one day to go across it. When they pass by a glacier they bundled up grass. They tied it [grass] into packs to prevent the ones following behind from falling into the glacier. It is a long way across that canyon, and when someone ran out of grass, another one packing it would take over. They would drop it across the glacier [to walk on].»"

9.19 **Ts'ilu Tayena** • 'Straight Hand Straight Stretch'
open place on the Chulitna River, above the Tokositna River
Shem Pete: "That's above **Tuqashitnu**. «Straight across from the end of **Ts'ilu Dghelaya** is **Ts'ilu Tayena**.» Big open place. You can see for miles."

9.20 **Betnu Detniyitnu** • 'Creek That Roars'
Coffee River
Shem Pete: "«Further upriver is the mouth of a stream. That creek they call **Betnu Detniyitnu**. That's another name that I remember.»"

Shem Pete recalled the prospector John Coffee for whom this stream was named in English. John Coffee appears on the 1920 census for Susitna Station. Shem also remembers another white man from this area named **Hudlach** who "talked native" and was thought by the Dena'ina to be a medicine man. Browne met Coffee and his partners, the Wells brothers, in 1912, and stated that they "knew more about the Chulitna country than any other men" (Browne 1956:216).

9.21 **Detniyi** • 'The One That Roars'
mountain, possibly between Coffee River and Spink Lake

‡9.40 **[Dnigi Ghi]** • 'Moose's Tooth'
The Mooses Tooth
We had overlooked this from Orth (1971:657): "A translation of the original Athabaskan Indian name obtained in 1953 by USGS." Kari once suggested **Dnigi Ghi** to Shem, but he did not know the name, nor was he able to distinguish this mountain in the profile of the Alaska Range. See Plate 12 and Figs. 24 and 130.

9.22 **Quntughet'ut** • 'Where Water Comes up from Below'
Byers Creek

9.23 **Quntughet'ut Bena** • 'Lake of Where Water Comes up from Below'
Byers Lake
Shem Pete: "«We came to **Quntughet'ut** on the way up **K'esugi** [9.7].» You see that lake has deep water."

9.24 **Dghelay Beq'e Nuhdagheltunt** • 'Mountain upon Which Canyon Crosses'
pass across K'esugi toward Gold Creek

9.25 **Łi Tayena** • 'Glacier Straight Stretch'
Eldridge Glacier and Fountain River
The following anecdote Shem Pete associated with one of the glaciers west of the Chulitna River.

FIGURE 131

Quntughet'ut (9.24, Byers Lake) with **K'esugi** 'The Ancient One' (9.7, K'esugi Ridge) extending to the south.
PHOTO BY JAMES KARI

FIGURE 132

Qununahdghashjuy Betnu (9.28, Hurricane Creek) at its confluence with **Ts'ilutnu** (9.1, the Chulitna River).
PHOTO BY MARK STASIK

FIGURE 133
Denyih T'u (9.32, Broad Pass), looking west into the West Fork of the Chulitna River near the boundary of Denali National Park, circa 1983. The West Fork has no recorded Native place name.
PHOTO BY LORRAINE BASNAR ELDER

Shem Pete: "«A man named **Batninch'ey** ['Wind Blows against Him,' Alexandra Allowan's father's brother] fell into a glacier. He had a stone axe in his shirt. He chopped out steps, and he climbed back out. That **Batninch'ey** came back out from the glacier's mouth [crevasse].»"

§9.36 **Łi Tayena Dghelaya** • 'Glacier Straight Stretch Mountain'
Mount Deception

9.26 **Łch'ibay Ka'a** • 'Big Whirlwind'
§possibly mountain 4680 feet up Coal Creek (revised location)
Shem Pete said that this mountain, the northernmost one of the central Alaska Range whose name he knows, is "like a razor." We called this Moose's Tooth in the first edition. However, we now think that mountain names that Shem knew are closer to the course of the Chulitna.

§9.37 **Łch'ibay Ka'a Betnu** • 'Big Whirlwind Stream'
§possibly Coal Creek

9.27 **Ałtnu** • 'Deadfall Trap Creek'
Pass Creek
The pass here leads to Indian River. See 10.9.

9.28 **Qununahch'dghashjuy Betnu** • 'Creek of the One That We Go Up to Watch (for Game)'
Hurricane Gulch

9.29 **Qununahch'dghashjuy** • 'That Which We Go Up to Watch (for Game)'
mountain, elev. 4665', north of Chulitna Pass
Shem Pete: "«Going up there they can see upriver.» Lookout [a game lookout], that's how they use it. «That is the Mountain People's country.»"

9.30 **Benench'iltledi Betnu** • 'Creek of Land That We Slide Down'
Honolulu Creek

9.31 **Benench'iltledi** • 'Land That We Slide Down'
mountain north of Honolulu Creek
Shem Pete: "«We skid down dragging a spear. We jump down the mountain.»"

§(9.38) **Lushelatnu** • '-?- Stream'
stream into Chulitna from east, possibly East Fork of the Chulitna
Only mentioned once by Shem Pete to Kari and Dave Johnston, in August of 1977 while driving north on the Parks Highway. Not recognized by Jake Tansy.

§(9.39) **Hulatnu** • '-?- Stream'
stream into upper Chulitna from east, possibly upper fork of Middle Fork of the Chiulita
Also only mentioned once by Shem Pete to Kari and Dave Johnston. Not recognized by Jake Tansy.

Shem Pete: "«Where that **K'esugi** ridge extends upriver, the [upper Chulitna] river flows through a straight stretch. Upriver from there the water flows among the **Gheltsana** [Tanana River Athabascans].... Wherever that **Ts'ilutnu** flows from, the **Gheltsana** had a trail. They had a trail through **Denyiht'u** where the train goes in that low country.» You go to Cantwell. Then you get to that [Nenana] river."

9.32 **Denyiht'u** • 'Enclosed Canyon'
Broad Pass area
Learnard (1900:664–5) in 1898 summarized travel between the Tanana Valley and Cook Inlet: "During the winter the Tanana Indians travel to the Susitna store to trade, and are said to make the trip in thirteen days, using

PLATE 1

(Above) Peter Kalifornsky, Katherine Nicolie, and Shem Pete in 1983.

PHOTO BY PRISCILLA RUSSELL

PLATE 2

(Below) Billy Pete tests the terrain on a Cook Inlet mudflat near **Susni Kaq'**, (2.3, mouth of the Susitna River) in June of 1977. Katherine Nicolie is standing in the distance.

PHOTO BY PRISCILLA RUSSELL

PLATE 3

(Above) **Łich'antnu Łi'a** (1.77), Capps Glacier, with the higher Tordrillo Mountains. **T'etniya** (1.78) Mt. Torbert is at the left side of the picture. The nunatak on the right **Łik'a Kin'i** (1.116, Dogshead) is a translation of the Dena'ina name 'dog's head.'

PHOTO BY FRED HIRSCHMANN, AK-7001

PLATE 4

(Opposite) Spectacular aerial view looking northwest up Coal Creek above Beluga Lake to **Tubughna Katidiłtuni** 'the Tyonek people's upriver trail' (6.17, Hayes River Pass). Visible west of the pass in the distance are Trimble Glacier and **Denyih T'u** (6.16, Spring Creek). See also the discussion of this pass at 6.17.

Shem Pete: "«Across from **Kech'itnu** [Happy River, 6.22] the stream with the name **Tubughna Katidiłtuni** flows into the Skwentna. The Tyonek people used to walk up that stream.»"

PHOTO BY FRED HIRSCHMANN, 2-8547

PLATE 5

An important lake district for the Sustina Dena'ina is shown here in this aerial photo taken just west of the town of Willow and east of **Tanłtun Bena** (3.19, Red Shirt Lake). In the foreground is **Nich'ghilen Bena** (3.24, Lynx Lake). **Unqeghnit Skitnu Bena** (12.24, Butterfly Lake—shaped like a butterfly) in the upper left. To its west is **Delindin Bena** (12.7, Delyndia Lake), which was named for Shem Pete by his Russian name. The southernmost end of **Tanłtun Bena** (3.19, Red Shirt Lake) and the village site **Tanłtunt** (3.18) is at the right edge of the picture in a line straight below **Dghelishla** (4.9, Mt. Susitna). Below Red Shirt Lake is the outline of **Tl'eghesh Bena** (3.16, Cow Lake), which has many ancient Dena'ina house sites. Fig. 61 is an index of this photo. This photo is also on the front cover.

PHOTO BY FRED HIRSCHMANN, AK-6838

PLATE 6

Aerial view of **Hnidi Bena** (6.19, Finger Lake) looking south with **Sheshjesh** (6.13, Porcupine Butte) in the distance shown beneath the taller Dickason Mountain. Finger Lake is north of the Skwentna River and near the Iditarod Trail. **Kiq'eh Dghlaya Bena** (6.20, Red Lake) and **Kiq'eh Dghelaya** (6.23, McDoel Mountain and ridge) are just to the west of **Hnidi Bena**.

PHOTO BY FRED HIRSCHMANN, AK-13081

PLATE 7

K'ichatnu Tl'u (7.26, the upper Kichatna River) looking SW toward the Kichatna Spires or Cathedral Spires. In the distance is Cul de Sac Glacier in the direction of **Tetno' Hwchwx Dotis** (6.59, Shellabarger Pass).

PHOTO BY MARK STASIK

PLATE 8

(Opposite, top) Mt. Russell (7.59) is **Ch'ighu' Tsats'ela'**, 'the fang' in the Upper Kuskokwim language, viewed near the base of the mountain from the Swift Fork by a bend of Chedotlothna Glacier.

PHOTO BY MARK STASIK, 1996

PLATE 9

(Opposite, bottom) Aerial view looking to the south above **Suyitnu** (2.1, the Sustina River), several miles above the mouth of Kroto Creek. The drainage of **Dashq'e Betnu** or **Tuqentnu** (8.10, Kroto Creek) is just above the more conspicuous **Beq'e Tach'itqeyi Q'eghtsi** (8.4, Kroto Slough). The site of **Dashq'e** (8.12, Kroto Village) is on the south bank. The lake to the west of the slough is Whitsol Lake. In the distance is **Dghelishla** (4.9, Mt. Susitna). On the east bank at the junction of the two large branches is **Niqagheleɫt** (8.35).

PHOTO BY FRED HIRSCHMANN, AK-6833

PLATE 10

(Above right) A beaver dam on upper **Untuhtay'untnu** (8.33, Moose Creek) off the Petersville Road.

PHOTO BY FRED HIRSCHMANN, 2509B

PLATE 11

(Right) **Dghelay Ka'a** (7.51, Denali) viewed from **K'esugi** (9.7, K'esugi Ridge) looking up Hidden River.

PHOTO BY DAVE JOHNSTON, 1983

‡PLATE 12

(Above) View of the west ridge of the Mooses Tooth (9.40, **Dnigi Ghi**) near the summit of the peak around 10,300 ft. The southeast face and summit of Denali looms above in the center of the photo, approximately 16 miles away as the crow flies.

PHOTO BY CHRIS CANNON, MAY 2, 2009

PLATE 13

(Below) The tall mountains of the Central Alaska Range **Be'u** (7.49, Mount Foraker), **Begguya** (7.50, Mount Hunter), and **Dghelay Ka'a** (7.51, Denali). Viewed from a ridge south of the upper **Tuqashitnu** (9.10, Tokasitna River). The valley in the left foreground is from **K'enik'ela Łi'a** (9.16, Kenikula Glacier and its stream).

PHOTO BY FRED HIRSCHMANN, AK-1968B

PLATE 14

The valley above Archangel Creek on **Tsałtastnu Tl'u** (12.21, the upper Little Sustina River) looking to the west toward peaks north of Hatcher Pass.

PHOTO BY FRED HIRSCHMANN, 1536A

PLATE 15

(Opposite) The spectacular mountains and passes above the Chickaloon area are shown in an aerial view taken from about ten miles up **Nay'dini'aa Na'** (14.31, Chickaloon River). The mountain in the foreground is **Ts'es Nay'detkayi** (14.92, Puddingstone Hill). Beyond this is the valley of **Łtaege' Na'** (14.32, Boulder Creek) and the northern side of **Tsaghedzigi** (14.43, Anthracite Ridge). In the distance is **Ch'atanhtnu Łi'a** (14.57, Matanuska Glacier).

PHOTO BY FRED HIRSCHMANN, AK-7968

PLATE 16

(Right, above) At the very head of **Ch'atanhtnu** (14.1, the Matanuska River) is **Hwyiis Tes Bene'** ('mirage hill lake,' 14.117, Knob Lake). Looking to the southwest over the valley of **Dzeł Ghaan' Na'** (14.69, the South Fork of the Matanuska River). The mountain on the far side of the South Fork is **Dzeł Ghaan'**, 'Half A Mountain' (14.70). Also see the discussion of 14.70, **Dzel Ghaan'** on p. 309.

PHOTO BY FRED HIRSCHMANN, AK-40179A

PLATE 17

(Right, below) Looking southwest down Knik Arm in winter from just below **Chuqilin Kaq'** (13.56, the mouth of Wasilla Creek). Silhouetted on the horizon are **Dghelishla** (4.9, Mount Susitna) and beyond this the outline of **K'idazq'eni** (1.17, Mt. Spurr). Mt. Spurr is about 120 miles from where this picture was taken.

PHOTO BY FRED HIRSCHMANN, AK-2655A

PLATE 18

The north shore of Knik Arm from Cottonwood Creek to Fish Creek must have had a very high aboriginal population. Looking south from the low ridge above Reedy Lake, just east of **Nik'udatl'ech'a** (13.43). On the opposite side of Knik Arm is a clear view showing the **Idluytnu** (15.24, Eklutna River valley). Features in the distance, left to right, are: **Bentułik'alashi** (15.28, the ridge tapering from the left edge of the frame); the small peak with the sun shining just on its tip **Kuy'inshla** (15.27); **Chishkatnu** (15.25, Thunderbird Creek valley); and, at the ridge edge of the frame, **Snutnadzeni** (15.52, Mt. Eklutna). Fig. 175 is an index for this photo. Also cf. Fig. 204, which shows some of the same features.

PHOTO BY RANDI HIRSCHMANN, AK-R1074B

PLATE 19

Idlishla (15.22, the north Knob at Eklutna) illuminated by the light of sunset, looking up Knik Arm at high tide.

PHOTO BY FRED HIRSCHMANN, AK-40050

PLATE 20

Cottonwood Lake (13.40) in Wasilla may be called **Baqutsaghi'i Bena** 'Lake in Which a Rock Sticks Up'. It is in the site complex know as **Benteh** 'among the lakes'. The view here with autumn colors has **Dnal'iy** (15.7, Pioneer Peak) in the distance.

PHOTO BY FRED HIRSCHMANN, AK-2020A

PLATE 21

Qunsghitnu (13.44, Rabbit Slough) in the foreground is near the village site of **Niteh** (14.4). Across the valley is a view of the mountains including **Dnal'iy** (15.7, Pioneer Peak), the canyon of **Łdagheltnu** (15.6 Goat Creek), and 15.34 **Łach Q'a** (15.34, Twin Peaks).

PHOTO BY RANDI HIRSCHMANN, FHR10844C

PLATE 22

A winter view to the north across **Nuti** (13.1, Knik Arm) from Anchorage toward **K'enakanen** (13.1, the west Knik Arm area). In the distance the high mountains of the Alaska Range (7.61, **Dghelay Teh)** are partially obscured by the curvature of the earth, being about 140 miles away.

PHOTO BY MARK STASIK

PLATE 23

This view of **Skitnu** (15.2, the Knik River Valley) was taken from the summit of **Dnal'iy** (15.7, Pioneer Peak). At the center of the frame are **Skitnu Łi'a**, (15.5, Knik Glacier) and **Skitnu Dghelaya** (15.16, Mt. Goode). Fig. 20 has a more detailed caption.

PHOTO BY LORRAINE BASNAR ELDER, 1982

PLATE 24

(Above) An aerial viewing approaching downtown Anchorage from the south with the moon rising over the profile of the Chugach Mountains. The radio tower is near **Chansh Kaq'** (15.83, the mouth of Chester Creek). The second mountain to the left of the moon is **Qin Cheghi,** 'Crying Ridge' (15.98, Tanaina Peak). Refer to Chapter 15 for more information on these places.

PHOTO BY FRED HIRSCHMANN, 341A-F

PLATE 25

(Below) Winter view, looking north from **Nen Ghiłgedi** (15.90, the beach at Earthquake Park), just north of **Nuch'ishtunt** (15.91, Pt. Wornzoff). In the right foreground is **Chansh Kaq'** (15.83, mouth of Chester Creek), the downtown Anchorage skyline, and the Chugach Mountains. The mountain valley in the center of the picture is **Dgheyay Tl'u** (15.80, upper Ship Creek and Arctic Valley).

PHOTO BY FRED HIRSCHMANN, AK-7203

PLATE 26

(Above) A winter view from above Chickaloon Bay and **Tutsahtnu Kaq'** (16.28, the mouth of Chickaloon River) looking across Turnagain Arm. In the distance at the east edge of Anchorage Bowl is **Q'isqa Dghelaya** (15.103, McHugh Peak) and the drainage of **Ggeh Betnu** (15.100, Rabbit Creek).

PHOTO BY FRED HIRSCHMANN, AK-7470

PLATE 27

(Below) A view to the south across **Tutl'uh** (16.1, Turnagain Arm) toward **Tutsilitnu** (16.9, Resurrection Creek) and the Hope townsite.

PHOTO BY FRED HIRSCHMANN, 29-1531B

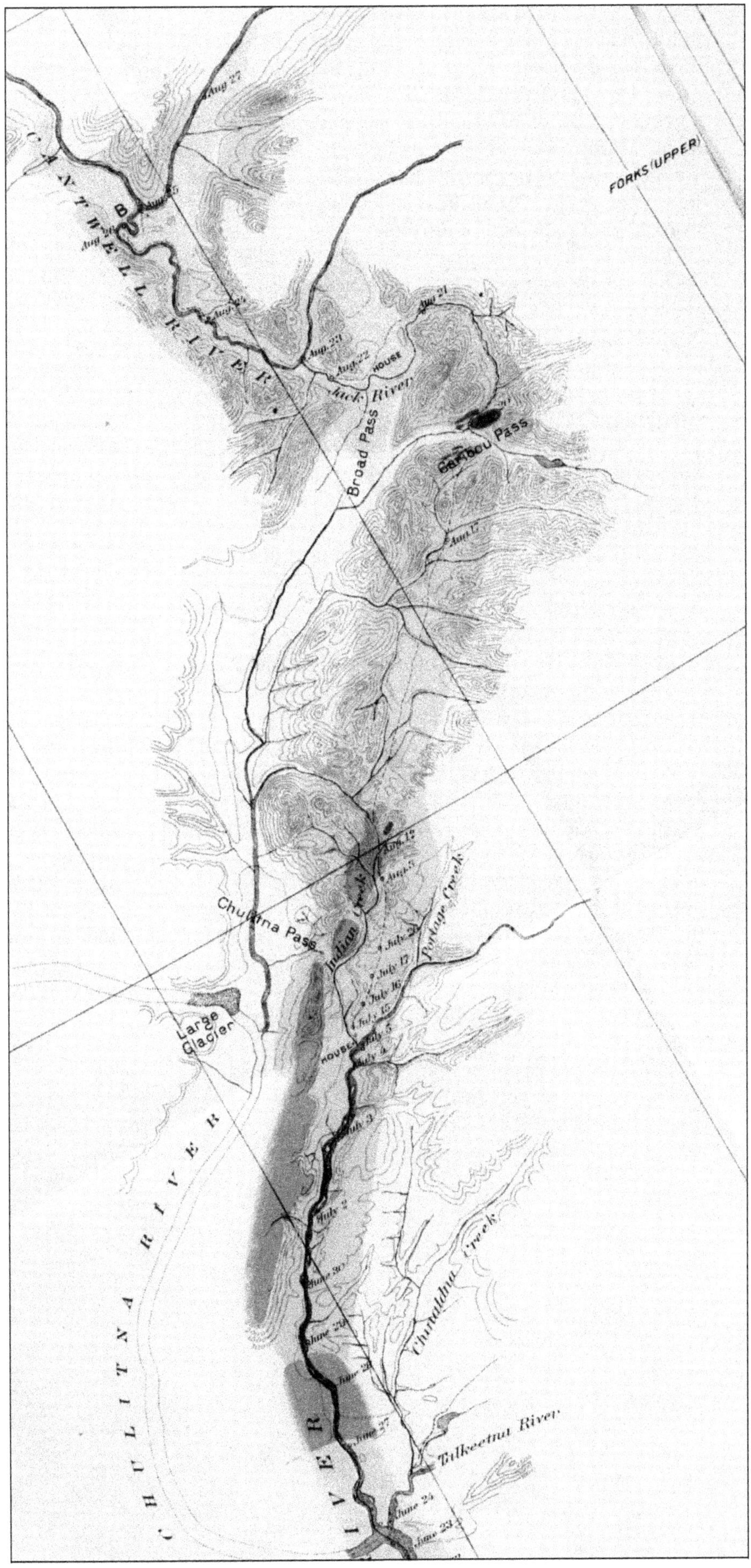

MAP 39

Detail from the Eldridge and Muldrow map of 1898: Talkeetna to Broad Pass.

The Eldridge-Muldrow party reached the Jack River and Cantwell [or Nenana] River in August of 1898 and marked a house here. Eldridge (1900:27) wrote, "On both the Sushitna and Cantwell (Nenana) rivers, however, in the heart of the mountains, cabins were seen—the homes of the Indian hunters in winter. On the Cantwell River these were particularly numerous and were said to be occupied by the Tananas—reputed great hunters—who came up from their valley when travel over the snow and frozen streams is rendered easy." The Eldridge-Muldrow survey of 1898 is the first source on the names Chulitna River and Chinaldna [Chunilna] Creek (11.4 **Ch'aniltnu**).

ARCHIVES, ALASKA AND POLAR REGIONS DEPT., RASMUSON LIBRARY, UNIVERSITY OF ALASKA FAIRBANKS

dog team, by which means they often travel from 35 to 40 miles a day, according to reports. The route followed by them is up the Susitna on the ice to the Forks, and then up the Chulitna across the divide to the tributary of the Tanana that Sergeant Yanert has mapped. This would seem to afford a very feasible route to the Tanana and Yukon in winter time, providing one is on the Sushitna River or at Tyoonok, as he can readily reach the Sushitna from the latter any time of the year."

The following statement by Van Schoonhoven in 1899 (1900:736) is the northernmost attribution of early Dena'ina land use: "The Jack River country is a good one for game and the Sushitna Indians make this their hunting ground for caribou and sheep."

Brooks, writing in 1899, made the following remarks about travel to Cook Inlet by the Tanana Indians: "They also have more or less intercourse with the Indians of the Sushitna, the traveling between the two basins being done chiefly in winter. In former years the visits to Cook Inlet must have been infrequent, for Ivan Petroff makes special note of the arrival of two Tanana Indians on Cook Inlet in 1865. Petroff states that the oldest man of the coast Indians remembered only two previous visits by the interior Indians to the Inlet" (Brooks 1900:491).

In 1899 Yanert (1900:678) wrote about Broad Pass: "A well-worn foot path leads over the divide, which the guide assured me was made and used by Indians going to and from the Tanana. He also pointed out the frames of two Indian houses north of the divide, stating that these were used by the Tanana Indians during hunting season."

This statement by the geologist Moffit, who had extensive experience in this area from about 1910 to 1915, adds independent corroboration of the territory as defined by Shem Pete through the place names inventory: "Formerly the lower Susitna natives also hunted in the Broad Pass region, coming into it by way of the Chulitna River or the valley leading northeast from Indian Creek. Broad Pass itself seems to be the northern limit of their territory" (Moffit 1915:20).

The lack of Ahtna place names in the Summit-Broad Pass area contrasts with the detailed Ahtna name system immediately east and north of Cantwell. Cantwell people do not use Dena'ina names such as **Denyih Ht'u** (9.32, Broad Pass). On the other hand, the Cantwell people have used the middle Nenana River much more than the Summit- Broad Pass area. Cantwell Ahtna elders Jake Tansy and the late Henry Peters know the upper Nenana River area in fine detail (Kari 1983, 1999).

‡**9.41 Dghelaay Nhwtnestc'oxi Na'** *(Ahtna)* • 'Pointed Mountains Stream'
Bull River
A name reported by Charlie Hubbard of Cantwell/Sterling in 2014, one of the few upper Chulitna River tributaries with an Ahtna name. Charlie hunted here with Jake Tansy.

‡**9.42 Dghelaay Nhwtnestc'oxi** *(Ahtna)* • 'Pointed Mountains'
mountains at head of Bull River
Charlie Hubbard noted in 2015: "That must have been an ancient pass to the Kantishna River area. You just go to the right of that pyramid mountain."

‡**9.43 Tsaani Na'** *(Ahtna)* • 'Brown Bear Creek'
Tsaani Creek into Middle Fork of Chulitna River
This name was suggested by the Cantwell Village Council in 2009 to replace the name Squaw Creek.

‡**(9.44) Denyishla** • 'Little Canyon'
location uncertain, canyon in Broad Pass area
The name is implied from a personal name, **Denyishla Iden**, the chief of the Mountain People, who originally was from Kroto village. According to Shem Pete, this man used to hunt in **Denyiht'u**, Broad Pass, every year, and died there on the trail in about 1905 in the winter. McKinney 1985: "Shem Pete remembered the story of **Denyishla Iden**, 'the person of little canyon.' **Denyishla Iden** died around the turn of the century. Because trees did not grow tall in his canyon, [when he died] his body couldn't be placed up high above the ground and was eaten by dogs."

FIGURE 134

This 1915 photo scores the railroad corridor along the Chulitna River, as it goes north through **Denyih T'u** (9.32, Broad Pass). From the Alaska Engineering Commission Report of 1916, Plate 27.

‡Names for Denali in Alaska Native Languages and the Denali Name Change of 2015

by James Kari

Five Athabascan (or Dene) language areas have had some territory in the stream drainages that surround Denali National Park and Preserve: Ahtna to the east, Dena'ina) to the south, Upper Kuskokwim to the west, Koyukon to the north, and Lower Tanana to the northeast. Athabascan travel and place naming are purposeful, and there is an extensive network of Athabascan place names surrounding the Central Alaska Range in the traditional land use areas for streams, lakes, and accessible mountains and ridges.

The name "Denali" is based upon the Koyukon place name as used by the people north of the mountain. Table 14 shows the two different names for the tallest mountains of the Central Alaska Range, one in the languages to the north and west of the range, and one in the languages to the south. These names can apply to the peak Denali/Mount McKinley, but more generally they apply to all of the high peaks of the Central Alaska Range. The names in Table 14 are spelled in the local practical alphabets, in a standardized alphabet, and in the International Phonetic Alphabet (or IPA). The five names closest to Denali are also summarized on Map 41. There are no clearly aboriginal names for Denali recorded in other Alaska Native languages.

The entire Alaska Range is commonly referred to as **Deghi:lo:yi** (see 7.62) 'the objects that are in a line' or 'the plural objects that are suspended.' Athabascan people have a quiet reverence for Denali. They tend to avoid talking about the mountain much like they avoid mentioning the names of their ancestors. Place names for major streams and landmarks or for various sacred hills and ridges near the old village sites are mentioned much more frequently than are the names for Denali.

In 1903 James Wickersham heard a Koyukon legend from the blind chief Koonah on the middle Kantishna River. The chapter in Wickersham (1938:238–254) has the story of the giant Yacko (**Yokuh** or 'Big Sky') that begins: "Long before Denali, the high one, was raised to the sky, Yako dwelt in the land where the Tena live." There are other recordings of 'Big Sky' stories by Athabascan experts such as Hester Evan, Peter John, and Katie John. The narrative told in 1903 by Koonah seems to be the only

TABLE 14A. ATHABASCAN NAMES FOR DENALI/MT. MCKINLEY

North of the Alaska Range: literally 'the tall one'

Native language	spelled in local practical alphabets	spelled in a standardized alphabet	spelled in the IPA
Koyukon	Deenaalee	Diinaalii	/di'næli/
Lower Tanana	‡Dinadhi, Dinadhedi	Diinaadhi, Diinaadhedi	/di'næði/
Middle Tanana	Diineezi	Diinaadhi	/di'næði/
Upper Kuskokwim	Denaze	Diinaazii	/di'næzi/
Ingalik (Deg Hit'an)	Dengadh, Dengadhi	Dengadh, Dengadhe	/dɛ'ŋað, dɛ'ŋaðɛ/
Holikachuk	Denadhe	Diinaadhii	/di'næði/

South of the Alaska Range: literally 'mountain-big'

Native language	spelled in local practical alphabets	spelled in a standardized alphabet	spelled in the IPA
Ahtna	Dghelaay Ce'e, Deghilaay Ce'e	Dgheloy Ke'e, Deghiloy Ke'e	/dɣɛ'lɔy 'kɛʔɛ/
Dena'ina (Upper Inlet)	Dghelay Ka'a	Dghelay Ka'a	/dɣə'lay 'kaʔa/
Dena'ina (Lower Inlet)	Dghili Ka'a	Dghili Ka'a	/'dɣili 'kaʔa/

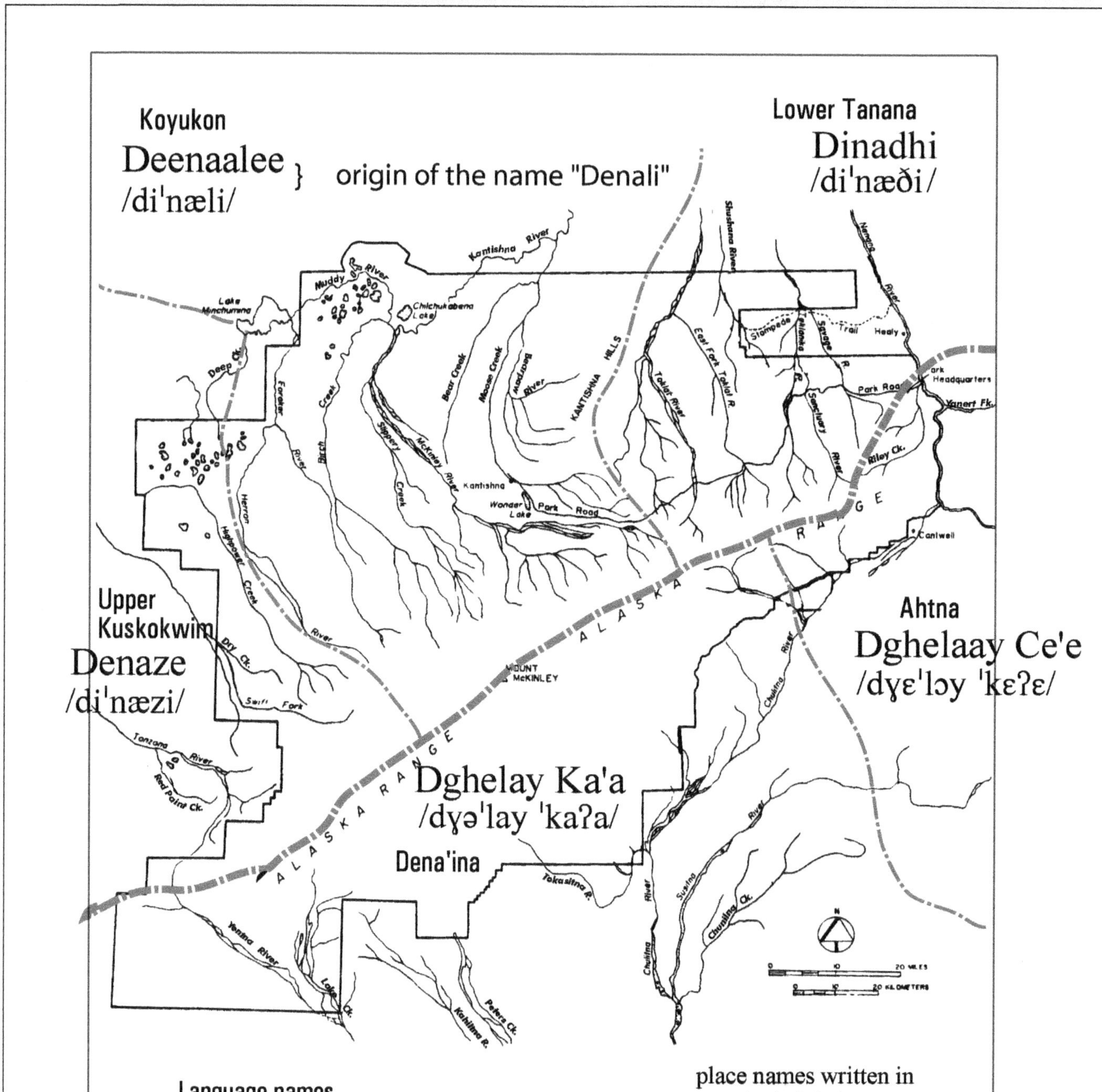

MAP 40

Athabascan names for Denali.

MAP BY JAMES KARI

TABLE 14B. ANALYSIS OF KOYUKON *DEENAALEE*

The Koyukon name **deenaalee** is a nominalized verb derived from the commonly used verb theme **Ø + naał** 'to be long, tall.' The word is composed of four morphemes:

d	+	ee	+	naał	+	ee
gender prefix		neuter prefix		verb stem 'tall, long'		nominalizing suffix 'the one that'

one that is centered on the origin of Denali. Shem Pete did not have a story about Denali.

The name "Denali" does not literally mean 'The Great One,' as is commonly stated, but is instead based upon the verb theme (see Table 14B) that means 'high' or 'tall.' Alaskan scholars Jules Jetté and James Wickersham correctly translated Denali as 'the high one' (Jetté and Jones 2000:432, Wickersham 1938:243). William Dickey's statement, "The Indians of Cook Inlet have always called this the Bulshaia (great) mountain" (1897:325), is not factually correct. Dickey recorded the Russian word for 'big' from some Dena'ina men, but I have never heard that term applied to Denali by Shem Pete or other Dena'ina speakers.

The first documented sighting of the mountain was on March 7, 1834 when Alaska Native Andrei Glazunov saw a high mountain from the mouth of the Stony River in the middle Kuskokwim River area. He recorded the name as "Tenada" (VanStone 1959). This is clearly a Deg Hit'an (Ingalik) name, probably from the McGrath area, **Dengadh**. Glazunov was a Russian creole and a speaker of the Kodiak Alutiiq language. He was literate in Russian, and he was formally documenting previously unexplored areas of the Kuskokwim and Yukon rivers at the direction of Admiral Ferdinand von Wrangell. Tenada and other westerly names from Glazunov's journal appear on the 1839 Wrangell map, considered the best map of its time of west and southcentral Alaska (Wrangell 1980 [1839]; see Map 17, p. 86).

William Dickey assumed that his sketch map of the Susitna River (Dickey 1897a; see Map 43) was the first to record a name for the tallest mountain of the Central Alaska Range. Alfred H. Brooks, to enhance the case for the name "Mount McKinley," claimed that there was no Russian map with names on the tallest mountains of the Alaska Range (Brooks 1911:24, 1953:230). However, "Tenada" on the Wrangell map of 1839 was the first time one of the Athabascan versions of "Denali" appeared on a prominent map (Kari 1986b).

The choice for a name for the tallest mountain has long been controversial. Since the early 1900s most Alaskans, Native and non-Native, have adopted the name Denali. Hudson Stuck (1914:vii-xi) made a passionate case for "Denali" in his account of the first ascent of the mountain.

Donald Orth, former secretary of the U.S. Board of Geographic Names (USBGN), summarized the Denali-McKinley name change controversy (Orth 1980, 1985). There has been vocal civic support in Alaska for the name change for over forty years. In 1975 the Alaska Legislature officially adopted the name Denali for the mountain and recommended that name to the USBGN. However, the Board could not issue a ruling because annually from 1977 to 2015 a bill had been introduced in Congress by members of the Ohio congressional delegation to retain the name Mount McKinley (Ohio being President McKinley's home state).

Since 2012 a Wikipedia entry, "The Denali/Mount McKinley Naming Dispute," has been a source for historical information and news items. In the summer of 2015 the Denali-McKinley name change issue was getting renewed attention. On August 28, 2015 Secretary of the Interior Sally Jewell issued a secretarial order with the approval of President Barack Obama to change the official name from Mount McKinley to Denali. The Department of Interior press release of September 1 noted that the repeated introduction of legislation by the Ohio delegation (1977–2015) had the effect of indefinitely deferring any further consideration of the McKinley-Denali controversy by the USBGN. "The 38-year impasse between the BGN and Congress was unique in BGN history, a situation that was never anticipated when the policy was adopted," said Doug Caldwell, the Chair of the U.S. Board on Geographic Names.

The restoration of Denali as the official place name has been applauded by a broad spectrum of Alaskans. In the days following Denali name change, Alaska's governor and congressional delegation, tribal leaders and many other Alaskans stated that the name change is a sign of recognition and respect for Athabascan and other Alaska Native languages and traditions.

Denali is Alaska's most visible mountain and most prominent place name. The Denali name change will enhance people's awareness of the concept of indigenous geographic knowledge. It introduces to the public basic concepts such as official place names, Native-origin place names (Denali), and authentic Native language names (such as Koyukon **Deenaalee**).

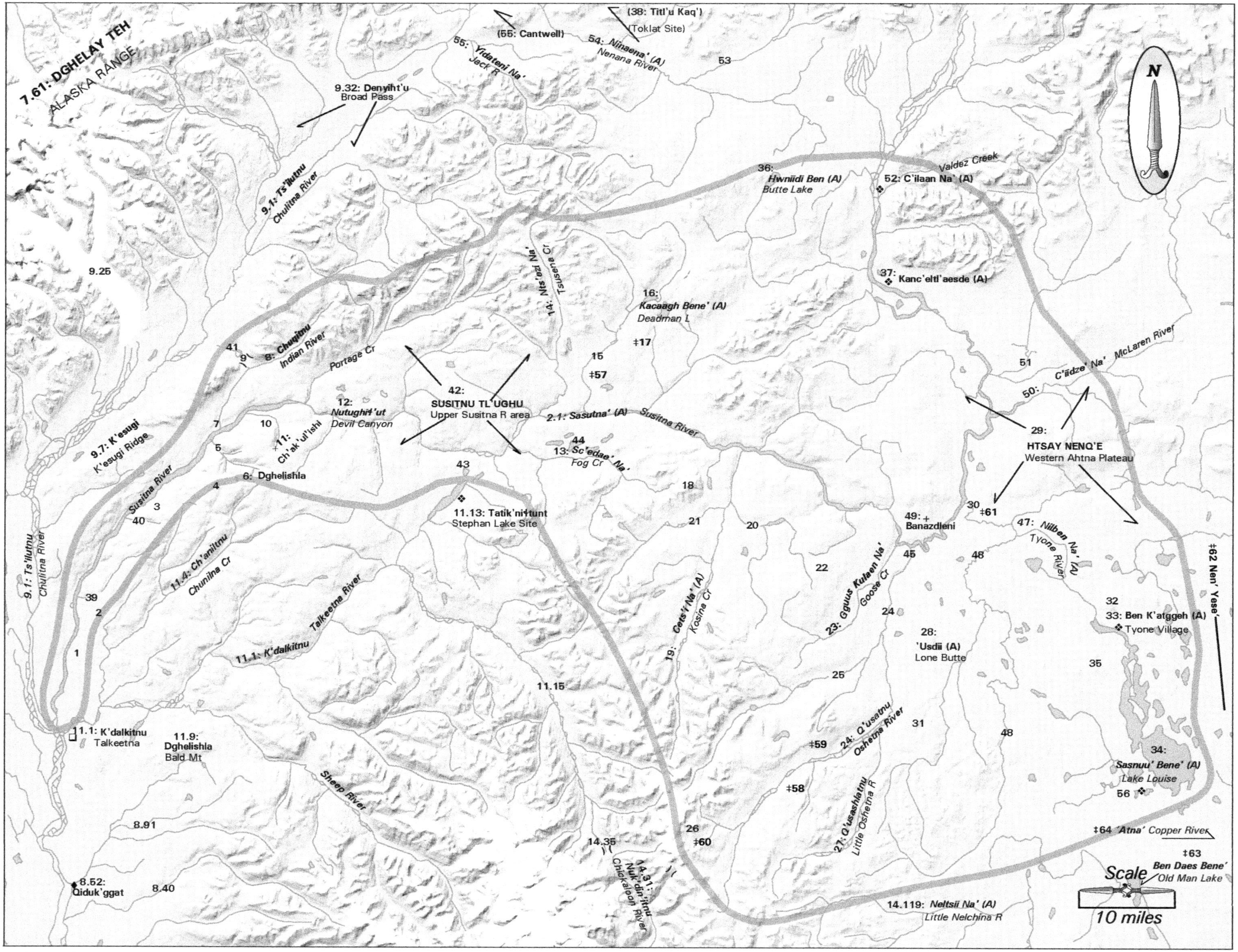
7.61: DGHELAY TEH
ALASKA RANGE
(38: Titl'u Kaq')
(Toklat Site)
(55: Cantwell)
54: Ninaena' (A)
Nenana River
55: Yidateni Na'
Jack R
53
9.32: Denyiht'u
Broad Pass
9.1: Ts'ilutnu
Chulitna River
9.25
36:
Hwniidi Ben (A)
Butte Lake
52: C'ilaan Na' (A)
Valdez Creek
37: Kanc'eltl'aesde (A)
14: Nts'ezi Na'
Tsusena Cr
16:
Kacaagh Bene' (A)
Deadman L
‡17
15
‡57
41
9
8: Chuqitnu
Indian River
Portage Cr
42:
SUSITNU TL'UGHU
Upper Susitna R area
12:
Nutughit'ut
Devil Canyon
10
11:
Ch'ak'ul'ishi
7
5
9.7: K'esugi
K'esugi Ridge
2.1: Sasutna' (A)
Susitna River
44
13: Sc'edae' Na'
Fog Cr
43
6: Dghelishla
4
Susitna River
3
40
11.13: Tatik'nitunt
Stephan Lake Site
18
21
20
51
50:
C'iidze' Na'
McLaren River
29:
HTSAY NENQ'E
Western Ahtna Plateau
30
‡61
49:
Banazdleni
47: Nilben Na' (A)
Tyone River
45
48
22
23: Gguus Kulaen Na'
Goose Cr
24
19: Cets'i Na' (A)
Kosina Cr
9.1: Ts'ilutnu
Chulitna River
11.4: Ch'anitnu
Chunilna Cr
39
2
1
11.1: K'dalkitnu
Talkeetna River
28:
'Usdii (A)
Lone Butte
32
33: Ben K'atggeh (A)
Tyone Village
35
11.15
25
1.1: K'dalkitnu
Talkeetna
11.9:
Dghelishla
Bald Mt
31
48
‡59
24: Q'usatnu
Oshetna River
34:
Sasnuu' Bene' (A)
Lake Louise
56
Sheep River
‡58
27: Q'usashlatnu
Little Oshetna R
8.91
26
‡60
14.35
14.31:
Nuk'din'itnu
Chickaloon River
‡62 Nen' Yese'
‡64 'Atna' Copper River
‡63
Ben Daes Bene'
Old Man Lake
8.52:
Qiduk'ggat
8.40
14.119: Neltsii Na' (A)
Little Nelchina R
Scale
10 miles
N

10 Upper Susitna River

from Talkeetna to Devil Canyon and Above

‡As of 2015 over 380 Ahtna names have been recorded on the upper Susitna River and over 600 for the Western Ahtna dialect area (Kari 2008, 2014). For the 2016 edition we added Ahtna names to Chap. 10 that offer insights into ancient Dene/Ahtna prehistory. Eleven names from Chap. 10 are grouped as Å[2] on Table 12 (pp. 145–146), to indicate these are potentially the second oldest Dene names surrounding the Alaska Range. See the place annotations at Fig. 135A (10.12), 10. 29, 10.34, 10.57, 10. 58, 10.61, 10.62, and 10.64.

Devil Canyon was the Ahtna-Dena'ina boundary on the main river, although the Dena'ina regularly hunted in the Oshetna River country. Included in this section are all of the names in the upper Susitna area remembered by Shem Pete as well as a selection of Ahtna names between Devil Canyon and head of the Susitna River. Shem never traveled on the Susitna above **Ch'ak'ul'ishi** (10.11), but he had been on the Oshetna River trail to Tyone Lake.

The Tyone River system was the focal area or the **Hwtsaay Hwt'aene** 'Small Timber People' (Ahtna). The Ahtna recognize that the central Talkeetna Mountains, including the Oshetna River drainage, used to be Dena'ina country, and that they, the Ahtna, have also been incursive into the upper Nenana River area. Based upon an analysis of the Athabascan-origin place names and descriptions in Wrangell (1980 [1839]), it appears that the upper Nenana River was, as of 1830, mainly Lower Tanana territory, rather than Dena'ina or Ahtna territory. Also see 10.29 **Htsay Nenq'e** and p. 145.

Reckord (1983:30): "The Western Ahtna, the **Hwtsaay Hwt'aene** or 'Little Tree People,' inhabited an area not dominated by the Copper River. During the nineteenth century, their location near the upper Susitna and Matanuska rivers encouraged trading at Russian posts on Cook Inlet. As a result a few western **denaes** [chiefs] became middlemen in the trading network."

Reckord (1983:76): "In several cases [Western Ahtna] main fishing sites, permanent winter villages, and hunting camps were all located in close proximity along lakeshores."

Irving (1957:38–40) has a detailed geographic description of the Western Ahtna country and its resources. "The lakes country is strongly marked by the effects of relatively recent glaciation. Much of the topography in the vicinity of Lake Louise consists of steep, densely wooded ridges and knobs of till. Interspersed are numerous small ponds and creeks following erratic courses among drift remnants. Most of the remaining portion here is taken up by partly forested hills with long, low slopes, broad treeless marshes, meadows and many large ponds....

"Food resources available to aboriginals, in order of importance are fish, especially whitefish, but also lake trout, ling cod, a type of herring [round whitefish], and grayling. In the way of large game, there are caribou, moose, black and grizzly bears. Of the rest, muskrats, beaver, rabbits, ducks, geese, grouse, and ptarmigan probably were important. Such animals as porcupines and squirrels, although present, apparently did not figure importantly in the menu. Generally most of the land-dwellers were taken individually although, in the case

MAP 41

(Opposite) Place names map of the Upper Susitna River, showing Nos. 10.1 to 10.64.

MAP BY MATT GANLEY

Sources: Shem Pete, Johnny Shaginoff, Annie Ronning, Jack Tyone, Jim Tyone, Jake Tansy, Henry Peters, Jim Sinyon, Jimmy Secondchief, Dick Secondchief, and Charlie Hubbard

2003 revisions: names revised 10.39–10.56; locations revised 10.3, 10.4.

‡2016 revisions: names added 10.57–64; names revised 10.13–10.17, 10.21, 10.22, 10.28, 10.29, 10.32, 10.37, 10.42, 10.44, 10.50, 10.54; figures added 135A, 140A; figure replaced 139; map revised 43; map replaced 45.

of the caribou, the drive was used in several forms. Fish traps accounted for large quantities of whitefish from late summer until January. Salmon do not occur in this part of the Susitna system.

"Blueberries and cranberries are abundant on hillsides and a number of edible roots and herbs are present. Generally speaking, on a year-round basis, the country is not rich enough in these food resources to sustain large villages. On the basis of recent houses discovered and information from local informants, it would appear that the early post-contact population was no more than one hundred persons. Presumably, these were living in scattered groups of five to thirty individuals following a semi-nomadic existence....

"They would go into the hill country often as far as the Talkeetna Mountains. They would remain hunting caribou until midsummer, when they returned for fishing. Travel was usually on foot; infrequently by canoe.... Vestiges of an elaborate system of trails may still be seen, and even now foot travel for distances of forty or fifty miles is routine." See also 10.34 for further quotes from Irving (1957).

Most of the Russian trade items and loanwords noted in Kari (1990:628–32) entered the Copper River area by means of Upper Inlet Dena'ina or Western Ahtna traveling the Matanuska trail to either Tyone Lake or Tazlina Lake.

Griffen (1990:69–70) has summarized the upper Susitna River archaeological work of the 1980s:

> Most of the archaeological research conducted with the Susitna drainage, located southeast of DENA [Denali National Park], has been associated with hydroelectric development....
>
> By far, the most intensive phase of Susitna research was accomplished during the Susitna Hydroelectric Project cultural resource program undertaken by the University of Alaska Museum between 1979 and 1985 (Dixon et al. 1985). A major goal of the research was to establish a preliminary cultural history sequence within the study area, which extended along the middle Susitna River.
>
> Nearly 250 new archeological sites were located during five field seasons of archeological survey. Ten sites/loci were assigned to the Euroamerican tradition (AD 1900 to present), 114 sites/loci were assigned to the Athabascan tradition (1,500 BP to approximately 100 BP), 38 sites/loci were assigned to the Late Denali complex (3,500 BP to 1,500 BP), six sites/loci were assigned to the Northern Archaic tradition (approximately 5,200 to 3,500 BP), and seven sites/loci were assigned to the American Paleoarctic tradition (5,200 to 10,500 BP) (Dixon et al. 1985: 172–186).
>
> Probably the most important result of the [University of Alaska] museum's research was the formation of a regional stratigraphic chronology based on a sequence of three distinct, prehistoric volcanic tephras (volcanic ash deposits) found in the area; Devil tephra, dated from 1,400–1,500 BP, Watana tephra, dated from 1,800–2,700 BP, and Oshetna tephra, dated from 5,200–5,900 BP. When the tephras are present in an archeological site, they are sufficiently distinct from other sediments and from one another that the archeologist can date the cultural strata in relation to the tephras.

‡Continuing archaeological research in the middle Susitna River basin continues to be primarily associated with ongoing hydroelectric explorations. During three field seasons, the cultural resource management firm Northern Land Use Research (2012 and 2013), and subsequently Northern Land Use Research Alaska (2014) were able to report an additional 151 previously undiscovered sites. 127 of these new sites were prehistoric in nature, with preserved technocomplexes representing preservation from the Northern Archaic tradition to the protohistoric period. (Gerad M. Smith p.c.)

10.1 Łch'ibay Keght • 'At the Big Whirlwind'
bluff on Susitna River near Chase

FIGURE 135

Annie Ronning, originally of Talkeetna, was a source of information about the Mountain People. Photo taken in Palmer in 1981.

PHOTO BY PRISCILLA RUSSELL

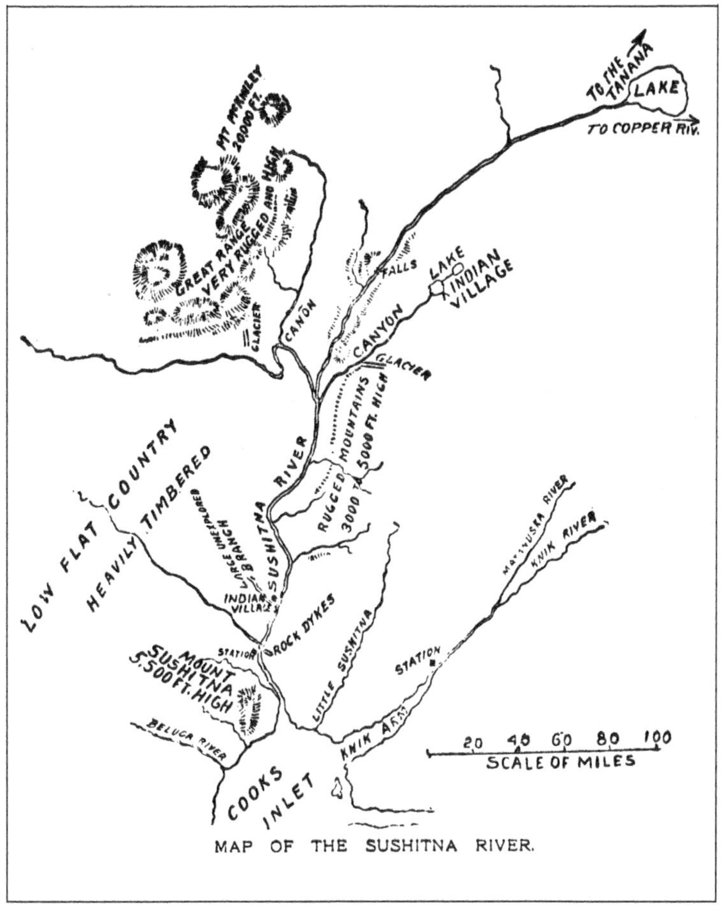

MAP 42

The Dickey sketch map of 1896.

The Dickey party ascended the Susitna River to Devil Canyon in 1896, some of the first Euro-Americans to ascend that far up the Susitna (Cole 1983:74–75). In this area they met one group of the Mountain People, perhaps at Indian River, which is marked "Indian village" on Dickey's sketch map.

Note this early documentation of salmon fishing here at the upper limits of the Susitna River salmon run. Dickey: "About seventy miles from the great forks [at Talkeetna] we came to a small village of the Kuilchau [**Gheltsana**] or Copper River Indians, tall and fine looking, and great hunters. Throughout the long and arduous winter they camp on the trail of the caribou. They build huge fires of logs, then erect a reflector of skins back from the fire between which reflector and the fire they sleep, practically out of doors, although the temperature reaches 50° below zero. We were surprised to find them outfitted with cooking stoves, planes, saws, axes, knives, sleds sixteen feet in length, 1894 model rifles, etc. They were encamped near a fish trap which they had constructed across a small side stream, and were catching and drying red salmon. They had no permanent houses, living in Russian tents.... They informed us that we could go no further with our boats, as the Susitna now entered an impassable canyon" (Dickey 1897b, cited in Moore 1981:14). In 1897 Dickey returned to this area and made a marker at Portage Creek.

ARCHIVES, ALASKA AND POLAR REGIONS DEPT., RASMUSON LIBRARY, UNIVERSITY OF ALASKA FAIRBANKS

‡FIG. 135A

Aerial view of 10.12, Devil Canyon, a treacherous 20 mile stretch of the Susitna River. The Ahtna name **Nataghiłʼaade** employs an innovated Ahtna verb theme for 'current flows.' Kari has recently noted that this name is also used for Baird Canyon/Abercrombie Rapids on the lower Copper River, the area where the glacial ice of Lake Ahtna breeched. This is a case of a *patterned duplication* among Ahtna names. Also we conclude that the Ahtna name for Devil Canyon preceded the name **Nataghiłʼaade** for Baird Canyon.

PHOTO BY BILL SIMEONE

FIGURE 136

The steep northern face of **K'esugi** 'The Ancient One' (9.7 K'esugi Ridge), viewed from **Chuqitnu Tustes** (10.9, Chulitna Pass) on the Alaska Railroad.

PHOTO BY JAMES KARI

FIGURE 137

Photo engraving made in 1898. Pass at the head of Indian Creek. Near **Chuqitnu Tustes** (10.9, Chulitna Pass).

FROM ELDRIDGE 1900:18

10.2 Ts'estałki • 'Flat Rock Point'
mountain "Lane" east of Chase
This name was reported by the late Annie Ronning, whose father **Shik'u,** or Nick Nicoli, used to hunt here. Katherine Nicolie mentioned that she (Katherine) was born at **Ts'estałki.**

§10.39 Ts'estałkitnu • 'Flat Rock Point Creek'
Lane Creek

§10.40 Sheshjeshtnu • 'Rescued, Saved Creek'
creek from mountain north of Curry, at Mile 252

10.3 Sheshjesh • 'Rescued, Saved'
§mountain north of Curry (revised location)

10.4 Dnelbu'i • 'The Grey One'
§mountain east of Susitna River, "Chunilna" 3710' east of ***K'esugi*** *(revised location)*
See also 11.23, **Dnelbu'i Betnu.**

10.5 Quht'anagga K'etnu K'ilani • 'Creek That Belongs to the Little People'
Gold Creek. See Map 37.
This place name is derived from rocks which have concretions that look like little people, dogs, animals, and other things. Shem Pete calls these "good luck rocks."

Shem Pete: "«We came onto a lot of caribou [in the **K'esugi** area, 9.6]. We killed them all and packed them down to the people staying at **Quht'anagga K'etnu K'ilani** and **Chuqitnu**. That's Alex and Wasidi Tukda. I saw Katherine Nicolie's mother there in 1914. And **Ch'k'idetnishen** [Talkeetna Nicholie, Katherine Nicolie's father].» I had a big gun already."

Johnny Shaginoff: "There is a trail from Gold Creek to upper Chunilna Creek along that "Boulder Creek" [locally named tributary of Chunilna Creek, 11.4]. It's 12 to 14 miles. The lake on the top there has fish in it. There's another trail to the north in open country across the mountain to Stephan Lake. It's about 20 miles. It's good on the north side."

Katherine Nicolie: "There was a camp at the mouth of Gold Creek where people caught trouts. The steamboat came up that far." When she was 14 years old, Katherine walked there from Talkeetna with Pete Alec's sister Christine (who was named after Katherine's mother). They camped overnight twice on the way. "Chada" (Talkeetna Alec) told them not to collect the rock figures of human beings, horses, and other creatures that can be found up Gold Creek. Katherine once picked up a figurine of a pregnant woman with a hair bun. Her older sister filled her pockets with these rock figures. Chada found out and made them return them. Otherwise, there would have been bad weather, Chada told them.

10.6 Dghelishla • 'Little Mountain'
mountain at the head of Gold Creek
This is a reduplicated place name, cf. Mount Susitna 4.9 and Bald Mountain 11.9.

10.7 Chuqikaq' • 'Beaver Lodge Mouth'
mouth of Indian River
Shem Pete: "«John Stump's father, **Ts'iduyuł Tu**, stayed at **Chuqikaq'**.» He stayed there year round. He got married to a woman from Susitna and went back up there. They moved down to Knik, and John Stump was born in Knik [in about 1898]."

10.8 Chuqitnu • 'Beaver Lodge Creek'
Indian River. See Map 37.
In the summer of 1906 the Cook party passed through this area. Charles Sheldon wrote, "A miner asked one [Indian] about a lot of suspicious bones he saw at Indian Creek, and he was promptly told that here even to this

day the raven made Indians, and that these bones were the leavings" (Sheldon 1908:272).

10.9 Chuqitnu Tustes • 'Beaver Lodge Creek Pass'
Chulitna Pass
Shem Pete: "«They boat down the **Ts'ilutnu** [9.1]. They portage to the Susitna. They go over the pass at the upper end of **K'esugi** [9.6]. There's a pass. We went over the pass. We came to some caribou toward **Chuqitnu**. We packed the meat down to **Quht'anagga K'etnu K'ilant** [Gold Creek, 10.5].»"

§10.41 Chuqitnu Bena • 'Beaver Lodge Lake'
Summit Lake
In the summer of 1898 Eldridge and Muldrow ascended the Susitna River to Chulitna Pass, the upper Chulitna River, and on to the Nenana River. Eldridge noted a visible Indian trail through these areas (1900:12) See Map 39. The trail to Broad Pass via Indian Creek is also noted on maps by Sleem (Map 38) and Moffit (1915:20).

Eldridge (1900:19,28): "An instance of secondary fold occurs in the ridge between the Sushitna River and its tributary the Chulitna on the other—an anticline with granite core and fringing slate and quartzite, the latter locally extending across the summit. Even in this secondary fold unevenness of development has been displayed, for opposite a point midway the length of Indian Creek is a most remarkable structural pass, a veritable synclinal crumple in the anticline of the main ridge.... From here (Indian Creek) an old and very obscure Indian trail was taken across the upland east of Indian Creek to the head of this stream, distant from the mouth about 20 miles."

10.10 Ch'ak'ul'ishitnu • 'Creek Where Lead Caribou Moves Out'
creek into Susitna River from mountain marked as "Clear" at Devil Canyon
This appears to be the same stream that Johnny Shaginoff called Cheechako Creek.

10.11 Ch'ak'ul'ishi • 'Lead Caribou Moves Out'
mountain marked as "Clear" between Devil Canyon and upper Chunilna Creek
Shem Pete said that this name is metaphoric. The western Talkeetna Mountains along the Susitna River valley are thought to look like a herd of caribou, with this mountain being the leader (Kari and Kari 1982:52). The mountain **Ch'ak'ul'ishi** is the upper limit of Shem Pete's first-hand knowledge of the Susitna River.

10.12 Nutughił'ut *(Dena'ina);* **Nataghił'aade** *(Ahtna)* • 'Where Current Flows Down'
Devil Canyon. See Fig. 135A, p. 217.
Devil Canyon forms a clear boundary between the Ahtna and Dena'ina language areas. This canyon seems to have been avoided by both the Ahtna and the Dena'ina.

These falls, noted as "Fall," are marked on the 1839 Wrangell map (Map 17), and are also noted on the 1897 Dickey map (Map 42), and the 1904 Moffit map (Map 44).

We have no Dena'na or Ahtna name for Portage Creek. The Spillum-Ladd party in the spring of 1894 found a cabin at Portage Creek where two white men were weak from scurvy. Bayou (1946:13,42): "About ten miles farther [before Devil Canyon] they met several Indians with their dog teams. One understood English a little. They explained as well they could about the two starving prospectors, and the Indians said they understood and would take them to Susitna. As a matter of fact old Reno did get back to Seattle. They prospected up as far as Valdez Creek. The next summer they cut lumber for a large dory at Portage Creek. The swift current carried them along, and they reached Susitna Station in a matter of hours. Jim Cleghorn and the Indians were on the bank to greet them."

§10.42 Susitnu Tl'ughu, ‡Sasutna' Tl'aa *(Ahtna)* • 'Sand River Headwaters'
the upper Susitna River area
A regional place name.

§10.43 Deniigi De' Bene' *(Ahtna)* • 'Moosehorn Lake'
lake northeast of Stephan Lake, (no. 1852 on USGS maps)
Johnny Shaginoff had a camp here as well as at Fog Lakes. Beyond there the trail went to Fog Creek.

10.13 Sc'edae' Na' *(Ahtna)* • possibly 'My Blanket Creek'
Fog Creek

FIGURE 138

Johnny Shaginoff (left) and Pete Nikolai in February of 1924 at **Nay'dini'aa Na'** (14.31, Chickaloon).

FROM THE MARY SHAGINOFF COLLECTION AND COURTESY OF CHICKALOON VILLAGE TRADITIONAL COUNCIL

‡This would be the only name in Ahtna or Dena'ina with the **sh-, s-** 'my' prefix. This is the first distinctly Ahtna place name without a known Dena'ina variant on the Susitna River. The name was contributed by Johnny Shaginoff.

Johnny Shaginoff traveled the portage between Stephan Lake and the Susitna River to Fog Creek. "The valley runs all the way to Fog Lake. I figure it is a 10 to 15 mile wide valley you know. I figure Stephan Lake to Fog Lake the way I have a trail must be about 28 miles maybe." He also noted that two other trails lead up Fog Creek, one to lower Tsiisi Creek and Mount Watana, and one to upper Tsiisi Creek. In the 1930s Shaginoff had two camps in the Fog Creek-Fog Lakes area.

§10.44 Sc'edae' Bene' *(Ahtna)* • possibly 'My Blanket Lake'
Fog Lakes
Johnny Shaginoff had a cabin here.

10.14 Nts'ezi Na' *(Ahtna)* • possibly 'The Pit (Seed) Creek'
Tsusena Creek
In the winter of 1927–28 and in 1937 Johnny Shaginoff walked here from his camp at Fog Lake and visited Jake Tansy and his family in the Deadman Lake area.

‡10.57 Nts'ezi *(Ahtna)* • 'The Pit (Seed)'
Tsusena Butte
In Upper Kuskokwim and Ahtna several place names with **nts'ezi** are for isolated conical-shaped mountains. 10. 57, 10.58, and Pyramid Mountain (also called **Nts'ezi**) on the Yanert Fork appear to be a set of western boundary marker place names.

10.15 Kacaagh Na' *(Ahtna)* • 'Large Area Creek'
Kacaagh Creek (formerly Deadman Creek)

10.16 Kacaagh Bene' *(Ahtna)*, **Qukugh Bena (Dena'ina)** • 'Large Area Lake'
Upland Kacaagh Lake and Lowland Kacaagh Lake (formerly Deadman Lake and Big Lake)
In 2015 name changes for Deadman Creek, Deadman Lake, and Big Lake were approved by USBGN. This name is listed on the 1839 Wrangell map (Map 17), probably in Dena'ina, as "Kochobena" and is transposed with the name for Butte Lake (10.36).

Jake Tansy commented that when he was trapping here in the winter of 1927–28, Johnny Shaginoff found his trail and came visiting.

10.17 Debae Tse' Na' *(Ahtna)* • 'Sheep Head Creek'
‡*west fork of Watana River*
Henry Peters noted that the name Watana was formerly said Watsena, which is more like the Native name.

10.18 Łts'ibaay *(Ahtna)* • 'Whirlwind'
Mt. Watana

10.19 Cets'i Na' *(Ahtna)* • 'Spearing Creek'
Kosina Creek

10.20 Cets'i Sletna' *(Ahtna)* • 'Little Spearing Creek'
Gilbert Creek
This is a Dena'ina-origin place name, as indicated by the stems **sle** 'little' and **-tna'** 'stream,' which are not used in Ahtna. Cf. also 10.27, the Little Oshetna River.

10.21 Tes Na'? *(Ahtna)* • 'Hill Creek'
Tsisi Creek
‡A name tentatively reported in 1983 by John Shaginoff who had been here. Orth (1971:988): "Tsisi Creek, Indian name reported in 1951 by USGS."

10.22 Tsiyese' *(Ahtna)* • 'Head Ridge'
‡*mountain 5603' <Goose> between Kosina and Goose Creek*
Name via Jack Tyone. "That's not our language. **Tsiyese'**, that's their language too. That's Eklutna's [language], Tyonek."

‡10.58 Nts'ezi *(Ahtna)* • 'Twin Hills'
'The Pit (Seed)'

‡10.59 Ht'u Ben • **'Beneath Area Lake'**
Square Lake west of Oshetna River
This name and 10.60 are from a 1982 SP text **Tiduhuk'dnelyeden** 'the one who pretended to be incompetent.' ‡Also this name seems likely to be displayed on the Wrangell map as "Htuben," see Map 17. Wrangell (1980:58) describes "Htuben" as being "on a plateau not far from the source of the Sushitna." He states, "Here the Cook Inlet Dena'ina are said to meet with the Ahtna, who assemble from Mantylbana [**Bendiil Bene'**, 14.120, Tazlina Lake], and Nutatlgat [the Dena'ina name **Nutał Kaq'** for Batzulnetas village], to hunt caribou and to trade. The distance between Lake Htuben and the northern corner of Cook's Inlet is 14 days' journey."

‡10.60 Nihałqelashtnu • 'Stream They Pack Things to'
stream, pass on upper Oshetna River, on trail to Chickaloon River

10.23 Gguus Kulaen Na' *(Ahtna)* • 'Creek Where There Is Celery'
Goose Creek
"Goose" is actually derived from the Ahtna word **gguus** 'wild celery,' the plant *Heracleum lanatum.*

10.24 Q'usatnu *(Dena'ina);* **K'aasi Na'** *(Ahtna)* • 'Quiver River' or 'Cliff River'
Oshetna River
The trail up the Chickaloon River to the Oshetna River is noted on the 1839 Wrangell map (Map 17). Also see 14.37.

The following quote by Wrangell from the 1830s is the earliest description of the trail to the north on the Matanuska and Oshetna rivers. This trail is shown on the Wrangell map (Map 17) beginning at **Niteh** (14.4), the village at the head of Knik Arm.

Wrangell (1980:58): "The Kenai [Dena'ina] living to the north, along the Knyk and the Sushitna, on the other hand, undertake a much longer journey. They go northeastwards from the northern angle of the straits and travel 7 days' fast march, or 10 days at the usual speed, through the mountain canyons as far as a very high ridge; the women and children and the poorer hunters stay at its foot while the rest travel 7 days farther to the small lake Chtuben which lies on a plateau not far from the source of the Sushitna." See also 10.34.

Shem Pete also walked this trail: "«[Coming from Matanuska River] we went over the mountains to **Q'usatnu** and to **Benq'etgge** [Tyone Lake, 10.33].

"«The Ahtna would leave and go upriver. They came to the Oshetna River and they stopped somewhere up there. They had a village there, and they hunted. That is a big river, the Oshetna. On the upriver side there is a lake [probably Crater Lake, Kari 1983:76]. They used to chase caribou into that lake.»" Knik and Eklutna Dena'ina continued to hunt caribou and sheep in the Oshetna country until the 1920s.

Jack Tyone, speaking in 1983: "We just crossed that **Segeli Na'** [Tyone Creek]. We not go up the creek though. Go to **K'aasi Na'** [Oshetna River]. We go north side, past there we hit the **K'aastle Na'** [Little Osheta River] and then goes in that big Oshetna."

§10.45 **K'aas Cae'e** *(Ahtna)* • 'Quiver Mouth' or 'Cliff Mouth'
mouth of Oshetna River
James Sinyon, interviewed by Lillian Boston in September 1973 for West (1973): Q: "Where were you born?" JS: "It's on the river, just about six or seven miles below mouth of Tyone River, on the Susitna River. My daddy was coming back from Susitna Station, woman that time was just about cramping, she got the pain. They just been waiting and camp right there on the island in the river. There I was born, some day in March 1894. Nobody live there, just the country... nobody go around there. **K'aas Cae'e** [mouth of Oshetna River]. Oshetna whiteman call it.... There's lota game in that creek. They came right straight over the mountains from Chickaloon when I was born."

Jim Tyone mentioned to Kari in 1981 that the farthest he had been from Tyone Lake down the Sustina River was to the mouth of the Oshetna River.

10.25 **Tułchuntnu** *(Dena'ina);* **Tełdzaan Na'** *(Ahtna)* • 'Dark Water River'
Black River
This is the most northeasterly Dena'ina-pronounced name reported by Johnny Shaginoff in March of 1985. The English name is a translation of the Dena'ina/Ahtna name.

10.26 **Q'usa Dhelaya** or **Q'usałtqest** • 'Quiver Mountain' or 'Cliff Mountain; '-?-'
mountain, elev. 7055', at head of Oshetna River
Shem Pete: "That mountain, every time they walk that way they drag [?] up and down on their back. Nice clear place. No brush. Lots of caribou."

Shem Pete mentioned both names. The second name is not analyzable. This may be the "high ridge" referred to in the passage from Wrangell cited in 10.24.

‡FIGURE 139
Jake and Lily Tansy in Cantwell, in the 1960s. Jake Tansy (1906–2003), the expert traveler and storyteller of the Valdez Creek-Cantwell Ahtna, is the strongest speaker on record for the Ahtna language.
PHOTO COURTESY OF ROY TANSY

§(10.46) **Ben Ghetgge** • 'Between the Lakes'
unidentified location in upper Oshetna River area
Shem Pete knew of this place through a story of the 'The One Who Died at Between the Lakes.' A man was getting sheep in the mountains when he got covered in an avalanche. A rock at this lake looks like the head of this man with his hair tangled in the alders.

10.27 **Q'usashlatnu** *(Dena'ina);* **K'aasi Sletna', K'aastle Na'** *(Ahtna)* • 'Little Quiver River' or 'Little Cliff River'
Little Oshetna River
Since the Ahtna name has both the stem **-sle** 'little' and the stem **tna'** rather than **na'** for 'river,' we can conclude that this is originally a Dena'ina place name. This name and the following place name provide evidence that the Dena'ina boundary once extended at least to here.

10.28 **Yusdi** *(Dena'ina);* **'Usdii, 'Usdicde** *(Ahtna)* • ‡'Ahead in the Distance'
Lone Butte
The trail to the Oshetna area passed north of here. Jim and Jack Tyone said that this is originally a Dena'ina name, and this ridge formerly was a boundary between Ahtna and Dena'ina territory. Moreover, both this name and 10.35 **Xensdii,** contain the directional root ***nes,** that means 'ahead, perimeter,' with **nes** reducing to **ns** or **s.** ‡The pair of names 10.28 and 10.35 are on Table 12 as a *resemblent pair* of names. This is a boundary region between Ahtna and Dena'ina and these two names are overt boundary-marking place names.

Glenn (1900a: 640): "The trail from Bubb River passes along the divide between the Copper and Sushitna Rivers. In returning to my own trail of last summer and fall it is only necessary to add that it leads through a very good pass in the Alaska Range, and showed evident signs of having been used by the natives from the Copper, Sushitna and Tanana rivers for an indefinite period. This was apparent from the number of trails we found leading into it."

10.29 Htsay Nenq'e *(Dena'ina);* **Hwtsaay Nene'** *(Ahtna)* • ‡'Dwarf Tree Country'
‡Western Ahtna uplands (upper Susitna-upper West Fork Gulkana river)
‡One of three cognate *distant patterned duplications* for ecoregions. See discussion on pp. 144–147. These three distant cognate place names provided some of the initial data for the theory PDLL. This term is used to designate the **Hwtsaay Hwt'aene** *(Ahtna)*, the Western Ahtna band. The Western Ahtna note that this area lacks birch, large spruce, and salmon, and has vast stretches of tundra with abundant caribou. ‡Also see Kari 2010a:71.

Shem Pete: "«Tyone country, **Htsay Nenq'e**, I stayed there one month. That's Jim Tyone's father's country.»

"They make caches there, just like beaver house. It freezes up. Four, five, six pile up. They put in fish eggs. They keep it for two, three years. «It dries and they use it.» No trees around there."

10.30 Nilben Caek'e *(Ahtna)* • 'Mouth of Water-Surges'
site at mouth of Tyone River
Hickok (1968:260): "A site at the confluence of the Tyone and Susitna Rivers is reported to be one of the largest inland Athapascan villages prior to 1500 AD" This site is also mentioned in Reckord (1983:179).

The 1904 Moffit map (Map 44) indicates a house on the Susitna River between the Tyone and McLaren rivers as "second chiefs house." Moffit on his 1904 map refers to the Tyone River as "Tyone Creek."

Moffit (1915:21): "The Indians who hunt on the Jack River and Yanert Fork also have their cabins on Valdez Creek. Formerly they lived in the vicinity of Tyone River and the big bend of the Susitna."

Jack Tyone: "In 1908 I see that place, Jimmy Secondchief's daddy and Oly Nikolai's daddy, two families there."

James Sinyon (West 1973): "There used to be village this way from there. Mouth of Tyone River. Used to be village there.... That's Secondchief's family used to live there, and Cantwell Nikolai was there, and then another Valdez Creek Jack, they used to call em. Him and his mother and brother used to live, they had a big village there."

‡Jake Tansy: "«**Nilben Caek'e** when I was small was covered with houses. In summer, in 'moulting feathers month' (August), 'leaves red month' (September) they would leave in a group. Every family they would walk about the glaciers (at heads of Susitna and Nenana Rivers). They would kill bull caribou that were moving through in the uplands. Then they made the dry meat. The skin boats were assembled with a willow pole-frame. The women would sew together the skins.... All of the meat, everything was stuffed inside (the skin boats). Then they came back in several boats to **Nilben Caek'e**. As they returned back downstream there, they put everything up in elevated caches. Then with the snowfall they would harvest marten; they would harvest fox too»" (Kari 2014).

§10.47 Nilben Na' *(Ahtna)* • 'Water Surges Stream'
Tyone River

‡10.61 K'ey Tsaaygha *(Ahtna)* • 'By the Dwarf Birch'
hill north of Tyone River
The name is a significant *patterned duplication.* It is the same as the name for Hogan Hill. Hogan Hill was an island in glacial Lake Ahtna, whereas this hill on Tyone River is northwest of the outlet of Glacial Lake Ahtna. Also **tsaay** 'Dwarf Tree' is cognate with the root in **Hwtsaay Nene'**.

§10.48 Snuu Na' *(Ahtna)* • 'Brushy Stream'
Sanona Creek
West (1973:37) via James Sinyon: "A village was located on the Tyone River six or seven miles upstream from its mouth. Mr. Jim Secondchief with his family and Mr. Valdez Creek Jack with his mother and brother lived here." This may be near the mouth of Sanona Creek.

West (1973:32) via James Sinyon: "A cache was seen still standing along the Tyone River by Mr. Sinyon where his mother's family and Mr. Tom Neely were raised. The place is called In-u-ind-na. In 1907 there was a big fish camp there."

10.31 Snuuni *(Ahtna)* • 'Brushy One'
Big Bones Ridge
Shem Pete: "I been all over that country, trapping beaver. I learned this name there. «I know that area.»"

10.32 Saltigi *(Ahtna)* • ‡'Sun Protrusion'
unnamed hill, elev. 3537', marked as "Tyone." See Fig. 141.
This is the major spiritual location for the **Tsaay Hwt'aene** and an important site and game lookout. The Tyone Village chieftainship, recently held by the late Jim Tyone, is referred to as **Saltigi Ghaxen** 'Person of **Saltigi**'. This is the westernmost of the titled Ahtna chieftainships (Kari 1986:15).

This is also Irving's site #9, about which he comments, "Nearby on the Tyone River are salt licks and a caribou crossing. That locality seems to be a concentration point for game of all sorts. The hill top affords an excellent outlook over the nearly flat surrounding country.... Most of the material was found on the southern side of the knob, which suggests use of the site during the winter months when this section would be favored by the low sun" (Irving 1957:43).

West (1973:34): "A single house depression is located about two-thirds of the way up a hill called Su-sta-ki. It is said to have been occupied by a powerful war leader."

A Trip from Tyone Village to Knik in 1912

by Jim Tyone

Recorded with Jim Tyone in Gulkana by Jim Kari on 6/26/81. Translated with Andy Tyone and Fred Ewan in 2001. Recording is ANLC0809. The segment is 9 minutes and 53 seconds long.

Jim Tyone was born at Tyone Lake in 1898. He was married to Annie Ewan Tyone and lived at Gulkana after the 1920s. Jim last walked the trail from Tyone Lake to Knik down the Matanuska Valley in 1912. This segment is a fine example of an Athabascan travel narrative. The story highlights camping spots that are at the end of each day of travel. The trail from Tyone Lake to Knik was about 170 miles in length. The places numbered here to correspond with features in Chapters 10, 13, and 14. Several places he mentions in the Little Nelchina River drainage are not in this book.

Jim Tyone spoke Dena'ina well. He was Shem Pete's cousin and a member of the Tulchina/Taltsiine clan. Jim knew many other locations in the Knik-Wasilla-Palmer area. This story is typical of the travel narratives that Jim and Shem would tell one another. Jim Tyone passed away in 1988.

‡In 2013 the text was reviewed with Andy Tyone and Fred Ewan. We did a GIS mapping of Jim's route, and we refined several locations for this edition (in Chap. 14). Jim Tyone mentioned thirty-eight place names in Ahtna or English, and he makes note of thirteen camping places (noted by a † symbol). Also see pp. 232–234 for further discussion of *place-intensive narratives* by Jim Tyone and Jake Tansy.

Ben K'atgge, that's what they call Tyone Lake [village].
[1] 'between the lakes' is what they call Tyone (Lake) Village (10.33).

Ben k'edaa'a, 'udaat ben k'edaadze' 'udaa' Nidaeggi Cii hwdi'aande yet hnighiyeł †.
Downstream on the lake, down the lake they camped at a place called [2] 'point of fallen objects' (island on north end of Lake Louise).

Yet su on a sled nahwluude about November c'a nen su xona Knik xu ts'e' ts'ikideł. Knik xu ts'e' ts'ihghideł dze'.
In the fall in about November month they would leave from there to Knik. They would leave for Knik (13.15).

And next day łu xona Lake Louise yi hdidełi, katggu yae' de.
And the next day then they would enter [3] Lake Louise (10.34) on the upper end.

Skosii'den yet hnighiyeł †.
They would camp at [4] 'where we draw birch sap' (10.56 lake and site near southwest end of Lake Louise).

Yehwts'en ye xuc'a 'unse nahdeł dze' tkutgge' Neltsii Na' 'unse tene xona.
From there they would go out ahead, up to [5] 'one-that-is-made creek' (14.119, Little Nelchina River), to the trail out there.

Tene kughił'aen'. I forget that name.
They had a trail. I forget that name.

Na xutgge' 'utgge' cu yet hnighiyeł †, one one another next day ts'ihdeł dze' xona, ba'aat Neltsii Na' yet ka'aa cu yet hnighiyeł. †
They spent the night up there, and in another day they came out [6] beyond 'one-that-is-made creek,' and they camped again the next place beyond there.

Xona xełts'e' de Kentsii Na' kahghideł.
Then by evening they came up to [7] 'Kentsii creek' (creek into Little Nelchina River, between Old Man and Crooked creeks).

Kentsii Na' łu tayenk'e daa'a htedeł dze' 'udaat Una' Cenaeł'sdildełi Na' yi caek'e łu xona c'ena' ngge' yii caek'e yet łu hnighiyeł.
They would go downstream on the straight bar of 'Kentsii creek,' and downstream at the mouth of [8] 'its-creek the-one-we-move-upriver-upon creek' (14.121, Old Man Creek) they would camp upland of its mouth.

Fall now. Skosii'den su fall hnighiyeł. †
It is fall time. It was fall time when they camped at [4] 'where we draw birch sap' (10.56, lake at south end of Lake Louise).

Now next morning xona k'adii Eureka hwdi'aande, Eureka hwdi'aande, C'enaen' N'aatde dae' hwdighi'a'.

And the next morning then at where now is named Eureka, the place named Eureka is named [9] 'where a face is in position' (14.76 hill at Tahneta Pass).

K'adii Eureka kaniide. C'enaen' N'aatde yet hnighiyeł. †

They camped there at the place now named Eureka at 'where a face is in position.'

Yet satggan ts'ihdeł dze' xona katsii that lake, what he call it?

They left there early in the morning then the next place downland, what do they call it?

Xelt'aats'i, that's what they call it Xelt'aats'i.

'water lily,' they call it [10] 'water lily' (14.64 ‡Fish Lake).

K'adii Tsendil'aats Kulaende k'aa ghayedu' cu tighita'.

Now at [11] 'where game migrate downland' (14.114, Trail Creek) that is where another trail used to be. [‡At this point the group enters the Matanuska River drainage.]

Ye kadaa'a 'udaa'a Unatadeł'aade yet ts'inaane.

There downstream down at [12] 'where the water flows around' (14.115 hill near Sheep Mountain) and straight across.

Ghat yet dghelaay nez'aan dze' Siz'aani udi'aan sunt'ae.

There is that mountain, the one named [13] 'my heart' (14.71, Gunsight Mountain).

Gunsight kiiłnii. Siz'aani.

They call it Gunsight, 'my heart.'

Siz'aani ubene' katsii big lake that time dełtaan, yet k'enaane'.

At 'my heart' downland there is a big lake ‡[13a] (14.126, Lake Leila) across the way.

Xona yet łu ic'a' natsene xał htelaes 'utsene.

So leaving from there downland, they would pull sleds.

No timber, nothing. Just all canyon.

'Utsene katsii xał htetiisi tighiyaałi k'etat'iił.

They would be walking and pulling sleds, if it would be possible.

Dii c'ena' kulaendze' ku'eł skotniic.

They never know how the river is going to be.

Skuz'aade tetiisi kughistle'i

FIGURE 140

Jim Tyone at his home in Gulkana in about 1980.

PHOTO COURTESY OF ANDY TYONE

In places it might not be conditions for pulling (sleds).

Xona yene xał c'atiili c'a daygge' nyet tkot'ae, tsene.

Then they would pull the sleds as it drops down, to the lowlands.

Ts'i kutene pretty soon 'unsogho river xona Ts'itonhna' ye k'ehdeł, yet hnighiyeł †.

And out ahead on the trail they would come out on [14] 'trail comes out river' (14.1, Matanuska River), and they would camp there.

Xona yet su satggan tedze tah early in the morning, na'aay tez'aani Ts'itonhna' k'ehdeł dze'.

Early the morning, as the sun is coming up, they come into 'trail comes out river.'

He go fast. Xantaey xona na'stedeł.

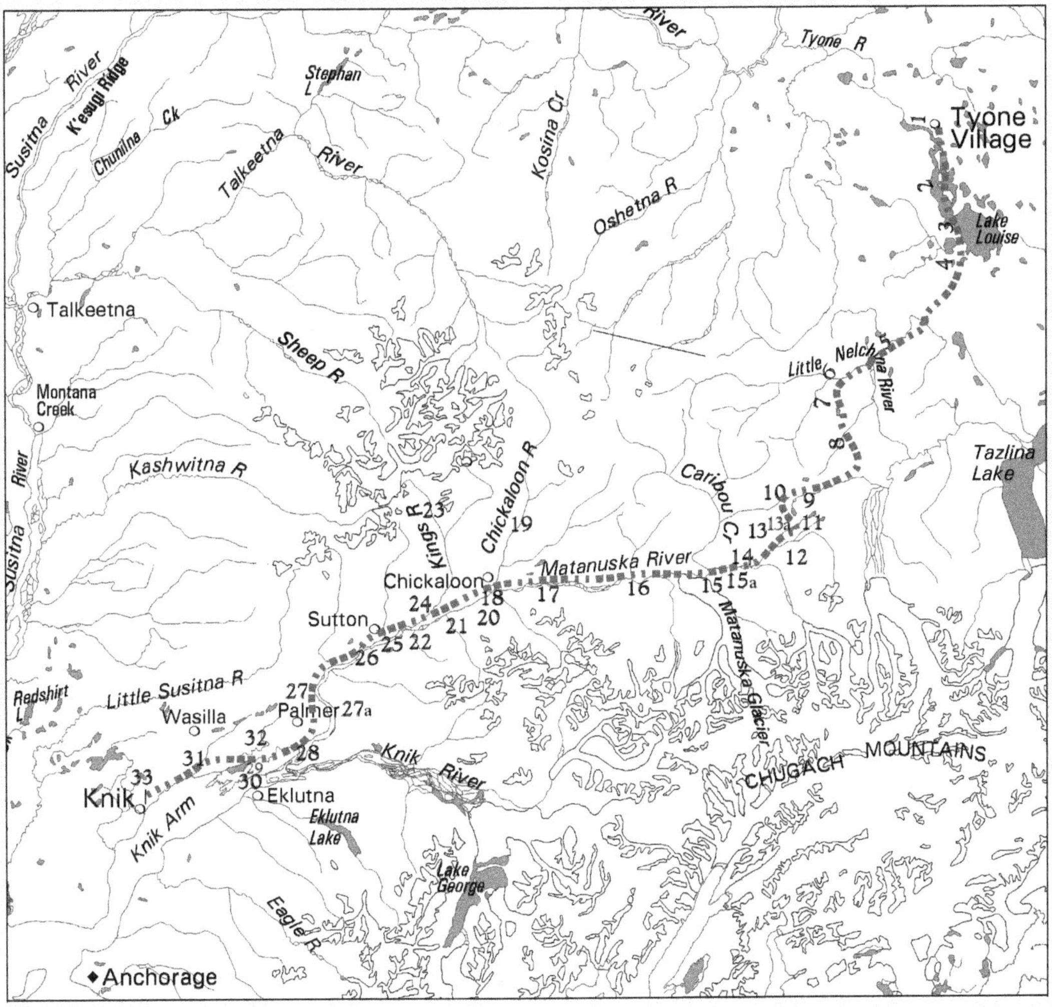

MAP 43

Jim Tyone's 1912 travel route from Tyone Village to Knik.

MAP BY JIM KARI

We were going fast then.

Yehwts'en 'adaa'a ten Natsede'aayi, what he call that, Natsede'aayi su

From there downstream on the trail is [15] 'Rock That Is Standing' (14.59, Lion Head, or Glacier Point).

'Adaa'a station gha kulaen I think. Natsede'aayi udi'aan.

There was a station by there. It is named 'Rock That Is Standing.'

Yet t'aa 'udaa'a, yet 'udaa' dae' xona Łuu K'ae hnighiyeł †.

They would camp beneath there downstream 'Glacier Place'; [15a] (14.125, camp at foot of Matanuska Glacier) at the base of the [Matanuska] glacier.

Cu yet camp tkusiix.

They would fix a camp there.

Yehwts'en xona tayen hdideł dze' ten k'edaa'a 'udaa'a Taałtaande cu yet hnighiyeł †.

From there they came onto the river bar going on the ice, and they camped at [16] 'Enclosed Water Place' (14.106, Tatonden Lake camp)

Three now uk'etl'aa first yihwts'en.

It has been three (days) since the first departure.

Yet hwts'en next next, Tandze Laedze' ałk'e yet hnighiyeł †, five four.

From there then they camped right at [17] 'Middle Sand'

(14.40, Windy Point below Riley Creek), the fifth day.

C'a next day łu xona Nay'dini'aa Caek'e, Chickaloon, Nay'dini'aa Na'.

And the next day they reached the [18] 'mouth of bridge extends across' (14.91, mouth of Chickaloon River), at [19] 'bridge extends across river (14.31, Chickaloon River).

Nay'dini'aa Caek'e xona yet su xona uts'its'ehghidełi k'e nihdghił'aax †.

When at 'mouth of bridge extends across' (14.91, mouth of Chickaloon River), they feel like they have already arrived. ‡[They were among relatives, an interesting statement.]

About five yehwts'en c'a su, fast he go.

So then we go fast for about five days.

K'adii King Mountain gha tiye kudeset dze' tkut'ae.

Now it was still quite a ways to King Mountain.

King Mountain, Chickaloon ts'en King Mountain kadaa'a Bes Tl'ets', King Mountain Bes Tl'ets'.

Next downstream from Chickaloon is King Mountain [20] (14.28, 'black stone'), King mountain is 'black stone.'

Kadaat T'aay Caek'e that creek, T'aay Caek'e yet hnighiyeł †.

The next place downstream they camped at is [21] 'chest mouth' (14.25, mouth of Carpenter Creek).

Yehwts'en kadaa'a Tsiis T'el'iixden keniide tsiis tsiis kughines.

From there the next place downstream they call, [22] 'where ochre is gathered' (14.21, canyon opposite King River), here they got ochre.

Dase ts'ihtedełde nitsiis kunes. He got pail (he pick it up), he come back.

They came out beyond there and they got ochre. They pick it up in a pail and come back.

Katsii nihghidełi tsiis kughile'.

Downland from there they stopped where the ochre was.

Xona xuk'a yet 'unaan' dae' King Creek, Staeł Na', Staeł Caek'e udi'aan.

Then right across there is [23] Kings River (14.20), 'wide place river,' it was named [24] 'wide place mouth.'

Yet Hdighilende yet c'a hnighiyeł †.

Then they camped there at [25] 'where current flows in (canyon)' (14.19, site at Granite Creek).

U'eł Naak' Dghiłtaazi 'adii gha Sutton hwniide su.

And then they camped by what is now Sutton at [26] 'The Bar that is Turning with it' (14.81 location on Matanuska River at Sutton).

Xuk'a su 'unggat ts'ihghideł dze' two one week, ten days I guess, more than ten days.

They had left from the uplands two weeks before, or ten days or more.

K'adii Palmer ts'eniide ‡Cetsii T'aade xona yet,

Now where we call Palmer, there is [27] ‡'beneath base of lowlands' (14.7, campsite at base of ridge, north bank of Matanuska River along Glenn Highway)

Palmer k'adii bridge nani'aat yet su xona tayen k'e.

there is [27a] 'where rocks come together' (14.9), where now the bridge goes across the stretch of river. ‡[Implied Nił'e Tse'it'aaden, 14.9, Palmer Canyon above bridge.]

Naane' 'unaane' Nuutah.

Across there is [28]) 'between the islands' (14.4 Matanuska village site).

Nic'adatl'ets'i 'unaan' k'adii koht'aene k'e you ever heard of Nic'adatl'ets'i?

And across from there in the Native language is [29] 'dark color extends from shore' (13.43, site on point above Weinie Lake off Fairview Loop).

Nic'adatl'ets'i, it's across Eklutna, I guess, across the river.

'Dark color extends from shore' (13.43) is across (Knik Arm) from [30] Eklutna.

Yet hwts'en xona T'aghes Konk'ae xu, That's what you call, Cottonwood, Cottonwood.

From there then is [31] 'cottonwood house' (13.35, site possibly at Cottonwood Slough).

I forget the name (of Cottonwood Creek). [JT added Łaets'i Caek'e (13.35), mouth of Cottonwood Creek, Kari's notebook #10.]

There's Chiqilintnu. He go Wasilla, that's Chiqilintnu, Wasilli. Tsikilintna'.

The is [32] 'fermented fish creek,' that is in Wasilla, that is 'fermented fish creek' (13.46, Wasilla Creek). ‡[1st two versions are Dena'ina, the 3rd is Ahtnaized, showing Jim's bilingual facility.]

Dzenax koniidze' chiqilin, chiqilin, fish yet łuk'ae yizti-isi, Tsikilintna'.

What they (Dena'ina) call fermented fish is chiqilin, they freeze the salmon like that ‡at 'fermented fish creek.'

De xona yet su xona C'enacetna' xona ts'ihghideł, ts'ikideł. C'enacetna'.

Then the came to [33] 'c'enacet stream' (13.15 Fish Creek in Knik), C'enacetna'

Big Store. Only Alaska big store.

Jack Tyone: "«My grandparents stayed at **Sałtigi**. There was no village at **Ben K'atgge**. They had a village on top of **Sałtigi**, my great grandfather.»"

10.33 Ben Q'etgge *(Dena'ina);* **Ben K'atgge** *(Ahtna)* •
'Between the Lakes'
Tyone Village
"Chiefs house" is noted here on the 1904 Moffit map (Map 44) and "Tyon's House" is shown on the 1899 Johnston and Herning map (Map 45) and the 1906 Herning map (Map 59). This village is also mentioned in de Laguna (1970:38), West (1973:33), and Reckord (1983:181).

Shem Pete: "Tyone Village was below that mountain [**Sałtigi**]. Tyone had a big house. I stay in there, 1945. John Shaginoff and I, we go up. We stay one month. Right next to Susitna Lake. That's where Mrs. Ezi was raised. Johnny and I sledded house logs there from **Snuuni** [10.31]. Haul it a long ways to Tyone house."

Johnny Shaginoff reported that this is good caribou country. The people of this village maintained a caribou fence which funneled the caribou to the shore of Lake Louise. Men chased the caribou into the lake and then speared them from canoes. "That's how they got meat for the village."

Shem Pete recalled trapping muskrats with Johnny Shaginoff here, staying for one month in the spring of 1945. Eagles stole the muskrats Shem and Johnny had caught and brought them to their nests. The eagles even took their traps. Shem Pete: "I don't know why they take the traps. Maybe for souvenir."

10.34 Susni Bena *(Dena'ina);* **Sasnuu' Bene'** *(Ahtna)* •
'Sand Island Lake'
Lake Louise, locally "Susitna Lake"
This place name designates this lake as the source of the Susitna River. Compare the related name for the Susitna Delta, **Susni Kaq'** 'Sand Island Mouth' (2.3). Note that the uppermost lake in the Gulkana River drainage, Summit Lake, is also named **Sasnuu' Bene'.** This duplication of names of the largest lakes at the heads of Gulkana and Susitna rivers appears to have been intentional and reflects Dene planning of the name system at the time these names were coined by the ancient Dene. Kari refers to such noticeable duplications in names as *geoduplicates.*

Jack Tyone: "**Sasnuu'**. That's islands, got three on there, **Sasnuu' Bene'**."

Lake Louise is shown on the 1898 Mendenhall map and 1900 Meiklejohn map from the 1898 surveys as well as on the 1904 Moffit map (Map 45), where it is labeled "Sushitna Lakes or L. Louise."

This is an area rich in Athna lore and history. The fishery in the area Lake Louise area was used nearly year round and was especially important during fall and winter. Irving (1957:40) has a good summary of the subsistence round for the Ahtna of Tyone Lake and Lake Louise:

"Jimmy Second Chief, a willing and able informant, the following was learned. The annual cycle was divided into two major phases, dependent upon the feasibility of fishing. From midsummer through December, the principal activity was fishing. The group at this time would accordingly locate near spots suitable for using 'V' and basket traps.

‡FIGURE 140A

Tyone Village **Ben K'atggeh,** (10.33) the hill to the right is **Sałtigi** (10.32). The photographer notes that the only residents at the village were Johnny Tyone and Jimmy Secondchief. Also see Kari 2010a:58.

PHOTO BY J. R. WILLIAMS, BUREAU OF INDIAN AFFAIRS

"Caribou and moose would be killed from time to time throughout the year, but were given particular attention in late summer and early fall. At this time bulls were fat and skins most suitable for clothing. Fish, however, formed the most important food item. By midwinter, shallow places in the lake would freeze to the bottom and fishing would no longer be profitable. By this time, also. the meat stores from the previous fall would be exhausted It was then necessary that extensive hunting of moose, bear, and beaver be carried out. It is not known whether this involved actual breaking up of the small community or whether it merely entailed groups of hunters fanning out over the countryside. Moose and caribou fences, in conjunction with snares and the surround, were used. This would continue until breakup, after which the hunters would go into the lakes and creek valleys."

§10.56 'Skosii'den *(Ahtna)* • 'Where We Peel Birch Sap'
lake at southwest end of Lake Louise
This name always brings a smile to Ahtna speakers. It refers to the peeling of birch trees for sap in springtime. Jack Tyone and Johnny Tyone were the most recent residents of this old fishing site.

Andy Tyone: "Good place for whitefish. Catch them

with fishtrap and with fence. Cover it up and one place open, put fish trap in there. They fish from first part of August until creek freeze up."

10.35 Xensdii *(Ahtna)* • 'The Next One Ahead'
mountain, elev. 3350', west of Susitna Lake
This is listed on the 1904 Moffit map (Map 45) as "Kunstee Country," with his comment "North of the Kunstee Country and east of the Sushitna is a rolling country."

‡10.62 Nen' Yese' • 'Land Ridge'
Nen' Yese' Ridge
An iconic and informative name for a ridge that was a shoreline or isthmus of Glacial Lake Ahtna 11,000 to 12,000 years ago. On Table 12 this is marked with ₪ to indicate a name that denotes environmental change. Also notable is a low north-south esker c. 3 miles to the east called **Nen' Yese' Ggaay** 'little land ridge,' so this pair of names mark two shorelines of Glacial Lake Ahtna.

‡10.63 Ben Daes Bene' *(Ahtna)* • 'Shallows Lake Lake'
Old Man Lake and village site. *See Map 56.*
A popular ancient Dene place name; cognate names include Mentasta Lake, Healy Lake, Cooper Lake, Fish Lake (near Tanana), and Tundra Lake (Lime Village); see p. 146.

‡10.64 Utnu *(Dena'ina),* **'Atna'** *(Ahtna)* • 'Beyond River'
Copper River
For years Kari treated the syllable **'at-** in 'Atna' as unanalyzable. But it is clear that **'at-** is from the directional root set **'ane'**, **'aat**, **'aax** 'beyond, over, outside.' The stream name **'Atna'** 'beyond (the Range)' is *overtly informative* (☼). The name was coined by the Tanana Valley Dene prior to earliest expansion of the Dene into Copper River Basin, perhaps over 11,000 years ago. Kari considers **'Atna'** to be the oldest Dene name on Table 12.

§10.49 Banazdleni *(Ahtna)* • 'The One That Current Flows Around'
mountain, elev. 4503', "Oshetna," at the "Big Bend" of the Susitna River
Annabel (1938:88–89) mentions killing a caribou here with a Talkeetna Indian man.

10.50 C'iidze' Na' *(Ahtna)* • "Fierce Stream'
McLaren River
C'iidze' is a rare Ahtna term applied to fiercely cold winds. This name is written on the Moffit map (Map 45) as "Ka–cha–nah."

10.51 Snuu Na' *(Ahtna)* • 'Brushy Stream'
lower Clearwater Creek

10.36 Hwniidi Ben *(Ahtna)* • 'Upriver Lake'
Butte Lake, formerly Nadiwen Lake
This lake appears on the 1839 Wrangell map as "Knitiben" (Map 17). It is to this lake that Wrangell says that the Galtsan [Tanana River Athabascans] "travel ten days over the mountains to the Lake Knitiben. The Kenai also travel to this lake to trade with the people of Titlogat [Toklat, 10.38, north of the Alaska Range]" (1980:52). Before 1951 this lake was known as Nadiwen Lake, a name based upon the Ahtna place name. The historic association of the place is now erased by the English name, Butte Lake.

The following additional information on **Hwniidi Ben** was obtained by Kari from Jake Tansy in 1983. A rack at the site at the head of the lake was still visible when Jake first came to this lake in about 1910. Jake's mother remarked that the lake used to be a **Ghaltsaane** (or Lower Tanana) camp. Jake heard that the **Ghaltsaane** carried the poles to Butte Lake on their shoulders from the timber on the upper Nenana River. Jake thinks that the nearest **Gheltsaane** location with timber was the whitefish camp known as **Ghaltsaane Ciisi K'ae** 'Lower Tanana dipnet place' on the Nenana River near Monahan Flat.

The account by Wrangell from the early 1830s, combined with Jake Tansy's information, suggest that in the early nineteenth century the entire Nenana River was Lower Tanana territory. The Ahtna based in the

FIGURE 141

Hwniidi Ben (10.36, Butte Lake) in 1981. Jake Tansy has recorded detailed information about Ahtna life and land use here.
PHOTO BY PRISCILLA RUSSELL

FIGURE 142

Cabins at the village of Cantwell in 1930. The man in the foreground is young Henry Peters, then age 18. Photo by Stephan R. Capps, Jr.
STEPHAN R. CAPPS, JR. COLLECTION (#83-149-2891), ARCHIVES, ALASKA AND POLAR REGIONS DEPT., RASMUSON LIBRARY, UNIVERSITY OF ALASKA FAIRBANKS

FIGURE 143

Henry Peters (1912–1999) of Valdez Creek and Cantwell was a major contributor to Ahtna language and traditions. He and his mother Jenny Peters told the story of the war at **Nay'nadełi** (Peters 1977). Henry also discussed details about life at Valdez Creek in Dessauer and Harvey (1980).

PHOTO BY JAMES KARI IN 1981

FIGURE 144

Hester Evan of Nenana was born at Toklat village in January of 1906 and died in February of 2002. A master storyteller, she has been the major contributor for the Toklat dialect, a Koyukonized variant of the Lower Tanana language (see Jetté and Jones 2000).

PHOTO BY JAMES KARI IN 1993

Tyone Lake area were pressed to increase their hunting territories. This created tension over places such as Butte Lake, and a caribou fence down the Nenana River at **Hwditsicghi'aaden**. A skirmish at **Nay'nadełi,** a hill west of Butte Lake, in about 1865 (described in Peters 1977), resulted in several deaths and forced the Nenana River Athabascans to retreat downriver. Shem Pete was not familiar with the details of these territorial shifts in this area.

‡The multi-component site Butte Lake Northeast was first described by Bob Betts (1987) and recently by Michael Wendt (2013). Four components (Northern Archaic to Ahtna) date from 10,000 BP until historic times and prompt discussions of site use, technology and climate change. Jake Tansy was Bob Betts' source for information on Ahtna use of the area.

10.37 Qunk'eltl'asht *(Dena'ina);* **Kanc'eltl'aesde** *(Ahtna)* • 'Where the Game (Caribou) Migrate Through'
‡sites on Lake Creek, 1 mile west of Swampbuggy Lake, locally called "Swampbuggy Lake"
The north-most features on the 1904 Moffit map (Map 45) are in this area. This important Western Ahtna hunting location is described in Reckord (1983:177–178). Archaeologists have called this place the "Ratekin site" after a Bureau of Land Management employee. This site was incorrectly located at Swampbuggy Lake in Kari (1983) and in Reckord (1983). Apparently this lake along Lake Creek has receded. "The upper Susitna Indians report that this site has probably been used by their ancestors for generations" (Reckord 1983:177). Henry Peters described this as being the caribou hunting site most valued by the Ahtna. The Nenana River people were approaching here when the battle took place at **Nay'nadełi** in about 1865 (Peters 1977). This site is described by Jake Tansy as his uncle Peter Secondchief's camp in the early 1900s. It is both a whitefish camp and as a major caribou harvesting area

‡Jake Tansy (Kari 2014): "«Right now at **Kanc'elts'esde** they do not migrate, but the caribou always used to migrate back there. That is why it is called 'where something (caribou herd) moves up'. Above there is a mountain extending out there they named **K'a' K'ae** 'arrow cavity' (hunting blind) (mountain "Gate" & ledges, & benches). Above on the mountain is there is a series of rocks in a circle [a rock blind]; they stay inside there (waiting) for them (caribou).»"

Shem Pete: "That is the farthest village I know on the Susitna River. It was about four or five days above Talkeetna. **Sghay Tu'** was the last man from **Qunk'eltl'asht**. He died in 1917. I know his song.

Qunk'eltl'asht means where the caribou go in springtime. They stay there waiting at **Qunk'eltl'asht.**" Shem Pete said that this was the northern extent of the travels of the nomadic Mountain People. He speculated that they had moved down the Susitna River into the Talkeetna area in the mid-nineteenth century. ‡Also see Kari 2010a:62.

§10.52 C'ilaan Na' *(Ahtna)* • 'Things Are Abundant-Stream'
Valdez Creek and village site
The modern town at Valdez Creek began in 1903. Prior to this time **C'ilaan Na'** was an important area for caribou and whitefish to the Western Ahtna. Moffit (1915:20): "Before the discovery of gold on Valdez Creek the upper Susitna natives depended on the country for most of their food and clothing. Valdez Creek was a favorite hunting ground; in fact, the native name for Valdez Creek (Galena) signifies a river where game abounds" (Moffit 1915:20).

Reckord (1983:171–177) summarizes Valdez Creek history. Dessauer and Harvey 1980 has a detailed account of Ahtna involvement in the early mining here.

10.53 Łuyinanest'aani Na' *(Ahtna)* • 'One That Extends into Glaciers - Stream'
upper Nenana River (above Brushkana River mouth)
Named for the ridge between the heads of the Nenana River and the West Fork of the Susitna River, and south of Nenana Glacier.

10.54 Ninena', Ninaena', Ninaes Na', Ninaenena' *(Ahtna)*, **Ninayh No'** *(Lower Tanana)* • 'Stop While Moving Nomadically - River'
Nenana River, Nenana River, below Brushkana River, formerly called Cantwell River
This name is not commonly used by the Western Ahtna. The Nenana River above Brushkana River is called **Łuyinanest'aani Na'**.

Yanert descended the Nenana River to the mouth of Yanert Fork in 1899 and then turned back south, having been deserted by his guide named Bate who was a "Skitig" Indian (possibly a Dena'ina from **Shk'ituk'** village at Kenai). Yanert (1900: 678–79) notes, "Upon reaching the tributary of the Tanana, the guide informed me that he was not acquainted with the trail from here on and gave me to understand that he made the trips only during the winter on snowshoes. The Indian intimated to me that the Tanana could be reached in three and a half days from where this river was struck.... As concerns the Indian's refusal to remain in service as a guide, I feel certain that his unwillingness to do so was prompted by fear of the Tanana Indians who he frequently assured me were numerous and bad."

Moffit (1915:20) makes this statement concerning the hunting areas used by the Ahtna who were then based at **C'ilaan Na'** (10.52, Valdez Creek): "The Indians of the upper Susitna spend a large part of the year hunting on the Jack River and on the Yanert Fork of the Nenana River. These two localities are considered the choice hunting grounds of the regions, and the Yanert Fork is the better of the two."

10.55 Yidateni Na' *(Ahtna)*; **Beyada' Tene No'** *(Lower Tanana)* • reanalyzed from 'Jaw Trail - Creek'
Jack River; Cantwell village
The name is in a set of names that includes Reindeer Hill, **Yidateni.** In Ahtna this name is often associated with the verb 'to be cold,' e.g., as 'cold inside (an area).' However, the Ahtna name is actually reanalyzed from the Lower Tanana name **Beyada' Tene** 'jaw trail' as reported by Hester Evan, Celia Peterson and others from Nenana. The meaning 'jaw trail' is novel to Cantwell speakers.

Eldridge reached the Jack River in August of 1898 and marked a house here on his map. See Map 39. (1900:27).

On Cantwell village de Laguna (1970:40) states, "The settlement was started only about 1916, by Indians (mostly half-blood) from Valdez Creek when the mine there closed. They were originally from Copper River, and still maintain connections with relatives there."

10.38 Titl'u Kaq' *(Dena'ina)*; **Tutl'o Chaget** *(Lower Tanana)*; **Tutl'aa Caek'e** *(Ahtna)* • 'Headwaters Mouth'
Toklat village site
Wrangell (1980:52): "The Galtsan village north of the Kenai is Titlogat." This is the northernmost place on the 1839 Wrangell map (#4 on Map 17). It is significant that this name appears on the map in its Cook Inlet Dena'ina pronunciation, indicating that this information was supplied by a Dena'ina speaker, probably a middleman in trade with both the Ahtna and the Athabascans north of the Alaska Range. Shem Pete did not know this name.

Hester Evan reported that three sisters of the Mountain People, including **Ts'enkut** (Lower Tanana for **Ch'anqet'**) visited Toklat when her mother was young, perhaps in the 1880s. This is the farthest north mention of travel by Dena'ina in the latenineteenth century. Hester also noted that several of her relatives of her grandparents' generation, such as Old Esau, named **Degge' Yenooł'o',** were men or women who came over from the Susitna River to get married in the Toklat River/ Kantishna River area.

‡Lower Tanana place names have been consolidated and mapped in Kari (2012). Hester Evan, Matthew Titus, and Al John were the main sources for names on the Nenana River. The center of the LT place names network is the Tolovana River.

‡Recent Advances in Ethnogeographic Research Methods

by James Kari

Ahtna place names have been maintained in the same drainage-based lists since the 1980s. New versions of Ahtna place names were published in Kari (2008 and 2013). During 2012–2014 an "ethnogeography phase" was included as part of the sponsored research for the Susitna Hydroelectric Project. From 2008 to 2015 the Ahtna place name inventory increased 8.7 percent (from 2208 to 2515 records) as we added names on audio recordings and as

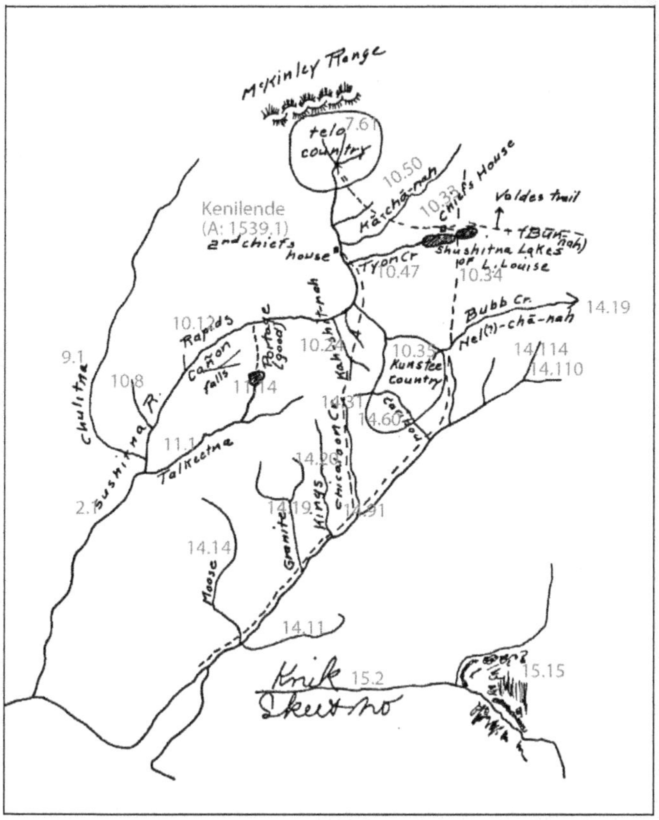

‡MAP 44

1904 Moffit sketch map with feature numbers from *SPA*.

Geologist Fred W. Moffit and an unnamed Ahtna speaker collaborated on this sketch map in Moffit's 1904 field notebook. Moffit labeled the map with 25 place names in English, Ahtna or Dena'ina. In probably 15 or 20 minutes an Ahtna expert from the Tyone Village area sketched out over 300 miles of drainages and intersecting trail routes. (See the 2003:231–32 edition for further details.)

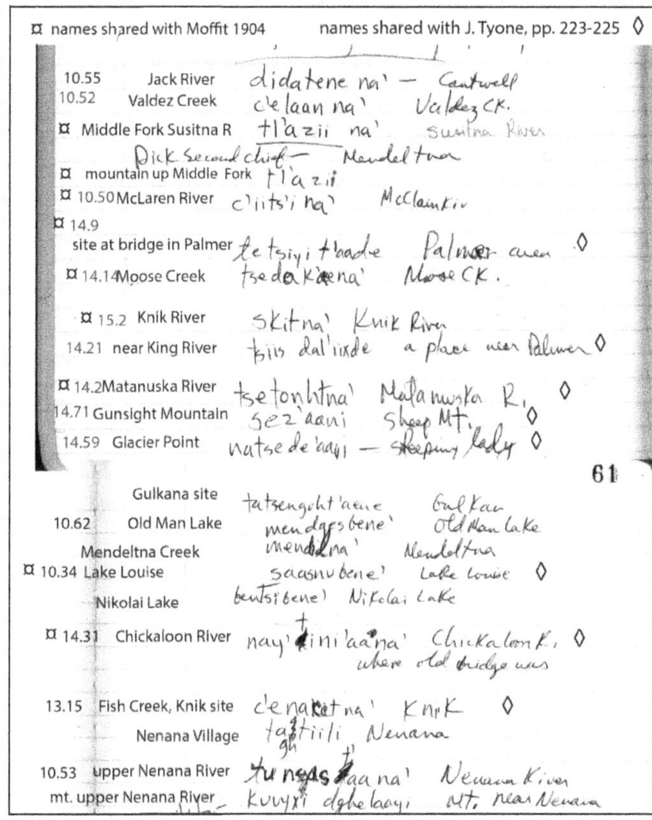

FIG144A

Kari's notes with Dick Secondchief, March 5, 1975, with feature numbers from *SPA* and compared with J. Tyone text.

On March 5, 1975, Dick Secondchief of Tyone Lake gave this list of place names in a brief encounter with Kari in Copper Center. Secondchief mentioned 22 names that extend from the east near Gulkana; to the north at Nenana Village, and to the south, a name for Knik River. (If plotted as a triangle, this is an area about 300 miles on the west, 180 miles north-to-east, and 200 miles south-to east). The symbol ¤ marks nine features shared between Secondchief's list and the Moffit map; marked with ◊ are eight features shared with the Jim Tyone text (p. 223–25). Such repeated confirmations (Moffit-Secondchief-Tyone) are the hallmark of the shared Dene geographic names and evidence for the antiquity of the rule-driven Dene names. We can generate maps and tables to display these place name arrays.

we reviewed and mapped lists with Ahtna experts. The two most important features of the recent Ahtna geography research are a) the use of database formats with ARC-GIS mapping, and b) the incorporation of place-intensive narratives—audio recordings by Ahtna experts who know the geography well (Kari 2010b and 2014).

The database format promotes editorial consistency and expands cross-disciplinary research options. Some of the fields being used are: *Ftype* (feature type) for sorts on features lakes, landforms, villages, trails, etc. *Stype* (semantic type) for analysis of name meanings (hydrology, plant, event, technology, metaphor, etc.). A field *match* tracks traits of significance within Ahtna names or in neighboring Dene languages. (See pp. 144–147 or the *patterned duplications* noted at 10.12, 10.29, 10.57, 10.58, 10.60, 10.63, 14.70, and 14.71, and *geoduplicates,* discussed at 10.34.) An *array* field allows for comparisons of lists of place names on maps, field notes, audio segments, or texts (see Map 44 and caption). Also included with draft materials for the Susitna Hydro project are maps that combine displays of archaeological sites, with Ahtna place names and several types trail data. The Western Ahtna place names are very informative in the search for undiscovered archaeological sites.

A high priority for specialized language work on Alaska Dene languages should be careful and enhanced editing of *place-intensive narratives* by Dene experts who have had the linguistic and physical skills to travel and to describe the landscape spontaneously. One fine example, on pp. 223–226, is Jim Tyone's detailed 210-mile route from Tyone Lake to Knik.

For the 2012–14 Susitna Hydroelectric Project we gave special attention to two sets of *travel routes*—thirteen by Jake Tansy and nine by Jim Tyone. Jake Tansy's thirteen routes are all within the range of the Cantwell-Valdez Creek band. Jim Tyone's nine routes are centered at Tyone Village, Crosswind Lake, or Gulkana. In contrast to Jake, Jim's routes ranged beyond his local into neighboring band territories (Cantwell, Tangle Lakes) and his long trip to Knik.

Map 45 presents the Tansy and Tyone routes with two dashed line styles. At a larger map scale and with colored routes it is possible to track the Tansy and Tyone routes

text	route	area described	audio time	p.n./repeats (total)	distance	landmarks ǂ	riv dir//lscp descript
JAKE TANSY ROUTES							
A1.1	1	Banazdleni vista	0:48	7/1 (8)	161 km (100 mi)	2 ǂ	6//1
A1.2	2	Brushkana-Yanert Fork-Valdez Ck routes	3:02	24/13 (37)	201 km (127 mi)	5 ǂ	20//15
A1.3	3	Brushkana to mid Susitna	3:16	11/21 (32)	157 km (108 mi)	3 ǂ	23//10
A1.4	4	Watana R-Jay Ck loop	1:50	13/7 (20)	88 km (56 mi)	5 ǂ	10//12
A1.5	5	upper Susitna R-W Fork McLaren loop	0:46	12/1 (13)	134 km (84 mi)	4 ǂ	8//3
A2.1	6	Valdez Cr-Tyone L; mid Su-Stephan L	7:30	28/11 (39)	217 km (134 mi)	6 ǂ	41//26
A2.2	7	Valdez C-mid Su R loops	7:06	27/20 (47)	237 km (147 mi)	4 ǂ	27//24
A2.3	8	Cantwell area loops	12:25	38/27 (65)	204 km (127 mi)	10 ǂ	52//26
A3.1	9	Carlo Ck-Yanert Fork	2:15	8/3 (11)	53 km (33 mi)	2 ǂ	14//12
A3.1	10	Cantwell-Tsusena Ck	0:46	5/1 (6)	71 km (44 mi)	0	0//1
A3.1	11	Wells Ck - Yanert Fork	3:21	12/9 (21)	65 km (40 mi)	7 ǂ	21//26
A3.1	12	Upper Nenana R loops	4:19	18/17 (35)	121 km (75 mi)	8 ǂ	28//17
A3.1	13	Caribou Pass-Tsusena Ck	0:55	7/2 (9)	65 km (40 mi)	2 ǂ	1//3
subtotals	13		48:21	210 (343)	1742 km (1115 mi)	59 ǂ	251//126
JIM TYONE ROUTES							
A4.1	1	Tyone Lake to Knik	9:53	36/19 (55)	334 km (208 mi)	5 ǂ	45//37
A4.2	2	mid and upper-Susitna R trails	5:35	18/10 (28)	78 km (109 mi)	5 ǂ	25//7
A4.3	3	Tyone Lake to Tangle Lakes and Valdez Creek	3:50	19/8 (27)	185 km (115 mi)	4 ǂ	15//9
A4.4	4	Tyone Lake to Gulkana, summer trail	3:34	13/2 (15)	159 km (99 mi)	5 ǂ	7//5
A4.5	5	Tyone Lake to Gulkana, winter trail	2:36	10/3 (13)	124 km (77 mi)	4 ǂ	16//7
A5.1	6	Tyone Lake west to Talkeetna Mountains	7:00	17/17 (34)	184 km (114 mi)	3 ǂ	8//13
A5.2	7	Hogan Hill Vista	0:57	8/2 (9)	68 km (42 mi)	5 ǂ	8//3
A6.2	8	Bear Creek Trail	3:15	20/8 (28)	66 km (41 mi)		11//10
A7	9	Hwnax Ggaay to upper West Fork	1:10	10/1 (11)	21 km (13 mi)	1 ǂ	2//5
subtotals	9		37:28	151(207)	1219 km (818 mi)	34 ǂ	178//132

ǂTABLE 15

Summary of thirteen routes by Jake Tansy and nine by Jim Tyone.

KARI 2014

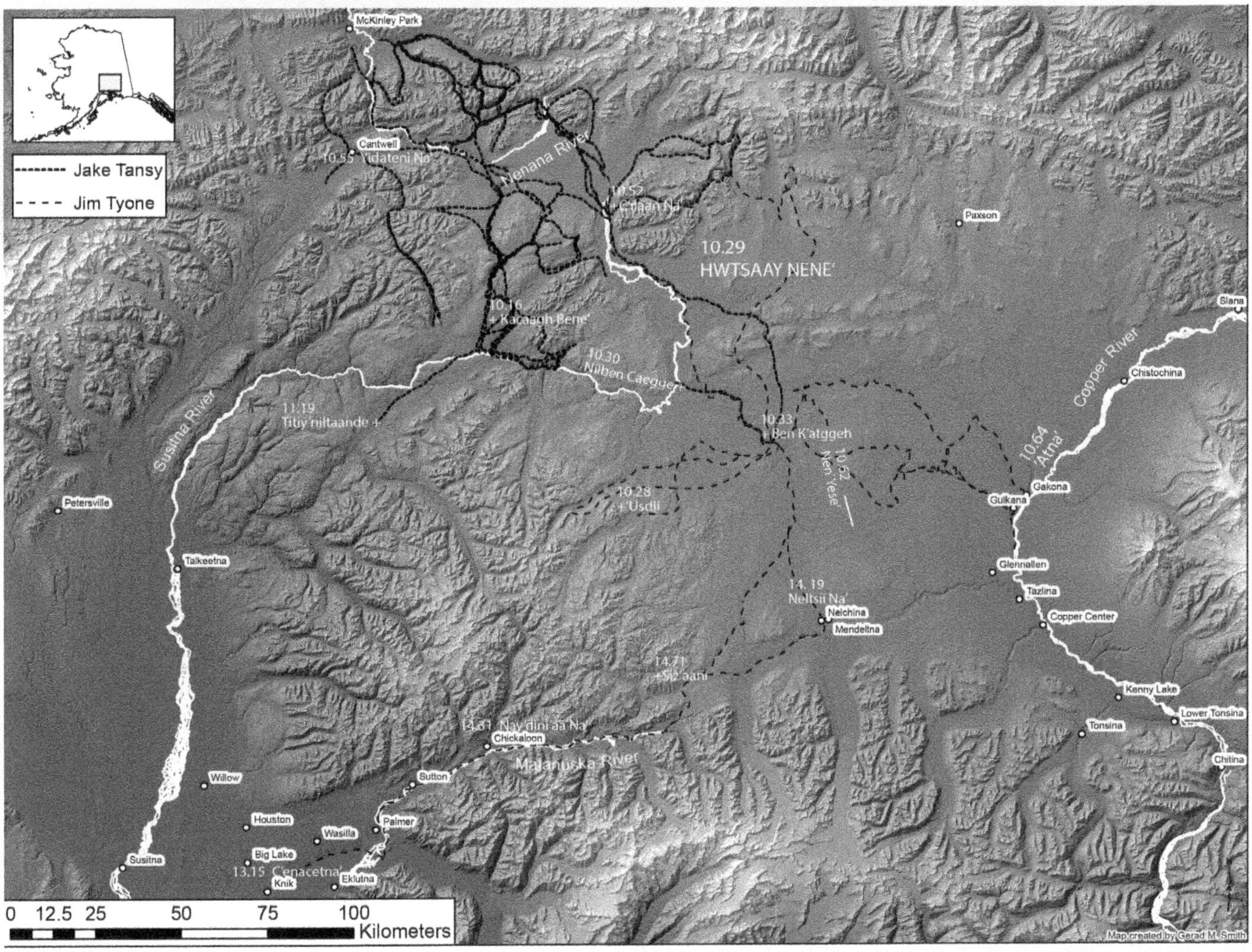

ǂMAP 45

Comparison of two sets of travel routes: thirteen by Jake Tansy and nine by Jim Tyone.

KARI 2014; MAP BY GERAD M. SMITH

rather closely. Jake Tansy, in 48 minutes of speech, summarizes 1115 miles on his 13 routes and mentions 210 places 343 times. Jim Tyone, in over 37 minutes, summarizes 818 miles on his nine routes and mentions 151 places 207 times. Table 15 presents the locations for these routes. In Kari (2014) we experimented with four mark-up features (see below).

From Kari (2014): "Tansy and Tyone have constant awareness of the flow of water. In blue highlight color we marked their use of riverine directional words. When Jake or Jim uses two and three directionals in one sentence, we try to translate each one. The red highlight color marks are Tansy and Tyone's use of landscape descriptors. They often makes note of various land features (a ledge, a mountainside, eskers, gorges, trails, mineral licks, vegetation). These areas typically do *not* have place names. Also we find it useful to mark salient landmarks ǂ that they mention. These tend to be off the trail and are being kept in sight as Jake or Jim determines junctions with streams and alternate trails. When Jake or Jim mentions man-made structures (camps, cache, weir, rock blind, tent frame) these features usually do not have distinct place names."

On a worldwide basis (with ground rules for valid comparisons!), Jake Tansy's thirteen routes certainly can be considered to be among the most precisely detailed travel narratives that have been edited and mapped with some accuracy. Furthermore, the confidence, precision, and facility of Jake Tansy's knowledge is evident in his voice, as he uses place names plus the riverine directionals, and in his reconfirmations and successive refinements to the landscape. The text marking conventions and the GIS route maps give us a sense of Tansy's expertise. The audio files and time-markings provide access to and authentication of these highly elite Ahtna travel narratives. In the future, perhaps with text-audio-geographic visualization, we can more fully convey the Jake's cognition of his band territory.

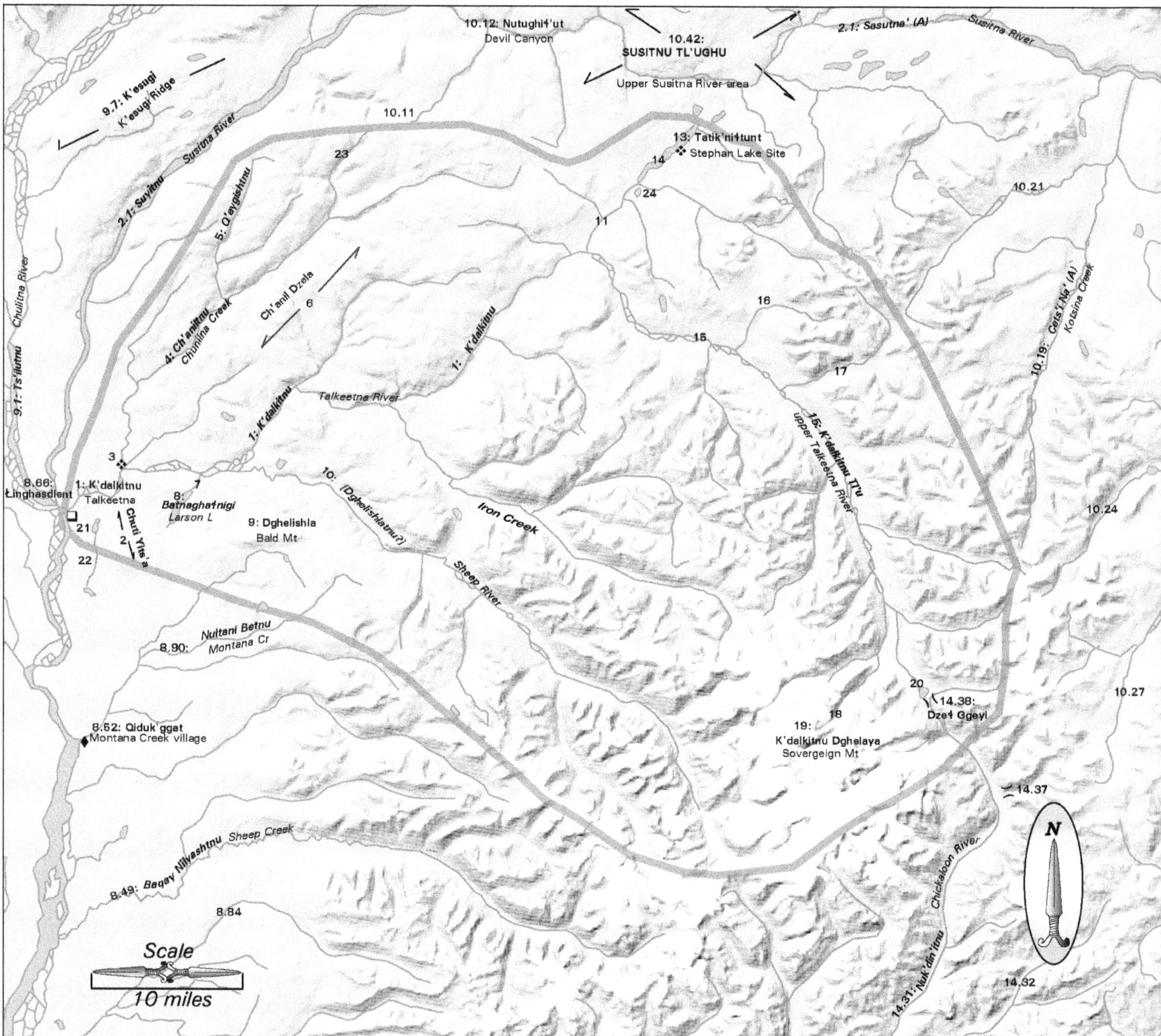

MAP 46

Place names map of the Talkeetna River, showing Nos. 11.1 to 11.24.

MAP BY MATT GANLEY

11 Talkeetna River

Kari (1977a:278): "The Mountain People are said to be an Ahtna band that had no permanent village and who migrated into the Talkeetna River drainage from the upper Susitna River perhaps 150 years ago.... The Tanaina [who are] descended from this group say that their ancestors used to fish on the Talkeetna River at Chunilna Creek, as far up the Talkeetna River as Stephan Lake, and on the Susitna River in the vicinity of Sunshine and Montana creeks, and they hunted caribou in the mountain country along the lower Talkeetna River and on the Chulitna River at least as far north as Indian River." Shem Pete and Katherine Nicolie made extensive commentary on the people, language, and land use of the Mountain People. A century ago this band was speaking both the Dena'ina and Ahtna languages. The first published source on the Mountain People was Kari (1977a). See also Sheldon (1995:1–4).

Shem Pete was of the opinion that the nomadic Mountain People used to be centered at the head of the Susitna River at **Qunk'eltl'asht** (10.37) and that they moved into the Talkeetna River region in the mid-nineteenth century.

De Laguna and McClellan (1981:654) have noted that the Mountain People are treated by the Ahtna as a small clan within the Raven moiety. There are several versions of a Mountain People origin story which involve the migration of a group of **Tulchina** water clan people from Cook Inlet to the Talkeetna Mountains.

According to Mentasta Pete (via deLaguna, personal communication), "Most of the **Taltsiine** [**Tulchina** clan] came straight to the Copper River Valley, but some went north, up the Chickaloon [River] and over the Talkeetna Mountains. Those are the ones we call **Dghelaay Tahwt'aene**."

11.1 K'dalkitnu *(Dena'ina);* **I'delcuut Na'** *(Ahtna)* • 'He Is Keeping Something (Food) Stored for Himself-River'
Talkeetna River; Talkeetna townsite
The name "Talkeetna" is from the verb theme **O+ł+kit** 'to keep object (food).' The specific verb form is **k'dalkit**, which has a literal meaning "s/he is keeping something (food) stored for himself" (third person benefactive in the stative-neuter aspect). Orth (1971:945) reported a figurative translation: "Tanaina Indian name reported in 1898 to mean 'river of plenty' by G. H. Eldridge and Robert Muldrow." Shem Pete: "**K'dalkitnu**, they got just like a cache there, that's what the name means."

The 1839 Wrangell map (Map 17) shows a dot for a village near the present town of Talkeetna, north of the mouth of the stream flowing from "Tatikniltunbena" (Stephan Lake, 11.14).

The modern town of Talkeetna had been the home of many of the last members of the Mountain People band. See the conclusion of the story of the woman named **Ch'anqet'**, p. 253, for the names of her six sons.

The chief of the Talkeetna Dena'ina from about 1908 to 1918 was Talkeetna Nicholie, **Ch'k'idetnishen**, or **Dech' k'idetnishen** 'The One Who Acquires Things for Himself,' the second oldest son of **Ch'anqet'** and Katherine Nicolie's father. Most of the place names Shem Pete knew above Talkeetna were told to him by Talkeetna Nicholie. See Figs. 145 and 146.

The 1910 census lists sixteen persons for the community of Talkeetna, nine of whom are Native. In 1910 Talkeetna Nicholie's family is listed as: Chief Nicholi, age 50; his wife Christina, age 26; daughters Alexan age 4 and Mytrona, age10; and "lodger" Olexia (?) age 46, possibly the chief's older wife. In the 1920 census 69 per-

Sources: Shem Pete, Johnny Shaginoff, Katherine Nicolie, Pete Stephan, Jack Tyone, Jake Tansy, and Charlie Hubbard

2003 revisions: names added 11.21–11.24.
‡2016 revisions: figures replaced 134a, 151, 154; figure added 151A; map revised 47.

FIGURES 145, 146

These two remarkable photos of Talkeetna people were taken by Ward Hall of the Alaska Railroad Commission in the summer of 1916. The pictures were taken on different days at Chief Talkeetna Nicholie's home. Fig. 145 has fourteen people. It appears to have been taken a few days prior to Fig. 146, with twelve people and three dogs on the roof of the chief's house. This photo actually was taken to document Talkeetna Nicholie's claim that his house was on the railroad easement.

Katherine Nicholie's comments on Fig. 146, Lillian Theodore's comments on Fig. 145, and a comparison of the photos with the 1910 and 1920 census records for Talkeetna allow us to make a number of identifications. It appears that all twelve people in Fig. 146 are in Fig. 145; ‡also cf. Fig. 151, p. 245.

One and a half-year old Katherine Nicolie is probably the child being held by her mother, Christine (**Nidinłna**) in both photos. The woman in the center of the group in Fig. 146, wearing a white blouse and checkered skirt, is Katherine's older sister Mytrona or **Ts'itaya**, and seems to be the woman at the far right in Fig. 145. The tall man in Fig. 145 remains unidentified, and he does not appear in Fig. 146.

Katherine Nicolie said that the house in Fig. 146 was the second house her father had built at Talkeetna. Seager-Boss (1996:34) has further information on the locations and status of the sites of the Indian cabins in Talkeetna.

FIGURE 145: PHOTO BY WARD HALL OF THE ALASKA RAILROAD COMMISSION, COURTESY OF BARBARA LANGLOIS AND ROBERTA SHELDON

FIGURE 146, 146A: ‡PHOTO BY SYDNEY LAURENCE, FROM THE NATIONAL ARCHIVES (126-AR-72A)

FIGURE 146A

Chief Talkeetna Nicholie's home in the summer of 1916. The people standing on the roof are shown in more detail in Fig. 146.

sons are listed for Talkeetna, eleven of whom are Native. In 1920 no names appear for anyone from Talkeetna Nicholie's family. His widow Christine must have then been living at Kroto Creek where she had remarried to **Chijuk.** Kroto village seems not to have been surveyed for the 1920 census.

Sheldon (1995:16–17), citing Ward Hall of the Alaska Engineering Commission in 1916: "At Talkeetna a small group of Indians had established a settlement. Nicholi was their chief. Nicholi had come from ... about 50 miles down the Susitna River.... He paddled up the river with his two wives, the old [woman] and Christine, and several children. One other family had accompanied him.

"The Indians provided most of their living by hunting and fishing. During the salmon run, they trapped enough salmon to last them and their dogs all winter. The salmon was smoked and dried and stored like cord-wood in the cabin. In the fall Indians made a trip to the area where the caribou are likely to run to get a supply of meat and hides. It was an interesting sight to see them on their way to the hunting grounds. Nicolie was in the lead carrying a rifle, next the old (woman) with a big pack. The other women and children had packs commensurate with their size. Even the dogs had packs." This was a poor fall for hunting [in 1916], and the Indians returned with little meat and few hides.

"Talkeetna Indians lived in a log cabin immediately south of the Talkeetna Warehouse. For the Commission to better prosecute its work, it was necessary to move the Indians to a new location. To their satisfaction and approval a plot of ground consisting of one acre was cleared, one-half mile south of Talkeetna. Upon this plot a substantial cabin was built, having the same dimensions as the old one. The Indians are now living comfortably in the new location."

Talkeetna Nicholie was described by Browne in 1910 (1956:179): "I had many an interesting talk with old Talkeetna Nicolae, chief of the Talkeetnas. Sitting cross-legged on the floor of his cabin with the smell of tanning moose-hide in my nostrils, I listened to weird stories of the olden days, and it was there that he told me of the Russian trader—possibly one of Malakoff's men—who died in the Kichatna swamps. Later he posed proudly before my camera, his chest liberally decorated with watches—that had long since ceased to work."

Johnny Shaginoff: "**Ts'ec'udetniisen** [Talkeetna Nicholie] and his mother were the real Mountain People. They go mostly from **Titiy'niłtaan Bene'** [11.14 Stephan Lake] over to Cantwell, like around Windy. They call them **dghelaay tahwt'aene**. Their main locations were any where from Talkeetna to let's say around the Alaska Range. That not really too far you know."

Sheldon (1995:3) reproduced a 1948 romantic poem by Will Johnson, "The Saga of Christine," which is about Christine, Talkeetna Nicholie's wife. See also Figs. 145 and 146.

Recalling other Mountain People, Shem Pete noted that Talkeetna Alec's name was **Htenususełen** 'The One That Reminds Me.' Katherine Nicolie referred to him as Chada 'Grandpa.' His son, Pete Alec, was **Basihdi'ushen**. Shem also noted that Christine's mother was from Talkeetna and was called **Ch'anst'a Gga** 'little old lady.'

Katherine Nicolie remembered the following women of her mother's generation who were Mountain People and had lived in Talkeetna: A) **Du'inałna** married Bill Larson's father before 1910. She died in 1928. She was Katherine Nicolie's father's niece. B) **Hna'estał**, the grandmother of the Standifer family of Tyonek who died in Kenai. C) **Dutnałna**, Elmer Hedberg's mother, who died in 1939. D) **Nuhnałchek'a**, Pete Alec's mother, who died in 1942. The latter three were sisters and were of the **Nulchina** clan.

Shem Pete was in Talkeetna in 1917 working on the Alaska Railroad. He did some interpreting between the local Indians and the railroad officials. Shem and Anderson Stephan got married in Talkeetna in 1920 in a double wedding.

Sava Stephan: "I went all the way up to Talkeetna on Susitna River in dory, with a motor on that. First time, I was fourteen, fifteen years old [in 1934]. I went from Susitna Station to Kroto and then from Kroto. Joe Nicolie and Alec Nicolie came with us. They had their sister up there [at Montana Creek]. Basili's wife, Katherine Nicolie's oldest sister, at Montana Station. Then they walked me up there to Talkeetna. Took us about two hours, on the track.... My auntie Annie Dahl was at Talkeetna. I don't remember her Indian name.

"Nagley had a store there, and Mrs. Lee had a store and a hotel and restaurant. Only one Dena'ina family at that time. His name was Alec. He killed his own brother and father. I would say I was about 11 years old [in 1931] when that happened. My dad went to funeral [at Montana Creek] and I went with him.... [A]t funeral, went up in canoe to Montana, people came down from mountains when he got shot, with a moose skin boat and with meat. They had dinner and sang. **Łału** was the name of that man. The old lady of the guy that got killed was at **Ch'aniltnu** (11.4).

"I went as far as Talkeetna on that Iditarod Trail [*sic*] with my three dogs. By myself with my dad. We come up to Talkeetna. We run out of groceries. Come up there. I had one sled. Yukon sled, gee pole on it. Twelve horses meet me. All on the harness. Draggin a sled, big sled, dragging it just like a little coaster. Then going on road there and we were off the road away from the horse. I didn't want my dogs to bother them. I keep them quiet. And someone killed moose on road and covered it up. Horse seen that, stacked up meat. And they got wild. They got crazy and tore up all their harness. Finally that guy there got a hold of it, chain him down. Me, I keep a going to Talkeetna. I stayed there about three days. My aunties was there, two of them, Mary Ephim and Annie Ephim. She got married in Talkeetna and that name of it was Dahl. Mike Dahl, her name was Annie Dahl. He give me a house. 'You can have that house.' By golly I was in there I don't know long, every year I comes over there I got my own house. Now he's gone and that house is gone too."

In 1980 the Cooperative Park Studies Unit crew concluded that the Dena'ina cemetery in Talkeetna townsite near the end of the airstrip had probably eroded away in the 1940s (Cooperative Park Studies Unit 1980).

11.2 Chuti Yits'a • 'Beaver Stream Ridge'
§Bartlett Hills east of Talkeetna Lakes
Shem Pete: "«**Chuti Yits'a** is below Talkeetna village about a mile and extends off from **Dghelishla** [Bald Mountain, 11.9].»"

Note that the names 11.2, 11.21, and 11.22 drain into the Susitna River and could have been placed in Chapter 8.

§11.21 Chuti Yits'a Bena • 'Beaver Water Ridge Lake'
Talkeetna Lakes

§11.22 Chuti Yits'a Betnu • 'Beaver Water Ridge Stream'
stream through Talkeetna Lakes

11.3 Ch'anilkaq' • 'Mouth of Flows Out'
mouth of Chunilna Creek
This is the main base camp of **Ch'anqet'** of the Mountain People. Shem Pete: "«That **Ch'anqet'** and her sons made a fish fence at **Ch'aniltnu**.» They put up dog fish for winter with all her six kids. That creek they put a fish trap across. That's the way they used to catch fish. They got no net, nothing them days. That old lady was there. There were six of them in her family.

"«They catch fish and they built a big smokehouse. They stayed there in the summer. She had lots of dogs. And from here the mother would backpack up into the mountains. Seven or eight dogs would pack grub up into the mountains. They would kill caribou. They would bring the meat back down to **Ch'aten Kaq'**» [mouth of Birch Creek, Fish Lake outlet stream, 8.62]. According to Shem, king, red, and silver salmon were caught in a fish trap in this creek. The fish "were still a little greasy yet." Lots of salmon were dried for winter here.

FIGURE 147
K'dalkitnu, (11.1, Talkeetna River) above Disappointment Creek and below Yellowjacket Creek.
PHOTO COURTESY OF COOK INLET REGION, INC.

Bagg (1900:683): "This spot is a favorite rendevous for Indians in the hunting season. A well constructed cache and many old frames for stretching skins were seen."

While camped here with some of the Mountain People in 1898, Learnard (1900:667) noted, "The Indians drew several maps of the country and said that it would take fifteen days to go [to the Tanana River] and about twelve to return, as on the return trip a raft could be made and used at the crossing of the Sushitna." Learnard concluded that this trail was on the Delta River. An Ahtna, Adam Sanford, described this trail through Isabel Pass in Kari (2010b:91–128).

‡In the past ten years the Mat-Su Borough has sponsored archaeological survey work at Ch'anqet's village **Ch'anilkaq'**. B. Wygal and K. Krasinski (p.c.): "We documented 67 surface features including caches and a single bear deadfall pit as described by Osgood (1937:96–98). Test excavations yielded hearth smears and a small collection of salmonid vertebrae submitted for AMS dating (Beta- 331339). A detailed analysis by the lab indicated the samples possessed 100 percent modern carbon (100.4 +/-0.3 pMC) or a potential age of 56 years ago which may indicate that [Ahtna/Dena'ina] people were using the site much later than expected. Charred material from a potential house feature produced an earlier age of 400 + 60 cal BP (340+40 BP, Beta-10001)."

11.4 Ch'aniltnu *(Dena'ina);* **Ts'anilna'** *(Ahtna)* • 'Creek That Flows Out'
Chunilna Creek, "Clear Creek"
In 1898 Learnard, calling this creek Chinaldna, said, "This stream marked the beginning of the old Indian trail across the mountains to the upper waters of the Talkeetna" (Learnard 1900:656).

In 1898 Yanert (1900:678) noted "Under the guidance of the Indian Bate... proceeded in a NW direction along the left bank of the Chaniltna.... The ascent of the mountains crossed between this and the third fork of the Sushitna was laborious. The Indian trail leading to the pass was apparently chosen on account of directness rather than ease."

11.5 Q'eygishtnu • 'Willow Creek'
creek into Chunilna Creek from west, locally called "Boulder Creek"
Shem Pete: "«That creek flows out from that **Ch'ak'ul'ishi**» [10.11]."

Katherine Nicolie: "Old lady, Pete Alec's mom, used to talk about it. That's my mother's uncle's wife."

According to Johnny Shaginoff, a trail led up this

creek ("Boulder Creek") to Gold Creek, twelve or fourteen miles distant, then along the ridgeline northeast to Stephan Lake. Johnny did some prospecting on this creek. This is called "Fuller Creek" on the 1910a Sleem map (Map 38). See also 10.5.

11.6 Ch'anil Dzela *(Dena'ina);* **Ts'anil Dzele'** *(Ahtna)* • 'Mountain of Flows Out'
mountain "Curry" 3631' east of upper Chunilna Creek

§11.23 Dnelbu'i Betnu • 'The Grey One Stream'
stream into Chunilna Creek from "Chunilna" 3710' east of K'esugi
See also 10.4, **Dnelbu'i,** the mountain.

11.7 Batnaghałnigi Betnu • 'Creek of That Which Has a Body in It'
Larson Lake outlet

11.8 Batnaghałnigi • 'That Which Has a Body in It'
Larson Lake
Shem Pete: "«Towards the mountains there is a big lake.» It's on the map. «There is a monster in it. Billy's grandmother saw it. Two miles down on the lower end it sticks its head out. On the upper end it sticks its head out.» That's a big animal. At **Batnaghałnigi** a guy went out hunting. He kill caribou. Then he kill ptarmigan. They was starving. They cook that ptarmigan, might be half raw. He swallow the bone, and it kill him. So they find his body alongside the big caribou, his foot sticking out. They find him on end of that lake there. So they call em **Batnaghałnigi**. They cremated him right there."

Katherine Nicolie: "Mom and that old man used to cry for that lake, the one they call **Batnaghałnigi**. Some guy starved to death there. In the springtime he got lost.

FIGURE 148
Batnaghałnigi (11.8, Larson Lake) looking east from near **Batnaghałnigi Betnu** (11.7, Larson Creek).
PHOTO BY MARK STASIK

FIGURE 149
Dghelisha 'little mountain,' (11.9, Bald Mountain) as viewed looking east from Question Lake. One can speculate about duplication in Dena'ina in place names. Bald Mountain, 4.9 Mount Susitna, and 10.6, the mountain at the head of Gold Creek, have the same name, **Dghelisha.** Is this due to similarity in the geomorphology of these mountains? Or that they are navigational landmarks? Or that they are intervisible? Or that they are named to contrast with 'big mountain,' **Dghelay Ka'a** (7.51, Denali) and the high mountains of the Alaska Range?
PHOTO BY MARK STASIK

Ch'anqet' and the Mountain People

by Shem Pete

The best source of information on the Mountain People is Shem Pete's biography of the woman **Ch'anqet'**. Shem estimated that this woman from the Talkeetna Mountains was born between 1810 and 1820 and that she died in Tyonek in 1904. Her name means 'She pats her face,' moving the hands away from the face with both hands cupped, apparently a shamanistic gesture. Shem assembled this biography of **Ch'anqet'** from stories about her that were told to him by his mother. His telling of the story is highly dramatic and theatrical. Katherine Nicolie once commented that this story about her grandmother was so realistic, with its detailed descriptions and imitations of the speech of the Mountain People, that it was as if Shem had actually been there. "How can he do that? He wasn't there," she said.

The story was recorded by Jim Kari on January 31, 1977, in Willow. It was translated with Shem and Billy Pete and Katherine Nicolie in 1977. Sheldon (1995:1) has a synopsis of the story of Ch'anqet'.

One further lead about Ch'anqet' came in 2001 from 95-year old Hester Evan, an expert storyteller from Toklat and Nenana. Hester mentioned that there were three sisters from somewhere south of Cantwell who were known to have come to Toklat village on the Kantishna River (see 10.38). Hester's grandmother, Old Alice, and her mother, Eliza Esau John, recalled meeting them, perhaps in the 1880s or so. Two of the three sisters' names reported by Hester are cognate with names known by Shem Pete for these sisters. The name **Ya' Talno** was not mentioned by Shem Pete.

Dena'ina name from Shem Pete	Lower Tanana/Koyukon name from Hester Evan
Ch'anqet':	**Ts'enkut**
Tes Gun	**Huteɫjon'** (Ch'anqet's younger sister)
not known	**Ya' Talno** (a "Cantwell" woman)

Ighi shi Shem Pete eɫan shit'i.
Well, I am Shem Pete.

Ki tsukdu eɫ nuhtghelnek.
I will tell another story.

Shchikdakda k'ghila.
I had a dear grandmother.

Shik'a nch'uk'a shchikda gheli.
She wasn't my real grandmother.

Katherine Nicolie betukda'ina ghuna yina qubunkda.
She was Katherine Nicolie's father's mother.

Yin tsukda beɫ nuhtghelnek.
I'll tell her story.

Ch'anqet'.
Ch'anqet' (was her name).

T'ada ghila dghu ɫu K'entl'u Bena hyighiɫ'an.
When she was a young girl, they hunted at 'Cheek Lakes' (11.12 off Prairie Creek, exact location uncertain).

Quht'ana kisht'a gheli q'aniɫnalggeyna, ghuna ghenuy qeytl'u'iltlet.
The people would run very fast in a group, and they would chase down those caribou.

Yina shughu K'entl'u Bena, K'entl'u Bena nelan heɫ dghinih,
Well, at those 'Cheek Lakes,' at where they call it 'Cheek Lakes,'

yaqech' t'ghit'a.
this is how it was done.

Ghenuy ghini yeh ch'a'iltlet ch'u yetl'uyiyush.
A caribou would run out and she would follow it.

Bet'uy nuytejih "Yehay!" yeɫni.
She would run up to it, saying "Yehay!"

Niɫq'agh tets' nudutiɫ.
She carried a double-ended spear.

Yequk'teɫt'ih.
She stabbed it.

Q'u tsukdi k'isen eydlan.
She already was an old woman.

Bech'enaqa q'a'idaq di.
Her children were all grown.

Q'anshełdultishen dek'isen ghila.
She was a fast-running woman.

Ghenuy tsiyildił.
Those caribou would try to scare her away.

Yin k'ghidlih shlagga, "Ehehehey ghenay snatsich'ildił,
She would laugh, that little one, "Hey, the caribou try to scare me away,

nishich'dełteł ch'u yeden łdi' ben atughełyik,"
but I cause them to be winded and then I run them into the lake." [1]

u yeł dghinih łu.
That's what she used to say.

Ben yindi K'entl'u Bena ghila.
Those were those 'Cheek Lakes.'

Q'u qichi taydlan hdi,
Well, she started to become an old lady and,

bech'enaqa ghuna Ch'aniltnu nunutsahdnghichesh ch'u,
her children drove in stakes (for a fish fence) across 'Creek That Flows Out' (Chunilna Creek, 11.3, 11.4),

tay'in qeyetadghichet.
and they set a fish trap.

"Sh'eł tay'in qił'ish."
"Take care of the fish trap for me (she told them)."

Tay'in k'a qeyet'ehł'ish.
They would fix the fish trap.

Dghelay qubeł aghiyik.
Then she would go to the mountains with them (her dogs).

Belik'aqa dinult'a ch'u belik'aqa łighala.
She had lots of dogs and dog packs.

Łuht'enudiłtesh ch'u yada łuq'u qada qilan.
She filled the dog packs, with whatever food there was.

Łuq'u dghelay ahałhyełdeł.
They would pack everything to the mountains.

Yi ghini, łik'aqa ghini yaqahneyuh ch'u,
She would walk ahead of those ones, those dogs, and,

qeyetl'uh ghu qeyanik'et' t'et'ah.
they would follow her single file.

Ch'u dghelay dech'enaqa ghuna ahałk'qełdeł.
And her "kids" (the dogs) would pack (her things) to the mountains.

Yada shahal buga ghudehdi, idiłti ch'elqadi ghini dnighichek' ch'u,
Sugar, flour, and whatever, and food was cheap then, and,

chayu ghudehdi eł dghelay hegh hałk'ełdeł.
they packed tea, etc. to the mountains.

Belik'aqa ghini dghelay egh hałk'ełdeł.
Those dogs packed (that food) to the mountains.

Ch'u ki kiq'u shan qiydlan iłhdi
And then another summer came and

ghu Ch'aniltnu qinunutsahdnechesh
they put in a fish fence again at 'Creek That Flows Out' (Chunilna Creek, 11.3) and

tay'in ghin k'a qeyet'hyił'ish t'ehyiluq.
and they fixed that fish trap.

Ghun "Dghelaych' belik'aqa ghini nagh nuhtulyani," qeyełni.
They said, "Her dogs will bring back things to us from the mountains."

"Hey'! Ugheli," hełnih.
"Yes! Good," she told them.

"Shik'a dghelay nunghel'an din?" ni ch'u
"Should I see the mountains again?"

"Shik'a dghelay nunghel'anni!"
"Let me see the mountains again!"

Nayna k'uch'q'u qenahdulghuy.
They talked different from us.

Utnuht'anaq' qenahdulghuy ch'u.
They spoke Ahtna.

Ghu dghelay belik'aqa ghini ahałk'nildatl'.
Those dogs packed (her supplies) to the mountains.

Ch'u dghelay q'u ndahqugh k'a dghelay q'e heł ghidu'en din?
And how long would she stay up in the mountains with them?

1. In this section Shem imitated the speech of the Mountain People, who spoke a dialect of Ahtna. He placed primary stress on stem syllables, and he used some Ahtna vowel qualities.

FIGURE 150

Tatik'niłtun Bena (11.14, Stephan Lake) near its outlet with**Tatik'niłtuntnu** (11.11, Prairie Creek). In the distance can be seen the mountains of the Alaska Range above the Nenana River.
PHOTO BY MARK STASIK

Yech' ghenuy chihghił'ik.
They would kill some caribou.

Ghu dik'a k'tsen ghini yidałyeshi.
She would wind-dry that meat.

Yaghelisht'a łik'aqa denłdesi łuq'u hen'iłghal ch'u
She would bundle it up nicely in dog packs and

"Q'u shi łiq'a na'a k'iydlan shi," heyełni.
"Now the fish have come to us," she said (to the dogs).

Ch'u nutashju.
And she started back.

Yehqugh łik'aqa qeyetl'u ghu denłdesi k'tsen nuhałquldeł.
The dogs would pack that heavy meat, following her.

Yethdi yulqedi ghuda.
That was for food.

Henda q'u betl'uyeh ghu łidilghuy.
All of a sudden they started barking behind her.

Chinshla hdi t'eghel'u, tl'ił eł hdi deseydghelyu.
She had a stone axe tucked in her belt, and she had a rope tied around her waist.

Naqanak'dalt'eq' ch'u.
She tapped around (with her cane).

Yethdi yesbula k'ilan qenen t'uh ghu.
There was a cutbank there at the base of the hill.

Kisht'a qenq'a gheli hqugh t'ghit'a.
It was like a very big house.

Ht'uh ch'atahdinłnen.
Water came out from beneath there.

Ht'uh ch'aqichuh t'qit'a.
Rocks had slid down below.

Yaqech' shughu yesbula hełnih.
This is what they call ***yesbula*** *(large hollow in a cutbank).*

Yada yit'uh hech' ki hyicheghdelghesh ki.
They (the dogs) were yelping at something at that place.

Ghu gheyułkda gheli ch'u hegh qiqighaghichet.
She, that dear one, walked there and then crawled in.

Yethdi dech'enaqa ghuna łuq'u hdelghesh dusa yun'eh,
Then, while all her "kids" were yelping out there,

ghuhdi beq'e ch'etniyi nughejeh.
there were wolves walking around.

K'enagha gheli yan qilan.
Only their eyes were showing.

Tiqundi tiqundi nuhdghiluyi łughu qeyedelghesh heł q'enutashju ch'u,
A wolf, a wolf with pups, was howling and pacing back and forth and,

łik'aqa hdelghesh.
the dogs were yelping.

Quqighaghichet ch'q'u chinshla ghini,
She crawled up there, and that stone axe,

tiqundi ghini yech' deyeneł'eq' ch'u.
she waved it at those wolves.

"Shch'enaqa shegh dnayiłdu ch'q'u, nch'enaqa ghini łuq'u qubegh nitsak'tidagheses.
"If you hurt my kids, I'll club all your kids.

"Sch'enaqa shetni'iłduhi lagi!"
"Don't hurt my kids!" she said.

Łuq'u yech' qenash wolf ghini.
She talked to all of them, to those wolves.

Łik'aqa ghini yehghu henuqitghechet ch'u heteqat-sak'itniyuch'.
Then she protected the dogs there and she tied them up together.

Yethdi qunubes-huldatl'.
Then she dragged them back out by herself.

Łuq'u quhdghiłtuk'.
She pulled them all out.

Łik'aqa ghini dehałk'qułdeł heł nuneju.
Those dogs, all with packs on, followed her.

Ndahqugh k'a heł ninu'ijun din łik'aqa ghini.
She went back so far with those dogs!

Tl'ił ghini daq'nanheyggey ch'u qeyetl'uyeh ch'anadalggey,
She untied that rope and they followed behind her,

qeyetl'uyeh ch'anadalggey ch'u.
and they followed her.

Ghedghu Ch'aniltnu yet heł nu'iju.
They returned with her there to 'Creek That Flows Out' (11.4).

Yethdi łiq'a łiq'a q'ushla dahdi shla k'ahdi q'uyehdi ghi'an.
Then salmon, she then saw just a few salmon.

Yethdi tay'in ghini tunuydghichet ch'q'u
Then she put in a fish trap, and

belik'aqa ghu k'tsen nuhał'ildatl'i ghini k'tsen
the meat that the dogs had packed,

yutgge yudeh ghu dunuyiłdatl'.
she hung it up high.

K'qeyedulghashi yaghelisht'a chaqenq'a qeyeqiłchin,
And then they built a nice smokehouse for putting up fish,

dghu k'tsen ghu degge yanananiłchet.
and she hung up that meat.

Łik'aqa nułtu k'et'us, k'et'us, k'et'us ch'q'u.
For her dogs she cut (fish) and cut and cut.

Łik'aqa ghu nuyilyuyi ghindi yi ki yenghełggen.
The dogs brought it (fish) back, and she dried it in batches.

Dahqugh gheli heyi edałt'ayi hqugh łiq'a yeydalghan
She harvested several winters' supply of fish

bech'enaqa yulqadi ghudi belik'aqa yulqadi ghudi eł!
for her children's food and her dogs' food!

Ghu hey dahqugh naqeli qeydlant idiłti qeyenishnughedatl'.
So then many fall seasons passed, and they came downriver (on the Susitna River).

Yethdi kanastan.
She was still living there modestly.

Qeyiqu nuhnil'ani ełdi ki kisht'a gheli k'eydalghan.
They looked for her and she had really put up a lot of fish.

Łik'aqa ghini hey itidułt'ah hqugh old lady qeyechaqenq'a dahdnaltlet gheli t'qiluq.
The old lady's smokehouse was full enough for several years' (food) supply for those dogs.

Bech'enaqa dehdunkda ghunen nuhyighetneq,
Her children took their mother back (to live with them) then,

yethdi q'u hushlaq'u beteya qustlagh.
because her strength was fading a little.

Dahdi heya k'a t'et'anen din ndi beteya qilal?
How old was she then when her strength gave out?

Ts'iłde Susitnu qeyeł nishdeł.
One time they came downriver the Susitna River with her (to Susitna Station, 2.25).

Nuk'eghutił t'et'ish.
She was barely limping around.

"Shich'anadelnehniłi!" nih.
"Take some of my blood out again!" she said.

Qeyets'ila ghini qeyeghuk'idiyesh ch'u q'itsey qeyeł dghinihi eł q'ank'dghiłqik.
They bandaged up her forearm and (they took) an awl that they sew with.

Q'u qeyets'ila qeyeghu nuk'idides tl'ił eł hnu'u,
When they wrapped up her forearm with rope,

benk'isa yudeh gheli nghik'et' qayaht'et'ish.
her veins really showed up.

Yethdi ghudehdi ha nilani k'ta'a qeyełchish.
Then they made some soup with lard.

Ha nilani sht'a k'ta'a' qeyedułtl'it'.
They poured out some greasy soup.

Qeyenk'isa ghini q'itsey qeyek'nełkes.
They poked her veins with that awl.

Dach' gheli del ghini niłq'ach' gheli bech'ałetnk'iynałdets t'et'ish.
Thus that blood really gushed out on both sides (of her arm).

Qeyenił'ih qeyenił'ih ch'u del ghini ha betenk'enałk'et' t'et'ish.
They watched and watched and they mixed the blood with the grease.

"Q'u, shijenhqugh bech'anadelnehnel.
"Enough, you've let out enough blood.

"Keshch'a badanłdał," hełnih.
"Put feathers on it," she told them.

Keshch'a dutdzel.
Feathers were chopped up.

Bech'adelnilen dghu keshch'a ghini qeyaqitnghilts'eł
Where the blood came out, they stuck on those feathers,

qeyeł qeyq'ek'iduyesh.
and they bandaged her.

Betets'akda yach' itdełt'eh.
She threw away her little old cane.

Ye'uh nuteltletkda gheli.
She could really hop around out there.

Yehech' heyut'et'an hnu'u!
She was brilliant!

Dahdi heyi k'a ki ninuk'ghatnu'en din
How many more years did she keep on working

q'u beteya gheli k'qilal?
before her strength disappeared?

Yethdi bech'enaqa ghuna Susitnu Station nishnuq-eye-taltan.
Then her children brought her down to Susitna Station again.[2]

Ch'u T'eghes Tuhdatbut Tayena qeyełnihi ghini yet *eight, ten miles* k'ashi qilan ch'u
And where they call it 'Cottonwood Bleached in Water-Straight Stretch' there, it's eight, ten miles (from Kroto Village; see 8.42).

yehqugh qubeł qubegh ninilghatl' ch'u
and they went that far with her, and it got dark on them and

yethdi quchitl'dghiłnen ch'u nichił t'uh eł nihdełdeł ch'u.
it snowed heavily and they put spruce boughs into an old house pit.

Yet k'a ełyus.
There it snowed.

Yedghu qeyeł na…qeyeł nayul.
There they camped with her.

Yekda tsułi ch'da t'uh ghu kanastan ch'u
That poor one, she lay meekly beneath a caribou-fawn skin blanket and

bech'eda ghinihdi ghenuy deyes tudujuni,
on that blanket, a tanned caribou skin,

bech'dakda nlan, yighini yedghu yekda kanastan ch'u
there she lay meekly on that old blanket, and

nichił ghini qeyeq'e nunuqeyeghiłchesh bech'enaqa ghuna.
her children had taken it (the skin) off the side of the old house.

Qeyek'u tahdilggey.
They left her behind.

Yet q'u kisht'a ełdukahnalghel ch'u tiqeli tihqutses.
There was really deep snow there and they broke trail.

Q'u nughiłghatl'i k'ashi Dashq'e nishqghidatl'.
Just as it got dark they came down to 'On the Shoal' (Kroto Creek village, 8.12).

K'qulqet'.
They ate.

Tuhna k'i ch'u k'qulqet' ch'u daha qahdelyu.
Three of them ate and they lay down somewhere.

"Ey hey hey! Ey hey hey! Na'unkdakda bech'ach'ninłneq k'unde q'u.
"We abandoned our dear mother because of starvation.

"Nanit gu T'eghes Tuhdatbut Tayena yet kanastankda ch'u
"She is staying up there at 'Cottonwood Bleached in Water Straight Stretch' (8.42) and

"bech'ach'dalggey.
"we left her behind.

"Ch'adach' q'u gudeh naqa'itidghulyeshen din?
"How can she be brought back here?

"Yik'i beyich' k'tulał, beyich' k'i k'ilan," qetni.
"She will live, she is still alive," they said.

Ghunen Naqaydałna bunkdashla ghun yen betukda.
That man was Naqaydałna's (Alexandra Allowan's) little mother's father.

Starikgga be'iyi k'dighila.
His name was 'Little Old Man.'

Nughiłghatl' ch'u kisht'a nughiłghatl' ch'u gga'ilnik ch'u be'u k'ilan.
It was dark, very dark, and he got up, and he had a wife.

Bech'enaqa k'ilan.
He had children.

Yet q'u hetl niniłggat ch'u
He put out a sled and

baba ghudehdi k'enut' ghudehdi eł yaghelisht'a hetl q'eduqiłdatl'
he packed the sled well with dry fish, and filleted salmon, and

2. Shem thought that this incident occurred in the 1890s.

‡FIGURE 151

Photo taken near Talkeetna, 1915–17 by August Cohn, an engineer for the Alaska Engineering Commission; cf. Fig 145, p. 236. The adult woman on left is **Nuhnałchek'a**, Ofelia, and the young woman on the right appears to be **Ts'itaya,** Mytrona Nicolie.
AMRC-B1997-022-16

keliba ghuhdi chayu ghuhdi eł.
with bread and with tea.

Nichił k'a hetl q'eduy'et.
He also put a birchbark tarp on the sled.

Nachishghedeh hqugh nikahnalghel.
The snow lay deep, all the way up to one's knees.

Ch'u takahetldghinlkit yun'e.
And he drove the sled upriver.

Qebeq'e tiqela ghudi ki jitshla q'u qayahdut'an.
The tracks of their trail just barely showed.

Q'udi nachishghedeh hqugh gheli ni'ushnighel.
Now he broke a trail with snowshoes, up to his knees (in snow).

Dghiłchek'a t'ghit'a en'ushen Starikgga shla.
He was small, that old man little Starikgga.

Ighi Starikgga ghunhdi yeh ghu tinqetsey tinqetsey.
Then that Starikgga broke trail and broke trail.

Tinqetsey hełch' gheli qiydlani ełdi.
He broke trail and it got very dark.

Ghu tutiytun dghu qayahdut'an.
There a trail was visible going upward there.

Yeh ghu nutsidulyeshi ełdi hetsit dghu,
As he turned his head there towards the river,

quchitl'hghilut dghu biłni q'a qayahdut'an.
where they had dug out some snow, a water hole was visible.

Gu łu ghu hnayult niyen.
He knew that they had camped here.

Tl'uduq' quyu łdi quk'itsay k'a hetl q'edełtun.
He went up on the bank and he had a shovel on the sled.

Quk'itsay ghini hetl ghe nuyghulkit ch'u,
He took that shovel from the sled and,

tl'uduq' quyu ełdi qenq'a qeni'uyi qeni'uyi ghini yedghi'an.
he went up the bank and he saw a house-pole frame—a frame.

Ch'u yet hch'aqadghildatl' ch'u,
And there he took off his snowshoes and,

yeh ghu nuyesdedush ch'u quk'itsay nih hninyełgush.
there he waded through the snow, and he poked his shovel around.

"Bach'a! Bach'a!," ni.
"Auntie! Auntie!" he said.

Chitl' t'u hech' k'i, "Ay!
From beneath the snow, "Ay!

"Shey'a nen nelan hu łu kdi! Qadandayeshnesh!
"My son, it's you! I can hear you!

"Yeshjesh! Yeshjesh!" ni chitl' t'u hech' q'u qetni.
"I'm saved! I'm saved!" she said from beneath the snow.

Nqełqa nqełqa nqełqa ch'u i'uh ninuqinituk' ch'u
He dug and dug and dug and he shoveled the snow away and

eł ghini quydghiłtuk'.
he shook off those spruce boughs.

Ghun k'a tsukdi k'isenkda ghun k'a.
There was that dear old lady.

Łuq'u gheli tuhyan ninuyniłghel.
He set her down in a clear spot.

Yethdi ch'dakda ghini yeq'enuyghulkit yedayghet.
Then he took that old blanket and shook it off.

Yet qanayni'et ch'u tiniyu ch'q'u.
He covered her there and he went out.

Ghu t'ghes ghini T'eghes Tuhdatbut Tayena t'ghes 'un k'dilan.
There are cottonwood there at 'Cottonwood Bleached in Water Straight Stretch.'

Yetsał yetsał yetsał ch'u chik'a nitnat'ech' gheli yak-en-dinyel.
He chopped and chopped and chopped and he made a big pile of wood.

Biłni yegh tuyequn.
He brought her water.

K'tnałghech.
He boiled (some tea).

"Bach'a deqenqighichet," yełni.
"Auntie, crawl up," he said.

"K'tnayełghech," yełni.
"I boiled something (tea)," he said.

"Yeshjesh! Shey'a yeshjesh," yełni ch'u.
"I'm safe! My son, I'm safe," she said.

"Deqenqighichet."
"Crawl up."

K'enut' ghudehdi łiq'aka'a baba ghuhdi eł yaghelisht'a yegh niqiniłdatl'.
He carefully put by her some filleted salmon and dry king salmon.

K'elqat ch'u k'teltlet.
She ate and she sipped.

"Chin'an, chin'an shey'a.
"Thank you, thank you, my son.

"Shighu nik'dansh'un hqugh nik'daghi'uyi lagi," yełni.
"You should not try to become as old as I am," she told him.

Ch'u q'u yuhdalnen.
And then the sky cleared up.

Yi k'a taghetneq.
He was exhausted.

Ts'iłq'i jani q'e gheli tinqiytsey.
He had broken trail for a whole day.

Nachish hqugh ghedeh ush eytunh.
The snowshoes broke through down to the depth of one's knees.

Hetl k'a besghilis ch'u t'uh niqildatl' ch'u
He dragged the sled and he made a bed, and

"Oh!" yedghu hech' qihudult'eq'.
"Oh!" he threw himself down there.

Old ladykda hdi, tsukdi k'isen dahqugh k'a nikanal-ghelen din.
The dear old lady, that old lady lay down for some time.

Baba ghuhdi k'enut' ghuhdi yaghelisht'a k'ulqet' ch'u
She ate well on dry fish and salmon meat, and

yikda q'u chayu nuniłqin nuk'ujey k'a shida.
that dear one, she warmed up the tea and drank again.

Utnuht'ana shin'i.
She was an Ahtna.

Q'ut'en janq'u nughiłghatl' hq'u deqenuneltlet desnuk'dnghiłt'ech'.
In the morning, when it was still dark, he jumped up and he built a big fire.

Chayu nutnałghech.
He made tea again.

Yaghelisht'a yegh niqiniłdatl' hliba hdi eł k'ulqet' ch'u diki nch'uk'a k'ilqeł.
He put things by her carefully, bread and things, and she ate, but he didn't eat.

"Hliba shi nulqet shida,"
"Maybe she should eat some bread," (he said).

Ch'u Dutna ghedla qeyeł dghinihi nubesghelis.
And he dragged what they call a Yup'ik Eskimo sled.

Ighi hetl q'e dukaynałghel.
And he laid her down on the sled.

Bech'dakda yet'uh nishqugh ghu yet niduł'uh ghuhdi.
Her mouth stuck halfway out from beneath that old blanket.

Tsitsa batnatqunh t'ghit'a.
He put cloth over her (mouth).

Yet ki yagheli tiqela ghini ninghalten ch'u ughasht'a t'an.
The trail had frozen over nicely and they made good time.

Ughasht'a nuhetlnyelchush.
He pulled the sled quickly.

Tsukdi k'isen nch'uk'a t'iłdes.
The old lady wasn't heavy.

Nch'uk'a t'iłkegh ch'u
She wasn't big, and

kisht'a nuk'dulnen hdi k'ashi nishnuhetlyultun.
as the sun set, he dragged the sled down the river.

Ch'adach' ghu t'ghił'an juq.
That was how he did it.

Dashq'e ghu tl'uduq' qunuhetlqeyeghalkit.
At 'On the Bar' (Kroto Creek village, 8.12) they dragged the sled up the bank.

Hdakaq' qeyeł nihetlniłggat ch'u yuh qibesqeyeghulkit.
They parked it at the doorway, and they dragged her inside.

Starikgga qenq'a yuyeh ghu qibesqeyghulkit.
They dragged her inside Starikgga's house.

Yet q'u kanastan.
And there she lay meekly.

Bech'enaqa ghuna heyi q'u k'kidza qeyiqughel'ani ghuda,
Her children, because of the winter's fur supply (that they needed to sell),

Yusdishlach' blahga nich'taydatl'.
had left downriver for the Susitna Station store (at Yusdishlaq', 2.26).

Yitkda kanastan ch'q'u qeyech'adalggey.
That one lay there meekly; they had left her behind.

Yeh yut'e yuh dalts'ih hnuq'u nu'uy yudeh gheli nutdalnen.
Downriver there they stayed indoors until the days got longer.

Yethdi ch'elqadi kenuhetlqilyu ch'u
Then they hauled food on a sled back up (to Kroto Creek) and

"Ena, q'u nuch'tetnash," qeyełni.
"Mama, let's move back now," they said.

Dehdunkda ghun deqenqighichet ch'u
Their mother crawled up and

dech'dakda besyulis ch'u qebegh qughiyu.
she dragged that old blanket, and she came out to them.

Dech'dakda dech'enaqa ghedla ghu q'ehetl-'itay'et ch'u
Her children laid her old blanket on the sled and

hetl tl'u hetl tl'u ghini yitih.
the sled handlebar, she held that handlebar.

Ch'u dahak'a ghudeh q'u ch'adelyish hnuq'u
And sometimes if she toppled off,

ki ts'iłt'an hetl yen beghedla hetl tl'u ghini yiłkit.
another one would grab her on the sled.

T'ghet'ih.
He did that.

Q'uyehdi yedeghu kanastan ch'u qeyekenuhetllyu.
Then there she lay meekly and they brought their sleds back upriver.

‡FIGURE 151A

A portrait of Chief Nicholie of Talkeetna, taken by Sydney Laurence c. 1917. Nicholie seems to be wearing a ground squirrel skin coat.
ANCHORAGE MUSEUM PHOTO AMRC B1983.146.104

Yethdi bech'enaqa ghuna qughedla denłdes.
Then her children's sleds were heavy.

Ki ghetna hetl tl'u itih ch'u nunhyiltan.
One after the other, they held the handlebars and they brought her back.

Ghu K'dalkitnu kenunhyiltan.
They brought her back upriver to 'River Where Food Is Stored' (Talkeetna River 11.1).

Ch'u daha gheli k'a hey hghidehna.
They spent the winter somewhere around there.

Tik'uteh hey hghideh.
They spent the winter out in the country.

Daha chiqeł'ish qebeqayeh.
Wherever they killed something was (where they made) their village.

Dgheli Teht'ana qebe'iyi k'dilan.
The Mountain People was their name.

Ts'iłde gheli k'a nch'uk'a hdilts'il.
They didn't stay in just one place.

Daha chiqeł'ish yet niqenash ch'u
Wherever they killed game they camped, and

łuq'u gheli dnigi suhyelt'eh hnuq'u ki ghel'eh di daha deh chik'qeł'ish
when they had eaten up the whole moose, then to another place, wherever they killed something else,

yiłq'a nuqudeł ch'u.
they would go to that camp.

Ghedeghu qebeł tuhdghiłggen.
And there it became spring.

K'enuy'a hdi eł ghedishla hdi eł yaghelisht'a chinuk'hdul'ik.
They killed for themselves a good amount of beaver and black bear.

Bargas qubargasakda k'ilan.
A boat, they had a flimsy boat.

Qeyaqighiłghel ch'u
They put her in and

"Yusdishla nik'unuch'ghutnishni," qeyełni.
"Let's go down to 'Little Point' (Susitna Station, 2.26)," they said.

Danakaqeyeghiłghel Yusdishla nishnuqeydul'un.
They laid her in the boat and took her down to 'Little Point.'

Qil gheli eydlan.
She became very sick.

Q'u dghasdlin heyi q'u dałchin hnes.
She was then over one hundred years old.

Q'uyethdi nch'uk'a danahyiłgheł ch'u bargaskda yehu qeyenahghiłdatl' ch'u
Then they didn't put her in the boat, and they loaded their old boat and

qeyeł ch'anatadalggey.
they hauled it with lines through the water (going to Tyonek without her).

Yedghu bargaskda Mergansina yach' qeytałdatl'ikda.
There were some old boats that had been thrown away by some Americans.

Yeh qahdnaydlu.
There they lay upside down.

Yet t'uh q'u kanastan.
And she lay meekly beneath there.

Bech'enaqa ghuna nuhtastnu.
Her children moved back.

Dahdi k'a hnayul hyiłtan.
After spending several days they (her children) found her.

Yusdishla q'u hdalts'ina ghuna
The people who lived at 'Little Point'

yada ghuhdi k'enut' ghudehdi k'iytin yada ghuhdi qeyelaq'a qeyeghiłdeł ch'u.
they gave her whatever they had, salmon and backbones.

Yehdi k'ulqet'.
There she ate.

Yehq'u nch'uk'a qubete q'anyesdik.
She couldn't go around visiting among them there.

Nch'uk'a qebeqiyelggesh.
She couldn't visit them.

Qilkda gheli eydlan.
She became very sick.

Dghasdlin hnes q'u heyi dałchin ch'u.
She was more than a hundred years old.

Idiłdi Susitnuht'ana łuq'u yun'eh q'ahdinłnen.
At that time the Susitna people had all gone upriver.

Łuq'u gheli dghelaych' htaydatl' ghenuy idiłti.
All of them had gone to the mountains for caribou.

Tubughnenq' Yegashchik qeyeł dghinihen ha
From Tyonek, the one they called Second Chief,

FIGURE 152

Looking west from Denali View North campground in Denali State Park just south of **Ałtnu** (9.27, Pass Creek). The valley to the right is the West Fork of the Chulitna with **Łi Tayena Dghelaya** (9.36, Mt. Deception) above the valley. Visible at left center is **Dghelay Ka'a** (7.51, Denali).

PHOTO BY JAMES KARI

dihdi "tlegh" yeł dghinih yi.
that guy would say "tlegh." [3]

Qelun gasa at dak'tnintsegi quyushi q'eh stq'eshi beł eydluh.
He poured mixed (kneaded) beluga fat into a ten-gallon gas can.

Yet quydal'un beyaqah q'u ch'akahdalnen.
He brought it there (by boat to sell) after they had gone upriver.

Yethdi "Ch'adach'?"
Then, "How is it?" (he said to her).

Ghu "Yagheli" ni.
"Good," she said.

Chayu qeyedaghinel ch'u Suyitnuht'ana chayu ghuna qeyunghiqun.
They poured her tea, and the Susitna people had left her some tea.

K'eyey.
She sipped.

K'i iłdi dach' qeyłnih:
And then they said this to him:

"A Ch'anqet' bach'akda ghun
"Yes, Ch'anqet', our auntie,

"ighi bargaskda t'uh kanastan ch'iłtan.
"we found her lying meekly under that old dory.

"Gudeh k'a nch'uk'a ts'es'igh.
"We have not seen her around here (before).

"Yada ghuhdi k'enut' k'iytin ghudehdi beł belaq'a eł ch'delchet ch'u
"We gave her fish meat, backbone, whatever,

"k'du'uł janq'u," qeyłni.
"she could still chew that," they said to him.

"Chayu ghini ts'ełq'i chashga yan k'a shi ghiyey."
"She drank maybe just one cup of that tea."

Bech'a'iltlet ch'u
He (Second Chief from Tyonek) ran out, and

yehghu tabagh yeh hqugh nushełdeltesh ch'u ki ghedi bargas t'uyesałges.
he ran there as far as the beach, and he peered under the boat.

Ch'u yedghu ki tał dałkits.
And there another mat was spread out.

Gu łu ghu yitni.
She recognized him there.

"Bach'a, bach'a," ni.
"Auntie, auntie," he said.

"Aa' shey'a nen łu nen nenq'u tghilał.
"Yes, my son, you, you, it would be you.

"Tubughnenq'e shey'a nen din?" yełni.
"My Tyonek son, is it you?" she said.

"Aa'," yełni.
"Yes," he said.

"Yeshjesh!"
"I'm safe!"

Ch'u yetq'u blahga qeł shełdałtuk'.
And he ran to the store.

Suxali shahal gusuk nlani ghuhdi k'ighiqat ch'u yenich nuqulyu. Yehghu hushełdeltesh.
He bought crackers, sugar, cube sugar, and they brought that back to her. He ran back up there.

3. This is the word for 'grease' in the Kenai-Kustatan dialect.

Tudla ggahdi q'ishtik ghuhdi eł niqendinyel ch'u chayu yet dnałghech.
He built a fire with small driftwood and dry alder, and he boiled tea there.

"Bach'a k'iyiy," yełni.
"Auntie, you drink," he said.

Yethdi baba eł Tubughna kisht'a k'qeyeghiłghak.
Then those Tyonek people had put up a lot of fish.

Dahqugh gheli k'a baba bekilaqa eł qadil'anen din.
He and his helpers had put up a great deal of dry fish.

Q'udik'a en'ushen gheli eydlan, q'uyehdi didghiłtey.
Then he had become an old man, but he was still strong.

Bech'enaqa ghuna q'aqidaq.
His children were all grown up.

Ch'u bekilaqa ghuna yach' hełni, "Tlegh ghini
And he told his helpers, "That (beluga) grease,

"daha łik'aqay nch'uk'a yi yitułkeł t'qit'a yeh shu ninłdał.
"put it where the dogs won't get it.

"Shbach'akda gun Tubughnen ch'andghel'unni.
"My auntie, let me take you to Tyonek by boat.

"Tubughnenh q'atnułneh ughasht'a," hełni.
"She might not last until Tyonek—hurry," he told them.

"Dach' nch'uk'a qit'aniyen t'ejuq q'et'ent'a.
"She doesn't seem to know anything.

"Tubughnenq' shi q'atnułneh ghu.
"She may not make it to Tyonek.

"Tebughnen hq'ayi hqugh chituniłkda," heyełni.
"She'll die before Tyonek," they told him.

Ch'u "Tlegh" ghu heyełnihi ni qelun five gallon cans ch'qilu
And that (substance) they call "Tlegh" (oil), ten five-gallon cans, five

"can" ch'qilu…
can, five…

(five-gallon can shu Dena'ina iyi nch'uk'a qit'a'ideshni.)
(I don't know the Dena'ina name for "five-gallon can.")

Gas yagh'a tlegh ghini stq'esi ghini badandalkit t'en'it'a.
They filled gas cans with that kneaded beluga oil.

Yaghelisht'a qeyeniqeyedinłdatl'.
They put it away safely.

Heyniqidala hnuq'u ghu nushełdułtuk'
When they were pouring it in, he ran back there,

k'chan yedet'us yedet'us k'eyagi eł yet'us ch'u
and he cut grass—cut it with a knife—and he cut and

k'chan ghini bargas aydnghiłt'ech'.
he filled that boat with grass.

Ch'u "Ughasht'a," hełni.
And "Hurry," he told them.

Ch'u bech'dakda ghini yedghi'et.
And he brought an old blanket.

N'ushen nik'uyghilkit.
The old man lifted her up.

Dora ayghi'et ch'u nik'uyghilkit.
He put a blanket in the boat and he put her on it.

Ch'q'u didghiłtey nik'uyghilkit ch'u bargas, bargas ayghiłghel.
And he was strong and he lifted her up and he put her in the boat.

Yeł nughetnesh, yeł nughetnesh ch'u
He traveled with her; he went with her and

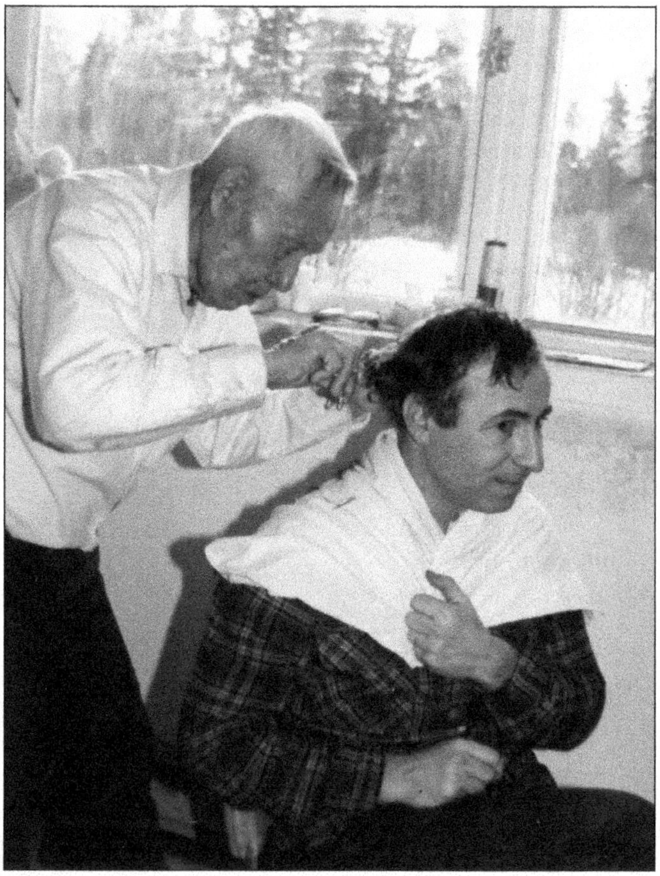

FIGURE 153
Shem Pete was giving haircuts in Anchorage and Susitna Station since about 1915. Here he is at his home in Tyonek in 1981, giving Jim Kari a haircut.
PHOTO BY PRISCILLA RUSSELL

Tebughnenq'e tunuydal'un.
he brought her to Tyonek (1.30).

Tubughnen ghe tunushełdaltuk' ch'q'u
He ran up to the village of Tyonek, and

"Shbach'akda hu tundayel'un," yełni.
"I brought my auntie back for you," he said.

"Nch'uk'a qit'aniyen q'et'ent'a.
"She doesn't seem to know anything.

"Ughasht'a beghu tudghilada," yełni.
"Hurry, give her a bath," he said.

Yejennushełdiltuk'.
He ran back over to her.

Nik'uyghilkit ch'u Tubughnen q'u gheqinuyultan ch'u
He picked her up and he brought her inside at Tyonek, and

bet'uh already yaghelisht'a niqeyenilu ghun.
they had already made a nice bed.

Yen ghun be'iya qit'a'ideshni.
I know her name.

Balbala qeył dghinih, Yagashchik be'u ghun.
She was called Balbala, that Second Chief's wife.

Ch'u be'u ghunen tuniłggin ch'u yeghu tudilu.
And his wife made some lukewarm water and she washed her (Ch'anqet').

Tatsiyniłtsey.
She washed her hair.

Yaghelisht'a begges qisen t'yiluq.
She made her very clean.

Gu q'udidi dghak yendghiggey.
She put a new dress on her.

Tubughna dek'isna ghuna łuq'u gheli qeyeqighidatl' gheli.
Those Tyonek women all came in to her.

Qeya'inasht'ech.
They crowded around her.

Yethdi yehqugh en'ushen eydlani nch'u qes'igh.
They had never seen a person that old before.

Łuq'u qeydghaga ghun ch'u niłq'e qeyenk'dela.
They put all kinds of clothing on her.

"Taneghesht'u shughu ben'eł'eni'i," hełni.
"I've been waiting to be baptized," she told them.

Gu Dichuk ghun qeyeł dghini natanin'ush.
Here one they called Dichuk ('Church reader') baptized her.

Yagashchik ghun di quqeshqa duyuq, quduyuq ghila qit'a din,
That Second Chief was their chief it seems,

Yagashchik ghunen.
that Second Chief.

Yaghelina Tebughnen q'u hqugh hnuq'u tsilgu k'delyal.
Those Tyonek people are good people, and then the church bell rang.

Q'u yeh kiq'u yiniłtan ch'u dahdnelnesh ch'u
And he carried her there and he made the sign of the cross, and

bresdi t'hghił'an bresdi t'hghił'an.
he forgave her (her sins), he forgave her.

Dichuk ghun taynin'un.
The reader baptized her.

Taynin'un ch'u yet k'a kanastan ch'u qachishyeł.
He baptized her and there she kneeled meekly.

Ch'iłch'en qałnish ch'u ch'iłch'en ghu datnelnesh
They held her on one side, and with one hand she made the sign of the cross

tanat'unh hnu'u.
as she was baptized.

Qeyenidelggesh ch'u łuq'u bresdi t'ehyiluq.
They went up to her and everyone made a blessing.

Ch'u nik'unuyghilkit ch'u Yagashchik ghunen deqenq'a ghu qinuyultan.
And he picked her up again and that Second Chief brought her into his house.

Yaghelisht'a bet'uh qiydlu ninuqiniłghel.
He laid her back down on a nice bed.

Tebughna'ina dek'isna ghuna ki nch'uk'a qeyech'adelggesh ch'u,
Those Tyonek women didn't leave her and,

qeyedghaga ghun niłq'e qeyenk'delash.
they dressed her with one garment after another.

Gu hqughkda gheli dghiłtsuy t'ehyiluq.
They made her just so big around.

Q'u yethdi niłghena gheli qeyenusaldeł.
And then, one after another, they came in to look at her.

Kiq'u qeyeninusa'itsey eł hdi beyich' ki qisen ki.
They all looked at her again, and she was not breathing any longer.

Tanat'uni ghini yen'ighil'en.
She had waited to be baptized.

Tsilgu qiqeyghiltan dghu "Ey tanaghesht'ugi en'eł'en hnuyu,
When they had brought her into church, "Yes, I have waited to be baptized,

"Tanaghesht'uni nideshni ch'u yada sbiduy tsilgu k'a nch'uk'a qanaytdelyesh.
"I want to be baptized, and I have never had holy water before.

"Q'udehdi yeshjesh," ni.
"Now I am saved," she had said.

Tuqeyeghiłghel.
They put her in water.

Tanat'un.
She was baptized.

Qinuhyultan, en'ikda kanastan,
They had brought her back into the house—the poor one was laying meekly—

dach'u beyich' ghini dałteł.
and then her breath expired.

Dnaldaqna q'et'ejuq.
She looked like one who is sleeping.

Yaghelisht'a qeyyashiga dnunluq.
They made a nice coffin.

Łuq'u gelis beq'e deydluh t'ehyiluq.
They fixed a cross on it.

Qeyegelisa nudałchin.
And they made another cross.

Ch'u yaghelisht'a yutsih qeyeł nidalnik.
And they buried her nicely toward the lower side.

Qeyegelisahdi yaghelisht'a nuhyiluq.
They made a nice cross for her.

Hey hnuq'u bech'enaqa ghuna nich'hghidatl'.
That winter her sons came downriver (to Susitna Station).

Duyuq shi shingha ghila'en ghunen.
That chief (Evan of Susitna) was my older brother.

Betukda ghunen qil eydlan hnuq'u,
When his father (Shem Pete's stepfather) died,

yen ghunen k'ingha gheli ghunen duyuq nuqełchin.
they made my older brother chief.

Yen duyuq nlan.
He was the chief.[4]

Yen deqenq'a t'qidghiłkegh niłkiqighet'u.
His house was big inside with an addition on it.

Yutgge shineh ka'a t'qighiłkegh ka'a gheli niłkiqighet'u t'qighit'a.
There was a big porch and an addition.

Nelni k'a qadanił'u t'qighit'a.
There also was a steambath built onto it.

Nich'hghidatl' ch'q'u chayu hghu'iqush.
They (Ch'anqet''s sons) came downriver and he gave them tea.

K'hghiyey ch'u dach' hełni:
They drank (tea) and he told them this:

"Hunkdakda ghunen ki Tebughnenq'e Yagashchik, naqeli ghu
"Your mother—that Tyonek Second Chief, last fall,

"gu hqugh ghaynik ch'u yiłtan ch'u belaq'a yedulnen ch'u
"he came as far as here—and he found her and he got her,

"Tebughnenq'e ch'anaydal'un.
"and he brought her to Tyonek (by boat).

"Yet tanat'un.
"She was baptized there.

"'Tanaghesht'uni en'eł'en hnu'u aq'a'idayelnen.'
"(She had said) 'I was waiting to be baptized and I have done it.'

"Ch'u datnelnesh ghu t'ejuq gu tanat'un hnuq'u.
"And she made the sign of the cross when she was baptized.

"Yekda kanastan ghu Tebughnen dek'isna ghuna qeye'unghasht'ech' ch'u
"That poor thing lay there meekly, and the Tyonek women crowded around her, and

"niłghena q'u qeyeninusaldeł.
"one after another they came to see her.

"Kiq'u qeyeninutsa'itsey łdi beyich' ki qisen.
"They looked at her again, and then her breath was gone.

"Yethdi shughu ełnench' qeyniłnik.
"Then they buried her.

"Dach' beqenga k'ilan.
"That is the news about her.

"Yaghelisht'a qeył nidalnik hunkdakda ghunen."
"They buried her nicely, that dear mother of yours."

4. This is Chief Evan of Susitna, who informed **Ch'anqet'**'s sons of her death. See Fig. 122.

‡FIGURE 154
Photo of Talkeetna Nicholie's yard with a boat and skin-boat frames with his house in the distance, taken on the same day in 1916 as was Fig146A.
PHOTO BY SYDNEY LAURENCE, ANCHORAGE MUSEUM B1983.005.58; PHOTO FOUND BY AARON LEGGETT.

"Heyhey…chin'an chin'an."
"Oh, thank you, thank you," (they said).

Yet q'u dunkda ghunen yeghititl'.
Then he (the oldest son named K'uk'enesh) made a potlatch for his mother.

Nuta k'eli q'u dałchin.
He made two songs.

Ts'ełq'i k'eli ghini yi ki be'elnesh.
One song, I remember it.

Qendugh qeyenaqaqułdełi k'eli dałchin.
They moved around the floor and he made a song.

Qeyeniłłulditl' ch'u:
They clapped their hands together and (sang):

(Song 1)

Gini yeq'adałchin.
He made this song for her.

Qendugh ghu qeyenaqaqułdełi.
They moved around the floor.

Q'u t'ełkighkda gheli.
Then I was just so big (dancing on the floor) there.

Qendugh ghu shi k'a qubeł k'eljesh.
I too danced on the floor with them.

Qubeł naqagheltlełkda gheli.
I really hopped around with them.

Ki k'dałchin.
And he made another song.

Yik'i dighun utnuht'ana nlanch' gheli k'dałchin.
He made a real Ahtna song.

(Song 2)

Yi gini k'eli dałchini gini yeghititl'.
He made this song and potlatched for her.

Dach' łu t'ejuq łu q'u.
That's how it happened.

Ch'anqet' k'uych'ena kiłqay hdi k'ghila.
Ch'anqet' had six sons.

Beqen ghunen be'iyi nch'u qit'a'ideshne.
I don't know what her husband's name was.

Undatna Dgheli Teht'ana hghila.
These were the last Mountain People.

Łuq'u nineteen-eighteen hdi qil eydlan.
They all died in the 1918 flu.

K'dalkitnu qil qeydlan.
They died in Talkeetna.

K'uk'enesh… Itegheyuł Tu',
(The names of her six sons were) K'uk'enesh or Itegheyuł Tu' [John Stump's father, who had two names],

Ch'k'idetnishen, Shik'u, Sinidegga, Nits'usełen, Kila Tlaq'a.
[Talkeetna Nicholie], Shik'u [Nick Nickoli, Annie Ronning's father], Sinidegga, Nits'usełen, Kila Tlaq'a.

FIGURE 155

View to the south with the lower end of **Tatik'niłtun Bena** (11.14, Stephan Lake), and with "Murder Lake" on the left.

Jack and Bill Larson's mother, **Du'inałna,** came from the Stephan Lake village. Her father, **Sghay Tu,** Talkeetna Stephan, was murdered near Stephan Lake in June of 1917. The small lake at the outlet of Stephan Lake, locally called "Murder Lake," is where **Sghay Tu**'s place was located. This site is noted in West (1973).

PHOTO BY MARK STASIK

FIGURE 156

The head of **Tatik'niłtun Bena** (11.14, Stephan Lake) and mountains to the east.

PHOTO BY MARK STASIK

They found him. He was eating half a fish. He must have been my stepfather's relation."

11.9 Dghelishla • 'Little Mountain'

Bald Mountain

Shem Pete: "«On the upriver end [of **Nultani**, 8.56] is **Dghelishla**.»"

‡**11.10 Dghelishlatnu ?** • 'Little Mountain Stream'

Sheep River

Shem Pete once speculated that a name for this major stream could be derived from the name for Bald Mountain. Johnny Shaginoff did not confirm this name, however.

Learnard (1900:663) at mouth of Talkeetna River in 1898: "At this place we met Stephan, our former guide, who was bound for the head waters of the first southern tributary of the Talkeetna River on a mining trip."

Lillian Theodore recalls that her father Wasilla Stephan's trail from Montana Creek to the northeast went up from where Yoder Road is, up the mountain there, to beyond Bald Mountain. Then he might return by skin boat. Wasilla Stephan used to point that out in the distance to her. He said that the last times he went that way was before Lillian was born in the 1920s and early 1930s.

Annabel (1948:199): "My friend Wasila Stepan told me once that a blue bear circled him repeatedly in an alder jungle on the upper Talkeetna River, roaring and popping its teeth threateningly. 'I got one shot at him,' Wasilla said, 'and I didn't hear him any more, but I don't know whether I killed him or not. I didn't try to find out. I went away from there as fast as I could.'"

11.11 Tatik'niłtuntnu • 'Creek of Game Trail Goes into Water'

Prairie Creek

De Laguna (1970:41) writes, "Camp site of the 'Midnooskies' was noted by Learnard in 1898 (1900: 659–660) at what I believe to be Prairie Creek, near Daneka or Stephan Lake. At this settlement were 3 men, 7 women, and 20 children, hunting caribou. Wasili's home, which Learnard failed to reach, was 20 miles above this village on the Talkeetna. About 1 mile away from the the caribou hunters' village was a winter village, but the Indians had gone to the middle fork of the Susitna."

In the Prairie Creek area Learnard said that this village was about 50 miles above the camp at Chunilna Creek. The location of Wasili's cabin has not been determined. Learnard 1900:661–62: "On the eighth day from camp the former Midnooskie village was met. To my surprise there were no Indians there, although the party of miners left the Indians there, and reported that they agreed to take me to Wasili's cabin. The packs were left at the fishing village, and we proceeded to follow their trial, which, in about a mile from there brought us to the Indians' winter cabins.

"From the mountains along the tributary of the Talkeetna, on which the Indian village was located, an extended view could be obtained up the valley of the tributary.... The valley varies in width from 1 to10 miles and was well timbered and full of small lakes. The trail followed when looking for Indians was fairly good, well-worn, and one over which pack animals could be taken without difficulty as far as we traveled. On our first trip to the Indian village they informed me that it was three sleeps to the middle fork of the Sushitna at the bend. The bend referred to could be seen from the mountains, and was very sharp.

"The difference in elevation between the Talkeetna

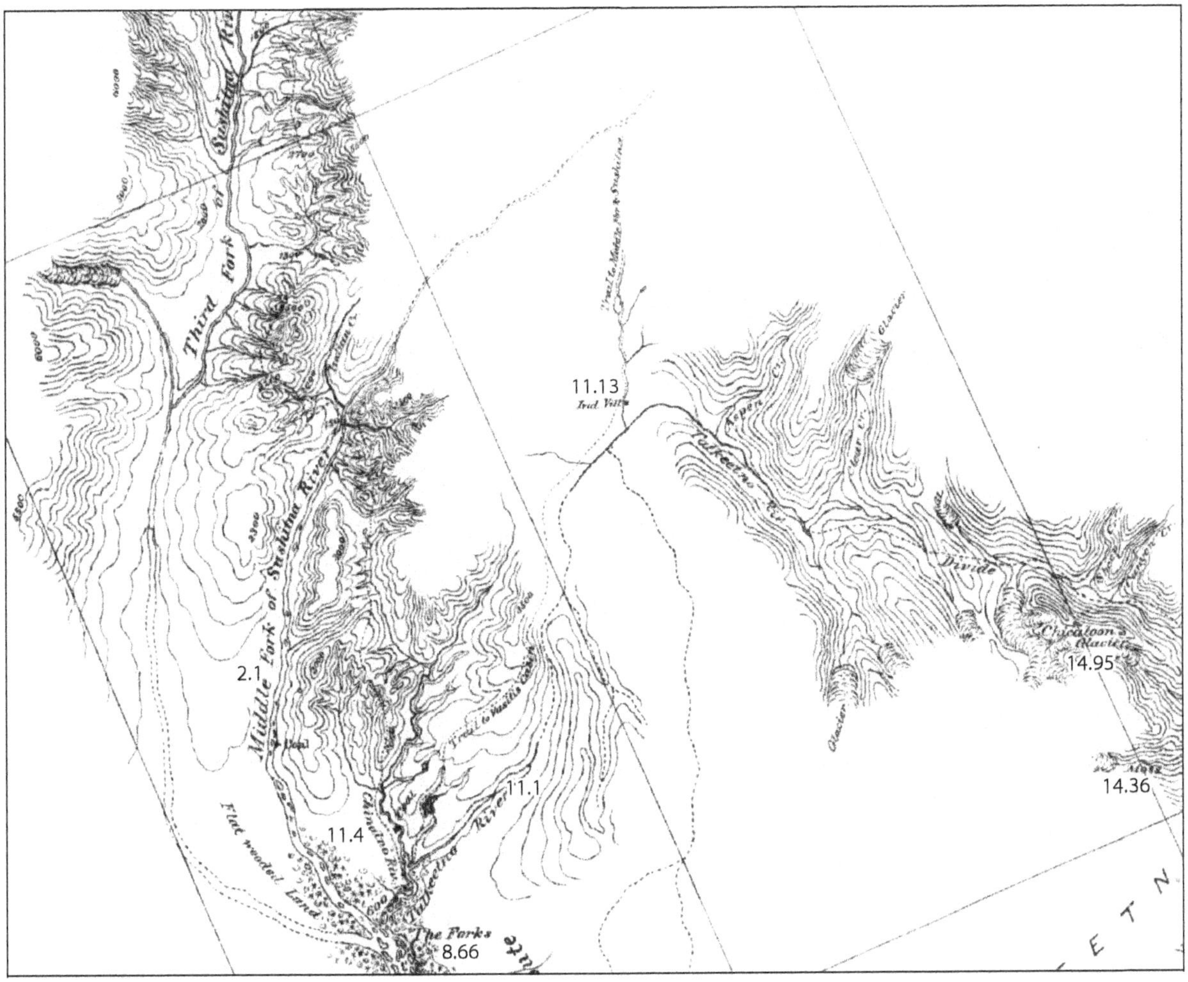

MAP 47

Detail from the 1900 Meiklejohn Map: Talkeetna River and Chickaloon River ‡with *SPA* feature numbers.

This map is the geographic compilation of the surveys of Learnard and Yanert in 1898, and Yanert, Mathys, and Vanschoonhoven in 1899 on the upper Susitna, the Talkeetna and the Chickaloon Rivers. Note the trail up Chunilna Creek (Chinaldna), the trail to "Wasilis Cabin," going to Prairie Creek, with a portage over to the Susitna River, and the trail and pass over to the Chickaloon River.

ARCHIVES, ALASKA AND POLAR REGIONS DEPT., RASMUSON LIBRARY, UNIVERSITY OF ALASKA FAIRBANKS

River at the mouth of the Chinaldna river and the Indian village about 50 miles away is approximately 1200 feet.... I could not learn if there were falls on the stream, but when questioned they said it was not good for a boat."

Johnny Shaginoff noted that he had hunted from Disappointment Creek over to Cache Creek. He did not know Native names for these streams.

(11.12) K'entl'u Bena • 'Cheek Lake'
location uncertain, perhaps general lake area in Prairie Creek area, or perhaps Daneka Lake
Shem Pete mentioned this area in the story of **Ch'anqet'** (p. 240). The Mountain People used to hunt caribou here.

§11.24 [Deniigi Bene'] *(Ahtna)* • 'Moose Lake'
Daneka Lake
A likely Ahtna-origin place name, but not re-elicited.

11.13 Tatik'niltunt *(Dena'ina)*; **Titi'niltaande** *(Ahtna)* • 'Where Game Trail Goes in the Water'
Stephan Lake village
Shem Pete: "That was **Ch'anqet'**'s village. «This was **Sghay Tu**'s [Talkeetna Stephan's] village.» He got a big cache. They club him there. They kill him. They bury him there [in June 1917]."

Jack Tyone said that Talkeetna Nicholie was the last Native resident of Stephan Lake. Jack saw him there in 1915 when Nicolie was then about sixty years old. He is said to have been from a lost tribe, **C'eltagi**, or sharp-tailed grouse, in Ahtna. He had one brother, **Sghaay Ta'**. They would go to Knik to trade. He is said to have "no power" because he had no relatives. They had previously fought over the country, but they were too small a group to continue the fight. Jack Tyone: "They just lay down their arms."

Jack Tyone: "Frank Secondchief's grandpa's brother, chief used to be of that village there. **Titiy'niltaande.**

Ts'e' C'udetniisen. Always chief. In 1908 Henry Peters' grandpa and grandma, they told story about that chief. **Ts'e' C'udetniisen.** And he had a box full of gold and twenty dollar, five dollar, ten. Nobody had that much money. I don't know how many thousands dollars maybe more. He hunting, he packing it round. So nobody see, can't leave it in home, somebody see it. Stephan Lake, **Tity'niłtaan Bene'**."

Jim Tyone noted that Frank Secondchief's mother, Fannie, lived at Stephan Lake and that there was only one house there.

11.14 Tatik'niłtun Bena *(Dena'ina);* **Titiy'niłtaan Bene'** *(Ahtna)* • 'Lake of Game Trail Goes into Water'
Stephan Lake
Katherine Nicolie: "Caribou got a trail right to the water. That's what the name means."

Note that Stephan Lake is shown as "Tatikniltubena" on the 1839 map by Wrangell (Map 17). This is the Dena'ina and not the Ahtna pronunication of the name.

This seems to be "Indian village" marked in this area on the 1896 sketch by William A. Dickey (Map 42, and "Ind. Vil." on the 1900 Meiklejohn map (Map 47).

West (1973:37–38): "A number of sites were found around Stephan Lake in 1971 by Dr. Frederick H. West. Four sites were located surrounding the lake. One site (TM 1) was tested extensively and revealed at least two separate cultural levels; the lower level contained a notched implement and flakes, and the upper layer contained only flakes. A radiocarbon assay on the lowest level gave a date of approximately 6000 years ago (F.W., p.c.)." These sites are mapped as location No. 135 in West (1973).

Johnny Shaginoff of Sutton, whose mother was of the Mountain People, trapped at Stephan Lake through the 1930s. He would travel from Chickaloon through the pass to the upper Talkeetna River and north to Stephan Lake. Johnny Shaginoff: "Salmon run right into that lake. They're still good when they get there."

Jake Tansy says that on occasion some Western Ahtna would go as far as Stephan Lake to harvest some salmon. Pete Stephan of Montana Creek said that he used to hunt here, and then drift down by boat to Talkeetna with meat.

On the 1904 map by Moffit (Map 44) a trail is marked from Stephan Lake north to the Susitna River. This is labeled "Portage (good)." Johnny Shaginoff has described the trail system in this area.

In 1953 John Nicklie of Valdez Creek and Cantwell reported to Ivar Skarland the trail from the upper Susitna to Susitna Station via Stephan Lake, Prairie Creek, and the Talkeetna River (Dixon et al. 1985:3–45).

11.15 K'dalkitnu Tl'u • 'Headwaters of Food Is Stored River'
upper Talkeetna River
Certainly much detail of the ethnogeography of the Talkeetna River and Talkeetna Mountains has been lost. Learnard noted that the trail system in the area was well used in 1898. On Talkeetna River travel he wrote, "They said that in winter time they traveled up and down the river.... From the Indian village to Wasili's cabin the Indians sometimes use canoes in going up the river, but generally they make a portage because of swift current" (Learnard 1900:662).

‡Jim Sinyon (West 1973): "at head of Chickaloon, where the Oshetna are all connected, right on that pass, the old people used to get sheep there. From there used to go down to the headwaters of the Talkeetna. There's sheep there too."

11.16 (Native name not remembered)
creek into Talkeetna River from the north, locally called "Pedro Creek"
Johnny Shaginoff: "Pedro was an Indian. That was Johnny Bull's step-father. He was **Dghelaay Tahwt'aene** [Mountain People]. He died in 1918, and he is buried by the bridge at Chickaloon. ‡Pedro was Talkeetna Stephan's nephew."

Johnny Shaginoff reported that the trail led north up Pedro Creek to the head of Tsisi Creek or **Tes Na'** (10.21). Then another trail branched to the northwest to Fog Lakes (10.44) and northeast to the Susitna River.

11.17 (Native name not remembered)
creek into Talkeetna River from north, opposite Yellowjacket Creek, locally called "Red Shirt Creek"

11.18 K'dalkitnu Łi'a • 'Glacier of Food Is Stored River'
Talkeetna Glacier
Mathys (1900: 680, 681): "I calculated from this point to Wasili's cabin it would require twenty-five days travel with a pack train.... The Indian also informed me that the other Indians will not stay in this section of the country for fear of getting snowed in [near Talkeetna Glacier].

"Aug. 19: Large quantities of berries and currants were found, and also an old Indian cache. As the stumps of the trees that had been cut down were very high, I inferred that the Indians used this as a winter camping place."

11.19 K'dalkitnu Dghelaya • 'Mountain of Food Is Stored River'
Sovereign Mountain

11.20 Dzeł Ggeyi Bena *(Dena'ina);* **Dzeł Ggezi Bene'** *(Ahtna)* • 'Mountain Gap Lake'
lake at head of Talkeetna River in pass
The pass called **Dzeł Ggeyi** leads from the upper Chickaloon River to the upper Talkeetna River. See 14.38.

Johnny Shaginoff: "We go by that lake here. It's only about eight miles from there at the head of Chickaloon River to the head of Talkeetna River."

Mathys and Bagg followed the visible trail this way in 1898 (Mathys 1900; Bagg 1900).

John Shaginoff

Johnny Shaginoff was a major contributor to this book. From his personal travels as a hunter and trapper, he knew a very large area from Knik Arm, the Matanuska River valley, and a good part of the the Talkeetna Mountains, between the Talkeetna River and the Tyone Lake area. In one session recorded in March of 1985, Johnny mentioned about seventy place names and detailed descriptions of travel from Cottonwood on Knik Arm, up the Matanuska River, to north of the Susitina River in the Deadman Lake area. Johnny Shaginoff passed away in 2001 at the age of ninety-two. An article about Johnny Shaginoff by Robert Tucker entitled "Mountain Man" appeared in the *Ruralite Magazine* in 1978. Tucker wrote:

FIGURE 157

Portrait of Johnny Shaginoff drawn by his granddaughter Sondra Shaginoff Stuart. See also Fig. 139, showing John as a young teenager.

> Aside from the fact that John Shaginoff was immensely powerful and possessed incredible stamina, he was not much different from any other big man. Yet his forays into the wilds, his great knowledge as a guide, and his capacity for hard physical labor caused him to become something of a legend during his own lifetime.
>
> The large size 'Trapper Nelson' packboard was too small and flimsy for John. He had a home-made model fashioned from tough birch, moose-hide and canvas. With this he packed huge loads, although few were documented. There was one time, though, that might serve as an example. It was a fall day and John was leaving a hunting camp high in the Talkeetnas. He tied one large ram and half of another on his board and started off the mountain, traveling all day with his heavy load. The pack was weighed for shipment that evening at the railroad station in Matanuska. It tipped the scales at 206 pounds.
>
> John Shaginoff was born in Cottonwood Village, a small settlement five miles east of Knik, on December 5, 1911 [1909]. His father was mostly of Russian descent, but his mother was Athabascan. The Alaska Commercial Company sent John's father to school. Later, he managed trading posts for them at Knik, Sunrise and at their main headquarters at Susitna Station. When John was eight or nine years old he left his home at Knik for the first time to live with his grandmother at Chickaloon, in order to attend the Territorial school there.
>
> In the summer of 1927 John [Shagnioff] was sixteen years old. He moved to Talkeetna with his parents that same year and his father died soon after. 'I was grown up then,' he said philosophically. 'It was time that I started making a living for myself.' The next fifteen years were to be the most interesting, lucrative and adventurous of John Shaginoff's life.... John ran a trapline while going to school. Then, beginning in 1927, his winters were occupied with six-month trapping expeditions into the Talkeetna Mountains. Fur was plentiful and selling for the highest prices in history. In November he left Talkeetna with his dogs for the Stephan Lake area, sixty trail miles to the east. In the spring he came out, down the Matanuska River, loaded with fur.
>
> John trapped alone, with only his dogs for companionship. 'I always liked trapping,' he said, 'When I was about twenty years old I caught more fur than anyone else in the country.' John's main cabin was located about half way between Clear Creek and Stephan Lake. He kept his fur and most of his supplies there. He also had smaller cabins at Stephan Lake, Clear Creek and Fog Lakes.

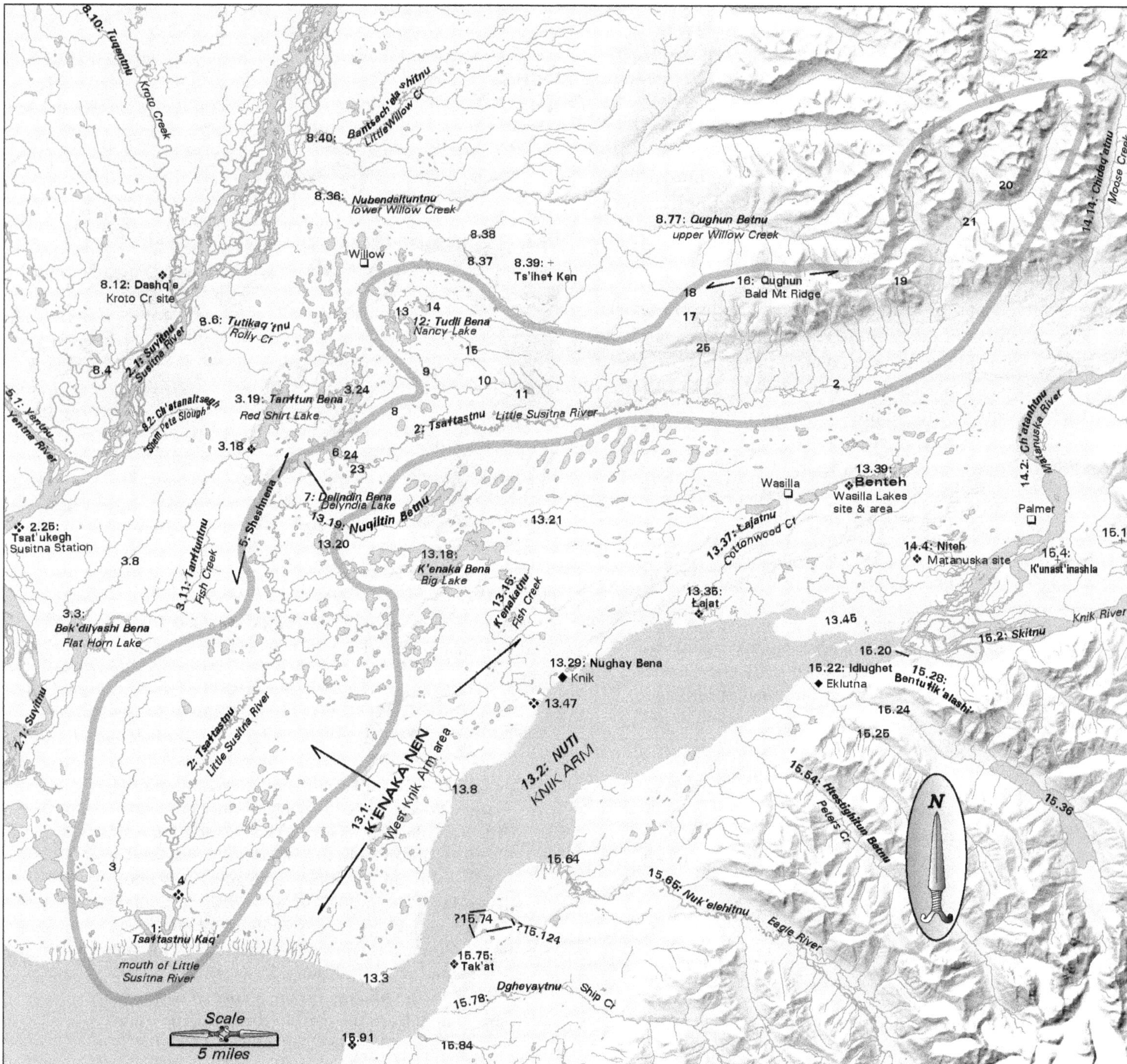

MAP 48

Place names map of the Little Susitna River, showing Nos. 12.1 to 12.25.

MAP BY MATT GANLEY

12 Little Susitna River

to Bald Mountain Ridge

Many features in the Little Susitna drainage, such as the numerous lakes in the Nancy Lake area, were used by the Susitna and Knik people, but the Dena'ina place names have been lost.

12.1 Tsałtastnu Kaq' • '-Ω- River Mouth'
mouth of Little Susitna River
The flats and lake country south of Flat Horn Lake to the mouth of the Little Susitna were not used much because the country is said to be too flat and wet. Billy Pete says that women used to snare geese here in the spring. There are no recorded names for the many small lakes in this area.

In the summer of 1906, Shem Pete saw **Dusgeda Tukda**, chief of Knik, coming by this area going toward **Susni Kaq'** (2.3). Shem says, "«He was coming in a big umiak. Way out there in the saltwater they were singing. The sound was wavering up and down. Then they heard them well.... They were coming around the point. On one side sixteen men were rowing. On the other side another sixteen men were rowing.... The one called **Dusgeda Tukda** stood in the bow. He was holding his arms out. He was swaying in order for them to see him. He was really making medicine»" (Pete 1977:16–17).

12.2 Tsałtastnu, ‡Tsełtestna' *(Ahtna)* • '-Ω- Stream'
Little Susitna River
‡Kari discussed the meaning of this name with Shem numerous times. No clear etymology is possible. The Ahtna name is from Jim Tyone.

Billy Pete noted that **Tsałtastnu** was used by the people who lived at Red Shirt Lake. When he trapped in this area, Billy sometimes traveled to **Tsałtastnu** to get fish. The otters left trout on the frozen river after taking a small bite out of them. Billy snared them with a hook and line to avoid breaking through the ice, chopped off the part the otters had fed on, packed them back to his camp, and cooked them up.

FIGURE 158
Tsałtastnu (12.2, Little Susitna River), as viewed above the bridge at the Alaska Railroad in April of 2000.
PHOTO BY JAMES KARI

12.3 (no recorded name)
Maguire Creek
A trail to Flat Horn Lake follows this creek. People would paddle up Maguire Creek going north to Flat Horn Lake.

Annabel (1948:293): "I first learned about milt from a gentle racketeer of a Tena Indian known as Siwash Jim.... I was fishing a tidewater of the Little Susitna River

Sources: Shem Pete, Billy Pete, Katherine Nicolie, Jim Tyone, and Johnny Shaginoff

2003 revisions: names added 12.6, 12.23–12.25; locations revised 12.11,12.15, 12.20.
‡2016 revisions: revised names 12.2, 12.5; figure replaced162.

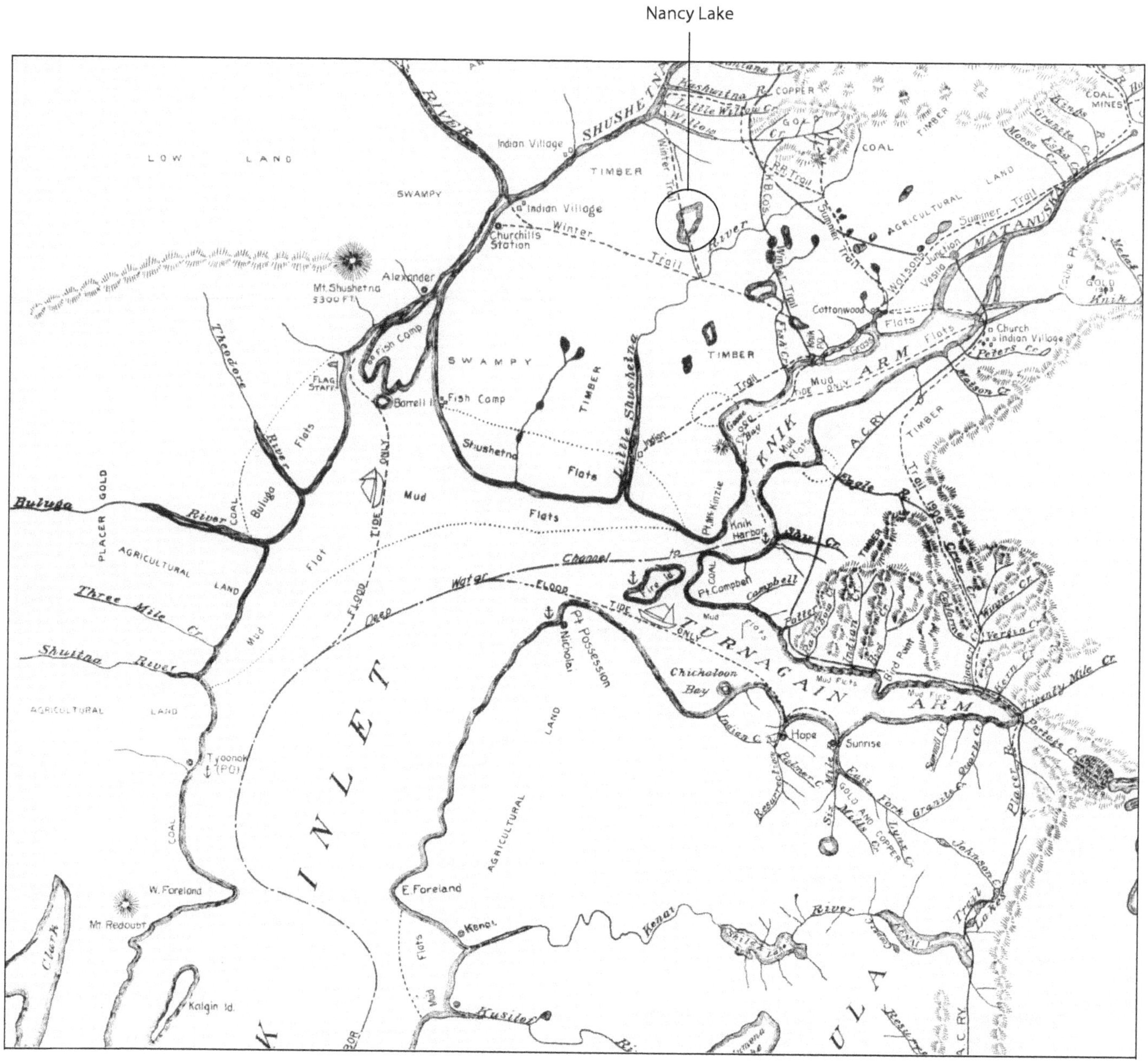

MAP 49

Detail from 1906 Herning map, Lower Susitna to Knik Arm.

This map has the first representation of Nancy Lake, with a trail junction at the mouth of Lake Creek. Also note the "Indian Trail" going from Knik to Goose Bay, with a structure shown at the lower Little Susitna River.

and had killed two male kings, intending to have them kippered at the cannery the next morning. Siwash Jim, watched me awhile, then asked if he might clean the fish for me.... He dressed the fish expertly and packed them in the grass, but as he was departing he picked up the rolls of milt and put them in his packsack. I asked him what he was going to do with them and he grinned and replied they were the best part of the salmon and he was going to eat them. So I experimented with the milt of the next salmon I killed. Maybe I should explain that the milt is the sperm of the male salmon. It lies in the fish in two thick milk-white rolls, about a foot long, and has the texture of fresh liver. Sliced and breaded or dusted with flour and fried in deep smoking fat, it is food to delight epicures."

12.4 Dusgeda Tukda Ti'iltant • 'Where Father of Dusgeda Was Carried Out'

site two miles up from the mouth of the Little Susitna River on the east bank

Shem does not remember the actual place name of this site. Chief **Dusgeda Tukda** died here, and the name

FIGURE 159

Left to right: John Stump, Nickalaska Stephan, and McGinty Stephan, in about 1930. The woman at the right and the child are not known. Kari recorded numerous Dena'ina place names with John Stump in the Wasilla and Anchorage areas on two occasions in 1976 and 1977. John Stump and his father were among the last Dena'ina to utilize the Wasilla Lakes area. John's father, **K'uk'enesh** or **Itegheyuł Tu',** was the oldest son of **Ch'anqet'.** John Stump's nickname was **Ch'em** from **ch'qałch'ema** 'butterfly.' He died in June of 1977. See Chapter 13 and the entry for **Benteh** (13.49, Wasilla Lakes) for other information via John Stump.

PHOTO COURTESY OF GEORGE AND SUSIE ONDOLA

refers to his being carried out of the bathhouse. This man's Russian name was Affinasa.

Shem Pete: "From there they used to go to that Flat Horn Lake trail and hike over to the Susitna.

"«There is a creek that flows into **Tsałtastnu** [Little Susitna River, 12.2] about two miles up. There on the right-hand side going up is a hill. I saw a village site there. That's where a village used to be. There weren't any people there then, but I know a story they told me about it. I saw that hill [in 1914]. On the hilltop there was a village. That is where **Dusgeda Tukda** [chief of Knik] was carried out they say.»"

"At Knik was **Dusgeda Tukda**. He was so rich nobody even counted his money. He had a bunch of blankets and stuff. Nobody knows how rich he was. «He had eight caches for his wealth. He had so much gold money it took two men to lift it up.» And he was a bad man. Those poor people—if he didn't like them, he kicked them. He kicked them in the face and everything. He had big old army shoes. After a while he got poor, and he had no clothes or nothing, just what other people threw away. Those medicine men tried to make bad luck—wish him bad luck all the time—and finally he went broke. They killed him without water in a bathhouse. They nailed the door and windows so he couldn't get out [he was too weak to escape]."

‡Coleen Mielke's research on the George Holt murder (see p. 278), documents the role of Knik Chief Affanasii as instigator of tensions between the Ahtna and the ACC Company, and the person who goaded an Ahtna man Nicolai to shoot Holt. Dusgeda Tukda, aka Afanasii, in fact is the same person. See Mielke's 2010 articles on Holt and Afanasii at her web link. See 16.8 for comments on a Chief Affinasa who died in Kenai in 1909, probably a different man. On the 1906 Herning map (Map 49) a structure at the trail crossing the Little Susitna River is shown in this area.

12.5 Shesh Nena • 'Saving Land' or 'Rescue Land' or 'Lucky Land'

low ridge extending from Cow Lake south to the Little Susitna River

Shem Pete: "«**Shesh Nena** is its name because they go there in springtime and autumn to kill bear in that country. That's why it is 'Saving Land.'» On that hill we save ourselves. That's its name. «There is good birch at that **Shesh Nena**, and those Dena'ina would go there in the spring to gather canoe birchbark.» That one part they pick 'em up that kind of birch. «They are long and tall. They pack that birch down to the Susitna. There is good birch on it. They gather canoe birch on it.»"

This low ridge is part of an intersecting trail system that ran from Susitna Station to Knik Arm and north to Red Shirt Lake or Cow Lake.

Shem Pete provided additional commentary while flying over the country between Anchorage and Red Shirt Lake with Fall and Greiser in 1986: "That hill down there, **Shesh Nena**. There's moose around that area there.

FIGURE 160

Sava Stephan and Lily Stump at Tyonek in 1975. Lily Stump, originally from Knik, was the wife of John Stump.
PHOTO BY THOMAS F. JOHNSTON

FIGURE 161

Shem Pete at his cabin at **Tudli Bena** (12.12, Nancy Lake) in 1975.
PHOTO BY PRISCILLA RUSSELL

That's bear country. And they hunt bears too. **Shesh Nena** they call it.... Not much snow on that hill and lota bear and moose. You would catch something. Even they pack the dogs and dog can't hardly live. He pack him... and when the dog move around, you let them lay down you know. Go for bear."

"The Hunting Dog Story" by Shem Pete (1989a) has an account of this method for hunting bears in times of starvation.

§12.23 Skitnu • 'Brushy Stream'
Skeetna Lake outlet stream
This Dena'ina-origin name did not get reviewed with Shem Pete. Sava Stephan stated that it is authentic.

§12.24 Skitnu Bena, Unqeghdut Skitnu Bena • '(Downstream) Brushy Stream Lake'
Skeetna Lake

§12.6 Unqeghnit Skitnu Bena • 'Upsteam Brushy Stream Lake'
Butterfly Lake
The name is derived from the stream name **Skitnu.**

Shem Pete: "«In 1945 we had a tent pitched there, and we hunted for beaver.»"

12.7 Delindin Bena • 'Derenty's Lake'
Delyndia Lake. See Plate 5 and Fig. 61.
Shem Pete: "That's my Russian name, **Delindin** [Derenty]. That's my name on it. They put my name on it. No **nichił** there."

Billy Pete: "I trapped all over that country."

The name Delyndia Lake was established in 1958 based upon Shem Pete's Russian name (Orth 1971:266). Shem could not remember the original name.

12.8 Utiditin • 'Trail Goes to It'
swamp between Little Susitna River and Nancy Lake

12.9 Tudli Betnu • 'Cold Water Creek'
Lake Creek
Some house pits are reported on the right bank of Lake Creek (Reger 1983). Shem Pete knew no specific information about them.

12.10 Betnu Hghiłgeditnu • 'Rotten Area Creek'
outlet stream into Lake Creek from Zero Lake northeast of Houston

12.11 Betnu Hghiłgedi Bena • 'Lake of Rotten Area Creek'
Zero Lake northeast of Houston
Shem Pete: "«That lake upland from Houston has a name, **Betnu Hghiłgeditnu,**» a little lake from Houston toward the mountain, above the Little Susitna."

Billy Pete: "Everyone, Native or white man, go to that lake they go crazy."

12.12 Tudli Bena • 'Cold Water Lake'
Nancy Lake
Fall (1981:385): "A second old village site is at the outlet

‡FIGURE 162

Shem and Billy Pete lived at several locations on Nancy Lake between 1944 and 1978. This previously unpublished photo is of Shem at the cabin that he built in 1948 near the mouth of Nancy Creek 12.15, **Betnu K'etelihitnu**, likely in the 1960s.

PHOTO COURTESY OF KNIK TRIBAL COUNCIL.

FIGURE 163

The iconic landform on the north side of the Matanuska Valley is **Qughun,** 'The Hump,' (12.16, Bald Mountain Ridge). Viewed from **K'unast'inshla** (15.4, Bodenberg Butte). At the west and lower end of Bald Mountain Ridge is **Ts'ihełken** (8.39) at the head of Deception Creek in the Willow area. **Tsałtastnu** (12.2, Little Susitna River) runs along **Qughun.**

Shem Pete: "«They go up on that mountain, and they kill bear on it. They call it **Qughun**. They go up there when the bears are fat. **Qughun Dghelaya**. That was **Chijuk** [Katherine Nicolie's stepfather]'s country.»"

PHOTO BY PRISCILLA RUSSELL IN 1977

No Room in the Homeland... Willow's First Citizen Looks for Home

by James Kari and Priscilla Russell

In 1978 Shem and Billy Pete were told that they had to move off the land they had been living on near Nancy Lake. This article is reprinted with minor revisions from the Alaska Advocate, *September 14, 1978.*

A prominent Tanaina tradition bearer, Shem Pete of Nancy Lake, is looking for a place to live once again. Shem is undoubtedly the Willow area's first and most resilient citizen. Born at Susitna Station in about 1898, he is the recognized leader of the Susitna Tanaina Indians. The lower Susitna River had been an area of high population until early in this century when Susitna Station and several surrounding villages were decimated by flu epidemics. Shem's mother and his older brother, who was the last village chief, died at Susitna in 1918, along with three other members of his family and 200 or more Susitna-area Natives. Susitna Station dissolved in the 1930s when most of the people moved to Tyonek.

Still very active and ebullient, Shem has lived, hunted, fished, trapped and panned for gold all over upper Cook Inlet. He is the foremost Tanaina storyteller and one of the outstanding Native language storytellers in Alaska. He is also the last Tanaina potlatch song leader, and is an expert on the culture of the Upper Inlet Tanainas and on the modern history of upper Cook Inlet.... He is one of the few Tanainas who know the aboriginal names in the proposed state capital area.

Shem's main area of residence has been the country between Susitna Station and Nancy Lake. His mother packed him in a cradle to their Red Shirt Lake village in about 1900. The Tanainas, like other Athabascans, had camps in several areas to make best use of seasonal resources. They had no private ownership of land, but instead had individual and family use areas. Shem decided, in about 1944, to settle at Nancy Lake rather than move to Tyonek. He heard that a road would parallel the train someday. He built the first of three residences on the big peninsula on Nancy Lake. Shem never owned or filed for that land. Since he was the first person to build on Nancy Lake, he thought he was staking land. His mother had told him that that point was an old Tanaina village site.

In about 1950 he learned that someone had homesteaded his land, and he was forced to move. Then he bought a three and one-half acre lot nearby and built a second cabin. In about 1965 this cabin was apparently swindled from him. A man showed him a paper with Shem's signature, a bill of sale for $500, and he was forced to move.

Shem's third residence is off the lakeshore but still on Nancy Lake Peninsula. He built a pre-cut cabin on land leased from a private party in 1965. This is the little cabin Shem lives in today with his son, Billy. They haul their water from the lake, set out a few rabbit snares, and burn wood. But this spring, the owner of the property gave Shem and Billy an eviction notice. Shem claims that he was told he could live on this land for the rest of his life, but the lease has a 30-day notice clause.

Shem cannot afford to buy land at today's prices and he adamantly rejects any suggestion that he move to a Pioneer Home.

Shem may now move onto someone else's land in the Willow area, and, if he lives long enough, he may get some Native Land Claims land to live on. He is an at-large member of Cook Inlet Region, Inc. and is not a member of either of the nearest Tanaina village corporations, Knik and Eklutna. Shem has told Cook Inlet Region, Inc. of his eviction notice, and it is possible that the corporation will be able to help him. There are many people in the Willow community who sympathize with Shem and have offered to help him move his cabin.

While some neighbors may tend to blame Shem and Billy Pete for their lack of foresight, the fact remains that many early Willow residents have made fortunes on land sales, and the only Natives from that community own no land. In the 1940s and 1950s no one helped Shem to file for a Native allotment. He continued to use his country as he always had, and later discovered that all the rules had been changed. He still has a traditional Native view, focusing on the utility of a general resource area rather than the monetary value of a plot of land....

On August 25, 1978, Shem and Billy Pete were in a car accident when being driven home. Shem cracked a bone in his right shoulder. After three days in the hospital he was back home. Within a few more days he was hauling water from Nancy Lake using his left arm. With a smile, Shem said, "I'll be all right in a few weeks. Good thing I didn't hurt my legs; I can still run."

Being With Shem Pete

by Priscilla Russell

FIGURE 164

Shem Pete's house after it was moved next to the Willow Post Office in 1978. In the winter of 1978–79 several Willow residents helped Shem move his cabin onto a lot next to the Willow post office. However, Shem missed being near **Tudli Bena**, Nancy Lake, and in the summer of 1979 he and Billy moved to Tyonek, where they resided until 1987.

PHOTO BY JAMES FALL

In the twelve years that I have known Shem Pete, certain outstanding characteristics of his have continued to impress me. The one that comes to mind first is his desire to share, which is a traditional Dena'ina value. It is not his sharing of material goods, however, that is so remarkable but rather his sharing of himself with others. Whenever Shem is a participant in a time of grief or hardship or crisis, he so overwhelms it with his songs and stories and personal words of encouragement that he helps the difficulty to pass, at least for the moment, and transforms the situation into a time of hope and strength. For example, a family summoned Shem to the hospital when their child was lying seriously ill in a coma. Besides comforting the family, Shem also attempted to encourage the boy's doctor by saying, "Oh, I've heard of you. You're the one trying to help all the people." At other times Shem turns ordinary occasions into festive ones through his use of powerful songs and words.

Another trait of Shem's is a strong sense of pride in being a Dena'ina and his dedication to living a Dena'ina-oriented life no matter what the circumstances are. In the early years of his life at Red Shirt Lake and Susitna Station, traditional values of the larger Dena'ina society were still

FIGURE 165

Billy Pete, Shem Pete, and Priscilla Russell along the Richardson Highway in 1979.

PHOTO BY JAMES KARI

intact. His mother and others of the community supplied him with the resources of the land and educated him in the skills, customs, and stories of his culture. Later, in the 1940s, when he decided to return to the country of his childhood and settle in Willow, he found that very little had remained the same because of development in the Willow area. In spite of this he kept trying to do what he had been brought up to do in the Dena'ina way. Besides hunting, trapping, gathering wood, and hauling water, he traveled to wherever people needed him to uplift their spirits. When possible, he attended potlatches and in general attempted to keep in touch with the now largely scattered Upper Inlet Dena'ina community, which looked to him for leadership.

This book is a product not only of Shem's remarkable memory but also of his ability to organize and synthesize the components of his knowledge in a very reflective and precise way, and of his willingness to communicate this knowledge to others. After work sessions with Shem, we would invariably have some unanswered questions. When we next saw him, he would have come up with answers to those questions and would proudly share them with us. He is in all senses both a great teacher and a great student.

I want to mention Shem's ability to identify and use plants that are significant in his culture. Much of this knowledge has been recorded in P. R. Kari (1991), so I will relate only one incident here. When Shem was a young man, he developed blood poisoning in one of his index fingers. He went to a medical doctor who said it was serious and who wanted to amputate a portion of the finger. Shem refused to allow this and went home, where he doctored his finger with the root of *Angelica* (**ggis kena** in Dena'ina) and with wormwood leaves (*Artemesia,* **ts'elbeni** in Dena'ina). He continued this treatment for a number of days until his finger healed, and he was able to return to the doctor to show him the results.

It is obvious from the scope of his travels documented in this book that Shem has a strong sense of adventure and a curiosity about the world around him. What may not be so obvious is his ability to meet the demands of a situation in a creative and innovative way. Nor has his sense of adventure ended with old age, but on the contrary, is very much alive today. Jim and I have had the good fortune to accompany him on a number of adventures, two of which I relate below.

Shem and his son, Billy, had not been back to their old country on the Susitna River for over twenty years when we all decided to go by boat to the area on a Memorial Day weekend in 1977.

Shem's niece, Katherine Nicolie, accompanied us on this adventure, which started in Anchorage and was supposed to end at Susitna Station. Our first difficulty was a leaky dory, which we continuously bailed in order to keep afloat. We were too late for the high tide at the mouth of the Susitna River, which made it impossible for us enter the river. Instead, we became soundly stranded on the mudflats with no hope of leaving until the next high tide at midnight, approximately 12 hours later. Of course, Shem was the first one out of the boat, and with a stick in hand, he was immediately off exploring. After finding us a proper place to set our windbreak on this extremely windy but sunny day, he took off again, exploring. He returned with with gull eggs that he had found on the mudflat. We promptly boiled them and ate them with our crackers and tea. After supplying lunch, he went down to the boat to oversee our patching it. Finally the midnight tide set us free and we cruised towards the lights of Anchorage, which looked good after our adventuring with Shem.

At another time, on a visit to Lime Village, Shem went with us and two Lime Village people to climb **Q'in Tetl'i,** a hill west of the village. Halfway up the hill it began to hail, and we huddled together under a tree and a plastic tarp. When the storm subsided, we suggested to Shem that he wait there for the rest of us, while we hurry to the top for a look. He agreed and graciously gave me his walking stick. Less than two minutes after we reached the top of **Q'in Tetl'i,** we heard a noise behind us. Turning around we found Shem, a broad smile on his face, taking his last step to the top.

of Nancy Lake.... One informant [Shem Pete] recalled hearing about 'a big **nichił**' and fish traps at this location."

Capps (1929:78): "The old winter dog trail from the Alaska Railroad at Nancy to the Kuskokwim by way of Rainy Pass is still open and may be used during the winter to points on the Skwentna as far west as the mouth of the Happy River. In summer the winter trail from Susitna Station to the Skwentna at Skwentna Crossing is said to be too swampy for travel by loaded pack horses."

12.13 K'itudaghi'ut • 'Where Water Extends in (to Land)'
"Indian Bay," "Indian Cove," middle bay on the east side of Nancy Lake
Shem Pete: "«There was a village at **Tudli Bena**. We used to stay where they had the fish fence. At Indian Bay there used to be **nichił** and they had fish traps there.» "That was the most important place for the Indians up there. They catch lots of fish over there. «And they [non-Native fishermen] remove that fish fence.» They pull out those stakes that they had driven in there. They would spoil motor. They put them fish trap poles in about one hundred years ago. They just pull it out about twenty years ago.

"«The village was at the head of this bay near a spring. Old man Bill Pete [not Shem's son, Billy] had a house there, the last one. There were half a dozen **nichił** there. The fish trap site was at the narrows at the mouth of the bay.»"

The Cook Inlet Historic Sites Project (1975:94) says that "A reported winter village [was] at Nancy Lake. According to Mr. [Mike] Ardaw, the natives of this village vacated during the summer months for fish camp at Pt. Possession. The population at its height was estimated at fifty persons in 1932. Mr. Ardaw also described a large flat rock which was the focal point for much of the social and economic activity in the village. Women would go there to clean and cook the fish which was brought home." This is also noted by Fall (1981:384–385).

Shem Pete recalled that Knik Arm Dena'ina from **Niteh** [14.4] and Eklutna [15.21], including the Ezis, regularly came up here around March to hunt and fish. They continued this until the 1930s.

Shem and Billy provided additional details in an interview with Fall and Greiser in 1986: Shem: "That bay there [**K'itudaghi'ut** at Nancy Lake], they used to put up part [of] their fish."

Billy: "I think they used those willow bark fish nets for just probably one guy, you know, he can tie it around.... Where he see lots of fish, he set the net out there. That's free fishing; bury them here and there."

Shem: "They used to be got fish traps there too. Mouth [of] the river too. They got two big traps for all the people."

Billy: "They never let no fish go by. Oh, when they catch enough fish, why the chief lift the trap up. Let the fish go by for next year."

12.14 Tudli Bena Dunich'di • 'The One Upriver from Cold Water Lake'
Frying Pan Lake or "Lynx Lake"
Shem Pete: "«There is another one that flows in [to Nancy Lake] on the upriver side. **Dunich'di**, that's the name.»"

12.15 Betnu K'etelehitnu • 'Fish Run Creek'
§Nancy Creek into east end of Nancy Lake
Shem Pete: "«Red salmon spawn here. The Dena'ina would spear fish here.»"

Shem Pete stated that the road from White's Crossing that crosses this creek passes over some Dena'ina graves.

This the closest drainage with a Dena'ina name from Shem Pete's cabin. Fall and Greiser (1986): Shem: "Yeah, 1948 we moved to Nancy Lake. And I built a cabin there, wintertime."

12.16 Qughun or **Qughun Dghelaya** • 'The Hump,' 'Hump Mountain'
Bald Mountain Ridge, "Willow Mountain"
See also 8.72 for Qughun Betnu, South Fork of Willow Creek, based upon this name. **Qughuna** 'humpback salmon' is a similar word. While living at Nancy Lake, Shem and Billy Pete frequently hunted on this ridge. Billy Pete said, "We go up there all the time just to enjoy our lives."

Katherine Nicolie: "My stepdad said Qughun was shortened from **beq'e nuch'k'esdghani** ['We Pack Something Back Up On it']. You talk about it, and it gets bad weather, they say. My stepdad got caribou in back of **Qughun** in his day. All gone in my time."

It was on **Qughun** (which she refers to as "Willow Mountain") that Katherine Nicolie first heard the **K'eq'a Tsukdu'a** (Pika Story) as a small girl from her mother. The story relates how a young man disrespectfully wounded a pika and consequently was transformed into one himself. Katherine Nicolie: "Then we go back to Willow Mountain. And poor Mom. They were catching those ground squirrel. Make a coat for us. Make a blanket for us. Make a parka for her husband. They didn't have no shoepack or nothing. Mooseskin moccasin. That's all we used to wear" (McClanahan 1986:133).

A section of Chandonnet's 1989 fictionalized story *Chief Stephen's Parky* is set on **Qughun.**

12.17 Qughun Tał • 'Hump Flat Place'
large flat westerly slope of Bald Mountain Ridge

§12.25 Qughun Tał Betnu • 'Hump Flat Place - Stream'
second stream west of Coal Creek, crossing Sitze Road

12.18 Ggisgaht'in K'ilant • 'Where There Is Pyrite'
point, elev. 3137', on west end of Bald Mountain Ridge
Shem Pete: "«Way up **Qughun** above the Little Susitna, there is a place where there is pyrite, so they call it **Ggisgaht'in K'ilant**.»"

"From **Ts'iheł** [8.39, hill at west end of Bald Mountain Ridge] there up to **Qughun** at **Ggisgaht'in K'ilant** is a seven or eight-foot long pyrite on the side toward Little Susitna.

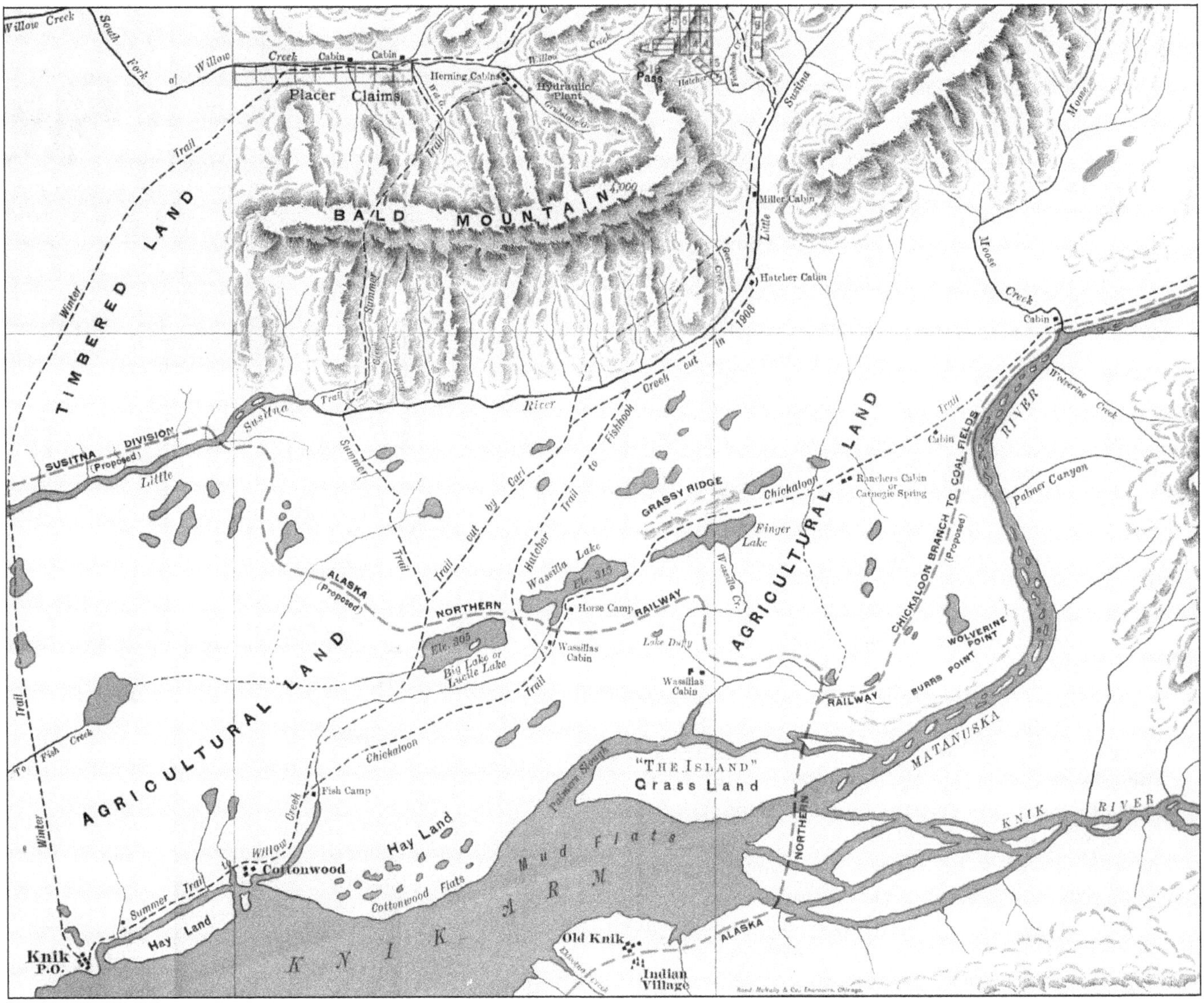

MAP 50

Detail from 1910b Sleem map of Willow Creek Mining District: Knik Arm.

This "Map of Willow Creek Mining District" is another fine map printed in Seward by D.H. Sleem. This is the south half of the map, showing the trail system, the proposed railway corridor, the Wasilla Lakes, and numerous structures ("Wasillas Cache," "Wasillas Cabin"), as well as many locally used place names from the 1900s and 1910s.

ARCHIVES, ALASKA AND POLAR REGIONS DEPT., RASMUSON LIBRARY, UNIVERSITY OF ALASKA FAIRBANKS

If we find it we make money. They dig down seven or eight feet, no bottom to it. They take axe and take seeds out of it. I don't think any good. I go through from Willow and go across over the mountain. I come out at Wasilla."

12.19 K'eda Beq'e Nay'uni • 'The One That Has a Horn on It'
Government Peak
Shem Pete: "«On **Qughun** they say there is a horn. Those hills are caribou horns.» They found caribou horns on it all over. «They seem to be rocks. I think they turned to rock.»

"And there's another one [rock] that looks like a porcupine standing on a rock. It wiggles in the wintertime."

12.20 Beq'e Ndnadalyut • 'Where Men Are Standing on It'
§possibly Idaho Peak (revised location)
Katherine Nicolie: "There is a story about two rocks standing there that look like humans. **Beq'e Ndnadalyut** back in there over **Qughun**. They hunt groundhog. When folks come back the kids turned to rock. They don't go close to 'em on account of bad weather."

12.21 Tsałtastnu Tl'u • '-Ω- River Headwaters'
upper Little Susitna River above canyon, in Independence Mine area
Potter (1967:23) noted that one summer trail used by Indians shown on the Johnston and Herning map of 1899 (Maps 45 and 52) went from the Matanuska River to the upper Little Susitna River, and over the pass to upper Willow Creek.

12.22 Tsałtastnu Dghelaya • '-Ω- River Mountain
Montana Peak

FIGURE 166

Valley above Archangel Creek on **Tsałtastnu Tl'u** (12.21, upper Little Susitna River). The mountain on the east bank is the north side of **Tside K'ae Dghelaaye'** (14.79), the Ahtna name for Arkose Peak and surrounding ridges.
PHOTO BY FRED HIRSCHMANN #2912A

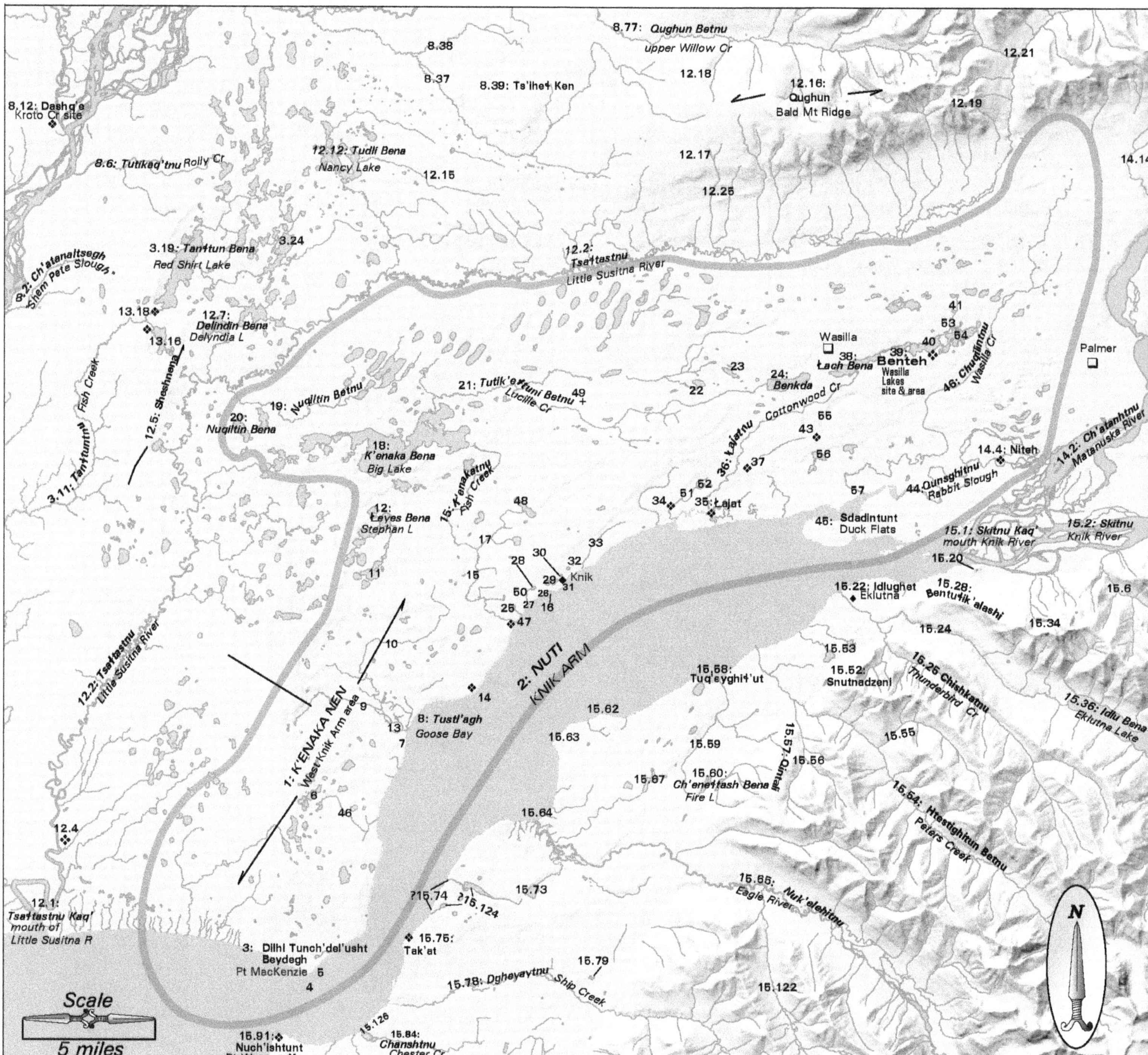

MAP 51

Place names map of the Western Knik Arm, showing Nos. 13.1 to 13.57.

MAP BY MATT GANLEY

13 Western Knik Arm

to mouth of Matanuska River

Osgood (1937:18): "The center of the Upper Inlet country is Knik Arm, a once populous region. Grassy meadows and shelving flat land lie between the arm and the Chugach Mountains, while the valleys of streams flowing from the northward offer opportunities for pleasant settlements. Tremendous tides, the second greatest in the world, characterize the Upper Inlet, making sea travel difficult.... The climate is colder [than that of lower Cook Inlet] but yet tempered by the sea. The land hunting is good but the salt water fauna is less rich because of the influx of glacial streams."

Fall (1981:178, 181, 203): "Most of the permanent villages were on the upper portions of Knik Arm, near red or silver salmon streams. Defense was also probably an important consideration in the choice of sites.... The Knik Arm Tanaina lacked beluga, and their runs of king salmon and eulachon were poorer than those to the west.... Along Knik Arm there was a more pronounced movement in spring... to establish [king salmon] fish camps on the lower parts of Knik Arm and Fire Island."

Travel from Knik Arm to the Oshetna and upper Susitna River area was summarized nicely by Wrangell in the 1830s: "The Kenai [Dena'ina] living to the north, along the Knyk and the Sushitna, on the other hand, undertake a much longer journey. They go northeastwards from the northern angle of the straits and travel 7 days' fast march, or 10 days at the usual speed, through the mountain canyons as far as a very high ridge; the women and children and the poorer hunters stay at its foot while the rest travel 7 days farther to the small lake Chluben [name not certain, in the Tyone Lake area] which lies on a plateau not far from the source of the Sushitna. Here there are large herd of reindeer [caribou] which also come to spend the winter in this locality. The hunters drive them in bands out of the woods into the lake, where they stab them from their canoes. The Ahtnas come here too, from Lake Mantylbana [Tazlina Lake], 14 days' journey away, as do the Galtsans from the [upper] Copper River, 10 days' distance by the fastest march over the mountains. The Kenai [Dena'ina] travel for 6 days farther to a small lake, in order to meet and trade with the western Galtsans [Lower Tanana Athabascans from Toklat or the Tanana River]. All these tribes depend on one another in trading their products, and display expert knowledge in their choice and purchases. After the hunting ends, usually at the end of September or in October, they travel the four days down the rapid river Sushitna to Cook's Inlet, in canoes covered with untreated reindeer hides. The families left at the foot of the mountain return home by the way they came" (1980:58).

See also comments on the Wasilla area in 13.39, the Matanuska River Valley at the start of Chapter 14, the Eklutna area in 15.21, the Anchorage area in 15.78, and the Point Possession area in 16.21.

13.1 K'enaka Nen • '-Ω- Land'
general Knik-Big Lake area
‡**K'enaka** resists usual analysis. The name is an archaism, and may be an early founding Dene place name that has been reshaped. The name has not been definitely translated by Upper Inlet speakers nor by Kari. It is in a set of names: **K'enakatnu**, Fish Creek (13.15), and **K'enaka Bena**, Big Lake (13.18). Also the Knik area Dena'ina people are known as the **K'enaht'ana**. The word **k'enah** could be translated as 'eyes' or 'vision,' though an Athabascan ethnonym that means 'vision people' would be somewhat unusual.

Variant spellings of the name "Knik" appeared on

Sources: Bailey Theodore, Johnny Shaginoff, John Stump, Shem Pete, Mike Alex, Mike Theodore, Arthur Theodore

2003 revisions: names added 13.46–13.57; locations revised 13.6, 13.16, 13.23, 13.31, 13.32, 13.36, 13.40, 13.41, 13.43, 13.45.
‡2016 revisions: names revised 13.1, 13.15, 13.35, 13.46, 13.47.

maps for Knik River as early as 1852 by Tebenkov and 1870 by Dall, and for Knik Arm by Davidson in 1869. Katherine Arndt (personal communication) notes that "five villages in the Orthodox Church confessional lists are listed simply as Knykovskoe 1st settlement through Knykovskoe 5th settlement from 1846 through 1876. In 1877 through 1881 there are only four villages, and from 1882 onward just one." There is a good discussion in Fall 1981:391–394 of the various uses of the names Knik, New Knik, and Old Knik (Eklutna) in the American period. Fall notes that "the term 'Knik' is not a Dena'ina name for any one place, but rather a Euro-American designation for an area or group of villages and their inhabitants" (1981:391).

Dall (1870:272), Baker (1906:373), Hodge (1907:717), and Orth (1971:533) have suggested that Knik derives from an Eskimo word for 'fire,' such as Alutiiq/Central Yup'ik *keneq*. Hodge (1907:717) states: "Knik (Eskimo: 'fire,' a name given by the Eskimo of Kodiak because, having no seaworthy boats of their own, they signaled other tribes across the bay to send aid." Hodge (1907:716) also notes that in 1882 Hoffman (in an ms. for the Bueau of American Ethnlogy) gave Chugach Eskimo (or Alutiiq) names for five divisions of the "Knaiakhotana," i.e., the Cook Inlet Dena'ina, one of which is "*Knikamut* (=Knik, Fire-signal people)." However, this may not be a true Chugach Eskimo ethnonym, and is more likely a mid-nineteenth century folk etymology with Alutiiq words for 'fire' or 'fire people.'

We speculated in the first edition that the name was reshaped from **K'enaht'ana,** the name for the Knik Arm Dena'ina band, or from **K'enakanen**, (13.1) the name for the Knik Arm area, and this still appears to be the best explanation. The name "Knik" is not derived from the Dena'ina names for Knik River (Skitnu 'brush river,' see 15.2), or Knik Arm (Nuti see 13.2).

FIGURE 167

Dilhi Tunch'del'usht Beydegh, 'Point Where We Transport Hooligans' (13.3, Point MacKenzie) with a view up **Nuti** (13.2, Knik Arm). The Knik Arm and Susitna Dena'ina used to catch hooligan (eulachon, *Thaleichtys pacificus*) in the Susitna Delta or Ship Creek areas and transport them here. The Knik Arm Dena'ina would come here in boats to relay the fish.

PHOTO BY PRISCILLA RUSSELL

13.2 Nuti • 'Salt Water'

Knik Arm and Cook Inlet

DeLaguna (1934:140): "Knik Arm is called Qay'tnu (Nikita) or Qi'tnu (Theodore, Eklutna)." This name via de Laguna was not re-elicited, but cf. **Skitnu** 15.2, the name for Knik River. In the 1970s the most commonly used Upper Inlet term for Knik Arm was simply **Nuti** 'Salt Water,' the same term that is used to refer to Cook Inlet.

Nellie Chickalusion has told the story of the founding of the **Yusdi Kinughelchina** or **Dusduyghelchina**, 'The Point Clan' (Kari 1980:47–50). In this story two sisters at Eklutna get caught on an ice floe while fishing in the winter in Knik Arm. They drift down Cook Inlet to Kustatan where people helped them ashore. There the Point Clan was founded. The Point Clan was a small clan that only occured in Cook Inlet Dena'ina. When discussing this story, Billy Pete once stated, "That happened about 1,000 years ago." Shem Pete then commented, "No, more like 1,500 years ago."

In 1914–1915 George Palmer gave a summary of the channels in Knik Arm based upon 30 years of his observations to engineer R.S. Patton:

"Mr. Palmer states that these channels are constantly changing and that the changes are of two kinds. First there is a gradual change, which is going on all the time; channel deepening in one place and filling in in another or shifting slightly in position, the amount of change depending upon the amount of rainfall in the basin drained by the various streams....

"Second, the arm is liable to be visited by a flood of considerable proportion, which, in a few hours, will change its entire configuration. These floods have their origin in a large lake drained by the Knik River... [see 15.18, Lake George].

"About fifteen years ago the waters of this lake burst through the ice barrier which confined them and flooded the arm. Previous to that time the channel up the arm had followed the coast of the north shore until up to, or a little above, the present town of Knik, then turned toward the center of the arm, which it followed to the river. The debris carried down by this flood entirely filled up all the channels, so that the present ones have been cut since that time. The Indians of this region state that these floods are liable to occur about every 15 to 20 years" (Alaska Engineering Commission 1916:127–28).

13.3 Dilhi Tunch'del'usht Beydegh • 'Point Where We Transport Hooligans'
Point MacKenzie
Shem Pete: "«From MacKenzie across to Dgheyay Leht [Ship Creek mouth, 15.78] used to be a short distance, like a river, they used to tell me. They cut fish with an ulu knife out there. They used to speak to them and toss the ulu back and forth, they told me. 'Impossible,' I told them. But then it happened that it got wider. It might have eroded out about a mile. But before, the banks were close together and they used to toss the ulu back and forth. I heard that from those old people.»"

Spurr (1900:65): "In the early part of June great schools of a small, oily fish known as the candle-fish enter the Sushitna River and ascend the Skwentna at least as far as the first snag flats....

"For a short season these candle-fish are so abundant as to almost entirely fill the river in places, so that it is impossible to wade without treading upon them, and they can be dipped in large quantities with common dip nets, or even with baskets. The candle-fish annually supplies a large quantity of food of the natives, who lay up a store for a long season. The salmon and other fish also ascend the Sushitna, although not in so large quantities as in the famous salmon rivers."

See 2.3 for other descriptions of the Dena'ina hooligan harvest.

13.4 Q'ech'nilent • 'Where Current Flows Back'
tide rip off Point MacKenzie
This and 13.5 are some of the few special current-condition features in Cook Inlet for which there are recorded place names. See also 15.94.

13.5 Tułtsedza • 'Swirling Water'
tide rip off Point MacKenzie

13.6 K'teleh Bena • 'Fish Run Lake'
§Lost Lake (revised location)

§13.46 K'telehtnu • 'Fish Run Stream'
Mule Creek

13.7 Hnihighil'iy • 'Tooth That Is Embedded'
hill on south side of Goose Bay

13.8 Tustl'agh • §'Rear Portage'
Goose Bay
Tustl'agh, Goose Bay was a popular goose hunting area for the Knik Dena'ina. Art Theodore: "I asked them one time I said, 'How did you guys used to get them geese a long time ago if you didn't shoot them out of the air?' and... I asked my uncle and he said, "Well you go down there and they'd set out snares on sticks and put them about where they thought they'd be." And they put kinda like little feed out there, and they get geese in there. And then they'd club them. And they'd club them. And he said that somehow when he was like four or five [years old] [the geese] would be bigger than him and he'd have a hard time.... He told me they'd put out snares. They'd drive in stakes and later on they used traps. But they didn't use the metal traps. They'd wrap like cloth or rope around the jaws of it so it wouldn't cut through. Cause if it [the trap] broke its foot, it would just fly away."

Shem Pete: "«In 1915 I left Susitna in a boat and came over to the Goose Bay cannery. They had just built a cannery there. There were Chinamen there.» Lot of people there. «I saw that cannery there in 1914 and 1915. We went by boat to George Palmer's [store] and sold fur.»"

13.9 Tustl'aghtnu • 'Rear Pass Creek'
south fork of Goose Creek
This name refers to a set of trails and portages from Goose Bay north to Red Shirt Lake, passing Sevenmile Lake, Big Lake, Papoose Twin Lake, and the Little Susitna River.

13.10 Łeyestnu • 'Dwarf Birch Creek'
Goose Creek
Shem Pete: "«The trail [from the Little Susitna to Knik Arm] went on **Łeyestnu**.»"

13.11 Biłni Dnaghelggey Bena • 'White Water Lake'
Sevenmile Lake
Art Theodore: "The water comes from Sevenmile, what they call Sevenmile Lake. Brian Road, is probably about the highest point in this area. And given its height, water running downhill. Then most of these lakes here are at a lower level than the one on the other side, like Threemile [Lake]. Sevenmile Lake is like seven miles from Knik. And that kinda run off like.... My dad had a trapper's cabin on Sevenmile Lake.

"Well I went there and I checked the traps one time. My dad had 13 dogs and we used to come from Knik and we'd go. His line kinda went like this. So anyway we went Threemile Lake and then he'd go around the outside and go to Sevenmile Lake and get beaver. And then he'd come back down Fish Creek."

FIGURE 168

Art Theodore of Knik, reading a copy of *SPA* at **Tustl'agh** (13.8, Goose Bay) in May of 2001. The point to the left is **Hnihighil'iy** (13.7).

PHOTO BY JAMES KARI

13.12 Łeyes Bena • 'Dwarf Birch Lake'
Stephan Lake
John Stump: "«They used to use that **łeyes** for tea, those little willows.»"

Shem Pete: "I guess they had **nichił** there a long time ago."

13.13 Ełnen Ghiłget • 'Rotten Ground'
swamp on Goose Bay side of Mosquito Point
Name contributed by John Stump.

13.14 Ts'es I'unt • 'Where There Is a Rock'
"Mosquito Point," between Fish Creek and Goose Bay
It is interesting that this place name contains the Ahtna word **ts'es** 'rock.'

Shem Pete: "«Red Jack, [Jack Bartell] and his daughter Minnie had a village at Mosquito Point. They say that there were lots of salmon there.» Where Army take it over there used to be a village. «There was a village there with **nichił**. Red Jack was called **Bushuldi**.» They were last there in 1927 or so. Then they moved down to Tyonek."

13.15 K'enakatnu *(Dena'ina);* **C'enacetna'** *(Ahtna)* • '-Ω- Stream'
Fish Creek; village site near mouth of Fish Creek
This Dena'ina name has also been used for Knik village and townsite located at Knik Lake, 13.29. The Ahtna also called the Knik Station trading post and town site, which was located a mile north by Knik Lake, by this name.

This was a major Dena'ina village on western Knik Arm and the most well known place name in this area. Perhaps the first recording of this name was "Knukhitnu" in the Wrangell notes from the 1830s (Arndt 1985). This settlement is also noted on Petroff's 1884 map (Map 6) as "Knakatnuk." Potter 1967:9 notes the Petroff source as "Knadatnuk, pop. 57, Goose Bay-Fish Creek area." Four sites are listed in this area in Cook Inlet Historic Sites Project (1975:85–86).

DeLaguna (1934:141): "He (Nikita of Knik) showed us a former village site ... on a low terrace on the north bank of the stream, about a mile above the mouth.... The old village is marked by the frame of a modern smoke house and a modern bath house, the latter made of branches bent over to form an inverted basket large enough to admit a single person. Nikita told me that this village was called Knakha'tnu, and was supposed to have been only a summer camp, though from the house pits he imagined it must originally have been a winter village."

It was the finding of a stone lamp by a homesteader here at Fish Creek in 1913 (Mason 1928) that promted de Laguna's hypothesis that the Upper Inlet had formerly been occupied by an Eskimo people. Excavating here in 1966, Dumond and Mace (1968) saw affinities between labrets and clay pottery from Naknek on the Alaska Peninsula and those found here. They suggested that Knik Arm may have been used intermittently by Eskimos in AD 1000 and later, and that the Dena'ina began using this area no earlier than AD 1650. On the other hand, Kari (1977a,1988a, 1996b) feels that differentiation among the Dena'ina dialects implies that the Dena'ina were in the Upper Cook Inlet area at a much earlier date. The Dena'ina word for stone lamp, **nayneq,** is a loan word from Eskimo.

Fish Creek is apparently the location of the Knik chief **Dusgeda Tukda**'s camp. Shem Pete: "«**Dusgeda Tukda** had eight caches. He used to come over to **Susni Kaq'** [Susitna Delta] in a big umiak in the spring for hooligan and beluga.»" Shem gives a detailed profile of **Dusgeda Tukda** in Fall (1981:280–281). See also 12.4 and Fall (1987:49,66).

Bailey Theodore stated that fish traps were used on Fish Creek until about 1916. Victor McNeil, the last Dena'ina to use one there, died in the early 1970s. He had a smokehouse alongside the creek.

Shem Pete: "«Joe Chilligan had a mother [Minnie Bartell], in one day she could cut I don't know how many hundred fish.» She cut up. Some them other girls cut one fish, she cut « three.» She's champion cutter of fish, they call em. She was from **K'enakatnu** where the fish run, she could cut. «In one day her big smokehouse would be packed full,» she quit."

13.47 K'enakatnu Kaq' • '-Ω- Stream-Mouth'
mouth of Fish Creek
Shem Pete: "Nick Alaska's camp was down that old place right over the bank. Down the Inlet, at **K'enakatnu Kaq'.** Right at mouth of Fish Creek there was an old house there." Nick Alaska died in about 1955 at the age of about seventy-five. See Fig. 159.

Art Theodore: "Right after I was born I came here to fish because I know that they've been dipping, I know that's how them people, Stephan, Nikita and all them

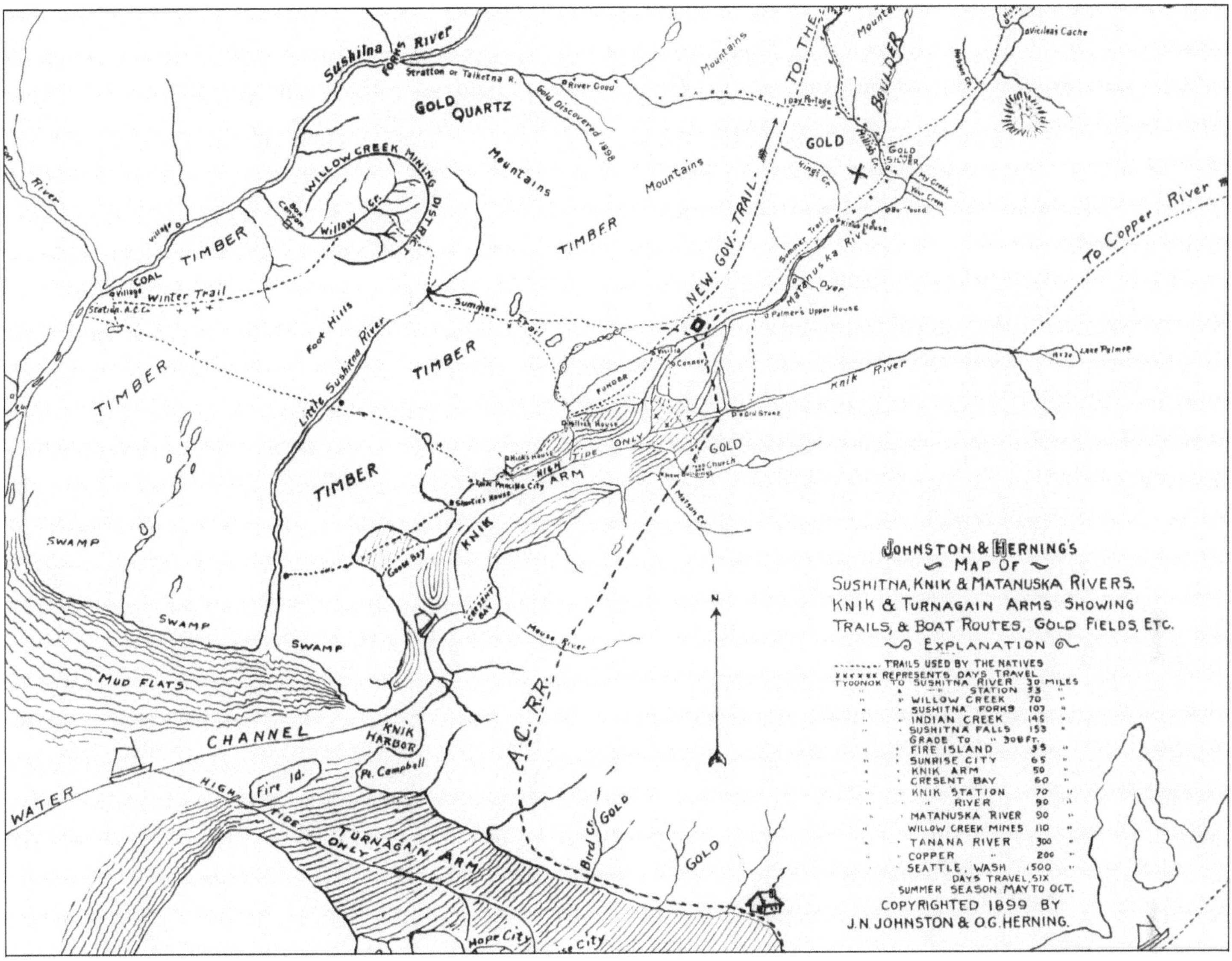

MAP 52

Detail from the 1899 Johnston and Herning Map: Knik Arm and lower Susitna River.

An important and frequently cited source on Knik Arm. The "trails used by natives" are marked by a fine dashed line. Note the various structures, such as the church at Eklutna, "Palmer's Upper House" on the south bank of the Matanuska River, and "Vasilia" in the Wasilla Lake area. A prospective rail route, A.C.R.R., is suggested.

ARCHIVES, ALASKA AND POLAR REGIONS DEPT., RASMUSON LIBRARY, UNIVERSITY OF ALASKA FAIRBANKS

‡The Point MacKenzie Rail Extension has been in development in the Matanuska-Susitna Borough since 2005. A 2008 survey of four possible routes found 29 new sites and a total of 56 prehistoric sites (fish caches or house pits). An appendix of 88 Dena'ina place names from the 2003 edition was included. The Houston-Houston South ROW (Houston-west of Horsehoe Lake-between Papoose Twin Lake and Big Lake) was chosen in consultation with Knik Tribal Council because it had the least potential for impacting historic or cultural sites (US Surface Transportation Board, 2011).

were.... They had a large family, and they were getting all their things from this little area here. They were all good hunters even later on. But they would gather their fish there."

13.16 K'eyghashtnu • 'Fish Harvest Creek'
§channel in Knik Arm tide flat paralleling the bank, between mouth of Fish Creek past Soldiers Creek to Knik Lake outlet (revised location)
Shem Pete: "«Fish are really crowded there. The fish run in there.» They can't go across without touch the fish."

13.17 Niłq'adaydleni Betnu • 'Joining Streams Creek'
Threemile Creek

§13.48 Niłq'adaydleni Bena • 'Joining Streams Lake'
Threemile Lake
Art Theodore:"This little lake on the left here is probably about as the bird flies probably about a mile from Knik. It's Threemile Lake trail, and we used to pick berries on the other side of it. It's kinda like a point for going, Threemile Lake then it kinda goes off toward Sevenmile Lake [13.11] from here. And it's kinda like a hunting and berry picking trail.... On your left here are tree stands where we used to hunt in here. And you could get up high here and look down and you could see the swamp from up here, it's kinda high and then it goes to low."

13.18 K'enaka Bena • '-Ω- Lake'
Big Lake
Bailey Theodore: "The [Knik Arm Dena'ina] had a village at Big Lake. Rich people owned it. They caught fish there year round. They couldn't starve. Even in February month they got silver salmon that were dark fish but lively. And lots of trout too. They could spot the fish under the ice. In two days I once got eighty pounds of trout from Big Lake. There's ling cod there, three feet long. They set hooks overnight for the ling cod. They were all rich people there. It belonged to the **Chishyi** clan." Bailey Theodore also reported that "Aleuts" [Alutiiq] once attacked the Dena'ina village at Big Lake.

John Stump: "That's where they [the Dena'ina of the past] used to have races."

Billy Pete: "**K'enaka Bena** last, last time they were using it for fishing and stuff around 1915, yeah somewhere around, maybe a few years after 1915. They used to bury those fish and make **chuqilin** and put up some fall fish too. They never got enough of fish, they always run short of fish all the time at Knik. Those Knik people used to go to mouth of Susitnu spring time, early in the spring so they can catch hooligan and eat hooligan and kill beluga."

Shem Pete: "«On **K'enakatnu** [Fish Creek] there is a big lake, **K'enaka Bena**. From **K'enaka Bena** to **Susitnu** [Susitna Station] there was just one trail that crossed the Little Susitna. They would catch fall fish there and make **chuqilin** [fermented fish]. The **nichił** were at the outlet. The trail through here went to the Little Susitna and then to **Tanłtunt** [Red Shirt Lake].»"

FIGURE 169

K'enakatnu (13.15, Fish Creek) flows out from **K'enaka Bena** (13.18, Big Lake). These two names and the regional name **K'enaka Nen** (13.1) are the most famous Dena'ina names from the west side of Knik Arm. We can't fully analyze the syllables **-naka-**.
PHOTO BY JAMES KARI

13.19 Nuqiltin Betnu • 'They Found a Place Creek'
outlet stream of West Papoose Twin Lake and stream from Hourglass Lake
This stream actually is in the Little Susitna River drainage.

13.20 Nuqiltin Bena • 'They Found a Place Lake'
West Papoose Twin Lake
Shem Pete: "«Towards Knik, when you leave **Tsałtastnu** [Little Susitna River, 12.2], the trail goes by **Nuqiltin Bena.**» I guess they had **nichił** there long time ago. «The one on the other side of **Nuqiltin Bena** is **Łeyes Bena** [Stephan Lake, 13.12]. **Nuqiltin Bena** is right next to the Little Susitna. There was a trail there. The trail went on **Łeyestnu** [Goose Creek, 13.10].»"

§13.49 possibly **Nuqenduggesh** • 'Lightning Strikes'
hill off Meadow Creek, near Theodore homestead
Name suggested by Art Theodore.

13.21 Tutik'ełtuni Betnu • 'Creek of Ponds Extend Down'
Lucille Creek
Bailey Theodore said that fish traps were used on this creek for both trout and salmon.

13.22 Tunilch'eli Bena • 'Clear Water Lake'
Clear Lake or perhaps "Wallace Lake" on some maps
At mile 73 on the railroad. Both this name and 13.23 were obtained from John Stump.

13.23 Hey Gega Bena • 'Lowbush Cranberry Lake'
§Jacobsen Lake at mile 70 on the railroad, west of Lake Lucille

13.24 Benkda • 'No-Good Lake'
Lake Lucille, Lucile Lake
Baker said of Lake Lucille, "Locally the prospectors and others call it Wasilla's Lake, after the chief of the Knik Indians who lives there" (1906:415).

Bailey Theodore: "Our great-great-grandfather bought this lake for us people to fish in, for the **Nulchina** people. They had their own lakes."

Mike Theodore: "They paid for that lake with **k'enq'ena** [dentalia beads]."

The outlet of this lake was a good fishing location (Fall 1987:36).

Heinie Snider (1966:64): "Before the coming of the whiteman the population of the Matanuska and Susitna Valleys was made up of Alaskan Indians. They were hunters, trappers and fishermen. On our homestead on Lake Lucille, you can still see the trail leading to the outlet and a small creek where large salmon and trout were caught. Using a trap made of willows, they also were able to catch migrating muskrats."

See Sleem (1910b) (Map 50) and Davidson (1911) (Map 54) for the Cottonwood Creek trail going past both ends of Lucile Lake and another trail above the lake that lead to the upper Little Susitna River.

FIGURE 170
K'enaka Bena (13.18, Big Lake) at its outlet into Fish Creek.
PHOTO BY JAMES KARI

13.25 Hnits'uk'nilut, §Hnits'uk'nilut Bena • 'Where Dishes Are Embedded,' 'Where Dishes Are Embedded Lake'
Caves Lake

13.26 Tuq'ets'ghet • 'By Spring Water'
site one mile below Knik, opposite Rohn Road turnoff
Shem Pete: "«'At the spring water' is the name where the one they called Aruf had a village. 'At the spring water.'» That's below Knik. Big town about a mile at least, about a mile far down the Inlet. «His house was up on the bank.» All Susitna people used to be living there. "«[Aruf's] Indian name was **Tenqa**. He was the last chief. He died in about 1913. His wife was **Łquqaghetna**. She was a Susitna woman. She was the mother of Jack Healy and Danya.»"

13.27 Ch'ak'nileght • 'Where Fish Swim Out'
mouth of "Soldiers Creek," 2 miles south of Knik
It is possible that a name noted in the Wrangell papers as "chuliuh" refers to this site (Arndt 1985).

§13.50 Ch'ak'nileghtnu • 'Fish Swim Out-Stream'
"Soldiers Creek," White Lake outlet stream, 2 miles south of Knik
Bailey Theodore reported that there were some **nichił** on this creek.

Art Theodore: "This is where the Nikitas and Nick Alaska used to be.... They used to live right in there. There's a cabin still in there. And it's falling in right now."

The Fisher-Hong archaeological site is on this outlet stream of White Lake (Dumond and Mace 1968).

13.28 Ggih Qughijaq Bena • 'Lake Where a Monster Came Up'
White Lake

FIGURE 171

‡Chief Stephan and family, photo taken on June 8, 1906. Herning: "Took picture of Stephan's family in sloop." (Via C. Mielke, p.c.)

O. G. HERNING COLLECTION (#74-65-5), ARCHIVES, ALASKA AND POLAR REGIONS DEPT., RASMUSON LIBRARY, UNIVERSITY OF ALASKA FAIRBANKS

13.29 Nughay Bena • 'Frog Lake'
Knik Lake; Knik townsite, "New Knik"
Usually the Dena'ina applied the name **K'enakatnu** to both Fish Creek and Knik town.

De Laguna (1934:141): "There are several house ruins at Knik Lake. This is probably the site of Cun'ta (Nikita). The houses measure 12 feet square (House I and II), and 25 by 30 feet (House III). The doorways are in the longer sides facing the lake. There were hearths in each house, and shallow piles of scorched rocks outside. I do not think the houses are very old." This site is also surveyed in Dumond and Mace (1968), and it is listed in Cook Inlet Historic Sites Project (1975:85) as site No. 147. The name "Cun'ta" via deLaguna is not recognized by contemporary speakers.

According to Shem Pete, one of the first Russians to live in the upper inlet was a storekeeper who was here around the time of the purchase (1867). He was called **Galeq Q'echishen** 'The One Who Wrote on Paper.' Although Chandonnet has stated that an Orthodox church was established in Knik as early as 1835 (1979:12), we have found no documentary evidence to support this, and it seems that no church was built here until 1870 or later.

Znamenski (1996:13) has noted that a log frame for the first Orthodox church in this area began in 1881, and a chapel was built in 1889. In 1897 the logs and fixtures of this building were moved to Eklutna.

George Palmer opened his store here in ‡1893 (C. Mielke, p.c.), and then the place became known as "New Knik," distinguishing it from the older store up Knik Arm at the mouth of the Knik River, **Niteh** (see 14.4 and Fall 1981:393). The town of Knik thrived between 1895 and 1915.

Irwin 1968:13: "Two years later [after founding a store a the mouth of the Matanuska River in 1885], 1887, [George] Palmer constructed a store at New Knik, on tide water at the west end of the Matanuska Valley. Here was deep water for boats and many Indians came from the Matanuska, the Susitna, and the Copper River Basins to catch and dry fish for their yearly supply of food.... Palmer continued his business in his Knik store and adjoining saloon until 1919 when his building burned. He then moved to Kenai, opened a store and died there in 1929.

‡In *SPA* 2003:278 we noted that Shem Pete had told a long narrative about the 1885 murder of George Holt, the Alaska Commercial Company trader at Knik, by an Ahtna man. Colleen Mielke (2010) has assembled a detailed account of the incident based on a remarkable array of primary sources, including her synopsis of Shem Pete's narrative (Pete 1985). Shem's story does not mention scene of the Holt murder; it focuses on the time of the 1891 citizens' arrest and hanging of the murderer, an Ahtna man Nicolai. Mielke also has extensive material on Knik Chief Afanasii (aka **Dusgeda Tukda** or Alexander) who provoked discontent in Knik for several years and instigated Holt's murder. See Mielke's 2010 articles at her web page; also see p. 261.

Knik's history is traced in Potter 1963 and 1967. Cole et al. (1985:31–43) has a nicely illustrated history of Knik. Especially useful is the sketch map (Map 52) of the town as of 1912 drawn by Stanley Herning, the son of Orville Herning, in 1978. The map (op.cit.:36) notes "Indian Chief Stephan's home" and three other groups of "Indian houses" or "Indian homes."

Potter collected a list of surnames for the Indians at Knik at the turn of the century. She writes, "By this time [turn of the century], too, at least five of the Inlet Indians were prosperous enough to own their own boats.... Several carried the government mail between Sunrise and Knik. When the gold miners came into the country, Indians were employed to cut mine timbers, house logs, and birch firewood. They also helped to brush out trails and served as guides. Others made and sold snowshoes, trapped for furs, hunted and sold moose meat (at 5 cents per pound in 1901!), fished and sold both fresh and dried fish, often used for dog food. Their women made fur robes, moccasins, mitts, and trinkets for sale, and picked barrels of cranberries . . . which were shipped through the Inlet trading posts to Seattle and beyond" (1967:11).

Chandonnet's 1989 story "Chief Stephen's Parky" is set in Knik in 1898. The main figures are **Qatsen,** Chief Stephen or Big Stephan who worked for Herning, and his fictionalized wife Olga.

‡C. Mielke has numerous articles on Knik: A history of Knik(2007), on O.J. Herning (2014), and on George Palmer (2007).

Art Theodore: "Right here is where Chief Stephan used to live, had a house right here. Right here on this hill here. And that was higher because it doesn't show. You know because it kinda filled in there. Okay there's spring water run out here and the white man gravesite right here. From here to this corner. And that's Knik [village corporation] land now.... But there's a spring water runs down, that's the one I think where they talk about getting water. Take a right. But it's right over that hill. See that kinda like a house like thing? See there was houses there, but there's graveyards there."

Writing in 1897, Bortnovksy noted: "The time the Copper River people usually descend to the village of Knik is the period between the end of December and the beginning of January. Before or after this time they hardly show up there. They come not all together, but in small groups of about nine to ten people.... The Copper Natives get along with the Kenaitze quite well, and when they come to Knik, they are usually provided with free accomodation in the Kenaitze houses and baraboras.... This winter about eighty Copper Natives visited Knik" (Znamenski 1998:11–12–13).

James Sinyon (West tapes 1973): "They always go to Knik [to trade]. They went down Matanuska River, go to mouth of it, and then they go to Matanuska Bay. They go down there with caribou skins and fox. Every winter the people go there. Sometimes some them go over Chickaloon Pass and down into Matanuska Bay. The first store built in Knik was somebody by name of George Palmer. They buy tea, tobacco. The last time I was down there was 1906. We stayed there just the side of that farmer John. While most of the time we was there we just camp there and sit around and eat. We don't know the winter went by. We finally moved one day this way, you see that, just right at mouth of Chickaloon. We use sled and we go up. We come back ‡with a sled yoke around our neck. We just don't know what to do. Well, we just went on up the Chickaloon River, and we come over the pass into Oshetna River, and when we come to the Susitna River we thought we get on the ice in that river. When we come there gee, gee the ice was just full in there too. There [is] my sled. I think that sled is still there. Because somebody been back there where we just stop and unload our sled and pack. We leave that sled. Our dog hates them days. We pack our dog and we pack ourselves. That was the last time I been to Knik in 1906."

FIGURE 172

Qatsen, chief of Knik, and his family, at their fish camp on lower **Chanshtnu** (15.84, Chester Creek).

PHOTO COURTESY OF ALEXANDRA ALLOWAN

13.30 Kidaghił'i, Niłkidaghel'uyi • 'The Ones That Are Connected Together'

first overflow marsh below Knik Lake

Shem Pete: "«Right in the village of Knik is 'the ones that are connected together,' little lakes are there. That lake come right up to the village. There were **nichił** there.» Quite a few. Three or four or five. «The creek that comes out and upstream» you can't wade across the water, the fish are so thick. «That is a sockeye stream. As they run they come to the point. This is why there were **nichił** there.»"

Art Theodore: "And this **Kidaghił'iy**, we used to come down here and when the tide would go down far enough it made a lake. And farther on down there we used to go on the other side of the lake like and we'd get Indian potatoes. **Ktl'ila** or whatever you call it. **K'tl'ila**, more like string, but it was white and it was kinda underneath like flower. And we used to swim in Knik Lake. The water would run free and we would set a small like a hooligan net and we'd catch salmon. I don't remember king salmon come in there but I know that other salmon came in the Knik Lake."

13.31 Bekidaghił'uyi Gga • 'Little One That Is Connected to the End'

§second lower salt marsh to the east of Knik Lake (location revised)

Shem Pete: "The farthest one to the east is «'Little One That Is Connected to the End.'»

13.32 Biłni Ch'unaghelqeni • 'Bitter Water'
§site and pond three-fourths of a mile north of Knik, on Knik Arm, on point below O'Brien Creek mouth (revised location)
Bailey Theodore: "There are all kinds of springs on that hill. There was a winter village there."

Fall (1981:395): "An important **qeshqa** who figures in the story of a battle with the Chugach Eskimo at Point Woronzof [15.91] had his winter village here."

Art Theodore: "They describe it as a lake above **Kidaghił'iy** sort of like a marker how far it was. And then the water would run off from like Threemile Lake, kinda like go underground and then come back up again so that it kinda ran along the bank too, along the bank, and then the bank kinda run back into O'Brien Creek too. Had like little small streams runoff. And in the springtime the lake would rise and go back down. Would get bigger. And they'd get ducks out of there and they'd get moose down in that area. And it was real good habitat for game."

13.33 Ch'ak'dinłent • 'Where Current Flows Out'
O'Brien Creek

13.34 Htidaghitunt • 'Where the Trail Meets the Place'
site on hill east of mouth of Crocker Creek, at what is locally called "Hughes Creek," creek headed by Lucy Lake
Shem Pete: "«There were four or five **nichił** at **Htidaghitunt**.» There are big spruce there, lots of wood. They say there were **nichił** all over for three, four, or five hundred years."

Johnny Shaginoff was born here in 1909. He reports that "Fifteen or twenty native families used to camp there in the winter; they lived in good log houses. The camp was one of several on the McKinnon and Bill Hughes' homesteads.... McKinnon used to run a restaraunt there" (Chandonnet 1979:18, Tucker 1978:24).

Johnny Shaginoff: "Right close to Crocker Creek, towards Wasilla. Right below, right down the chain [of hills]. Here's another creek. Hughes Creek there in between Cottonwood and Crocker Creek. I think that's where **Htidaghitunt** is."

This area may be the location of "Duck Creek," mentioned by Castner as being by a "trail going toward the Susitna River used by Indians" (1984:15).

Shem Pete: "«From **Htidaghitunt** the used to go straight across to Eklutna, via **Nik'udatl'ech'a** [13.43],» on the flat."

Shem Pete: "Tommy Nikolai's father, an Eklutna chief, was from **Htidaghitunt**. They had four, five **nichił** there. His name was **Benitnalchinen** 'the one with a birthmark.' **Benitnalchinen** married a girl from **Nik'udatl'ech'a**. He kept her at Knik in early years of Knik town. **Htidaghitun** was eight or so miles from **Nik'udatl'ech'a**."

A trail on the Johnston and Herning map (Map 52) leads from this area to the Little Susitna and beyond to upper Willow Creek.

§13.51 Htidaghituntnu • 'Stream of Trail Meets the Place'
"Hughes Creek," stream from Lucy Lake

§13.52 Htidaghitun Bena • 'Lake of Trail Meets the Place'
Lucy Lake

13.35 Łajat *(Dena'ina);* **Łaets Caek'e** *(Ahtna)* • 'Silt Place'
site complex on lower Cottonwood Creek, formerly called "Cottonwood Village"
This name was first recorded as "Khliagia" in the Wrangell notes from the 1830s (Arndt 1985). The Dena'ina term **łach** in the names on Cottonwood Creek refers to fine soil, silt, clay, or loess.

Shem Pete: "«That was an old village. They made **nichił** there.» That's all I heard about it. I didn't see it. Before my time. I think that was the first village [in this area] that went down [was depopulated]. «Eklutna John, whose name was **Qalbis**, and their older brother [Eklutna Theodore] **Kala Łchun**, were born at **Łajat**.»"

De Laguna (1934:140): "At Cottonwood Creek, above Knik on the west shore of Knik Arm, there was an old village site on a high hill, called Tladje't. The name is derived from tlatc, 'sand,' and the stream is called Tladjau'tnu (Nikita). Theodore of Eklutna told me that this was both a summer and a winter village. It was one mile above the mouth of the stream."

"Cottonwood" is noted on the 1910a and 1910b Sleem maps (Map 51) west of Cottonwood Creek. The "Knik-Cottonwood trail," both summer and winter routes are depicted on Davidson (1914) (Map 55, which was surveyed in 1911). The name mentioned by Jim Tyone, p. 226, **T'eghes Konk'ae** 'Cottonwood House,' likely refers to 13.35 but may be for 13.36.

Potter (1967:37): "This village, on Cottonwood Creek a mile from the Inlet, was the junction point of several of the oldest trails out of Knik.... It had a number of white as well as Indian residents."

‡**Łajat** (silt place) is an extensive Dena'ina village including 138 semi-subterranean houses and over 1500 caches. Single and multi-roomed structures have yielded debitage, burned caribou and fish bone, a bone bead, and fire cracked rock. Five houses have been radiocarbon dated between AD 1490–1890. Matanuska-Susitna Borough in collaboration with Knik Tribe is nominating the village as an Archaeological District spanning the pre-contact, Russian, and American periods. (K. Krasinski, p.c., Alaska Archaeology Month [poster], 2007).

13.36 Łajatnu, Łashch'itnu, Łashch'i Betnu *(Dena'ina);* **Łaedzi Na'** *(Ahtna)* • 'Silt (Mud) Place Creek,' or 'Ashes Creek'
Cottonwood Creek
In 1898 Castner noted two streams in this area that "drain a series of lakes in which the Indians fish" (1984:15). There are two variations of this name recorded by Kari, one with the stem 'silt, mud' and another with the word for 'ashes.'

Knik Archaeological Excavations

by Fran Seager-Boss

Fran Seager-Boss is an archaeologist and is the Cultural Resource Specialist with the Matanuska-Susitna Borough. For the past five years she has directed the archaeological work at the Knik townsite.

Over a four year period, between 1998 through 2001, the Matanuska-Susitna Borough, University of Alaska Anchorage, and Matanuska-Susitna College have participated in an archaeological excavation at the former Knik Townsite. The site is situated on the west coast of Knik Arm. The site under investigation is a portion of Knik's residential area situated east of Knik's former commercial center. A trail depicted on a 1911 map divides the site and crosses a small cemetery at the edge of the property under investigation. Archaeological excavations have revealed important data concerning the relationship between early gold miners of the region and the Dena'ina. The following information, gained from the historical record and Herning's diaries, demonstrates the importance of Native trade in Knik at the turn of the twentieth century.

FIGURE 173

Unidentified Dena'ina men at Knik circa 1900.

O. G. HERNING COLLECTION (#74-64-21), ARCHIVES, ALASKA AND POLAR REGIONS DEPT., RASMUSON LIBRARY, UNIVERSITY OF ALASKA FAIRBANKS

George Palmer, a trading post operator, moved his store, in 1887, from the mouth of Knik River (Old Knik) to the western shores of Knik Arm. The move was made to take advantage of the annual gathering of many Indians who came from the Matanuska, Susitna, and Copper River Basins to catch and dry fish for their yearly supply of food (Irwin 1968:13). He was primarily a fur trader until the aftermath of the 1896 Klondike gold strikes. The promise of gold triggered a stream of prospectors into Upper Cook Inlet. It was not long before Knik became a major distribution center for miners plying the tributaries of the Susitna and Matanuska Rivers in search of gold. A number of Dena'ina families of Russian Orthodox faith moved to Eklutna, in 1897, to distance themselves from the traders and miners at Knik, while others stayed (Bortnovsky: Yarborough 1993:5). Orville G. Herning, a prospector representing the Klondike Boston Company, placer mined in the Willow Creek district. He left the company in 1905 and opened his own mercantile store (Herning's diary). The town grew in importance as gold mining opened up in the northern regions of Iditarod and Innoko. The Iditarod Trail, constructed in 1908, traversed through Knik, connecting Seward to Nome with branches leading to several other northern gold mining regions. This brought increased traffic to Knik as a stampede of 10,000 new prospectors flowed through the town over the next four years. Throughout the growth of the town the Dena'ina played an important role in its development, serving as freighters, carpenters, guides, and lumbermen. Six Natives lightered passengers from ship to shore in their own boats. Chief Nicolai owned a boat. Stephan of Knik owned the *Ruby L.* Affinassa and Goosmar of Knik owned a sloop and sailboat respectively. Both Esi (possibly Simeon) and Elie Vacilla of Old Knik also owned boats on the inlet. The latter owned a dory. A Dena'ina won a contract to deliver government mail from Hope and Sunrise to Knik. Others bartered and sold goods to the commercial stores for retail and in some instances for export to Seattle (Herning). Dena'ina men provided dried fish, wild meat, and snowshoes. The women contributed furs, mittens, parkeys, robes, moccasins, and dried fruit for retail and export. The following diary entries indicate the volume of snowshoes the Dena'ina were providing Herning for export.

> March 18, "Theodore was down with snow shoes. Baled up 82 pair of snowshoes...." April 10, "sent 80 pr. Snowshoes to Seattle Hardware Co...." April 30, bought several pair of snowshoes...." May 2, bought 9pr. snowshoes...." May 7, "Buying lots of snowshoes from natives, 78pr. Bundled up...." May

> 11, "Bought 6pr. Snowshoes making 84pr. Ready to ship out...." May 12, "busy in store cash sales $84.30. Mostly native trade. Got 26 more pair of snowshoes making 100pr. Ready to ship on next boat...." May 27 "...shipped another 50pr. Snowshoes...."

The Copper River Ahtna also assisted in providing hides and robes to the commercial stores for retail. Herning noted on February 3, 1908 that "2 Matanuska women arrived, bought $19 fur." On the same date he noted, "Matanuska Natives in town to sell rabbit robes." It was not unusual for the Matanuska, Ahtna natives to spend several months during the winter at Knik (Herning).

Archaeological excavations carried out at the site revealed that a number of natives lived within an area Stanley Herning noted as "Family and Batchelor Homes (right side of Map 53)." The first year test excavations took place in an area immediately adjacent to the commercial district. House features were small, possibly representative of single miner cabins. Contents of the houses and middens yielded utilitarian enamel-ware, various types of tobacco cans, coffee cans, numerous milk cans, medicinal bottles, and alcohol beverage bottles. Larger house features appeared to have supported integrated households. The site has revealed elements of both Euro-American and Dena'ina cultures. Herning's diary recounts several occasions when the Orthodox priest visited Knik and conducted marriage ceremonies for integrated couples—Euro-American miners and Dena'ina women. Artifacts retrieved from features adjacent to a house foundation reflect tools and equipment commonly used by an assayer. A slight distance away from the house, two birchbark lined cache pits were uncovered superimposed by Euro-American goods. Initially used to cache food, its later use was as a midden. Two very large subterranean basements associated with the house feature revealed more assaying tools and numerous pieces of utilitarian ware. From Herning's diary and photograph collection, it is evident that Mr. Patchell, one of the assayers at Knik, was married to a local Dena'ina woman. The feature associated with assaying equipment and cache pits may represent the Patchell home. Another large house feature with a deep, subterranean rolled asphalt lined basement encompassed numerous utilitarian Euro-American goods. Although all the goods recovered from within and immediately outside the house are Euro-American, a short distance from the house foundation twelve white glass trade beads were recovered. This too may indicate occupancy by an integrated couple.

Strung along, north of the trail, are a series of cache pits of indeterminate age. Most have numerous birchbark linings. Each lining is separated by a thin layer of sand and pebbles, indicating reuse through time. One small cabin associated with the cache pits is still in the process of being uncovered. Several soil samples have been taken for flotation purposes, and samples of organic material have been collected for C-14 dating. Flotation samples already processed from a number of cache pits excavated in 1999 have indicated storage of caribou meat and raspberries. Small fish vertebrae have been recovered in one of the cache pits located north of the trail. Similar to caches located outside the Assayer's house feature, cache pits located north of the trail were used as a midden, filled with Euro-American goods in their upper levels. A very large depression encompassing a series of deep cache pits with adjacent smaller ones resemble the same configuration as described by Elizabeth Arndt for the Ahtna. This may indicate a bi-directional communication between the Ahtna and Dena'ina. A couple of house features, located on the bluff above Knik Lake, resemble the characteristic outline of a Dena'ina house owned by a wealthy chief described by both de Laguna and Osgood. There is a strong possibility that these features predate the Euro-American era of the townsite. They are semi-subterranean in nature with a number of cache pits adjacent to the exterior walls. One of the features is composed of two very large central rooms that open up into smaller rooms. The two house features appear to be in line with an older trail now covered with alders that terminates into the current Knik–Goose Bay road. Further investigation may shed light on the occupancy of these large features. Test excavations at Knik townsite are on-going. It is hoped that this will result in a better understanding of the people who inhabited the site.

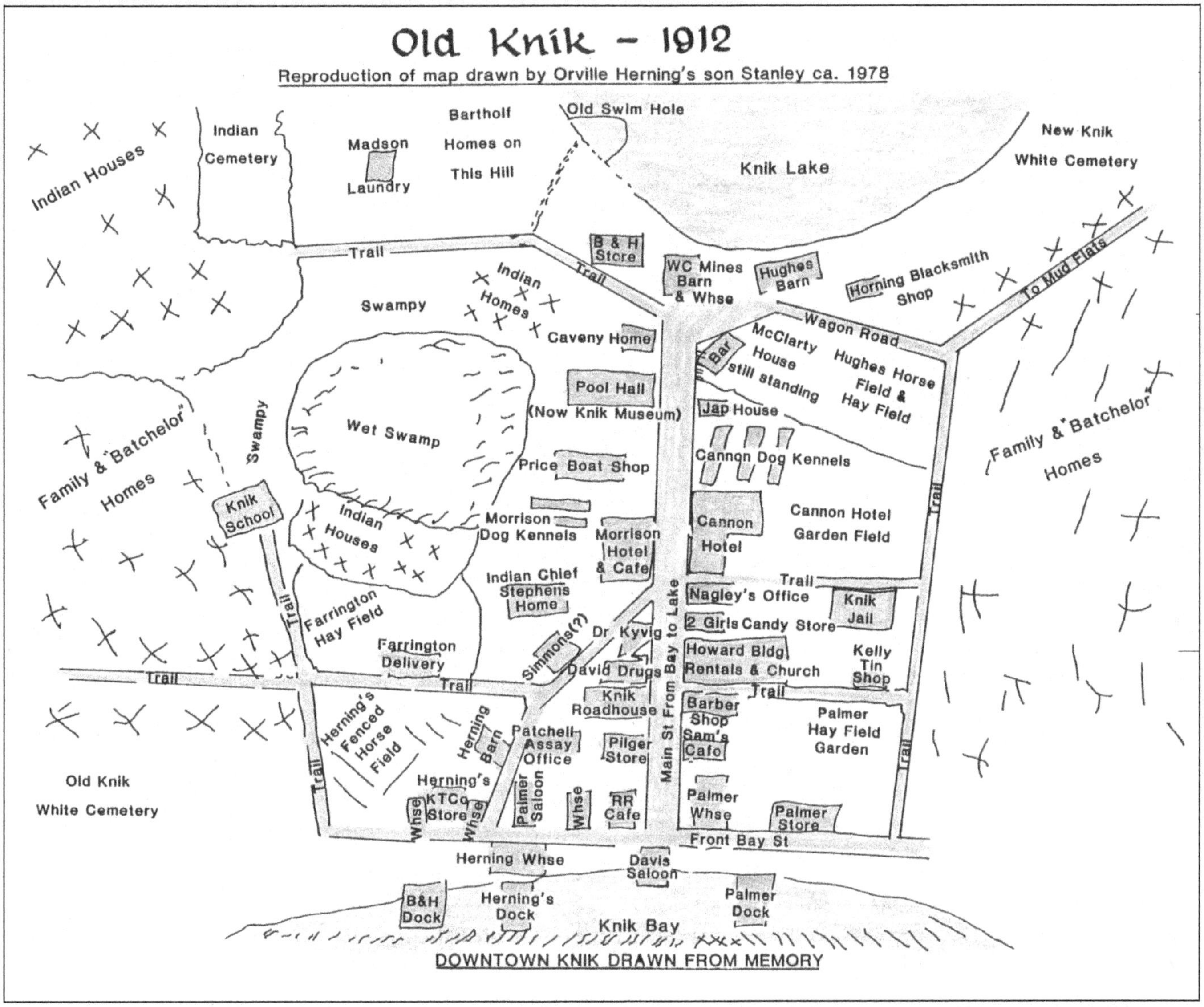

MAP 53

Old Knik in 1912 as drawn by Stanley Herning.

O. J. Herning's son Stanley left Knik in 1917 as a young boy 13 years of age. He drew a map of Knik in 1978 from memory for the Wasilla-Knik-Willow Creek Historical Society. Stanley depicted the location of Chief Stephan's house, and in three other areas he indicated groups of Indian houses. This is a redrawing of Stanley Herning's map.

COURTESY OF FRAN SEAGER-BOSS AND THE MATANUSKA-SUSITNA BOROUGH

FIGURE 174

Chief Wasilla, circa 1906, with his wife, **Undudya**, and their son, perhaps at Wasilla's house at **Benteh** (13.39).

Shem Pete confirmed that the Chief Wasilla pictured here with his wife in about 1906 is the man for whom the town of Wasilla is named. His wife's name was **Undudya** and she was a sister to **Batninch'ey** and **Qatsen**. Chief Wasilla was of the **Nulchina** clan. He commited suicide in 1907 after the death of his young son. On Sleem (1910b) (Map 50) "Wasilla's cabin" is shown south of Wasilla Lake at a junction in the trails. Also see 13.46, a second "Wasilla's cabin" was located to the east off Wasilla Creek

Potter (1963:12–13): "An old Chickaloon Indian chief bearing the name of Wasilla, and remembered by many of the town's 'old timers,' is buried on Cottonwood Creek (back of what now is the valley Christian Home) where there were once a few small Indian cabins." Seager-Boss (1995) is a full report on the 1995 excavations at the Chief Wasilla grave site. The statement that appears in Chandonnet (1979:40 and repeated in 1991:50) that the man named Wasilla was Theodore Vasili or Wasilla Theodore is not correct.

PHOTO COURTESY OF THE ANCHORAGE MUSEUM OF HISTORY AND ART (#B82.52.273)

13.37 T'ghes Hnidaghi'ut • 'Where a Cottonwood Is Embedded'

§site, near Cottonwood Slough, perhaps Cottonwood Slough (revised location)

The large-scale map by Sleem (1910b) (Map 50) shows a trail up the west bank of Cottonwood Creek and a "Fish Camp," at a fork in the trails, probably near the mouth of Cottonwood Slough. Large house pits are reported near the upper end of Cottonwood Slough (Seager-Boss, personal communication).

13.38 Łach Bena • 'Silt (Mud) Lake'

Wasilla Lake

A trail to the upper Little Susitna River and Hatcher Pass area passes by Wasilla Lake on the 1910a and 1910b maps by Sleem (Map 50). Note that Mud Lake is a translation of the Dena'ina name.

13.39 Benteh • 'Among the Lakes,' 'Lake Country'

Wasilla area; area between Wasilla Lake and Cottonwood lakes

Fall (1981:402): "Several informants believe that **Benteh** refers to a large Indian village on the creek between Wasilla Lake and Cottonwood Lake."

Wasilla is a Russian-origin personal name. Potter (1963:12–13) stated that "Wasilla" is from a Dena'ina name meaning "breath of air." This was reiterated by Snider (1966:109): "Wasilla was named after a chief of the Knik Indians, 'Vasili'... and is, perhaps, a corruption of the Russian given name 'Valili.' John Stump, one of the Knik Indians, told me that Vasili means breath of air, such a noise as air taken in by a Beluga whale when surfacing." Stump's account is interesting. Checking on words for the breathing of belugas with Sava Stephan, we found a word **bashelda'u** 'it is inhaling.' We suspect that John Stump was matching some such Dena'ina word with the word 'Wasilla" and came up with the folk etymology.

Snider (1966:109): "Fisherman who have fished in Wasilla Lake know that there is more than one lake and that there are at least three good lakes—connected to each other by a small stream. Between lake number one and number two, some time ago there stood some old buildings—known to the old timers as the Wasilla cabins. Old chief Vasili's grave was there, surrounded by a small broken down fence while an old rusty gun and a Master's Voice Gramaphone with a long horn was laying on the mound as a grave decoration. Indian folklore has it that when he arrived at the Happy Hunting Ground, he would have a gun to use and the gramaphone to listen to."

Katherine Nicolie: "He raised lots of kids that had no home. He saved lots of people that way. He took those kids hunting. He got rich from hunting."

Shem Pete gave the following description of another chief from this area, **Bentehen**. "**Bentehen** was a very rich man who lived and died before my time. He had a big **nichił** at a narrow place between Wasilla Lake and a lake close to it. There were four or five **nichił** in this area, all full of his **ukilaqa** [helpers]. In spring he would send three or four hundred [*sic*] of his people down to Fire Island to get king salmon. Then later in the summer the red and silver salmon come up to the Wasilla area, and they put up lots of fish. Later [trout] came, in the fall. They had year round trout at **Benteh**. He told the young men to go out trapping" (Fall 1981:265, 1987:45).

The name **Bentehen** is an inherited chief's title, similar to the title **Nitehen** for the chief of **Niteh,** Matanuska village (14.4). Thus several men may have held this title, including the man for whom the Wasilla townsite was named.

Shem Pete: "«**Ts'iduyuł Tu,** John Stump's father was the chief there.»" John Stump is said to be the last Dena'ina person who regularly camped and hunted in the Wasilla and Cottonwood lakes area. See Fig. 159, a picture of John Stump.

13.40 Baqutsaghi'i Bena • 'Lake in Which a Rock Sticks Up'
§lake, possibly Cottonwood Lake (revised location)
Possibly Cottonwood Lake, which has a prominent island, assuming the names that we have are from the series of lakes from Lucille Lake to Finger Lake.

§13.53 Hundadi Betnu • 'Last Stream'
§upper Cottonwood Creek, from Nikleson Lake

13.41 Hundadi Bena • 'Last Lake'
§Nikleson Lake (revised location)
Name mentioned by John Stump to Kari in 1976. Fran Seager-Boss has told us about a recognizable Dena'ina fishing site at the upper end of Nikleson Lake.

§13.54 Baqay Tuch'elisht Bena • 'Where We Put Birchbark Canoes in Water - Lake'
Finger Lake
Noted in Mendenhall's 1898 notes as "Bakiatutsilictmuna—Finger Lake." Name suggested by Sava Stephan.

13.43 Nik'udatl'ech'a *(Dena'ina);* **Nic'adatl'ets'i** *(Ahtna)* • 'Dark Color [spruce timber] Extends from Shore'
§site possibly on point above "Dinkle Lake," north of Wienie Lake off Fairview Loop
This was off the trail around the shore of Knik Arm, between Knik and Eklutna. See Map 54.

Shem Pete: "«From there they go straight across to Eklutna on the flat. Up there, there were four or five big **nichił**. Spruce extends out there in a dark strip like charcoal.» Big village there for timber. «Dark patch of spruce.» There were people there for firewood and salmon."

Johnny Shaginoff: "**Nik'udatl'ech'a**, that's between there (Rabbit Slough) and Knik. You go down there

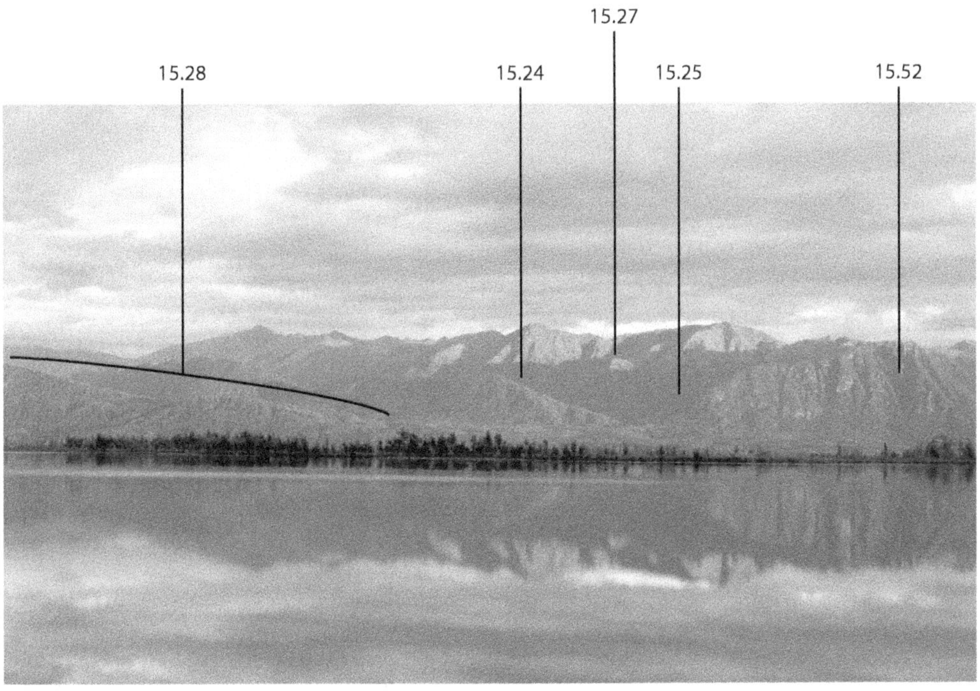

FIGURE 175

The north shore of Knik Arm from Cottonwood Creek to Fish Creek must have had a very high aboriginal population. Looking south from the low ridge above Reedy Lake, just east of **Nik'udatl'ech'a** (13.43). On the other side of Knik Arm is a clear and detailed view showing the **Idluytnu** (15.24, Eklutna River valley). Features in the distance, left to right are **Bentułik'alashi**, (15.28, the ridge tapering from the left edge of the frame); the small peak with the sun shining just on its tip **Kuy'inshla** (15.27); **Chishkatnu** (15.25, Thunderbird Creek valley); and at the ridge edge of the frame **Snutnadzeni** (15.52, Mt. Eklutna). Cf. Plate 18.
PHOTO BY RANDI HIRSCHMANN, #AK-R1074B

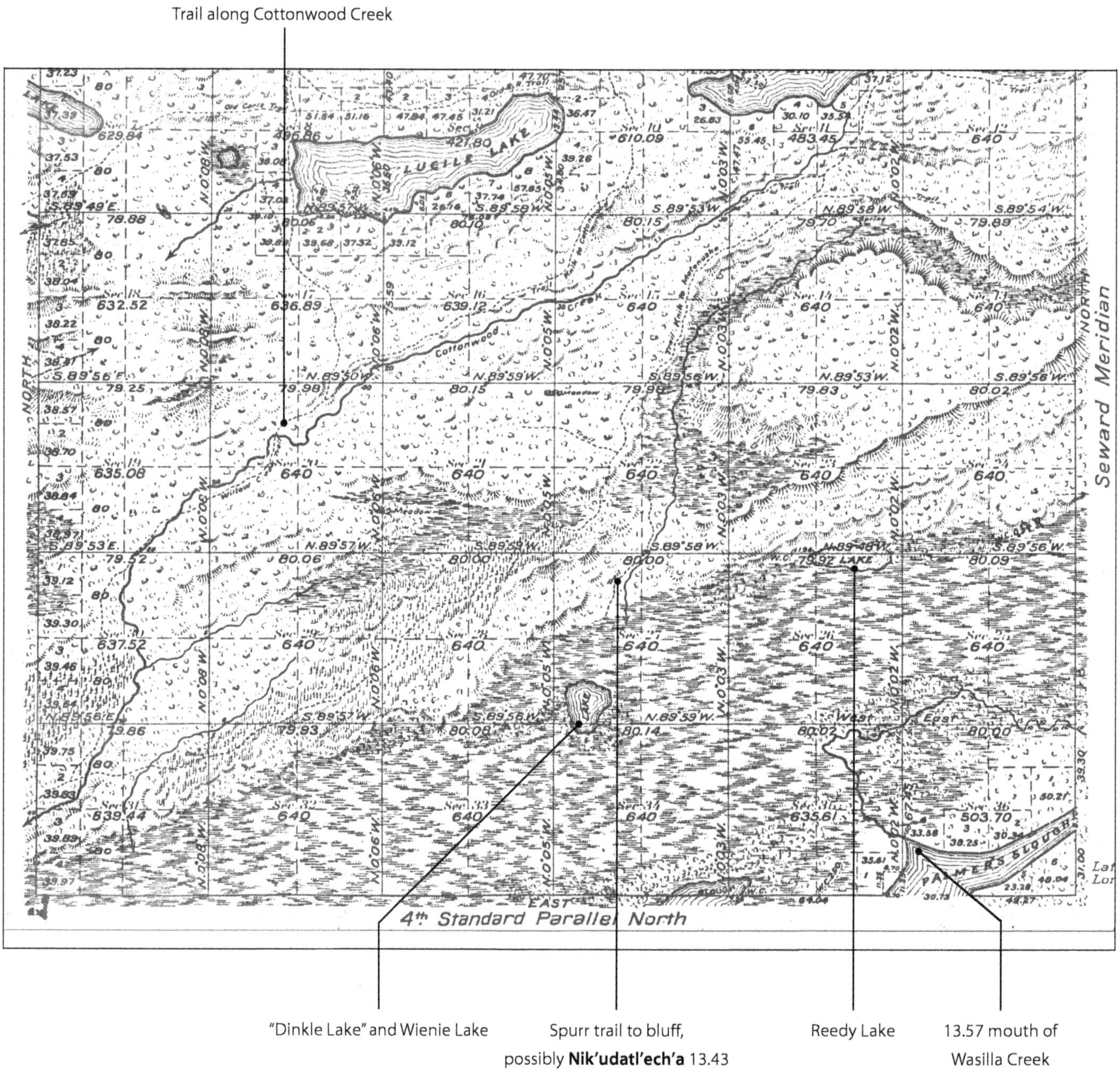

MAP 54

Detail from Davidson 1915 cadastral map of Cottonwood Creek area.

The first cadastral maps of the Knik area, made by Surveyor General Charles E. Davidson in 1911, have finely detailed topography and hydrography. The scale of these maps is large, one half mile to the inch. These early cadastral maps are good sources on trails and structures. This map of Knik area shows a short trail leading from upper Cottonwood Slough to the north side of a lake ("Dinkle Lake" and Wienie Lake). This appears to be **Nik'udatl'ech'a** (13.43).

MAP COURTESY OF FRAN SEAGER-BOSS AND THE MATANUSKA-SUSITNA BOROUGH

about this side of Cottonwood Creek and past Wasilla Creek. Must be about half way in there. You can't help from seeing it. There's a spruce timber point right out you know. You can see it for long ways either side. Good high ground and good protection. This was a popular stopping place. Only one day over to Knik."

§13.55 Nik'udatl'ech'a Betnu • 'Stream of Dark Color [spruce timber] Extends from Shore'
stream into "Dinkle Lake"

§13.56 Nik'udatl'ech'a Bena • 'Lake of Dark Color [spruce timber] Extends from Shore'
"Dinkle Lake," lake north of Wienie Lake

§13.57 Chuqilin Kaq' • 'Fermented Fish Creek-Mouth'
mouth of Wasilla Creek on Palmer Slough

13.46 Chuqilintnu *(Dena'ina),* **Tsikiliintna'** *(Ahtna)* •
'Fermented Fish Creek'
Wasilla Creek
Fall (1981:401): "There was once a large village at the mouth of Wasilla Creek... where it enters Palmer Slough.... In pre-contact times this village and its 'chief' were destroyed by 'medicine' sent from Eklutna. After this it was deserted."

Bailey Theodore: "There used to be a lot of people there. They had trouble with Eklutna, and they killed each other off. All the weapons were thrown away. Then it was a ghost town, and my father told me not to go around there. This wasn't too long ago, after the Russians came."

Shem Pete: "«One chief there was **Benitnanilchinen**, the one who had a design [birthmark] on his forehead.» He had pictures of little people on his skull. He was a big medicine man, five or six hundred years ago."

Fish traps were used for salmon here, according to Bailey Theodore.

On Sleem (1910b) "Wasilla's cabin" (see Map 50) is located to the west of Wasilla Creek near the big bend in the railroad grade. House pits are reported here (Seager-Boss, p.c.).

13.44 Qunsghitnu *(Dena'ina),* **Kansghuytna'** *(Ahtna)* •
'Creek Farthest Ahead'
Palmer Slough and Rabbit Slough
This name is reported by Jim Tyone and Johnny Shaginoff. Shem Pete did not recognize the name. Johnny Shaginoff: "In August salmon run there. I fished there."

13.45 Sdadintunt • 'Where a Point Extends'
point and marsh from Coffee Point to Duck Flats

FIGURE 176

Blind Nick's 1940 cabin on upper **Qunsghitnu** (13.44, upper Rabbit Slough), near the Matanuska townsite (see 14.4). The cabin was built with creosoted railroad ties.

Nick McNeil, known as Blind Nick, lived on upper Rabbit Slough near Old Matanuska. In stories by Russell Annabel he was frequently portrayed as a charismatic blind shaman (e.g., 1953a, 1997b:81, 1987:233–47). In a letter to the editor of *Sports Afield,* Annabel (1953b) wrote: "Blind Nick still lives on Rabbit Slough, or did last summer. He may have died in the meantime, but I doubt it. The Indian shamans are not well known to the whites, nor are the Eskimo angioks. There aren't probably half a dozen business men in Anchorage who have heard of Blind Nick or know that he is a medicine man. Yet mere mention of his name among the Indians will get you a lot of attention instantly. He possesses strange powers, as do all shamans and angioks." Jeff Davis (2002:223–26) gives an account of Blind Nick and his place in Russell Annabel's fiction.

‡C. Mielke has compiled articles about Blind Nick (1880–1953) and his brother Capt. Alex Slivers McNeil (1886–1946). From a 1948 Anchorage newspaper article (but see the entire article!): "Icy roads or darkness do not keep 73 year old "Blind Nick" from making his almost daily trek to the little town of Wasilla from his cabin 3/4 of a mile down the road. With his trusty two sticks to guide him and creepers fitted over his shoe packs, "Blind Nick" walks the distance in half an hour with ease. He buys groceries in small quantities and carries them home in a pack on his back. In his cabin, where he lives alone, he cooks his own food on a wood heater, cuts kindling and packs water from a nearby well.... "Blind Nick" has his own system for getting around, which no doubt takes experience and patience but the main thing is that it works. He has various markers along the way. By the side of the road, in front of his cabin he has a stick marker and here he turns into the path which leads him home, about one hundred feet off the road. The Community Hall, a large log structure at the end of Wasilla's main street is one of his landmarks. A little further down it, is the telephone pole near the coffee shop. From here on, there's nothing to it. He walks straight to the local store. Here telephone poles a few feet from the building and the end of the sidewalk act as guides."

PHOTO BY JEFF DAVIS

11.1: K'dalkitnu
Talkeetna River
8.43: K'itbitnu
Kashwitna River
10.24: Q'usatnu
Oshetna River
10.27: Q'usashitnu
Little Oshetna River
10.48
10.26
38: Dzeł Ggeyi
8.48
8.36
8.47
119: Neltsii Na' (A)
Little Nelchina R
Bakaey Ts'elaas Na' (A)
Crooked Cr
32: Łtagetnu
Boulder Cr
60: Nataghilen Na' (A)
Caribou Cr
66: Tsedghaazi (A)
121: Una' Cenaeł'sdiłdeł i Na' (A)
Old Man Cr
120: Bendil Bene' (A)
Tazlina Lake
20: Ch'tet'mu Kings River
31: Nuk'din'itnu
Chickaloon River
50: Hdgheltnu
Hicks Cr
2: Ch'atanhtnu
Matanuska River
28: Bashtl'ech'
King Mt
12.22
12.21
12.16: Qughun
Bald Mt Ridge
12.1
14: Chidaq'atnu
Moose Cr
Sutton
2: Ch'atanhtnu
57: Ch'atnahnu Ł'i'a
Matanuska Glacier
53: Ts'en Dabaas Na' (A)
Gravel Cr
70: Dzeł Ghaan' (A)
109: 'Atciis Dghelaaye' (A)
Mt Sergeant Robinson
106: Ts'en Dabaas (A)
58: Ch'atanhtnu Dghelaya
Mt Marcus Baker
13.39: Benteh
13.46: Chuqilintnu
Wasilla Cr
5: Dnal'iy Kena
Palmer
4: Niteh
Matanuska Site
13.45: Sdadintunt
15.2: Skitnu
Knik River
15.7: Dnal'iy
Pioneer Peak
15.12
15.106
15.11
15.4
15.3
15.13: Ts'itnu
Friday Cr
15.113: [Yuyantnu ?]
Metal Creek
Scale
10 miles
N

14 Matanuska River

The place names data on the Matanuska River nicely illustrate Athabascan place names usage across a language boundary. There is a single system of names, pronounced with regular phonological adjustments. This reflects the close association between the Upper Inlet Dena'ina and the Ahtna. Many people spoke both languages (as did Shem Pete, Jim Tyone, and Johnny Shaginoff), and there was overlapping territory with no rigid boundary. See Jim Tyone's account of travel along the Matanuska River from Tyone Lake to Knik, pp. 223–226.

This close association between the Ahtna and the Upper Inlet Dena'ina is discussed in detail in Kari (1977a). Both the Dena'ina and the Ahtna report that the Ahtna have moved farther to the west and northwest in the past 150 years. The Chickaloon and Oshetna areas were formerly used by Dena'ina, but mainly Ahtna have used these places since the mid-nineteenth century. Similarly, Ahtna were also expanding into the Talkeetna River region at this time. The Ahtna-Dena'ina relations contrast with the more formal boundary, with very little joint land use or bilingualism, between the Dena'ina and the Upper Kuskokwim people west of the Alaska Range. See 6.42.

Mendenhall (1900:294): "Mr. Handmore, the Indian agent at Tyonek, courteously furnished me with a copy of a map in his possession, based upon an old Russian chart and with such additions as he was able to make by carefully sifting the reports of Indian traders. This chart, while not correct in detail, gave a very good idea of the course of the Matanuska River and was much more nearly correct than any of the published Government maps."

‡See p. 310, Kari's 2008 summary of documentary sources on Native place names along the Matanuska-Tazlina river trail.

14.1 Ch'atan Kaq' • 'Mouth of Trail Comes Out'
mouth of Matanuska River

14.2 Ch'atanhtnu *(Dena'ina);* **Ts'itonhna', Ts'etuunh Na'** *(Ahtna)* • 'River from Which Trail Comes Out'
Matanuska River
Shem Pete and others have said that this place name is shortened from the word **ch'atinitun** 'trail comes out' + **tnu**. Both the Dena'ina and the Ahtna names have irregular stem vowels. Also the suffix **-h** before the stem 'river' is unusual. Mary Shaginoff once remarked that **Ts'etuunh Na'** would be in Ahtna **Una' Ts'etinitaan Na'** 'its stream-trail comes out from-stream.'

The Ahtna version of this place name was documented very early, in 1797, by Dmitrii Tarkhanov. A name west of Tazlina Lake is transliterated as "tsetenkunna" in Black (2008:79). Writing in the 1850s, Doroshin stated, "The Goltsani in the middle Copper River and the Kenaitsi from the head of Cook Inlet follow the Matanuska and Tazlina common trail and speak the same language" (Doroshin n.d.:9; cf. Mendenhall 1900:303). Doroshin also noted that the first Russian to travel from Cook Inlet

Sources: Johnny Shaginoff, Shem Pete, Mary Shaginoff, Jack Tyone, Jim Tyone, Jim McKinley, Bailey Theodore, Katie Wade, Morrie Secondchief, Dick Secondchief, Jim Sinyon, Frank Stickwan, Alberta Stephan, Leo Stephan, and Fred Ewan

2003 revisions: names added 14.77–14.122; revised locations 14.33, 14.67, 14.72 and 14.73.

‡2016 revisions: names added 14.123–14.126; names revised 14.7, 14.32, 14.46, 14.47–52, 14.61, 14.62, 14.63, 14.64, 14.72, 14.74, 14.81, 14.101, 14.122; map revised 56; map replaced 58; figures added 179A, 190A.

MAP 55

(Opposite) Place names map of the Matanuska River, showing Nos. 14.1 to 14.126.

MAP BY MATT GANLEY

FIGURE 177

Looking across **Ch'atanhtnu** (14.1, the lower Matanuska River) with **Dnal'iy** (15.7, Pioneer Peak) and **Łdagheltnu** (15.6, Goat Creek) in the distance.
PHOTO BY JEFF DAVIS

to the Copper River was a man named Bajenov, who made the trip in about 1804. Bajenov had a Dena'ina wife and child, and he traveled in the company of Dena'ina from Knik Arm (n.d.:38).

In the 1860s Dall (1870:272) and others called this the "Knik River." The name Matanuska does not appear on the first nineteenth-century maps (e.g., see Map 17: Wrangell 1839 and Map 6: Petroff 1884). It is a Russian-origin name, probably a variant of the Russian term for the Ahtna, *Mednovtsy*, literally 'people of the Copper River' (Katherine Arndt, personal communication).

Shem Pete said that no one used boats on the Matanuska River because it is much too swift and rocky. People traveled on the Matanuska trail mainly from late fall until spring when they could move their supplies by sled. Jim McKinley said that the Ahtna did the same: "Them days they waited till late in the fall and then started pulling the sled. They pull the sled over the pass just about where the road is running today, down the Matanuska River, and into the Knik" (McKinley 1980:195).

Castner (1984:10, 12) remarked that in 1898 his guide, Hicks, was the only white man who had ever been to the upper Matanuska River, and that no white man had gone beyond "Canyon Gulch" (Hicks Creek, 14.50). Note however that in 1905 Addison Powell interviewed 62-year-old James Germansen in Valdez. Germansen dictated a narrative of his life travels throughout the plains and western Canada. Germansen commented, "I was in the Cook Inlet country in 1895. I hired two Indians to pack for me up the Matanuska, and we passed over to the Tazlina slope of the Copper River country where we killed a moose. I was told the Indians would kill me, when we started on that trip, but I lived to follow the Yukon from its headwaters to the sea, and enjoy life on Middleton Island, the gem of the Northern Pacific Ocean" (Powell 1910:325).

The prevailing wind from the Matanuska River is known as **Ch'atanhtnu hch'anich'ey**.

14.3 Tuhnaghiłkitst *(Dena'ina);* **Tahwnighiłciitsde** *(Ahtna)* • 'Where Bank Extends (fabric-like)'
bluffs and site at lakes near Parks-Glenn Highway junction
De Laguna (1934:140): "Near the site of the Knik and Matanuska Rivers there is said to be a village site called To'xnaytlkitc (Theodore, Eklutna). His [Theodore's] placing of this village and of Nitak are not very certain, however. This is probably the 'Kinik' of Petroff's map."

Osgood lists the people of this village as "Toxnaikicdana" (1937:216).

Jack Tyone marked the location of this site. Mike Alex, Bailey Theodore, and Mike Theodore had heard of the site but could not locate it.

Johnny Shaginoff: "That's one of them hills. I know I heard that name a lota times. I think he [Jack Tyone] is right because that hill comes down there [at junction], high hill. That's what it means you know."

According to Bailey Theodore, this is probably the place where his grandfather died. He was the first Upper Inlet Dena'ina to have a tent frame cover made of moose hide. At his potlatch, which also took place at **Tuhnaghiłkitst,** this moose hide was cut up into small pieces and distributed. Each person received enough for the soles of their moccasins, "enough for the bottoms of their feet."

Cook Inlet Historic Sites Project lists this as site no. 158 (1975: 87).

§14.77 Tuhnaghiłkits Bena • 'Where Bank Extends (fabric-like) Lake'
Kepler Lake, Bradley Lake, Matanuska Lake at Parks-Glenn Highway junction

14.4 Niteh *(Dena'ina);* **Nuu Tah** *(Ahtna)* • 'Between Islands,' 'Among Islands'
Matanuska village site, Old Knik; general delta area between the Matanuska and Knik rivers
Johnny Shaginoff: "Old **Niteh** is about a mile up from the old railroad bridge near the Matanuska River. That's the real **Niteh**. That's where the Matanuska Indians came down to the trading post. After that they [Ezi family] moved between the highway and railroad bridge [toward the Knik River]. That's 'New **Niteh**.'" Shaginoff added that the village moved periodically because of flooding from the ice-dammed Lake George.

Niteh is probably also the site of a winter post of the Russian-America Company as described by Khlebnikov in the 1820s (Liapunova and Fedorova 1979:18; see quote p. 19). It is noted as "Nuchta" on the 1839 Wrangell map (Map 17) and with variant spellings on the 1847 Zagoskin map and the 1854 Holmberg map. It is called "Nytyk" in

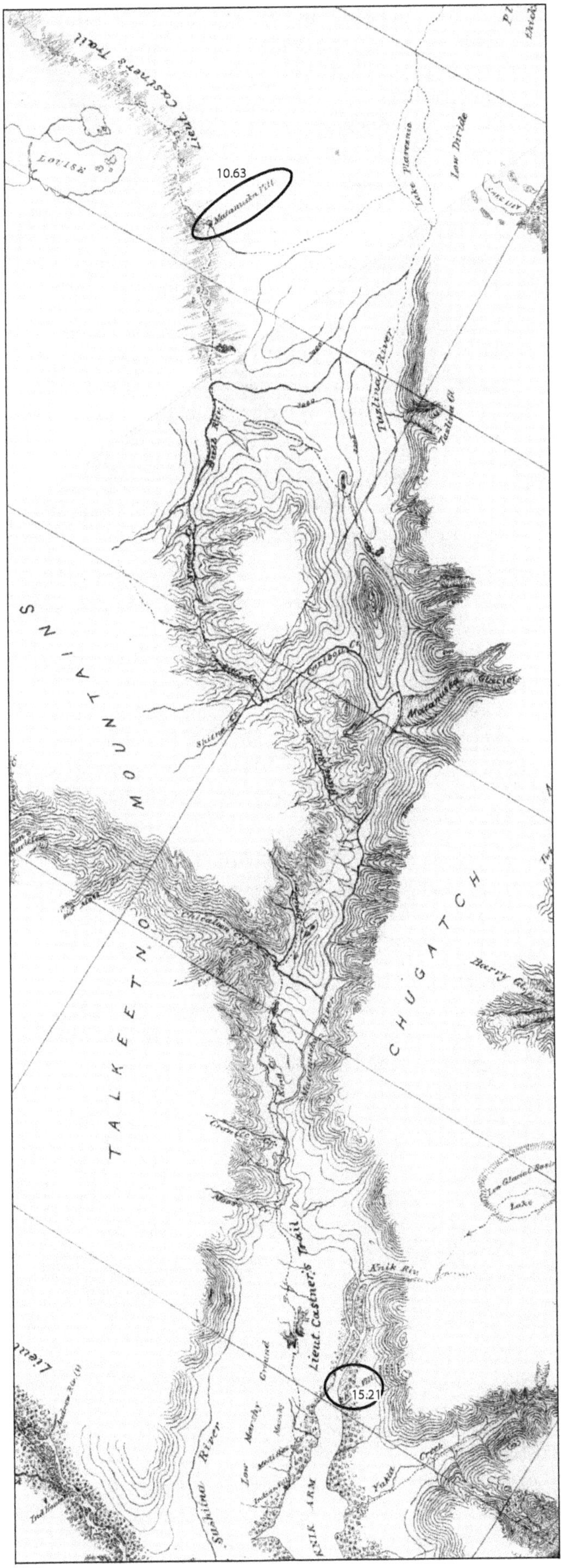

MAP 56

Detail from the 1900 Meiklejohn Map: Matanuska River.

The rarely cited Meiklejohn map of 1900 is a compilation of the several U.S. Army survey expeditions of 1898 and 1899. This detail traces the Castner and Glenn trail from Knik Arm up the Matanuska River. Circled at the south end of the map is "Knik Vil," 15.21 **Idlughet** Eklutna village, and at the top of the map is "Matanuska Vill," 10.63 **Ben Daes Bene'**, the Ahtna village at Old Man Lake. Cf. also the detail of Map 47 on the Chickaloon and Talkeetna rivers from this same map.

ARCHIVES, ALASKA AND POLAR REGIONS DEPT., RASMUSON LIBRARY, UNIVERSITY OF ALASKA FAIRBANKS

the Wrangell collection notes with the following note: "Nytyk is an islet at the very head of Kenai Bay up to where the tide reaches; from the shore side [north] it is formed by the mouths of several streams, very swift" (Arndt 1985).

In the late 1840s Doroshin made a vague reference to a recently established agricultural community which was probably near the Russian-America Company post (n.d.:3).

Writing in the early 1880s, Petroff said, "These people of Kinnick in olden times and even to the transfer of the Territory, have conserved and claimed the profits of middle-men, or commission merchants, in the trade which the Indians of the far interior brought down to the coast" (1884:39).

Irwin (1968:12) "The Alaska Commercial Co. had a store at Old Knik (Eklutna) from 1875 to 1882, operated by George Palmer as agent. George Palmer noticed that prospectors, trappers, and Indians came to trade from the Copper River country. He constructed a store of his own, locating it on the Matanuska River, a short distance above where the present Anchorage-Palmer highway bridge crosses that river. It is said that this store was unattended.... At Palmer's Matanuska River store trade increased and that of the ACC at Old Knik diminished.... In 1885, the Lake George breakup, combined with heavy rains caused the water in Knik Arm to be at record height. It overflowed the tide flats, undercut Palmer's store and the building and contents were washed into the inlet." Also see 3.29, New Knik. This is the "old store" on the 1899 Johnston and Herning map (Map 52).

Glenn (1899:41): "I learned from reliable sources that about two years ago the navigable channel of the inlet passed directly in front of and close to the trading station. But it seems that at that time an immense body of water came down, apparently from the Knik River, destroying not only the trading station establishment of the Alaska Commercial Company, located on the opposite bank of the inlet, but also a number of Indian houses."

The chief of **Niteh** had the title **Nitehen**. According to the late Bailey Theodore, one chief of **Niteh,** named **Qa Dyiluggen,** was killed in a snowslide on the upper Knik River. A later chief of **Niteh** was named **Betsik'nughesalen**.

Snider (1966:104): "The first time I heard about Knik was in the year 1924. From Old Indian Jim I learned that Old Sunny Knik, located on Knik Arm which is the head of ocean navigation and 200 miles up Cook Inlet, is really New Knik.... Old Knik, however, was located on the site where the present Matanuska Railroad Bridge is located. There, many years ago, stood a thriving Indian village. One spring, when the break-up came, so old Indian Jim told me, the waters of the Matanuska River were very high. A flood came suddenly and many Natives were drowned. He showed me some pilings where once stood their houses and caches. He told me also that according to Indian legend, there was a small village at the mouth of the Eklutna which also was washed away. The survivors of both villages started what is not Old Knik, but New Knik."

Annabel (1997d:319): "Twelve years ago Chilligan's Uncle Esai, the aging Knik-Denna prophet, had been crowded off his ancestral homesite down near the mouth of the river. The way it happened, government railroad contractors were going to dynamite a butte there for track ballast. A siding had been laid. Steam shovels were standing by. The boss contractor, a cheechako from the States, wanted to pitch additional bunk tents on the grass flat where Esai's log cabin stood. He told Esai that the flat was government land and, sorry, the government needed it. Chilligan, nine years old and an orphan, was living with Esai. Yielding to authority, the pair loaded their household equipment and woods gear into a borrowed freight canoe, and headed upriver to resettle."

Alberta Stephan (2001) describes growing up at **Niteh** and the way of life of the Dena'ina living there from 1900 to about 1950. Her family lived next to the house of her grandparents Simeon and Olga Nicholi Ezi, which was built in 1897 (Stephan 2001:5). Subsistence activities based out of **Niteh** in the early and mid-twentieth century included trapping beaver and muskrats; hunting rabbits, porcupines, ducks, geese, swans, moose, sheep, and goats; fishing for salmon and trout; picking berries and other wild plants; and tanning moose hides.

In 2000 archaeologists from Northern Land Use Research surveyed the site of **Niteh** with Leo Stephan (Potter et al. 2000:20–21): "Leo Stephan located a habitation site used by his family and other families during the 1930s and early 1940s. The site, identified as ANC-286 (AKRR-2), Niteh or Nitakh (so called "Old Old Matanuska")... consists of two cabins, a bathhouse, a raised cache (now fallen), berm remains of another structure, a boat, a possible bridge/dock remnant, a number of cache pits, and, reportedly, approximately five graves with associated spirit houses located nearby, though unobserved by archaeologists and Mr. Stephan in the field.... Most significant is the presence of graves in the site vicinity.... All of the structures are in some state of decay, exacerbated by long sinuous water-filled cracks approximately 2–4 meters wide, which according to Mr. Stephan, were caused by the 1964 earthquake. Though there is considerable damage to the site, the site integrity is deemed to be high with no human-related disturbance in the form of modern debris. Although the site lies outside of the ARRC project area, we recommend continued avoidance of this area as this site is clearly eligible for the National Register of Historic Places, and because it is of considerable significance to Eklutna residents. Mr. Stephan related to NLUR archaeologists another habitation dating to the 1930s and located just north and east of the railroad bridge spanning the Matanuska River. However, during the brief survey, we determined that the site had been totally eroded by the river."

14.5 Denal'i Kena • 'Flat of the One That Is Standing Still' or 'Flat of The One That Is Watching Us'
general Palmer townsite and lower Matanuska Valley area
This name is based upon the name for Pioneer Peak. See 15.7.

14.6 Gelis Hnidaghi'ut • 'Where a Cross Stands'
site on Matanuska River two miles below old highway bridge
This apparently is a cemetery.

14.7 ‡Cetsii T'aade *(Ahtna)* • "Beneath base of Lowlands'
campsite at base of ridge, N bank of Matanuska River along Glenn Highway, perhaps near Arctic Ave. intersection.
Spelling and map location revised in 2014, on north side of Matanuska River on the main trail. Jim Tyone's version is audible on recording and the location now is accurate. Cf. 2003 **Kents'iis T'aa, Kentsiis T'aa**. This suggests that John Shaginoff was tentative on this name. Johnny Shaginoff and Mike Alex stated that this was a Dena'ina village.

‡14.123 Cetsii *(Ahtna)* • 'Base of the Lowlands'
ridge on north bank of Matanuska River along Glenn Highway Fishhook Road to Arctic Avenue
Implied from Jim Tyone text.

14.8 Saeł Ciik'e *(Ahtna)* • 'Box Point'
point on north side of river one to two miles below old bridge
Name reported by Jim Tyone. Shem Pete had heard the name mentioned but did not know the place.

FIGURE 178

Nił'atsa'it'ut 'where rocks come together' (14.9, the gorge in the Matanuska River by the Old Glenn Highway bridge near Palmer).
PHOTO BY PRISCILLA RUSSELL

Basdut—Old Man Ezi

told in Dena'ina by Shem Pete

translated by Billy Pete

FIGURE 179

Bill Ezi, Sr., in the 1960s.

From 1951 to 1972 a group of Dena'ina in Palmer, through Chief William Ezi, Sr., and others who lived at **Niteh**, had a claim for lands before the U.S. Indian Claims Commission. This claim extended around the shores of Knik Arm to the headwaters of the Knik and Matanuska rivers. The claim was voided with the passage of the Alaska Native Land Claims legislation (Indian Claims Commission, Docket No. 370; Chandonnet 1985:60–63). William Ezi, Sr. (1898–1971) is profiled in Chandonnet (1991:60–63).

PHOTO COURTESY OF ALBERTA STEPHAN

"Now there was a man whose name was Ezi. He lived at **Niteh**. They used to call that Old Man Ezi **Basdut** in Native. There was a rich man at **Niteh** whose name was **Nitehen**. Ezi got to be chief after him. I'm going to tell you a little story about this man, Ezi. I don't want his story to die. That's why I am saying these few words about him. Maybe somebody will hear this story.

"His name was Ezi. Up north, around Tyone Lake, a woman came from there. Lake Louise, she's from. There was a big medicine man up there. His daughter heard about these Cook Inlet people, that they were the best looking people. So she made a little pack for herself and took off for Cook Inlet. She had fallen in love with a man from **Niteh** [14.4]. That's why she walked all the way down there. She was a real pretty woman. That man called **Basdut** was just a young fellow at that time. He fell in love with that woman, and he took her and got married to her before she found that other man that she came down for. That woman's father was a big medicine man [at Tyone Lake], and she just stayed at **Niteh** with Ezi. "Then she got pregnant, and when the baby was born, it was a boy. And about one hour later a girl was born. They were twins. One was Bill Ezi [Sr.], and his sister was Mary Ezi. A man named Billy Pete [not Shem Pete's son] married her when she was old enough. When she [Mary Ezi's mother] first had the babies, she kept staying down at **Niteh** with **Basdut**. She stayed down there a year or two, and pretty soon her father came down to **Niteh** to find his daughter.

"There was a big glacier broke up [at Lake George], and all the houses at **Niteh,** and the store, washed away. They had a big flood. That store drifted up on Fire Island. The Eklutna and Knik people were down at Fire Island putting up fish for themselves. And they found that big store on the beach. Nothing had washed away from inside the store. It was just full. Some of those people wore two sets of suspenders, and everbody wore two or three neckties. Those women wore neckties too. And some of them wore big cowboy hats, the men and the women. Any color hat they wanted, they just took that kind. That's the way they were.

"And after that, the woman's father, the big medicine man, came down to **Niteh**. By that time **Basdut** had built a two-room house, and they were staying in that two-room house. When her father came down, it must have been wintertime. And he stayed with them all summer.

"That safe that had been in the store washed out somehow and drifted away. Nobody knew how far that store drifted before that big bank [safe] fell out of the store. Clothes and all drifted to the topside, and nothing washed away from the store except the bank. What was heavy washed away. All the guns and axes had washed away. That big safe got buried underneath the sand. And that girl's father told his daughter, 'Tell your husband to look for that bank.' And he gave Old Man Ezi a staff. He told him, 'Take that staff and poke it in the sand here and there all over.'

"Down the creek, the main channel of the Matanuska River, it is just like quicksand. He told him, 'Push the stick down eight or ten inches away from each hole you make. Keep going like that, and each evening when you get through just leave the stick in the last place you poked it down.' He kept going like that. Maybe he poked the stick down two feet. He was a strong man. He just kept going like that. And that medicine man told him, 'You're getting a little closer. That last place you poked the stick down, just leave it there so I can take a look with the medicine.' If he thought he should go east or west, he told him, 'You're going the wrong way. Back up and keep going the other way.'

"Pretty soon he kept going like that, and one day he found that bank. He poked it with his staff, and he knew he found that bank. And he dug it up and filled his pockets with a bunch of 20-dollar gold pieces. After all his pockets were full he covered that box up and went home. When he found the bank, he couldn't even lift it up. It was too heavy. When he dug it up, the keys were tied onto the safe's handle. He took that key off the handle and opened the box. Just thousands of dollars of 20-dollar gold pieces in that safe.

"That storekeeper had got all that money that year to buy furs and snowshoes, but he didn't do that because before the people came down, the store washed away. When that glacier busted, it might have been July month or so.

"He [Ezi] kept packing all the gold home, and pretty soon he could pack that bank home on his back. It was summertime, and he couldn't use a sled or anything. That's how he got rich, from finding all that gold. Maybe two or three years later he made a big potlatch at **Niteh**. He was **Chishyi**. That's my **Shtukda Ka'a**, 'my big dad.' He wasn't my dad, but that's what I called him. Old Lady Ezi was **Tulchina**. She was Johnny Shaginoff's grandmother. That's a long story. I don't want this story to die. That's why I am telling this story. If I die, who is going to tell this story? Nobody. You people are going to hear it. My name is Shem Pete. That's enough."

FIGURE 179A

Portrait of Olga Ezi, date unknown.
PHOTO COURTESY OF ALBERTA STEPHAN.

FIGURE 180

Simeon (**Basdut**) Ezi, Olga Ezi, Pete Ezi, and Anderson Stephan (Sava Stephan's father) on the right in 1921.

Niteh village is said to have been large in the past, but at the turn of the century it was mainly occupied by the Ezi family. Shem Pete stated that this used to be excellent country for hunting moose and rabbit. The Ezis would go up the Knik River in fall to hunt sheep. See also 15.11 and 15.14 on the Ezis' house and camp locations up the Knik River.
PHOTO COURTESY OF ALBERTA STEPHAN

Chief Ezi

by Alberta Stephan

Alberta Stephan (née Ezi) of Eklutna is Shem Pete's grandniece. After reading Shem's story about Old Man Ezi (p. 293), she added this about the Ezi family (with revisions for the second edition). Alberta Stephan is the author of three books (Stephan 1993, 1996a, and 2002).

This story is about Chief Ezi (Esi Esia, 1870–1935). Picture the area from Seward to Fairbanks with no highways or railroad tracks. In the summertime the only way people traveled from one place to another was by walking or canoes. Right up to the early 1920s there used to be a seasonal migration of Athabascan Natives from the north: Gulkana, Tyone Lake, Copper Center, Valdez Creek, and those areas. They came down by the hundreds in the spring to put up their winter supply of dried fish. The trail of the spring migration went right by the Chickaloon area. The single-file trail is said to have been three feet deep—there were so many Athabascan people walking back and forth to Cook Inlet.

From the many stories my Grandma told me, I know that this was how the various villages were started along the Knik Arm and Cook Inlet areas.

When the white people started running steamships to Anchorage (let me explain that the name Anchorage came from the boats anchoring here to unload supplies and mail), the supplies and mail had to be delivered by smaller boats to Knik, Sunrise, and other places. The mail carriers were also using horses and foot trails to deliver the mail. What is now Eklutna, *Idloitnu* in Athabascan, because of the fresh water in the rivers, was a resting place for both the great migration in the spring time and later the mail carriers for the gold rush.

Grandma Ezi [see Fig. 179] was from the Copper Center area. Her father and stepmother had a fish camp at Point Woronzof. When Olga was eighteen years old, she came with her parents to put up their fish. The year was approximately 1896. She met this big, handsome guy that ran one of the smaller steam-driven boats that delivered supplies from the big steamboats anchored at Anchorage to places like Knik and other places. His name was Simeon Esia. His Native name was *Bastute* **[Basdut].** Olga and her parents packed their dried fish back to their home up north for the winter. Olga decided she wanted to marry that big, handsome guy that she met, so after talking to her father, she packed her things on her back and walked back down the trail of the great migration all by herself. She married Simeon Esia, and they built their home at Nitak.

Simeon Esia's last name was changed to Ezi by the people that came from the Eklutna Vocational School. He was the last recognized chief of upper Cook Inlet. He was the chief of the Natives. Simeon Ezi inherited a document that was given by the dominating foreign people stating that he was in charge of the Natives of upper Cook Inlet.

Chief Ezi and his wife Olga had their first house on the north side of the Matanuska River. Their first son, Bill Ezi, was born in December of 1898. Five of their children grew up to be adults. Today [2001] there are seven of us grandchildren left, and many great-grandchildren. Olga and Chief Ezi took in many orphans and raised other children, not their own. That was a tradition among the Athabascans. Chief Ezi carried on the fish camp at Point Woronzof, as did his sons, Bill, Pete, and Jack Ezi.

In the 1930s, they were allowed to commercial fish for Emard Packing Company. In about 1945, the area of Point Woronzof was closed to commercial fishing. There was an elder fishing around Campbell Point, and his name was John Hedberg. Some of them found other sites down the Inlet to fish; some had to give up commercial fishing.

The Ezis also had a hunting and trapping home at Jim Creek [15.9] at the headwaters of Knik Arm. They stayed at Jim Creek in the fall time to hunt goat, Dall sheep, moose, ducks, geese, and porcupine.

Simeon and Olga's first home was flooded by the annual dumping of Knik Lake, later named Lake George. The flooding washed away many homes. There was a store built in the 1920s north of the Matanuska that also washed away. Everything in that store was lost, including a wooden barrel filled with silver coins used for a cash register. In the 1930s there was a little town that was built at the junction of the railroad was also ruined by the annual flood.

Chief Ezi died on January 18, 1935. There was an article in the *Anchorage Times* about it.

Bill Ezi filed the Palmer Land Claims in 1953, and many people did not understand why anyone would expect money for the land that was lost to the Natives. He lived to be enrolled in the Alaska Native Land Claims. He died in 1971.

My mother, Ruth Ezi (Mrs. Pete Ezi), was Shem Pete's niece by marriage. Shem Pete's half-brother married one of Chief Ezi's daughters, named Annie. His name was Bill Pete. He died in 1940.

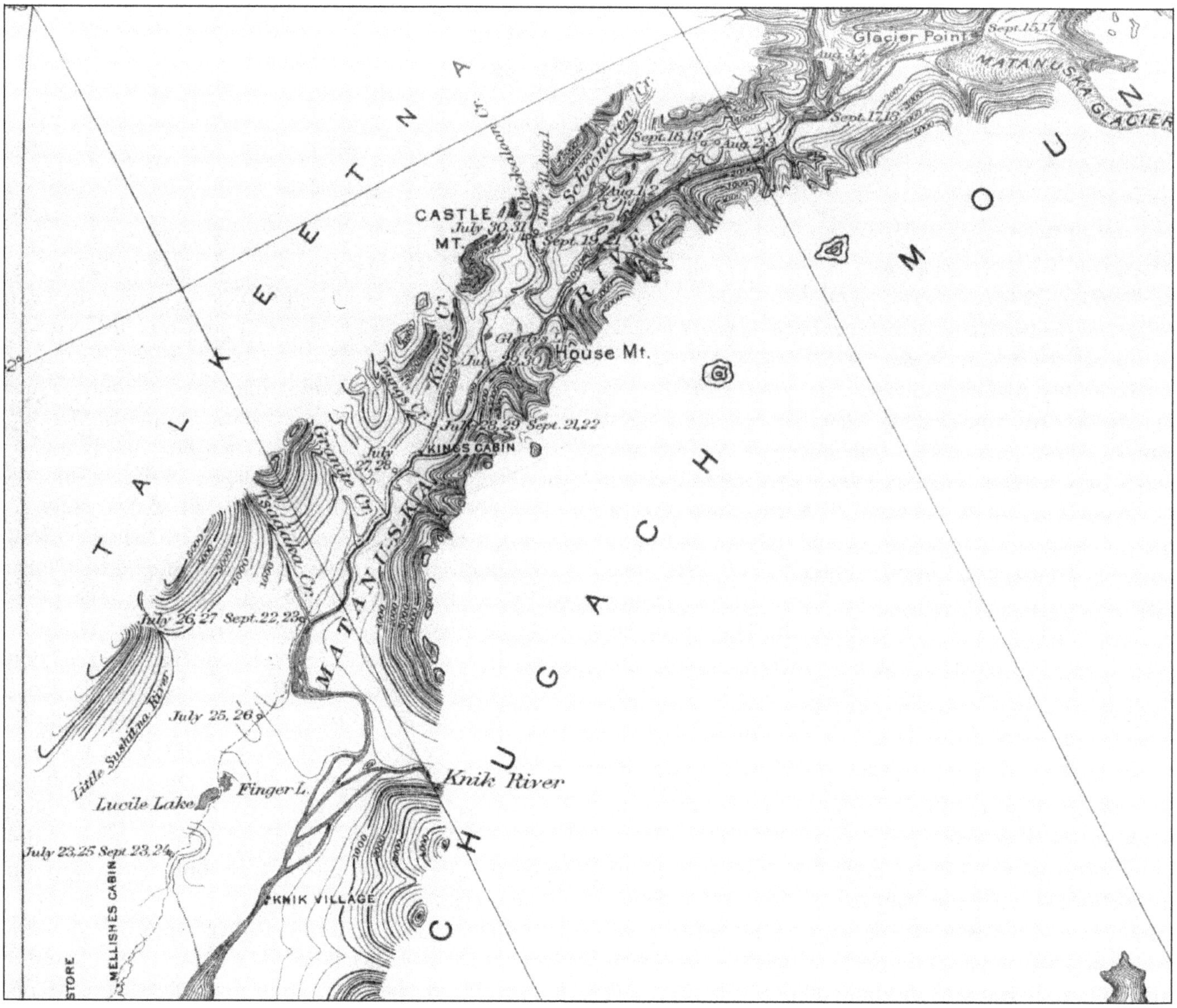

MAP 57

Detail from Mendenhall map of 1898: Matanuska River.

USGS geologist William Mendenhall was on loan to the U.S. Army during their 1898 expedition. His map with his 1900 report accurately depicts topography from Resurrection Bay north through Isabel Pass. In his field notebook of 1898, Mendenhall recorded several Dena'ina place names between Finger Lake and Chickaloon. This was the best map of the Matanuska River of that period.

ARCHIVES, ALASKA AND POLAR REGIONS DEPT., RASMUSON LIBRARY, UNIVERSITY OF ALASKA FAIRBANKS

14.9 Nil'atsa'it'ut *(Dena'ina);* **Nil'etse'it'aade** *(Ahtna)* • 'Where Boulders Come Together'
site at old Matanuska River bridge at "Palmer Canyon"
The late Mike Alex reported that this site was just above the bridge. The late Bailey Theodore said that his grandfather was buried near here.

14.10 Kiydlent *(Dena'ina);* **Cizdlende, Cisidlende** *(Ahtna)* • 'Where Current Flows to a Point'
site below confluence of Wolverine Creek and Matanuska River
Johnny Shaginoff: "Two or three miles below Wolverine Creek. When Matanuska [Ahtna] Indians used to come down the river, those people used to meet 'em there. That's the name of the old village there. Big patch of timber below Wolverine Creek. I don't know how far it is. Maybe two or three miles. There's a little stream runs through timber there. That's why they call it **Cizdlenden**.

Kind of a hot spring through the timber in there, and it's kind of a village meeting place."

14.11 Kisidlentnu • 'Point Current Creek'
Wolverine Creek

14.12 Kisidlen Bena • 'Point Current Lake'
Wolverine Lake

14.13 C'ek'aali Cene' *(Ahtna)* • 'Whetstone Flat'
bluff on north side of Matanuska River between Palmer and Moose Creek
Jim Tyone: "It is like it has been filed by the wind."

Johnny Shaginoff reported that a village site was located on this bluff near the mouth of Moose Creek. "It was a well-known place for Natives. All big high bluffs have names."

14.14 Chidaq'atnu *(Dena'ina);* **Tsidek'etna'** *(Ahtna)* • 'Grandmother's Place Creek'
Moose Creek, formerly called Tsadaka Creek
This name is distinctively Dena'ina in origin, based upon the word **chida** 'old lady, grandma.' Note however that Orth (1971:987) stated, "Tanaina Indian name meaning "moose," reported in 1898 by Capt Glenn." Mendenhall (1898, Map 58) wrote this as "Tsadaka."

Castner (1899:199): "Above Moose Creek on our [north] side of the Matanuska was an old camping place of the Matanuskas used in their journeys up and down the river."

According to Johnny Shaginoff and Katie Wade, there are burials on both sides of the mouth of Moose Creek. Some graves have washed out. Several people died here during the 1918 flu epidemic.

There is a modest king salmon run in Moose Creek. The fish were harvested with spears, according to Katie Wade.

§14.78 Chidaq'a Denyi *(Dena'ina);* **Tsidek'e Dyii** *(Ahtna)* • 'Grandmother's Place Canyon'
Tsadaka Canyon on Moose Creek
Cole et al. (1985:75): "As early as 1894, trappers and prospectors heard about the rich coal veins in the Matanuska Valley from local Indians."

In the 1940s the Wade and Larson families lived near the Premier Mine and hunted and harvested berries throughout this area.

14.15 Chidaq'ashla Bena • 'Lake of Grandmother's Little Place'
Wishbone Lake
A trail leads up from the Moose Creek homestead of the Shaginoffs and Wades up to Wishbone Lake, a popular fishing spot.

14.16 Chidaq'ashla • 'Grandmother's Little Place'
Wishbone Hill
Katie Wade said that this is thought of as a dangerous area. Many hunters have gotten lost here. A giant with feet that are turned backwards is said to have lived in the area.

§14.79 Tsida K'ae Dghilaaye' *(Ahtna)* • 'Grandmother's Place Mountain'
Arkose Peak and ridge
The name of this ridge at the head of Moose Creek is implied from the suffix **-shla**, 'small, little' for 14.16, Wishbone Hill. Typically a hill or mountain noted as 'small' is paired with a nearby larger named feature.

According to Johnny Shaginoff, a trail led up Moose Creek and over the mountains to the upper Kashwitna River. The Larsons from Talkeetna used to travel this trail. "I know some people went through. Jack Larson went up Moose Creek, came down Kashwitna. He used to trap beaver someplace on Kashwitna." See 8.44.

§14.80 Tanilent • 'Where Current Flows to Water'
rapids probably above Moose Creek
Name provided by John Stump.

§14.81 ‡U'eł Naak' Dghiłtaazi *(Ahtna)* • 'Bar That Is Turning With It'
bar on Matanuska River at Sutton
Name from the text by Jim Tyone. See p. 226.

14.17 Ts'es Tuk'ilaght *(Dena'ina);* **Ts'es Tac'ilaexde** *(Ahtna)* • 'Where Fish Run Among Rocks'
Eska Creek; Sutton
A name written by Mendenhall in 1898 as "Chistookalat," or "Spring Creek," is clearly the Dena'ina name for Eska Creek.

The salmon fishery on the Matanuska River was on a much smaller scale than it was for the Dena'ina peoples on Knik Arm or for the Ahtna on the Copper River (for which see Simeone and Kari 2002.). The Chickaloon Ahtna did not spend much time salmon fishing. Some salmon were harvested here and at a small stream now called Mile Seventeen Creek (ponds near Eska Creek mouth) and at Little Granite Creek. Mary Shaginoff noted that she did little fishing following her family's move to Chickaloon in 1915. Johnny Shaginoff said that the salmon are good only the first two or three days of the run. In the past, salmon from the Eska area were mainly used as dog feed. The people in this area obtained dried salmon through trade with the people downstream at **Niteh**. See also Fall (1981:178, 203–205, and 1987:31, 36).

Katie Wade notes that the main traditional method of harvesting the salmon in the sidestreams and ponds along the Matanuska River was the fish spear. She also notes that the Ahtna-style **ciisi** or dipnet did not seem to have been used for any salmon fishing on the Matanuska River. Katie has noted that along the Matanuska River **ba'** or spread and scored dry fish was made only when there were enough good quality fish, and that they did not make **dzenax** or **nełk'oli**, the two styles of fermented fish that are made by the Ahtna on the Copper River.

14.18 Neltsii Ce'e *(Ahtna)* • 'Big One That Is Made Like a Face'
"Mount Sutton," mountain elev. 4415', "Crag"

The Chickaloon Ahtna Country

by Katie Wade and the Chickaloon Village Traditional Council

FIGURE 181

Katie Wade at her home at **Tsidek'etna'** (14.14, Moose Creek).

PHOTO BY KARI SHAGINOFF

Selected from Burkett (2001) and Wade (2004). ‡Katie Wade passed away on March 23, 2009.

FROM BURKETT (2001:D-6):

It would be difficult to understand Chickaloon without understanding Katie Wade's role in the day-to-day life of the tribe. At 78, Wade is not only respected as an elder but as "Clan Grandmother"—that's an official title. Almost everyone in the tribe is related to her, and most refer to her as "Aunt Katie."

A warm woman with flowing white hair, a fiery temper and little reserve, Wade is widely credited by tribe members as being the force behind much of Chickaloon's renaissance. It was Wade who founded Ya Ne Dah Ah School in an attempt to save the Ahtna language, now spoken fluently by only a handful of people, most of them her age. It was Wade who first ran head-on against the Matanuska-Susitna Borough's attempts to tax tribal properties shortly after the borough was founded in 1965.

In the Chickaloon hierarchy, the citizens of Chickaloon—as in any democracy—are the absolute authority, but many of the tribe's decisions are colored by Wade's opinions. It is her experience from which they draw. Unlike many younger members, she still remembers many of the tribe's traditions and knows much of its history. Her decisions aren't always appreciated at first—such as when she decided that. the tribe's peace officers shouldn't carry weapons.

Several officers argued with her, she said, but ultimately Wade prevailed. Ask just about anyone in Chickaloon's administration about that issue now and they'll concede the wisdom in her decision.

"Aunt Katie is the teacher, and we are her students," said Gary Harrison, her nephew and Chickaloon's chief.

FROM WADE (2004:V):

Katherine is an honored Elder of the traditional village of Chickaloon. She serves as the Chickaloon Traditional Council Advisor as the official Clan Grandmother. Aunt Katie, as most members know her, has dedicated her life to the preservation of her Ahtna Athabascan language, culture, and heritage. She is an eloquent Ahtna storyteller, a true Ahtna historian, and a respected Ahtna Athabascan teacher who visualized the preservation of the culture and was instrumental in the creation of the Ya Ne Dah Ah School for the village children of Chickaloon. In the past, as she continues to do today, Aunt Katie has always held fast to her Ahtna Athabascan rights, morals, and beliefs. She has passed these unique traits on to her children, grandchildren, and most members of the Chickaloon Tribe.

"May Creator Guide Your Footsteps"

WADE (2004:51):

Traditionally, Chickaloon territory was a center of trade for copper, sheep, and goats from the north; and salmon, beluga, fur seals, and dentalium from the south.... The Ahtna [and formerly the Dena'ina] of Chickaloon traveled extensively within the Copper River and Cook Inlet areas. Winter houses set in the forest were temporarily left in the spring when many Ahtna moved to their summer fish camps. Winter houses were semi-subterranean, built with logs and roofed with sod. Summer camps were built dome-shaped and were covered with birch bark and moose or caribou skins. The people moved from camp to camp depending upon what food source they were pursuing.

They had camps along the rivers and streams for various kinds of fish and then into the mountains for berries, ground squirrels, caribou, sheep and bears. Some camps were used only for a few days and others were used for weeks. Each resource that was collected from these camps was important to Ahtna survival. The Ahtna often did not return to their winter villages until the snow fell.

WADE (2004:80–81):

A special note written by Katherine Wade: In the winter there is nothing like a hot soup and stew made out of smoked-dried meat, that was soaked overnight to soften before cooking. The animals were so plentiful. For fresh game we had spruce hens, rabbits, ptarmigan, ducks, and geese in the spring and fall. Once in a while someone would get a sheep or goat and pass it around to all the families. We gathered berries. By the time I was growing up everyone had a garden of potatoes, turnips, cabbage, carrots, and lettuce, also rhubarb and strawberries.

We also went ice fishing in the winter and summer. We had Fish Lake full of silvers and rainbows, and dollies in the creeks and Chickaloon River. We felt very rich, we were taught not to kill any more game than we could use, one never knows when there might be a shortage of food. You always have to leave some fish in the creeks and lakes. They also believed in keeping the land clean. As human beings it's their duty to show gratitude to our Creator for putting us on this beautiful land. The men walked in the forest to chop down old rotten trees and burn the dead spruce trees.

Remember do not use up all the resources.

‡In 2015 the Chickaloon Village Traditional Council has ten departments and numerous projects that make use of Ahtna names. In the past decade Markle Pete of Tazlina and Jeannie Maxim of Gulkana have been teaching Ahtna at the Ya Ne Dah Ah School. See www.chickaloon.org.

FIGURE 182

Hdighilen Dghilaaye' (14.83, Granite Peak) with **Hdighlen Na'** (14.19, Granite Creek) in the foreground.

PHOTO TAKEN AT SUTTON BY KARI SHAGINOFF

§14.82 Neltsii Ce'e Na' *(Ahtna)* • 'Stream of Big One That Is Made Like a Face'
creek above Wolverine Creek, off mountain elev. 4415', "Crag"

14.19 Hdighilentnu *(Dena'ina);* **Hdighilen Na'** *(Ahtna)* • 'Creek That Flows In (canyon)'
Granite Creek
Johnny Shaginoff said that there was a good source of ochre paint on this creek. Johnny Shaginoff: "A guy told me, a Russian guy long time ago, I used to work for him when I was a kid, named Frank Lee. He said after '98 there were horses went up through, went clear to the Yukon. He said he went up Granite Creek into Talkeetna River. I don't know who started that. Maybe he went over to Sheep River."

§14.122 [Hech' Taytin] • 'The Long Object That Extends to the Place'
possibly ridge between Little Granite Creek and Granite Creek
A name for "Granite Creek" in geologist Mendenhall's 1898 notes is written as "Hachtaytin." This is a close rendition of a Dena'ina name for a ridge or mountain. The name has not been re-elicited.

14.83 Hdighilen Dghilaaye' *(Ahtna)* • 'Creek That Flows in (canyon) Mountain'
Granite Peak

§14.84 Ch'tałtnu Tayena *(Dena'ina);* **Staeł Na' Tayene'** *(Ahtna)* • 'Wide River Straight Stretch'
"Kings River straight stretch," bench on north side of the river below Kings River
The salmon run in ponds along Little Granite Creek, now diverted by culverts, used to be the last accessible run on the river. The ponds had sockeyes, pinks, and silvers. This run was important for the Chickaloon area people as a source of food for dogs.

Katie Wade: "We used to camp down here by Little Granite and catch our supply of fish for dogs. They weren't that good to where we could use them for people. They were kind of dried up when they got here. We cut them for dog food. They tried to make **ba'** [flat dried fish] out of the ones that are good, but they're very few. Most of them are pretty well chewed up by the time they get to where we were catching them. Moose Creek fish are a lot fresher than the ones we got way up here."

14.20 Ch'tałtnu *(Dena'ina);* **Staeł Na'** *(Ahtna)* • 'Wide River'
Kings River
Johnny Shaginoff: "You can go up King River and come over to Chickaloon River. I did that. Good sheep hunting. You come out fourteen, fifteen miles up Chickaloon River. There's two forks up there. Came across at near Fourteenmile cabin [on Chickaloon River.] East Fork, just a little narrow, just a mountain. You can stand up there and look both sides, down King River and Chickaloon River. There's only one spot there."

"The historic Chickaloon-Knik-Nelchina trail system, begins at Kings River and runs all the way to Eureka and the Nelchina gold fields.... Chickaloon-Knik-Nelchina trail...was originally an Indian trail system.... The trail extends over 60 miles in length and has numerous spurs and branches" (Bauer 1987:14).

§14.85 Staeł Dghilaaye' *(Ahtna)* • 'Wide Mountain'
mountain up Kings River

14.21 Chish T'el'iht *(Dena'ina);* **Tsiis T'el'iixden** *(Ahtna)* • 'Where Ochre Is Gathered'
creek opposite mouth of Kings River
This place is of special prehistoric significance. It is noted as the home of the **Chishyi** 'Ochre Paint' clan in the clan origin story (Kari and Kari 1982:62).

Johnny Shaginoff: "A woman was born there or was from there. Her name will be **tsiis ts'aey** ['ochre paint woman']. Woman you know come from here, so they named the tribe after her [the **chishyi/tsisyu** Ochre Paint Clan.]. There is a vein of Indian snowshoe paint there, one inch wide. All the people go there to pick up what they need. It grows every year and pops out."

In 1981 Jack Tyone told Jim Kari a brief outline of the clan origin story. It is noteworthy that Jack associated *three* clans with events in this area. He said that the **Tsisyu** were formed at this canyon opposite King River, that the **Hwggaexyu** Snowbird Clan [Dena'ina **Ggahyi** Raven Clan] were formed when a girl found a snowbird feather at King River, and that the **C'ecela'yu** were formed when a fish tail was found at Eska Creek. (Jack used the Ahtna clan names.) See also Fall (1981:409–427).

14.86 Tsiis T'el'iix Deyii *(Ahtna)* • 'Where Ochre Is Gathered-Canyon'
canyon opposite mouth of Kings River

14.22 Neltsii Sle, Neltsii Ggaay *(Ahtna)* • 'Little One That Is Made Like a Face'
Pinnacle Mountain

FIGURE 183

Hnu Ch'k'eł'iht 'where we do work,' (14.30, Castle Mountain). Johnny Shaginoff: "I guess that mean they climb up that mountain. That mountain is steep; they work to go up it. That's a good sheep hunting area."

PHOTO BY KARI SHAGINOFF

§14.87 Neltsii Ggaay Na' *(Ahtna)* • 'Stream of Little One That Is Made Like a Face'
creek off Pinnacle Mountain, below Carpenter Creek

14.23 Staeł Bene' *(Ahtna)* • 'Wide Lake'
Fish Lake
Fish Lake and Ida Lake (locally called "Thirtymile Lake") were popular fishing spots for people from Chickaloon Village. Katie Wade said ice fishing from February through April was especially good. Rainbows and Dolly Varden were caught, and especially good were the kokanee or landlocked silver that Katie said her father, Jesse Wickersham, planted in the Fish Lake in the 1920s.

Katie Wade: "We used to set up a tent at Fish Lake and we'd go down there and start a fire, cook our lunch, and then fish all day. We used to go ice fishing every spring, starting late March, till the ice goes away."

§14.88 Bet'uyedi Tayena • 'Necklace Straight Stretch'
stretch of Matanuska River between Kings River and Carpenter Creek

14.25 T'uy Kaq' *(Dena'ina);* **T'aay Caek'e** *(Ahtna)* • 'Chest Mouth'
mouth of Carpenter Creek
Annabel (1938:129 and1947:20–21) has descriptions of the topography and hunting on upper Carpenter Creek.

14.26 T'u'itnu, T'uytnu *(Dena'ina);* **T'aa'itna'** *(Ahtna)* • 'Enclosed Creek' or 'Chest Creek'
Carpenter Creek

14.27 Bes Tl'ets' Deyii *(Ahtna)* • 'Black Stone Canyon'
Linquist Creek
This is the home of the family of ten giant brothers in the story called **Dnigi Gich** recorded by Shem Pete.

Shem Pete: "«They had a **nichił** at a lake in the mountains. That **Dnigi Gich** was a seven- or eight-foot tall man.» He come down the mountain with sheep tied to his belt just like rabbits."

Johnny Shaginoff: "There were ten people there, ten brothers, really big people. There was a **Dastnaey** [Dena'ina] base camp at the foot of that [King] mountain. And people had a village there. They get a sheep. They used to carry them you know. They could carry a couple of them [sheep] you know, they were so big and strong."

14.28 Bashtl'ech', Bashtl'esh *(Dena'ina);* **Bes Tl'ets'** *(Ahtna)* • 'Black Stone'
King Mountain

14.29 Bashtl'ech'tnu • 'Black Stone Creek'
Carbon Creek

§(14.89) Deniigi I'niggoxe' *(Ahtna)* • 'Moose Snout'
near Castle Mountain, location uncertain

14.30 Hnu Ch'k'eł'iht • 'Where We Do Work'
Castle Mountain

§14.90 Hnu Ch'k'eł'ihtnu • 'Where We Do Work-Stream'
California Creek
From 1915 until the 1920s several older Ahtna lived in cabins at California Creek.

14.31 Nuk'din'itnu *(Dena'ina);* **Nay'dini'aa Na'** *(Ahtna)* • 'River That Bridge Extends Across'
Chickaloon River; Chickaloon village site
Shem Pete: "«They say that the place is **Nuk'din'itnu**. They put a log bridge across there. They would cover the women's heads with coats, and they would hold their hands as they brought them across.»"

The Ahtna name **Nay'dini'aa Na'** is being used in publications and correspondence of the Chickaloon Village Traditional Council.

The main precontact site was on the north bank above the mouth of the Chickaloon River. The last Dena'ina chief here was named **Chiklu**, who became known as Chief Chickaloon. Mary Shaginoff thought that this was a Russian personal name. It is said that he moved from here to Point Possession in the mid to late nineteenth century. He was still living at Point Possession in 1899 and is remembered by Kenai people (Barry 1973:40; Kalifornsky 1991:314–15).

The two distinct names for "Chickaloon River," here and in Turnagain Arm (16.12) seem to be based upon the personal name of the same individual. According to Baker (1902:176) this feature here in the Matanuska River was first documented in 1898 (though it was in local usage for some time before then). The Chickaloon River on Turnagain Arm was first recorded in 1895. See 16.20 for further discussion of the name "Chickaloon."

Johnny Shaginoff: "Chickaloon was quite a man. He was **Tulchina** [clan]. Everybody knew him. [Formerly] Chickaloon people spoke the Knik language."

FIGURE 184

Balasculya Nickolai, Frank Nickolai, Olga Nickolai, and children Herb Balenger and Paul Goodlataw in 1932.

PHOTO FROM THE PAUL GOODLATAW COLLECTION, AND COURTESY OF CHICKALOON VILLAGE TRADITIONAL COUNCIL

FIGURE 185

Balasculya Nickolai, Frank Nickolai. and their dog Queeny at **Nay'dini'aa Na'** (14.31, Chickaloon). Note the dog pack on Queeny.

From Chickaloon Village Traditional Council (1998:16): "Frank, Balasculya, and Queeny are ready to begin their journey for the mountains to spend the summer filling their winter cache. They would fill the cache with sheep, caribou, moose, and goat meat and use the hides to make parkas. This was also a sad occasion, since they had to leave their children behind to gather food for the winter."

FROM THE PAUL GOODLATAW COLLECTION, AND COURTESY OF CHICKALOON VILLAGE TRADITIONAL COUNCIL

The U.S. Navy sponsored a coal mining boom in Chickaloon drainage between 1915 and 1923 (Cole et al. 1985:83–87). In 1915 several Ahtna families from Tyone Lake and Old Man Lake moved to Chickaloon when the coal mining began. The cemetery on the road dates from this period. Numerous Ahtna and Dena'ina are buried there. Their descendents live in this area today.

On September 22, 1898, Glenn (1899:87) noted that an Indian boy was spearing a late-spawning salmon in the Chickaloon River. A run of king salmon, perhaps similar in size to the Moose Creek run, occurred in the Chickaloon River, prior to the coal mining activity according to Katie Wade and Gary Harrison.

§14.91 Nuk'din'itnu Kaq' *(Dena'ina);* **Nay'dini'aa Cae'e** *(Ahtna)* • 'Mouth of Bridge Extends Across'
mouth of Chickaloon River
Mary Shaginoff said that the oldest site by this name was located on the south bank opposite the mouth of the Chickaloon River.

14.32 Łtagetnu *(Dena'ina);* **Łtaege' Na'** *(Ahtna)* • ‡'Carcass Stream'
Boulder Creek
Johnny Shaginoff: "Knik Indian call it **Łtagetnu**. Matanuska Indian call it **Łtaege' Na'**."

Frank Nickolai, Mary Shaginoff's father, had several caches on this creek.

According to Katie Wade, in late June the Chickaloon Ahtna would go through here into the Talkeetna Mountains, where they would spend the whole summer. They would cache dry caribou and sheep meat and berries. In the winter they would relay the food by sled down to Chickaloon village.

§14.92 Ts'es Nay'detkay *(Ahtna)* • 'Rocks Blocked Across'
Puddingstone Hill
See Plate 15 for an aerial view of this area.

14.33 Ts'es Nay'detkay Na' *(Ahtna)* • 'Rocks Blocked Across Creek'
§creek into Boulder Creek behind Puddingstone Hill (location revised)

§14.93 Ts'etsiis Na' *(Ahtna)* • 'From Ochre Stream'
East Fork of Boulder Creek
Name via Katie Wade. A trail here leads to upper Caribou Creek via Chitna Pass, also called Dreese Pass locally, after prospector Al Dreese.

14.34 Chun eł Duk'eldesht • 'Where Arrows with Excrement Are Shot Down'
"Table Mountain" (local name) on east side of Chickaloon River below Fourteenmile Cabin, mt. 6180' "Suicide"
Shem Pete: "«They hunt for sheep on that mountain. The sheep keep away from them so they move up above them and defecate, and then they shoot that arrow [rubbed] with excrement, and it causes the sheep to move.»"

Johnny Shaginoff: "That Table Mountain they call **Chun eł Duk'eldesht**. That's on the right hand side as you go up. That's where they shoot arrow to scare game [sheep or caribou] that they can't get to. And when they do that, the animal gets the scent you know. Smell it and run off, down where they can get em. Somebody else be waiting. That what that mean."

Bagg (1900:682): "We advanced on August 8 9 miles over an easy trail, most of the way in a river bottom. Camp was made at the mouth of Canyon Creek. The Indian guide stated that this was a favorite hunting place during fall and winter.... The point between the two streams contains about 160 acres, and forms an ideal camping spot."

14.35 Nuk'eldeshtnu • 'Creek Where Arrows Are Shot Across'
creek at Fourteenmile Cabin
Johnny Shaginoff said that here and further up at Twentymile Creek there used to be cabins built by Indians.

Johnny Shaginoff: "You know that hill between "Table Mountain" and that other mountain, there's a good size stream running out. They call it **Nuk'eldestnu.**"

14.36 Staq'ay K'ilantnu *(Dena'ina);* **Stak'aey C'ilaen Na'** *(Ahtna)* • 'Creek Where There Is a White Mineral'
Moss Creek, formerly "Thirtymile Creek"
Johnny Shaginoff: "There's a fish stream here, opposite. Comes from Talkeetna [Sovereign] Mountain, Moss Creek. **Staq'ay** is some kind of rock. It grows out of the rock just like white flour. It's a hard granite rock and this stuff grows right out of it. You can see it from quite a ways off that white stuff. You go right up and you can scrape them off. Like a flour stuff. That's what **staq'ay** means."

Interestingly, the 1906 Herning map (Map 59) shows a trail probably up Moss Creek over to Sheep River on the Talkeetna River, marked "one day portage." This is in addition to the trail indicated on this map between the Chickaloon and Talkeetna rivers.

§14.94 Staq'ay K'ilant • 'Creek Where There Is a White Mineral'
mountain up Moss Creek

14.37 Ucaek'e Hwdezk'aani Na' *(Ahtna)* • 'Creek That Has a Burned Mouth'
Pass Creek, Chickaloon Pass (to Oshetna River)
Aboriginally, the trail along Pass Creek to the Oshetna River and on to the upper Susitna and upper Gulkana areas was the major north-south transportation corridor in this region. The 1839 Wrangell map (Map 17) shows this trail through the Talkeetna Mountains to the upper Susitna area. Also see Wrangell's quote in 10.24. This trail is also marked on the 1899 Johnston and Herning map (Map 52), the 1904 Moffit map (Map 44), and the 1906 Herning map (Map 59).

Jim Sinyon interviewed by Lillian Boston in September 1973 (West tapes, 1973) [quote incorrectly attributed to Jimmy Secondchief in the first edition]: "A trail ran from Susitna Lake down the Tyone River, to the headwaters of the Chickaloon River, and over Chickaloon Pass to the Matanuska River and Knik. An old style house about fourteen feet by sixteen feet with a sweat house attached was seen in the pass in 1906. The walls were built two logs wide for warmth and insulated with bark, a smoke hole was left open in the roof, and it had a moosehide door.

"I remember they go that way, they got a trail right there, they got a bridge to Susitna, they used to go that way, they got a foot trail right down from there, right down that way. They used to go into Chickaloon headwaters. For sheep and caribou.

"[For] sheep, yeah, [they] go [to] Susitna [to] **Kanc'eltl'aesde** (10.37) down that way, and at head of Chickaloon and Chickaloon there they are all connected, right on that pass, the old people used to get sheep, from there we used to go down to the head of Talkeetna, there's sheep there too."

§14.95 Nuk'din'itnu Łi'a *(Dena'ina);* **Nay'dini'aa Na' Luu'** *(Ahtna)* • 'Glacier of Bridge Extends Across'
Chickaloon Glacier

14.38 Dzeł Ggeyi *(Dena'ina);* **Dzeł Ggezi** *(Ahtna)* • 'Mountain Gap'
pass from Chickaloon River to Talkeetna River
Johnny Shaginoff: "You go through by that lake there. It's only about eight miles from here to the head of the Talkeetna."

In 1898 Mathys (1900:679–681) followed a well-defined Indian trail through this pass to the Talkeetna River. Mathys (1900: 679): "The trail went in a northerly direction along the Chicaloon river. Being an old Indian trail it was in good condition, except in a few places where the river had destroyed the banks entirely.... There is an Indian or game trail that leads down [the Talkeetna R] at this point to a low, flat country, which is well timbered with spruce and cottonwood."

The best early map of the Chickaloon River and trail is Meiklejohn (1900) (see Map 47). This trail is also marked on the 1899 Johnston and Herning map (Map 45) as a "one day portage."

Leo Stephan recalls traveling by foot as a young man with Johnny Shaginoff far up the Chickaloon River before crossing it. This was a very wide trail, like a road. In some places, the trail was very deep. He asked Johnny, "What made this trail? What could it be?" Johnny replied, "That's your ancestors made that trail. They made that trail by walking it." Leo: "That's what he told me. This was a human footpath. Had to be a lot of people for a long time [using that trail]."

14.39 K'eyah Betnu Nughik'et' • §possibly 'Creek of Skin Shavings Hang Downward'
possibly Coal Creek Valley

14.40 Tandze Laedze' *(Ahtna)* • 'Middle Sand'
"Windy Point" on Matanuska River below Riley Creek
Johnny Shaginoff: "It is really windy there. This is the last place the river freezes. They had to pack their stuff around this place all the time."

FIGURE 186

Mary Nickolai Goodlataw (later Mary Shaginoff) and Paul Goodlataw with a bull moose circa 1934.

Mary Nickolai was born at Lake Louise in 1907, the daughter of Balasculya and Frank Nickolai. She and her family were the last Ahtna residents of 10.64 **Ben Daes Bene'** Old Man Lake and Nickolai Lake in the plateau country between Lake Louise and Tazlina Lake. As a girl Mary fished and hunted in the Old Man Lake and Little Nelchina River area. She once recalled to Kari a goat hunting trip with her father in 1914 at **Xez Ghae** (the upper Nelchina River south of Tazlina Lake). She moved with her family to Chickaloon in 1918. She was first married to John Goodlataw of Chitina and then to Johnny Shaginoff. After she was married she lived at Moose Creek in the summer and at Eska and Chickaloon in the winter. She also had a cabin at Purinton Creek. A great wit and expert on Ahtna language and history, Mary passed away in 1983.

FROM THE PAUL GOODLATAW COLLECTION, AND COURTESY OF CHICKALOON VILLAGE TRADITIONAL COUNCIL

14.41 Tandze Laedze' Na' *(Ahtna)* • 'Middle Sand Creek'
Riley Creek

14.42 Tsaghedzigi Tah *(Ahtna)* • 'Among Rocks -?-'
general area below Anthracite Ridge, from Long Lake to Hicks Creek
Johnny Shaginoff: "Indians were superstitious of that area. A lot of old timers were really scared of something. People used to live there long ago."

Artifacts about 6,000 years old have been found here (West 1981).

14.43 Tsaghedzigi *(Ahtna)* • 'Rocks-?'
Anthracite Ridge
Several areas of this ridge have distinct names. Johnny Shaginoff said that an old sheep camp is located at the upriver end of this ridge. Glenn (1900:722): "Wild goat is much more scarce [than sheep]. The only place I have known them to be found was in the valley of the Matanuska River, where the Indians kill a few each season."

14.44 Tsaghedzigi Bene' *(Ahtna)* • 'Rocks -?- Lake'
Long Lake

§14.96 Staghatggadi *(Ahtna)* • 'The One away from and in Between'
possibly west end of Anthracite Ridge

§14.97 Staghatggadi Tayene' *(Ahtna)* • 'The One away from and in Between-Straight Stretch'
stretch of river above Long Lake

§14.98 Tanidzehi *(Ahtna)* • 'The One in the Middle'
section of Anthracite Ridge, possibly between Purintan Creek and Cascade Creek

§14.99 Kaniidi *(Ahtna)* • 'The Next One Upriver'
east peak on mountain off Anthracite Ridge

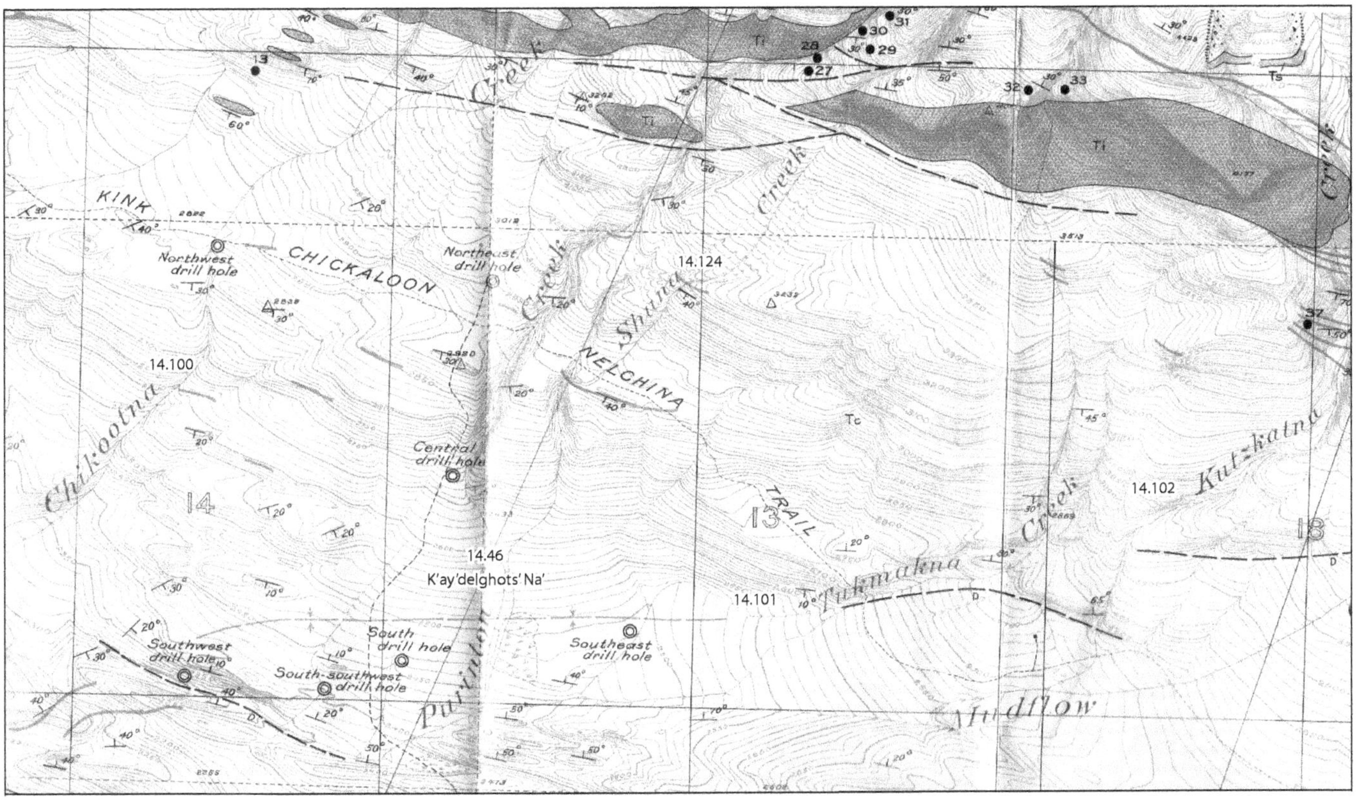

14.45 K'ay'delghots' Tayene' *(Ahtna)* • 'Willow Gap Straight Stretch'
section of river between Long Lake and Cascade Creek

14.46 K'ay'delghots' Na' *(Ahtna)* • 'Willow Gap Creek'
Purinton Creek, locally "Puritan Creek"
This is an old campsite. Mary Shaginoff stayed here when she was young. She and Johnny Shaginoff had a cabin here until the late 1940s.

Johnny Shaginoff: "That's on the Matanuska River where them is, all them willow. There's quite a few hundreds of acres, a timbered area there. You can see that."

§14.100 "Chikootna'"
Chikootna Creek
This and the following three names are Dena'ina-origin names (rather than Ahtna names) recorded in 1932 but that have not been re-elicited. Orth (1971:209) "BGN 1932, (map 69). Tanaina Indian name reported in 1932 by G. A. Waring and L. O. Newsome, USGS." See Map 58.

‡14.124 "Shuna" • meaning unknown
"Shuna Creek," upper east fork of Purinton Creek
Only on the 1936 Waring map.

‡§14.101 [Tuk'ebeq'tnu ?]
Tukmakna Creek
Orth (1971:989): "BGN 1932 (map 69). Reported in 1932 by a USGS field party." See Map 58.

‡MAP 58

‡Four Dena'ina/Ahtna-origin names on Waring 1936.

On this excellent geologic map are *SPA* numbers for Dena'ina or Ahtna-origin names in the Purinton Creek drainage on the Knik-Chickaloon-Nelchina Trail: 14.124 "Shuna," an upper east fork of Purinton Creek, 14.100 Chikootna Creek, 14.101 Tukmakna Creek, and 14.102 Kutzkatna Creek. These names and the names for sections of Anthracite Ridge (14.96–99) via Johnny Shaginoff, show that this area was on well-known hunting trails.

§14.102 [Q'ech' K'etnu ?]
Kutzkatna Creek
Orth (1971:556): "BGN 1932 (map 69). Tanaina Indian name meaning "canyon river" reported in 1932 by a USGS field party." See Map 58. ‡Waring (1936): "Two cabins [are] on this trail, one on Boulder Creek and one near Kutskatna creek, were used as stopping places by travelers."

14.47 Hdghelshlatnu • ‡'Little Area Is Pounded-Stream'
Packsaddle Gulch, "Little Hicks Creek," creek above Muddy Creek

14.48 Hdghelshla • ‡'Little Area Is Pounded'
Strelshla Mountain
Orth (1971:922): "Tanaina Indian name meaning "humped," reported in 1933 by USGS."

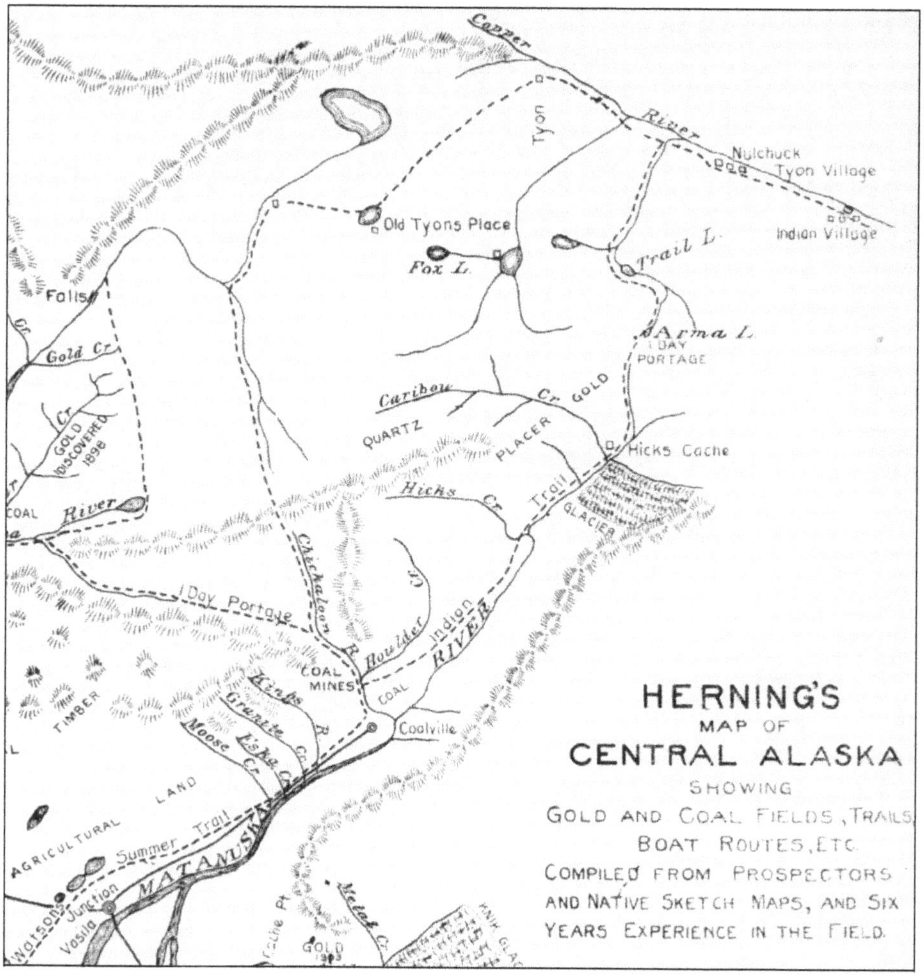

MAP 59

Detail from the 1906 Herning map: Matanuska River.

Herning's 1906 map has a good depiction of the trail system in the upper Matanuka River and areas to the north. The villages shown here on the Copper River appear to be in the Gulkana area. The system of Native trails is fairly similar for the Matanuska Valley on the 1899 Johnston and Herning maps (Map 45) and the 1904 Moffit map (Map 44).

ARCHIVES, ALASKA AND POLAR REGIONS DEPT., RASMUSON LIBRARY, UNIVERSITY OF ALASKA FAIRBANKS

14.49 Hdghel Kaq' *(Dena'ina);* **Hdghil Caek'e** *(Ahtna)* • ‡'Little Area Is Pounded-Mouth'
mouth of Hicks Creek
The Johnston and Herning map of 1899 (Map 46) indicates "Hicks' cache" on lower Hicks Creek and "Vicilea's cache" opposite the mouth of Hicks Creek. The latter cache is not shown on the 1906 Herning map (Map 59).

14.50 Hdgheltnu • ‡'Area Is Pounded-Stream'
Hicks Creek
The form **hdghel-** appears in several names. We treat this as unanalyzable. This seems to be the stream known in 1898 as "Canyon Gulch." The Hicks Creek trail through here was documented in 1898 by Castner and Mendenhall. Led by a Knik Indian, Billy, the Castner party went on to Caribou Creek, Billy Creek, Bubb Creek, and Nelchina River. They reached Chief Andre's village, on Old Man Lake. This apparently was the first time white people had entered this part of Western Ahtna territory (see Castner 1984:25–31).

Johnny Shaginoff commented that a trail runs along Pinochole Creek to Hicks Creek then on to the Oshetna River country. This was a good area for hunting sheep.

14.51 Hdghel Bena • ‡'Area Is Pounded-Lake'
Hicks Lake

14.52 Hdghel Bene' Beł Inakudzeden *(Ahtna)* • ‡'The One Who Returned at Area Is Pounded-Lake'
rock that looks like man near Hicks Lake
Shem Pete said this rock looks like a man smiling, wearing a hat. As you pass by, it looks as if the "man" tips his hat.

Johnny Shaginoff: "There's one [lake] between Pinochle Creek and Hicks Creek, that lake in there. They bury people on it. Native people have a superstition about it. That's a rock that look like a man or something, the way Shem Pete described it. That's a **Dastnaey** [Dena'ina]. He come back to the country he like."

§14.103 Tsitna' *(Ahtna)* • 'Head Creek'
Chitna Creek
Perhaps there is a mountain by the name **Tsitna' Dghelaaye'**. Cf. Horn Mountains off Caribou Creek, **Tsiyese',** 10.22. Written on the Meiklejohn map of 1900 (Map 56) as "Shitna."

§14.104 Tsitna' Tates *(Ahtna)* • 'Head Creek Pass'
"Drease Pass," East Boulder Creek to Caribou Creek Pass
Johnny Shaginoff: "You can go through Dreese Pass there. From East Boulder Creek. That creek down there is alright, they call it Chitna Creek. Al Dreese, he was

a prospector. He died not too long ago, thirty or forty years ago."

§14.105 Nataghilen Na' Tates *(Ahtna)* • 'River Where Water Flows Down'
Chitna Pass (Boulder Creek-Caribou Creek Pass)

14.53 Ts'en Dabaas Na' *(Ahtna)* • possibly 'Gray Bone River'
Gravel Creek
Katie Wade's father, Jesse Wickersham, had a cabin here, and her sister Helen was born here in 1921.

§14.106 Ts'en Dabaas *(Ahtna)* • possibly 'Gray Bone'
mountain up Gravel Creek

14.54 Łaltaan Bene' *(Ahtna)* • §'Enclosed Water Lake'
Tatonden Lake
This is an old campsite on the Matanuska trail. The last Ahtna cabin there belonged to Annie Nickolie. This was an important fishing district in pre-contact times. This is the uppermost sockeye and coho lake on the Matanuska River (ADF&G 1998). According to Katie Wade, salmon reach here. ‡Waring (1936): "At Tatondan Lake...there was a trapper's cabin."

De Laguna (1970): "Allen (1887:66) [see Map 60] published an Indian's sketch map of the route to Tasnai (Dasnei "Knik people") via Tazlina River and Lake. A village on Tazlina Lake is shown..., and another seems to be at Tatonden Lake, south side of the Glenn Highway, west of the pass at Sheep Mountain."

14.107 Łaltaanden *(Ahtna)* • ''Enclosed Water Place'
camp at Tatonden Lake

14.108 Łaltaan Tayene' *(Ahtna)* • 'Enclosed Water Straight Stretch'
stretch of Matanuska River near Tatonden Lake

14.55 Łaltaan Na' *(Ahtna)* • 'Enclosed Water Creek'
Lake Creek

14.56 'Ałciis Na' *(Ahtna)* • perhaps 'Bag Creek'
Glacier Creek
This name may contain the Ahtna/Dena'ina word for bag **'ałcesi** or **ułkesa.**

14.109 'Ałciis Dghilaaye' *(Ahtna)* • perhaps 'Bag Mountain'
Mount Sergeant Robertson

14.57 Ch'atanhtnu Łi'a • 'Glacier of River That Trail Comes out From'
Matanuska Glacier
Mendenhall (1900:299): "One of the guides, Andrew, told us that a glacier discharges bergs into its [Matanuska River] upriver end."

‡14.125 Ts'itonhna' Łuu K'aet *(Ahtna)* • 'Trail Comes out River Glacier Place'
campsite at Matanuska Glacier
Noted in Jim Tyone text, p. 225.

FIGURE 187

Hdgheltnu, (14.50, the valley of upper Hicks Creek).

PHOTO COURTESY OF COOK INLET REGION, INC.

FIGURE 188

Ch'atanhtnu Łi'a, (14.57, Matanuska Glacier).

PHOTO TAKEN IN 1982 BY LORRAINE BASNAR ELDER

FIGURE 189

Looking downstream toward **Natsede'aayi** (14.59, Lion Head or Glacier Point).

PHOTO BY JAMES KARI

14.58 Ch'atanhtnu Dghelaya • 'Mountain of River That Trail Comes out From'
Mount Marcus Baker and surrounding peaks

14.59 Nutsada'iy *(Dena'ina);* **Natsede'aayi** *(Ahtna)* • 'Rock That Is Standing'
Lion Head, formerly called Glacier Point
De Laguna (1970:40): "Glacier Point at the end of Matanuska Glacier represents a Tcisyu **[Tsisyu]** girl and her baby who were coming from Chitina and turned to stone."

Ben Neeley (2000:4): "**Tsisyu ts'akaey** [paint clan women], three sisters started walking. One sister was packing a baby. They sat down and took a rest. They had left their country and I guess the lord had led them to an unknown country. So they sat down. All of a sudden they turned into big rocks, the sisters. **Natsede'aayi,** that's what they call it. Two of the sisters kept going on down to around King River to **Tsiis T'el'iixden"** (14.21).

Reckord (1983:53): "One Ahtna informant cited the location of **Natsede'aayi,** which is a humped mountain called Glacier Point between the Glenn Highway and the Matanuska River near Sheep Mountain, where the present-day Indians believe that a **Tsisyu** woman and her baby were turned to stone. Big trading parties are said to have been held there, although it is not known if such parties occurred before contact."

§14.110 Natsede'aayi Na' *(Ahtna)* • 'Rock That Is Standing Across-Stream'
Rock Glacier Creek

14.60 Nutughilentnu *(Dena'ina);* **Nataghilen Na'** *(Ahtna)* • 'River Where Water Flows Down'
Caribou Creek
One trail up Caribou Creek leads to the upper Oshetna River. Other trails off Billy Creek go to the Little Oshetna or to the Little Nelchina headwaters. Another trail leads west to East Boulder Creek.

Mendenhall (1900:303): "Hicks to Caribou to Bubb or Tahneta Pass. This route has been followed by the Copper River Indians in their annual trading rips to the stores on Cook Inlet." Trails up Caribou Creek and Squaw Creek are shown on both the Mendenhall and the Meiklejohn maps of 1900 (Maps 56 and 57).

Glenn (1899:85): "At the mouth of the Caribou was located the cache of our guide, Mr. Hicks, which had been used by him for two or three years to cache stores that he traded with the Indians." The 1906 Herning map indicates "Hicks' cache" on lower Caribou Creek. Cf. 14.49 above.

As the Glenn and Mendenhall parties headed northeast in August of 1898, the first clearly Ahtna (i.e., non-Dena'ina) stream names they recorded were in the Bubb Creek/Little Nelchina drainage (Glenn 1899:60), "Taiklano" and "Taikano." Their guide, Big Stephan, of Knik/Wasilla, would have been bilingual in Ahtna and Dena'ina.

14.61 Hnilges Na' *(Ahtna)* • ‡'They Slide Creek'
Fortress Creek

14.62 Hnilges *(Ahtna)* • ‡'They Slide'
Fortress Ridge

14.63 Xelt'aats'i Na' *(Ahtna)* • 'Water Lily Creek'
‡Fish Lake outlet stream
This is on the trail system to Old Man Lake and Tyone Lake.

14.64 Xelt'aats'i Bene' *(Ahtna)* • 'Water Lily Lake'
‡Fish Lake
Location revised via Jim Tyone text.

FIGURE 190 AND 190A

Siz'aani, (14.71, Gunsight Mountain) and mountain north of Copper Glacier.

Another *patterned duplication* that provokes thought: why should two mountains have the same Ahtna name, **Siz'aani**? viz, Gunsight Mountain and the distinctive 6580' unnamed mountain at the head of the Copper River, (Fig. 190A just N of Copper Glacier). This name is metaphoric, 'Inside Me,' and is a pun on the word **sciz'aani** 'my heart.' Gunsight Mountain can be seen from a large radius, but the mountain at Copper Glacier can only be seen from nearby to the north (e.g., the Slana area). This duplication must have been pragmatic and intentional.

LEFT: PHOTO BY LORRAINE BASNAR ELDER IN 1981 RIGHT: PHOTO BY CARL BENSON, UAF GEOPHYSICAL INSTITUTE

14.65 Tsedghaazi Na' *(Ahtna)* • 'Rough Rock Creek'
Alfred Creek
The trail here went on to **Neltsii Na',** (14.119) the Little Nelchina River via Crooked Creek, **Bakaey Ts'elaes Na',** and has been mentioned by Johnny Shaginoff and Jack Tyone.

14.66 Tsedghaazi *(Ahtna)* • 'Rough Rock'
Syncline Mountains

14.67 Nalk'uugi *(Ahtna)* • 'Jagged One'
mountain at the head of Caribou Creek, possibly west of Billy Creek

§14.111 Nalk'uugi Na' *(Ahtna)* • 'Jagged One Creek'
Billy Creek
Johnny Shaginoff knew the pass from Billy Creek to the Little Oshetna River.

14.68 Beznae *(Ahtna)* • '(A type of) Stone '
Sheep Mountain
Jim Tyone noted that the name refers to a specific type of stone.

Frank Stickwan (West tapes 1973): "Grandpa hunted from Tyone Lake to Tazlina Lake, Tazlina Glacier. That way they used to hunt for sheep. Some they go to Sheep Mountain on Glenn Highway. Sheep Mountain. That's where they hunt sheep."

§14.112 Beznae Na' *(Ahtna)* • '(A type of) Stone Creek'
Gypsum Creek

14.69 Dzeł Ghaan' Na' *(Ahtna)* • 'Half Mountain River'
South Fork of Matanuska River

§14.113 Dzeł Ghaan' Luu' *(Ahtna)* • 'Half Mountain Glacier'
Powell Glacier

14.70 Dzeł Ghaan' *(Ahtna)* • 'Half Mountain'
mountain between the Nelchina River and the South Fork of the Matanuska River. See Plate 16.
‡Another mountain named **Dzeł Ghaan'** is on the Delta River west of North Tangle Lake. This name is likely a patterned duplication with 14.70. This duplication calls one's attention to intervisible mountains at the west and north edges of Ahtna territory.

‡14.126 Siz'aani Bene' *(Ahtna)* • 'Heart Lake'
Lake Leila

14.71 Siz'aani *(Ahtna)* • 'Heart'
Gunsight Mountain. See Figs. 190 and 190A.

14.72 Siz'aani Na' *(Ahtna)* • 'Heart Creek'
‡Gunsight Creek (location revised)

§14.73 Tsendil'aats Kulaen Bene' *(Ahtna)* • 'Heart Lake'
Trail Lake

§14.114 Tsendil'aats Kulaende *(Ahtna)* • 'Where Game Migrate Downland'
Trail Creek
Revisions in 14.72 and 14.73 and this location are based upon the travel narrative by Jim Tyone (p. 223): "«Now at 'where game migrate downland' that is where the trail used to be.»"

§14.115 Unatadeł'aade *(Ahtna)* • 'Where The Water Flows Around'
hill near Sheep Mountain and Trail Creek
Mentioned by Jim Tyone, see p. 223 and Map 43.

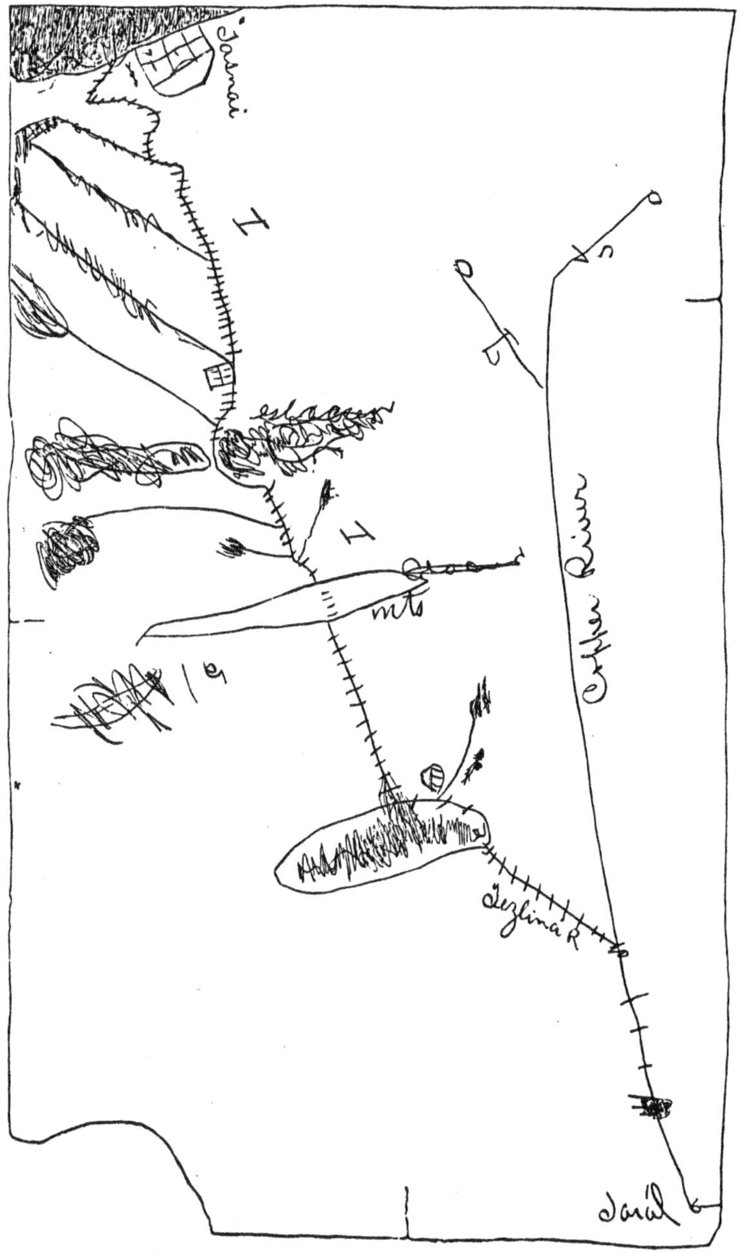

MAP 60

The 1885 Ahtna Sketch annotated by Allen.

Allen (1887:61): "I had frequent maps made by the natives to show us the trail over the Alaskan Mountains and down the Tanana to the Yukon River, all of which indicated the route to be via the Tazlina River to Tasnai. The accompanying sketch represents one of the maps thus made.... It was not until we reached the Tezlina that I felt sure that the trail up it could not lead over the Alaskan Mountains, but rather to Cook's Inlet."

On the map Allen wrote the names or words "Taral," "Tezlina R," "Copper River," "mts," and "Tasnai." The latter is the Ahtna word for the Dena'ina: **Dastnaey**. The first lake on the Tazlina river is Tazlina Lake, with a structure noted on the north bank. The map seems to mark the Nelchina and Matanuska Glaciers. The loop in the trail may be at Glacier Point. Note that one structure is noted on the south bank of the Matanuska River above a left-hand stream.

‡The Tazlina-Matanuska River trail system (i.e., the Glenn Highway route) is one of the best documented aboriginal trails in Alaska. Kari (2008:11) has a table of sixteen sources on this trail (e.g., Tarkhanov, Wrangell, Allen, Moffit, early mining maps and journals, a series of USGS maps, as well as anthropologists' and linguists' notes). There is some overlap and repetition between all of these sources on sequences of Ahtna or Dena'ina names along the main trail, and on intersecting routes and trails. Such repeated confirmations via geographic particularism is the hallmark of shared Athabascan geographic knowledge. Since antiquity, foot travel has been facilitated by the memorization of place names and vice versa. Such reconfirmations are a measure of the conservative nature of the verbally transmitted Athabascan place names system.

ARCHIVES, ALASKA AND POLAR REGIONS DEPT., RASMUSON LIBRARY, UNIVERSITY OF ALASKA FAIRBANKS

§14.116 Naghilenden *(Ahtna)* • 'Where Current Flows Down'
East Fork of Matanuska River
Name via Frank Stickwan

14.74 Hwyiis Tes *(Ahtna)* • 'Mirage Hill'
‡hill 3447' by Knob Lake
‡It is remarkable that the name for this hill was documented in 1797 by Tarkhanov, among the earliest documented Ahtna place names (Black 2008:79). This visible hill at this divide was a key name for the learning Athabascan place names and trail system. See 14.120.

§14.117 Hwyiis Tes Bene' *(Ahtna)* • 'Mirage Hill Lake'
Knob Lake. See Plate 16.

14.75 Nekets'alyaexden *(Ahtna)* • 'Where We Turn Around'
Tahneta Pass
Walter Charley reported: "People used to carry a handful of soil from their homes as they left to go down the Matanuska River to Cook Inlet. At **Nekets'alyaexden**, 'where we turn around,' they had their last view of the Copper River country. Here they turned and scattered the handful of soil and made a prayer for a safe journey" (Kari 1983:viii).

14.76 C'enaen' 'Aaxden *(Ahtna)* • §'Where a Face Is in Position'
hill at Tahneta Pass
The name "Tahneta,"recorded by Glenn and others in 1898, has not been re-elicited and is perhaps a vague rendition of this aboriginal name. This is on intersecting trails to the Ahtna villages at Tazlina Lake, Old Man Lake, and Tyone Lake. Other names in this area are in Kari (1983 and 2001).

Johnny Shaginoff: "People from Old Man Lake used the Matanuska country for trails, summer and winter. They all hunted there. There was lots of fur, and they had summer salmon at Tazlina Lake. Those people used to walk down to Knik every year."

§14.118 C'enaen' 'Aax Bene' *(Ahtna)* • 'Where a Face Is in Position-Lake'
Tahneta Lake

§14.119 Neltsii Na', Neltsiin Na', Neltsiigi Na' *(Ahtna)* • 'Stream That Is Made,' 'Stream That Is Yellow'
Little Nelchina River
Three versions of this name have been recorded with Ahtna speakers. This place name may have been documented as early as 1797 by Dmitrii Tarkhonov. A name west of Tazlina Lake is transliterated as "nechinenna" in Halamaa (2001).

§14.121 Una' Cenaeł'sdildełi Na' *(Ahtna)*
Old Man Creek • 'Its-Creek The-One-We-Move-Upriver-Upon Creek'
Jim Tyone: "«They would go downstream on the straight bar of 'Kentsii creek,' and they would camp downstream at the mouth of **Una' Cenaeł'sdildełi Na'** (Old Man Creek).»" The name is emblematic of this stream being on the main trail toward the Matanuska River. The derivational prefix **ce-** means 'downstream.'

§14.120 Bendiil Bene' *(Ahtna)* • 'Lake Current Lake'
Tazlina Lake
‡The earliest historic account recorded on the Copper River is that of Dmitrii Tarkhanov. Early in the winter of 1797 he stayed for about two months in the vicinity of Chitina and Lower Tonsina. Tarkhanov recorded about thirteen Ahtna place names (Kari and Tuttle 2005, Kari 2008).

From Lydia Black's (2008:79) translation of the Tarkhanov journal.

> These Kelkheni (group name not recognized) live from [this] village one day's march distant. They have no toens (chiefs) and are subject to no one. In winter, they go to the lake Baltybele* (**Bendiil Bene'**) to trade with others who come there from another village... The distance from the Ahtna people to the first barabora of the Kelkhleni is fifty or forty-five verst. The Tezlenna River (Tezdlen Na' Tazlina River) is a day and a half march from the last, the eighth, barabora. One may estimate the distance to about seventy-five verst. They [Ahtna] live in a treeless area beyond the rivers Tezlenna and Copper. A large lake, their Baltylbele, according to them, the [other] shore of it cannot be seen. The Tezlenna River flows from this lake into the Copper. The Nelchinenna River (**Neltsii Na'**, Little Nelchina River, 14.119) flows from Kuesteshe Mountain (**Hwyiis Tes** 14.74); its mouth enters the [Tazlina] lake across from the Tezlenna. The Tsetenkunna River (**Ts'itonh Na'** 14.2, Matanuska River) flows from the other side of the same mountain. Its mouth is at the Meltkhna River (Possibly **Benteh** 13.39 name for Wasilla area + 'stream'). Its course, source, and where it empties are unknown.

Tazlina Lake is prominently noted on the Wrangell map of 1839 (Map 17) as "Mantilbana." It is also on the 1854 Holmberg map.

Mendenhall (1900:339): "The Matanuska [Western Ahtna] dwell on the southern edge of the Copper River Plateau, generally on the Copper River drainage. They are more active than the coast tribes and are held in much awe by them. Once or twice during each winter season they come down the Matanuska River on the ice to exchange furs with the traders at the head of Knik Arm for firearms ammunition, clothing or food. The journey of more than 100 miles is usually very leisurely performed and occupies several weeks."

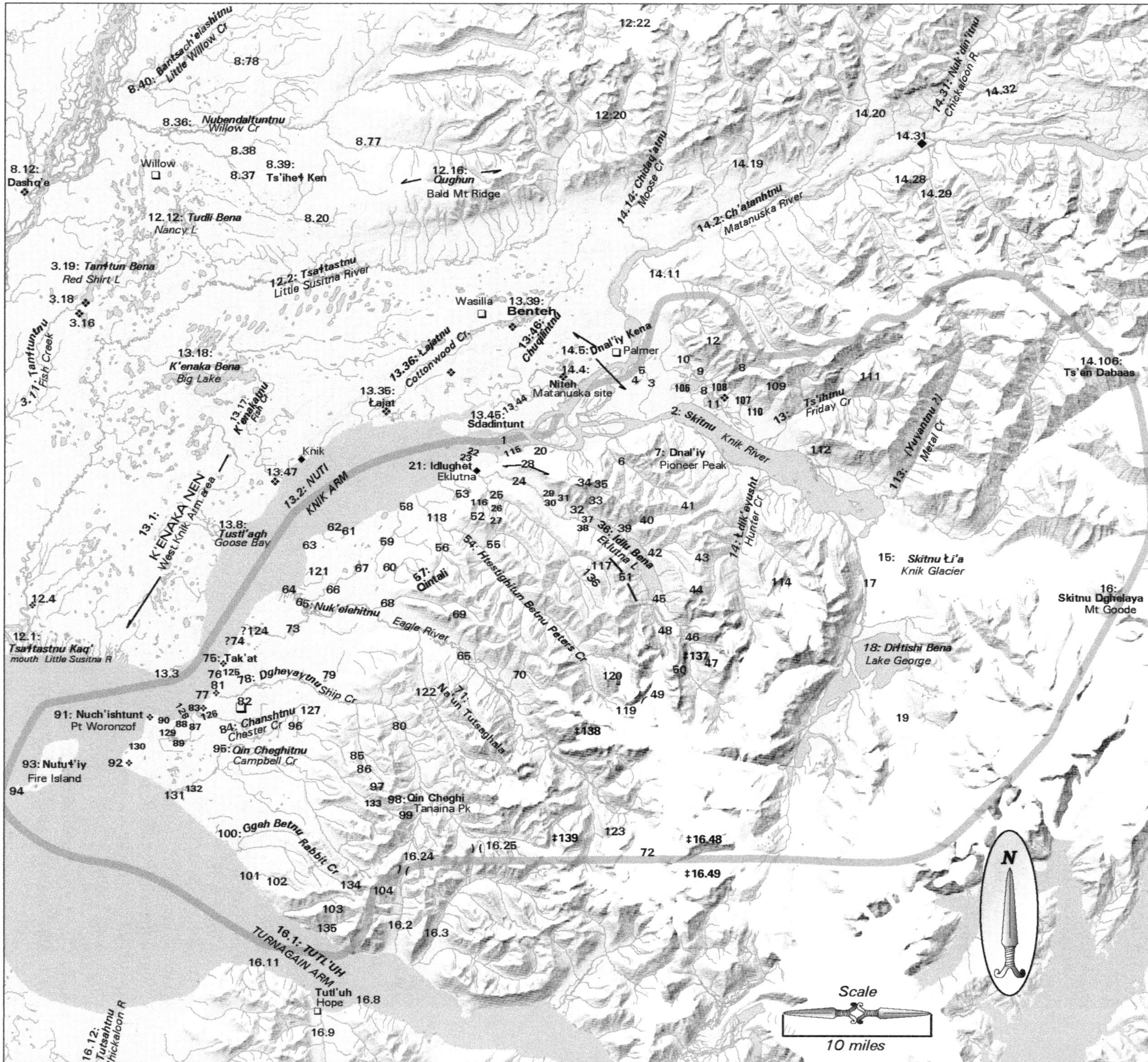
8.40: Bantsach'elashitnu
Little Willow Cr
8.36: Nubendaltuntnu
Willow Cr
Willow
8.12: Dashq'e
8.39: Ts'ihet Ken
12.16: Qughun
Bald Mt Ridge
12.12: Tudli Bena
Nancy L
3.19: Tantun Bena
Red Shirt L
12.2: Tsattastnu
Little Susitna River
3.71: Tantuntnu
Fish Creek
13.18: K'enaka Bena
Big Lake
13.17: K'enakatnu
Fish Cr
Wasilla
13.39: Benteh
13.46: Chuqilintnu
13.36: Łajatnu
Cottonwood Cr.
13.35: Łajat
13.45: Sdadintunt
14.4: Niteh
Matanuska site
14.5: Dnal'iy Kena
Palmer
14.14: Chidaq'atnu
Moose Cr
14.2: Ch'atanhtnu
Matanuska River
14.31: Nuk'din'itnu
Chickaloon R.
14.106: Ts'en Dabaas
13: Ts'ihtnu
Friday Cr
2: Skitnu
Knik River
113: (Yuyantnu ?)
Metal Cr
7: Dnal'iy
Pioneer Peak
Knik
13.2: NUTI
KNIK ARM
13.1: K'ENAKA NEN
West Knik Arm area
13.8: Tustl'agh
Goose Bay
21: Idlughet
Eklutna
36: Idlu Bena
Eklutna L
14: Łdik'eyusht
Hunter Cr
15: Skitnu Łi'a
Knik Glacier
16: Skitnu Dghelaya
Mt Goode
54: Htestighitun Betnu Peters Cr
57: Qintali
65: Nuk'elehitnu
Eagle River
12.1: Tsattastnu Kaq'
mouth Little Susitna R
75: Tak'at
78: Dgheyaytnu
Ship Cr
71: Na'un Tutsaghala
18: Dihtishi Bena
Lake George
91: Nuch'ishtunt
Pt Woronzof
84: Chanshtnu
Chester Cr
95: Qin Cheghitnu
Campbell Cr
93: Nutuł'iy
Fire Island
98: Qin Cheghi
Tanaina Pk
100: Ggeh Betnu
Rabbit Cr
16.1: TUTL'UH
TURNAGAIN ARM
Tutl'uh
Hope
16.12: Tutsahtnu
Chickaloon R
N
Scale
10 miles

15 Eastern Knik Arm and the Anchorage area

Knik River to Anchorage (Potter Marsh)

15.1 Skitnu Hdakaq' • 'Mouth of Brush River'
mouth of Knik River

15.2 Skitnu *(Dena'ina)*; **Scitna'** *(Ahtna)* • 'Brush River'
Knik River
The name "Knik" is not based upon the Dena'ina name for Knik River, **Skitnu** (see 13.1). This name was recorded as "Skeetno" on the 1904 Moffit sketch map (Map 44). The prevailing wind from the Knik River is known as **Skitnu hch'anich'ey**.

Leo Stephan regarding walking from **Niteh** [14.4] up the Knik River: "We used to start next to the river. We followed Matanuska River all the way over to this Ezi Slough. And then this sand bar on the river bed, all the way up to this Knik River bridge. There used to be a house that Old Billy Ezi used to live in. We call that Halfway House. Then we'd follow the river and get into Jim Creek, and go across the swamp right here and get into this lake (**Skintuk'ełaha**, 13.12). That was a regular summer/winter trail. Last time I walked up there I was pretty young. Took me seven hours to get all the way to Jim Creek. But then there was about a foot and half of snow, walking in the snow."

In September 1913 Herning (n.d.) wrote, "The Ezi family had left in a boat for the Knik River to go hunting."

15.3 K'unast'in Shlatnu • 'Creek of Little One That Stands Apart'
Bodenberg Creek, formerly Palmer Creek
A trail is shown on the Johnston and Herning map of 1899 (Map 52) leading from the Knik River, up Palmer Creek, to "Palmer's Upper House" on the Matanuska

FIGURE 191
Skitnu Kaq' (15.1, the mouth of Knik River) and in the distance **Ch'atan Kaq'** (14.1, the mouth of the Matanuska River), as seen from the summit of **Denal'iy** (15.7, Pioneer Peak) in 1982. The general area of the lower Knik-Matanuska rivers in Palmer area is called **Denal'iy Kena** (14.5).
PHOTO BY LORRAINE BASNAR ELDER

MAP 61
(Opposite) Place names map of the Eastern Knik Arm, showing Nos. 15.1 to 15.139. Note that several features in Chapter 15 along east Knik Arm are more legible on Maps 49 (Chapter 12) and 51 (Chapter 13) than on Map 61. ‡This map was reproduced in Tobias (2009:327). Since 2014 The Alaska Gallery at the Anchorage Museum has an interactive map that displays eleven Dena'ina place names in the Anchorage bowl.
MAP BY MATT GANLEY

Sources: Mike Alex, John Stump, Bailey Theodore, Mike Theodore, Johnny Shaginoff, Shem Pete, Leo Stephan, Alberta Stephan, Sava Stephan, Billy Pete

2003 revisions: names added 15.105–15.136; revised locations 15.14, 15.19, 15.71, 15.74, 15.90, 15.96 and 15.128; revised spelling 15.71.
‡2016 revisions: names added 15.137, 15.138, 15.139; names revised 15.28, 15.33, 15.71, 15.79, 15.113, 15.122.

FIGURE 192

(Above) **Skitnu** (15.2, the lower Knik River) with **Denal'iy** (15.7, Pioneer Peak) and one side of **Łach Q'a** (15.34, Twin Peaks).
PHOTO BY JAMES KARI

FIGURE 193

(Right) **Dnal'iy** or **Denal'iy**, (15.7, Pioneer Peak), with **K'unast'inshla** (15.4, Bodenberg Butte) beneath it, viewed looking south on the east bank Matasnuska River above Palmer.

Mike Theodore: "They say that it is a bear's face watching us."

Mary Shaginoff: "[It is] the one leaning with its head held in position."

Shem Pete: "«Regarding that **Dnal'iy**, that **Qalbisgga** and his older brother **Qatsen**—those two Eklutna medicine men—used to say that when the town [Palmer] was formed, and they got rock sidewalks, that mountain was starting to break. 'We see it starting to break,' they said to me. 'I don't know. Another 100 years more, maybe, the mountain will break up.' They said it will break. It is breaking upriver from **Niteh** village [14.4].» I think they're right, but I don't know. I got to see where it coming down. It's a really big mountain, that **Dnal'iy**. They said that it's going to break down pretty soon, those medicine men."
PHOTO BY LORRAINE BASNAR ELDER

River. This likely refers to the original store founded by George Palmer

15.4 K'unast'in Gga or **K'unast'inshla** • 'The Little One That Stands Apart'
Bodenberg Butte
John Stump: "Those three hills in the valley [Bodenberg Butte; the hill to the north, 15.11; and the hill **Hninaghi'iy Ka'a**, 15.20], they were people. Three of them coming down the river, old man, old lady, and one son."

15.5 Hutnaynut'i • 'That Which Is Shining'
site in Bodenberg Butte area
Eklutna Alex, Mike Alex's father, was born here in about 1865.

Fall (1981:399): "People from this village fished near the mouth of Palmer [Bodenberg] Creek on the Knik River, but built their **nichił** inland to avoid flooding."

This site is listed in Cook Inlet Historic Sites Project (1975:87) as No. 157. Mike Alex and Bailey Theodore reported that this site was razed during early homesteading.

15.6 Łdagheltnu, Hdagheltnu • '-Ω- River'
Goat Creek

15.7 Dnal'iy, Denal'iy *(Dena'ina);* **Tnel'aay** *(Ahtna)* • 'The Object That Is Standing Still' or 'The One That Watches Us'
Pioneer Peak
The name is a pun in Dena'ina, and could be given either analysis. The Ahtna name would translate as 'The object that is standing still.' People often ask if there is a connection between this place name and "Denali," the Koyukon-origin name for Mount McKinley. There is no etymological connection.

Leo Stephan: "Old Bill Ezi used to have a cabin [at the base of Pioneer Peak, at a pond, two to three miles east of the bridge] about one hundred fifty to two hundred feet up, facing this way. We come from Knik River and we come visit him. I remember the lake."

15.8 Dghełtayi Betnu, Dghiłtayen Betnu • 'Creek of the One That Is Strong'
Jim Creek

FIGURE 194

A view looking up the north side of the Knik River valley beyond **Dghełtayi Betnu** (15.8, Jim Creek). The mountain at the left edge is **Xazggezi** (15.12), and the mountain in the center is **Ts'ihtnu Dghelaya** (15.111). Also seen are the valleys of Jim Creek, **Ts'ihtnu** (15.13, Friday Creek), and 15.113, Metal Creek which is possibly called **Yuyantnu.**

PHOTO BY JEFF DAVIS

Dghełtayi is said to be the personal name of Indian Jim Nikita of Eklutna, who was Cornelius Osgood's main consultant at Eklutna in 1931. ‡C. Mielke (2013) has profiled the life Jim Nikita.

This was a summer and fall fishing location of the **Niteh** band.

Alberta Stephan (1996:149): "After Simeon Esia stopped working with his steam boat, he made his living trapping. His trap line was in the Jim Creek, Friday Creek area."

Alberta Stephan (2001:15–16) describes the Ezi family's subsistence activities in the Jim Creek area in the 1930s, when the family was living at **Niteh**. They traveled up Knik River in an open dory. The men walked the boat to the mouth of Jim Creek when the water became shallow, while the women and children walked along the sandbars. After reaching their hunting cabin at Jim Creek, hunters scanned the mountainsides for sheep and goat with binoculars. Younger men fished for salmon with a short gill net. Children fished for trout. The family remained at Jim Creek until all the meat and fish was dried. Alberta Stephan (2001:15) recalled that, "Those times in late August was the happiest times for the whole Esi family. They did things the old traditional way, working together and putting up food. They used the sheep and goat skins for their mattress and rugs. The meat of these animals would be dried for their cache back home."

Leo Stephan: "There is a certain type of fish in Jim Creek I never seen any place else. They look like a king salmon. They are probably some kind of mountain trout. They come right off Jim Creek."

Annabel (1948:192, 1971, 1987:79–89) set several of his adventure stories in the Jim Creek area with characters who seem to be composites of several Dena'ina he knew from the Knik River area.

15.9 Dghełtayi Bena • 'Lake of the One That Is Strong'
Jim Lake

§15.106 Quggesh Bena • 'Swan Lake'
Mud Lake, lake west of Jim Lake

15.10 K'unast'in Ka'a • 'The Big One That Stands Apart'
hill, elev. 541', "Burnt Butte" or "Swan"

15.11 Skintuk'ełaha • 'Fish Run Through Brush'
Swan Lake and village site

Shem Pete: "«That's where Old Man Ezi's last village was. I saw the house there. There are salmon there. There is a lake on the east side [of the Knik River]. The trail is

FIGURE 195

Peter Ezi at the Ezi cache in 1968 at **Skintuk'ełaha** (15.11, Swan Lake) with **Ts'ihtnu Dghelaya** (15.111) in the background.

This was the upland camp of the Ezi family. It was still used until Billy Ezi, Sr., died in 1971. The camp on the upper end of the lake was located close to the base a mountain where sheep were often available. This was also good moose hunting country.

PHOTO BY ALBERTA STEPHAN

on the left-hand side going up. The trail goes up to the mountain. Old Man Ezi would go up there in a boat. There were **nichił** there long ago. They wait for the sheep to come down, and they kill them. And there are king salmon there.» Good place to get by. "«There were nice steambaths there and a good cabin. Afterwards Bill Ezi took it, and there is still a house there yet. If we see it,» we got a place to stop.

"«I do not know where Indian Jim's place is. I think it is further up the Knik River.» That's Jim [Nikita]'s country, but I never been there.

"«I went to Old Man Ezi's with a message in 1926 or 1927. His grandchild was about to die in Eklutna. He was up there, and he left from there in a boat. When he came downstream he was transporting a moose down to us, that Old Man Esi. That child recovered and did not die.»"

15.12 Xazggezi *(Ahtna)* • possibly 'Rough' or 'Worn'
mountain between Jim Creek and Wolverine Creek, Matanuska Peak and lower ridges
After considerable effort, Johnny Shaginoff in 1985 recalled this name: "There's a name to that mountain there. Steep mountain right along. Beside the camp, toward Matanuska River. That's a big mountain there. It's got a name. That mountain. Wolverine Creek there."

This southern side is the sheep hunting area used by the Swan Lake people. This is an Ahtna name with the consonant **z**. The name has not been reconfirmed since then.

§15.107 Baquch'k'ilyuyi Bena • 'In it We Butcher Something-Lake'
"Butcher Lake," lake at base of mountains on stream north of Swan Lake
Leo Stephan: "The reason they call that Butcher Lake is that they hunt up here on the mountain, and then they go to work, and they drag the animals down here to that lake and they butcher them on that."

"They were spear catching those fish. Last time I seen them I was really young. We had a boat close to that Butcher Lake. They [salmon] go into that Butcher Lake, a bunch of them.... When those fish took off we almost went dry. It just took the water and make one big swell. It just red all the way across the bottom."

§15.108 Nik'uleh Bena • 'End of Fish Run-Lake'
spawning lake off Jim Creek, perhaps lake north of Swan Lake
Leo Stephan: "These are little lakes. We used to ice fish in them all the time. In wintertime there is spring water coming off the mountains, and they don't freeze all the way solid, and there is fish in them."

§15.109 Łaqinaltl'il • 'Braided into a Fan'
mountain and slope west of Friday Creek
Leo Stephan: "Back behind Jim Creek and around towards Friday Creek there used to be quite a lot of sheep in there." See Fig. 195.

§15.110 Łaqinaltl'iltnu • 'Braided into a Fan-Stream'
upper fork of Jim Creek emanating from springs west of Friday Creek

15.13 Ts'ihtnu • 'Straight Creek'
Friday Creek

§15.111 Ts'ihtnu Dghelaya • 'Straight Creek Mountain'
mountain 7060' up Friday Creek
Leo Stephan: "You see that mountain valley way back there? That's where I told you there was sheep. It was hard to get up there because of that canyon. It is straight up and down on both sides."

§15.112 (no recorded name)
Wolf Point
Johnny Shaginoff: "They got a couple places in there where they hunt and chase the moose. I think the white people call it Wolf Point around there.... I went to chase them when I was young kid there one time. Right close to Wolf Point there."

Writing in 1900 biologist Wilfred Osgood (1901:62) wrote: "Mountain goat.... A small band is known to inhabit a district of the headwaters of the Matanuska and Knik rivers. Mr. Hanmore [at Tyonekl] knows the animals thoroughly and says he has seen skins and horns from this place and often heard of them from the Indians who hunt in that vicinity. As far as I can learn, this is the northernmost occurrence of the mountain goat."

FIGURE 196

(Left) An upper fork of Jim Creek is called **Łaqinaltl'iltnu** (15.110) with lakes above Swan Lake such as **Nik'uleh Bena** (15.108). The mountain in the center is **Ts'ihtnu Dghelaya** (15.111).

Leo Stephan: "Part of the mountain up here is a bunch of little springs, straight up and down, **Łaqinaltl'il** (15.109). They look like that, and they come down into one. That means 'all things come together at one point.'"

PHOTO COURTESY OF COOK INLET REGION, INC.

FIGURE 197

(Below) A view from **K'unast'inshla**, (15.4, Bodenberg Butte) of the upper **Skitnu** (15.2, Knik River valley) and **Skitnu Łi'a** (15.15, Knik Glacier). At the upper center of the frame is **Skitnu Dghelaya** (15.16, Mt. Goode). The two lakes at the left edge are **Skintuk'ełaha** (15.11, Swan Lake) and **Quggesh Bena** (15.106, Mud Lake).

PHOTO BY PRISCILLA RUSSELL

FIGURE 198

The Ezi cabin site on a pond off the Knik River a few miles below **Łdik'eyusht** (15.8, Hunter Creek).

Shem Pete: "«Ezi had a house at **Łdik'eyusht**. Sheep move down toward the water there, and they [**Niteh** people] kill sheep. . . . I saw the house by the river. He had a house at **Łdik'eyusht** and sheep would come to them, and they would kill sheep all the time. Salmon would run in the lake. He had some steambaths. . . . I have been up to Old Man Ezi's upstream of **Dnal'iy**. That's as far as I have gone (on the Knik River).»"

PHOTO BY JAMES KARI

FIGURE 199

Alberta and Leo Stephan at **Łdik'eyusht** (15.8, Hunter Creek).

Alberta Stephan: "My mother used to mention that place. She used to go up there and help them to drive the moose."

PHOTO BY JAMES KARI

The following passages culled from the voluminous writings of Russell Annabel seem to be fairly authentic documentation of Dena'ina goat hunting in the Knik River valley. Annabel (1987:304) "Although you don't see many of them any more, there used to be a race of Indians who called themselves the Goat Eater Denna. They were a rugged outfit, sure-enough mountaineers. They depended on goats for red meat, made clothes and bedding from their hides, ate with goat horn spoons, and petitioned their tribal demons with the aid of goat masks and goat-hock rattles." Annabel (1997a:212): "They [goat horns] project straight up from the goat's skull, with a slight backward curve at the tips, and are so keenly pointed that the Indians used them as awls in sewing leather." Annabel (1997e:144): "I resorted to a Goat-Eater Denna Indian trick. Cupping my hands at my mouth, I imitated the grunts of a panicked kid. I got action. A female trotted out of the alders and halted to stare."

When asked to comment on Annabel's "Goat Eater" band, Leo Stephan remarked: "The goat is a lot fatter than the sheep. I used to like to hunt them. I like to eat them. Maybe those people are right that they called us the Goat Eaters. They don't jump around like sheep. Sheep sometimes get too skinny. We used to eat the whole thing, the head and everything. We ate the head [while] on the mountains. We roast them and eat them and take the fat and meat home, back to camp."

§15.113 possibly **[Yuyantnu]** • 'Cloud Creek'
Metal Creek
The name 'Cloud Creek' was called to our attention by Jeff Davis based upon his studies of the writings of Russell Annabel. In a passage from one of Annabel's early stories set in the 1920s, the Dena'ina shaman Blind Nick sent Annabel to 'Cloud Creek' to find Tex Cobb, the well-known trapper and outdoorsman, who had cabins and camps on Metal Creek (Annabel 1997b:220 also 1987:208–09). Other stories by Annabel (*e.g.*, 1997d: 340, 1997e:143–44) feature Dena'ina characters planning gold and hunting goats up Metal Creek.

Leo Stephan: "I should have heard that ['Cloud Creek']. Because our tribe like to hunt goat and sheep, and lotta times when we're up in the mountains, we get closed in with clouds you know. We're way up there and cloud is all around us and we can't see."

It is possible that a seasonal trail across the range between Metal Creek and Carpenter Creek offered a short cut to Knik River for Dena'ina or Ahtna traveling down the Matanuska River. Alberta Stephan has heard mention of such a travel route from her grandmother. Note that Glenn (1899:32), writing in 1898 at Twentymile River on Turnagain Arm had heard of a trail that led from Turnagain Arm and then on to Copper River: "Our information up to this point was that the Indians used a trail down some stream that brought them into the waters of Turnagain Arm from the Copper River." It is curious that the 1899 Johnston and Herning map indicates a trail

15.16

FIGURE 200

A close-up of **Skitnu Łi'a** (15.15, Knik Glacier) with **Skitnu Dghelaya** (15.16, Mt. Goode) in the distance.

PHOTO BY JEFF DAVIS

"to Copper River" leading northeast from somewhere off the upper Knik River (Map 52).

15.14 Łdik'eyusht • 'Where Animals Go In'
§Hunter Creek (location corrected for second edition)
The name "Hunter Creek" is an indirect reference to the Dena'ina place name.

Johnny Shaginoff: "That's on the Knik River, Pioneer Peak side. That means they chase the moose when they hunt. Couple of us, you know where they're crossing is the runway you know. A guy there waits for moose and the other guy chases it. When the moose comes in already **udi dik'ghiyu** ['it has come in']. That mean he got the bull. He get in this [canyon]."

§15.114 Łdik'eyusht Dghelaya • 'Where Animals Go In-Mountain'
mountain on upper Hunter Creek

15.15 Skitnu Łi'a • 'Brush River Glacier'
Knik Glacier
Note that these glaciers were sketched by the Ahtna man who drew the 1904 Moffit map (Map 44).

15.16 Skitnu Dghelaya • 'Brush River Mountain'
Mount Goode

15.17 Diłtishi Betnu • 'Stream That Freezes In'
Lake Fork, the Gorge

15.18 Diłtishi Bena • 'Lake That Freezes In'
Lake George
Shem Pete: "That means glacier's water breaks out sometimes. «Upstream of Old Man Ezi's village there was that lake that would erode through.»"

Hulsing (1977:10): "Just before 1900, three Indian villages along the Knik River were destroyed by a great flood, which was believed to be the result of the breakout of Lake George. No previous flood damage along Knik River had been recorded, although the lake emptied once every 15 to 20 years according to Indians living in the area."

Alberta Stephan (1996:22): "Many of the Indians from his area were drowned by the bursting waters of Knik Lake (Lake George) in the 1800s. Some Indians who were out trapping disappeared and never returned home with their catch."

Snider (1966:41): "Self-dumping Lake George is a remnant of the ice age. Chief Nicoly told me they found [ice] worms on the glacier, six to ten inches long. He said they were white, not red."

Alberta Stephan (2001:16) describes the Ezi family's hunting of moose at Lake George in the 1920s and 1930s. "All of the hunters and young people would go out and when they found a moose the sharp shooter would sit in the area where the moose would run. Then the rest of the party would circle the animals and chase it towards the man with the gun."

15.19 Diłtishi Bena Łi'a • 'Glacier of Lake That Freezes In'
§Colony Glacier (location revised)
There is no specific evidence that the Dena'ina formerly went from the Knik or Matanuska rivers over the mountains to Prince William Sound. Osgood wrote: "In the Upper Inlet country, the mountains prove too high and the glaciers too forbidding. For them there is no direct Eskimo contact except for the sudden attacks of raiding parties which come up the inlet" (1937:74–75). However, see 16.4, the Twentymile River.

Annabel (1938b) is a story told to Annabel by "Barsilla," a Knik Indian hunter who stayed on Cottonwood Creek. In his younger years on the upper Knik River Barsilla trapped "a reddish animal, larger than a fox but smaller than a wolf, with sharp pointed ears and a lean muzzle." Such an animal that had never been seen before in the country, a coyote. This story may be built around an authentic Dena'ina account about the first appearance of coyotes in their country. The Upper Inlet Dena'ina name for coyote is **tiqin gga**, 'little wolf.'

Annabel (1997d:304): "Well, a moment later the grizzly of a lifetime hove into sight on the game trails ahead of the goats. The bear was no giant of his race, not heavier than seven hundred pounds, but he had a freak grayish pelt with cream points. I had, during my nomad career as a working woodsman, seen only two other gray grizzlies, both of them in this remote sector of the Chugaches. The Knik Indians report having sighted several of these remarkable bears, and call them cloudy grizzlies."

15.20 Hninaghi'iy Ka'a • 'Big One That Is Embedded'
hill at junction of Glenn Highway and Old Palmer Highway

§15.115 Hninaghi'iy Kena • 'One That Is Embedded-Flat'
eastern end of Eklutna Flats
Kari (1978b:3): "Mike [Alex] would sometimes tell how his mother would gather **k'tl'ila**, Indian potatoes *(Hedysarum alpinum)* with a stick around Eklutna Flat.

FIGURE 201

Hninighi'iy Ka'a (15.20), the unnamed hill at the old and new Glenn Highway junction. The Alaska Railroad goes close by this hill close by on its east side. The flat in the foreground is **Hninighi'iy Kena** (15.115).

Johnny Shaginoff: "I never heard of village in this area. Natives were scared to climb **Hninaghi'iy Ka'a**. They said it was dead people's house. They saw smoke [of ghosts] there all the time." Cf. Fall (1981:397).

PHOTO BY JAMES KARI

FIGURE 202

Chief Mike Alex (center) for many years gave talks about the Russian Orthodox church at Eklutna (15.21). The children here are from Lime Village.

PHOTO TAKEN IN 1976 BY PRISCILLA RUSSELL

Sometimes in the spring or fall she would dig all day long and would store the potatoes underground."

Osgood (1937:75): "Edible roots, common in the country around Knik Arm, are sold to the Indians farther down the inlet. They pack the roots in covered baskets about three feet in diameter and as many deep. One fur blanket is given for one basket of roots or a quantity of dry fish may be preferred by the vendors of the roots."

15.21 Idlughet *(Dena'ina);* **Zdlaaygha** *(Ahtna)* • 'By the Objects'

Eklutna village, "Old Knik," "Knik Village"

The story of the giant fish in Eklutna Lake (pp. 326–327) gives the origin of this name. Several hills on the shore of the inlet here are said to have washed out from Eklutna Lake.

The earliest recording of this name is "Izliueskoe" in the Wrangell collection notes from the 1830s (Arndt 1985), based on the Lower Cook Inlet Dena'ina pronunciation, **Ezdlughet**, for **Idlughet**; *-skoe* is a Russian suffix 'village.' This name is recorded as "Zdluiat" and is mislocated several miles to the south on the 1884 Petroff map (Map 6). The Mendenhall and Meiklejohn maps of 1900 label Eklutna as "Knik Village." Chandonnet (1979:11) and Fall (1981:396) trace the early recordings of the names "Knik" and "Old Knik" for the village now known as Eklutna.

The first *Handbook for North American Indians,* Hodge (1907:717), has an entry for "Knik" which applies to Old Knik/Eklutna:: "A Knaiakhotana [Dena'ina] settlement of several villages on Knik r. at the head of Cook Inlet.

The chief village had 46 people in 1880 (Petroff, 1884); in 1900 the population was 160 in 31 houses. This branch of the tribe numbers altogether between 200 and 300, who obtain their subsistence from hunting and trapping and by bartering with the Ahtena....

"Their houses are built above ground of logs tightly calked [*sic*] with moss and covered with bark. They use the birch bark canoe on the inland rivers but purchase skin bidarkas of the Kenai or Nikishka people to fish and travel along the coast."

Shem Pete: "They [Eklutna people] caught fish at Knik River, and they were close to the mountains. They go to the mountains to catch bear, sheep, and ground squirrel. And there used to be caribou around Anchorage in those mountains."

Glenn (1899:89) noted "from the Indian fishing village, just below the station, which is the head of navigation, a good trail over high ground could be opened to connect with my trail."

As Browne passed through Eklutna on the sled trail in the spring of 1912 (1956:204), he noted a large number of recent graves and the sickly condition of the people in the village.

Billy Pete: "Eklutna is an old, old village. Nobody knows when they first moved there. People came down the Matanuska River then they returned to Cook Inlet after the Ice Age."

Johnny Shaginoff: "Eklutna was always an old village. Years ago there was many people there, but many moved away or died. Later some people moved back from Knik."

Yarborough (1996) discusses the "founding" of Eklutna in 1897 with the relocation of ten Dena'ina families from Knik, along with the "dismantling" of the Russian Orthodox chapel at Knik and the construction of a new one at Eklutna. This relocation was documented by the Russian Orthodox priest John Bortnovsky in his travel journal (Yarborough 1996:116–119; Znamenski 1998:10–11). According to the priest, ten Indian families moved from "Old Knik" (that is, the place now known as Knik) to "New Knik" (that is, Eklutna) in order to distance themselves from white traders who were exploiting them at their former village. The Indians at first had intended to reconstruct the dismantled old church at Eklutna, but Bortnovsky persuaded them to build a new church instead. Icons from the old church were installed in the new building, perhaps accounting for the tradition that the older building had itself been moved to a new site. Cf. Davis (1965:14); Carberry (1979:140); Chandonnet (1985:45–48). Note that Bortnovsky's calling the site to which the families moved "New Knik" is confusing in that Eklutna has also been called "Old Knik." For example, in 1979 Bailey Theodore noted that, "Eklutna used to be called Old Knik." See also Sleem (1910a) (Map 63). Because Eklutna had been occupied formerly, the 1897 move from Knik is best viewed as a "re-founding" of the village of Eklutna, much in the way that, traditionally, old village sites were "recycled" (see Fall 1987:29).

Alberta Stephan (1996) has provided details about the Dena'ina families of Eklutna, their homes, and their seasonal camps. For example (p. 148):

Eklutna Alex, who might have been listed as Alec Vasilly in the 1910 census, lived in one of the older little houses [in Eklutna] that is falling down now. He also had a cabin up past the bench on the hill above where we used to get spring water. That is where Mike Alex was born. They also had the hunting cabin located on the far east end of Eklutna Lake. (The cabin is still there, maintained by Chugach State Park.)

Annabel (1938a:91–93) is a humourous account of an Eklutna Indian named Johnny Bull who tracked a moose with one gigantic footprint. The moose had gotten its foot stuck in a bucket.

The restored church at Eklutna is the oldest standing building in the Anchorage area. "The Eklutna village site was at the junction of several traditional Indian trails–some later used as gold rush trails and mail trails.... As a crossroads Eklutna was a perfect site for a religious meeting place" (Chandonnet 1991:46). The recent history of Eklutna, a profile of Eklutna Alex (1866–1953), an interview with the late chief, Mike Alex, and a description of the restoration of the church building in the winter of 1976–77 are included in Chandonnet (1979, 1985 and 1991). Also Davis (1965) presents an overview of Eklutna history, including a summary of the loss of traditional lands as Anchorage, Eagle River, and the Matanuska Valley became populated. Kari (1978b) is an obituary of the late Mike Alex, along with his mourning song, composed by Shem Pete, and a list of local Dena'ina place names.

15.22 Idlishla • 'Small Plural Objects'
north hill on Eklutna Flat, "The Knobs"
Today, Eklutna people refer to this and the larger adjacent hill **Idlika'a,** as "The Knobs." Both served as navigational aides for Dena'ina on the land and the water. Travelers used them to gauge travel time and determine their location. They marked a source of water, shelter, and hospitality.

This and the larger knob, **Idlika'a,** served as lookout sites to guard the Knik Arm Dena'ina villages against attack from the **Ułchena** (Alutiiq). They figure in the story of the last series of battles between the Dena'ina and the **Ułchena**, which ended with a Dena'ina victory at Point Campbell (15.92). They were also game lookouts.

15.23 Idlika'a • 'Big Plural Objects'
south hill with gravel quarry on Eklutna Flat, "The Knobs"
Both hills (15.22, 15.23) played a role in traditional Dena'ina subsistence activities, such as hunting small game (porcupines, hares) and moose, harvesting edible wild plants, and gathering wood for fuel, smoking fish, construction, and manufacture of tools. Eklutna village's educational fishery takes place in Knik Arm just southwest of this hill.

Since at least the 1940s, the Alaska Railroad has quarried rock from its property at **Idlika'a**. The remainder of the hill is owned by the National Bank of Alaska, which in the 1990s began developing plans to mine the rock as well. In 1996 and 1997, the Eklutna Tribal Council voiced objections to continued mining at the railroad quarry and further development of the bank property (O'Harra 1996) because of the importance of this small hill as a landmark and a symbol of identity for the people of Eklutna. Leo Stephan (in Fall 1997) explained:

"Well, the thing here is that we as Native people, we belong to the land and a lot of these landmarks and stuff is almost like what they have in Washington, DC. We don't go down to Washington DC and try to dismantle the Capitol and all the monuments. I'm not very eloquent, but hopefully we can get across somehow that the name of the village here is those two knobs, plural, **Idluytnu**, meaning two things laying by a river. And it's a landmark. It's a place. And it's always been that way. You probably go to around the Yukon, the Tanana River, all places like that, if you go and say "**Idluytnu**," they know where that is. Now if you come over and say, "Washington DC," people are certainly going to say, "Oh, yeah. That's the place where the nation's Capitol is." It's the same thing with us. We have places. Instead of building stuff to ourselves, monuments, we just use natural things. Either to identify ourselves, or to identify where we come from, or where we are. Like the word "Talkeetna," for instance. It's not "Talkeetna," it's "**K'dalkitnu**." It means they got cache there, food cache. These are [our] monuments. You can't take them away. You can't take the river away and say, "Hey, we're going to use this for something else." That's what they are doing to our knobs here. After that's gone, what are we going to call ourselves? How are we going to call Eklutna if it's not there no more? There is no such thing as **Idluytnu**. There is no two things laying there no more. It's gone."

On February 5, 2000, the Alaska Supreme Court ruled that the City of Anchorage had erred in issuing a permit to the National Bank of Alaska to operate a quarry at this site because of inadequate consideration of the potential damage to archaeological and historical resources. It ordered the city's planning commission to conduct a more thorough analysis and weigh the value of preserving the cultural values against the potential economic benefits of mining the rock.

‡In 2014 Wells Fargo Bank (who bought NBA) donated the 143-acre tract of land back to Eklutna village through a conservation easement (Herz, 2014).

15.24 Idluytnu • 'Plural Objects River'
Eklutna River
The name Eklutna is derived from this name for Eklutna River.

15.25 Chishkatnu • 'Big Ochre Creek'
Thunderbird Creek

§15.136 Chishkatnu Dghelaya • 'Big Ochre Creek Mountain'
Thunderbird Peak

15.26 Kuy'inshla Betnu • 'Little Heart Creek'
creek into Thunderbird Creek

15.27 Kuy'inshla • 'Little Heart'
small peak 4009' east of Mount Eklutna
When viewed from Eklutna village, this peak looks like a heart tucked among the mountains. Mike Alex often indicated that this mountain was important and that it used to be mentioned in potlatch speeches. He was implying that it was a sacred mountain for Eklutna.

§15.116 Snutnadzenitnu • 'Stream of That Which Extends away Steeply'
stream off Mount Eklutna into Thunderbird Creek

15.28 Bentułik'elashi • 'The One That Dogs Are Driven Up'
ridge extending ‡west of Twin Peaks
This name refers to the use of dogs during sheep hunts. See Fig. 204.

15.29 Ghetgge Daydlent • 'Where It Flows Between'
creek that crosses Eklutna Lake Road at Chugach State Park boundary

15.30 K'enan Qetni'unt • 'Where There Is a Face'
on Eklutna Lake Trail, five to six miles from village

15.31 Benshla • 'Little Lake'
Lake Barbara

15.32 Huch'iydelq'uht • 'Where We Build a Fire for Ourselves'
creek from West Twin Peak into Eklutna River
Mike Alex stated that a trail at this campsite led up the ridge **Bentułik'elashi**, (15.28).

15.33 Łach Q'atnu • 'Clay Hole Creek'
‡Łach Q'atnu Creek
Thachkatnu Creek along Twin Peaks Trail had been an official name since 2000. In 2015 this was changed to reflect correct Dena'ina spelling.

15.34 Łach Q'a • 'Clay Hole'
Twin Peaks

15.35 Dnasan • 'A Man Is Standing'
rock pinnacle between Twin Peaks
This colorful name refers to a protruding rock that looks like a man.

15.36 Idlu Bena • 'Plural Objects Lake'
Eklutna Lake
This was the upland hunting territory of the Eklutna people. Eklutna people continued to hunt sheep here until the 1950s (Davis 1965:17).

15.37 Ben Q'estsiq' • 'Lake Outlet'
outlet of Eklutna Lake

15.38 Łachda • 'Silt Place'
mineral lick south of Eklutna Lake outlet

FIGURE 203

(Right) **Chishkatnu** (15.25, Thunderbird Creek).

PHOTO BY LORRAINE BASNAR ELDER

FIGURE 204

(Below) Looking southwest from Eklutna Flats, one can view, from left to right: **Hninighi'iy Ka'a** (15.20, hill at Glenn Highway junction), **Bentułik'alashi** (15.28, the ridge at the left edge of the frame), **Idluytnu** (15.24, the Eklutna River valley) with the small peak 15.27 **Kuy'inshla**, which is beneath the tallest mountain on the north side of **Chishkatnu** (15.25, Thunderbird Creek valley), and the steep slope of **Snutnadzeni** (15.52, Mount Eklutna). Cf. this view with Plate 18, a photo of this area from the other side of Knik Arm.

PHOTO BY PRISCILLA RUSSELL

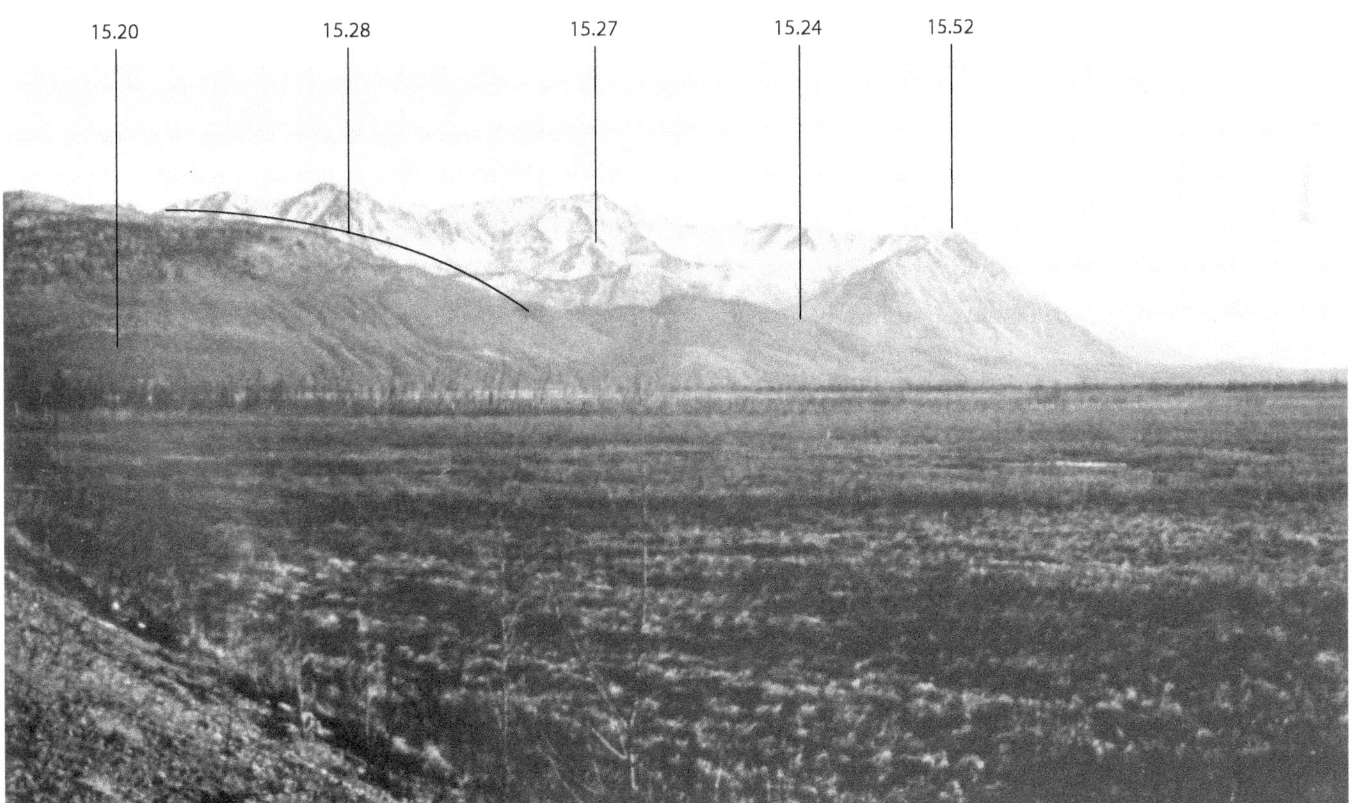

FIGURE 205

Idlu Bena (15.36, Eklutna Lake) in winter and **Nuji Qeneh**, (15.44, Bold Peak).

PHOTO BY LORRAINE BASNAR ELDER

15.39 Ts'inshla • 'Little -Ω- '
rocks on north shore of Eklutna Lake before ***Yuditnu***

15.40 Yuditnu • 'Golden Eagle Creek'
creek at large point on north shore of Eklutna Lake

15.41 Yudi Qeneh • 'Golden Eagle House'
Black Peak, mountain at head of ***Yuditnu***

15.42 Sdayłent • 'Where Current Flows at the Point'
creek into Eklutna Lake in the middle of the north shore

15.43 Qunsha Qeneh • 'Ground Squirrel House'
mountain, elev. 3000', east of Sdayłent
This name refers to the shelter the Dena'ina used in the mountains when hunting ground squirrel. See the story of the giant fish in Eklutna Lake, p. 326.

15.44 Nuji Qeneh • 'Sheep House'
Bold Peak
We note the misplacement and misspelling of 15.41, 15.43, and 15.44 and on the map of Chugach State Park by Imus Geographics (2000 and 2006).

15.45 Nuhałch'k'eldełt • 'Where We Return with Packs'
site at start of east fork trail at head of Eklutna Lake

15.46 Niłtanikda Betnu • 'Creek of the One That Is Leaning'
East Fork of Eklutna River

15.47 Niłtani, Niłtanikda • 'The One That Is Leaning'
hill elev. 3000', north of East Fork trail

‡15.137 [Tulchina Nudghiłent] • 'Water Clan – Place Current Flows Down'
"Tulchina Falls" at the north of the head of Eklutna Lake
Tulchina Falls is noted on the 2006 Imus Geographics map. A possible aboriginal name that has been used in Chugach State Park since the 1990s. According to park staff, this name was provided by Alice Debbie Fullenwider of Eklutna.

15.48 Bendilent • 'Where It Flows into Lake'
creek from Eklutna Glacier, West Fork of Eklutna River
This is the site of Eklutna Alex's hunting cabin.

Shem Pete: "He [Eklutna Alex in 1927] just pack a little grub and went up to upper end of the lake. And he build a cabin there. That's why he never come back for a month. His wife worry about him. He build a big house on the upper end the lake. He's living in the cabin already when I find him...." «I walked the length of Eklutna Lake. It had gotten dark previously and it was night time. Around that lake shore it is seven miles. There were all kinds of rocks and boulders. Those glacial rocks are no good. Since it was nighttime we could not do anything else. We did not recognize anything.» I make it seven mile. «At the head of the lake where the stream flows in there are sheep. They used to kill them. There are lots of sheep there.» Good country."

Mike Alex said that in the fall of 1933 he and his father killed thirty-three sheep in the mountains around Eklutna Lake (Kari 1978b:4).

According to the late Mike Theodore, there is gold at the head of Eklutna Lake. The medicine men protect it. If someone looks for it, rain will come.

15.49 Idlu Bena Łi'a • 'Glacier of Plural Objects Lake'
Eklutna Glacier

15.50 Idlu Bena Dghelaya • 'Mountain of Plural Objects Lake'
The Mitre

15.51 Nuhdaltunt • 'Ridge That Extends Across'
ridge on south shore of Eklutna Lake
Kari (1978b): "Just three days before his [Mike Alex's] death we reviewed the Knik Arm place names list. The day before he died, and the last time I saw him, he greeted me in the morning with a broad smile. The night before he remembered a name for a mountain at the head of Eklutna Lake, **Nuhdaltunt**. This name had been eluding him for some months."

§15.117 Nuhdaltuntnu • 'Ridge That Extends Across'
upper north fork of Thunderbird Creek

15.52 Snutnadzeni • 'That Which Extends away Steeply'
Mount Eklutna
In November of 1975 Mike Alex told this anecdote to Kari in Dena'ina: "«In fall time we used to go to **Snudnadzeni** hunting for sheep. I saw some sheep going around on the mountain, and I went towards them. I got close, and I shot and killed some. And then I butchered them. Then I built a fire and roasted some for myself. Then I bundled it up, and I packed it back.»"

15.53 Snutnadzeni T'ugh Daydliyi Ben • 'Lakes Beneath That Which Extends away Steeply'
Mirror Lake and Edmonds Lake

§15.118 **K'anakatnu** • '-Ω- Creek'
lower Peters Creek
This name was mentioned by Mike Theodore and Mike Alex on two different occasions. They seem to have been referring to Peters Creek as it enters Knik Arm, so we conclude that the name contributed by John Stump (15.55) refers to upper Peters Creek and its trail to the uplands. Kari heard this name as being similar to the name for Fish Creek (13.15), **K'enakatnu**, however it is distinct.

15.54 **Htestighitun Betnu** • 'Creek of Trail Goes Through Pass' (translation revised)
upper Peters Creek (location revised)
John Stump: "Dog team used to come right through that mountain there."

Shem Pete: "«I saw a salmon from Peters Creek that was eight feet long. We measured it.»"

Bailey Theodore had a sheep hunting camp up Peters Creek.

Annabel (1948:51 and 1997a:127) describes Eklutna John, who hunted for bear and moose on upper Peters Creek and elsewhere in the Chugach Mountains.

§15.119 **Htestighitun Tustes** • 'Pass of Trail Goes Through Pass'
Rumble Pass at head of Peters Creek
Mike Alex once commented about a trail between upper Peters Creek to upper Eklutna Lake.

FIGURE 206

Katherine Nicolie, Katherine Theodore, and Mike Theodore visited **Idlu Bena Łi'a** Eklutna Glacier (15.49) in 1976.

PHOTO BY PRISCILLA RUSSELL

§15.120 **Htestighitun Dghelaya** • 'Mountain of Trail Goes Through Pass'
Mount Rumble

15.55 **Dkenyi Betnu** • 'Underground Cache Creek'
creek into Peters Creek from north, "Fourmile Creek"
Bailey Theodore said that his father had a sheep camp in this area.

15.56 **Qintali Betnu** • 'Wide Ridge Creek'
Little Peters Creek

15.57 **Qintali** • 'Wide Ridge'
mountain, elev. 4786', east of Chugiak
This prominent mountain east of the town of Chugiak still is officially unnamed. Summits are marked with unofficial names "Roundtop" and "Mt. Baldy" on the 2000 Imus Geographics map.

15.58 **Tuq'eyghil'ut** • 'Where Water Flows Through Birch'
point on beach at Birchwood, between Fire Creek and Peters Creek
Bailey Theodore: "There was no village located there."

We consider the name "Birchwood" to be an approximate translation of the Dena'ina place name.

15.59 **Ch'eneltash Betnu** • 'Creek Where We Sleep'
Fire Creek

15.60 **Ch'eneltash Bena** • 'Lake Where We Sleep'
Fire Lake, Lower Fire Lake
Name mentioned by John Stump.

15.61 **Nutl'eghghulk'et'** • 'Sedge Extends Down'
§fish site at the NE corner of Whitney Point, formerly Eklutna School fish camp
Davis and the Dena'ina Team (1994:52–56, 117–118) visited this site in 1994. Leo Stephan located the site of the large smokehouse, about 14' by 20' that was used

FIGURE 207

Qintali (15.57) as viewed from Chugiak High School.

PHOTO BY JAMES KARI

Dach' Idlughet Hyighiyih—How Eklutna Got Its Name

by Shem Pete

Eklutna Alex told Shem Pete this story about the giant fish in Eklutna Lake and the formation of the hills near the village of Eklutna. The story was recorded by Jim Kari on February 7, 1985, in Fairbanks. It was translated with Billy Pete. The narrative is five minutes and ten seconds long.

Ekluktna Utnuht'ana hch'anaghedeł.
The Ahtna used to come out to Eklutna.

Niłdajaqa ighi yedghu Eklutna Lake ghin q'estsiq' ghu shagela ghe k'undet yan ch'aqideł ch'u
Two sisters came out to the outlet of Eklutna Lake for trout, being without food, and

shagela ghuda yet quqidatl'.
they had gone up there for trout.

Shagela qubedighilagh.
A trout swam into their trap.

Shagela dghiłchek'a k'uda yet ts'in'e tunuyiłghel.
It was a little trout, and they threw it back in the water upstream.

Ben ghinhdi seven mile hqugh daghiłney.
The lake is seven miles long.

Daghiłkegh.
It is large.

Utnuht'ana dek'isna shagela gga ts'in'e tsighel'unh tunuqeyghiłghel ch'u
Those Ahtna women threw the little fish back in with its head facing upstream and [they said to it]

"Nunkdach' ntukdach' nutitnash.
"You go back to your mother and father.

Nech' ch'ujeshi ghuda.
We might have saved ourselves [from starvation] by [eating] you.

Kitigi ghuda dghinłchek' beł dini," qyełni.
You tell him that you are too small," they told it.

"Qech'u bedghinni da beghe nanidyaa da."
"You tell him that when you return to him."

Yet Utnuht'ana q'u hyech' qenash ch'u
They spoke to it there in the Ahtna language, and

tunuqeyghiłghel ch'u yun'e qinughedlagh.
they threw it back in the water, and it swam back up the lake.

Tatl'ah beł qi'uni ghinhdi little trout gga beł nuqelnek hnuq'u kadilagh.
When that little trout told that [giant] underwater creature [what they had said], it [a giant fish] swam downstream.

Qughilagh.
It swam up from the bottom.

Ts'iłq'i yan q'u yet idu.
Only one creature stayed there.

Biłni badahdetnesh.
A noise was heard in the water.

Ghu tatl'ah beł qi'uni ghini łuhtalghel.
That creature under the water was starting to move around.

Dghelay egh hnijaq'.
They [the girls] ran to the mountain.

Yet dghelay q'aghtgge ghu dałtun ch'u
That lake is between mountains, and

łiq'a ghini qughilagh ch'u
then a [giant] fish swam up from below, and

ben q'estsiq' ch'dudilagh.
it swam out through the lake outlet.

Ghelugh k'enulq'eł ch'u
It floundered along the creek;

k'etnu yet niłtsatnetun ka'a t'qit'a.
downstream the cliffs form a big canyon.

Yet denyi ghilagh.
It swam into that canyon.

Yeh hqugh nutidulnen ch'u chijuq.
The water level dropped there and it died.

Beq'estsiq' ghu kadilagh ghu yet ełnen hch'ataghilagi shughu
As it swam through the outlet, the water washed out the land, and

łuq'u ełnen idlu qit'a all over Eklutna.
all over Eklutna [pieces of] all of that land remained.

Idlughet yet ghuda h'iyi k'dilan.
That is why its name is 'By the Plural Objects.'[1]

Dach' shnughel qeynuqulnek.
That is what they told me about it.

Dach' qit'anesen Eklutna story'a.
That is the Eklutna story that I know.

Ki ch'adach' ghu heł dgheshniy.
I will tell you a little more.

Łuq'u jitgga qit'anesen shnughel nuhqelnekt'i about some country anyway q'u yagheli.
I know a little that they used to tell me about some country anyway, and that is good.

Yik'a qeyegh batahdałnen shida.
It [that giant fish] made it start to go dry.

Eklutna Lake batihdalnishi.
Eklutna Lake started to go dry.

K'chan yan bak'dilan.
Just grass is in there.

Ghinhdi tatl'ah beł qi'uni ghini elugh k'a bayahdist'ik.
The underwater creature has not appeared again since.

Henda q'u bayahtidut'ił.
It might show up, though.

Ribs, bekaq'a ghini ki qunsha qeneh łuq'u qeyeł qighilu łu.
They [Dena'ina] built ground squirrel hunting shelters with those ribs [of the giant fish], they say.

Ighi all over Eklutna Mountain ch'u
All over Eklutna Mountain

shagela kaq'a ghini łuq'u little brush camp gga denqidałkeght ka'a qeyeł qighisen.
they made sizeable brush camps with that fish's ribs.

Denqidałkegh ka'a eight, nine, ten, twenty ghuh qihdalts'ih hqugh.
They were large enough for eight, nine, ten, or twenty [people] to stay inside.

Qunsha qeneh ghini qeyeł qighilu łu.
They built ground squirrel hunting shelters with it, they say.[2]

Eklutna Alex ghun janq'u ghu qayeh ka'a qit'anesen.
I still know Eklutna Alex's big village [at Eklutna Lake; see 15.48].

"Yeh ts'en ghinhdi biqunghel'ani.
[Eklutna Alex said,] "I should go look for those bones.

"Yeh janq'u kisht'a denłneyi ni'u shida," dghini q'u chijuq.
"They are really long," he said, but then he died.

"Nhin dahdi nhyituqadiyi bech' tayu da," beł dgheshni.
I had told him, "They might buy them from you if you go for them."

Too late ch'u he don't know what's gonna coming.

Dach' stroke ghu chijuq.
He died of a stroke.

He never sick.

Dach' yeqech' qit'anesen Eklutna story'a.
That is the Eklutna story that I know.

1. Shem and Billy Pete added these comments: "That big monster trout hit the mouth of the lake, the outlet. Then high water—200, 300 feet—with the trout jammed into the canyon. In about two or three months or one year, water running too high. Then the fish rotted away, and the dam busted, and those chunks drifted down. They had a big flood when the dam busted. Eklutna village is nothing but glacier ground now. There's lots of lumps at Eklutna and that's why they call it 'lump station.' Before that it had another name."

2. A **qunsha qeneh** is a brush camp above timberline, used when hunting sheep and ground squirrel. One of the mountains on the north shore of Eklutna Lake is named **Qunsha Qeneh** (15.43).

Shem and Billy Pete noted that "When that big trout died, everything got back to normal. They cut the ribs as big as they need for **qunsha qeneh** frame, and they pack them up into the mountains. They used them for thousands of years. They didn't have to pack wood up there for **qunsha qeneh**; they just covered it with birchbark."

to put up fish by the students of the Eklutna Vocational School, which operated between 1924 and 1946. This place is mentioned in Chandonnet (1979:37).

15.62 K'qiydulghakt • 'Where We Harvest Fish'
point marked as "Whitney," north of Eagle Bay
Eklutna people used to put up fish in this area.

Shem Pete: "«They used to dig up **k'tl'ila** [*Hedysarum alpinum*] here. And they used to put up dry fish for winter. They also made **chuqilin** [fermented fish].»"

15.63 K'eł Taydeght • §'With It - Water - Point'
bluff and point two miles north of the mouth of Eagle River
This officially unnamed point is shown on the map by Imus Geographics (2000 and 2006) with the odd spelling "Kethtaydut".

§15.121 Tsał Tl'u • 'Box Headwaters'
gulley ½ mile north of Eagle River flats
Name recalled by Mike Theodore.

15.64 Nuk'elehitnu Kaq' • 'Mouth of Fish Run Again Creek'
Eagle Bay, mouth of Eagle River

15.65 Nuk'elehitnu • 'Fish Run Again Creek'
Eagle River
In 1898 Luther Kelly, a member of the Glenn party, recorded the name "Yukla-hitna" for this river. He noted that the trail along the river was well defined (Kelly 1900:685). Glenn abbreviated this name to Yukla Creek (Map 62). Later this name was applied to Mount Yukla on the upper Eagle River (15.117).

In 1898 Mendenhall (1900:279) encountered a group of Dena'ina camps several miles up from the mouth of Eagle River. "On the second day of travel on Yukla Creek we entered a region of forest fires.... Several hunting shacks, built during the fall and winter seasons by the Indians, were passed and were usually surrounded by evidence of success in the chase–moose antlers and bones and sheep pelt being plentiful.... Now and again we would find an old Indian or game trail, only to have it fade away within a mile."

15.66 T'usq'a • 'Cutting Place'
small creek into Eagle River, possibly Clunie Creek
Bailey Theodore said that there were fish camps along this creek that were used mainly for harvesting silver salmon.

15.67 Ben Ka'a • 'Big Lake'
Lake Clunie
The name "Clunie" potentially is a Dena'ina-origin name, but we never were able to re-elicit it. This lake was named and mapped early; see Brooks (1911) (Map 15) and Sleem (1910a) (Map 63). Mike Alex once commented that this lake was a stopping point on the winter trail that came through Eklutna to Anchorage.

15.68 K'ulch'eytnu • 'Creek of Wind Blows Against It'
Meadow Creek

15.69 K'ulch'ey • 'Wind Blows Against It'
Mount Magnificent

15.70 Łiq'a Ta'a Bugh • 'Fish Soup Shore'
Falling Water Creek from Mt. Yukla into Eagle River

15.71 §Na'un Tutsaghala (revised spelling, from notes) • ‡'Beyond Water-Rock-Pack'
ridge from Contata Peak to Organ Mountain south of upper Eagle River (revised location)
These names on upper Eagle River were supplied by the late Bailey Theodore. Bailey described this as a bald mountain on the south side of upper Eagle River.

Shem Pete: "«Old Man [Wassila] Theodore used to kill lots of moose and sheep in that country up at the head of Eagle River. They would come down the river in a skin boat. They say that it is strong current.»"

Art Theodore: "My dad [Bailey Theodore] ... used to go up in Eagle River. It was burnt out in this area and he said go over the hill, go over the mountains and get the moose. And then they'd pack them back and make

FIGURE 208

Near the headwaters of **Nuk'elehitnu** (15.65, Eagle River).
PHOTO BY LORRAINE BASNAR

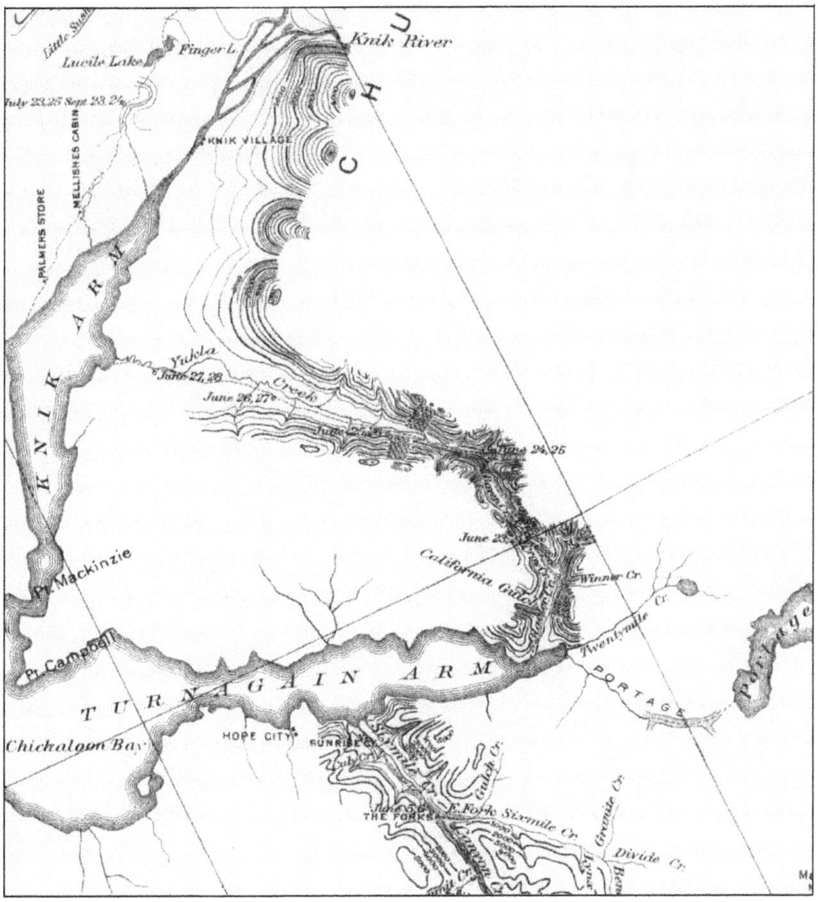

MAP 62

Detail from the Mendenhall map of 1898: Eagle River.

The route of Kelly and Mendenhall along "Yukla Creek," the Eagle River Valley in 1898 is shown in this detail.

ARCHIVES, ALASKA AND POLAR REGIONS DEPT., RASMUSON LIBRARY, UNIVERSITY OF ALASKA FAIRBANKS

a frame out of wood and then they'd put skins on it and then they'd load up five or six moose he said. And then they'd float it down to the Inlet. And then they'd make a sturdier craft and come across. I asked him why they were hunting over there all the time they said it was burned out here before. There wasn't no good hunting on this [Knik Arm, west] side."

§15.122 Na'un Tutsaghala Betnu • ‡'Beyond Water-Rock-Pack Stream'
South Fork of Eagle River

‡15.138 Nant'ina • 'Woodsman, Bogeyman'
"Nantina Point," south of Kiliak Glacier
A Dena'ina-origin name, lit. 'the one who steals people,' has been in use since the early 1990s by the Mountaineering Club of Alaska. Cited on map by Imus Geographics 2006.

‡15.139 Delgga Dghelaya • 'Raven's Mountain'
"Delgga Mountain"
A name coined by the Mountaineering Club of Alaska on Imus Geographics 2006.

15.72 Nuk'elehitnu Łi'a • 'Glacier of Fish Run Again River'
Eagle Glacier

§15.123 Nuk'elehitnu Dghelaya • 'Fish Run Again Creek-Mountain'
Raven Ridge and "Saghala Peak" south of Eagle Glacier
Crossing through Crow Creek Pass from Turnagain Arm in 1898, Mendenhall reported on the upper Eagle River: "Several hunting shacks, built during the fall and winter seasons by the Indians, were passed and were usually surrounded by evidence of success in the chase—moose antlers and bones, and sheep pelts being plentiful" (1900:279). Also see 16.4.

15.73 K'ka Bena • 'Tail Lake'
Otter Lake

FIGURE 209

The Dena'ina Team in 1994: Lester Stephan, Alberta Stephan, Leo Stephan, Susie Ondola, George Ondola.
PHOTO BY NANCY YAW DAVIS

15.74 Ch'ak'dinłenghet • 'By the Current That Flows Out'
either a site at the mouth of the creek from Green Lake, now locally known as "Moonshine Creek" or a site at the mouth of Six-Mile Creek. See Maps 48 and 51.
The location of this site is uncertain. De Laguna (1934:140) reported that a Dena'ina village called "Tcukti'ntlinat" was located on the north bank of a stream called "Moonshine Creek," and that "Theodore of Eklutna found a T-shaped hunting adze or pick here." At some point during the period of homesteading in this vicinity, the Green Lake outlet stream came to be known as "Moonshine Creek." The first edition of *Shem Pete's Alaska* placed this site at the mouth of this stream. However, the map accompanying de Laguna's report (1934:Plate 1) shows "Moonshine Creek" flowing northwesterly into Knik Arm between "Anchorage" and Eagle River, and not draining from a lake. The Green Lake outlet stream flows southwesterly and the lake itself is natural, while Six-Mile Lake was created in 1951 when the creek was dammed to create a landing facility for float planes (McMahan and Holmes 1996:7), and the stream flows in a northwesterly direction. Also, Jack and Nellie Brown, who homesteaded at the mouth of the Green Lake outlet stream in January 1916 and lived there until 1923, called their homestead "Alderbrook" (Barry 2000:54), which might have been an early name for the stream as well, rather than Moonshine Creek. This leaves open the possibility that the site mentioned by de Laguna was at the mouth of Six-Mile Creek.

Davis and the Dena'ina Team (1994:107) also conjectured that "Moonshine Creek" refers to Six-Mile Creek rather than the Green Lake outlet stream. They pointed out that there are salmon runs in this stream, making it a likely location for a Dena'ina village or fish camp. They suggested that this is the site that de Laguna referred to as "Tcukti'ntlinat." This was also the location of homesteading activity beginning in the 1910s that obscures any prior evidence of Dena'ina use.

This was an important Knik Arm fishing site. The Alex family of Eklutna fished at the mouth of the Green Lake outlet stream until 1918 (Kari 1978:15). Davis and the Dena'ina Team in 1994 (1994:97–99) located pits and house depressions north of the Green Lake outlet stream along the Knik Arm bluff, which were later examined by McMahan and Holmes (1996:38). The latter noted that "It is likely that this location... was used for a range of activities during late prehistoric and historic times." As noted, this site was occupied by Jack and Nellie Brown's homestead from 1916 to 1923, and the cabin remains date from this period. However, the pit features near the bluff might be former Dena'ina fish pits (Daugherty and Saleeby 1998:66–67).

§15.124 Ch'ak'dinłen Bena • 'Lake of Current That Flows Out'
perhaps Green Lake; or Six-Mile Lake
Dan Alex recalls a story told to him by his father, Mike Alex, about a battle between the Knik Arm Dena'ina and the Alutiiq of lower Cook Inlet that took place at Green Lake. The battle took place in the nineteenth century when Mike Alex's father, Eklutna Alex, was a young man. The Alutiiq customarily raided Dena'ina villages to take slaves. The Dena'ina ambushed the Alutiiq war party at Green Lake, killing all but one. The survivor was sent back to his people to tell them it was not a good idea to attack the Indian villages. The remains of all those killed in the battle from both sides were cremated at the Green Lake battle site. This was the last battle between the Upper Inlet Dena'ina and the Alutiiq.

This name is based on Dena'ina naming conventions, and is appropriate if **Ch'ak'dinłenghet** was at the mouth of the Green Lake outlet stream. If **Ch'ak'dinłenghet** was at the mouth of Six-Mile Creek, however, then **Ch'ak'dinłen Bena** is an appropriate name for Six-Mile Lake, created in 1951.

15.75 Tak'at • 'Dipnet Platform'
site immediately north of Ocean Dock No. 7, also Cairn Point
Mike Alex: "Before Anchorage there was a big native fish camp settlement stretching up from Ocean Dock to Eastchester" (Chandonnet 1979:15, 1991:38).

Shem Pete: "«At **Tak'at** the water [in the inlet] swirls around. I used to walk over there on the trail [from the Ship Creek-downtown Anchorage area]. That **Stepankda** had a cabin upriver from where Ship Creek flows out, at the Army camp. His village was there in that elevated clearing [apparently just inland from **Tak'at**]. They say that there were **nichił** there, above Government Hill. That was when the people were not very old. Some people killed each other off here. And the people disappeared, and there were very few people left in the time since I was born. They had a cemetery there. **Stepankda** told me that there were big **nichił** there. They used to use that place a lot. They say there were **nichił** there, but I didn't see any. It was already clear when I saw the place. But **Stepankda** told me that he had seen the [occupied] **nichił** there.»

"He owned that country there. Last man. «The soldiers took it.» They [Dena'ina] don't get no money for it. «He [**Stepankda**] was asleep» [i.e., politically unaware]."

The possible precise location of **Tak'at** about one half mile north of Ocean Dock was identified by Nancy Yaw Davis and the Dena'ina Team on July 20, 1994 (Davis and the Dena'ina Team 1994:25–28). They discovered a cluster of large stones at about three-quarters tide level that may be supports for a dip net platform as described by Nikafor Alexan (1981). Also located by the Dena'ina Team was a single piece of a Blue Willow pattern plate, which they identified as a type used by Knik Arm Den'aina. Upon returning to this site, Leo Stephan recalled visiting the Rufe Stephan family there in the 1930s. Use of this area as a dump by the military has likely obscured physical evidence of its former use as a Dena'ina fishcamp (McMahan and Holmes 1996:28).

Billy Pete visited the fish camp at **Tak'at** while he lived with his grandmother during the summers in Anchorage, from the early 1920s until about 1931. During an interview with Nancy Yaw Davis in 1994, Billy recalled: "From Fourth Avenue they had a back road. They used to go across Government Hill and then they had a back road. Once in a while we used to take a taxi down there. And it used to cost the big money of fifty cents. And we used to go down there and visit Rufe Stephan's wife (Annie).... Early in the morning we used to go down there, about nine o'clock. And we used to stay there until about four o'clock in the evening. We used to walk back. It was about a pretty good two-and-a-half mile walk, I believe. We used to follow the road. I was about nine years old I guess. As far as I can remember, we used to spend all summer here in Anchorage after my grandma put up king salmon at Susitna Station. And then we'd come to Anchorage here and spend the summer in Anchorage. And we just used to go to **Tak'at,** and we used to go to Point Woronzof and just visit around. My grandma used to rent a house for fifteen dollars a month, I think it was.

"There was just a smokehouse there and Old Man Rufe Stephan used to have a tent set over there. There was about two or three tents sent over there. I don't know who used to own those other tents. He (Rufe Stephan) used to have one or two nets set over there. When there's too many fish, why they just put half a net out. That was good enough, when there was lots of fish. There used to be lots of fish (at **Tak'at**) a long time ago.... In 1929 or 1930 in the summer the last Dena'ina potlatch was held there at **Tak'at. Stepankda** had the potlatch. People were there from Eklutna, Knik, and Susitna."

Billy Pete recalled attending this potlatch as a young boy with his grandmother. Billy's grandmother brought bundles of fish and loaves of bread. Billy: "They call us and give us soup and tea and lots of bread and things. Then we (all the children) run back out and play." The potlatch lasted three days. There was singing and drumming on a seven-foot-long plank—this was before it was common for the Upper Inlet Dena'ina to use skin drums.

FIGURE 210

Tak'at (15.75, Cairn Point) with **Tak'at Qenuts'en** (15.76) in the foreground. This was the northernmost site on Knik Arm at which a **tanik'edi** (log fish dock, pp. 64–65) was used. The place name is a variation of the word **tanik'edi**. The traditional fishery here last belonged to **Stepankda**, Rufe Stephan, who was Alice Theodore's father. According to Katherine Nicolie, the bluff is steep here, and people lived mainly on the beach in the summer. Wasilla Theodore had a tent site carved out by a spring in a notch on the bluff.
PHOTO BY NANCY YAW DAVIS

Billy Pete: "About 1936 was the last time I visit that place there. [Billy was working at the Emard cannery.] I used to walk the beach (to **Tak'at**) at that time. And Rufe Stephan's wife used to stay there with all her kids. And she used to put up fish. Old man Rufe Stephan used to work on the railroad. And when I'm not working I used to go up there and play with the kids up there."

Billy Pete recalled that because there was a road to the bluff at **Tak'at** already, the military began using the area as a dump. The smokehouse was burned down. The area where the smokehouse and tents had been became covered with refuse. Billy: "The army guys burned that smokehouse down and they used that place for garbage dump. **Tak'at** is right where that army dump used to be. And that **Tak'at**, 1941, that's the last time they use that place and after that there was nothing over there. The army destroyed that smokehouse, so they (Rufe Stephan's family) used to go up Montana Creek to put up fish, after there was no more smokehouse at **Tak'at.**"

Alice Theodore, Rufe Stephan's daughter, recalled her father and oldest brother rowing her mother and sisters from Knik to **Tak'at** in the spring, where the women stayed all summer putting up fish. There were three smokehouses there, belonging to her mother and her mother's two sisters. There was also a steambath. Alice Theodore remembered the many Dena'ina visitors to the camp, who came to take a steambath and eat smoked fish soup. She believed that she last stayed at **Tak'at** in the summer of 1938, where her first child was born. When she returned several years later, "Everything was torn down. It didn't look like a fish camp any more."

Fall, Davis, and the Denaina Team (2003) is a recent compilation of information about former Dena'ina uses of present-day Elmendorf Air Force Base. ‡Fall (2009:73–75) has a synopsis of the **Tak'at** site.

§15.125 Tak'atnu • 'Dipnet Platform Stream'
stream or spring near Cairn Point

15.76 Tak'at Qenuch'en • 'Across from Dipnet Platform'
site one-quarter of a mile south of Tak'at
After the 1910s the name **Dgheyay Kaq'** was used by the Dena'ina to refer to Anchorage townsite. See also 15.82.

Carberry (1979:141): "The Tanaina were known to have fish camps near the mouth of Ship Creek. In the early days of Anchorage existence, cabins and the remains of cabins were noted to exist in the Ship Creek and Bootlegger Cove area."

15.77 Dgheyay Kaq' • 'Stickleback Mouth'
mouth of Ship Creek; early name for Anchorage
Davis (1965:15, 18): "Ship Creek was the hereditary fish camp site for several Eklutna families.... In 1915 the Indians were moved off their traditional site on Ship Creek."

Chandonnet (1991:60): "Mike Alex recalled an epidemic at the Ship Creek fish camp during the summer of 1916, and the 1918 Spanish flu epidemic. Both, he said, 'wiped out lots of Denna.' In both cases, the diminution of the Denna (Tanaina) population corresponds with the swelling of the Caucasian population of Anchorage."

15.78 Dgheyaytnu, Dgheyay Leht *(Dena'ina)*; **Dghayitna'** *(Ahtna)* • 'Stickleback Creek' or 'Where Stickleback Run'
Ship Creek, original Anchorage townsite
De Laguna (1934:140): "House pits or 'fortifications' have been seen, on the north bank of Ship Creek opposite Anchorage."

Shem Pete: "«They talk about **Dgheyay Leht**. That was a good place to save ourselves [from starvation]. A lot of king salmon swim in there, and they still go upstream there. Needlefish [stickleback] run along with them.» You put your hand in, it is just full of needle fish. «No one uses this anymore. They used to survive on needlefish. And salmon spawn there, and they used to put up salmon.

"«That Eklutna Alex and Old Man Theodore put up salmon there. Some of the Knik Arm Dena'ina used to go over to **Susni Kaq'** [mouth of Susitna River, 2.3] in a **badi** [umiak, large skin boat]. Over there and here [at Ship Creek] the hooligan and the needlefish run first. They run mixed together. No one went to bed at this season, they say. They may have been starving and may have barely survived [the winter]. Wherever they had stopped in the uplands—Yentna, Susitna, or Kichatna—when some of the people feel sorry for themselves, they drag themselves down here and they become really satisfied. At that **Dgheyay Leht** we save ourselves nicely. Those Knik Arm Dena'ina bring themselves there and survive on needlefish. After the needlefish, they put up salmon. That is the only place like this. When there were too many people for Ship Creek and Point Woronzof, they would spread out and go over to **Susni Kaq'** in an umiak. Perhaps half of them. Over there they would stay beneath the umiaks.»"

Alberta Stephan (1996a:18): "Each spring the Indians had used all their supplies and begun looking for food. They knew the first fresh fish in the spring would be stickle-back fish, which they boiled for soup. Then hooligan (smelt) would become available. Ducks and other migrating birds came back in the early spring, and the Indian were able to gather duck and sea gull eggs. Trout were also caught in traps."

15.79 ‡[Deshtnu Bena?] • possibly 'Spruce Hen Stream Lake'
Dishno Pond
This pond is off upper Ship Creek on the military's Moose Run Golf Course. This may be an Athabascan-origin place name. Orth (1971:274): "Local name reported in 1962 by USGS." ‡The name Dishno Pond was not recognized by Mike Alex.

15.80 Dgheyay Tl'u • 'Stickleback Headwaters'
upper Ship Creek, Arctic Valley
Shem Pete: "«On upper Ship Creek, in that large, level area, that one called Deafy Dan [Bigoff] used to walk around. He told me that he used to see caribou horns up there. He said that they were sticking up there all over. Long ago there were caribou there, but I never killed any there. Now there are none. He saw one place with many caribou horns, so many that you could not sit down. So many bones there.»"

15.81 Tl'egh Dink'et' • 'Sedge Extends'
Standard Oil dock area north of mouth of Ship Creek
For some Dena'ina speakers from the Kenai area, this place name came to be used to refer to the town of Anchorage.

15.82 Angits; Tan; Qatuk'e'usht; Ves Dnaghiłdeqt • loanwords from English; 'Something Drifts Up to It,' 'High Bank'
Anchorage
Angits is the early Dena'ina pronunciation of the name "Anchorage." The name **Tan** from "town" is frequently used as well. The Dena'ina name for the Anchorage area, **Qatuk'e'usht** 'Something Drifts Up to It' was reported by Peter Kalifornsky of Kenai, upon Kari's reading to him the following passage from de Laguna (1934:140): "The native name for Anchorage is Xa'tikiuct (Theodore Sasha, Kenai)." It refers to travel toward Anchorage on the incoming tide. However, this name was not known

FIGURE 211

Dgheyay Tl'u (15.80, upper Ship Creek, Arctic Valley).

PHOTO BY LORRAINE BASNAR ELDER

FIGURE 212

Westchester Lagoon (15.126), the popular pond, park, and recreational site near downtown Anchorage, was created in 1973 when a small dam was built at the mouth of Chester Creek. Following Dena'ina place name conventions, we offer **Chansh Kaq' Bena** here as an addition to the set of Dena'ina names in the Anchorage bowl. Although **Chansh Kaq' Bena** is not a traditional Dena'ina place name, it is an authentic Dena'ina name.

PHOTO BY JAMES KARI

FIGURE 213

Dgheyay Kaq' (15.77, the mouth of Ship Creek), in the summer of 1914, from the Alaska Engineering Commission Report of 1916, Plate 48.

ARCHIVES, ALASKA AND POLAR REGIONS DEPT., RASMUSON LIBRARY, UNIVERSITY OF ALASKA FAIRBANKS

to Mike Alex, John Stump, or other speakers from Eklutna and Knik. Iliamna and Nondalton Dena'ina have referred to the Anchorage area as **Ves Dnaghiłdeqt** 'High Bank.' See also 15.77.

15.83 Chansh Kaq' • 'Grass Mouth'
mouth of Chester Creek
Several Dena'ina used to fish for salmon here. Bailey Theodore said that his father and Bobby Stephan fished for king salmon here, as did John Stump. Alberta Stephan (1996:149) notes that Eklutna Alex had a fish camp near Chester Creek mouth, "but he had to move to Fire Island when Anchorage became a town."

§15.126 Chansh Kaq' Bena • 'Grass Mouth Lake'
Westchester Lagoon
See Fig. 212.

15.84 Chanshtnu • 'Grass Creek'
Chester Creek
John Stump: "Lots of grass with a creek coming through. That [name] means 'Grass Creek.'"

Bailey Theodore noted that the name "Chester" derives from **Chanshtnu**. The name Chester Creek was first recorded in 1906 by T. G. Gerdine and R. H. Sargant (Orth 1971:205). Chester Creek is shown on the 1911 Brooks map (Map 15).

Chandonnet (1985:67): "Bailey Theodore recalled that his father was cheated out of a big house on Chester Creek in Anchorage where the family resided from about 1918 to 1927."

Quite a few Dena'ina people had cabins and houses on lower Chester Creek from the 1920s to 1940s. See also the stories by Sava Stephan in "Early Days in Anchorage."

Shem Pete: "«That was a Dena'ina village. The Americans took it.» They get it for nothing anyway. That Jilubech Pete was his partner. And Paul Nikolai. They used to hunt all over for moose and sheep. They had moose and sheep meat all the time. And beaver meat too. They dry that meat in the summer. This was up until about 1930."

Billy Pete: "Old Man Mike Peteroff built a nice cabin down Chester Creek, about a half a mile where there was good spring water."

Interestingly, the most recent archaeological dating of a wood bison *(Bison priscus)* in Alaska was a discovery of a bison skull on Chester Creek in the 1960s by Fred Hadleigh-West. The skull was dated as being only 170±30 years old (Stephenson et al. 2001:135). We never had the opportunity to discuss this with Shem Pete.

‡Langdon and Leggett (2009:174): "On the UAA campus Langdon and Leggett have been working on having *Chanshtnu* signs placed at key locations along the route of the creek as it flows through campus."

§15.127 Nungge Betnu • 'Upland Area Creek'
South Fork of Chester Creek
See 15.96 **Nungge,** Nunaka Valley below.

15.85 Qanchi • 'Porcupine'
"Kanchee Point," mountain, elev. 4310', at head of South Fork of Chester Creek
Kanchee, from Dena'ina **Qanchi,** is not an official name nor an aboriginal place name. The Dena'ina-origin name was suggested by the Mountaineering Club of Alaska in 1965 based upon vocabulary provided by Mike Alex, chief of Eklutna. Cf. 15.86, 15.97, and 15.99.

15.86 K'nuy'a • 'Beaver'
"Knoya Peak," mountain, elev. 4650', at head of South Fork of Chester Creek
Knoya, **K'nuy'a** is also not an official name nor an aboriginal place name. The Dena'ina-based English name was suggested by the Mountaineering Club of Alaska in 1965.

15.87 Ch'atanaltsegh • 'Yellow Water Comes Out'
Fish Creek
We conclude that 15.87 and 15.135 are two different locations. Mike Alex suggested 15.87 and John Stump 15.128.

15.128 Łiq'aka Betnu • 'King Salmon Creek'
§Fish Creek slough and mouth (revised location)

15.88 Unqetsit Ch'atanaltsegh • 'Next Place Below Yellow Water Comes Out'
small creek east of Fish Creek

§15.129 Niłkidal'iy Betnu • 'Stream of The Ones (Lakes) That Are Joined Together'
Hood Creek

15.89 Niłkidal'iy • 'The Ones (Lakes) That Are Joined Together'
Lake Spenard and Lake Hood
This name was reported by John Stump in 1976.

15.90 Nen Ghiłgedi • 'Rotten Land'
§bank in Earthquake Park east of Hood Creek (location revised)
Alberta Stephan recalls that this was a berry picking area for the Dena'ina fishing at Point Woronzof.

15.91 Nuch'ishtunt • 'Place Protected from Wind'
Point Woronzof. See Plate 25.
De Laguna reported a site here: "Point Woronzof: There was a summer fishing camp about one mile south of the point, called Nuti'ctunt" (1934:140).

Two sites reported by Leo Stephan are also noted here in Cook Inlet Historic Sites Project: "Pt. Woronzof No. 1: Pits on bluff south of Pt. Woronzof.... Pt. Woronzof No. 2: Site contains remains of fish camps, smokehouse, bath house and graves; site area utilized by Natives from Knik, Susitna, and Matanuska areas for at least 100 years" (1975:84,162).

Carberry (1978:143): "Along the bluff facing Fire Island there is evidence of native occupation. A graveyard exists in the meadow near the bluff. (The top of a spirit house was still there in recent years.) The remaining logs of a sweat house are near the shoreline.... There were as many as six houses along the bluff facing Fire Island.

Early Days in Anchorage

by Shem Pete and §Sava Stephan

‡This section of the book was the basis for the first chapter of Charles Wohlforth's 2014 book From the Shores of Ship Creek, Stories of Anchorage's First 100 Years.

"I was a young feller when, in 1914, my mother buy me .30-30. I think I'm going to kill all the animals in Cook Inlet, in Alaska. The bear—five dollars a skin. The black bear skin, 1914. We went up to, from Susitna Station, up to Talkeetna. In the sleigh, we're going way up, ahead. And we went up there, and I killed fourteen black bear that spring. And we all dry 'em, take 'em down in dory, and row to Anchorage. But no Anchorage that time. No buildings. And that first street, it was right up top of the hill there. They're trying to make a street there. And lots of tents.

"They had the store in the tent. They carry the coat, dress, pants, and shirt. They put it over our neck. They hold our back. 'That's big enough for you. Just right. Just right. Fifty cents. Sixty cents. Nice one seventy-five cents.' We buy, and I got a job in the restaurant. I was fourteen years old. They give me four dollars a day. And them old people, we went down to Anchorage with them. We see the car running. 'Oh gee, that's something!' We get in there. A dollar a minute. And, oh, lots of tent. And they burn and cut the trees. It's full of smoke, fire, nighttime. They like to work the nighttime too. It's too hot day time, June month, so a lot of people working. And I work in the restaurant. For about two weeks. And they play cards. Lots of gambling in the tent.

"So we stay there I don't know how many days, 'cause I work, get four dollars a day. I don't give them money. And so we go back to Susitna in the dory. We tell the story, 'We see lots of white people. There's smoke all over in Anchorage there now.' At that time it was all full of trees and willows. Everything they cut down. Nights and days they work.

"And in 1917 we see the first boat, big steamer. Steam boat. Go 'Choo, choo, choo.' Big steamboat.... And that go up Susitna Station. Go up to Kroto, 1917. I went up there, and they take me up to Talkeetna. Montana Creek. Below Montana Creek, big village. Number one, number two, number three, government boat. They put the rails and everything and a lot of stuff. They freighting all summer. I work there as a mail carrier. I mail carrier for government on horseback. We got no power, nothing... only... power is the horses them days. No train coming up, so they can't bring nothing up, the piles of stuff. There's two cars, that's all, in Anchorage.

FIGURE 214

Shem Pete in Anchorage in the early 1920s.

PHOTO COURTESY OF ALEXANDRA ALLOWAN

"And 1918, World War One, and I don't like to go back as a mail carrier. I was all alone. I was only a kid, fifteen [*sic*] years old. So they put me to work on the railroad. We connect the rail up in the Seward line, around there someplace. We connect the rail together. We see the train coming. Gee, that's the first train we see. Just like a snake. Go around, 'Whooo, whooo, whooo, whoooo0!' Gee whiz. We all quit working because we win. They beat the Seward crew. So I was a barber for six hundred people. There was six hundred crew...

"They bring some more people from Anchorage. All over. Knik, Eklutna, Susitna, Tyonek, Kenai, Kustatan. Lots of Kustatan people there—a big village. Nobody know how many people. Lots of Natives working. We make a banyo [steambath]. And lot of porcupine, gee whiz. We left a

FIGURE 215

Sava Stephan with his three sons Isaac, Sava, Jr., and Ralph, in Valdez in 1949.

PHOTO COURTESY OF ISAAC STEPHAN

FIGURE 216

Juliana Stephan took this portrait of her grandfather Sava Stephan in 2001.

pick and jack handle and shovel handle. We just throw it away when we quit. We get in the hand car. We go like hell. And when we come back the next day, porcupine so many they chew our shovel—we got our name on it. And the handle, the porcupine chew them up. And sometime I hang it up, mine, up on the tree [or] brush, so I'm okay. And I'm a barber too. Sometimes I cut four guys' hair and lots of daylight left behind. I just go to town too. I was a young feller. I like to work alright. Fifty cents a haircut I charged them. Them days were the good old days.

"And we see train coming. And then pretty soon we see the airplane. Little cub airplane. A dollar a minute to go up in the air. Impossible to go up in the air, everybody say in Alaska, 1918. That year was 1918. We go up in the air for five minutes. Five dollars. So we fly up, and we come back down. Oh, we was up in the air! We thought it was impossible that somebody could go up in the air, that time. And a lot more car coming in when the rail connected together. Quite a few car. There's a little town there already. They're building the cabins. Well, we had lots of fun there. A lot of things we don't see [before], we see them days."

Sava Stephan frequently reminisces about the Dena'ina people that lived in Anchorage in the 1920s to 1940s. His stories offer a uniquely Dena'ina view of Anchorage. Also see other recollections by Sava at 15.91, 15.93, 15.121, and 15.96.

"**Chidashla** ('Little Old Lady') they called her, I don't know what they called her, that's all I know. She was close related to my grandma. Our grandma used to go from Anchorage to Point Woronzoff. They pack up. Both of them [women] was same age. They were pretty strong legs anyway. They go to Point Woronzoff. You know how they do, old timers, they set net, they catch geese, ducks, everything like that, by set net on the beach at Point Woronzoff. Grandma sometime she take me to Point Woronzoff porcupine hunting. Sometime they come home with two, three geese. They got nothin to do in town here. They just work everyday trying to get some food. My grandma and that **chidashla** they used to go together, they used to be friends.... They travel around. They used to take gunny sack for their pack. Packing on their back, they put a little tea in there and sugar, and tea kettle and pot. They goes to this side of that Fire Island, [Point Woronzoff]. They go duck hunting together they got no gun. "Our Little Grandma" they used to call [her]. And they kill the ducks all the time. **Chida** and **Chidashla**. «The one called **Chidashla** had kids. One was name of Paul Stephan. Another one is Alex **Łedehen** they called him,» and his English name was Alec [Nikolai].

And the youngest one is Tommy. He had a little humpback on his back. They used to stay in Anchorage here. That was **Chidashla**'s kids, three boys. And one girl, name of her is Marion, she died too. They not related to us, but my grandmother and this lady called **Chidashla** was closely related. She was from Susitna Station, and she [the other woman] was from Eklutna.

"[They lived] at Chester Creek, by the railroad bridge, you know by the railroad bridge. That's where they had a cabin. That's where their house was. Big house. That old girl let me sleep with her, she take me around town. **Chidashla** died in the '40s, our grandma [died] too.1 **Chidashla** died first, during the war. In the 1950s their home was still there. When I was about ten years old (in 1930) they were about thirty years old. Their house was in town, close to Chester Creek. They had a real house [frame house]. Had running water, lights and everything.

"«The one they call **Stepankda** stayed there.» **Qatsen** I think his name was **Stepankda.** He lived in Anchorage, his home was at Chester Creek, on Anchorage side. They had a building house for him. Just on the side of the hill up Chester Creek. We had to go over the railroad and on the other side is a sand bar. And Inlet was there already. I was two or three years old. That's [he is from] Old Knik, old fella. I think he got about eleven or twelve girls. All his daughters. We come there, and we stayed there with my dad. And **Chidashla** and my grandma we walked there next. Back trail and they know where they go. They drag us over there. They had a couple of cabins there. Them ladies they walked the beach on the mud flat. We come back there [to Chester Creek].

"[Later in 1940s] the old ladies, one of them was his wife I think, I don't know, his widow. I remember about five or six years after that we come back to them, my dad, my grandma took me over to that place over there next. Same one, same guy. He got about five or six girls and about three boys. They got a whole bunch of kids out of him. **Stepankda**, he was from Knik. He had a house up Knik too. And down Chester Creek that's where he built a house.

"There were lots of Dena'ina [living in Anchorage]. That's when I first met my uncle, Aruf Ephim, and Andrew Ephim. Two of them was pretty old. I think they were older than my dad. And my dad's wife, my mother you know, she was the only one, the youngest one. And in the '40s Bobby Ephim died. He had stroke on Fourth Avenue. Buster Ephim, I was mostly with him all the time."

1. Shem Pete once mentioned that **Chidashla**, Tommy Nikolai's mother, died in 1944. See also 16.2 Indian Creek on Turnagain Arm, where **Chidashla** used to have a cabin.

A Sign of War

The following story by Sava, "A Sign of War," was prompted by a thick reddish-colored fog that covered Anchorage town one afternoon in the early 1940s.

Nachikda gun uyich' qilan Fourth Ave na'eł nugheyuł q'u.
Our grandmother was still alive then, and she was walking along Fourth Avenue with us.

Jan dach' tqijuq. Nice day gheli, yethdi about ten o'clock.
This is what happened that day. It was a nice day, about ten a.m.

Dach'u del ghu ununik'et' hq'u na'eł qbichuq'. Blood.
They was blood [in a low reddish fog] extending across. It covered us (the red fog). Blood.

Everybody all the ladies, girls that took me around, Mary you know, she was so scared.

She can't take me home.

White man gu qit'ayitninen taxi driver ghilanen una yiłkit na'a ni'iltlet hnu.
A white man that she knew, a taxi driver, stopped to pick us up.

Duntnatilya.
We were transported back.

"H'i'elnit," yełni,
"I am scared," she told him.

Blood ghin na'a ighalnik, natsendechuh, just like snow.
We had been covered with blood, it had been piled over us, like snow.

What I mean is you know when the war gonna start. World War II. That's what happened.

That's why that happened,

Del nunik'et'h t'yiłyuq du.
That is what made the blood extend across like that.

They can tell by that war gonna start again.

Sava offered further explanation:

"First world war start, she and I went to town, Fourth Avenue, only one street. They used to call it Chauncy Peterson's [a club], we go in there all the time. We sit there, all of a sudden it got kinda dark, and you see this blood, them people blood. There they get shot, all the blood is hanging down, right down to the ground. From that blood it got dark and we can't see the road. They can hardly see anything. That's when the war gonna start. That's why that happened."

FIGURE 217

Ezi fish camp at **Nuch'ishtunt** (15.91, Point Woronzof) in 1942 or 1943. Pete Ezi, Sr., Knik Prince, Pete Ezi, Jr., Margie Rousseau Rosser.

PHOTO COURTESY OF ALBERTA STEPHAN

FIGURE 218

Dena'ina commercial salmon fishing at **Nuch'ishtunt,** (15.91, Point Woronzof) in the late 1930s. From left: Mike Yakasoff, Sr., Jimmy Ezi, Mike Yakasoff, Jr., Felix Yakasoff.

PHOTO COURTESY OF GEORGE AND SUZIE ONDOLA

This could have been a permanent winter camp at one point in time."

Shem Pete stated that in the early nineteenth century this was a **tanik'edi** fishing site. A log fish dock was set in the mud flats for dipnetting salmon.

Shem Pete: "This was Ezi's fishcamp and also **Qalbis**, Wassilli Theodore. There was a steambath and five or six smokehouses there. Billy Ezi stayed there until 1945 or 1946."

Alberta Stephan (1996a:149): "The father and stepmother of Olga Ezi, Alberta Stephan's grandmother, used to put up fish at Point Woronzof, coming down by foot from Tyone Lake."

Alberta Stephan (2001:12,14) recalled that every spring, her family moved to their Point Woronzof fish camp from their winter home at **Niteh**. They preferred the salmon from salt water because they tasted "fresher." The Ezi family and other Dena'ina at the Point Woronzof fish camps dried and smoked king salmon, making **baba**, **k'enut'**, and **balik**. They also dried sockeye salmon. They ate the salmon heads, tails, eggs, and livers while living at the camp.

Sava Stephan: "**Hk'uydeshnin** a man's name, was from Point Woronzof, that's where he had a cabin there. I barely remember this guy. He was from Eklutna. He fished up here in Anchorage. At Point Woronzof. And old Ezi was there too. My Dad paddled. **Nuch'ishtunt**, that's the name of it.... Old Ezi was there, he had one or two kids there. I was a little kid, I barely remember that."

Leo Stephan: "They would all come up from **Niteh**. They might stay from May until August. They used to row down here in a dory, catching the tide.... All the way out to end of where of this grass there used to be ten, fifteen other fish camps.... My grandfather was here. There was a bath house right here. That was the last thing standing, and it's gone. There used to be a tent frame right here.

That's the wall of the bath house.... The smoke house they burned down here was made out of big logs, like this, and no nails. They used wooden pins [dowels] to hold them together."

§15.130 Q'is Kaq' • 'Birchbark Mouth'
creek half mile beyond Point Woronzof, creek at the end of east-west runway
This was the main source of drinking water for those fishing at **Nuch'ishtunt** just to the north.

Sava Stephan: "Another name, something like **Q'is Kaq'** over there. Below it. Below **Nuch'ishtunt**. Not very far, about 100 feet (yards) from Point Woronzof, **Q'is Kaq' ghe** they go over there. Ezi, they used to use that for fish camp. From there they row to cannery at Ship Creek. They never used to go on the beach. They left their dory at Ship Creek. They used to go by [along the] railroad."

15.92 Ułchena Huch'ilyut, Ułchena Bada Huch'ilyut • 'Where We Pulled up the Alutiiqs' (umiak)'
Campbell Point
The final battle in a war story took place here. The Alutiiqs came from Prince William sound and attacked a Dena'ina village on upper Knik Arm. As they went home, they were attacked here. Mike Alex and Shem Pete recorded versions of this story in Dena'ina.

15.93 Nutuł'iy • 'Object That Stands in the Water'
Fire Island
According to Orth (1971:334) the name Turnagain Island was first applied by Vancouver in 1794 and the name Fire Island was established in 1895. A Tanaina Indian name for Fire Island was published in 1847 as "Os[trov] Mushukhli," or "Mushukhli Island," on Russian Hydrographic Dept. Chart 1378. This seems to be an approximation of **Nutuł'iy**.

Shem Pete: "There's water all around. It's just sitting in the water."

Kalifornsky (1991:205): "«When they [Nulchina clan] were living in the sky on the frozen clouds, they stayed on an island they called **hagi** ['basket']. That island was a basket, they say. When they landed on Mount Susitna, on top of the mountain, a whirlwind struck the basket-island they lived on, and it was blown off the mountain and landed in Cook Inlet, where it turned into **Nutuł'iy** [Fire Island].»"

"[Note] Mr. Palmer's statement that 20 years ago the present flats on the north side of the arm opposite Fire Island did not exist, the channel at the time being close along the north shore to the mouth of the Susitna River" (Alaska Engineering Commission 1916:128).

De Laguna (1934:136) reported that Theodore of Eklutna told her that an epidemic had destroyed a village on Fire Island and that the survivors moved to Point Possession.

Shem Pete said that before contact with non-Natives, the Knik Arm Dena'ina had a **tanik'edi** or fishing dock on the west shore of Fire Island.

The Alex and Theodore families maintained fish camps here from about 1918 to the 1970s. They came here especially after Ship Creek was closed to fishing in 1951. Davis (1965:18) notes that after a Nike-Hercules station was located here, access to the higher portions of the island was restricted.

Sava Stephan: "We got caught by storm a few times. That Fire Island was the main thing to them when they are going to Tyonek. When they storm bound they got to come right ashore and stay over night."

The Dena'ina's intricate knowledge about Cook Inlet's tides, currents, winds, and channels was demonstrated during a search for a downed helicopter off the coast of Fire Island in October 2001 (Porco 2001:B1,B3). After several days of fruitless searching, and following a suggestion by anthropologist Nancy Yaw Davis, rescue officials consulted Leo Stephan, who has traveled the Upper Inlet by boat for decades and has fished at Point Woronzof and Point Possession, George Ondola, who fished for many years on Fire Island, and Susie Yakasoff Ondola, who was born at Point Woronzof. Leo, George, and Susie applied their experiences to predict that the tides and currents would push the helicopter towards North Point, the tip of Fire Island. This information was instrumental in the ultimate discovery of the aircraft.

15.94 Tudzedza • 'Swirling Water'
West Point on Fire Island
Shem and Billy Pete remarked that the most dangerous place in Cook Inlet is between Fire Island and Point Possession.

§15.131 Qin Cheghi Kaq' • 'Crying Ridge Mouth'
mouth of Campbell Creek

FIGURE 219

Leo Stephan pointing toward **Q'is Kaq'** (15.129) in August, 2001.

Leo Stephan: "Way back there in the bend where this swamp ends, that's where the drinking water was.... I know where it is because when I was a little boy I fetch a lotta water."

PHOTO BY JAMES KARI

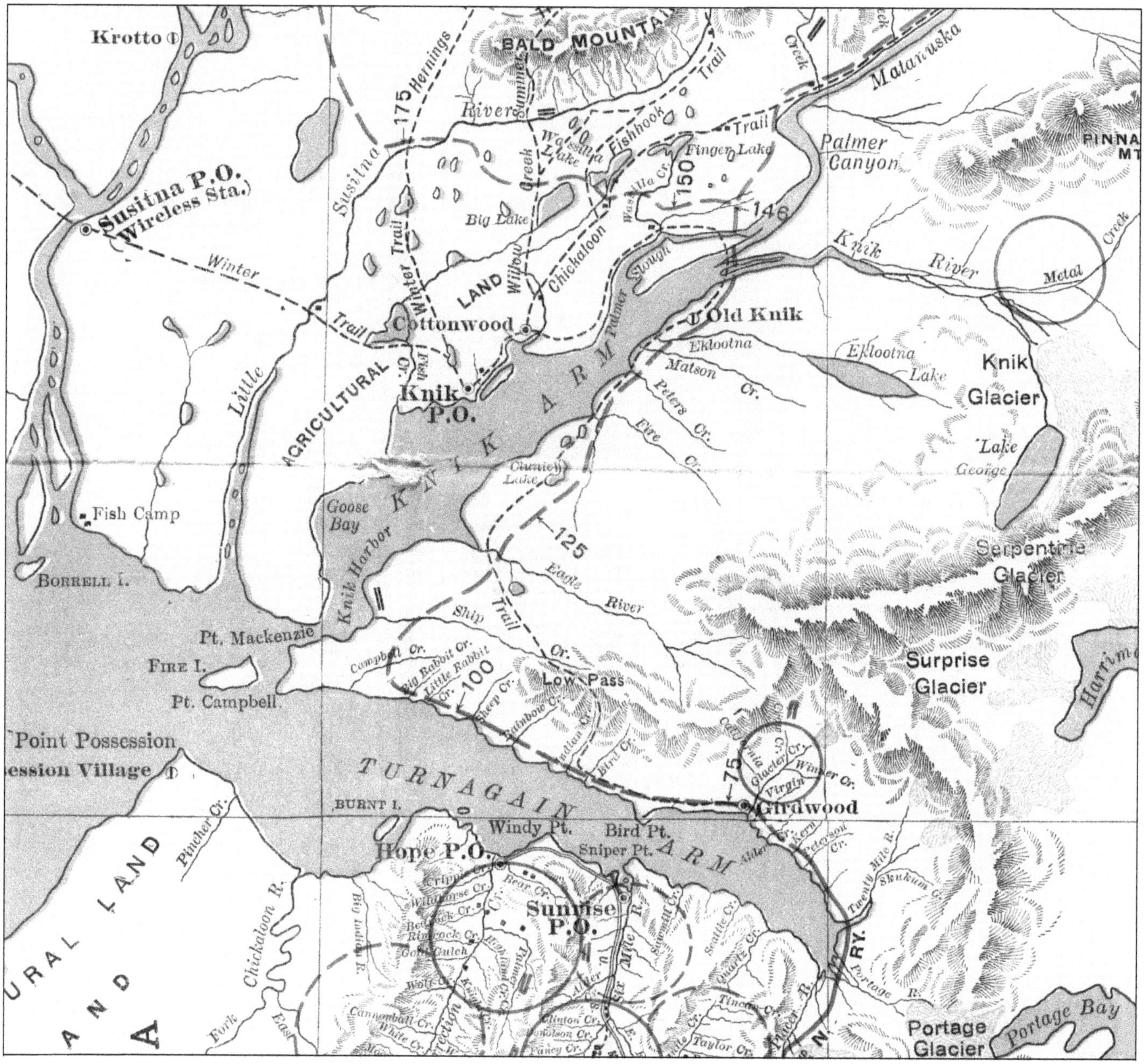

MAP 63

Detail from the 1910a Sleem Map: Anchorage area and Turnagain Arm.

The rarest and most interesting map of the early twentieth century for Southcentral Alaska is the 1910 map by D. H. Sleem, who was an M.D. in Seward. Sleem had talent as a draftsman and cartographer. The large map (32" x 45") was printed in Seward and is at the scale of 1:625,000 or about ten miles to the inch. The map was printed in three colors of ink, blue, black, and red, on a mauve paper. The map is very handsome, with attention to detail for all of the mining districts and a good though approximate rendering of relief and drainages. The map's projection is very interesting, showing all of Cook Inlet and the Kenai Peninsula, the Central Alaska Range and part of the Tanana drainage between the Melozitna River and Salcha River, and an inset map of the Iditarod mining district.

The Sleem map is a fascinating compilation of the available information on place names and trails to the mining districts in Southcentral Alaska. It is interesting to compare the 1910a Sleem map with the 1906 map by O.G. Herning, the storekeeper at Knik (Maps 32, 49, and 59). The 1906 Herning map has a similar projection as the 1910a Sleem map, showing all of Cook Inlet and the Kenai Peninsula and the Central Alaska Range with the Tanana River in the Fairbanks are in the north. Sleem incorporated many details from Herning's 1906 map into his 1910 map.

ARCHIVES, ALASKA AND POLAR REGIONS DEPT., RASMUSON LIBRARY, UNIVERSITY OF ALASKA FAIRBANKS

Alberta Stephan recalls "In about 1945, the area of Point Woronzof was closed to commercial fishing. There was an elder fishing around Campbell Point, and his name was John Hedberg. Some of them found other sites down the Inlet to fish; some had to give up commercial fishing." Hedberg, known as "Moose Meat John," was married to a ‡Talkeetna Dena'ina woman.

§15.132 Qin Cheghi Kaq' Bena • 'Crying Ridge Mouth Lake'
Campbell Lake
Campbell Lake was created in the 1960s when a small dam was placed on Campbell Creek. **Qin Cheghi Bena** is not an aboriginal Dena'ina place name, but following traditional naming conventions, we offer it here as an addition to the set of Dena'ina names in the Anchorage bowl.

15.95 Qin Cheghitnu • 'Crying Ridge Creek'
Campbell Creek

15.96 Nungge, Nunegge • 'Upland Area'
Nunaka Valley §and possibly South Fork of Chester Creek (revised location)
Perhaps an aboriginal Dena'ina place name. This is a Dena'ina directional word for the upland direction, away from the Inlet.

Sava Stephan: "My dad used to go out on this mountain around here [above Anchorage]. He killed caribou in Anchorage back of this mountain here. When my dad was alive all he would do would grab a gun and hunt. He would walk up the mountain. He put a little tea in his bag and go.... This mountain, we almost come to it. Picking berries. We would go with our grandmother. We pick, that was all I used to do is put a berry pack on my back. That's all I used to do, me and Billy Pete. This mountain we come to it, [in Anchorage] on top of it."

15.97 Ghedishla • 'Black Bear'
"Mount Tikishla," mountain, elev. 5150', on north fork of Campbell Creek
Tikishla, from **ghedishla** 'black bear,' is not an official name nor an aboriginal place name. The Dena'ina-based place name was suggested by the Mountaineering Club of Alaska in 1965.

15.98 Qin Cheghi • 'Crying Ridge'
Tanaina Peak and ridge along north side of upper Campbell Creek
The Dena'ina place name implies that this was a mourning place. Cf. 1.87 **Ch'chihi Ken**, the ridge south of Mount Susitna. Tanaina Peak, an official name, was suggested by the Mountaineering Club of Alaska. Porco 1985: "'Tanaina,' the anglicized version of Dena'ina, translates as 'the people' and is one of five Indian words picked by Rodman Wilson in 1965 for peaks on this ridge."

§15.133 Qin Cheghi Bena • 'Crying Ridge Lake'
Long Lake at the head of the middle fork of Campbell Creek

15.99 K'uhda'i • 'Moose'
"Koktaya Peak," mountain, elev. 5148', east of Tanaina Peak
This is another unofficial name suggested by the Mountaineering Club of Alaska in 1965, based upon Dena'ina vocabulary supplied by the late Mike Alex.

15.100 Ggeh Betnu • 'Rabbit Creek'
Rabbit Creek
This name, reported by John Stump in 1976, is probably an aboriginal place name. The name Rabbit Creek was first recorded in 1906 (Orth 1971:789).

§15.134 Ggeh Bena • 'Rabbit Lake'
Rabbit Lake

15.101 Hkaditali • 'Drift Lumber'
Potter Marsh
The beach here is a good place to collect material that drifts in on the tide, thus the name. The Dena'ina knew of metal prior to Euro-American contact. The Dena'ina name for metal that drifts to shore on planks is **beł tituqiz'in**.

15.102 Hkaditali Betnu • 'Drift Lumber Creek'
Potter Creek

15.103 Q'isqa Dghelaya • 'Banjo Snowshoe Mountain'
McHugh Peak
Q'isqa are temporary snowshoes made of lashed brush.

§15.135 Q'isqa Betnu • 'Banjo Snowshoe Stream Mountain'
McHugh Creek

15.104 Ułchena Tich'qiluqt • 'Where We Killed Alutiiq People'
mountain near Potter Marsh, location uncertain; possibly Suicide Peak
John Stump mentioned that this was a battle site.

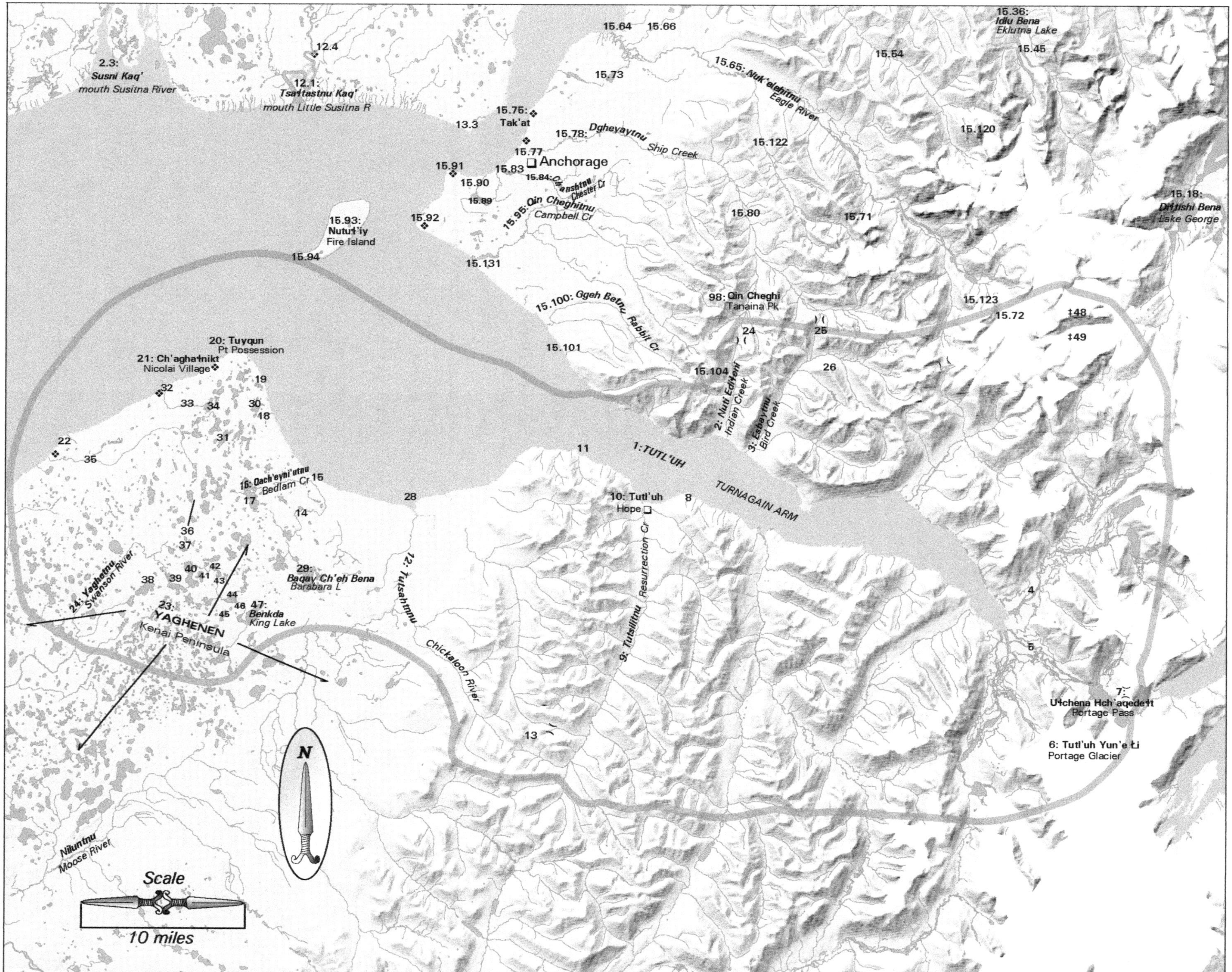
2.3: Susni Kaq'
mouth Susitna River
12.4
12.1: Tsaɬtastnu Kaq'
mouth Little Susitna R
15.64 15.66
15.73
15.36: Idlu Bena
Eklutna Lake
15.45
15.54
15.65: Nuk'elehitnu
Eagle River
15.120
15.76: Tak'at
13.3
15.78: Dgheyaytnu Ship Creek
15.122
15.77
Anchorage
15.91
15.90
15.83
15.84: Ch'anshtnu Chester Cr
15.89
15.95: Qin Cheghitnu Campbell Cr
15.80
15.71
15.18: Diɬtishi Bena
Lake George
15.93: Nutuɬ'iy
Fire Island
15.92
15.94
15.131
15.100: Ggeh Betnu Rabbit Cr
98: Qin Cheghi
Tanaina Pk
15.123
15.72
48
49
20: Tuyqun
Pt Possession
21: Ch'aghaɬnikt
Nicolai Village
15.101
24
25
26
15.104
2: Nuti Edɬeni
Indian Creek
3: Esbaytnu
Bird Creek
19
32
33
34
30
18
31
22
35
11
1: TUTL'UH
TURNAGAIN ARM
16: Qach'eyni'utnu
Bedlam Cr
15
17
14
28
10: Tutl'uh
Hope
8
36
37
40
42
41
43
38
39
24: Yaghetnu
Swanson River
29: Baqay Ch'eh Bena
Barabara L
12: Tutsahtnu
Chickaloon River
9: Tutsilitnu
Resurrection Cr
4
44
46
45
47: Benkda
King Lake
23: YAGHENEN
Kenai Peninsula
5
7: Uɬchena Hch'aqedeɬt
Portage Pass
13
6: Tutl'uh Yun'e Ɫi
Portage Glacier
N
Niluntnu
Moose River
Scale
10 miles

16 Turnagain Arm and Point Possession

16.1 Tutl'uh • 'Back Water, Headwaters'

Turnagain Arm; also used for Hope townsite, 16.10. See Plate 27.352.

This name indicates that the Dena'ina treat Turnagain Arm as the head of Cook Inlet.

Koman's 1989 guide to Turnagain Arm quotes extensively from the 1987 edition of *Shem Pete's Alaska.*

Shem Pete noted that the word for the bore tide in Turnagain Arm, **nudidghul**, is onomatopoetic of the roar of the water. He emphasized how dangerous these tides were to traditional Dena'ina boats. "That tide killed a lot of people." Dena'ina terms for tides are discussed in Kari and Kari (1982:93).

Billy Pete recounted a story about the swamping of a **badi** on its way across Turnagain Arm to Sunrise for moose hunting. A tidal bore caught the group by surprise, and they had no time to bail out the boat with their birch bark baskets. Most of the crew swam to shore. He also remarked that because of the Dena'ina knowledge of the tides and currents, such incidents were uncommon. "Those Indians were seafaring people."

Henry T. Elliott wrote (1897:84): "The northeastern extremity of this large arm of the sea, which Cook entered with the confident hope of finding a watery circuit of the continent, and, being disappointed, applied to it the name of 'Turnagain,' presents a tidal phenomenon equal to that so well reconized in the Bay of Fundy. Here the tide comes in with a thundering roar, raising a 'bore' wave that advances like an express train in rapidity, carrying everything before it in its resistless onward, upward sweep. High banks of clay and gravel, which at low tide seem as though they were far removed form submersion, are flooded instantly, to remain so until the ebb takes its place. The natives never fail to remember the angry warning of the incoming tide; they always

FIGURE 220

A view looking up the north side of **Tutl'uh** (16.1, Turnagain Arm).
PHOTO BY LORRAINE BASNAR ELDER

Sources: Mike Theodore, John Stump, Shem Pete, Peter Kalifornsky, Billy Pete, Leo Stephan, Betty Gilcrist

2003 revisions: names added 16.24–16.47.
‡2016 revisions: names added 16.48, 16.49; names revised 16.18, 16.30.

MAP 64

(Opposite) Place names map of Turnagain Arm and Point Possession, showing Nos. 16.1 to 16.49.
MAP BY MATT GANLEY

FIGURE 221

Tutl'uh Yun'e Łi (16.6, Portage Glacier), in 1978.
PHOTO BY PRISCILLA RUSSELL

hurriedly rush out of their huts, scan quickly everything surrounding, lest some utensil, some canoe, or basket weir be thoughtlessly left within the remorseless rush of that swift coming flood."

16.2 Nuti Edilłeni • 'That Which Flows into Salt Water'
Indian Creek
Shem Pete: "In 1918, when the rail go through, I seen that house where all the Dena'ina used to stay [not quite two miles north of the Indian section house]. That was Tom Nikolai's mother's house, **Chidashla**. She was from Knik. She died in 1944. In 1918 the cabin could have been thirty years old. They had a good cabin and a steambath. In 1918 all the Natives from Knik, Tyonek, and Kenai used to hang out there. Good porcupine hunting. And sheep. They say that there used to be **nichił** there. There are salmon there too."

Billy Pete: "My mother packed me there [in the early 1920s]. In 1931 that house was still there. We lived there hunting porcupine."

§16.24 Nuti Edilłeni Tustes • 'That Which Flows into Salt Water-Pass'
Indian Creek Pass
The Indian Creek trail to Knik Arm is noted on Sleem (1910a) (Map 63).

16.3 Esbaytnu • 'Goat Creek'
Bird Creek
Shem Pete: "«Eklutna Alex was the first man to kill a goat they say. There were no goats before. The first moose came here about two hundred years ago, and the goat came about one hundred fifty years later.»"

Learnard (1900:648) and Castner (1984:10) noted in 1898 that the trails up Bird and Indian creeks to upper Ship Creek and Knik Arm were used by Indians.

The Dena'ina of today do not recollect any use of Beluga Point, an important archaeological site near the mouth of Bird Creek (Reger 1985, 1996).

§16.25 Esbaytnu Tustes • 'Goat Creek Pass'
Bird Creek Pass

§16.26 Esbaytnu Dghelaya • 'Goat Creek Mountain'
"Esbay Peak"
The name "Esbay Peak" is in use by the Mountaineering Club of Alaska.

‡16.48 Yudi Dghelaya • 'Golden Eagle Mountain'
mountain 6540' between Eagle Glacier and Yudi Glacier
This and 16.49 cited on the map by Imus Geographics (2006)

‡16.49 Yudi Łi'a • 'Golden Eagle Glacier'
"Yudi Glacier" at the head of Glacier Creek
Cited on the map by Imus Geographics (2006)

16.4 (no recorded name)
Twentymile River
While in Port Wells in 1898 Glenn (1899:28) wrote "Mr. Hunt a prospector and miner from Sunrise, informed me that there was an Indian trail from Portage Bay by which one could reach both the city of Sunrise and Knik Arm.... He was informed that it passed over a watershed that separates some stream flowing into Portage Bay

Captain Cook's Arrival in Cook Inlet in 1778

by James Kari

The first certain contact between Euro-Americans and Native peoples in Cook Inlet took place in late May of 1778 when two small British ships, captained by James Cook on his third voyage of the Pacific, entered what Cook had hoped would be a passage to the north (Cook 1967:360–372). Between May 26 and June 6, the Cook party and the ships Endeavor and Resolution explored and mapped the inlet.

On May 30 two kayak-style canoes paddled by Natives approached the ships, coming from the Kustatan or Tyonek areas on the west shore, but Cook's ships did not land there. On May 31, near North Foreland or Tyonek, a group of men, women, and children approached Cook's

MAP 65

The 1778 Chart of Cooks River.

James Cook's landmark voyage of 1778 resulted in the first maps of Prince William Sound and Cook Inlet. This map shows the routes his ships made past Kalgin Island to Fire Island and Point Possession. The only place names on this map in Upper Inlet are Point Possession and R. Turnagain. Compare this with the Vancouver map of 1794 (Map 15), both of which are famous examples of maritime (or ship-based) cartography. The Vancouver map is more detailed in topography and several more names have been assigned. Neither map has any Native place names in Cook Inlet. ‡Also discussed in Postnikov and Falk (2015:129–131).

ARCHIVES, ALASKA AND POLAR REGIONS DEPT., RASMUSON LIBRARY, UNIVERSITY OF ALASKA FAIRBANKS

ships in one large boat or umiak and several small kayaks, displaying a leather garment on a pole, apparently as a sign of friendship. The Natives then boarded the ships. On June 1 the ships anchored off Point Possession where a party led by Lt. James King went ashore, and before a group of about forty Natives, they displayed the English flag and buried a bottle attesting their claim to these lands at the place Cook named "Point Possession." A dog bit the ship's surgeon, Mr. Law; to display their firearms, Cook's men shot the dog.

Lt. King then entered Knik Arm in a small boat, landing at Fire Island. (Fire Island first was named Currant Island; in 1794 Vancouver renamed it Turnagain Island. The name Fire Island was reported by the U.S. Coast and Geodetic Survey in 1895.) On June 2, the ships still anchored off Point Possession, the men traded clothing for salmon, halibut, and skins.

As they sailed down the inlet, Cook's crew met Natives from the east shore, probably from around Kenai. Cook remarked, "All the people we have met with in this River are of the same Nation as those who inhabit Sandwich Sound [Prince William Sound]" (1967:371).

The identity of the Natives that the Cook party met in upper Cook Inlet has been controversial. Bancroft sug-

[column headings from manuscript]

English	Oonalaska		Sandwich Sound [Cook Inlet]		Norton Sound	Greenland from Emnik	Esquimaux
No	Not				Ena	Nag	
Yes, or Aye	Āh	aa'	Aā		Eh	Ilisve	
What call you that		? yaha shu	Ahā'shou	'? possibly'	–	Kina	
1	Turadac	ts'ełq'i	Chilki		Aduwjac	Attousek	Attouset
2	Alac	nutiha (O) nuta (U	Taiha		Aiba	Arlak	Mardluk
3	Canoogin	tuq'i	Tokke		Pingashooe	Pingajuak	Pingasut
4	Sceh'in	ch'qilu	Cheekels	'five'	Shetamee	Sissamat	Sissamat
5	Chang	k'uzhch'eni (O) k'uych'eni (U)	Kocheene	'six'	Dallemie	Tellimat	Tellimat
6	Aloo	łtaqul'i (O)	Takulai	'eight'	In counting more		Arbangot
7	Ooloo	łq'ich'idi	Kleichilko	'nine'	than 5 they re-		{Arbangot-Attousek
8	Kamchung	qelun (U)	Klieu	'ten'	peat the same		{Arbangek-mun-dlik
9	Sechiny				[illegible] over again		Kollin illoct
10	Kuse						Kollit
'four'		denk'i	***denki*** *(Cook 1784:376)*				

TABLE 15. DENA'INA WORDS ON THE 1778 ANDERSON VOCABULARY

The nine numerals listed (1, 2, 3, 4, 5, 6, 8, 9, 10) are definitely Dena'ina. The number four is in Cook 1784 but is not in the clerk's copy of the Anderson list. One numeral, **łtaqul'i** "six" (actually 'eight') is diagnostic of the Outer Inlet dialect. The last numeral listed, "Klu" or "Kliew," "eight" **qelun** (actually 'ten') is diagnostic of the Upper Inlet dialect (cf. Lower Inlet **qeluzhun**). One of the items, 'what call you that' may contain **shu** 'possibly, perhaps' which is diagnostic of the Outer Inlet dialect (cf. Upper Inlet **shi**).

gested that the people at Point Possession were Eskimo and that "the Innuit in those days occupied more of the coast of Cook Inlet than they do today" (1886:207). De Laguna (1934:14–15) cautioned that Cook's descriptions of the Cook Inlet peoples could fit either the Tanaina Athabascans or the Chugach or Koniag Eskimos. Mishler (1985a:10–13) examined the mention of clothing in Cook's records, and noted that Cook observed both bird-feather parkas, which are a known Koniag Eskimo item of apparel, and marten- and hare-skin coats, which are Athabascan but are not known to have been used by the Koniag.

However, conclusive proof that the Cook expedition did in fact meet Dena'ina is the eleven-word vocabulary collected by William Anderson, the surgeon for the Cook party. These are the first words written in the Dena'ina language (and in any Alaska Athabascan language). Anderson's original notebooks have not been located and what survives is a clerk's copy of Anderson's notebooks, which we show with the retranscribed Dena'ina words (M. E. Krauss, personal communication). The 1784 publication of this word list (Cook 1784:375–376) obscured the identity of the languages by merging the eleven-word Dena'ina list with other word lists that were elicited from Prince William Sound Alutiiq. However, the copy of the Anderson comparative vocabulary (Anderson 1778) has a column of ten items from "Sandwich Sound," i.e., Cook Inlet (Figure 222). There is nothing to indicate exactly where this word list was recorded; it could be from Point Possession or Trading Bay. It appears that the Cook party encountered speakers of both the Outer and Upper Inlet dialects.

The Dena'ina in their own historical traditions assert that they occupied Cook Inlet at the time the first Euro-Americans arrived. The following story, as told by Simeon Chickalusion, is presented in brief in Carlson (1972): "It [the ship] was like a giant bird with great white wings.... All the Tyonek people were very frightened and ran and hid in the woods, except one brave man. He paddled out in his bidarka to see what it was, the strange people on the boat traded him some of their clothes for what he was wearing. When the courageous native returned to the shore he was a hero to his people, and the costume he brought back with him was faithfully copied down through the years, to wear in ceremonial dances." Carlson adds, "It was the uniform of an English sailor, for it was Captain Cook's good ship Resolution beating its way up the Inlet in 1778 that the natives had mistaken for the giant bird."

Wilson and Crews (1999:32) cited geologist Josiah Spurr's notes from Tyonek in 1898. "Clearly, he communicated with Natives upon his arrival there April 26, 1898, for he records in his field notes (p. 1), interestingly, that the Indians 'preserved the tradition of Captain Cook entering the Inlet' more than a century earlier."

The Point Possession Dena'ina have oral traditions about Cook's arrival. The following account appears in Cook Inlet Historic Sites Project (1975:59) based upon an interview with Feodoria Pennington of Point Possession: "Chief Jimmy Nicolai and... Doris Nicolai related stories of the meeting with the English. The people of the village saw Cook's men coming and thought it might mean war, so they got their spears and weapons ready and went down to meet the English. The Natives ended up giving the English a porcupine or a deer, and the English buried a jar of coins with a proclamation of ownership. The small children of the village would always take a jar or can they found floating on the beach to Doris Nicolai to see if it was Captain Cook's."

‡In 2015, the Anchorage Museum presented an exhibition on Cook's Alaska explorations entitled "Arctic Ambitions: Captain Cook and the Northwest Passage." Several essays in the book that was produced in connection with the exhibition describe Cook's explorations of Cook Inlet and encounters with the Dena'ina (Barnett and Nicandri 2015). Also note discussions of Cook and the Cook artifact collections in Jones, Fall, and Leggett (2013).

Nutuł'iy ch'u Tutl'uh—
Fire Island and Turnagain Arm

by Shem Pete

Shem Pete was positive that the people whom Cook met in the Inlet in 1778 were Dena'ina. Shem told the following story about the Cook party's visit and the origins of English names "Fire Island" and "Turnagain Arm." Recorded by Jim Kari on February 8, 1985, in Fairbanks.

Captain Cook nqaniyu ghedghu Fire Island huydilq'un.
Captain Cook came ashore and built a fire there at Fire Island.

Yet huqeydilq'un ch'u yet k'qulqet'.
They built a fire for themselves there and they ate there.

Yeh hqugh nihghinnik, nqahghinnik.
They [Cook's men] came that far by boat and landed.

K'qulqet'.
They ate.

Dach' ghuda shughu Fire Island h'iyi dilan.
That is why its name is Fire Island.

Dach'u hqu'uyi ghuda.
That is so that they could find the place.

Qeyq'e niqendinłtsiyi ghuda yedahdi Fire Island beq'e dayq'eni Island yadin'un.
In order for them to light that fire on it, he named Fire Island, 'that which is burning on it.'

How you call 'em, Turnagain Arm?

Yeh qubeł hkayiqats' yun'e.
There they went by boat in the upriver direction.

"Qil," ni.
"No good," he said.

"Naqandghelghełni,"
"I should turn back,"

"I turn around,"

Turnagain Arm h'iyi dałchin.
He made the name Turnagain Arm.

"Niqandghelghel," ni.
"I turned around," he said.

Turnaround,

Turnagain Arm h'iyi dilan.
Its name is Turnagain Arm.

Point Possession yet hnayul.
They camped there at Point Possession.

from the Twenty-Mile River, that there were no glaciers on this route." Glenn gives more detail (op. cit.:104): "This route runs from Portage Bay on the coast, up Cabin Creek, over the divide, to the head of Twenty-Mile River; thence up the west fork across to Winner Creek; down this and across California Creek; thence up Crow Creek, a tributary of California Creek, to Raven Creek; thence down it and the Yukla River [Eagle River] to Knik Arm." Glenn (op. cit.:32) explored the divide at the head of the Twentymile River near the Twentymile Glacier which may be approached from either Eagle River or Knik River and speculated that Copper River Indians could reach Turnagain Arm via Knik River and this trail. See 15.113, Metal Creek, a possible route for this trail.

In May 1899 Herron ascended the Twentymile River, then crossed over the Chugach mountains to the Eagle River drainage. In the Lake Glenn area he noted "Signs of two Indian camps were found near the west end of Lake Glenn. One of them was only a few days old and had been used by a solitary hunter for a night's camp, the remains of an eagle showing his bill of fare" (1901:15).

Driving past here in October of 1982, Shem Pete recalled that Jim Moccasin, a Dena'ina from Kenai, had a hunting cabin on the Twentymile River in the 1950s.

16.5 Tutl'uh Betnu • 'Backwater Creek'
Portage Creek

16.6 Tutl'uh Yun'e Łi • 'Glacier Upriver from Backwater'
Portage Glacier

16.7 Ułchena Hch'aqedełt • 'Where the Alutiiqs Came Out'
Portage Pass
Shem Pete: "«That's where the Alutiiq came over the pass.»" In the war story that concludes at Campbell Point (15.92), the Alutiiq are said to have dragged a large umiak over this portage to Turnagain Arm.

Osgood (1937:74): "The Kenai people go over the mountain passes to meet the Eskimo [Alutiiq] of the east coast of the peninsula as do the Kachemak Bay people."

The Dena'ina of today know few Native place names in Prince William Sound. A few Dena'ina names have been recorded, such as **Tl'ubugh** 'Back Shore' for Seward and Resurrection Bay (Kalifornsky 1991:350).

§(16.27) Tuł'itnu • 'Stream of the One in Water'
unlocated name of stream into Turnagain Arm
Name mentioned once by Peter Kalifornsky in 1976. This stream name implies that it is named for a mountain that is near Turnagain Arm.

16.8 (no recorded Dena'ina name)
Ephanasy Point or Affanasi Point, north of the mouth of Bear Creek
According to long-time Hope resident Carl Clark, as summarized in Cook Inlet Historic Sites Project (1975:62): "The Ephanasy community area and cemetery... is importantly associated with an historic figure, Chief Ephanasy, and with several historic events in Tyonek and Hope [during the gold rush at Hope in the 1890s]. The presence of these Native people further contributed... meat, hides, snowshoes and moccasins to the townspeople.... Many years later there was an epidemic and a large proportion of this Indian settlement died. Five were buried at the Ephanasy Point cemetery and the survivors moved away."

Mishler (1985a:42): "At one time there were three or four houses on Affanasi Point, but white people later moved into the cabins and eventually burned everything down."

In 1904 O. G. Herning, storekeeper at Knik, noted in his diary that a Dena'ina named Affinasi owned a sloop. At that time several Knik Dena'ina owned sailboats and transported goods between Knik and Hope for Herning. See Fig. 171.

A 1909 issue of the *Seward Weekly Gateway* ran an obituary of Chief "Affanacy": "Affanacy once had his headquarters at Old Knik [Eklutna].... Time was when Chief Affanacy was a power—a veritable monarch—among his people.... When he died a few days ago at Kenai he was living in poverty, shorn of his power" (Mishler 1985a:41).

Fall (1981:432) notes that two chiefs named Affinasi or Affinasa have been associated with Knik or Eklutna. Shem Pete has said that Affinasi was the Russian name of **Dusgeda Tukda** of Knik. It is possible that the chief who died in 1909 was the same man. Shem Pete, however, feels that **Dusgeda Tukda** died on the Little Susitna River. See 12.4.

16.9 Tutsilitnu • 'River of Water Head Flows'
Resurrection Creek. See Plate 27.

16.10 Tutl'uh • 'Back Water'
Hope-Sunrise townsites
The general name for Turnagain Arm, **Tutl'uh**, also refers to the Hope and Sunrise townsites.

Mishler (1985b): "Of the 27 persons counted at Hope City in 1900, 14 were Indians, all identified as having come from Knik. These Indians were probably all in Chief Affanasi's band."

Shem Pete: "«When the Americans came, they found a lot of gold there. Some Dena'ina were there, and Ahtna. Johnny White's mother and father lived there. And Steve Bismark and his wife. They were from the Wasilla Lake village, and they moved to Hope and Point Possession.»" Shem also noted that Eklutna Alex knew Turnagain Arm well and that he sold sheep meat to the miners at Hope.

Annabel, writing in the 1920s at Hope (1997d:108): "I had a launch standing by, the thirty-foot Western Maid, skippered by a Denna Indian named Simeon Chickaloosun."

‡C. Mielke has compiled the 1900 and 1910 censuses for Hope and Sunrise.

16.11 Qeshqa Eł Tak'niqats't • 'Where the Rich Man Sank'
point by Gull Rock
Shem Pete: "«A Knik chief was crossing here in a skin

FIGURE 222

Johnny Nicholai of Point Possession with his nieces Feodoria Kallander, Anna Kallander, Mary Kallander, and Minnie Kallander in Anchorage in 1928.

PHOTO COURTESY OF FEODORIA KALLANDER PENNINGTON

badi [umiak] as he returned from the Russian post at Kenai. His boat swamped across from **Tutsahtnu** [16.12], and they drowned. His hat floated up to Knik, and they found it.»"

§16.28 Tutsahtnu Kaq' • 'Water Canyon River-Mouth'
Chickaloon River mouth, Chickaloon Bay. See Plate 26.

16.12 Tutsahtnu • 'Water Canyon River'
Chickaloon River
Shem Pete says that there was a small village here. "«That's the last place the Dena'ina used [in pre-contact times]. I don't think anyone was farther up Turnagain Arm.»"

The grave of Chief Chickaloon, according to Carl Clark, is on the west bank of the Chickaloon River on the first timber patch up from the mouth. Clark says that the cross from the grave was removed by a white man in the 1920s. In 1980 Cooperative Park Studies Unit archaeologists could not locate this grave. ‡This gravesite is also noted in Rabich (1977:147).

Cook Inlet Historic Sites Project (1975:63): "After Chief Chickaloon was buried here, his spirit is said to have haunted the Chickaloon River in order to eat the white men who went into the country. Several people did disappear in that area; it is thought they were eaten by a large brown bear known to live in the vicinity."

Mike Theodore remarked that the old Dena'ina from this area, the Kenai Mountains band, were called **Tsaht'ana**.

Barry states that the Tyonek Indians regularly raided the people at Chickaloon Bay, taking their women (1973:40). The raids ceased after a storm destroyed a fleet of one hundred Tyonek bidarkas.

Peter Kalifornsky of Kenai was familiar with the upper reaches of the Chickaloon River, which is on the trail system that leads to the lake country in the upper Swanson River region via Barabara Lake. See Kalifornsky (1991:331).

16.13 Tsik'el'unt, Chik'el'unt • §possibly 'Where a Head Is in Position'
ridges at head of Chickaloon River, American Pass
Kalifornsky (1991:331): "«Long ago they traveled through there to the village here at Kenai or to the trails to **Tsik'el'unt**....»"

Often we have been asked about the similarities between the place names "Chickaloon," for two rivers (16.12 and 14.31) and the well-known Dena'ina surname of "Chickalusion." We feel that the similarity is a coincidence. "Chickaloon" apparently is from a Dena'ina chief named **Chiklu** (perhaps a Russian-origin name) who spent his earlier years on the middle Matanuska River and his later years on the south shore of Turnagain Arm. Baker (1902:176) notes that the name "Chickaloon" was first recorded here in 1895 by G. F. Becker as "Chic Loon." However, Peter Kalifornsky felt that the name "Chickaloon" was from this Dena'ina place name **Tsik'el'unt** (Kalifornsky 1982:131, 1984:91, 1991:315.) "Chickalusion" derives from the name of a Kustatan chief of the 1880s–90s whose Dena'ina name was **Begh Chik'el'ishen**, which means 'the one that kills something for him/her." Also see 16.21 about Chief Chickaloon.

16.14 Baqay Ch'ehtnu • 'Canoe Folded (Birchbark) Creek'
Pincer Creek

§16.29 Baqay Ch'eh Bena • 'Canoe Folded (Birchbark) Lake'
Barabara Lake
The name for Pincer Creek implies that this was along a canoe trail system. We have assigned this name to the largest lake in that drainage, Barabara Lake, which is just two or so miles from **Benkda** (16.45, King Lake) in the Swanson River drainage.

16.15 Qach'eyni'ut • 'Where Wind Is Against Place'
flat at mouth of Bedlam Creek
A village site was reported here as No. 87 in Cook Inlet Historic Sites Project 1975. In 1980 Cooperative Park Studies Unit archaeologists spent two days on this creek but could not locate the site. Cook Inlet Historic Sites Project (1975:61): "Mysterious location in swampy depression. Old rectangular and circular depressions reported by Mr. Julius Kallander. Possible a way camp for Turnagain Arm crossing, in an area of historic occupation by Chickaloon Indians (Barry 1973:40). Also near an historic Native pile cutting operation."

‡A site on lower Bedlam Creek was noted in Rabich (1977:147–48). In 2002 the BIA ANSCA group tested house pits and cache pits near lower Bedlam Creek one of which yielded rather early dates for north Kenai Peninsula of 1820 ± 60 BP (O'Leary 2002).

FIGURE 223

(Above) Grant Brown (left) and Billy Nicholai rowing a dory at **Tuyqun** (16.20, Point Possession) in the late 1930s.

PHOTO COURTESY OF FEODORIA KALLANDER PENNINGTON

FIGURE 224

(Below) Aerial view of **Tuyqun** (16.20, Point Possession) looking east toward **Tutsahtnu Kaq'** (16.28, Chickaloon Bay). The site of **Ch'aghałnikt** (16.21) is near the beach to the right of the frame. The largest lake is Diamond Lake, locally known as "Diamond Kid Lake."

A small pond just to the right of the frame has been known as "Shem Pete Lake." Shem Pete: "That Shem Pete Lake, that was just recently named, around 1935. I kill a lot of moose around there all the time. That's why they call it that."

.PHOTO BY BETTY GILCRIST

16.16 Qach'eyni'utnu, Qach'eytnu • 'Creek of Wind Against Place'
Bedlam Creek

16.17 Qach'eyni'u Bena, Qach'eytnu Bena • 'Lake of Wind Is Against Place'
Mull Lake, at head of Bedlam Creek
Cook Inlet Historic Sites Project (1975:59): "Back among the lakes at Pt. Possession the people had secret cellars where women and children might hide during hostile attacks. An acquaintance of Mr. Kallander, George Kail (also known as Russian George), once accidentally fell into one of these cellars. He said it contained dry meat and berries, and might have been hundreds of years old. Russian George sealed the place back up, but thought the contents might be ruined because of the air let in when he fell through. Nobody knows where these places are located anymore, they are so well concealed."

16.18 Shqit • '-∞-'
creek from Dipper Lake
‡One of three names with **shqit,** an obscure word in Dena'ina that is in three distant place names. Neither Shem Pete nor Peter Kalifornsky provided translations. **Shqit** is one of a small number of Dena'ina names that we mark as a substrate place name from a language that preceded Dena'ina; cf. 6.2 **Shqitnu** Skwentna River. See pp. 144–147.

§16.30 Shqit Bena • '-∞- Lake'
Dipper Lake

§16.31 (Dena'ina name not known)
Neckshortka Lake
This name, established in 1961 (Orth 1971:679), has the feel of being a translation of a Dena'ina place name combined with the suffix **-ka** 'big.' This name has not been re-elicited.

16.19 Quch'k'eshtisht • 'Where We Carry Something [canoe] Up'
bank one mile east of Point Possession

16.20 Tuyqun *(U)*, **Tuzqun** *(O)* • 'Calm Water'
Point Possession, locally "Point Station"
Billy Pete: "The water don't go anyplace when tide goes in or out. That's why they call it that. But it gets really rough." This name was recorded by de Laguna (1934:136) as "Tucqant." Point Possession has also been known as Nicolai Point.

The name "Point Possession" was given on June first of 1778 by James Cook and Lt. James King with the intention of claiming Cook Inlet for the British crown. Of this event, the historian Bancroft (most likely in the words of ghost writer Ivan Petroff) remarked, "Some lords aboriginal were present, but it is nowhere written that King asked their permission to take possession of the country, as the admiralty had ordered" (1959[1887]:208).

In April of 1794, Lt. Whidbey of George Vancouver's expedition (Vancouver 1801:203), in a small boat, met a party of fifteen Dena'ina south of Point Possession. The Dena'ina gave the British sailors some dried fish and took them to see two houses that they had recently built. Each was occupied by a family of about fifteen persons of different ages and both sexes.

FIGURE 225
At Point Possession in 1940 are Nayna Snodgrass, Katherine Nicolie, and Katherine's mother, Christine Nicolie. They had moved from Kroto Creek Village to Point Possession in 1937.
PHOTO COURTESY OF LILLIAN THEODORE

16.21 Ch'aghałnikt • 'Where Fabric Extends Out'
Point Possession village, Nicolai Village
The 1906 Herning map notes this as "Nicolai Village," and the 1910a Sleem map as "Possession Village" (Map 63).

Cook Inlet Historic Sites Project (1975:58) compiled some interesting facts about the logistical aspects of prehistoric raids between the Dena'ina and the Alutiiq in the Point Possession area from the Kallander family: "Long ago the Aleuts [Alutiiq] came up the Inlet in bidarkis, and set up places at each point or promontory, usually on the southern side. After the Athabascans moved into the area there was sometimes raiding and women stealing between them and the Aleuts to the southwest. The Indians had pretty good control of the Upper Inlet region by holding the East and West Forelands, which constitute "the bottleneck of the Inlet." At least one big battle took place near there at Boulder Point."

Shem Pete has recorded a detailed story about a sickness that devastated a Dena'ina village at Point Possession before contact with the Russians.

Shem Pete: "«There were lots of people there before. There was a village at Point Station, they say. The people died off sometime before the Russians came, and time passed. A big village died out. Nobody knows where the disease came from. This was 300 years ago.»" Shem added that these people were Kenai Dena'ina. Afterwards many other Dena'ina moved there from all over the Upper Inlet region.

Shem also stated that one of the Dena'ina battles with Russians occurred here, probably in the 1780s or 1790s. Three or four Dena'ina men were killed and their women were taken. The Dena'ina regrouped, killed the Russian men, and got their women back. Also see 16.25 below.

De Laguna (1934:136): "The village Tca'tliniq't (Nikita), is modern, and is said to have been founded by the survivors from the epidemic which destroyed a village on Fire Island, Nututli (Theodore, Eklutna)."

The 1900 census showed fifteen people at Point Possession in three families (Mishler 1985b:13). It seems that all of the recent Dena'ina residents of Point Possession spoke the Upper Inlet dialect of Dena'ina.

Kalifornsky (1991:315): "«He [Chickaloon] was the last Dena'ina to have two wives.... In wintertime he would come here to Kenai, with his wives, for the holidays. Then when spring came, they would move to Pt. Possession to put up fish. He himself and his followers would go around to Kustatan and Kalgin Island, hunting seal and beluga, putting up provisions for the winter.»"

There is a good discussion of this area in Cook Inlet Historic Sites Project (1975:58–60) based on interviews with Feodoria Pennington, Julius Kallander, Jr., and others: "Pt. Possession has figured significantly in the Native history and lifeways of a large part of the Cook Inlet region. It has long been a summer meeting place for family and friends from other villages, in addition to seeing its share of regional conflict and warfare.

"At the turn of the twentieth century there were about fifty people at Nicolai village. Travel...between there and Kenai was common, with some Russian people and others having moved into the Pt. Possession area over the years.... In addition to fishing, there was hunting and trapping along the coast and in the lake country back to the mountains.... Some of the place names of the area honor people of Nicolai village families, such as Shem Pete Lake and Diamond Kid Lake. The Nicolai family had traditionally trapped and hunted all across that part of the peninsula, and many old cabin sites are to be found on the lakes and rivers from Mystery Creek to Swanson River and north to Turnagain Arm.... The original village has almost all washed over the bank.... Grandma Doris Nicolai died in 1933, which to some meant the death of village life as it had been for generations.... After she died most of the people moved to Anchorage, but continued to live at Pt. Possession part of the year for fishing and hunting.... Today family members still live at Pt. Possession during the fishing season, and some stay on into the fall."

Feodoria Pennington gives a nice description of the annual round of activities at Point Possession village in the 1920s and 30s in McClanahan (1986:22–30).

Billy Pete: "We spent about twenty-five years there at

Cora Nicholai Kallander
Gus Nicholai
Grandma Doris Nicholai ‡(b. 1878)
Julius Kallander, Sr.
Billy Nicholai
Doris Nicholai Bismark
‡Steve Bismark (b. 1880)

FIGURE 226

Three generations from Point Possession village in the 1920s at the wedding of Julius Kallander, Sr., and Cora Nicholai Kallander. Grandma Doris Nicholai wears the white scarf. Also present are her sons Gus and Billy Nicholai and her daughter, Doris Nicholai Bismark, and her husband, Steve Bismark.

Shem Pete: "«Billy Nicholai's mother's husband—his name was Chickaloon—went there with a Susitna woman. This was at least 100 years ago. They say that he came from Chickaloon [14.31, in the Matanuska Valley], but I don't know. Too far back. They lived in the woods. Then they started to repopulate. The Kallanders were born there. Billy Nicholai and others used to stay there year round. That was their home. And Old Man Kallander.»" Billy Nicholai was chief of Point Possession in the 1940s. He died in 1952.

PHOTO COURTESY OF FEODORIA KALLANDER PENNINGTON

Point Station just commercial fishing. 1936 was my first year. My father was there since about 1910."

Bailey Theodore reported that his father, Theodore Vasily, used to spend summers at Point Possession fishing when Bailey was a boy. The family traveled between Knik and Point Possession in an old cannery scow powered by oars and a sail (Chandonnet 1985:66).

Sava Stephan: "I been to Point Possession lota times. Old timers, I think that's where they all come from, like Pedro Goozmer, him and his wife.... They came from there. It was a big city way back long time ago. That's where the groceries came from. And Nick McCord and his wife. Old Steve Bismark, that's where he was from. I brought them back to Point Possession in a boat.... Shem Pete fished at Point Possession with the Nicholai brothers.... [They were] related to Mrs. [Doris Nicholai Bismark] Nikanorga, Fred Bismark's mother. I took them back across from Point Possession to Tyonek. Took about two hours coming across Inlet. Cut across at Fire Island."

‡C. Mielke's pages have complete Point Possession village census information and various notes.

§16.32 Nuch'ishtunt • 'Protected from Wind Place'
site near mouth of Miller Creek, Vogel Lake outlet stream
This may be the village listed as Nukitun in the Wrangell notes of the 1830s, said to be "near Point Possession" (Arndt 1985). Note that this is also the Dena'ina name for 15.91, Point Woronzof.

This is probably near the mouth of Miller Creek, the stream that drains Vogel Lake, south of Point Possession, where Oscar Vogel used to fish. In Shem Pete's "Point Possession War Story" the Russians built a large house or fort here, where they held Dena'ina women they had kidnapped. The Point Possession Dena'ina drove the Russians out of their shelter by shooting burning **k'adatsayi** (black birch burl) onto it. As the Russians escaped from the burning building, the Indians killed them.

§16.33 Nuch'ishtuntnu • 'Protected from Wind Stream'
Miller Creek

§16.34 Nuch'ishtun Bena • 'Protected from Wind Lake'
Vogel Lake

16.22 Hnik'daghi'ut • 'Where Something Is Embedded'
Moose Point
Shem Pete and Peter Kalifornsky noted that long ago there were many Dena'ina sites on the north coast of the western Kenai Peninsula. There were many **tanik'edi** (fish dock) sites in this area.

§16.35 Quqegh Nik'eteleht • 'Fish Run up Through Place'
Seven Egg Creek, formerly "Libby Creek"
Name from Peter Kalifornsky. A site explored by de Laguna in 1932. She noted (1934:135): "There is a village site of five houses on the right bank of the stream, ¼ mile above the mouth. The name of the stream is Qoqani'ktalik (Theodore Sasha, Kenai). These houses are so well preserved that I doubt if they can be very old."

16.23 Yaghenen • 'Good Land'
Kenai Peninsula, western Kenai Peninsula
‡**Yaghenen,** an Å4 name on Table 12, is a significant early Dena'ina name on Cook Inlet, surely a founding place name. The regional name **Yaghenen** is derived from the name for the Swanson River. The Kenai Peninsula Dena'ina people are called **Yaghedna** 'Good [Land] People.' These names imply that this area was an early central base for the Kenai Peninsula Dena'ina. This

FIGURE 227

Julius Kallander, Sr., with Feodoria Kallander, Roy Kallander, and Cora Kallander at their fishtrap at **Hnik'daghi'ut** (16.22, Moose Point) in 1943.
PHOTO COURTESY OF FEODORIA KALLANDER PENNINGTON

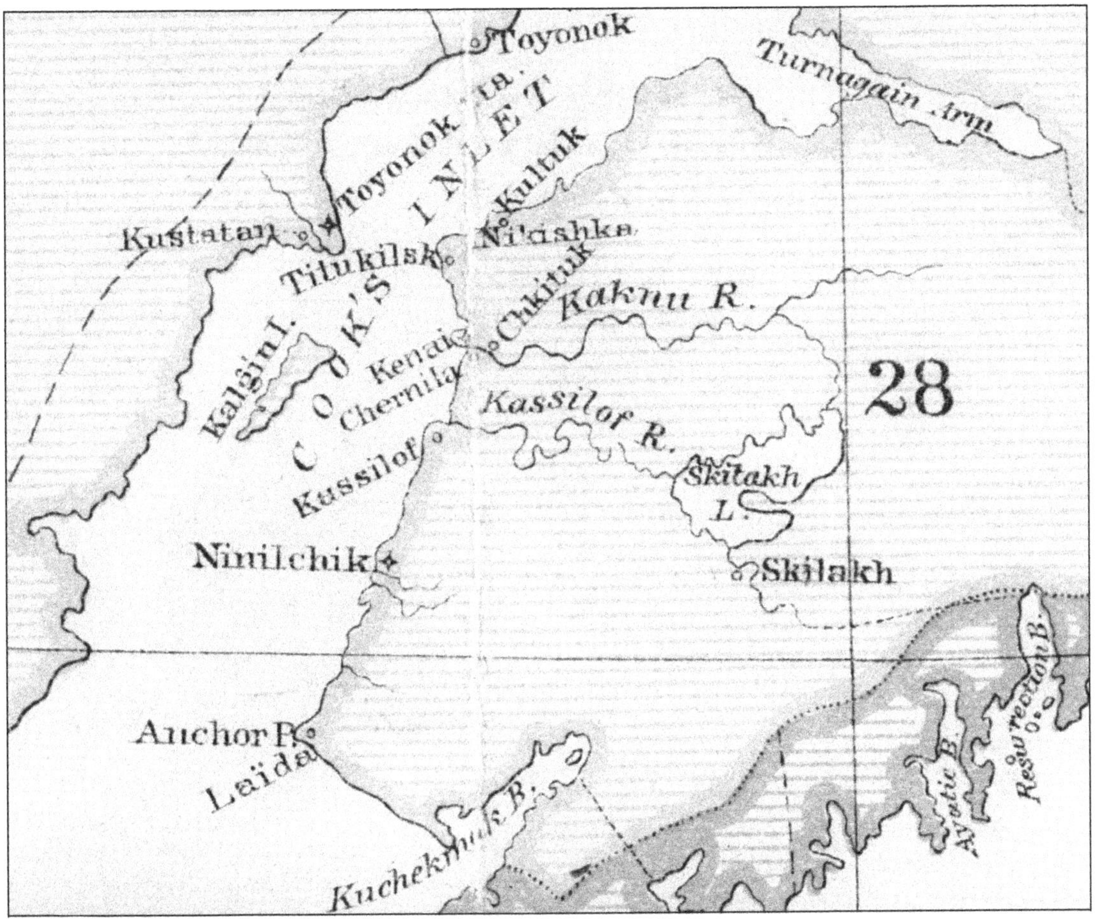

name is associated by speakers with the common greeting **yagheli** 'it is good,' and is translated as 'good land' (Kalifornsky 1991:310). However, in the place name, **yagheli** truncated to **yaghe** gives the word a language-internal obscurity.

The following are some early sources on game and Dena'ina hunting on the Kenai Peninsula and middle Cook Inlet. Ivan Petroff provided this discussion of Dena'ina bear hunting in Cook Inlet in the 1880s (Petroff 1884:57–58): "Bears both brown and black—the former of great size and ferocity; frequently from 10 to 12 feet in length, strongly suggestive of the grizzly—are killed in large numbers by the hunters every year....

"On the steep sides of the volcanic range of mountains on the west side of Cook's inlet, brown bears can be seen in herds of twenty or thirty. Their skins are not very valuable, and, owing to this fact and to the fierce disposition of the animals, they are not commonly hunted. All natives of Alaska respect them, and it is the universal custom of hunters to address a few complimentary remarks to the intended victims before attempting to kill them. Perhaps the skins of fully one-half of the brown bears killed throughout Alaska are retained by the natives for bedding and to hang before the entrances of houses in the place of doors. The smaller skins are tanned and cut up into straps and lines, and the natives of the interior

MAP 66

Detail from the 1884 Petroff map of Middle Cook Inlet.

Ivan Petroff (1842–1896) was born in St. Petersburg Russia and in 1861 came to America, where he fought in the Civil War for the U.S. Army (Sherwood 1965:57–69). A colorful character, Petroff was a journalist and translator of Russian, and he was the main researcher for the 1880 and 1890 Alaska censuses and for H. H. Bancroft's *History of Alaska* (1887). Petroff spent considerable time in Kenai in the 1870s and 1880s. Petroff's research on place names is reflected in this detail from the map from the 1880 census. This section of this map has fourteen non-English place names, most of which are documented Dena'ina place names. Also cf. Map 6, another detail from the 1884 Petroff map. ‡Postnikov and Falk (2015:453–456) have a thorough summary of Petroff's historical contributions. ‡Also see Jones, Fall, and Leggett (2013:53).

Unhsah Tahna'ina
The First Underwater People

by Fedosia Sacaloff

Feodosia Sacaloff of Kenai (1922–89), an expert speaker of the Kenai Dena'ina dialect, told this story in 1975. The Dena'ina gave the name ***tahdna*** *'underwater people' to the first people who arrived in the Inlet by ship. The name later came to be used to refer to the Russians. This story shows that the Dena'ina have maintained a historical story of the Cook party's arrival in Cook Inlet. The incident in which a dog is shot is strong evidence that the story refers to Cook's party. The story seems to blend Cook's encounter on the western shore, where the canoes first approached his ships, with his landing at Point Possession, where a dog was shot.*

FIGURE 228

Katherine Nicolie, Fedosia Sacaloff, and Peter Kalifornsky, on the beach at Kenai in August of 1979. Peter and Fedosia were siblings and outstanding speakers of the Kenai dialect of Dena'ina. Kalifornsky (1911–93) was the author of several books, including the award-winning collection of his writings, Kalifornsky 1991.
PHOTO BY PRISCILLA RUSSELL

Unhsahgheli shlup Qezdeghnenh tults'et.
The very first ship sailed into Kustatan [1.119].

Tahna'ina shlup tults'et da łuq'u hqilnit.
When the Underwater People's ship sailed in, everyone was afraid.

Ts'iłt'an quht'ana hyanq'u k'usht'a h'ilnigh ch'u shlup'a nuk'ughinik.
There was only one man who never was afraid, and he went out to the ship.

Baydalgi eł ts'iłq'u daqeyghiłtan.
They picked him up together with his boat.

Saldatinaq' qeynunk'ghilu.
They dressed him like a soldier.

Łuq'u niłk'uch't'a qyudiqghilu ch'u naqank'dal'un.
They filled his boat with all kinds of things, and he brought them back ashore.

Yethdi Tahna'ina hdghini.
And they were called the Underwater People.

Unhsahgheli Tahna'ina tughaznik yethdi tl'inqin ghuduhdi.
After the Underwater People first came, there were sewing needles.

Yeki ughasht'a qeyq'aynidulnen.
These they [Dena'ina] learned to use quickly.

Nuzhnich yethdi k'usht'a qeyq'aynidilnil.
But they could not figure out the scissors.

Tl'ił qyaninggezh ch'u qeył nusank'nalyu qeyiluq.
They strung a rope through them and hung them around their necks.

Qeył ghetnuyi niłk'uch' yethdi shughu nak'qizdlant'i.
At that time we also acquired different kinds of tools.

Izin k'u qwa qizdlan.
They also got guns.

Łik'a qeył chiłyuq.
They killed a dog [with a gun].

Ts'iłt'an quht'ana dich'anulchiłi ghuda yetnul'ani ghuda ya nitsaniyel.
One man, in order to see how the bullet comes out, put his head to the gun.

Yedałtetl'.
Someone fired.

Yetq'u quht'ana qeył chiłyuq.
And they killed the man with it [the gun].

utilize them for manufacturing sledge fastenings and the net-work bottoms of snow-shoes, because this leather does not stretch when exposed to moisture as moose- and deer-skins do."

Biologist Wilfred Osgood (1901:61–62) writing in 1900 noted: "According to reports the moose has but recently appeared in the Cook Inlet region; the older Indians say no moose were there when they were boys; and even within the memory of white men it has moved westward, now being known as far out on the Alaska Peninsula as Katmai.

"It is quite common in many places about Cook Inlet, but is hunted most successfully in the Knik district, and on the north shore of the Kenai Peninsula, from Kussilof and Fort Kenai to Point Possession at the north of Turnagain Arm. A few Indians hunt moose here practically all the year round, making a living by selling the meat in the mining camps of Hope and Sunrise. Several carcasses were brought in during our stay and the meat was quickly sold at 10 cents pound. On the northwest side of the inlet moose are less common than on the Kenai Peninsula, but occur sparingly.

"Caribou are rare on the Kenai Peninsula. I saw a pair of weather beaten antlers said to have been picked up on the peninsula side near the mouth of Turnagain Arm and heard an unsatisfactory report of a large buck but beyond this could obtain no evidence of the animal's occurrence in this region near the coast.... Caribou in the southern and western part of the Kenai Peninsula... are 'already very scarce and will doubtless be soon exterminated.' ... They are more or less common a short distance in the interior and are often killed near the Sushitna River, whence their skins are brought to the coast to be traded.

"Dall sheep were formerly common in the mountains on both sides of Turnagain Arm, but since active mining began there they have retreated to the interior of the peninsula, where they still occur in large numbers. They are also common in the mountains near the Knik river, from which place several heads were brought in by Indians while we were at Sunrise City. According to apparently a reliable report, these sheep in the interior of the Kenai Peninsula gather into very large flocks in fall, as many as three hundred individuals having been seen together at one time."

Annabel (1997d:113): "Early in autumn of 1897 a forest fire wiped the caribou out to the ultimate animal. No survivors—the whole species destroyed, rushed into oblivion. I mean, there is no reliable record that anybody, after the smoke lifted, ever saw another caribou on the Kenai Peninsula.

"According to the Indians, the tragedy took place in six days. The fire, they say, started on the coast of Turnagain Arm and, driven by high winds, went greyhounding viciously south until rainfall stopped it near Tustamena Lake."

16.24 Yaghetnu • 'Good River'
Swanson River

The following eleven names (16.34–45) in the upper Swanson River drainage are selected from Kalifornsky (1991:330–35 and 352–353). In the 1970s and 80s Peter Kalifornsky and James Kari were documenting Kenai Peninsula Dena'ina place names. The most complete published source on these names is Kalifornsky (1991:338–353) which lists over two hundred fifty Dena'ina place names between Portage and English Bay. Fred Mammaloff of Kenai has recently contributed several more names. Kalifornsky had a continuous sequence of names to the head of Swanson River, but he knew only a few major names in the Point Possession area. Shem Pete and Mike Theodore reported most of the minor place names there. ‡Several sites on Swanson River are noted in Rabich (1977:203–06).

§16.36 Sus Q'anch'edełt • 'Where We Walk Through Portage'
trail from Wild Lake to Point Possession
This was the most northerly name in the Swanson River drainage contributed by Peter Kalifornsky.

§16.37 Sus Q'anch'edeł Bena • 'Where We Walk Through Portage'
Wild Lake

§16.38 K'jech'a Dałtuni • 'Kidney That Lies'
Swanson Lake

§16.39 Niłq'a Tighitun Bena • 'Trails Intersect Lake'
Gene Lake
Kalifornsky 1991:331: "«And up there in the years 1920 to 1925 my father trapped at **Niłq'a Tighitun Bena.** From 1929 to 1936 I trapped there.»"

§16.40 Gidara Q'dalchini • 'The One That Is Made Like a Guitar'
Pepper Lake

§16.41 Unhtsahdi • 'The First One'
Eider Lake

§16.42 Uch'eh Dałtuni • 'The One That Lies Obscured'
Olsjold Lake

§16.43 Qeyach'en Dałtun • 'It Lies on Other Side'
Wonder Lake

§16.44 Benkda Ch'en Dałtuni • 'The One That Lies on the Side of Benkda'
Wilderness Lake

§16.45 Q'es Dileni • 'The One That Flows to Outlet'
Wren Lake

§16.46 Benkda Q'estsiq' • 'No-good Lake Outlet Stream'
King Lake outlet stream

§16.47 Benkda • 'No-good Lake'
King Lake
Kalifornsky (1991:331): "«**Benkda** 'no good lake' is big and doesn't freeze up well, so it's dangerous, so they call it 'bad' or 'dangerous' lake in Dena'ina.»"

2003 Bibliography

Afable, Patricia O. and Madison S. Beeler. 1996. Place-Names. In *Handbook of North American Indians, vol. 17. Languages.* Ed. by Ives Goddard. pp. 185–199. Washington: The Smithsonian Institution.

Alaska Road & Recreation Maps. 1995. Big Lake and Point MacKenzie, Road & Recreation Map. Anchorage: Todd Communications.
———. 1995. Parks Highway Road & Recreation Map. Anchorage: Todd Communications.
———. 1997. Matanuska Valley Road & Recreation Map. Anchorage: Todd Communications.
———. 2000. Anchorage & Vicinity Road & Recreation Map. Anchorage: Todd Communications.

Alexan, Nickafor. 1965a. How Tyonek People Use to Eat. *Alaska Sportsman* 31(1):38–39.
———. 1965b. Stories About How to Raise Children. *Alaska Sportsman* 31(4):13–14.
———. 1981. *The Last Indian War in Tyonek and Other History.* Kenai: Kenai Peninsula Borough School District.
———. n.d. Nickafor Alexan, Photographs and Writings; 1938, ca 1957. Typescript on file in the archives of the Library of the University of Alaska, Anchorage.

Alaska Engineering Commission. 1916. *Reports of the Alaska Engineering Commission for the Period from March 12, 1914 to December 31, 1915.* Washington: Government Printing Office.

Alaska Native Language Center. 1979. *Talking Alaska* (videotape). No. 6, Dena'ina.

Alaska Weekly. 1926. Geological Survey Party Come South. October 8, 1926. S. R. Capps Collection, Alaska and Polar Regions Department, Rasmuson Library, University of Alaska, Fairbanks.

Allen, Henry T. 1887. *Report of* an *Expedition to the Copper, Tanana, and Koyukuk Rivers in the Territory of Alaska in the Year 1885.* Washington: U.S. Government Printing Office.

Alpha, Tau Rho, Janis S. Detterman, and James M. Morley. 1988. *Atlas of Oblique Maps.* U.S. Geological Survey Miscellaneous Investigations. Series I–1799.

Anchorage Daily Times. 1926. Geologists Map Skwentna Region; Cover Big Area. September 18, 1926. S. R. Capps Collection, Alaska and Polar Regions Department, Rasmuson Library, University of Alaska, Fairbanks.

Anderson, William. 1778. Vocabulary of "Sandwich Sound." Public Records Office, British Admiralty ms. 55/113, folios 59v–60v. Clerk's copy of Cook's journal.

Annabel, Russell. 1938a. *Tales of a Big Game Guide.* New York: The Derrydale Press
———. 1938b. The Red Wolfer. *National Sportsman* 9.
———. 1939a. A Dog Named Dan. *Hunting and Fishing Magazine.* March.
———. 1939b. Mishka's Beads. *Field and Stream.* October 1939.
———. 1948. *Hunting and Fishing in Alaska.* New York: Alred A. Knopf.
———. 1953a. *Alaskan Tales.* New York: A. S. Barnes and Co.
———. 1953b. Letter to Lurton Blasingame of *Sports Afield.* 4 pp.
———. 1971. Wacky Bandits of the Wilderness. *Sports Afield.*
———. 1987. *Alaskan Days, Mexican Nights.* Clinton New Jersey: The Amwell Press.
———. 1997a. *Alaskan Adventures: The Early Years.* Long Beach: Safari Press Inc.
———. 1997b. *Adventure is My Business, 1951–55.* Long Beach: Safari Press Inc.
———. 1997c. *Adventure is in My Blood, 1957–64.* Long Beach: Safari Press Inc.
———. 1997d. *The High Road to Adventure, 1964–70.* Long Beach: Safari Press Inc.
———. 1997e. *The Way We Were, 1970–79.* Long Beach: Safari Press Inc.

Arndt, Katherine. 1985. Translation of F. Wrangell n.d. Two manuscript maps of Russian America with notes and explanations. Shur Collection (reel 7, item 63), Alaska and Polar Regions Department, University of Alaska, Fairbanks. Original in Arkhiv Geograficheskogo, R. 99, d. 122, Leningrad.

Bacon, Glenn. 1983. (ed.) *Susitna River Basin Study, Cultural Resource Assessment of Willow-Talkeetna-Beluga Areas.* Anchorage: U.S. Department of Agriculture, Soil Conservation Service.

Bagg, John S. 1900. A Trip Up the Chicaloon. In *Compilation of Narratives of the Exploration of* Alaska, pp. 682–84. Washington: U.S. Government Printing Office.

Baker, Marcus. 1906. *Geographic Dictionary of Alaska* (2nd ed.) U.S. Geological Survey Bulletin 299. Washington: U.S. Government Printing Office.

Bancroft, Hubert Howe. 1886. *The History of Alaska, 1730–1885.* A. L. Bancroft.
———. 1959. [1886] *The History of Alaska, 1730–1885.* New York: Antiquarian Press.

Barry, Mary J. 1973. *A History of Mining on the Kenai Peninsula.* Anchorage: Alaska Northwest Publishing Co.
———. 2000. *Jack and Nellie Brown: Pioneer Settlers of Anchorage Alaska, A Pictorial History.* Anchorage. Privately Published.

Bauer, Mary Craft. 1987. *The Glenn Highway, the Story of its Past, a Guide to its Present.* Sutton: Brentwood Press.

Bayou, Katherine. 1946. First up the Susitna. *Alaska Sportsman* 12(11):10–13, 40–42.

Beach, William N. 1931. *In the Shadow of Mt. McKinley.* New York: The Derrydale Press.

Bean, Tarlton H. 1887. The Fishery Resources and Fishing Grounds of Alaska. In *The Fisheries and Fishery Industries of the United States.* Ed. by G. B. Goode. Sec. III. pp. 81–116. Washington: Government Printing Office.

Beard, D. C. 1914 [1972]. *Shelters, Shacks, and Shanties.* New York: Charles Scribner's Sons.

Begét, J. E., R. D. Reger, D. Pinney, T. Gillispie, and K. Campbell. 1991. Correlation of the Holocene Jarvis Creek, Tangle Lakes, Cantwell, and Hayes Tephras in Southcentral and Central Alaska. *Quaternary Research* 35: 174–189.

Begét, J. E. 1993. Personal Communication to Greg Dixon.

Bergsland, Knut. 1959. Aleut Dialects of Atka and Attu. *Transactions of the American Philosophical Society,* n.s. 49.
———. 1994. *Aleut Dictionary.* Fairbanks: Alaska Native Language Center.

Brink, Frank and Jo Brink. 1988. Tubughna: The Beach People. Filmed and narrated by Frank and Jo Brink. Tyonek Film Project Supervisor: Emil McCord Sr. Anchorage: The CIRI Foundation.

Brooks, Alfred H. 1900 A *Reconnaissance in the Tanana and White River Basins,* Alaska, *in 1898.* U.S. Geological Survey Annual Report No. 20:441–469.
———. 1911. *The Mount McKinley Region, Alaska.* U.S. Geological Survey Professional Paper 70. Washington: U.S. Government Printing Office.
———. 1953. *Blazing Alaska's Trails.* College: University of Alaska and Arctic Institute of North America.

Browne, Belmore. 1956 [1913]. *The Conquest of Mount McKinley.* Cambridge, Mass: Houghton Mifflin Company.

Buck, Mildred and James Kari. 1975. *Ahtna Noun Dictionary.* Fairbanks: Alaska Native Language Center.

Bureau of Soils. 1914. Soil Map. Alaska, Cook Inlet-Susitna Region. U.S. Geological Survey. Washington: U.S. Government Printing Office.

Burkett, Eric. 2001. Katie Wade, Clan Grandmother. *Anchorage Daily News,* Aug. 12, 2001. D–6.

Capps, Stephen R. 1913. *The Yentna District, Alaska.* U.S. Geological Survey, Bulletin 534. Washington: U.S. Government Printing Office.
———. 1915. *The Willow Creek District, Alaska.* U.S. Geological Survey, Bulletin 607. Washington: U.S. Government Printing Office.
———. 1929a. *The Skwentna Region.* U.S. Geological Survey, Bulletin 797–B. Washington: U.S. Government Printing Office.
———. 1929b. *The Mount Spurr Region, Alaska.* Washington: U.S. Geological Survey Bulletin #810–C. Washington: U.S. Government Printing Office.
———.1935. *The Southern Alaska Range.* U.S. Geological Survey, Bulletin 862. Washington: U.S. Government Printing Office.
———. 1940. *Geology of the Alaska Railroad Region.* Washington: 1940, Government Printing Office. U.S. Geological Survey Bulletin 907. 201 pp.
———. n.d. Stephen R. Capps Collection. Alaska and Polar Regions Dept., UAF.

Carberry, Michael E. 1979. *Patterns of the Past: An Inventory of Anchorage's Heritage Resources.* Anchorage: The Municipality of Anchorage.

Carlson, Phyllis D. 1972. Chief Simeon Chickalusion, A Wise Old Chief. *The Great Lander,* November 1, 1972. Alaska Press Women Series.

Castner, Joseph C. 1899. Report of Lieut. J. C. Castner, Fourth U.S. Infantry. In *Reports of Explorations in the Territory of Alaska.* Ed. by E. F. Glenn and W. R. Abercrombie. U.S. Adjutant General's Office, Military Information Division, Publication 25. War Department Document 102. pp. 189–267. Washington: U.S. Government Printing Office.
———. 1984. Lieutenant Castner's Alaskan Exploration, 1898. *Alaska Historical Commission Studies in History No. 125.* Lyman L. Woodman, ed. Anchorage: Cook Inlet Historical Society.

Chandonnet, Ann. 1979. *The Once and Future Village of Iklu-at-Eklutna.* Chicago: Adams Press.
———. 1985. *On the Trail of Eklutna.* Anchorage: User Friendly Press.
———. 1989. C*hief Stephen's Parky, One Year in the Life of an Athapascan Girl.* Billings: Council for Indian Education.

Chickalusion, Maxim. 1982. *Qezdeghnen Ggagga, The Kustatan Bear Story.* Fairbanks: Alaska Native Language Center.

Chickalusion, Maxim and Nellie Chickalusion. 1979. *Tubughna Elnena, The Tyonek People's Country.* Fairbanks: Alaska Native Language Center.

Cole, Terrence. 1979. The History and Use of the Upper Susitna River, Indian River to the Headwaters. Ms. Anchorage: Alaska Department of Natural Resources.
——— 1983. Historical Survey of the Talkeetna-Susitna River Drainages. In *Susitna River Basin Study,* Glenn Bacon, ed., pp. 72–117. Anchorage: U.S. Department of Agriculture, Soil Conservation Service.

Cole, Vickie et al. 1985. *Knik, Matanuska, Susitna: a Visual History of the Valleys.* Sutton: Matanuska-Susitna Borough.

Collins, Raymond. 1985. Place Names in the Upper Kuskokwim. Appendix 1 in Stokes 1985, pp. 320–372.
———. 2004. *Dichina Nek' Hwt'ana, a History of the People of the Upper Kuskokwim who Live in Nikolai and Telida Alaska.* Anchorage: National Park Service.
——— and Betty Petruska. 1979. *Dinak'i (Our Words), Upper Kuskokwim Junior Dictionary.* Anchorage: National Bilingual Materials Development Center.

Cook, Frederick A. 1904. Round Mount McKinley. *Bulletin of the American Geographical Society* 6:321–327.
———. 1907. Miner's Map of the Mt. McKinley Region, Alaska. In *To the Top of the Continent* by F. A. Cook. Ninetieth Anniversary Edition. Hurleyville New York: Alpen Books (1994). P. 96 (1/5).
———. 1908. *To the Top of the Continent.* New York: Doubleday, Page, and Company.

Cook Inlet Historic Sites Project. 1975. Cook Inlet Region Inventory of Native Historic Sites and Cemeteries. Anchorage: Cook Inlet Native Association.

Cook Inlet Region, Inc. [CIRI] 1989. "Shem Pete Receives First Shareholder of the Year Award." Cook Inlet Region, Inc. Newsletter. June 1989. Vol.15, No. 6, page 6. Anchorage.

CIRI Foundation. 1990. Shem Pete Memorial Potlatch. Videotape.

Cook, James. *A Voyage to the Pacific* Ocean. 1784. Vol. II, pp. 375–376. London: Lords Commissioners of the Admiralty, G. Nichol and T. Cadell.
———. 1967. [1776–8] *The Journals of Captain James Cook on His Voyages of Discovery.* Vol. III: The Voyage of the Resolution and Discovery, 1776–1780. J. C. Beaglehole, ed. Cambridge: University Press.

Cooperative Parks Studies Unit. 1980. Notes from 1980 field survey in Cook Inlet Region. Alaska and Polar Regions Department, University of Alaska, Fairbanks.

Dall, William H. 1870. *Alaska and Its Resources.* Boston: Lee and Shepard.

Daugherty, Paula M. and Becky M. Saleeby. 1998. Elmendorf Air Force Base Homestead Study. Anchorage: National Park Service, Alaska Support Office.

Davidson, Charles E. 1914. Townships No. 16 and 17, West of Seward. [Knik area cadastral maps on file at Matanuska-Sutistna Borough Office, Palmer.]

Davidson, George. 1869. Coast Pilot of Alaska, first part, from southern boundary to Cook's Inlet. U.S. Coast and Geodetic Survey.

Davis, Jeff. 2002. *Return to Toonaklut—The Russell Annabel Story.* Long Beach: The Safari Press.

Davis, Nancy Yaw. 1965. *A Tanaina Indian Village.* Unpublished M.A. thesis, University of Chicago.
———. 1994. Audiotaped Interview with Billy Pete. Conducted in Anchorage, AK, August 19, 1994.

Davis, Nancy Yaw and the Dena'ina Team. 1994. Draft Report: Ethnohistoric Land Use Patterns: Elmendorf Air Force Base (Knik Arm) Area, Alaska. Report prepared for the National Park Service and Elmendorf Air Force Base. Anchorage.

Davydov, Gavriil I. 1977 [1810–1812] *Two Voyages to Russian America, 1802–1807.* Translated by Colin Bearne. R. Pierce, ed. Kingston, Ontario: The Limestone Press.

Deaphon, Miska. 1980. *Nikolai Hwch'izoya' [Stories from Nikolai].* Anchorage: National Bilingual Materials Development Center.

Deaphon, Miska and Bobby Esai. 1981. *Beliefs From Nikolai.* Anchorage: National Bilingual Materials Development Center.

Delorme Mapping.1992. *Alaska Atlas and Gazetteer.* 1st edition. Freeport Maine: Delorme Mapping.

Dessaur, Peter F. and David W. Harvey. 1980. An Historical Resource Study of the Valdez Creek Mining District, Alaska–1977. Anchorage District Office. Bureau of Land Management.

Dickey, William A. 1897. The Sushitna River, Alaska. *National Geographic Magazine* 8:322–327.
———. 1897b. Discoveries in Alaska. *The Sun,* New York, Sun. January 24. Reprinted in Washburn 1951:81–88.

Dixon, Ann. 1994. *The Sleeping Lady.* Anchorage: Alaska Northwest Books.

Dixon, E. James 1985. Cultural Chronology of Central Interior Alaska. *Arctic Anthropology* 22(1):47–66.

Dixon, E. J. Jr., G. S. Smith, W. A. Andrefsky, B. M. Saleeby, and C. J. Utermohle. 1985. Draft Report. *Susitna Hydroelectric Project, Cultural Resources Investigations 1979–1985.* Anchorage: Alaska Power Authority.

Dixon, R. Greg. 1990. Archaeological Investigation of Cook Inlet Aquaculture Association's Proposed Hewitt Creek Weir Camp. Ms. Anchorage: Alaska Division of Parks and Outdoor Recreation, Office of History and Archaeology.
———. 1991. Tiq'atl'ena Betnu (Hewitt Lake) Archaeological Research. Proposal submitted in partial fulfillment of requirements for the course Archaeological Method and Theory. Ms. Department of Anthropology. University of Alaska Fairbanks.
———. 1992. Analysis of Tiq'atl'ena Betnu Collections. Submitted in partial fulfillment of requirements for the course Archaeology Proseminar. Ms. Department of Anthropology. University of Alaska Fairbanks.
———. 1996. Tiq'atl'ena Bena (Hewitt Lake) Archaeological Research Project, 1992 Investigations. In *Adventures Through Time: Readings in the Anthropology of Cook Inlet, Alaska,* Nancy Yaw Davis and William E. Davis, editors, pp. 95–107. Anchorage: Cook Inlet Historical Society.

Doroshin, Petr P. n.d. Doroshin, a Russian Engineer, Prospected for Gold in Russian America, 1848–1858. Translated by an unknown editor from "Iz zapisok vedennykh v Russkoi Amerike" *Gornyi Zhurnal* 3(iii):365–400, (1866). Manuscript in Consortium Library, University of Alaska, Anchorage.

Dumond, Don E. and Robert Mace. 1968. An Archaeological Survey Along Knik Arm. *Anthropological Papers of the University of Alaska* 14(1):1–21.

Eldridge, George Homans. 1900. *A Reconnaissance in the Sushitna Basin and Adjacent Territory in 1898.* U.S. Geological Survey, 20th Annual Report, Part 7:1–29. Washington: U.S. Government Printing Office.

Fall, James A. 1978–79. Unpublished fieldnotes on the Upper Inlet Tanaina. Typescript.
———. 1981. Patterns of Upper Inlet Tanaina Leadership, 1741–1918. Ph.D. dissertation, University of Wisconsin Madison.
———. 1987. The Upper Inlet Tanaina: Patterns of Leadership Among an Alaskan Athabaskan People, 1741–1918. *Anthropological Papers of the University of Alaska,* vol. 21.
———. 1990. Upper Cook Inlet Dena'ina Oral Traditions: An Introduction to the Narrative Art of an Alaskan Athabaskan People. Report to the Alaska Humanities Forum.

———. 1997. A Review of Ethnographic Information Concerning Two Small Hills at Eklutna, Alaska. A report prepared for the Alaska Railroad Corporation under a reimburseable services agreement. Division of Subsistence, Alaska Department of Fish and Game, Anchorage.

Fall, James A., Nancy Yaw Davis, and the Denaina Team. 2003. An Overview of Dena'ina Athabascan Uses of Sites on and near Elmendorf Air Force Base, Alaska. Report prepared for the U.S. Army Corps of Engineers.

Fall, James A., Dan J. Foster, and Ronald T. Stanek. 1984 *The Use of Fish and Wildlife Resources in Tyonek, Alaska.* Alaska Department of Fish and Game, Division of Subsistence. Technical Paper No. 105. Juneau.

Fall, James A. and T. Weber Greiser. 1986. Interview with Shem and Billy Pete. Susitna hydroelectric Project, Phase II Final Report. Historical Research Associates, Prepared for Alaska Power Authority.

Fall, James A. and James Kari. 1987. Dena'ina Place Names in the Upper Cook Inlet Region. *Alaska Fish & Game* 19(6):19–22.

Fattig, Paul. 1985. Native Storyteller Lives His Legends. *Anchorage Times,* Oct. 19.

Gillette, Helen. 1978. Simeon Chickalusion. *Anchorage Times,* June 11, 1978, B–4.

Glenn, Edward F. 1900a. A Trip to the Tanana Region, 1898. In *Compilation of Narratives of the Exploration of Alaska, pp.* 629–647. Washington: U.S. Government Printing Office.

———. 1900b. Explorations in and about Cook Inlet, 1899. In *Compilation of Narratives of the Exploration of Alaska,* pp. 713–724. Washington: U.S. Government Printing Office.

Glenn, Edward F. and William R. Abercrombie. 1899. *Reports of Explorations in the Territory of Alaska.* U.S. Adjutant General's Office, Military Information Division, Publication 25. War Department Document 102. Washington: U.S. Government Printing Office.

Governor's Commission on Tolerance. 2001. *Ten Ways to a More Tolerant Alaska That Celebrates Our Diversity of People and Cultures.* Juneau: State of Alaska.

Grinev, A. V. 1997. The Forgotten Expedition of Dmitrii Tarkhonov on the Copper River. *Alaska History* 12:1–16.

Griffin, Kristen. 1990. *An Overview and Assessment of Archeological Resources, Denali National Park and Preserve, Alaska.* Anchorage: National Park Service.

Griffiths, C. E. 1900. From Knik Station to Eagle City. In *Compilation of Narratives of the Exploration of Alaska.* Washington: U.S. Government Printing Office. pp. 724–733.

Gudgel-Holmes, Dianne. 1990a. *Native Place Names of the Kantishna Drainage, Alaska.* Anchorage: National Park Service.

———. 1990b. Language, Territory and Seasonal Round of the Athabaskans of Denali National Park and Preserve. In Griffin, K. 1990, pp. 271–306.

Hadleigh-West, Frederick 1981. *The Archaeology of Beringia.* New York: Columbia University Press.

———. (editor). 1996. *American Beginnings: the Prehistory and Palaeoecology of Beringia.* Chicago:University of Chicago Press.

Hall, Ward. 1916. Report of the Resident Engineer. Alaska Engineering Commission.

Harrington, John P. 1916. Ethnogeography of the Tewa Indians. *29th Annual Report of the Bureau of American Ethnology.* pp. 29–618. Washington.

Hays, Lydia L. 1989. Shem Pete. Shem Pete Memorial Potlatch Program. Oct. 7, 1989.

Herning, Orvel G. n. d. The Diaries of O. G. Herning, 1898–1946. Four Volumes. Manuscript typed from original materials by Louise Potter. Anchorage: Cook Inlet Historical Society.

———. 1906. Herning's Map of Central Alaska. Unpublished. [reproduced in Irwin 1968 and Bauer 1987].

Herron, Joseph S. 1901. *Explorations in Alaska, 1899.* U.S. Adjutant General's Office, Military Information Division, Publication 31. Washington: U.S. Government Printing Office.

Hickok, David M. 1968. Land and Ethnic Relationships. In *Alaska Natives and the Land,* pp. 85–285. Anchorage: Federal Field Committee for Development Planning in Alaska.

Hodge, Frederick Webb. 1907. *Handbook of North American Indians North of Mexico.* Bureau of American Ethnology Bulletin 30. Washington: U.S. Government Printing Office.

Holmberg, Henrik Johan. 1985. *Holmberg's ethnographic sketches.* Edited by Marvin W. Falk, translated by Fritz Jaensch. Fairbanks: The University of Alaska Press.

Hosley, Edward Howard. 1966a. Factionalism and Acculturation in an Alaskan Athapaskan Community. Unpublished Ph.D. dissertation, University of California at Los Angeles.

——— 1966b. Kolchan: Athapaskans of the Upper Kuskokwim. Ms. UAF Rasmussen Library.

———. 1981. Kolchan. In *Handbook of North American Indians, Volume 6: Subarctic,* June Helm, ed., pp. 618–22. Washington: The Smithsonian Institution.

Hubback, Theodore R. 1929. *To Far Western Alaska For Big Game.* New York: Charles Scribner's Sons.

Hulen, David. 1989a. A Region Loses a Rare Storyteller: Shem Pete Passes on History, Tradition. *Anchorage Daily News,* Vol. XLIV, No. 185, pages A1, A8. July 4, 1989.

———. 1989b. Death of a Storyteller: Goodbye Shem Pete. *We Alaskans. Anchorage Daily News.* XXX

Hulsing, Harry. 1977. The Breakout of Alaska's Lake George. U.S. Geological Survey, Stock no. 024-001-00310-4. Washington, D.C.: U.S. Government Printing Office.

Hunn, Eugene. 1994. Place-Names, Population Density, and the Magic Number 500. *Current Anthropology* 35(1):81–85.

Imus Geographics. 2000. Map of Chugach State Park, Chugach Mountains, Alaska. Eugene, Oregon.

Indian Claims Commission. 1951–71 Docket No. 37, Natives of Palmer v. The United States of America. Documents on file at Eklutna Inc., Anchorage.

Irving, William. 1957. An Archaeological Survey of the Susitna Valley. *Anthropological Papers of the University of Alaska* 6(1):37–52.

Irwin, Don L. 1968. *The Colorful Matanuska Valley.* Palmer. Privately published.

Jacobsen, Johan Adrian. 1977 [1884]. *Alaskan Voyage, 1881–1883.* Translated by Ema Gunther. Chicago and London: The University of Chicago Press.

Jacobsson, Mildred. 1976. *Legend of Sleeping Lady.* Anchorage: Adult Literacy Laboratory.

Jetté, Jules. 1910. On the Geographical Names of the Ten'a. Spokane: Gonzaga University, Ms. file 14, drawer 13.

Johnson, Will A. 1948. *Untrodden Trails.* New York: Exposition Press.

Johnston, J. N. and O. G. Herning. 1899. Johnston and Herning's Map of Sushitna, Knik, and Matanuska Rivers, Knik and Turnagain Arms. Copy in University of Alaska, Alaska and Polar Regions Department, Rasmuson Library, University of Alaska, Fairbanks. (Reprinted in Potter 1967).

Johnston, Thomas F. 1979. Music of the Tanaina Indians of South-Central Alaska. *Tennessee Folklore Society Bulletin* 45(1):12–16.

Kalifornsky, Peter. 1975. Qunshi Uqu Ch'el'ani, Beluga Hunting. In *Dena'ina T'qit'ach', The Way the Tanainas Are,* James Kari, ed., pp. 16–18. Fairbanks: Alaska Native Language Center.

———. 1982 [1977]. *Kahtnuhtana Qenaga, The Kenai People's Language.* Second edition. Fairbanks: Alaska Native Language Center.

———. 1984. *K'tl'eghi Sukdu, Remaining Stories.* Fairbanks: Alaska Native Language Center.

———. 1991. *A Dena'ina Legacy, K'tl'egh'i Sukdu: The Collected Writings of Peter Kalifornsky.* Fairbanks: Alaska Native Language Center.

Kari, James. 1975a. A classification of Tanaina dialects. *Anthropological Papers of the University of Alaska* 17(2):49–53.

———. 1975b. (ed.) *Dena'ina T'qit'ach': The Way the Tanainas Are.* Fairbanks: Alaska Native Language Center.

———. 1977a. Linguistic diffusion between Ahtna and Tanaina. *International Journal of American Linguistics* 43:274–289.

———. 1977b. *Dena'na Noun Dictionary.* Fairbanks: Alaska Native Language Center.

———. 1978a. *K'qizaghetnu Ht'ana, The Stony River People.* Anchorage: National Bilingual Materials Development Center.

———. 1978b. *The Heritage of Eklutna: Mike Alex, 1908–1977.* Eklutna: Eklutna-Alex Associates.

———. 1980. (ed.) *Qudi Heyi Nitch'diluyi Sukdu'a, This Year's Collected Stories (Tyonek and Iliamna Lake).* Anchorage: National Bilingual Materials Development Center.

———. 1981. Native names celebrate the mountain's grandeur. *Now in the North,* February.

———. 1982a. Dena'ina Place Names in the Talkeetna Study Area. In *Cultural Resource Assessment: Part One: Talkeetna-Lower Susitna River Basin.* Glenn Bacon, ed., pp. 1665. Report to the U.S. Department of Agriculture, Soil Conservation Service. Fairbanks: Alaskarctic. (Reprinted in Bacon 1983.).

———. 1982b. Dena'ina Place Names in and Adjacent to the Beluga Study Area. In *Cultural Resource Assessment: Part Two: Beluga Study Area.* Glenn Bacon, ed., pp. 2666. Report to the U.S. Department of Agriculture, Soil Conservation Service. Fairbanks: Alaskarctic. (Reprinted in Bacon 1983.).

———. 1983. *Ahtna Place Names Lists.* Fairbanks: Copper River Native Association and Alaska Native Language Center.

———. 1985. Can Native Place Names be Preserved? *Alaska Native News.* July. pp. 8–14, 27.

———. 1986a (ed.) *Tatl'ahwtaenn Nenn', The Headwaters People's Country.* Fairbanks: Alaska Native Language Center.

———. 1986b. The Tenada-Denali-McKinley Controversy. *Names* 34(2):241–244.

———. 1988. Some Linguistic Insights into Dena'ina Prehistory. In *The Late Prehistoric Development of Alaska's Native People,* ed. by R. D. Shaw, R. K. Harritt, and D. E. Dumond. Aurora, Alaska Anthropological Association Monograph Series 4, pp. 319–39.

———. 1989. Some Principles of Alaskan Athabaskan Toponymic Knowledge. In *General and Amerindian Ethnolinguistics, In Remembrance of Stanley Newman,* ed. by M. R. Key and H. Hoenigswald. Berlin: Walter de Gruyter, pp. 129–151.

———. 1990. *Ahtna Athabaskan Dictionary.* ANLC.

———. 1994. *Dictionary of Dena'ina Athabaskan, Vol. 1: Topical Vocabulary.* ANLC. 333 pp. (draft).

———. 1996a. Names as Signs: the Distribution of 'Stream' and 'Mountain' in Alaskan Athabaskan. In *Athabaskan Language Studies, Essays in Honor of Robert W. Young,* ed. by E. Jelinek, S. Midgette, K. Rice, and L. Saxon. Albuquerque: The University of New Mexico Press. pp. 443–475.

———. 1996b. Linguistic Traces of Dena'ina Strategy at the Archaic Periphery. In *Adventures Through Time: Readings in the Anthropology of Cook Inlet.* Edited by Davis, N. Y. and W. Davis. Anchorage: the Cook Inlet Historical Society. pp. 49–64.

———. 1996c. A Preliminary View of Hydronymic Districts in Northern Athabaskan Prehistory. *Names* 44:253–271.

———. 1999. Draft Final Report: Native Place Names Mapping in Denali National Park and Preserve. Anchorage: National Park Service.

———. 2002. Ahtna Place Names Lists. Draft ms.

Kari, James and James A. Fall. 1987. *Shem Pete's Alaska, the Territory of the Upper Cook Inlet Dena'ina.* Fairbanks: Alaska Native Language Center.

———. 1998. Index of Upper Inlet Dena'ina Recordings. Ms.

Kari, James and Priscilla Russell Kari. 1982. *Dena'ina Elnena, Tanaina Country.* Fairbanks: Alaska Native Language Center.

Kari, Priscilla Russell. 1975–85. Upper Inlet Dena'na field-notes.
———. 1991. *Dena'ina K'et'una, Tanaina Plantlore, An Ethnobotany of the Dena'ina Indians of Southcentral Alaska.* Third Edition. Fairbanks: Alaska Native Language Center with Alaska Natural History Association and National Park Service.

Kelly, Luther S. 1900. Subreport of Luther S. Kelly. In *Compilation of Narratives of the Exploration of Alaska,* pp. 684–686. Washington: U.S. Government Printing Office.

Ketz, James A. 1983. *Paxson Lake, Two Nineteenth Century Ahtna Sites in the Copper River Basin, Alaska.* Occasional Paper No. 33. Fairbanks: Cooperative Park Studies Unit.

Khlebnikov, Kiril T. 1994. *Notes on Russian America.* Edited by Richard Pierce. Kingston, Ontario: Limestone Press.

Koman, John. 1989. *Alaska's Tunragain Arm and the Road to Hope.* Anchorage: Ram Publications.

Krauss, Michael E. 1973. Na-Dene. *Current Trends in Linguistics,* vol 6: 903–978
———. 1982. *Native Peoples and Languages of Alaska* (map). Fairbanks: Alaska Native Language Center. Kroll Map Co. 1945. Alaska [map]. Seattle: Kroll Map Co.
———. 1995. Alaska [map]. Seattle: Kroll Map Co.

de Laguna, Frederica. 1934. *The Archaeology of Cook Inlet, Alaska.* Philadelphia: University of Pennsylvania Press.
———. 1970. Unpublished fieldnotes on Ahtna sites. Typescript.

de Laguna, Frederica and Catharine McClellan. 1981. Ahtna. In *Handbook of North American Indians, Volume 6, the Subarctic,* June Helm, ed., pp. 641–664. Washington: The Smithsonian Institution.

Laws of Alaska. 1982: CSSB 727(SA), An act relating to the duties of the State Geographic Board.

Learnard, H. G. 1900. A trip from Portage Bay to Turnagain Arm and up the Sushitna. In *Compilation of Narratives of the Exploration of Alaska,* pp. 648–676. Washington: U.S. Government Printing Office.

Lee, S. 1987. 1987 Hewitt Lake Excursion. Matanuska-Susitna Borough History Division Newsletter. 1(5):1.

Liapunova, R. G. and S. G. Fedorova. 1979. *Russkaia Amerika v Neopublikovannykh Zapiskakh K. T. Khelbnikova,* [Russian America in unpublished notes of K. T. Khlebnikov]. Leningrad:Nauka.

Mahoney, Barbara A. and Kim E. W. Shelden. 2000. Harvest History of Belugas, *Delphinapterus leucas,* in Cook Inlet, Alaska. *Marine Fisheries Review* 62(3):124–133.

Mason, J. Alden. 1928. A Remarkable Stone Lamp from Alaska. *The Museum Journal* 19(2): 170–194. Philadelphia: University of Pennsylvania Museum.

Mathys, Frederick. 1900. Up the Chickaloon and Down the Talkeetna. In *Compilation of Narratives of the Exploration of Alaska,* pp. 679–681. Washington: U.S. Government Printing Office.

McKinley, Jim. 1980. Four Views of the Effects of Exploration on Alaska Natives: Jim McKinley. In *Exploration in Alaska, Captain Cook Commemorative Lecture Series,* Antoinette Shalkop, ed., pp. 193–194. Anchorage: Cook Inlet Historical Society.

McKinney, Debbie. 1985. An Elder's Tradition. *Anchorage Daily News.* Oct. 25.

McMahan, J. David and Charles E. Holmes. 1996. Archaeological Survey of Elmendorf Air Force Base, Alaska: Final Report. Alaska Department of Natural Resources, Office of History and Archaeology Report Number 61. Anchorage.

McClanahan, A. J. 1986. *Our Stories, Our Lives.* Anchorage: The CIRI Foundation.

Meiklejohn, G. D. 1900. Map of Alaskan Military Reconnaissance of 1898. In *Compilation of Narratives of the Exploration of Alaska.* Washington: U.S. Government Printing Office.

Mendenhall, W. C. 1898. Reconnaissances from Resurrection Bay to the Tanana River, Note Book. USGS, Denver, [Dena'ina and Russian vocabulary], ms. 3 pp.
———. 1900 A Reconnaissance from Resurrection Bay to the Tanana River, Alaska, in 1898. U.S. Geological Survey Annual Report 20(7):265–340.

Metcalf, Gertrude. 1910. Mount McKinley and the Mazama Expedition. *The Pacific Monthly, a Magazine of Education and Progress.* Sept.:55–65. Portland, Oregon.

Mills, R. D. 1994. Radiocarbon Calibration of Archaeological Dates from the Central Gulf of Alaska. *Arctic Anthropology* 31:126–149.

Mishler, Craig. 1985a. Tanaina Ethnohistory on the Northern Kenai Peninsula. In *Progress Report, Sterling Highway Archaeological Mitigation,* Charles E. Holmes, ed., pp. 8–53. Anchorage: Alaska Division of Geological and Geophysical Surveys.
———. 1985b. Historical Demography and Genealogy, the Decline of the Kenai Peninsula Tanaina. Ms. Anchorage: Alaska Division of Geological and Geophysical Surveys.

Moffit, Fred H. 1904. Map of Matanuska–Susitna rivers, drawn by a local Ahtna–Dena'ina person, inside front cover of field notebook 89. U.S. Geological Survey Archives, Menlo Park.
———. 1912. *The Headwater Regions of Gulkana and Susitna Rivers.* U.S. Geological Survey Bulletin 498. Washington: U.S. Government Printing Office.
———. 1915. *The Broad Pass Region, Alaska.* U.S. Geological Survey Bulletin 608. Washington: U.S. Government Printing Office.

Moore, Terris. 1981, *Mt. McKinley, the Pioneer Climbs.* Fairbanks: University of Alaska Press.

Murkowski, Carol. 1987. Place Names: Mapping the Homeland. *Anchorage Times.* Nov. 21.

National Marine Fisheries Service. 2000. [Draft] Federal Actions Associated with Management and Recovery of Cook Inlet Beluga Whales: Environmental Impact Statement. Alaska Regional Office. Juneau.

Neely, Ben. 2000. Interview at Gulkana, April 10, 2000. Recorded by Chickaloon Village Staff. Ms.

O'Harra, Doug. 1996. Rock of Contention. We Alaskans. *Anchorage Daily News.* May 19, 1996. G7–G14.

O'Leary, Matt. 2002. Draft Report of Investigation for AA-11819. Ms. BIA ANCSA Office, Anchorage.

Orth, Donald J. 1971. *Dictionary of Alaska Place Names.* Geological Survey Professional Paper 567. Washington: U.S. Government Printing Office.

———. 1980. Report on the Proposal to Change the Name of the Alaska Mountain from Mount McKinley to Denali. Typescript. United States Board of Geographic Names.

———. 1985. The Story of the Naming of Mt. Rainier and Other Domestic Names Activities of the U.S. Board of Geographic Names. *Names* 32.4:428–434.

Osgood, Cornelius. 1937. *The Ethnography of the Tanaina.* Yale University Publications in Anthropology, No. 16. New Haven: Yale University Press.

———. 1940. *Ingalik Material Culture.* Yale University Publications in Anthropology, No. 22. New Haven: Yale University Press.

Osgood, Wilfred A. 1901. *Natural History of the Cook Inlet Region.* U.S. Dept of Agriculture Biological Survey, North American Fauna No. 21. Washington: U.S. Govt. Printing Office.

Pete, Shem. 1975. *Susitnu Htsukdu'a, Susitna Story.* Fairbanks: Alaska Native Language Center. [reprinted in Cole et al. 1985:24–26.]

———. 1977. *Diqelas Tukda: The Story of a Tanaina Chief.* Fairbanks: Alaska Native Language Center.

———. 1980a. Four Views of the Effects of Exploration on Alaska Natives: Shem Pete. In *Exploration in Alaska, Captain Cook Commemorative Lecture Series,* Antoinette Shalkop, ed., pp. 196–197. Anchorage: Cook Inlet Historical Society.

———. 1980b. Beluga Hunting, In *Qudi Heyi Nitch'diluyi Sukdu'a, This Year's Collected Stories (Tyonek and Iliamna Lake),* James Kari, ed., pp. 6–13. Anchorage: National Bilingual Materials Development Center.

———. 1989. The Hunting Dog: A Dena'ina Tale of Subsistence Values. Introduction by James Fall. Translation by Billy Pete, James Kari, and James Fall. *Alaska Fish and Game* 21(6):2–7.

———. 2000. Shq'uła Tsukdu: The "Whistler" (Hoary Marmot) Story. In *Denali: A Literary Anthology,* Bill Sherwonit, editor, pp. 35–50. Seattle: The Mountaineers Books.

Peters, Henry and Jennie Peters 1977. *Nay'nadeli I'ghaan Dghat'aen'den (The War at Nay'nadeli).* Fairbanks: Alaska Native Language Center.

Petroff, Ivan. 1884. Report on the Population and Resources of Alaska, 1880. In *10th Census of the United States, 1880,* Volume 8. Washington: U.S. Government Printing Office.

———. 1900. Report on the Population and Resources of Alaska. 1880. In *Compilation of Narratives of the Exploration of Alaska,* pp. 55–284. Washington: U.S. Government Printing Office.

Pierce, Richard A. 1996. Tyonek in the 1880s: From the Diary of V. V. Stafeev. In *Adventures Through Time: Readings in the Anthropology of Cook Inlet, Alaska.* Nancy Yaw Davis and William E. Davis, editors, pp. 175–179. Anchorage: Cook Inlet Historical Society.

Porco, Peter. 1985. The Chugach, a Mountain Saga. *Anchorage Daily News.* March 2, 1985.

———. 2001. Native Ways: Dena'ina Fishermen Aided in Search for Helicopter Missing in Cook Inlet. *Anchorage Daily News.* December 10, 2001. Section B, pp. B1, B3.

Portlock, Nathaniel. 1789. *A Voyage Around the World.* London: J. Stockdale, and G. Goulding.

Potter, Ben A. Peter M. Bowers, Stacie J. McIntosh, and S. Craig Gerlach. 2000. Cultural Resource Survey of Proposed Realignments for the Alaska Railroad, Milepost 105.7 to 110.1 and 146.4 to 158.6. Prepared for Alaska Railroad Corporation. Fairbanks: Northern Land Use.

Potter, Louise. 1963. *Early Days in Wasilla, A Study of a Frontier Town in Alaska: Wasilla to 1959.* Privately published.

———. 1967. *Old Times on Upper Cook's Inlet.* Anchorage: The Book Cache.

Pratt, Kenneth L. 1998. Copper, Trade and Tradition Among the Lower Ahtna of the Chitina River Basin: the Nicholai Era, 1884–1900. *Arctic Anthropology* 35:77–98.

Pulu, Tupou (ed.). 1975. *Nikolai Reader.* Anchorage: Alaska State Operated School System.

Radloff, Leopold and Anton Schiefner. 1874. Leopold Radloff's Worterbuch der Kinai-Sprache. *Memoires de lAcademia Imperiale des Sciences de St. Petersbourg* XXI:8:1–33.

Reckord, Holly. 1983. *Where Raven Stood, Cultural Resources of the Ahtna Region.* Fairbanks: Cooperative Park Studies Unit.

Reger, Douglas R. 1981. A Model for Culture History in Upper Cook Inlet. Unpublished Ph.D. dissertation. Washington State University.

———. 1983[1978]. Willow-Wasilla-Lower Susitna River Basin, Southcentral Alaska. In *Susitna River Basin Study,* Glenn Bacon, ed., pp. 1–22. Anchorage: U.S. Department of Agriculture, Soil Conservation Service.

———. 1985. Beluga Point in Prehistory. *Heritage* No. 23, January-March, 1985.

———. 1996. Beluga Point. In: *American Beginnings: the Prehistory and Palaeoecology of Beringia,* edited by Frederick Hadleigh-West, pp. 433–436. University of Chicago Press, Chicago.

———. 1998. Archaeology of the Northern Kenai Peninsula and Upper Cook Inlet. *Arctic Anthropology* 35(1):160–171.

Reger, Douglas R. and Alan Boraas. 1996. An Overview of the Radiocarbon Chronology in Cook Inlet Prehistory. In *Adventures through Time: Readings in the Anthropology of Cook Inlet.* Edited by Davis, N. Y. and W. Davis. Anchorage: the Cook Inlet Historical Society. pp. 155–172.

Reger, Douglas R. and Mark E. Pipkin. 1996. Round Mountain Microblade Locality. In *American Beginnings: the Prehistory and Palaeoecology of Beringia,* edited by Frederick Hadleigh-West, pp. 430–433. University of Chicago Press, Chicago.

Reger, Richard D., and DeAnne S. Pinney. 1996. Late Wisconsin Glaciation of the Cook Inlet Region with Emphasis on Kenai Lowland and Implications for Early Peopling. In *Adventures Through Time: Readings in the Anthropology of Cook Inlet, Alaska,* edited by Nancy Davis and William Davis, pp. 157–171. Cook Inlet Historical Society, Anchorage.

Riehle, J. R. and P. M. Bowers. 1990. The Hayes Tephra Deposits, an Upper Holocene Marker Horizon in Southcentral Alaska. *Quaternary Research* 33:276–290.

Ross, Ernest A. 1989. Letter to James Kari.

Roy, Skip. 1987. *Southcentral Alaskan Salmon Streams: an Atlas.* Anchorage: Salmon Atlas.

Rusk, C. E. 1910. [1945] On the Trail of Dr. Cook. *Pacific Monthly,* reprinted in *Mazama* 27(13), 1945.

Russian-America Company Records (RACR). 1844. Excerpt by A. K. Etolin, October 18, 1844. Translated by Katherine Arndt. Reel 47 (vol. 22), f. 549v.-552v. Alaska and Polar Regions Department, Rasmuson Library, University of Alaska, Fairbanks.

———. 1847. Excerpt by M. D. Tebenkov, May 12, 1847. Translated by Katherine Arndt. M-F roll 52, pp. 461–465. Vol. 27. Alaska and Polar Regions Department, Rasmuson Library, University of Alaska, Fairbanks.

Sacaloff, Fedosia. 1975. Unhsah Tahna'ina, the First Russians. In *Denaina T'qit'ach', The Way the Tanainas Are,* James Kari, ed., pp. 20–24. Fairbanks: Alaska Native Language Center.

Schneider, William, Dianne Gudgel-Holmes, and John Dalle-Molle. 1984. *Land Use in the North Additions of Denali National Park and Preserve: an Historical Perspective.* Research-Resources Management, no. 9. Anchorage: U.S. Department of Interior, National Park Service.

Seager-Boss, Fran. 1995. *Survey and Inventory of Chief Wasilla House Site.* Palmer: Matanuska-Susitna Borough.

———. 1996. *Talkeetna Middle-Sustina Region Archaeological Survey & Inventory.* Palmer: Matanuska-Susitna Borough.

———. 2000. Old Knik Townsite Archaeological Survey and Inventory Phase II. Palmer: Matanuska-Susitna Borough Planning Department, Cultural Resource Division.

Shalkop, Antoinette. 1980. (Ed.) *Exploration in Alaska, Captain Cook Commemorative Lectures.* Anchorage: Cook Inlet Historical Society.

Sheldon, Charles. 1908. The Cook Inlet Aborigines. In *To the Top of the Continent.* Appendix C, by Frederick Cook, pp. 269–77. New York: Doubleday, Page and Company.

Sheldon, Roberta. 1995. *The Heritage of Talkeetna.* Talkeetna, Alaska: Talkeetna Editions.

Sherwonit, Bill (editor). 2000. Denali: A Literary Anthology. Seattle: The Mountaineers Books.

Sherwood, Morgan. 1965. *Exploration of Alaska, 1865–1900.* New Haven: Yale University Press.

Simpson, Ronald N. 2001. *Legacy of the Chief.* Anchorage: Publications Consultants.

Simeone, William E. and James Kari. 2002. Traditional Knowledge and Fishing Practices of the Ahtna of Copper River, Alaska. Alaska Department of Fish and Game, Division of Subsistence Technical Paper No. 270.

Sleem, D. H. 1910a. Sleem's Map of Central Alaska, Iditarod. Seward. Copy at Alaska and Polar Regions Dept., University of Alaska, Fairbanks.

———. 1910b. Map of Willow Creek Mining District. Seward. Copy at Alaska and Polar Regions Dept., University of Alaska, Fairbanks.

Snider, Gerrit Heinie. 1966. *100 Stories of Alaska.* Anchorage: Color Art Printing Co.

Spurr, Josiah Edward. 1900. A Reconnaissance in Southwestern Alaska in 1898. *United States Geological Survey 20th Annual Report.* Part 7:31–264. Washington: U.S. Government Printing Office.

———. 1950. The Log of the Kuskokwim, An Exploration in Alaska. Typescript. Rasmusson Library, UAF. Typescript. 173 pp.

Stafeev, Vladimir. n.d. The Devastation of the Russians in Tuyunok. In Papers, 1869–1895. Russian Manuscript Number 6. Juneau: Alaska Historical Library. Translated from Russian by Janet Crayne, University of Wisconsin Madison, in possession of the editors.

Steensby, H. P. 1917. An Anthropogeographical Study of the Origin of Eskimo Culture. *Meddelelser om Gronland.* Vol 53(2). Copenhagen.

Stephan, Alberta E. 1993. Traditional Athabascan Fish Recipes. Eklutna: Traditional Native Village of Eklutna.

———. 1996a. *The First Athabascans of Alaska: Strawberries.* Pittsburgh: Dorrance Publishing Co.

———. 1996b. Athabaskan Natives of Upper Cook Inlet. *In* Adventures Through Time: Readings in the Anthropology of Cook Inlet, Alaska, Nancy Yaw Davis and William E. Davis, editors, pp. 147–150. Anchorage: Cook Inlet Historical Society.

———. 2001. *Cheda (Athabascan for Grandma).* Anchorage: Todd Communications.

Stephan, Sava. 1980. Htal, Rainy Pass. In *Q'udi Heyi Nilch'diluyi Sukdu'a, This Year's Collected Stories (Tyonek and Iliamna Lake),* James Kari, ed., pp. 23–24. Anchorage: National Bilingual Materials Development Center.

———. 2005. Upper Inlet Dena'ina Language Lessons. Transcribed and edited by James Kari. Dena'inaq' Titaztunt and Alaska Native Heritage Center.

Stephenson, Robert O., S. Craig Gerlach, R. Dale Guthrie, C. Richard Harrington, Robin O. Mills, and Gregory Hare. 2001. Wood Bison in Late Holocene Alaska and Adjacent Canada: Paleontological, Archaeological and Historical Records. In *People and Wildlife in Norther North America, Essays in Honor of R. Dale Guthrie.* Ed. by S. Craig Gerlach and Maribeth S. Murray. BARS 944. Oxford: Archaeopress. pp. 124–158.

Sterritt, Neil J., Susan Marsden, Robert Galois, Peter R. Grant, and Richard Overstall. 1998. *Tribal Boundaries in the Nass Watershed.* Vancouver: UBC Press.

Stokes, Jeff. 1985. *Resource Utilization of Four Upper Kuskokwim Communities.* Alaska Department of Fish and Game, Subsistence Division, Technical Paper, 86.

Stuck, Hudson. 1914 [1977]. *The Ascent of Denali.* Seattle: The Mountaineers Books.

Teben'kov, M.D.1981 [1852]. *Atlas of the Northwest Coasts of America from Bering Strait to Cape Corrientes, and the Aleutian Islands, with Several Sheets on the Northeast Coast of Asia.* Kingston, Ontario: The Limestone Press.

Thomas, George B. 1900. From the Middle Fork of the Sushitna to Indian Creek In *Compilation of Narratives of the Exploration of Alaska.* pp. 733–735. Washington: U.S. Government Printing Office.

Tenenbaum, Joan. 1984. *Dena'ina Sukdu'a, Traditional Stories of the Tanaina Athabaskans.* Fairbanks: Alaska Native Language Center.

Tikhmenov, P. A. 1978 [1861–1863] *A History of the Russian-American Company.* Translated by Richard A. Pierce and Alton S. Donnelly. Seattle: University of Washington Press.

Toomey, Sheila. 2000. Court Rules Against City on Eklutna Quarry Permit. Anchorage Daily News, February 5, 2000, pages B-1, B-2.

Townsend, Joan B. 1970. The Archaeology of Pedro Bay, Alaska. Paper presented at the 35th Annual Meeting of the Society for American Archaeology, Mexico City.
———.1974. Journals of Nineteenth Century Russian Priests to the Tanaina. *Arctic Anthropology* 11(1):1 29.
———. 1981. Tanaina. In *Handbook of North American Indians, Volume 6: Subarctic,* June Helm, ed., pp. 623–641. Washington: The Smithsonian Institution.

Tyonek. 1989. Shem Pete Memorial Potlatch Program. Oct. 7, 1989.

United States Board On Geographic Names, Domestic Names Committee. October 10, 2002. Docket 380, K'esugi Ridge, Alaska

United States Daily. 1928. Airplanes Facilitate Mapping of Alaska, October 10, 1928. S. R. Capps Collection, Alaska and Polar Regions Department, Rasmuson Library, University of Alaska, Fairbanks. United States Bureau of the Census. 1910. Thirteenth Census of the United States.
———. 1920. Fourteenth Census of the United States.

United States Geological Survey. 2001. Geographical Names Information System. [Online database]. U.S. Mapping Center.

Unrau, Harlan D. 1994. *Lake Clark National Park and Preserve, Alaska: Historic Resource Study.* Anchorage, Alaska: U.S. Dept. of the Interior, National Park Service.

Vancouver, George. 1801. *A Voyage of Discovery to the North Pacific Ocean, and Around the World.* In six volumes. London: John Stockdale.

VanStone, James W. 1959. Russian Exploration in Interior Alaska, an Extract from the Journal of Andrei Glazunov. *Pacific Northwest Quarterly* 50.2:37–42.

Vanschoonhoven, George. 1900. A Quest for the Tanana. In *Compilation of Narratives of the Exploration of Alaska,* pp. 736–737. Washington: U.S. Government Printing Office.

Wade, Katherine Wickersham. 2004. *Chickaloon Spirit: the Life and Times of Katherine Wade.* Chickaloon Village Traditional Council.

Wahrhaftig, Clyde. 1965. *Physiographic Divisions of Alaska.* Washington: U.S. Government Printing Office.

Washburn, Bradford. 1951. *Mount McKinley and the Alaska Range in Literature; a Descriptive Bibliography.* Boston: Museum of Science.
——— and David Roberts. 1991. *Mount McKinley, the Conquest of Denali.* New York: Harry N. Abrams, Inc.

Waterman, T. T. 1920. *Yurok Geography.* University of California Publications in American Archaeology and Ethnology. Vol 16.

West, Constance F. 1973. An Inventory of Trails and Habitation Sites in the Ahtna Region. Unpublished ms. [with audio tape collection].

Williams, Howel. Ed. 1958. *Landscapes of Alaska, Their Geologic Evolution.* Berkeley and Los Angeles: University of California Press.

Wilson, Rodman and Paul Crews Sr. 1999. *Tordrillo, Pioneer Climbs and Flights in the Tordrillo Mountains of Alaska.* Anchorage: Todd Communications.

Workman, Karen W. 1996. Toward an Archaeological Definition of Dena'ina. In *Adventures Through Time: Readings in the Anthropology of Cook Inlet.* Edited by Davis, N. Y. and W. Davis. Anchorage: The Cook Inlet Historical Society. pp. 207–220.

Workman, William B., Janet Klein, Marlene Testaguzza and Peter Zollars. 1993. 1992 Test Excavations at the Sylva Lake Site (SEL 245): A Stratified Late Ocean Bay Occupation in Upper Kachemak Bay, Kenai Peninsula. Paper presented at the 20th Annual Meeting of the Alaska Anthropological Association, Anchorage.

Wrangell, Ferdinand Petrovich von. 1839. Statitische und Ethnographische Nachrichten Uber die Russischen Bisitzungen an der Nordwestkiiste von Amerika. In *Beitrdge zur Kenntniss des Russischen Reiches und der Angrdnzenden Lander Asiens,* bd. 1. St. Petersberg.

———. 1970[1839]. The Inhabitants of the Northwest Coast of America. Translated and edited by James VanStone. *Arctic Anthropology* 6(2):5–20.

———. 1980. [1839] *Russian America, Statistical and Ethnographic Information.* Translated from the German edition of 1839 by Mary Sadousld. Richard Pierce, ed. Kingston, Ontario: The Limestone Press.

Yanert, William. 1900a. Subreport of Sergt. William Yanert. In *Compilation of Narratives of the Exploration of Alaska,* pp. 677–679. Washington: U.S. Government Printing Office.

———. 1900b. Subreport of Sergt. William Yanert. In *Compilation of Narratives of the Exploration of Alaska,* pp. 736–737. Washington: U.S. Government Printing Office.

Yarborough, Michael R. 1996. "A Village which Sprang Up Before My Very Eyes": An Historical Account of the Founding of Eklutna. In *Adventures Through Time: Readings in the Anthropology of Cook Inlet, Alaska.* Nancy Yaw Davis and William E. Davis, editors, pp. 111–122. Anchorage: Cook Inlet Historical Society.

Young, Robert W. and William Morgan. 1980. *The Navajo Language: A Grammar and Colloquial Dictionary.* Albuquerque: University of New Mexico Press.

Zagoskin, L. A. 1967. [1847] *Lieutenant Zagoskin's Travels in Russian America, 1842–1844.* Henry N. Michael, ed. Toronto: University of Toronto Press.

Zimmerly, David W. 2000. *Qayaq, Kayaks of Alaska and Siberia.* Fairbanks: University of Alaska Press.

Znamenski, Andrei A. 1996. Athapaskan Church, Russian Ortho-dox: the Tanainas' Encounter with Russian Orthodox Missionaries, 1893–1917. *Alaska History* 11:26–44.

———. 1998. Native Culture Through Orthodox Eyes: Russian Missionary Ioann Bortnovsky on the Dena'ina and Ahtna, 1896–1907. *Alaska History* 13:1–27.

———. 2000. Dena'ina Orthodox Chapels as a Native Institution, 1871–1917. *Acta Americana* 8(2):5–22.

———. 2003. *Through Orthodox Eyes: Russian Missionary Narratives of Travels to the Dena'ina and Ahtna, 1850s–1930s.* Fairbanks: University of Alaska Press.

2016 Bibliography

Ackerman, R.A. 1996. Lime Hills, Cave 1. In *American Beginnings: The Prehistory and Paleoecology of Beringia.* West, F.H. (editor). Chicago, IL. University of Chicago Press. pp. 456–460.

Alaska Archaeology Month. 2007. Culture & Change, Maintaining Values. K'enaht'ana, Knik people, Nay'dini'aa Na' Hwt'aene, Chickaloon people. [poster]. Public Education Group.

Anderson, Douglas D. 2008. A Current Synthesis of the Northern Archaic. *Arctic Anthropology* 45(2):169–178.

Balluta, Andrew. 2008. *Shtutda'ina Da'a Shet Qudel, My Forefathers are Still Walking with Me, Verbal Essays on Tsaynen and Qizhjeh Traditions.* Anchorage: National Park Service.

Barnett, James K. and David L. Nicandri. 2015. *Arctic Ambitions: Captain Cook and the Northwest Passage.* Seattle and London: University of Washington Press.

Betts, Robert C. 1987. Archaeological Investigations at Butte Lake, Alaska: A Report to the University of Alaska Museum Geist Fund. M.A., Department of Anthropology, University of Alaska Fairbanks, Fairbanks, Alaska.

Black, Lydia. 2008. Commentary on Journal of 1796 by Dmitrii Tarkhanov. In *Anooshi Lingit Aani Ka, Russians in Tlingit America, The Battles of Sitka, 1802 and 1804.* Ed. by N. M. Dauenhauer, R. Dauenhauer, and L. Black. Seattle: University of Washington Press, 67–90.

Boas, Franz. 1934. *Geographical Names of the Kwakiutl Indians.* New York: Columbia University Press.

Boraas, Alan S. and Aaron Leggett. 2013. Dena'ina Resistance to Russian hegemony, Late Eighteenth and Nineteenth Centuries: Cook Inlet, Alaska. *Ethnohistory* 60:3: 485–504.

Boraas, Alan S., Ronald T. Stanek, Douglas R. Reger, and Thomas F. King. 2015. The Ch'u'itnu Traditional Cultural Landscape. Native American Rights Fund on behalf of the Native Village of Tyonek. Anchorage, Alaska.

Bright, William (editor) 2004. *Native American Placenames of the United States.* Norman: University of Oklahoma Press.

Brooks, Alfred H. 1904. An exploration to Mount McKinley, America's highest mountain. *Smithsonian Report for 1903.* Washington: Government Printing Office. pp. 407–425.

Braund, Stephen R. and Associates. 2007. PacRim Coal Ch'uit'nu Coal Project West Cook Inlet, Alaska: Subsistence and Traditional Knowledge Studies: Subsistence Use Areas and Traditional Knowledge Studies for Tyonek and Beluga, Alaska. Prepared for DRven Corporation, Anchorage, Alaska by Stephen R. Braund and Associates. February 28, 2007.

Braund, Stephen R. and Associates and Huntington Consulting. 2011. Relationship between the Native Village of Tyonek, Alaska and Beluga Whales in Cook Inlet, Alaska. Report submitted to NOAA Fisheries. Anchorage.

Chickaloon Village Traditional Council. n.d. www.chickaloon.org.

CIRI, an Alaska Native Corporation. n.d. www.ciri.com.

Collins, Raymond. 2015. Raymond Collins Collection 2015. Alaska Native Language Archive, ANLA. UK964C2015.

Cooper, H. Kory. 2012. Innovation and prestige among Northern hunter-gatherers: late prehistoric native copper use in Alaska and Yukon. *American Antiquity,* 77(3):565–590.

Deaphon, Miska. 2015. [Collected Stories.] Ms. Draft in progress by Ray Collins, Betty Petruska, and James Kari.

Esdale, Julie A. 2008. A Current Synthesis of the Northern Archaic. *Arctic Anthropology* 45(2):3–38.

Evanoff, Karen. 2010. *Dena'ina Ełnena, a Celebration.* Anchorage: National Park Service.

Fall, James A. 2009. Dena'ina ełnena, Dena'ina country: the Dena'ina in Anchorage. In *The Alaska Native Reader, History Culture, Politics.* Ed. by Maria Williams. pp. 67–84. Durham: Duke University Press.

Fortescue, Michael. 1998. *Language Relations across Bering Strait: Reappraising the Archaeological and Linguistic Evidence.* London and New York: Cassell.

Helm, June (editor) 1981. *Handbook of North American Indians, Volume 6: Subarctic.* Washington: The Smithsonian Institution.

Herz, Nathaniel. 2014. Wells Fargo to repatriate traditional Dena'ina land. *Anchorage Daily News.* June 6, 2014.

Jetté, Jules and Eliza Jones. 2000. *Koyukon Athabaskan Dictionary.* Edited by James Kari. Fairbanks: ANLC.

Jones, Suzie, James A. Fall, and Aaron Leggett (editors) 2013. *Dena'inaq' Huch'ulyeshi: The Dena'ina Way of Living.* Fairbanks: University of Alaska Press.

Kari, James. 2007 and 2013. *Dena'ina Topical Dictionary.* Fairbanks: ANLC. Revised edition 2013.

———. 1993. Local vs. regional place naming conventions in Alaskan Athbaskan languages. In *Proceedings of the 23rd Western Conference on Linguistics,* Vol. 6, WECOL 93. S. Hargus, G. R. McMenamin, and V. Samiian, eds., pp. 233–251. Fresno, CA: California State University, Fresno, Department of Linguistics.

———. 2008. Ahtna Place Names Lists. Revised 2nd edition. Fairbanks: Alaska Native Language Center.

———. 2010a. *Ahtna Travel Narratives, a Demonstration of Shared Geographic Knowledge among Alaska Athabascans.* Fairbanks: Alaska Native Language Center.

———. 2010b. The Concept of Geolinguistic Conservatism in Na-Dene Prehistory. In *The Dene-Yeniseian Connection,* ed. by J. Kari and B. Potter. *Anthropological Papers of the University of Alaska.* New Series, vol 5:194–222.

———.2011. A Case Study in Ahtna Athabascan Geographic Knowledge. In *Landscape in Language, Transdisciplinary Perspectives,* ed. by D.M. Mark, A.G. Turk, N. Burenhult and D. Stea. Amsterdam: John Benjamins, pp. 239–260.

———. 2012. *Lower Tanana Athabascan Place Names Lists.* Fairbanks: Alaska Native Language Center.

———. 2013. Ahtna Place Names Lists and Maps, version 3.1. Fairbanks: Alaska Native Language Center. CD, 17 pdf files.

———. 2014. Appendix E. Selected Western Ahtna Narratives Grouped by Genre. Report by Northern Land Use Research Alaska to Alaska Office of History and Archaeology, the Bureau of Land Management, and URS Corp, Anchorage, Anchorage, Alaska. Ms. 403 pp.

———. 2015. Upper Kuskokwim Athabascan Place Names Lists, vers. 3.32, April 24, 2015. Ms. Alaska Native Language Center.

Kari, James and Ben A. Potter. 2010. (editors) *The Dene-Yeniseian Connection. Anthropological Papers of the University of Alaska,* new series, vol. 5.

Kari, James and Siri G. Tuttle. 2005. Copper River Native Places, Report on Culturally Important Places to Alaska Native Tribes of Southcentral Alaska, BLM Alaska Technical Report 56. BLM Glennallen Field Office. 43 pp.

Kari, James, R. Greg Dixon, Alan Boraas and Aaron Leggett. 2012. Bibliography of Sources on Dena'ina and Cook Inlet Anthropology Version, 3.1; 165 pp. www.kpc.alaska.edu/files/resources/denaina-bibliography-version-3-1-g.pdf.

Knik Tribal Council. n.d. www.kniktribalcouncil.org.

Langdon, Stephen J., and Aaron Leggett. 2009. Dena'ina Heritage and Representation in Anchorage: A Collaborative Project. In *The Alaska Native Reader, History Culture, Politics.* Ed. by Maria Williams. pp. 163–175. Durham: Duke University Press.

Leggett, Aaron 2009. Dena'ina Lifeways [radio series] www.denainalifeways.org/ Kohanic Broadcast Corp.

Lopez, Barry. H. 2004. Review of *Shem Pete's Alaska. Orion* Jan-Feb.: 74–75.

Mielke, Colleen. 2000–. Matanuska-Susitna Valley, Alaska, Researching Our South Central Alaska Roots. http://freepages.genealogy.rootsweb.ancestry.com/~coleen/south_central_alaska.html.

———. 2010. George Holt, What led up to his 1885 Murder. Ms.

———. 2010. Who was Afanasii? the Man Who Instigated Holt's Murder?

Neely, Burr, Patrick Hall, and Gerad Smith. 2016. 2012–2014 Cultural Resources Summary Report for the Susitna-Watana Hydroelectric Project, Susitna River, Alaska. Report prepared for Alaska Energy Authority by Northern Land Use Research Alaska, Fairbanks.

National Marine Fisheries Service. 2015. Draft Recovery Plan for the Cook Inlet Beluga Whale. National Marine Fisheries Service, Alaska Regional Office, Protected Resources Division, Juneau, AK.

Nichols, Johanna. 1992. *Linguistic Diversity in Space and Time.* Chicago: University of Chicago Press.

Pete, Shem. 2010. The George Holt Story. Ms. ANLC 3702. ANLCA.

Postinikov, Alexey and Marvin Falk. 2015. *Exploring and Mapping Alaska, The Russian America Era, 1741–1867*. Fairbanks: University of Alaska Press.

Potter, Ben A. 2010. Archaeological Patterning in Northeast Asia and Northwest North America: An Examination of the Dene-Yeniseian Hypothesis. IN *The Dene-Yeniseian Connection*, ed. by J. Kari and B. Potter. *Anthropological Papers of the University of Alaska*. New Series, vol. 5:138–167.

Rabich, Joyce Chris. 1977. The Anthropology of the Cook Inlet Region: A Synthesis. An Annual Report Submitted to Cooperative Parks Study Unit and Cook Inlet Region, Inc. Ms. 216 pp.

Schneider, William H. 2013. Hewitt Lake (Tiq'atl'ena Bena) archaeological nvestigations. M.A. thesis. University of Alaska Anchorage.

Reger, Douglas. 2013. Dena'ina Archaeology. In *Dena'inaq' Huch'uyeshi, The Dena'ina Way of Living*. Fairbanks: University of Alaska Press. pp. 63–71.

Reger, R. D., Lowell, T., and Evenson, E. B. 2011. Discussion of "Late Quaternary megafloods from Glacial Lake Atna, Southcentral Alaska, U.S.A." *Quaternary Research* 75:301–302.

Rogers, Monty Joe. 2015. The Role of Quartz in the Lithic Technology of the Western Upper Cook Inlet Ancestral Dena'ina. MA Thesis, University of Alaska, Anchorage.

Shimer, Grant. 2009. Holocene vegetation and climate change at Copper River Basin. MA Thesis, University of Alaska, Fairbanks.

Smith, A. Beverly. 1899. In the Wilds of Alaska. *Wide World Magazine, an Illustrated Monthly of True Narrative*. Vol. 3, pp. 424–433.

Stanek, Ronald T, James A. Fall, and Davin L. Holen. 2006. *West Cook Inlet Ethnographic Overview and Assessment for Lake Clark National Park & Preserve*. Anchorage: National Park Service.

Tobias, N. Terry. 2009. *Living Proof, the Essential Data-Collection Guide for Indigenous Use-and-Occupancy Map Surveys*. Vancouver: Ecotrust Canada & Union of BC Indian Chiefs.

U.S. Army Corps of Engineers. 2015. Chp. 3.20 Cultural Resources. Donlin Gold Project, Draft Environmental Impact Statement. Anchorage: CEPOA-RD. JBER, AK, November. www.donlingoldeis.com/EISDocuments.aspx

U.S. Dept. of Interior. 2015. Old Name Officially Returns to Nation's Highest Peak. Press release, Sept. 1, 2015.

United States Surface Transportation Board. 2011. Chp. 6. Cultural Resources. IN Final environmental impact statement: Alaska Railroad Corporation construction and operation of a rail line extension to Port MacKenzie, Alaska. Docket no. FD 35095. pp. 6-1 to 6-37.

Vajda Edward J. 2010. A Siberian Link with Na-Dene Languages. IN *The Dene-Yeniseian Connection*, ed. by J. Kari and B. Potter *Anthropological Papers of the University of Alaska*. New Series, vol 5:33–99.

VanStone, J. W., and Townsend, J. B. 1970. *Kijik: An Historic Tanaina Indian Settlement* (Vol. 59). Field Museum of Natural History, Chicago.

Waring, Gerald A. 1936. Geology of the Anthracite Ridge Coal district. USGS Bull. 861.

Wendt, Michael L. 2013. Integrating Climate Change with Human Use Patterns: Archaeology of Butte Lake Northeast. M.A Thesis, University of Alaska Fairbanks.

Wickersham, James. 1938. *Old Yukon, Tails, Trails, Trials*. Washington DC: Washington Law Book Co.

Wikipedia. 2012. The Denali/Mount McKinley Naming Dispute. en.wikipedia.org/wiki/Denali–Mount_McKinley_naming_dispute.

Wohlforth, Charles. 2014. *From the Shores of Ship Creek, Stories of Anchorage's First 100 Years*. Anchorage: Todd Communications.

Workman, William B. 1978. Prehistory of the Aishihik-Kluane area, southwest Yukon Territory. *National Museum of Man*, Mercury Series No. 74.

Workman, W. B., and Workman, K. W. 2010. The end of the Kachemak tradition on the Kenai Peninsula, southcentral Alaska. *Arctic Anthropology*. 47(2):90–96.

Wygal, B. T. and Goebel, T. 2012. Early Prehistoric Archaeology of The Middle Susitna Valley, Alaska. *Arctic Anthropology*, 49(1):45–67.

Geographic Name Index

This is an alphabetical index of *a)* the official place names that are presented in the book, *b)* the better-known unofficial English place names, and *c)* the more prominent Dena'ina or Ahtna names for unnamed features. Within parentheses, following the official name and a comma, are the chapter and number of the feature. In **boldface** are the Dena'ina or Ahtna place names. After a colon the page numbers are indicated. If there is a photograph or illustration with a place or place name, the page number is in *italic type*. Many lesser known unnamed features with Dena'ina names are not in this index. The chapter place name maps and most of the names on historic maps are not included in this index.

196 Mile Creek, now called Grey's Creek, (8.81 **Q'istnu**): 191

Abercrombie Rapids, 217
Alaska Range, (7.61 **Dghelay Teh**): *ix*, 10, 13, 16, 32, 33, 40, *46*, 73, 85, 110, 142, 144, 149, 159, 167, *170*, *199*, 211, 213, 230, 232, *242*, 289, 340, *plates 11, 22. Also see* Southern Alaska Range.
Alexander Creek, (4.1 **Tuqentnu**): 70, 83, 88, 89, 108–114, *110*
Alexander Creek village site, (4.2 **Tuqen Kaq'**): 10, 14, 26, 27, 28, 81, 85, 96, 107, 109, *110, 113*
Alexander Lake, (4.23 **Deldida Bena**): 114
Alfred Creek, (14.65 **Tsedghaazi Na'**): 308
American Pass, (16.13 **Tsik'el'unt, Chik'el'unt**): 350
Anchorage, (15.77 **Dgheyay Kaq'**, 15.82 **Angits**; **Tan**; **Qatuk'e'usht**; **Ves Dnaghiłdeqt**): 3, 4, 7–9, 13, 14, 25, 40, 47, 169, 178, 179, 250, 261, 295, 321, 330–37, *335*, 340, 353, *plates 24, 25*
Anderson Creek, (2.18 **Q'eysestnu**): 89
Anderson Creek site, (2.17 **Q'eyses Kaq'**): 89
Anthracite Ridge, (14.43 **Tsaghedzigi**): 304, 305, *plate 15*
Archangel Creek, *plate 14*
Arctic Valley, (15.80 **Dgheyay Tl'u**): 332, *333, plates 24, 25*
Arkose Peak and ridge, (14.79 **Tsida K'ae Dghilaaye'**): 269, 297
Augustine Island: 87
Avalanche Spire, (9.35 **K'enik'ela**): 46, *205*

Baird Canyon, 217
Bak'nin'iy (mountain, caribou fence, site north of Puntilla Mt), (6.31): 137
"Bald Hills," (1.25 **Nuntnalyiy**): 34, 114
Bald Mountain, (11.9 **Dghelishla**): 218, 239, 254
Bald Mountain Ridge, (12.16 **Qughun**): 173, 178, 191, 202, 263, 267, 269
Barabara Lake, (16.29 **Baqay Ch'eh Bena**): 350
Bartlett Hills, (11.2 **Chuti Yits'a**): 238
Batzulnetas, Tanada Creek site: 17, 87, 220
Bear Creek (4.19 **Hniditnu**): 113
Bedlam Creek, (16.16 **Qach'eyni'utnu**): 350
Beluga Lake, (1.75 **Unqeghnit Nughiltnu Bena**): *71*, 72, 134
  Lower Beluga Lake (1.114 **Unqeghdut Nughiltnu Bena**): 70
Beluga Mountain, (4.20 **Hnidi**): 7, 23, 37, 70, 72, *113, 114*, 133, 134
Beluga Point: 15–16, 344
Beluga River, (1.70 **Nughiltnu**): 68, 69, 70, *71*, 72, 73
Beluga River, mouth of, (1.110 **Nughiltnu Kaq', Nughil Kaq'**): 56, *70*, 73, *81*
Beluga Slough, (2.36 **Bech'didatl'tnu**): 84
Benka Lake, (8.61 **Ben Ka'a**): 198
Bentułik'alashi (ridge west of Twin Peaks), (15.28): *285*, 322, *323, plate 19*
Beshta Bay, (1.40 **Bashda Q'atl'u, Bashda Ch'atl'utnił'u**): 62
"Big Bend" mountain (10.49 **Banazdleni**), 228, 232
Big Island, (2.34 **Susni Kaq' Hni'a**): 83
Big Lake, (13.18 **K'enaka Bena**): 100, 102, 271, *276–77*
Big River (Kuskokwim River): 143, 155
Billy Creek, (14.111 **Nalk'uugi Na'**): 305, 307, 308
Birch Creek (Talkeetna), (8.64 **Ch'atentnu**): 198, 238
Birchwood, (15.58 **Tuq'eyghił'ut**): 44, 324
Bird Creek, (16.3 **Esbaytnu**): 344
Bird Creek Pass, (16.3 **Esbaytnu Tustes**): 344
Bishop Creek, (1.113 **K'q'uya Betnu**): 70
Bishop Lake, (1.74 **K'q'uya Bena**): 70
Black Peak, (15.41 **Yudi Qeneh**): 324
Black River, (10.25 **Tułchuntnu**): 221
Bodenberg Butte, (15.4 **K'unast'in Shla**): *263, 314, 317*
Bodenberg Creek, (15.3 **K'unast'in Shlatnu**): 313
Bold Peak, (15.44 **Nuji Qeneh**): *324*
Boulder Creek (Chickaloon), (14.32 **Łtagetnu**): 238, 302, 306, 307, *plate 15*
  East Fork of Boulder Creek, (14.93 **Ts'etsiis Na'**): 302, 303
Broad Pass, Broad Pass area, (9.32 **Denyiht'u**): 33, *208, 209, 210*, 219
Bubb Creek: 232, 305, 308
Bulchitna Lake, (7.35 **Hneh'itnu Bena**): 47, 159
Bull River, (9.41, **Dghelaay Nhwtnestc'oxi Na'**): 210
Bunco Creek, (9.34 **Ben Ka'a Betnu**): 205
Bunco Lake, (9.13 **Ben Ka'a**): *46*, 205
Bunka Lake, (1.49 **Ben Ka'a**): 66
"Butcher Lake," (15.107 **Baquch'k'ilyuyi Bena**): 316
Butte Lake, (10.36 **Hwniidi Ben**): 85,87, 220, *228, 229*
Butterfly Lake, (12.6 **Unqeghnit Skitnu Bena**): 100, 262, *plate 5*
Byers Creek, (9.22 **Quntughet'ut Betnu**): 207
Byers Lake, (9.23 **Quntughet'ut Bena**): *207*

Cache Creek, (7.47 **Delggematnu**): 89, 161, 162, *165*, 203, *204*, 259, 325
Cairn Point and site, (15.75 **Tak'at**): 330, *331*
California Creek, (14.90 **Hnu Ch'k'eł'ihtnu**): 301, 344
Camp Creek (Yentna River), (7.38 **Hdaq K'ilantnu**): 161, *168*
Campbell Creek, (15.95 **Qin Cheghitnu**): 339, 341
Campbell Lake, (15.95 **Qin Cheghitnu**): 339
Campbell Point, (15.92 **Ułchena Huch'ilyut**): 63, 104, 295, 321, 338, 339, 349
Canyon Creek (Skwentna River), (6.49 **Denyihtnu**): 73, 134, 303
Cantwell, (10.55 **Yidateni Na'**): 228, 230, 232
Capps Glacier, (1.77 **Łich'antnu Łi'a**): *43, 72, plate 3*
Carbon Creek, (14.29 **Bashtl'ech'tnu**): 301
Caribou Creek (upper Matanuska River), (14.60 **Nutughilentnu**): 233, 302, 305, 306, 307, 308
Carpenter Creek, (14.26 **T'u'itnu**): 226, 232, 300, 301, 318
Castle Mountain, (14.30 **Hnu Ch'k'eł'iht**): *301*
Caswell Creek, (8.86 **Q'uch'u'itnu**): 192, 193 *19*

Caves Lake, (13.25 **Hnits'uk'nilut**): 277
Chakachatna River, (1.13 **Ch'akajatnu**): *51, 52*
Ch'akajabena Lake, (1.16 **Ch'akaja Bena**): 23, *25*, 47, 51, 53, 54
Ch'akajabena Mountain (1.126: **Ch'akaja Bena Dghil'u**):
Ch'ani'iy (<McArthur> ridge between McArthur River and Chakachatna River), (1.9): *51*
Ch'chihi Ken (ridge south of Mt. Susitna), (1.87): *13, 74, 81, 110*, 112, 341
Chedatna Lakes, (1.118 **Tl'equkena Bena**): *74*
Chedatna Lakes Flat, (1.84 **Tl'equkena**): 74
Chedotlothna Glacier: *plate 8*
Chelatna Lake, (7.40 **Ht'u Bena**): *160, 161*
Chester Creek, (15.84 **Chanshtnu**): 6, 8, 47, *279*, 332, *333*, 334, 337, 339, *plates 24, 25*
South Fork of Chester Creek, (15.127 **Nungge Betnu**): 334, 339
Chichantna River, (1.76 **Łich'antnu**): *71*, 72
Chickaloon Bay, (16.28 **Tutsahtnu Kaq'**): 349, 350, *351, plate 26*
Chickaloon Glacier, (14.95 **Nuk'din'itnu Łi'a**): 255, 303
Chickaloon Pass (to Oshetna River), (14.37 **Ucaek'e Hwdezk'aani Na'**): 279, 303
Chickaloon River (Turnagain Arm), (16.12 **Tutsahtnu**): 349, 350, *plate 26*
Chickaloon River; Chickaloon village, (14.31 **Nuk'din'itnu**): 220, 225, 226, 232, 233, 235, 255, 256, 257, 279, 291, 296, 298–303, *304*, 350, *plate 15*
Chijuk Creek, (8.30 **Hneh'itnu**): 182
Chikootna Creek, (14.100 [**Chikootna'** ?]): *305*
Chitina River: 87
Chitna Creek, (14.103 **Tsitna'**): 306
Chitna Pass, (14.105 **Nataghilen Na' Tates**): 302, 306
Chuitbuna Lake, (1.68 **Ben Ka'a, Ch'u'itnu Bena**): 70
Chuitbuna Lake outlet stream, (1.27 **Ben Ka'a Betnu**): 70
Chuitkilnachna Creek, (1.22 **Ch'k'e'uła Betnu**): 47, *54, 114*
Chuitt River, Chuitna River, (1.59 **Ch'u'itnu, Ch'ubetnu**): 44, 68, *69*, 78, 134
mouth of Chuitna River, (1.58 **Ch'u'itnu Hdakaq'**): 68
Chuitt Creek, (1.64 **Dghelikda Nutentnu**): *69*
Chulitna Pass, (10.9 **Chuqitnu Tustes**): 202, *218*, 219
Chulitna River, (9.1 **Ts'ilutnu**): 43, 46, 104, 199, 200–210, *207, 208, 210*, 232, 235
Chunilna Creek, also "Clear Creek," (11.4 **Ch'aniltnu**): 204, 209, 219, 235, 238, 241, 254, 255
mouth of Chunilna Creek and site, (11.3 **Ch'anilkaq'**): 238, 241
Clear Lake (Wasilla), (13.22 **Tunilch'eli Bena**): 277
Clearwater Creek (Yentna River), (7.29 **Tseles Qantnu**): 156, *158*
Clearwater Creek (Upper Susitna River), (10.51 **Snuu Na'**): 227
Clunie Creek, (15.66 **T'usq'a**): 328
Coal Creek (Beluga Lake): 71, *133, plate 4*
Coal Creek (Chickaloon), (14.39 **K'eyah Betnu Nughik'et'**): 303
Coal Creek (Chulitna River), (9.37 **Łch'ibay Ka'a Betnu**): 207
Coffee Creek (into Chuitt River), (1.73 **Esni Ghiłent**): 70
Coffee Creek (into Chelatna Lake), (7.59 **Ch'alentnu**): *160*, 161
Coffee Point to Duck Flats, (13.45 **Sdadintunt**): 298
Coffee River, (9.20 **Betnu Detniyitnu**): *206*, 207
Colony Glacier, (15.19 **Diłtishi Bena Łi'a**): 319
Columbia Peak, (6.24 **Beq'e Nutistuni**): 135
Congahbuna Lake, "Peter's Lake" or "Bird's Lake," (1.39 **K'enq'a Bena**): 44, 62
Constantine Harbor, Redoubt (Hinchinbrook Island): 87
Cook Inlet, (1.1 **Tikahtnu** or **Nuti**): 10, 50, 62, 63, 75–77, 85, 104, 112, 145–146, 272, 343, 345–347, 352, 354, 355, 357, *map 2*
Lower Cook Inlet: 13, 14
Outer Inlet dialect: 14, 56, *map 2*
Upper Cook Inlet: *See* Upper Cook Inlet
Western Cook Inlet: 48–74, *50*, 354
Copper River, (10.64 **Utnu**): 16, 17, 18, 28, 82, 85, 87, 88, 145, 180, 184, 215, 216, 221, 230, 232, 235, 271, 279, 282, 289, 290, 291, 297, 299, 306, 309, 310, 311, 313, 349
Cottonwood Creek, (13.36 **Łajatnu**): 277, 280, 285, *286*, 287, 319
Cottonwood Creek site, Cottonwood Village, (13.35 **Łajat**): 14, 226, 257, 280
Cottonwood Lake, (13.40 **Baqutsaghi'i Bena**): 284, 285, *plate 20*
Cottonwood Slough (Knik), (13.37 **T'ghes Hnidaghi'ut**): 226, 280, *286*
Cottonwood Slough (McArthur River), (1.12 **Tudesi Betnu**): 51
Cow Lake, (3.16 **Tl'eghes Bena**): *100*, 105, 261, 262, *plate 5*
Curry Ridge, (9.6 **K'esugi Ken**): *46*, 202

Daneka Lake, (11.24 **Deniigi Bene'**): 254
Deadman Creek, Deadman Lake. *See* Kacaagh Creek, Kacaagh Lake(s)
Deception Creek, (8.37 **Hech' Nuydlentnu**): 191, 263
Deep Creek, (4.27 **Deldida Bena Dinłent**): 114
"Delgga Mountain," (15.139, **Delgga Dghelaya**): 329
Delta Island, (2.2 **Buk'ghidaggi, Tuy'ingga**): 83
Delta River: 238
Delyndia Lake, (12.7 **Delindin Bena**): 1, 40, *100*, 262, *plate 5*
Dena'ina language area: 10–13, 147, *map 2*
Denali, Mt. McKinley, (7.51 **Dghelay Ka'a**): ix, *xiv, 46*, 87, 112, 113, 155, 159, 162, 163, *168, 199*, 201, 202, 211–213, 239, *249, plates 11, 13, 22*
Denali National Park and Preserve: xv, 208, 212, 216
Denali State Park: 201, 202, 249
Deshka River. *See* Kroto Creek.
Denyishla, (9.44, loc. in Broad Pass): 210
Devil Canyon, (10.12 **Nutughił'ut**): 18, 87, 145, 216, *217*, 219, 232
Diamond Lake, "Diamond Kid Lake": *351*
Dickason Mountain: *plate 6*
Dillinger River, (6.44 **Tetno' Hwchwh**): 143, 155, 159
Dinglishna Hill, (4.3 **Dinlishla**): *81, 110*, 111, 113
"Dinkle Lake," (13.56 **Nik'udatl'ech'a Bena**): 205, 207, 286
Dipper Lake, (16.30 **Shqit Bena**): 352
Disappointment Creek: 42, 238, 254
Dishno Pond, (15.79 [**Deshtnu Bena?**]): 332
Dogshead, (1.116 **Łik'a Kin'i**): *43*, 72, *plate 3*
Dogshead Glacier, (1.117 **Łik'a Kin'i Łi'a**): 44, 72
Donkey Creek, (7.12 **Keshch'a Betnu**):154
Donkey Creek Lake, (7.13 **Keshch'a Bena**): 154
"Dreese Pass," (14.104 **Tsitna' Tates**): 306
Drill Creek, (1.115 **Tahelitnu**): *71*, 72
Duck Flats, (13.45 **Sdadintunt**): 287
Dzeł Ggeyi (pass from Chickaloon River to Talkeetna River), (14.38): 256, 303

Eagle Bay, (15.64 **Nuk'elehitnu Kaq'**): 47, 328
Eagle Glacier, (15.72 **Nuk'elehitnu Łi'a**): 329
Eagle River, (15.65 **Nuk'elehitnu**): *328*, 321, 329, 344, 349
South Fork of Eagle River, (15.122 **Na'un Tutsaghala Betnu**): 329
Earthquake Park area, (15.90 **Nen Ghiłgedi**): 334, *plate 25*
East Foreland: 352
Edmonds Lake, (15.53 **Snutnadzeni T'ugh Daydliyi Ben**): 324
Egypt Mountain, (6.60 **Toy'draya'**): 142, 143, 155
Eider Lake, (16.41 **Unhtsahdi**): 357
Eightmile Creek, (6.3 **Ts'ahshlatnu**): 114, 131
Eightmile Lake, (6.4 **Ts'ahshlatnu Bena**): 131
Eklutna, (15.21 **Idlughet**): 3, 7, 10, 19, *20*, *25*, 25–28, 44, 47, 104, 267, 272, 275, 278, 280, 281, 285, 291, 292, 293, 295, 315, *320*, 321, 325–328, 331, 335
Eklutna Glacier, (15.49 **Idlu Bena Łi'a**): 324, *325*
Eklutna Lake, (15.36 **Idlu Bena**): 47, 322, *324*
Eklutna River, (15.24 **Idluytnu**): *285*, *323*, 324, *plate 18*
East Fork of Eklutna River, (15.46 **Niłtanikda Betnu**): 324
West Fork of Eklutna River, (15.48 **Bendilent**): 324
Eldridge Glacier and Fountain River, (9.25 **Łi Tayena**): *206*, 207, *plate 12*
Emil Lake: 197
Ephanasy Point, (16.8): 349
"Esbay Peak," (16.26 **Esbaytnu Dghelaya**): 344
Eska Creek, (14.17 **Ts'es Tuk'ilaght**): 297, 300
Eyak site: 87
Ezi Slough: 313

Falling Water Creek, (15.70 **Łiq'a Ta'a Bugh**): 328
Felt Lake: 71
Finger Lake (Skwentna River), (6.19 **Hnidi Bena**): 135, *plate 6*
Finger Lake (Wasilla), (13.54 **Baqay Tuch'elisht Bena**): 285, 296
Fire Creek, (15.59 **Ch'enełtash Betnu**): 325
Fire Island, (15.93 **Nutuł'iy**): 339, 348
Fire Lake, (15.60 **Ch'enełtash Bena**): 325
First Lake (Tyonek), (1.55 **Qaggeyshla Bena**): 68
Fish Creek (Anchorage), (15.87 **Ch'atanaltsegh**): 334
Fish Creek (from Red Shirt Lake), (3.11 **Tanłtun Betnu, Tanłtuntnu**): 99–106, 173
Fish Creek (Knik), (13.15 **K'enakatnu**): 14–16, 27, 28, 226, 271, 274, *276*, *277*, 278, 285, 324
Fish Creek (lower Yentna River), (5.3 **Ch'atanjeghet**): 121
Fish Lake (Chickaloon), (14.23 **Staeł Bene'**): 299, 300, 301
Fish Lake (Talkeetna), (8.63 **Ch'atem Bena**): 198
Fish Lake (upper Matanuska River), (14.64): 224, 308
Fish Lake Creek, (5.20 **Bentalitnu**): 123
Fish Lake villages, (5.21 **Bentalit**): 81, *124*, 123, 183
Flat Horn Lake, (3.3 **Bek'dilyashi Bena**): 99, 100, 259
Fog Creek, (10.13 **Sc'edae' Na'**): 219, 220
Fog Lakes, (10.44 **Sc'edae' Bene'**): 219, 220, 256, 257
"The Forks" (Talkeetna), (8.66 **Łinghasdlent**): *46*, 193, 194, 198, *199*, 201, 208, 255
Fort Alexander, (English Bay): 87
Fortress Creek, (14.61 **Hnilges Na'**): 308
Fortress Ridge, (14.62 **Hnilges**): 308
Fountain River, (9.25 **Łi Tayena**): *206*, 207
"Fourmile Creek," (15.55 **Dkenyi Betnu**): 325
Friday Creek, (15.13 **Ts'ihtnu**): *315*, 316
Frying Pan Lake, (12.14 **Tudli Bena Dunich'di**): 267

Gene Lake, (16.39 **Niłq'a Tighitun Bena**): 357
Gillbert Creek, (10.20 **Cets'i Sletna'**): 220, 232
Glacier Creek (Matanuska River), (14.56 **'Ałciis Na'**): 307
Glacier Point, (14.59 **Nutsada'iy**): 224, 231, 307, *308*, 310
Goat Creek, (15.6 **Łdagheltnu, Hdagheltnu**): 314, *plate 21*
Gold Creek, (10.5 **Quht'anagga K'etnu K'ilani**): 203, 207, 218, 219, 238
Goose Bay, (13.8 **Tustl'agh**): *260*, 273, *274*, 282
Goose Creek (Knik), (13.10 **Łeyestnu**): 220, 277
South fork of Goose Creek (Knik), (13.9 **Tustl'aghtnu**): 273
Goose Creek (upper Susitna River), (10.23 **Gguus Kulaen Na'**): 47, 220
Goose Creek (Willow), (8.87 **Tunadlut'**; 8.51 **K'eł Tuqishlatnu**): *193*, 195
Government Peak, (12.19 **K'eda Beq'e Nay'uni**): 269
Granite Creek (Alexander Creek), (4.5 **Dinlishlatnu**): *110*, 111
Granite Creek (Sutton), (14.19 **Hdighilentnu**): 226, 232, 297, *300*
Granite Peak, (14.83 **Hdighilen Dghilaaye'**): *300*
Granite Point, (1.27 **Badi Dulyasht**): *55*, 56, 60, 62, 104
Gravel Creek (Matanuska River), (14.53 **Ts'en Dabaas Na'**): 306
Green Lake, (15.124 **Ch'ak'dinłen Bena**): 329, 330
Grey's Creek, (8.81 **Q'istnu**): 191
Gulkana(village): 223, 231, 232, 295, 209, 306
Gulkana River: 222, 227, 303 221, 223, 224, 227, 232, 295, 303
Gull Rock, (16.11 **Qeshqa Eł Tak'niqats't**): 349
Gunsight Creek, (14.72 **Siz'aani Na'**): 309
Gunsight Mountain, (14.71 **Siz'aani**): 145, 224,231, *309*
Gypsum Creek, (14.112 **Beznae Na'**): 308

Happy River, (6.22 **Kech'itnu**): 32, 132, 135–137, 156, 157, 161, 267, *plate 4*
Hatcher Pass: 280
Hayes River, (6.15 **Tubughna Katidiłtuni Betnu**): 134, 135, *plate 4*
Hayes River Pass, (6.17 **Tubughna Katidiłtuni**): 23, 71, 134, *plate 4*
Hayes Volcano: 153
Hellsgate or "Ptarmigan Pass," (6.39 **Nik'uhhay Niłjenghiyut**): 139, *141*
Hewitt Creek, (7.1 **Tiq'atl'ena Betnu**): 151, *154*
Hewitt Lake, (7.3 **Tiq'atl'ena Bena**): 15, 16, 104, 119, 131, 134, *149*
Hewitt Lake village site, (7.2 **Tiq'atl'ena**): 134, 146, *149*–153
Hicks Creek, (14.50 **Hdgheltnu**): 290, 305, 306, *307*
Hicks Lake, (14.51 **Hdghel Bena**): 304, 305
Hidden River: *plate 11*
Highpower Creek, (**Tsat'asr Nek'**): 146
Hiline Lake, (6.9 **Bak'elghiłi Bena**): 23, 133
Hninaghi'iy Ka'a (hill at Glenn Highway/Old Palmer Highway junction), (15.20): 319, *320*
Hogan Hill, (**K'ey Tsaagha**): 221
Holitna River: 142, 145
Honolulu Creek, (9.30 **Benench'iltledi Betnu**): 208
Hood Creek, (15.129 **Niłkidal'iy Betnu**): 334
Hook Creek, (**Tałchatnaq'**): 146
Hope-Sunrise townsites, (16.10 **Tutl'uh**): 349
Htidaghitunt (site east of mouth of Crocker Creek), (13.34): 280
Htsay Nenq' plateau at upper Stony-Holitna-Mulchatna rivers: 14, 146, 222
Htsay Nenq'e, (10.29 West Ahtna Uplands): 145, 146, 222, 233

"Hughes Creek" (from Lucy Lake), (13.51 **Htidaghituntnu**): 280
Hunter Creek, (15.14 **Łdik'eyusht**): *318*, 319
Hurricane Creek, Hurricane Gulch, (9.28 **Qununahch'dghashjuy Betnu**): *207*, 208

Ida Lake: 300
Idaho Peak, (12.20 **Beq'e Ndnadalyut**): 269
Iditarod Trail: 89, 135, 141, 157, 170, 237, 281
Iliamna Lake: 10, 49
"Indian Bay" (Nancy Lake), (12.13 **K'itudaghi'ut**): 267
Indian Creek (Turnagain Arm), (16.2 **Nuti Ediłeni**): 337, 344
Indian Creek (Tyonek), (1.51 **Qaggeyshlat Betnu**): 66
Indian Creek (Yentna River), (5.15 **Jan Bughutnu**): 123
Indian Creek Pass, (16.24 **Nuti Ediłeni Tustes**): 344
Indian River (upper Susitna River), (10.8 **Chuqitnu**): 203, 210, *218*, 219
Inland dialect: 10, *map 2*
Iron Creek, (8.78 **Nudayk'et'i Betnu**): 191
Isabel Pass: 238, 296
Ivan River, (1.86 **Ch'qi'untnu**): 74

Jack River, (10.55 **Yidateni Na'**): *209*, 210, 230
Jacobsen Lake, (13.23 **Hey Gega Bena**): 277
Jim Creek, (15.8 **Dghełtayi Betnu**): 40, 295, 313–317, *315*
Jim Lake, (15.9 **Dghełtayi Bena**): 315
Johnson Creek (7.17 **Tuk'elehtnu**), 154, 164-
Jones River, (6.58 **Tetno' Hwgoya**): 142, 143
Judd Lake, (6.47 **Tununiłch'ulyutnu Bena**): *133*, 134

Kacaagh Creek (formerly Deadman Creek), (10.15 **Kacaagh Na'**): 220
Kachemak Bay: 14, 27, 153, 349
Kahiltna Glacier, (7.48 **Kagheltnu Łi'a**): 162
Kahiltna River, (7.42 **Kagheltnu**): 119, 123, 149, *160*, 161, 162, 163, 182, 183, 203
Kaldachabuna Lake, (1.44 **Batutnalyuy Bena, Batunk'elyashi Bena**): 44, 63
Kalgin Island: 109, 245, 353, 355
Kalifornsky site and stream, (**Unhghenesditnu**): 147
Kamishak Bay: 87
"Kanchee Point," (15.85 **Qanchi**): xvii, 334
Kanikula Glacier, (9.16 **K'enik'ela Łi'a**): *205*, *plate 13*
Kashwitna Glacier, (8.47 **Kiłbitnu Łi'a**): 192
Kashwitna Knobs, (8.82 **Hnibes**): 191
Kashwitna Lake: 177
Kashwitna River, (8.43 **Kiłbitnu**): 102, 178, 191, *193*
  mouth of Kashwitna River, (8.83 **Kiłbitnu Kaq'**): 191
  North Fork of Kashwitna River, (8.84 [**Yus Tutay'uhtnu** (?)]): 192
  upper Kashwitna River, (8.44 **Kiłbitnu Tl'u**): 177, 191, *193*
Kasilof River, (**Ggasilatnu**): 17, 147
K'chanli (hill north of Old Tyonek), (1.32): 55
K'eł Taydeght (bluff two miles north of the mouth of Eagle River), (15.63): 47, 328
Kenai: 9, 10, 13, 17, 19, 21, 27, 32, 37, 50, 59, 60, 68, 83, 87, 109, 125, 179, 195, 220, 227, 229, 237, 261, 271, 278, 301, 311, 321, 335, 339, 344, 346, 349, 350, *356*
Kenai Bay: 290
Kenai Mountains: 350
Kenai Peninsula, (16.23 **Yaghenen**): 28, 62, 76, 102, 147, 153, 340, 354
Kenai River: 14, 15, 16, 63, 75, 87
Kenibuna Lake, (1.20 **Hni Bena**): 54
Kepler Lake, Bradley Lake, Matanuska Lake (14.77 **Tuhnaghiłkits Bena**): 290
K'esugi Ridge, (9.7 **K'esugi**): 40, 47, 173, 202, *203*, *207*, *208*, *218*, 219, *plate 12*
Ketchumstock Uplands, (**Hwtthaayh Nénn'** Tc):145, 222
K'ey Tsaaygha (10.61 hill N of Tyone River) 145, 222
Kichatna Mountains, (7.28 **K'its'atnu Dghelaya**): 156
Kichatna River, (7.19 **K'its'atnu**): 18, 32, 120, 138, 147, 154–156, 159, 161, 167, 237, 332
  upper Kichatna River, (7.26 **K'its'atnu Tl'u**): *156*
K'idazq'eni Glacier, formerly Kidazqeni Glacier, (1.91 **K'idazq'eni Łi'a**): 47, *53*, 53, 54
Kijik site: 16
King Lake, (16.47 **Benkda**): 357
King Mountain, (14.28 **Bashtl'ech'**): 226, 301
Kings River, (14.20 **Ch'tałtnu**): 226, 300
Knik, Knik townsite, New Knik, (13.29 **Nughay Bena**, 13.16 **K'enakatnu**): 10, 14, 17, 19, 25–28, 32, 81, 91, 100, *103*, 107, 161, 218, 225, 226, 255, 257, 259, 261, 272, 274, 275, 277, 278, *281–283*, 286, 287, 289, 291, 292, 293, 295, 303, 309, 321, 331, 332, 337, 344, 349, 353, 355
  Old Knik. *See* Eklutna
Knik Arm, (13.2 **Nuti**): ix, *xiv*, 13, 14, 15, 18, 19, 22, 24, 25, 28, 44, 85, 104, 257, 259, 268, 271, 272, 278, 275, *285*, 312–342, *plates 19, 22*
  Western Knik Arm area, Knik-Big Lake area, (13.1 **K'enaka Nen**): *xiv*, 14, 102, 270–287, 328, *plate 22*
  Knik Arm and Cook Inlet, (13.2 **Nuti**): 272
Knik Glacier, (15.15 **Skitnu Łi'a**): *35*, 231, 317, 319, *plate 23*
Knik Lake, (13.29 **Nughay Bena**): 278
Knik River, (15.2 **Skitnu**): 24, 25, 27, *35*, 231, 290, 291, 294, 295, *313*, *314*, *plate 23*
"The Knobs" (Eklutna), (15.22 **Idlishla**, 15.23 **Idlika'a**): 321, 322, *plate 19*
Knob Hill, (14.74 **Hwyiis Tes**): 309
Knob Lake, (14.117 **Hwyiis Tes Bene'**): 309, *plate 15*
"Knoya Peak," (15.86 **K'nuy'a**): 47, 334
Kohlsaat Peak, (6.54 **Qułtsadi**): 40, 122, 132, 138
"Koktaya Peak," (15.99 **K'uhda'i**): 47, 341
Kosina Creek, (10.19 **Cets'i Na'**): 220
Kroto Creek, (8.10 **Tuqentnu, Dashq'e Betnu**): 9, 13, 14, 16, 19, 41, 82, 109, *174*, 175–183, 193, *plate 9*
  mouth of Kroto Creek, (8.9 **Dashq'e Kaq'**): 175, *plate 9*
  upper Kroto Creek area, (8.34 **Tuqentnu Tl'u**): 183
Kroto Slough, (8.4 **Beq'e Tach'itqeyi Q'eghtsi**): *174*, 175, *plate 9*
Kroto village, Kroto Creek village, (8.12 **Dashq'e**): 8, 10, 26, 27, 28, 85, 90, 101, 104, 107, 116, 121, 161, 173, 175–180, 184–191, 193, 195, 201–203, 237, 244, 247, 335
Kuskokwim River, (6.61 **Dichina Nek', Kenaniq'**): 10, 33, 120, 121, 143, 146, 159, 267
  South Fork of Kuskokwim River, (6.42 **Idzitnu**): 70, 119, 132, 135, 136, 139, *141*, 142, 143, 146, 156
Kustatan Peninsula, Kustatan village site, (1.121 **Qezdeghnen, Qeydeghnen**): 10, 13, 28, 44, 49, *50*, 51, 53, 58, 62, 59, 60, 62, 147, 248, 272, 335, 345, 350, 353, 357
Kutna Creek, (5.12 **K'etnu**): 123
Kutzkatna Creek, (14.102 [**Q'ech' K'etnu** ?]): 305

Łach Q'atnu Creek, (15.33 **Łach Q'atnu**): 47, 322
Ladd, (1.58 **Ch'u'itnu Hdakaq'**): 68
Lake Barbara, (15.31 **Benshla**): 322

Lake Ahtna, Glacial Lake Ahtna: 145, 217, 222, 228
Lake Clark: 13, 142
Lake Clunie, (15.67 **Ben Ka'a**): 328
Lake Creek (from Chelatna Lake), (7.39 **Ht'u Bena Q'estsiq'**, 7.34 **Hneh'itnu**): 123, 159, 161
Lake Creek (from Nancy Lake), (12.9 **Tudli Betnu**): 260, 262
Lake Creek (Matanuska River), (14.55 **Tałtaan Na'**): 307
Lake Creek (upper Susitna River): 328
Lake Fork, (15.17 **Diłtishi Betnu**): 319
Lake George, (15.18 **Diłtishi Bena**): 273, 290, 291, 293, 295, 319
Lake Leila, (14.126 **Siz'aani Bene'** : 224, 309
Lake Louise, "Susitna Lake," (10.34 **Susni Bena**): 145, 215, 222, 223, 227, 231, 293, 304
Lake Lucille, Lucile Lake, (13.24 **Benkda**): 277, 285
Lake Spenard and Lake Hood, (15.89 **Niłkidal'iy Bena**): 334
Lane Creek, (10.39 **Ts'estałkitnu**): 218
Larson Lake, (11.8 **Batnaghałnigi**): *239*
Leech Lake, (2.30 **Ha Bena**): 93
Lewis River, (1.85 **Ts'idatnu**): 74
Lime Village: 10, 31, 42, 53, 54, 143, 266, 320
Linquist Creek, (14.27 **Bes Tl'ests' Deyii**): 301
Lion Head, formerly Glacier Point, (14.59 **Nutsada'iy**): 224, 307, *308*, 310
Little Jack Slough: 49
Little Montana Creek, (8.89 **Qiduk'ggatnu**): 43, 193, 194
Little Montana Creek Lake, (8.90 **Qiduk'ggat Bena**): 194
Little Mt. Susitna, (1.83 **Henq'e Dishla**): *74, 81, 114, 174, plate 9*
Little Nelchina River, (14.119 **Neltsii Na', Neltsiin Na'**): 223, 232, 304, 308, 309
Little Oshetna River, (10.27 **Q'usashlatnu**): 220, 221, 308
Little Peters Creek, (15.56 **Qintali Betnu**): 325
Little Susitna River, (12.2 **Tsałtastnu**): 19, 42, 100, 192, 258–269, *269*, 273, 277, 280, 349, *plate 14*
Little Willow Creek, (8.40 **Bantsach'elashitnu**): 191, 192
Lockwood Lake, (5.4 **Qanłik'edlis Bena**): 121
Lone Butte (Oshetna River), (10.28 **Yusdi**): 145, 221, 232
Lone Creek, (1.64 **Dghelikda Nutentnu**): 69
Lone Ridge, (1.65 **Dghelikda Nuten**): *69*, 134
Long Lake (Matanuska River), (14.44 **Tsaghedzigi Bene'**): 304
Long Lake (Campbell Creek), (15.133 **Qin Cheghi Bena**): 341
Long Lake Hills, (6.27 **Sandalyut**): 136
Lost Lake, (13.6 **K'teleh Bena**): 273
Lowland Kacaagh Lake (formerly Deadman Lake), (10.16, **Qukugh Bena**): 47, 87, 220
Lucile Lake, (13.24 **Benkda**): *See* Lake Lucille
Lucille Creek, (13.21 **Tutik'ełtuni Betnu**): 277
Lucy Lake, (13.52 **Htidaghitun Bena**): 280
Lynx Creek and site, (3.23 **Nich'ghilentnu**): 101, 105
Lynx Lake, (3.24 **Nich'ghilen Bena**): *100*, 105, *plate 5*

Maguire Creek, (12.3): 259
Matanuska Glacier, (14.57 **Ch'atanhtnu Łi'a**): 225, *307*, *plate 15*
Matanuska Lake, (14.77 **Tuhnaghiłkits Bena**): 290
Matanuska River, (14.2 **Ch'atanhtnu**): 14, 15, 17, 21, 22, 24, 27, 35, 41, 42,145, 215, 216, 220, 223–226, 231, 232, 233, 257, 269, 275, 277, 278, 279, 281, 288–311, *313*, 316, 318, 321, 350, *plate 15*
East Fork of Matanuska River, (14.116 **Naghilenden**): 309
South Fork of Matanuska River, (14.69 **Dzeł Ghaan' Na'**): 308, *plate 16*
Matanuska Valley area, lower Matanuska River and Palmer area, (14.5 **Denal'i Kena**): 257, *263*, 275, 292, 321, 324, 353
Matanuska village site, (14.4 **Niteh**): 18, 22, 26–28, 52, 87, 178, *195*, 220, 257, 267, 278, 285, 290–295, *294*, 297, 313–315, 318, 334, 338, 339, *plate 21*
McArthur Glacier and/or Blockade Glacier, (1.10 **Nadudiltnu Łi'a**): 51
McArthur River, (1.2 **Nadudiltnu**) : 49, *50*, 60, 68
McDoel Mountain or ridge, (6.23 **Kiq'eh Dghelaya**): 135, 161, *plate 6*
McDougall, (5.17 **Hneh'itnu Kaq'**): 123, 159, 161
McHugh Creek, (15.135 **Q'isqa Betnu**): 341
McHugh Peak, (15.103 **Q'isqa Dghelaya**): 341, *plate 26*
McLaren River, (10.50 **C'iidze' Na'**): 222, 227, 231
Meadow Creek, (15.68 **K'ulch'eytnu**): 277, 328
Mendeltna Creek: 311
Merrill Pass, (**Tutnutl'ech'a Tustes**): 13, 53
Metal Creek, (15.110 **[Yuyantnu?]**): 44, *315*, 318, 349
Middle Fork and Windy Fork of Big River: 143, 145, 155
Middle River, "Allowan River," (1.122 **Jateghił'iy Betnu**): 51
Middleton Island: 87
Miller Creek, (16.33 **Nuch'ishtuntnu**): 354
Mirror Lake and Edmonds Lake, (15.53 **Snutnadzeni T'ugh Daydliyi Ben**): 324
The Mitre, (15.50 **Idlu Bena Dghelaya**): 324
Montana Creek, (8.91 **Nultani Betnu**): 173, 191, 193, *199*, 235, 237, 239
North Fork of Montana Creek, (8.93 **Nuch'elehitnu**): 197
South Fork of Montana Creek, (8.54 **Tsit'untali Betnu**): 197
Montana Creek village, (8.52 **Qiduk'ggat**): 10, 28, 181, 193, *194–197*, 199, 237, 256, 331, 335
Montana Peak, (12.22 **Tsałtastnu Dghelaya**): 269
"Moonshine Creek," (15.74 **Ch'ak'dinłenghet**): 329, 330
Moose Creek (into Kroto Creek), (8.33 **Untuhtay'untnu**): 183, 232, *plate 10*
Moose Creek (Rainy Pass), (6.32 **Chuqitnu**): 137, 138
Moose Creek (Sutton), (14.14 **Chidaq'atnu**): 231, 296, 297, *298*, 300, 302, *304*
Moose Creek (Yentna River), (5.10 **Denyiht'u**): 123
Moose Creek Lake (Rainy Pass), (6.33 **Ch'dat'ana Bena**): 137
Moose Point, (16.22 **Hnik'daghi'ut**): 354
Mooses Tooth (9.40 **[Dnighi Ghi]**): *46*, *plate 12*, *206*, **207**
Moquawkie Indian Reservation: 62
"Mosquito Point," (13.14 **Ts'es I'unt**): 274
Moss Creek, formerly "Thirtymile Creek," (14.36 **Staq'ay K'ilantnu**): 255, 303
Mt. Deception, (9.36 **Łi Tayena Dghelaya**): *46*, *206*, 207, *249*
Mt. Eklutna, (15.52 **Snutnadzeni**): *323*, 324, *plate 19*
Mt. Foraker, (7.49 **Be'u**): *46*, 162, *163*, *168*, *170*, *plate 13*
Mt. Gerdine, (1.80 **Qayeh Dghelaya**): 72
Mt. Goode, (15.16 **Skitnu Dghelaya**): *35*, *317*, *319*, *plate 23*
Mt. Hunter, (7.50 **Begguya**): *46*, 162, *plate 13*
Mt. Kliskon, (7.30 **Tseles Qan**): *158*, 161
Mt. Magnificent, (15.69 **K'ulch'ey**): 328
Mt. Marcus Baker, (14.58 **Ch'atanhtnu Dghelaya**): *35*, 307, *plate 23*
Mt. McKinley, Denali, (7.51 **Dghelay Ka'a**): *See* Denali
Mt. Rumble, (15.120 **Htestighitun Dghelaya**): 325
Mt. Russell, (7.60 **Ch'ighu' Tsats'ela**): 162, *170*, *plate 8*
Mt. Sergeant Robertson, (14.109 **'Ałciis Dghilaaye'**): 307
Mt. Spurr, (1.17 **K'idazq'eni** *(O)*, **K'idayq'eni** *(U)*): *52*, 53, 54, *plate 17*

Mt. Susitna, (4.9 **Dghelishla**): *13*, 37, *64*, 70, *74*, *81*, *92*, 109, *110*, 111, *112–114*, 162, 218, 239, 339, 341, *plates 5, 9, 17*
"Mt. Sutton," (14.18 **Neltsii Ce'e**): 297
"Mt. Tikishla," (15.97 **Ghedishla**): 341
Mt. Torbert, (1.78 **T'etniya**): *72*, *plate 3*
Mt. Watana, (10.18 **Łts'ibaay**): 47, 220
Mt. Yenlo, (7.14 **Dghelikda**): *154*, *158*, 161
Mt. Yukla, (15.123 **Nuk'elehitnu Dghelaya**): 47, 328
Mud Lake, (15.106 **Quggesh Bena**): 280, 315, *317*
Mulchatna River, (**Vałts'atnaq'**): 60, 146
Mule Creek, (13.46 **K'telehtnu**): 273
Mull Lake, (16.17 **Qach'eyni'u Bena**): 350
"Murder Lake": *254*
Mystic Pass, (7.58 **Ch'idotl'uł No' Dotis**): *159*

Nagishlamina River, (1.19 **Nahq'ashla Betnu**): 43, 54
Nakochna River, (7.20 **Nanquq'tnu, Nunquhtnu** [?]): 155, 156
Nancy Creek, (12.15 **Betnu K'etelehitnu**): 263, 267
Nancy Lake, (12.12 **Tudli Bena**): 1, 2, 3, 5, 7, 100, 101, 102, 105, 173, 175, 192, 193, 259, *260*, 262, *263*, 264, *265*, 267
"Nantina Point," (15.138, **Nant'ina**): 329
Neacola River, (1.21 **Nikugh Betnu**): 54
Neckshortka Lake, (16.31): 352
Neil Lake, (8.32 **Benteh**): 182, 183
Nelchina River: 223, 300, 304, 305, 309, 310
Nen' Yese' Ridge, (10.62, **Nen' Yese'**): 47, 145, 228, 233
Nenana River, (10.54 **Ninena'**, 10.53 **Łuyinanest'aani Na'**): 204, 208, 209, 210, 215, 219, 221, 228, 231, 242
New Knik. *See* Knik
Nicolai Village (Point Possession), (16.21 **Ch'aghałnikt**): 26, 351–353
Nikiski, Nikishka: 28, 104, 321
Nikleson Lake, (13.41 **Hundadi Bena**): 285
Nikolaevsk, (Kenai): 19, 143, 311
Nikolai Creek, (1.24 **Sdidahtnu**): *54*, *114*
Nikolai Village: 145, 146, 162
Nik'udatl'ech'a (site at "Dinkle Lake"), (13.54): 285, *286*, 287, *plate 19*
Nilben Caegge (site at mouth of Tyone River), (10.30): 222
Nin Ridge, (7.25 [**Nen** ?]): 156
Niteh, (14.4). *See* Matasnuska site
Noaukta Slough, (1.3 **Nughi'ukda**): 50, *51*
Nondalton: 10, 13, 31, 42, 103, 332
North Foreland, (1.48 **Batl'eghdink'et'**): 50, *63*, 66, 345
North Rolly Lake, (8.7 **Tutikaq' Bena**): 105, 175
Nudinli (ridge between Beluga Mt. and Mt. Susitna), (4.18): *71*, *113*, *114*
Nultani (mountains on upper middle fork of Montana Creek), (8.56): 194, *197*, 239
Nunaka Valley, (15.96 **Nungge, Nunegge**): 334, 339
Nunhdat'unh (Alaska Range between East and West Forks of the Yentna River), (7.33): 158, 159, *170*
Nuntnalyiy ("Bald Hills"), (1.25): 55, *114*
Nunutsahdnulchet (site on lower Kroto Creek), (8.22): 181, 182, 188
Nutnasdlenitnu (upper Talachulitna River), (6.10): 72, 114, 133, 134

O'Brien Creek, (13.33 **Ch'ak'dinłent**): 279, 280
Ocean Bay (Kodiak): 15
Old Knik. *See* Eklutna; *also see* Matanuska site.
Old Man Creek, (14.121 **Una' Cenael'sdildeli Na'**): 223, 311
Old Man Lake, (10.63 **Ben Daes Bene'**): 145, 228, 291, 304
Old Tyonek, (1.30 **Tubughnenq'**): *56–59*, 63, *64*, 66, 78
Old Tyonek Creek, "Robert's Creek," (1.29 **Ch'elehtnu**): 44, 56, 62, 66
Olsjold Lake, (16.42 **Uch'eh Dałtuni**): 357
Olson Creek, (1.71 **Q'aghiltnu**): 70
Oshetna River, (10.24 **Q'usatnu**): 215, 216, 220, 221, 232, 279, 303
Otter Lake, (15.73 **K'ka Bena**): 329
Out Lake, (3.13 **K'enuq' Bena**): 100, 121
Outer Inlet dialect area: 10, 13, 49, 57, 59, 346, *map 2*

Packsaddle Gulch, (14.47 **Hdghelshlatnu**): 305
Palmer area, Palmer town, (14.5 **Denal'i Kena**): 216, 223, 226, 275, 292, 293, 295, 305, *313*, *314*
"Palmer Canyon," (14.9 **Nil'atsa'it'ut**): 226, *292*
Palmer Slough: 287
Pass Creek (Chulitna River), (9.27 **Ałtnu**): 208, *249*
Pass Creek (Rainy Pass), (6.38 **Niljentnu**): 139
Pass Creek, Chickaloon Pass (to Oshetna River), (14.37 **Ucaek'e Hwdezk'aani Na'**): 303
"Pedro Creek," (11.16): 256
Pepper Lake, (16.40 **Gidara Q'dalchini**): 357
"Peter's Creek" (Tyonek), (1.39 **K'enq'a Betnu**): 62
Peters Creek (Chugiak), (15.118 **K'anakatnu**, 15.54 **Htestighitun Betnu**): 324, 325
Peters Creek (Kahiltna River), (7.45 **K'enuqak'itnetan Betnu**): *160*, 162
Peters Creek (Willow Creek), (8.36 **Nubendaltuntnu**): 183
Peters Hills, (7.46 **K'enuqak'itnetant**): 41, *46*, *157*, *162*, 202, 203, 204
"Pete's Slough": 194, *196*
Pierce Creek, (4.8 **Etl' Ghiłgetnu**): 88, 111, 112
Pincer Creek, (16.14 **Baqay Ch'ehtnu**): 350
Pinnacle Mountain, (14.22 **Neltsii Sle**): 300
Pioneer Peak, (15.7 **Dnal'iy**, **Denal'iy**): *35*, *290*, 292, *313*, *314*, *plates 20, 21*
"Pirate Lake": 206
Point Harriet: 49, 55
Point MacKenzie, (13.3 **Dilhi Tunch'del'usht Beydegh**): 14, *272*, 273
Point Possession, (16.20 **Tuyqun**): 5, 7, 9, 17, 26 28, 49, *190*, 267, 301, 339, *345*, 346–349, *350–352*, 354–357
Point Possession village, Nicolai village, (16.21 **Ch'aghałnikt**): 26, *103*, 180, 349, 351–*353*
Point Woronzof, (15.91 **Nuch'ishtunt**): 6, *112*, 295, 331, 334, 336, *338*, 339, 354, *plate 25*
Polly Creek, (**Tałin Ch'iłtant**): 10, 49, 55, 60, 75
Porcupine Butte, (6.13 **Sheshjesh**): 134
Portage Creek (Happy River), (6.28 **Tus Nuch'k'elyashtnu**): 136, 137, 217, 219
Portage Creek (Turnagain Arm), (16.5 **Tutl'uh Betnu**): 349
Portage Creek (upper Susitna River): 217, 219
Portage Glacier, (16.6 **Tutl'uh Yun'e Łi**): *344*, 349
Portage Pass, (16.7 **Ułchena Hch'aqedełt**): 135, 349
Portage Pass (to Styx River), (6.52 **Tus Nuch'k'elyasht**): 136
Port Wells: 344
Post River: 142
Potter Creek, (15.102 **Hkaditali Betnu**): 341
Potter Marsh, (15.101 **Hkaditali**): 341
Powell Glacier, (14.113 **Dzeł Ghaan' Luu'**): 308
Prairie Creek, (11.11 **Tatik'niłtuntnu**): 35, 232, 240, *242*, 254, *255*, 256
Prince William Sound: 87

Ptarmigan Creek, (6.57 **Htal Betnu**): 139, *141*, 162
"Ptarmigan Pass," (6.39 **Nik'uhhay Niłjenghiyut**): 10, 139, *141*
Ptarmigan Valley and the Rainy Pass area, (6.35 **Htal**): *See* Rainy Pass
Puddingstone Hill, (14.92 **Ts'es Nay'detkay**): 302, *plate 15*
Puntilla Lake, (6.30 **Kech'itnu Bena, Bendiltunt**): 137
Purinton Creek, locally "Puritan Creek," (14.46 **K'ay'delghots' Na'**): *304*, 305

Qintali (mountain, elev. 4786', east of Chugiak), (15.57): *325*
Qunk'eltl'asht (sites on upper Susitna River, near Lake Creek), (10.37): 229

Rabbit Creek, (15.100 **Ggeh Betnu**): 341, *plate 26*
Rabbit Lake, (15.134 **Ggeh Bena**): 341
Rabbit Slough, (13.44 **Qunsghitnu**): 232, *287*, *plate 21*
"Railroad Creek," (9.4 **Tuch'etl'ghi'ut**): 201
Rainy Pass, (6.56 **Niłjentnu Tustes**): 139, 143
Rainy Pass area, (6.35 **Htal**): 2, 9, 10, 28, 30, 33, 50, 70, 81, 97, 132, 138, 140, *141*, 142–146, 149, 154, 159, 164, 267
Raven Ridge, (15.123 **Nuk'elehitnu Dghelaya**): 329
Red Creek, (7.16 **K'qiy'untnu**): 154
Red Lake, (6.20 **Kiq'eh Dghelaya Bena**): 135, *plate 6*
Red Salmon Lake, (6.14 **Shesh Bena, Seshjesh Bena**): 134
"Red Shirt Creek," (11.17): 256
Red Shirt Lake, (3.19 **Tanłtun Bena**): 17, 23, 81, 93, 99, 100–102, 105–107, 150, 173, *174*, 259, 262, 264, 265, 273, 277, *plate 5*
Red Shirt Lake village site, (3.18 **Tanłtunt**): *101*
Redoubt Bay: 23
Reedy Lake: *285*, *286*, *plate 18*
Reindeer Hill, (**Yidateni**): 230
Resurrection Creek, (16.9 **Tutsilitnu**): 349, *plate 27*
Riley Creek, (14.41 **Tandze Laedze' Na'**): 225, 304
"Robert's Creek," (1.29 **Ch'elehtnu**): 44, 57
Robideaux Creek, (8.94 **Tuqentnu**): 198
Rock Glacier Creek, (14.110 **Natsede'aayi Na'**): 307
Rolly Creek, (8.6 **Tutikaq'tnu**): 175
"Rohn River," (6.43 possibly [**Duditnu**]): 142
Rumble Pass, (15.119 **Htestighitun Tustes**): 325
Ruth Glacier, (9.18 **Dghelay Ka'a Łi'a**): 43, *46*, 163, *199*, 201, 203, 205

Saltigi (hill, elev. 3537', <Tyone>), (10.32): 222, *227*
Sanona Creek, (10.48 **Snuu Na'**): 222
Sdak'dal'iy (bend on lower Yentna River), (5.8): 89, 122, 123, 150, 181
Second Lake (Tyonek), (1.56 **Tuk'eleh Bena**): 68
Seldovia: 10
Seven Egg Creek, (16.35 **Quqegh Nik'eteleht**): 354
Sevenmile Lake, (13.11 **Biłni Dnaghelggey Bena**): 273, 274
Sheep Creek (Willow), (8.49 **Baqay Nilyashtnu**): 192, 197
Sheep Mountain (Matanuska River), (14.68 **Beznae**): 224, 306, 307, 308
Sheep River, (11.10 [**Dghelishlatnu** (?)]): 42, 239, 300, 303
Shell Hill, (6.11 **Nusdatl'na Nichila**): 134, *149*
Shell Lake, (6.12 **Nusdatl'na Nichila Bena**): 134
Shellabarger Pass, (6.59 **Tetno' Hwchwh Dotis**): 142, *156*, 159, *plate 7*
"Shem Pete Lake": *357*
"Shem Pete Slough," (8.2 **Ch'atanaltsegh**): 173
Shesh Nena (ridge between Cow Lake and Little Susitna River), (12.5): 101, 261, 262
Seward: 7, 268, 281, 285, 335, 340, 349
Ship Creek, (15.78 **Dgheyaytnu**): 272, 332, 338, 339, 344
  mouth of Ship Creek, (15.77 **Dgheyay Kaq'**): 273, 330, 332, *333*
  upper Ship Creek, Arctic Valley, (15.80 **Dgheyay Tl'u**): 332, *333*, 344, *plates 24, 25*
(lake above) Shirley Lake, (6.25 **Beq'e Nutistin Bena**): 135
Shulin Lake, (7.44 **Chulyin Bena**): *160*, 162
Simpson Pass, (7.27 **K'ich'atnu Tustes**): 139, 142, *155*, 156
Sixmile Creek, (15.74 **Ch'ak'dinłenghet**): 329, 330
Six-Mile Lake, (15.124 **Ch'ak'dinłen Bena**): 329, 330
Skeetna Lake, (12.24 **Skitnu Bena**): 44, 262
"Ski Hill," (8.65 **Hnibes Ka'a**): *46*, 198
'Skosii'den (lake, site southwest Lake Louise), (10.56): 223, 227
Skwentna River, (6.2 **Shqitnu**): 10, 13, 23, 54, 69, 70, *73*, 130–139, *132*, 141,147, 149, 164, 352
  upper Skwentna River, (6.29 **Shqitnu Tl'u**): *136*, 137, *138*, 146
"Soldiers Creek," (13.50 **Ch'ak'nileghtnu**): 276, 277
Southern Alaska Range, (6.41 **Dzeł Ken**): 50, 59, 87, 139, 142, 146
South Peak Canyon, (4.7 **Tsedi Bak'ilani**): 111
Sovereign Mountain, (11.19 **K'dalkitnu Dghelaya**): 256, 303
Spring Creek, (6.16 **Denyiht'u**): 134
Square Lake, (10.59 **Ht'u Ben**): 42, 85, 86, 220
Stephan Lake (Knik), (13.12 **Łeyes Bena**): 274, 277
Stephan Lake, (11.14 **Tatik'niłtun Bena**): *18*, 35, 87, 193, 218, 220, 225, 233, 238, *242*, *254*, 256
Stephan Lake village site, (11.13 **Tatik'niłtunt**): 31, 232, 255, 256, 257
Stetatna Creek, (1.95 **Batuk'elehtnu**): 54
Stony River, (**K'qizaghetnu**): 10, 53, 87, 146, 213
Straight Creek, (1.15 **Ch'atanalch'elt**): 51, *52*
Strelshla Mountain, (14.48 **Hdghelshla**): 305
Stump Lake, (2.4 **Nuk'ests'ey Bena**): *82*, 83, 84
Styx River, (6.40 **Qułch'ishtnu**): 30, 141
Sucker Creek, (4.14 **Niłq'aghedlentnu**): 112, 113
Sucker Lake, (4.23 **Deldida Bena**): 112, 113
Suicide Peak, (15.104 **Ułchena Tich'qiluqt**): 341
Summit Lake (at Chulitna Pass), (10.41 **Chuqitnu Bena**): 219, 227
Summit Lake (head of Gulkana River), (**Sasnuu' Bene'**): 145
Sunrise townsite, (16.10 **Tutl'uh**): 349
Sunshine Creek, (8.60 **K't'usq'atnu**): 198
Sunshine Lake, (8.95 **K't'usq'a Bena**): 198
Susitna Basin upland area, (2.39 **Yunggech'**): 93
Susitna River, (2.1 **Suyitnu, Susitnu**): 3, 6, 9, 13, 14, 17, 18, 19, 22, 23, 24, 27, 28, 40, *46*, 49, 74, *82*, 80–97, 99, 102, 109, 113, 119, 134, 164, *174*, 177, *186*, 199, 81–96, 173–200, 215–230
  east channel of lower Susitna River, (2.6 **Yach'ditnu**): 84
  middle Susitna River area, (8.67 **Dun'e**): 32, 172–199, *174*, 213, *plate 9*
  mouth of Susitna River, Susitna Delta, (2.3 **Susni Kaq'**): 23, 24, 80, *82*, 119, 222, 235, 259, 271, 332, 339
  upper Susitna River, (10.1 **Susitnu Tl'ughu**): 214–230, 235, 271
Susitna Station, (2.25 **Tsat'ukegh**): xx, 1, 2, 6, 8, 14, 19, 21, 26–28, 55, *84*, *88*, 89, *92*, *107*, 109, 114, 116, 119–124, 126, 132, 143, 156, 158, 164, 170, *171*, 175, 178, 183, 191, 203, 207, 219, 220, 237, 243, 244, 247, 248, 250, 252, 262, 264, 266, 277, 311, 331

Susitna Station village hill, (2.25 **Tsat'ukegh**): 26, 89, *92*
Sutton, (14.17 **Ts'es Tuk'ilaght**): 226, 256, 297
Swan Lake and village site, (15.11 **Skintuk'ełaha**): 315, 316, *317*
Swanson Lake, (16.38 **K'jech'a Dałtuni**): 357
Swanson River, (16.24 **Yaghetnu**): 28, 350, 353, 354, 357
Syncline Mountains, (14.66 **Tsedghaazi**): 308

Tahneta Lake, (14.118 **C'enaen' 'Aax Bene'**): 309
Tahneta Pass, (14.75 **Nekets'alyaexden**): 224, 308, 309
Tak'at (Cairn Point site), (15.75): 6, 7, 330, *331*
Talachulitna River, (6.7 **Tununiłch'ulyutnu**): 69, 72, 73, 131, *133*, 134
Talkeetna (town), (11.1 **K'dalkitnu**): 3, 7, 8, 10, 14, 22, 24, 28, 32, *42*, 43, 44, 46, 47, 83, 112, 170, 173, 177, 178, 181, 182, 183, 191, *193*, 198, 199, 201–204, *209*, 228, 232, 235–238, *253*, 297, 300, 303, 322, 335
Talkeetna Glacier, (11.18 **K'dalkitnu Łi'a**): 256
Talkeetna Lakes, (11.21 **Chuti Yits'a Bena**): 238
Talkeetna Mountains: xv, 7, 24, 163
Talkeetna River, (11.1 **K'dalkitnu**): 173, 199, 234–256
Tanaina Peak, (15.91 **Qin Cheghi**): 44, 341, *plate 24*
Tanana River, Tanana Valley: 15, 19, 32, 37, 39, 40, 82, 87, 145, 146, 163, 208, 209, 210, 222, 228, 230, 238, 271, 310, 322, 340
Tangle Lake(s): 232, 309
Tani'i (site opposite Susitna Station), (2.28): 26, 93, 109
Tank'its'a (ridge north of Old Tyonek Creek), (1.46): 66
Tanłtunt. *See* Red Shirt Lake site
Tatina River, (6.43 possibly[**Duditnu**]): 120, 142
Tatonden Lake, (14.54 **Tałtaan Bene'**): 225, 306, 307
Tazlina Lake, (14.120 **Bendil Bene'**): 17, 18, 87, 216, 227, 271, 289, 304, 306, 308, 309, 310, 311
Tazlina River: 87, 306, 310
Telaquana Mt., (**Nduk'eyux Dghil'u**): 146
Telaquana Pass, (**Dilah Vena Tustes**): 13, 53
Terra Cotta Mountains: 155
Texas Creek, (4.22 **K'kuy'inshla Betnu**): 114
Theodore River, (1.81 **T'ghesitnu**): 70, 72, 73, 74, 134
Third Lake, (1.57 **Chuqan Baydli Bena**): 68
Three Mile Creek (Tyonek), (1.66 **Tuk'elehtnu**): 69
Threemile Creek (Knik), (13.17 **Niłq'adaydleni Betnu**): 274, 376
Threemile Creek (Rainy Pass), (6.37 **Chish T'el'iht**): 139
Threemile Lake, (13.48 **Niłq'adaydleni Bena**): 280
Thunderbird Creek, (15.25 **Chishkatnu**): *285*, 322, *323*, *plate 18*
Thunderbird Peak, (15.136 **Chishkatnu Dghelaya**): 322
T'ighis Nungi (site on the lower Windy Fork): 143
"Tobona," (1.45 **Tank'itnu**): 57, 66
Tokasha Mountains, (9.14 **Tuqashi**): 203, *205*
Toklat village, (10.38 **Titl'u Kaq'**): 30, 87,202, 227, 229, 240, 271
Tokositna Glacier, (9.15 **Tuqashi Łi'a**): 205
Tokositna River, (9.10 **Tuqashitnu**): 24, 157, *161*, 162, 201–203, 205, *plate 13*
"Tontatin," (6.62 [**Tuntaytin**]): 135
Tordrillo Mountains, (6.18): 53, *72*, 134, *135*
Trading Bay: 50, 347
Trail Creek (Matanuska River), (14.114 **Tsendil'aats Kulaende**): 224, 309
Trail Creek (Mt. Susitna), (4.11 **T'eghes Untnu**): 112
Trail Lake (14.73 **Tsendil'aats Kulaen Bene'**): 309
Trail Ridge, (2.19 **Yen Ses**): 89, 119
(lower) Trapper Creek, (8.28 **Nuch'ulghełatnu**): 182
Trapper Lake, (8.29 **Ben Taydlent**): 182, 193
Triumvirate Glacier, (1.79 **Nughiltnu Łi'a**): *71*, 72
Troublesome Creek, (9.8 **Nelnikda Ey'unt**): 202
Tsaani Creek, (9:43 **Tsaani Na'**): 47, 210
Tsadaka Canyon, (14.78 **Chidaq'a Denyi**): 297
Tsadaka Creek, (14.14 **Chidaq'atnu**): 297
Tsat'ukegh. *See* Susitna Station village (2.25)
Ts'ihełken (ridge, elev. 1500', <Bullion> at base of Bald Mountain Ridge), (8.39): 191, *263*
Ts'ilu Dghelaya (mountain elev. 4270', <Alder> west of Chulitna River), (9.17): 205, *206*
Tsisi Creek, (10.21 **Tes Na'**): 220, 256
Tsuk Qayeh (site on lower Yentna R), (5.6): 26, 27, 28, 121
Tsuk Qayeh (site opposite Sunshine Creek mouth (Talkeetna), (8.58): 198
Tsusena Butte, (10.57 **Nts'ezi**): 220
Tsusena Creek, (10.14 **Nts'ezi Na'**): 220
Tuhnaghiłkitst (site at lakes near Parks-Glenn Highway junction), (14.3): 290
"Tulchina Falls," (15.137 [**Tulchina Nudghilent**], 324
Tukallah Lake, (1.67 **Tuk'eleh Bena**): 69
Tukmakna Creek, (14.101 [**Tuk'ebeq'tnu** ?]): 305
Turnagain Arm, (16.1 **Tutl'uh**): 28, 47, 104, 110, 301, 318, 329, 337, *340*, 342–350, 353, 357, *plates 26, 27*
Tuxedni Bay: 23
Twenty Mile Slough, (5.11 **Ninatnu**): 123
Twentymile River, (16.4): 318, 319, 344
Twin Hills, (10.58 **Nts'ezi**): 220
Twin Peaks, (15.34 **Łach Q'a**): *314*, 322, *plate 21*
Tyone Lake (**Hwtsuughi Ben Ce'e**): 31, 145, 215, 216, 221, 223, 227, 228, 231, 232, 257, 289, 293, 295, 302, 308, 309, 311, 338
Tyone River, (10.47 **Nilben Na'**): 215, 220, 222, 303
Tyone Village, (10.33 **Ben Q'etgge**): 222, 223, *227*, 231, 232
Tyonek Creek, (1.45 **Tank'itnu**): 55, 57, 62, 66
Tyonek Reservation (south boundary), (1.26 **Qunduk'elyasht**): 55, 62
Tyonek, Tyonek area, (1.30 **Tubughnenq'**): 1, 3, *4*, 6, 7, 8, 9, 10, 13, 14, 17, 23, 24, *25*, 26, 28, 42, 43, 44, 49–80, 57*(Map 13)*, *67*, *76*, 81, 83, 84, 91, 92, 97, *114*, 115, 116, 120, 125, 126, *129*, 133, 134, 147, 156, 162, 178, 179, 180, *188*, 237, 240, 248–252, 264, 265, 274, 289, 311, 316, 335, 339, 344, 345, 347, 349, 350, 354
  First Tyonek, First Village: 68
  New Tyonek, (1.52 **Qaggeyshlat**): *6*, 66, *67*, 68, *262*
  Old Tyonek, (1.30 **Tubughnenq'**): 19, 21 *57*, 58, 66
  "Second Tyonek," (1.45 **Tank'itnu**): 66

Upland Kacaagh Lake (formerly Big Lake), (10.16 **Qukugh Bena**): 47, 220
Upper Cook Inlet: xi, xii, xv, 6, 10, 13–29, 30, 45–47, 66, 73, 85, 144, 274, 281, 293, 295, 340, *maps 1, 2*
Uq'e Tsits'ełdatl'i (ridge between Kroto Creek and Kahiltna River), (8.27): 182

Valdez Creek and village site, (10.52 **C'ilaan Na'**): *221*, 229
Viapan Lake, (1.109 **Batuk'iydlaghi**): 69
Vogel Lake, (16.34 **Nuch'ishtun Bena**): 354

Wasilla area, (13.39 **Benteh**): 14, 26, 28, 128, 261, 271, 275, 284, 285, *plate 20*
Wasilla Creek, (13.46 **Chuqilintnu**): 226, 232, *284*, 287, *plate 17*

Wasilla Lake, (13.38 **Łach Bena**): 14, 26, 268, 280, 284, 285, 349
Watana Creek, west fork of, (10.17 **Debae Tse' Na'**): 220
West Foreland: 50, 352
West Papoose Twin Lake, (13.20 **Nuqiltin Bena**): 275, 277
West Point (Fire Island), (15.94 **Tudzedza**): 339
Westchester Lagoon, (15.126 **Chansh Kaq' Bena**): 43, 332, *333*
"West Ahtna uplands," (10.29 **Htsay Nenq'e**): 221
Whiskey Lake, (7.10 **Qutsas Bena**): 150
White Lake, (13.28 **Ggih Qughijaq Bena**): 278
Whitsol Lake: *plate 9*
Wienie Lake: 285
Wild Lake, (16.37 **Sus Q'anch'edeł Bena**): 357
Wilderness Lake, (16.43 **Qeyach'en Dałtun**): 357
Willow (town): 1, 6, 106, 115, *177*, 178, 181, 184, 191, 240, *263*, 264–266, 269, *plate 5*
Willow Creek, lower Willow Creek, (8.36 **Nubendaltuntnu**): 177, 183, 191, 192, 268, 269, 280, 283
  upper Willow Creek, (8.77 **Qughun Betnu**): 191, 269, 280
Willow Mountain: 161
Wishbone Hill, (14.16 **Chidaq'ashla**): 297
Wishbone Lake, (14.15 **Chidaq'ashla Bena**): 297
Wolf Lakes, (4.26 **Nudinli Bena**): 113
Wolf Point, (15.112): 360
Wolverine Creek (Mt. Susitna), (4.15 **Hghetgge Ch'aydinłeni**): 112
Wolverine Creek (Palmer), (14.11 **Kisidlentnu**): 292, 296, 297, 316
Wolverine Lake, (14.12 **Kisidlen Bena**): 296
Wonder Lake, (16.43 **Qeyach'en Dałtun**): 357
Wrangell Volcano: 87
Wren Lake, (16.45 **Q'es Dileni**): 357

Xensdii (mountain, elev. 3350', west of Susitna Lake), (10.35): 145, 221, 227, 231

Yenlo Creek, (7.36 **Dghelikda T'uh Ch'adinłeni**): 159
Yensus Lake, (2.21 **Kala Ch'aq'a Bena**): 89
Yentna Glacier, (7.32 **Yentnu Łi'a**): 158
Yentna River, (5.1 **Yentnu**): 3, 13, 14, 15, 21, 22, 23, 28, 41, 81, 82, 85, 89, 106, 110, *118*, 119, *120*, 122, 123, *132*, 133, 140, *148*, *154*, 155, 156, *157*, 158, 160, 161, 173, 183, 203
  lower Yentna River: 26, 118–124, 133, 137, 139
  mouth of Yentna River, (5.2 **Yan Kaq'**): 119, 121
  upper Yentna River area, (7.11 **Yentl'u**): 148–163
  West Fork of Yentna River, (7.57 **Nunhdat'unhtnu**): 158, 159, *170*, *plate 7*
"Yudi Glacier," (16.49 **Yudi Łi'a**): 344
Yusdishlaq', (site and island opposite Susitna Station), (2.26): 92, 247, 248

Zero Lake, (12.11 **Betnu Hghiłgedi Bena**): 262

Personal Name Index

Personal names in this book are listed below. Dena'ina names are in **boldface** type. Page numbers in *italic* indicate a photo of the person. *Aka* = also known as.

As noted in the introduction (page 30), Shem Pete contributed over 650 place names to this book as well as much of the background information, and he is present on almost every page. This index therefore includes only a selective subject index for Shem. We have not, for example, tried to list all the pages that document his hunting, fishing, and trapping activities.

Afanasii. *See* **Dusgeda Tukda**
Affanacy. *See* Affanasi
Affanasi, Chief, 349. *Aka* Ephanasy, Affanacy
Affanassia, 26
Affinassa, 26, 349
Alec, Christine, 218
Alec, Pete, 218
Alec, Pete **Basihdi'ushen**, 181, 218, 236, 237, 238
Aleck, 202, 203, 204. *Aka* Indian Aleck
Alex family, 303, 339
Alex, Dan, 88, 330
Alex, Mike, *20*, *25*, 26, 88, 290, 292, 314, *320*, 321, 322, 324, 325, 328, 330, 332, 334, 338, 341
Alexan, Martha, *4*
Alexan, Nikafor, 25, 43, 53, 59, 64, 66, 68, 70, 72, 77, 116, 184
Alexander. *See* **Diqelas Tukda**
Alexie, Emma, ix, *112*
Allen, Henry T., 85, 310
Allowan, Alexandra **Naqaydałna**, 88, *90*, 93, 183, 191, 207, 244
Allowan, Pete, *90*
Allowan, Robert, 51, 72, 90, 113, 114
Allowan, Tommy, 4, 77, *84*, *90*, 92
Anderson, William, 346–347
Andre, Chief, 305
An Ka'a. *See* Big Evan
Annabel, Russell, *xv*, 42, 44, 91, 163, 192, 193, 194–195, 197,228, 254, 259, 287, 292, 301, 315, 316, 318, 319, 321, 325, 349, 357
Annie, *xx*
Antone, Victor, 99
Ardaw, Mike, 267
Arndt, Katherine, 171, 282
Aruf. *See* **Tenqa**

Bagg, John S., 238, 256, 303
Baird, Gronia, *20*
Baird, Margaret June, *20*
Baker, Marcus, 44, 272, 277, 301, 350
Balasgulya. *See* **K'eludghiłna**
Bałaytninłna. *See* Nicolie, Katherine
Balbala, 251
Balenger, Herb, *302*
Balluta, Andrew
Balluta, Duane, *frontispiece*
Balluta, Harry, *frontispiece*, 103
Balluta, Liz, *frontispiece*
Balluta, Margaret, *frontispiece*
Balluta, Sophie, *frontispiece*
Bancroft, Hubert Howe, 346, 352, 355
Barbol, Nikolai, 90, 92, 109
Barry, Mary J., 350
Bartell, Jack **Bushuldi**, 274. *Aka* Red Jack
Bartell, Minnie, 274
Basdut. *See* Ezi, Simeon
Basihdi'ushen. *See* Alec, Pete
Basili. *See* Red Shirt; Stephan, Wasilla
Bate, 229, 238
Batninch'ey, 106, 207, 284
Bayou, Catherine, 91
Baytnidahen, 26, 106–107
Bazhenov, 17, 289
Beach, William, 91, 159
Beard, D. C., 94, 95
Becker, G. F., 350
Begh Chik'eł'ishen. *See* Chickalusion, Chief Peter
Beghuduch'di'ishen. *See* Phillip, Chilligan
Beł K'ighił'ishen. *See* Eklutna Alex
Benił'a Ch'ulyałen. *See* Pete, Chief
Benitnanilchinen (a **qeshqa** at **Chuqilintnu**), 26, 287
Benitnanilchinen. *See* Nikolai, Chief (of Eklutna)
Bentehen, 26, 285
Beq'e Nuqeyedghulya Tukda. *See* Ephim, Chief
Betuyelash, 63
Betsik'nughesalen, 26, 291
Bidyaka'a, 76, 79
Big Ghilligan. *See* Phillip, Chilligan
Big Ephim. *See* Ephim, Chief
Big Evan **An Ka'a**, 121, 122, 133. *Aka* Evan **Ka'a**
Big Stephan. *See* Stephan, Chief
Bigoff, "Deafy Dan," 332
Billy, 305
Bismark, Doris Nicholai, *353*, 354
Bismark, Fred, 354
Bismark, Steve, 349, 353
Black, Lydia, 21
Blind Nick. *See* McNeil, Nick
Boas, Franz, xii
Bobby, Pete, 54, 131, *188*
Bortnovsky, Ioann (John), 19, 68, 91, 321
Boston, Lillian, 220, 303
Bowen Affanassia. *See* Affanassia
Bright, William, xi, 62, 139
Brink, Frank, 68
Brink, Jo, 68
Brooks, Alfred H., 17, 32, 33, 69, 70, 72, 73, 112, 134, 139, 142, 156, 163, 203, 210, 213
Brown, Grant, *351*
Brown, Jack, 329, 330
Brown, Nellie, 329, 330
Browne, Belmore, 91, 94, 112, 154, 203, 205
Bull, Johnny, 256, 321
Bushuldi. *See* Bartell, Jack
Caldwell, Doug, 213
Californsky, Sergei, 62, *129*, *188*
Cantwell Nicolai, 222
Capps, Stephen R., Jr., 159
Carlson, Phyllis D., 59

Carltikoff (Willis), Jeanne, *frontispiece*
Castner, Joseph C., 280, 290, 291, 297, 305, 344
Chada. *See* Talkeetna Alec (as referred to by Katherine Nicolie)
Chadaka'a, 26
Chadalasla, 90
Chambers, Natasya, *frontispiece*
Chandonnet, Ann, 267, 279, 320, 332, 334
Ch'anqet', 191, 198, 201, 230, 235, 238, 240–253, 254, 255, 261
Ch'anst'a Gga, 237
Charley, Walter, 309
Ch'em. *See* Stump, John Chickaloon, Chief. *See* **Chiklu**
Chickaloosun, Simeon. *See* Chickalusion, Simeon
Chickalusion family, 53
Chickalusion, Anna. *See* Stephan, Anna Chickalusion
Chickalusion, Annie, 8, *59*, *60*, 92
Chickalusion, Chief Peter (of Kustatan) **Begh Chik'eł'ishen**, 59, 60, 109, 350
Chickalusion, Chief Simeon, 3, 8, 9, 26, 51, 53, *59*, *60*, 62, 68, 77, 91, 97, 109, 115, 116, 117, 347, 349
Chickalusion, Maxim Sr., 4, 51, 62, *129*, *188*
Chickalusion, Nellie, 88, *90*, *124*, 136, 272
Chickalusion, Theodore, 59, 60
Chickalusion, Theodore "Chad," *129*
Chidashla, 336, 337, 344
Chijuk, 26, *90*, *180*, 182, *186*, 237, 263. *Aka* **Tsilałen**
Chiklu, 26, 301, 350, 353. *Aka* Chickaloon, Chief
Chilligan **Tsilgi**, 164–166, 169
Chilligan, Chief. *See* Phillip, Chief Chilligan
Chilligan family, 19
Chilligan, Joe, 274
Ch'k'idetnishen. *See* Talkeetna Nicholie
Chuitt family, 19, 49, 69, 70
Chuitt, Ella, 66, 69, 70
Chuitt, Pat, 69
Chuitt, Paul, 66, 69, 79, 92, 114
Chuitt, Polly, 92
Chuitt, Steve, 72
Clark, Carl, 349
Cleghorn, Jim, 1, 51, 219. Also "Cleghourn"
Cleghourn, Jim. *See* Cleghorn, Jim
Cobb, Tex, 195–196, 318
Coffee, John, 207
Collins, Ray, xv, 120, 142, 143, 155
Constantine, Fedora, 4, 88, *90*, *129*
Constantine, Keith, *129*
Constantine, Nestor, 56
Constantine, Peter, 50, 51, 53, 56, *58*, 66, 69, 72
Cook, Frederick A., 110, 134, 156, 161, 162, 163, 218
Cook, John P., 153
Cook, Captain James, 96, 343, 345, 346, 347, 348, 352, 357
Crews, Paul Sr., 53, 135, 347
C'uket Ta', 17

Dahl, Annie Ephim, *102*, 237
Dahl, Mike, 237
Dall, William H., 19, 271, 272, 289
Danya, 277
Davidson, Charles E., 286
Davis, Clark, 179
Davis, Jeff, 195, 287, 318
Davis, Nancy Yaw, 7, 329, 331
Davydov, Gavriil, 82
Dech'k'idetnishen. *See* Talkeetna Nicolie
Deaphon, Miska, xv, 131, 135, 139, 142, 143, 149, 162, 199
Deck, Leona, 116
Degge' Yenooł'o'. *See* Old Esau
de Laguna, Frederica, 68, 109, 230, 235, 254, 272, 274, 278, 280, 282, 290, 306, 307, 329, 330, 332, 334, 339, 352
Delendii, Delindin. *See* Pete, Shem
Dennis, Nick, 162
Dennison, Bill, 122
Denyishla Iden, 26, 210
Derenty. *See* Pete, Shem
Dgheltayi. *See* Nikita, Jim
Dickey, William, 32, 213
Dillinger, Gilbert 142
Diqelas Tukda, (5, 26, 83, 109, 143, 154, 261, 278. *Aka* Afanasii, Alexander
Dixon, Ann, 112
Dixon, R. Greg, 151, 280
Doroshin, Petr P., 149, 289, 290, 311
Dreese, Al, 302, 306
Dryer, Jim, 192
Duggel. *See* Stephan, Sava
Du'inałna, 237
Dumond, Don, 274, 280
Dunder, Fred, 192
Dusgeda Tukda, 26, 40, 259, 261, 274, 349. *Aka* Affinasi
Dutnałna, 237
Dzeniskevich, Galina I., 75

Eklutna Alex **Beł K'ighił'ishen**, 26, 314, 321, 324, 326, 327, 330, 332, 344, 349
Eklutna Jim. *See* Nikita, Jim
Eklutna John **Kala Łchun**, 280
Eklutna Theodore. *See* Theodore, Wasilla
Eldridge, George, 111
Elliott, Henry W., 32, 50, 64, 343
Ephanasy, Chief. *See* Afanassi
Ephim, Andrew, 337
Ephim, Annie. *See* Dahl, Annie
Ephim, Aruf, 337
Ephim, Bobby, 337
Ephim, Buster, 9, 337
Ephim, Chief **Beq'e Nuqeyedghulya Tukda** (of Susitna Station), 2, 26, *88*, 89, 115, 116, 155
Ephim, Evgenia. *See* Stephan, Inga
Ephim, Irene, *84*, *90*
Ephim, Jimmy, 92
Ephim, Mary, 237
Ephim, Mattie, *90*
Ephim, Nellie (wife of Buster Ephim), 9
Ephim, Vasca, *90*
Esai, Bobby, 131, 142, 143, 159
Esia, Simeon. *See* Ezi, Simeon
Etolin, A. K., 18
Evan, Antone, *frontispiece*
Evan, Chief (of Susitna Station), 1, 2, 26, 32, 89, 103, 109, 117, *122*, 131, 132, 139, 252. *Aka* Evan **Duyeq**
Evan **Duyeq**. *See* Evan, Chief
Evan Longhair, 122
Evan, Hester, *229*, 230, 240
Ewan, Fred, 223
Ezi family, 294, 295, 313, 314, 315, 316, 318, 319, 334, 338
Ezi, Annie, 295

Ezi, Jack, 295
Ezi, Jimmy, *338*
Ezi, Mary, 293
Ezi, Olga Nicholi, 14, 222, 292, 293, *294*, 295, 33
Ezi, Peter Jr., 5, *338*
Ezi, Peter Sr., *294*, 295, *316*
Ezi, Ruth, 295
Ezi, Simeon **Basdut**, **Tsitnelggeyan**, 14, 26, 191, 292, 293, *294*, 295, 315, 316, 318, 319, 334
Ezi, William Sr. (Bill, Billy), 26, *293*, 295, 313, 316, 334

Fall, James A., 4, 7, *121*
Fisher, Mr., 83
Foster, Dan, 24, 176
Fullenwider (Baird), Alice Debbie, *20*, 325

Gadwalter (game warden), 178
Galeq Q'echishen, 278
Ganley, Matt, xv, 36, 43
George, Henry, *84*, *90*, 109
Gerdine, T. G., 332
Germanson, James, 21
Gilcrist, Betty Kallander, *20*
Gillette, Helen, 59
Glazunov, Andrei, 213
Glenn, Captain Edward F., 58, 62, 82, 89, 120, 134, 221, 291, 297, 302, 304, 308, 309, 318, 321, 328, 344
Goodlataw, John, 304
Goodlataw, Mary Nickolai. *See* Shaginoff, Mary
Goodlataw, Paul, *302*, *304*
Goosmar (of Knik), 281
Goozmer, Pedro, 70, 353
Greiser, T. Weber, 101, 175, 262, 267
Griffin, Kristen, 216

Hadleigh-West, Fred, 334
Hall, Ward, 236, 237
Handmore. *See* Hanmore
Hanmore, Mr. (Indian agent at Tyonek), 289, 316
Harrison, Gary, 298, 302
Hays, Lydia, 4, 125
Healy, Jack, 277
Healy, Rowland R., 91
Hedberg, Elmer, 237
Hedberg, John, 295, 339
Herndon, H., 183
Herning, Orville G., 35,171, 278, 279, 281, 282, 283, 313, 340, 349
Herning, Stanley, 278, 282, 283
Herron, Lieut. Joseph, 32, 69, 113, 120, 123, 134, 135, 139, 142, 154, 155, 156, 158, 159, 349
Hicks, H. H., 290, 308
Hk'uydeshnin, 334
Hna'estał, 237
Hobson, Macy, *frontispiece*
Hodge, Frederick Webb, 104, 272, 320
Hoehn, Dr., 192
Holmes, Charles E., 330
Holt, George, 278
Hosley, Edward, 142, 143,
Htenususeɫen. *See* Talkeetna Alec
Hubback, Theodore, 133, 137, 141
Hubbard, Charlie, xv, 201, 210, 215, 235
Hudlach, 207
Hughes, Bill, 280
Hu'idiłna, 8, 336–337. *Aka* **Nachikda**
Hulsing, Harry, 319
Hunt, Mr., 344
Huteljon'. *See* **Tes Gun**

Inda'i, 92, 180
Indian Jim. *See* Nikita, Jim
Indian Jimmie, 134
Irving, William, 215, 216, 222, 227
Irwin, Don, 278, 291
Itegheyuł Tu'. *See* **K'uk'enesh**
Ivan. *See* Evan, Chief (of Susitna Station)

Jacko, Annie, *90*, 164–170, 171, 330–331. *Aka* Joko, Annie
Jacobsen, Johan, 49, 56, 77
Jacobsson, Mildred, 112
Jetté, Jules, xiii, 213
Jewell, Sally, 213
Jilubech Pete, 334
John, Eliza Esau, 240
John, Fred, 17, 18
John, Katie, 17, 18
Johnson, Will, 237
Johnston, Dave, 43, 208
Johnston, J. N., 21
Johnston, Thomas F., 61, 125
Joko, Annie. *See* Jacko, Annie
Jones, Dixon, xv

Kail, George, 350, 352. *Aka* Russian George
Kala Łchun. *See* Eklutna John
Kalifornsky, Agrafena Chickalusion, 60
Kalifornsky, Peter, *frontispiece*, 4, 60, 112, *188*, 332, 339, 349, 350, 353, 354, *356*, 357, *plate 1*
Kallander family, 20, 352
Kallander, Anna, *350*
Kallander, Betty. *See* Gilcrist, Betty
Kallander, Bobby, *20*
Kallander, Cora Nicholai, *353*, *354*
Kallander, Feodoria. *See* Pennington, Feodoria Kallander
Kallander, Gilbert, *190*
Kallander, Jimmy, *20*
Kallander, Julius Jr., 2, 350, 353
Kallander, Julius Sr., *353*, *354*. *Aka* "Old Man Kallander
Kallander, Mary, *20*, *350*
Kallander, Minnie, *350*
Kallander, Norman, *20*
Kallander, "Old Man." *See* Kallander, Julius Sr.
Kallander, Roy, *354*
Kallander, Sammy, *20*
Kaloa, Alexandra, 58
Kane, Katherine, *107*
Kari, James, *frontispiece*, 4, 21, 36, *41*, 125, 223, 240, *250*, 326, 348
Kelly, Luther, 328
K'eł Nuts'ehen. *See* Red Shirt
K'eludghiłna (Shem Pete's mother), *xx*, 1, 3, 106–107, 264. *Aka* Balasgulya
K'etech'ayutiłen. *See* Pete, Shem
K'ghudu, 26, 44, 180, 181, 183
Khlebnikov, Kiril, 18, 290

Kiefer, Kathy, 22
Kila Tlaq'a, 253
Kiłkda, 192
King, James, 346, 352
Knik Prince, *338*
K'nuy'a Gga. *See* Stephan, Pete
Kroto, Chief. *See* **K'ghudu**
Krasinski, Katherine, xv, 182, 237, 280
Kroto, Charlie, 180
K'uk'enesh (John Stump's father, who had three names), 218, 253, 285. *Aka* **Itegheyuł Tu'**, **Ts'iduyuł Tu**
Kuliktukta, Nikolai, 58

Ladd, Charles D. 21, 91, 219
Larson family, 297
Larson, Bill, 237
Larson, Jack, 237, 297
Laurence, Sydney, 236, 247, 253
Law, Mr., 346
Learnard, H. G., 32, 74, 83, 92, 109, 119, 175, 181, 193, 208, 238, 239, 254, 255, 256, 344
Leggett, Aaron, xv, 79, 92, 253
Lee, Frank, 300
Lee, Susan, 151

Łału, 237
Łedehen. *See* Nikolai, Alec
Łquqaghetna, 277

Mace, Robert, 274, 278, 280
Madison, John, 122, 135
Malakhov, Petr, 18
Mammaloff, Fred, 357
"Mary," *xxvii*
Mathys, Frederick, 255, 256, 303
McClellan, Catharine, 235
McCord, Bonnie, 4, *129*
McCord, Emil Sr., 7
McCord, Nick, 353
McCord, Nora, *84, 90, 102*
McKinley, Jim, 290
McKinley, President William, 213
McKinnon, H., 280
McMahan, J. David, 330
McNeil, Nick, 287. *Aka* Blind Nick
McNeil, Victor, 274
Mendenhall, William C., 227, 232, 285, 289, 296, 297, 300, 305, 307, 308, 311, 320, 328, 329
Mentasta Pete, 235
Metcalf, Gertrude, 163
Mielke, Colleen, xv, 171, 287
Miller, Mr., 169, 170
Mishakoff, Dick, 179
"Mishkah" (fictional), 194
Mishler, Craig, 347, 349
Mitropolsky, Nikolai, 19
Moccasin, Jim, 349
Moffit, Fred W., 231, 310
Moon, Rupert Axley, 104
Morris, W. J., 183
Muldrow, Robert, 111, 235

Nachikda ("our grandmother": Sava Stephan's grandmother). *See* **Hu'idiłna**
Naqaydałna. *See* Allowan, Alexandra
"Nayna," *xx*
Nagley (Susitna and Talkeetna storekeeper), 123, 237. *Aka* Nickli
Neeley, Ben, 307, 311
Nelson, Charley, 159
Nicholai family (of Point Possession), 353
Nicholai Brothers, 353–354
Nicholai, Billy, 26, *103, 351, 353*
Nicholai, Chief (of Taral), 88
Nicholai, Doris, 347, *353*. *Aka* Grandma Doris
Nicholai, Gus, *353*
Nicholai, Jimmy, 26, 347
Nicholai, Johnny, *103, 350*
Nichols, Dallas, 151
Nichols, Judy, 151
Nickli. *See* Nagley
Nicklie, John, 256
Nickolai, Balasculya, *302*, 304
Nickolai, Frank, *302*, 304
Nickolai, Mary. *See* Shaginoff, Mary
Nickolai, Olga, *302*
Nickolai, Pete, *219*
Nickolie, Annie, 306
Nicolai (Ahtna man d. 1891), 278
Nicolai, Chief (of Eklutna). *See* Nikolai, Chief
Nicolie family (of Talkeetna and Kroto), 181
Nicolie, Alec (brother of Katherine Nicolie) **Q'untsila**, *90*, 177, 178, 197, *236*, 237
Nicolie, Alexan, 235, *236*
Nicolie, Ann, *236*
Nicolie, Christine **Nidinłna**, *90*, 177, *180*, 181, 218, 235, *236*, 237, *352*
Nicolie, Joe, *90, 180*, 182, *236*, 237
Nicolie, Katherine **Bałaytninłna**, 4, *90*, 94, 121, 123, 149, 173, 175, *177*, 180, 181, 182, 183, 184, 191, 192, 193, 198, 201, 202, 216, 218, 235, *236*, 237, 238, 239, 240, 245, 256, 263, 266, 267, 269, 284, *325*, 331, *352, 356, plates 1, 2*
Nicolie, Mytrona **Ts'itaya**, 235, *236*, 237, *245*
Nicolie, Nick **Shik'u**, 198, 216, 253
Nicolie, Wilson, 70, *90*, 191
Nicoly, Chief, 319
Nidinłna. *See* Nicolie, Christine
Nikanorga, Doris, 62, 354
Nikita (of Knik), 274, 276, 277
Nikita, Heirmonk, 19
Nikita, Jim **Dghełtayi**, 40, 182, 291, 315, 316. *Aka* Indian Jim, Eklutna Jim
Nikolai, Alec (grandfather of Sava Stephan), 140
Nikolai, Alex (Alec) **Łedehen** (son of **Chidashla**), 337
Nikolai, Chief (of Eklutna) **Benitnanilchinen**, 26, 88, 280, 281
Nikolai, Marion, 337
Nikolai, Oly, 222
Nikolai, Paul, 334
Nikolai, Tommy (Tom), 280, 337, 344
"Nikolai" **Nik'uhhay**, 139
Nik'uhhay. *See* "Nikolai"
Nitehen, 26, 27, 285, 291, 293
Nits'usełen, 253
Nugheldu Tukda, 26

Nuhnałchek'a (Pete Alec's mother), *236*, 237, 238, *245*
Nuhunulgak. *See* Oskolkoff, Nick
Nunk'ilash, 26, 72
Obama, President Barack, 213
Old Alice, 240
Old Esau **Degge' Yenooł'o'**, 230
Olexia, 235
Olga (sister to Nellie Ephim), 9
"Olga" (fictional), 280
Ondola, George, *330*, 339
Ondola, Susie Yakasoff, *330*, 339
Orth, Donald, 44, 213
Osgood, Cornelius, 14, 22, 60, 75, 76, 91, 102, 117, 145, 152, 182, 184, 188, 271, 282, 290, 315, 319, 320, 349
Osgood, Wilfred, 58, 16, 355
Oskolkoff, Mrs. Mike, *20*
Oskolkoff, Nick **Nuhunulgak**, *195*

Palmer, George, 107, 272, 273, 278, 279, 281, 291, 314
Patchell, Mr., 282
Patton, R. S., 273
Pedro, 256
Pennington, Feodoria Kallander, *20*, 343, 347, *350*, 353, *354*
Pete (Shem Pete's father, Chief at Susitna Station), 1, 26, 117. *Aka* "Susitna Pete," but not to be confused with Susitna Pete **Tsel Ch'a'ilk'elen**, Shem's former brother-in-law
Pete, Billy Shem, 2, 3, 4, *6*, 7, 8, *9*, *25*, 53, 59, 62, 69, 81, *84*, 88, *90*, 93, 99, 100, *101*, 105, 106, 111, 112, 114, 121, *125*, *129*, 133, 150, 159, 173, *174*, 175, 181, 182, 183, 184, 185–189, *190*, 205, 240, 259, 262, 263, 264, *265*, 267, 272, 276, 293, 321, 326, 327, 330, 331, 334, 339, 341, 343, 344, 352, 353, *plate 2*
Pete, Chief (of Tyonek) **Benił'a Ch'ulyałen**, 26, 58, 72, 76, 134
Pete, Inge **Tulałen** (Shem Pete's wife), 3, 8, 164, 168, 169, 170, 171
Pete, Mary, 3, 6, 8, *90*, 91
Pete, "Old Man" Bill, 267, 293, 295
Pete, Shem **K'etech'ayutiłen, Derenty, Delindin**
- as "chief," 2, 3, 60, 115
- birth and childhood, 1–2, 92, 106, 149
- biographic essay, 1–6
- commercial fishing, 5, 7, 273, 353
- death, funeral, and potlatch, 4
- extent of geographic knowledge (general and outer limits of travel), 3, *30*, 44, 158, 201, 203, 208, 216, 219, 220, 222, 228, 318, 324, 354
- hunting accounts, 2, 72, 114, 137, 141, 164–170, 202, 218, 316, 335, 351
- jobs (other than fishing, hunting, trapping, and prospecting), 1, 3, 237, 250, 335, 336
- marriage, 3, 8, 164, 169–170, 237
- multi-lingual abilities, 1–2, 14, 21, 237, 241
- personal names, 1, 4, 99, 262
- personality, 4–5, 264–266
- photographs of, *frontispiece*, *xi*, *2*, *4*, *5*, *9*, *20*, *41*, *68*, *76*, *101*, *105*, *107*, *115*, *121*, *125*, *129*, *165*, *188*, *250*, *262*, *265*, *335*, *plate 1*
- prospecting, 5, 7, 114
- relatives, 2, 161, 162, 171. *See* also Ephim, Chief (step-brother); Evan, Chief (step-brother); **K'eludghiłna** (mother); Pete, Billy (son); Pete, Inge (wife); Pete, Mary (daughter); "Pete" (Step-father); Stephan, Sava ("son")
- residences, 1–6, 100, 101, 263, 264, 267
- Shem Pete Day, xi, 4, 9
- singer, songs, composer, and dancer, 2, 3, 74, 115, *129*, *188*, 125–129, 264
- story-telling ability and range (some examples), xv, 3–6, 17, 66, 76, 106, 109, 122, 139, 161, 184, 240, 264, 272, 273, 354.
- *See* also the specific Dena'ina stories told by Shem Pete

Peter, Alec, 68, 70
Peteroff, "Old Man" Mike, 334
Peters, Henry, 210, 220, *228*, *229*, 255
Peters, Jennie, 163, 229
Peterson, Celia, 230
Petroff, Ivan, 19, 50, 75, 109, 210, 291, 352, 354, 355
Phillip, Chief Chilligan **Beghuduch'di'ishen**, *25*, 26, 51, 53, 54, 59, 60, 116, 117, 178, 181. *Aka* Big Chilligan
Phillip, Olga, *25*
Pierce, Richard, 58
Pontella, 137
Potter, Ben A., 14, 145
Potter, Louise, 269, 274, 278, 280, 284
Powell, Addison, 290
Pratt, Ken, 88

Qa Dyiluggen, 26, 291
Qalbis. *See* Theodore, Wasilla
Qalbisgga, 314
Qatsen. *See* Stephan, Chief
Q'untsila. *See* Nicolie, Alec
Quq'ey, 63, 66

Reckord, Holly, 215, 222, 228, 229, 307
Red Jack. *See* Bartell, Jack
Red Shirt **K'eł Nuts'ehen**, 26, 44, 106, 107, 150
Red Shirt, Evan, 107
Reger, Douglas, 15
Reno, 219
Robinson, Roger, *160*
Rogers, Monty, 68
Rohn, Oscar, 137
Rojec, F. H., 103
Ronning, Annie, 198, *216*, 235, 253
Ross, Ernest A., 91
Rosser, Margi Rousseau, *338*
Rozell, Don, 115
Rozell, Tina, 115
Rusk, C. E., 201
Russell, Priscilla, *265*–266
Russian George. *See* Kail, George

Sacaloff, Fedosia, 21, *356*
Sal-tart, 50
Sanford, Adam, 238
Sargent, R. H., 332
Sasha, Theodore, 332, 354
Savage, Leonard, 75, 140
Scottie, 197
Sdigel, 21, 40, 88
Seager-Boss, Fran, 193, 236, 281, 284, 285
Secondchief family, 222
Secondchief, Dick, 215, 231, 289
Secondchief, Fannie, 256
Secondchief, Frank, 255, 256

Secondchief, Jim (Jimmy), 222, 227, 303
Secondchief, Morrie, 289
Secondchief, Peter, 228
Serebrennikov, Ruf, 18
Sesui, Carl, 162
Sesui, Chief, 137, 142
Sidel Bunkda, 162
Sghay Tu. *See* Talkeetna Stephan
Shaginoff, Johnny, 14, 42, 218, *219*, 220, 221, 222, 237, 238, 239, 254, 256, *257*, 280, 287, 289, 290, 292, 294, 297, 300, 301, 302, 303, 304, 305, 306, 308, 309, 316, 319, 320, 321
Shaginoff, Mary, 289, 301, 302, *304*, 305, 324
Sheldon, Charles, 19, 163, 181, 218
Sheldon, Roberta, 235, 237, 240
Sherwood, Morgan, 111
Shik'u. *See* Nicolie, Nick
Shilligan. *See* Phillip, Chilligan
Sinidegga, 253
Sinyon, Jim (James), 215,. 220, 222, 228, 279, 303
Skarland, Ivar, 256
Sleem, D. H., 72, 162, 175, 180, 204, 219, 268, 280, 340
Slinkta, 120, 142
Smith, A. Beverly, 92, 93
Smith, Gerad M., 216
Snider, Gerrit Heinie, 183, 277, 284, 291, 319
Snodgrass, Nayna, *90*, *352*
Spillum, Chris 21, 91, 219
Spurr, Josiah, 32, 42, 54, 70, 81, 83, 102, 111, 119, 122, 123, 131, 132, 134, 135, 136, 137, 138, 139, 141, 155, 163, 273, 347
Stafeev, Vladimir V., 17, 58, 66
Standifer family, 237
Starikgga, 244–247. *Aka* "Little Old Man"
Steensby, H. P., 76
Stefano, 122
Stepan, Nick, 194
Stepan, Wasilla. *See* Stephan, Wasilla
Stepan (guide for Herron), 120, 142
Stepankda. *See* Stephan, Chief; Stephan, Rufe
Stephan (son-in-law to Talkeetna Nicholie), 201, 239
Stephan, Alberta Ezi, 292, 295, 315, *318*, 319, 321, *330*, 332, 334, 339
Stephan, Anderson, 8, 89, *90*, *124*, 140, 183, 237, *294*
Stephan, Anna Chickalusion, 8
Stephan, Annie, 331
Stephan, Bobby (brother of Anderson Stephan), 56, *90*, *124*, 139, 140, 332
Stephan, Bobby (brother to Lillian Stephan Theodore), *194*, *199*
Stephan, Chief (of Knik) **Qatsen**, 26, *278*, *279*, 281, 283, 284, 308, 314, 337. *Aka* Big Stephan, **Stepankda**
Stephan, Ely, 117
Stephan, Mrs. Ely, 117
Stephan, Inga, 8, *124*
Stephan, Isaac, 8,*60*, *336*
Stephan, Jacob. *See* Stephan, Yagu
Stephan, John, 181, 197
Stephan, Juliana, 336
Stephan, Katherine, *90*
Stephan, Lee, 322
Stephan, Leo, 5, 42, 292, 303, 313, 314, 315, 316, 317, *318*, 322, 325, *330*, 334, 338, *339*
Stephan, Lester, *330*
Stephan, McGinty, *261*
Stephan, Nick, *261*, 275–277. *Aka* Nickalasky
Stephan, Olga, *90*
Stephan, Pete **K'nuy'a Gga**, 181, 192, 193, 194, 195, 196, 197, 198, *199*, 256
Stephan, Ralph, *336*
Stephan, Richard, *90*
Stephan, Rufe, 330, 331. *Aka* **Stepankda**
Stephan, Sava, Jr., 8, *336*
Stephan, Sava Sr., *frontispiece*, xv, xx, 3, 4, 6, *8*, *9*, 41, 42, 43, 44, 51, 54, 55, 59, *60*, 62, 68, 69, 70, 72, 74, 83, 84, 89, *90*, 92, 93, 104, 110, 112, 121, 123, *124*, *129*, 131, 136, 138, 139, 140, 159, 164, 183, 184, 185, *188*, 191, 192, 193, 197, 205, 237, *262*, 284, 285, 294, 334, 335, *336*, 338, 339, 341, 353
Stephan, Susie, *194*
Stephan, Terry, 63
Stephan, Wasilla, 182, 193, *195*, 197, 239, 254
Stephan, Yacob, *90*
Stephan, Yagu (Jacob) (Tommy Allowan's father), 164–167
Stickwan, Frank, 308, 309
Stuart, Sondra Shaginoff, 257
Stuck, Hudson, 32, 213
Stump, John, 149, 163, 218, 253, *261*, 262, 274, 276, 277, 284, 285, 297, 314, 324, 325, 332, 334, 341
Stump, Lily, *262*
Sunrise, Archie, 62
Susitna Pete **Tsel Ch'a'ilk'elen**, 161, 162, 203

Talkeetna Alec **Htenususełen**, **Chada** (as referred to by Katherine Nicolie), 104, 178, 237
Talkeetna Nicholie **Ch'k'idetnishen**, 17, 26, 154, 177, 198, 201, 218, 235, *236*, 237, 240, *247*, *253*, 255. *Aka* **Dech'k'idetnishen**, **Ts'e' C'udetniisen** (Ahtna)
Talkeetna Stephan **Sghay Tu**, 228, 254, 255
Tansy, Jake, 201, 208,215, 220, *221*,222, 227, 228, 232–233, 256
Tarkhanov, Dimitrii, 17, 289, 309, 310, 311
Taylor, Tom, 43, 44
Teben'kov, M. D., 17, 18
Tenqa, 26, 277. *Aka* Aruf
Terentij. *See* Pete, Shem
Tes Gun, 240. *Aka* **Hutełjon'**
Theide, Diane L., 64
Theodore. *See* Theodore, Wasilla
Theodore family, 277, 339
Theodore, Alice, 331
Theodore, Art, 273, *274*, 276–279, 328
Theodore, Bailey, 50, 192, 274, 276, 277, 279, 287, 290, 291, 292, 314, 321, 325, 328, 332, 334, 353
Theodore, Katherine, *325*
Theodore, Lillian Stephan, 43, *177*, 182, 193, *194*, 195, 197, 198, *199*, 236, 239
Theodore, Mike, 197, 277, 290, 314, 324, *325*, 328, 350, 357
Theodore, Paul, 5
Theodore, Wasilla **Qalbis**, 280, 284, 328, 331, 332, 334, 339, 353. *Aka* Eklutna Theodore, Theodore Vasily, Wassilli Theodore, Theodore
Thurston, Jim, 152
Toughluck, George, 182
Toughluck, Johnny, 192
Trefon, Ada, *frontispiece*
Trefon, Chuck, *frontispiece*

Trefon, Clyde, *frontispiece*
Trefon, Melvin, *frontispiece*
Trefon, Pete Sr., *frontispiece*
Trefon, Pete Jr., *frontispiece*
Trenton family, 49
Trenton, Harry, 51
Ts'e' C'udetniisen. *See* Talkeetna Nicholie
Tsel Ch'a'ilk'elen. *See* Susitna Pete
Ts'enkut. *See* **Ch'anqet'**
Tsilałen. *See* **Chijuk**
Tsilgi. *See* Chilligan
Ts'iduyuł Tu. *See* **K'uk'enesh**
Ts'inst'a Gga Tukda, 96
Ts'itaya. *See* Nicolie, Mytrona
Tsitnelggeyan. *See* Ezi, Simeon
Tsuk Qayeh Ka'a Iden, 26, 121
Tucker, Robert, 257
Tulałen. *See* Pete, Inge
Tuts', *90*
Twitchell, Hollis, 43
Tyone (Chief Tyon), 222
Tyone, Andy, 223, 227
Tyone, Annie Ewan, 223
Tyone, Jack, 220, 221, 222, 227, 255, 290, 300, 308
Tyone, Jim, 14, 42, 221, 222, 223, *224*, 232, 256, 280, 287, 289, 292, 296, 297, 308, 309, 311
Tyone, Johnny, 227

Undudya, *284*

Vacilla, Elie, 281
Vajda, Edward, 14, 144
Valdez Creek Jack, 222
Vancouver, George, 17, 50, 63, 66, 339, 345, 346, 352
Van Horn, Walter, 104
Van Schoonhoven, George, 210
Vasili. *See* Wasilla, Chief
Vasily, Theodore. *See* Theodore, Wasilla
Vogel, Oscar, 354

Wade family, 297
Wade, Katie, 42, 297, *298*, 300, 301, 302, 306
Washburn, Bradford, 46, 163
Wassillie, Albert, *frontispiece*
Wasidi Tukda, 218
Wasihdi Tukda, 26, 109
Wasili, 254, 256
Wasilla, Chief, 26, 44, 277, *284*, 287
Wells brothers, 207
Whidbey, Lt. Joseph, 66, 352
Wickersham, Helen, 306
Wickersham, James, 211
Wickersham, Jesse, 301, 306
White, Johnny, 349
Wilson, Rodman, 53, 135, 341, 347
Workman, Karen Wood, 152
Wrangell, Ferdinand von, 58, 75, 76, 85–87, 88, 119, 180, 213, 220, 227, 228, 230, 271, 274, 277, 280, 290, 311, 320, 354
Wrathall, Grant, 151
Wygal, Brian, xv, 182, 237

Yagu, 133, 150
Yakasoff, Felix, *338*
Yakasoff, Mike Jr., *338*
Yakasoff, Mike Sr., *338*
Yanert, William, 82, 193, 208, 210, 229, 238, 255
Yarborough, Michael, 321
Ya' Talno, 240
Yentna Evan, 109

Zagoskin, L. A., 142, 143
Znamenski, Andrei, 19, 58, 278

Subject Index

Also see the Personal Name Index for topics about Shem Pete. Pages that have a figure, table, or map on the topic are noted in *italic.*

Ahtna (the people), 16, 17, 18, 58, 184, 210, 215, 227, 271, 274, 279, 282, 289, 299, 326, 349. *See also discussions in Chaps. 10 and 14*
Ahtna language, 13, 14, 42, 82, 158, 211, 219, 220, 235, 241, 274, 289, 298–299
  orthography and sound system, xix–*xx*
  Ahtna place names, 31, 37–38, 145, 215. *See also Chaps. 10 and 14*
airplanes, 1, 2, 53, 92, 96, 145, 336,
Alaska Commercial Company, 1, 21, 49, 56, 58, 88, 91, 92, 257, 278, 291
Alaska Railroad, 6, 7, 21, 181, 183, 193, 203, 210, 218, 236, 237, 253, 259, 267, 277, 287, 290, 291, 292, 320, 321, 331, 335
Alaska State Board of Geographic Names, 47, 53
Aleuts. *See* Alutiiq
Alutiiq (**Ułchena;** Chugach Eskimo, & previous peoples), 14, 16, 22, 75, 89, 93, 147, 154, 182, 272, 276, 321, 330, 347, 349, 352
archaeology
  surveys, investigations, 14, 68, 146, 151, 216, 256, 281–282, 292
  sites, 15–16, 62, 66, 68, 146, 151–153, *153,* 175, 182, 229, 232, 237, 238, 262, 274, 277, 280, 287, 292, 301, 304, 330, 332, 334, 344, 350, 354
archaisms, linguistic archaisms, 144, 145

armor, slat, 145
Athabascan (Dene) peoples, Athabascan (Dene) language family, xiii, xx, 10, *12 (Map 5),* 27, 31, 35, 37, 39–41, 43, 102, 135, 211, 223, 264, 289
  Dene (Athabascan) prehistory, 14, 39, 144–147, 221–222, 227–229

band names (ethnonyms), 22, 27–*29; See also names of particular bands*
band territories, 22, 27–*29,* 144–147, 228
baptism, 251–152
barabara. *See* **nichił**
barbering, *25, 250,* 335–336
bashla (ulu), 14, 273
baskets, 58, 83, 112, 273, 320, 339, 343
bats, little brown bat, 201
beads, trade, 3, 16, 115, 116, 151, 153, 177, 282
bear (black, brown, & unspecified), 49, 123, 124, 142, 150, 153, 154, 189, 195–196, 197, 215, 254, 314, 319, 335, 350
  bear hunting, 7, 23, 25, 53, 70, 81, 101, 105, 112, 123, 133–134, 149, 155–156, 169, 175, 181, 202, 227, 248, 261, 262, 299, 321, 325, 354–355
beaver, 16, 49, 110, 133, 134, 143, 151, 153, 180, 182, 215
  beaver hunting and trapping, *2,* 5, 7, 23, 50, 58, 68, 69, 72, 99, 101, 107, 114, 119, 149, 173, 175, 178–179, 191, 194, 201, 222, 227, 248, 262, 263, 274, 292, 297, 334
Beł Dink'udlaghen (Salmon Boy; *Aka* **Taltashen**), 13–14, 41, 182, 184–189
beluga, 23, 49, 50, 77, 83, 190, 271, 284
  beluga fat, grease, 23, 49, 77, 81, 119, 149, 248–250
  beluga hunting, 56, 66, 70, *75,* 75–79, 276, 353
  Cook Inlet beluga population, 77
  beluga spearing platform (**yuyqul**), 23, *75,* 75–*79*
berries, 59, 84, 110, 134, 155, 191, 215, 256, 282, 292, 352
  berry picking, 99, 276, 297, 299, 302, 334
bilingualism
  between Dena'ina and Ahtna, 14, 235, 241, 289, 308
  between Dena'ina and Russian, 21, 59
  bilingual place names, 37
birch bark, 58, 102, 153, 261, 327, 350
birch sap, 59, 227
bison, wood bison, 334
black bear. *See* bears and bear hunting
blood letting, 243
boats. *See* watercraft
bow and arrow, 56, 191, 203
bridges (traditional Dena'ina), 99, 173, 301
brown bear. *See* bears and bear hunting
buildings. *See* houses, cabins, and buildings (made by Dena'ina)

cabins. *See* houses, cabins, and buildings (made by Dena'ina)
canneries, 6, 21, 273, 295, 331, 338
caribou, 49, 50, 56, 97, 100, 124, *138,* 142, 145, 153, 161, 189, 215, 217, 219, 221, 222, 256, 269, 282, 332, 357
  caribou fences, 137, 138, 193, 222, 227, 228
  caribou hides, skins, 2, 119, 149, 279, 299
  caribou hunting, 2, 16, 23, 24, 25, 53, 74, 77, 134, 137, *140,* 141, 154, 161, 162, 164, 173, 177, 182, 192, 202, 210, 216, 218, 219, 220, 227, 228, 229, 235, 237, 238, 239, 240–242, 248, 254, 267, 271, 299, 302, 303, 311, 321, 341
cartography (mapping), 17–18, 31–36, 63, 73, 85–86, 111, 275, 286, 289, 296, 306, 310, *340,* 345
  list of maps, vii, 36–37
  place name mapping methods, 36, 42, 43
  sketch maps by Dena'ina or Ahtna, 32, 35, 85, 132, 136, *231,* 232, 238, 275, 289
  symbols on maps, xvii, *maps 1, 2*
  typology of historic maps, *33–35*
celery, wild celery, wild parsnip (**ggis**), 181, 188, 220
C'ełtagi (Sharp Tailed Grouse Clan), 255
census and geneology research, 171
"champion," "strongman" (Dena'ina warriors), 131
chapter guide for book, *map 1* (inside front cover)
chiefs (general), 2, 3, *26,* 44, 59–60, 101. *Also see individual chiefs,* **qeshqa, duyeq**
  chiefs' regalia, *xi,* 3, *9, 59,* 60, *115–117,* 125
  chieftainships (inherited), 222, 285, 291
  duyeq (chief, chiefs), 88, 89, 115, 122
  yagashchik, "second chief," 106
chinook salmon. *See* king salmon
Chishyi (clan), 23, 276, 294, 300, 307
Chugach Eskimo. *See* Alutiiq
Chuitna Coal Mine project, 68
Ch'u'itnu Archaeological District, 68
chum (dog) salmon, 89

churches, church buildings, 2, 9, 19, 58, 59, *68*, 91, 92, 251, 275, 278, *320*, 321
cinnabar, 139
CIRI (Cook Inlet Region, Inc.), xi, xv, 4, 5, 264
CIRI Foundation, xi, 4, 6, 7
clams, 23, 49, 55
clans (general), 14, 22–23, 26, 300. *See also* **Chishyi**, **Ggahyi**, **K'kalayi**, **Nulchina**, **Tulchina**
clubbing salmon, 133
coal, coal mining, 41, 62, 121, 297, 301, 302
coho salmon. *See* silver salmon
commercial fishing, 7, 8, 295, *338*, 339, *353*
Cook Inlet Historical Society, 4
copper, copper working, 16, 106, 111, 290, 299
coyote, 319
  coyote trapping, 7
cranes, sandhill crane, 73, 189
cremation, 175, 330, 383

dance. *See* songs, singing, and dancing
deadfalls, 23, 114
Deg Hit'an language (Ingalik), 76
Dena'ina geographical knowledge (general), 30–41, 120, 121, 141, 142
Dena'ina language. *See also* place names
  audio recordings (inventory), 5–6
  dialects, xix, 10, 11, 13, 14, 49, 56, 346, *maps 1, 2*
  directional system, 40, 50, 113, 221, 339
  distribution, 10–14, 143, 347, *maps 1, 2*
  major Dena'ina villages, *maps 1 and 2, 26, 28*
  month names, 23, *24*
  orthography, sound system, xix-xx, 13
  proto-Dena'ina, 10, 14, 146
  special mountain language, 149
  status, xv, 5, 10, 42
  stress system, xx
Dena'ina population, 10, 14, 89–91, 96–97, 119, *171*, 181, 349, *plate 19*
Dena'ina prehistory, 10–14, 15–16, 31, 144–147, 151–153, 274, 321
Dena'ina Team, The, *330*
Dene languages. *See Athabascan languages*
Dene-Yeniseian, xvii, 14, 144
dentalium, 115, 116, 277, 299, 311
dip net platform (**tanik'edi**), 23, 25, 64–65, *65*, 66, 75, 330, 334, 339, 354
dogs
  Gemuk, *20*
  packing, 101, 177, 237, 238, 241–243, *302*
  sleds, teams, 51, 69–70, 72, 114, 173, 183, 219, 237
  use in hunting bears, 23, 124, 262
  use in hunting sheep, 322
Dolly Varden, 69, 150, 299, 301
Donlin Gold Pipeline, 70, 142
drums
  plank drum, *188*, 331
  skin drum, *125*, 331
dry fish (**baba**), 49, 119, 244, 246, 249, 325, 334
ducks, 73, 182, 215, 292, 295, 299, 332
  duck eggs, 332
  duck hunting, 3, 66, 83, 99, 121, 280, 336
duyeq. *See* chiefs

eagles, 222, 349
  eagle feathers, 116, 117
eels, 188
Eklutna Vocational School, 295, 325
Elmendorf Air Force Base, 6, 331
epidemics, pre-contact, 339, 352
Eskimos, 14, 16, 75, 77, 144, 145, 274, 347
ethnogeography, ethnogeographic research, xi, xii, xiii, xiv, 30, 41, 144, 231–233, 256
eulachon (hooligan), 7, 23, 24, 55, 83, 91, 122, 271, 272, 273, 274, 276, 332
  eulachon (hooligan) oil, 119, 149
exploration of Upper Inlet (general), 21, 31, 39, 91, 290, 345–347, 348, 352, 356. *See also names of individual explorers*

fermented fish (**chuqilin**), 133, 226, 276, 277, 287, 297, 325
first salmon ceremony, 182, 184, 194
fish (general), 1, 3, 49, 68–69, 91, 97, 123, 131, 146, 235, 249
  fish caches, pits, 16, 68, 101, 109, 133, 146, 151, 177, 181, 183, 191, 198, 221
  fish eggs, 221
  fish head oil, 119, 149
  fish processing, 83, 101, 133, 181, 243, 267, 274, 276, 297, 300, 334
fish traps and weirs (general), 23, 50
  locations, 60, 62, 66, 68, 99, 101, 105, 106, 109, 110, 123, 150, 181, 182, 183, 184–190, 198, 217, 227, 238, 241, 267, 274, 277, *354*
fishing (general), 81, 113, 149, 175. *See also particular fish; see* ice fishing
fishing sites, fish camps, 6, 7, 16, 23, 55, 56, 60, *62*, 66, 68,69, 70, 83, 84, 89, 101, 105, 121, 123, 131, 133, 173, 175, 181–183, 222, 228, 267, 271, 276, 277, *279*, 280, 284, 295, 297, 299, 303, 304, 314, 315, 316, 321, 325, *328*, 331, 332, 334, 336, *338*, 339, 353, *354*. *See also particular fish*
floods, 58, 92–93, 183, 273, 290, 291, 292, 293, 295, 314, 319, 327
fox, red fox, 137, 279
  fox trapping, 111
fungus, bracket fungus, 111
furs, trapping (general), 3, 6, 49, 173
fur trade, fur trading, 17, 50, 83, 107, 121, 123, 273, 279, 281–282, 291

game laws, 178–179
game lookouts (**dehq'a**, **nahq'a**), 54, 75, 105, 158, 208, 222
gardens, 109, 299 geese. *See* goose
generic geographic terms. *See* place names
Ggahyi clan, 22–23, 300
ghosts, 175, 320, 350
ghuliy (potlatch wealth and regalia), *115–117*
giants
  giants in human form, 297, 301
  giant brown bear, 161
  giant fish, 161, 320, 324, 325, 326–327
  giant ground squirrel, 138
  giant leech, 161
glaciers, 15, *43*, 120, *205*, *206*, 207, 273, *307*, 319, 324, *325*, *plate 3*
  glacier people (supernatural) (**Łi Dnay**), 205
goats, mountain goat, 316, 319
  goat hunting, 292, 295, 299, 302, 304, 315, 318, 344

goat skins, 315
gold, gold rush, 21, 88, 89, 91, 110, 278, 281–282, 295, 300, 349
general, 156, 157, 162, 183, 192, 229, 230, 255, 261, 268, 294, 324, 340
prospecting, mining, 7, 59, 114, 204, 207, 238, 318
goose, 23, 73, 184–186, 215, 259
goose feathers, 117
goose hunting, 66, 99, 114, 138, 273, 292, 295, 299, 336
graves, graveyards, 62, 92, 93, 107, 109, 175, 182, 193, 198, 238, 256, 267, 279, 284, 292, 297, 301–302, 306, 330, 334, 349, 350
grayling, 112, 114, 193, 215
grease (general), 81, 93, 182, 248
ground squirrel. *See* squirrel, ground squirrel
gull eggs, 83, 84, 266, 332

halibut, 346
hand game (**ch'enlahi**), *129*
headdress, 116–117
hill people (supernatural), 142
hooligan. *See* eulachon
houses, cabins, buildings (built by Dena'ina, when discussed), 22, *56*, 59, 66, 89, 91, *94–95*, 175, *180*, 181, 222, 236, 237, *253*, 278, 279, 282, *283*, *284*, 291, 297, 303, 315, *316*, 320, 324, 329–330, 344. *See also* **nichił** winter house
hot springs, 54, 138
hunting (general), 1. 3. 8. 50, 72, 89, 99, 100, 105, 114, 121, 136, 141, 158, 197, 216, 228, 276, 285, 297, 303, 309, 321, 349, 353, 354. *See also specific animals, e.g.,* moose hunting, caribou hunting
hunting camps, hunting shelters, 9, 15, 16, 22, 23, 25, 32, 33, 51–54, 60, 66, 68, 69, 215, 257, 325, 327, 328, 334, 336, 341, 343, 344, 378, 379
Hunting Dog Story, 4, 7
hydronymns, hydronymic districts, 38–39, 144–147
Hwggaexyu (Ahtna Snowbird Clan), 300
Hwtsaay Hwt'aene (western Ahtna band), 28, 145, 215, 221, 232

ice, ice conditions, 23, 54, 69, 70, 81, 83, 92, 121, 123, 159, 161, 173, 177, 178, 183, 194, 208, 225, 259, 263, 272, 276, 279, 290, 300, 331
ice fishing, 128, 299, 300, 316
Iliamna Lake Dena'ina, 49
Indian potato, 84, 88, 279, 319, 320, 325
influenza ("flu"), 2–3, 21, 66, 91, 96, 170, 192, 253, 264, 297, 332
Ingalik people and language. *See* Deg Hit'an.
iron pyrite, 99, 269

jellyfish, 55, 68
jiggi (child of **qeshqa**), 112, 154
Jiggi Baneyaht story, 154

Kachemak tradition, 15, 147
Kenai Peninsula Dena'ina, 9, 13, 14, 19, 28, 32, 50, 142, 220, 271, 279, 301, 339, 349, 352, 354, 356. *See Chap. 16*
Kenaitze. *See* Kenai Peninsula Dena'ina
K'eq'a Tsukdu'a (Pika Story), 267
king salmon (chinook), 23, 24, 25, 55, 56, 154, 182, 238, 246, 259–260, 271, 279, 297, 315, 316, 331
king salmon fishing, *6*, 66, 83, 119, 124, 150, 177, 181, 182, 184, 193, 198, 285, 302, 332, 334

K'kalayi (clan), 1, 3, 6, 23, 106, 131, 300
Knik Arm band (**K'enaht'ana**), 24–25, 81, 271, 276. *See also Chaps. 13, 14, and 15*
Kolchan. *See* Upper Kuskokwim Athabascans
Koniag (Kodiak Island Alutiiq), 22, 347
Koyukon language, 211
Kroto Creek band, **Dashq'ehtana**, 22, 23, 24, 28, 81, 82, 175, 177–179, 202. *See also Chaps. 8 and 9*
Kustatan Bear Story, 50
Kustatan people, band, 13, 49, 50, 51, 53, 59, 356

Ladd Company (saltery), 68
lake monster, 239, 278, 326–327. *See also* giant fish, giant leech
lake trout, 99, 183, 215. *See also* trout
land claim, 293, 295
land marks, 13, 46, 70, 156, 211, 239, 321, 322
landforms (in Dena'ina place names), 38
Lebedev-Lastochkin Company, 66
Lime Hills Cave site, 146
Lime Village Dena'ina, 10, 53, 142, 143, 163, 266, 320
ling cod (burbot), 215, 276
log structures, *94–95*
Lower Tanana language, 37, 40, 144, 202, 211, 215, 228, 230, 240. *See also* Tanana Valley Athabascans
luck, hunting ("power"), 58, 72, 111, 112, 136, 218
lynx, 49
lynx stick, *174*
lynx trapping, 7, 101, 173, 175

maps. *See* cartography
marmot ("whistler," "groundhog"), 49, 190
marmot hunting, 133, 269
marmot skins, 199
marsh violet, 84
marten, 49
marten skins, 50, 119, 143, 149
marten trapping, 7, 23, 101, 113–114, 162
measles, 2, 68, 96
mineral licks, 100, 191–192, 222
mining. *See* gold, gold rush
mink, 7, 143
months, Dena'ina, 23
moose, 1, 2, 56, 84, 100, 114, 124, 140, 153, 191–192, 194, 201, 215, 262, 290, 344, 355
moose hunting, 7, 9, 16, 23, 24, 50, 53, 54, 68, 69, 89, 99, 100, 107, *124*, 135, 139, 141, 150, 156, 158, 162, 173, 177, 178, 227, 237, 247, 280, 292, 294, 302, 303, *304*, 311, 316, 319, 321, 325, 328, 334, 343, 351
moose fences, 227
moose skins, 267, 299
mosquitoes, 97
Mountain People (Talkeetna Mountains band), 28, 208, 210, 217, 228, 230, 235, 237, 238, 240–253, 256. *See also Chaps. 10 and 11*
Mountaineering Club of Alaska, 47, 329, 334, 341, 344
mountains
special behavior in, 149, 163, 192, 267, 304
sacred, 211, 222, 322
subsistence activities (general), 32–33
mountain people (supernatural), 142, 163
mourning sites, 74, 112, 341
mourning song, 60–61, 126
music. *See* songs, singing, and dancing

muskrat, 194, 215, 222, 277, 292
mussels, 55

Na-Dene languages, 12
names. *See* place names, personal names
Naq'eltani ("God"), 185
narratives (stories), xiv, 1, 4, 5, 23, 233, 326
travel narratives, place-intensive narratives, 5, 143, 164–170, 223–226, 231–233
Navajo language, 76
nch'eł'eni (Brush Man), 123
necklaces, 115, 116
needlefish (stickleback), 55, 83, 332
nichił (traditional multi-family houses; barabara), 16, *22*, 56, 81, 83, 89, 93, 99, 100, 101, 105, 109, 113, 114, 121, 123, 131, 138, 150, 151–152, 159, 173, 175, 180–181, 182, 186, 189, 191, 267, 274, 277, 279, 280, 285, 303, 311, 314, 330, 344. *See also* houses, cabins, and buildings
Northern Archaic tradition, 14, 15, 145, 216, 229
Northern Athabascans (Dene), 37, 39, 85
Nulchina (clan), 1, 4, 22–23, 106, 112, 131, 277, 311, 339

Ojibwa language, 62
onions, wild onions, 135
otter, land otter, 259
otter trapping, 101

parka squirrel. *See* squirrel, ground squirrel
passes, mountain pass, xv, 32–35, 38, 40, 45, 53, 60, 71, 120, 134–139, 141, 142, 147, 156, 158, 159, 202, 207, 208, 218, 219, 221, 238, 256, 269, 279, 290, 302, 303, 306, 308, 309, 325, 329, 344, 349, 350, *plate 4*
PDLL (Proto-Dene *Lex Loci*), xii, 14, 39, 141, 144–147, 154, 214–215, 217, 221–222, 227–229, 309
personal names (in Dena'ina), 1, 40, 240, 253, 278. *See also Dena'ina names in bold in the Personal Name Index*
pika, collared pika, 267
pink salmon, 154, 193, 267, 300
place names, Dena'ina place names
as folk poetry, 31, *passim*
as source of knowledge and information, xv, 30–47
Dena'ina and Athabascan naming principles, xvi, 30–37, *38*, 39–47, 50, *113*, 144–147, 232, 239, 289, 385
Dena'ina knowledge of place names (reconfirmation of), 30–33, 85, 231–233, 310
founding place names, 14, 144–147
inventory in book, xii, xiii, *37*
mountains, oronymns (in Dena'ina place names), 37, 143, 163
official naming, recognition of Alaska Native place names, xiii, 44, 47, 53, 54, 62, 204, 213
opaque place names (-Ω-, significance of), xvi, 141, 146, 154
patterned duplications, 37, 141, 144–147, 217, 222, 227, 232, 239
place name ensemble, 37, 50, 113, 144, 147
research and documentation methods, xiii, 31–35, 37–47, 85–87, 231–234
semantic analysis summary, xvi, *40*
streams, hydronymns (in Dena'ina or Dene place names), 37, 39, 144–147
substrate place names, xvi, 14, 37, 40, 131, 144–147, 352
types of place names and conventions and symbols used in book, xvi, xvii, 144.
watershed tenure, 39, 144–147, 215. *See also* ethnogeography
plants, medicinal plants, 66, 181, 188, 220, 266, 274
Point MacKenzie Rail Extension, 275
porcupine, 7, 16, 23, 89, 111, 114, 134, 142, 162, 192, 215, 269, 292, 295, 321, 335, 336, 344, 347
porcupine quill (giant quill), 72
portages, 38, 76, 88, 89, 99, 122, 132, 136, 141, 150, 219, 220, 232, 255, 256, 273, 303, 349, 357
potlatch, potlatching, 2, 3, 7, 23, 60, 116, 117, 179, 252, 266, 290, 294, 322, 331
prophesy, 91, 93, 96–97, 138, 314, 337
proto-Dene, proto-Athabascan, 144–147
ptarmigan, 23, 113, 203, 215, 299
ptarmigan hunting, 191, 239
puffin beaks, 116, 117

qeshqa ("rich man," leader, chief), 22, 23, 25, *26*, 32, 81, 88, 106, 109, 122, 143, 154, 180, 261, 274, 279, 285, 349. *See also* chief. *Also see names of particular chiefs and leaders*
as "storekeepers," 89, 91, 122
managing fish traps, 23, 267
role in fur trade as middlemen, 18–19, 58, 215

rabbit, snowshoe hare, 16, 23, 110, 173, 175, 215, 264, 282, 292, 294, 299, 301, 321
radium, 141
rainbow trout, 69, 150, 299, 301. *See also* trout
rattles, dance rattles, 115–117
raven (**Delgga**; culture hero, trickster), 60, 163, 219
red ochre, 139, 161, 226, 297, 300, 311
retreat (refuge) sites, 111, 182, 350
rock cairn, 154
Russian-American Company, 58, 290–291
Russian Orthodoxy, churches, 2, 9, 17, 19, *20*, 21, 58, 68, 92, 251, 278, 320, 321. *See also* churches
Russians
in Upper Cook Inlet area, 17–21, 31, 55, 66, 85, 154–155, 278, 289, 290–291, 309, 311, 356
intermarriage with Dena'ina, 19
Russian language, 19, 21, 50
Russian loan words, 21, 40, 88, 216

salmon (general), 64, 70, 75, 100, 110, 123, 131, 133, 146, 169, 248, 256, 274, 287, 299, 330, 341. *See also particular salmon species*
Salmon Boy. *See* **Beł Dink'udlaghen**
salmon fishing, 81, 99, 101, 105, 109, 173, 184–190, 217, 237, 277, 292, 297, 309, 315, 332, 334, 338, 344. *See also particular salmon species*
salt fish, 69
sea anemone, 55
sea snails, 55, 84
sea urchins, 55
seals, 49, 50, 53, 68, 77, 190, 299
seal hunting, 23, 24, 110, 131, 167–169, 353
seal oil, 81, 104, 119, 149
seal skins, 119
shamans, "medicine men," 55, 59, 93, 96, 109, 117, 178, 184, 188–189, 259, 261, 287, 293–294, 314, 318
Shandała Nununk'dnelghuyna (Dena'ina band), 28, 138

sheep, Dall sheep, 97, 139, 141, 142, 145, 299, 300, 301, 349, 355
sheep hunting, 16, 23, 25, 53, 77, 134, 142–143, 150, 159, 210, 220, 221, 228, 292, 294, 295, 302, 303, 304, 305, 308, 315, 316, 318, 321, 322, 324, 325,328, 334, 344
shirts, dancing shirts, 116
Shq'uła Tsukdu (Marmot Story), 4
silver (coho) salmon, 7, 23, 25, 53, 56, 68, 69, 101, 105, 106, 123, 131, 133, 165, 193, 195, 198, 238, 271, 276, 285, 299, 300, 301, 306, 328
skis, 7
sleds, 162, 201, 202, 224, 246–247, 290
Sleeping Lady legend, *13*, 112
smokehouses, *xx*, 83, 84, 101, 105, 106, 121, 123, 181, 184, 188, 194, 195, *196*, 238, 243, 274, 325, 331, 334, 338
snowshoes, snowshoeing, 7, 54, 91, 245, 281–282, 341
sockeye (red) salmon, 7, 23, 25, 53, 69, 101, 105, 123, 150, 154, 185, 194, 238, 267, 271, 279, 285, 300, 306, 334
social organization of Dena'ina, 22–23. *See also* clans
solstice, winter solstice, 188–189
songs, singing and dancing, 1, *4*, 60, 68, 74, 106, 115, 116, 125–129, *129*, 149, 179, *188*, 252, 253, 259, 321
spears, spearing, 23, 240, 267, 297, 302, 316
spruce grouse (spruce hen), 7, 105, 107, 110, 114, 167, 215, 299
squirrel, ground (parka squirrel), 7, 24, 25, 49, 50, 53, 58, 69, 112, 158, 177, 190, 215, 267
coats, blankets 83, 119, 131, *247*
ground squirrel hunting, 133, 149, 299, 321, 324, 327
squirrel, red, 16
starvation, 25, 121, 123, 167–169, 186–187, 239, 244, 332
steambath, sweat house (**nelni**, banya, banyo), 55, 56, 83, 84, 101, 135, 141, 152, 163, 184, 188, 202, 252, 261, 274, 303, 316, 318, 331, 334, 335, 338, 344
steelhead, 7, 101, 123. *See also* trout
stickleback. *See* needlefish
stone lamps, 274
stone tools, 15–16, 151–*153*, 242, 256, 329
stores, trading posts, 123, 226, 278, 281–282, 290, 291, 293, 295, 314
stories, story telling, 6, 7, 23, 106, 298–299. *See* Pete, Shem, storytelling *in Personal Name Index*
subsistence. *See also specific activities and resources, such as moose hunting, salmon, seals*
general patterns of Upper Inlet Dena'ina, 10, 22–25, 75
Chulitna River (general), 210. *See Chap. 9*
Knik Arm (general), 24–25, 271, 276, 292, 295, 313, 321. *See Chaps. 13 and 15*
Kroto Creek area (general), 172, 175, 177–178, 180–181, 183. *See Chaps. 8 and 9*
Lower Susitna River (general), 81, 110. *See Chaps. 2, 3, and 4*
Matanuska River (general), 299, 302. *See Chap. 14*
Mountain People (Talkeetna Mountains), 235, 237, 238, 240–248. *See Chap. 11*
Nancy Lake area, 7. *See Chap. 12*
seasonal round of subsistence activities, 23–25, 81, 292, 295, 315, 353
Susitna River (general), 23, 49, 82, 119, 175, 227. *See Chaps. 2, 8, and 10*
Tyone Lake area, 222, 227–228. *See Chap. 10*
Tyonek area (general), 3, 23, 49, 51, 52, 53, 55, 58, 68, 69. *See Chap. 1*
Upper Susitna River, 215–216, 222, 229, 230. *See Chap. 10*
women's activities, 49, 178
Yentna River (general), 119, 133, 149, 156, 164–170. *See Chaps. 5, 6, and 7*
substrate place names, substrate languages. *See* place names
Susitna Hydroelectric Project, 216, 231, 232
Susitna River band (**Susitnuht'ana**), 22, 23, 82. *See also Chaps. 2, 3, 4, and 12*
swans, 84, 182
swan hunting, 121, 292 symbols and abbreviations, xix

Tanana River Athabascans, 31, 40, 42, 144, 208, 209, 210, 215, 227, 230, 238, 271
territories, as reflected in place name knowledge, 14, 18, *30*, 30–35, 37–47, 120, 146, 221, 289
tide flats (on or near Cook Inlet), 23, 70, 75, 76, 78, 82, 84, 266, 273, 276, 279, 291, 319, 334, 339, 343
tides, tide conditions, 55, 56, 64, 66, 70, 75 78, 79, 83, 110, 266, 271, 273, 279, 290, 330, 332, 339, 343, 378, 341, 352
toponymy. *See* place names
trade
pre-Russian (aboriginal, between Dena'ina groups), 23–25, 49, 53, 74, 77, 83, 119, 149, 297, 299, 320
between Dena'ina and miners, 278, 281–282, 349, 355
between Dena'ina and Ahtna, 19, 227, 230, 271, 296, 311, 321
trails (when described), 31–34, 38, 53, 69–70, 72–74, 99, 112, 132, 134, 156, 183, 192, 197, 203, 210, 216, 218–221, 223–226, 233, 238, 255–256, 262, 277, 297, 300, 303, 306, 308–310, 318, 344
Trapper Creek Overlook site, 182
trapping, furbearer, general, 23, 50, 285. *See also specific animals*
locations, 8, 9, 51, 113, 123, 183, 191, 197, 220, 257, 259, 273, 274, 295, 309, 311, 315, 353, 357
pre-Russian trapping, 23, 114
travel (general mention), 30, 31–34, 69, 70, 208, 220, *passim*
travel narratives, 164–170, 223–226, 295, *passim*
trout, 3, 7, 16, 23, 50, 62, 66, 68, 101, 105, 106, 110, 113, 123, 150, 175, 182, 185, 198, 218, 259, 276, 277, 278, 285, 292, 315, 326, 332. *See also* lake trout; rainbow trout; steelhead
tsukdu (legendary stories), 6, 41, 107. *See also* Salmon Boy story
tuberculosis (t.b.), 3, 169
Tulchina clan, 60, 223, 235, 294, 301, 311
Tyonek band (**Tubughna**), 22, 23, 25, 28, 68, 81, 83, *plate 4*
Tyonek Singers and Dancers, 4, 7, 9, *129*

Upper Kuskokwim Athabascans (**Gheltsana**), 32, 139, 141–147, 155, 156, 159, 289
Upper Kuskokwim language, 139, 142, 143, 158, 211, 220
Upper Kuskokwim place names work: 143
U.S. Board of Geographic Names, 47, 53, 202

villages, village sites, Dena'ina settlements, 10, 13, *26*, 28, 49, 50, 55, 56, 58, 59, 66, *67*, 68, 69, 81, 85, 89, 91, 92, 93, 96, 109, 121, 124, 137, 138, 149, 150, 154, 162, 180, 192, 193, 198, 222, 232, 237, 254, 255, 256, 261, 267, 271, 272, 274, 276, 277, 279, 284, 290, 292, 297, 301, 305, 309, 311, 314, 315, 320, 321, 329, 330, 334, 339, 349, 350, 352–353, 354. *See also* **nichił**. *Also see the chapter maps and maps 1 and 2*
volcano, 52, 53, 152, 153, 216

warfare, wars
  between Alaska Native groups, 16, 62, 63, 89, 111, 131, 145–146, 154, 182, 228, 229, 279, 287, 319, 321, 330, 338, 341, 349, 350, 352
  between Dena'ina and Russians, 17, 66, 352, 354
  World War II, 337
watercraft, water travel
  general, 76, *102–104*, 290, 339, 343
  canoes (**baqay**), 83, 89, 102, 109, 119, 123, 131, 154, 155, 156, 161, 173, 177, 182, 186, 192, 203, 216, 222, 237, 271, 350
  dories, 97, 164, 237, 281, 315, 335, 338, *351*
  gas boats, 9, 295, 315
  kayaks, baidarkas (**biqidin**), 19, 21, 23, 58, 75, 76, 79, *102–104*, 122, 154, 182, 345, 350
  moose or caribou skin boats (**elgheji**), 55, 64, 68, 81, 84, 102, 119, 133, 134, 136, 156, 161, 164, 173, 177, 191, 201, 202, 203, 237, 254, 328
  rafts (**hnes**), 102, 104, 131, 203, 238
  sailboats, *103*, *278*, 281, 349, 353
  sternwheelers, steamboats, 74, 110, 121, 183, 218, 335
  umiaks (seal skin boat) (**badi**), 55, 102, 104, 119, 149, 259, 274, 332, 343, 346, 349
waterfowl (general), 24, 50, 54, 70. *See also specific fowl*
watershed tenure. *See* place names
weather lore, 163, 192, 218, 267, 269, 324. *See also* mountains, special behavior in
weasel, least weasel, 58
whales, 7, 75
whitefish, 183, 193, 215, 227, 228, 229
whooping cough, 2
wind, winds, 84, 106, 110, 137, 141, 168, 196, 296, 304, 313
wolf, wolves, 191, 192, 242
wristlets, *116–117*

Yentna River band **Yentnuht'ana**, 22, 23, 24,28, 82, 119. *See also Chaps. 5, 6, and 7*
Yubugh Tayqan (culture hero), 93, 107, 109, 122
Yusdi Kinughelchina (**Dusduyghelchina**) (Point Clan), 272

MAP 2

The Dena'ina language area showing dialects and surrounding languages

MAP BY MATT GANLEY AND JAMES KARI

Language names (**BOLD**) and boundaries

Dena'ina dialect names (*Italic*) and boundaries

Modern settlements with Dena'ina population

Some former Dena'ina settlements of the historic period (now abandoned)

Other modern towns and villages

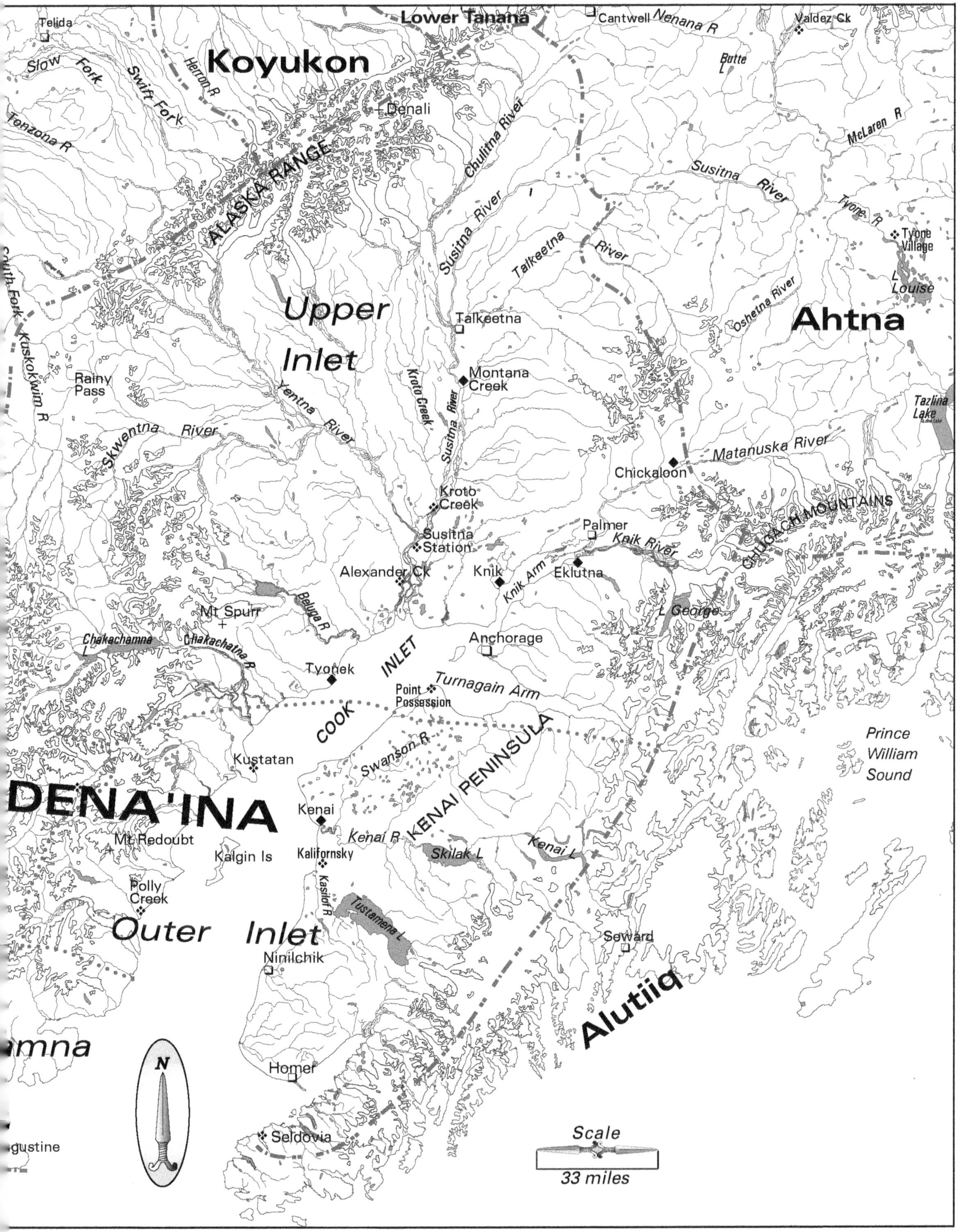
Telida
Lower Tanana
Cantwell
Nenana R
Valdez Ck
Koyukon
Slow Fork
Swift Fork
Herron R
Butte L
Denali
Tonzona R
Chulitna River
McLaren R
ALASKA RANGE
Susitna River
Tyone R
Tyone Village
Susitna River
Talkeetna
River
L Louise
South Fork Kuskokwim R
Upper Inlet
Oshetna River
Talkeetna
Ahtna
Rainy Pass
Montana Creek
Kroto Creek
Susitna River
Yentna River
Tazlina Lake
Skwentna River
Matanuska River
Chickaloon
Kroto Creek
CHUGACH MOUNTAINS
Palmer
Susitna Station
Knik River
Alexander Ck
Knik
Eklutna
Knik Arm
Beluga R
Mt Spurr
L George
Chakachamna L
Chakachatna R
Anchorage
Tyonek
INLET
Point Possession
Turnagain Arm
COOK
Prince William Sound
Kustatan
Swanson R
KENAI PENINSULA
DENA'INA
Kenai
Kenai R
Mt Redoubt
Kenai L
Kalgin Is
Kalifornsky
Skilak L
Kasilof R
Polly Creek
Tustamena L
Outer Inlet
Seward
Ninilchik
Alutiiq
amna
N
Homer
gustine
Seldovia
Scale
33 miles

‡One of the best portraits of Shem Pete, likely taken at Willow in the 1960s. PHOTO COURTESY OF KNIK TRIBAL COUNCIL.

ABOUT THE AUTHORS

James Kari is professor emeritus of linguistics, Alaska Native Language Center, University of Alaska Fairbanks and author or editor of numerous publications on Athabascan languages and peoples. He is the co-editor of *The Dene-Yeniseian Connection* (Anthropological Papers of the University of Alaska, 2010)

James A. Fall is a cultural anthropologist at the Division of Subsistence of the Alaska Department of Fish and Game. He is the author of *The Upper Inlet Tanaina: Patterns of Leadership Among an Alaska Athabaskan People* (Anthropological Papers of the University of Alaska, 1987), which was based on research with Shem Pete and other Dena'ina elders.